Religion, War, and Ethics

A Sourcebook of Textual Traditions

Religion, War, and Ethics is a collection of primary sources from the world's major religions on the ethics of war. Each chapter brings together annotated texts – scriptural, theological, ethical, and legal – from a variety of historical periods that reflect each tradition's response to perennial questions about the nature of war: When, if ever, is recourse to arms morally justifiable? What moral constraints should apply to military conduct? Can a lasting earthly peace be achieved? Are there sacred reasons for waging war, and special rewards for those who do the fighting? The religions covered include Sunni and Shiite Islam; Judaism; Roman Catholic, Eastern Orthodox, and Protestant Christianity; Theravada Buddhism; East Asian religious traditions (Confucianism, Shinto, Japanese and Korean Buddhism); Hinduism; and Sikhism. Each section is compiled by a specialist, recognized within his or her respective religious tradition, who has also written a commentary on the historical and textual context of the passages selected.

Gregory M. Reichberg is Research Professor at the Peace Research Institute Oslo (PRIO). He is leader of the Oslo-based Research School in Peace and Conflict, adjunct Professor in the Department of Political Science at the University of Oslo, and associate editor of the *Journal of Military Ethics*. He is co-editor of *World Religions and Norms of War* (2009); *Ethics, Nationalism, and Just War: Medieval and Contemporary Perspectives* (2007); and *The Ethics of War: Classic and Contemporary Readings* (2006).

Henrik Syse is Senior Researcher at the Peace Research Institute Oslo (PRIO). He is also co–editor-in-chief of the *Journal of Military Ethics* and teaches at the Norwegian Defense University College and Bjørknes College. He is the author of *Natural Law, Religion, and Rights* (2007) as well as several books in Norwegian on topics such as war, the virtue of moderation, and the relationship between faith and philosophy. He is the co-editor, with Gregory M. Reichberg and Endre Begby, of *The Ethics of War: Classic and Contemporary Readings* (2006) and, with Reichberg, of *Ethics, Nationalism, and Just War* (2007).

Nicole M. Hartwell is a DPhil candidate in History at the University of Oxford (Lincoln College), an Associate Researcher at the Peace Research Institute Oslo (PRIO), and a managing editor of the *Journal of Military Ethics*.

D0073726

Religion, War, and Ethics

A Sourcebook of Textual Traditions

Edited by

Gregory M. Reichberg
Peace Research Institute Oslo

Henrik Syse
Peace Research Institute Oslo

with the assistance of Nicole M. Hartwell

CAMBRIDGE
UNIVERSITY PRESS

CAMBRIDGE
UNIVERSITY PRESS

32 Avenue of the Americas, New York, NY 10013-2473, USA

Cambridge University Press is part of the University of Cambridge.

It furthers the University's mission by disseminating knowledge in the pursuit of education, learning, and research at the highest international levels of excellence.

www.cambridge.org
Information on this title: www.cambridge.org/9780521738279

© Cambridge University Press 2014

First published 2014

Printed in the United States of America

A catalog record for this publication is available from the British Library.

Library of Congress Cataloging in Publication data
Reichberg, Gregory M.
Religion, war, and ethics : a sourcebook of textual traditions / Gregory M. Reichberg, Peace Research Institute Oslo (PRIO), Henrik Syse, Peace Research Institute Oslo (PRIO); with the editorial assistance of Nicole Monique Hartwell.
    pages   cm
Includes bibliographical references and index.
ISBN 978-0-521-45038-6 (hardback)
1. War – Religious aspects.   2. War – Moral and religious aspects.
3. Just war doctrine.   I. Title.
BL65.W2R385 2014
205'.6242–dc23   2013030383

ISBN 978-0-521-45038-6 Hardback
ISBN 978-0-521-73827-9 Paperback

Contents

Notes on Contributors

Adam Afterman is a Senior Lecturer in the Department of Hebrew Culture Studies at Tel Aviv University. He serves as a Senior Research Fellow at the Shalom Hartman Institute in Jerusalem and the John Paul II Center for Interreligious Dialogue in Rome.

Gedaliah Afterman is Research Fellow at the Jewish People Policy Institute in Jerusalem.

Robert John Araujo, S.J., is the John Courtney Murray, S.J., University Professor at Loyola University, Chicago. He is co-author of a two-volume study, *Papal Diplomacy and the Quest for Peace* (2004, 2010).

Nesrine Badawi is Assistant Professor of Public and International Law in the Political Science Department of the American University in Cairo. She received her PhD in law at the School of Oriental and African Studies at the University of London. Her work focuses on the history and development of Islamic jurisprudence on the regulation of armed conflict.

Torkel Brekke teaches Religious Studies in the Faculty of Theology at the University of Oxford and is a Fellow of Pembroke College. He has written extensively on religious trends in Asia, including *Makers of Modern Indian Religion* (2002). His most recent book is *Fundamentalism: Prophecy and Protest in an Age of Globalization* (2012).

Mahinda Deegalle is Senior Lecturer in the School of Humanities and Cultural Industries at Bath Spa University. He is the author of *Popularizing Buddhism* (2006) and the editor of *Dharma to the UK* (2008) and *Buddhism, Conflict and Violence in Modern Sri Lanka* (2006). He held the NEH Professorship in Humanities at Colgate University in the spring semester of 2013.

Mohammad H. Faghfoory is Professor of Islamic Studies at George Washington University in Washington, DC. His most recent publication, in addition to several articles, is a translation and annotation of Abu Hamid al-Ghazzali's last treatise on Sufism, *The Path of Worshippers to the Paradise of the Lord of the Worlds* (2012). In addition to teaching and writing, Professor Faghfoory has been active in interfaith dialogue in the Washington Metropolitan area.

Nicole M. Hartwell is a DPhil candidate in History at the University of Oxford (Lincoln College), an Associate Researcher at the Peace Research Institute Oslo (PRIO), and a managing editor of the *Journal of Military Ethics*.

John Kelsay is Distinguished Research Professor of Religion at Florida State University in Tallahassee. A Guggenheim Fellow in 2002–2003, Professor Kelsay's publications include *Arguing the Just War in Islam* (2007).

Soho Machida is Professor and Director of the Center for Ecological Peace Studies in the Graduate School of Integrated Arts and Sciences at Hiroshima University. Among his many books are *Renegade Monk: Hōnen and Japanese Pure Land Buddhism* (1999) and *Why Does Religion Prevent Peace?* (2004).

Valerie Ona Morkevicius is Assistant Professor of Political Science at Colgate University. She is the author of several articles on Protestant approaches to the ethics of conflict, including "Changing the Rules of the Game: A Just Peace Critique of Just War Thought," *Nova et Vetera* 10(4), 2011, and "Ethics of War in Protestant Christianity," in *World Religions and Norms of War* (2009), as well as essays on Hindu and Shi'i just war thinking in *The Prism of Just War: Asian and Western Perspectives on the Legitimate Use of Military Force* (2010).

Gregory M. Reichberg is Research Professor at the Peace Research Institute Oslo (PRIO), where he specializes in the history of ethical thinking about peace and war. Over the last few years he has co-edited several volumes, including *World Religions and Norms of War* (2009) and *The Ethics of War: Classic and Contemporary Readings* (2006). He heads the Research School on Peace and Conflict (a consortium for doctoral students based at the University of Oslo) and is currently writing a monograph, *War and Peace in the Ethics of Thomas Aquinas*, which will be published by Cambridge University Press.

Kaushik Roy is Guru Nanak Professor in the Department of History at Jadavpur University, Kolkata, and Global Fellow at the Peace Research Institute Oslo (PRIO), Norway. His latest publication is *Hinduism and the Ethics of Warfare in South Asia* (2012).

Yuri Stoyanov is a Research Fellow in the Department of the Near and Middle East, School of Oriental and African Studies, University of London, and a Senior Associate Fellow at the Albright Institute, Jerusalem. His latest book is *Defenders and Enemies of the True Cross* (2011).

Henrik Syse is a Senior Researcher at the Peace Research Institute Oslo (PRIO), where he specializes in ethics, including the ethics of war and peace. He has written books about ethics, politics, and religion and has co-edited several volumes, including *The Ethics of War: Classic and Contemporary Readings* (2006). He is currently co–editor-in-chief of the *Journal of Military Ethics*.

Vladimir Tikhonov (Korean name: Pak Noja) is Professor of Korean and East Asian studies at the University of Oslo, Norway. He is co-editor of and contributor to *Buddhism and Violence: Militarism and Buddhism in Modern Asia* (2012). His book *Pak Noja's Ten Thousand Feelings Diary* (*Pak Noja ŭi Mangam ilgi*, 2008) was officially recommended as "excellent reading for general knowledge" by the South Korean Culture Ministry.

Preface

The events of 11 September 2001 cast a harsh new light on links between religion and violence. While much of the attention was initially directed toward Islam, it was not long before parallels were explored within Christianity, Judaism, Hinduism, and other mainstream religious traditions. This coincided with a sharp rise of philosophical interest over the past decades in the ethics of war, particularly within the confines of what is standardly termed the Western "just war tradition." Consequently, among scholars certainly, but also among the general public, there is now a wider recognition that religion has the dual potential to encourage and to restrain violence. While some religious adherents urge a complete renunciation of violence (pacifism), more often there can be found a mixed approach in which the resort to force is excluded under certain conditions but allowed and perhaps even enjoined in others. Some have looked for ethical alternatives to limit war; others have sought to justify acts of violence to make these acceptable in ethical terms; while still others have sought to use religious symbols and ideals to foment conflict in pursuit of political agendas.

Despite the accrued interest in religion, violence, war, and ethics, the source texts in which these issues are expounded have often remained inaccessible to all but a handful of specialists. This is especially true of traditions such as Islam, Hinduism, and Judaism, where the key authoritative treatments are often embedded in texts (e.g., *Qur'anic* jurisprudence, religious epics, or Halakhic commentary) that are not overtly about matters pertaining to the ethics of war, thus requiring a difficult process of interpretation and selection, and for which English translations frequently do not exist. Since debate in the public arena (on, for instance, what Islam does or does not teach regarding participation in violence) often hinges on a proper knowledge of the relevant textual traditions, the quality of such debate would be significantly enhanced if the most important texts could be made available, under a single cover, in English, to a broader reading public. It is with this goal in mind that the present book was conceived.[1] A generous grant from the Research Council of Norway, for a four-year project on "Comparative Ethics of War," enabled the idea to become a reality.

The volume that thus emerged – this sourcebook – explores how the world's leading religious traditions have approached the normative problems associated with war and armed conflict. While nonviolent approaches have been taken into account, the book's main focus is on "the just-war outlook in the generic sense of the term."[2] This is the idea that the use of armed force may be justifiable within determinable limits, in order to uphold fundamental human values, such as protection of one's homeland from attack, defense of the innocent, or preservation of the rule of law.

If "just war" designates the search for a middle ground between "no violence whatsoever" and "anything goes," then it can be a useful term for designating the abundant literature that arose first in Hindu culture, then among the ancient Israelites and Chinese, to a certain extent among Buddhists and Sikhs, and finally with more explicit articulation by Christians and Muslims.

Some may find this focus on "just war" surprising in a volume that purports to study specifically how *religious traditions* have assessed the normative dimensions of armed conflict. For many, "just war" has come to signify a secular Western discourse (of the sort exemplified by Michael Walzer's widely cited book *Just and Unjust Wars*) that is ill suited for describing properly religious attitudes toward the phenomenon in question. Moreover, on the theme of religion and war the reading public has grown accustomed to apparently contradictory attitudes. On the one hand, it is often assumed that religion requires a renunciation of violence; on the other hand, it seems equally true that when individuals enter war with religious motivations their use of force will know no limits. Hence the freighted term "holy war," long associated with historical excesses such as the medieval crusades or the Reformation-era wars of religion, has newly found application to a wide range of violent struggles in which religious identities are taken to be a key factor. The discourse about religion and war thus swings from principled pacifism to violent extremism. The ground traditionally occupied by the world's great religious traditions – wherein over the centuries a network of overlapping distinctions has been drawn concerning the difference between justifiable and unjustifiable uses of force – is often sidelined in favor of the more dramatic discourse that alternates between the opposing poles of nonviolence and militant extremism.

The present volume aims to remedy this neglect by making available, under a single cover, the key texts on "just war" that may be found within the world's major religions. Nonviolent and "extremist" alternatives have not thereby been excluded, as some if not all of the chapters include at least some texts that reflect these viewpoints. The book's center of gravity does nonetheless remain within the orbit of "just war." Since the cultural matrix for millions of people in the world today is infused with ideas, sentiments, images, and expectations that originate from their respective religious traditions, if norms of war are to have real traction, if they are to have a hold on the minds and hearts of believers, it is important that they be associated with long-standing norms of peace and war that can be found within each of these traditions.

It was impossible within the confines of a single volume to provide exhaustive coverage of all relevant texts within each religious tradition. Difficult choices were forced upon the contributors, each of whom was given strict limits on the size of his or her respective chapter. By the same token, space constraints were such that some religious traditions could not be represented herein. Had the total number of pages not been a consideration, the by-no-means-insignificant developments within, say, Coptic and Armenian Christianity, Ismaili Islam, Native American and African spirituality, Tibetan Buddhism, and Zoroastrianism would certainly have found their rightful place. Let it be added that our focus on textual traditions has implied that nearly all of the historical sources reproduced in this volume have originated from male authors. This is certainly a problem and challenge worth noting.

The book has been designed according to a set of guiding principles that have been applied in the measure possible throughout each of its eleven chapters.

First, in commissioning contributors for the different chapters, we sought to identify scholars who could provide an internal viewpoint on the traditions to be represented in the volume or who know the tradition truly well based on long-standing scholarship – under the supposition that linguistic and religious familiarity would promote a keen grasp of delicate and often controversial issues. Second, it was understood that each of the chapters would be free-standing so they could be read independently of each other. Similarly, it was acknowledged that the treatment of war within these traditions was sufficiently diverse that no common set of categories – for instance, the Western just war terminology of *jus ad bellum* and *jus in bello* – could be imposed throughout. Some shared rules were nonetheless apposite in order that the book might cohere as a single unit. Each chapter, for instance, begins with a general introduction. In some cases this sufficed to present and to contextualize the sources reproduced. In other cases, the contributors interspersed commentary throughout their chapters or more frequently paraphrased material that could not readily be detached from its surroundings. A careful typographical differentiation was established between editorial commentary on the one hand and original texts on the other, thereby enabling our readers to understand at any point whether they are hearing the chapter editor's voice or reading an actual text from the tradition in question. All passages reproduced verbatim or closely paraphrased include an initial statement that identifies the source – book, article, manuscript, poem, epic, sacred scripture – from which the passage is taken. When translations were needed – as was most often the case – these were ordinarily drawn from previously published materials. Our colleagues at Cambridge University Press, especially Anastasia Graf and Emily Spangler, are to be praised for their painstaking efforts at identifying and contacting the relevant copyright holders. At other times, the chapter editors translated passages themselves or entrusted others with this task. For works not in the public domain, copyright holders of the original versions were able to review these translations so that their consent could be given.

All of the contributors were urged to include source materials across a broad time span, thus from ancient, modern, and contemporary periods, although it was understood that depending on the contours of each tradition the emphasis would be placed differently from case to case. Moreover, within each chapter it was expected that a range of different sources would be represented – epical, scriptural, theological, jurisprudential, patristic, liturgical, pastoral, and the like – depending in each instance on the special characteristics of the tradition in question. Let us note that the relevant Scriptural passages related to Christianity are assembled at the beginning of the Catholic chapter. These passages are also relevant for the discussions and texts in the Orthodox and Protestant chapters. (Furthermore, texts from Hebrew Scriptures found in the Judaism chapter are of relevance to the chapters on Christianity; some passages will indeed be found both there and in the Catholic chapter.) In the case of the Muslim and Buddhist sources, the basic texts from those traditions have to a larger extent been divided between the relevant chapters (i.e., Sunni and Shia for Islam, and Theravada Buddhist and Japanese traditions for Buddhism).

We have given our contributors the option of expressing their own considered judgment on the texts included within their respective chapters. Thus, in some cases, the reader will find that the chapter editor has taken a stand on controversial issues, while in other chapters the editor has retained more of a distance from personal views. In all of the chapters care has nonetheless been taken to provide a representative sampling of diverse views on war and ethics that can be found within each of the traditions.

Finally, while writings on peace could not be ignored altogether – virtually all religious traditions acknowledge that peace is the normative horizon for reflection – it was recognized from the outset that the preponderance of citations would necessarily have to be drawn from writings about war and violence. By the same token, the many metaphorical uses of "war" and related concepts – which in some traditions can be quite extensive – were largely set aside as outside the scope of this volume.

An undertaking such as this could not succeed without indispensable support from many quarters. First and foremost there was the indefatigable editorial assistance of Nicole M. Hartwell, who coordinated the flow of numerous drafts from our contributors. She kept careful track of their successive revisions; attentively read the manuscript through its various transformations; offered many valuable suggestions, stylistic and substantive; and was of great help to the contributors in finalizing their chapters. Our committee of external readers, Timothy J. Demy (United States Naval War College), Glenn "Chip" Hughes (St. Mary's University, San Antonio), Matthew Levering (University of Saint Mary of the Lake), Ayatollah Mostafa Mohaghegh Damad (Shahid Beheshti University, Teheran), and Josef Stern (University of Chicago), enhanced the accuracy and scope of this volume through their perceptive comments. Much praise is likewise due to our copy editor, Stephanie Sakson, and Cambridge University Press senior editor Beatrice Rehl, who enthusiastically embraced the project from the outset, attending our workshops in Oslo and Paphos, and providing invaluable guidance over the last six years. Considerable thanks are also due to our indexer, Tobiah Waldron, for carefully putting together the index. Without the institutional support of our home institution, the Peace Research Institute Oslo (PRIO), encouragement from our friends in the section on Peace and Reconciliation at the Norwegian Ministry of Foreign Affairs, and the financial contribution of the Research Council of Norway, this project would not have seen the light of day. Very special mention is lastly reserved for our contributors, who made the book what it is. From our communion in the ethics of war may there emerge some durable roots of peace. To all of the above, we the editors-in-chief express our heartfelt gratitude and thanks.

Gregory M. Reichberg
Henrik Syse

NOTES

1 The idea emerged at a conference organized by the Peace Research Institute Oslo (PRIO) in Rome (March 2006) on "Conceptions of Peace and War in the Abrahamic Religions." The ground for the present volume was prepared when a group of scholars at that conference contributed essays to a book, *World Religions and Norms of War*, edited by Vesselin Popovski, Gregory M. Reichberg, and Nicolas Turner, which was subsequently published by United Nations University Press (Tokyo, 2009). We, the editors, thank UNU Press for allowing us to reproduce in this preface some passages that originally appeared in the conclusion to the aforementioned volume, "Norms of War in Cross-Religious Perspective."

2 Stephen Neff, *War and the Law of Nations* (Cambridge: Cambridge University Press, 2005), p. 34.

Introduction
Nicole M. Hartwell and Henrik Syse

Does Religion Cause War? Or Does Religion Promote Peace and Restrain War?

Within the pages of this book the reader will discover a rich array of texts that, in their different ways, throw light on a range of religious attitudes toward violence and war. The challenge inherent in such a collection of texts lies in their divergence – both the divergence between texts from different religions on the one hand, and the different, partly conflicting views found within the same religion or branches of a religion on the other. To draw a single overarching conclusion about the relationship between religion, war, and ethics is well-nigh impossible. Does religion cause war? Yes. Does religion promote peace and restrain war? Yes. Both – and more – are true. Much depends on the conflict in question, the historical situation, the people and beliefs involved, and – not least important for this book – the interpretation of texts. Yet in spite of this diversity there do exist common tensions and questions that can be found throughout the materials gathered herein. In highlighting these, our purpose in this Introduction is to facilitate the reading of the texts on war, violence, and religion found in this book.

What Is Our Subject Matter?

Before we go any further, let us start with a very basic question: What is religion? In other words, what is the basic point of departure for this book? This is not easy to answer, since there are so many nuances and differences within and between religions, such as the following:

- between monotheism and polytheism;
- between belief in a god who reveals him- or herself through history and belief in karma or other more impersonal forces that influence our lives;
- between the belief that earthly life is lived only once and the belief that any one human life is part of a long cycle of lives lived;
- between belief in an overarching, omnipotent power or principle and belief in several competing powers or principles who (or which) can challenge and potentially defeat each other;

- between belief in a strict dividing line between earthly and heavenly existence and beliefs that do not as clearly distinguish between the two; and
- between belief in a set of canonical texts that express divine truth and belief in less text-oriented and less canonical approaches to the tenets of a religion.

For these very reasons – and several others – it is difficult to draw *one* conclusion about religion and participation in violence and war. We must, in short, be aware of the basic differences confronting us. Furthermore, religions change over time, in their expressions of their beliefs, and sometimes in their basic creeds. There is not *one* Christianity or *one* Hinduism. By saying this, we are not implying that there cannot be truth in a real, metaphysical sense in one or more religions; it is fully possible to champion this critical-analytical stance toward religions as we find them in this world and still maintain religious belief. In addition, we are not taking any stand here on what *common* truths different religions may express or whether there is possibly a basic equivalence of symbolization between religious systems and beliefs, in the sense that several religions, on a deeper level, may be carriers (partly or wholly) of the same truth, with different levels of differentiation.[1] In an academic work such as this, it is not our task to evaluate the truth claims of religious beliefs but rather to remind the reader of the complexity of religious traditions and to understand better what they say. For this reason we have not sought to formulate a single or unifying definition of religion for the purposes of this book. The traditions covered are ones that are standardly included under the heading of "religion," as implying some *relation to the transcendent*. We are aware, however, that even this very broad designation may not fit all traditions, as witnessed by, for instance, Confucianism or even Zen Buddhism.

Ethics, War, and Violence

Religion, as a tradition or communal activity or set of beliefs, has often had (and still has) a significant influence on many communities' ways of conceptualizing right and wrong in interpersonal affairs – that is, on ethics. It follows that religion will naturally play a role in shaping the views of any given community as it grapples with one of the most challenging of all ethical questions: when and how it is right to employ violence against other human beings. There exist long-standing traditions around the world for judging when it may be right to do so, and many of these have their roots in religious belief.

Following from this, the basic questions we should ask as we read these texts are: *How is the nature of a religious tradition's set of beliefs and practices related to the views within that religion about war and peace?* And: *Can differences between the different religions and confessions on the question of war be related to the underlying philosophies and/or theologies that shape the religious beliefs and practices in question?*

These questions cannot be answered in one sentence, not least since the answers will be different for each of the religious traditions in this book. However, by framing the basic problem in this way, we are led to a number of related questions, which we will now mention in turn, and which attempt to sum up the challenges we face in the study of these texts.

Permission, Encouragement, or Restraint

First, we have the question of whether the religious beliefs and practices we are dealing with serve *to permit* and maybe even *to encourage* the use of armed force or whether they rather and primarily function as a *restraint on* or even *prohibition against* such force – or whether they do both, depending on the time, problem at hand, and context.[2] This question, and the underlying tension between the religious approval and the religious abhorrence of war, is one that runs through a number of the texts gathered herein; and it is one where different texts can pull in different directions even within one and the same tradition. We have those texts that identify a sacred ground for – or hallowed examples of – use of armed force and from which we can draw, more or less directly, the conclusion that such use of armed force is not only to be sanctioned, but probably even looked up to and used as an example. And then there are those texts where violence is condemned, more or less directly, and where ideals strongly in tension with violence and war-fighting are extolled as the true virtues of a right believer.

Multiple Interpretations

Second, we are confronted with the challenge that one and the same text may be, and often has been, susceptible to multiple interpretations, pertaining not only to the reasons that can be put forward in order to justify the use of armed force, but also to the question of how and against whom such force can be used. This hermeneutical challenge takes on a grave character when parts of a text are selectively utilized in order to endorse the use of armed force for reasons that seem contrary to its whole, or possibly even contrary to the nature of the religious tradition that it is said to represent.

A number of chapters in this volume show that in some cases religious texts have been reinterpreted or, arguably, taken out of their literary and historical context by both religious and secular authorities in order to exercise control over populations or to provide religious justification for political ends, such as military expansion and conquest. It is imperative to consider how we as readers, from both within and outside these traditions, can navigate through such hermeneutical challenges. Can we self-assuredly say that there is an "essence" to each religious tradition, against which interpretations of canonical or other texts can be measured (and condemned) if they seem to serve particularly intolerant or violent purposes? Are there, in the words of the French philosopher Pierre Bayle, "clear and distinct notions of natural light" that can guide us when we are confronted with diverging interpretations? Or will the work of interpretation never be finished and always be colored by the context in which the interpreter finds him- or herself?

Who Interprets?

This leads us to our third challenging point: *Who* is to participate in and contribute to the endeavor of interpreting religious texts? Should this be the exclusive domain of members of a particular religious faith, maybe even of just a few select members of that faith? Or should such a discussion take place between insiders and outsiders, possibly constituting a precursor toward greater religious tolerance and dialogue between individuals of diverging faiths? If we embrace the latter approach – for instance, with a view to utilizing classical texts to address our present-day political realities – it is important to bear in mind the need to be attentive to and respectful of the conventions of interpretation embedded within the religious traditions themselves, especially when we approach them as outsiders.

Examples or Injunctions

Fourth, reflecting on the nature and purpose of each text found in this volume, we are led to see the tension between texts that relate narratives that are supposed to work as *examples* of what we should do (or not do), on the one hand, and those that contain *direct injunctions* to act in a certain way (and not in others), on the other. The former will tell us (mythically or historically) what certain people in certain situations thought was the right or wrong thing to do, or were led or forced to do, whereas the second will, through some authority, give us principled guidance or commandments related to war or violence. In the terms of moral philosophy, the first kind of text will often be closer to a "virtue" ethics, whereas the second will more rightly be called a "duty" or "deontological" ethics. By the first we mean texts that tell us something about what sort of persons we ought to be; with the second, the concern is with norms or rules that should guide our behavior.

All or Some

Fifth, we should be aware as we read these texts that sometimes they hold forth examples and principles that are meant to apply to *all* human beings, regardless of their religious belief or belonging, while others draw a sharper line between those within a religious community and those outside it. In the latter case, this may lead to the creation of different rules for how to treat human beings in the respective spheres. Is an insider meant to be treated differently from and better than an outsider? In some cases, the answer to this question will be clearly specified; in other cases, one has to infer from the context what is meant, or whether any such distinction is implied at all.

There are also cases in which a text has to be understood in terms of which sector(s) of society it is addressing. For instance, if a text is directed to a group of monks, we can assume that the ethical ideals espoused are meant to apply primarily to the life of the monks and not to everyone equally. This also shows the danger of quoting a text out of context: it may be that what is held forth is not meant to apply as generally as an out-of-context quote may imply.

Ideal or Directly Action-Guiding

Sixth, there is the difference between religion representing an ideal, referred to and talked about as something to be strived for and aspired to, but hardly shaping concrete events, and religion informing political life and the vicissitudes of history much more directly. This is related to the difference between virtue-ethical ideals and duty-ethical rules mentioned above. A general ideal of peacefulness will often fall into the first category, whereas political injunctions from a religious authority at some specific moment concerning some specific action will, at least at the moment in question, fall into the second category.

Regarding the first – the ideal that is strived for – we can sometimes see a tension developing between what the religious tradition would see as the best way to live in this world, on the one hand, and what actually happens in society, on the other; as, for instance, in the case of a religion preaching peacefulness and good will toward all yet engaging in, recommending, or at least accepting some acts of violence.

Arguably, to the extent that a religious tradition sees itself as *not* having much to say about the concrete dealings of politics – that is, its ideals are of another world or primarily meant as aspirations for the religious individual or community, not for political life – it may come to advance religious and ethical ideals sharply different from those that it directly or indirectly supports or accepts, politically speaking, faced with the exigencies of everyday life (including war). At one and the same time, then, a religion can be seen as extolling ideals that are in strong tension with political practices, while actually endorsing those very same political practices, if nothing else, because it has little to say about them yet seems willing to live with them. In some such cases, religion can function as a general motivator for the use of armed force – for instance, through the promotion of patriotism – even if what it says about violence and war is actually quite abstract or even in strong tension with the conduct of martial affairs.

On the other hand, we have instances where religion and religious texts clearly guide action directly, as when they express very concrete norms or laws about social and political life. In this case, there will normally be less of a tension between the religion's ultimate aims and ideals on the one hand and the practices it endorses with reference to its sacred texts on the other, the two presumably being in line with each other. If such a struggle nonetheless occurs (say, between seemingly pacific rules or texts on the one hand and injunctions to fight violently on the other), most likely one will either end up prioritizing texts that sanction the practices actually going on or come to criticize those practices and seek to change them in the light of other texts. In such cases, we are, of course, led back to the problem of interpretation.

Political Insider or Outsider

This leads to a related challenge – number seven on our list – namely, the tension between religion as tied to a political agenda and religion as not playing any official role in shaping politics. Here again, one and the same religious tradition may exhibit different traits at different times. Indeed, in traditions that are marked by a plurality of branches or confessions, history has sometimes shown that representatives of the differing branches have found themselves in competition with one another to attain recognition and support from the state or the people. Sometimes, one branch or confession may have political power and the other not, leading to strong tensions that become tied to or interpreted in light of religious differences. We should note that the meaning of the text(s) we are reading will often be better understood once we know what this particular relationship consists in – that is, whether the text came from a religious tradition (or a religious denomination or branch) that saw itself as political or apolitical – and also what the role of the author or editor of the text was vis-à-vis the political authorities of his or her time.

Atrocities

Finally, we come to one of the most perplexing questions that we confront in this volume: the ambivalent relationship between religion and the undertaking of what we would normally call atrocities. In some cases we find that in order for soldiers to commit manifestly brutal acts, the values of a religious faith are called upon and even used as a motivation, sometimes in a way that seems to overpower and set aside the actual moral guidelines espoused by the religion itself. In other cases, a political system may draw upon religious elements in order to "sacralize" its ideological cause, through attempts to justify all actions of extremity for the good of the nation or some other, higher cause. The "*Gott mit uns*" of German National Socialism chillingly comes to mind.

Yet as we struggle to comprehend historical events such as the Rape of Nanking and the Holocaust, events that have been analyzed by scholars in light of their complex relationships with Buddhist and Christian culture, respectively, we must endeavor to draw a line between the historical representation of a religious faith and the ideals that it espouses from within. Admitting that persons who identify themselves as religious have committed acts of great brutality, even believing that they have been so commanded by the tenets of their religion, is not the same as saying that these acts truly represent the tradition to which they appeal. Indeed, many such atrocities have been perpetrated by people and parties with no inner concern for religion or religious faith but who see great utility in aligning themselves with a religious tradition.

Conclusion

By bringing to light the tensions and challenges that we confront when reading and interpreting the religious texts found in this volume, it has been our ambition in this introduction to assist the reader in comprehending the complex inter-relationship between religion, war, and ethics. As we have seen, religions can be both defenders of peace and promoters of war, noble protectors of the weak and innocent, and motivators for brutal attacks in the name of God or gods, even against human beings who could not possibly know that they had done anything wrong or believed anything erroneously. By learning from these contrasting sides of religion, one may also learn to practice one's faith in ways that incline more toward peacefulness and legitimate, measured defense than brutality.

We have, on purpose, not given references to or examples from particular texts in this introduction. That would have brought us into the field of concrete interpretation and would have presented us with a great problem of fair representation. Furthermore, it could have constrained the reader in his or her reading of the texts. Nevertheless, the introduction has of course been written with the texts of this book clearly in mind. Hence, it will not be hard for the reader to recognize the challenges and questions we have identified above in the individual chapters and texts of the book.

We began this introduction from a cautionary perspective, emphasizing that the religious traditions and texts gathered within this volume are marked by their diversity. Yet if we delve more deeply into each religious tradition, we can arguably find at least one common thread between the mainstreams of these traditions: namely, that they profess a strong presumption against injustice and the accompanying understanding that, in some circumstances, action must be taken to defend human dignity. What constitutes injustice and how action should be taken are defined and understood differently, of course, yet these are common assumptions found across the traditions.

In the philosophy of religion, some scholars have professed that acknowledgment of a plurality of religious traditions has the potential to foster greater *in*tolerance. According to this argument, when plurality is openly embraced by some, it will seem to others that their own deeply held truths are by the same token diminished. Following such a line of reasoning,[3] it is inferred that competing sets of believers will press their exclusivist claims against each other. By contrast, it is hoped that, with a volume such as this, by opening ourselves to a greater understanding of other religious faiths, we will be more inclined to express not only humility with regard to articulating our own beliefs, even when they are steadfastly held, but also a greater appreciation and respect for the human dignity of those whose belief systems are unfamiliar to and different from our own.

NOTES

1 See Eric Voegelin, "Equivalences of Experience and Symbolization in History," in *Published Essays, 1966–1985*, Ellis Sandoz (ed.), vol. 12 of *The Collected Works of Eric Voegelin* (Baton Rouge: Louisiana State University Press, 1990), pp. 115–133.

2 See Paul Gordon Lauren, Gordon A. Craig, and Alexander L. George, *Force and Statecraft: Diplomatic Challenges for Our Time* (New York: Oxford University Press, 2007), pp. 252–255, for a succinct and heartfelt formulation of this very problem.

3 The contours of this argument are explored by Alvin Plantinga in "Pluralism: A Defense of Religious Exclusivism," in *The Philosophical Challenge of Religious Diversity*, Philip Quinn and Kevin Meeker (eds.) (New York: Oxford University Press, 2000), pp. 172–192.

1

Judaism

Adam Afterman and Gedaliah Afterman

Judaism, the oldest surviving monotheistic religion, traces its origins to the cultic practices and rites of ancient Israel. According to its scripture, the Tanakh, or Hebrew Bible, the nation of Israel consisted of descendants of the patriarch Abraham the Hebrew and was then led from bondage in Egypt to the land of Canaan by the prophet Moses to whom the Torah (Pentateuch), the Law, was revealed by God at Mount Sinai. Although relatively little is known about the development of its practices until 70 CE when the Second Temple in Jerusalem was destroyed by Rome, Ancient Judaism subsequently evolved into what is now known as Rabbinic Judaism whose oral and written traditions were eventually composed and redacted in the Mishnah (ca. 220 CE) and the Talmud (ca. 500 CE). The Tanakh, Mishnah, and Talmud remain the three core canonical texts of Jewish law, or halakhah, although they have been supplemented and enriched through the centuries by a wealth of later commentaries, codes, and legal compilations.

Introduction

The debate within Judaism regarding the ethics and conduct of war has always been a marginal one. Jewish attitudes toward issues of war in general and the ethics of war in particular were almost completely theoretical. The Jewish people, certainly since the second-century rebellion of Bar Kochba, were victims of war rather than agents of war. Without a state and an army, Jews, with a diaspora mentality, did not have the privilege or the need to articulate views on the ethics of war.[1] Indeed, discussions of this issue throughout the centuries have been almost purely theoretical and not prescriptive, usually introduced as part of rabbinical interpretation of Biblical law.

That normative reflection on war has taken the form of a theoretical typology rather than a practical effort can be deduced from the fact that, up until modern times, one can hardly find an attempt to develop a category of banned or forbidden war within the framework of Judaism.[2] The omission of a forbidden war category, however, should not lead one to conclude that the Rabbis denied the soundness of such a category, that is, that they were permitted all forms of warfare; this omission seems to result from the fact that Jews were unable to initiate wars, hence the ad hoc approach to this topic.[3]

Indeed, even the more theoretical discussions of war-related matters were not systematic, centering on one or two chapters from the *Book of Deuteronomy*. The Rabbis, with the exception of the medieval rabbinical authority Maimonides, did not attempt to reflect systematically on the subject in order to create a system of norms, but rather touched on this topic as part of their interest in the biblical laws.

As we will see, another motivation that led rabbinical authorities to debate matters related to war was their interest in the hypothetical (but politically important) question of relations between the monarch and the rabbinical institutions such as the Sanhedrin, the rabbinical Supreme Court that functioned also as a "Parliament." It is in this context that an effort was made to distinguish between a war commanded directly by God and executed by the king as a "holy war" and a political war initiated by the king to advance his own earthly interests. Rabbinical discussions were focused mainly on the circumstances under which a war could be considered a religious duty and much less on the actual conduct of such (or another kind of) war.

This state of affairs changed somewhat with the advent of Jewish nationalism and the establishment of the modern State of Israel. The emergence of Zionism, and with it the possibility of a Jewish state becoming more tangible, led some religious scholars to draw on the sporadic, theoretical, and hermeneutical debates of the previous two millennia of Jewish thought, in an attempt to establish more practical guidelines regarding war and its conduct. Other scholars, meanwhile, attempted to provide practical answers to concrete and specific dilemmas as they arose. Such efforts intensified with the founding of the State of Israel (1948) and the establishment of the Israel Defence Forces (IDF). These contemporary attempts to create a "Jewish" code, however, while interesting, are in no way complete nor are they authoritative. Some of these attempts should be seen as part of the traditional halakhic discourse, namely as an effort to provide an adequate response to the emerging circumstances. Other contemporary attempts undertaken by secular institutions, such as the IDF, while drawing on rabbinical sources, should not however be categorized as "Jewish halakhic texts" or as an integrated part of the Jewish halakhic tradition. In other words, a clear distinction should be made between the traditional Rabbinic halakhic discourses and the modern attempts by institutions of the State of Israel to create a code of ethics of war. While a multifaceted relationship exists in modern Israel between religion and state, it must be said that the state has an inherently secular character, as does its army.[4]

Some examples of the aforementioned contemporary attempts to establish a Jewish practical ethical code for the conduct of war are presented later in this chapter. However, in order to adequately understand the background as well as the issues faced by these contemporary thinkers in their ongoing efforts to transform a theoretical and limited debate into a practical ethical code, we first discuss some of the main and most influential traditional sources regarding these matters.

Discussions within Judaism regarding the conduct of war can be broadly divided into two categories. The first aspect of the debate focuses on the reasons or justifications for going to war, that is, the circumstances that allow, indeed at times compel, one to launch war (*jus ad bellum*). The second aspect of the debate outlines proper conduct of a war once it has commenced (*jus in bello*). As we will see, discussions regarding the more practical questions of *jus in bello* were first introduced in one section of the Book of Deuteronomy and revisited much later in modern times in response to new circumstances demanding a more practical approach to issues arising apropos of the conduct of war. The rabbinical discussions, meanwhile, have focused primarily on the *jus ad bellum*, differentiating between a religious or holy war commanded directly by God, and a "regular" political war.

This chapter is not intended to provide an analysis of war in Jewish apocalyptic texts or of metaphorical speech about war.[5] The aim is rather to survey only those debates focused on the normative dimensions of war. Conceptual discussions on the nature and interrelationship of war and peace, on Jewish discourses that employ "war" as a metaphor for internal or spiritual struggles, or commentaries regarding the subject of purity and war, as in Deuteronomy (23:10–15) accordingly fall outside the scope of this chapter.

The development of the conceptual debate regarding the ethics of war in Judaism has several defining stages: from the introduction of basic ethical guidelines for the conduct of war and the concept of divinely decreed wars in the Bible to the more complex discussions by the Rabbis in the first centuries CE, as well as debates in noncanonical texts such as the Temple Scroll and the exegesis of Philo. Discussions among medieval rabbinic authorities such as Rashi (Rabbi Shlomo Yitzhaki, 1040–1105), Maimonides (Rabbi Moshe ben Maimon, 1138–1204), and Nachmanides (Rabbi Moshe ben Nachman, 1194–1270), and their varying perceptions of norms of war, introduce yet another layer of interpretation. Modernity, the emergence of Jewish nationalism, and the establishment of the State of Israel instituted, for the first time, the need for a more practical debate.

When approaching the literature on this topic, one should remain cognizant of the fact that the discussions in question all refer to wars that either have occurred in the past (or mythical past) or will occur in some theoretical future.[6] These debates, therefore, as Michael Walzer has argued,[7] should be seen not as prescriptive or as outlining actual policy for conducting warfare nor, indeed, as an accurate description of the historical events in question, but rather as having an academic or hermeneutical role. It should be understood that at least part of the rabbinic enterprise was in the realm of rabbinic imagination, including detailed discussions of institutions and procedures that either no longer existed or never existed at all.

Likewise, discussions regarding the legal procedures of conducting war can be considered part of an imagined and perhaps utopian world. The rabbinical interpretations are focused mainly on the institution of monarchy and its functions, which included the initiation and conduct of war. This led the Rabbis to reflect on the procedures that might govern participation in war. Given that these rabbinical reflections were introduced after the destruction of the Second Temple and the shattering of Jewish sovereignty in the Holy Land, thus a time when no king or Sanhedrin existed, this discourse regarding war was part and parcel of the much wider phenomenon of rabbinical fantasy that characterizes many of their writings.

The lack of practical relevance of Jewish debates on the issue of war is even more striking when it comes to the debates that engaged Maimonides, the foremost twelfth-century rabbinical halakhic authority. Maimonides fled Andalusia as a child, seeking refuge in the Middle East and North Africa, and finally settling in Egypt where he became a leader of the community. Powerless in political terms, he experienced not only the destruction of Jewish communities in Spain but also the vulnerability and helplessness of the Jewish communities in Africa, especially Yemen.[8] Despite or perhaps as a result of his experience, Maimonides wrote extensively on the laws of war as part of his magisterial legal codification. Of a piece with an elaborate discussion of issues relating to the king and procedures of relevance to that institution, including the conduct of war, his presentation can be compared to his similarly unparalleled achievement in codifying the procedures of temple worship (more than a millennium after the destruction of the Second Temple).[9]

The pages that follow present a brief outline of some of the central themes introduced in each of these periods. The discussion concludes with an examination of the ways in which these classical debates have been used in modern attempts to provide practical advice regarding dilemmas arising from the conduct of war.

I

Biblical References

The Hebrew Bible includes a few short sections in which codes of war are discussed; these discussions, in turn, are divided into two categories.[10] The first is a code regarding a special type of war, commanded directly by God, targeting specific enemies. The second code concerns wars commanded not by God, but rather by a human authority engaged in a political war that is aimed at serving the authority's own interests. The Bible refrains from providing a special code for wars of defense and from introducing the category of forbidden war.

The first code of war, war commanded directly by God, concerns the conquering of the Promised Land as a religious duty. The People of Israel are commanded to launch a war of total extermination against the Seven Nations,[11] who occupied the Land of Israel.[12] While this concept is of interest to us historically and intellectually, it should be noted that the Bible itself casts doubt on whether this kind of total war actually took place.[13] Moreover, the Rabbis were quick to rule that the historic Seven Nations could no longer be identified,[14] thus eliminating any practical role for this decree in the future.[15]

A similar type of war was commanded by God against another ancient nation, Amalek. This commandment was not limited to a specific geographic locale, as it was stated that this nation should be annihilated wherever it may be found.[16] This extreme decree, we are told, is punishment for Amalek's terrible attacks against the People of Israel while they were fleeing from Egypt.[17] The totality of the religious duty to annihilate not only the Amalek nation but even the memory of the nation is demonstrated clearly in the story of King Saul, who failed to comply with this special norm of war, by sparing the life of the Amalekite king and the lives of their livestock. King Saul's hesitation to execute such extreme measures, not then part of the conventional practice of war, led to severe punishment, with Saul losing his throne to King David.[18] As in the case of the Seven Nations, the fact that Amalekites are no longer traceable has emptied this category of any practical relevance in modern times.[19]

The second biblical code of war applies to wars initiated against enemies other than the Seven Nations and Amalek. For this type of war, initiated by a political rather than a divine authority, a different code of behavior is stipulated. This code, articulated in Deuteronomy 20, is among the most detailed biblical discussions on norms of warfare. The text contains a detailed list of principles relating to behavior in times of war. The first section of chapter 20 presents a set of persons who should be exempt from conscription and participation in war. The list of exemptions includes the cowardly, those lacking faith in God, and those who have other commitments to keep, such as toward a wife, a new house, or the maintenance of a newly planted vineyard.[20]

The text then focuses on the conduct of war itself: any besieged city should be offered terms of peace. If this offer is rejected, the city's men are to be killed while the women and children are to be captured. The city is to be looted. Further details regarding the way in which women captives should be treated and issues relating to ceremonial purity are provided in following chapters.[21] The biblical concern for the need to avoid targeting the innocent is symbolically exemplified by the precept forbidding the destruction of besieged cities' fruit trees. The fighters are forbidden to destroy them, as they are defenseless in the face of the attacking force.[22]

The text distinguishes, however, between cases of normal war, to which the above principles apply, and the war commanded by God against the Seven Nations, which is to be conducted under much harsher terms.[23] The harsh treatment of the Seven Nations, however, is justified not solely by the fact that it was commanded directly by God; rather, God justifies this severe treatment by arguing that if not annihilated, they will defile the souls of the People of Israel through their practice of idolatry.[24] Thus, we learn that the religious war is aimed not only at conquering the Promised Land or maintaining its integrity, but also against idolatrous practices.

II

Pre-Rabbinical and Rabbinical Debates

Early attempts to explain the biblical text can be found in the writings of Philo; in the *Temple Scroll* (found among the *Dead Sea Scrolls*, a collection of approximately 900 documents including texts from the Hebrew Bible discovered between 1947 and 1956 in eleven caves near the Dead Sea); in the early Rabbinical commentary of Deuteronomy (also known as *Sifre*); as well as in the Mishnah and Talmud.

Philo (20 BCE–AD 50), known also as Philo of Alexandria, was a Hellenistic Jewish philosopher born in Alexandria who wrote extensive commentaries on Jewish law and the Torah in Greek. In his *On the Special Laws*, Philo presents his commentary of the biblical code. Philo ignores the special code of war conduct against Amalek and the Seven Nations. In Philo's view, the Deuteronomy code refers not to initiated wars of aggression but rather to warfare against an enemy that has "renounced its alliance" with the Nation of Israel. Philo argues that the biblical code is both rational and merciful, ensuring that war did not deteriorate into irrational and unnecessary bloodshed. The biblical code, he argues further, is proof of the peaceful nature of the People of Israel, who, while not seeking conflict, do not cower when faced with a savage enemy that fundamentally rejects peace.[25]

The *Temple Scroll* 11QT (11Q19–20), discovered in 1956 in cave 11 in Qumran, is a long scroll describing an idealized temple, yet it also contains some discussion of the issue of conduct during war.[26] The last section of the scroll analyzes the status of the king and his army. The scroll discusses the procedures for mobilization of the king's army when faced with a foreign military threat. Following from Deuteronomy, the scroll distinguishes between two codes of conduct in war: the first code, employed in wars initiated by the king against distant enemies beyond the borders, sanctions a procedure for allowing the enemy to surrender peacefully and regulates punitive action in cases where the offer has been denied. The second type of war is a "holy war" against the Seven Nations inhabiting the Promised Land – to which a special protocol of behavior is applied.

According to the Scroll, the war against the inhabiting nations is religiously justified because their life of idolatry may spiritually contaminate the spiritual integrity of the Israelites. A holy war of total extermination against these nations is, therefore, demanded. Such a war of extermination, however, is not sanctioned in the case of war against distant cities (where the justification is political and military rather than religious). Given that those cities do not threaten the religious integrity of the nation, the war against them is to be conducted under the "normal" code of war.

The Temple Scroll emphasizes that the criterion for distinguishing between a holy war and a regular war is the manner in which the enemy might affect not only the physical well-being of the People of Israel but, more important, their faith and religious behavior. Against near enemies, the battle is over a way of life and worship, marking the war a religious war. Against distant enemies, the war is over physical well-being, and as such the normal code of conduct of war is to be applied. The scroll also describes the procedure to be followed in distributing of the booty.[27] The Qumran texts include other discussions known as the "War Texts,"[28] but we consider these to be nonnormative, as they focus wholly on descriptions of apocalyptic war (thus falling outside the scope of this chapter, as indicated above).

The *Sifre*, which is an anthology of rabbinic Midrashic exegesis on the book of Deuteronomy, engages in characteristic word-by-word analysis of the biblical texts on war. The *Sifre* puts forward two new interpretations concerning the categories of religious and "permitted" wars. According to the *Sifre*, the focus of the religious war (or commanded war) against the inhabitants is not the military threat posed by those nations, but rather the religious threat posed by their idolatry. The *Sifre* adds a caveat, however, in arguing that if these nations were to agree to change their idolatrous ways and thereby desist from posing a spiritual threat to the People of Israel, there would no longer be justification for the radical measures of extreme war.

Based on the biblical code in Deuteronomy 20 that refers to the nonobligatory war, the *Sifre* substantially expands the list of exemptions from participation in an "optional" war. The Rabbis argue that the norms detailed in Deuteronomy 20 concerning the category of permitted war should be carried out only against true "enemies, who would not have mercy on you" and stress that such permitted war must be aimed at achieving peace not only as a political goal but also as a religious value. In contrast, the Rabbis maintain that when a religious war is declared, even "the bridegroom from his chamber and the bride from her bridal canopy" must participate in the war effort. We see then that the Rabbis espouse a dual attitude toward war: while demanding total commitment and, at times, extreme action in cases of religious war, they allow for much more freedom of choice when it comes to political wars.

The *Sifre* adds many details and qualifiers to the biblical code,[29] but its most significant contribution is the assertion that even in the case of the war on the inhabitants of the Promised Land – a religious war of extermination commanded by God – the nations in question are to be given an opportunity to repent, and thus to avoid death. The conclusion is that religious war is aimed not against the enemy's population but rather against the threat of idolatry.[30]

Rabbinical Discussions in the Mishnah and Talmud

The Rabbis of the Mishnah and Talmud interpret the biblical codes of war using halakhic categories of commanded and optional war. As we will see, the commanded war category is expanded to include wars not only against the Seven Nations and Amalek but also against other enemies in cases of self-defense or in wars aimed at preserving the geographical integrity of the Land of Israel. The second biblical code relates to permitted or optional war that is to be launched by a king, with the permission of the Sanhedrin, for political purposes.[31] Participation in these wars of choice was not considered to be a religious obligation. The Rabbis accordingly provided plenty of room for those uninterested in participation to be legally discharged. The fact that a war is merely "permitted" means that, from the religious point of view, there is no halakhic obligation to participate and, on the other hand, no halakhic prohibition – this kind of war is, in other words, halakhically neutral.

One may ask, How can a war be permitted or optional and at the same time be just?[32] The Rabbis were not part of a "just war" tradition. Instead, in line with the Hebrew Bible, their distinction between a permitted war and an "obligatory" war marks the contrast between wars mandated by God and wars mandated by human kings. Permitted war simply refers to a war initiated by the human king for his own purposes. By contrast, an obligatory war is one commanded by God and not by a human king. The difference between wars initiated and authorized by the heavenly king and by the earthly king is thus articulated in halakhic terms. That wars initiated by human kings are only permitted underscores the fact that the king cannot force people to fight his war using religious arguments; from the halakhic point of view, the war is optional. However, using his political authority, he can obligate the people to fight and contribute to the war effort.

To summarize, Mishnaic and Talmudic debates distinguish between three categories of war:

1. Obligatory war: a slightly expanded interpretation of a divinely commanded war of the Bible.
2. Optional war: a political war initiated by the king that is nevertheless to be authorized by the Sanhedrin, the authoritative religious council that existed presumably in the time of the Temple. In addition, this authorization requires the stamp of the

Urim ve Tumim, an oracle type device in the temple, transmitting God's will and approval. As the Bible does not show much faith in kings, the Rabbis made sure that under no circumstances could a king wage his own wars independently, that is, without the approval of the Rabbis and the priest. The point of the authorization by the Sanhedrin and by the *Urim ve Tumim* was not to provide religious or divine justification or authorization to the king's independently initiated wars, but just the opposite: approval by the Sanhedrin and *Urim ve Tumim* was meant to be a constraint by which the Rabbis hoped to prevent and control kings from going to war at all.

Participation in such a war is not a religious duty, and the Rabbis provided ample pretexts for those who cared not to participate.
3. Preventive war: a war of self-defense.

The Rabbis accepted the biblical category of obligatory war, while arguing that the main target of such a war, the Seven Nations, was no longer traceable. In addition, the Rabbis slightly expanded the category of Joshua's biblical conquest to include future defense of the Land of Israel. In other words, it seems that the Rabbis understood the concept of obligatory war as being closely related to the commandment of the conquest of the Land of Israel, rather than being focused on the no longer existent biblical Seven Nations. The concept of obligatory war was further developed by a rabbinical distinction between Joshua's war of conquest, which is unequivocally perceived as an obligatory war, and the later wars of expansion carried out by King David, which are described as merely permitted.[33] This interpretation of King David's wars seems to indicate that not every case of the conquest of the Land of Israel (or its neighboring lands) falls unequivocally under the category of religious obligatory war.

The Rabbis also added the category of "defensive" war to the earlier discussions. Such a war they classified under the category of obligatory war, on the reasoning that self-defense is itself a religious obligation. The Rabbis crystallized this religious principle in the famous saying "If someone comes to kill you, kill him first!"[34]

As in the case of the wars against the Seven Nations and Amalek, the rabbinical category of optional (permitted or political) war was, already at the time of development, without any practical relevance. While conceding that a political leader may be permitted to launch war under some circumstances, the Rabbis conditioned the initiation of such a war on the approval of the Sanhedrin. The requirement for the Sanhedrin to authorize the launching of war was designed presumably to counter misguided ambitions of political leaders striving for power and land. The fact, however, that both the Jewish Monarchy and the Sanhedrin were no longer in existence at the time of writing and, in addition, the procedure required seeking the oracle's approval using a device long lost, in a temple long destroyed, leads one to conclude that this too was no more than a theoretical category.

Medieval Halakhic Authorities: Maimonides

Rabbi Moses Maimonides is considered the greatest medieval Jewish philosopher and one of the most important halakhic authorities. He is best known for writing the magisterial *Mishneh Torah*, a fourteen-volume compendium of Jewish law; the first comprehensive commentary on the Mishnah; and the *Guide of the Perplexed*, the greatest medieval Jewish philosophical work. His codification of the law was very different from the Mishnah and the Talmud, as Maimonides aimed to present the reader with the "bottom line" codex of the law. To this end, he omitted much of the argumentation and the presentation of multiple legal (including minority and rejected) opinions characteristic of Talmudic discourse.

Maimonides was the first to codify the biblical and rabbinic discussion of norms of war into a halakhic code. But Maimonides' interpretation embodied a perspective different from that of his rabbinic predecessors. While the Bible and the Rabbis showed considerable reserve toward the monarch and his motivations, Maimonides celebrates the ideal motive of the righteous king when going to war. The king's "sole aim," Maimonides argues, "should be to uplift the true religion, to fill the world with righteousness ... and to fight the battles of the Lord."[35] Indeed, in his understanding of an ideal reality only commanded wars are permitted, as the wishes of God and those of the righteous king are identical. Transforming the king into a righteous agent allows Maimonides to reclassify the permitted war as a religious duty conditioned on its *telos*. Maimonides both conceptualizes and classifies war under his laws of the messianic age. So the king he is speaking of is a messianic ruler, of the Davidic line. Maimonides thinks of the king as a philosopher, yet at the same time the role of the philosopher-king is to spread truth and knowledge, especially knowledge of God. In that way the aspirations and wishes of God and of the king coincide because both of them have to do with truth and knowledge.[36]

While giving precedence to the commanded wars, Maimonides, who himself lived in exile, and was well aware of the constraints of reality, broadened the category of optional wars and changed the focus of the commanded wars. While adhering to the rabbinic trio – the wars against the Seven Nations, Amalek, and the war of self-defense (like the Rabbis, Maimonides argues that the first two entities can no longer be identified and therefore be targets of war) – Maimonides changed the focus from wars to conquer the Land of Israel, as argued by the Rabbis, to the war against idolatry.

On the conception introduced by Maimonides, warfare was transformed into a battle of mind and consciousness, rather than a battle for land and resources. Previously, the historical battles between the nation of Israel and its archetypal enemies had been centered on the Land of Israel, but after being exiled from the land, the focus shifted to the monotheistic truth, a truth that Israel's enemies were making every effort to deny and to undermine. Maimonides typology of war is part of his messianic vision, and as such he shifts the emphasis to an ideological war between truth (identified with monotheism) and polytheism (or any form of idol worship). Maimonides concluded accordingly that all the wars of Israel (even those initiated by a king) were religious wars by nature, and for that reason he contends that the battle of God executed by the righteous king ought to be fought between monotheism and idolatry.[37] This is further illuminated by Maimonides' perception of holiness. According to Maimonides, holiness is a nominal halakhic category and not an intrinsic quality.[38] He therefore argued that the Promised Land serves the purpose of creating a political entity that will be able to transmit and embody the monotheistic truth, but does not in itself have intrinsic "magical" or "mystical" qualities. Maimonides seems to consider war justified only when it is waged against idolatry specifically in the land of Israel because he is concerned to create a divine community in a particular locale; thus Maimonides' war against idolatry is not the universal *jihad* that we find in certain streams of Islam.

Nachmanides and the Land of Israel

This change in focus derives from Maimonides' perception that the obligation to fulfill the commandment of the settlement of the Land and the other commandments that are unique to the Land of Israel stems not from any intrinsic holiness of the land, but rather from the nominal halakhic category. The sanctity of the land, then, derives from the Jews' obligation to live as a Jewish society.[39] Put in a different way, Maimonides appears to deem the spiritual war against idolatry as more befitting "the battles of God" than the physical conquest of the Land of Israel.[40]

As we have seen, rabbinical interpretations shifted the focus of the commanded wars of the Bible and the annihilation of the Seven Nations to the fulfillment of the commandment of the conquest of the Land of Israel. This understanding, perhaps an expression of hope of a nation to return to its homeland, had become the accepted view in Judaism. Maimonides' contrasting interpretation, further amplified by his omission of the settling of the Land of Israel from the list of the commandments of Judaism, led another prominent scholar, Rabbi Moses Nachmanides, to confront him on this very point.

Moses Nachmanides, also known as Rabbi Moses ben Nachman Girondi (Gerona, 1194–Land of Israel, 1270), was the most important rabbinic authority of his time. A Catalan Rabbi and mystic, Nachmanides is best known for his biblical and Talmudic commentaries. Living after Maimonides, he was known to be one of his most important admirers and, at the same time, critic.

The concept of the Land of Israel played a central role in the theology of Nachmanides. Indeed, he perceived the laws relating to the Land of Israel as constituting the essence of the Torah.[41] According to him, settling the Land of Israel is an unambiguous commandment that can be practiced and performed even after the Destruction of the Temple.[42] Nachmanides criticized Maimonides for neglecting to include the commandment to settle the Land of Israel in his Book of Commandments that enumerates the commandments of the Torah.[43] Nachmanides argued that this was a definite commandment, not a mere promise or prophecy, and for this reason he asserted that "our sages termed [it] a holy war."[44]

Nachmanides goes on to argue, in contrast to Maimonides, that the commandment regarding the treatment of the Seven Nations who occupied the Land of Israel in the time of Joshua did not have merely symbolic value later; on the contrary, it represented an obligation that should be fulfilled by all succeeding generations.[45] Taking the rabbinical interpretation to its extreme, Nachmanides maintained that the unique holiness of the Land of Israel and the importance of the commandment to settle it make the conquering of the Land of Israel, and, if necessary, annihilation of its occupants, an eternal commandment. Moreover, Nachmanides believed that some of the inhabitants of the Land would engage in a continuous fight with the People of Israel, thus evoking presumably the need for the People of Israel to defend themselves – a commanded war by all accounts.[46]

III

Contemporary Texts

The emergence of Zionism and the establishment of the State of Israel provided a further theological challenge to religious scholars, who thereby attempted to put the new reality in halakhic context. Broadly speaking, attitudes among Orthodox Jews toward the Zionist ideology and the establishment of a secular state can be divided into two. The majority view led by the ultra-Orthodox community was vehemently opposed to Zionism and the establishment of a Jewish state.

According to this conservative, "passive" view, Jewish sovereignty can be established only as part of an all-encompassing messianic process of redemption. This view holds that redemption is exclusively in the realm of the divine, and humans should not interfere or hasten that process by re-establishing a Jewish sovereign state in the Holy Land. Such acts are seen as a blatant interference in the messianic process.[47] Thus, Jews should not use active power or build institutions of organized power even for self-defense; they should instead rely on God's providence.

Other Orthodox held a more pragmatic view, believing that the process of redemption was a gradual process that advanced slowly toward the end goal of salvation. According to this view, the process of redemption commenced with the establishment of the State of Israel, despite its secular nature. Serving and advancing the state is therefore a religious duty that directly influences the process of redemption.

These fundamentally differing theological approaches are also of significance to our discussion of the ethics of war in Judaism. This new reality also brought with it more practical halakhic debates as well as calls – and some attempts – to develop a code of ethics for the conduct of war. These discussions, however, were conducted by individual Rabbis with varying levels of authority, both within their respective communities and more broadly.

While modern debates on the issue of norms of war can be divided into a number of groups, it appears that all streams of thought share one basic assumption: halakhic debates throughout the centuries regarding the norms of war, while insightful, do not provide adequate guidance for practical implementation.[48] They differ, however, in the conclusions they each derive from this assumption.

According to the conservative, ultra-Orthodox position, the fact that norms of war do not exist in the halakhic debate in Judaism signifies that Jews should not be involved in nor initiate war until the time of redemption, when Jewish sovereignty is reinstalled by God. Given the lack of halakhic guidance on this matter, proponents of this view argue that the Jewish people should not initiate any acts of war and, by extension, not establish institutions capable of waging war (such as an army or a state) until the time of redemption.

The two other approaches found among modern thinkers can be termed "exclusive" and "inclusive." Those advocating an exclusive approach argue that the establishment of the State of Israel calls for the development of new halakhic categories, including those relating to the norms of war, in order to provide answers to the emerging reality of Jewish sovereignty. Scholars such as Shlomo Goren and Yishayahu Leibowitz argue that this process of development and interpretation should be done from within, and on the basis of, the existent halakhic debates. This ethical construct, they argue, should be distinctly and exclusively "Jewish." In his capacity as chief Military Rabbi of the IDF for twenty years, and subsequently as Israel's chief Rabbi, Schlomo Goren sought to establish a halakhic code for the operation of the IDF, which would cover normative issues arising in warfare.

The inclusive approach, led by Rabbi Shaul Yisraeli, a leading rabbi in the Religious Zionist movement,[49] understood the lack of a developed normative doctrine on war within Judaism to suggest that this area should be dealt with in accordance with internationally accepted norms. Using the halakhic concept of *dina de malchutah dina* (the law of the king is your law), Rabbi Yisraeli argued that this widely accepted principle, usually applied to Jewish communities in the Diaspora, not only applied to individual Jews, but, regarding the conduct of war, should apply to the Jewish state as well. Thus instead of developing norms of warfare from within Jewish law, he maintained that the State of Israel should adopt standards of warfare that are derived from customary conventions and international law.

Both theoretical approaches were used by rabbis when analyzing military events and issues related to proper ethical conduct in war. Recently, there have been fewer ambitious attempts to provide halakhic solutions to dilemmas arising from events such as the first Palestinian *intifada* and other ethically challenging events. As we have mentioned previously, however, such modern debates should be seen as part of the internal halakhic debate conducted by individual rabbis, with very limited influence on the actual practical conduct of war. It is telling that the IDF ethical code was authored not by rabbis but rather by internationally recognized ethicists. While not clashing with the "Jewish tradition" (which it cites as one of its sources), it is clearly more influenced by Western norms and discussions than the texts of Deuteronomy, Maimonides, and Nachmanides.

IV

Classical Sources

From: Hebrew Bible (JPS 1917), Translation from the New King James Version (NKJV)

Exodus 17:8–16. Now Amalek came and fought with Israel in Rephidim. And Moses said to Joshua, "Choose us some men and go out, fight with Amalek. Tomorrow I will stand on the top of the hill with the rod of God in my hand." So Joshua did as Moses said to him, and fought with Amalek. And Moses, Aaron, and Hur went up to the top of the hill. And so it was, when Moses held up his hand, that Israel prevailed; and when he let down his hand, Amalek prevailed. But Moses' hands became heavy; so they took a stone and put it under him, and he sat on it. And Aaron and Hur supported his hands, one on one side, and the other on the other side; and his hands were steady until the going down of the sun. So Joshua defeated Amalek and his people with the edge of the sword. Then the Lord said to Moses, "Write this for a memorial in the book and recount it in the hearing of Joshua, that I will utterly blot out the remembrance of Amalek from under heaven." And Moses built an altar and called its name, The-Lord-Is-My-Banner; for he said, "Because the Lord has sworn: the Lord will have war with Amalek from generation to generation."

Deuteronomy 20:1–15. When you go out to battle against your enemies, and see horses and chariots and people more numerous than you, do not be afraid of them; for the Lord your God is with you, would brought you up from the land of Egypt. So it shall be, when you are on the verge of battle, that the priest shall approach and speak to the people. And he shall say to them, "Hear, O Israel: Today you are on the verge of battle with your enemies. Do not let your heart faint, do not be afraid, and do not tremble or be terrified because of them; for the Lord your God is He who goes with you, to fight for you against your enemies, to save you." The officers shall speak to the people, saying: "What man is there who has built a new house and has not dedicated it? Let him go and return to his house, lest he die in the battle and another man dedicate it. Also what man is there who has planted a vineyard, and has not eaten of it? Let him go and return to his house, lest he die in the battle and another man eat of it. And what man is there who is betrothed to a woman and has not married her? Let him go and return to his house, lest he die in the battle and another man marry her."

The officers shall speak further to the people, and say, "What man is there who is fearful and fainthearted? Let him go and return to his house, lest the heart of his brethren faint like his heart." And so it shall be, when the officers have finished speaking to the people, that they shall make captains of the armies to lead the people.

When you go near a city to fight against it, then proclaim an offer of peace to it. And it shall be that if they accept your offer of peace, and open to you, then all the people who are found in it shall be placed under tribute to you, and serve you. Now if the city will not make peace with you, but war against you, then you shall besiege it. And when the Lord your God delivers it into your hands, you shall strike every male in it with the edge of the sword. But the women, the little ones, the livestock, and all that is in the city, all its spoil, you shall plunder for yourself; and you shall eat the enemies' plunder which the Lord your God gives you. Thus you shall do to all the cities which are very far from you, which are not of the cities of these nations.

Deuteronomy 20:16–20. But of the cities of these peoples which the Lord your God gives you as an inheritance, you shall let nothing that breathes remain alive, but you shall utterly destroy them: the Hittite and the Amorite and the Canaanite and the Perizzite and the Hivite and the Jebusite, just as the Lord your God has commanded you, lest they teach you to do according to all their abominations which they have done for their gods, and you sin against the Lord your God. When you besiege a city for a long time, while making war against it to take it, you shall not destroy its trees by wielding an ax against them; if you can eat of them, do not cut them down to use in the siege, for the tree of the field is man's food. Only the trees which you know are not trees for food you may destroy and cut down, to build seigeworks against the city that makes war with you, until it is subdued.

Deuteronomy 21:10–14. When you go out to war against your enemies, and the Lord your God delivers them into your hand, and you take them captive, and you see among the captives a beautiful woman, and desire her and would take her for your wife, then you shall bring her home to your house, and she shall shave her head and trim her nails. She shall put off the clothes of her captivity, remain in your house, and mourn her father and her mother a full month; after that you may go in to her and be her husband, and she shall be your wife. And it shall be, if you have no delight in her, then you shall set her free, but you certainly shall not sell her for money; you shall not treat her brutally, because you have humbled her.

Deuteronomy 23:9–14. When the army goes out against your enemies, then keep yourself from every wicked thing. If there is any man among you who becomes unclean by some occurrence in the night, then he shall go outside the camp; he shall not come inside the camp. But it shall be, when evening comes, that he shall wash with water; and when the sun sets, he may come into the camp. Also you shall have a place outside the camp, where you may go out; and you shall have an implement among your equipment, and when you sit down outside, you shall dig with it and turn and cover your refuse. For the Lord your God walks in the midst of your camp, to deliver you and give your enemies over to you; therefore your camp shall be holy, that He may see no unclean thing among you, and turn away from you.

Deuteronomy 25:17–19. Remember what Amalek did to you on the way as you were coming out of Egypt, how he met you on the way and attacked your rear ranks, all the stragglers at your rear, when you were tired and weary; and he did not fear God. Therefore it shall be, when the Lord your God has given you rest from your enemies all around, in the land which the Lord your God is giving you to possess as an inheritance, that you will blot out the remembrance of Amalek from under heaven. You shall not forget.

Isaiah 2:1–4. The word that Isaiah the son of Amoz saw concerning Judah and Jerusalem. Now it shall come to pass in the latter days That the mountain of the Lord's house Shall be established on the top of the mountains. And shall be exalted above the hills; And all nations shall flow to it. Many people shall come and say, "Come, and let us go up to the mountain of the Lord, To the house of the God of Jacob; He will teach us His ways, And we shall walk in His paths." For out of Zion shall go forth the law, And the word of the Lord from Jerusalem. He shall judge between the nations, And rebuke many people; They shall beat their swords into plowshares, And their spears into pruning hooks; Nation shall not lift up sword against nation, Neither shall they learn war anymore.

Book of Maccabees (ca. 100 BC)[50]

From: Maccabees I, 2:29–41[51]

Then many that sought after judgment, and justice, went down into the desert, and they abode there, they and their children, and their wives, and their cattle: because afflictions increased upon them. And it was told to the king's men, and to the army that was in Jerusalem in the city of David, that certain men who had broken the king's commandment, were gone away into the secret places in the wilderness, and that many had gone after them. And forthwith they went out toward them, and made war against them on the Sabbath day. And they said to them: Do you still resist? Come forth, and do according to the edict of King Antiochus, and you shall live. And they said: We will not come forth, neither will we obey the king's edict, to profane the Sabbath day. And they made haste to give them battle. But they answered them not, neither did they cast a stone at them, nor stopped up the secret places, saying: Let us all die in our innocency: and heaven and earth shall be witnesses for us, that you put us to death wrongfully. So they gave them battle on the Sabbath: and they were slain, with their wives and their children, and their cattle, to the number of a thousand persons. And Mathathias and his friends heard of it, and they mourned for them exceedingly. And every man said to his neighbor: If we shall all do as our brethren have done, and not fight against the heathens for our lives, and our justifications, they will now quickly root us out of the earth. And they determined in that day, saying: Whosoever shall come up against us to fight on the Sabbath day, we will fight against him: and we will not all die, as our brethren that were slain in the secret places.

Philo of Alexandria (20 BCE–AD 50)[52]

From: Philo, *On the Special Laws*, IV 4:219–229[53]

XLI. These laws he gives to each single person but there are other more general commands which he addresses to the whole nation in common, advising them how to behave not only to friends and allies but also to those who renounce their alliance. For if these revolt, he tells us, and shut themselves up within their walls your well-armed fighting force should advance with its armaments and encamp around them, then wait for a time, not letting anger have free play at the expense of reason, in order that they may take in hand what they have to do in a firmer and steadier spirit. They must therefore at once send heralds to propose terms of agreement and at the same time point out the military efficiency of the besieging power. And if their opponents repent of their rebellious conduct and give way and show an inclination to peace, the others must accept and welcome the treaty, for peace, even if it involves great sacrifices, is more advantageous than war. But if the adversaries persist in their rashness to the point of madness, they must proceed to the attack invigorated by enthusiasm and having in the justice of their cause an invincible ally. They will plant their engines to command the walls.

And when they have made breaches in some parts of the walls, they will pour in altogether and with well-aimed volleys of javelins and with swords which deal death all around them they will wreak their vengeance without stint, doing to their enemies as the enemies would have done to them, until they have laid the whole opposing army low in a general slaughter. Then after taking the silver and gold and the rest of the spoil they must set fire to the city and burn it up, in order that the same city may not after a breathing space rise up and renew its sedition, and also to intimidate and so admonish the neighboring peoples, for men learn to behave wisely from the sufferings of others.

But they must spare the women, married and unmarried, since these do not expect to experience at their hands any of the shocks of war as in virtue of their natural weakness they have the privilege of exemption from war service. All this shows clearly that the Jewish nation is ready for agreement and friendship with all like-minded nations whose intentions are peaceful, yet is not of the contemptible kind which surrenders through cowardice to wrongful aggression. When it takes up arms it distinguishes between those whose life is one of hostility and the reverse. For to breathe slaughter against all, even those who have done very little or nothing amiss, shows what I should call a savage and brutal soul, and the same may be said of counting women, whose life is naturally peaceful and domestic, to be accessories to men who have brought about the war.

Indeed so great a love for justice does the law instill into those who live under its constitution that it does not even permit the fertile soil of a hostile city to be outraged by devastation or by cutting down trees to destroy the fruits. "For why," it says, "do you bear a grudge against things which though lifeless are kindly in nature and produce kindly fruits?" Does a tree, I ask you, show ill will to the human enemy that it should be pulled up roots and all, to punish it for ill which it has done or is ready to do to you? On the contrary it benefits you by providing the victors with abundance both of necessaries and of the comforts which ensure a life of luxury. For not only men but plants also pay tributes to their lords as the seasons come round, and theirs are the more profitable since without them life is impossible. But as to the trees which have never had or have lost the power to bear fruit and all the wild type there should be no stinting in cutting them down at will for siege works and stakes and pales for entrenchment and when necessary for constructing ladders and wooden towers. For these and similar purposes will be a fitting use to which to put them."

The Dead Sea Scrolls (150 BCE–70 CE)[54]

From: *The Temple Scroll*[55]

Col. LVII: 1–21. And this is the law of the priests. On the day when they proclaim [him] king, [they shall muster] the children of Israel, from twenty years old to sixty years old, according to their banners. And [they] shall appoint at their head chiefs of thousands, chiefs of hundreds, chiefs of fifties and chiefs of tens in all their cities. And [the chief] shall select for himself a thousand of them, a thousand from each tribe, to be with him: twelve thousand men of war who shall not leave him alone and will be seized by the hands of the nations. And all the selected whom he has selected, shall be men of truth, God-fearers, enemies of bribery, skilled men in war; and they shall continuously be with him, day and night, and they shall guard him from every act of sin and from the foreign nations so that he does not fall into their hands. And twelve princes of his people shall be with him, and twelve priests and twelve levites, who shall sit together with him for judgment and for the law. And he shall not rise his heart above them nor shall he do anything in all his councils outside of them.

And he shall not take a wife from among all the daughters of the nations, but instead take for himself a wife from his father's house from his father's family. And he shall take no other wife in addition to her for she alone will be with him all the days of her life. And if she dies, he shall take for himself another from his father's house, from his family. And he shall not pervert justice, and he shall not accept a bribe to pervert righteous judgment. And he shall not crave a field, a vineyard, any wealth, a house or any valuable thing in Israel and seize their men.

Col. LXI: 13–LXII: 13–15. When you go out to war against your enemies, and you see horses and chariots and a people more numerous than you, do not be afraid of them, because I, he who made you come up from the land of Egypt, am with you. And when you advance to battle, the priest shall come forward and he will speak to the people and shall say to them: "Listen, Israel, you are approaching [the enemy]."

Col. LXII: 1–16, 9–15. . . .[A]gain the judges . . . shall speak to the people and . . . say: "Who is a coward and feeble of heart? He should go and return to his house, lest he weaken the heart of his brother like his own heart."

And when the judges have finished speaking to the people, they shall appoint military commanders at the head of the people.

When you approach a city to fight against it, you shall offer it peace; if it answers you with peace and opens up to you, all the people that are in it shall be tributaries to you and shall serve you; however, if it does not make peace with you and makes war against you, you shall besiege it; and I shall put it into your hand. And you shall put its males to the sword; but the women, the children, the flocks and all that there is in the city, all its booty, you shall capture for yourself and / you/ shall consume the booty of your enemies whom I deliver to you. Thus shall you act with the cities which are very far from you. . . . However, from the cities of the peoples which I grant to you as inheritance, you shall not leave alive anything that breathes, because you must carry out the ban of extermination against the Hittites, the Amorites and the Canaanites, the Hivites and the Jebusites and the Gergasites and the Perizzites, as I have commanded you, so that they do not teach you to do in accordance with all the abominations which they do for their gods.

When you go ... to war against your enemies and I place them in your hands, and you make prisoners, and you see among the prisoners a woman of beautiful appearance, and you desire her, and you take her as a wife for yourself, you shall bring her into your house, and shave her head and cut her nail/s/, and you shall remove the prisoner's clothes from her. And she will live in your house, and she will weep for her father and her mother a full month. Afterwards you shall enter her, /and/ marry her, and she will become your wife. But she may not touch your purities for seven years, nor may she eat the peace offering until seven years pass; afterwards she may eat.

Sifre: A Tannaitic Commentary on the Book of Deuteronomy[56]
From: *Sifre*: Sections 190, 192, 194, 198–200[57]

Section 190

R. Jose the Galilean says: Whence do we learn that a man should not go forth to war unless he has arms, legs, eyes, and teeth? From the verse, *And thine eye shall not pity: life for life, (eye for eye, tooth for tooth, hand for hand, foot for foot,) when thou goest forth to battle* (19:21–20:1). [R. Judah said: To what kind of war does this apply? To a war prescribed by a commandment; in a defensive war, everyone must go forth, even the groom from his bridal chamber and the bride from her bridal canopy.

(*Horse and chariot*) (20:1): When Israel does God's will, all the nations become as one horse before them, as it is said, *The horse and his rider hath he thrown into the sea* (Exod. 15:1) – was there only one horse there?, etc.]

When thou goest forth to battle against thine enemies (20:1): This refers to a non-obligatory war. *Against thine enemies* – you are fighting against your own enemies.

And seest horse and chariot (and many people) (20:1): Just as these go out against you with horse and chariot, so shall you go out against them with horse and chariot; just as they go out against you with many people, so shall you go out against them with many people.

Thou shalt not be afraid of them; for the Lord thy God is with thee, who brought thee out of the land of Egypt (20:1): He who had brought you out of the land of Egypt is with you in time of trouble.

Section 192

What man is there that is fearful and faint-hearted (20:8): *And the officers shall speaker further* (20:8): Why were all these matters spoken of? So that the cities of Israel should not become desolate; so taught R. Johanan ben Zakkai. Come and see how considerate God is for the honor of His creatures, even such as are fearful and faint-hearted, so that when such a person returns, the others would say,

"Perhaps he left to build a house, or to plant a vineyard, or to wed a wife." Other absentees had to present valid proof, but not the fearful and faint-hearted, in whose case the proof is self-evident: he heard the crashing of shields and was terrified, he heard the neighing of horses and trembled, he heard the piercing sound of trumpets and was frightened, he saw the unsheathing of swords and water ran down between his knees. Another interpretation: *And shall say unto them: Hear, O Israel, ye draw nigh this day unto battle against your enemies* (20:3): Not against your brothers – not Judah against Simeon nor Simeon against Judah – for if you fall into their hands, they will have mercy on you, as witness (the case of Benjamin), of whom it is said, *And they said: "O Lord, the God of Israel, why is this come to pass in Israel, (that there should be today one Tribe lacking in Israel?"* (Judg. 21:3), whereupon they restored the Tribe (of Benjamin), to its former place, and not as in the matter of which it is said, *And the children of Israel carried away captive of their brethren two hundred thousand women, sons, and daughters, and took also away much spoil from them, and brought the spoil to Samaria. But a prophet of the Lord was there, whose name was Oded; and he went out to meet the host that came to Samaria, and said unto them: "Behold, because the Lord, the God of your fathers, was wroth with Judah, He hath delivered them into your hand, and ye have slain them in a rage which hath reached up unto heaven. And now ye purpose to bring the children of Judah and Jerusalem (into subjection for bondmen and bondwomen unto you; but are there not even with you acts of guilt of your own against the Lord your God?) Now hear me therefore, and send back the captives that ye have taken captive of your brethren"* (2 Chron. 28:8–11). And it is said further, *And the men that have been mentioned by name rose up, and took the captives, and with the spoil clothed all that were naked among them, and arrayed them, and shod them, and gave them to eat and to drink, and anointed them, and carried all the feeble of them upon asses, and brought them to Jericho, the city of palm trees, unto their brethren; then they returned to Samaria* (2 Chron. 28:15). You are now going against your enemies, who, should you fall into their hands, will have no mercy on you.

Let not your heart faint; fear not, nor be alarmed, neither be ye affrighted at them (20:3): *Let not your heart faint* at the neighing of their horses, *fear not* the crashing of their shields and the tramp of their nail-studded shoes, *nor be alarmed* at the sound of the trumpets, *neither be ye affrighted* at the sound of their shouting. This refers to the four methods used by the nations of the world (to frighten their enemies): crashing (shields), trumpeting, shouting (battle cries), and stamping (their heavy shoes).

For the Lord your God is He that goeth with you (20:4): The enemies come (trusting) in the triumph of flesh and blood, but you come (trusting) in the triumph of the Omnipresent One.

Section 194

What man is there that hath built (a new house) (20:5): This obviously refers only to one who has built it. Whence do we learn that this applies also to one who has inherited a house, or purchased it, or was given it as a gift? From the expression, *What man is there that hath built*.

A house: This obviously means only a dwelling house. Whence do we learn that this includes also a hut for straw, a barn for cattle, a shed for wood, or a store-house? From the phrase *that hath built*. One might think that this includes also one who has built a gatehouse, an exedra, or a balcony; therefore the verse uses the term *house* – "house" is generally understood as a dwelling place, hence places that are not suitable for dwelling are excluded.

And hath not dedicated it – thus excluding one who has acquired it by robbery – *let him go and return to his house* – let him go and listen to the priest of the armies of battle, and then return home – *lest he die in the battle* – if he does not obey the words of the priest, he will in the end die in battle – *and another man dedicate it* (20:5) – one might think that this refers to his uncle or his cousin; but Scripture says here *another* and says elsewhere *another* (28:30): just as *another* there refers to a stranger, so does *another* here refer to a stranger.

Section 198

And it shall be, when the officers have made an end (20:9): The officers should post guards in front of them and behind them with iron axes in their hands, and if anyone tries to return, they are permitted to smite them sorely on the thigh, for flight is the beginning of defeat, as it is said, *Israel is fled before the Philistines, and there hath been also a great slaughter among the people* (I Sam. 4:17). When does this apply? In the case of a non-obligatory war. In the case of an obligatory war, everyone must go forth (to battle), even the bridegroom from his chamber and the bride from her bridal canopy.

Section 199

When thou drawest nigh unto a city – Scripture speaks here of a non-obligatory war – *unto a city* – not to a metropolis, nor to a village – *to fight against it* – not to reduce it through lack of food or water, nor to slay its inhabitants through disease – *then proclaim peace unto it* (20:10) – great is peace, for even the dead require peace. Great is peace, for even in their war Israel requires peace. Great is peace, for even those who dwell on high require peace, as it is said, *He maketh peace in His high places* (Job 25:2). Great is peace, for the priestly blessing concludes with it. And even Moses was a lover of peace, as it is said, *And I sent messengers out of the wilderness of Kedemoth unto Sihon king of Heshbon with words of peace* (2:26).

Section 200

And it shall be, if it make thee answer of peace (20:11): One might think that this applies even when only some of the inhabitants (make answer of peace);

therefore the verse goes on to say, *and open unto thee* – meaning the entire city does so, and not only some of its inhabitants.

(Then it shall be) that all the people that were found therein – including the Canaanites that are within – *shall become tributary unto thee, and shall serve thee* (20:11): If they say, "We are willing to pay tribute to you but not to serve you," or "We will serve you but not pay tribute to you," they are not to be heeded. They must accept both conditions.

And if it will make no peace with thee, but will make war against thee – Scripture informs you that if it will not make peace with you, it will eventually make war against you – *then thou shalt besiege it* (20:12) – even by reducing it through lack of food or water or by slaying its inhabitants through disease.

And when the Lord thy God delivereth it into thy hand – if you do everything that is prescribed in this matter. . . .

Tosefta (220 CE)[58]

From: *Tosefta, Tractate Erubin* Chapter 3:5–8[59]

A. Gentiles who came against Israelite towns [cf. M. Erub. 4:1A] – they go forth to do battle against them carrying weapons,

B. and they violate the prohibitions of the Sabbath on their account.

C. Under what circumstances?

D. When they came for blood.

E. But if they did not come for blood,

F. they do not go forth against them carrying weapons, and they do not violate the prohibitions of the Sabbath on their account.

G. [If, however,] they came against towns located near the frontier, even to grab straw, even to grab a loaf of bread,

H. they go forth against them carrying weapons, and they violate the prohibitions of the Sabbath on their account.

3:6 A. At first they would leave their weapons in the house nearest the wall.

B. One time they ran about and were in haste to grab their weapons, and they ended up killing one another.

C. They made an ordinance that each one should go home [to get his weapon].

3:7 A. A detachment which goes out to fight an optional war does not besiege a gentile town less than three days before the Sabbath.

B. But if they began the siege, even on the Sabbath they do not interrupt it.

C. And thus did Shammai the Elder expound, "[That you may build siege works against the city that makes war with you,] until it falls (Deut. 20:20) – even on the Sabbath."

3:8   A.   A town which gentiles besieged,

    B.   or a river,

    C.   and so too, a ship sinking at sea,

    D.   and so an individual who was running away from gentiles or from thugs or from an even spirit –

    E.   lo, these sorts of people should violate the prohibitions of the Sabbath,

    F.   and save themselves.

From: *Tosefta, Tractate Sotah* Chapter 7:18–24[60]

7:18 A.   R. Judah b. Laqish says, "There were two arks, one which went out with them to battle, and one which stayed with them in the camp.

    B.   "In the one which went out with them to battle there was a scroll of the Torah, as it is said, *And the ark of the covenant of the Lord went before them three days' journey* (Num. 10:33).

    C.   "And this one which stayed with them in the camp, this is the one in which were the tablets and the sherds of the tablets, as it is said, *Neither the ark of the covenant of the Lord nor Moses departed out of the camp* (Num. 14:44)" [cf. M Sot. 8:1R-S].

    D.   Two times does he go out and talk with them, once on the boundary [before invading the enemy's territory] and once on the battlefield.

    E.   On the boundary what does he say? "Hear the words of the priest['s war-regulations] and return [home]."

    F.   On the battlefield what does he say? *What man is there that has built a new house and has not dedicated it?* (Deut. 20:5)

    G.   [If] his house fell down and he built it up again, lo, this one goes home.

    H.   R. Judah says, "If he did something new in connection with the house, he goes home, but if not, he does not go home" [cf. M. Sot. 8:3G].

    I.   R. Eliezer says, "The men of the Sharon did not go home to their houses, because they do something new to their houses once in every seven years" [M. Sot. 8:3H].

    J.   *And what man is there that has planted a vineyard and has not enjoyed its fruit? Let him go back to his house, lest he die in the battle and another man enjoy its fruit* (Deut. 20:6).

    K.   All the same are the one who plants a vineyard and the one who plants five fruit-trees of five different kinds, even in five distinct rows – lo, such a one goes home [M. Sot. 8:2E-F]. L. R. Eliezer b. Jacob says, "I find implied in this Scripture only one who has planted a vineyard."

7:19 A.   *And what man is there that had betrothed a wife and has not taken her? Let him go back to his house, lest he dies in the battle and another man takes her* (Deut. 29:7).

    B. All the same is he who betrothed and he who enters into Levirate mar-
riage, and even if there is a woman awaiting Levirate marriage with one
of five brothers,

    C. and even if there are five brothers who heard that their brother has died
in battle, all of them return and come home [M. Sot. 8:2J-K].

7:20 A. I know only that the law applies to one who builds his house but has not
dedicated it, planted a vineyard but has not eaten the fruit, betrothed a
wife but has not taken her.

Mishnah (ca. 220 CE)[61]

From: Mishnah, *Tractate Sotah*: Chapter 8[62]

8.   1. When the Anointed for Battle[63] speaks unto the people he speaks in the
Holy Language, for it is written, *And it shall be when ye draw nigh unto the battle,
that the priest shall approach* (this is the priest anointed for the battle) *and shall
speak unto the people* (in the Holy Language), *and shall say unto them, Hear, O
Israel, ye draw nigh unto battle this day against your enemies* – and not against
your brethren, not Judah against Simeon, and not Simeon against Benjamin, for
if ye fall into their hands they will have mercy upon you, for it is written, *And the
men which have been expressed by name rose up and took the captives and with
the spoil clothed all that were naked among them, and arrayed them and shod
them and gave them to eat and to drink and anointed them and carried all the
feeble of them upon asses and brought them to Jericho, the city of palm trees,
unto their brethren: then they returned to Samaria.* Against your enemies do ye
go, therefore if ye fall into their hands they will not have mercy upon you. *Let not
your heart be faint, fear not nor tremble, neither be ye affrighted.... Let not your
heart be faint* at the neighing of the horses and the flashing of the swords; *fear
not* at the clashing of shields and the rushing of the tramping shoes; *nor tremble*
at the sound of the trumpets, *neither be ye affrighted* at the sound of the shouting; *for the Lord your God is he that goeth with you.* They come in the strength of
flesh and blood, but ye come in the strength of the Almighty. The Philistines came
in the strength of Goliath. What was his end? In the end he fell by the sword and
they fell with him. But not so are ye, *for the Lord your God is he that goeth with
you, to fight for you....* This is the Camp of the Ark.

2. *And the officers shall speak unto the people, saying, What man is there that
hath built a new house and hath not dedicated it, let him go and return to his
house....* It is all one whether he builds a house for straw, a house for cattle, a
house for wood, or a house for stores; it is all one whether he builds or buys or
inherits [a house] or whether it is given [to] him as a gift. *And what man is there
that hath planted a vineyard and hath not used the fruit thereof....* It is all one
whether he plants a vineyard or plants five fruit-trees, even if they are of five kinds.

It is all one whether he plants vines or sinks them into the ground or grafts them; it is all one whether he buys a vineyard or inherits it or whether it is given [to] him as a gift. *And what man is there that hath betrothed a wife.* . . . It is all one whether he betrothed a virgin or a widow, or even one that awaits levirate marriage,* or whether he hears that his brother has died in battle – let him return home. These all hearken to the words of the priest concerning the ordinances of battle; and they return home and provide water and food and repair the roads.

3. And these are they that may not return: he that builds a gate-house or portico or gallery, or plants but four fruit-trees, or five trees that do not bear fruit; or he that takes back his divorced wife; or a High Priest that marries a widow, or a common priest that marries a woman that was divorced or that performed *halitzah*,† or an Israelite that marries a bastard or a *Nethinah*,‡ or a bastard or a *Nathin* that marries the daughter of an Israelite – these may not return. R. Judah says: He also that rebuilds his house as it was before may not return. R. Eliezer says: He also that builds a house of bricks in Sharon may not return.

4. And these are they that stir not from their place: he that built a house and dedicated it, he that planted a vineyard and used the fruits thereof, he that married his betrothed wife, or he that consummated his union with his deceased brother's wife, for it is written, *He shall be free for his house one year: for his house* – this applied to his house; *he shall be* – this is [to include also] his vineyard; and *shall cheer his wife* – this applies to his own wife; *whom he hath taken* – this is to include also his decreased brother's wife. These do not provide water and food and do not repair the roads.

5. *And the officers shall speak further unto the people* [*and they shall say, What man is there that is fearful and fainthearted?*] R. Akiba says: *Fearful and fainthearted* is meant literally – he cannot endure the armies joined in battle or bear to see a drawn sword. R. Jose the Galilean says: The *fearful and fainthearted* is he that is afraid for the transgressions that he had committed; wherefore the Law has held his punishment in suspense [and included him] together with these others, so that he may return because of his transgressions. R. Jose says: If a widow is married to a High Priest, or a woman that was divorced or that had performed *halitzah* is married to a common Priest, or a bastard or a *Nethinah* to an Israelite, or the daughter of an Israelite to a bastard or a *Nathin* – such a one it is that is *fearful and fainthearted*.

---

* Levirate marriage is a marriage in which the brother of a deceased man is obligated to marry his brother's widow, and the widow is obligated to marry her deceased husband's brother.

† Under the Biblical system of levirate marriage (Deuteronomy 25:5–10) *halitzah* is the ceremony by which a widow and her husband's brother could avoid the duty to marry after the husband's death.

‡ A *Nathin* is a man or woman from the Gibeonites who converted to Judaism in the time of Joshua. See Joshua 9:27. Later during the period of King David it was prohibited for the *Nathinim* to marry Jews.

6. *And it shall be when the officers have made an end of speaking unto the people that they shall appoint captains of hosts at the head of the people*, and at the rearward of the people; they stationed warriors in front of them and others behind them with axes of iron in their hands, and if any sought to turn back, the warrior was empowered to break his legs, for with a beginning in flight comes defeat, as it is written: *Israel is fled before the Philistines, and there hath been also a great slaughter among the people.* And there again it is written, *And the men of Israel fled from before the Philistines and fell down slain....*

7. What has been said applies to a battle waged of free choice; but in a battle waged in a religious cause all go forth, even the bridegroom out of his chamber and the bride out of her bride chamber. R. Judah said: What has been said applies to a battle waged in a religious cause; but in a battle waged in duty bound all go forth, even the bridegroom out of his chamber and the bride out of her bride chamber.

From: Mishnah, *Tractate Sanhedrin*: 1:5[64]

5. A tribe, a false prophet, or the High Priest may not be tried save by the court of one and seventy; they may not send forth [the people] to a battle waged of free choice save by the decision of the court of one and seventy; they may not add to the City or the Courts of the Temple save by the decision of the court of one and seventy; they may not set up *sanhedrins* for the several tribes save by the decision of the court of one and seventy; and they may not proclaim [any city to be] an Apostate City save by the decision of the court of one and seventy. No city on the frontier should be proclaimed an Apostate City, nor three together, but only one or two.

From: Mishnah, *Tractate Sanhedrin*: 2:4[65]

4. He may send forth [the people] to a battle waged of free choice by the decision of the court of one and seventy.

V

Talmudic Sources[66]

Babylonian Talmud (ca. 500 CE)

From: *Babylonian Talmud, Tractate Sanhedrin*: 16a–b[67]

Mishnah: War of free choice etc. [see above].

Whence do we deduce this? – Said R. Abbahu: Scripture states, And he shall stand before Eleazar the Priest [who shall inquire for him by the judgment of the Urim before the Lord. At his word shall they go out and at his word they shall come in, both he and all the children of Israel with him even all the Congregation]. "He," refers to the King; "And all the children of Israel with him," to the Priest anointed for the conduct of war; and, "all the Congregation," means the Sanhedrin. But perhaps it is the Sanhedrin whom the Divine Law instructs to inquire of the Urim and Tummim*? – But [it may be deduced] from the story related by R. Aha b. Bizna in the name of R. Simeon the Pious: A harp hung over David's bed, and as soon as midnight arrived, a northerly wind blew upon its strings and caused it to play of its own accord. Immediately David arose and studied the Torah until the break of dawn. At the coming of dawn, the Sages of Israel entered into his presence and said unto him: "Our Sovereign King, thy people [of] Israel need sustenance." "Go and support yourselves by mutual trading," David replied, "But," said they, "a handful does not satisfy the lion, nor can a pit be filled with its own clods." Whereupon David said to them: "Go and stretch forth your hands with a troop [of soldiers]." Immediately they held counsel with Ahitophel and took advice from the Sanhedrin and inquired of the Urim and Tummim. R. Joseph said: What passage [states this]?

16b – *And after Ahitophel was Benaiah the son of Jehoiada and Abiathar; and the captain of the king's host was Joab. "Ahitophel" is the adviser,* even as it is written, *And the counsel of Ahitophel which he counselled in those days, was as if a man inquired from the word of God. "Benaiah the son of Jehoiada,"* refers to the Sanhedrin, and *"Abiathar"* to the *Urim and Tummim.* And so it is written, *And Benaiah the son of Jehoiada was over the Kerethites and Pelethites.* And why were they termed *Kerethites?* – Because they gave definite instructions, And *Pelethites?* – Because their acts were wonderful. Only after this [is it written], *And the captain of the king's host was Joab.* R. Issac the son of R. Adda, – others state, R. Issac b. Abudimi – said: What verse [tells us of the harp hanging over David's bed]? – *Awake my glory, awake psaltery and harp; I will wake the dawn.*

From: *Babylonian Talmud, Tractate Sanhedrin*: 20b[68]

Mishnah. He [the King] may lead forth [the host] to a voluntary war, on the decision of a court of seventy-one. He may force a way through private property and none may oppose him. There is no limitation to the King's way. The plunder taken by the people [in war] must be given to him, and he receives the first choice [when it is divided].

Gemara.[†] But we have already once learnt it. A voluntary war may be declared only by the permission of a court of seventy-one? – As the Tanna deals with all matters pertaining to the king, he also states [the law] concerning the declaration of a voluntary war.

---

* The *Urim* and *Tummim* were oracular devices used by the priests in the temple.
† The Talmud first quotes a short portion from the Mishnah and then embarks in the Gemara in a detailed commentary of the Mishnah, drawing on many other sources. The Talmud therefore is the combination of the Mishnah and its extended commentary in the Gemara.

Rab Judah said in Samuel's name: All that is set out in the chapter [dealing with the actions] of a king, he is permitted to do. Rab said: That chapter was intended only to inspire them with awe, for it is written, Thou shalt in any wise set him king over thee; [i.e.,] his awe should be over thee.

[The same point of difference is found among the following] Tannaim; R. Jose said: All that is set out in the Chapter [relating to the king], the king is permitted to do. R. Judah said: That section was stated only to inspire them with awe, for it is written, Thou shalt in anywise set him king over thee, [meaning], that his awe should be over thee. And thus R. Judah said; Three commandments were given to Israel when they entered the land: [i] to appoint a king, [ii] to cut off the seed of Amalek, and [iii] to build themselves the chosen house. While R. Nehorai said: This section was spoken only in anticipation of their future murmurings, as it is written, And shalt say, I will set a king over me etc.

It has been taught: R. Eliezer said: The elders of the generation made a fit request, as it is written, Give us a king to judge us. But the *am ha-arez* acted unworthily, as it is written, That we also may be like all the nations and that our king may judge us and go before us.

It has been taught: R. Jose said: Three commandments were given to Israel when they entered the land; [i] to appoint a king; [ii] to cut off the seed of Amalek; [iii] and to build themselves the chosen house [i.e., The Temple] and I do not know which of them has priority. But, when it is said: The hand upon the throne of the Lord, the Lord will have war with Amalek from generation to generation, we must infer that they had first to set up a king, for "throne" implies a king, as it is written, Then Solomon sat on the throne of the Lord as king. Yet I still do not know which [of the other two] comes first, the building of the chosen Temple or the cutting off of the seed of Amalek. Hence, when it is written, And when He giveth you rest from all your enemies round about etc., and then [Scripture proceeds], Then it shall come to pass that the place which the Lord your God shall choose, it is to be inferred that the extermination of Amalek is first. And so it is written of David, And it came to pass when the king dwelt in his house, and the Lord had given him rest from his enemies round about, and the passage continues; that the king said unto Nathan the Prophet: See now, I dwell in a house of cedars etc.

Resh Lakish said: At first, Solomon reigned over the higher beings, as it is written, Then Solomon sat on the throne of the Lord as king; afterwards, [having sinned,] he reigned [only] over the lower, as it is written, For he had dominion over all the region on this side [of] the river, from Tifsah even to Gaza.

Rab and Samuel [explain this verse in different ways]: One says, Tifsah was situated at one end of the world and Gaza at the other. The other says: Tifsah and Gaza were beside each other, and just as he reigned over these, so did he reign over the whole world. But eventually his reign was restricted to Israel, as it is written, I Koheleth have been king over Israel etc. Later, his reign was confined to Jerusalem alone, even as it is written, The words of Koheleth, son of David, king in Jerusalem. And still later he reigned only over his couch, as it is written, Behold it is the litter of Solomon, three-score mighty men are about it etc. And finally, he reigned only over his staff as it is written, This was my portion from all my labor.

Rab and Samuel [explain this differently]: One says: His staff [was all that was left him]; the other: His Gunda.

Did he regain his first power, or not? Rab and Samuel [differ]: One maintains that he did; the other, that he did not. The one who says that he did not, agrees with the view that Solomon was first a king and then a commoner; the other, who says that he did, agrees with the view that he was first king, then commoner and finally king again.

From: *Babylonian Talmud, Tractate Sotah*: **44b**[69]

Mishnah. Because the beginning of flight is falling, as it is said, Israel is fled before the Philistines, and there hath been a great slaughter among the people; and further on it states, and the men of Israel fled from before the Philistines and fell down slain etc.

To what does all the foregoing apply? To voluntary wars, but in the wars commanded by the Torah all go forth, even a bridegroom from his chamber and a bride from her canopy. R. Judah says: To what does all the foregoing apply? To the wars commanded by the Torah; but in obligatory wars all go forth, even a bridegroom from his chamber and a bride from her canopy.

Gemara. What is the difference between R. Jose and R. Jose the Galilean? – The issue between them is the transgression of a Rabbinical ordinance. With whom does the following teaching accord: He who speaks between [donning] one phylactery and the other has committed a transgression and returns home under the war-regulations? With whom [does it accord]? With R. Jose the Galilean. Who is the Tanna of the following: Our Rabbis taught: If he heard the sound of trumpets and was terror-stricken, or the crash of shields and was terror-stricken, or [beheld] the brandishing of swords and the urine discharged itself upon his knees, he returns home? With whom [does it accord]? Are we to say that it is with R. Akiba and R. Jose the Galilean? – In such a circumstance even R. Jose the Galilean admits [that he returns home], because it is written: Lest his brethren's heart melt as his heart.

And it shall be, when the officers have made an end etc. The phrase, because the beginning of flight is falling, should be, "because falling is the beginning of flight"! Read [in the Mishnah]: Because falling is the beginning of flight.

To what does all the foregoing apply? To voluntary wars etc. R. Johanan said: [A war] which is [designated] voluntary according to the Rabbis is commanded according to R. Judah, and [a war] which is [designated] commanded according to the rabbis is obligatory according to R. Judah. Raba said: The wars waged by Joshua to conquer [Canaan] were obligatory in the opinion of all; the wars waged by the House of David[70] for territorial expansion were voluntary in the opinion of all; where they differ is with regard to [wars] against heathens so that these should not march against them. One calls them commanded and the other voluntary, the practical issue being that one who is engaged in the performance of a commandment is exempt from the performance of another commandment.

Maimonides, Mishneh Torah (1170–1180)[71]

From: Maimonides, *Kings and Wars*, Chapter 4[72]

1. It is within the province of the King to levy taxes upon the people for his own needs or for war purposes....

2. He may send (messengers) throughout all of the borders of Israel, take from the people the strong and valiant men, place some of them in the chariots and among his horsemen, appoint others to attend to him, and still others to run before him....

5. Similarly, he may draft those capable of holding office, appoint them heads of groups of thousands, and of groups of fifties....

6. He may seize fields, oliveyards, and vineyards, and give them to his servants when they go forth to war and are encamped around those places and have no other supply of food, and he pays for what he seizes....

From: Maimonides, *Kings and Wars*, Chapter 5[73]

1. The primary war which the king wages is a war for a religious cause. Which may be denominated a war for a religious cause? It includes the war against the seven nations, that against Amalek, and a war to deliver Israel from the enemy attacking him. There-after he may engage in an optional war, that is, a war against neighboring nations to extend the borders of Israel and to enhance his greatness and prestige.

2. For a war waged for a religious cause, the king need not obtain the sanction of the court. He may at any time go forth of his own accord and compel the people to go with him. But in case of an optional war, he may not lead forth the people save by a decision of the court of seventy-one.

3. He may break through (private property) to make a road for himself, and none may protest against it. No limit can be prescribed for the king's road; he expropriates as much as is needed. He does not have to make detours because someone's vineyard or field (is in his way). He takes the straight route and attacks the enemy.

4. It is a positive command to destroy the seven nations, as it is said: *But thou shalt utterly destroy them* (Deut. 20:17). If one does not put to death any of them that falls into one's power, one transgresses a negative command, as it is said: *Thou*

shalt save alive nothing that breatheth (Deut. 20:16). But their memory has long perished.

5. So too, it is a positive command to destroy the memory of Amalek, as it is said: *Thou shalt blot out the remembrance of Amalek* (Deut. 25:19). It is a positive command always to bear in mind his evil deeds, the waylaying (he resorted to), so that we keep fresh the memory of the hatred manifested by him, as it is said: *Remember what Amalek did unto thee* (Deut. 25:17). The traditional interpretation of this injunction is: *Remember*, by word of mouth; *do not forget*, out of mind.

6. All provinces conquered by the king at the decision of the court are deemed a national conquest and become in all respects an integral part of the Land of Israel conquered by Joshua, provided that they are annexed after the whole of Palestine, the boundaries of which are specified in the Bible, has been reconquered.

From: Maimonides, *Kings and Wars*, Chapter 6[74]

1. No war is declared against any nation before peace offers are made to it. This obtains both in an optional war and a war for a religious cause, as it is said: *When thou drawest nigh unto a city to fight against it, then proclaim peace unto it* (Deut. 20:10). If the inhabitants make peace and accept the seven commandments enjoined upon the descendents of Noah, none of them is slain, but they become tributary, as it is said: *They shall become tributary unto thee, and shall serve thee* (Deut. 20:11). If they agree to pay the tribute levied on them but refuse to submit to servitude, or if they yield to servitude but refuse to pay the tribute levied on them, their overtures are rejected – they must accept both terms of peace.

The servitude imposed on them is that they are given an inferior status, that they lift not up their heads in Israel but be subjected to them, that they be not appointed to any office that will put them in charge of Israel. The terms of the levy are that they be prepared to serve the king with their body and their money, such as building walls, fortifying strongholds, constructing the king's palace, and similar services, as it is written: *And this is the account of the levy which King Solomon raised; to build the house of the Lord, and his own house, and Millo,[75] and the walls of Jerusalem ... and all the store cities that Solomon had.... All the people that were left of the Amorites ... of them did Solomon raise a levy of bond servants, unto this day. But of the children of Israel did Solomon make no bond servants, but they were the men of war, and his servants, and his princes, and his captains, and rulers of his chariots and of his horsemen* (I Kings 9:15, 19–22).

2. The king may lay down as a condition of peace that he take half their money or land and leave in their possession all chattel, or that he take all their chattel and leave the land in their possession.

3. Once they make peace and take upon themselves the seven commandments, it is forbidden to deceive them and prove false to the covenant made with them.

4. If they refuse to accept the offer of peace, or if they accept the offer of peace but not the seven commandments, war is made with them; all adult males are put to death; all their money and little ones are taken as plunder, but no woman or minor is slain, as it is said: *But the women and the little ones . . . shalt thou take as a prey unto thyself* (Deut. 20:14); the phrase *the little ones* refers to male minors.

This applies only to an optional war, that is, a war against any other nation; but in war waged against the seven nations or against Amalek, if these refuse to accept the terms of peace, none of them is spared, as it is said: *Thus shalt thou do unto all the cities which are very far off from thee. . . . Howbeit of the cities of these peoples . . . thou shalt save alive nothing that breatheth* (Deut. 20:15, 16). So too, with respect to Amalek, it is said: *Thou shalt blot out the remembrance of Amalek* (Deut. 25:19).

Whence do we derive that the (above-cited) command refers only to those who refuse to accept terms of peace? Because it is written: *There was not a city that made peace with the children of Israel, save the Hivites the inhabitants of Gibeon; they took all in battle. For it was of the Lord to harden their hearts, to come against Israel in battle, that they might be utterly destroyed* (Josh. II:19–20), We infer therefrom that the offer of peace had been made, but they did not accept it.

5. Three proclamations Joshua sent (to the inhabitants of Canaan) before he entered the land. The first read: "Whoever wishes to emigrate, let him emigrate"; this was followed by a second which read: "Whoever wishes to make peace, let him do so"; the third proclamation read: "Whoever wants war may have war."

Why then did the Gibeonites resort to stratagem? Because they had first ignored the proclamation (issued to the seven nations) in general, and, not knowing the law of Israel, they thought that the opportunity for making peace was gone. Why did the princes find the case of the Gibeonites difficult, arguing that but for the oath, the latter deserved to be smitten with the edge of the sword? Because the princes had made a covenant with them, which was contrary to the injunction *Thou shalt make no covenant with them* (Exod. 23:32); they should have made them servants, doing task work.

From: Maimonides, *Kings and Wars*, Chapter 8[76]

1. The armed men who invade heathen territory, conquer the (enemy) forces, and take captives are permitted to eat *nebelah*, *terfah*, pork, and the like, if no other articles of food are available to them. So too, they may drink forbidden wine. . . .

2. A soldier in the invading army may also, if overpowered by passion, cohabit with a captive woman. He may not, however, leave her after cohabiting with her. He must take her into his house. . . . He is forbidden to cohabit with her a second time before he marries her.

3. Coition with her is permitted only at the time when she is taken captive. . . . It is all one whether she is still a virgin, or is no longer a virgin, or is a married woman. For the marriage of a heathen does not give the woman a legal martial status. . . .

How do we know that he must not force her (to yield to him) in the open field of battle? Because it is said: *Then thou shalt bring her home to thy house*, that is, he shall take her to a private place and cohabit with her....

9. A captive woman who refuses, after the lapse of twelve months, to renounce idolatry, is put to death. Likewise, if a city sues for peace, no covenant is made with it, unless the inhabitants repudiate idolatry, destroy all places of idol worship and accept the other commandants mandatory upon the descendants of Noah, for any heathen who refuses to accept those seven commandments is put to death if he is under our control.

10. Moses our teacher, bequeathed the Law and commandments to Israel ... and to those of other nations who are willing to be converted (to Judaism).... But no coercion to accept the Law and commandments is practiced on those who are unwilling to do so. Moreover, Moses, our teacher, was commanded by God to compel all human beings to accept the commandments enjoined upon the descendants of Noah. Anyone who does not accept them is put to death. He who does accept them is invariably styled a resident alien. He must declare his acceptance in the presence of three associates. Anyone who has declared his intention to be circumcised and fails to do so within twelve months is treated like a heathen infidel.

From: Maimonides, *Kings and Wars*, Chapter 11[77]

1. King Messiah will arise and restore the Kingdom of David to its former state and original sovereignty. He will rebuild the sanctuary and gather the dispersed of Israel. All the ancient laws will be reinstituted in his days; sacrifices will again be offered; the Sabbatical and Jubilee years will again be observed in accordance with the commandments set forth in the Law....

4. If there arise a King from the House of David who meditates on the Torah, occupies himself with the commandments, as did his ancestor David, observes the precepts prescribed in the Written and the Oral law, prevails upon Israel to walk in the way of the Torah and to repair its breaches, and fights the battles of the Lord, it may be assumed that he is the Messiah.... He will prepare the whole world to serve the Lord with one accord, as it is written: *For then will I turn to the peoples a pure language, that they may call upon the name of the Lord to serve Him with one consent* (Zeph. 3:9).

From: Maimonides, *Shmita and Yovel Laws*, Chapter 13[78]

10. The entire Tribe of Levi was enjoined to have no share in the Land of Canaan. They were likewise enjoined to seize no share in the spoils of war while the cities were being conquered, as it is said, *The priests, the Levites, even all the Tribe of Levi, shall have no portion nor inheritance with Israel* (Deut. 18:1), implying, *no portion* in the spoils *nor inheritance* in the Land. Similarly it is said of Aaron, *Thou shalt have no inheritance in their land, neither shalt thou have any portion among*

them (Num. 18:20), *portion* referring to spoils of war. If a Levite or a priest seizes a share in the spoils, he is liable to a flogging, and if he takes a share in the Land, it must be taken away from him.

11. It would appear to me that this rule applied only to the Land which is subject to the covenant made with Abraham, Isaac, and Jacob, and which was inherited by their children and was divided among them. As for other lands conquered by one of the kings of Israel, the priests and the Levites have the same share in them and in their spoils as do all other Israelites.

12. Why was the Tribe of Levi granted no right to a share in the Land of Israel and in its spoils, together with his brothers? Because they were set apart to worship the Lord, to serve Him, and to teach His upright ways and His righteous judgments to the many, as it is said, *They shall teach Jacob Thine ordinances, and Israel Thy law* (Deut. 33:10). They were consequently set apart from the ways of the world: they may not wage war as do the rest of Israel, they have no share in the Land, and they may acquire nothing for themselves by physical force. They are rather the host of the Holy Name, as it is said, *Bless, Lord, his host* (Deut. 33:11). It is He, blessed be He, who acquires for them, as it is said, *I am thy portion and thine inheritance* (Num. 18:20).

13. Not only the Tribe of Levi, but also each and every individual of those who come into the world, whose spirit moves him and whose knowledge gives him understanding to set himself apart in order to stand before the Lord, to serve Him, to worship Him, and to know Him, who walks upright as God had made him to do, and releases his neck from the yoke of the many speculations that the children of man are wont to pursue – such an individual is consecrated in the Holy of Holies, and his portion and inheritance shall be in the Lord forever and ever-more. The Lord will grant in this world whatsoever is sufficient for him, the same as He had granted to the priests and to the Levites. Thus indeed did David, upon whom be peace, say, *O Lord, the portion of mine inheritance and of my cup, Thou maintainest my lot* (Ps. 16:5).

Rabbi Moshe ben Nachman (Nachmanides) (1194–1270)

From: Nachmanides, *Commentary on the Torah, Deuteronomy 20:10*[79]

10. When thou drawest near unto a city to fight against it, then proclaim peace unto it. "Scripture is speaking of a permissible war [rather than a war required by the Torah, such as the invasion of the seven nations of Canaan], as it is expressly stated in this section, *Thus shalt thou do unto all the cities which are very far off from thee.*" This is Rashi's language. The Rabbi [Rashi]* wrote this based on the

---

* Rabbi Shlomo Yitzhaki (1040–1105), better known by the name Rashi, was the first to write a comprehensive commentary on the Talmud, as well as a comprehensive commentary on the Tanakh (Hebrew Bible).

Sifre where a similar text is taught: "Scripture is speaking of a battle waged of free choice." But the intent of our Rabbis with reference to this verse [before us, was not to say that the requirement of proclaiming peace applies exclusively to permissible, but not to obligatory, wars; rather, their teaching in the Sifre] refers only to the later section wherein there is a differentiation between the two kinds of wars [i.e., in Verses 13–14 declaring that if the enemy insists on war, then only the men are to be killed, but the women and children are to be spared – that law applies only to a permissible but not to an obligatory war]. But the call for peace applies even to an obligatory war. It requires us to offer peace-terms even to the seven nations [of Canaan], for Moses proclaimed peace to Sihon, king of the Amorites, and he would not have transgressed both the positive and negative commandments in this section: *but thou shalt utterly destroy them*, and *thou shalt save alive nothing that breatheth!* Rather, the difference between them [i.e., obligatory and permissible wars] is when the enemy does not make peace and continues to make war. Then, in the case of the *cities which are very far off*, Scripture commanded us to *smite every male thereof* and keep alive the women and male children, but in *the cities of these peoples* [i.e., the seven nations of Canaan in the event they refuse the call to peace], it commanded us to destroy even the women and children. And so did our Rabbis say in the Midrash of Eileh Hadevarim Rabbah,* and it is found also in Tanchuma† and in the Gemara Yerushalmi:‡ "Rabbi Shmuel the son of Rabbi Nachmani said: Joshua the son of Nun fulfilled the laws of this section. What did Joshua do? Wherever he went to conquer, he would send a proclamation in which he wrote: 'He who wishes to make peace let him come forward and make peace; he who wishes to leave, let him leave, and he who wishes to make war, let him make war.' The Girgashite left. With the Gibeonites who made peace, Joshua made peace. The thirty-one kings who came to wage war – the Holy One, blessed be He, chase them down etc." And so indeed Scripture states with reference to all cities [including those of the seven nations], *There was not a city that made peace with the children of Israel, save the Hivites the inhabitants of Gibeon; they took all in battle. For it was of the Eternal to harden their hearts, to come against Israel in battle, that they might be utterly destroyed.* Obviously if they had wanted to make peace, the Israelites would have made peace with them.

It appears that regarding the terms of peace, there were differences [between what was offered *the very far off cities* and what was offered the seven nations], for, with reference to the distant cities, we ask that they make peace and become tributary to us and serve, but, regarding *the cities of these peoples* [the seven nations] we request of them peace, tribute and service, on the condition that they agree not to worship idols. Scripture does not mention it in this section, because concerning idolaters, it has already given the prohibition, *They shall not dwell in thy Land, lest they make thee sin against Me, for thou wilt serve their gods.* It is possible that we must inform them only of the peace offer, tribute and service;

---

* An early rabbinic commentary on the book of Deuteronomy.
† *Tanchuma* is an early rabbinic commentary on the Torah.
‡ The Palestinian Talmud.

after they are subject to us, we tell them that we execute judgment upon idols and their worshippers, whether individuals or the community. Similarly, that which is stated here, *That they teach you not to do after all their abominations*, and with reference to it the Rabbis said in the Sifre, "But if they repent [of their idol-worship] they are not to be killed" – this refers to the seven nations. The "repentance" is that they accept upon themselves the seven commandments in which "the sons of Noah" were commanded, but not that they must convert to become righteous proselytes.

Now, in Tractate Sotah the Rabbis have said that "they [i.e., the Israelites upon coming into the Land] inscribed the Torah upon stones in seventy languages and that, below, they wrote, *That they teach you not to do*. However, [we deduce,] if the peoples were to repent, the Israelites would accept them." Rashi explained this text as follows: ["This verse was written upon the stones below] to inform the nations that dwelled outside the border of the Land of Israel that they [i.e., the Israelites] were not commanded to destroy [populations] except for those [the seven nations] that dwell within the borders in order that they [the Canaanites] should not teach them their perverted practices. But as to those who dwell outside [the boundaries] we tell them, 'If you repent, we accept you,' Those who dwell within the Land we do not accept because their repentance was due to fear." This is the language of the Rabbi [Rashi]. But it is not correct, for it was with reference to *the cities of these peoples, that the Eternal thy God giveth thee for an inheritance* – it was of them that he said *that they teach you not* thus indicating that if they do repent [thereby negating the fear that they may *teach you*] they are not to be slain. Similarly He said of them, *They shall not dwell in thy Land, lest they make thee sin against Me, for thou wilt serve their gods*, which indicates that if they abandon their gods they are permitted to dwell there.

This is the project of Solomon concerning which it is written, *And this is the account of the levy which King Solomon raised; to build the House of the Eternal, and his own house, and Millo, and the wall of Jerusalem etc. All the people that were left of the Amorites, the Hittites, the Perizzites, the Hivites, and the Jebusites, who were not of the children of Israel; even their children that were left after them in the Land, whom the children of Israel were not able utterly to destroy, of them did Solomon raise a levy of bondservants, unto this day. But of the children of Israel did Solomon make no bondservants*. This project he did in accordance with the Law, for they accepted the observance of the seven commandments upon themselves. Now it is clear that since Solomon was able to draft them as his labourers, he had power over them and he could have destroyed them, except that it was permissible to let them live, as we have written.

From: Nachmanides, *Commentary on the Torah, Genesis 34:13*[80]

13. And the sons of Jacob answered Shechem and Hamor his father with subtlety. Now Hamor and Schechem spoke to her father and her brothers, but the patriarch did not answer them at all as his sons spoke in his place on this matter out

of respect for him for since the affair was a source of shame to them, they did not want him to speak about it at all.

There is a question which may be raised here. It would appear that they answered with the concurrence of her father and his advice for they were in his presence, and it was he who understood the answer which they spoke with subtlety, and, if so, why was he angry afterwards? Moreover, it is inconceivable that Jacob would have consented to give his daughter in marriage to a Canaanite who had defiled her. Now surely all the brothers gave that answer with subtlety, while Simeon and Levi alone executed the deed, and the father cursed only their wrath. [But if all the brothers shared responsibility for the answer and the plan, why did Jacob single out only Simeon and Levi for chastisement?] The answer is that the craftiness lay in their saying that every male of theirs be circumcised, as they thought that the people of the city will not consent to it. Even if perchance they will listen to their prince and they will all become circumcised, they will come *on the third day, when they were in pain*, and will take their laughter from the house of Shechem. Now this was the advice of all the brothers and with the permission of their father, but Simeon and Levi wanted to take revenge on them and so they killed all the men of the city.

It is possible that Jacob's anger in cursing their wrath was because they killed the men of the city who had committed no sin against him; they should have killed Shechem alone. It is this which Scripture says, *And the sons of Jacob answered Shechem and Hamor his father with subtlety, and spoke, because he had defiled Dinah their sister*, for they all agreed to speak to him craftily because of the base deed which he had done to them.

Now many people ask: "But how did the righteous sons of Jacob commit this deed, spilling innocent blood?" The Rabbi (Moshe ben Maimon) answered in his Book of Judges, saying that "sons of Noah" are commanded concerning Laws, and thus they are required to appoint judges in each and every district to give judgment concerning their six commandments which are obligatory upon all mankind. "And a Noachide* who transgresses one of them is subject to the death-penalty by the sword. If he sees a person transgressing one of these seven laws and does not bring him to trial for a capital crime, he who saw him is subject to the same death-penalty. It was on account of this that the people of Shechem had incurred the death-penalty because Shechem committed an act of robbery and they saw and knew of it, but they did not bring him to trial."

But these words do not appear to me to be correct for if so, our father Jacob should have been the first to obtain the merit of causing their death, and if he was afraid of them, why was he angry at his sons and why did he curse their wrath a long time after that and punish them by dividing them and scattering them in

---

* A Noachide is a gentile observing the seven Noachide commandments. The Noachide commandments apply to all humanity through humankind's descent from Noah. They include prohibitions of idolatry, murder, theft, sexual immorality, blasphemy, and eating flesh taken from an animal while it is still alive.

Israel? Were they not meritorious, fulfilling a commandment and trusting in G-d Who saved them?

In my opinion, the meaning of "Laws" which the Rabbis have counted among their seven Noachidic commandments is not just that they are to appoint judges in each and every district, but He commanded them concerning the laws of theft, overcharge, wronging, and a hired man's wages; the laws of guardians of property, forceful violation of a woman, seduction, principles of damage and wounding a fellowman; laws of creditors and debtors, and laws of buying and selling, and their like, similar in scope to the laws with which Israel was charged, and involving the death-penalty for stealing, wronging or violating or seducing the daughter of his fellowman, or kindling his stack, or wounding him, and their like. And it is also included in this commandment that they appoint judges for each and every city, just as Israel was commanded to do, but if they failed to do so they are free of the death-penalty since this is a positive precept of theirs [and failing to fulfill a positive precept does not incur the death-penalty]. The Rabbis have only said: "For violation of their admonishments there is the death-penalty," and only a prohibition against doing something is called an "admonishment." And such is the purport of the Gemara in Tractate Sanhedrin.

And in the Jerusalem Talmud [the Palestinian Talmud] they have said: "With respect to Noachide laws, a judge who perverts justice is to be slain. If he took a bribe he is to be slain. With respect to Jewish laws, [if after having heard both parties] you know perfectly well what the proper legal decision should be, you are not permitted to withdraw from the case without rendering a decision, and if you know that it is not perfectly clear to you, you may withdraw from the case. But with respect to their laws, even though you know the law perfectly well you may withdraw from it." From this it would appear that a non-Jewish judge may say to the litigants, "I am not beholden to you," for it is only in Israel that there is an additional admonishment – "*Lo thaguru" (ye shall not be afraid) of the face of any man*, meaning, "You shall not gather in, [i.e., restrain], your words before any man" – and surely he is not to be slain for failing to make himself *chief, overseer, or ruler* in order to judge superiors. [Ramban thus disagrees with Rambam, who writes that the people of Shechem had incurred the death-penalty by not having brought Shechem to justice.] Moreover, why does the Rabbi … [Maimonides] have to seek to establish their guilt? Were not the people of Shechem and all seven nations idol worshippers, perpetrators of unchaste acts, and practitioners of all things that are abominable to G-d? In many places Scripture loudly proclaims concerning them: *Upon the high mountains, and upon their hills, and under every leafy tree*, etc.; *Thou shalt not learn to do after the abominations*, etc.? *For all these abominations have the men of the land done, etc.* However, it was not the responsibility of Jacob and his sons to bring them to justice.

But the matter of Shechem was that the people of Shechem were wicked [by virtue of their violation of the seven Noachide laws] and had thereby forfeited their lives. Therefore Jacob's sons wanted to take vengeance [on] them with a vengeful sword, and so they killed the king and all the men of his city who were his subjects, obeying his commands. The covenant represented by the circumcision of the inhabitants of Shechem had no validity in the eyes of Jacob's sons for it was done to curry favor with their master [and did not represent a genuine conversion]. But Jacob told them here that they had placed him in danger, as it is said, *You have troubled me, to make me odious*, and there, [i.e., at the time he blessed the other children], he cursed the wrath of Simeon and Levi for they had done violence to the men of the city whom they had told in his presence, *And we will dwell with you, and we will become one people*. They would have chosen to believe in G-d and trust their word, and perhaps they might have indeed returned to G-d and thus Simeon and Levi killed them without cause for the people who had done them no evil at all. It is this which Jacob said; *Weapons of violence are their kinship.*

And if we are to believe in the book, "The Wars of the Sons of Jacob," their father's fear was due to the fact that the neighbors of Schechem gathered together and waged three major wars against them, and were it not for their father who also donned his weapons and warred against them, they would have been in danger, as is related in that book. Our Rabbis have mentioned something of this conflict in their commentary on the verse, *Which I took out of the hand of the Amorite with my sword and with my bow*. They said, "All the surrounding nations gathered together to join in battle against them, and Jacob donned his weapons to war against them," just as Rashi writes there. Scripture, however, is brief about this because it was a hidden miracle, for the sons of Jacob were valiant men, and it appeared as *if their own arm saved them*. Scripture is similarly brief about the matter of Abraham in Ur of the Chaldees, and it did not at all mention Esau's wars with the Horites. Instead, Scripture mentions here that *there was the terror of G-d upon the cities that were round them*, and they did not all assemble to *pursue after the sons of Jacob* for they would have fallen upon them *as the sand which is on the sea-shore in multitude*. And this is the meaning of *the terror of G-d*, for the terror and dread of the military prowess they had seen fell upon them. Therefore Scripture says, *And Jacob came to Luz . . . he and all the people that were with him*, in order to inform us that not one man among them or their servants was lost in warfare.

VI

Modern Debates before the Founding of the State of Israel (1948)

Avraham Yeshaya Karelitz (1878–1953)

Avraham Yeshaya Karelitz, popularly known by his literary name Chazon Ish, was a Belarusian-born rabbi who later became a leader of the ultra-Orthodox community in Palestine (later Israel), where he spent his final twenty years. While Karelitz never held an official position, he became recognized as a worldwide authority on matters relating to Jewish law.

From: Avraham Yeshaya Karelitz, Laws Regarding the Jewish Calendar[81]

(*Orach Hayim*, 1911)*

Maimonides, Ch. 5 of the Laws of Kings, art. 1, writes that helping Israel from the hand of an enemy that has come upon it (in other words, has already come upon it) is included in [the category of] a "divinely commanded war." Maimonides omitted the rule of war regarding [preventive war against] Samaritans that had not yet come [upon Israel]. And he interpreted [the concept of] "optional war" as David's war to expand the borders of Israel, and in Ch. 7, art. 5, he wrote about those exempted [from conscription], that is, during an "optional war." In a "divinely commanded war," even a groom from his chamber and a bride from her canopy [are required to assist]. And he did not expound on the nature of a "divinely commanded war," and on the nature of an "optional [war]," and he relied on what he wrote here [in 5:1]. One may conclude from the wording: "helping Israel from the hand of an enemy *that has come upon it* [emphasis added]" that this means "has already come upon them." In any case from the wording "that David's war to expand [borders] is an 'optional war,'" you could conclude that preventive war against the Samaritans that has not yet come is a "divinely commanded war." And in any case, there must be a reason for the omission, because it is not usual [for Maimonides] to omit a law that appears in the Mishnah and is expounded upon in the Talmud, and what the Lehem Mishneh [commentary on Maimonides] wrote – that this issue is implied in the text – does not make sense.

It seems that the Mishnah's teaching that in a "divinely commanded war," even a groom [is taken] from his chamber does not refer to a time when his help is needed for victory in the war, since it is obvious that for the sake of saving a life and saving the people, all are obligated. But rather [it refers] to a case when, though only a certain number [of soldiers] are needed (and most of their wars were such that there was only capacity for a particular number of soldiers), it was permissible to take a groom from his chamber, since those meriting exemption have no such rights in a "divinely commanded war," while in an "optional war," they are not exempt except when victory for Israel is not dependent on them when the number needed by the army is reached without them. But if they are needed, they must come to the succor of their brothers, and then the war becomes a "divinely commanded war." But this obtains [only] if the "optional war" is already under way. But ex ante, one should not enter an "optional war" if it cannot be fought without those in the exempt category. And after an "optional war" has commenced with a force of a particular size, if it is seen that additional soldiers are necessary, then those that we are commanded to exempt are not drafted as long as the requisite number is fulfilled without them.

And even if they [the enemy soldiers] are now coming upon us, had they come upon us at the outset, it would have been considered a "divinely commanded war." In any case, because they embarked upon it as an "optional war"

---

* *Orach Hayim* is a section of classic codification of Jewish law that treats all aspects of Jewish law primarily pertinent to the Hebrew calendar.

from the outset, those in the exempt category have their right, as long as the fighting can be done by others. But if they are needed for victory in the war, even a groom must set out from his chamber, even though it was originally an "optional war."

Rabbi Chaim Hirschensohn (1857–1935)

Rabbi Chaim Hirschensohn was born in the city of Sefad in the Galilee. After a period in Jerusalem where he worked to revive the Hebrew language with Eliezer Ben Yehudah, Hirschensohn was appointed in 1904 as the chief rabbi of Hoboken, New Jersey, where he remained until his death. While Hirschensohn wrote on many subjects, including the relationship between Judaism and democracy, the status of women, and conflicts between traditional Judaism and modern scholarship and science, he is best known for *Malki Ba-Kodesh*, a six-volume work he published between 1919 and 1928, in which he attempted to create a halakhic corpus for a future Jewish state.

From: Rabbi Chaim Hirschensohn, *The Holy Kingdom or Ruling with Holiness* (*Malki Ba-Kodesh*), Chapter 2[82]

We see from this that Rava's opinion is that it is inconceivable that the Sages believed that it is imperative that Israel embark on a war in the case of "non-Jews who have not ['yet'] come upon them," and that even a groom from his chamber and bride from her canopy would be obligated to join on its behalf. Since after the Jews upheld the commandment to conquer and dispossess the seven nations, it is written: *For I will dispossess nations before you, and I will widen your territory and no man will covet your land when you go up to appear in the presence of the Lord three times in the year* (Ex. 34:24). And when a Jew performs the will of God he need not fear at all that the nations will rise up against him. Such a matter could not possibly be conceived of as an obligatory war for which a groom must leave his chamber and a bride her canopy. And yet, it is not prohibited, and the King is authorized to call [persons] up for a war when such a fear is aroused in him. Here the intention of the word "optional" is to distinguish it from [a] prohibited [war], under the reasoning that since war itself is the murder of others, and a danger to oneself, it cannot be an option at all. For this reason the Sages took care to inform us that it is optional, i.e. that it is permissible since such is the way of the world, and it is the nature of the individual and the nation to fear and to entertain political thoughts against the increasing power of a neighboring nation, and as long as the nations have not beaten their swords into plowshares and their spears into pruning hooks, Israel has the option, when it sees a nation taking in its midst, and it fears that the nation will rise up against it, it has the option of taking the first step and declaring war against it. But in the opinion of the Sages, this is not a divine commandment regarding which one who is engaged in one *mitzvah* is exempt from another. Nevertheless in the opinion of Rabbi Yehudah, it is a divine commandment to protect Israel from any fear, even though it is not requisite that the groom leave his chamber and the bride her canopy. [However], the law that "one engaging in a *mitzvah* is exempt from another *mitzvah*" does apply to it, as shall be clarified below in chapters 5–6, with God's help.

From: Rabbi Chaim Hirschensohn, *The Holy Kingdom* or *Ruling with Holiness* (*Malki Ba-Kodesh*), Chapter 3

Out of a concern for this prohibition [of proceeding to an "optional war" without the consent of a court of seventy-one], the mishnah teaches that only a court of seventy-one can declare an optional war (Mishnah Sanhedrin. 2a). In other words, there must be a court order permitting it, and the court must comprise seventy-one qualified persons, as is the Law of the Sanhedrin as enumerated in that pericope (ibid). And that is what Rashi of blessed memory writes in San. 16a, regarding what is related there regarding the wars of King David, peace unto him, [that they were] "advised by Ahitofel[83] and crowned by the Sanhedrin." Rashi explains [the meaning of the words "crowned by the Sanhedrin"] as follows: "they receive permission from them – i.e. as stated in our mishnah" (Rashi's quote ends here). In other words, according to what is taught in the mishnah, one does not embark on an optional war except according to a court of seventy-one, i.e. to receive permission from them so they can [issue an] order as to whether the [particular] war is permitted or forbidden.

Following from the general discussion above, Hirschensohn seeks to provide halakhic legitimation for the Jewish Legion (five battalions of Jewish volunteers established by the British Army in 1914–1915 as part of their war against the Ottoman Empire, which Zionists saw as an opportunity to promote the idea of a Jewish homeland in Palestine) and their participation in the war within the British Army.

From: Rabbi Chaim Hirschensohn, *The Holy Kingdom* or *Ruling with Holiness* (*Malki Ba-Kodesh*), Chapter 7

Indeed, everything that we have written until now relating to the Jewish Legion is according to its preliminary concept, i.e. in line with those members of our people in America who classified it as an optional war. We discussed its halakhic foundation in the law of optional war, and due to this conceptualization, they sought rabbinic approval to remove it from the category of a prohibited war, which some mistakenly thought it to be, as we explained. However, if we consider its true foundation, it is in fact an "obligatory war," but in any case, it still does not require a groom to leave his chamber and a bride her canopy. However, those of the nation who volunteer are upholding the commandment of an "obligatory war," "*at a time of disorder in Israel, When people dedicate themselves, Bless the Lord!*" (Jud. 5:2).

The basis of the matter is what Nachmanides wrote regarding the fourth of the positive commandments that he believed Maimonides of blessed memory to have forgotten to enumerate. . . . To paraphrase his words, the commandment of conquering Eretz Israel is a commandment that is effective for all generations, and every commandment that applies to all generations must be counted among the commandments, and this is why he believed that Maimonides of blessed memory forgot to enumerate it based on error and oversight, which every mortal creature is likely to commit. And the Gaon [R. Isaac de Leon] of blessed memory, author of the *Scroll of Esther* [commentary on Nachmanides' critique of *Sefer ha-Mitzvot*[84]], who took [it] upon himself to substantiate all of Nachmanides' reservations regarding Maimonides, said, "I believe that the reason he did not include it was that the commandment of inheriting and settling the land was only practiced in the days of Moses and Joshua and David, as long as they were not exiled. But after they were exiled from their land, this commandment ceased to be in practice for all generations until the time that the Messiah comes. To the contrary, we were commanded according to what is written at the end of *Ketubot*[85] (110a) not to rebel against the nations and set out to conquer the land by force, supported by the verse: 'I adjure you, O maidens of Jerusalem . . .' etc., requiring that they not ascend to Eretz Israel en-masse [Heb. *be-homa*]. And [de Leon claims that] what Nachmanides said in the name of the Sages, that conquest of the land is a 'divinely commanded war' – applies to when we are no longer subordinated by the nations. He further said that the Sages' exaggerated praise of living in the land refers specifically for the time when the Temple is standing, but now there is no commandment to live there etc." (end of his words).

And my master this brilliant rabbi [de Leon] should forgive me: [but it is] because of his own shortcoming regarding respect for settling in Eretz Israel [he did not live there!] that he erred in an obvious case . . . in his desire to explain why Maimonides of blessed memory did not include this commandment in thinking that it is not a commandment applicable to all generations and thus not numbered among the commandments as explained in the Book of Commandments, under "principle [root] 3." No one would make a mistake on such a matter, to think that a commandment in practice during the days of Moses and Joshua and David and in the future [during the Messianic era] and only annulled while the Temple is not standing would not be considered a commandment applicable to all generations, since according to this, there would be no need to include the precepts relating to the sacrifices and the commandment of the punishments and the blotting out of Amalek and the like, among the commandments, which Maimonides, of blessed memory, did include. He would not commit such an error unless he was misled by Heaven on account of his shortcoming in terms of respect for the commandment of settling the Land of Israel on which all commandments depend, and would not write that they are not in practice during these times. He presents the pericope from Ketubot [110a–b] but fails to see how the Sages strongly emphasized in it the greatness of the commandment to ascend to Eretz Israel. In this manner, R. Yehudah,[86] regarding the settling of Bavel,[87] for all of his Torah study, said in the name of Shmuel that just as it is prohibited to leave Eretz Israel for Bavel, so is it prohibited to leave Bavel for other countries [i.e., using Eretz Israel as the standard].

Yeshayahu Leibowitz (1903–1994)

Yeshayahu Leibowitz was a leading Israeli philosopher and scientist known for his out-spoken, often controversial opinions on Judaism, ethics, religion, and politics. An ultra-Orthodox Jew, Leibowitz also held controversial views on the subject of halakhah. He argued that the sole purpose of religious commandments was to obey God and not to receive any kind of reward in this world or in the world to come. He maintained that the reasons for religious commandments were beyond human understanding, as well as irrelevant, and any attempt to attribute emotional significance to the performance of commandments was misguided and akin to idolatry.

In an essay dedicated to the Kibiyeh incident (1953), in which IDF soldiers acting in response to several deadly attacks against Israeli civilians, carried out a reprisal operation against the village from which the perpetrators of the attacks originated, leaving more than fifty inhabitants of the village dead, Leibowitz wrote the following.

From: Yeshayahu Leibowitz, *After Kibiyeh* (1953–1954)[88]

Kibiyeh, its causes, implications, and the action itself are part of the great test to which we as a nation are put as a result of national liberation, political independence, and our military power – for we were bearers of a culture which, for many generations, derived certain spiritual benefits from conditions of exile, foreign rule, and political impotence. Our morality and conscience were conditioned by an insulated existence in which we could cultivate values and sensibilities that did not have to be tested in the crucible of reality. In our own eyes, and, to some extent in those of others as well, we appeared to have gained control over one of the terrible drives to which human nature is subject, and to abhor the atrocities to which it impels all human societies – impulse to communal murder. While congratulating ourselves upon this, we ignored, or attempted to ignore, that in our historical situation such mass-murder was not one of the means at our disposal for self-defense or for the attainment of collective aspirations. From the standpoint of both moral vocation and religious action, exilic existence enabled us to evade the decisive test. Attachment to the *Galuth* (Diaspora) and the opposition of many of the best representatives of Judaism to political redemption within historic reality was, in no small measure, a form of escapism reflecting the unconscious fear of such a test – fear of the loss of religious-moral superiority, which is easy to maintain in the absence of temptation and easy to lose in other circumstances....

Only the decision of one who is capable of acting and on whom rests the responsibility for acting or refraining from action can pass the genuine test of morality. We, the bearers of a morality which abominates the spilling of innocent blood, face our acid test only now that we have become capable of defending ourselves and responsible for our own security. Defense and security often appear to require the spilling of innocent blood.

This moral problem did not arise in connection with the war we conducted for our liberation and national restoration.... We accept war – without enthusiasm or admiration, but also without bitterness or protest – just as we accept many repulsive manifestations of human biological reality. In declaring our will to live as a real historic nation – not a meta-historical and metaphysical one – we took upon ourselves the functions of national life we had shunned when we were not bound by the tasks and concerts of normal national existence. By the logic of history and of moral evaluation, our war of independence was a necessary consequence of our two-thousand-year exile. Only one prepared to justify historically, religiously, or morally the continuation of the exilic existence could refuse to take upon himself the moral responsibility for using the sword to restore freedom.

Therefore, in our religious-moral stocktaking, we neither justify the bloodshed of the war (in which our blood was spilled no less than that of our enemies) nor do we apologize for it. The problematic issues concern the *manner* of conducting that war, which goes on to this very day, and what is to be done after this war will be over. . . .

We can, indeed, justify the action of Kibiyeh before "the world.". . .

[B]ut let us not try to do so. Let us rather recognize its distressing nature. There is an instructive precedent for Kibiyeh: the story of Shekhem and Dinah.[89] The sons of Jacob did not act as they did out of pure wickedness and malice. They had a decisive justification: "should one deal with our sister as with a harlot?!" The Torah, which narrates the actions of Simeon and Levi in Shekhem, adds to the description of the atrocity only three words (in the Hebrew text) in which apparently it conveyed the moral judgment of their behavior: "and came upon the city unawares, and slew all the males." "The sons of Jacob came upon the slain, and spoiled the city, *because they had defiled their sister*" (Gen. 34:25, 27). Nevertheless, because of this action, two tribes in Israel were cursed for generations by their father Jacob.

Although there are good reasons and ethical justifications for the Shekhem-Kibiyeh action, there is also an ethical postulate which is not itself a matter of rationalization and which calls forth a curse upon all these justified and valid considerations. The Shekhem operation and the curse of Jacob when he told his children what would befall them in the "end of days" is an example of the frightening problematic ethical reality: there may well be actions which can be vindicated and even justified – and are nevertheless accursed.

Citation of this example from the Torah does not reflect belief in the uniqueness of the "morality of Judaism." It does not imply that the action is forbidden for us as Jews. It is intended to indicate that the action is forbidden per se. "The morality of Judaism" is a most questionable concept – not only because morality does not admit a modifying attribute and cannot be "Jewish" or "not Jewish." The concept is self-contradictory for anyone who does not deliberately ignore its religious content.

There is, however, a specifically Jewish aspect to the Kibiyeh incident, not as a moral problem but an authentically religious one. We must ask ourselves: what produced this generation of youth, which felt no inhibition or inner compunction in performing the atrocity when given the inner urge and external occasion for retaliation?... The answer is that the events at Kibiyeh were a consequence of applying the religious category of holiness to social, national, and political values and interests − a usage prevalent in the education of young people as well as in the dissemination of public information. The concept of holiness − the concept of the absolute which is beyond all categories of human thought and evaluation − is transferred to the profane. From a religious standpoint only God is holy, and only His imperative is absolute. All human values and all obligations and undertakings derived from them are profane and have no absolute validity. Country, state, and nation impose pressing obligations and tasks which are sometimes very difficult. They do not, on that account, acquire sanctity. They are always subject to judgment and criticism from a higher standpoint. For the sake of that which is holy and perhaps only for its sake − man is capable of acting without any restraint. In our discourse and practice we have uprooted the category of holiness from its authentic location and transferred it to inappropriate objects, thus incurring all the dangers involved in such a distorted use of the concept....

This is the terrible punishment for transgressing the stringent prohibition: "Thou shalt not take the name of the Lord thy God in vain." The transgression may cause our third commonwealth to incur the curse of our father Jacob.

Shlomo Goren (1917–1994)

Shlomo Goren was a leading Religious Zionist rabbi who founded and served as the first head of the Military Rabbinate of the IDF. Born in Poland, Goren immigrated with his family to Palestine in 1925. He served in the IDF during three wars and wrote several award-winning books on Jewish law including his three-volume *Meshiv Milchama*,[90] the most thorough effort to provide halakhic answers to issues related to the military and the conduct of war to date. Goren was appointed as the third Ashkenazi Chief Rabbi of Tel Aviv in 1968 and later served as Chief Rabbi of Israel from 1973 to 1983.

From: Shlomo Goren, "The Ethics of War in light of the Halakhah" (1983)[91]

There is no doubt that the preservation of human life is the highest principle in the Torah, the halakhah and the ethical teachings of the Prophets. It is not limited to the preservation of Jewish lives but rather to all humans created in the image of God.

It is forbidden to harm the civilian population; we should not take instruction from the wars of ancient days.

Despite the unequivocal commandment of fighting in the Torah, we are commanded to have mercy even on our enemies and refrain from killing them even during times of war, unless in acts of self-defense or if this is necessary to secure a conquest and victory. It is forbidden to harm the non-combatant population and it is, of course, forbidden to harm women and children that are not participating in the fighting. This applies for all wars with the exception of the "commanded wars" of ancient times on which we were specifically commanded "you should not spare any soul." The Torah commanded such harsh treatment of these enemies due to their harsh treatment of others. But we should not deduce, God forbid, from these, as we have seen God has mercy also on idol worshippers and does not rejoice in their demise and is pained by their loss. We are commanded to follow His ways and pity his creatures. . . .

Goren goes on to debate a saying, which seems to contradict his judgment, by the leading Tanaic Rabbi Shimon Bar Yochai: "[Even] the best amongst the idol worshippers should be killed in times of war." Following a textual based discussion, Goren concludes:

It is clear this applies only in times of war and only when the people in question pose a direct threat to us . . . the intention of the saying was not, heaven forbid, to imply that it is permitted to kill them when they are not participating in the fighting and do not pose a threat to us. . . . There is neither justification nor permission [in this saying] to kill even in times of war those who are not actively engaged in war against us and even our enemies when they do not constitute a direct threat to us.

The treatment of prisoners of war and enemy remains.

The ethics of war of any military in the world is demonstrated primarily by two categories: (a) the treatment of war prisoners; (b) the treatment of enemy remains. The contrast between the behavior of the People of Israel's army and the other armies at the time, regarding both these issues, is outlined in the Bible and the Talmud . . . there is clear evidence in the scriptures that the People of Israel treated prisoners of war, including those of foreign armies, mercifully. This was true also in cases where the enemy waged war against us and was defeated and captured by [the nation of] Israel. This behavior was well known among the nations of the world which were neighbors of the people of Israel. . . .

Affording proper burial to enemy fatalities gives a man a good name, honor, and the title righteous.

As for the treatment of enemy fatalities, we have clear evidence for the high level of humanity and righteousness that was prevalent within the Army of Israel in ancient times. As it says in Samuel 2 (8:13) *And David made himself a name when he returned from killing eighteen thousand Syrians in the Valley of Salt*. And Rashi explained there: *And David made himself a name* – this was because David buried the enemy soldiers he killed at Adom and created a good name for the People of Israel who are known to bury their enemies. . . . As we are loyal to the sanctified heritage and righteousness of the army of Israel in ancient times, we have established during my service in the IDF special burial units whose role it is to identify and bury the remains of enemy fatalities in times of war. This is also in line with our earlier comment that the verse *For in the image of God He made man* (Genesis 9:6) applies to all humans without difference between nations or races, with faith and confidence in the prophetic vision for the end of days: *For then I will restore to the peoples a pure language, That they all may call on the name of the Lord, To serve Him with one accord.*

Shlomo Aviner (b. 1943)

Shlomo Aviner, head of the Ateret Cohanim *yeshiva*[92] in Jerusalem and rabbi of the settlement of Beit El. Aviner, is considered one of the spiritual leaders of the Religious Zionist movement. The following excerpts are from a booklet published in an attempt to provide halakhic responses to issues that arose as a result of the First Intifada (1988).

From: Shlomo Aviner, "Questions and Answers from the First Intifada" (1988)[93]

Response against Rioters

Does the Torah teach us how to act against rioters?

Maimonides points out that Joshua, in his day, sent three epistles to the inhabitants of Eretz Israel: Joshua, before entering Eretz Israel, sent three epistles. The first stated: "Anyone who wishes to take flight [from the oncoming army] should take flight." He sent another: "Anyone who wishes to make peace should make peace." He sent another: "Anyone who wishes to make war should do so."[94]

What is told of Joshua in the Bible still has value as divine [word]. Initially, Joshua announced: If you are intending to flee, we will not pursue you. This is what the Gergashites did: "The Gergashite cleared out, trusting in the Holy One."[95]

In his second epistle he wrote: "We need to enter this land and to set it up under our governance. If you desire to live with us in peace, you may remain therein. This land is ours, it is under our rule. If you decide to remain in it, you may, but the one condition for this is that you accept our governance."[96]

Therefore, even today, if the Ishmaelites are not busy murdering us and acting as our foes, they may remain under our governance. But if they act as our foes through all kinds of violent disturbances, we will be unable to leave them among us, as it is written: "And if you do not dispossess the inhabitants of the land from before you, it will come about that those of them you leave will become stings in your eyes and thorns in your sides, and they will be foes to you on the land in which you dwell" (Num. 33:55).

"One who tries to kill you, rise up and kill him first" (Ha-ba le-horgekha, hashkem le-horgo)

"When someone tries to kill you, rise up and kill him first."[97] When must I arise? After he threw a stone, Molotov cocktail at me, or before and am I permitted to pursue and kill him?

The Shulhan Arukh[98] ruled thus: "One who pursues an associate to kill him, and this assailant has been warned and continues in his pursuit, even if he is a minor, all of Israel is commanded to save him [the potential victim], by injuring one of the assailant's limbs; and if they cannot aim and save [the potential victim] without killing the assailant, they should kill the assailant even though he has not yet killed."[99] From this we conclude that it is forbidden to kill a pursuer who is trying to kill you unless there is no other way to save oneself or the assailant himself.

If he [the assailant] already threw the stone, it is not permissible to kill him, but of course he must be caught and brought to trial. However, in most cases, one who threw a stone once will continue to throw [it] additional times and therefore – ostensibly – there is cause for killing him after he threw once, in order to save others from future occasions. Similarly, we found regarding the Law Regarding the *moseir* [one who hands over a Jew or his goods to a non-Jew, enacted in order to prevent harm coming to additional members of the community]: "If there is a legal presumption [regarding someone that he is] *moseir* – he should be killed, lest he inform on others."[100] Rabbeinu Asher [the "Rosh"][101] also wrote: "They are taking counsel and scheming to eradicate him from the world, in order to limit the damage [or: set limits or rules – put their foot down; lit. 'put a fence around the matter'] so that others are warned and to prevent the proliferation of *mosrim* in Israel, and also to save all of Israel from being persecuted by him."[102] Yet, of course, this is not a matter that can be carried out by an individual, since at the present he himself is not in danger. In all likelihood, there is indeed a future danger to others, and still, it is a matter that the army and police need to address and decide what should be done.

And here, regarding what is written in the Gemara: "When someone tries to kill you, rise up and kill him first," the medieval Sages [Rishonim] commented on the place where this is written in the Torah. According to Rashi, it is inferred from the story of the burglar breaking into one's house [who presumably poses a life danger] (*ha-ba be-mahteret*). Rabbi Menahem Ha-Meiri[103] wrote: "And where did he state it? It was elucidated in Midrash Tanhuma: 'Be foes to the Midianites[104] and strike them, for they have been foes to you.'"[105] Thus did our Sages of blessed memory state: "When someone tries to kill you, rise up and kill him first," in other words they always act as your foes, and now be foes unto them since they seek to be foes unto you." Regarding one whom we know for certain is our foe, and intends to be our foe in the future, we must act as his foe in order to prevent him from doing so.[106]

Deterrence

Is it permissible for the army to carry out activities the aim of which is deterrence, in the midst of a hostile population?

Not only may the army do so, but it is obligated to do so since it is the appointed guardian of preserving the peace, calm and security of civilians, as Maimonides writes of the task of a king in Israel: "to fill the world with justice and to break the arms of the wicked,"[107] to work for the betterment of society, and "to abolish the wrongdoing of one against another.... This is tantamount to every individual among the people not being permitted to act according to his will and up to the limits of his power."[108]

Of course: If it is possible to arrange the matter with subtlety and pleasant-ness – that is surely fine; but if not, it is obligatory to employ punishment and deterrence, as in the words of Maimonides: "[It is] unsustainable without punish-ments and laws, and thus unsustainable without stationing judges dispersed in each and every city … and unsustainable without a king, who should inspire fear and take varied preventative measures, and strengthen the hand of the judges and vest them with authority."[109]

What extent of severity is permissible for the army to employ in deterrence activities?

Everything possible must be done to deter, and this depends on the particular mat-ter. Maimonides explains that there are four criteria for determining the extent of the punishment:

a. **Greatness of the crime**: the greater the crime, the heavier the penalty.

b. **Frequency of the occurrence of the crime**: the more often the crime is com-mitted, the heavier the penalty necessary. And if it is rare, a slight penalty is sufficient.

c. **Strength of incitement**: The more that the crime incites the person because he has a great desire to commit it, or because great pressure is enacted upon him to commit it, the heavier the penalty must be, in order to serve as a deterrent.

d. **Ease with which the action can be committed [in secret]**: If it is easy to carry out the crime without being caught, only a harsh and threatening pun-ishment can prevent it from recurring.[110]

Is such punishment not lacking in compassion to some degree?

When punishment is necessary, avoiding it is not compassion but the opposite: it constitutes cruelty toward the innocent citizens who suffer harm at the hands of evil-doers. According to Maimonides, "If the guilty person is not punished, the damage will never be abolished, and anyone who thinks to do evil will not be prevented. And it is not as the foolishness of the nations who think that abandon-ing punishment is compassion toward human beings; rather, it is the epitome of cruelty and a loss of state order. Rather, compassion is as the Creator commanded: "Judges and overseers you should set for yourself."[111] "Since compassion toward destructive evildoers constitutes cruelty against all creatures."[112]

Collective Punishment

Is it permissible to carry out retaliatory activities on villages from which stones were thrown, even against people who themselves did not throw stones?

Simply speaking, it is impossible to punish people for a crime they did not com-mit. The Rivash, Rabbi Yitzhak bar Sheshet,[113] one of the great Sages of Spain five hundred years ago, tells of a case of "two or three Jews who were responsible for the King's counting house, when a counterfeit coin was found under their watch. The king was furious and his rage burned within him to deport all the Jews in his kingdom. And after much labor and trouble they bargained with the king that he not send them in exchange for such and such thousand gold coins.[114] In other words, because of the sin of a few Jews a heavy fine was imposed on all of the Jewish communities, in exchange for canceling the punishment of deportation. The Rivash writes that this was an unjust and illegal step that deviated from the authority of the king: "Because of two or three who spoiled things in the matter of the coin, he would rage at all the Jews, and with a strong hand would deport them from his land to the point that they need to compromise over a few thousand gold coins?" Regarding the like, Abraham the Patriarch, peace unto him, said to the Holy One: "Far be it from You to do such a thing, to put to death the innocent with the guilty, making innocent and guilty the same. Far be it from You! Will not the Judge of all the earth do justice?"[115] And Moses our Teacher, peace unto him, said, "Should one man offend and against all the community You rage?"[116]

And he also relies on the known Aramaic saying: "Tuvia sinned, and Zigod was punished" (i.e. the innocent take the punishment).[117]

All of the aforesaid relates to regular times of peace. So certainly, during war between one nation and another it is not thus, because everyone who belongs to the enemy nation is considered an enemy and can, in an instant, become an enemy, and therefore, it is impossible to distinguish between one who has been actually sent out against you, and one who is numbered among your enemies but has not fought to this day. Moreover, when Saul set out to war against the Amalekites, *Saul said to the Kenites, "Come, withdraw at once from among the Amalekites, that I may not destroy you along with them; for you showed kindness to all the Israelites when they left Egypt." So the Kenites withdrew from among the Amalekites.*[118] Because during wartime, it is impossible to distinguish between one person and another, and if the Kenite, from Jethro's family, had not withdrawn from the Amalekites, he would have been destroyed with them. But during peacetime, when there is no war between one nation and another, but rather lone murderers, certainly a person who has committed no wrongdoing should not be punished simply because he belongs to that people, or to that village of murderers.

All of the above supposes that the people of said village are, truly, innocent. But if they give cover to murderers, protect them or encourage them, and even if they know their whereabouts and do not inform the police, they are committing a grave ethical transgression against the laws of the state, and must be punished. Of course, not to the same severity of punishment that the murderers themselves are punished, but rather with a light punishment for an accomplice and the like.

If, indeed, the reality is that when a person throws stones his family knows about it, and all members of the village know about it and do not report it to the police, they are also deserving of punishment.

Ill-Treatment of Arabs

Is it necessary, or permissible, to ill-treat Arabs?

It is clear that ill-treatment of any person in the world is prohibited. To the contrary, one should act toward him with respect, whether he is a Jew or a non-Jew, since he was created in the image of God. True, sometimes the police are obliged to act with a heavy hand against all manner of criminals who are dangerous to society – but here as well, caution is mandated, to the extent possible, so as to not detract from a person's dignity. Maimonides ruled that a judge has the authority to use severe methods of punishment even though they are not mentioned in the Torah, if the situation demands it. *"Whenever the court sees that a command has fallen into general disuse, the duty devolves upon it to safeguard and strengthen the command in any way which in its judgment will achieve the desired result . . . to flog . . . to expropriate money . . . to lay the ban and invoke the major excommunication upon him . . . to quarrel with him who deserves to be quarreled with, to smite him . . . to pluck his hair . . . to fetter the hands and feet of the offender, to imprison him, to sock him down and drag him to the ground."*[119]

However, Maimonides adds, "all his deeds should be done for the sake of Heaven. Let not human dignity be light in his eyes. This applies with even greater force to the dignity of the children of Abraham, Isaac and Jacob, who adhere to the True Law."[120]

This is for you [to know] that every person must be respected, and Jews all the more so.

Yuval Sherlo (b. 1957)

Yuval Sherlo, the head of the Petah Tikva *yeshiva*, is a pragmatic Religious Zionist Rabbi. Sherlo is a leading member of Tzohar, a liberal young rabbinical movement, and the Ma'aglei Tzedek movement for social justice. The following essay was written in the aftermath of Operation Defensive Shield, a large-scale military operation conducted by the IDF in 2002, at the height of the Second Intifada. It was the largest military operation in the West Bank since the 1967 Six-Day War. The operation, aimed at stopping the increasing civilian deaths in Israel from Palestinian terrorist attacks, especially suicide bombings, resulted in the death and injury of many Palestinians as well as considerable damage to property.

From: Yuval Sherlo, "Questions on the Ethics of War" (She'elot Al Musar HaMilchama), (2002)[121]

Operation "Defensive Shield" led to the resurfacing of a discussion on the Jewish laws of war. I refer not to laws applied during a time of war, as in the question of exemption of combatants from the obligation of phylacteries* or an *eruv*† in

---

* Observant Jews are obliged to wear the phylacteries (Tefilin) during morning prayers on weekdays.

† *Eruv* is a symbolic enclosure around a home, community, or even a military camp. It enables the carrying of objects in public places during the Sabbath, when this would otherwise be forbidden by Jewish law.

a military camp, but rather to questions pertaining to the Jewish collective (*klal Yisrael*) in terms of the way war itself is conducted. For many generations, we were denied the privilege of clarifying these questions and therefore, the Torah offers little guidance. We are forced to discuss the questions regarding the Laws of Capital Offenses [*dinei nefashot*] with very limited sources, and in the absence of a jurisprudential tradition. Therefore, all who deal in these issues are forced to appeal to sources that are not usually invoked in halakhic deliberations, such as the straightforward biblical text, and *midrashic* texts.

One of the main topics that arose for discussion during this war was the question of war ethics. The Torah categorically rejects the unnatural pseudo-morality of turning the other cheek. The Torah itself is full of instructions for war; we are not prohibited from taking revenge and bringing murderers to justice. On the contrary, it teaches us that there is law and order, and that the world is not a free-for-all, but rather the world of the Holy One whose signature is truth, and where true justice is rendered. The question of whether war against those who seek our demise is at all ethical is entirely not negotiable. It is a matter of simple justice, divine morality, and in effect, the Torah precept of delivering Israel from the hand of the enemy.

The question on which the discussion focuses is whether we are obligated to fulfill additional [ethical] foundations, beyond our will and obligation to achieve victory in war....

Today, obligations regarding the conduct of war often find their source in the legal agreements that the nations of the world have formally ratified. In this connection there is little reason to repeat that which is commonly known, namely that these conventions accepted by the nations are in partial use, and in most cases, each nation demands that its fellow [nations] uphold them while it simultaneously engages in indiscriminate killing. The international judicial institutions are also unfair and politically tainted, and serve as a tool for the achievement of political aims rather than as an arm of justice. However, our vision of repairing the world – *tikkun olam* – in the Kingdom of G-d obligates us to ask the question at the theoretical level, and not to abdicate responsibility for fear of being condemned by the nations of the world. It is imperative that we ask these questions internally and consider: Is it the Torah's intent that our message to the nations be a recognition of the ethical boundaries during war, and that not everything is permissible; or is the thrust of our message to the world that if indeed you come in the name of truth and justice, you must not enact limitations during war against wickedness and evil, and the army waging combat is not required to restrain itself from doing anything in order to achieve victory – mainly it must not refrain from actions that would prevent it from endangering itself.

Many obligations are officially accepted in our world, some formulated in the Geneva Conventions, some in various international conventions, and some in international law. Among those with which we disagree in conducting our wars against our enemies are the obligations not to harm those outside the arena of combat, and the distinction between combatants and non-combatants. Likewise, it is internationally prohibited to exile a civilian population.

The struggle of the IDF against terrorists has raised mainly, in a practical sense, the question of taking precautions against harming people who are outside of the direct arena of combat. The army has often been caught in this dilemma. For example, in the planning stage concerning the allocation of forces for missions, one can [plan to] enter a refugee camp with the help of ground forces, which enable slow and precise work, while greatly endangering the combatants, and in contrast, one can use artillery or the air force, corps which entail low risk to self, where the likelihood of harming people outside the arena of combat is high. At the operational stage, we encounter these questions when a terrorist makes his hiding place using pregnant women who are not part of the arena of combat, or when children constitute a living barricade, sometimes against their will, and so forth. The common aspect to all of the questions is that on one side of the balance is certainly the endangerment of soldiers' lives, and the question we are asking is whether there is another side to the balance that must be considered, and if sometimes soldiers' lives must even be endangered in order to avoid killing, or is it that the other side of the balance contains nothing, and we must fight G-d's war, no holds barred?

Ethics of Combat in Jewish Sources

The Bible contains no explicit [ethical] requirements beyond defining absolute victory in war. Regarding war against the seven nations, the text sets forth the requirement to destroy and kill the nations of the Land; in the war against the Midianites, the text speaks of passing through the prisoner camp and killing every woman who has lain with a man; it speaks of annihilating the seed of Amalek; King David, in his offensive against Moab, measures off two-thirds using a rope and kills them (II Sam. 8); the prophet criticizes King Ahab of Israel for setting free the defeated King of Aram (I Kings 20), as well as many other examples.

Common to all is the requirement for victory in war, with no limitations.... It is rare to find in the Bible any demands vis-à-vis soldiers who have exceeded the limits. To the contrary, it seems that when compassion is shown toward enemies, we encounter the prophet's vehement criticism....

The *midrashic* rabbinic literature also lacks the foundations for preventing excessive harm to those outside of the arena of combat. The Sages addressed the topic of war frequently in the various *midrashic* texts, but in their words there is almost no reference to an obligatory act of loving-kindness or compassion toward enemies. However, it is difficult to draw far-reaching conclusions from this, since, to our dismay, when the Oral Torah was recorded, such a question was not relevant, both due to the loss of halakhic independence and also due to the cruelty of the Roman army and our struggle against it.

Considerations Regarding the Determination of Ethical Boundaries

In light of all this, why might we suppose that we are likely to find – at the other end of the balance – ethical obligations or behaviours toward an enemy that limit the intensity of the war waged against it, which prohibit us from killing those outside of the war arena? What might be the source of limitations on the force used in war?

In what follows, we will consider the various halakhic foundations that are likely to occupy the other side of the balance.

I. *The Status of Natural Morality*

Two assumptions form the basis for clarifying this point, namely, the status of natural morality. The first determines that natural morality opposes the killing of those who are not in the arena of combat. . . . It is likely that what we call natural morality is actually Christian morality, and it is distorted and alien to natural morality. This morality is the morality of the weak, which dictates the turning of the other cheek, and is not the morality of justice and law (*tzedek u-mishpat*). Even if we seek to determine natural morality as the morality accepted today by human beings, it will be difficult in light of the great hypocrisy that characterizes the various positions accepted today in the world. However, the assertion that there is no natural morality today in its contemporary known sense is erroneous, both as a reading of the state of the world, as an understanding of the human soul, and as a highly negative estimation of the essence of the human race.

A second assumption is that the Torah recognizes natural morality. The recognition of natural morality can be induced from many dilemmas, which might be presented according to three categories.

a. First among them is the straightforward meaning of the text – we find that the Torah itself often uses the language of natural morality. Sometimes it positions humans against the Holy One, such as: "Will not the Judge of all the earth do justice?" [Gen. 18:25] which is a kind of justice whose source is in natural morality and not in a divine command, because it ostensibly contradicts Him; "Should one man offend and against all the community You rage?" [Num. 16:22], or the words of the Holy One Himself, which emphasize the horror of burning children alive on arguments derived from the natural world of man, "For even their sons and their daughters they burn in fire to their gods" [Deut. 12:31]. The words of Nachmanides on natural ethics during war are also explicit. Nachmanides viewed the commandment uttered at Mara: "There did He set him a statute and law, and there did He test him" [Ex. 15:25], as encapsulating the rules of behavior during wartime. . . .

b. The second is the broad use of ethical considerations found in many *midrashic* texts and in medieval commentaries (*Rishonim*) of the various commandments. In this context we invoke the words of Maimonides in the Laws of the

Sabbath, regarding the saving of a human life (*pikuah nefesh*): "From this you learn that the laws of the Torah are not revenge against the world, but rather mercy and compassion and peace in the world."

In Torah commentaries we also find these principles touted as the obvious, and additionally, many commentators raise the question of morality vis-à-vis the nations (*goyim*). The first member of the *goyim* to raise the issue was Abimelekh: "Will you slay a nation even if innocent?" (Gen. 20:4), and the Sovereign of the Universe thanked him by saying, "Indeed, I know that with a pure heart you have done this" (ibid. 20:6). However, the question of acting deceitfully toward the *goy* also arises frequently in Torah commentary.

c. Third among them is the introduction of these rules into halakhic consider-
    ations. We often find the rule "Her ways are pleasant ways / And all her paths,
    peaceful," (Prov. 3:17) [referring to the Torah] as a halakhic rule, as well as
    other similar rules. We who follow the teachings of Rabbi Abraham Isaac Kook*
    cannot but account for the tremendous extent of his words in praise of natural
    morality....

II. *The Prohibition against Killing a Person*

Upon Noah's exit from the ark, he was told that, "He who sheds human blood /by humans his blood shall be shed" (Gen. 9:6). This statement stipulated the prohibi-tion against the shedding of blood as one of the Noahide commandments, and as a basic foundation on which the world was created. The Ten Commandments, as well, also state the categorical command: "You shall not murder." In effect, this commandment does not distinguish between men and women, Jew and non-Jew, adult or child – it is an absolute command.

However, in the Torah's system of punishment, there is, apparently, a distinc-tion between the punishment prescribed for killing a Jew, and the punishment for killing a non-Jew. However, the penal system is not the measure for determining the severity of the matter....

It should be noted that ... killing a *goy* [Gentile] is graver than killing a Jew, since it also embodies the commandment of desecrating G-d's name [i.e., as if the murderer took matters pertaining to heaven into his own hands]. This is how he interpreted the words of the Torah in his gloss on the weekly Torah reading of *Mishpatim*.

As stated, it is understood that the prohibition against killing a person instructs one to avoid killing a *goy*. It is difficult to say that all of the laws apply to this prohibition, to the extent that one should submit to martyrdom in order to avoid killing a *goy*. As everyone knows, if one tells a Jew to kill or else he will be killed,

---

* Rabbi Abraham Isaac Kook (1865–1935) was the first Ashkenazi chief rabbi of the British Mandate for Palestine, the founder of the Religious Zionist Yeshiva Merkaz HaRav, a Jewish thinker, halakhic authority, and a renowned Torah scholar.

he is obligated to be killed, and from explications of the issue in the Talmud, it appears – at least, simply understood – that if the person to be killed is a *goy*, this law does not apply. And yet, the very caution against and careful avoidance of killing a person for no reason is a Torah commandment....

The prohibition against killing a person therefore mandates caution in not killing too much in war. As stated above in the words of R. David Kimhi (*Radak*), one who kills in the storm of battle during war is not to be judged for it. However, this exemption does not compensate for the fact that this is something that must be avoided. In this context one must recall that in the *midrash* (Deut. Rabbah, *Az Yavdil*), we see that Moses viewed himself as one who had murdered in error when he killed the Egyptian (!).

Samuel Dov Rosenberg

The issue of Jewish ethics of war has also been addressed in recent years by IDF officers in the *Military Defense Force Rabbinate Journal*. One such example can be found in an article by Major Rabbi Samuel Dov Rosenberg.

From: Samuel Dov Rosenberg, "The Ethics of War and the Treatment of the Enemy and His Surroundings According to the Halakhah" (2008)[122]

Combat – National Struggle

It is a known rule in our Torah that, "Nothing stands before saving life except for idolatry, incest and bloodshed."[*]

If so, from whence does the Israeli combatant in war assume divine authority or the authority of the Judge (known in the Torah as "Elokim") to harm and kill human beings created in G-d's image? The responsibility for preserving life and the prohibition against endangering [life] are entirely undermined during war, and if so, what is the source of the halakhic allowance to fight and to enter into danger?

Rabbi Abraham Isaac Kook writes in his article (*Mishpat Kohen*,[†] 142–44) that although war endangers those who participate in it, it is permissible and is even a commandment. This is because going to war arises from the status of sovereignty, and since a king in Israel is authorized to issue a temporary ordinance to have people executed, he is also authorized to endanger combatants in battle. There is an absolute connection between the king and going out to war, since by power of his authority a special halakhic dimension is created, such that when he declares a state of war, all citizens of the kingdom must apply themselves to this situation with all of its ramifications. It is no coincidence that Maimonides in *Yad*

---

[*] Babylonian Talmud, Tractate Ketubot 19a.
[†] In Hebrew, lit. "the laws of the priest."

Ha-hazakah[*] linked the two essentially different concepts of "The Laws of Kings and their Wars" under a single heading.

According to these foundations, we can conclude that in a war, the collective of Israel is rendered a single body, and then every individual is required to devote himself to the life of the collective, without taking into account his entering into danger.[†]

And when he enters [the] relations of war, his heart should be devoted to everything relating to the war (as appears in the halakhah determined by Maimonides, Laws of Kings, ch. 7, law 15), and he should not think of his wife, or of his children, but should blot out their memory from his heart. This arises from the necessity of distinguishing between private affiliation, and absolute devotion to the collective.

From this it follows that all of the foundations of [the laws of] preserving lives that we know from the Torah deal expressly with the individual or with a collection of individuals considered to be individuals, which is not the case with the essence of war which is public, an activity of the kingdom and the entire nation; and it is irrelevant to discuss and to deal with the act and the results of war in terms of the individual.

The Wars of Israel in Our Day

After having stated the types of wars we find discussed among the Sages and the halakhic authorities, we must consider the halakhic status of Israel's war today.

With the beginning of the process of Israel's return to its land and the overall threat by the Arabs of the area against the people residing in Zion, the great men of Israel meditated on the problem and discussed how to define the situation that was created, since one can conclude from the Laws of war that a war lacking a "king" or a "Sanhedrin" is prohibited.

Rabbi Abraham Isaac Kook (*Mishpetei Kohen*, art. 144) introduced the opinion that even when there is no king in Israel, when the laws of the kingdom in all that relates to the general state of the nation are determined by it and its representatives, their decision and stipulation are as equally valid as those of a king.

Rabbi Yisraeli's student also expanded (*Amud Ha-yemini*, art. 9) with the assertion that a leader in Israel whom the masses have appointed is given a status identical to the Laws of Kings.

In addition, we find in the words of the Sages (*Horayot* 3)[‡] a clarification that "the community of the Land of Israel is called a community and that community living in the Diaspora is not called a community." Therefore, confrontation vis-à-vis the Jewish community in Israel has a special validity for the sake of the entire community of Israel.[123]

---

[*] Maimonides' codex of the law, also known also as the *Mishneh Torah*.

[†] Rabbi Shaul Yisraeli, *Amud Ha-yemini* (in Hebrew, lit. the "right pillar"), a tractate dedicated to the religious laws of the state, art. 14.

[‡] *Horayot* (*Decisions*) is a tractate in the Talmud dedicated to laws pertaining to errors in jurist procedures and systems.

Rabbi Herzog,[*] who was the First Chief Rabbi of the State of Israel, determined with certainty at the time of the outbreak of the War of Independence, that the war coming upon us is a "divinely commanded war" (Rabbi Yitzhak HaLevi Herzog in his article about the establishment of the State and its wars, *Tehumin* 4:19), obligatory beyond any doubt, both in the opinion of Maimonides who states that "helping Israel from the hand of an enemy that has come upon them" is a "divinely commanded war," since the goal of our Arab neighbors is to leave no memory or remnant of the Jews in Israel, and to remove us by force and destroy us. Also, of course, in the opinion of Nachmanides, who emphasizes that the commandment to conquer Eretz Israel applies to every generation, since it is a commandment from the Torah, and also, many sages of Israel in that same generation instructed thus.[†]

After the War of Independence as well, when Israel's boundaries had already been determined, the eternal struggle against the enemies who attack and harm us continued, and therefore, every war based on the conquest of the Land is a "divinely commanded war."[‡]

Likewise, an offensive – and not just a defensive – war, is included in the category of "divinely commanded war," when the enemy intends to attack in the future.[§] As found in the *Shulhan Arukh* (*Orah Hayyim*, 329:6 and according to Rabbi Moses Isserles – The Rama, ibid.) regarding permission to desecrate the Sabbath when fighting enemies who attack Jewish towns, the Rama adds "even if they have not yet come, but intend to come."

It can arise that limited fighting carried out by individuals, when the entire nation is not devoted to the effort, is also considered a "divinely commanded war,"[**] since we found that in the war against Amalek, it says explicitly (Ex. 17:9) "Choose men for us and go out to battle Amalek"; that is most certainly a case of "divinely commanded war."

One of the great rabbis of the last generation[††] wanted to introduce the idea that a Jewish war in our day included all the foundations of a "divinely commanded war," whether [those deriving from war] against the seven nations, or

---

[*] Rabbi Yitzhak HaLevi Herzog (1888–1959) was the first Chief Rabbi of Ireland. From 1937 until his death in 1959, he was Ashkenazi Chief Rabbi of the British Mandate of Palestine and of Israel after its independence in 1948.

[†] See Rabbi Shlomo Yosef Zevin (1888–1978), "Ha-Milhamah" (The War) in *Le-or Ha-halakhah* (*In Light of the Law*), p. 65.

[‡] Rabbi Shaul Yisraeli (1909–1995), "Peulot Tagmul Le-Or Ha-halakhah" (Acts of Retaliation in Light of Jewish Law), in *Tzomet Ha-Torah ve-Ha-Medinah* (*The Crossroad between the Torah and the State*), Part 3, p. 253. R. Rabbi Katriel Fishel Tchors (1895–1979) wrote the same in his article "Milhemet Reshut Mitzvah o Hova?" (Optional War: A Religious Duty or Obligatory War?), in *Tzomet Ha-Torah ve-Ha-Medinah*, Part 3, p. 243.

[§] Responsa *Heikhal Yitzhak*, "Orekh Hayyim," 37, as well as Rabbi Shaul Yisraeli, in *Tzomet Ha-Torah ve-Ha-Medinah*.

[**] Responsa by Rabbin Yechiel Yaakov Weinberg (1884–1966), *Seridei Eish* (*Remnants of the Fire*), Part 1, p. 314.

[††] Rabbi Yehudah Gershuni, *Kol Tzofayikh*, p. 175.

against Amalek, or coming to the aid of Israel at the hand of an enemy, but we do not need this [claim] to conclude that this war, even when its extent is limited both in terms of the limited forces engaged in fighting and the fighting in a limited area, is a "divinely ordained war."

Harming a Civilian Population during Wartime

According to guidelines set by the Torah, one cannot apply the rule "When someone tries to kill you, rise up and kill him first" (*Ha-ba le-horgekha, hashkem le-horgo*) to a population of tens of thousands, even if situated in an environment hostile to us, and even if they view us as an occupier, since it is a small minority that is harming us and seeks to kill us.* Even in a "divinely commanded war," with the exception of those places where the Torah instructed us "You shall let no breathing creature live" (Deut. 20:16), we are commanded to have mercy and not to kill a civilian population, and certainly one must not harm women and children, except for when self-defense is necessary, and for purposes of conquest and victory.†

On the other hand, when there is actual and apparent danger in the eyes of the combatant, there is a strong and sound basis for war requiring that every action must be carried out such that no soldier or civilian on the combatants' side be harmed, and in this situation one must not compare the number of our soldiers likely to be harmed with civilians of the Israel-hating enemy who are likely to pay the price of this war with their lives.‡

Even if we had found that it was suitable to fastidiously adhere to the laws of the "pursuer" (*rodef*) who must be stopped by damaging only one of his limbs [if possible], in war we have already mentioned above (end of Ch. 3) the case is different than for individuals; but rather, this is a fight for national survival (*malkhut*), and should not be limited to a consideration of one individual or another who is harmed on the enemy's side or under his protection.§ Moreover, it appears that in a war, it is more important for those under attack to fight and kill their pursuers even if the latter retreat midway, in contrast to the law in the case of a burglar breaking into one's house [who presumably poses a life danger] (*ha-ba be-mahteret*), since that is the practice in wars,** as King David said, "I pursued my enemies and wiped them out / I did not turn back till I destroyed them" (2 Sam. 22:38).

---

* Rabbi Hayyim David HaLevi (1924–1998), "Ha-ba le-horgekha, hashkem le-horgo be-hayyenu ha-tziboriyyim" (Principles of Self-Defense), *Tehumin*, 1:343.

† Rabbi Shlomo Goren, *Meshiv Milhama* (A War Responsa), Part 1, p. 14.

‡ Rabbi Abraham Shapira (1914–2007), "Milhama ve-Musar" (War and Ethics), *Tehumin* 4:182.

§ Rabbi Yoezer Ariel, "Haravot ve-Itim" (Swords and Plowshares), *Tehumin*, 4:189.

** Ariel, "Haravot ve-Itim," p. 190.

This is what we find in Saul's appeal to the Kenites during the fighting against the Amalekites, '"Come, withdraw at once from among the Amalekites, that I may not destroy you along with them" (I Sam. 15:6). From this we learn that had the Kenites not left the Amalekites, they would have likely perished with them, and Saul would therefore have been deterred from fighting against Amalek.

In the case of a local civilian population that offers cover to the enemy, even if they offer no assistance to the fighters or to the government, and even if they are not sentenced before the fact as murderers themselves, they must know that they are taking their lives into their own hands, and that the hands of one who harms them are clean.[*]

Based on his detailed halakhic discussion, Rosenberg goes on to conclude the following:

Summary and Conclusions

1. In the opinion of Maimonides, coming to the aid of Israel against an assailant is defined as a "divinely commanded war." It seems that also Nachmanides maintains that every war for the conquest of Eretz Israel in every generation is a "divinely commanded war."
2. The halakhic authority of the government to declare and launch a "divinely commanded war" is identical to that of a king.
3. It is not relevant to consider killing during war at the level of the individual, since the obligation to preserve life from any danger is waived during wartime for the needs of the nation.
4. The rabbis of Eretz Israel determined during the War of Independence, with total certainty, that our war was a "divinely commanded war."
5. Ongoing war as well, which is more complex than a circumscribed war, as well as offensive operations, are included in the rubric of a "divinely commanded war."
6. The prohibition against besieging an enemy city from all directions does not apply in a "divinely commanded war," in the opinion of most of the medieval sages (*Rishonim*).
7. The prohibition against destroying fruit trees during a siege against the enemy applies to destruction that would serve no purpose or destruction as an end in itself.
8. It is fitting and proper that while deliberating over a decision as to whether to go to war, the component of emotional harm and the devaluation of human life is to be considered.
9. Despite this, it can be reckoned that during a "divinely commanded war," when the combatants are convinced of the righteousness and the religious obligation that they are upholding, their emotional health and moral character will not be compromised.
10. The Laws of the Assailant (*dinei rodef*) cannot be applied to a hostile population numbering in the tens of thousands.

---

[*] R. Shlomo Aviner, *Responsa on the Intifada*, p. 24.

11. There is nothing that prevents harming the house of a terrorist, even if his neighbor will be harmed by destruction of the building.

12. When a terrorist's neighbor helps him or even ignores his neighbor's activity, he is not considered innocent and he is taking his life into his own hands.

13. Civilians situated near terrorists and who do not move away from them are endangering their lives, and our forces have no responsibility to avoid harming them due to their proximity to civilians.

14. A soldier who senses actual life danger during his operational activity will do all that is necessary to protect himself from harm, and will not be deterred by fear of harming civilians on the enemy side.

15. During combat against terrorists in a populated area, it is proper to warn civilians in the area who are not involved [in the fighting], to distance themselves from the place of combat activity.

NOTES

1 Some would argue that as a general rule the rabbinical debates did not create any structured or systematic discussion on any matter; the issue of the ethics of war was no exception in that regard. Regardless of whether this approach is correct, it is clear that the amount of halakhic effort put into this subject is marginal in comparison to other legal matters debated.

2 See Michael Walzer, "War and Peace in the Jewish Tradition," in Terry Nardin (ed.), *The Ethics of War and Peace: Religious and Secular Perspectives* (Princeton, N.J.: Princeton University Press, 1996), pp. 95–114. For an important response to this claim, see A. Ravitzky, "Prohibited Wars in the Jewish Tradition," in ibid., pp. 115–127.

3 An example of this sort of discussion, one focusing more on religious practice than on moral norms, can be found in a debate about the permissibility of fighting on the Sabbath (Shabbat). Jews fighting the Greeks and later the Romans faced complicated dilemmas as to whether this should be forbidden. The view that eventually emerged was that war could be waged on the day of rest only if the Greeks had taken advantage of this day to launch an attack. A forcible response was accordingly permitted, but strictly within the limits of self-defense. This condition, in turn, allowed the Romans much later to take advantage of the Shabbat not for direct combat with the Jews but rather for other warfare manoeuvres that were not considered direct fighting; as a result the Jews were forbidden to react. See I Maccabees, 2:29–41; Josephus, *Antiquities*, 12: 272–277; 14:63–65.

4 This link between religion and state has mainly to do with issues such as marriage, divorce, and funerals. A separate question is the status of the rabbis that serve in the army providing religious services.

5 See Jack Bemporad, "Norms of War in Judaism," in Vesselin Popovski, Gregory M. Reichberg, and Nicholas Turner (eds.), *World Religions and Norms of War* (Tokyo: United Nations University Press, 2009), pp. 106–141; John Ferguson, *War and Peace in the World's Religions* (New York: Oxford University Press, 1978), pp. 78–98; Norman Solomon, "The Ethics of War in Judaism," in Torkel Brekke (ed.), *The Ethics of War in Asian Civilizations: A Comparative Perspective* (New York: Routledge, 2006), pp. 39–80; Norman Solomon, "The Ethics of War: Judaism," in Richard Sorabji and David Rodin (eds.), *The Ethics of War: Shared Problems in Different Traditions* (Aldershot: Ashgate, 2006), pp. 108–137; Aviezer Ravitzky, "Peace: Historical versus Utopian Models in Jewish Thought," in J. C. Gieben (ed.), *History and Faith: Studies in Jewish Philosophy* (Amsterdam: Brill, 1996), pp. 22–45; and the collections of papers in A. Bar-Levav (ed.), *Peace and War in Jewish Culture* (Jerusalem and

Haifa: University of Haifa, Center for the Study of Jewish Culture, 2006) (in Hebrew), and Lawrence Schiffman and Joel Wolowelsky (eds.), *War and Peace in the Jewish Tradition* (The Orthodox Forum Series) (New York: Yeshiva University Press, 2007).

6 The Deuteronomy chapters (20, 23) were written centuries after the actual or imagined wars described. The same refers to the rabbinical discussions and categories referring to national institutions such as the king and the Sanhedrin, institutions that had long disappeared by this time. The attempt of the Rabbis was first to analyze the biblical text in a way similar to their attempt to analyze many other theoretical issues. Later attempts should be seen as an analysis of both the biblical and the rabbinical commentaries done in an academic fashion. An interesting exception to this is found in the Palestinian Talmud where the Rabbis are critical of the Bar Kochba rebellion against the Roman Empire, indicating explicitly that this action was against God's will (see *The Palestinian Talmud*, "Tractate Ta'anit, 60b-d" (Jerusalem: The Academy of Hebrew Language, 2001), pp. 733–734). One may therefore conclude that it is rare to find a debate or discussion in Jewish sources regarding an actual conduct of war up until modern Israel. See Walzer, "War and Peace in the Jewish Tradition," pp. 95–96

7 Walzer, "War and Peace in the Jewish Tradition," pp. 95–96.

8 Moses Maimonides, *Epistles of Maimonides: Crisis and Leadership*, Abraham Halkin (trans.) and David Hartman (disc.) (Philadelphia: Jewish Publication Society of America, 1985).

9 Interestingly, as we will see, some of these intellectual debates, despite their completely non-practical nature at the time of writing, would under very different circumstances come to be seen as authoritative and prescriptive texts.

10 For a general survey of the topic of war in the Hebrew Bible, see Susan Niditch, *War in the Hebrew Bible: A Study in the Ethics of Violence* (New York: Oxford University Press, 1993); Philip R. Davies, "The Biblical and Qumranic Concept of War," in James H. Charlesworth (ed.), *The Bible and the Dead Sea Scrolls* (N. Richland Hills, Texas: BIBAL Press, 1999), pp. 275–306.

11 The Seven Nations are the earliest inhabitants of the land of Canaan.

12 Deuteronomy 20:17.

13 This is indicated in I Kings 9:20–21, and II Chronicles 8:7–8.

14 See Mishnah Yadayim 4:4.

15 While this position is without doubt the prevailing opinion in Judaism, there have been recent attempts, as we have shown elsewhere, by religious extremists such as Meir Kahane at reviving the concept of the war against the Seven Nations and applying it to the contemporary political reality by equating the Seven Nations to current-day Palestinians. For more on this issue, see Gedaliah Afterman, "Understanding the Theology of Israel's Extreme Religious Right: 'The Chosen People' and 'The Land of Israel' from the Bible to the 'Expulsion from Gush Katif,'" PhD dissertation, The University of Melbourne, 2007, pp. 134–161; Elliott Horowitz, *Reckless Rites: Purim and the Legacy of Jewish Violence* (Princeton, N.J.: Princeton University Press, 2006).

16 See Exodus 17:8–16; Deuteronomy 25:17–19; I Samuel, 30:1–16.

17 See Exodus 17.

18 I Samuel, chapter 15.

19 Ibid.; see the discussion by Horowitz, *Reckless Rites*, 107–146, who traces the history of "Amalek" and the different ethnic groups who were imaginatively identified with Amalek. While both the Seven Nations and Amalek can no longer be identified, Amalek has consistently been appropriated by Jews as the forefather of every Jewish persecutor and Anti-Semite, from Haman to Hitler. In this way, the image of Amalek has played both an important psychological and political role, as analyzed in detail by Horowitz.

20 Deuteronomy 20:1–10. See also Norman Solomon, "Judaism and the Ethics of War," *International Review of the Red Cross* 87 (2005), 296.

21 See: Deuteronomy 21:10–15 and 23:10–15.

22 Deuteronomy 20:19–20.

23 Deuteronomy 20:15–18. For the original commitment to the People of Israel, see Genesis 18–21.

24 Deuteronomy 20:18.

25 Philo of Alexandria, *Philo*, vol. 7, Greek and English edition, 10 vols., F. H. Colson (trans.), G. P. Goold (ed.) (Cambridge: Loeb Classical Library and Harvard University Press, 1999), pp. 219–229.

26 The temple scroll was published by Yigael Yadin, *The Temple Scroll*, 3 vols. (Jerusalem: Israel Exploration Society, 1977–1983). The second part of the manuscript was published in Florentino Garcia Martínez, Eibert J. C. Tigchelaar, and A. S. van der Woude, *Qumran Cave 11 2, 11Q2–18 and 11Q20–31* (Oxford: Clarendon, 1998).

27 Yigael Yadin (ed.), *The Temple Scroll*, Hebrew edition (Jerusalem: Israel Exploration Society, 1977), vol. 1, pp. 274–275.

28 See Jean Duhaime, *The War Texts: 1QM and Related Manuscripts* (New York: T&T Clark International, 2004).

29 For example, the *Sifre* makes it clear that in the case of an optional war against a city that is distant or remote from the boundaries of Israel or Judea, a city that includes inhabitants of the Seven Nations, these populations should not be subjected to harsher treatment but should rather be treated in the same way as the rest of the city's population.

30 This is underlined by the *Sifre*'s determination that if the populations in question were to repent, their lives are to be spared. Furthermore, in the case of cities that are distant from the borders, their lives are to be spared even if they do not repent because they do not pose a direct religious threat.

31 The halakhic categories of "obligatory" and "permitted" are different from and should not be confused with these categories in the Christian tradition of "just war."

32 See the important discussion by Noam J. Zohar, "Can a War Be Morally 'Optional'?," *Journal of Political Philosophy* 4:3 (1996), 229–241.

33 *The Babylonian Talmud*, "Tractate Sotah": 44b.

34 Ibid., "Tractate Sanhedrin": 72a.

35 Maimonides, *Hilchot Melachim*: The Code of Maimonides Book XIV – The Book of Judges, Treatise V – Laws Concerning Kings and Wars, Chapter 4:10.

36 Sarah Stroumsa, *Maimonides in His World: Portrait of a Mediterranean Thinker* (Princeton, N.J.: Princeton University Press, 2009), pp. 53–81.

37 See Moshe Halbertal and Avishai Margalit, *Idolatry*, Naomi Goldblum (trans.) (Cambridge: Harvard University Press, 1992), pp. 108–136; G. J. Blidstein, "Spreading the Faith as a Goal of War in the Doctrine of Maimonides," in *Peace and War in Jewish Culture*, A. Bar-Levav (ed.), Hebrew edition (Jerusalem and Haifa: Center for the Study of Jewish Culture, 2006), pp. 85–98; G. J. Blidstein, "Holy War in Maimonidean Law," in J. Kraemer (ed.), *Perspectives on Maimonides* (Oxford: Littman Library of Jewish Civilization, 1991), pp. 209–220; Noah Feldman, "War and Reason in Maimonides and Averroes," in Sorabji and Rodin, *The Ethics of War*, pp. 92–107; Josef Stern, "Maimonides on Amalek, Self-Corrective Mechanisms, and the War against Idolatry," in Jonathan Malino (ed.), *Judaism and Modernity: The Religious Philosophy of David Hartman* (London: Ashgate, 2004), pp. 371–410.

38 See Menachem Marc Kellner, *Maimonides' Confrontation with Mysticism* (London: Littman Library of Jewish Civilization, 2006).

39 Rabbi Moses Maimonides, "Hilchot Melachim," *Mishneh Torah*, Chapter 5:6–12. And compare with Eliezer Schweid, *The Land of Israel: National Home or Land of Destiny* (London: Associated University Press, 1985), p. 64.

40 Furthermore, the Jewish mission of embodying and spreading the monotheistic truth depended not necessarily on the re-establishment of the Jewish kingdom in the Holy Land, but on the fact that the Jews were spread across the world and could serve that purpose even more effectively.

41 See, e.g., Nachmanides, *Commentary on the Torah*, Genesis 24:3, 28:21, 26:5; Aviezer Ravitzky, "Waymarks to Zion: The History of an Idea," in Moshe Hallamish and Aviezer Ravitzky (eds.), *The Land of Israel in Medieval Jewish Thought*, Hebrew edition (Jerusalem: Yad Itzhak Ben-Zvi, 1991); and Moshe Halbertal, *By Way of Truth: Nachmanides and the Creation of Tradition*, Hebrew edition (Jerusalem: Hartman Institute, 2006), pp. 173–176.

42 Nachmanides, *Commentary on the Torah*, Numbers 33:53.

43 Aryeh Newman, "The Centrality of Eretz Yisrael in Nachmanides," *Tradition* 10:1 (1968), 23.

44 Nachmanides, Commentary on Maimonides' *Sefer Hamitzvot* (Book of Commandments), positive commandment, number 4.

45 Ibid., *Mitzvat Asseh*, positive commandment, number 4.

46 Nachmanides, *Commentary on the Torah*, Leviticus 26:42.

47 For a detailed survey of the arguments of those in the ultra-Orthodox community fiercely opposed to Zionism, see Aviezer Ravitzky, *Messianism, Zionism, and Jewish Religious Radicalism*, Michael Swirsky and Jonathan Chipman (trans.) (Tel Aviv: Am Oved Publishers, 1993), pp. 40–78.

48 For a detailed outline of this matter, see Arye Edrei, "Law, Interpretation, and Ideology: The Renewal of the Jewish Laws of War in the State of Israel," *Cardozo Law Review* 28:1 (October 2006), 198–208; Noam J. Zohar, "Morality and War: A Critique of Bleich's Oracular Halakhah," in *Commandment and Community: New Essays in Jewish Legal and Political Philosophy*, Daniel H. Frank (ed.) (Albany: State University of New York Press, 1995), pp. 245–258.

49 Religious Zionism is an ideological movement that combines Zionism and Judaism and whose members mostly adhere to Modern Orthodox Judaism, in contrast to ultra-Orthodox Judaism.

50 The first book of Maccabees was written by a Jewish author after the restoration of an independent Jewish kingdom, probably about 100 BCE. This book is included within the Catholic Bible but does not enjoy canonical status within the Jewish and Protestant traditions. The setting of the book is about a century after the conquest of Judea by the Greeks under Alexander the Great. It tells how the Greek ruler Antiochus IV Epiphanes attempted to suppress the practice of Jewish religious law, resulting in a Jewish revolt against Seleucid rule. The book covers the whole of the revolt, from 175 to 134 BCE, highlighting how the salvation of the Jewish people in this crisis came from God through Mattahias' family.

51 Douay-Rheims Bible.

52 Philo of Alexandria was a Hellenistic Jewish philosopher born in Alexandria who wrote extensive commentaries on Jewish law and the Septuagint in Greek.

53 Philo of Alexandria, *Philo*, vol. 7, Colson (trans.), G. P. Goold (ed.), pp. 145, 147, 149, 151 (translation slightly modified).

54 The Dead Sea Scrolls are of great religious and historical significance, as they include the oldest known surviving copies of the biblical and extra-biblical documents and preserve evidence of great diversity in late Second Temple Judaism. They are written in Hebrew, Aramaic, and Greek, mostly on parchment, but with some written on papyrus. These manuscripts generally date between 150 BCE to 70 CE and were discovered in the twentieth century near the Dead Sea.

55 *The Dead Sea Scrolls: Study Edition*, Florentino Garcia Martinez and Eibert J. C. Tigchelaar (eds.) (Boston: Brill, 1997), vol. 2, 11Q19, pp. 1279–1280, 1285, 1287 (translation slightly modified).

56 A rabbinic commentary on Deuteronomy written proximally during the second half of the third century.

57 *Sifre: A Tannaitic Commentary on the Book of Deuteronomy*, Reuven Hammer (trans.) (New Haven, Conn.: Yale University Press, 1986), pp. 211–217.

58 The *Tosefta* is an early rabbinical legal text corresponding to the Mishnah (220 CE).

59 The *Tosefta*, Jacob Neusner (trans.), 2 vols. (Peabody, Mass. Hendrickson Publishers, 2002), vol. 1, pp. 437–438.

60 Ibid., vol. 1, pp. 865–868.

61 The Mishnah is the main compilation of rabbinical law, compiled out of oral traditions around 220 CE.

62 "Tractate Sotah," in *Mishnah*, Herbert Danby (trans.) (London: Oxford University Press, 1933), pp. 301–303.

63 A special priest with a mission to inspire the army before leaving to the battlefield.

64 "Tractate Sanhedrin," in *Mishnah*, p. 383.

65 Ibid., p. 384.

66 The Palestinian Talmud (ca. 400 CE) and the Babylonian Talmud (ca. 500 CE) include the record of thousands of discussions of generations of rabbinic scholars interpreting the Jewish law incorporated in the Torah, the Mishnah, and other early rabbinic writings including the *Tosefta*.

67 "Tractate Sanhedrin 16 a–b," from *The Babylonian Talmud*, Rabbi Dr. Isidore Epstein (ed.), Come and Hear: An Educational Forum for the Examinations of Religious Truth and Religious Tolerance Web site, http://www.come-and-hear.com/sanhedrin/sanhedrin_16.html.

68 "Tractate Sanhedrin 20b," from *The Babylonian Talmud*, Rabbi Dr. Isidore Epstein (ed.), Come and Hear Web site, http://www.come-and-hear.com/sanhedrin/sanhedrin_20.html#PARTb.

69 "Tractate Sotah: 44b," from *The Babylonian Talmud*, Rev. A. Cohen (trans.), Rabbi Dr. I. Epstein (ed.), Come and Hear Web site, http://www.come-and-hear.com/sotah/sotah_44.html.

70 "House of David" refers to the lineage of kings starting from King David.

71 The *Mishneh Torah* (*The Code of Maimonides*) is a systematic codification of Jewish law authored by the great scholar and philosopher Moses Maimonides between 1170 and 1180.

72 "Kings and Wars: Chapter 4," in *The Code of Maimonides – Book 14: The Book of Judges*, Abraham M. Hershman (trans.) (New Haven, Conn.: Yale University Press, 1949), vol. 3, pp. 214–216.

73 Ibid., chapter 5, pp. 217–218.

74 Ibid., chapter 6, pp. 220–221.

75 The *Millo* was a structure in Jerusalem built by King Solomon and repaired by King Hezekiah.

76 "Kings and Wars: Chapter 8," in *The Code of Maimonides – Book 14*, pp. 228, 230.

77 Ibid., chapter 11, pp. 238, 240.

78 *The Code of Maimonides – Book 7: The Book of Agriculture*, Issac Klein (trans.) (New Haven, Conn.: Yale University Press, 1979), pp. 402–403.

79 Ramban (Nachmanides), *Commentary on the Torah – Deuteronomy XX*, in Charles B. Chavel (trans.) (New York: Shilo Publishing House, 1976), pp. 238–241.

80 Ramban (Nachmanides), *Commentary on the Torah – Genesis XXXIV, Vayishlach*, Charles B. Chavel (trans.) (New York: Shilo Publishing House, 1971), pp. 416–420.

81 *Orach Hayim*, Rabbi Shmuel Grinman (ed.) (Bnei Brak, Israel: n.p., 1994), pp. 332, 333. Translated from the original Hebrew by A. Afterman and G. Afterman.

82 C. Hirschensohn, *Malki Ba-Kodesh* (Jerusalem: Bar Ilan University, Shecter Institute for Jewish Studies and the Shalom Hartman Institute, 2007), pp. 143–144, 146, 148–149, 156–160. Translated from the original Hebrew by A. Afterman and G. Afterman.

83 Ahitofel ("Brother of Insipidity" or "Impiety") was a counselor of King David.

84 The *Scroll of Esther* was wrongly associated with the Spanish author R. Isaac de Leon, who lived in Spain in the fifteenth century. The *Scroll of Esther* is a commentary on Nachmanides' critical commentary of Maimonides' *Sefer ha-Mitzvot (the Book of Commandments)*.

85 *Babylonian Talmud*, Tractate Ketubot (lit. "prenuptial agreements").

86 Rabbi Yehudah Ha-Nasi was a key leader of the Jewish community of Judea toward the end of the second century CE. He is best known as the chief editor of the Mishnah.

87 Bavel is the Hebrew name for Babylon.

88 Yeshayahu Leibowitz, "After Kibiyeh (1953–54)," in *Judaism, Human Values and the Jewish State*, Eliezer Goldman (ed.) (Cambridge: Harvard University Press, 1992), pp. 185–186, 187–190.

89 Genesis 34.

90 *Meshiv Milchama* is a treatise of halakhic responsa regarding war. In Hebrew, literally a "war response."

91 Shlomo Goren, "The Ethics of War in Light of the Halakhah," in *Meshiv Milchama* (Jerusalem: Idra Raba, 1983), vol. 1, pp. 14, 38. Translated from the original Hebrew by A. Afterman and G. Afterman.

92 A *yeshiva* is a seminary dedicated to religious studies.

93 Shlomo Aviner, *Shut Intifada* (Responsa on the Intifada) (Beit El, Israel: Sifriyat Hava, 1995), pp. 9, 13, 17, 23. Translated by the authors of this chapter from the original Hebrew.

94 Maimonides, "Laws of Kings," 6:5.

95 Palestinian Talmud, Tractate Shev'it, p. 6a.

96 See Maimonides, "Laws of Kings," 6:1.

97 Babylonian Talmud, Tractate Sanhedrin, Folio 72a.

98 The *Shulhan Arukh* (lit. the "set table") is a codification of Jewish law, written and published by Rabbi Yosef Karo in the sixteenth century. Together with its commentaries, it is generally considered the most widely accepted and authoritative compilation of Jewish law since the twelfth-century *Mishneh Torah* by Maimonides. The "Hoshen Mishpat" is one of its four parts dedicated to laws of finance, financial responsibility, and damages (personal and financial).

99 *Shulhan Arukh*: Hoshen Mishpat, 425a.

100 Ibid., 388:11.

101 Asher ben Yechiel (1250/1259–1327) was an eminent rabbi and Talmudist best known for his abstract of Talmudic law. He is often referred to as Rabbenu Asher, "our Rabbi Asher," or by the Hebrew abbreviation for this title, the HaROSH (which also means "the head or leader").

102 HaRosh, *Responsa*, Rule 19.

103 Rabbi Menachem Meiri (1249–c. 1310) was a famous Catalan rabbi, Talmudist, and Maimonidean.

104 Midian was the son of Abraham and Keturah. His five sons, Ephah, Epher, Hanoch, Abidah (R. V. "Abida"), and Eldaah, were the progenitors of the Midianites (Genesis 26:1–4; I Chronicles: 32–33). It appears that the Midianites dwelt in the Sinai Peninsula. Later, in the period of the Kings, Midian seems to have occupied a tract of land between Edom and Paran, on the way to Egypt (I Kings 11: 18). Midian is likewise described as in the vicinity of Moab: the Midianites

were beaten by the Edomite king Hadad "in the field of Moab" (Genesis 36: 35), and in the account of Balaam it is said that the elders of both Moab and Midian called upon him to curse Israel (Numbers 22:4, 7).

105 Numbers 25:17–18.
106 Midrash Tanhuma on the portion of Pinhas (Numbers 25:10–30:1), 3.
107 Maimonides, "Laws of Kings," 4:10.
108 Maimonides, "Guide," 3:27.
109 Ibid., 3:41.
110 Ibid.
111 Deuteronomy 16:18.
112 Maimonides, "Guide," 3:39.
113 *The Rivash*, Rabbi Yitzhak bar Sheshet (1326–1408), a Spanish Talmudic authority and the author of 518 responsa.
114 *Teshubot ha-Ribash ha-Hadashot* (*The Rivash responsa*), 60:9 (original text in Hebrew).
115 Genesis 18:25.
116 Numbers 16:22.
117 Pes. 113b.
118 I Samuel 15:6.
119 Maimonides, "Laws of the Sanhedrin," 24:4–10.
120 Ibid.
121 Yuval Sherlo, "Questions on the Ethics of War" (She'elot Al Musar HaMilchama), *Tzohar* 11 (Summer 2002), pp. 97–98, 99–101. Translated from the original Hebrew by A. Afterman and G. Afterman.
122 Samuel Dov Rosenberg, "The Ethics of War and the Treatment of the Enemy and His Surroundings According to the Halakhah," *The Israeli Defence Force Rabbinate Journal* 2 (Autumn 2008), pp. 301–311. Citations from pp. 302–303, 306–308. Translated from the original Hebrew by A. Afterman and G. Afterman.
123 Rabbi Y. Ariel, "Arakhim Be-Mivhan Milhamah" (Ethical Values in the Test of War), *Alon Shvut* (*Alumni Journal*) 18 (2003), p. 82.

SELECT BIBLIOGRAPHY

Bemporad, Jack, "Norms of War in Judaism," in Vesselin Popovski, Gregory M. Reichberg, and Nicholas Turner (eds.), *World Religions and Norms of War* (Tokyo: United Nations University Press, 2009), pp. 106–141.

Blidstein, G. J., "Holy War in Maimonidean Law," in J. Kraemer (ed.), *Perspectives on Maimonides* (Oxford: Littman Library of Jewish Civilization, 1991), pp. 209–220.

Davies, Philip R., "The Biblical and Qumranic Concept of War," in James H. Charlesworth (ed.), *The Bible and the Dead Sea Scrolls* (N. Richland Hills, Texas: BIBAL Press, 1999), pp. 275–306.

Duhaime, Jean, *The War Texts: 1QM and Related Manuscripts* (New York: T&T Clark International, 2004).

Feldman, Noah, "War and Reason in Maimonides and Averroes," in Richard Sorabji and David Rodin (eds.), *The Ethics of War: Shared Problems in Different Traditions* (Aldershot: Ashgate, 2006), pp. 92–107.

Ferguson, John, *War and Peace in the World's Religions* (New York: Oxford University Press, 1978), pp. 78–98.

Niditch, Susan, *War in the Hebrew Bible: A Study in the Ethics of Violence* (New York: Oxford University Press, 1993).

Ravitzky, Aviezer, "Prohibited Wars in the Jewish Tradition," in Terry Nardin (ed.), *The Ethics of War and Peace: Religious and Secular Perspectives* (Princeton, N.J.: Princeton University Press, 1996), pp. 115–127.

Schiffman, Lawrence, and Joel Wolowelsky (eds.), *War and Peace in the Jewish Tradition* (The Orthodox Forum Series) (New York: Yeshiva University Press, 2007).

Solomon, Norman, "The Ethics of War: Judaism," in Richard Sorabji and David Rodin (eds.), *The Ethics of War: Shared Problems in Different Traditions* (Aldershot: Ashgate, 2006), pp. 108–137.

Stern, Josef, "Maimonides on Amalek, Self-Corrective Mechanisms, and the War against Idolatry," in Jonathan Malino (ed.), *Judaism and Modernity: The Religious Philosophy of David Hartman* (London: Ashgate, 2004), pp. 371–410.

Stern, Josef, "Maimonides on Wars and Their Justification," *Journal of Military Ethics* 11.3 (2012), 245–263.

Walzer, Michael, "War and Peace in the Jewish Tradition," in Terry Nardin (ed.), *The Ethics of War and Peace: Religious and Secular Perspectives* (Princeton, N.J.: Princeton University Press, 1996), pp. 95–114.

2

Catholic Christianity

Part I: Historical Development

Gregory M. Reichberg

Catholic Christianity has existed institutionally for almost two thousand years. Founded on the life and teaching of Jesus Christ, it is organized as a society of believers (an ecclesia), under the jurisdiction of its bishops, with primacy accorded to the bishop of Rome (the pope), who is viewed as the direct successor of Saint Peter, the apostle whom Jesus designated the first leader of the Church.

Old and New Testaments

The New Testament contains very few statements on permissible violence. Jesus Christ refused to defend himself (nor did he allow himself to be defended) by force of arms. And his precepts admonishing patience in the face of evil seem inimical to warfare and organized fighting of any sort. Yet in its doctrine and practice the Catholic Church has rarely drawn out this implication. To the contrary, its standard teaching is that resort to armed force can have a valid place in human affairs. This teaching was derived from passages of the New Testament (in particular, Romans 13:4 and I Peter 2:13–14) that affirm how God has instituted civil authority to maintain order in human affairs. In fact, the very notion of *bellum justum* ("just war") has become common coinage within Western civilization precisely after being adopted by a long line of Church ("canon") lawyers and theologians.

The doctrinal affirmation of just war within the Catholic Church[1] can be explained by the belief that the New Testament contains a body of consistent teachings that are in harmony with the Old Testament. Since the New Testament countenanced resort to the sword by civil authorities, while the Old Testament gave ample instruction on war, formative Christian authors such as St. Augustine and St. Thomas Aquinas found in both scriptures a permanently valid scriptural source for the doctrine of just war.

Below is a representative sampling of scriptural passages that were often cited by theologians and canon lawyers in their discussions of war. The appeal to the Bible could be made to serve a number of quite different ends. Sometimes the point was to reconcile the seeming inconsistency between the passages (mainly drawn from the New Testament) urging nonviolence and the contrasting passages (mainly from the Old Testament) that seemed to endorse resort to armed force. In other instances, sacred Scripture supplied a basis for religiously sanctioned warfare. These same passages could also be read with a "spiritual" or allegorical meaning, so that they referred to the soul's struggle with wayward passions, worldly attractions, or demonic powers. Other passages were thought to contain a literal teaching about just war, thereby offering instruction on right and wrong reasons for waging war or the proper mode of conduct to be observed therein. Finally, defeat in war was sometimes taken to be a punishment that God inflicted (by means of the victorious army) for idolatry or other sins. By the same token, victory could be regarded as proof of divine approval for one's cause.

From: Standard Revised Version of the Bible

Genesis 14:19–20. And he blessed him and said, "Blessed be Abram by God Most High, maker of heaven and earth; and blessed be God Most High, who has delivered your enemies into your hand! . . ."

Exodus 2:11–12. One day, when Moses had grown up, he went out to his people and looked on their burdens; and he saw an Egyptian beating a Hebrew, one of his people. He looked this way and that, and seeing no one he killed the Egyptian and hid him in the sand.

Exodus 17:16. "A hand upon the banner of the LORD! The LORD will have war with Am'alek from generation to generation."

Numbers 21:21–25. Then Israel sent messengers to Sihon king of the Amorites, saying, "Let me pass through your land; we will not turn aside into field or vineyard; we will not drink the water of a well; we will go by the King's Highway, until we have passed through your territory." But Sihon would not allow Israel to pass through his territory. He gathered all his men together, and went out against Israel to the wilderness, and came to Jahaz, and fought against Israel. And Israel slew him with the edge of the sword, and took possession of his land from the Arnon to the Jabbok, and far as to the Ammonites; for Jazer was the boundary of the Ammonites. And Israel took all these cities, and Israel settled in all the cities of the Amorites, in Heshbon, and in all its villages.

Deuteronomy 20:1–4. When you go forth to war against your enemies, and see horses and chariots and an army larger than your own, you shall not be afraid of them; for the LORD your God is with you, who brought you up out of the land of Egypt. And when you draw near to the battle, the priest shall come forward and speak to the people, and shall say to them, "Hear, O Israel, you draw near this day to battle against your enemies: let not your heart faint; do not fear, or tremble, or be in dread of them; for the LORD your God is he that goes with you, to fight for you against your enemies, to give you the victory."

Deuteronomy 20:10–15. When you draw near to a city to fight against it, offer terms of peace to it. And if its answer to you is peace and it opens to you, then all the people who are found in it shall do forced labor for you and shall serve you. But if it makes no peace with you, but makes war against you, then you shall besiege it; and when the LORD your God gives it into your hand you shall put all its males to the sword, but the women and the little ones, the cattle, and everything else in the city, all its spoil, you shall take as booty for yourselves; and you shall enjoy the spoil of your enemies, which the LORD your God has given you. Thus you shall do to all the cities which are very far from you, which are not cities of the nations here.

Deuteronomy 20:19–20. When you besiege a city for a long time, making war against it in order to take it, you shall not destroy its trees by wielding an axe against them; for you may eat of them, but you shall not cut them down. Are the trees in the field men that they should be besieged by you? Only the trees which you know are not trees for food you may destroy and cut down that you may build siegeworks against the city that makes war with you, until it falls.

Joshua 8:1–9. And the LORD said to Joshua, "Do not fear or be dismayed; take all the fighting men with you, and arise, go up to Ai; see, I have given into your hand the king of Ai, and his people, his city, and his land; and you shall do to Ai and its kings as you did to Jericho and its king; only its spoil and its cattle you shall take as booty for yourselves; lay an ambush against the city, behind it." So Joshua arose, and all the fighting men, to go up to Ai; and Joshua chose thirty thousand mighty men of valor, and sent them forth by night. And he commanded them, "Behold, you shall lie in ambush against the city, behind it; do not go very far from the city, but hold yourselves all in readiness; and I, and all the people who are with me, will approach the city. And when they come out against us, as before, we shall flee before them; and they will come out after us, till we have drawn them away from the city; for they will say, 'They are fleeing from us, as before.' So we will flee from them; then you shall rise up from the ambush, and seize the city; for the LORD your God will give it into your hand. And when you have taken the city, you shall set the city on fire, doing so as the LORD has bidden; see, I have commanded you." So Joshua sent them forth; and they went to the place of ambush, and lay between Bethel and Ai, to the west of Ai; but Joshua spent that night among the people.

Judges 10:6–8. And the people of Israel again did what was evil in the sight of the LORD, and served the Ba'als and the Ash'taroth, the gods of Syria, the gods of Sidon, the gods of Moab, the gods of the Ammonites, and the gods of the Philistines; and they forsook the LORD, and did not serve him. And the anger of the LORD was kindled against Israel, and he sold them into the hand of the Philistines and into the hand of the Ammonites, and they crushed and oppressed the children of Israel that year. For eighteen years they oppressed all the people of Israel that were beyond the Jordan in the land of the Amorites, which is in Gilead.

II Samuel 8:2. And he defeated Moab, and measured them with a line, making them lie down on the ground; two lines he measured to be put to death, and one full line to be spared. And the Moabites became servants to David and brought tribute.

Psalm 68:1–2. Let God arise, let his enemies be scattered; let those who hate him flee before him! As smoke is driven away, so drive them away; as wax melts before fire, let the wicked perish before God!

Psalm 82:4. Rescue the weak and the needy; deliver them from the hand of the wicked.

Psalm 144:1. Blessed be the LORD, my rock, who trains my hands for war, and my fingers for battle.

Ecclesiastes 3:1–8. For everything there is a season, and a time for every matter under heaven ... a time for war, and a time for peace.

Isaiah 2:4. He shall judge between the nations, and shall decide for many peoples; and they shall beat their swords into plowshares, and their spears into pruning hooks; nation shall not lift up sword against nation, neither shall they learn war any more.

Jeremiah 48:10. Cursed is he who does the work of the LORD with slackness; and cursed is he who keeps back his sword from bloodshed.

1 Maccabees 2:41. "... Let us fight against every man who comes to attack us on the Sabbath day; let us not all die as our brethren died in their hiding places."

Matthew 5:39. But I say to you, Do not resist one who is evil. But if any one strikes you on the right cheek, turn to him the other also.

Matthew 8:5–10. As he entered Caper'na-um, a centurion came forward to him, beseeching him and saying, "Lord, my servant is lying paralyzed at home, in terrible distress." And he said to him, "I will come and heal him." But the centurion answered him, "Lord, I am not worthy to have you come under my roof; but only say the word, and my servant will be healed. For I am a man under authority, with soldiers under me; and I say to one, 'Go,' and he goes, and to another, 'Come,' and he comes, and to my slave, 'Do this,' and he does it." When Jesus heard him, he marveled, and said to those who followed him, "Truly, I say to you, not even in Israel have I found such faith."

Matthew 10:34. Do not think that I have come to bring peace on earth; I have not come to bring peace, but a sword.

Matthew 22:19–21. "Show me the money for the tax." And they brought him a coin. And Jesus said to them, "Whose likeness and inscription is this?" They said, "Caesar's." Then he said to them, "Render therefore to Caesar the things that are Caesar's, and to God the things that are God's."

Matthew 26:51–54. And behold, one of those who were with Jesus stretched out his hand and drew his sword, and struck the slave of the high priest, and cut off his ear. Then Jesus said to him, "Put your sword back into its place; for all who take the sword will perish by the sword. Do you think that I cannot appeal to my Father, and he will at once send me more than twelve legions of angels? But how then should the scriptures be fulfilled, that it must be so?"

Luke 3:14. Soldiers also asked him, "And we, what shall we do?" And he said to them, "Rob no one by violence or by false accusation, and be content with your wages."

Luke 14:23–24. And the master said to the servant, "Go out to the highways and hedges, and compel people to come in, that my house may be filled...."

Luke 14:31–32. Or what king, going to encounter another king in war, will not sit down first and take counsel whether he is able with ten thousand to meet him who comes against him with twenty thousand? And if not, while the other is yet a great way off, he sends an embassy and asks terms of peace.

Luke 22:36–38. He said to them, "But now, let him who has a purse take it, and likewise a bag. And let him who has no sword sell his mantle and buy one...." And they said, "Look, Lord, here are two swords." And he said to them, "It is enough."

John 2:14–17. In the temple he found those who were selling oxen and sheep and pigeons, and the money-changers at their business. And making a whip of cords, he drove them all, with the sheep and oxen, out of the temple; and he poured out the coins of the money-changers and overturned their tables. And he told those who sold the pigeons, "Take these things away; you shall not make my Father's house a house of trade." His disciples remembered that it was written, "Zeal for thy house will consume me."

John 15:13. Greater love hath no man than this, that a man lay down his life for his friends.

John 18:36. Jesus answered, "My kingship is not of this world; If my kingship were of this world, my servants would fight, that I might not be handed over to the Jews; but my kingship is not from the world."

Romans 12:21. Do not be overcome by evil, but overcome evil with good.

Romans 13:4. [F]or he is God's servant for your good. But if you do wrong, be afraid, for he does not bear the sword in vain; he is the servant of God to execute his wrath on the wrongdoer.

II Corinthians 12:10. For the sake of Christ, then, I am content with weaknesses, insults, hardships, persecutions, and calamities. For when I am weak, then I am strong.

Ephesians 6:11. Put on the whole armor of God, that you may be able to stand against the wiles of the devil.

Hebrews 11:32–34. And what more shall I say? For time would fail me to tell of Gideon, Barak, Samson and Jephthah, of David and Samuel and the prophets, who through faith conquered kingdoms, enforced justice, received promises, stopped the mouths of lions, quenched raging fire, escaped the edge of the sword, won strength out of weakness, became mighty in war, put foreign armies to flight.

Hebrews 12:14. Strive for peace with all men, and for the holiness without which no one will see the Lord.

I Peter 2:13–14. Be subject for the Lord's sake to every human institution, whether it be to the emperor as supreme, or to governors as sent by him to punish those who do wrong and to praise those who do right.

I John 3:16. By this we know love, that he laid down his life for us; and we ought to lay down our lives for the brethren.

Revelation 19:11–16. Then I saw heaven opened, and behold, a white horse! He who sat upon it is called Faithful and True, and in righteousness he judges and makes war. His eyes are like a flame of fire, and on his head are many diadems; and he has a name inscribed which no one knows but himself. He is clad in a robe dipped in blood, and the name by which he is called is The Word of God. And the armies of heaven, arrayed in fine linen, white and pure, followed him on white horses. From his mouth issues a sharp sword with which to smite the nations, and he will rule them with a rod of iron; he will tread the wine press of the fury of the wrath of God the Almighty. On his robe and on his thigh he has a name inscribed, King of kings, and Lord of lords.

To demonstrate the concordance of the Old and New Testaments on the question of armed force, a leading strategy was to differentiate the respective functions of state and Church within the economy of salvation (God's plan for humanity as revealed in the Scriptures). Distinguishing the "things of Caesar" from the "things of God" (Matt. 22:21), theologians explained that while wars could rightly be waged to protect the temporal order of the state (the domain of "Caesar") from unjust violence, within the spiritual order of the Church (the domain of "God") there could be no place for resort to the sword. Both orders, temporal and spiritual, were considered inherently good and thus worthy of the Christian's participation and concern. It was nonetheless acknowledged that the Church represented a beginning on Earth of a perfect society (a "kingdom of God") that would come to full completion only in Heaven. The precepts of the Gospel (the "New Law") were especially directed to life within the Church. Since in Heaven there will be no violence of any sort, so too, even now within the Church, there should be no resort to force. The reality of the state, by contrast, was understood to be firmly anchored in this world. Having no transcendent ordering, a different set of norms, designated under the heading "natural law," were taken to be the proximate guide for worldly activities. In principle accessible to all human beings, Catholic theologians held that the natural law included a teaching on just war. They presumed that key elements of this teaching had already been conveyed within the Old Law of the ancient Israelites.

Pacifism in the Early Church

The differentiation between the respective domains of Church and state, the spiritual and the temporal, kingdoms of the earth and the kingdom of God, was not explicitly drawn in Catholic theology until the fourth century. In the earlier period, Christians often refused to serve in the Roman army so as to avoid taking part in pagan rituals. Pacifism – the renunciation of armed force – was thus an acknowledged viewpoint within the Church in its first three centuries. It must be said however that this was more of a lived reality than a deliberately argued theological position.[2] With the collapse of the Roman Empire, and the rise of Christian civilization under the emperor Constantine, this early pacifism lost much of its appeal for the mainstream Church. And indeed, up until quite recently,[3] pacifism was present in Catholicism mainly as a foil against which the just war doctrine would be compared.

Justin Martyr (ca. 100–ca. 165)

From: Justin Martyr, *First Apology*, 39.2–3[4]

When the Prophetic Spirit speaks and foretells the future, he says, "The Law shall come out of Sion and the Lord's word from Jerusalem. And he will judge the Gentiles and reproach many people, and they will beat their swords into plows and their spears into pruning hooks. And nation will not raise its sword against nation, and they will no longer learn the arts of war" [Isaiah 2:4]. You can believe that this prophecy, too, was fulfilled. For twelve men, ignorant and unskilled in speaking as they were, went out from Jerusalem to the world, and with the help of God announced to every race of men that they had been sent by Christ to teach the word of God to everyone, and we who formerly killed one another not only refuse to make war on our enemies but in order to avoid lying to our interrogators or deceiving them, we freely go to our deaths confessing Christ.

Tertullian (ca. 160–ca. 220)

From: Tertullian, *On Idolatry*, 19.1–3[5]

But the question now is whether a member of the faithful can become a soldier and whether a soldier can be admitted to the Faith even if he is a member of the rank and file who are not required to offer sacrifice or decide capital cases. There can be no compatibility between an oath made to God and one made to man, between the standard of Christ and that of the devil, between the camp of light and the camp of darkness. The soul cannot be beholden to two masters, God and Caesar. Moses, to be sure, carried a rod; Aaron wore a military belt and John had a breast plate. If one wants to play around with the topic, Jesus, son of Nun [i.e., Joshua] led an army and the Jewish nation went to war. But how will a Christian do so? Indeed how will he serve in the army even during peacetime without the sword that Jesus Christ has taken away? Even if soldiers came to John and got advice on how they ought to act, even if the centurion became a believer, the Lord, by taking away Peter's sword, disarmed every soldier thereafter. We are not allowed to wear any uniform that symbolizes a sinful act.

From Augustine and Ambrose to Medieval Canon Law

The just war idea emerged at a time (fourth century) when Christians had begun to assume positions of leadership within the temporal sphere. The defense of homeland from attack, the repression of criminality, and protection of the innocent were now contemplated as live issues for Christians in positions of power, thus requiring a reappraisal of Christ's example and teaching in the light of these changed historical circumstances. Spearheading this reappraisal were two Latin bishops who were keenly aware of the new political role that Christians had begun to assume in the waning years of the Roman Empire: St. Ambrose (ca. 339–397) and St. Augustine (354–430). Neither wrote a treatise or even a section of a treatise on the moral problem of war, but the theme was nevertheless addressed by them in numerous passages, including some quite long digressions, wherein the justifiability of engagement in war was clearly enunciated.

The emergent just war doctrine was oriented around two key presuppositions. First, peace was considered the normative, baseline condition of humanity. In line with the fundamental goodness of a world created by God, it was believed that God had intended human beings and their respective communities to live together harmoniously, bound together by ties of mutual assistance and friendship. This condition of harmony was represented by the biblical narration of the Garden of Eden (Gen. 2:8–25), where interhuman violence had no place. Yet it was also believed (second presupposition) that God's original plan for humanity had been contravened by human sin. The biblical story of humanity's fall from grace (Genesis 3), was summed up in the dogma of "original sin," according to which the transgression of Adam and Eve has had an enduring effect on their descendants (the universality of human beings), all of whom are born with a susceptibility to evil. While war is not specifically mentioned, Cain's killing of his brother Abel (Gen. 4:1–16) and related stories, such as the Tower of Babel (Gen. 11:1–9), were meant to illustrate how violence and related forms of evil are endemic to our "fallen" world.

Although Christians held that restoration was possible through the redemptive action of Jesus Christ, it was also recognized that evil would endure in this world until his messianic return at the end of time. Initially, many who belonged to the Christian community awaited the imminent coming of Christ, believing his messianic return to be near. But by the time of Ambrose and Augustine, it was more commonly held that this time horizon need not be so very short. Humanity had indeed entered the final times after the resurrection and ascension of Christ, but whether these times would last a year or thousands of years, we would have to adjust to life in this world and organize ourselves accordingly.

As agents cooperating in God's governance of a fallen world, Christians, especially those charged with the duties of public authority, were expected to resist evil actively, especially when grave injustice was directed against the weak and defenseless. At the limit, this would entail using armed force against those, whether internal malefactors or external enemies, who had disrupted the peace. This was famously summed up by Augustine when he wrote, "It is iniquity on the part of the adversary that forces a just war upon the wise man."[6] On this understanding, "just war" was derivative from the more fundamental concept of "peace" (*pax*). Armed force could be viewed as having a positive value (thereby warranting the designation "just") insofar as it contributed toward restoring a peace that had been violated by prior wrongdoing. By extension, since injustice could be expected to occur on a regular basis, officers of the law (police and soldiers) were deemed necessary in order to hold it in check. In line with our fallen condition, the preservation of peace thus required just war as its unavoidable counterpoint.

While the Catholic teaching on just war is ordinarily traced to the seminal writings of Ambrose and Augustine, the tradition as it later emerged in the medieval Church did not result from a direct reading of their disparate passages on war in the original texts. The articulation of a just war theory in the thirteenth century was based rather on compilations, the most famous of which was the *Decretum Gratiani* (ca. 1140), which had organized the earlier materials on war and violence into an articulated body of doctrine.[7] In this last-named work, the Italian canon lawyer Gratian devoted an entire chapter (*causa* 23) to problems associated with force and armed coercion from a Christian perspective. Based almost entirely on citations, with brief interjectory comments by Gratian, *causa* 23 brought together the building blocks that succeeding generations of Church lawyers and theologians would use to erect their own theoretical constructions on the ethics and legality of war. In addition to passages from Ambrose and Augustine, the *causa* included numerous citations from scripture (both the Old and New Testaments); other early Church theologians, for instance Isidore of Seville; as well as Church councils and papal statements. To illustrate how these texts on war were made available to successive generations of medieval thinkers, we reproduce below a sampling taken directly from the *Decretum*.

Gratian himself engaged in little independent theorizing. However, having become the main textbook for the emerging law schools of the Latin West, his *Decretum* gave rise to commentaries in which important new views on war and coercion were put forward, usually by reference to Roman law. The thinkers who wrote these commentaries were called Decretists, and among their writings we find the first explicit normative theories on topics such as the scope of self-defense and legitimate war-making authority. Around the middle of the thirteenth century, the interest of Church lawyers shifted to the newly gathered collections of papal legislation, called "decretals," hence those who commented on them were termed Decretalists.[8] Among the most famous of these commentators was Pope Innocent IV (1180–1254). In his *Apparatus in quinque libros Decretalium*, which is thought to have been written in the early years of his pontificate, he carefully distinguished war from other forms of licit violence (self-defense by private individuals and internal police-action by princes) thereby carving out the *jus ad bellum* as a distinctive sphere of normative reflection. Innocent also proposed an influential justification for the crusades that were then waged to recover Jerusalem and surrounding areas from the control of Muslim rulers: the land had been "unjustly expropriated and despoiled by those who have no right to it," and the attempt to retake the land therefore constituted a just war against an unjust occupation.[9]

Alongside Innocent, another Decretalist, the Dominican Raymond of Peñafort (1180–1275), wrote a treatise (*Summa de casibus poenitentiae*) that was intended to serve as a guide for confessors. By virtue of their power to absolve penitents from their sins, confessors exercised a role akin to judges and were expected to apply the law within a special jurisdiction: the inner domain of conscience. Since many of the individuals who came to confession had contact of one sort or another with problems relating to war, this theme would receive careful treatment within Raymond's work. We thereby find him offering significant comments on a wide range of topics, including the conditions that cumulatively must be fulfilled if a war is to be considered just: legitimate self-defense, the seizure of booty, and civilian immunity.

The early legal writings on just war often discussed the topic in relation to specifically religious ends. Indeed, Gratian began his *causa* 23 with consideration of "a case of heresy into which certain bishops had lapsed, and its repression by their Catholic counterparts, acting upon orders from the pope."[10] A counterpoint to this teaching was expressed, however, by (*inter alia*) Pope Innocent IV, who denied that force could rightly be used against nonbelievers to compel their conversion to the Christian faith.[11] That armed force could be placed at the service of Church interests would remain a live issue for many centuries. For instance, as late as the mid-nineteenth century, Pope Pius IX encouraged a military intervention by Catholic princes to support his army in protecting the Pontifical States against the invasion of Italian nationalists.[12] This sort of appeal definitively came to an end with the loss of the Papal States in 1870, after which time Church leaders increasingly emphasized the peace-making role of the papacy.

Alongside the canon law developments mentioned above, also important in the Middle Ages was the emergence in the tenth century of a popular movement, "the Peace of God" (*Pax Dei*) to limit the depredations of private warfare, then endemic to Europe. As the movement began to wane in the mid-eleventh century, a new initiative arose on the part of the clergy and the higher nobility to limit warfare to certain times and periods. This was termed the "Truce of God" (*Treuga Dei*). It called for the cessation of warfare during certain days of the week, on specified religious festivals, and even for several weeks during Advent and other periods in the religious calendar. The Truce also adopted the central restrictions of the Peace regarding persons and property that ought not to be attacked. To the list of protected persons and things were added women, travelers, merchants, persons engaged in agriculture, shepherds tending their flocks, animals that are used to till the soil, olive trees, and others. The main tenets of the two movements were summed up at the Second Lateran Council (1123), which also issued a ban on using certain weapons against fellow Christians. This was one of the first attempts at what centuries later would be termed "arms control."

Concern with placing restrictions on the actual conduct of warfare (*jus in bello*) became prominent again in the fourteenth century, at which time there arose a literature geared to knightly practitioners of just war. Focusing on the principles of chivalry – the virtues and rules applicable to right conduct in war – the authors exhibiting this orientation (*inter alia* John of Legnano, Honoré Bonet, and Christine of Pizan) did much to promote the idea that laws of war should guide all combatants on the battlefield. In so doing they gave Christian form to the ancient Roman ideal of "public war," a war that could be deemed just on both sides in the measure that the belligerents adhered to a standard set of procedures (hence the term "regular war" that would later be adopted by Protestant thinkers such as Vattel).[13]

Finally, during the Middle Ages there emerged (especially in connection with the crusades to recapture the Holy land) a conception of "holy war." Although the term itself came to be coined much later, this was the idea that "war was not merely justifiable but justifying and spiritually beneficial to those who participated in it."[14] It was manifested, for instance, in the conviction that those who died in battle "for the faith" would be given a heavenly reward. Arguably, the most famous articulation of this idea may be found in a work that the great Cistercian mystic St. Bernard of Clairvaux wrote (ca. 1150) to a fellow Cistercian who had recently become Pope Eugene III. Using a phrase that would be much cited subsequently, he asserted that the pope possessed "two swords," one representing spiritual power, the other material power. By virtue of the latter, the pope (and also to a certain extent lower ecclesial authorities) was deemed to possess "an inherent right to use physical coercion as well as spiritual censures in the exercise of his jurisdiction. But since it was forbidden for a priest to shed blood it was necessary for the pope to summon the secular princes of Christendom to aid him in such matters and to exercise the 'material sword' on his behalf."[15]

Canons of the Second Lateran Council (1123)

From: H. J. Schroeder, *Disciplinary Decrees of the General Councils: Text, Translation and Commentary*[16]

Canon 11: We command also that priests, clerics, monks, travelers, merchants, country people going and returning, and those engaged in agriculture, as well as the animals with which they till the soil and that carry the seeds to the field, and also their sheep, shall at all times be secure.

Canon 12: We decree that the truce of God be strictly observed by all from the setting of the sun on Wednesday to its rising on Monday, and from Advent to the octave of Epiphany and from Quinquagesima to the octave of Easter. If anyone shall violate it and does not make satisfaction after the third admonition, the bishop shall direct against him the sentence of excommunication and in writing shall announce his action to the neighboring bishops....

Canon 18: By the authority of God and of the blessed Apostles Peter and Paul we absolutely condemn and prohibit that most wicked, devastating, horrible, and malicious work of incendiaries; for this pest, this hostile waste, surpasses all other depredations. No one is ignorant of how detrimental this is to the people of God and what injury it inflicts on souls and bodies. Every means must be employed, therefore, and no effort must be spared that for the welfare of the people such ruin and such destruction may be eradicated and extirpated....

Canon 29: We forbid under penalty of anathema that the deadly and God-detested art of slingers and archers be in the future exercised against Christians and Catholics.

Gratian (Twelfth Century)

From: Gratian, *Decretum*, book II, *causa* 23[17]

Certain bishops have fallen into heresy with the people in their charge. They began with threats and tortures to force neighboring Catholics into adopting this heresy. Having learned of this, the pope ordered the Catholic bishops of the neighboring regions, who had received temporal jurisdiction from the emperor, to defend the Catholics from the heretics, and to compel them by any means possible to return to the true faith.... At this stage we ask in the first place whether it is a sin to serve as a soldier (*militare*). Second, what sort of war is just, and how the children of Israel fought just wars. Third, whether an injury inflicted upon our associates (*sociorum*) ought to be repelled with arms. Fourth, whether vengeance (*vindicta*) is permissible. Fifth, whether it is a sin for a judge or minister to execute a guilty person. Sixth, whether the wicked may be forced to do good. Seventh, whether heretics ought to be despoiled of their property, and whether he who gains possession of property taken from heretics is to be considered as possessing things belonging to others. Eighth, whether it is permitted for bishops, or any sort of cleric, to take up arms on the authority of the pope or by command of the emperor.

Question I . . .

Gratian: Here is how we answer these arguments: The precepts of patience have to prevail less in outward deed than in the preparation of the heart.

Hence Augustine said in his *Sermon on the Child of the Centurion*:

Canon 2. The precepts of patience have to be observed through firmness of the mind, not in outward attitude. The just and pious man ought to be ready to put up with the malice of those he wants to become good, in order that the number of the good may increase, instead of adding himself by equal malice to the number of the wicked. In sum, these precepts are rather for the preparation of the heart which is internal, than for the deed which is in the open; so that patience and benevolence are to be confined to the secret of the mind, while that has to show in the open what would seem to profit to those we want to become better. . . .

Likewise, [Augustine] to Boniface:

Canon 3. Many can please God in the profession of arms. Do not think that none can please God while serving in arms. . . . Therefore keep this in mind first of all, when you prepare to fight, that your valor, including your bodily courage, is a gift of God. Thus you will care not to use a gift of God against the Lord. For, when it has been vowed, faith is to be kept even toward the enemy against whom war is being waged; how much more toward a friend whom one is fighting for? To strive for peace is a matter of willing, but war should be of necessity, so that God may free us from necessity and conserve us in peace. For peace is not pursued in order to wage war, but war is waged in order to gain peace. Be therefore peaceful while you wage war, so that you may in winning lead over to the benefit of peace those whom you defeat. . . . It is therefore necessity, not will, that crushes the fighting enemy. Just as he who fights and resists is checked by violence, mercy is due to the vanquished, to the captive, mostly when no trouble to the peace is to be feared on his part.

Likewise, [Augustine] said against the Manicheans:

Canon 4. What is rightfully to be blamed in war. What is to be blamed in war? Is it the death of some who are to die in any case, so that others may be forced to peaceful subjection? To reprove this is cowardice, not religion. What is rightly reproved in war are love of mischief, revengeful cruelty, fierce and implacable enmity, wild resistance, lust of power, and such like. And it is generally to punish these things, when force is required to inflict punishment, that, in obedience to God or some lawful authority, good men undertake wars, when they find themselves in such a position as regards the conduct of human affairs, that this very position justly compels them either to give such orders or to obey them. Thus John does not order soldiers to lay down their arms, and Christ urges that money be given to Caesar, because soldiers need to get their pay on account of war. For this natural order which seeks the peace of mankind ordains that the authority and resolve to undertake war lie with the princes. . . .

Gratian: From all this we gather that soldiering is not a sin, and that the precepts of patience are to be observed in the preparation of the heart, not in the ostentation of the body.

Question II . . .

Gratian: Now, as to what constitutes a just war, Isidore in *Twenty Books of Etymologies* says . . .

Canon 1. What is a just war. That war is just which is waged by an edict in order to regain what has been stolen or to repel the attack of enemies. . . .

Likewise, Augustine in *Seven Questions Concerning the Heptateuch* says:

Canon 2. It is of no concern to justice whether one fights openly or by ambushes. Our Lord God himself gave the order to Joshua to set up an ambush behind him, that is, to arrange his warriors so as to trap the enemy in an ambush. This teaches us that such things are not done unjustly by those who fight a just war; so that the just man doesn't need particularly to worry about this, except that war be undertaken by one who has the right to do so. For this right does not belong to everyone. Yet when a just war is undertaken, it does not affect justice whether one fights openly or by ambushes. Just wars are usually defined as those which have for their end the avenging of injuries, when it is necessary by war to constrain a nation or a city which has either neglected to punish an evil action committed by its citizens, or to restore what has been taken unjustly. But also this kind of war is certainly just which is ordered by God, who knows what is owed to everyone; in which case the leader of the army or the people itself are not to be deemed authors but agents of the war.

Gratian: Since therefore the just war is one which is waged by an edict, or by which injustices are avenged, it is asked how the children of Israel fought just wars.

On this subject, Augustine wrote in his *Questions on* [*the book of*] *Numbers* that

Canon 3. The sons of Israel were refused innocent passage, and therefore they waged just wars. One ought indeed to note how just wars were waged by the sons of Israel against the Amorites. For they were denied innocent passage, which ought to have been granted according to the most equitable law governing human society. . . .

Likewise, Ambrose [writes] in the first book of [his work] *On the Duties* [*of Ministers*]:

Canon 7. He who does not ward off an injury from an associate is similar to him who caused it. The law of valor lies not in inflicting injury but in repelling it; for he who fails to ward off injury from an associate if he can do so, is quite as blamable as he who inflicts it. It is here, therefore, that Moses the saint gave the first proofs of his courage at war. For when he saw a Hebrew being mistreated by an Egyptian, he defended him by striking the Egyptian and hiding him in the sand. Solomon too said: Deliver him who is being led to death. . . .

Question VI

Gratian: As to the question whether the wicked ought to be compelled the good, the answer is obvious. The Ancient People were indeed compelled by the fear of punishments to observe the law. In the Gospel, too, the Lord said to his disciples: "Be not afraid of those who kill the body, while they cannot kill the soul, be rather afraid of him" – that is, serve him in awe – "who can kill the soul and the body in hell" (Matt. 10:28). Paul, too, when he persecuted God's Church, was blinded on his way and forced to convert to God. . . . Hence Augustine wrote to Boniface [letter 185]:

Canon 1. The Church must compel the wicked to the good, as Christ compelled Paul. The schismatics say: To whom did Christ do violence, whom did he compel? Let them take the apostle Paul as an example. Let them recognize in him Christ, first compelling, then teaching; first striking, then comforting. It is indeed remarkable how this man, who came to the Gospel through corporal punishment, was to labor more than all those who were called to the Gospel only through words; and he who was forced to charity by great fear, was to banish fear through his perfect charity. Why therefore should the Church not compel the lost sons, when the lost sons compelled others to perdition? Yet, even when those who were not compelled but only seduced, are called back by severe but salutary laws into the bosom of their pious mother, she will lovingly receive them and rejoice much more with them than with those whom she never lost. §1. Is it not part of the vigilance owed by the shepherd even to those sheep who have left their flock and come to be possessed by others, not by being violently drawn off but blandly and softly seduced – once he finds them, to drive them back to the flock under the threat and even the pain of flogging? – Likewise: §2. We have referred to the example of Paul compelled by Christ. The Church has therefore imitated her Lord in applying coercion, when she first waited, in order not to compel anybody, so that the prophecies concerning the faith of the kings and peoples may be fulfilled. §3. Nor is it absurd to refer to this apostolic sentence where Saint Paul said: "We are ready to avenge any disobedience, when your obedience will first be complete" (II Cor. 10:4). Therefore the Lord himself ordered the guests first to be invited, then to be compelled to his great meal. For when the servants answered him: "Lord, what you ordered has been done and there is still room," he said: "Go out by the ways and paths, and compel whomsoever you meet to enter" (Luke 14:22–23). In those, therefore, who were first gently brought along, prior obedience was fulfilled; but in those who were compelled, disobedience was curbed. – Likewise: §5. If, by the power the Church received in its time as a divine gift through the religion and the faith of the kings, those who are found on the ways and paths, that is, in the heresies and schisms, are compelled to enter, they should not reprehend being compelled but rather ask themselves to what purpose they are being compelled. . . .

Gratian. [dictum post can. 4]: From all this one gathers that the wicked must be compelled to the good. §1. But it is objected that nobody is to be uselessly compelled to anything. But it is useless to compel anybody to the good, since God disdains forced worship.... §5. These [objections] we answer thus: If the wicked were always to suffer unwillingly the good which they are forced to, without ever serving it willingly, they would have been uselessly compelled to it. But since human nature tends to dislike what it gets out of habit and rather likes what it is used to, the wicked have to be removed from evil by the lash of tribulation and called to the good, so that, evil falling into disuse through the fear of punishment, it is rejected, while the good becomes agreeable owing to habit....

Question VIII

Gratian: We answer this as follows: Priests may not take up arms themselves; but they are allowed to exhort others to do so in order to defend the oppressed and to fight the enemies of God.

Hence pope Leo IV wrote to emperor Louis: ...

Canon 8. The pope has to be the defender and protector of his flock. You must know that we shall never suffer our men to be oppressed by anyone; but should there arise some necessity, then we shall presently react, because we have to defend our flock against everybody and be its foremost protectors.

The same, to the army of the Franks:

Canon 9. He shall obtain the heavenly kingdom from God who dies in defense of the Christians. Having relinquished all fright and terror, do combat with all your strength the enemies of the holy faith and the adversaries of all religions. For, if any one of you dies, the Almighty knows that he died for the truth of the faith, for the salvation of the country and the defense of the Christians, and he will therefore obtain celestial reward.

Bernard of Clairvaux (1090–1153)

From: Bernard of Clairvaux, *Treatise on Consideration*, book 4, chap. 3[18]

[H]e who would deny that the sword belongs to thee [the pope, as successor of the apostle Peter], has not, as I conceive, sufficiently weighed the words of the Lord, where He said, speaking to Peter, "Put up *thy* sword into the scabbard" (John 18:11). For it is here plainly implied that even the material sword is thine, to be drawn at thy bidding, although not by thy hand. Besides, unless this sword also appertained to thee in some sense, when the disciples said to Christ, "Lord, behold here are two swords" (Luke 22:38), He would never have answered as He did, "It is enough," but rather, "it is too much." We can therefore conclude that both swords, namely the spiritual and the material, belong to the Church, and that although only the former is to be wielded by her own hand, the two are to be employed in her service. It is for the priest to use the sword of the word, but to strike with the sword of steel belongs to the soldier, yet this must be by the authority and will (*ad nutum*) of the priest and by the direct command of the emperor, as I have said elsewhere.[19]

Raymond of Peñafort (ca. 1180–1275)

From: Raymond of Peñafort, *Summa de casibus poenitentiae*, II, §17[20]

Now in order to gain complete clarity concerning war, note that five conditions are required for a war to be just, namely person (*persona*), object (*res*), cause (*causa*), state of mind (*animus*), and authority (*auctoritas*): The *person* [engaged in war] must be a secular, for whom it is permitted to shed blood, and not a cleric, for whom this is prohibited unless under necessity.... The *object* [of war must be] the recovery of property and the defense of the fatherland.... The *cause* [requires] that [the war] be fought out of necessity, so that peace is achieved by the fighting.... The *state of mind* [requires] that [war be waged] not because of hatred, revenge, or greed, but because of piety, justice, and obedience ... and to serve as a soldier is not wrong, but to do so for the sake of booty "is a sin." ... *Authority* [requires] that [war be] waged by the authority of the Church, particularly if it is fought for the faith; or by the authority of the prince.... If any of these conditions be lacking, the war will be called unjust.

Innocent IV (1180–1254)

From: Innocent IV, *Apparatus in quinque libros Decretalium*, "On the Restitution of Spoils," Decretal "Olim causam inter vos" (*Decretals*, II, 13, 12), n. 8 (f. 89vb)[21]

[8] It is permissible for anyone to wage war in self-defense or to protect property. Nor is this properly called "war" (*bellum*), but rather "defense" (*defensio*). And when someone has been ejected, he may lawfully fight back on the spot (*incontinenti*), that is, before he has turned his attention to other matters. And since this is permitted by law, authorization by the prince is not required....

War, properly speaking, can only be declared by a prince who does not have a superior. He can declare war against those who would not be liable to an execution of jurisdiction, for example, against those who fall under the rule of some other prince.

From: Innocent IV, "On Vows and the Fulfilling of Vows," Decretal "Quod super his" (*Decretals*, III, 34, 8), nn. 7–8 (f. 164vb)[22]

[7] The pope may grant indulgences to those who act to recover the Holy Land, even though the Saracens occupy it. The pope may also declare war and grant indulgences to those who occupy the Holy Land which the infidels illegally possess. All this has

a [good] cause, for the pope acts justly when he strives to recover the Holy Land – which is consecrated by the birth, life, and death of Jesus Christ, yet where not Christ but Mohammed is being worshipped – in order that it be inhabited by Christians.

Furthermore, the Holy Land was conquered in a just war by the Roman emperor after the death of Christ. Thus it is legitimate for the pope, by reason of the Roman Empire which he obtained, to return it to his jurisdiction, since it was unjustly expropriated and despoiled by those who have no right to it. This same reason holds for all other lands in which the Roman emperors had jurisdiction, although it might be said that he cannot do it on the basis of this right, that is, by reason of the Roman Empire, because the Church has dominion only in the West.... But if he cannot do it as emperor, he can do it according to the aforesaid reasons. At the very least the emperor can do it in the capacity of the King of Jerusalem, which belongs to him by law – which we believe and ought to believe, since the contrary is not obvious to us.

Yet the pope may also justly lay down rules and decrees against other infidels, who now hold the land where Christian princes had jurisdiction, in order that they do not unjustly persecute the Christians who find themselves under their jurisdiction. What is more, he may even exempt them entirely from their jurisdiction and dominion.... Indeed, if they maltreat Christians he may by a pronouncement deprive them of the jurisdiction and dominion they have over Christians, but it would require an extreme necessity to bring this about. The pope ought to put up with them insofar as he can, provided there is no great danger to Christians, or there is no great offense done to them.

[8] Furthermore, although infidels ought not be forced to accept the faith, since everyone's free will ought to be respected, and this conversion should [come about] only by the grace of God ... yet the pope may command the infidels to admit preachers of the Gospel to the lands under their jurisdiction; for, since every rational creature is created to praise God, they sin if they stop the preachers from preaching, and therefore they ought to be punished.

Scholastic Theologians

Concurrently with the work of the Decretalists, theologians in the thirteenth century also began to write on problems associated with war. Most famous among them was undoubtedly St. Thomas Aquinas (ca. 1224–1274), whose division of just war criteria into legitimate authority, just cause, and right intention has served as the basic armature for Western moral reflection on war up to the present day. From the sixteenth century onward, Aquinas' *Quaestio de bello* became the principal locus for theological discussions on war. The most famous of Aquinas' commentators was Thomas de Vio (1468–1524), better known by the name "Cajetan"), who established a close linkage between just war and punishment. The Italian cardinal argued that no political community could be deemed self-sufficient if it did not possess the power to exact just revenge against its internal and external foes.

Spain's colonization of the Americas in the sixteenth century dramatically stimulated Catholic reflection on norms of war. Reports of indiscriminate killing, forced labor, and confiscation of land had raised doubts about the fast-growing colonies. Since it was by resort to arms that Catholic Spain had come to exercise dominion over the indigenous peoples of the Americas, the theologians who were then debating this involvement would have to assess, *inter alia*, whether religious motives – for instance, a desire to convert the Amerindians to Christianity – could provide moral warrant for the employment of these coercive measures. It was in this period that one of the first full-fledged theological treatises on the problem of war between nations appeared in the Latin West: the lectures on war by Francisco de Vitoria (ca. 1492–1546), especially famous for their criticism of the behavior of the Spanish conquistadors and the accompanying defense of the rights of the American Indians.[23] In this connection, Vitoria was influenced by a text from Cajetan's commentary to the *Summa theologiae* where the learned cardinal had sharply chastised those Christians who would justify the conquest of pagan lands by appeal to the inhabitants' condition of unbelief.

Of particular importance in Vitoria's treatment of war was the establishment of a tight conceptual linkage between the moral problem of conquest and war, on the one hand, and the norms of natural law, on the other. Appealing to a set of unwritten moral imperatives rooted in a source antecedent to human deliberation and choice, namely God, yet which do not depend on a special religious revelation (a holy book), Vitoria viewed these norms as applicable to all men, in whatever lands they may find themselves. His focus on natural law had a formative influence on the development of the modern Catholic conception of resort to armed force, which henceforth would be framed in terms of secular ("natural") rather than specifically religious (revealed) principles.

Vitoria was moreover one of the first Christian thinkers to discuss war and peace with explicit reference to the common good, not only of an individual nation or people, but of "the whole world" (*bonum totius orbis*). In a famous passage he similarly suggested that just war was akin to an act of policing to be undertaken by the authority of the international community.

Vitoria's line of thought was further developed by two fellow Spaniards, both Jesuits. The first, Luis de Molina (1535–1600), was instrumental in reformulating the notion of just cause so that it no longer presupposed personal guilt on the part of the adversary. This he termed "material injury"; such an injury would arise if the offender carried out a wrongful act while in a state of "invincible ignorance."[24] If the injury was of sufficient gravity, the offended party could have just cause to seek redress through resort to armed force. This resort would count as an instance of offensive war, yet, since it was not predicated on the culpability of the adversary, it could not be waged in view of punishment. By distinguishing just war from punishment, Molina thereby established one of the central premises on which the modern *ius in bello* came to be built. Henceforth any damage caused in war would have to be justified at a minimum by the requirement of military necessity. Harm inflicted solely with the intent of making the adversary suffer pain would eventually be deemed incompatible with the laws of war.

The second of the two Jesuits, Francisco Suarez (1548–1617), wrote a systematic treatise, *De bello*, which covered in some detail (and with numerous original arguments of his own) many of the points earlier treated by Vitoria. In a famous passage he asserted that human beings are not condemned to settle their disputes by war since God has provided us with other means – including arbitration – to resolve controversies between commonwealths.[25] He insisted, likewise, that political and military leaders have obligations not only toward the well-being of their own polity but vis-à-vis the enemy commonwealth as well. Before declaring war such leaders must make their grievances known to the latter, providing it an opportunity to avoid war by offering satisfaction for the wrong done. Suarez is also noteworthy for the very careful treatment that he gave to the problem of side-effect harm in war (collateral damage), which he applied by reference to what has since become known as the "principle of double effect."[26]

Thomas Aquinas (1225–1274)

From: Thomas Aquinas, *Summa theologiae*, part II-II, question 40, a. 1, "Whether any war is permissible?"[27]

... In order for a war to be just, three things are necessary. First, the authority of the prince by whose command the war is to be waged. For it is not the business of a private person to declare war, because he can seek for redress of his rights (*ius suum prosequi*) from the tribunal of his superior. Moreover it is not the business of a private person to summon together the people, which has to be done in wartime. And as the care of the common weal is committed to those who are in authority, it is their business to watch over the common weal of the city, kingdom or province subject to them. And just as it is permissible for them to have recourse to the material sword in defending that common weal against internal disturbances, when they punish evil-doers, according to the words of the Apostle (Rom. 13:4): *He beareth not the sword in vain: for he is God's minister, an avenger to execute wrath upon him that doth evil*; so too, it is their business to have recourse to the sword of war in defending the common weal against external enemies....

Secondly, a just cause is required, namely that those who are attacked should be attacked because they deserve it on account of some fault (*culpa*). Therefore Augustine says (*Questions in Hept.*, q. X, *super Jos.*): "A just war is usually described as one that avenges wrongs, when a nation or state has to be punished, for refusing to make amends for the wrongs inflicted by its subjects, or to restore what it has seized unjustly."

Thirdly, it is necessary that the belligerents should have a right intention, so that they intend the advancement of good, or the avoidance of evil.... For it may happen that the war is declared by the legitimate authority, and for a just cause, and yet be rendered illicit through a wicked intention.

Thomas de Vio (Cajetan) (1468–1534)

From: Thomas de Vio, *Summula*, "When war should be called just or unjust, licit or illicit"[28]

After [the war] has been fought a while, and human casualties have occurred on both sides, he who has a just war is not required to end the war, merely because the enemy now offers satisfaction. The reason for this is that the prosecutor of the just war functions as a judge of criminal proceedings. That he functions as a judge of criminal proceedings is clear from the fact that a just combat is an act of vindicative justice (*actus vindicativae iustitiae*), which is properly within the power of a prince or judge. A private person is not empowered to seek vengeance, for it is written, "Vengeance is mine."[29] That it is a criminal matter is clear from the fact that it leads to the killing and enslavement of persons and the destruction of goods, for all of these things result from a just war – although today slavery is avoided among Christians. It is also clear that he who has a just war is not a party, but becomes, by the very reason that impelled him to make war, the judge of his enemies; for the same reason a prince can resort to the sword against internal and external disturbers of the commonwealth, that is, owing to the nature of a perfect commonwealth. For it is not a perfect commonwealth if it lacks the ability to exercise vindicative justice, either against internal disturbers of the commonwealth or external disturbers.

From: Thomas de Vio, Commentary (ca. 1515) to Thomas Aquinas, *Summa theologiae* II-II, q. 66, a. 8[30]

Some unbelievers (*infideles*) are neither *de jure* nor *de facto* under the temporal jurisdiction of Christian princes: such would be the case if there were found unbelievers who have never been subjects of the Roman Empire and who inhabit lands where the name *Christian* has remained unknown. Such people, despite being unbelievers, nonetheless have legitimate dominion over their own affairs, which are governed by monarchy or by political rule. They are not to be deprived of dominion by reason of their unbelief, for dominion is a matter of positive right (*ex jure positivo*) while unbelief pertains to divine right (*ex divino jure*). Divine right does not eliminate positive right as was said above [apropos *Summa theologiae* II-II, q. 10, a. 10]. . . . No [Christian] king or emperor, nor the Roman [Catholic] Church is entitled to initiate war against these unbelievers, occupying their lands or subjecting them to temporal rule. There is no just cause for war against them, for Jesus Christ, King of Kings, to whom all power has been given on heaven and earth, has sent out to gain possession of the world, not soldiers and armies, but holy preachers as sheep among wolves. That is why even in the Old Testament, which was a time of armed conquest, I do not see that war was ever declared against a land because its inhabitants were not believers. War was waged against them because they denied free passage, or attacked first . . . or to regain from them things that had been given [to the Israelites] by divine concession. That is why we would sin very gravely should we seek to spread the faith of Christ in such a way. Far from having legitimate dominion over these unbelievers, we would have committed robbery and as a result would have an obligation to make restitution, as are all those who have unjustly waged a war or occupied a land. To these unbelievers we should send not conquerors who oppress and scandalize them . . . but holy preachers who are able to convert them to God by their word and example.

Francisco de Vitoria (ca. 1492–1546)

From: Francisco de Vitoria, *On the American Indians*, question 2, article 4: "Fourth unjust title, that they refuse to accept the faith of Christ, although they have been told about it and insistently pressed to accept it"[31]

[H]owever probably and sufficiently the [Christian] faith may have been announced to the barbarians and then rejected by them, *this is still no reason to declare war on them and despoil them of their goods*.... The proof is that belief is a matter of will, but fear considerably diminishes the freedom of will.... The proposition is also proved by the use and custom of the Church, since no Christian emperor, with the benefit of the advice of the most holy and wise popes, has ever declared war on unbelievers simply because they refused to accept the Christian religion.

From: Francisco de Vitoria, *On the Law of War*, question 1, article 3: "What are the permissible reasons and causes of just war?"[32]

First, *difference of religion cannot be a cause of just war*. This proposition was amply proved in the previous relection [*de Indis*]....

Second, *enlargement of empire cannot be a cause of just war*. This proposition is too well known to require further proof....

Third, *the personal glory or convenience of the prince is not a cause of just war*. This proposition is also well established. The prince must order war and peace for the common good of the commonwealth; he may not appropriate public revenues for his own aggrandisement or convenience, still less expose his subjects to danger. This is the difference between a legitimate king and a tyrant....

Fourth, *the sole and only just cause for waging war is when harm has been inflicted*....

Fifth, *not every or any injury gives sufficient grounds for waging war*.... [S]ince all the effects of war are cruel and horrible – slaughter, fire, devastation – it is not lawful to persecute those responsible for trivial offenses by waging war upon them....

Therefore it is not lawful to start war for every reason or injury.

From: Francisco de Vitoria, *On the Law of War*, question 1, article 4: "What and how much, may be done in a just war?"[33]

[T]he prince has the authority not only over his own people but also over foreigners to force them to abstain from harming others; this is his right by the law of nations and the authority of the whole world. Indeed, it seems he has this right by natural law: the world could not exist unless some men had the power and authority to deter the wicked by force from doing harm to the good and the innocent.

Luis de Molina (1535–1600)

From: Luis de Molina, *On Justice and Law*, tract II, disputation 102: "A common just cause of war, comprising all of the others"[34]

Notice, however, that it is sometimes sufficient for a just war that there be injury [committed] materially (*iniuria materialiter*), which involves no sin. For owing to the very fact that God granted the lands of the Canaanites and the Amorites to the children of Israel [Deut. 1:7], they had the right to expel by war those peoples who resisted them, in order to occupy the land that God had given to them – even if those peoples were ignorant of God's gift, and were thereby without blame in resisting and trying to retain these lands; and therefore they inflicted only a material injury upon the children of Israel. For this reason ... this war was just on both sides: materially and formally on the side of the children of Israel, but only formally on the side of those peoples, inasmuch as they defended themselves and their property without sin, being invincibly ignorant of God's donation and will.

Francisco Suarez (1548–1617)

From: Francisco Suarez, On War (*De bello*),[35] Section VI, "What certitude as to the just cause of war is required in order that war may be just?"[36]

[I]t is impossible that the Author of nature should have left human affairs, governed as they are by conjecture more frequently than by any sure reason, in such a critical condition that all controversies between supreme princes and commonwealths should be settled only by war; for such a condition would be contrary to wisdom and the common good of the human race; and therefore it would be contrary to justice. Furthermore, if this condition prevailed, those persons would as a rule possess the greater right who were the more powerful, and [this right] would have to be measured by arms, which is manifestly a barbarous and absurd supposition.

From: Francisco Suarez, *On War*, Section VII, "What is the proper mode of conducting war?"[37]

I hold that the innocent as such (*per se*) may under no condition be killed, even if the punishment inflicted upon their commonwealth would, otherwise, be deemed inadequate; but incidentally (*per accidens*) they may be slain, when such an act is necessary in order to secure victory.

The reason supporting this conclusion is that the killing of innocent persons is intrinsically evil....

The conclusion is confirmed by the difference existing between life and other possessions. For the latter fall under human dominion, and the commonwealth as a whole has a greater right to them than do individual persons. Hence, such persons may be deprived of [their] property because of the fault of the whole commonwealth. But life does not fall under human dominion, and therefore, no one may be deprived of his life save by reason of his own fault....

But one may ask, who actually are the innocent, with respect to this issue? My reply is that they include not only the persons enumerated above [§10, children, women, and all unable to bear arms, diplomats, members of religious order, priests, etc.], but also those who are able to bear arms, if it is evident that, in other respects, they have not shared in the crime nor in the unjust war....

These arguments prove beyond a doubt that, after victory has been attained, only those who are known to be guilty may be slain.... [T]he slaughter of all those whose innocence is not clearly evident by reason of age or sex is, in general, permitted, as long as the actual combat continues; but the case will be otherwise after the cessation of combat, and the attainment of victory.

The latter part of the [sixth] conclusion is also commonly accepted [it is just to visit upon the enemy all losses which may seem necessary either for obtaining satisfaction or for securing victory, provided that these losses do not involve direct intrinsic injury to innocent persons, which would be intrinsically evil] and is clearly true in the case of certain means essential to victory, which, however, necessarily involve the death of the innocent, as in the burning of cities and the destruction of fortresses. For, strictly speaking, whoever has the right to attain the end sought by a war, has the right to use the means to that end. Moreover, in such a case, the death of the innocent is not directly intended (*per se intenta*), it follows rather as an incidental consequence (*per accidens sequitur*). Hence, it is not considered voluntary, rather it is permitted by one who exercises his right in a time of necessity. A confirmation of this argument lies in the fact that it would [otherwise] be impossible to conclude the war. In like manner, a pregnant woman may use medicine necessary to preserve her own life, even if she knows that this will result in the death of her unborn child. From these arguments it is to be inferred that, save out of necessity, the means in question are not permissible.

Modernity

Despite its vigor and the new perspectives that it opened up, the "golden age" of Spanish theorizing on war came to a close toward the middle of the seventeenth century. During the next three centuries, the Catholic teaching on war would enter a period of sterility. Apart from the work of Luigi Taparelli d'Azeglio (1793–1862),[38] who updated just war theory to deal with problems such as preventive war, and whose strong endorsement of international society, arbitration, and arms reduction would contribute toward the papacy's later embrace of these ideas, most authors merely repeated points made by earlier just war theorists such as Aquinas, with few attempting to apply these ideas to current events. This was the heyday of *raison d'état* (classical international law), when it was generally assumed that individual sovereign states had full discretion in waging war to serve their interests. Matters of ethics were relegated to the private conscience of political leaders and were not thought to be a fit topic for public discourse.

The normative landscape began to change, however, when journalists reported on the large casualties associated with the Crimean (1854–1856) and Franco-Prussian (1870–1871) wars. A wave of pacifist sentiment rose, making inroads among some Catholic organizations. The First World War, in particular, made manifest the disastrous consequences of an unbridled *jus ad bellum*. The League of Nations Covenant (1919) sought to remedy this state of affairs by establishing a system of obligatory arbitration, with the aim of preventing states from resorting to force to resolve their differences.

The legal regime established by the League stood in a somewhat ambiguous relation to the just war outlook of the Catholic tradition. On the one hand, in its underlying supposition that "the normal state of international relations is one of peace, with war permitted only as an exceptional act requiring affirmative justification,"[39] the League represented a rejection of *raison d'état* and a return to the classical just war point of view. Likewise, in its strong endorsement of arbitration as a method for limiting resort to war, the League renewed ties with an approach that had traditionally been advocated by the popes and leading theologians such as Suarez. On the other hand, the League showed discontinuity with the earlier tradition of just war in the measure that it largely excluded the problematic of just cause from its deliberations. Built up around a set of rules that dictated what *procedural* conditions (chief among them the submission of disputes to arbitration) had to be met before a resort to force could be deemed lawful, the League could side-step the question "as to which side had legal right on its side."[40]

This change in outlook from just war idea to the legal regime of the Covenant presented an obvious challenge to Catholic thinkers, who engaged in two lines of response. Some sought to minimize the difference between the two outlooks, by arguing that the normative conception underlying the League was in fundamental continuity with the outlook of the traditional just war theorists (Vitoria, etc.). This argument was typically made in historical studies,[41] where the main tenets of earlier just war thinking were explained in some detail.

The other approach was to call for a reformulation of Catholic teaching on war and peace, to render it more consistent with the contemporary outlook.[42] An emphasis on arbitration, arms reduction, nonviolent peace-making strategies, and supranational institutions would outflank the earlier preoccupation with just cause and legitimate authority. This was the path marked out by a group of Catholic theologians who issued a document, the "Fribourg Conventus"[43] (after the Swiss city where they had assembled in 1931), which discussed the morality of war in light of the most recent developments on the world scene.

Fribourg Conventus (1931)

From: "Conclusions of the Theological Conventus at Fribourg upon War"[44]

[N]o civilized State could in these days attain its own end, fulfill its own duties and vindicate its own rights without associating and co-ordinating its own life with that of other nations. This being the case, the question of the morality of war cannot rightly be studied in the abstract without relation to that natural society toward which tends the natural sociability of States or the juridical form which international relations are seen to have assumed.

If, as was once the case, any juridical organization of the society of nations were lacking and the conditions in which States existed implied their full independence, it would indeed be possible for a war declared by the supreme authority of some one State to be sometimes considered *positis ponendis* a lawful war. And that is the kind of war which the older school of theologians and moralists who were almost exclusively concerned with determining the conditions of just war generally had in mind. But once with the growth of international relations the natural society of nations has received a structure through certain instruments adapted to that end; once it has assumed in public law a form more in accord with the rational nature of man the question to be solved is whether this *accidental* legitimacy of war can in fact still exist. That is the only way in which the problem of the morality of war can be stated at the present time. . . .

Although international society does not enjoy the full authority which it might well possess, both from the very nature of things and from the consent of men, yet it is clear that it has now been developed into a form of positive law in such a way that it is consolidated by many juridical and political instruments which are designed to establish human order and peace. Because of this *a war declared by a State on its own authority without previous recourse to the international institutions which exist cannot be a lawful social process.* It would be repugnant to the dictates both of public law and of conscience, for at the start it would involve a violation of that general or legal justice which requires that the State should not only not offend the rights of other peoples which are equal to its own, but should also subordinate its own national end to the more general end of international society. *A fortiori,* modern war, that is war as understood and waged nowadays, could not be a legitimate social process.

Reaction to Nazi aggression and the subsequent occupation of Europe led to a revival of just war discourse among some French Catholic thinkers, for instance, Jacques Maritain, who in 1940 published a set of essays on this theme.[45]

Jacques Maritain (1882–1973)

From: Jacques Maritain, "Just War,"[46] *Commonweal* (22 December 1939)

Many people thought that under modern world conditions there could no longer be a just war; this idea seemed to them tenable in the abstract, yet it was false. Of course it is true that the criteria for a just war established by the theologians of the classic age need revision, for war itself has radically changed: the war of armies has become the war of peoples, and is something which more closely resembles a cosmic cataclysm than the "last recourse" (*ultima ratio*) of those theologians. Yet in this cosmic cataclysm human beings are engaged, and hence the rules governing what is just and what is unjust remain. Confronted with the joint action by which the two peoples of France and of England – in order to challenge the frightful passion of violence and pride which thrust out against Poland and in order to prevent the world from being enslaved to the lust for brutal domination by which Hitler's totalitarianism is obsessed – decided to go to war against Germany, what man of right judgment would not say in conscience: this war against Germany is a just war?

Here is no question of an ideological war. It is not to serve an Idea or a divinized abstract Principle that France and Great Britain are giving the blood of their children and jeopardizing their heritage of civilization. It is rather for the elementary realities in the absence of which human life ceases to be human....

Nor is there here any question of a holy war. The people of this country have enough common sense, they know well enough what every war brings with it and after it, in misery and in poison and in the intensification of the most vile as well as the exaltation of the most noble in our earthly life, to guard themselves against enlisting the sanctity of the ineffable Name in the temporal war which they are fighting.

It is a question of a just war. Fighting for justice – suffering and dying so that a bestial barbarism may not rule over the earth – they know (at least those who have the light of faith know) that they may count upon the help of God. They do not say: our cause is divine, our cause is the cause of God, we are the soldiers of God. They say: our cause is human, it is the cause of that human community desired by God in the natural order and which is called our fatherland, and which, hating war, has been forced to resort to war against an iniquitous aggressor; and because our cause is just, God will have pity on us....

What I would now like to point out is that the question of the justice of a war – which relates to a specific act and a dispute between men – and the question of its distant origins – which relate to the endless concatenations and crisscrossings of many acts and a dispute between the human conscience and the Master of history – are two quite different questions. For one thing, we know that all sin is the cause of all the evil that happens on earth and that all men are sinners; for another thing, we know that a man may defend a just cause against an unjust adversary. And these two things are both true at the same time.

That which makes a war either just or unjust is, in essence, the immediate purpose and motive which determined it. The war against German National Socialism has for its immediately determining purpose and motive to resist the aggression of which Poland has been the victim, and to resist unbridled imperialist greed: it is a just war....

Germany wages an unjust – a manifestly, monstrously unjust – war; and to the extent that she has yielded to Hitler and given herself over to him, her part in the underlying causes and the remote origins of the war is enormous. Yet she is not alone in carrying the burden of the sins from which the war sprung. That her war should be unjust and criminal does not free the other peoples from the duty of making themselves humble before God. That the other peoples should have some share before God in the remote origins of the war in no way makes Germany innocent of the crime of the unjust war she is waging nor of the barbarous fashion in which she is waging it.

However, as the Second World War came to an end, several Catholic thinkers raised critical questions about the Allied strategy of attacks on densely populated urban centers. Two names stand out in this connection: the American Jesuit John C. Ford and the British philosopher Elizabeth Anscombe. Both appealed to just war principles in condemning obliteration bombing, which, in the words of Ford, constituted "an immoral attack on the rights of the innocent."[47]

John C. Ford (1903–1989)

From: John C. Ford, "The Morality of Obliteration Bombing" (1944)[48]

Obliteration bombing is the strategic bombing, by means of incendiaries and explosives, of industrial centers of population in which the target to be wiped out is not a definite factory, bridge, or similar object, but a large area of a whole city, comprising one-third to two-thirds of its whole built-up area, and including by design the residential districts of workingmen and their families. If this kind of bombing is not taking place, so much the better. But we have such compelling reasons for thinking it does, that the following discussion of its morality is necessary.

The Moral Problem Raised by Obliteration Bombing

I do not intend to discuss here the question: Can any modern war be morally justified? The overwhelming majority of Catholic theologians would answer, I am sure, that there can be a justifiable modern war. And the practically unanimous voice of American Catholicism, including that of the hierarchy, assures us that we are fighting a just war at present. I accept that position. Our question deals rather with the morality of a given means made use of in the prosecution of a war which itself is justified....

The morality of obliteration bombing can be looked at from the point of view of the bombardier who asks in confession whether he may execute the orders of his military leaders, or it may be looked at from the viewpoint of the leaders who are responsible for the adoption of obliteration bombing as a recognized instrument of the general strategy of war. The present paper takes the latter viewpoint. It is not aimed at settling difficulties of the individual soldier's conscience....

The conclusion of this paper can be stated briefly. Obliteration bombing, as defined, is an immoral attack on the rights of the innocent. It includes a direct intent to do them injury. Even if this were not true, it would still be immoral, because no proportionate cause could justify the evil done; and to make it legitimate would soon lead the world to the immoral barbarity of total war. The voice of the Pope and the fundamental laws of the charity of Christ confirm this condemnation.

In the period after the Second World War, Catholic reflection on war was increasingly directed to the risks posed by nuclear weapons and the need for international restrictions on the use of force. The teaching authority of the Church (the Magisterium) issued numerous statements supporting the United Nations, which was founded in 1945.[49] The division of Europe and the subsequent Cold War made the threat of a nuclear holocaust especially acute, which in turn led to a reassessment of the traditional just war doctrine. In an encyclical published in 1963 (*Pacem in Terris*), Pope John XIII famously wrote how "in this age which boasts of its atomic power, it no longer makes sense to maintain that war is a fit instrument with which to repair the violation of justice."[50] A survey of these developments, and a selection of primary sources, is provided in the next section of this chapter.

Part II: Contemporary Sources
Robert John Araujo, S.J.

We may recall the Biblical prophecy that Jesus Christ is the Prince of Peace,[51] a point worthy of consideration in this chapter. Nonetheless, while the teachings of the Catholic Church condemn the use of military force when it constitutes a "useless slaughter,"[52] it would be mistaken to conclude that Catholic teaching is essentially pacifist in its nature – for such a conclusion would betray the long-held principle that a nation, through its civil authorities, has a prerogative to defend itself, its citizens, and other innocents against the actions of an aggressor whose use of force is unjustifiable on legal and moral grounds. It is evident that the Church's teachings on the use of force and just war theory over the past century have emphasized that reliance on legitimate force is a last resort for addressing threats to which there can be a military response. It remains however that the principal means of resolving disputes or addressing conflicts is through the juridical institutions of international law and diplomacy.

Moreover, the tradition of Catholic teaching on the use of force is also concerned with how to end conflicts that employ the use of force just as it is with the considerations involving its employment in the first place and its conduct once force has been employed – for the Catholic position on the use of force does not contend that armed conflict must be viewed as a permanent fixture in the relations between peoples and states.

For centuries, the Church has expressed teachings based on the classical principles of just war theory.[53] Of course it needs to be recognized that these principles are a *means* to guide those who, by exercise of their legitimate public office, can authorize the use of legitimate force; therefore, these principles do not determine the outcome of how a proper authority is to apply them in an actual circumstance. In this introduction, these principles are briefly outlined in order to assist the reader toward a better understanding of the contemporary Catholic teaching on armed force.[54] The emphasis will be on developments concerning weapons of mass destruction, terrorism, genocide, and the proliferation of nuclear weapons. These have generated a pressing need to reformulate the traditional Catholic teaching for this new context.

As has already been suggested, it would be erroneous to conclude that the Church teaches pacifism as its core doctrine regarding the legitimate use of force. While the Fifth Commandment of the Decalogue asserts that one shall not kill,[55] it is relevant to note that Catholic teaching and generally accepted principles of public international law parallel one another in arguing that disputes between nations ought preferably to be settled through peaceful means. The Church's contemporary teachings on the use of force in the age of modern weaponry emphasize, based on right reason, reliance on juridical means for relieving tensions and problems that might otherwise be resolved by the use of force. The parallel between international law and the Church's teachings is evident from the various exhortations issued by the popes beginning with Benedict XV during World War I.[56]

But as both the Church and public international law authorities recognize, the preference for peaceful means of dispute resolution is not always possible, especially when some nations honor the prescription that favors peaceful means of resolving disputes but others do not. A further consideration surfaces when nongovernment agents such as terror cells rely on violence in the pursuit of their objectives – whatever they may be. In these circumstances, the use of force may be permissible, even necessary, under prescribed conditions when it becomes clear that peaceful means are not only ineffective but may further endanger innocents.

It is pivotal to acknowledge a further parallel that both the Church and international law share: that in the age of weapons of mass destruction, "it is hardly possible to imagine that … war could be used as an instrument of justice."[57] The modern means of massive devastation represent a particularly serious threat to humanity, and those entities that possess these weapons have an enormous responsibility before God and all of humanity.[58] However, the practice of nuclear deterrence, as will be seen, necessitates the evaluation also of other factors, noted by several influential bishops' conferences in the early 1980s.

The Catholic Church, along with established legal principles accepted in the international order, recognizes that nations (and peoples) reserve the right to use the amount of force necessary to muster self-defense. This is both permissible and lawful.[59] To suggest that there is a strong presumption against the use of force would be inaccurate in view of the fact that there is, in reality, a presumption that civil authorities must act justly because of their responsibility to protect those whom they are called to serve.[60] The responsibility to protect has expanded as developments in recent years have demonstrated that the subjects of this protection, that is, natural persons, may not have governments of their own to protect them. Their government may be incapable of rendering assistance, or it may be the very agent of their persecution and responsible for jeopardizing the welfare of these innocents. As with respected principles of public international law, the Catholic Church acknowledges that there are forces in the world – be they states or cells such as terrorist groups – that threaten peace because they do not respect or practice norms designed to govern relations between peoples by resolving disagreements by peaceful means – a fundamental principle of the Church's social doctrine. Pope Paul's celebrated plea at the United Nations made in his October 1965 address to that body – "never again one against another, never, never again! ... never again war, war never again!" – must be understood in this context.[61] Any consideration of his noble words must take into account that there are agents in the world who do not abide by the applicable legal and moral norms that regulate the use of force. As Pope Paul stated in his first World Day of Peace Message of 1968, "it is to be hoped that the exaltation of the ideal of Peace may not favor the cowardice of those who fear it may be their duty to give their life for the service of their own country and of their own brothers, when these are engaged in the defense of justice and liberty."[62]

The traditional guidelines governing the use of force that reflect Catholic teachings mandate considerations and application of moral legitimacy. The essential and general principles constitutive of the Catholic view of the legitimate use of force or just war, which must be considered together, are the following:[63]

1. There is or will be damage inflicted by the aggressor on the nation or community of nations that must be lasting, grave, and certain;
2. All other means of putting an end to the threats and improper actions of the aggressor, such as diplomacy, must have been shown to be impractical or ineffective;
3. There must be genuine prospects of success in achieving the objectives that the use of force are designed to realize; and
4. The use of arms must not produce evils and disorders graver than the evil to be eliminated (thus, considerations of the destructive power of modem methods of using force, i.e., weapons of mass destruction, weigh very heavily in evaluating this final condition).

It is crucial to the Catholic perspective on the use of force that these four interrelated principles be utilized for advancement of the common good[64] through the exercise of the prudential judgment of the properly constituted civil authority, which is typically some designated organ of the state. It is generally regarded in the Catholic tradition on the legitimate use of force that the public authority, that is, the servant state, has the responsibility to exercise this power.[65] In order to assist the public authority in fulfilling its obligations, the authority also retains the additional right and duty to impose on its citizens those obligations and contributions from them essential to a legitimate defense or exercise of protection. The public authority must necessarily take stock of alternatives that may obviate the need for the use of force and that are premised upon an understanding of the underlying causes of armed conflict. In short, the public authority should ascertain whether the catalysts for reverting to the use of force in an armed conflict are rooted in injustice, poverty, or other exploitations that can be resolved in a more appropriate fashion by means other than using armed force.

The concurrent duties of the public authority and the citizenry who may serve in the armed forces or in another defense-related capacity make those who participate at all levels in the national defense the "servants of the security and freedom of nations."[66] By carrying out their responsibilities with honor, the state and those who have a role in its defense contribute to the common good and the maintenance of international peace.[67] It is consistent within these particular teachings pertaining to the use of force that individual conscience be respected by those who direct and exercise the legitimate use of force so that citizens will not be forced against their will to bear arms since they can serve their nation in alternative ways; however, the citizen's duty to serve in some appropriate capacity for the lawful defense remains inviolate.

Once resort to force has been justified (*jus ad bellum*), moral principles regarding the actual use of force (*jus in bello*) come into play. In this subsequent context, the Church's teachings necessitate the utilization of sound human reason and rely on objective moral considerations necessary to guide the exercise of armed force so that only licit means of waging war are employed. This means that, in accordance with modern-day humanitarian principles (e.g., the four Geneva Conventions of 1948), noncombatants, wounded combatants, and prisoners of war must be cared for and preserved from further harm during the conflict. Military actions that contravene these humanitarian principles, whether undertaken by the public authority or by persons acting on its behalf, may be considered crimes of war or crimes against humanity. The Church endorses the principles that those individuals who violate the objective moral standards essential to using military force (once the reasons for its use have been established), be they commanders or those who follow orders, and contravene accepted humanitarian principles, will be subjected to accountability before impartial tribunals in accordance with the due process of law and upon these widely accepted legal norms regarding the permissible use of force. Under Catholic teachings there can never be justification of actions that constitute "ethnic cleansing" or genocide, for these acts contravene established juridical norms and constitute mortal sin, the most grievous offenses against God and the neighbor.

The application of force that is justified in principle, as outlined by the standards identified and discussed so far, must simultaneously take account of two additional considerations: (1) the exercise of force must use only proportionate methods (only that force that is necessary to accomplish that which is permissible), and (2) the application of the methods used must be discriminate so that only those targets that are well-defined and constitute legitimate military objectives may be the targets of the force used. The use of modern weapons may or may not be legitimate in the implementing of these two elements as the following distinctions should illustrate. For example, the field use of weapons of mass destruction (such as atomic, chemical, and biological weapons) would most likely violate these inextricably related criteria of proportionality and discrimination because the force released would be disproportionate to the target and, in all probability, affect areas adjacent to the target inhabited by noncombatants. This does not exclude, however, that the use of "smart weapons" could conceivably meet these criteria if their precision complies with the proportionate and discriminating mandates long held to be a part of the Roman Catholic teachings on the use of force. Under such a scenario, their permissibility would still be subject to a further consideration: namely, that the acquisition of such weapons represents a prudent use of public funds. True enough, the high cost of developing and stockpiling such weapons may in itself be legitimate, as a means of deterring armed attack. But under some circumstances this could represent a misuse of public funds, if, as a result of acquiring such weapons, other more important social needs go neglected, thus leading to an unnecessary aggravation of poverty.

Before concluding this introduction to Catholic teachings on just war theory, several points that provide an overview of these teachings as they apply to the contemporary age can now be identified and briefly explained.[68]

1. The Right and Duty of Legitimate Self-Defense (and the Duty to Protect)

The use of force must always be used in the name of legitimate self-defense or the defense of others and never employed to further the interests of aggression against other members of the world community. Any use of force that constitutes a war of aggression (sometimes referred to as the crime against peace), which is not a legitimate use of force for self-defense or other permissible reason, is intrinsically immoral and would conflict with the first principles of the Church's teachings. The history of aggression demonstrates that it inevitably leads to tragedy for all concerned – it often depletes the resources of the aggressor nation and subjugates, by devastation and humiliation, the nation or region that is the aggressor's target.

When planning for any self-defense or defense of others that will require the use of force, the public authority must carefully evaluate the destructive potential of the modern means of conducting war – which can be disproportionate or nondiscriminating. The evaluation of the four principles listed above[69] must be considered by the public authority in assessing the moral legitimacy of using military force; moreover, the responsibility of pursuing this consideration belongs to the prudential judgment of the public authority that has the duty to defend its people or others for the common good.

In the present day, there has been much discussion about whether the use of military force designed to execute a "preventive war" can be justified.[70] This subject raises grave moral and serious juridical questions; however, it may be possible for the competent public authority to demonstrate that the use of force to prevent further bloodshed is justified for self-defense or the protection of others and preservation of the common good if such a use of force is consistent with and adheres to the four essential principles identified earlier. Nonetheless, the burden of complying with this benchmark is stringent and difficult to meet. Typically, preventive war would not comply with the traditional understanding of the first principle (i.e., legitimate self-defense) of Catholic thinking on the use of force.[71] However, there could be a narrow justification for initiating the use of force where it is essential to effectuate the duty to protect or defend.

2. Actions Necessary to Defend the Peace and to Protect the Innocent

The legitimate use of force necessitates the existence of an armed force that is the servant of those who are to be protected by it. The sole justification for the existence of a standing military force is legitimate defense or protection; therefore, the fundamental mission of this force is to preserve the peace by affording protection from the aggressor without provoking or prolonging conflict. The authentic mission of defensive armed force is to protect noncombatants and to promote peace and justice, the counterpoints to conflict, by arresting the unlawful aims and actions of any aggressor who threatens innocents, peace, or security. Those who direct or serve in the armed force are never permitted to perpetrate infractions of the laws of war recognized by civilized peoples or to violate the humanitarian principles that must guide their every action. If they do, they must be held accountable, be accorded due process of law, and be given the opportunity to defend their actions in accordance with objectively reasoned legal principles.

3. The Responsibility to Protect the Innocent

By way of supplement to traditional self-defense, there is growing recognition of the justification of using force in order to protect those incapable of resisting acts of aggression. Sadly, in the present age, the aggressor often targets innocent[72] civilian populations rather than the armed forces of a competent public authority. Nothing can ever justify acts against innocent civilians (e.g., Rwanda and Darfur); therefore, it becomes the duty of the competent public authority (or associations of public authorities) to protect the innocent by using proportionate and discriminating force to repel or contain aggressive acts directed against innocents. It is becoming increasingly important to recognize that this duty to protect includes offering assistance to those who become refugees from their homeland in order to escape victimization by aggressor forces. The principle of national sovereignty cannot be relied on to prevent a military intervention whose sole purpose is to defend innocent victims.[73]

4. Only Permissible Actions Are to Be Directed against Those Who Threaten the Peace

Within the realm of international organizations, such as the United Nations, sanctions are frequently viewed as a method for correcting the behavior of states that jeopardize international peace and security. But the intended objectives of sanctions can be blunted or negated when the leadership of sanctioned states find ways of escaping their impact while large segments of their populations become the indirect victims of the effects of sanctions that were never intended to harm innocent civilians. As a result, the purpose of sanctions must be clearly defined, and measures must be adopted enabling regular and periodic evaluation by competent bodies to ensure compliance with the sanctions' objectives so that any sanction that is utilized will be effective in achieving its objectives without having adverse consequences on the innocent civilian population.

It follows that sanctions must never be used as a means of direct punishment of an entire population: it is not licit that entire populations, and above all their most vulnerable members, be made to suffer as a consequence of the imposition of sanctions.[74] As is the case with the use of force, the impact of sanctions must be carefully circumscribed so that their effect is proportionate and discriminate. Otherwise, the good that they may achieve will be offset by the suffering of those who should not be made to suffer.

5. Considerations about Disarmament and Deterrence

This issue has existed and been debated for some time; however, it has achieved greater significance given the widespread presence of weapons of mass destruction intensified by the mid-twentieth-century arms race that existed during the Cold War. The development and stockpiling of nuclear weapons, in particular, raised new and seemingly unprecedented questions. While weapons of mass destruction were traditionally the subject of public debate concerning disarmament, a more recent concern has evolved regarding the proliferation of small arms and light weapons that have been expanding in recent times in many regions of the world.

The sharp increase of these conventional and affordable arms represents a grave threat to stability and peace throughout the world. Under Catholic teaching, the *principle of sufficiency* mandates that each state possess only those means and in those quantities necessary for legitimate self-defense. Moreover, this principle must be applied not only to those states that buy and stock arms but also to those that produce and furnish them to others. The principles of proportionality and discrimination apply to the manufacturing, stockpiling, and trading in all arms; therefore, manufacturing, stockpiling, or trading that exceeds reasonable limits necessary for legitimate self-defense cannot be morally justified.

The proliferation of conventional weapons, which include antipersonnel mines that continue to threaten communities long after hostilities cease, cannot be justified, according to Catholic teaching. Once placed into a field of operation, antipersonnel mines continue to deliver their hideously debilitating and deadly force for years, sometimes decades, after hostilities have ceased. It is virtually impossible to justify their manufacture and deployment since antipersonnel ordnance is neither proportionate nor discriminate. Too often their victims are innocent civilians – often children – who enter harm's way years after hostilities responsible for their deployment have ceased.

What is increasingly alarming in the early twenty-first century is that weapons of mass destruction are beginning to proliferate once again even though the competition between the superpowers has largely come to an end. While superpowers have agreed to reduce their arsenals of such devastating weaponry, these weapons are now finding their way into the hands of smaller states and, quite possibly, nonstate entities. It has become a perverse "badge of honor" for even the poorest of countries to possess such means of destruction. It is claimed that the possession of weapons of mass destruction make smaller states the equal of larger, more powerful states. But this view of the world order is fallacious and filled with peril. The Church is clear in its teaching that "Any act of war aimed indiscriminately at the destruction of entire cities or extensive areas along with their population is a crime against God and man himself. It merits unequivocal and unhesitating condemnation."[75]

The Church's teachings condemn in the strongest manner possible a new development that has come to the world's attention and speaks to the cause for disarmament: the recruitment and use of children as soldiers. Child soldiers are victimized on many fronts: they are deprived of education and normal childhood activities and are forced into a destructive and dehumanizing lifestyle for themselves and for those whom they encounter. They are maliciously transformed from children into killing automatons for whom the value of life has no meaning. The use of child soldiers in combat forces of any kind must be stopped, and, at the same time, all possible assistance must be given to the care, education, and rehabilitation of those children who have been recruited for combat.[76]

Since the evolution of weapons of mass destruction, debates about the deterrent effect of such weapons, especially thermonuclear ones, have arisen. Thus, in addition to questioning the legitimacy of their use, there has also been questioning about the moral legitimacy of their existence. The fact of the matter is that they do exist, and Catholic teaching is clear on arguing against their use. The more difficult questions emerge from their possession as a deterrent. As will be seen, substantive questions have emerged in Catholic teaching regarding the moral legitimacy of their existence as a deterrent against the "other side" from using its weapons of mass destruction. In spite of these questions, it is generally regarded that a unilateral disarmament, while noble, may be fraught with peril.

Therefore, it is evident that the most prudent manner for the disarmament of weapons of mass destruction is to have those who possess these devices mutually eliminate them in a progressive manner so that at the conclusion of the negotiated process, no party possesses them or the infrastructure needed for their reconstruction. With just some parties possessing them, the threat of Armageddon remains; but with the removal and disappearance of these weapons from every arsenal, the threat of Armageddon also vanishes.

6. The Matter of Terrorism

Simply put, the Church teaches that terrorism – indiscriminate attacks upon noncombatants in order to sow fear in the populace – is one of the most brutal and barbaric forms of violence traumatizing the international community today. It can never be a legitimate basis for justifying the use of force. Terrorism is based on no understandable or rational political, social, economic, or religious perspective that has previously been considered in the development of just war theory and the legitimate use of force. Rather, terrorism is based on the most vulgar of ideologies designed to sow hatred, death, and an urge for revenge and reprisal. Under Roman Catholic teachings, terrorism has no role in legitimate society due to the chaotic disruption or societal dissolution it may cause. The reality of terrorism becomes a justification for the use of force by civilized society to defend itself.

In recent times, those responsible for terrorism have acquired the means of sophisticated technology to implement their misbegotten activities. Those misguided individuals who mastermind terrorist activities have often devised means to obtain extensive economic resources to finance the ensuing malevolence. Because terrorism operates in accordance with no known or accepted rubrics of civil society, the means necessary to muster proper defenses against it must be manifold and flexible. However, those who are responsible for providing these defenses against terrorism are nonetheless required to rely only on those discriminate and proportionate methods that will be effective in combating it. Although terrorism proceeds without any consideration of moral and legal norms, the use of force directed to combat it must exercise respect for human rights and never dispense with the rule of law and the due process from which the rule of law cannot be separated. When the use of force is necessary to combat and eradicate terrorism, it must never be repressive or punitive.

Part II of this chapter is organized as follows: (1) papal sources (typically those relied upon as the source of greatest authority); (2) curial sources (or bishops' conferences); and (3) the *Catechism of the Catholic Church* and Church Council sources.

Papal Sources

In the present age, there is a natural inclination and a juridical impulse to consult papal literature for direction on issues important to the Catholic community. The authority of the popes to address theological as well as temporal matters has its juridical foundation in their primacy as the successors of St. Peter. As the Second Vatican Council concluded, "[In] virtue of his office, as the Vicar of Christ and Pastor of the whole Church, the Roman Pontiff possesses full, supreme, universal power over the Church, and he is always able to exercise it without impediment."[77] These provisions are reflected in the Church's law wherein it is specified that the pope has and exercises complete authority in the Church from which there is no earthly appeal or review.[78] The pope's actions are subject to Christ and divine authority but not to human power.

Consequently, papal statements on the use of force must be considered as the most authoritative statements and directives that the Church can promulgate. In view of this reality, we begin with consideration of papal statements that have addressed the use of force. It is this corpus of the Church's writings that provides the most authoritative instruction regarding when the use of force is legitimate and when it is not.[79]

While Benedict XV (1914–1922) was clearly not the first pope to discuss the use of force, he broke new ground in his examination of modern weapons that could cause destruction on a global scale. While Pope Pius X had earlier touched on this theme in his exhortation to the Apostolic Delegate in the United States in June 1911,[80] it was Benedict XV, Supreme Pontiff during most of the First World War,[81] who recognized that the ability to forgive was crucial to maintaining stability and peace in a world filled with recurrent tensions between and among states, especially those most powerful in temporal matters. He saw that averting war was not the only challenge laid upon civil leaders. If the use of force became necessary, then it was incumbent on civil leaders to ensure that those who suffered from it would be cared for upon the immediate cessation of hostilities. The exercise of charity in postconflict theaters would promote reconciliation that he considered essential to avoiding or minimizing the likelihood of war in the future.

Benedict XV's successor, Pius XI, was to reign from 1922 until 1939. Unlike his immediate predecessor and successor (Pius XII), Pius XI was an academic and not a veteran of the Vatican Diplomatic Service.[82] Notwithstanding his background, he found himself thrust into the emerging conflicts of Europe and the rest of the world that would culminate in the Second World War. In his 1930 Christmas Eve allocution to the College of Cardinals, "Benedetto il Natale," he acknowledged the growing tensions that would lead to the outbreak of another world conflict in a decade's time. The excerpt from his allocution suggests that Pius XI was not a pacifist; moreover, he understood the need for peoples and their governments to muster a defense against aggressors. However, in 1930 he thought it incredulous that any state would precipitate another global conflagration since the world was still reeling from the aftermath of the "Great War."[83]

With the death of Pius XI in 1939, his successor the Secretary of State Eugenio Cardinal Pacelli ascended to the Chair of Peter as Pius XII (1939–1958). He wasted little time in crafting a major encyclical, *Summi Pontificatus* (1939), which would address the new world conflict and the legitimacy and illegitimacy of the use of force. His papal prose reflected the mind and pen of the skilled and discreet diplomat. Consequently, his presentation was circumspect, but he still conveyed a strong message of how Catholic teachings favored diplomacy and peaceful means of resolving disputes; moreover, he hoped and prayed for an international organization that could one day serve as the guarantor of peace that would eliminate the need and, therefore, the legality of the use of force. Nonetheless, he understood well the sufferings of peoples at the hands of aggressors, for instance, Poland at the hands of the Nazis. As he said, "The blood of countless human beings, even noncombatants, raises a piteous dirge over a nation such as Our dear Poland, which, for its fidelity to the Church, for its services in the defense of Christian civilization, written in indelible characters in the annals of history, has a right to the generous and brotherly sympathy of the whole world...."[84] This language does not criticize or condemn the defense that the Poles tried to muster; in fact, it praises the Poles and their resistance to Nazi aggression. Pius XII exhorted prayers and penance, but he did not forget the "courageous profession of the Faith" and the "heroic sacrifices" made by the "suffering and agonizing members of the Church."[85]

While Pope Pius XII favored peaceful means of resolving conflict, he commended those who were willing to make the necessary sacrifice in the call of duty; he praised heroism in the trials of dangerous times; and he admired the virtuous who conquered the evildoer in the hope of converting him or her to more "amiable" ways. Thus, in his 1941 allocution to Italian university students in the movement Catholic Action, he acknowledged the possibility of "a truly just war" in which honor and the efforts to save one's country from the armed adversary were a noble enterprise. He cautioned that the virtuous warrior was forbidden to employ means of "cruelty against innocent persons" or "punish the guilty beyond the limits of justice."[86] Perhaps in this regard he foreshadowed Pope Paul VI, who coined the expression "If you want peace, work for justice."[87] But the labor for justice, which will ensure peace, may come at great expense. As Pius XII noted in his Christmas Message of 1942, "Mankind owes that vow to the countless dead who lie buried on the field of battle: The sacrifice of their lives in the fulfillment of their duty is a holocaust offered for a new and better social order."[88] While he knew that the law of nations condemned wars of aggression, he recognized that aggression necessitates a "war on war," as he suggested in his Christmas Message of 1944. Although war is generally an outmoded means of resolving international conflict, he recognized that to prevent aggression, a first use of force might sometimes be necessary. As he later noted, the peace to be established at the end of the Second World War may entail mutual guarantees, economic sanctions, and "even armed intervention."[89] After the close of the war, Pius XII was subjected to criticism on grounds that he had been insufficiently vocal in condemning the Nazi persecution of the Jews. While a detailed discussion of the role and attitude of Pius XII cannot be explored here, two essential points must be made. The first is that Pius XII was a consummate diplomat who saw the wisdom of diplomacy as the means to come to the aid of those in need, that is, the Jews and other persecuted groups. Second, it is crucial to remember that German military forces were ready and able to invade the Vatican City and the Apostolic Palace. To remain effective, Pius XII knew he did not have the means to repel an invasion; consequently, he had to rely on the sole earthly means at his disposal: diplomacy and the political skills that accompany it.

Pius XII's immediate successor, Pope John XXIII (1958–1963), another seasoned diplomat who spent decades in the papal service, penned the famous encyclical *Pacem in Terris*, Peace on Earth. In the time of his pontificate, humanity was imperiled by the escalation in the arms race between the superpowers, which included increased arsenals of thermonuclear weapons made all the more concrete by the Cuban Missile Crisis of 1962. For Pope John XXIII, "justice, right reason, and the recognition of man's dignity cry out insistently for a cessation to the arms race."[90] Thus, nuclear arms had to be eliminated; moreover, the acquisition of arms for the purpose of serving as a deterrent was highly dubious. As Pope John argued, "even though the monstrous power of modern weapons does indeed act as a deterrent, there is reason to fear that the very testing of nuclear devices for war purposes can, if continued, lead to serious danger for various forms of life on earth."[91]

Pope John XXIII was succeeded by another prelate who had spent a considerable number of years as a papal diplomat, Pope Paul VI (1963–1978). During his pontificate, Pope Paul was confronted with the increasing tensions between the East and West that was manifested in the conflict in Vietnam. As an emissary trained in the art of diplomacy, Paul VI traveled to the United Nations headquarters in New York in October 1965 to meet the nations of the world and to endorse strongly the work of the organization. As the institution was about to enter its third decade of existence, he conveyed his profound respect for those who pursue diplomacy in resolving the conflicts that emerge in the world. During his address to the General Assembly, he proclaimed the essence of his message: "Never again war, war never again! Peace, it is peace, which must guide the destiny of the peoples and of all mankind!"[92]

However, in just three years' time, Paul VI expressed a very different sentiment when he issued the first World Day of Peace message that would be continued annually by him and by his successors. In the inaugural address issued in 1968, he stated that the ideal of peace was not to be an excuse for cowardice of those who had the responsibility to defend their nations. As he put it, those called to this important duty are defenders of "justice and liberty." He asserted with clarity that the pursuit of peace was not to be confused with pacifism. Rather, peace is the quest for "truth, justice, freedom, and love," and this search may require those who pursue it seriously and with honor to sacrifice themselves so that others may live.[93]

The papacy of Pope John Paul I lasted a short thirty-three days; consequently, he was unable to issue any pertinent statement regarding just war and the use of force. His successor, by contrast, served in the Petrine Office for over a quarter of a century. Thus during his pontificate (1978–2005) John Paul II not only had ample opportunity but in fact contributed immensely to those who spoke on these matters of just war and the use of force. As he noted in his encyclical letter *Centesimus Annus*, caution must be used in exercising armed force against evil or corrupt political institutions and the states they control. He took this opportunity to express his evaluation of the post–World War II era in which a semblance of peace was characterized by growing distrust among the great powers that led to the appropriation of scientific advances to generate new weapons of overwhelmingly destructive capacity. In this development, advances that could have been better used to bring peoples together and solidify peace were being used to drive them apart. The promotion of legitimate self-defense must not be an excuse of intensifying mistrust and prolonging conflict, as was the case with the Cold War. John Paul II would sometimes refer to the wisdom of Pius XII, who stated, "The danger is imminent, but there is yet time. Nothing is lost with peace; all may be lost with war. Let men return to mutual understanding. Let them begin negotiations anew."[94]

For John Paul II, "[P]roblems are not resolved with arms, but ... new and greater tensions among peoples are thus created."[95] And what is key to the success of a durable peace is not the presence and reliance on arms, even if they are intended for self-defense, but an understanding and acceptance of the reality that there can be no peace without justice, and there can be no justice without forgiveness.

Pope John Paul II had the occasion to address twice the emerging conflicts in Iraq. The 1991 war was short-lived and largely guided by broad international consensus. That same consensus was not present in the second armed conflict that would take place in Iraq beginning in March 2003. Just prior to the outbreak of that conflict, the Pope addressed the Diplomatic Corps accredited to the Holy See on January 13, 2003, and asserted that war is not simply a means for resolving international disputes; rather, it is the means of last resort, "the very last option" to be used "in accordance with very strict conditions."[96] For this force to be permissible, it must take stock of its effect on the well-being of civilian populations that would be affected.

While an intervention made by the Holy See's Permanent Observer to the United Nations may be more appropriately discussed elsewhere in this chapter, it seems relevant to include it in this section as it is probable that such an intervention would most certainly have been approved at the highest levels in the Vatican, if not by John Paul II himself. Addressing the U.N. Security Council on February 19, 2003, just as it was deliberating a proposed military action against Iraq, the Permanent Observer (Archbishop Celestino Migliore) stressed that because the "peaceful tools provided by the international law" were still viable, the "resort to force would not be a just one."[97] His words reflect the sentiments expressed by Popes Benedict XV and Pius XII that they issued before the outbreaks of the First and Second World Wars, respectively.

Apart from two short passages from newly elected Pope Francis, this section on papal texts concludes with the address given by Pope Benedict XVI (2005–2013) to the U.N. General Assembly on April 18, 2008. This provided him with an opportunity to discuss the "responsibility to protect," now an official U.N. doctrine: the primary duty of every state to protect its own population. But if a state is incapable or unwilling to respond in the affirmative to this duty, then the obligation is transferred to the international community via juridical means, as the pope further noted. But the question remains: What happens if the international community is also incapable of responding in a timely manner to a humanitarian crisis? This situation generates the need to pause and consider whether the use of force may be required to contend with a human agent that threatens the security and peace of innocents. As His Holiness suggested, it is indifference or failure to intervene that can compromise their safety when "real damage" follows.[98]

Logic would necessitate consideration of the use of force, particularly in those instances where an aggressive agent relies on the slowness of diplomacy and negotiation to attack innocents. Indeed, there are entities in the world for whom diplomacy and juridical mechanisms mean little or nothing. Pope Benedict acknowledged that "natural reason [can be] abandoned," and, as a consequence, "freedom and human dignity [are] grossly violated."[99] In such cases, must sovereign states and the international community stand by and allow the aggressor who abides not by the instruments of peace to erase from the face of this earth his aggressors' victims? I do not believe so, for that is why there has remained in Catholic teaching the duty to use that force that is necessary, carefully directed, and proportional to protect those who *must* be defended and protected.

Pope Benedict XV (1854–1922)

Pope Benedict XV and his papacy were consumed by the events of the First World War. It may well have been this experience that shaped the one pope of modern times whose views came close to being pacifist. As the following excerpt demonstrates, Benedict XV was of the view that, for all states, mutual suspicion had to be put aside so that they could unite into a league, a family of peoples, in order to maintain their own independence and to safeguard human society. He concluded that an international organization consisting in its membership of all nations would be the best human method to abolish or reduce the enormous burden of the military expenditures that states could no longer bear, in order to prevent disastrous wars or at least remove the danger of them occurring again as far as possible. In addition to securing the independence of nations, such an association would also provide for the integrity of national territories within just frontiers.

From: Pope Benedict XV, *Pacem, Dei Munus Pulcherrimum* (1920)[100]

8. Our Lord Jesus Christ, in teaching us how to pray to God, makes us say that we wish for pardon as we forgive others: "Forgive us our trespasses as we forgive them that trespass against us." And if the observance of this law is sometimes hard and difficult, we have not only the timely assistance of the grace of Our Divine Redeemer, but also His example to help us to overcome the difficulty.... We then, who should be the first to imitate the piety and loving kindness of Jesus Christ, whose Vicar, without any merit of Our own, We are; with all Our heart, and following His example, We forgive all Our enemies who knowingly or unknowingly have heaped and are still heaping on our person and Our work every sort of vituperation, and We embrace all in Our charity and benevolence, and neglect no opportunity to do them all the good in Our power. That is indeed what Christians worthy of the name ought to do toward those who during the war have done them wrong....

13. Therefore, Venerable Brethren, We pray you and exhort you in the mercy and charity of Jesus Christ, strive with all zeal and diligence not only to urge the faithful entrusted to your care to abandon hatred and to pardon offenses; but, and what is more immediately practical, to promote all those works of Christian benevolence which bring aid to the needy, comfort to the afflicted and protection to the weak, and to give opportune and appropriate assistance of every kind to all who have suffered from the war. It is Our especial wish that you should exhort your priests, as the ministers of peace, to be assiduous in urging this love of one's neighbor and even of enemies which is the essence of the Christian life, and by "being all things to all men" and giving an example to others, *wage war everywhere on enmity and hatred*, thus doing a thing most agreeable to the loving Heart of Jesus and to him who, however unworthy, holds His place on earth.... [Emphasis added]

14. All that We have said here to individuals about the duty of charity We wish to say also to the peoples who have been delivered from the burden of a long war, in order that, when every cause of disagreement has been, as far as possible,

removed, and *without prejudice to the rights of justice*, they may resume friendly relations among themselves.... [Emphasis added]

15. Truly, as We have already said, this Apostolic See has never wearied of teaching during the war such pardon of offenses and the fraternal reconciliation of the peoples, in conformity with the most holy law of Jesus Christ, and in agreement with the needs of civil life and human intercourse; nor did it allow that amid dissension and hate these moral principles should be forgotten. With all the more reason then, now that the Treaties of Peace are signed, does it proclaim these principles as, for example, it did a short time ago in the Letter to the Bishops of Germany, and in that addressed to the Archbishop of Paris....

17. Things being thus restored, the order required by justice and charity reestablished and the nations reconciled, it is much to be desired, Venerable Brethren, that *all States, putting aside mutual suspicion, should unite in one league, or rather a sort of family of peoples, calculated both to maintain their own independence and safeguard the order of human society. What specially, among other reasons, calls for such an association of nations, is the need generally recognized of making every effort to abolish or reduce the enormous burden of the military expenditure which States can no longer bear, in order to prevent these disastrous wars or at least to remove the danger of them as far as possible. So would each nation be assured not only of its independence but also of the integrity of its territory within its just frontiers.* [Emphasis added]

Pope Pius XI (1857–1939)

Pius XI stood in contrast to his predecessor Benedict XV for making the stronger case for the just use of force. While his pontificate did not extend into either of the world wars, he observed the growing tensions in Europe that would lead to the Second World War. As a result, he exhorted that the proper Christian attitude of peace and the disfavoring of war as a means of conflict resolution must not be understood as a sentimental, confused, or unwise pacifism. He indicated that tranquillity in the world could best be assured by having the means to engage in a just self-defense.

From: Pope Pius XI, Allocution *Benedetto il Natale* to the College of Cardinals

(24 December 1930)[101]

916. ... *We wish you the "Peace of Christ," not a sentimental, confused, unwise pacifism, because that only is true peace that comes from God and that bears the essential and indispensable marks and priceless fruits of true peace.* [Emphasis added]

917. The Peace of Christ, the true peace, transcends, therefore, the senses. It is a grave error to believe that true and lasting peace can rule among men and among

peoples so long as they turn first and foremost and avidly in search of sensible, material, earthly things. . . .

920. Even more difficult – not to say impossible – is it for peace to last between peoples and States if, in the place of true and genuine love of country, there rules and abounds a hard and selfish nationalism, which is the same as saying hatred and envy, in place of mutual desire for the good, distrust and suspicion in place of the confidence of brothers, competition and struggle in place of willing co-operation, ambition for hegemony and mastery in place of respect and care for the rights of all, even those of the weak and the small.

921. *It is totally impossible for peoples to possess and enjoy that tranquillity in order and freedom, which is the essence of peace, so long as they are beset at home and abroad by threats and dangers which are not balanced by sufficient measures and provisions for defense.* [Emphasis added] And certainly threats and dangers are inseparable from anti-social and anti-religious propaganda; yet not with material defenses alone can they be scattered and conquered.

922. *As for threats of new wars, while the peoples of the world are still feeling so deeply the scourge of the last merciless war, We cannot believe they are real, because We are unable to believe any civilized State exists which would become so monstrously murderous and almost certainly suicidal.* [Emphasis added] If We should even only suspect the existence of such a State, We should turn to God with the inspired prayer of the Prophet-King, who indeed knew both war and victory: Scatter Thou the nations that delight in wars [Psalms LXVII:31], and the daily and universal prayer of the Church: "Give us peace!"

Pope Pius XII (1876–1958)

Pius XII was one of the most skilled diplomats to sit on the Chair of Peter. In his earlier diplomatic career, he had carefully observed conditions in Europe and around the world that fueled unnecessary conflict. Because of his legal and diplomatic training, he urged peaceful means of dispute resolution between and among states under the rule of law, that is, international law and the natural moral law. However, he did not dismiss the possibility of the use of a proper and just force to deal with the aggressor who had no respect for international agreements and the rule of law. Thus, armed intervention might be necessary to curb the aggressor's unjust appetite for conquest.

From: Pope Pius XII, Encyclical Letter, *Summi Pontificatus* (20 October 1939)[102]

23. Venerable Brethren, as We write these lines the terrible news comes to Us that the dread tempest of war is already raging despite all Our efforts to avert it. When We think of the wave of suffering that has come on countless people who but yesterday enjoyed in the environment of their homes some little degree of well-being, We are tempted to lay down Our pen. Our paternal heart is torn by anguish as We

look ahead to all that will yet come forth from the baneful seed of violence and of hatred for which the sword today plows the blood-drenched furrow. . . .

74. *[I]t is indispensable for the existence of harmonious and lasting contacts and of fruitful relations, that the peoples recognize and observe these principles of international natural law which regulate their normal development and activity.* [Emphasis added] Such principles demand respect for corresponding rights to independence, to life and to the possibility of continuous development in the paths of civilization; they demand, further, fidelity to compacts agreed upon and sanctioned in conformity with the principles of the law of nations.

75. The indispensable presupposition, without doubt, of all peaceful intercourse between nations, and the very soul of the juridical relations in force among them, is mutual trust: the expectation and conviction that each party will respect its plighted word; the certainty that both sides are convinced that "better is wisdom, than weapons of war" and are ready to enter into discussion and to avoid recourse to force or to threats of force in case of delays, hindrances, changes or disputes, because all these things can be the result not of bad will, but of changed circumstances and of genuine interests in conflict.

76. But on the other hand, to tear the law of nations from its anchor in Divine law, to base it on the autonomous will of States, is to dethrone that very law and deprive it of its noblest and strongest qualities. Thus it would stand abandoned to the fatal drive of private interest and collective selfishness exclusively intent on the assertion of its own rights and ignoring those of others.

77. Now, it is true that with the passage of time and the substantial change of circumstances, which were not and perhaps could not have been foreseen in the making of a treaty, such a treaty or some of its clauses can in fact become, or at least seem to become unjust, impracticable or too burdensome for one of the parties. It is obvious that should such be the case, recourse should be had in good time to a frank discussion with a view to modifying the treaty or making another in its stead. But to consider treaties on principle as ephemeral and tacitly to assume the authority of rescinding them unilaterally when they are no longer to one's advantage, would be to abolish all mutual trust among States. In this way, natural order would be destroyed and there would be seen dug between different peoples and nations trenches of division impossible to refill. . . .

81. No, Venerable Brethren, safety does not come to peoples from external means, from the sword which can impose conditions of peace but does not create peace. Forces that are to renew the face of the earth should proceed from within, from the spirit.

82. *Once the bitterness and the cruel strifes of the present have ceased, the new order of the world, of national and international life, must rest no longer on the quicksands of changeable and ephemeral standards that depend only on the selfish interests of groups and individuals. No, they must rest on the unshakeable foundation, on the solid rock of natural law and of Divine Revelation.* [Emphasis added] There the human legislator must attain to that balance, that keen sense of

moral responsibility, without which it is easy to mistake the boundary between the legitimate use and the abuse of power. Thus only will his decisions have internal consistency, noble dignity and religious sanction, and be immune from selfishness and passion.

102. *The Church preaches and inculcates obedience and respect for earthly authority which derives from God its whole origin and holds to the teaching of her Divine Master Who said: "Render therefore to Caesar the things that are Caesar's"*; she has no desire to usurp, and sings in the liturgy: "He takes away no earthly realms who gives us the celestial." [Emphasis added] She does not suppress human energies but lifts them up to all that is noble and generous and forms characters which do not compromise with conscience. Nor has she who civilizes the nations ever retarded the civil progress of mankind, at which on the contrary she is pleased and glad with a mother's pride. The end of her activity was admirably expressed by the Angels over the cradle of the Word Incarnate, when they sang of glory to God and announced peace to men of good will: "Glory to God in the highest; and on earth peace to men of good will" (Saint Luke ii. 14).

106. . . . Our paternal heart is close to all Our children in compassionate love, and especially to the afflicted, the oppressed, the persecuted. The nations swept into the tragic whirlpool of war are perhaps as yet only at the "beginnings of sorrows," but even now there reigns in thousands of families death and desolation, lamentation and misery. *The blood of countless human beings, even noncombatants, raises a piteous dirge over a nation such as Our dear Poland, which, for its fidelity to the Church, for its services in the defense of Christian civilization, written in indelible characters in the annals of history, has a right to the generous and brotherly sympathy of the whole world*, while it awaits, relying on the powerful intercession of Mary, Help of Christians, the hour of a resurrection in harmony with the principles of justice and true peace. [Emphasis added]

109. In the meantime however, Venerable Brethren, the world and all those who are stricken by the calamity of the war must know that the obligation of Christian love, the very foundation of the Kingdom of Christ, is not an empty word, but a living reality. A vast field opens up for Christian Charity in all its forms. We have full confidence that all Our sons, especially those who are not being tried by the scourge of war, will be mindful in imitation of the Divine Samaritan, of all these who, as victims of the war, have a right to compassion and help.

From: Pope Pius XII, Allocution *Nei Tesori* to Italian University Students in Catholic Action (1941)[103]

In your world overturned and torn asunder by struggles and wars, what lesson is more necessary than that of humility and charity inculcated by word and example with so much solicitude by the Divine Master, Meek and Humble of Heart . . . ? Teach not pride, which is weak, which puffs up but does not edify, which is a vain respecter of persons; but teach a sense of duty, the conquering of self, courage, heroism in trials and dangers, that virtue which does not become proud in victory and which renders the conqueror more amiable. . . .

These virtues of humility and charity . . . are not enemies, nor are they out of keeping with human dignity. They do not lessen one's love of country. They do not diminish courage or impede a citizen who, in a truly just war, struggles for the defense, honor and salvation of his country, fights with full fortitude against an adversary armed to overcome him. But beneficent charity finds no pleasure in iniquity, not even on the battlefield nor in the most difficult vicissitudes; it forbids those who fight with cruelty against innocent persons or who punish the guilty beyond the limits of justice. . . . [Emphasis added]

From: Pope Pius XII, "Christmas Broadcast to the Whole World" (24 December 1942)[104]

1859. . . . What is this world war, with all its attendant circumstances, whether they be remote or proximate causes, its progress and material, legal and moral effects? What is it but the crumbling process, not expected, perhaps, by the thoughtless but seen and deprecated by those whose gaze penetrated into the realities of a social order which . . . hid its mortal weakness and its unbridled lust for gain and power?

1860. That which in peace-time lay coiled up, broke loose at the outbreak of war in a sad succession of acts at variance with the human and Christian sense. *International agreements to make war less inhuman by confining it to the combatants, to regulate the procedure of occupation and the imprisonment of the conquered remained in various places a dead letter. . . .* [Emphasis added]

1861. *Mankind owes that vow to the countless dead who lie buried on the field of battle: The sacrifice of their lives in the fulfillment of their duty is a holocaust offered for a new and better social order.* [Emphasis added] Mankind owes that vow to the innumerable host of sorrowing mothers, widows and orphans who have seen the light, the solace and the support of their lives wrenched from them. Mankind owes that vow to those numberless exiles whom the hurricane of war has torn from their native land and scattered in the land of the stranger; who can make their own the lament of the Prophet: "*Our inheritance is turned to aliens; our house to strangers.*" Mankind owes that vow to the hundreds of thousands of persons who, without any fault on their part, sometimes only because of their nationality or race, have been consigned to death or to a slow decline. Mankind owes that vow to the many thousands of non-combatants, women, children, sick and aged, *from whom aerial warfare – whose horrors We have from the beginning frequently denounced – has, without discrimination or through inadequate precautions,* taken life, goods, health, home, charitable refuge, or house of prayer. [Emphasis added] Mankind owes that vow to the flood of tears and bitterness, to the accumulation of sorrow and suffering, emanating from the murderous ruin of the dreadful conflict and crying to Heaven to send down the Holy Spirit to liberate the world from the inundation of violence and terror. . . .

1862. .... His light can overcome the darkness, the rays of His love can conquer the icy egoism which holds so many back from becoming great and conspicuous in their higher life.

1863. Do you, crusader-volunteers of a distinguished new society, lift up the new call for moral and Christian rebirth, *declare war on the darkness which comes from deserting God*, on the coldness that comes from strife between brothers. It is a fight for the human race, which is gravely ill and must be healed in the name of conscience ennobled by Christianity. [Emphasis added]

From: Pope Pius XII, "Christmas Message of 1944 – Addressed to All People of the World on the Subject of Democracy and a Lasting Peace"[105]

58. There is a duty, besides, imposed on all, a duty which brooks no delay, no procrastination, no hesitation, no subterfuge: It is the duty to do everything *to ban once and for all wars of aggression* as legitimate solutions of international disputes and as a means toward realizing national aspirations. [Emphasis added]

59. Many attempts in this direction have been seen in the past. They all failed. And they will all fail always, until the saner section of mankind has the firm determination, the holy obstinacy, like an obligation in conscience, to fulfill the mission which past ages have not undertaken with sufficient gravity and resolution.

60. *If ever a generation has had to appreciate in the depths of its conscience the call: "war on war," it is certainly the present generation.* ... [Emphasis added]

62. The decisions already published by international commissions permit one to conclude that an essential point in any future international arrangement would be the formation of an organ for the maintenance of peace, of an organ invested by common consent with supreme power to whose office it would also pertain to smother in its germinal state any threat of isolated or collective aggression.

63. *No one could hail this development with greater joy than he who has long upheld the principle that the idea of war as an apt and proportionate means of solving international conflicts is now out of date.* [Emphasis added]

64. No one could wish success to this common effort, to be undertaken with a seriousness of purpose never before known, with greater enthusiasm, than he who has conscientiously striven to make the Christian and religious mentality reject modern war with its monstrous means of conducting hostilities. ...

66. *But by that very fact the immorality of the war of aggression has been made ever more evident.* [Emphasis added] And if now, to the recognition of this immorality there is to be added the threat of a judicial intervention by the nations and of chastisement inflicted on the aggressor by the society of States, so that war will always be subject to the stigma of proscription, always under surveillance and liable to preventive measures, then mankind, as it emerges from the dark night in which it has been so long submerged will be able to hail the dawn of a new and better era of its history.

67. But only on one condition: namely that the peace settlement which should be strengthened and made more stable by mutual guarantees and, where necessary, economic sanctions and *even armed intervention*, should not give definite countenance to any injustice, does not imply any derogation of any right to the detriment of any nation (whether it be on the side of the victors, the vanquished, or the neutrals), and does not impose any perpetual burden, which can only be allowed for a time as reparation for war damages. [Emphasis added]

From: Pope Pius XII, "To the Armed Services Committee of the U.S.A.," 8 October 1947[106]

An Armed Services Committee of a legislative body is a happy augury. It suggests a mutual dependence that is very healthy. Law and order may at times have need of the strong arm of force. Some enemies of justice can be brought to terms only by force. But force should be held always in check by law and order and be exercised only in their defense. Nor is any man law unto himself. If that principle were everywhere accepted and acted on, there would be a greater sense of security among peoples today.

So We greet the honorable legislators and the distinguished members of the armed forces. May God's blessing be upon your friendly cooperation for the greater good of your own beloved country and of the entire world. We pray Him also to bless you and all who are near and dear to you.

From: Pope Pius XII, "Christmas Message of 1948, on the Two-Fold Duty of All Christians"[107]

4. . . . The genuine Christian will for peace means strength, not weakness or weary resignation. It is completely one with the will for peace of Eternal and Almighty God. Every war of aggression against these goods which the Divine plan for peace obliges men unconditionally to respect and guarantee and accordingly to protect and defend, is a sin, a crime, an outrage against the majesty of God, the Creator and Ordainer of the world.

A people threatened with an unjust aggression, or already its victim, may not remain passively indifferent, if it would think and act as befits Christians. All the more does the solidarity of the family of nations forbid others to behave as mere spectators, in an attitude of apathetic neutrality. Who will ever measure the harm already caused in the past by such indifference to war of aggression, which is quite alien to the Christian instinct? How much more keenly has it brought home to the "great" and specially to the "small," the sense of their insecurity? Has it brought any advantage in recompense? On the contrary; it has only reassured and encouraged the authors and fomenters of aggression, while it obliges the several peoples, left to themselves, to increase their armaments indefinitely.

Resting for support on God and on the order He established, the Christian will for peace is thus as strong as steel. Its temper is quite different from mere humanitarian sentiment, too often little more than a matter of pure impression, which detests war only because of its horrors and atrocities, its destruction and its aftermath, but not for the added reason of its injustice. Such a sentiment, under a hedonistic and utilitarian disguise, and materialistic in its source, lacks the solid foundation of a strict and unqualified obligation. It creates conditions which encourage the deception resulting from sterile compromise, the attempt to save oneself at the expense of others, and the success in every case of the aggressor.

This is so true that neither the sole consideration of the sorrows and evils resulting from war, nor the careful weighing of the act against the advantage, avail to determine finally, whether it is morally licit, or even in certain concrete circumstances obligatory (provided always there be solid probability of success) to repel an aggressor by force of arms.

One thing, however, is certain: the commandment of peace is a matter of Divine law. Its purpose is the protection of the goods of humanity, inasmuch as they are gifts of the Creator. Among these goods some are of such importance for society, that it is perfectly lawful to defend them against unjust aggression. Their defense is even an obligation for the nations as a whole who have a duty not to abandon a nation that is attacked.

The certainty that this duty will not go unfulfilled will serve to discourage the aggressor and thus war will be avoided or, if the worst should come, its sufferings will at least be lessened.

In this way, a better meaning is given to the dictum, *si vis pacem para bellum* [if you seek peace, prepare for war], as also to the phrase "peace at all costs." What really matters is the sincere and Christian will for peace. We are compelled to it surely by the following considerations: The spectacle of the ruins of the last war, the silent reproach which rises from the great cemeteries where the tombs of the victims of war are marshaled in endless ranks, the still unsatisfied longing of prisoners and refugees to return home, the anguish and dereliction of many political captives, worry of unjust persecution. But we ought to find a still greater incentive in the potent word of the Divine commandment of peace – the gently penetrating glance of the Divine Child in the manger.

Pope John XXIII (1881–1963)

Another seasoned diplomat to occupy the Chair of Peter in the twentieth century was Pope John XXIII. Even though he was to occupy the papacy for a brief five years, his memorable writings exhorted the world to a place where justice and peace were attainable goals. While not dismissing the possibility of necessary and just self-defense, he strongly counseled people of good will to choose the path of peace. Methods he suggested in doing so were built upon the principles of international law as buttressed by truth, justice, freedom, and charity – the four pillars of the social order. One of the most important points made in his pontificate was the pressing need to curtail and, then, eliminate thermonuclear weapons from the arsenals of the world. The wisdom of this point was emphasized by the Cuban Missile Crisis that brought the United States and the Soviet Union to the brink of a nuclear war.

From: Pope John XXIII, Encyclical Letter, *Pacem in Terris* (1963)[108]

109. . . . We are deeply distressed to see the enormous stocks of armaments that have been, and continue to be, manufactured in the economically more developed countries. This policy is involving a vast outlay of intellectual and material resources, with the result that the people of these countries are saddled with a great burden, while other countries lack the help they need for their economic and social development.

110. There is a common belief that under modern conditions peace cannot be assured except on the basis of an equal balance of armaments and that this factor is the probable cause of this stockpiling of armaments. Thus, if one country increases its military strength, others are immediately roused by a competitive spirit to augment their own supply of armaments. And if one country is equipped with atomic weapons, others consider themselves justified in producing such weapons themselves, equal in destructive force. . . .

Moreover, *even though the monstrous power of modern weapons does indeed act as a deterrent, there is reason to fear that the very testing of nuclear devices for war purposes can, if continued, lead to serious danger for various forms of life on earth.* [Emphasis added]

Need for Disarmament

112. Hence justice, right reason, and the recognition of man's dignity cry out insistently for a cessation to the arms race. The stock-piles of armaments which have been built up in various countries must be reduced all round and simultaneously by the parties concerned. *Nuclear weapons must be banned. A general agreement must be reached on a suitable disarmament program, with an effective system of mutual control.* In the words of Pope Pius XII: "The calamity of a world war, with the economic and social ruin and the moral excesses and dissolution that accompany it, must not on any account be permitted to engulf the human race for a third time." [Emphasis added]

113. Everyone, however, must realize that, unless this process of disarmament be thoroughgoing and complete, and reach men's very souls, it is impossible to stop the arms race, or to reduce armaments, or – and this is the main thing – ultimately to abolish them entirely. Everyone must sincerely co-operate in the effort to banish fear and the anxious expectation of war from men's minds. But this requires that the fundamental principles upon which peace is based in today's world be replaced by an altogether different one, namely, the realization that true and lasting peace among nations cannot consist in the possession of an equal supply of armaments but only in mutual trust. And We are confident that this can be achieved, for it is a thing which not only is dictated by common sense, but is in itself most desirable and most fruitful of good.

Three Motives

114. Here, then, *we have an objective dictated first of all by reason. There is general agreement – or at least there should be – that relations between States, as between individuals, must be regulated not by armed force, but in accordance with the principles of right reason: the principles, that is, of truth, justice and vigorous and sincere co-operation.* [Emphasis added]

115. Secondly, it is an objective which We maintain is more earnestly to be desired. For who is there who does not feel the craving to be rid of the threat of war, and to see peace preserved and made daily more secure?

116. And finally it is an objective which is rich with possibilities for good. Its advantages will be felt everywhere, by individuals, by families, by nations, by the whole human race. The warning of Pope Pius XII still rings in our ears: "Nothing is lost by peace; everything may be lost by war.". . .

Signs of the Times

126. Men nowadays are becoming more and more convinced that any disputes which may arise between nations must be resolved by negotiation and agreement, and not by recourse to arms.

127. We acknowledge that this conviction owes its origin chiefly to the terrifying destructive force of modern weapons. It arises from fear of the ghastly and catastrophic consequences of their use. Thus, in this age which boasts of its atomic power, it no longer makes sense to maintain that war is a fit instrument with which to repair the violation of justice.

128. And yet, unhappily, we often find the law of fear reigning supreme among nations and causing them to spend enormous sums on armaments. Their object is not aggression, so they say – and there is no reason for disbelieving them – but to deter others from aggression.

129. Nevertheless, We are hopeful that, by establishing contact with one another and by a policy of negotiation, nations will come to a better recognition of the natural ties that bind them together as men. We are hopeful, too, that they will come to a fairer realization of one of the cardinal duties deriving from our common nature: namely, that love, not fear, must dominate the relationships between individuals and between nations. It is principally characteristic of love that it draws men together in all sorts of ways, sincerely united in the bonds of mind and matter; and this is a union from which countless blessings can flow.

Pope Paul VI (1897–1978)

The middle decades of the twentieth century saw three popes who spent most of their priestly lives in the diplomatic service of the Church. The third pope in this series was Paul VI. But his diplomatic skills, which led to the assignment of a Permanent Observer of the Holy See to the United Nations, did not preclude him from announcing before this premier international organization the famous words: "Never again war, war never again! Peace, it is peace, which must guide the destiny of the peoples and of all mankind!" However, he astutely made the distinction between weapons of aggression and weapons of legitimate self-defense. Paul VI also inaugurated in 1968 a tradition, the issuance of the World Day of Peace Message, that has robustly continued in the pontificates of John Paul II and Benedict XVI. In the inaugural message of 1968, he clearly acknowledged that self-sacrifice in the call of duty to a just cause is not inconsistent with the desire for peace. Moreover, he intensified his position that the duty to give one's life in the noble cause of defending justice and the liberty of others may be required. He observed that the desire for peace is not to be confused with pacifism, for the desire for true peace must be founded on John XXIII's four pillars of truth, justice, freedom, and charity. And these may require self-sacrifice when those in the world choose not to honor or respect these essential principles of the social order.

From: Pope Paul VI, "Address to the General Assembly of the United Nations" (4 October 1965)[109]

1. We wish Our message first of all to be a moral and solemn ratification of this high Institution. The message comes of Our experience of history. It is as an "expert in humanity" that We bring to this Organization the voices of Our latest Predecessors, those of the whole Catholic Episcopate, and Our own, convinced as We are that this Organization represents the obligatory road of modern civilization and of world peace. . . .

2. We know that you are fully aware of this. Listen now to the rest of Our message. It looks wholly to the future. The building you have made must never again fall in ruins; it must be perfected and conformed to the demands world history will make. You mark a stage in the development of mankind: henceforth no turning back, you must go forward. . . .

   You give sanction to the great principle that relations between the peoples should be regulated by reason, by justice, by law, by negotiation; not by force nor by violence nor by war, neither by fear nor by fraud.

   So it should be. . . .

5. And here Our message reaches its highest point. Negatively, at first. It is the word you are expecting from Us and We cannot utter it without being conscious of its gravity and solemnity: *never again one against another*, never, never again! Is it not to this end above all that the United Nations was born: against war and for peace? Listen to the lucid words of a great man now departed, John Kennedy, who declared four years ago: "Mankind must put an end to war, or war will put an end to mankind." There is no need of long speeches to proclaim the supreme finality of this Institution. Suffice it to recall that the blood of millions of men, that countless and unheard-of sufferings, that useless massacres and fearful ruins have sealed the pact uniting you, with a vow which must change the future history of the world: never again war, war never again! Peace, it is peace, which must guide the destiny of the peoples and of all mankind!

Thanks to you, glory to you, who for twenty years have labored for peace and have even given illustrious victims to this holy cause. Thanks to you and glory to you for the conflicts you have prevented and for those you have settled. The results of your efforts for peace, up to these last days, even if not yet decisive, deserve that We venture to interpret the feelings of the whole world and in its name express to you both congratulations and gratitude.

You, gentlemen, have done and are doing a great work: you are teaching men peace. The United Nations is the great school where that education is acquired, and We are here in the *Aula Magna* [Assembly Hall] of that school. Whoever takes a place here becomes both pupil and teacher in the art of building peace. And when you leave this hall, the world looks to you as to the architects, the builders of peace.

Peace, as you know, is built not only by means of politics and the balance of forces and interests. It is built with the spirit, with ideas, with works of peace. You are laboring at this great work. But you are as yet only at the beginning of your labors. Will the world ever succeed in changing the exclusive and bellicose state of mind which up to now has woven so much of its history? This is hard to foresee; but it is easy to affirm that we must resolutely take the road toward a new history, a peaceful history, one that will be truly and fully human, the very history God promised to men of goodwill. The roads to it are mapped for you: the first is that of disarmament.

If you wish to be brothers, let the weapons fall from your hands. You cannot love with offensive weapons in your hands. Even before they cause victims and ruins, weapons, especially the terrible weapons modern science has given you, beget bad dreams, nourish bad feelings, create nightmares, mistrust and somber resolves; they exact enormous expenditures; they bring to a halt projects of useful work undertaken in solidarity; they warp the psychology of peoples. So long as man remains the weak, changeable and even wicked being that he often shows himself to be, defensive arms will, alas! be necessary. But you, your courage and valor spur you to study ways of guaranteeing the security of international life without recourse to arms: this is an aim worthy of your efforts, this is what the peoples expect of you. This is what must be attained. And for this, unanimous trust in this Institution must grow; its authority must grow; and the goal, it is to be hoped, will then be reached. Then you will win the gratitude of all peoples, relieved of the crushing expense of armaments and delivered from the nightmare of ever-imminent war.

From: Pope Paul VI, "Message for the Observance of a Day of Peace," 1 January 1968 (released 8 December 1967)[110]

Accordingly, in conclusion, it is to be hoped that the exaltation of the ideal of Peace may not favor the cowardice of those who fear it may be their duty to give their life for the service of their own country and of their own brothers, when these are engaged in the defense of justice and liberty, and who seek only a flight from their responsibility, from the risks that are necessarily involved in the accomplishment of great duties and generous exploits. Peace is not pacifism; it does not mask a base and slothful concept of life, but it proclaims the highest and most universal values of life: truth, justice, freedom, love.

Pope John Paul II (1920–2005)

Unlike his predecessors who were raised in Italy and had served in the Holy See's diplomatic service, John Paul II grew up in Poland under the Nazi occupation, and later under Soviet-dominated Polish Communism. He thus became intimately familiar with the totalitarian brutality of states that indiscriminately relied on the use of force as a principle means of implementing the will of the government. He astutely observed that in more recent times there exist serious grievances and injustices and exploitations that are at the source of war. The answers to these problems that are often at the root of conflict are genuine human development that contains the promise of long-lasting peace and the avoidance of war as a means of conflict resolution. Like most of his twentieth-century predecessors who occupied the Chair of Peter, John Paul II acknowledged and exhorted that innocent civilians may require armed protection and defense against the acts of unjust aggressors; thus, the purpose of armed force was both for protection and disarming the aggressor. Moreover, such military interventions, to be considered just, must be carried out in full respect of international law and just agreements.

From: Pope John Paul II, Encyclical Letter *Centesimus Annus* (1 May 1991)[111]

18. While it is true that since 1945 weapons have been silent on the European continent, it must be remembered that true peace is never simply the result of military victory, but rather implies both the removal of the causes of war and genuine reconciliation between peoples. For many years there has been in Europe and the world a situation of non-war rather than genuine peace. Half of the continent fell under the domination of a communist dictatorship, while the other half organized itself in defense against this threat. . . .

An insane arms race swallowed up the resources needed for the development of national economies and for assistance to the less developed nations. Scientific and technological progress, which should have contributed to man's well-being, was transformed into an instrument of war: Science and technology were directed to the production of ever more efficient and destructive weapons. Meanwhile, an ideology, a perversion of authentic philosophy, was called upon to provide doctrinal justification for the new war. And this war was not simply expected and prepared for, but was actually fought with enormous bloodshed in various parts of the world. The logic of power blocs or empires, denounced in various Church documents and recently in the Encyclical *Sollicitudo Rei Socialis*, led to a situation in which controversies and disagreements among Third World countries were systematically aggravated and exploited in order to create difficulties for the adversary.

Extremist groups, seeking to resolve such controversies through the use of arms, found ready political and military support and were equipped and trained for war; those who tried to find peaceful and humane solutions, with respect for the legitimate interests of all parties, remained isolated and often fell victim to their opponents. In addition, the precariousness of the peace which followed World War II was one of the principal causes of the militarization of many Third World countries and the fratricidal conflicts which afflicted them as well as of the spread of terrorism and of increasingly barbaric means of political and military conflict. Moreover, the whole world was oppressed by the threat of an atomic war capable of leading to the extinction of humanity. Science used for military purposes had placed this decisive instrument at the disposal of hatred strengthened by ideology. But if war can end without winners or losers in a suicide of humanity, then we must repudiate the logic which leads to it: the idea that the effort to destroy the enemy, confrontation and war itself are factors of progress and historical advancement. When the need for this repudiation is understood, the concepts of "total war" and "class struggle" must necessarily be called into question. . . .

52. [O]n the occasion of the recent tragic war in the Persian Gulf, [I] repeated the cry: "Never again war!" No, never again war, which destroys the lives of innocent people, teaches how to kill, throws into upheaval even the lives of those who do the killing and leaves behind a trail of resentment and hatred, thus making it all the more difficult to find a just solution of the very problems which provoked the war. Just as the time has finally come when in individual states a system of private vendetta and reprisal has given way to the rule of law, so too a similar step forward is now urgently needed in the international community. Furthermore, it must not be forgotten that at the root of war there are usually real and serious grievances: injustices suffered, legitimate aspirations frustrated, poverty and the exploitation of multitudes of desperate people who see no real possibility of improving their lot by peaceful means.

For this reason, another name for peace is development. Just as there is a collective responsibility for avoiding war, so too there is a collective responsibility for promoting development. Just as within individual societies it is possible and right to organize a solid economy which will direct the functioning of the market to the common good, so too there is a similar need for adequate interventions on the international level. For this to happen, a great effort must be made to enhance mutual understanding and knowledge, and to increase the sensitivity of consciences. This is the culture which is hoped for, one which fosters trust in the human potential of the poor and consequently in their ability to improve their condition through work or to make a positive contribution to economic prosperity. But to accomplish this, the poor – be they individuals or nations – need to be provided with realistic opportunities. Creating such conditions calls for a concerted worldwide effort to promote development, an effort which also involves sacrificing the positions of income and of power enjoyed by the more developed economies.

From: Pope John Paul II, "The 50th Anniversary of War's End in Europe" (8 May 1995)[112]

9. The divisions caused by the Second World War make us realize that force in the service of the "will to power" is an inadequate means for building true justice. Instead, it sets in motion a sinister process with unforeseeable consequences for men, women and whole peoples, who risk the complete loss of their dignity, together with their property and life itself. We can still appreciate the stern warning which Pope Pius XII of venerable memory voiced in August 1939, on the very eve of that tragic conflict, in a last-minute attempt to prevent recourse to arms: "The danger is imminent, but there is yet time. Nothing is lost with peace; all may be lost with war. Let men return to mutual understanding. Let them begin negotiations anew." Pius XII was here following in the footsteps of Pope Benedict XV who, after making every effort to prevent the First World War, did not hesitate to brand it "a useless slaughter." I myself reaffirmed these principles when on January 20, 1991, on the eve of the Gulf War, I observed that "the tragic situation of recent days makes it even more evident that problems are not resolved with arms, but that new and greater tensions among peoples are thus created." This is something which the passing of the years proves even more correct, although in some regions of Europe and elsewhere in the world fresh outbreaks of war continue to occur. Pope John XXIII, in his Encyclical Letter *Pacem in Terris*, listed as one of the signs of the time the growing conviction that "disputes which may arise between nations must be resolved by negotiation and agreement, not by recourse to arms." Despite all human failures, there are many events, even in recent times, which serve to show that honest, patient negotiations which respect the rights and aspirations of all involved can lead to a peaceful resolution of even highly complex situations. In this spirit I express my deep appreciation and strong support to all modern peacemakers.

I do so especially by reason of the haunting memory of the atomic explosions which struck first Hiroshima and then Nagasaki in August 1945. They bear witness to the overwhelming horror and suffering caused by war: the final toll of that tragedy – as I recalled during my visit to Hiroshima – has not yet been entirely determined nor has its total cost in human terms yet been calculated, particularly when we consider what effect nuclear war has had and could still have on our thinking, our attitudes and our civilization. "To remember the past is to commit oneself to the future. To remember Hiroshima is to abhor nuclear war. To remember Hiroshima is to commit oneself to peace. To remember what the people of this city suffered is to renew our faith in man, in his capacity to do what is good, in his freedom to choose what is right, in his determination to turn disaster into a new beginning."

Fifty years after that tragic conflict, which ended some months later also in the Pacific with the terrible events of Hiroshima and Nagasaki and with the subsequent surrender of Japan, it appears ever more clearly as "a self-destruction of mankind." War is in fact, if we look at it clearly, as much a tragedy for the victors as for the vanquished.

The Propaganda Machine

10. A further reflection is called for. During the Second World War, in addition to conventional, chemical, biological and nuclear weapons, there was widespread use of another deadly instrument of war: propaganda. Before striking the enemy with weapons aimed at his physical destruction, efforts were made to annihilate him morally by defamation, false accusations and the inculcation of an irrational intolerance by means of a thorough program of indoctrination directed especially at the young. It is in fact characteristic of all totalitarian regimes to create an enormous propaganda machine in order to justify their own crimes and to provoke ideological intolerance and racial violence against those who do not deserve – it is claimed – to be considered an integral part of the community. How distant all this is from the authentic culture of peace! ...

The perverse techniques of propaganda do not stop at falsifying reality; they also distort information about where the responsibility lies, thus making an informed moral and political judgment extremely difficult. War gives rise to a propaganda which leaves no room for different interpretations, critical analysis of the causes of conflict and the attribution of real responsibility. This emerges quite clearly from our information about the years 1939–1945, and from the documentation concerning other wars which broke out in subsequent years. In every society war leads to a totalitarian use of the means of communication and propaganda which fails to inculcate respect for others and esteem for dialogue, but rather encourages suspicion and a desire for reprisals.

From: Pope John Paul II, "Peace on Earth to Those Whom God Loves: Message for the World Day of Peace" (1 January 2000)[113]

Humanitarian Intervention

11. *Clearly, when a civilian population risks being overcome by the attacks of an unjust aggressor and political efforts and non-violent defense prove to be of no avail, it is legitimate and even obligatory to take concrete measures to disarm the aggressor. These measures, however, must be limited in time and precise in their aims. They must be carried out in full respect for international law, guaranteed by an authority that is internationally recognized and, in any event, never left to the outcome of armed intervention alone.* [Emphasis added]

The fullest and the best use must therefore be made of all the provisions of the United Nations Charter, further defining effective instruments and modes of intervention within the framework of international law. In this regard, the United Nations [Organization] itself must offer all its member states an equal opportunity to be part of the decision-making process, eliminating privileges and discriminations which weaken its role and its credibility.

12. This opens a new field of reflection and discussion both for politics and for law, a field which we all hope will be earnestly and wisely cultivated. What is needed

without delay is a renewal of international law and international institutions, a renewal whose starting point and basic organizing principle should be the primacy of the good of humanity and of the human person over every other consideration. Such a renewal is all the more urgent if we consider the paradox of contemporary warfare in which, as recent conflicts have shown, armies enjoy maximum security while the civilian population lives in frightening situations of danger. In no kind of conflict is it permissible to ignore the right of civilians to safety.

From: Pope John Paul II, World Day of Peace Message 1 January 2002: "No Peace without Justice, No Justice without Forgiveness"[114]

1. The World Day of Peace this year is being celebrated in the shadow of the dramatic events of last 11 September. On that day, a terrible crime was committed: in a few brief hours thousands of innocent people of many ethnic backgrounds were slaughtered. Since then, people throughout the world have felt a profound personal vulnerability and a new fear for the future. Addressing this state of mind, the Church testifies to her hope, based on the conviction that evil, the *mysterium iniquitatis*, does not have the final word in human affairs. The history of salvation, narrated in Sacred Scripture, sheds clear light on the entire history of the world and shows us that human events are always accompanied by the merciful Providence of God, who knows how to touch even the most hardened of hearts and bring good fruits even from what seems utterly barren soil. . . .

2. Recent events, including the terrible killings just mentioned, move me to return to a theme which often stirs in the depths of my heart when I remember the events of history which have marked my life, especially my youth.

The enormous suffering of peoples and individuals, even among my own friends and acquaintances, caused by Nazi and Communist totalitarianism, has never been far from my thoughts and prayers. I have often paused to reflect on the persistent question: *how do we restore the moral and social order subjected to such horrific violence?* My reasoned conviction, confirmed in turn by biblical revelation, is that the shattered order cannot be fully restored except by a response that combines justice with forgiveness. *The pillars of true peace are justice and that form of love which is forgiveness.* [Emphasis added]

3. But in the present circumstances, how can we speak of justice and forgiveness as the source and condition of peace? *We can and we must*, no matter how difficult this may be; a difficulty which often comes from thinking that justice and forgiveness are irreconcilable. But forgiveness is the opposite of resentment and revenge, not of justice. In fact, true peace is "the work of justice" (Isa. 32:17). As the Second Vatican Council put it, peace is "the fruit of that right ordering of things with which the divine founder has invested human society and which must be actualized by man thirsting for an ever more perfect reign of justice" (Pastoral Constitution *Gaudium et Spes*, 78). For more than fifteen hundred years, the Catholic Church has repeated the teaching of Saint Augustine of Hippo on this

point. He reminds us that the peace which can and must be built in this world is the peace of right order – *tranquillitas ordinis*, the tranquillity of order (cf. *De Civitate Dei*, 19, 13).

True peace therefore is the fruit of justice, that moral virtue and legal guarantee which ensures full respect for rights and responsibilities, and the just distribution of benefits and burdens. But because human justice is always fragile and imperfect, subject as it is to the limitations and egoism of individuals and groups, it must include and, as it were, be completed by the *forgiveness which heals and rebuilds troubled human relations from their foundations*. This is true in circumstances great and small, at the personal level or on a wider, even international scale. Forgiveness is in no way opposed to justice, as if to forgive meant to overlook the need to right the wrong done. It is rather the fullness of justice, leading to that tranquillity of order which is much more than a fragile and temporary cessation of hostilities, involving as it does the deepest healing of the wounds which fester in human hearts. Justice and forgiveness are both essential to such healing. . . .

4. It is precisely peace born of justice and forgiveness that is under assault today by international terrorism. . . . When terrorist organizations use their own followers as weapons to be launched against defenseless and unsuspecting people they show clearly the death-wish that feeds them. Terrorism springs from hatred, and it generates isolation, mistrust and closure. Violence is added to violence in a tragic sequence that exasperates successive generations, each one inheriting the hatred which divided those that went before. *Terrorism is built on contempt for human life.* For this reason, not only does it commit intolerable crimes, but because it resorts to terror as a political and military means it is itself *a true crime against humanity.*

5. *There exists therefore a right to defend oneself against terrorism, a right which, as always, must be exercised with respect for moral and legal limits in the choice of ends and means. The guilty must be correctly identified, since criminal culpability is always personal and cannot be extended to the nation, ethnic group or religion to which the terrorists may belong.* [Emphasis added] International cooperation in the fight against terrorist activities must also include a courageous and resolute political, diplomatic and economic commitment to relieving situations of oppression and marginalization which facilitate the designs of terrorists. The recruitment of terrorists in fact is easier in situations where rights are trampled upon and injustices tolerated over a long period of time. . . .

6. Those who kill by acts of terrorism actually despair of humanity, of life, of the future. In their view, everything is to be hated and destroyed. Terrorists hold that the truth in which they believe or the suffering that they have undergone are so absolute that their reaction in destroying even innocent lives is justified. Terrorism is often the outcome of that fanatic *fundamentalism* which springs from the conviction that one's own vision of the truth must be forced upon everyone else. Instead, even when the truth has been reached – and this can happen only in a limited and imperfect way – it can never be imposed. Respect for a person's conscience, where the image of God himself is reflected (cf. Gen. 1:26–27), means that we can only propose the truth to others, who are then responsible for accepting it. To try to

impose on others by violent means what we consider to be the truth is an offense against human dignity, and ultimately an offense against God whose image that person bears. For this reason, what is usually referred to as fundamentalism is an attitude radically opposed to belief in God. *Terrorism exploits not just people, it exploits God*: it ends by making him an idol to be used for one's own purposes....

10. Forgiveness is not a proposal that can be immediately understood or easily accepted; in many ways it is a paradoxical message. Forgiveness in fact always involves an *apparent* short-term loss for a *real* long-term gain. Violence is the exact opposite; opting as it does for an apparent short-term gain, it involves a real and permanent loss. Forgiveness may seem like weakness, but it demands great spiritual strength and moral courage, both in granting it and in accepting it. It may seem in some way to diminish us, but in fact it leads us to a fuller and richer humanity, more radiant with the splendor of the Creator....

15. ... *No peace without justice, no justice without forgiveness*: I shall not tire of repeating this warning to those who, for one reason or another, nourish feelings of hatred, a desire for revenge or the will to destroy.

From: Pope John Paul II, "The International Situation Today": Address of Pope John Paul II to the Diplomatic Corps Accredited to the Holy See (13 January 2003)[115]

War is never just another means that one can choose to employ for settling differences between nations. As the Charter of the United Nations and international law itself remind us, war cannot be decided upon, even when it is a matter of ensuring the common good, *except as the very last option and in accordance with very strict conditions*, without ignoring the consequences for the civilian population both during and after the military operations. [Emphasis added]

On the eve of the 2003 War in Iraq, the Holy See's Permanent Observer to the United Nations, Archbishop Celestino Migliore intervened before the Security Council at the United Nations Headquarters. Speaking as the diplomatic representative of the Holy See, which was then under the pontificate of Pope John Paul II (for this reason his words are included in this section), the Archbishop emphasized that international conflicts are best resolved by peaceful means, especially the mechanisms available through the application of international law. If these methods are not first explored and exhausted, the resort to force will not be just.

From: Archbishop Celestino Migliore, Permanent Observer of the Holy See to the United Nations, before the Security Council, "Preventing a Possible War in Iraq" (19 February 2003)[116]

Thank you for giving me this opportunity to express the Holy See's deep concern and solicitude on the Iraqi issue also in this chamber of the Security Council, where the issues related to international peace and security are debated, to prevent the world from the scourge of war. I am pleased to recall on this occasion, Mr. President, the successful meeting of Secretary General Kofi Annan with His Holiness Pope John Paul II yesterday evening at the Vatican....

[S]ince the very beginning, the Holy See has always recognized the international community's irreplaceable role in solving the issue of Iraq's compliance with the provisions of U.N. resolutions.

In this regard, the Holy See realizes that the international community is rightly worried and is addressing a just and urgent cause: the disarmament of arsenals of mass destruction, a threat surfacing not just in a single region but unfortunately in other parts of our world. *The Holy See is convinced that in the efforts to draw strength from the wealth of peaceful tools provided by international law, to resort to force would not be a just one.* [Emphasis added] To the grave consequences for a civilian population that has already been tested long enough are added the dark prospects of tensions and conflicts between peoples and cultures, and the deprecated reintroduction of war as a way to resolve untenable situations.

The Holy See is closely following the developments on the ground and expresses its support for the efforts of the international community toward resolving the crisis within the sphere of international legality. For this purpose and with this in mind, His Holiness Pope John Paul II has recently sent a Special Envoy to Baghdad who met with President Saddam Hussein and delivered to him a message from the Pope stressing, *inter alia*, the need for concrete commitments in faithful adherence to the relevant resolutions of the United Nations. A similar message has also been conveyed to Mr. Tariq Aziz, Iraqi Deputy Prime Minister, who visited the Pope on February 14 last. Moreover, in view of the devastating aftermath of a possible military intervention, the Special Envoy of the Pope made an appeal to the conscience of all those who have a role to play in determining the future of the crisis in these coming decisive days, "because, in the end, it is conscience that will have the last word, stronger than all strategies, all ideologies and also all religions."

[T]he Holy See is convinced that even though the process of inspections appears somewhat slow, it still remains an effective path that could lead to the building of a consensus which, if widely shared by nations, would make it almost impossible for any government to act otherwise without risking international isolation. The Holy See is therefore of the view that it is also the proper path that would lead to an agreed and honorable resolution to the problem, which, in turn, could provide the basis for a real and lasting peace.

"War is never just another means that one can choose to employ for settling differences between nations. As the Charter of the U.N. organization and international law itself remind us, *war cannot be decided upon, even when it is a matter of ensuring the common good, except as the very last option and in accordance with very strict conditions, without ignoring the consequences for the civilian population both during and after the military operations*" (Address of Pope John Paul II to the Diplomatic Corps, January 13, 2003). [Emphasis added]

On the issue of Iraq, the vast majority of the international community is calling for a diplomatic resolution of the dispute and for exploring all avenues for a peaceful settlement. That call should not be ignored. The Holy See encourages the parties concerned to keep the dialogue open that could bring about solutions in preventing a possible war and urges the international community to assume its responsibility in dealing with any failings by Iraq.

Mr. President, before concluding this statement, allow me to echo in this chamber of peace the hope-inspiring words of John Paul II's Special Envoy to Iraq: "Peace is still possible in Iraq and for Iraq. The smallest step over the next few days is worth a great leap toward peace."

From: Pope John Paul II, World Day of Peace Message, "An Ever Timely Commitment: Teaching Peace" (1 January 2004)[117]

1. ... In the 25 years of pontificate which the Lord has thus far granted me, I have not failed to speak out before the Church and the world, inviting believers and all persons of good will to take up the cause of peace and to help bring about this fundamental good, thereby assuring the world a better future, one marked by peaceful coexistence and mutual respect....

4. In my message for the World Day of Peace on January 1, 1979, I made this appeal: To reach peace, teach peace. Today that appeal is more urgent than ever because men and women, in the face of the tragedies which continue to afflict humanity, are tempted to yield to fatalism, as if peace were an unattainable ideal.

The Church, on the other hand, has always taught and continues today to teach a very simple axiom: Peace is possible. Indeed, the Church does not tire of repeating that peace is a duty. It must be built on the four pillars indicated by Blessed John XXIII in his encyclical *Pacem in Terris*: truth, justice, love and freedom. A duty is thus imposed upon all those who love peace: that of teaching these ideals to new generations, in order to prepare a better future for all mankind.

5. In this task of teaching peace there is a particularly urgent need to lead individuals and peoples to respect the international order and to respect the commitments assumed by the authorities which legitimately represent them. Peace and international law are closely linked to each another: Law favors peace.

From the very dawn of civilization, developing human communities sought to establish agreements and pacts which would avoid the arbitrary use of force and enable them to seek a peaceful solution of any controversies which might arise. Alongside the legal systems of the individual peoples, there progressively grew up another set of norms which came to be known as *ius gentium* (the law of the nations). With the passage of time, this body of law gradually expanded and was refined in the light of the historical experiences of the different peoples....

This process led with increasing force to the formulation of universal principles which are prior to and superior to the internal law of states and which take into account the unity and the common vocation of the human family.

Central among all these is surely the principle that *pacta sunt servanda*: Accords freely signed must be honored. This is the pivotal and exceptionless presupposition of every relationship between responsible contracting parties. The violation of this principle necessarily leads to a situation of illegality and consequently to friction and disputes which would not fail to have lasting negative repercussions. It is appropriate to recall this fundamental rule, especially at times when there is a temptation to appeal to the law of force rather than to the force of law....

6. That war, with the horrors and the appalling violations of human dignity which it occasioned, led to a profound renewal of the international legal order. The defense and promotion of peace were set at the center of a broadly modernized system of norms and institutions. The task of watching over global peace and security, and with encouraging the efforts of states to preserve and guarantee these fundamental goods of humanity was entrusted by governments to an organization established for this purpose – the United Nations – with a Security Council invested with broad discretionary power. Pivotal to the system was the prohibition of the use of force. This prohibition, according to the well-known Chapter VII of the U.N. Charter, makes provision for only two exceptions. *The first confirms the natural right to legitimate defense*, to be exercised in specific ways and in the context of the United Nations – and consequently also within the traditional limits of necessity and proportionality. [Emphasis added]

The other exception is represented by the system of collective security, which gives the Security Council competence and responsibility for the preservation of peace, with power of decision and ample discretion.

The system developed with the U.N. Charter was meant "to save succeeding generations from the scourge of war, which twice in our lifetime has brought untold sorrow to mankind." In the decades which followed, however, the division of the international community into opposing blocs, the Cold War in one part of the world, the outbreak of violent conflicts in other areas and the phenomenon of terrorism produced a growing break with the ideas and expectations of the immediate post-war period....

8. Today international law is hard pressed to provide solutions to situations of conflict arising from the changed landscape of the contemporary world. These situations of conflict frequently involve agents which are not themselves states but rather entities derived from the collapse of states, or connected to independence movements, or linked to trained criminal organizations. A legal system made up of norms established down the centuries as a means of disciplining relations between sovereign states finds it difficult to deal with conflicts which also involve entities incapable of being considered states in the traditional sense. This is particularly the case with terrorist groups.

The scourge of terrorism has become more virulent in recent years and has produced brutal massacres which have in turn put even greater obstacles in the way of dialogue and negotiation, increasing tensions and aggravating problems, especially in the Middle East.

Even so, if it is to be won, the fight against terrorism cannot be limited solely to repressive and punitive operations. It is essential that the use of force, even when necessary, be accompanied by a courageous and lucid analysis of the reasons behind terrorist attacks. The fight against terrorism must be conducted also on the political and educational levels: on the one hand, by eliminating the underlying causes of situations of injustice which frequently drive people to more desperate and violent acts; and on the other hand, by insisting on an education inspired by respect for human life in every situation: The unity of the human race is a more powerful reality than any contingent divisions separating individuals and people.

In the necessary fight against terrorism, international law is now called to develop legal instruments provided with effective means for the prevention, monitoring and suppression of crime. In any event, democratic governments know well that the use of force against terrorists cannot justify a renunciation of the principles of the rule of law. Political decisions would be unacceptable were they to seek success without consideration for fundamental human rights, since the end never justifies the means.

Pope Benedict XVI (b. 1927)

Like his immediate predecessor John Paul II, Benedict XVI was not a member of the Holy See's diplomatic service. Nonetheless, he quickly responded to the call and challenges of his new office as successor to the Chair of Peter. In doing so, he followed the footsteps of Paul VI and John Paul II and traveled to the U.N. headquarters to deliver a major address to the General Assembly and to the world. While he emphasized the primacy of peaceful means of disputes, he acknowledged that the states of the world have the duty to protect their populations from grave and sustained violations of human rights. If states fail in their responsibility to protect, then the international community must intervene in accordance with the principles of the Charter of the United Nations.

From: Pope Benedict XVI, "Address to the United Nations General Assembly" (2008)[118]

Recognition of the unity of the human family and attention to the innate dignity of every man and woman today find renewed emphasis in the principle of the responsibility to protect. This has only recently been defined, but it was already present implicitly at the origins of the United Nations and is now increasingly characteristic of its activity. *Every State has the primary duty to protect its own population from grave and sustained violations of human rights as well as from the consequences of humanitarian crises, whether natural or man-made.*

If States are unable to guarantee such protection, the international community must intervene with the juridical means provided in the U.N. Charter and in other international instruments. [Emphasis added] The action of the international community and its institutions, provided that it respects the principles undergirding the international order, should never be interpreted as an unwarranted imposition or a limitation of sovereignty. On the contrary, it is indifference or failure to intervene that does the real damage. What is needed is a deeper search for ways of pre-empting and managing conflicts by exploring every possible diplomatic avenue, and giving attention and encouragement to even the faintest sign of dialogue or desire for reconciliation.[119]

The principle of *"responsibility to protect"* was considered by the ancient *ius gentium* as the foundation of every action taken by those in government with regard to the governed: At the time when the concept of national sovereign states was first developing, the Dominican Friar Francisco de Vitoria, rightly considered as a precursor of the idea of the United Nations, *described this responsibility as an aspect of natural reason shared by all nations and the result of an international order whose task it was to regulate relations between peoples.* [Emphasis added] Now, as then, this principle has to invoke the idea of the person as image of the Creator, the desire for the absolute and the essence of freedom.

Pope Francis (b. 1936)

Elected to the pontificate on 13 March 2013, after the surprise resignation of Benedict XVI, Pope Francis's first extended statements on peace and war were issued in September of the same year, apropos the civil war in Syria. Alluding to calls for a punitive strike against the Assad regime, in reaction to its alleged use of chemical weapons against civilians, Pope Francis sent a letter to Russian President Vladimir Putin, who was then hosting a meeting of heads of state. In his letter the pope cautioned against forcible external intervention in the Syria conflict.

From: Pope Francis, "Letter to H.E. Mr. Vladimir Putin, President of the Russian Federation, on the Occasion of the G20 St. Petersburg Summit" (4 September 2013)[120]

[I]t is clear that, for the world's peoples, armed conflicts are always a deliberate negation of international harmony, and create profound divisions and deep wounds which require many years to heal. Wars are a concrete refusal to pursue the great economic and social goals that the international community has set itself.... Unfortunately, the many armed conflicts which continue to afflict the world today present us daily with dramatic images of misery, hunger, illness and death. Without peace, there can be no form of economic development. Violence never begets peace, the necessary condition for development....

It is regrettable that, from the very beginning of the conflict in Syria, one-sided interests have prevailed and in fact hindered the search for a solution that would have avoided the senseless massacre now unfolding. The leaders of the G20 cannot remain indifferent to the dramatic situation of the beloved Syrian people which has lasted far too long, and even risks bringing greater suffering to a region bitterly tested by strife and needful of peace. To the leaders present, to each and every one, I make a heartfelt appeal for them to help find ways to overcome the conflicting positions and to lay aside the futile pursuit of a military solution. Rather, let there be a renewed commitment to seek, with courage and determination, a peaceful solution through dialogue and negotiation of the parties, unanimously supported by the international community. Moreover, all governments have the moral duty to do everything possible to ensure humanitarian assistance to those suffering because of the conflict, both within and beyond the country's borders.

Several days afterward, a "vigil of prayer for peace" was held in St. Peter's Square, Rome. At this event Pope Francis offered some words on the prospect of humanity living together in peace.

From: Pope Francis, "Words to the Vigil of Prayer for Peace" (9 September 2013)[121]

I ask myself: Is it possible to walk the path of peace? Can we get out of this spiral of sorrow and death? Can we learn once again to walk and live in the ways of peace? Invoking the help of God, under the maternal gaze of the *Salus Populi Romani*, Queen of Peace, I say: Yes, it is possible for everyone! From every corner of the world tonight, I would like to hear us cry out: Yes, it is possible for everyone! Or even better, I would like for each one of us, from the least to the greatest, including those called to govern nations, to respond: Yes, we want it! My Christian faith urges me to look to the Cross. How I wish that all men and women of good will would look to the Cross if only for a moment! There, we can see God's reply: violence is not answered with violence, death is not answered with the language of death. In the silence of the Cross, the uproar of weapons ceases and the language of reconciliation, forgiveness, dialogue, and peace is spoken. This evening, I ask the Lord that we Christians, and our brothers and sisters of other religions, and every man and woman of good will, cry out forcefully: violence and war are never the way to peace! Let everyone be moved to look into the depths of his or her conscience and listen to that word which says: Leave behind the self-interest that hardens your heart, overcome the indifference that makes your heart insensitive toward others, conquer your deadly reasoning, and open yourself to dialogue and reconciliation. Look upon your brother's sorrow – I think of the children: look upon these ... look at the sorrow of your brother, stay your hand and do not add to it, rebuild the harmony that has been shattered; and all this achieved not by conflict but by encounter! May the noise of weapons cease! War always marks the failure of peace, it is always a defeat for humanity.... Brothers and Sisters, forgiveness, dialogue, reconciliation – these are the words of peace, in beloved Syria, in the Middle East, in all the world! Let us pray this evening for reconciliation and peace, let us work for reconciliation and peace, and let us all become, in every place, men and women of reconciliation and peace! So may it be.

Bishops' Conferences Sources

During the Second Vatican Council (1962–1965), the Roman Catholic Church acknowledged, in the Decree Concerning the Pastoral Office of Bishops in the Church, *Christus Dominus*, the role of national conferences of Catholic bishops as an important mechanism within the Church's juridical structure.[122] As the Council fathers stated, "An episcopal conference is, as it were, a council in which the bishops of a given nation or territory jointly exercise their pastoral office to promote the greater good which the Church offers mankind, especially through the forms and methods of the apostolate fittingly adapted to the circumstances of the age."[123] In the early 1980s, during the last but nevertheless very tense years of the Cold War, the episcopal conferences of two nuclear powers, the United States and France, issued statements concerning the use of force that included the nuclear deterrent. Although not a nuclear power, the German episcopal conference also issued a statement. Moreover, the Archbishop of Westminster, Basil Cardinal Hume, O.S.B., representing a major see of another nuclear power, the United Kingdom, issued his own letter on the role of nuclear deterrence. Each of these texts presents an accurate assessment of the inevitable tragedy of a nuclear exchange. However, each specifies in its own way an acknowledgment that a unilateral elimination by one nuclear power of its arsenal could pose a new danger to peace and security. There was a common acknowledgment that the world would be far better off with the elimination of nuclear weapons, yet each of these statements presents a nuanced view about the inherent dangers associated with the elimination of such weapons of mass destruction while other powers would still possess them in their arsenals. A theme common to these statements is that the threat of the use of nuclear weapons could be eliminated responsibly if a mutual agreement of progressive elimination could be achieved by good faith negotiation.

The statements acknowledge that the horror of nuclear exchange would be unlike the horror of any previous conflict, thereby making the use of thermonuclear weapons all the more reprehensible. However, these texts recognize that the need to resort to force as a last resort may be the only way to preserve future options for securing peace. These authoritative statements also reflect an important pragmatic note, directly or indirectly, that it would be unwise to insist that those states willing to disarm may place themselves in harm's way if the adversary, potential or present, is unwilling to reciprocate. The restriction on the use of force and the elimination of weapons of mass destruction is a crucial goal. But if it is to be achieved, it must be done with prudence and the participation of all rather than just some.

United States Conference of Catholic Bishops

The United States Conference of Catholic Bishops has in recent times (1983 and 1993) issued statements concerning the use of force. The 1983 document acknowledged the traditional guidelines for a just war. At the same time, it held that there is a presumption against war.[124] The 1983 document clearly stated that the bishops could not conceive of any circumstance in which the use of thermonuclear weapons could be justified. In the 1993 text, the bishops pointed out that in addition to the just war tradition there is another strain of thought that is based on the principles of pacifism. In this document the bishops of the United State appeared to suggest that both strains, that is, the just war tradition and pacifism, were elements of different Catholic approaches to the use of force.

From: United States Conference of Catholic Bishops, *The Challenge of Peace* (1983)[125]

9. In this pastoral letter, too, we address many concrete questions concerning the arms race, contemporary warfare, weapons systems, and negotiating strategies. We do not intend that our treatment of each of these issues [should] carry the same moral authority as our statement of universal moral principles and formal Church teaching. Indeed, we stress here at the beginning that not every statement in this letter has the same moral authority. At times we reassert universally binding moral principles (e.g., non-combatant immunity and proportionality). At still other times we reaffirm statements of recent popes and the teaching of Vatican II. Again, at other times we apply moral principles to specific cases.

10. When making applications of these principles, we realize – and we wish readers to recognize – that prudential judgments are involved based on specific circumstances which can change or which can be interpreted differently by people of good will (e.g., the treatment of "no first use"). However, the moral judgments that we make in specific cases, while not binding in conscience, are to be given serious attention and consideration by Catholics as they determine whether their moral judgments are consistent with the Gospel....

12. ... *The experience of preparing this pastoral letter has shown us the range of strongly held opinion[s] in the Catholic community on questions of war and peace.* [Emphasis added] Obviously, as bishops we believe that such differences should be expressed within the framework of Catholic moral teaching. We urge mutual respect among different groups in the Church as they analyze this letter and the issues it addresses. Not only conviction and commitment are needed in the Church, but also civility and charity.

The *Pastoral Constitution* calls us to bring the light of the gospel to bear upon "the signs of the times." Three signs of the times have particularly influenced the writing of this letter. The first, to quote Pope John Paul II at the United Nations, is that "the world wants peace, the world needs peace." The second is the judgment of Vatican II about the arms race: "The arms race is one of the greatest curses on the human race and the harm it inflicts upon the poor is more than can be endured." The third is the way in which the unique dangers and dynamics of the nuclear arms race present qualitatively new problems which must be addressed by fresh applications of traditional moral principles. In light of these three characteristics, we wish to examine Catholic teaching on peace and war....

24. ... This pastoral letter is more an invitation to continue the new appraisal of war and peace than a final synthesis of the results of such an appraisal. We have some sense of the characteristics of a theology of peace, but not a systematic statement of their relationships.

After an elaboration of the proposal for a "theology of peace," the bishops address the issue of when the use of force is permissible and how it is permissible.

Jus ad Bellum
85. Why and when recourse to war is permissible.

86a. Just Cause
War is permissible only to confront "a real and certain danger," i.e., to protect innocent life, to preserve conditions necessary for decent human existence, and to secure basic human rights. As both Pope Pius XII and Pope John XXIII made clear, if war of retribution was ever justifiable, the risks of modern war negate such a claim today.

87b. Competent Authority
In the Catholic tradition the right to use force has always been joined to the common good; war must be declared by those with responsibility for public order, not by private groups or individuals.

88. The requirement that a decision to go to war must be made by [a] competent authority is particularly important in a democratic society. It needs detailed treatment here since it involves a broad spectrum of related issues. Some of the bitterest divisions of society in our own nation's history, for example, have been evoked over the question of whether or not a president of the United States has acted constitutionally and legally in involving our country in a *de facto* war, even if − indeed, especially if − war was never formally declared. Equally perplexing problems of conscience can be raised for individuals expected or legally required to go to war even though our duly elected representatives in Congress have in fact voted for war.

89. The criterion of competent authority is of further importance in a day when revolutionary war has become commonplace. Historically, the just-war tradition has been open to a "just revolution" position, recognizing that an oppressive government may lose its claim to legitimacy. Insufficient analytical attention has been given to the moral issues of revolutionary warfare. The mere possession of sufficient weaponry, for example, does not legitimize the initiation of war by "insurgents" against an established government, any more than the government's systematic oppression of its people can be carried out under the doctrine of "national security.". . .

92c. Comparative Justice
Questions concerning the *means* of waging war today, particularly in view of the destructive potential of weapons, have tended to override questions concerning the comparative justice of the positions of respective adversaries or enemies. In essence: Which side is sufficiently "right" in a dispute, and are the values at stake critical enough to override the presumption against war? The question in its most basic form is this: Do the rights and values involved justify killing? For whatever the means used, war, by definition, involves violence, destruction, suffering and death.

93. *The category of comparative justice is designed to emphasize the presumption against war which stands at the beginning of just-war teaching.* [Emphasis added]

In a world of sovereign states recognizing neither a common moral authority nor a central political authority, comparative justice stresses that no state should act on the basis that it has "absolute justice" on its side. Every party to a conflict should acknowledge the limits of its "just cause" and the consequent requirement to use *only* limited means in pursuit of its objectives. Far from legitimizing a crusade mentality, comparative justice is designed to relativize absolute claims and to restrain the use of force even in a "justified" conflict. . . .

95d. Right Intention

Right intention is related to just cause – war can be legitimately intended only for the reasons set forth above as a just cause. During the conflict, right intention means pursuit of peace and reconciliation, including avoiding unnecessarily destructive acts or imposing unreasonable conditions (e.g., unconditional surrender).

96e. Last Resort

For resort to war to be justified, all peaceful alternatives must have been exhausted. There are formidable problems in this requirement. No international organization currently in existence has exercised sufficient internationally recognized authority to be able either to mediate effectively in most cases or to prevent conflict by the intervention of U.N. or other peacekeeping forces. Furthermore, there is a tendency for nations or peoples which perceive conflict between or among other nations as advantageous to themselves to attempt to prevent a peaceful settlement rather than advance it. . . .

98f. Probability of Success

This is a difficult criterion to apply, but its purpose is to prevent irrational resort to force or hopeless resistance when the outcome of either will clearly be disproportionate or futile. The determination includes a recognition that at times defense of key values, even against great odds, may be a "proportionate" witness.

99g. Proportionality

In terms of the *jus ad bellum* criteria, proportionality means that the damage to be inflicted and the costs incurred by war must be proportionate to the good expected by taking up arms. Nor should judgments concerning proportionality be limited to the temporal order without regard to a spiritual dimension in terms of "damage," "cost," and "the good expected." In today's interdependent world even a local conflict can affect people everywhere; this is particularly the case when the nuclear powers are involved. Hence a nation cannot justly go to war today without considering the effect of its action on others and on the international community.

100. This principle of proportionality applies throughout the conduct of the war as well as to the decision to begin warfare. During the Vietnam War our bishops' conference ultimately concluded that the conflict had reached such a level of devastation to the adversary and damage to our own society that continuing it could not be justified.

Jus in Bello

101. Even when the stringent conditions which justify resort to war are met, the conduct of war (i.e., strategy, tactics and individual actions) remains subject to

continuous scrutiny in light of two principles which have special significance today precisely because of the destructive capability of modern technological warfare. These principles are proportionality and discrimination. In discussing them here we shall apply them to the question of *jus ad bellum* as well as *jus in bello*; for today it becomes increasingly difficult to make a decision to use any kind of armed force, however limited initially in intention and in the destructive power of the weapons employed, without facing at least the possibility of escalation to broader, or even total, war and to the use of weapons of horrendous destructive potential. This is especially the case when adversaries are "superpowers," as the council clearly envisioned:

"Indeed, if the kind of weapons now stocked in the arsenals of the great powers were to be employed to the fullest, the result would be the almost complete reciprocal slaughter of one side by the other, not to speak of the widespread devastation that would follow in the world and the deadly after-effects resulting from the use of such weapons." . . .

The Initiation of Nuclear War

150. *We do not perceive any situation in which the deliberate initiation of nuclear warfare, on however restricted a scale, can be morally justified.* [Emphasis added] Non-nuclear attacks by another state must be resisted by other than nuclear means. Therefore, *a serious moral obligation exists to develop non-nuclear defensive strategies as rapidly as possible.* [Emphasis added]

From: U.S. Catholic Bishops, *The Harvest of Justice Is Sown in Peace* (1993)[126]

An essential component of a spirituality for peacemaking is an ethic for dealing with conflict in a sinful world. The Christian tradition possesses two ways to address conflict: nonviolence and just war. They both share the common goal: to diminish violence in this world. . . . We take up this dual tradition again recognizing, on the one hand, the success of nonviolent methods in recent history and, on the other, the increasing disorder of the post–Cold War world with its pressures for limited military engagement and humanitarian intervention. . . .

The devastation wrought by . . . recent wars reinforces and strengthens for us the strong presumption against the use of force, which is shared by both traditions. . . .

[T]here are diverse points of view within the Catholic community on the moral meaning and efficacy of a total commitment to nonviolence in an unjust world. Clearly some believe that a full commitment to nonviolence best reflects the Gospel commitment to peace. Others argue that such an approach ignores the reality of grave evil in the world and avoids the moral responsibility to actively resist and confront injustice with military force if other means fail. Both the just-war and nonviolent traditions offer significant moral insight, but continue to face difficult tests in a world marked by so much violence and injustice. Acknowledging this diversity of opinion, we reaffirm the Church's traditional teaching on the ethical conditions for the use of force by public authority.

Ten years after our pastoral letter, recent events raise new questions and concerns which need to be addressed:

Nonviolence: New Importance

As *The Challenge of Peace* observed, "The vision of Christian nonviolence is not passive about injustice and the defense of the rights of others." It ought not be confused with popular notions of nonresisting pacifism. For it consists of a commitment to resist manifest injustice and public evil with means other than force. These include dialogue, negotiations, protests, strikes, boycotts, civil disobedience and civilian resistance. Although nonviolence has often been regarded as simply a personal option or vocation, recent history suggests that in some circumstances it can be an effective public undertaking as well. Dramatic political transitions in places as diverse as the Philippines and Eastern Europe demonstrate the power of nonviolent action, even against dictatorial and totalitarian regimes. Writing about the events of 1989, Pope John Paul II said:

"It seemed that the European order resulting from the Second World War ... could only be overturned by another war. Instead, it has been overcome by the nonviolent commitment of people who, while always refusing to yield to the force of power, succeeded time after time in finding effective ways of bearing witness to the truth."

These nonviolent revolutions challenge us to find ways to take into full account the power of organized, active nonviolence. What is the real potential power of serious nonviolent strategies and tactics – and their limits? What are the ethical requirements when organized nonviolence fails to overcome evil and when totalitarian powers inflict massive injustice on an entire people? What are the responsibilities of and limits on the international community?

One must ask, in light of recent history, whether nonviolence should be restricted to personal commitments or whether it also should have a place in the public order with the tradition of justified and limited war. National leaders bear a moral obligation to see that nonviolent alternatives are seriously considered for dealing with conflicts. New styles of preventative diplomacy and conflict resolution ought to be explored, tried, improved and supported. As a nation we should promote research, education and training in nonviolent means of resisting evil. Nonviolent strategies need greater attention in international affairs.

Such obligations do not detract from a state's right and duty to defend against aggression as a last resort. They do, however, raise the threshold for the recourse to force by establishing institutions which promote nonviolent solutions of disputes and nurturing political commitment to such efforts. In some future conflicts, strikes and people power could be more effective than guns and bullets.

German Bishops

The following text of the German Bishops' pastoral letter is an interesting synthesis of just war theory based on the teaching of the Church that it may be necessary to rely on reasonable force to protect innocent populations against brutality and oppression. Thus they understood that military service is a noble profession in which the soldier has the responsibility to protect the innocent so as to ensure justice and peace.

From: German Bishops' Pastoral Letter, *Gerechtigkeit schafft Frieden* (18 April 1983)[127]

(61) These observations [Thomas Aquinas, Article 40] on a just war are completely incorporated within the doctrine of moral action. The subject is dealt with by Thomas Aquinas in his comprehensive chapter on the virtue of love. War as such appears, to begin with, as a vice which runs counter to the love entrusted to man and bestowed upon him by God. War is only permissible in order to establish a peace, which in turn restores the order disturbed by a grave injustice or protects us against a grave injustice....

(104) [Due to the existence of forces of darkness in the world], *the Church has always adhered to the necessity of protecting the innocent against brutality and oppression, combating injustice and defending justice and righteousness.* [Emphasis added] As we know from the lessons of history, a universal renunciation of this protection and resistance may be understood as weakness and possibly as an invitation to perpetrate political blackmail. In fact, *such a renunciation may foster the very things which it is designed to prevent, namely, the oppression of the innocent and the infliction of suffering and brutality upon them.* [Emphasis added]

(203) [W]e acknowledge the mandate and the service of soldiers in the German Armed Forces. *The state, society and also the Church rely on soldiers performing their duties with expert skill and personal courage.* [Emphasis added] The soldier makes a personal contribution to service on behalf of peace by a keen awareness of his moral responsibility to perform that service. Participation in the formation of political and ethical opinions and judgments represents an expression of his awareness of responsibility.

French Bishops

The French Bishops' pastoral letter also acknowledged that lawful political authorities have a duty to protect, which includes the use of force in situations that are warranted. They seem to eschew a pacifist stance by the assertion that individuals may choose the path of nonviolence, but lawful authorities may not have this luxury in order to comply with their duty to defend peace against the aggressor. The French bishops address the existence and use of nuclear weapons. They make a careful distinction between having such weapons, which is not synonymous with their use, and their actual use. They conclude that the possession of such weapons as a deterrent against unjust aggressors may be legitimate.

From: French Bishops' Pastoral Letter, *Gagner la paix* (8 November 1983)[128]

(12) The nonresistance of Christ, the pardon that he offers, is the salt which alone can save the world from the corruption of violence. Nonviolence remains a summons to each man and even to human communities. But can nonviolence be a policy for states? *The Church has always recognized the right that political powers have to respond to violence by means of force. . . . Nonviolence is a risk which individuals can take. Can states, whose function is to defend peace, take this risk?* [Emphasis added]

Threat Is Not Use

(26) This logic is, to be sure, a logic of distress: It cannot hide or conceal its congenital weakness. Certainly, it is in order not to wage war that nations seek to show themselves capable of waging it. *Peace is still being served when the aggressor is discouraged and constrained to the beginning of wisdom as a result of an appropriate fear. The threat of force is not the use of force. It is the basis of deterrence, and this is often forgotten when the same moral qualification is attributed to the threat as to the use of force.* [Emphasis added]

(27) Nevertheless, the danger of the logic of deterrence is immediately evident. In order not to allow a possible aggressor to have illusions about the credibility of our defenses, we must show ourselves ready to use our weapons if deterrence should fail.

(28) But the moral legitimacy of this move from possession to use is more than problematical. This is all the more true in France because our deterrence is a "deterrence of the strong by the weak," a poor man's deterrence: Because of the lack of diversified means of deterrence, our deterrence still rests on an anti-city strategy, itself clearly condemned, without appeal, by the Council: "Every act of war directed to the indiscriminate destruction of whole cities or vast areas with their inhabitants is a crime against God and man, which merits firm and unequivocal condemnation." [*Gaudium et Spes*, N. 80]

(29) *But threat is not use. Does the immorality of use render the threat immoral? This is not evident.* [Emphasis added] For, as the Council says, "they cannot ignore the complexity of the situation as it stands." [*Gaudium et Spes*, N. 82] . . .

(30) *Faced with a choice between two evils, both of them all but unavoidable, capitulations or counter-threats, one chooses the lesser without pretending that one is choosing a moral good.* [Emphasis added] It is clear what recourse to nuclear deterrence supposes, if it is to be morally acceptable: that it applies only to defense; that over-arming be avoided − deterrence is reached at the moment when the formulated threat renders unreasonable the aggression of a third party; that all precautions be taken to avoid a "mistake" or the intervention of a madman, or of

a terrorist, and so on; that the nation which takes the risk of nuclear deterrence likewise pursue a constructive policy in favor of peace.

Basil Cardinal Hume

Although the English and Welsh bishops did not issue in 1983 any pastoral letter regarding the use of force as did the German, French, and American bishops, the Archbishop of Westminster issued his own letter covering the use of force and the possession of nuclear weapons. In his letter, he emphasized that the state retains the right to exercise its authority in providing for a legitimate self-defense against any aggressor. While the first use of nuclear weapons could never be justified, he indicated that their unilateral abandonment might prove to be foolish without reciprocity by those considered to be potential adversaries. In his estimation, unilateral disarmament could prove to be a source of conflict rather than a means to avoid conflict in the future. His reasoning for this was based on the belief that unilateral disarmament could destabilize existing political and military positions that would increase rather than decrease the risk of "nuclear blackmail."

From: Basil Cardinal Hume, *Towards Nuclear Morality* (17 November 1983)[129]

(5) Inevitably, though, the peace movements bring pressure to bear primarily on the governments of the West and not on those of the East. In communist regimes movements critical of official policy are rarely tolerated. There are different perceptions in East and West about the threat to peace.

(6) No one can deny the moral dilemma which faces us today. On the one hand we have a grave obligation to prevent nuclear war from ever occurring. On the other hand, *the state has the right and duty of legitimate self-defense*, thus ensuring for its citizens justice, freedom and independence. *Although nothing could ever justify the use of nuclear arms as weapons of massive and indiscriminate slaughter, yet to abandon them without adequate safeguards may help to destabilize the existing situation and may dramatically increase the risk of nuclear blackmail.* [Emphasis added] . . .

(12) *The acceptance of deterrence on strict conditions and as a temporary expedient leading to progressive disarmament is emerging as the most widely accepted view of the Roman Catholic Church.*[130] [Emphasis added]

The *Catechism of the Catholic Church* and the Second Vatican Council Sources

The *Catechism of the Catholic Church* had its birth in the Synod of Bishops that Pope John Paul II convened in 1985. During that important meeting, the Synod stated, "Very many have expressed the desire that a catechism or compendium of all Catholic doctrine regarding both faith and morals be composed.... It must be sound doctrine suited to the present life of Christians."[131] The work on the catechism thus began. Its fruit was presented to Pope John Paul II in 1992, and he issued his Apostolic Constitution, *Fidei Despositum*, approving the publication of the Catechism on 11 October 1992.[132] The following excerpts are those addressing Catholic doctrine regarding the use of force.

From: *The Catechism of the Catholic Church*[133]

2302. By recalling the commandment, "You shall not kill," our Lord asked for peace of heart and denounced murderous anger and hatred as immoral.

Anger is a desire for revenge. "To desire vengeance in order to do evil to someone who should be punished is illicit," but it is praiseworthy to impose restitution "to correct vices and maintain justice." If anger reaches the point of a deliberate desire to kill or seriously wound a neighbor, it is gravely against charity; it is a mortal sin. The Lord says, "Everyone who is angry with his brother shall be liable to judgment."

2303. Deliberate *hatred* is contrary to charity. Hatred of the neighbor is a sin when one deliberately wishes him evil. Hatred of the neighbor is a grave sin when one deliberately desires him grave harm. "But I say to you, Love your enemies and pray for those who persecute you, so that you may be sons of your Father who is in heaven."

2304. Respect for and development of human life require *peace*. Peace is not merely the absence of war, and it is not limited to maintaining a balance of powers between adversaries. Peace cannot be attained on earth without safeguarding the goods of persons, free communication among men, respect for the dignity of persons and peoples, and the assiduous practice of fraternity. Peace is "the tranquillity of order." Peace is the work of justice and the effect of charity.

2305. Earthly peace is the image and fruit of the *peace of Christ*, the messianic "Prince of Peace." By the blood of his Cross, "in his own person he killed the hostility," he reconciled men with God and made his Church the sacrament of the unity of the human race and of its union with God. "He is our peace." He has declared: "Blessed are the peacemakers."

2306. Those who renounce violence and bloodshed and, in order to safeguard human rights, make use of those means of defense available to the weakest, bear witness to evangelical charity, provided they do so without harming the rights and obligations of other men and societies. They bear legitimate witness to the gravity of the physical and moral risks of recourse to violence, with all its destruction and death.

Avoiding War

2307. The fifth commandment forbids the intentional destruction of human life. Because of the evils and injustices that accompany all war, the Church insistently urges everyone to prayer and to action so that the divine Goodness may free us from the ancient bondage of war.

2308. All citizens and all governments are obliged to work for the avoidance of war.

However, "as long as the danger of war persists and there is no international authority with the necessary competence and power, governments cannot be denied the right of lawful self-defense, once all peace efforts have failed."

2309. The strict conditions for *legitimate defense by military force* require rigorous consideration. The gravity of such a decision makes it subject to rigorous conditions of moral legitimacy. At one and the same time:

- the damage inflicted by the aggressor on the nation or community of nations must be lasting, grave, and certain;
- all other means of putting an end to it must have been shown to be impractical or ineffective;
- there must be serious prospects of success;
- the use of arms must not produce evils and disorders graver than the evil to be eliminated. The power of modern means of destruction weighs very heavily in evaluating this condition.

These are the traditional elements enumerated in what is called the "just war" doctrine.

The evaluation of these conditions for moral legitimacy belongs to the prudential judgment of those who have responsibility for the common good.

2310. Public authorities, in this case, have the right and duty to impose on citizens the *obligations necessary for national defense*. Those who are sworn to serve their country in the armed forces are servants of the security and freedom of nations. If they carry out their duty honorably, they truly contribute to the common good of the nation and the maintenance of peace.

2311. Public authorities should make equitable provision for those who for reasons of conscience refuse to bear arms; these are nonetheless obliged to serve the human community in some other way.

2312. The Church and human reason both assert the permanent validity of the *moral law during armed conflict*. "The mere fact that war has regrettably broken out does not mean that everything becomes licit between the warring parties."

2313. Non-combatants, wounded soldiers, and prisoners must be respected and treated humanely. Actions deliberately contrary to the law of nations and to its universal principles are crimes, as are the orders that command such actions. Blind obedience does not suffice to excuse those who carry them out. Thus the extermination of a people, nation, or ethnic minority must be condemned as a mortal sin. One is morally bound to resist orders that command genocide.

2314. "Every act of war directed to the indiscriminate destruction of whole cities or vast areas with their inhabitants is a crime against God and man, which merits firm and unequivocal condemnation." A danger of modern warfare is that it provides the opportunity to those who possess modern scientific weapons — especially atomic, biological, or chemical weapons — to commit such crimes.

2315. The *accumulation of arms* strikes many as a paradoxically suitable way of deterring potential adversaries from war. They see it as the most effective means of ensuring peace among nations. This method of deterrence gives rise to strong moral reservations. The *arms race* does not ensure peace. Far from eliminating the causes of war, it risks aggravating them. Spending enormous sums to produce ever new types of weapons impedes efforts to aid needy populations; it thwarts the development of peoples. *Over-armament* multiplies reasons for conflict and increases the danger of escalation.

2316. The *production and the sale of arms* affect the common good of nations and of the international community. Hence public authorities have the right and duty to regulate them. The short-term pursuit of private or collective interests cannot legitimate undertakings that promote violence and conflict among nations and compromise the international juridical order.

2317. Injustice, excessive economic or social inequalities, envy, distrust, and pride raging among men and nations constantly threaten peace and cause wars. Everything done to overcome these disorders contributes to building up peace and avoiding war:

Insofar as men are sinners, the threat of war hangs over them and will so continue until Christ comes again; but insofar as they can vanquish sin by coming together in charity, violence itself will be vanquished and these words will be fulfilled: "they shall beat their swords into plowshares, and their spears into pruning hooks; nation shall not lift up sword against nation, neither shall they learn war anymore."

The Second Vatican Council

The Second Vatican Council was convened during the papacy of Blessed John XXIII in 1962. It ended during the pontificate of Pope Paul VI in December 1965. The Council issued over a dozen important documents regarding the Church's teachings. The text addressing the Church's social teachings, including the use of force, is the Pastoral Constitution of the Church in the Modern World, *Gaudium et Spes* (Latin, meaning "Joy and Hope"). The relevant provisions of the Pastoral Constitution took into account the traditional teachings of the Church regarding the use of force and just war theory; however, it did so in the atmosphere of the Cold War and the aftermath of the Cuban Missile Crisis of 1962, the year the Council convened and began its work. The relevant elements of the Pastoral Constitution now follow.

From: Second Vatican Council: The Pastoral Constitution on the Church in the Modern World, *Gaudium et Spes* (1965)[134]

77. During these current years, in which the gravest distress and anxieties persist among men because of war either raging or threatening, the entire human family has reached a supremely critical moment in its progress toward maturity. It is gradually being unified and everywhere better realizing its unity; but it is unable to

carry out the task which weighs on it, of building a more humane world, unless all are renewed in mind and converted to the cause of peace. . . .

78. Peace is not the mere absence of war. It cannot be reduced to mere balance of power. It does not come of tyrannical domination. It is rightly and properly called "the work of justice" (Isa. 32:7). It exists as the fruit of the order built into human society by its divine Founder, an order to be given practical expression by men ever thirsting for more perfect justice. . . .

There can be no peace on earth unless personal welfare is safeguarded and men spontaneously and confidently exchange the riches of their minds and genius. The construction of peace absolutely demands a firm resolve to respect other men and peoples, and the practical determination to be brothers. Thus peace is also the fruit of love, which advances beyond what justice can supply. . . .

Section 1: Avoiding War

79. In spite of the fact that recent wars have inflicted the greatest material and moral damage on our world, every day, in some part of the world, war continues its devastations. In fact while scientific weapons of any kind are employed in war, its savage character threatens to reduce the combatants to a barbarism far beyond that of past times. Besides, the complexity of present-day conditions and the intimate relations between nations allow concealed wars to drag on by new, insidious and subversive methods. In many cases the use of terrorism is considered a new way of waging war. . . .

There exist various international agreements about war, to which a large number of nations have subscribed, for the purpose of humanizing military action and its consequences: e.g., agreements about the treatment of prisoners and wounded, and the like. These agreements are to be observed, in fact governments and experts are bound to do everything possible to improve them, so that they may check the frightfulness of war more effectively. It seems fair moreover that laws should make humane provision for conscientious objectors, so long as they accept another form of service to the human community.

War has decidedly not been eradicated from human affairs. So long as the danger of it persists and we have no competent international authority equipped with adequate force, it will not be possible to deny governments the right of legitimate self-defense, given that they have exhausted every peaceful means of settlement. [Emphasis added]

Rules and others sharing the responsibility have the duty of looking to the safety of those in their charge, and must handle such grave matters with proper seriousness. But military policy based on rightful defense is one thing, to want to subdue other nations is quite another. Nor does the possession of war potential make every military or political use of it lawful. Nor does everything between the belligerents become lawful once war has unhappily broken out.

Those who are serving their country in the armed forces should regard themselves as servants of the people's security and liberty. While they are fulfilling this duty they are genuinely contributing to the establishment of peace.

80.... All this forces us to examine war in an entirely new frame of mind. Our contemporaries should know that they will have to give a very serious account of their waging war. The future will hang very largely on their present decisions.

Bearing this in mind, the Council makes its own, the condemnations of total war already issued by recent Popes and declares: All warfare which tends indiscriminately to the destruction of entire cities or wide areas with their inhabitants is a crime against God and man, to be firmly and unhesitatingly condemned.

The peril peculiar to war today is this: that it offers to those who possess the latest scientific weapons occasion to commit such crimes and can by a kind of inexorable escalation drive men to the most atrocious decisions. Lest this should ever happen, the assembled bishops of the world implore all, especially statesmen and military leaders, never to stop pondering such a responsibility before God and humanity.

81. Scientific weapons are not accumulated only to be used in war. Since the defensive strength of either side is reckoned to depend on its being equipped for lightning reprisals; stockpiling of arms, heavier year by year, helps in a novel way to deter likely enemies. Many think this the most effective of all ways of keeping international peace nowadays.

Whatever may be thought of this method of dissuasion, men should be convinced that the armaments race in which so many nations compete is no safe way to guarantee peace, nor is the "balance" resulting from it sure and genuine peace. It slowly aggravates the causes of war instead of doing away with them. While vast wealth is spent on new weapons it is impossible to provide adequate remedies for so much destitution throughout the world....

Hence we must declare afresh: the arms race is a most serious injury to humanity and an intolerable one to the poor. It is greatly to be feared that if it lasts it will bring fatal disaster, the means of which it is already preparing.

The calamities mankind has made possible should be a severe warning to us. Providentially we are allowed a breathing space: we should use it more responsibly to find ways of settling our differences in a fashion more worthy of man. Divine Providence urgently commands us to rid ourselves of the ancient slavery of war. If we refuse to make the attempt, who knows where the evil road we have set out on will lead us?

82. It is clear that we should give all our energies to hastening the day when by common consent of the nations, war may be altogether banned. This obviously calls for the setting up of some universal public authority recognized by everybody, commanding effective power, to guarantee for everybody security, regard for justice and respect for rights. Before this authority can be set up, the present international bodies should devote themselves zealously to studying better ways of achieving general security. Peace must be born of mutual trust between nations, not imposed on them by armed terror. So all must work to see an end of the arms race and a real beginning of disarmament; to see, moreover, that this disarmament proceeds not unilaterally but *pari passu* and by agreement, and is protected by adequate guarantees.

NOTES

1 For a compilation of the most important texts in this tradition, with much fuller coverage of the primary sources than was possible in the present volume, see Gregory M. Reichberg, Henrik Syse, and Endre Begby (eds.), *The Ethics of War: Classic and Contemporary Readings* (Oxford: Blackwell Publishing, 2006).

2 See James Turner Johnson, *The Quest for Peace* (Princeton, N.J.: Princeton University Press, 1987), chapter 1, "Christian Attitudes toward War and Military Service in the First Four Centuries," pp. 3–66. For a more recent discussion of this theme, see Alan Kreider, "Military Service in the Church Orders," *Journal of Religious Ethics* 31:3 (2003), 415–442.

3 For a survey on pacifist thought in twentieth-century Catholicism, see George Weigel, *Tranquillitas Ordinis* (Oxford: Oxford University Press, 1987).

4 Louis J. Swift (ed. and trans.), *The Early Fathers on Law and Military Service* (Wilmington, Del.: Michael Glazier, 1983), pp. 34–35. Swift's excellent anthology contains a wide selection of other patristic writings on matters relating to war.

5 Tertullian, *On Idolatry*, 19.1–3, in Swift, *The Early Fathers on Law and Military Service*, pp. 41–42.

6 Augustine, *The City of God*, book 19, 7; cited in Ernest L. Fortin and Douglas Kries (eds.), *Augustine: Political Writings*, Michael W. Tkacz and Douglas Kries (trans.) (Indianapolis, Ind.: Hackett, 1994), p. 149.

7 For an overview of Gratian's approach to just war, see the editors' comments on "Gratian and the Decretists (Twelfth Century): War and Coercion in the *Decretum*," in Reichberg et al., *The Ethics of War*, pp. 104–108.

8 For a survey on the medieval canon law teaching on war, see Frederick H. Russell, *The Just War in the Middle Ages* (Cambridge: Cambridge University Press, 1975).

9 For a selection of texts on the crusades, see "The Crusades (Eleventh to Thirteenth Centuries): Christian Holy War," in Reichberg et al., *The Ethics of War*, pp. 98–103. The quoted passage is from Innocent's *Decretals*, III, 34, 8, also reproduced below.

10 See the first extract from Gratian reproduced below in this section.

11 Catholic authors of the period typically distinguished (a) apostates, schismatics, and heretics from (b) Jews, pagans, and other non-Christians. While it was thought that the former could be coerced back to a faith they had willingly abandoned, the latter were considered immune from coercion within the sphere of belief.

12 Pius IX, discourse to the College of Cardinals, 28 September 1860; the text is reproduced in Moines de Solesmes (ed.), *Les Enseignements Pontificaux*, vol. 1: *La Paix Internationale* (Paris: Desclée & Cie, 1956), pp. 24–25. For a related papal text (letter to the Syrian bishops, 29 July 1960), see Georges Minois, *L' Église et la guerre: De la Bible à l'ère atomique* (Paris: Fayard, 1994), p. 366. For an account of the military defense of papal states and related use of force under the direction of Church leaders, see D. S. Chambers, *Popes, Cardinals, and War: The Military Church in Renaissance and Early Modern Europe* (London: I. B. Tauris, 2006). A theological assessment may be found in Charles Journet, "Canonical Power and Political Power," chapter 6 in *Church of the Word Incarnate* (New York: Sheed and Ward, 1955), vol. 1, pp. 193–330.

13 On the tradition of regular war, see Peter Haggenmacher, "Just War and Regular War in Sixteenth Century Spanish Doctrine," *International Review of the Red Cross* 290 (September–October 1992), 434–445.

14 James A. Brundage, "Holy War and the Medieval Lawyers," in *The Holy War*, T. P. Murphy (ed.) (Columbus: Ohio State University Press, 1976), pp. 99–140, on p. 100. See also Carl

Erdmann's seminal study *Die Entstehung des Kreuzzugsgedankens* (1935), which was translated by M. W. Baldwin and W. Goffart as *The Origin of the Idea of Crusade* (Princeton, N.J.: Princeton University Press, 1977).

15 Brian Tierney, *The Crisis of Church and State 1050–1300* (Toronto: University of Toronto Press, 1988), p. 88.

16 H. J. Schroeder, *Disciplinary Decrees of the General Councils: Text, Translation and Commentary* (St. Louis, Mo.: B. Herder, 1937), pp. 202–203, 207, 213.

17 *Decretum Magistri Gratiani*, in E. Friedberg (ed.), *Corpus Iuris Canonici*, pars prior (Leipzig: Tauchnitz, 1879). Translation in Reichberg et al., *The Ethics of War*, pp. 109, 111–112, 112–115, 121–124.

18 St. Bernard's *Treatise on Consideration*, translated from the original Latin by "A priest of Mount Mellery" (Dublin: Browne and Nolan, 1921), pp. 119–120.

19 A letter written by Bernard to Pope Eugene III in 1146, urging him to assist the Christians in Palestine: "Now whilst Christ is enduring a second passion where He also endured His first, both swords, the material as well as the spiritual, must be unsheathed. And by whom but by thee? For the two swords are Peter's, to be drawn whenever necessary, the one by his own hand, the other by his authority (*ad nutum*)" (translation, ibid., p. 120, note).

20 Raymundus de Pennafort, *Summa de poenitentia, et matrimonio, cum glossis Ioannis de Friburgo* (Rome, 1603). Translation in Reichberg et al., *The Ethics of War*, pp. 134–135.

21 Lyon, 1535. Translation in Reichberg et al., *The Ethics of War*, pp. 150–151.

22 Lyon, 1535. Translation in ibid., pp. 153–154.

23 *Relectiones de Indis* and *De juri belli*. For a discussion of the main points covered in the two lectures, see Gregory M. Reichberg, "Philosophy Meets War: Francisco de Vitoria's *De Indis* and *De jure belli relectiones* (1557)," in Jorge J. E. Garcia, Gregory M. Reichberg, and Bernard N. Schumacher (eds.), *The Classics of Western Philosophy* (Oxford: Blackwell Publishers, 2003), pp. 197–204.

24 This scholastic term signifies an erroneous belief that results from an interplay of factors that are beyond an agent's voluntary control.

25 *De bello*, section VI, §5, translation in Gwladys L. Williams and Henry Davis (eds.), *Selections from Three Works of Francisco Suárez* (Oxford: Clarendon Press, 1944), p. 830.

26 For a general treatment of double-effect reasoning in the context of war, see Gregory M. Reichberg and Henrik Syse, "The Idea of Double Effect – in War and Business," in Lene Bomann-Larsen and Oddny Wiggen (eds.), *Responsibility in World Business: Managing Harmful Side-Effects of Corporate Activity* (Tokyo: United Nations University Press, 2004), pp. 17–38.

27 Translation in *The Summa Theologica of Saint Thomas Aquinas*, The Fathers of the English Dominican Province (trans.), Daniel J. Sullivan (rev.), vol. 2 (Chicago: William Benton, 1952), p. 578. This and most other editions of the *Summa theologiae* list "Whether it is always sinful to wage war?" as the title to q. 40, a. 1. However, it can be argued that "Whether any war is permissible" represents a more accurate rendition of the article's title, hence this is the version being used here; see Gregory M. Reichberg, "Thomas Aquinas between Just War and Pacifism," *Journal of Religious Ethics* 38:2 (2010), 219–241, at 220–221.

28 "Bellum quando dicatur iustum, vel iniustum, licitum vel illicitum," in *Summula Caietani* (Lyon: A. de Harsy, 1581). Translation in Reichberg et al., *The Ethics of War*, pp. 247–248.

29 Romans 12:9.

30 *Summa Thomae Aquinatis Doctoris Angelici Opera Omnia iussu impensaque Leonis XIII, cum commentariis Thomae de Vio Caietani Ordinis Praedicatorum*, vol. 9 (Rome: Editori di San Tommaso, 1895), p. 94. Translation by Gregory M. Reichberg.

31 Francisco de Vitoria, *Relectio de Indis*, L. Pereña and J. M. Pérez Prendes (eds.), Corpus hispanorum de pace V (Madrid: Consejo Superior de Investigaciones Científicas, 1967). Translation in Anthony Pagden and Jeremy Lawrance (eds.), *Francisco de Vitoria: Political Writings* (Cambridge: Cambridge University Press, 1991), pp. 271–272.

32 Francisco de Vitoria, *Relectio de iure belli; o, Paz dinámica*, L. Pereña, V. Abril, C. Baciero, A. García, and F. Maseda (eds.), Corpus hispanorum de pace VI (Madrid: Consejo Superior de Investigaciones Científicas, 1981). Translation in Pagden and Lawrance, *Francisco de Vitoria: Political Writings*, pp. 302–304.

33 Translation in Pagden and Lawrance, *Francisco de Vitoria: Political Writings*, p. 305.

34 Ludovicus Molina, *De Iustitia et Iure opera omnia* (Geneva: M. M. Bousquet, 1733). Translation in Reichberg et al., *The Ethics of War*, pp. 334–335.

35 Franciscus Suarius, *Disputatio de bello* in *Opera omnia*, vol. 12 (Paris: Vivès, 1858).

36 Translation in Williams and Davis (eds.), *Selections from Three Works of Francisco Suárez*, p. 830. Translation altered.

37 Translation in Reichberg et al., *The Ethics of War*, pp. 364–365.

38 Most notably, *Saggio teoretico di dritto naturale appoggiato sul fatto* (Theoretical Essay on Natural Law Based on Facts) (Palermo, 1840–1843).

39 Stephen C. Neff, *War and the Law of Nations* (Cambridge: Cambridge University Press, 2005), p. 279.

40 Ibid., p. 293.

41 The two most notable works in this genre were Alfred Vanderpol, *La doctrine scolastique du droit de la guerre* (Paris: Pedone, 1919), and Robert Regout, *La doctrine de la guerre juste de saint Augustin à nos jours d'après les théologiens et les canonists catholiques* (Paris: A. Pedone, 1935).

42 The work of the Italian priest-politician Luigi Sturzo was particularly important in this regard. See his *La comunità internazionale e il diritto di Guerra* (The International Community and the Right of War) (1928; revised ed., Bologna: Zanichelli, 1954).

43 "Conclusiones conventus theologici Friburgensis de bello," *Les documents de la vie intellectuelle*, 3 (1932), 199–213. Translation in John Eppstein, *The Catholic Tradition of the Law of Nations* (Washington, D.C.: Carnegie Endowment for International Peace, 1935), pp. 138–142.

44 Translation in Eppstein, *The Catholic Tradition of the Law of Nations*, pp. 138–142.

45 Jacques Maritain, *De la justice politique: Notes sur la présente guerre* (Paris: Plon, 1940).

46 Translation of "La guerre juste," *Commonweal* 31:9 (1939): 199–200; original French version subsequently published in Maritain, *De la justice politique: Notes sur la présente guerre*, pp. 17–29.

47 John C. Ford, "The Morality of Obliteration Bombing," *Theological Studies* 5 (1944), 261–309; for a selection of writings by Anscombe on war, see "G. E. M. Anscombe (1919–2001): The Moral Recklessness of Pacifism," in Reichberg et al., *The Ethics of War*, pp. 625–632.

48 Ford, "The Morality of Obliteration Bombing," 257, 268, 308–309.

49 For a detailed history of the Magisterium's endorsement of (and engagement with) the United Nations, see Robert John Araujo, S.J., and John A. Lucal, S.J., *Papal Diplomacy and the Quest for Peace: The United Nations from Pius XII to Paul VI* (Philadelphia: Saint Joseph's University Press, 2010).

50 *Pacem in Terris*, §127 in Claudia Carlen (ed.), *The Papal Encyclicals 1958–1981* (Raleigh: McGrath Publishing, 1981), p. 121.

51 Isaiah 9:6. The prophecy is fulfilled with the birth of Jesus and chronicled by St. Luke's Gospel, chapter 2, verses 13–14, "And suddenly there was with the angel a multitude of the heavenly host praising God and saying: 'Glory to God in the highest, and on earth peace,

goodwill toward men!'" And, as the life of Jesus progressed, He said, "Peace I leave with you; My peace I give to you; not as the world gives do I give to you." John 14:27.

52　Benedict XV, Exhortation, *Dès le début* (To the Belligerent Peoples and to Their Leaders), 1 August 1917, §532, in Reverend Harry C. Koenig (ed.), *Principles for Peace: Selections from Papal Documents Leo XIII to Pius XII* (Washington, D.C.: National Catholic Welfare Conference, 1943), p. 232.

53　The bibliography associated with this chapter presents a spectrum of useful perspectives addressing the use of force and just war theory in the Catholic tradition.

54　My guides for developing these principles are the *Catechism of the Catholic Church* (The Vatican: Libreria Editrice Vaticana, 1994); and Pontifical Council for Justice and Peace, *Compendium of the Social Doctrine of the Church* (The Vatican: Libreria Editrice Vaticana, 2004).

55　Deuteronomy 5:17.

56　It is interesting to see the two strands of thought that emerge in the New Testament. On the one hand, there is the Biblical exhortation to peace. We see this in Jesus' critique of Peter, who cuts off the ear of one of those about to apprehend Jesus, and Jesus tells Peter to put away his sword, John 18:11; moreover, in the Beatitudes, Jesus counsels, "Blessed are the peacemakers, for they shall be called sons of God," Matthew 5:9. But in contrast, we must acknowledge that Jesus did not condemn those who served in the military, as in the case of the centurion about whom He says, "not even in Israel have I found such faith," Luke 7:9. In one instance, we see Jesus himself fashioning crude weapons of whips and cords to drive out the merchants from the Temple, John 2:15. In addition, the Church permits the appointment of Catholic chaplains who serve in the armed forces of their countries. Moreover, it appoints bishops as military ordinaries to oversee the work of Catholic military chaplains.

57　*Pacem in Terris*, §127, in Carlen (ed.), *The Papal Encyclicals 1958–1981*, p. 121; International Court of Justice Advisory Opinion on the Use of Nuclear Weapons, 8 July 1996; available at http://www.un.org/law/icjsum/9623.htm.

58　*The Pastoral Constitution on the Church in the Modern World – Gaudium et Spes*, §80 (London: Catholic Truth Society, 1966), pp. 83–84. As a result of the saturation or obliteration bombing used by the Allies in World War II, the Rev. John Cuthbert Ford, S.J., published a famous article in 1944, "The Morality of Obliteration Bombing," in *Theological Studies* 5 (1944), 261–309. In his important article, Fr. Ford, a well-respected moral theologian, proffered the important distinction between precision bombing of definite, limited military targets and the bombing of a much larger area that could be an entire city or a very large section of a developed area that would include residential districts. For an excerpt from this article, see the first section of this chapter.

59　The United Nations Charter, "Chapter VII: Action with respect to threats to the peace, breaches of the peace, and acts of aggression," Article 51, available at http://www.un.org/en/documents/charter/chapter7.shtml.

60　See Gregory M. Reichberg, "Is There a 'Presumption against War' in Aquinas's Ethics?," in Henrik Syse and Gregory M. Reichberg, *Ethics, Nationalism, and Just War: Medieval and Contemporary Perspectives* (Washington, D.C.: Catholic University of America Press, 2007), pp. 72–98.

61　Pope Paul VI, "Speech to the United Nations," October 1965, §5 in *Never Again War! A Documented Account of the Visit to the United Nations of His Holiness Pope Paul VI* (New York: Office of Public Information, United Nations, 1965), pp. 37–39.

62　Pope Paul VI, "Message for the Observance of a Day of Peace," 1 January 1968; available at http://www.vatican.va/holy_father/paul_vi/messages/peace/documents/hf_p-vi_mes_19671208_i-world-day-for-peace_en.html.

63 *Catechism of the Catholic Church*, §2309 (New York: Burns and Oates, 2002), pp. 496–497.

64 The common good is understood to be: "the sum of those conditions of social life which allow social groups and their individual members relatively thorough and ready access to their own fulfillment," *The Pastoral Constitution of the Church in the Modern World – Gaudium et Spes*, §26.

65 Heinrich Rommen, *The State in Catholic Thought: A Treatise in Political Philosophy* (London: B. Herder, 1945), p. 657.

66 *Catechism of the Catholic Church*, §2310, p. 497.

67 See supra note 95.

68 These points are distilled from the *Compendium of the Social Doctrine of the Church*, pp. 279–290.

69 See supra footnote 94 and accompanying text.

70 "In the contemporary literature on just war, *prevention* is usually contrasted to *preemption*. While both sorts of defense are anticipatory (they aim at countering attacks that have not yet occurred), the latter is most often taken to designate an armed action against an offensive that, by demonstrable signs, is imminent, while the former presupposes a longer time frame. Prevention thus seeks to counter an adversary who either is preparing to mount an attack at a still undetermined point in the future, or, still more remotely, has acquired a military capability that, if exercised, would have devastating consequences for the defender" (Gregory M. Reichberg, "Jus ad Bellum," in Larry May (ed.), *War: Essays in Political Philosophy* [Cambridge: Cambridge University Press, 2008], 11–29, at pp. 25–26).

71 The noncompliance with Catholic teaching is suggested in the following passage of the *Compendium of the Social Doctrine of the Church*: "[E]ngaging in a preventive war without clear proof that the attack is imminent cannot fail to raise serious moral and juridical questions" (§501).

72 In Catholic traditional teaching on war, beginning as early as Vitoria, the term "the innocent" (Latin: *innocentes*, lit. "not causing harm") is standardly used as an equivalent for "noncombatants." As such it stands in opposition to *nocentes*, those who are noxious or actively causing harm.

73 Cf. Pope John Paul II, "'Principles Underlying a Stance toward Unjust Aggressors' – Address to the Diplomatic Corps Accredited to the Holy See," 16 January 1993, §13 in *Origins* 22:32 (4 February 1993), 583–587. Note on p. 587.

74 See Pope John Paul II, "'Averting Civilization's Ruin' – Address to the Diplomatic Corps (9 January 1995)," §7 in *Origins* 24:31 (19 January 1995), 520–522. Note on p. 521.

75 *The Pastoral Constitution of the Church in the Modern World – Gaudium et Spes*, §80.

76 Pope John Paul II, "'Respect for Human Rights: The Secret of True Peace' – Message for the 1999 World Day for Peace," §11 in *Origins* 28:28 (24 December 1998), 489–493. Note on p. 492.

77 *The Dogmatic Constitution on the Church – Lumen Gentium*, §22, Austin Garvey (trans.) (London: Catholic Truth Society, 1965), p. 33.

78 See Canon 331 of the *Code of Canon Law*, which states in pertinent part: "in virtue of his office he enjoys supreme, full, immediate and universal ordinary power in the Church, which he can always freely exercise." "Ordinary" does not mean here what it means in its conventional sense; here "ordinary" means by virtue of the office and is not delegated by some human power.

79 A valuable resource may be found in the anthology of modern papal writings on war and peace edited by the Benedictine monks of Solesmes (France): Moines de Solesmes (eds.),

Les Enseignements Pontificaux: La Paix Internationale, vol. 1: *La guerre moderne* (Tournai: Desclée & Cie, 1956).

80 "Pontifical Brief on International Peace, June 11, 1911 from Pope Pius X to the Apostolic Delegate in the United States of America," *American Journal of International Law* 5:3, Supplement: Official Documents (July 1911), 214–216.

81 His first encyclical letter, *Ad Beatissimi Apostolorum*, was issued on 1 November 1914, the first year of his pontificate. In it, he referred to the European conflagration as a "useless slaughter." He concluded this encyclical with an exhortation that he vigorously attempted to implement until his death in 1922: "we implore with our most earnest prayers the end of this most disastrous war for the sake of human society and for the sake of the Church; for human society, so that when peace shall have been concluded, it may go forward in every form of true progress; for the Church of Jesus Christ, that freed at length from all impediments it may go forth and bring comfort and salvation even to the most remote parts of the earth." §30 in Carlen (ed.), *The Papal Encyclicals 1903–1939*, p. 150.

82 Pius XI briefly served as Papal Nuncio to Poland from 1919 to 1921 when he was made Archbishop of Milan.

83 See later in this chapter, the first selection from Pope Pius XI (his allocution to the College of Cardinals, 24 December 1930)..

84 *Summi Pontificatus*, §106 in Carlen (ed.), *The Papal Encyclicals 1939–1958*, p. 19.

85 Ibid., p. 20.

86 See below, this chapter, Pope Pius's allocution to Italian University Students in Catholic Action (1941).

87 Pope Paul VI, "Message for the Celebration of the Day of Peace," 1 January 1972; available at http://www.vatican.va/holy_father/paul_vi/messages/peace/documents/hf_p-vi_mes_19711208_v-world-day-for-peace_en.html.

88 Pope Pius XII, "Christmas Broadcast to the Whole World, December 24, 1942," in Koenig (ed.), *Principles for Peace*, p. 803.

89 Pope Pius XII, "Christmas Message of 1944, Democracy and Peace," in Rev. Gerald C. Treacy, S.J. (disc.), *Four Great Encyclicals of Pope Pius XII* (New York: Deus Books / Paulist Press, 1961), pp. 194–208, §§60 and 67 on pp. 202, 204.

90 *Pacem in Terris*, §112 in Carlen (ed.), *The Papal Encyclicals 1958–1981*, p. 119.

91 *Pacem in Terris*, §111 in Carlen (ed.), *The Papal Encyclicals 1958– 981*, p. 119.

92 Pope Paul VI, "Address to United Nations Headquarters, 4 October 1965," in *Never Again War!*, p. 37.

93 Pope Paul VI, "Message for the Observance of a Day of Peace," 1 January 1968; available at http://www.vatican.va/holy_father/paul_vi/messages/peace/documents/hf_p-vi_mes_19671208_i-world-day-for-peace_en.html.

94 Pope John Paul II, "The 50th Anniversary of War's End in Europe," 8 May 1995, §9 in *Origins* 25:3 (1 June 1995), 33, 35–40. Note on pp. 36–37.

95 Pope John Paul II, "The 50th Anniversary of War's End in Europe," §9, pp. 36–37.

96 Pope John Paul II, "'The International Situation Today' – Address to Diplomatic Corps," *Origins* 32:33 (30 January 2003), 543–545. Citation on p. 543.

97 Archbishop Celestino Migliore, "Preventing a Possible War in Iraq," *Origins* 32:38 (6 March 2003), 625, 627. Citation on p. 625.

98 Pope Benedict XVI, "Address to the United Nations General Assembly," *Origins* 37:46 (1 May 2008), 747–750. Citation on p. 748.

99 Ibid., p. 749.

100 Pope Benedict XV, "*Pacem, Dei Munus Pulcherrimum* – Encyclical of Pope Benedict XV on Peace and Christian Reconciliation," 23 May 1920, in Carlen (ed.), *The Papal Encyclicals 1903–1939*, pp. 171–175. Citations on pp. 172–174.

101 Pope Pius XI, Allocution *Benedetto il Natale* to the College of Cardinals, 24 December 1930, in Koenig, *Principles for Peace*, pp. 395–396.

102 Pope Pius XII, "*Summi Pontificatus* – Encyclical of Pope Pius XII on the Unity of Human Society," 20 October 1939, in Carlen (ed.), *The Papal Encyclicals 1939–1958*, pp. 8–22. Citations on pp. 8, 15, 16, 19–20.

103 Pope Pius XII, "Allocution *Nei Tesori* to the Italian University Students in Catholic Action," in Koenig (ed.), *Principles for Peace*, pp. 717–718.

104 Pope Pius XII, "Christmas Broadcast to the Whole World, 24 December 1942," in Koenig (ed.), *Principles for Peace*, pp. 803–805.

105 Pope Pius XII, "Christmas Message of 1944 – Addressed to All People of the World on the Subject of Democracy and a Lasting Peace," in *Four Great Encyclicals of Pope Pius XII*, pp. 202, 203, 204.

106 Vincent A. Yzermans (ed.), *The Unwearied Advocate: Public Addresses of His Holiness Pope Pius XII* (St. Cloud, Minn.: Diocese of Saint Cloud, 1954), vol. 2, pp. 174–175.

107 Vincent A. Yzermans (ed.), *The Major Addresses of Pope Pius XII* (St. Paul, Minn.: North Central Publishing, 1961), pp. 124–125.

108 Pope John XXIII, "'*Pacem in Terris* – Encyclical on establishing universal peace in truth, justice, charity, and liberty,' 11 April 1963," in Carlen (ed.), *The Papal Encyclicals 1958–1981*, pp. 107–129. Citations on pp. 119, 120, 121.

109 Pope Paul VI, "Address to United Nations Headquarters, 4 October 1965," in *Never Again War!*, pp. 33–35, 37–39.

110 Pope Paul VI, "Message for the Observance of a Day of Peace," 1 January 1968; available at http://www.vatican.va/holy_father/paul_vi/messages/peace/documents/hf_p-vi_mes_19671208_i-world-day-for-peace_en.html.

111 Pope John Paul II, "Centesimus Annus – Encyclical on the 100th Anniversary of Rerum Novarum," *Origins* 21:1 (16 May 1991), 1, 3–24. Citations from pp. 8–9, 20.

112 Pope John Paul II, "The 50th Anniversary of War's End in Europe," pp. 36, 37.

113 Pope John Paul II, "'Peace on Earth to Those Whom God Loves': Message for the World Day of Peace," 1 January 2000, in *Origins* 29:28 (23 December 1999), 449, 451–455. Citations from pp. 452–453.

114 Pope John Paul II, "World Day of Peace Message 2002: No Peace without Justice, No Justice without Forgiveness," in *Origins* 31:28 (20 December 2001), 461, 463–466.

115 Pope John Paul II, "The International Situation Today," §4, p. 544.

116 Archbishop Celestino Migliore, "Preventing a Possible War in Iraq," pp. 625, 627.

117 Pope John Paul II, "Message for the 2004 World Day of Peace," *Origins* 33:29 (1 January 2004), 489, 491–494. Citations from pp. 491–493.

118 Pope Benedict XVI, "Address to the United Nations General Assembly," *Origins* 37:46 (1 May 2008), 747–750. Citations from pp. 747, 748–749.

119 See, e.g., the intervention of Archbishop Celestino Migliore, Permanent Observer of the Holy See to the United Nations during the General Debate of the General Assembly on 29 September 2008 on the matter of the "responsibility to protect"; available at http://www.holyseemission.org/29Sep2008.html. See also his 14 October 2008 intervention at the 63rd Session of the UN General Assembly on "The Rule of Law at the National and International Levels"; available at http://www.holyseemission.org/13Oct2008.html.

120 Pope Francis, "Letter to H. E. Mr. Vladimir Putin, President of the Russian Federation, on the Occasion of the G20 St. Petersburg Summit," 4 September 2013; available at http://www.vatican.va/holy_father/francesco/letters/2013/documents/papa-francesco_20130904_putin-g20._en.html.

121 Pope Francis, "Words to the Vigil of Prayer for Peace," 9 September 2013; available at http://www.vatican.va/holy_father/francesco/homilies/2013/documents/papa-francesco_20130907_veglia-pace_en.html.

122 *Decree Concerning the Pastoral Office of Bishops in the Church – Christus Dominus*, Proclaimed by His Holiness, Pope Paul VI, 28 October 1965; available at http://www.vatican.va/archive/hist_councils/ii_vatican_council/documents/vat-ii_decree_19651028_christus-dominus_en.html.

123 *Christus Dominus*, Chapter 3, "Concerning Bishops Cooperating for the Common Good of Many Churches," I. Synods, Councils and Especially Episcopal Conferences, §38.1.

124 This has proven to be a controversial claim. For discussion and references, see Gregory M. Reichberg, "Is There a 'Presumption against War' in Aquinas's Ethics?," in Syse and Reichberg, *Ethics, Nationalism, and Just War*, pp. 72–98.

125 U.S. Catholic Bishops, "The Pastoral Letter on War and Peace, the Challenge of Peace: God's Promise and Our Response," *Origins* 13:1 (19 May 1983), 1–32. Citations on pp. 2–4, 10–11, 15.

126 U.S. Catholic Bishops, "The Harvest of Justice Is Sown in Peace," *Origins* 23:26 (December 1993), pp. 449, 451–464. Citations on pp. 453–454.

127 Joint Pastoral Letter of the West German Bishops, "Out of Justice, Peace," in James V. Schall, S.J. (ed. and introduction), *Out of Justice, Peace and Winning the Peace* (San Francisco, Calif.: Ignatius Press, 1984), pp. 33–100. Citations from pp. 53, 68, 96.

128 Joint Pastoral Letter of the French Bishops, "Winning the Peace," in Schall (ed.), *Out of Justice, Peace and Winning the Peace*, pp. 101–120. Citations on pp. 105, 109–111.

129 Basil Cardinal Hume, "Appendix – Towards Nuclear Morality," in Schall (ed.), *Out of Justice, Peace and Winning the Peace*, pp. 121–124. Citations on pp. 121–122, 122–123.

130 See, e.g., Pope John Paul II, Message to the United Nations, 7 June 1982, "In current conditions 'deterrence' based on balance, certainly not as an end in itself but as a step on the way toward a progressive disarmament, may still be judged morally acceptable. Nonetheless in order to ensure peace, it is indispensable not to be satisfied with this minimum which is always susceptible to the real danger of explosion." §8.

131 Final Report of the Extraordinary Synod, 7 December 1985, II, B, a, n. 4: *Enchiridion Vaticanum*, vol. 9, p. 1758, n. 1797.

132 Pope John Paul II, "Apostolic Constitution *Fidei Depositum* on the Publication of the Catechism of the Catholic Church Prepared Following the Second Vatican Ecumenical Council"; available at http://www.vatican.va/archive/ccc_css/archive/catechism/apos-cons.htm.

133 *Catechism of the Catholic Church*, §§2302–2317.

134 *The Pastoral Constitution on the Church in the Modern World – Gaudium et Spes*, pp. 80–85.

SELECT BIBLIOGRAPHY

Araujo, Robert John, S.J., and John A. Lucal, S.J., *Papal Diplomacy and the Quest for Peace: The Vatican and International Organizations from the Early Years to the League of Nations* (Naples, Fla.: Sapientia Press, 2004).

Araujo, Robert John, S.J., and John A. Lucal, S.J., *Papal Diplomacy and the Quest for Peace: The United Nations from Pius XII to Paul VI* (Philadelphia: Saint Joseph's University Press, 2010).

Brundage, James A., *The Crusades, Holy War and Canon Law* (Burlington, Vt.: Ashgate, 1991).

Eppstein, John (ed.), *The Catholic Tradition of the Law of Nations* (Washington, D.C.: Carnegie Endowment for International Peace, 1935).

Erdmann, Carl, *The Origin of the Idea of Crusade* (original German: *Die Entstehung des Kreuzzugsgedankens*), M. W. Baldwin and W. Goffart, trans. (Princeton, N.J.: Princeton University Press, 1977).

Haggenmacher, Peter, *Grotius et la doctrine de la guerre juste* (Paris: PUF, 1983).

Joblin, Joseph, *L'Église et la guerre* (Paris: Desclée de Brouwer, 1988).

Kreider, Alan, "Military Service in the Church Orders," *Journal of Religious Ethics* 31:3 (2003), 415–442.

Madden, Thomas F. (ed.), *The Crusades: The Essential Readings* (Oxford: Blackwell Publishing, 2008).

Moines de Solesmes (eds.), *Les Enseignements Pontificaux*, vol. I, *La Paix Internationale* (Paris: Desclée & Cie, 1956).

Musto, Ronald G., *The Catholic Peace Tradition* (Maryknoll, N.Y.: Orbis Books, 1986).

Regout, Robert, *La doctrine de la guerre juste de saint Augustin à nos jours d'après les théologiens et les canonistes catholiques* (Paris: A. Pedone, 1935).

Reichberg, Gregory M., "Discontinuity in Catholic Just War? From Aquinas to the Contemporary Magisterium," *Nova & Vetera* (English Edition) 10:4 (2012), 1073–1097.

Reichberg, Gregory M., Henrik Syse, and Endre Begby (eds.), *The Ethics of War: Classic and Contemporary Readings* (Oxford: Blackwell Publishing, 2006).

Russell, Frederick H., *The Just War in the Middle Ages* (Cambridge: Cambridge University Press, 1975).

Swift, Louis J. (ed. and trans.), *The Early Fathers on Law and Military Service* (Wilmington, Del.: Michael Glazier, 1983).

3

Eastern Orthodox Christianity
Yuri Stoyanov

Eastern Orthodoxy represents one of the three principal branches of Christianity and the second largest Christian denomination. With its historical connections with the Eastern Roman/Byzantine Empire, the traditional and contemporary areas of its greatest spread and influence are in Eastern Europe, Russia, the Eastern Mediterranean, and the Near East. It represents a decentralized church organization of autocephalous (administratively independent) doctrinally and liturgically united ecclesial bodies. Among these ecclesial bodies the Ecumenical Patriarch of Constantinople has the honor of titular primacy, while several of them function in effect as national churches. The continuity of Eastern Orthodoxy with the apostolic church through the process of apostolic succession is strongly emphasized, with faith and worship being delineated and regulated by its adherence to and recognition of only the decisions and canons of the first seven ecumenical councils (325–787 CE).

Introduction

The provenance, historical trajectories, and modern transformations of Eastern Orthodox cultures vis-à-vis the ethics of war display both significant analogies and dissimilarities to the respective Western Christian developments but have received much less in-depth and comprehensive treatment. However, in the last three decades some intense debates have evolved among Eastern Orthodox theologians, Byzantinists, and historians of the modern period centered on the Eastern Orthodox Churches' and cultures' traditional and current stances on the legitimization and conduct of just, justifiable, and "holy" warfare, as well as on pacifism and nonresistance to violence. These debates have ranged from the scriptural and patristic substructures of these stances to their more recent reformulations and political instrumentalizations in modern ideologized, "nationalized," and reformist trends in Eastern Orthodox thought and societies.

The study of the Eastern Orthodox perspectives on the morality and justifiability of warfare, the principal stages of their evolution, and figures involved in their conceptualization and elaboration is still hampered by the fact that a good of deal of the relevant late antique, medieval, and early modern material has been neither edited and published nor translated into modern Western European languages and thus remains not sufficiently accessible and little known, not only to the general public but also to the larger scholarly audience.[1] While comprising predominantly texts already available in English translations, it is hoped that the present selection of sources will provide an informative and balanced picture of the normative and influential Eastern Orthodox perspectives on the nature and laws of war, as they evolved in diverse religio-historical contexts. It is also hoped that this selection will usefully complement the Orthodox resource book on war, peace, and nationalism published in 1999[2] in representing classical and modern theological, juridical, religio-philosophical, and ideological discourses on the problems of warfare in Eastern Orthodoxy as well as stimulate further efforts to gather and publish relevant source material essential for further study.

Similarly with Catholic and Protestant Christianity, the New Testament sources of the traditional approaches to the ethics of war and normativity of peace in Eastern Orthodoxy can be traced to the Gospel passages regarding the recourse to armed force and violence as well as to Christ's moral precepts and their underlying pacific perspectives (Matthew 5–7, 26:52, Luke 2:14, 3:14, 6:29, etc.). The pronouncements and exhortations of the early Church Fathers[3] on the questions of war, violence, nonretaliation, and nonviolent martyrdom, reflecting the prevalent antimilitarism and pacific views of the early Church, formed another authoritative resource of texts that, with its plurality of voices, had been continuously drawn on in early medieval as well as modern Eastern Orthodox thought in this sphere. The early Christian ideal of the normativity and affirmation of peace in all its dimensions, from the peace of the spirit to the peace among humans, as elaborated further during the patristic period, remained one of the preeminent themes and found some striking expressions in Eastern Orthodox theology, ethics, anthropology, hymnography, and hagiography.

As in Western Christianity the Old Testament accounts of righteous wars in the service of God in Deuteronomy, Numbers, Joshua, and the Maccabees provided a convenient normative source for justifying, sanctioning, and conducting warfare, especially in the sphere of imperial Byzantine political theology and the related Eastern Orthodox versions of rulership ideology, with their dependence on the Old Testament kingship models of Saul, David, and Solomon. Eastern Orthodoxy retained also the dichotomies and tensions between the notions of war and peace respectively in the Old and New Testament (which despite some evident continuities, differed in some important spheres), which were also reflected in the corresponding Old Testament–related imperial and more New Testament–based clerical attitudes to warfare in medieval Eastern Christendom.[4]

Apart from scriptural and patristic sources, early medieval Byzantine stances on warfare experienced also the formative impact of inherited Greco-Roman concepts, moral norms, and theorizing (including military manuals) concerning the legitimacy of and causes for resorting to military force, right conduct on the battlefield and in the wake of the cessation of the conflict, just and unjust wars, and so on. Some of these concepts such as self-defense and recovery of lost imperial territory and possessions entered imperial secular law books and collections such as the *Basilika* and *Epanagoge*.[5] The classical legacy of concepts and attitudes included the ever-influential Aristotelian precepts on the nature and morality of war and peace as the preferable condition and desired outcome of any warfare.

The process of the institutionalization of the Christian Church in the Roman Empire that began during the reign of Constantine the Great (306–337) led to various models of rapprochement between the imperial state and the church authorities. The newly developing consonance between the secular and ecclesiastical order in the sphere of the justification and sanctioning of warfare in some instances followed divergent trajectories in the West and East Roman Empire occasioned by the different evolution of church–state relations in the Latin West and Greek East. In the characteristic political and religious conditions in the Latin West St. Ambrose (ca. 339–397) and St. Augustine (354–430) were to lay the foundation of the medieval Catholic just war tradition. In the Greek East, adhering to a different corpus of patristic writings and a different model of relationships with the East Roman/Byzantine centralized imperial state and political theology, the Eastern Orthodox Church retained important elements from pre-Constantinian Christian pacific attitudes to war, its legitimation, and morality. In East Roman Christian/Byzantine culture and society these clerical attitudes coexisted with the inherited traditions of the pre-Christian just war tradition and the political and military needs of the imperial state, which preserved some central features of pre-Christian Roman military structures and ethos.

The Christian East Roman/Byzantine ideology of warfare was thus strongly indebted to the largely secular late Roman just war tradition but subjected it to an inevitable Christianization that began as early as the reign of Constantine. In the maturing Christianized version of this Byzantine ideology of warfare it was the divinely ordained mission of the Christian Romans (the new "chosen people") to safeguard Constantinople, seen as both the "New Rome" and the "New Jerusalem," and its single universal Christian empire, the "New Israel," against the encroachments of the new "barbarians": first pagans, in later periods Muslims, and, on occasion, West European Christians. Elaborating the notion of Byzantium representing the new "chosen people," Byzantine chroniclers, ideologues, and propagandists could depict Byzantine wars as God-guided campaigns against the new "infidel" enemies (often recognized as new versions of the Old Testament adversaries of the Israelites), in which successful warrior-emperors could be associated with the paradigmatic figures in the biblical Israelite God-commanded wars such as Moses, Joshua, or David.

The sources in the first section of the present anthology intend, therefore, to illustrate the synthesis and cross-fertilization of these diverse concepts, normative regulations, and imagery in the periods of the formation and maturing of imperial Christian ideology of warfare in Byzantium. The section includes extracts from Byzantine military manuals, with their Christian just war statements (acknowledging the "evil" or antinormative nature of war and the permissibility of defensive warfare) and emphasis on religious practices in the Byzantine army, imperial statements and military orations, as well as military religious services. While no evidence of a systematic attempt at formulating a just war theory coming from within the Byzantine Church has been unearthed as yet, the roots and precepts of the mature Byzantine just war theory developed by the imperial court and government are thus much easier to trace and categorize. Both more extensive and narrower categorizations of such just war theory have been proposed: in the former it can be defined as comprising generally five major types of justification of warfare: "self-defense," "recovery of lost territory," "breach of agreement," "averting a greater evil," and "pursuit of peace,"[6] most of which are indeed illustrated in the selected extracts.

As in Western Christendom, the responsibilities of the Eastern Orthodox Church in the practical spheres of medieval warfare were manifested in military religious services, the presence of military chaplains in the army, the celebration of Eucharistic liturgies in the field, the employment of Christian religious symbolism and relics for military purposes, prebattle blessings of standards and weapons, services for fallen soldiers, and thanksgiving ceremonies to commemorate victory.[7] At the same time, a series of rulings in Eastern Orthodox canon law unequivocally proscribe clerics and monks from bearing arms and taking part in any fighting or acts of violence, given the pacific nature of their vocation. While these canonic regulations made the nonparticipation of clergy and monks in warfare obligatory and unambiguous, throughout the medieval period a certain ambiguity persisted, in both canon law and Byzantine political military ideology, concerning the status of the Christian soldiers and whether their involvement in fighting on behalf of the Byzantine Empire could bring them spiritual recompense. Given their importance for understanding core notions and dichotomies in Byzantine clerical and secular attitudes regarding warfare and Christian soldiery, the principal statements in Eastern Orthodox canon law addressing these problems, beginning with those of St. Athansasios of Alexandria and St. Basil the Great, are reproduced in the present selection along with extracts from the debates that their pronouncements provoked.

During the pre-crusading period of the ninth and eleventh centuries when the first notions of absolution and heavenly rewards for fallen Christian soldiers were formulated by Pope Leo IV (847–855), Pope John (872–882), and Pope Leo IX (1049–1054),[8] the Eastern Orthodox Church by and large did not share the changing stances of Western Christendom on Christian involvement in warfare. Nonetheless, a conscious attempt to formulate a Christian just war theory and articulate the notion of a Christian military martyrdom can be discerned in a statement attributed to St. Constantine–Cyril the Philosopher (826/7–869), the celebrated missionary to the Slavs. This approach was not however affirmed or developed more systematically in the medieval period. With very few exceptions the mainstream followers of the Eastern Orthodox Church thought and practice, especially the ecclesiastical elites, remained opposed to the idea of Christian "military martyrdom" for fallen soldiers. At the same time, a number of assertions and allusions in Byzantine military manuals and services commemorating fallen soldiers indicate that vocabulary and imagery related to the notion of Byzantine Christian warriors receiving spiritual recompense for their fighting on behalf of Orthodoxy and their Christian brethren, including martyrdom status, was integrated into the military religious ideology evolving among the Byzantine military classes, becoming an important element of their distinctive lay piety. It is thus very likely that the imperial government attempted to foster and gain acceptance for such notions regarding the status of the Byzantine soldier in more cases and more energetically than the extant evidence suggests. Such developments can be detected especially in the Byzantine Anatolian frontier zones where the local church and hierarchs may have played some role in this process and where Byzantine troops and military formations continuously confronted the *ghazwa* warfare of advancing Turkoman groups from around the mid-eleventh century onward.[9] Moreover, in the evolution of the increasingly popular cult of military saints (such as St. George and St. Demetrius of Thessaloniki, widely adopted as patrons by the Byzantine military aristocracy), some of its earlier antiwarfare perspectives were tamed or neutralized. This shift arguably facilitated the development of its easier integration into Byzantine lay military piety.[10] Consequently, the extracts selected for the section on "Medieval Eastern Orthodox Perspectives on the Status of the Christian Soldier" intend to convey both the ecclesiastical perspectives in this sphere and those developed in Byzantine lay military piety, as they highlight the interrelations, interdependence, and occasional tensions between these two dominant trends in Byzantine ideologies of warfare.

From the First Crusade (1095–1099) onward, Byzantine theologians, canonists, and *literati* became acquainted with aspects of the war theology of the crusading movement, with its amalgamation of pilgrimage, just war, and religious (holy) war notions. However, no comparable innovations in canon law or theological attempts to systematize just and religious war doctrines were undertaken in high and late medieval Byzantium or the Byzantine Commonwealth of Southeastern Europe, Ukraine, and Russia. The debate on whether Byzantium ever conceptualized and put into practice elements (or a restricted version) of the ideology of the wars fought for ostensibly religious purposes in the contemporaneous Islamic and Western Christian worlds, which has developed among Byzantinists in the last twenty years or so,[11] has brought to the attention of a wider audience some important but less well-known evidence of the interrelations between Byzantine Orthodox Christianity, on the one hand, and Byzantine political and military ideology and warfare, on the other. The varying approaches to this religio-historic problem arise mainly from views concerning the applicability to the Eastern Orthodox world of criteria for wars fought with a religious rationale that had been voiced in medieval Western Christian and Islamic societies. The balance of argument and current state of evidence indicates that the religious elements and rhetoric present in the several Byzantine campaigns usually treated in this context were sporadic and not a consequence of a consistently and systematically developed ideology of religious war. It is also becoming increasingly evident that the Byzantine evidence should be treated on its own terms and within its own religio-political settings due to which, among other contrasts with the Latin West, the Byzantine Church entirely delegated the justification and practice of warfare to the secular imperial government and thus did not promulgate war or release warlike declarations. With this problematic finally receiving the attention it deserves, some of the extracts in the two sections on Byzantine ideology of warfare (such as the religiously charged orations of Herakleios or the texts dwelling on the spiritual recompense for fallen soldiers) have obvious implications for the pro and contra arguments in the above debate.

The classical Byzantine synthesis between inherited religious and political pacific models, the late Roman just war tradition, and some innovations in the theory and practice of warfare created an ambivalent and flexible system of nuanced attitudes to war in which various compromises were achieved to neutralize the inherent tensions between the various elements. The elaboration of more systematic theories for the religious and philosophical justification of war was apparently not seen as necessary; similarly, the *jus in bello* regulations in Byzantine military treatises often largely reproduced earlier Greco-Roman models. This synthesis was well suited to the religious and secular needs of an imperial state that viewed itself as the sole "holy and Orthodox universal empire"; it seemed sufficiently appropriate also to the Orthodox monarchies and principalities that emerged in the Byzantine Commonwealth in the Balkans, Ukraine, and Russia.

Russian secular and religious concepts of just war began to crystallize early in the history of Orthodox Russia. Defensive war was, as a rule, seen as justifiable, as were military conflicts aimed at regaining territories unjustly lost to an invader – they could be seen accordingly as wars of liberation. These notions of just war were intertwined with a commitment to the inviolability of frontiers and the belief that war represented the judgment of God. In the period following the beginning of the Christianization of Kievan Rus' in 988, religious components in the conflicts that arose between medieval Russian Christian princes and the nomadic Turkic Kumans (illustrated in the present anthology with several extracts from contemporaneous Russian historical records) and other Turkic nomadic and settled peoples seem largely comparable to those present in other medieval Christian ideologies of warfare, especially in the Byzantine version. As in Byzantium, such religious elements were not of central importance in justifications for engaging in the armed conflicts that preimperial Russian military power subsequently waged against the Mongols, Kazan, Astrakhan, and Crimean Tatars, as well as Russia's western Catholic neighbors. At the same time, on occasion Muscovite rulers could seek religious justification, principally the defense and protection of Orthodox peoples under "alien" rule, for military offensives against Catholic and Muslim powers – as exemplified by Grand Prince Ivan III's (1462–1505) campaign against Catholic Lithuania in 1500 and Tsar Ivan IV the Terrible's (1533–1584) offensive against the Muslim Kazan Khanate in 1552.

In the sphere of Russian military religious ideology, lay pacifism, as exemplified by the cult of the passion-bearer prince-martyrs of Kievan Rus', Saints Boris and Gleb (d. 1015), coexisted with the cult or high renown for warrior-princes, praised as defenders of Orthodoxy and subsequently declared saints, such as St. Alexander Nevskii (1236–1263, proclaimed a saint in 1547) and St. Dmitrii Donskoi (1359–1389, canonized as a saint in 1988). These two pious warrior-princes pursued their military feats in the period of Tatar Golden Horde's suzerainty over the Russian lands (1236–1452), during which the Russian Church played the role of the preeminent carrier of the cultural heritage and evolving ethno-religious consciousness in Russia. In the early stages of this era the Russian Church remained generally pacific, in harmony with prevailing Byzantine clerical attitudes of the period. But with the onset of the decline and fragmentation of the Golden Horde, Muscovite high ecclesiastical circles became crucially involved in the formulation and promotion of a militant anti-Tatar religio-political ideology. Coupled with intensely anti-Muslim rhetoric, this ideology is represented in the present anthology with several ecclesiastical and royal pronouncements made before and after the Russian conquest of Kazan in 1552. As a number of historians have approached the Kazan campaign as a crusade-like venture against a clear-cut "infidel" enemy,[12] these statements deserve closer critical scrutiny in the framework of earlier Christian anti-Muslim war efforts with an analogous religious justification and a comparable level of royal and clerical involvement in the process.

In the aftermath of the Ottoman conquests in Anatolia and the Balkans and the integration of these regions into the new Ottoman version of the Islamic caliphate in the fourteenth and fifteenth centuries, the Orthodox Churches in these regions, along with the Constantinople patriarchate, found themselves in completely new religious and polit-ical circumstances. In the wake of the fall of Constantinople to the Ottomans in 1453, an evolving Russian religio-political ideology came to claim the imperial leadership of the Orthodox Christian Commonwealth through the already adopted notion of Muscovy as "The New Israel" and the idea of "Moscow the Third Rome," which enjoyed a gradual, if not methodical elaboration.

This new Russian version of imperial Orthodox Christianity inevitably developed some new perspectives on the moral and religious issues of war and peace and legitimate frameworks for engaging in armed conflict. But the inherited and newly emerging con-cepts in this sphere were not systematically developed even in the period when Russian military thinking came under strong Western influence during and after the reforms of Peter the Great (1682–1725). This influence is particularly visible in the first original Russian tract on international law, written in 1717 by the prominent diplomat Baron Petr Shafirov, who discussed the just causes of Russia's war against Sweden (1701–1721). Extracts from this tract are reproduced below. Increasing Russian military involvement in Europe during the eighteenth and nineteenth centuries did not lead to further major developments in Russian military thought on conceptual guidelines related to *casus belli* issues and *jus in bello* regulations. Napoleon's invasion of Russia in 1812 enhanced belief in the defense of the homeland as the highest form of just war and the ultimate patriotic duty, notions articulated also in some of the orations of the influential theologian St. Filaret, Metropolitan of Moscow (1821–1867, canonized in 1994).

Russia's role as a protector of Eastern Orthodoxy in the Ottoman Empire was recog-nized in a peace treaty that was signed between the two imperial powers in 1774. This treaty was cited repeatedly in Russian foreign policy, providing legal grounds to inter-vene through diplomatic pressure or militarily in the turbulent processes that led to the formation of the post-Ottoman nation-states in Southeastern Europe. Russian inter-ventionism in the Balkans and the conflicts marking these state-formation processes coincided with the rise of Russian Slavophilism, European Pan-Slavism, and its Russian versions in the ideological, political, and religious spheres. Nineteenth-century Russo-Ottoman conflicts (both political and military), as well as the wide-ranging popularity and emotional appeal of Slavophilism and Pan-Slavism, generated discourses dwelling on the religious justification of military offensives against the Ottoman empire (repre-sented below by a selection of pertinent extracts). The conceptualization and spread of Tolstoiian pacifism from the 1880s onward provoked powerful opposition among Russian ecclesiastical and religiously oriented intellectual circles. This was accompanied by reassessments of Christian just war traditions and the morality of war – a process that continued into the interwar period and is illustrated here by an assortment of excerpts from writings exemplifying these Tolstoiian, anti-Tolstoiian, and just war reappraisal discourses.

Concurrent with the intensification of Russian interventionism in the late Ottoman Balkans the respective Orthodox Churches, after having acted during the Ottoman era as a nationally and culturally unifying force, inevitably played a crucial role in the forma-tion of the corresponding national ideologies. Orthodox ecclesiastical elites were directly involved in the nation/state-building processes and often in the legitimization of the mili-tary conflicts that accompanied these processes in the post-Ottoman Orthodox-majority states. The ecclesiastical, political, and national spheres in the Orthodox world in Southeastern Europe continued to merge and interact profoundly and unpredictably in the tense years preceding World War I and the equally tense interwar period, generating blends of nationalism, militarism, and Orthodoxy, which are represented in the current anthology by a small selection of excerpts from contemporaneous sources.

A selection of extracts from the sermons and pronouncements of leading Russian ecclesiastical figures from the period of the Russian Revolution (and the onset of Bolshevik antichurch campaigns) and World War II are intended to demonstrate some important continuities with preceding Russian and earlier Orthodox discourses on the legitimacy and morality of warfare, yet employed under the different circumstances of first a civil war and then a national defensive war.

Following World War II nearly all European Eastern Orthodox Churches (apart from the Ecumenical Patriarchate in Istanbul and the autocephalous Orthodox Churches of Greece and Cyprus) were forced to function and survive in the framework of the militantly secularist and repressive Communist regimes of Eastern Europe. After initial stages of anti-Church repression, Communist governments became aware of the potential of using the national Orthodox Churches as a tool of their foreign policy through the existing network of international Orthodoxy as well as the World Council of Churches and similar international ecclesiastical institutions. A small selection of excerpts from this period illustrates the participation of these Orthodox Churches in international ecclesiastical and lay peace initiatives during the Cold War period, a participation that the respective Communist governments endeavored to supervise and control.

The collapse of Communism in Eastern Europe in 1989 marked the beginning of a new period for the revitalization of the Orthodox Churches and the restoration of their traditional place in the social and religious life of the region. However, the military conflicts of Yugoslav Succession in the 1990s posed some obvious challenges to international Orthodoxy. The various meetings, initiatives, statements, and appeals organized and hosted by the Ecumenical Patriarchate and other Orthodox Churches in response to these and other contemporary conflicts intensified the debate on contemporary challenges to Eastern Orthodox views on the ethics of war and peace. Inevitably, the debate developed in the framework of newly actualized issues such as interreligious violence, ethnic cleansing, and the justification of humanitarian intervention.[13]

Against the backdrop of these developments and the rising prominence of a morality of war problematic in inter-Orthodox and ecumenical dialogues (as well as increasing contacts with institutions related to the implementation of the League of Nations Covenant, the U.N. Charter, etc.) in 2003 the ecumenical patriarch of Constantinople, Bartholomew, emphatically reiterated traditional pacific Eastern Orthodox patristic and clerical precepts on warfare. Meanwhile, after a decade of redefining its new models of relations with the state, and indeed the military, in 2000 the Jubilee Council of Russian Bishops issued a statement of faith that contains a section entitled "War and Peace." This section contains a systematic and up-to-date Orthodox reappraisal of the Christian just war tradition and its relevance to modernity. This chapter concludes with excerpts from these statements by Bartholomew and the Russian Bishops, in light of their importance for understanding the dispute on the existence or nonexistence of a just war tradition in Eastern Orthodoxy among Orthodox theologians and ecclesiastics.[14]

It is hoped that this chapter will broaden the study of the principal currents in Eastern Orthodox perspectives on warfare and their classification.[15] A related aim has been to show that the long-standing neglect of the problematic of nonmonolithic plurality of Eastern Orthodox attitudes to warfare[16] is undeserved. Further exploration of the theological, philosophical, and ideological roots of this Eastern Orthodox plurality will undoubtedly contribute to a better understanding of the diversity of Christian approaches to war and peace making. Likewise, it will bring to light their modern relevance and applicability to crucial problems in the ethics of war in the twenty-first century.

From Byzantium to the Rise of Muscovy

Imperial Christian Ideology of Warfare in Medieval Byzantium

Byzantine Military Treatises

In the late East Roman Christian/early Byzantine empire the formation and evolution of Christian theologies and general socio-cultural notions of war and peace inevitably developed under the impact of prevailing contemporaneous Church attitudes (which maintained some pre-Constantinian pacifistic perspectives in this sphere) and the inherited traditions of the political-military ideology of the Roman imperial state (which included core elements of the pre-Christian just war tradition of Greco-Roman antiquity). This progressively Christianized "just war" tradition (understood as intended to defend imperial territories, regain lost territories, and protect imperial subjects) became a fundamental part of Byzantine imperial ideology, closely interwoven with the reinterpreted and actualized Romano-Byzantine paradigms of God-guidedness in battle and imperial triumphalism, as manifested in the gradual Christianization of the traditional Roman victory parades.

Such Christianization of the inherited Roman political-military ideology can be discerned in Byzantine manuals such as the *Strategikon*, attributed to Emperor Maurice (582–602); the *Taktika*, ascribed to Emperor Leo VI the Wise (886–912); *Praecepta Militaria*, ascribed to Emperor Nikephoros II Phokas (963–969); and other texts belonging to this genre.[17] Drawing heavily on earlier Hellenistic and Roman authorities (highlighting thus the continuity of the tradition of tactical and strategic manuals from Greco-Roman antiquity to the Byzantine Middle Ages), these manuals inevitably contain much valuable material and advice reflecting the evolving Byzantine Christian stances on warfare. In the sphere of legitimization of warfare it is certainly important that an ancient and influential military tract such as Onasander's *Strategikos*, continuously used as a source for the medieval Byzantine military treatises, emphasizes how warfare should be motivated by a just cause and likewise that it should be waged justly – echoes of which are perceptible in the corresponding, more elaborate just war statements in one of the classical and authoritative Byzantine military tracts, the *Taktika*, ascribed to Leo VI.

From: Onasander, *Strategikos*, 10 (first century CE)[18]

It is most important that the cause of a war must be wisely constituted, and that it be evident to all that the war is being waged justly.

From: Leo VI, *Taktika*, Epilogue 169
(late ninth/early tenth century CE)[19]

Certainly justice must be at the beginning of every action. More than other actions, the beginnings of war must be just. Not only must it be just but the war must be conducted with prudence. For then God will become benevolent and will fight along with our armies. The men will be more enthusiastic, holding the shield of justice before them, with the realization that they are not initiating injustice but are warding off those committing unjust acts.

From: Leo VI, *Taktika*, 2.49–50[20]

For we have always welcomed peace, both for our subjects and for the barbarians, through Christ, God and ruler of all, if the foreigners enclosed within their own bounds are content, professing no injustice, while you yourself (the general) with-hold your hand from them, sprinkling the earth neither with foreign nor with our own blood. . . . But if the foe is not sensible, and himself commences the injustice, then indeed there is a just cause present – an unjust war having been begun by the enemy – to undertake war against them with good courage and with eagerness, since they furnish the causes, raising unjust hands against our subjects. So take courage, for you have the God of righteousness as a help, and taking up the fight on behalf of your brethren you will achieve a complete victory.

From: Leo VI, *Taktika*, Epilogue 14, 16[21]

14. . . . Do not act unjustly or initiate an unjust war. Do not launch unjust attacks or pillaging raids against people who have done you no wrong. Live in piety but also, as far as it depends on you, live in peace with your enemy. . . .

16 The belief that one is not acting unjustly but is being treated unjustly will bring [you] the Divinity as your general and leader, and you will be compelled to believe that God has obligated himself to bring a just war to a good conclusion, and an unjust one to the contrary.

Combining religious and secular notions, these just war statements in Leo VI's *Taktika* thus uphold the Christian ideal of the normativity of peace. Defensive warfare is legitimized only in response to hostilities unjustly initiated by imperial adversaries. In its prologue the tract declares that peace should be sought first and foremost. But should the peace be broken by warfare (whose origin is attributed to the devil), a defensive response will be necessary, thereby ensuring by military means the security and safety of those who have been attacked, and the subsequent reestablishment of peace.

From: Leo VI, *Taktika*, Prologue 4[22]

For honored by the image and word of God, all men ought to embrace peace and foster love for one another instead of taking up murderous weapons in their hands to use against their own people. But since the devil, the killer of men from the beginning, the enemy of our race, has made use of sin to bring men to the point of waging war against their own kind, it becomes entirely necessary for men to wage war making use of contrivances of the devil, developed through men and, without flinching, to take their stand against those nations that want war. They must then make provision for their security by military means, employing them to defend themselves against the onslaughts of the enemy, to take action against them, and to make them suffer what they may well deserve. . . . With everyone embracing his own safety, peace will be cherished by all and will become a way of life.

In Leo VI's *Taktika* war is defined thus as a necessary evil. A similar affirmation of peace as the archetypal and desirable norm and war as "a great evil" and even "the worst of all evils" is clearly articulated in another well-known Byzantine military tract, *Peri Strategikes* (*De Re Strategica*). In it, defensive war is considered a legitimate reaction against attacks that had been unleashed by Byzantium's enemies.

From: *Peri Strategikes* (*De Re Strategica*), 4:9–14 (sixth century CE)[23]

I know well that war is a great evil and the worst of all evils. But since our enemies clearly look upon the shedding of our blood as one of their basic duties and the height of virtue, and since each one must stand up for his own country and his own people with word, pen, and deed, we have decided to write about strategy. By putting it into practice we shall be able not only to resist our enemies but even to conquer them.

The articulation of this Christian rhetoric on war and peace in the framework of military strategy included the prerequisite, as asserted in Leo VI's *Taktika* and the *Strategikon* ascribed to Maurice, that the army commander's military ethics should be ruled by the love of God and justice, which would bring him divine favor and victory during his campaign.

From: Maurice, *Strategikon*, Prologue (late sixth/early seventh century CE)[24]

First, we urge upon the general that his most important concern be the love of God and justice; building on these, he should strive to win the favor of God, without which it is impossible to carry out any plan, however well devised it may seem, or to overcome any enemy, however weak he may be thought. For all things are ruled by the providence of God. . . . Armed with the favor of God and, without pausing to rest, employing his tactical and strategical skills, he manages the army entrusted to him with confidence and is able to counter the various machinations of the enemy.

From: Maurice, *Strategikon*, 8.2[25]

Before getting into danger, the general should worship God. When he does get into danger, then, he can with confidence pray to God as a friend.

From: Leo VI, *Taktika* 2:22–23[26]

22. Before everything else, O general … be concerned about the love of God and righteousness in such manner that you constantly have God before your eyes. Fear him. Love him with all your heart and all your soul…. Keep his commandments and, in turn, you will receive his favor….

23. For you must realize that, apart from God's favor, it is not possible to bring any plan to a successful conclusion, however intelligent you may seem to be; it is not possible to overcome the enemy, however weak they may be thought. Everything lies in the providence of God….

From: Leo VI *Taktika*, Epilogue 73[27]

And so, it is always necessary for you, O General, in a fitting, dutiful way, to devote yourself to prayer to God and to observe his commandments…. By so doing you will receive salvation and victory from above in Christ the true God and eternal Emperor of all….

The need to plead for divine help and favor in warfare remains thus an important theme in the Christian just war tradition articulated in Byzantine military manuals. Apart from conveying in general the *jus ad bellum* regulations of this evolving tradition, as well as specifying to some extent its *jus in bello* guidelines, these Byzantine military treatises do not aim to develop in greater depth a theory addressing more general questions raised by the need for a Christian justification of warfare. But as practical manuals dealing with the reality of warfare, they dwell in some detail on the religious practices that were prescribed in Byzantine military camps. These range from prebattle blessing of standards and Eucharistic liturgies to religious burials of fallen warriors, as well as the related religious duties of soldiers and priests.

From: Maurice's *Strategikon*, 2.18[28]

[P]rayers should be said in camp on the actual day of battle before anyone goes out the gate. All, led by the priests, the general, and the other officers, should recite the "Kyrie eleison" (Lord have mercy) for some time in unison. Then, in hopes of success, each meros* should shout the "Nobiscum Deus" (God is with us) three times as it marches out of camp.

From: Maurice's *Strategikon*, 7.17[29]

Whether the bandon† or tagma‡ is in service with the rest of the army or is camping someplace by itself, the "Trisagion"§ must be sung, and the other customary

---

* Military divison.
† Basic military unit.
‡ Military unit of regiment size.
§ The "Thrice-Holy" prayer.

practices observed, early in the morning before any other duty and again in the evening after supper and the dismissal.

From: Leo VI, *Taktika*, 14.1[30]

1. ... O general, before all else, we enjoin upon you that on the day of battle your army should be free from sin. The night before, the priests are to offer fervent prayers of intercession. Everyone should be sanctified and so, by words and deeds, they should be convinced that they have the help of God.

From: Leo VI, *Taktika* 13.1[31]

A day or two before combat, the tourmarchs* should see that the standards are blessed by the priests and then present them to the standard-bearers of the tagmata.

From: Leo VI, *Taktika* 16.11[32]

11. Show particular concern for the burial of the dead.... Reverence for those who have died is always good and holy. It is especially necessary in the case of those who have fallen in battle, for it is with them that piety must manifest itself.

From: *Praecepta Militaria*, 4.106–120 (ca. 963–969 CE)[33]

As the enemy draws near, the entire contingent of the host, every last one of them, must say the invincible prayer proper to Christians, "Lord Jesus Christ, our God, have mercy on us, Amen," and in this way let them begin their advance against the enemy.... Have the signal given to them either by trumpet or another instrument for them to repeat the same prayer at the signal's end, "Lord Jesus Christ, our God have mercy on us," and, "Come to the aid of us Christians, making us worthy to rise up and fight to the death for our faith and our brethren by fortifying and strengthening our souls, our hearts, and our whole body, the mighty Lord of battles, incomparable in power, through the intercession of the Mother of God Who bore Thee, and of all the saints, Amen."

Imperial Statements and Addresses

Statements and addresses attributed to Byzantine emperors reveal important (mainly secular) aspects of the Byzantine ideology of warfare. However, the ultimatum that, according to Anna Komnene's *Alexiad*, Emperor Alexios I Komnenos (1081–1118) delivered to the Seljuk Sultan Malik Shah, demonstrates that in such instances traditional secular concerns such as the inviolability of imperial frontiers could be combined with

---

* Byzantine military commanders in charge of a "tourma" (military detachment).

religiously motivated aims such as a demand for a halt in military aggression against Christian communities, as clearly articulated in the following text.

From: Anna Komnene (1083–1153), *Alexiad*, 15.6.5[34]

"If you are willing," he said, "to yield to the authority of Rome and to put an end to your raids on the Christians, you will enjoy favors and honor, living in freedom for the rest of your lives on lands set aside for you. I refer to the lands where you used to dwell before Romanus Diogenes became emperor and before he met the sultan in battle – an unfortunate and notorious clash which ended in the Roman's defeat and capture. It would be wise, therefore, to choose peace rather than war, to refrain from crossing the frontiers of the Empire and to be content with your own territories. The advice I give is in your interests.... On the other hand, if you reject it, you can be sure of this: I will exterminate your race."

Pre-Battle Military Orations

Pre-or postbattle orations delivered by (or on behalf of) Byzantine emperors or army commanders[35] also reveal much about the Christian ideology and justification of warfare that supported the Byzantine military efforts, especially against non-Christian adversaries. The first example of such a speech, attributed to the Roman army commander Justinian (supposedly delivered during Byzantine-Sasanian hostilities in 576) conflates just war with anti-Persian and anti-Zoroastrian rhetoric to highlight the contrasts between Christianity and the Persian belligerent "false religion" and its "unjust altars." Significantly, the oration introduces the notion of higher, heavenly recompense for the East Roman soldiers.

From: Theophylaktos Simokattes, *History*, 3.13.13–20 (early seventh century CE)[36]

The Romans have hired Justice as an ally, since they have once again sought peace; the Medes [Persians] have marshaled Justice in opposition to themselves, since they abhor peace virtually always and honor belligerence like an auspicious god. Ours is not a false religion, nor have we set up spurious gods as leaders ... we do not do obeisance to a god that turns to ashes, who is now ablaze but is soon not even visible; smoke and fuel do not constitute religion, but their fading proves their falsehood. The barbarian exults in cheerful circumstances, but success is unaccustomed to remain stable when it ascends unjust altars. Injustice is often successful, but is also turned toward destruction.... Today angels are recruiting you and are recording the souls of the dead, providing for them not a corresponding recompense, but one that infinitely exceeds in the weight of the gift.

The second selection of prebattle orations represents exhortations attributed to the Emperor Herakleios (610–641), which were supposedly delivered to his troops during the last Sasanian Persian-Byzantine conflict (603–628) – customarily seen as the last great war of antiquity. The orations highlight Herakleios' endeavor to magnify the religious dimension of this war, portraying the Sasanian enemies as implacable enemies of Christendom who have destroyed and defiled Christian sanctuaries. Significantly, apart from calling for self-sacrifice, the harangues ascribed to Herakleios go as far as to promise heavenly rewards (recompense from God) and even martyr's crowns to imperial Christian soldiers who fell in the battle for the salvation of their Christian brethren. This is arguably the first occurrence of such a promise in Byzantine sources. It must be said, however, that this sanctification of warfare did not find widespread acceptance among ecclesiastical elites or more generally within the medieval Byzantine ideology of warfare – see the section on the "Medieval Eastern Orthodox Perspectives on the Status of the Christian Soldier" below.

From: Theophanes the Confessor (ca. 760–ca. 817/18 CE), *Chronographia*, 303.12–304.13[37]

And he spoke to them those words of encouragement: "You see, O my brethren and children, how the enemies of God have trampled upon our land, have laid our cities waste, have burned our sanctuaries and have filled with the blood of murder the altars of the bloodless sacrifice; how they defile with their impassioned pleasures our churches. . . ."

From: Theophanes, *Chronographia*, 307.1–11[38]

As for Herakleios, he called together his troops and roused them with these words of exhortation: "Men, my brethren, let us keep in mind the fear of God and fight to avenge the insult done to God. Let us stand bravely against the enemy who have inflicted many terrible things on the Christians. Let us respect the sovereign state of the Romans and oppose the enemy who are armed with impiety. Let us be inspired with faith that defeats murder. Let us be mindful of the fact that we are within the Persian land and that flight carries a great danger. Let us avenge the rape of our virgins and be afflicted in our hearts as we see the severed limbs of our soldiers. The danger is not without recompense: nay, it leads to the eternal life. Let us stand bravely, and the Lord our God will assist us and destroy the enemy."

From: Theophanes, *Chronographia*, 310.25–311.2[39]

The emperor gathered his troops and gave them courage by assuaging them with these words of exhortation: "Be not disturbed, O brethren, by the multitude (of the enemy). For when God wills it, one man will rout a thousand. So, let us sacrifice ourselves to God for the salvation of our brothers. May we win the crown of martyrdom so that we may be praised in the future and receive our recompense from God."

The second half of the tenth century saw campaigns of Byzantine offensive warfare and expansion against its Near Eastern Muslim neighbors, accompanied by a heightened religious element in the rhetoric employed to conceptualize or justify these campaigns, as well as in contemporaneous military manuals.[40] Such enhanced religious sentiment is evident in two military orations ascribed to Constantine VII Porphyrogennetos (908–945, co-emperor; 945–959, emperor) that were delivered in the context of the unfolding Byzantine conflicts with the Muslim Hamdanid dynasty in eastern Anatolia and northern Syria. By framing the hostilities in religious terms, which included appealing to the powerful prayers of holy men, employing sacred relics, and anointing soldiers with "holy water," the emperor sought to infuse his troops with confidence in eventual victory of the imperial Christian cause.

From: Constantine VII, Postbattle Military Oration (ca. 950 CE)[41]

Therefore have no fear, my men, have no fear, fill your souls with zeal and show the enemy . . . what those who put their faith in Christ can accomplish. Be the avengers and champions not only of Christians but of Christ Himself. . . . Do men know that those who fight on their behalf are rewarded, and will Christ not stretch forth His hand to those girded for battle against His foes? . . . And so let us put all our hope in Him, and instead of our whole panoply let us arm ourselves with His cross, equipped with which you have lately made the fierce soldiers of the Hamdanid the victims of your swords. . . .

You know how virtuous it is to fight on behalf of Christians, and how much glory the man who does so achieves for himself. This is more profitable than all wealth, more praiseworthy than all other honor.

From: Constantine VII, Postbattle Oration 3, 8 (ca. 958 CE)[42]

[A]fter appealing to the most venerable and saintly fathers . . . and enjoining them to offer prayers of supplication, we have appointed them to pray incessantly and unstintingly on your behalf; but we have also directed those in the churches of the City guarded by God and the pious monasteries to perform the same task, so that as the entreaty of all those holy men rises up to the ears of the Lord God of hosts and is blended and united with your fervor and trust in us, the route before you may be easy and smooth. . . .

[A]s I devote my exertions to your salvation and to *prospering you*, behold, that after drawing holy water from the immaculate and most sacred relics of the Passion of Christ our true God – from the precious wooden fragments (of the True Cross) and the undefiled Lance, the precious Titulus, the wonder-working Reed, the life-giving blood which flowed from His precious rib, the most sacred Tunic, the holy swaddling clothes, the God-bearing winding sheet, and the other relics of His undefiled Passion – we have sent it to be sprinkled upon you, for you to be anointed by it and to garb yourselves with the divine power from on high. For I trust in my true God and Savior Christ, that just as He restored and endowed the human race with life through the blood and water which flowed from His precious rib, so will He through the sprinkling of this holy water quicken and restore you and furnish you with confidence and might and domination against the enemy.

Military Religious Services

The numerous invocations of peace in Byzantine liturgical and hymnographic literature occasionally coexist with prayers (and prayer services) for the safety and well-being
of Orthodox soldiers/armies and their victory in battle. Accompanied with military
imagery and symbolism, these prayers often allude to the empire's previous victories
on the battlefield, as aided by God. Characteristically, for example, the *Liturgy of St.
Basil* pleads for victory only over war-minded barbarian adversaries, so that lasting
peace may be achieved.[43] The following tenth-century military service characteristically conflates the constantly actualized inherited paradigms of imperial triumphalism (Christianized with invocations of the victory-giving powers of the cross) with
that of Byzantium as "The New Israel." Its related typology associates the archetypal
Old Testament protagonists of God-ordained, righteous wars such as David and the
Philistines with, respectively, the Byzantine warrior-emperors and their "barbarian"
enemies.

From: Military Religious Service (tenth century CE)[44]

Savior, who gave power to wise David,
cast down our adversaries as you did Goliath of old,
Compassionate One,
with your invisible slingshot, Christ,
crush their insolent acts and designs,
so that with faith we may honor you.

Life-giving son of God, by the prayers of your mother,
and by the divine supplications of the angels and gloriously triumphant martyrs,
gladden your faithful emperors,
shatter the throngs of barbarians, and to the army
that worships you, show mercy.

O Lord who showed to Constantine the first emperor of the Christians
the divine cross, and uttered from the heavens
"Trust in this sign,"
You, O Lord, by the power of the cross give now
victory and vigor and truly divine power
to your army in your compassion.

O Lord who fought with most gentle David
to defeat the Philistine,
fight beside your faithful emperors.
and armed with the cross
cast down their enemies.

Medieval Eastern Orthodox Perspectives on the Status of the Christian Soldier

Eastern Orthodox Canon Law

The codification of ecclesiastical legislation in the Eastern Roman Empire following the legalization of the status of the Christian Church by Constantine's Edict of Milan of 313 led to the compilations of the first Byzantine collections or synopses of the rulings of the so-called Apostolic Canons and those of the Ecumenical and Local Councils. The earliest of these collections date most likely from the sixth century and some of these synopses came to include also authoritative pronouncements of Eastern Church Fathers that were thus accorded a canonical status. A number of canons drawn from these regulations and patristic writings that formed the basis of Eastern Orthodox canon law (such as Canon 7 of the Fourth Ecumenical Council of Chalcedon of 451)[45] spell out prohibitions on Christian clergy and monks becoming involved in military service or the secular state administration and government.[46] Emphasizing the precepts of clerical and monastic nonresistance to violence, these canonical regulations enunciated that both clergy and monks were expected to maintain the pacific and pacifistic standards of the early Church. They were accordingly prohibited from any military activity, a domain that was strictly reserved to the laity. Within both the evolving canon law and political military ideology one can however detect symptomatic tensions and debates regarding the status of Christian soldiers and whether their participation in warfare could bring them spiritual rewards. The disputes within Byzantine canon law largely draw on the contrasting approaches of St. Basil the Great (ca. 330–379) and the influential Nicene theologian and anti-Arian polemicist, St. Athanasios of Alexandria (ca. 296–373). Enormously influential, St. Basil was counted in Eastern Orthodoxy as one of the "Three Holy Hierarchs," while in Roman Catholicism St. Athanasios was eventually recognized as one of the Four Great Doctors of the Eastern Church alongside the Three Hierarchs.

From: St. Athanasios of Alexandria, Epistle 48, *To Ammoun the Monk* (written before 357)[47]

Since in other transactions in life too we shall find differences to occur in some way or another: for instance, it is not permissible to murder anyone (Exod. 20:13), yet in war it is praiseworthy and lawful to slay the adversaries. Thus at any rate those who have distinguished themselves in war are entitled to and are accorded great honors, and columns are erected in memory of them reciting their exploits. So that the same matter in some respect and at some time or other is not permitted, but in another respect and at some other time when there is a good occasion for it, may be allowed and permitted.

Killing in war was considered both lawful and praiseworthy by St. Athanasios of Alexandria in his *Epistle to Ammoun the Monk* (one of his three epistles that have received the status of canons) and has inevitably been of central importance to Eastern Orthodox thought on the legality and justifiability of warfare in theological and canon law discussions, as will be shown below. While the epistle mainly concerns issues of sexual purity, when the passage in question is extracted as a separate assertion it can be read as a rare Eastern Christian patristic legitimization of slaying in war (albeit under determinate circumstances). Not only was such killing said to be permissible, but moreover it was characterized as a commendable deed that might bring honor and renown to the doer.[48] When, however, the pronouncement is considered in the overall context of the rhetoric and imagery of the epistle, it admittedly can allow for different readings, some of which cast doubt on its interpretation as a patristic justification of killing on the battlefield.[49] While the debates on the precise meaning and contextualization of St. Athanasios' statement seem certain to continue, it is equally certain that those who seek to recognize (at least elements of) a just war tradition in Eastern Orthodox religious thought will continue to use it as an authoritative patristic testimony for an early and important articulation of just war thinking in Eastern Christendom.

From: St. Basil the Great, *Epistle* 188.13 (ca. 374)[50]

> Our Fathers did not consider murders committed in the course of wars to be classifiable as murders at all, on the score, it seems to me, of allowing a pardon to men fighting in defense of sobriety and piety. Perhaps, though, it might be advisable to refuse them Communion for three years, on the ground that they are not clean-handed.

This well-known thirteenth canon of St. Basil the Great from his first Canonical Epistle to Amphilochus, Bishop of Iconium (378), clearly stipulates that the act of killing during war needs to be distinguished from voluntary murder, although it is advisable that the perpetrators should abstain from Communion for three years. The allusion to the "fathers" and their attitude with respect to killing in time of war evidently refer to the above statement of St Athanasios. The canon needs to be considered in the context of the evolving fourth-century Christian clerical attitudes with respect to the phenomenon of "involuntary murder" (treated in the preceding, eleventh canon of St. Basil) and the penance required for having shed blood in armed conflict, treated in Canon 14 from the fourth-century (or later) canons attributed to St. Hippolytus of Rome (ca. 170–ca. 235).[51] While clearly acknowledging the permissibility and occasional necessity of "fighting in defense of sobriety and piety," St. Basil refuses to recognize killing during war as a "praiseworthy" deed, advising that those responsible for such acts should abstain from Communion for three years. Hence St. Basil's canon has been often seen as forestalling the development of just war theory in Eastern Orthodox thought in late antiquity and the early Middle Ages, comparable to that conceptualized (in its early and formative stages) by St. Augustine and St. Ambrose in the contemporaneous Latin West.[52] At the same time, while condemning the praise and rewards bestowed during wars on the combatants in accordance with "the magnitude of the slaughter,"[53] St. Basil could also state that the military profession could be consonant with the Christian faith and "perfect love for God."[54]

Later Byzantine Canonists: Theodore Balsamon (ca. 1130/40–d. after 1195), Ioannes Zonaras (d. after 1159), Matthew Blastares (d. after 1346)

The interpretative commentary to St. Basil's thirteenth canon in the important and influential collection of Eastern Orthodox canon law from 1800, the *Pedalion* (The Rudder), specifies that this canon (and its stipulation that those who have slain adversaries during warfare should be prohibited from Communion for three years) has an "advisory and indecisive" character,[55] and this was indeed the way it was considered by the later, twelfth-century leading Byzantine canonists Theodore Balsamon and Ioannes Zonaras. At the same time, both canonists refer to the proceedings of a Church synod during the reign of the Byzantine Emperor Nikephoros II Phokas (963–969) during which Patriarch Polyeuktos (956–970) and the ecclesiastical hierarchy invoked the authority of St. Basil's thirteenth canon to deny the emperor's request that the Church should establish canonical regulations through which Byzantine soldiers who fell in warfare would begin to be honored on par with the holy martyrs and accordingly be celebrated with hymns and feast days, as recounted in Ioannes Scylitzes' *Synoposis Historiarum.*

From: Ioannes Scylitzes, *Synoposis Historiarum* (second half of the eleventh century CE)[56]

[Emperor Nikephoros II Phokas] was also eager to institute a law that the soldiers who perished in battle should be deemed worthy of the privileges of martyrs, placing the salvation of the soul in war alone and not in any other sphere. He urged the patriarch and the bishops to agree to this doctrine, but some of them nobly opposed him and frustrated his plan, putting forward the canon of the great [St.] Basil, which states that those who have slain an adversary in a battle should be debarred from Communion for three years.

This conflict over the military martyrdom status for Christian soldiers fallen on the battlefield requested by Nikephoros II Phokas is symptomatic of the enduring tension between Byzantine imperial and clerical approaches to the ideology of medieval Christian warfare.[57] Byzantine ecclesiastical perspectives on the legitimacy and consequences of Christian participation in warfare were themselves characterized by internal contradictions and disagreements. Contrasting positions on the applicability of St. Basil's thirteenth canon are illustrated in the passages below, from Theodore Balsamon and Ioannes Zonaras, on one hand, and the influential fourteenth-century canonist and hieromonk[58] Matthew Blastares, on the other.

From: Theodore Balsamon, *Commentary on St. Basil's Thirteenth Canon*[59]

This canon sets forth views in a manner proper to the holiness of the Divine Father, but is not in force, because, if it were established, soldiers who are engrossed with successive wars and slaying the enemy, would never partake of the divine

Sanctified Elements. Wherefore, it is unendurable. However, it is written that when that emperor Phokas deemed those slain in wars worthy to be numbered with the martyrs, the bishops at that time making use of this canon, silenced the imperial interference, saying, how will we number with the martyrs those who fall in wars. . . .

From: Ioannes Zonaras, *Commentary on St. Basil's Thirteenth Canon*[60]

The saint speaks not by command, that those who slay during wars refrain from Communion for three years, but according to counsel. In addition, such counsel appears to be burdensome. For it might follow from it that soldiers never partake of the Divine Gifts. . . . At any rate I think that this counsel of St. Basil never was in force. In the meantime, at the right moment it was profitable for those who refer to ecclesiastical traditions.

The views of Balsamon and Zonaras on the practical applicability of St. Basil's thirteenth canon were summarized in Matthew Blastares' systematic fourteenth-century encyclopedic collection, *Syntagma kata stoicheion* ("The Alphabetical Collection"), which was to become the standard reference work in the sphere of Eastern Orthodox canon law in the post-Byzantine period.

From: Matthew Blastares, *Commentary on St. Basil's Thirteenth Canon* (1355)[61]

For it will follow, they say, in consequence of this that the most brave of the soldiers by their way of life . . . will be deprived of the good participation, which is an unendurable punishment for Christians. For what reason, they say, are their hands not clean, which he himself testifies fight for chastity and piety, viewing this as best of all? If these men were not willing to come to blows with their opponents . . . might those things that ruin piety be hastened when the barbarians bring everything under their sway in the great absence of opposition, and when they zealously decide to strengthen their own worship? Who will be the one that pursues chastity, when all are compelled to live in accordance with those who have already become rulers?

Blastares also refers to the tenth-century synod that relied on the authority of St. Basil's thirteenth canon to thwart Phokas' attempts to secure martyrdom status for Byzantine soldiers slain in battle and the ecclesiastical arguments to achieve this: "How it is possible to number with the martyrs those who fell during war, whom Basil the Great excluded from the Sanctified Elements for three years since their hands were not clean?"[62] Both Balsamon and Blastares also recount (with some differences) another instance during the same synod when St. Basil's canon was applied to effect the defrocking of certain priests and bishops who were arraigned for having fought and killed enemies in battles.[63] Ultimately, Blastares rejects the arguments of Balsamon and Zonaras and confirms the validity and relevance of the three-year penance of exclusion from Communion recommended in St. Basil's canon on the basis of his own theological and scriptural arguments.[64] The scriptural arguments, according to Blastares, include allusions to and exegesis of the aftermath of the God-commanded war of obliteration of the Israelites against the Midianites, when Eleazar the priest ordered the Israelite soldiers who were returning from the bloodshed

> to remain outside the encampment for seven days, showing, I believe, that although slaughters against enemies are legal, nevertheless, the man who kills a human being … appears to be blameworthy. . . .[65]

Blastares thus reasserts the theological and ecclesiastical appropriateness of the prohibition envisaged in St. Basil's canon. At the same time, inevitably conscious of the existing patterns of justifying Byzantine Christian engagement in armed conflict on the basis of St. Athanasios' canonical epistle to Ammoun, he emphasizes also St. Basil's tribute to those who safeguard "the race of the Christians" and fight its enemies; indeed, drawing on it he proceeds to affirm the legitimacy of Christian defensive warfare by posing the rhetorical question: "[F]or what might be a more worthy reason for praise than to defend on behalf of chastity and piety?"[66]

There exist various records of strong Eastern Orthodox disquiet at the phenomenon of Western priests carrying arms and participating in fighting during the crusading era. The following extract from Anna Komnene's *Alexiad* highlights both the criticism of this "Latin" phenomenon and the view, shared in both Byzantine secular and ecclesiastical circles, that the pacifistic precepts in the New Testament and Eastern Orthodox canon law categorically disallow such a practice for Eastern Orthodox monks and priests.

From: Anna Komnene, *Alexiad*, 10.8.8[67]

The Latin customs with regard to priests differ from ours. We are bidden by canon law and the teaching of the Gospel, "Touch not, grumble not, attack not – for thou art consecrated."[68] But your Latin barbarian will at the same time handle sacred objects, fasten a shield to his left arm and grasp a spear in his right. He will communicate the Body and Blood of the Deity and meanwhile gaze on bloodshed and become himself "a man of blood" (as David says in the Psalms).[69] Thus the race is no less devoted to religion than to war. . . . Our rules, as I have just said, derive from Aaron, Moses and our first high priest.

The Vita of St. Constantine–Cyril the Philosopher (826/7–869)
The above discussions on the nature and implications of Christian involvement in warfare within the tradition of Byzantine canon law not only show a shift toward moderating the harshness of St. Basil's thirteenth canon (thereby considering it an advisory rather than a mandatory canonical requirement) but also betray a concern with the spiritual dimensions of engagement in warfare to shield fellow Christians from harm or, in the words of St. Basil, "on behalf of sobriety and piety." In Western Christendom an analogous concern with the potential spiritual rewards for those who have died defending the Church and Christian faith received dramatic and influential expression (especially in

settings where the papacy played a leading role) in the period leading to and during the crusading era. Within the Eastern Orthodox tradition, comparable notions are recorded to have been articulated (roughly one century before Phokas failed to win clerical support for his Christian military martyrdom initiative) during the ambassadorial visit of the celebrated missionary to the Slavs, St. Constantine–Cyril the Philosopher, to the court of the Abbasid caliph al-Mutawakkil (847–861) in 851. The ninth-century *Vita* of St. Constantine recounts his debates with Muslim (Hagarene) theologians at the Abbasid court during which they ask him why Christians do not apply in practice the precepts in the well-known verses in Matthew 5:38–44 teaching nonviolence and nonresistance to evil/evildoers, as well as love and prayer for one's enemies. In his reported reply, St. Constantine in effect gives priority to John 15:13 ("No one has greater love than this, to lay down one's life for one's friends"), arguing that as private people Christians can bear any offenses, but when in company they defend each other and sacrifice their lives in battle for their neighbors.

From: *Vita Constantini* (late ninth century)[70]

(The Muslim scribes ask St. Constantine–Cyril:) "Your God is Christ. He commanded you to pray for enemies, to do good to those who hate and persecute you and to offer the other cheek to those who hit you, but what do you actually do? If anyone offends you, you sharpen your sword and go into battle and kill. Why do you not obey your Christ?" Having heard this, St. Cyril asked his fellow-polemists: "If there are two commandments written in one law, who will be its best respecter – the one who obeys only one commandment or the one who obeys both?" When the Hagarenes said that the best respecter of law is the one who obeys both commandments, the holy preacher continued: "Christ is our God Who ordered us to pray for our offenders and to do good to them. He also said that no one of us can show greater love in life than he who gives his life for his friends (John 15:3). That is why we generously endure offenses caused us as private people. But in company we defend one another and give our lives in battle for our neighbors, so that you, having taken our fellows prisoners, could not imprison their souls together with their bodies by forcing them into renouncing their faith and into godless deeds. Our Christ-loving soldiers protect our Holy Church with arms in their hands. They safeguard the sovereign in whose sacred person they respect the image of the rule of the Heavenly King. They safeguard their land because with its fall the home authority will inevitably fall too and the evangelical faith will be shaken. These are precious pledges for which soldiers should fight to the last. And if they give their lives in battlefield, the Church will include them in the community of the holy martyrs and call them intercessors before God."

St. Constantine–Cyril's reply clearly interprets the martial feats of the "Christ-loving soldiers" in defense of their lands, the Church, and Christianity through the prism of the precept in John 15:3 as constituting paradigmatic Christian duties for which they should "fight to the last." What is more, after fulfilling these "precious pledges," the

Church would qualify these Christian soldiers as martyrs and intercessors before God. This explicit legitimization of Christian just war notions and the potential martyr status of the Christian warrior ascribed to St. Constantine–Cyril can perhaps be best understood within the religio-political framework of his mission to the court of al-Mutawakkil.[71] Unlike contemporary and later Catholicism, however, when such notions do appear on occasion in medieval Eastern Orthodoxy, they were not developed in any systematic fashion or integrated into a consistent theory. Overall, the concept of military martyrdom failed to find acceptance in the mainstream of Byzantine Church thought and practice.[72] At the same time, within the Byzantine Commonwealth (and particularly in the Slavonic Orthodox world), the continuing prestige of St. Constantine–Cyril's pronouncements made it possible for his proclamation at the Abbasid court, as narrated in his *Vita*, to be used as an authoritative basis for later Eastern Orthodox attempts to articulate and elaborate just war concepts (if not a structured theory).

Religious Services Commemorating Fallen Christian Soldiers

The Byzantine Church may have halted the Emperor Phokas' attempts to attribute martyrdom status to soldiers fallen in battle, but a number of indications suggest that the idea of Byzantine Christian warriors anticipating heavenly rewards for their defense of Orthodoxy, including the conferral of martyrdom status, became part of the evolving military religious ideology developed in the lay piety of the Byzantine military classes. Indeed, an ideology underpinned by such notions may have been encouraged more frequently by the imperial court than the only recorded case of such an imperial initiative during Phokas' reign would suggest. Certainly, the military treatise *Taktika*, ascribed to Emperor Leo VI (866–912), emphasized that in battling their Saracen (Muslim) adversaries, Byzantine Christian soldiers were also fighting for God, their Christian brethren, and the salvation of their souls.

From: Leo VI, *Taktika*, 18.127[73]

If we are well armed and drawn up in formation, with God fighting along beside us, we charge against them bravely and in good spirits on behalf of the salvation of our souls, and we carry on the struggle without hesitation on behalf of God himself, our kinsmen, and our brothers the other Christians, then we place our hopes in God. We shall not fail to achieve, rather, we shall certainly achieve the glory of victory over them.

The tract, moreover, evidently also envisages a religious service to commemorate soldiers who have sacrificed their lives for their faith and brethren. They are praised with the honorific "blessed" and their names are to be held in eternal memory.

From: Leo VI, *Taktika*, 14.31[74]

After the battle, O general, you are obliged to see to the comfort of the soldiers wounded in the action, as well as to provide proper burial for those who have fallen. Constantly pronounce them blessed because they have not preferred their own lives over their faith and their brothers. This is a religious act and it greatly helps the morale of the living.

From: Leo VI, *Taktika*, Epilogue 72[75]

The bodies of the soldiers who have been killed in battle are sacred, especially those who have been most valiant in the fight on behalf of Christians. By all means, it is necessary to honor them reverently and to dignify them with burial and eternal memory.

A service of the type prescribed in Leo VI's *Taktika* has been indeed uncovered in a tenth-century Greek version of the *Triodion* (the pre-Easter Orthodox liturgical service book) and is dedicated to those who have died in battle or as prisoners of war.

From: "All Souls Service for the Saturday of Meatfare Week" (tenth century)[76]

Let us gather together people of Christ
And celebrate the memory
Of our brothers who died in battle
And those who perished in intolerable captivity.
Let us entreat on their behalf.

They were valiant until their slaughter
Your servants, Lover of Man;
They received
Blows pitilessly
Persevering in fetters;
Let it be that these men for these things
Achieve atonement of their souls, Lover of Man.

You alone who are without sin,
Took in those
Who are your servants,
Illustrious generals,
Commanding commanders,
Brave soldiers,
Judge them worthy of your repose.

This service ultimately was not integrated within the Eastern Orthodox calendar. It indicates nonetheless a distinctive trend in the ethics and martyrology of Byzantine Christian warfare, elements of which, as already observed, can be traced to the Anatolian frontier zones of the empire. The evolution of this cult of the Byzantine warrior saints demonstrates much about the ritual and iconographic dimensions of the Byzantine lay military-religious ethos, some aspects of which the Church was patently not enthusiastic to support. Significantly, the canonization and widespread veneration of historical Orthodox warrior-princes in some of the late medieval cultures of the Byzantine Commonwealth (notably Russia, Ukraine, and Serbia), as well as the proliferation of hagiographical biographies, suggest that in these cultures the Orthodox Churches were more prepared to foster and cultivate lay military piety than was the Byzantine mother Church. At the same time both South Slavonic and Russian Orthodox cultures offer some early paradigmatic examples of saintly princes who accepted martyrdom without resorting to violence or self-defense – for example, St. John Vladimir, Prince of Duklja (d. 1016), and Saints Boris and Gleb, Princes of Kievan Rus' (d. 1015).

Eastern Orthodox Lay Pacifism

Saints Boris and Gleb, the first Russian saints to be canonized in 1072, represent also the paradigmatic figures of lay pacifism in the Eastern Slavonic Orthodox world. According to sources such as Nestor's *Lives of Boris and Gleb* and the Russian *Primary Chronicle*, upon the death of their father, Vladimir I (Grand Prince of Kiev), the two saints were killed by assassins who had been dispatched by their brother, Sviatopolk, who sought to remove them as rivals to the throne. In the face of this attack as passion-bearers and followers of Christ's example, they chose the path of nonresistance to evil. The martyrdom of Saints Boris and Gleb, and their exemplary nonretaliation to violence, have been repeatedly invoked in the tradition of Eastern Orthodox pacifism. At the same time, in the following extract from the Russian *Primary Chronicle* their intercession is sought for a victory of the princes of the new Christian nation over its "pagan" adversaries. Indeed, as early as the thirteenth century, their cult as protectors of Russia was mobilized to legitimate Russian war campaigns.[77]

From: The Russian *Primary Chronicle*, Laurentian Text, 137–139 (1337 CE)[78]

After Gleb had been slain ... they took him and carried him away, to bury him beside his brother Boris beside the Church of St. Basil.

United thus in body and still more in soul, ye dwell with the Lord and King of all, in eternal joy, ineffable light, bestowing salutary gifts upon the land of Rus'.... Rejoice, martyrs in Christ from the land of Rus', who gave healing in them who draw near to you in faith and love.... Rejoice, ye who have trampled the serpent of evil beneath your feet. Ye have appeared amid bright rays, enlightening like beacons the whole land of Rus'.... Ye, glorious ones, with the sacred drops of your blood ye have dyed a robe of purple which ye wear in beauty, and reign forevermore with Christ, interceding with him for his new Christian nation and for your fellows, for our land is hallowed by your blood. By virtue of your relics deposited in the church, ye illuminate it with the Holy Spirit, for there in heavenly bliss, as martyrs among the army of martyrs, ye intercede for your nation. Rejoice, bright day-springs, our Christ-loving martyrs and intercessors! Subject the pagans to our Princes, beseeching our Lord God that they may live in concord and in health, freed from intestine war and the crafts of the devil.

Religious Elements in Russian War Campaigns against the Polovtsians (Kumans)

Apart from resorting to just war precepts bearing on self-defense, the inviolability of frontiers, and punishment of oath-breaking adversaries, Russian medieval accounts of confrontations between Russia and the nomadic Turkic Polovtsians (Kumans), the Mongols, as well as the Kazan and Crimean Tatars, display on occasion (without being central to the justification of the war effort) a number of religious elements. Such elements can be detected in the following extracts from the Russian *Primary Chronicle* regarding Russian-Polovtsian fighting: defeat at the hands of the Polovtsians is interpreted as a divine chastisement for the sins of the Russian Christians; the Polovtsians are depicted as enemies of Christianity who have destroyed or defiled Christian shrines; divine inspiration is shown to move the Russian princes to initiate a campaign of war against the Polovtsians; the Cross is invoked to ensure success in battle; while ecclesiastical blessings are conferred on the Russian war effort.

From: The Russian *Primary Chronicle*, Laurentian Text, 172[79]

For great is the power of the Cross. By the Cross are vanquished the powers of the devil. The Cross helps our princes in combat, and the faithful who are protected by the Cross conquer in battle the foes who oppose them.

From: The Russian *Primary Chronicle*, Laurentian Text, 232–233[80]

The godless sons of Ishmael slew the brethren in the monastery. . . . Then they set fire to the shrine of the Holy Virgin. . . . [T]hey seized the eikons, burned the doors, and blasphemed against God and our faith. . . . Thus they said, "Where is their God? Let him come and deliver them,". . . they did not know that God punishes his servants by means of barbarian incursions that they may appear as gold which has been tried in the furnace.

From: The Russian *Primary Chronicle*, Laurentian Text, 276[81]

During the following year, God inspired the princes of Rus' with a noble project, for they resolved to attack the Polovcians and invade their territory, and this project was actually realized.

From: The Russian *Primary Chronicle*, Laurentian Text, 278–279[82]

The princes of Rus' and all the soldiery offered their prayers to God and made their vows to God and to the Blessed Virgin. . . .

Now God on high inspired an awful fear in the Polovcians, so that terror and trembling beset them at the sight of the Russian forces, and they wavered. . . .

On April 4, God thus performed a great salvation and bestowed upon us a mighty victory over our foes.

From: The Russian *Primary Chronicle*, Laurentian Text, 282[83]

On August 12, the Polovcians abandoned their camp, after the capture of which the Russian soldiery returned home with a great victory. Svyatopolk arrived before the Crypt Monastery at matins on the feast of the Assumption of the Blessed Virgin [August 15] and the brethren embraced him amid great rejoicing, because our enemies were overthrown through the prayers of the Holy Virgin and of our holy father Theodosius. For Svyatopolk, before he went forth to war or on some other mission, made it a habit to kneel beside the tomb of Theodosius, and after receiving the blessing of the prior who was present, he proceeded with his errand.

The Battle of Kulikovo

Medieval Russian accounts and reactions to the Battle of Kulikovo field (near the Don River) in 1380 in which the combined Russian troops of Dmitrii Donskoi (1350–1389, Prince of Moscow and Grand Prince of Vladimir) defeated the larger Tatar army of the Golden Horde and its allies (led by Mamai), also conflated just war rhetoric with a heightened religious sentiment, including the notion of divine support and ecclesiastical intercession for the Russian military victory. This is vividly demonstrated in the frequently cited encounter between Dmitrii Donskoi (proclaimed in 1988 a saint by the Russian Orthodox Church) and one of the most highly esteemed saints of Orthodox Russia, St. Sergius of Radonezh (ca. 1319/22–1392). The following account shows St. Sergius offering strong spiritual support for the Russian anti-Mongol war effort.[84]

From: *The Life of St. Sergius*, 8 (1430s)[85]

A rumor spread that Khan Mamai was raising a large army as a punishment for our sins and that with all his heathen Tatar hordes he would invade Russian soil.... The puissant and reigning prince, who held the scepter of all Russia, great Dmitry, having a great faith in the saint, came to ask him if he counseled him to go against the heathen. The saint, bestowing on him his blessing, and strengthened by prayer, said to him: "It behooveth you, Lord, to have a care for the lives of the flock committed to you by God. Go forth against the heathen; and upheld by the strong arm of God, conquer; and return to your country sound in health, and glorify God with loud praise."...

Assembling all his armies, he marched against the heathen Tatars; but, seeing the multitudes of them, he began to doubt.... Of a sudden, a courier from the saint arrived, in all haste, with the message, "Be in no doubt, Lord; go forward with faith and confront the enemy's ferocity; and fear not, for God will be on your side." Forthwith, the Grand Duke Dmitry and all his armies, were filled with a spirit of temerity; and went into battle against the pagans. They fought; many fell; but God was with them, and helped the great and invincible Dmitry, who vanquished the ungodly Tatars. In that same hour the saint was engaged with his brethren before God in prayer for victory over the pagans. Within an hour of the final defeat of the ungodly, the saint, who was a seer, announced to the brotherhood what had happened, the victory, the courage of the Grand Duke Dmitry, and the names, too, of those who had died at the hands of the pagans; and he made intercession for them to all-merciful God.

The Russian perception (contemporaneous or later) of the religious dimension of the Battle of Kulikovo is also evident in other chronicle and literary accounts such as the *Zadonshchina* ("The Tale of the Events beyond the Don"), which categorizes it as a self-sacrificial struggle on behalf of the Russian land and Christian faith against the "infidel" invader Mamai and his "Muslim Tatar" army.[86]

From: *Zadonshchina* (first half of fifteenth century CE)[87]

"Do you know, dear brothers, that Emperor Mamai
invaded the Russian land at the swift river Don...?

Let us lay down our lives for the Russian land and the Christian faith.
Let us encourage the Land of Russia...
Let us sing of the defeat of Mamai, the infidel....

"Lord, Great Prince, the infidel Tatars have begun
advancing into our lands....
We will put our brave warriors to the test
For the Russian land and the Christian faith."...

Oh, great princes of Russia,
fight the enemy with your valorous army,
Fight for the Russian land and the Christian faith,
fight against the infidel emperor, Mamai....

But God was merciful to the Russian land,
and still more Tatars fell on the battlefield.
And then Prince Dmitry Ivanovich addressed the dead: ...

"Here you gave your lives for the holy Church
for the Russian land and for the Christian faith.
Forgive me, brethren, and give me your blessing
For this life and for the life everlasting."

The Muscovite Anti-Tatar Ideology of Warfare

After the disintegration of the Golden Horde in the 1420s, the confrontation with its successor state (the Kazan, Astrakhan, and Crimean Khanates) led the Grand Duchy of Moscow (from 1547, Tsardom of Russia/Muscovy) to emphasize the religious dimensions of the conflict. In this connection, some circles in the Muscovite ecclesiastical elite played a major role in the conceptualization of anti-Tatar ideology,[88] an ideology that was used to justify military campaigns against the Khanates, in particular the Kazan one. In the preparatory stages and aftermath of Ivan IV the Terrible's (1533–1584) brutal conquest of Kazan in 1552, the anti-Tatar campaign was frequently legitimized as a just war to restore Muscovite suzerainty over the Kievan Rus', a patrimony that had been seized by the Tatars. Religious justification was also sought to further the political-military goals of conquest. This was articulated by prominent religious and secular publicists, whose arguments for a religiously oriented *casus belli* included mention of vengeance, the rescue of Russian Orthodox Christians from Muslim Tatar captivity, as well as the expansion of Russian Orthodoxy.

Following his move to Russia in 1515 the prominent Greek monk, scholar, and publicist Maxim the Greek (1475–1556) appealed to Vasilii III, Grand Prince of Moscow (1505–1533) not only to embrace the cause of the liberation of Byzantium from Ottoman Muslim oppression, but also to launch an offensive against the Kazan Khanate, offering him a war justification that combined a forceful religious rationale with *Realpolitik* considerations.

From: Maxim the Greek, *Epistle to Grand Prince Vasilii III* (1521/22)[89]

"Let us be exalted by holy zeal and avenge the blood of our many Orthodox brethren who were killed there, and we shall, in addition, not permit the godless abodes to boast against Christ and against the Orthodox who revere Him. . . ."

For as long as we have sufficient time, and as long as there is no pagan uprising to disturb us, let us advance against and attack the killers of the Christians from the city of Kazan, and let us not waste the time for action with sterile deeds. . . . When the abominable Kazan shall have disappeared, it shall be easier for us to oppose other [enemies] since we shall become formidable on this account.

A similar understanding of the struggle between Moscow and Kazan as a religious conflict to be solved by a Russian war of conquest partially underlies the justification for anti-Kazan warfare that the contemporary secular publicist Ivan Peresvetov proposed to Ivan IV. Ivan also urged the Russian ruler to expand the Christian faith by liberating the Orthodox people under Ottoman suzerainty.[90]

The conquest of the Kazan Khanate was legitimized by condemning it as an anti-Christian power that had destroyed Christian sanctuaries and oppressed numerous Christians. This sort of discourse was forcefully articulated in a number of official pronouncements that were attributed to Ivan IV and to the Metropolitan of Moscow and all Russia, Makarii (1542–1563).

From: Makarii, Metropolitan of Moscow and All Russia, *Second Epistle to Ivan IV* (13 July 1552)[91]

[Thou shouldst] in firm, tsar-like fashion take a stand with thy Christ-loving host against thy foes, the godless Kazanian Tatars, traitors and apostates, who continually shed innocent Christian blood and befoul and destroy the holy churches; the more so it is befitting for thee, O pious Tsar Ivan ... and all thy Christ-loving host, to struggle firmly, valiantly and courageously, with God's help, for God's holy churches and for all Orthodox Christians, innocently led into captivity, robbed, and tormented by them [Kazanians] ... it is most [befitting] for thee to struggle for our holy, pure and most honorable Christian faith of the Greek creed ... against her [the Orthodox faith] the dragon, the cunning enemy, the devil, haughtily becometh infuriated, and together with pagan tsars, thy foes, the Crimean tsar and his accomplices, the pagan peoples, the Crimean and Kazanian Tatars, taketh up a fierce battle against her....

From: Ivan IV, *Address to Metropolitan Makarii and the Ecclesiastical Assembly* (1553)[92]

[Not] long ago, I held council with thee [Makarii and with the Ecclesiastical assembly] about [the fact that] the Kazan tsars and all the people of Kazan have been betraying us for many years in spite of our benevolence toward them and that they are capturing [our] Christians. They have plundered many cities and villages of our God-given Russian state; in these cities several holy churches were destroyed and demolished, and venerable monasteries were plundered; and a multitude of Christian people from the clergy and the monastic order, princes and boyars, children and youths, of both male and female sex, were taken into captivity and scattered over the face of the whole world....

From: Ivan IV, *Address to Metropolitan Makarii and the Ecclesiastical Assembly* (October 1552)[93]

And the Almighty Lord looked upon us from Heaven.... He handed over to us the ruling capital, the populous city of Kazan, with all its inhabitants, and He removed [from there] Mohammed's deceit and erected the life-giving Cross in the desolated abomination of Kazan.... [B]y God's design and His holy will, and on account of thy [the Russian clergy's] holy prayers, the city of Kazan which was pagan before, we enlightened with Christianity in the name of the life-giving Trinity....

From: Metropolitan Makarii, *Address to Ivan IV* (October 1552)[94]

[A]nd God granted thee His mercy: He placed the city and tsardom of Kazan into thy hands, and he enlightened thee with His grace, as He had enlightened the previous pious tsars who acted according to His will, and He granted the victory of the Cross to the pious Tsar Constantine, co-equal to the Apostles, against his foes, and to other pious tsars, and also to thine ancestor, the Grand Prince Vladimir, who enlightened the Russian land with holy baptism and defeated many foreign nations [*inoplemennyx*], and to the praiseworthy Grand Prince Dmitrij (Donskoj) who defeated the barbarians on the Don river, and to the holy Alexander Nevskij who defeated the Latins. And upon thee, O pious Tsar, God's grace descended from above: Thou wert granted the ruling city of Kazan with all its environs, and the dragon, who had his lair there, and who was fiercely devouring us, was destroyed by thy piety and the power of the Cross, and on account of thee, O pious Tsar, the evil spirits were expelled and piety was introduced [in their place] and the life-giving Cross and the holy churches were erected [there] and by thine imperial hand many captive Christians were liberated from bondage.

Opinions vary as to what extent Ivan IV's conquest of Kazan was underpinned by a religious rationale. Some authors recognize it to be, at least partially, a "religious crusade,"[95] while others view the religious elements in the campaign as secondary and subordinate to its primarily secular military and political goals.[96] When seen against the background of medieval religious warfare, Ivan IV's campaign certainly does not realize all the characteristics of a crusade. At the same time, justifications for this campaign do evince an intensely religious rhetoric in which the local war effort is situated within the general contemporaneous Muslim-Christian conflict in Europe. This religious rhetoric appears vividly in the following diplomatic note, which was released in Moscow after the takeover of Kazan.

From: *Diplomatic Note to the Lithuanian Magnates* (1553)[97]

The Mussulman nation of Kazan which had shed Christian blood for many years and which had caused our Sovereign much annoyance before he reached his mature age, by God's grace, this Mussulman nation of Kazan died by the sword of our Sovereign; and our Sovereign appointed his viceroys and governors in Kazan, and he enlightened this Mussulman abode with the Orthodox Christian faith and he destroyed the mosques and built churches [in their place], and God's name is being glorified now in this city by the Christian faith.... And we praise God for this, and may God also grant in the future that Christian blood be avenged against other Mussulman nations.

Early Imperial Russia to Post-Communism

Russian Just War Tradition and International Law of War

Peter the Great's (1682–1725) policies of modernization of the Russian state included military reforms that drew on contemporaneous Western European models. The emergent international law was a point of reference, and translations were made of works such as Hugo Grotius' seminal *De iure belli ac pacis* ("On the Law of War and Peace," 1625). The impact of this European discourse on the norms of war and peace is clearly discernible in the first original treatise on international law (of unofficial character) to appear in Russian, *A Discourse Concerning the Just Reasons Which His Czarish Majesty, Peter I, Had for the Beginning of the War against the King of Sweden, Charles XII*, composed in 1717 by one of Peter's diplomats, Baron Petr Shafirov (1670–1739). The tract intended to present and promote the Russian case for the just causes and legality of Russia's initiation, along with its allies, of the Great Northern War against Sweden (1701–1721); hence the work was also translated into German and English.[98] Shafirov addresses the principal issues of contemporary international law of war (but not in a systematic fashion) from his formulation of an acceptable just war doctrine (reclaiming the hereditary Russian dominions that had been unjustly annexed by Sweden) to breaches of armistice agreements, as well as violations of *jus in bello* and the status of the prisoners of war, all attributed to the Swedish side. The following extracts reveal Shafirov's stance that the course of the conflict was determined by a divine providence favoring the Russian Tsar; in so doing the text sheds light on some of the religiously related episodes of the war (the Swedish King's alliances with the "hereditary" Turkish and Tatar enemies of Christendom and the alleged profanation of Orthodox churches by Swedish troops) so as to provide additional justification for the Russian war effort.

From: Baron Petr Shafirov, *A Discourse Concerning the Just Reasons Which His Czarish Majesty, Peter I, Had for the Beginning of the War against the King of Sweden, Charles XII* (1717), Article 1[99]

The ancient and modern Causes, for which his Czarish Majesty, as a Father of his Country, was in Justice obliged to make War against *Sweden*, and to recover the hereditary Dominions, which had been unjustly wrested from the Crown of *Russia.* . . .

Now, though all the ancient Causes above related, would have been weighty and urging enough for *Russia* to begin a War against the Crown of *Sweden*, yet his Czarish Majesty's equitable Mind did not permit him to do it, had not Sweden given new Causes for it; he sacredly and inviolably observed a Peace extorted from his Predecessors, and he chose rather to employ his Arms against the *Turks* and *Tatars*, the constant Enemies of Christendom, than to imbrue them with Christian Blood in revenging past Injuries. But God's just Judgment, who suffers no Injustice to go unpunished, hardened the Hearts of the *Swedes*, and gave them over to such a Blindness, that they themselves blew up the Fire of old Offences and Injuries, which seemed buried under the Ashes of Time and Oblivion, by a new Insult offered to his Czarish Majesty's own high Person. . . .

From: Petr Shafirov, *Rassuzhdenie* (A Discourse)[100]

[H]e [the king of Sweden] continued his wicked Intrigues against his Czarish Majesty to a degree, that during his Stay at *Bender* he stirred up against him the hereditary Enemy of the Christian Name, and a Rupture actually ensued in 1711.

Those Infidels broke the Peace of thirty Years they had made with his Czarish Majesty, and sent the *Tartar Can* to make a sudden Irruption into his Dominions, who carried away from the Lesser-Russian and Polish *Ukraina* a great number of Christians into Slavery.

From: Shafirov, *A Discourse*, Article 3[101]

[W]hen ... the Russians came to the Place where the Swedish Baggage stood, they saw with Astonishment, that the Stables of many of the Generals and Officers, for Horses and Cows, were filled with [an] abundance of Images, as that of our Savior, of the Holy Virgin, of the Apostles and other Saints, which had been taken out of the Churches to make Doors and Stalls for Horses ... which without doubt was done with no other Design than to scoff at and jest with Religion ... despoiling the Churches, and profaning sacred things.

Russian Pan-Slavism, the Crimean War, and the Russo-Ottoman War of 1877–1878

Russian victories in the Russo-Ottoman conflicts of the second half of the eighteenth century made it possible for Russia to demand and receive in the peace treaty of 1774 a de facto recognition of its self-declared mandate to protect the rights of Orthodox Christian communities under Ottoman suzerainty. Subsequent Russian interventionism in the Balkans on behalf of these communities became a tool of Russian foreign policy. But according to the ideology of Russian Slavophilism and Pan-Slavism, the self-determination and "liberation" of the various Slavonic peoples under foreign domination could be envisaged as possible only through Russian military aid or engagement, which in the case of the Orthodox Christians under Ottoman domination received also an additional religious justification. While never a dominant factor in Russian foreign policy formulation, this ideology occasionally exercised considerable influence within the Russian court, as well as in diplomatic and military circles. The following extracts represent some of the leading nineteenth-century representatives of these trends: Aleksei S. Khomiakov (1804–1860), Nikolai Y. Danilevskii (1822–1885), the prominent poet Fedor I. Tiutchev (1803–1873), Ivan S. Aksakov (1823–1886), as well as Tsar Alexander II's (1818–1881) "Kremlin Address" (1876). The extracts below illustrate some of the principal religiously based legitimacy frameworks in Pan-Slav discourse for the use of armed force against the Ottoman empire (in the case of the Crimean War, also against its Western allies and defined on occasions as a "holy undertaking" or "sacred mission"). This is accompanied in some cases by notions such as the providential destiny of Russia as the religio-military guardian or liberator of the Christian Orthodox East (based on and reviving the Byzantine imperial heritage) against both Ottoman Islam and the imperialism of an expansionist Europe (or revolution-plagued Europe of 1848).

From: Aleksei Khomiakov, "Letter to a Foreign Friend on the Eve of the Eastern (Crimean) War" (1854)[102]

The year which is just beginning will leave deep traces in history. The forces of all the nations advance and regard each other. A terrible struggle will begin....

Turkey has failed in its obligation toward us; it violated its promises, to the detriment of the rights of our brothers. Russia demanded guarantees; they were refused....

England and France have strengthened Turkey's hopes by their alliance and help; they have aroused the courage of the Mohammedans and fanaticized their passions....

Russia arms herself.... The Russian people do not think of conquests: conquests never had anything alluring for it.... It thinks of its duty, it thinks of a holy war. I shall not call it a crusade, I shall not dishonor it by this name. God has not given us the task of conquering far-off lands, however precious they may be to our religious feelings, but he does give us the task of saving brothers who are blood of our blood and heart of our heart. A war which would be criminal in the first case is holy in the second case. Thus Russia understands the struggle which she is about to enter. This is the reason why she arms with joy, ready, if need be, for the fullest mobilization....

[T]here is something unworthy in the attitude of men who call themselves Christians and who draw their sword to deprive Christians of the right to protect their brothers against the arbitrary cruelties of Mohammedans....

Whatever happens, Providence has marked out our time to become a decisive era in the destiny of the world.... Thanks should be given to the Western powers.... [U]nwittingly they push Russia herself to enter a new road on which she had been vainly invited for many years....

Human blood is precious, war is horrible – but the designs of Providence are inscrutable, and a task must be fulfilled whatever its rigors.

Wave flags! Sound, trumpets of battle! Nations, forward into battle! God orders mankind to march on!

From: Fedor Tiutchev, *Russia and Revolution* (1848)[103]

Besides – why hide it – it is hardly likely that all these earthquake shocks which are overturning the West are stopping at the threshold of the countries of the East; and how, in this war to the death, in this impious crusade that the Revolution, already mistress of three-quarters of Western Europe, is preparing against Russia, how could the Christian East, the Slav-Orthodox East whose life is indissolubly bound to ours not be behind us in the struggle, and the war may even begin through it....

In short, what would not be the terrible confusion into which these countries of the East at close quarters with the Revolution would fall if the legitimate sovereign, if the Orthodox Emperor of the East for long delayed his appearance!

No, it is impossible, the forewarnings of a thousand years are not deceptive. Russia, the country of faith, will not lack faith at the supreme moment. She will not be frightened of the splendor of her destiny and will not recoil before her mission.

From: Fedor Tiutchev, *Dawn* (1848/49)[104]

Arise, O Rus! The hour is near!
Arise to do Christ's service!
Is it not time, while crossing yourself,
To ring Byzantium's bells?

Now let the church bell sound ring out
And all the East resound!
It summons and awakens you –
Arise, take heart, to arms!

Enclothe your breast in the armor of faith,
And God be with you, stout giant!
O Rus, great is the coming day,
The worldwide, Orthodox day!

From: Fedor Tiutchev, *A Prophecy* (1850)[105]

When Byzantium is restored to us
The ancient vaults of Saint Sophia
Will shelter the altar of Christ anew.
Kneel them before it, O Tsar of Russia –
You will arise all Slavdom's Tsar!

From: Nikolai Danilevskii, *Russia and Europe* (1869)[106]

The religious aspect of the cultural activity belongs to the Slav cultural type and to Russia in particular; it is its inalienable achievement, founded on the psychology of its people and on its guardianship of religious truth....

The political independence of the race is the indispensable foundation of culture, and consequently all the Slav forces must be directed toward this goal....

But first, as a *sine qua non* condition of success, strong and powerful Russia has to face the difficult task of liberating her racial brothers; for this struggle, she must steel them and herself in the spirit of independence and Pan-Slav consciousness.

From: Danilevskii, *Russia and Europe*[107]

"Sooner or later, whether we like it or not ... a struggle with Europe (or at least with its most significant part) over the Eastern Question, that is, over the freedom and independence of the Slavs, over the possession of Constantinople – over all that which in Europe's opinion is the object of Russia's illicit ambition, and which, for every Russian worthy of the name, is the irresistible demand of its historical calling – is inevitable....

"We do not preach war ... we assert, and not merely assert but demonstrate, that a struggle is inevitable, and we submit that although war is a very great evil, there is something far worse than war, something for which war can also serve as a cure, for 'man shall not live by bread alone.'"

From: Ivan Aksakov, "On the Eastern Question" (1861)[108]

There too [i.e., in Austria] Russia will fulfill her mission of liberating the ethnically homogeneous and largely Orthodox peoples ... and the whole Slavonic world will breathe more easily under the patronage of Russia once she finally fulfills her Christian and fraternal duty.

From: Alexander II, Tsar of Russia, "Kremlin Address" (11 November 1876)[109]

I know that all Russia joins with me in taking the deepest interest in the sufferings of our brothers by faith and by origin.... I have striven and am continuing to strive to achieve by peaceful means a real improvement in the life of all the Christian inhabitants of the Balkan peninsula. Deliberations between the representatives of the six great powers are shortly to be begun at Constantinople for the determination of conditions of peace. I much desire that we shall reach a general agreement. If this is not attained and if I see that we are not gaining such guarantees as would assure the execution of our just demands upon the Porte, then I firmly intend to act independently and I am convinced that in such an eventuality all Russia will respond to my appeal, when I count it necessary and the honor of Russia requires it. I am convinced likewise that Moscow, as always, will set the example. May God help us to fulfill our sacred mission.

From: Ivan Aksakov, "Speech to the Slavonic Benevolent Committee" (Moscow, 26 September 1877)[110]

The Russian common people have little historical knowledge and no abstract conceptions about the mission of Russia in the Slavonic world; but they have historical instinct, and they clearly perceive one thing, that the war was caused neither by the caprice of an autocratic Tsar nor by unintelligible political considerations. Free from all ambition and all desire for military glory, they accepted the war as a moral duty imposed by Providence – a war for the faith, for Orthodox Christians of the same race as themselves, tortured by the wicked enemies of Christianity....

All the importance of Russia in the great world lies in her peculiar religious and national characteristics combined with external material force – in her Orthodoxy and Slavonism, which distinguish her from Western Europe. She cannot attain her full development without securing the triumph of those spiritual elements in their ancient homes and re-establishing equality of rights for races closely allied to her by blood and spirit. Without the emancipation of the orthodox East from the Turkish yoke, and from the material and moral encroachments of the West, Russia must remain forever mutilated and maimed. For her the war was a necessity, an act of self-defense, or rather the natural continuation of her historic organic development. Blessed is the country whose political missions coincide with the fulfillment of a high moral duty.

From: Ivan Aksakov, "Speech to the Slavonic Benevolent Committee" (Moscow, 4 July 1878)[111]

If the mere reading of the papers makes our blood boil in our veins, what, then, must experience the Sovereign of Russia, who bears the weight of the responsibility which history will lay on his shoulders? Did not he himself give the appellation of a "holy undertaking" to the war in question?... Terrible are the horrors of war, and the heart of our Sovereign cannot lightly call on his subjects for a renewal of deaths, and a fresh shedding of blood – on his subjects ready for all sacrifices. And yet it is not by concessions which are detrimental to the national honor and conscience that one can counteract disasters. Russia wishes not for war, but less still would she desire a peace which dishonors her....

Invincible, invulnerable is the Russian Czar, from the moment when, with a firm belief in the mission of his people, putting aside thoughts about the interests of Western Europe – interests hostile to our own – he will lift up, as say our ancient chronicles, "with dignity, severity, and honor," the standard of Russia, which is also the standard of the Slavs and of all Eastern Christians.

Tolstoiian Pacifism, Anti-Tolstoiism, and Just War Reappraisals

Lev Tolstoi's (1828–1910) reformulation and reassertion of Christian pacifism (developed from ca. 1880 onward) exercised a decisive impact on a number of major contemporaneous and later figures (such as Mahatma Gandhi and Martin Luther King, Jr.) as well as movements professing the ideals of nonviolence and nonresistance, including trends such as Christian anarchism and anarcho-pacifism. Apart from its eclectic conceptual roots (which absorbed the impact of Protestant pacifism), Tolstoiism also shows important continuities with the traditions of Eastern Orthodox pacifism.[112] Tolstoi actively campaigned, moreover, on behalf of Russian pacifistic and persecuted dissenting groups such as the Doukhobors. The following extracts are intended to provide a representative sampling of his eclectic pacifism. They illustrate his influential views on nonresistance to evil (and its Gospel provenance) and on national armies as instruments of organized mass murder.

From: Lev Tolstoi, *My Religion* (1884)[113]

This was the passage that gave me the key to the whole: "*Ye have heard that it hath been said, An eye for an eye, and a tooth for a tooth: But I say unto you, That ye resist not evil*" (Matthew 5:38–39)....

These words suddenly appeared to me as if I had never read them before....
[O]ften in speaking of this passage, Christians took up the Gospel to see for themselves if the words were really there. Through a similar neglect of these words I had failed to understand the words that follow: "*But whosoever shall smite thee on thy right cheek, turn to him the other also*" (Matthew 5:39).... For the first time I grasped the pivotal idea in the words "*Resist not evil*"; I saw that what followed was only a development of this command; I saw that Jesus did not exhort us to turn the other cheek that we might endure suffering, but that his exhortation was, "*Resist not evil*," and that he afterward declared suffering to be the possible consequence of the practice of this maxim.

From: Lev Tolstoi, *The Kingdom of God Is within You* (1893)[114]

The first and crudest form of reply consists in the bold assertion that the use of force is not opposed by the teaching of Christ; that it is permitted, and even enjoined, on the Christian by the Old and New Testaments....

The second, somewhat less gross form of argument, consists in declaring that, though Christ did indeed preach that we should turn the left cheek, and give the cloak also, and this is the highest moral duty; yet that there are wicked men in the world, and if these wicked men were not restrained by force, the whole world and all good men would come to ruin through them....

The third kind of answer, still more subtle than the preceding, consists in asserting that though the command of non-resistance to evil by force is binding on the Christian when the evil is directed against himself personally, it ceases to be binding when the evil is directed against his neighbors, and that then the Christian is not only not bound to fulfill the commandment, but is even bound to act in opposition to it in defense of his neighbors and to use force against transgressors by force....

A fourth, still more refined reply to the question, What ought to be the Christian's attitude to Christ's command of non-resistance to evil by force? consists in declaring that they do not deny the command of non-resistance to evil, but recognize it; but they only do not ascribe to this command the special exclusive value attached to it by sectarians. To regard this command as the indispensable condition of Christian life, as ... the Quakers, the Mennonites, and the Shakers do now, and as the Moravian brethren, the Waldenses, the Albigenses, the Bogomilites and the Paulicians did in the past, is a one-sided heresy.

From: Lev Tolstoy, *The Law of Love and the Law of Violence* (1908)[115]

It would seem natural that if the possibility is once admitted that men may torture or kill their fellow beings in the name of humanity, others may claim the same right to torture and kill in the name of some ideal of the future. The admission of a single exception to the law of love destroys entirely its beneficial effect, although it is the basis of all religious or moral doctrines....

But as soon as one is freed from the superstitions that attempt to justify violence, one understands all the horror of the crimes committed by one nation against another. . . .

[T]he need to oppose evil by violence is merely to provide justification for our habitual vices – of vengeance, cupidity, envy, ambition, pride, cowardice, and spite. . . .

Do not forget that what we all want in common is the union of men, and that this union can never be attained by means of violence. It is enough that everyone should observe the law of love, and this union will then be realized without the need to seek for it. This *supreme law*, alone, is the same for all of us and unites us all.

Revealed by Christ, it is recognized to-day by men, and its observance is obligatory as long as there is revealed to us no other law, a still clearer one, conforming better to the calls of the human conscience.

From: Lev Tolstoi, "Two Wars" (1898)[116]

The people of every nation are being deluded by their rulers, who say to them, "You, who are governed by us, are all in danger of being conquered by other nations; we are watching over your welfare and safety, and consequently we demand of you annually some millions of rubles – the fruit of your labor – to be used by us in the acquisition of arms, cannons, powder, and ships for your defense; we also demand that you yourselves shall enter institutions, organized by us, where you will become senseless particles of a huge machine – the army – which will be under our absolute control. On entering this army you will cease to be men with wills of your own; you will simply do what we require of you. But what we wish, above all else, is to exercise dominion; the means by which we dominate is killing, therefore we will instruct you to kill."

From: Lev Tolstoi, "Nobel's Bequest" (1897)[117]

So that, if peace has not yet been established, it is not because there does not exist among men the universal desire for it; it is not because there is no love for peace and abhorrence of war; but only because there exists the cunning deceit by which men have been, and are, persuaded that peace is impossible and war indispensable. And therefore, to establish peace among men, first of all among Christians, and to abolish war, it is not necessary to inculcate in men anything new; it is only necessary to liberate them from the deceit which has been instilled into them, causing them to act contrary to their general desire.

From: Lev Tolstoi, "Postscript to the 'Life and Death of Ivan Drozhin'" (1895)[118]

The suborned clergy preaches to the soldiers in the churches; suborned writers write books justifying the army; in the schools, those of higher and those of lower grade, false catechisms are made obligatory, and the children are taught in accordance with them that to kill in war and in executing justice is not only possible, but mandatory. All those that enter the army take the oath of allegiance; everything that might reveal the deception is sternly repressed and punished – the most terrible punishments are inflicted on men that refuse to carry out the demands of service in the army, that is, of murder.

From: Lev Tolstoi, "Letter to a Peace Conference" (1899)[119]

Armies can be reduced and abolished only in opposition to the will, but never by the will, of governments. . . .

Armies will first diminish, and then disappear, only when public opinion brands with contempt those who, whether from fear, or for advantage, sell their liberty and enter the ranks of those murderers, called soldiers; and when the men now ignored and even blamed – who, in despite of all the persecution and suffering they have borne – have refused to yield the control of their actions into the hands of others, and become the tools of murder – are recognized by public opinion, to be the foremost champions and benefactors of mankind. Only then will armies first diminish and then quite disappear, and a new era in the life of mankind will commence. And that time is near.

From: Lev Tolstoi, "Patriotism or Peace" (1896)[120]

It must be understood that, as long as we praise patriotism, and cultivate it in the young, so long will there be armaments to destroy the physical and spiritual life of nations; and wars, vast, awful wars, such as we are preparing for, and into the circle of which we are drawing, debauching them in our patriotism, the new and to be dreaded combatants of the far East.

Tolstoiism provoked powerful and long-lasting opposition both in Russia and internationally in circles ranging from ecclesiastical elites (Tolstoi was excommunicated by the Russian Orthodox Church in 1901) to Christian religious philosophers and theoreticians of war ethics; the following extracts demonstrate some of the main arguments of this anti-Tolstoiian/antipacifistic reaction. A forceful criticism of Tolstoiian views on war and government-organized warfare as well as an attempt to formulate a more "ecumenical" Christian just war theory can be discerned in the writings of the renowned Russian religious philosopher Vladimir Solov'ev (1853–1900).

From: Vladimir Solov'ev, *The Justification of the Good* (1895)[121]

Thus to the first question with regard to war there exists only one indisputable answer: *war is an evil*. Evil may be either absolute (such as deadly sin, eternal damnation) or relative, that is, it may be less than some other evil, and, as compared with it, may be regarded as a good (e.g., a surgical operation to save a patient's life).

The significance of war is not exhausted by the negative definition of it as an evil and a calamity. There is also a positive element in it – not in the sense that it can itself be normal, but in the sense that it may be actually necessary in the given condition. *This* way of regarding abnormal phenomena in general is not to be avoided and must be adopted in virtue of the direct demands of the moral ideal and not in contradiction to it. . . .

It is not a case of deviation from the moral norm but of actual realization of that norm in a way which, though dangerous and irregular, proves from real necessity to be the only possible one *under given conditions.*

It may be that war too depends upon a necessity which renders this essentially abnormal course of action permissible and even obligatory *under certain conditions.* . . .

Theories which take up an absolutely negative attitude toward war and maintain that it is the duty of every one to refuse the demand of the state for military service, altogether deny that the individual has any duties toward the state. . . . This view is particularly ill-founded when it appeals to Christianity.

Christianity has revealed to us our absolute dignity, the unconditional worth of the inner being or of the soul of man. This unconditional worth imposes upon us an unconditional duty – to realize the good in the whole of our life, both personal and collective. We know *for certain* that this task is impossible for the individual taken separately or in isolation, and that it can only be realized if the individual life finds its *completion* in the universal historical life of humanity. One of the means of such completion, one of the forms of the universal life – at the present moment of history the chief and the dominant form – is the *fatherland* definitely organized as the state. . . .

But successfully to defend all the weak and innocent against the attacks of evil-doers is impossible for isolated individuals or even groups of many men. Collective organization of such defense is precisely the destination of the military force of the state, and to support the state in one way or another in this work of pity is the moral duty of every one, which no abuses can render void. Just as the fact that ergot is poisonous does not prove that rye is injurious, so the burdens and dangers of *militarism* are no evidence against the necessity of armed forces. . . .

The military or indeed any compulsory organization is not an evil, but a consequence and a symptom of evil.

From: Vladimir Solov'ev, *Three Conversations* (1900)[122]

Prince. – . . . Only think of it: militarism brings forth as its extreme expression the system of universal military service, and, thanks just to that, there perish not only the most modern form of militarism, but all the ancient foundations of the military idea. Wonderful!. . .

Mr. Z. – There isn't the slightest doubt that militarism in Europe and in Russia will eat itself up and die of surfeit, but what sort of joys and triumphs will result from that fact remains to be seen.

Prince. – How? Do you mean to say that you have any doubt but that war and the military business is anything but an unconditional and extreme evil from which humanity has got to free itself absolutely, and as soon as it can? Do you mean to say you doubt that a complete and rapid disappearance of this cannibalism would not be, under any circumstances, a triumph of reason and goodness?

Mr. Z. – I am absolutely convinced to the contrary.

Prince. – That is to say?

Mr. Z. – … that war is not an unconditional evil, and that peace is not an unconditional good, or speaking more simply, it is possible to have a *good war*; it is also possible to have a *bad peace*.

Prince. – Oh, now I see the difference between your point of view and that of the General. He thinks that war is always good and that peace is always bad.

General. – No, no. I understand perfectly that war can be upon occasion a very bad affair, for instance, when we are beaten, as at Narva or Austerlitz; and peace can be splendid, as for instance, the peace of Nishstadt or Kutchuk-Kainardzh.

From: Vladimir Solov'ev, "Byzantinism and Russia" (1896)[123]

Finding the death penalty to be unjust, Vladimir also related to war with Christian nations negatively as well, preserving his retainers just for defense of the land against barbaric and rapacious nomads, who were amenable to no other arguments apart from armed force. . . .

Vladimir Monomakh, who like his great-grandfather was so suffused with Christian spirit that he considered it impermissible to kill even villains, had to live his entire life on horseback in perpetual campaigns, defending the nation from barbaric predators or pacifying internecine struggles among princes.

An influential theologian and polemicist (who was to take up leadership of the Russian Church in exile after the Russian revolution of 1917), Metropolitan Antonii Khrapovitskii of Kiev and Galicia (1863–1936) composed his "The Christian Faith and War" (1916) at the beginning of World War I. His evident intention was to use scriptural exegesis so as to refute Tolstoiian and related pacifist rejections of Christian participation in warfare (and disobedience to the warring state). He endorsed current and those previous Russian military campaigns as "lesser evils," justifiable by reference to Orthodoxy and Orthodox Slavdom. He does not, however, attempt to sanctify the Russian military effort as a "sacred" cause or obligation, unlike some other religiously oriented authors and clerics in Russia,[124] or indeed in Western Europe, during the war period. Invoking patristic authority for his defense of the Russian military effort, he employs the long-standing interpretation of St. Athanasios' canonical epistle to Ammoun (see section on "Eastern Orthodox Canon Law" above) as legitimizing Christian participation in warfare and the killing of adversaries in battle.

From: Metropolitan Antonii Khrapovitskii, *The Christian Faith and War* (1915)[125]

... Christ our Savior and the Apostles did not prohibit their followers from fulfilling their governmental obligations and commanded obedience even to pagan governments. Thus it is clear that although the Lord united His followers in a Churchly union, not in a governmental one, still He did not prohibit their forming a supplementary union for physical self-defense, i.e. a state; but there will never be a state without courts, prisons and wars, and the hopes of our contemporaries that the present war (World War I) will be the final one in history are in direct contradiction not only to reality with its intensifying nationalism, but also to the completely clear predictions of our Savior about the last times when kingdom will rise up against kingdom, and nation against nation (Matthew 24:6–21; cf. Luke 21:10–26)....

We hope that after what has been said all followers of Tolstoy, Pietists, and Mennonites will be obliged to recognize that neither in the Old nor in the New Testament is there any prohibition of participating in war....

They [the fighters for peace] may be ready to recognize that our war is unselfish and is no more than self-defense of the nation and its co-believers, the Slavs; but in the horrors of war they see a greater evil than in everything which might come about as the sad results of a peace such as we described above.... It would be difficult to weaken the force of such arguments if the contrast between war and peace-time were as extreme as it appears at first glance....

The moral elevation which followed the declaration of war and continues to a considerable extent even to the present is a copious redemption of those unavoidable moral crimes with which any war abounds. Take up the Book of Judges; there in the second chapter this law of national life is set forth: in times of political peace the Jews fell into depravity and idolatry; then the Lord sent hostile tribes against them; the people rose up in defense of their homeland and were transfigured morally, bewailing their former apostasy....

Even now there exist Christian communities to a greater or lesser degree foreign to physical self-defense: these are the monasteries and in general all clergymen, who are not permitted to defend themselves with weapons....

However, to impose the demand for such self-denial, of which are capable only exceptionally zealous believers who consciously have abandoned the world ... to a whole people including "those with child and those giving suck" ... such a prohibition would be absolutely unthinkable. War is an evil, but in the given case, and in the majority of Russian wars, a lesser evil than declining war and surrendering to the power of the barbarians either our holy homeland or the other Orthodox nations who are our brothers....

"I did not expect praise for war from a servant of God," a "Christian" of the Tolstoyan sect writes me. The Tolstoyans will respond in the same insincere spirit to this article too. But let them get it into their heads that I am not praising war nor justifying it, but that I consider it a lesser evil than if kings, governments, nations, and individual citizens had declined it in such a situation as that which prevailed two years ago....

Our soldiers going into the field of battle ... did not think about how they would kill, but about how they would die. In their eyes a soldier is not a self-satisfied conqueror, but a self-denying ascetic, laying down his life for the Faith, Tsar, and Fatherland....

I feel that the Tolstoyans will applaud spitefully when they read this canon [St. Basil's thirteenth canon][126] and will reproach our soldiers: "You do not have the right to communicate for three years"; but do not be spiteful, friends.... [T]he penance for soldiers was abolished by the Church at the time when great piety still existed, when the wars with the Moslems increased....

Finally, we have the perfectly clear teaching of the Church about murder in war which is set forth in the canonical epistle of St. Athanasius the Great to the monk Ammun and confirmed by the Sixth Ecumenical Council.[127] With these words of the Church, or more accurately of the Holy Spirit speaking through her mouth, we will conclude the present article....

Murder is reprehensible as an act of self-will and hatred, i.e. personal murder, but killing an enemy in battle "is tolerated and permitted."

Equally, if not more forceful, was the rejection of Tolstoiism that may be found in works on war ethics that were written by Russian émigrés such as Anton Kersnovskii (1905–1944) and Ivan Il'in (1883–1954). The latter published in 1925 his *On Resistance to Evil by Force* wherein he reaffirmed the necessity of war but questioned whether it can ever be defined as "just." This essay provoked intense disputes in Russian émigré lay intellectual and clerical circles.

From: Anton Kersnovskii, *The Philosophy of War* (1939)[128]

We have to denounce the pseudo-teaching of the "non-resistance to evil by force" as God-opposed, anti-church and in the final analysis – inhuman.

From: Ivan Il'in, *On Resistance to Evil by Force* (1925)[129]

[T]he teaching of Count L. N. Tolstoi and his followers attracted to itself weak and simple-minded people, and assuming a false appearance of a consonance with the spirit of Christ's teachings, has been poisoning Russian religious and political culture....

Resistance to evil by force and sword does not represent, therefore, a sinful action on all these occasions when it is objectively necessary or where it appears to be the only and least unrighteous alternative. Claims that such kind of resistance represents "evil," "sin," or "moral crime" reveal a paucity of moral experience or helpless obscurity of thought.

Nevertheless, this resistance carries out a moral unrighteousness.... The very act of *resistance* to evil as such always remains a good, righteous, and necessary deed. The more difficult the resistance, the greater the dangers and suffering which accompany it, the greater the feat and merit of the one who resists. But this *that* the resisting swordbearer does in the struggle with the evildoer does not represent perfect, nor holy, nor a righteous series of acts. Indeed only the naive rudeness of the doctrinaire moralist can define it as "evil" and "sin," since actually it represents an *unsinful* (!) enactment of unrighteousness. But it would be no less of a mistake to absolutely justify and sanctify the use of force and the sword, since in reality it is a deed which is an unsinful enactment of *unrighteousness* (!). An absolute ban on the sword and the use of force should not be imposed, as a resort to them can be religiously and morally necessary.

The issues of rejection, justifiability, and sanctification of war in earlier and modern Christian frameworks, going beyond the Eastern Orthodox experience, attracted the attention of other prominent Russian émigré figures such as the religious and political philosopher Nikolai Berdiaev (1874–1948), the influential theologian Vladimir Losskii (1903–1958), and Mother Maria Skobtsova (1891–1945, canonized in 2004).

From: Nikolai Berdiaev, *Slavery and Freedom* (1939)[130]

There never was a really "holy" state; still less can wars be "holy." But all this is intensified once we begin to speak in terms of modern times and modern wars, that more nearly resemble cosmic catastrophe. The military ideals of honor were always un-Christian, against the Gospel, but modern war is immeasurably lower than those concepts of honor....

There is nothing more monstrous than the blessing of war by Christian churches, than that awful combination of words, "Christ-loving soldiers." Man should be a warrior; he is called to warfare. But this has nothing to do with a corporation of the military which is an extreme form of human enslavement. We must clearly distinguish this viewpoint from bourgeois pacifism which is powerless to stop war and may even be a condition lower than war itself.... There is a peace more shameful than war: peace is not to be purchased at any price. True war against war is truly war, courage and readiness to sacrifice.... Many Christians turn away in horror from revolution because it implies killing and bloodshed, but they accept and even bless war which kills more people and sheds more blood than does revolution.... Revolution may be a far lesser evil than war. But only a Christianity purified and liberated from historical enslavement may put the question of war and revolution....

From: Nikolai Berdiaev, *The Divine and Human* (1947)[131]

The denunciation of the evil and sin of war should not be permitted to lead to absolute pacifism, to peace at any price. In the evil condition of our world, war may be the lesser of two evils. While a war of conquest or subjugation is absolute evil, protective or liberating war may be not only justified but hallowed.... Good is active in a concrete world-milieu, complex and indistinct, and the action of good may not always be in a direct line. Good may sometimes be compelled to struggle for the lesser evil. The final abolition of war is linked with a change in the spiritual condition of human society and the social order.

From: Vladimir Losskii, *Seven Days on Road of France* (1940)[132]

War is not fought for absolute values. This was the great error of the so-called "religious" wars and the main cause of their inhuman atrocities. War is equally not waged for relative values that we attempt to render absolute, for abstract concepts we cloak in religion. If we oppose the idol of the "pure race" with the more humane idols of law, liberty and humanity, they would not be any the less idols for it, ideas rendered hypostasized and absolute; the war would still be a war of idols, and not a human war. Human war, the only just war (inasmuch as any war may be called just) is a war for relative values, for values that we know to be relative. It is a war where man – a being called for an absolute goal – dedicates himself spontaneously and without hesitation for a relative value that he knows to be relative: the soil, the land, the Homeland. And this sacrifice acquires an absolute value, imperishable and eternal for the human person. . . .

We also talked about Justice, and even the justice of God, in the name of which we should fight so that justice (which is an attribute of God) would triumph in the face of our adversaries' iniquity. "Our cause is just. This is why God will grant us victory." This is how the prelates spoke, the people's spiritual leaders. The just cause often triumphed in "God's judgment," those judicial duels waged between two parties in conflict. But those two parties abandoned their justice, abandoned their just cause, to give place to divine justice alone – without possibility of appeal – which would manifest through their feat of arms. And again, the Church was obliged to oppose this practice eight hundred years ago. . . . His [God's] justice is not our justice, because His ways are not our ways. . . . We should have prayed for victory with tears and great contrition, bearing in mind this fearsome Justice, before which we are all unjust. We should not have called on Justice, which is beyond our measure, which we could not bear, but on the infinite mercy which made the Son of God descend from Heaven.

From: Mother Maria Skobtsova, "Insight in Wartime" (posth. 1947)[133]

I think that, in our notions of war, the definitions of attacking and defending sides are not sufficiently detailed. These notions are put in place at the beginning of a conflict with the aim of using them for diplomatic, political, and economic purposes. But in fact the real moral or even religious distinction has not been made. . . .

There is something in war that makes people listen – not all, but many – and suddenly, amid the roar of cannons, the rattle of machine guns, the groaning of the wounded, they hear something else, they hear the distant, warning trumpet of the archangel.

There is also, in a sense, a more terrible phenomenon, which cannot be accounted for by statistics: it is the brutalization of nations, the lowering of the cultural level, the loss of creative ability – the decadence of souls. Every war throws the whole of mankind back. . . .

The war demands of us, more than ever, that we mobilize absolutely all our spiritual powers and abilities. . . . In our time Christ and the life-giving Holy Spirit demand the whole person. The only difference from state mobilization is that the state enforces mobilization, while our faith waits for volunteers. And, in my view, the destiny of mankind depends on whether these volunteers exist and, if they do, how great their energy is, how ready they are for sacrifice.

Nationalism, Militarism, and Orthodoxy in Post-Ottoman Southeast Europe

The involvement of the Orthodox churches in the post-Ottoman state formations in Southeast Europe, as well as their attitudes to the military confrontations (including the legitimization of anti-Ottoman war efforts) and outbreaks of organized violence that accompanied these processes, have not yet received the close attention and comparative analysis they certainly deserve. One of the obvious instances of this coalescence of nationalism, militarism, and Orthodoxy was the newly established institution of military chaplains. Below are reproduced some statutes on their duties, from a Romanian document dated 1877.

From: Romanian Orthodox Church Statute on the Duties of Military Priests, "Address to Soldiers to Join Battle" (1877)[134]

Soldiers, beloved sons of this sacred Church! For the Fatherland and Church your parents fought until death. . . . We die or live, we belong to God. You should prefer an honored death to a shameful life and subsequently the enemy's powers will be diminished like the spiders' web. God is with you. Forward my sons. . . . Be convinced that God, who is the master of the people's life, will generously embrace your souls in his hands and full of glory you will return to your beloved fatherland, where you will be applauded by the whole people. God bless your arms, and let Him crown you with the glory of victory. Amen.

Some of the most far-reaching and symptomatic attempts to "update" Orthodox justifiable war ethics within nineteenth- and twentieth-century ethno-religious frameworks can be discerned in the writings of the influential Serbian hierarch, theologian, and preacher Bishop Nikolaj Velimirović (1880–1956, declared a saint of the Serbian Orthodox Church in 2003). The following extracts reveal the interweaving of notions from the Kosovo covenantal mythology (which had evolved in Serbian Orthodox readings of the religious dimension of the Battle of Kosovo in 1389); the Serbian religio-national ideology of "Svetosavlje" (the teachings of St. Sava (1174–1236), which emerged in the interwar period); and a "crusade"-oriented anti-Ottoman just war rhetoric that extolled the ethos of the Church Militant fighting physical battles against infidel enemies, "sword against the sword."

From: Bishop Nikolaj Velimirović, *Serbia in Light and Darkness* (1916)[135]

Our kings of old said very often that Serbia must fight on the side of justice, even if justice has for the moment no visible chance to be victorious. Our saint King, Lazar, refused on the eve of the battle of Kosovo to negotiate with the Turkish Sultan, whom he regarded as a bearer of injustice and an enemy of Christianity....

... King Lazar ... perished with all his army on the field of Kosovo fighting for Cross and Freedom against Islam rushing over Europe.

From: Bishop Nikolaj Velimirović, *Agony of the Church* (1917)[136]

Islam was another kind of Imperialism against which the Church fought. If the Roman Imperialism was cool, calculating, without any fanaticism, Islam was a unique form of religious, fanatical Imperialism, having in view world-conquest and world-dominion, like Rome and yet unlike Rome. Here the Church fought with the sword against the sword. Before the definite fall of the Roman Empire the crusades of Christianity against Islam began, and it has not been finished until this day. Very dramatic was this struggle in Palestine, under Western crusaders, in Spain and Russia. But I think the most dramatic act of this dramatic conflict happened in the Balkans, especially in Serbia, during the last five hundred years.

From: Bishop Nikolaj Velimirović, *The Serbian People as a Servant of God* 53 (pub. posth. 1984)[137]

[T]he leaders of the Serbian people – be they kings or tsars, or despots or commanders or military governors – served Christ their God from their thrones and seats of power; as founders of churches and monasteries, as defenders of the Orthodox faith, as helpers in defense of neighboring peoples, as protectors of the poor, and as cross-bearing warriors against the infidels.

From: Bishop Nikolaj Velimirović, "Kosovo and St. Vitus' Day" (1939)[138]

He [St. Sava] did not want only a holy church but also holy education, a holy culture, a holy dynasty, holy rule, a holy army, a holy country and a holy people. A holy army, entirely surrounded by a halo of sacredness; an army which fought for the sacrosanctity of the people, the sacrosanctity of Christendom, the sacrosanctity of Europe....

The people want with all their heart a holy church, holy schools, a holy culture, a holy dynasty, holy rule, a holy country and – a holy army. Yes, also a holy army. I.e. an army ... which heroically defends the truth and justice of God and – when needed – heroically sacrifices itself for the truth and justice of God.

In the following extract, Patriarch Gavrilo V of Serbia (1881–1950) sets the events of the Serbian military coup on 27 March 1941 (which deposed the Regent Prince Paul of Yugoslavia, two days after he had signed the Tripartite Pact with the Axis powers and was to be followed shortly by the German invasion and occupation of the country) in the framework of the "Kosovo ethics," symbolized by the military deeds of paradigmatic (historic and epic) figures of Serbian anti-Ottoman resistance (Obilić and Prince Marko) and the restoration of Serbian statehood (after anti-Ottoman revolts) by Karađorđe and Obrenović. Combining elements of the Kosovo covenantal mythology with militarist imagery and just war notions, Patriarch Gavrilo effectively ascribes to the Serbian military efforts a religio-historic salvific quality.

From: Patriarch Gavrilo V of Serbia, "What Is the significance of March 27?" (1941)[139]

[T]he Kosovo ethics ... has elevated our past and exalted the spirit of Obilić, who became an ideal and a model of heroism, as well as the scope of Prince Marko, a protector of justice and a hero who defeated the enemy.... The same Kosovo spirit inspired Karađorđe and Miloš [Obrenović] to build a new foundation for the Serbian state, which rose ever higher, and this clearly proves that the entire ascent of the Serbian people in history was won only and exclusively by the sword, in a sea of spilled blood and countless victims, which means that without all of this there is no victory, as there is no resurrection without death.

The Russian Orthodox Church during the Russian Civil War and World War II

Bolshevik legislation and measures against the Russian Orthodox Church began as early as the Russian civil war of 1917–1923. Despite his various pronouncements and protests against these measures, St. Tikhon, Patriarch of Moscow and all Russia (1918–1925), did not officially "sanctify" the anti-Bolshevik war effort of the White Army, appealing, along with influential preachers such as archpriest Ioann Vostorgov (1864–1918), for a nonviolent resistance to the suppression of Church institutions, hierarchy, and religious life. While condemning civil war as "fratricidal fury," Patriarkh Tikhon condemned the Bolsheviks for signing the Treaty of Brest-Litovsk (1918), defining it as "disgraceful" for extinguishing in the conscience of Russians the Christian warrior ethos, as legitimized through St. Constantine–Cyril's reading of John 15: 13 (see sections entitled "The *Vita* of St. Constantine–Cyril the Philosopher" and "Tolstoiian Pacifism, Anti-Tolstoiism, and Just War Reappraisals," above).

From: Archpriest Ioann Vostorgov, Sermon "The Struggle for Faith and the Church" (1918)[140]

By religious processions, petitions, declarations, protests, resolutions, messages to the authorities – by decisive force, by all that is permitted by Christian conscience, we can and are obliged to fight in the holy fight for faith and church, for the trampled treasures of our soul.... Let them cross our dead bodies. Let them shoot us, shoot innocent children and women. Let us go with crosses, icons, unarmed, with prayers and hymns – let Cain and Judas kill us! The time has come to go to martyrdom and suffering!

From: St. Tikhon, Patriarch of Moscow, "Pastoral Letter" (19 January/1 February 1918)[141]

And you, brothers archpastors and pastors, without delaying in your spiritual action for one hour, with burning faith call our sons to defend the trampled rights of the Orthodox church, immediately organize religious leagues, call them ... to range themselves in the ranks of the spiritual fighters, who to external force will oppose the strength of their holy inspiration, and we firmly trust that the enemies of the church of Christ will be broken and scattered by the strength of the Cross of Christ....

From: St. Tikhon, Patriarch of Moscow, "Letter to the Council of People's Commissars" (13/26 October 1918)[142]

... You have deprived our soldiers of everything for which they had fought bravely in the past. You have instructed them, who not so long ago were still valiant and unconquerable, to abandon the defense of the motherland, to escape from the battlefields. You have extinguished in their hearts the conscience which used to inspire them that "No one has greater love than this, to lay down one's life for one's friends" (John 15:13)....

Having given up the defense of the motherland from external enemies, you, however, are ceaselessly raising troops.

Against whom will you lead them?...

It was not Russia who needed the disgraceful peace with the external enemy concluded by you, but you yourself, who have contrived to finally destroy its internal peace.

... Celebrate the anniversary of taking the power by setting free the imprisoned, by putting an end to bloodshed, violence, ruination, constrains on faith; turn not to destruction, but to the institution of order and lawfulness, give to the people their yearned for and deserved respite from fratricidal conflict.

Paradoxically in Russia itself, World War II was to bring about a reinstatement of the Russian Church after several cycles of intensifying Soviet anti-Church repression. This ensued from Stalin's decision to engage the Church's support to boost national unity so as to mobilize for the massive war effort against Nazi Germany. The following extracts from sermons and pronouncements of leading Russian hierarchs during the war reveal that apart from blessing, praying for, and praising the heroic and just defensive war (which in some of the statements acquires a degree of "holiness") of the Russian army (enhanced by repeated invocations of John 15:13), they viewed the conflict as possessing universal religious and ethical dimensions. In their eyes it was fought on behalf of humanity against an inhuman and anti-Christian enemy.[143]

From: Metropolitan Sergii, "Sermon" (26.06.1941)[144]

A dark and wild storm is threatening our country. Our native land is in danger and calls to us: "All to the ranks, all to the defense of the native soil, its historical sanctuaries, its freedom from foreign enslavement." Shame on him, whoever he be, who remains indifferent to such a call, who leaves it to others to sacrifice themselves for the common cause of the people.... We are not taught to act thus by any of our Orthodox God-inspired people, who used not to hesitate to sacrifice themselves for their friends and thus achieved victory over ... foreign foe[s]....

Fear at an invasion of believers of another faith never has caused, and never will cause, our Orthodox people faintheartedly to betray their best historical traditions and hand over without a struggle both their country and their future destiny to the mercy of a sworn enemy.

From: Metropolitan Sergii, "Sermon" (12.08.1941)[145]

At the present time all our thoughts are turned to the West, to the places where our valiant soldiers are engaged in mortal battle with the enemy who has fallen on our Fatherland. Continually thinking of them, we pray God to give them strength, courage and patience to endure the heavy trials of war, and to crown their efforts with victory.

This time I should like to recall the prayer for those whom the Lord has called to lay down their lives in battle....

[T]here is ... sense and great hope in praying for those who have fallen in battle, and it is our brotherly duty to do this because they laid down their souls for us.

May then the just Judge in his ineffable mercy give to our warriors the crowns of immortality for their self-sacrificing heroic deeds....

From: Metropolitan Aleksei of Leningrad, "Sermon" (10.08.1941)[146]

And just as the Russian people were called during the Napoleonic era to liberate the whole world from the madness of tyranny, so today has fallen to our people the high mission of delivering humanity from the villainies of fascism, of giving back freedom to the enslaved countries and of establishing everywhere peace, which has been so insolently destroyed by fascism. The Russian people march to carry out this holy object with complete self-denial.

From: Metropolitan Nikolai of Kiev, "Sermon" (3 August 1941)[147]

Fulfilling their most holy duty, all the Orthodox believers of our country give all their efforts to defend the country at the present time.... The believers are encouraged to patriotic deeds not only by the consciousness of their civil and Christian duty, but also by that special blessing of the Holy Orthodox Church.

May the Lord Himself crown with the most complete success the holy labors of all who do not spare their lives for the sake of a more speedy victory over the monster of the human race!

From: Archpriest A. P. Smirnov, "Sermon" (4 December 1941)[148]

On 22 June 1941, our beautiful land put on a crown of thorns. From under the sharp needles, the first ruby drops of sacrificial blood fell over its face, fulfilling the Gospel precept: "Greater love hath no man than this, that he lay down his life for his friends" (John 15:13).

On that day our country and all who dwell in it took on their shoulders the great and glorious cross of the Holy War of Liberation.

From: Aleksei, Archbishop of Ufa, "On the Altar of the Fatherland" (27 March 1942)[149]

Young and old, the whole of the Orthodox community in Russia have risen for the defense of their Fatherland, and their arms have been blessed with the heavenly blessing conferred on them through the supreme hierarch of the Russian Orthodox Church, His Beatitude the Metropolitan Sergius....

Faithful sons of Orthodox Russia ... [t]hey display the loftiest self-abnegation and self-sacrifice, the spirit of the noblest Christian love.... [E]mbodying in their exploits the Gospel words: "Greater love hath no man than this, that a man lay down his life for his friends" (John 15:13)....

Everything in the Russian people is permeated and illuminated by holy prayer and Christian faith, and this faith will burn and consume those who have dared to invade our holy soil.

From: Pitirim, Bishop of Kaluga, "Praise to Thee, Holy Moscow!" (28 March 1942)[150]

Just wars have always called forth the heroism of the people, fighting forgetful of self....

We Russian people clearly recognize that the German Army is waging an unjust war.

Our Army is fighting for the rights of all humanity, for the righteousness of God, for eternal justice. The Lord God, who sent down on us this great trial, seeing our readiness to defend with our lives our native land, seeing our eager devotion to the noble and lofty aims of the war which we are waging, is giving us victory over the foe.

From: Aleksei, Metropolitan of Leningrad, "Eastertide in Leningrad" (09 April 1942)[151]

In this Easter message the Metropolitan Sergius speaks especially strongly of the base acts and plans of fascist Germany "which has dared to take as its banner the pagan swastika instead of the Cross of Christ." This is not the first time that the Metropolitan Sergius has borne witness, in the name of the Church, to the fact that the fascists and their bloodstained leader Hitler are savage enemies of Christianity, and that he deepens the conviction of believers that there can be no agreement between these bestial degenerates of the human race and Christians without a betrayal of Christ.

The Eastern Orthodox Churches and Peace-Making Initiatives during the Cold War

The following statements by three Eastern Orthodox Church patriarchs, enunciated during the Cold War period, highlight how peace-making activities (and related rhetoric) of the respective ecclesiastical hierarchies were carried through international bodies and networks such as the World Council of Churches, World Peace Council, and Christian Peace Conference. Such activities were also exercised within the Peace and Disarmament Campaign of the 1980s.[152]

From: Patriarch Justinian of Romania (1948–1977), "Evangelical Humanism and Christian Responsibility" (1967)[153]

The struggle for peace has become today an active testimony of God the Creator, Redeemer, and Comforter, namely: God the Father, the Son, and the Holy Spirit. These efforts reflect, in practice, one of the main means of proving one's active confession of the Christian faith. Acting through the World Council of Churches against a devastating war, Christianity thus witnesses its belief in the immeasurable value of the world, created and redeemed by God. . . .

Peace calls for equality between men and nations and equality rests on justice which in its turn derives from freedom. Peace in freedom is the only peace which ensures human dignity. Therefore, the World Council of Churches is striving for a peace that promotes the freedom of nations and men.

From: Patriarch Pimen I of Moscow (1971–1990), "An Orthodox View on Contemporary Ecumenism"[154]

Every good undertaking which furthers the cause of peace and friendship among peoples, which lowers international tension and opens a sphere of international collaboration and mutual understanding must call forth our warm support, encouragement, understanding and readiness to cooperate. . . .

We are ready to listen and are full of good will and desire to understand other points of view if their aim is the achievement of a stable and just peace among the nations.

Going on from there, we are assuming that it would be useful for the World Council of Churches and for the Ecumenical Movement as a whole to take note of the views of a large body of churches and numerous Christians, who have combined their efforts toward the building of peace within the framework of the Christian Peace Conference.

From: Patriarch Cyril of Bulgaria (1953–1971), "Address of Welcome to Dr. Eugene Blake" (1968)[155]

The problem of war and peace is still the outstanding problem.... [T]o work for peace, especially today, is one of the primary tasks of Christian ecumenicity.

The menace of war is constantly hanging over our heads and may overwhelm the world at any moment with all its forces of destruction. Can any duty be more important, therefore, than that of preventing the flames of war from developing into a world conflagration?

The issues of justifiability of warfare and whether just war theory was ever conceptualized in Eastern Orthodox traditions were treated in statements such as the "Orthodox Perspectives on Justice and Peace," issued after the meeting of Orthodox theologians in Minsk in May 1989.

From: "Orthodox Perspectives on Justice and Peace" (1989)[156]

Another problem, specific to the church, is the dilemma presented by the phenomenon of Christian participation in war. The Orthodox Church unreservedly condemns war as evil. Yet it also recognizes that in the defense of the innocent and the protection of one's people from unjust attack, criminal activity and the overthrowing of oppression, it is sometimes necessary, with reluctance, to resort to arms. In every case, such a decision must be taken with full consciousness of its tragic dimensions. Consequently, the Greek fathers of the Church have never developed a "just war theory," preferring rather to speak of the blessings of and the preference for peace.

The Post-Communist Period

In a succession of statements in the 1990s, excerpts from two of which are reproduced here, the Ecumenical Patriarch of Constantinople Bartholomew I addressed various issues related to the morality of modern warfare, interreligious violence, and militaristic religious nationalism. He focused in particular on the irrationality of war and its adverse impact on the physical and spiritual environment. Especially significant in this series of pronouncements was his reiteration of the traditional Eastern Orthodox patristic and ecclesiastical pacific stance that the Orthodox Church "forgives armed defense against oppression and violence" only in a limited set of cases.

From: Ecumenical Patriarch Bartholomew I, "Environment, Peace, and Economy" (24 May 1999)[157]

In particular, we would like to address the impact of war on the environment. For if ecological issues are acute even during times of peace, when the protection of human beings is perceived positively, then how much more critical are these issues during times of war, when the extermination of others and the destruction of their environment are the unfortunate objective?...

Indeed, if we consider the consequences of war at different historical periods, then we shall also observe the sad reality that, the closer one comes to our period, the more dramatic the effects of military clashes have been on the natural environment....

Finally, the spiritual atmosphere is inundated by boundless falsehoods of propaganda; passions are cultivated in people's souls; hatred and violence are justified. The effects of this spiritual "pollution" are manifested everywhere in the world, irrespective of distance....

This list of environmental effects that result from contemporary warfare clearly shows the irrationality of military conflict, which can only be explained as a paranoid act. For, while war is instigated supposedly in order to protect certain people who are provoked by their unjust treatment by other people, nevertheless warfare ensures that unjust treatment is extended to include numerous others....

Therefore, *the irrationality of war is evident from its effect on humanity and on the natural environment.* It is our duty to intervene, wherever possible, to persuade those who are responsible for making decisions to seek peaceful resolutions to human problems.... The choice of military violence as the sole method for resolving conflicts betrays a lack of imagination and intellectual laziness, as well as misplaced confidence in the erroneous notion that evil can be corrected by evil.

As heralds of the Gospel truth, which is the only complete truth, we repeat the words of the Apostle: "Do not be overcome by evil, but overcome evil with good" (Romans 12:21). We conclude with this exhortation, adding only our fervent prayers that irrational wars may cease as soon as possible and that the almighty and beneficent Lord may grant everyone the wisdom to understand that war is an impasse.

From: Ecumenical Patriarch Bartholomew I, "War and Suffering" (22 October 1999)[158]

War and violence are never means used by God in order to achieve a result. They are for the most part machinations of the devil used to achieve unlawful ends. We say "for the most part" because, as is well known, in a few specific cases the

Orthodox Church forgives an armed defense against oppression and violence. However, as a rule, peaceful resolution of differences and peaceful cooperation are more pleasing to God and more beneficial to humankind.

War and violence breed hatred and revenge, leading to an endless cycle of evil until opponents completely annihilate each other....

[O]ur main concern is not to impose our will on others, but to walk together with justice and not to act unjustly. In the long term, this will prove to be more advantageous, because whatever is built on injustice collapses with the passage of time. This is the reason why wars keep recurring, because after each war things are not regulated on the basis of right, but on the basis of might.

The Bases of the Social Concept of the Russian Church

It is difficult to overestimate the importance of the section on "War and Peace" in the statement of faith, *The Bases of the Social Concept of the Russian Church*, issued in 2000 by the Jubilee Council of Russian Bishops. It has even been proposed that this document should be adopted as a basis for the Russian state's religious policies. While reiterating the traditional Eastern Orthodox teaching on war as unconditionally evil and the divine, "grace-filled," and salvific gift of peace, the statement identifies the cases in which war must be deemed "necessary," despite its being evil and undesirable. To justify the resort to armed force in such instances the document reproduces the already quoted pronouncement of St. Constantine–Cyril (see section on "The *Vita* of St. Constantine–Cyril the Philosopher" above), which based, as in previous instances (see sections on "Tolstoiian Pacifism, Anti-Tolstoiism, and Just War Reappraisals" and "The Russian Orthodox Church during the Russian Civil War and World War II"), its justifiable war doctrine on John 15:13. Significantly, the statement reproduces the traditional *jus ad bellum* and *jus in bello* conditions of the Western Christian just war tradition (as modeled on St. Augustine's teachings), redefining some of them on the basis of scriptural exegesis. The document articulates the Russian Church's special concern for the Christian education of the military, the tasks of military chaplains, a commitment to international peace making, and opposition to any propaganda of war.

From: Jubilee Bishops' Council of the Russian Orthodox Church, "War and Peace" (2000)[159]

VIII. 1. War is a physical manifestation of the latent illness of humanity, which is fratricidal hatred (Gen. 4:3–12). Wars have accompanied human history since the fall and, according to the Gospel, will continue to accompany it: "And when ye hear of wars and rumors of wars, be ye not troubled: for such things must needs be" (Mark 13:7).... *War is evil. Just as the evil in man in general, war is caused by the sinful abuse of the God-given freedom*; "for out of the heart proceed evil thoughts, murder, adulteries, fornications, thefts, false witness, blasphemies" (Matt. 15:19)....

VIII. 2. Bringing to people the good news of reconciliation (Rom. 10:15), but being in "this world" lying in evil (1 John 5:19) and filled with violence, Christians involuntarily come to face the vital need to take part in various battles. *While recognizing war as evil, the Church does not prohibit her children from participating in hostilities if at stake is the security of their neighbors and the restoration of trampled justice. Then war is considered to be [a] necessary though undesirable means.* In all times, Orthodoxy has had profound respect for soldiers who gave their lives to protect the life and security of their neighbors. The Holy Church has canonized many soldiers, taking into account their Christian virtues and applying to them Christ's word: "Greater love hath no man but this, that a man lay down his life for his friends" (John 15:13). [Here the statement reproduces the relevant episode from St. Constantine–Cyril's *Vita*; see section on "The *Vita* of St. Constantine–Cyril the Philosopher" above.]

VIII. 3. **"**They that take the sword shall perish with the sword" (Matt. 26:52). These words of the Savior justify the idea of just war. From the Christian perspective, *the conception of moral justice in international relations should be based on the following basic principles: love of one's neighbors, people and Fatherland; understanding of the needs of other nations; conviction that it is impossible to serve one's country by immoral means....*

The development of high moral standards in international relations would have [been] impossible without that moral impact which Christianity made on people's hearts and minds. The requirements of justice in war were often far from being complied with, but the very posing of the question of justice sometimes restrained warring people from extreme violence.

In defining just war, the Western Christian tradition, which goes back to St. Augustine, usually puts forward a number of conditions on which war in one's own or others' territory is admissible. [Here the statement reproduces a summary of the relevant conditions of the Western Christian just war tradition.]

In the present system of international relations, *it is sometimes difficult to distinguish an aggressive war from a defensive war.* The distinction between the two is especially subtle where one or two states or the world community initiate hostilities on the ground that it is necessary to protect the people who fell victim to an aggression (see XV. 1). In this regard, the *question* whether the Church should support or deplore the hostilities *needs to be given a special consideration every time they are initiated or threaten to begin.*

Among obvious signs pointing to the equity or inequity of a warring party are *its war methods* and attitude toward its war prisoners and the civilians of the opposite side, especially children, women and elderly. Even in the defense from an aggression, every kind of evil can be done, making one's spiritual and moral stand not superior to that of the aggressor. *War should be waged with righteous indignation, not maliciousness, greed and lust (1 John 2:16) and other fruits of hell.* A war can be correctly assessed as a feat or a robbery only after an analysis is made of the moral state of the warring parties. "Rejoice not over thy greatest enemy being dead, but remember that we die all," Holy Scriptures says (Sirach

8:8). Christian humane attitude to the wounded and war prisoners is based on the words of St. Paul: "If thine enemy hunger, feed him; if he thirst, give him drink; for so doing thou shalt heap coals of fire on his head. Be not overcome of evil, but overcome evil with good" (Rom. 12:21–22).

VIII. 4 ... *The Church has a special concern for the military, trying to educate them for the faithfulness to lofty moral ideals.* The agreement concluded by the Russian Orthodox Church with the Armed Forces and law-enforcement agencies opens up considerable opportunities for overcoming the artificially created dividing walls, *for bringing the military back to the established Orthodox traditions of service to the fatherland.* Orthodox pastors, both those who perform special service in the army and those who serve in monasteries and parishes, are called to nourish the military strenuously, taking care of their moral condition.

NOTES

1 See, e.g., the brief and cautious overview of this field in Timothy S. Miller, "Introduction," in Timothy S. Miller and John Nesbit (eds.), *Peace and War in Byzantium. Essays in Honor of George T. Dennis* (Washington, D.C.: Catholic University of America Press, 1995), pp. 1–17, at pp. 11–12; cf. the comments in John Haldon, *Warfare, State and Society in the Byzantine World, 565–1204* (London: University College Press, 1999), pp. 2–7, passim.

2 Hildo Bos and Jim Forest (eds.), *For the Peace from Above: An Orthodox Resource Book on War, Peace and Nationalism* (Bialystok: Syndesmos Press, 1999); available at http://www.incommunion.org/2004/10/18/toc/

3 Such as St. Justin Martyr (ca. 100–ca. 165), Clement of Alexandria (ca. 150–ca. 215), St. Hippolytus (ca. 170–ca. 236), Tertullian (ca. 160–ca. 225), Origen (ca. 185–ca. 254), St. Cyprian of Carthage (d. 258), Arnobius (third to fourth century), and Lactantius (ca. 250–ca. 325).

4 See note 60 below.

5 On this process, see Hélène Ahrweiler, *L'Idéologie politique de l'empire byzantine* (Paris: P.U.F., 1975), pp. 42ff.; Angeliki E. Laiou, "On Just War in Byzantium," in J. Langdon et al. (eds.), *To Hellenikon*, vol. 1: *Hellenic Antiquity and Byzantium. Studies in Honor of Speros Vryonis Jr.* (New Rochelle, N.Y.: Aristide D. Caratzas, 1993), pp. 153–177, at pp. 163–164.

6 Laiou, "On Just War in Byzantium" (on the basis of an analysis focused especially on Anna Komnene's *Alexiad*); see the more restricted classification of Byzantine types of just war in W. Treadgold, "Byzantium, the Reluctant Warrior," in N. Christie and M. Yazigi (eds.), *Noble Ideals and Bloody Realities: Warfare in the Middle Ages* (Leiden: Brill, 2006), pp. 209–33, at pp. 212–213; cf. also Angeliki E. Laiou, "The Just War of Eastern Christians and the Holy War of the Crusaders," in Richard Sorabji and David Rodin (eds.), *The Ethics of War: Shared Problems in Different Traditions* (Aldershot, Hants: Ashgate, 2006), pp. 30–44, at pp. 33–34; George T. Dennis, "Defenders of the Christian People: Holy War in Byzantium," in Angeliki E. Laiou and Roy Parviz Mottaheden (eds.), *The Crusades from the Perspective of Byzantium and the Muslim World* (Washington, D.C.: Dumbarton Oaks Research Library and Collection, 2001), pp. 31–41, at pp. 37–38.

7 On the military religious services in the Byzantine army, see J.-R. Vieillefond, "Les pratiques religieuses dans l'armée byzantine d'après les traités militaires," *Revue des études anciennes* 37 (1935), 322–330; Michael McCormick, *Eternal Victory: Triumphal Rulership in Late Antiquity, Byzantium and the Early Medieval West* (Cambridge: Cambridge University Press,

1986), pp. 238–251; George T Dennis, "Religious Services in the Byzantine Army," in E. Carr et al. (eds.), *Eulogēma: Studies in Honor of Robert Taft, S.J.* (Rome: Pontificio Ateneo S. Anselmo, 1993), pp. 107–118.

8   See James A. Brundage, *Medieval Canon Law and the Crusader* (Madison: University of Wisconsin Press, 1969), pp. 22–26.

9   On these developments in the military religious ideology of the Byzantine military classes positioned along the Anatolian frontiers, see Gilbert Dagron and Haralambie Mihǎescu (eds.), *Le traité sur la guérilla (De velitatione) de l'empereur Nicéphore Phocas (963–969)* (Paris: Editions du CNRS, 1986), pp. 284–286; Tia M. Kolbaba, "Fighting for Christianity: Holy War in the Byzantine Empire," *Byzantion* 68 (1998), 194–221, at 206–207; John Haldon, *Warfare, State and Society in the Byzantine World, 565–1204* (London: University College Press, 1999), pp. 30–32.

10 On the rise, spread, and evolution of the cult of Byzantine military saints, see Hippolyte Delehaye, *Les légendes grecques des saints militaries* (Paris: Librairie A. Picard, 1909); Alexander F. C. Webster, "Varieties of Christian Military Saints: From Martyrs under Caesar to Warrior Princes," *St. Vladimir's Theological Quarterly* 24 (1980), 3–35; Christopher Walter, *The Warrior Saints in Byzantine Art and Tradition* (Aldershot: Ashgate, 2002).

11 Some of the relevant studies of this problematic have been reprinted in part 1 in John Haldon (ed.), *Byzantine Warfare* (Aldershot: Ashgate, 2007). For further references and summary of the arguments of both sides of the debate, see Yuri Stoyanov, "Norms of War in Eastern Orthodox Christianity," in G. Reichberg, V. Popovski, and N. Turner (eds.), *World Religions and Norms of War* (Tokyo: UNU Press, 2009), pp. 84–128, at pp. 176–180.

12 See, e.g., Henry Huttenbach, "The Origins of Russian Imperialism," in Taras Hunczak (ed.), *Russian Imperialism from Ivan the Great to the Revolution* (New Brunswick, N.J.: Rutgers University Press, 1974), pp. 18–44, at p. 25; Henri Troyat, *Ivan the Terrible*, trans. J. Pinkham (London: Phoenix, 2001), p. 65, and note 78 below.

13 For reasons of space the texts of the ecclesiastical appeals and statements resulting from these initiatives cannot be included here; a number of these documents (including texts highlighting some of the controversies related to the conduct of the Serbian Orthodox Church during the conflicts) have been conveniently assembled in Bos and Forest, *For the Peace*, ch. 9; also available at http://www.incommunion.org/2004/10/18/chapter-9/.

14 A recent issue of *St. Vladimir's Theological Quarterly* 47:1 (2003), was entirely devoted to these disputes. For a summary of the debate and its pro and contra arguments, see Stoyanov, "Norms," pp. 208–210.

15 For preliminary typologies of the main trends in Eastern Orthodox perspectives on warfare and their proposed elements, see Webster, *The Price of Prophecy*, pp. 20–23; Paul Robinson, "The Justification of War in Russian History and Philosophy," in Paul Robinson (ed.), *Just War in Comparative Perspective* (Aldershot: Ashgate, 2003), pp. 62–75.

16 On the modern Orthodox churches' "refusal to be monolithic" in their approaches to the use of force and the patristic roots of this "pluralistic" approach, see Grant White, "Orthodox Christian Positions on War and Peace," in Semegnish Asfaw, Guillermo Kerber, and Peter Weiderud (eds.), *The Responsibility to Protect: Ethical and Theological Reflections* (Geneva: WCC Publications, 2005), pp. 37–39, at p. 37.

17 For surveys of the principal texts of the genre and their literary and historical contexts, see, e.g., Alphonse Dain, "Les stratégistes byzantins," *Travaux et Mémoires* 2 (1967), 317–392; Edward N. Luttwak, *The Grand Strategy of the Byzantine Empire* (Cambridge, Mass.: Belknap Press of Harvard University Press, 2009), pp. 235–393 passim (with a discussion of the Greco-Roman classical inheritance reworked in the genre at pp. 239–266); Denis Sullivan,

"Byzantine Military Manuals: Prescriptions, Practice, and Pedagogy," in Paul Stephenson (ed.), *The Byzantine World* (London: Routledge, 2010), pp. 149–161.

18 E. Korzenszky and R. Vári (eds.), *Onasandri Strategicus* (Budapest: Typis Societatis Franklinianae, 1935), p. 10 (Greek text); English translation from: Laiou, "On Just War in Byzantium," p. 167. On the influence of the tract in medieval Byzantium and post-Renaissance Europe and the significance of the early articulation of its just war argument, see Luttwak, *The Grand Strategy*, pp. 253–254.

19 Leo VI, *Taktika*, Epilogue 169, *The Taktika of Leo VI*, George Dennis (ed. and trans.) (Washington, D.C.: Dumbarton Oaks Research Library and Collection, 2010), p. 594 (Greek text), p. 595 (English translation).

20 Leo VI, *Taktika*, 2.30–31 in *The Taktika of Leo VI*, pp. 34–36 (Greek text); English translation from Haldon, *Warfare*, p. 27.

21 Leo VI, *Taktika*, Epilogue 14, 16 in *The Taktika of Leo VI*, p. 624 (Greek text), p. 625 (English translation).

22 Leo VI, *Taktika*, Prologue 4, in *The Taktika of Leo VI*, pp. 2–4 (Greek text), pp. 3–5 (English translation).

23 *Peri Strategikes/De Re Strategica* ("The Anonymous Byzantine Treatise on Strategy"), 4:9–14, in George T. Dennis (ed. and trans.), *Three Byzantine Military Treatises* (Washington, D.C.: Dumbarton Oaks Research Library and Collection, 1985), p. 20 (Greek text), p. 21 (English translation). For an assessment that this statement, with its evident Christian provenance, marks the beginning of the process of "delegitimization of war as valid human undertaking," which has acquired a new impetus in the wake of the global wars of the twentieth century, see Luttwak, *The Grand Strategy*, p. 259.

24 *Strategikon*, Prologue, *Strategikon Arta militară. Mauricius*, H. Mihăescu (ed. and trans.) (Bucharest: Editura Academiei Republicii Socialiste România, 1970), p. 44 (Greek text); English translation from George T. Dennis (trans.), *Maurice's Strategikon: Handbook of Byzantine Military Strategy* (Philadelphia: University of Pennsylvania Press, 1984), p. 9.

25 *Strategikon* 8.2, Mihăescu (ed.), p. 204 (Greek text); English translation in Dennis, *Maurice's Strategikon*, p. 83.

26 Leo VI, *Taktika*, 2.22–23 in *The Taktika of Leo VI*, p. 30 (Greek text), p. 31 (English translation).

27 Leo VI, *Taktika*, Epilogue 73, in *The Taktika of Leo VI*, p. 642 (Greek text), p. 643 (English translation).

28 *Strategikon* 2.18, Mihăescu (ed.), pp. 94–95 (Greek text); English translation from Dennis, *Maurice's Strategikon*, pp. 33–34.

29 *Strategikon* 7.17, Mihăescu (ed.), p. 192 (Greek text); English translation from Dennis, *Maurice's Strategikon*, p. 77.

30 Leo VI, *Taktika*, 14.1, in *The Taktika of Leo VI*, p. 290 (Greek text), p. 291 (English translation).

31 Leo VI, Taktika 13.1, in *The Taktika of Leo VI*, p. 278 (Greek text), p. 279 (English translation). The analogous practice prescribed for the pre-combat blessing of the standards of the dromons (a type of Byzantine galley) is prescribed in 19:24.

32 Leo VI, *Taktika* 16.11 in *The Taktika of Leo VI*, p. 386 (Greek text), p. 387 (English translation). For the status of the fallen Christian soldiers and the related religious services, see the section on "Religious Services Commemorating Christian Soldiers" below.

33 *Praecepta Militaria* 4.106–120, in Eric McGeer (ed. and trans.), *Sowing the Dragon's Teeth: Byzantine Warfare in the Tenth Century* (Washington, D.C.: Dumbarton Oaks Research Library and Collection, 1995), pp. 13–61, at p. 44 (Greek text), p. 45 (English translation).

These prayer instructions are paraphrased in Nikephoros Ouranos' slightly later *Taktika*, 61.160–172 (999–1011 CE), p. 126 (Greek text), p. 127 (English translation).

34 Anna Komnene, *Alexiad*, 15.6.5; *Alexiade: règne de l'empereur Alexis I Comnène, 1081–1118*, B. Leib (ed. and trans.), vol. III, Books XI–XV (Paris: Les Belles Lettres, 1989), p. 209 (Greek text); English translation from *The Alexiad of Anna Comnena*, E. R. A. Sewter (trans.) (Harmondsworth: Penguin, 1969), p. 488.

35 On the genre and *raison d'être* of such military orations, see Eric McGeer, "Two Military Orations of Constantine VII," in John W. Nesbit (ed.), *Byzantine Authors: Literary Activities and Preoccupations: Texts and Translations Dedicated to the Memory of Nicolas Oikonomides* (Leiden: Brill, 2003), pp. 111–35, at pp. 113–117.

36 Theophylaktos Simokattes, *History*, 3.13.13–20, *Theophylacti Simocattae Historiarum*, I. Bekker (ed.) (Bonn: Weber, 1834), pp. 142–143 (Greek text); English translation from *The History of Theophylact Simocatta*, Michael Whitby (trans.) (Oxford: Clarendon Press, 1986), pp. 93–94. Given the period when Simokattes's work was written, it is possible that in Justinian's speech he may have actually projected back the notion of heavenly recompense for fallen Christian soldiers developed in the religiously charged wartime rhetoric of Herakleios' anti-Persian campaigns of the 620s (see the following selection of orations) to an earlier Persian-Roman military engagement – see Michael Whitby, "Deus Nobiscum: Christianity, Warfare, and Morale in Late Antiquity," in M. Austin, J. Harries, and C. Smith (eds.), *Modus Operandi: Essays in Honour of Geoffrey Rickman* (London: Institute of Classical Studies, SAS, University of London, 1998), pp. 191–208, at p. 194.

37 Theophanes the Confessor, "Chronographia," 303.12–304.13, *Theopahis Chronographia*, Carl de Boor (ed.), 2 vols. (Leipzig: Teubner 1883–1885); English translation from *The Chronicle of Theophanes Confessor: Byzantine and Near Eastern History, AD 284–813*, Cyril Mango and Roger Scott (trans.) (Oxford: Clarendon Press, 1997), p. 436.

38 Theophanes, "Chronographia," 307.10–11; English translation from Mango and Scott, *The Chronicle of Theophanes*, p. 439.

39 Theophanes, *Chronographia*, 310.25–311.2; English translation from Mango and Scott, *The Chronicle of Theophanes*, pp. 442–443. On the possible provenance of the introduction of the notion of military martyrdom in Herakleios' oration, see James Howard Johnston, "Heraclius' Persian Campaign and the Revival of the East Roman Empire," *War in History* 6 (1996), 1–44, at 40; cf. Yuri Stoyanov, *Defenders and Enemies of the True Cross* (Vienna: Austrian Academy of Science Press, 2011), ch. 3 passim.

40 Cf. Vieillefond, "Les pratiques religieuses"; Sullivan, "Byzantine Military Manuals," pp. 356–357.

41 Edited in Hélène Ahrweiler, "Un discours inédit de Constantin VII Porphyrogénète," *Travaux et Mémoires* 2 (1967), 393–404 (Greek text at 397–399), at 398 and 399; English translation from McGeer, "Two Military Orations," pp. 117–120, at pp. 118, 119.

42 Edited in R. Vári, "Zum historischen Exzerptenwerke des Konstantinos Porphyrogennetos," *Byzantinische Zeitschrift* 17:1 (1908), 75–85 (Greek text at 78–84, at 80, 83); English translation from McGeer, "Two Military Orations," pp. 127–134, at pp. 129, 132–133.

43 See Robert F. Taft, "War and Peace in the Byzantine Divine Liturgy," in Miller and Nesbit, *Peace and War*, pp. 17–33, at pp. 30–31.

44 Edited in A. Pertusi, "Una acolouthia militare inedita del X secolo," *Aevum* 22 (1948), 145–168; English translation from Paul Stephenson, available at http://homepage.mac.com/paulstephenson/military_texts.html.

45 "We have decreed in regard to those who have once been enrolled in the Clergy or who have become Monks shall not join the army nor obtain any secular position of dignity. Let those be

anathematized who dare to do this and fail to repent, so as to return to that which they had previously chosen on God's account." English translation from *The Pedalion (The Rudder) of the Orthodox Catholic Church: The Compilation of the Holy Canons by Saints Nicodemus and Agapius*, D. Cummings (trans.) (Chicago, Ill.: Orthodox Christian Educational Society, 1957; reprint New York 1983), p. 251 (English translation of the collection of Eastern Orthodox canon law, the *Pedalion (The Rudder)*, compiled by St. Nikodemos the Hagiorite (ca. 1749–1809) and the hieromonk Agapios, and published in 1800.

46 For other texts of some of the relevant canons, see Louis J. Swift (ed. and trans.), *The Early Fathers on Law and Military Service* (Wilmington, Del.: Michael Glazier, 1983), pp. 90–93. For further analysis of these canons, see Alexander F. C. Webster, *The Pacifist Option: The Moral Argument against War in Eastern Orthodox Theology* (Lanham, Md.: Rowman & Littlefield, 1998), pp. 165–181. On these canonical regulations as instituting a kind of "stratification of pacifism" in the post-Constantinian Christian Church and society, see Stanley S. Harakas, "The Morality of War," in Joseph J. Allen (ed.), *Orthodox Synthesis. The Unity of Theological Thought* (Crestwood, N.Y.: St. Vladimir Seminar Press, 1981), pp. 67–95, at pp. 85ff.

47 St. Athanasios of Alexandria, Epistle 48, *To Ammoun the Monk*, in Georgios A. Rhalles and Michael Potles, *Syntagma ton theion kai hieron kanonon* (Athens: G. Chartophylax, 1852), vol. 4, p. 69; English translation from *The Pedalion (The Rudder)*, Cummings (trans.), pp. 758–760, at pp. 759–760.

48 For this "just war" reading of St. Athanasios' statement, see Alexander F. C. Webster, "Justifiable War as a 'Lesser Good' in Eastern Orthodox Moral Tradition," *St. Vladimir's Theological Quarterly* 47:1 (2003), 3–59, at 25–27; Haldon, *Warfare*, pp. 16, 26.

49 For this line of interpretation of St. Athanasius' assertion, which also has been gaining currency, see Stanley S. Harakas, "The Teaching of Peace in the Fathers," in Stanley S. Harakas, *The Wholeness of Faith and Life: Orthodox Christian Ethics: Part One: Patristic Ethics* (Brookline, Mass.: Holy Orthodox Press), ch. 6, pp. 155–156; John A. McGuckin, "Non-Violence and Peace Traditions in Early and Eastern Christianity," in K. Kuriakose (ed.), *Religion, Terrorism and Globalisation: Non-Violence – A New Agenda* (New York: Nova Science Publishers, 2006), pp. 189–202; John A. McGuckin, *The Orthodox Church: An Introduction to Its History, Doctrine, and Spiritual Culture* (Oxford: Blackwell, 2008), pp. 403–404. Cf. Swift, *The Early Fathers*, p. 95.

50 St. Basil the Great, *Epistle* 188.13, Rhalles and Potles, *Syntagma*, vol. 4, p. 131; English translation from *Pedalion (The Rudder)*, Cummings (trans.), p. 801.

51 English translation and analysis of the canon in Swift, *The Early Fathers*, p. 93.

52 See, e.g., Harakas, "The Teaching of Peace"; McGuckin, *The Orthodox Church*, pp. 403–405.

53 St. Basil, *Homily 21 on Psalm 61*, 4; English translation from *Saint Basil Exegetic Homilies*, Sister Agnes C. Way (trans.) (Washington, D.C.: Catholic University of America Press, 1963), pp. 341–351, at pp. 345–346.

54 St. Basil, *Letter 106*: "I have become acquainted with a man who demonstrated that it is possible even in the military profession to maintain perfect love for God … ," *Patrologia Graeca*, vol. 32, col. 513; English translation from Swift, *The Early Fathers*, p. 94.

55 *Pedalion (The Rudder)*, Cummings (trans.), pp. 801–802.

56 Ioannes Scylitzes, *Synoposis Historiarum*, Hans Thurn (ed.) (New York and Berlin: Walter de Gruyter, 1973), pp. 274–275; English translation from Jonathan Shepard available at http://www.heacademy.ac.uk/assets/hca/classics/featureResources/practicalAdvice/NonLanguageTeaching/Teaching_Byzantium.pdf.

57 See the analysis of the differentiation between the imperial and clerical strands of Byzantine Christianity in the sphere of legitimizing warfare and the status of the Christian soldier in Paul Stephenson, "Imperial Christianity and Sacred War in Byzantium," in James K. Wellman, Jr. (ed.), *Belief and Bloodshed: Religion and Violence across Time and Tradition* (Lanham, Md.: Rowman & Littlefield, 2007), pp. 81–97, in which the differentiation between the "Old Testament in tone" imperial Christianity and the "more New Testament–oriented Christianity of the clergy" postulated in Gilbert Dagron, *Emperor and Priest. The Imperial Office in Byzantium*, J. Birrell (trans.) (Cambridge: Cambridge University Press, 2003), pp. 1, 103–104, passim, is applied to the sphere of the ideology of Byzantine warfare.

58 A monk ordained as a priest whose duties include conducting the services in the monastic church.

59 Theodore Balsamon, *Commentary on St. Basil's Thirteenth Canon*, Rhalles and Potles, *Syntagma*, vol. 4, p. 133 (Greek text); English translation from Patrick Viscuso, "Christian Participation in Warfare: A Byzantine View," in Miller and Nesbit, *Peace and War*, pp. 33–41, at p. 38.

60 Ioannes Zonaras, *Commentary on St. Basil's Thirteenth Canon*, Rhalles and Potles, *Syntagma*, vol. 4, p. 132 (Greek text); English translation from Viscuso, "Christian Participation," p. 38.

61 Matthew Blastares, *Commentary on St. Basil's Thirteenth Canon*, Rhalles and Potles, *Syntagma*, vol. 6, pp. 488–493, at p. 489 (Greek text); English translation from Viscuso, "Christian Participation," p. 34.

62 Blastares, *Commentary*, Rhalles and Potles, *Syntagma*, vol. 6, p. 492; English translation from Viscuso, "Christian Participation," p. 38.

63 Balsamon, *Commentary*, Rhalles and Potles, *Syntagma*, vol. 4, p. 133; Blastares, *Commentary*, Rhalles and Potles, *Syntagma*, vol. 6, p. 492.

64 For a lucid discussion of Blastares' theological and scriptural argumentation to affirm St. Basil's canon, see Viscuso, "Christian Participation."

65 Blastares, *Commentary*, Rhalles and Potles, *Syntagma*, vol. 6, pp. 491–492; English translation from Viscuso, "Christian Participation," p. 37.

66 Blastares, *Commentary*, Rhalles and Potles, *Syntagma*, vol. 6, p. 489; English translation from Viscuso, "Christian Participation," p. 34.

67 Anna Komnene, *Alexiad*, 10.8.8, *Alexiade: règne de l'empereur Alexis I Comnène, 1081–1118*, B. Leib (ed. and trans.), vol. 2, Books V–X (Paris: Société d'Édition "Les Belles Lettres," 1943), pp. 218–219 (Greek text); English translation from *The Alexiad*, Sewter (trans.), p. 317.

68 Colossians 2:21.

69 Psalms 59:2, 139:19.

70 *Vita Constantini*, in *Kliment Okhridskii. Săbrani săchineniia*, B. S. Angelov and K. Kodov (eds.) (Sofia: Izdatelstvo na Bŭlgarskata Akademiia na Naukite, 1973), vol. 3, pp. 89–109, at p. 93. English translation from *The Bases of the Social Concept of the Russian Orthodox Church*, available on the website of the Moscow patriarchate at http://www.mospat.ru/index.php?mid=90i.

71 See, e.g., the insightful analysis in David K. Goodin, "Just War Theory and Eastern Orthodox Christianity: A Theological Perspective on the Doctrinal Legacy of Chrysostom and Constantine-Cyril," *Theandros: An Online Journal of Orthodox Christian Theology and Philosophy* 2(3), 2005; available at http://www.theandros.com/justwar.html; cf. Marian Gh. Simion, "Seven Factors of Ambivalence in Defining a Just War Theory in Eastern Christianity,"

in Marian Gh. Simion and Ilie Tălpăşanu (eds.), *Proceedings of the 32nd Annual Congress of the American Romanian Academy of Arts and Sciences* (Montreal: Polytechnic International Press, 2008), pp. 537–543, at p. 539.

72 Despite becoming moderately and progressively more acquainted with crusading ideology in the era of the Crusades the Byzantine church elites retained a generally negative stance toward its principal notions regarding the status of the Christian warrior. This is also demonstrated by the fact that, in contrast to the high and late medieval Western Christendom, medieval Byzantine ecclesiastics took the formal step to respectively promise remission of sins and bestow martyrdom on Byzantine soldiers who died in battle only on two occasions which clearly represent exceptions to the prevalent clerical attitudes; on religious and historical context of these occasions, see Stoyanov, "Norms of War," pp. 171–172.

73 Leo VI, *Taktika*, 18.127, Dennis (ed. and trans.), respectively pp. 484 (Greek text) and 485 (English translation); see also the observations of Gilbert Dagron, "Byzance et le modèle islamique au Xe siècle, à propos des *Constitutions tactiques* de l'empereur Léon VI," *Comptes rendus des séances de l'Académie des Inscriptions et Belles-Lettres* 127 (4) (Paris, 1983), pp. 219–243, at p. 223.

74 Leo VI, *Taktika*, 14.31, Dennis (ed. and trans.), respectively pp. 306 (Greek text) and 307 (English translation); see also the observations of Dagron, "Byzance et le modèle islamique," pp. 230–231, and Stephenson, "Imperial Christianity," p. 89.

75 Leo VI, *Taktika*, Epilogue 72, Dennis (ed. and trans.), respectively pp. 560–562 (Greek text) and 561–563 (English translation).

76 T. Détorakis and J. Mossay, "Un office inédit pour ceux qui sont morts à la guerre, dans le Cod. Sin. Gr. 734–735," *Le Muséon* 101 (1988), 183–211; English translation from Paul Stephenson, "'About the emperor Nikephoros and how he leaves his bones in Bulgaria': A Context for the Controversial Chronicle of 811," *Dumbarton Oaks Papers* 60 (2006), 87–109, at 107–108.

77 See Mari Isoaho, *The Image of Aleksandr Nevskiy in Medieval Russia: Warrior and Saint* (Leiden: Brill, 2006), pp. 53–67.

78 *Povest' vremennykh let, Lavrent'evskaiia letopis'*, 137–139, *Polnoe sobranie russkikh letopisei*, vol. 1: *Lavrent'evskaia letopis'* (Leningrad: Izdatel'stvo Akademii Nauk SSSR, 1926), pp. 96–98 (Old Russian text); English translation from *The Russian Primary Chronicle, Laurentian Text*, Samuel H. Cross and Olgerd P. Sherbowitz-Wetzor (eds. and trans.) (Cambridge, Mass.: Mediaeval Academy of America, 1953), pp. 129–130.

79 *Primary Chronicle*, Laurentian Text, 172; *Polnoe sobranie*, p. 121 (Old Russian text); English translation from *The Russian Primary Chronicle*, Cross and Sherbowitz-Wetzor (eds. and trans.), p. 149.

80 *Primary Chronicle*, Laurentian Text, 232–233; *Polnoe sobranie*, pp. 162–163 (Old Russian text); English translation from *The Russian Primary Chronicle*, Cross and Sherbowitz-Wetzor (eds. and trans.), p. 183.

81 *Primary Chronicle*, 276; *Polnoe Sobranie*, p. 193 (Old Russian text); English translation from *The Russian Primary Chronicle*, Cross and Sherbowitz-Wetzor (eds. and trans.), p. 200.

82 *Chronicle*, 278–279; *Polnoe Sobranie*, pp. 194–195 (Old Russian text); English translation from *The Russian Primary Chronicle*, Cross and Sherbowitz-Wetzor (eds. and trans.), p. 201.

83 *Primary Chronicle*, 282; *Polnoe Sobranie*, p. 197 (Old Russian text); English translation from *The Russian Primary Chronicle*, Cross and Sherbowitz-Wetzor (eds. and trans.), pp. 203–204.

84 On the provenance of the report of this meeting and St. Sergius' reputed blessing of the campaign of the Golden Horde, the time of its introduction into the life of the saint and its

religio-political underpinnings, see David B. Miller, "The Cult of Saint Sergius of Radonezh and Its Political Uses," *Slavic Review* 52:4 (1993), 680–699, at 692–693.

85 *Life of St. Sergius of Radonezh* 8, *Zhitiia Sergiia Radonezhskogo*, L. A. Dmitriev and D. S. Likhachev (eds.), *Pamiatniki literatury Drevnei Rusi XIV-seredina XV veka* (Moscow: Khudozh. Literatura, 1981), pp. 256–429, at pp. 386–88 (Old Russian text); English translation from *Medieval Russia's Epics, Chronicles, and Tales*, Serge A. Zenkovsky (ed. and trans.) (New York: Dutton, 1963), pp. 208–236, at pp. 230–231.

86 For other contemporaneous and later Russian accounts and interpretations of the Battle of Kulikovo, which emphasize what they consider or reconstruct as its religious aspects, see Irina Moroz, "The Idea of the Holy War in the Orthodox World (on Russian Chronicles from the Twelfth-Sixteenth Century)," pp. 52–58, available at http://www.deremilitari.org/resources/pdfs/moroz.pdf. On pronouncements coming from within the modern Russian Orthodox Church regarding the just cause of Dmitrii Donskoi's campaign against the Golden Horde and the Russian Church's role in legitimizing his war effort, see Alexander F. C. Webster, *The Price of Prophecy: Orthodox Churches on Peace, Freedom, and Security* (Washington, D.C.: Ethics and Public Policy Center, 1993), pp. 203–204.

87 *Zadonshchina*, in *Skazaniia i povesti o Kulikovskoi bitve* (Tales and Stories of the Battle of Kulikov), L. A. Dmitriev and O. P. Likhacheva (eds.) (Leningrad: Nauka, 1982), pp. 369–374 (Old Russian text); English translation from *Medieval Russia's Epics*, Zenkovsky, pp. 186–198.

88 See the analysis of Jaroslaw Pelenski, *Russia and Kazan: Conquest and Imperial Ideology, 1438–1560s* (The Hague/Paris: Mouton, 1974), pp. 177–283; Donald Ostrowski, *Muscovy and the Mongols: Cross-Cultural Influences on the Steppe Frontier, 1304–1589* (Cambridge: Cambridge University Press, 1998), pp. 133–249.

89 Maxim the Greek, *Epistle to Grand Prince Vasilii III*, V. F. Ržiga (ed.), "Opity po istorii russkoi publitsistiki XVI veka" (Experimental Essays on the History of Russian Social and Political Journalism in the 16th century), *Trudy otdela drevnerusskoi literatury* 1 (1943), 111–116, at 113 and 115; English translation from Pelenski, *Russia and Kazan*, p. 185.

90 For analysis of and quotations from the aggressive plan for military-political action against the Kazan Khanate that Peresvetov proposed to Ivan IV and its religious components, see Pelenski, *Russia and Kazan*, pp. 190–192.

91 Makarii, Metropolitan of Moscow and all Russia, *Second Epistle to Ivan IV (13 July 1552)*, in *Letopisnyi sbornik, imenuemyi Patriarsheiu ili Nikonovskoiu letopis'iu* (Chronicle Collection Named Patriarch's or Nikon's Chronicle), *Polnoe sobranie russkikh letopisei* (Complete Collection of Russian Chronicles) (St. Petersburg: Tipografiia I. N. Skorokhodova, 1904; reprint Moscow: Nauka, 1965), pp. 192–197, at p. 193; English translation from Pelenski, *Russia and Kazan*, p. 199.

92 Ivan IV, *Address to Metropolitan Makarii and the Ecclesiastical Assembly*, in *Letopisnyi sbornik, imenuemyi Patriarsheiu ili Nikonovskoiu letopis'iu*, pp. 223–225, at p. 224; English translation from Pelenski, *Russia and Kazan*, pp. 242–243.

93 Ivan IV, *Address to Metropolitan Makarii*, in *Letopisnyi sbornik*, p. 225; English translation from Pelenski, *Russia and Kazan*, p. 207.

94 Metropolitan Makarii, *Address to Ivan IV* (October 1552), in *Letopisnyi sbornik*, pp. 225–227, at p. 226; English translation from Pelenski, *Russia and Kazan*, pp. 201–202.

95 For a recent reinstatement, see, among others, Andrei Pavlov and Maureen Perrie, *Ivan the Terrible* (London: Longman, 2003), pp. 47, 206; see also the analysis of the notion of heavenly rewards for Russian Christian warriors fighting in the campaigns against Kazan in Metropolitan Makarii's statements in Moroz, "The Idea of Holy War," pp. 62–63.

96 For a recent reinstatement, see, among others, Galina M. Yemelianova, *Russia and Islam: A Historical Survey* (New York: Palgrave, 2002), p. 30.

97 *Diplomatic Note to the Lithuanian Magnates*, in *Pamiatniki diplomaticheskikh snoshenii Moskovskogo gosudarstva s Pol'sko-Litovskom gosudarstvom* (Monuments of the Diplomatic Relations between the State of Muscovy and the United Kingdom of Poland and Lithuania), *Pt. 2 (1553–1560)*, G. F. Karpov (gen. ed.), *Sbornik Imperatorskogo Istoricheskogo Obshchestva*, 59 (1887), p. 372; English translation from Pelenski, *Russia and Kazan*, p. 208.

98 Petr P. Shafirov, *Razsuzhdenie kakie zakonnye prichiny Petr I, tsar' i povelitel' vserossiiskikh k nachatiiu voiny protiv Karla XII, korolia shvedskogo, v 1700 imel* (1717); both the Russian original text and anonymous English translation from 1722 are reproduced in an edition prepared by William E. Butler: Peter P. Shafirov, *A Discourse Concerning the Just Causes of the War between Sweden and Russia: 1700–1721* (Dobbs Ferry, N.Y: Oceana Publications, 1973), with an introduction by Butler that situates the tract within the context of contemporaneous international law of war and Russian just war thinking.

99 Shafirov, *A Discourse*, pp. 241, 273–274.

100 Petr Shafirov, *Rassuzhdenie, kakie zakonnye prichiny Petr I, tsar' i povelitel' vserossiĭskiĭ, k nachatiiu voĭny protiv Karla XII, korolia shvedskogo, v 1700 godu imel* (A Discourse Concerning the Just Reasons Which His Czarish Majesty, Peter I, Had for the Beginning of the War against the King of Sweden, Charles XII), V. Tomsinov (ed.) (Moscow: Zertsalo, 2008), p. 175; elsewhere in the tract Shafirov claims that the Swedish King dispatched Russian Christian civilian captives as a gift to the Sultan to serve as slaves on his galleys where half of them perished.

101 Shafirov, *A Discourse*, pp. 336–337.

102 Aleksei Khomiakov, "Pis'mo k priiateliu-inostrantsu pered' nachalom vostochnoi voiny" (Letter to a Foreign Friend on the Eve of the Eastern [Crimean] War), *Polnoe sobranie sochinenii Alekseia Stepanovicha Khomiakova*, 3rd ed. (Moscow: Universitetskaia tipografiia, 1900), vol. 3, pp. 187–205 (Russian text); English translation from *The Mind of Modern Russia: Historical and Political Thought of Russia's Great Age*, Hans Kohn (ed.) (New Brunswick, N.J.: Rutgers University Press, 1955), pp. 108–112. The letter articulates the general outrage in Russia provoked by Western powers (such as the British and French empires) joining the Ottoman empire in an anti-Russian coalition during the Crimean War.

103 Fedor Tiutchev, "Rossiia i Revoliutsiia," in *Polnoe sobranie sochinenii F.I. Tiutcheva*, P. V. Bikov (ed.) (St. Petersburg: Izd. T-va A. F. Marks, 1913), pp. 456–475 (Russian text); English translation from Jesse Zeldin, *Poems and Political Letters of F. I. Tyutchev* (Knoxville: University of Tennessee Press, 1973), pp. 176–187, at pp. 186–187.

104 Fedor Tiutchev, "Razsvet," in *Polnoe sobranie sochinenii F.I. Tiutcheva*, p. 293 (Russian text); English translation from Zeldin, *Poems*, pp. 131–132. Both "Dawn" and the following political poem, "A Prophecy," were written by Tiutchev in anticipation of a Russian-Ottoman conflict that materialized in the Crimean War.

105 Fedor Tiutchev, "Prorochestvo," in *Polnoe sobranie sochinenii F.I. Tiutcheva*, p. 294 (Russian text); English translation from Zeldin, *Poems*, p. 132.

106 Nikolai Danilevskii, *Rossiia i Evropa*, 5th ed. (St. Petersburg: Tip. brat. Panteleevykh, 1895); English translation from *The Mind*, Kohn, pp. 195–211, at pp. 201, 209, 210.

107 Danilevskii, *Rossiia i Evropa*, pp. 474–475 (Russian text); English translation from Michael B. Petrovich, *The Emergence of Russian Panslavism, 1856–1870* (New York: Columbia University Press, 1956), pp. 281–282.

108 Ivan Aksakov, "O vostochnom voprose" (On the Eastern Question), Tsentral'nyi gosudarstvennyi literaturnyi arkhiv/Rossiiskii Gosudarstvennyi Arkhiv Literatury i Iskusstva, fond

10, op.1/219; English translation from Andrzej Walicki, *The Slavophile Controversy*, Hilda Andrews-Rusiecka (trans.) (Oxford: Clarendon Press, 1975), p. 497.

109 Alexander II, Tsar of Russia, "Kremlin Address," in Sergei Tatishchev, *Imperator Aleksandr II, ego zhizn' i tsarstvovanie* (Emperor Alexander II, His Life and Reign) (St. Petersburg: Izd. A. S. Suvorina, 1903), vol. 1, pp. 335–336 (Russian text); English translation from Benedict Sumner, *Russia and the Balkans, 1870–1880* (Oxford: Clarendon Press, 1937), p. 227. The Tsar's address was delivered in the buildup to the Russo-Ottoman War of 1877–1878 and was greeted with euphoria in Russian Pan-Slav circles; few days after the speech Russia mobilized troops of 160,000 men.

110 *Sochineniia I. S. Aksakova, 1860–1886* (Moscow: Tip. M. G. Volchaninova, 1886), vol. 1, pp. 266–280, at pp. 273, 274–275 (Russian text); English translation from Ol'ga Novikova, *Russia and England from 1876 to 1880: A Protest and an Appeal* (London: Longmans, Green, 1880), pp. 52–61, at pp. 56, 57. The speech was delivered roughly five months after the beginning of the Russo-Ottoman War. For the continuous commemoration of the war by the Russian and Bulgarian Orthodox Churches as a "sacred cause"/"sacred war of liberation" and the contribution of the Russian and Bulgarian clergy to the war effort, see Webster, *The Price of Prophecy*, pp. 204–207.

111 *Sochineniia I. S. Aksakova*, pp. 297–308, at p. 307 (Russian text); English translation from Novikova, *Russia and England*, pp. 99–106, at pp. 105–106. The speech was delivered as a protest against the decisions of the Congress/Treaty of Berlin (13 June–13 July 1878), which was seen in Russian Pan-Slav circles as reversing many of the gains of the Russo-Ottoman War and betraying the Pan-Slav cause. Following his speech Aksakov was exiled for several months and the Pan-Slav Slavonic Benevolent Committee was closed down.

112 See, e.g., the analysis of Daniel Rancour-Laferriere, *Tolstoy's Quest for God* (New Brunswick, N.J.: Transaction Publishers, 2007), pp. 96–99.

113 Lev Tolstoi, *V chem moia vera?* (1884); English translation from Lev Tolstoi, *My Religion* (London: W. Scott, 1890), pp. 7–8.

114 Lev Tolstoi, *Tsarstvo Bozhie vnutri vas* (1893); English translation from: Lev Tolstoi, *The Kingdom of God Is within You*, Constance Garnett (trans.) (London: William Heinemann, 1894), pp. 45, 46, 47, 48, 50. In these passages Tolstoi summarizes the main negative responses to his ideas on nonviolence and pacifism, ideas that he considers a reflection and reinstatement of the Gospel precepts of nonresistance to evil by force.

115 Lev Tolstoy, *Zakon nasiliia i zakon liubvi* (1908); English translation from Lev Tolstoy, *The Law of Love and the Law of Violence*, Mary Tolstoy (trans.) (London: Anthony Blond, 1970), pp. 32, 92, 96.

116 Lev Tolstoi, "Dve voiny" (1898); English translation from *Tolstoy's Writings on Civil Disobedience and Non-Violence*, A. Maude (trans.) (New York: Bergman Publishers, 1967), pp. 21–29, at pp. 22–23.

117 Lev Tolstoi, "Po povodu zaveshchaniia Nobelia" (1897); English translation from Lev Tolstoi, "Nobel's Bequest," in *Tolstoy's Writings*, pp. 233–241, at p. 238.

118 Lev Tolstoi, "Posleslovie k 'Zhizn' i smert' Drozhina" (1895); English translation from Lev Tolstoi, "Postscript to the 'Life and Death of Ivan Drozhin,'" in *Tolstoy's Writings*, pp. 349–377, at p. 355.

119 Lev Tolstoi, "Po povodu kongressa o mire" (1899); English translation from Lev Tolstoi "Letter to a Peace Conference," in *Tolstoy's Writings*, pp. 149–159, at p. 156.

120 Lev Tolstoi, "Patriotism ili mir" (1896); English translation from Lev Tolstoi, "Patriotism or Peace," *Tolstoy's Writings*, pp. 137–149, at p. 145.

121 Vladimir Solov'ev, *Opravdanie dobra. Nravstvennaia filosofiia* (The Justification of the Good: An Essay on Moral Philosophy), in *Sochineniia V. S. Solov'eva*, S. Solov'ev and E. Radlov (eds.) (St. Petersburg: N. F. Merts, 1903), vol. 8 (Russian text); English translation from *The Justification of the Good: An Essay on Moral Philosophy*, Nathalie Duddington (trans.) (London: Constable, 1918), pp. 387, 404, 405, 406.

122 Vladimir Solov'ev, *Tri razgovora* (Three Conversations), in *Sochineniia* (Writings), Solov'ev and Radlov, vol. 10, pp. 81–197 (Russian text); English translation from *War and Christianity from the Russian Point of View: Three Conversations*, Stephen Graham (trans.) (London: Constable & Company, 1915), pp. 10–11. The book is written as a discussion between five characters; in the present extract the Prince represents Tolstoiism, the General militarism, and Mr. Z. the views of the author.

123 Vladimir Solov'ev, "Vizantinizm i Rossia" (Byzantinism and Russia), in *Sochineniia*, Solov'ev and Radlov, vol. 7, pp. 287–325 (Russian text); English translation from Vladimir Solov'ev, "Byzantinism and Russia," in *Freedom, Faith, and Dogma: Essays by V.S. Soloviev on Christianity and Judaism*, Vladimir Wozniuk (ed. and trans.) (Albany: State University of New York Press, 2008), pp. 191–229, at pp. 195, 196. Solov'ev is referring to the Grand Princes of Kievan Rus', Vladimir I (958–1015, who embraced Christianity in 988) and Vladimir II Monomakh (1053–1125).

124 See, e.g., Viacheslav Ivanov, "Vselenskoe delo (The Universal Task)," *Russkaia Mysl'* 12 (1914), 97–107.

125 Metropolitan Antonii Khrapovitskii, "Khristianskaiia vera i voina," *Russkii inok* 21 (November 1916), 872–877; English translation from Metropolitan Antony Khrapovitsky, *The Christian Faith and War* (Jordanville, N.Y.: Holy Trinity Monastery, 1973), pp. 5–6, 10, 11, 13, 15, 16.

126 See section on "Eastern Orthodox Canon Law" above.

127 Ibid.

128 Anton Kersnosvkii, *Filosofiia voiny* (The Philosophy of War) (Belgrade, 1939), p. 9. Translation by Y. Stoyanov.

129 Ivan Il'in, *O soprotivlenii zlu siloiu* (On Resistance to Evil by Force) (1925), in *Sochineniia v dvukh tomakh*, E. Antonova (ed.) (Moscow: Medium, 1993), pp. 301–480, at pp. 307, 454. Translation by Y. Stoyanov.

130 Nikolai Berdiaev, *O rabstve i svoboda cheloveka* (Slavery and Freedom) (1939); English translation from *Christian Existentialism: A Berdyaev Anthology*, Donald Lowrie (ed. and trans.) (London: G. Allen & Unwin, 1965), pp. 301, 302.

131 Nikolai Berdiaev, *Dialectique existentielle du divin et de l'humain* (Paris: J. B. Janin, 1947); English translation from *Christian Existentialism*, p. 303.

132 Vladimir Losskii, *Sept jours sur les routes de France* (Paris: Éditions du Cerf, 1998); English translation from *The Teachings of Modern Orthodox Christianity on Law, Politics, and Human Nature*, John Witte, Jr., and Frank Alexander (eds.) (New York: Columbia University Press, 2007), pp. 213, 214.

133 Mother Maria Skobtsova, "Prozrenie v voine" (Insight in Wartime), in *Mat' Mariia. Vospominaniia, stat'i, ocherki* (Mother Maria. Memoires, Articles and Essays) (Paris: YMCA Press, 1992), vol. 1, pp. 312–337 (Russian text); English translation from *The Teachings of Modern Orthodox Christianity*, pp. 288–290, at p. 289.

134 G. Răşcanu, *Biserica Ortodoxă Română. Jurnalul periodic ecclesiasticu* 4:3 (1877–1878), 178 (Romanian text); English translation from Silviu Hariton, "Religion, Nationalism and Militarism in Nineteenth Century Romania," *Études Balkaniques* 44:4 (2008), 9–36, at 22.

135 Bishop Nikolaj Velimirović, *Serbia in Light and Darkness* (London: Longmans, Green, 1916), p. 40.

136 Bishop Nikolaj Velimirović, *Agony of the Church* (London: Student Christian Movement, 1917), pp. 64–65.

137 Bishop Nikolaj Velimirović, *The Serbian People as a Servant of God* 53 (publ. posth. 1984); available at http://www.sv-luka.org/library/ServantOfGod.html.

138 Bishop Nikolaj Velimirović, "Kosovo i Vidovdan" (1939); available at http://www.svetosavlje. org/biblioteka/vlNikolaj/KosovoiVidovdan/KosovoiVidovdan10.htm (Serbian text). Translation by Y. Stoyanov.

139 Patriarch Gavrilo V of Serbia, "U čemu je značaj 27. marta," *Memoari patriarcha srpskog Gavrila* (Belgrade: Sfairos, 1991), p. 270; English translation from Branimir Anzulovic, *Heavenly Serbia* (New York: New York University Press, 1999), p. 17.

140 Archpriest Ioann Vostorgov, "Bor'ba za veru i tserkov" (The Struggle for Faith and Church), in A. I. Vvedenskii, *Tserkov' Patriarkha Tikhona* (The Church of Patriarch Tikhon) (Moscow, 1923), pp. 45–47; English translation from John S. Curtiss, *The Russian Church and the Soviet State, 1917–1950* (Boston: Little, Brown), p. 50.

141 St. Tikhon, Patriarch of Moscow, "Poslanie (19.01/01.02.1918)" (Pastoral Letter), in A. I. Vvedenskii, *Tserkov' i gosudarstvo* (Church and State) (Moscow, 1923), pp. 114–115; English translation from *The Russian Church and the Soviet State*, p. 49.

142 St. Tikhon, Patriarch of Moscow, "Poslanie patriarkha Tikohona Sovetu Narodnykh Komisarov" (Letter to the Council of People's Commissars [26 October 1918]), *Tserkovnye Vedomosti (Vysshee Russkoe Tserkovnoe Upravlenie za granitse)* 9–10 (1925), 20–21. Translation by Y. Stoyanov. In this letter St. Tikhon denounces the Treaty of Brest Litovsk (1918), whose terms were seen in Russia as humiliating and unfair.

143 On church–state relations in wartime Soviet Russia and their impact on the ideology of war-fare endorsed by the church, see Steven Miner, *Stalin's Holy War: Religion, Nationalism, and Alliance Politics, 1941–1945* (Chapel Hill: University of North Carolina Press, 2003).

144 Metropolitan Sergius, "Sermon" (12 August 1941), in Moskovskaiia Patriarkhiia, *The Truth about Religion in Russia* (London: Hutchinson, 1944), pp. 43, 44.

145 Ibid., pp. 46–47, 48.

146 Metropolitan Aleksei of Leningrad, "Sermon" (10 August 1941), in *The Truth about Religion in Russia*, p. 49.

147 Metropolitan Nikolai of Kiev, "Sermon" (3 August 1941), in *The Truth about Religion in Russia*, pp. 53–54.

148 Archpriest A. P. Smirnov, "Sermon" (4 December 1941), in *The Truth about Religion in Russia*, pp. 58–59.

149 Aleksei, Archbishop of Ufa, "On the Altar of the Fatherland" (27 March 1942), in *The Truth about Religion in Russia*, pp. 70, 71, 72.

150 Pitirim, Bishop of Kaluga, "Praise to Thee, Holy Moscow!" (28 March 1942), in *The Truth about Religion in Russia*, pp. 74, 77.

151 Aleksei, Metropolitan of Leningrad, "Eastertide in Leningrad" (9 April 1942), in *The Truth about Religion in Russia*, p. 107.

152 For an English-language account of the Patriarchate of Moscow's peace-making activities coming from within the church, see *Russkaia pravoslavnaia tserkov': The Russian Orthodox Church*, Doris Bradbury (trans.) (Moscow: Progress, 1982), pp. 112–135; for a critical account, see Webster, *The Price of Prophecy*, chs. 5 and 6 passim.

153 Patriarch Justinian of Romania, "Evangelical Humanism and Christian Responsibility," in *The Orthodox Church in the Ecumenical Movement: Documents and Statements 1902–1975*, Constantin Patelos (ed.) (Geneva: World Council of Churches, 1978), pp. 248–250, at p. 249.

154 Patriarch Pimen of Moscow, "An Orthodox View on Contemporary Ecumenism," in *The Orthodox Church*, pp. 325–337, at pp. 335, 336.

155   Patriarch Cyril of Bulgaria (1953–1971), "Address of Welcome to Dr. Eugene Blake," in *The Orthodox Church*, pp. 280–282, at p. 281.

156   "Orthodox Perspectives on Justice and Peace," in *Justice, Peace and Integrity of Creation: Insights from Orthodoxy*, Gennadios Limouris (ed.) (Geneva: WCC Publications), pp. 16–28, at pp. 17–18.

157   Patriarch Bartholomew I, "Environment, Peace and, Economy," in Bartholomew I, *Cosmic Grace – Humble Prayer: The Ecological Vision of the Green Patriarch Bartholomew*, John Chryssavgis (ed.) (Grand Rapids, Mich.: W. B. Eerdmans, 2003), pp. 237–243, at pp. 239–240, 241, 242.

158   Patriarch Bartholomew I, "War and Suffering," pp. 261–264, at pp. 262, 263.

159   Jubilee Bishops' Council of the Russian Orthodox Church, "War and Peace," in *The Orthodox Church and Society: The Bases of the Social Concept of the Russian Orthodox Church* (Belleville, Mich.: St. Innocent, Firebird Publishers, 2000), available at http://www.mospat.ru/index. php?mid=90.

ADDITIONAL READINGS

Due to limitations of space, the following list of readings includes only titles published shortly prior to or after the submission of the manuscript and thus could not be taken into account while completing the chapter.

Frankopan, Peter, *The First Crusade: The Call from the East* (London: Bodley Head, 2012).

Garena, Kamen (Petŭr), *Voennoto dukhovenstvo na Bŭlgaria* ("The Military Clergy of Bulgaria"), (Sofia: Gutenberg, 2008–2009), 2 vols.

Howard-Johnston, J. D., *Witnesses to a World Crisis: Historians and Histories of the Middle East in the Seventh Century* (Oxford: Oxford University Press, 2010).

Nichanian, M., "De la guerre 'antique' à la guerre 'médiévale' dans l'empire romain d'orient. Legitimite imperiale, ideologie des la guerre et revoltes militaries," in D. Barthélemy and J.-Cl. Cheynet (eds.), *Guerre et Société au Moyen Âge, Byzance – Occident (VIIIe–XIIIe siècle)* (Paris: ACHCByz, 2010), pp. 27–43.

Richters, Katja, *The Post-Soviet Russian Orthodox Church: Politics, Culture and Greater Russia* (London: Routledge, 2012).

Schean, J. F., *Soldiering for God: Christianity and the Roman Army* (Leiden: Brill, 2010).

Stephenson, Paul, "Religious Services for Byzantine Soldiers and the Possibility of Martyrdom, c. 400–1000 C.E.," in S. Hashmi (ed.), *Just Wars, Holy Wars, Jihads* (Oxford: Oxford University Press, 2012), pp. 25–46.

Stouraitis, Ioannis, *Krieg und Frieden in der politischen und ideologischen Wahrnehmung in Byzanz (7.–11. Jahrhundert)* (Vienna: Fassbaender, 2009).

Stouraitis, Ioannis, "Jihād and Crusade: Byzantine Positions towards the Notions of 'Holy War,'" *ByzantinaSymmeikta* 21 (2011), 11–63, available at http://www.byzsym.org/index.php/bz/ article/view/994/948.

Stouraitis, Ioannis, "'Just War' and 'Holy War' in the Middle Ages: Rethinking Theory through the Byzantine Case-Study," *Jahrbuch der Österreichischen Byzantinistik* 62 (2012), 227–264.

Stouraitis, Ioannis, and J. Koder (eds.), *Byzantine War Ideology between Roman Imperial Concept and Christian Religion* (Vienna: Österreichische Akademie der Wissenschaften, 2012).

Stoyanov, Yuri, *Defenders and Enemies of the True Cross* (Vienna: Austrian Academy of Science Press, 2011).

4

Protestant Christianity

Valerie Ona Morkevicius

Protestant Christianity emerged from the Roman Catholic tradition in the fifteenth century, spurred by the desire to "return" to the original precepts of Christianity. Its numerous denominations' histories, practices, and theologies differ, but all share a commitment to following the teachings of Christ as laid out in the Bible, which is understood to be the primary source of faith and practice. Protestants claim that all believers have the right and duty to interpret the Bible for themselves. Likewise, the role of individual conscience and a direct relationship with God are often emphasized. For this reason, although some denominations are hierarchically organized, their spiritual leaders tend to be seen as educated guides, rather than as possessing superior spiritual authority.

Introduction

Encapsulating a single Protestant perspective on just war is impossible. The multitude of Protestant denominations are united as much by what they are not (Catholic, Orthodox) as by what they are in terms of theology or practice. The emphasis placed on individual conscience adds further complexity. This chapter focuses on various denominations' *political* relations with their states as a framework for analyzing their perspectives on war. Denominations whose relations with governments are distant or troubled tend toward pacifistic stances. Denominations granting governments authority over the secular sphere, but within strictly defined limits, generally have perspectives resembling Catholic just war theory. Denominations preferring a government uniting the secular and theological spheres sometimes even express perspectives tantamount to holy war.

This framework expresses a correlation, not a causal relationship. Some pacifistic denominations run into trouble with governments *because* of their pacifist stance; others, already out of favor, adopt pacifism defensively. Furthermore, denominations may move within the framework: one that begins on society's fringes may later reach a détente with the government.

Nonetheless, this framework usefully highlights a central concern: just authority. The right that secular authorities have to govern domestically is closely linked to their right to use force internationally. The central question is, has God "given the sword" to earthly rulers? Do they have the right to use force (and, implicitly, from whom do they derive that right)? May Christians even participate in earthly governments?

Most Protestant denominations answer these questions positively. Some, such as the Lutheran and Anglican traditions (and their daughter churches), quarantined governmental authority to the political sphere, effectively separating church and state.[1] Others, notably the Calvinist tradition (including the Reformed churches and the English Puritans), envisioned an ideal government entrusted with both political and theological authority.[2] Still others, in the Anabaptist tradition, believed Christians should withdraw from participation in state affairs.[3] Differing perspectives on the right to govern lead to significant differences regarding just cause, the legitimacy of rebellion against tyranny, and conscientious objection.

This introduction explores each of these three broad perspectives, before turning to a discussion of the Restorationist movement and the Church of Latter-Day Saints, which do not fit quite as nicely into the schema developed here. Finally, it lays out the distinction between the evangelical and fundamentalist movements, and sketches their unique perspectives on the use of force.

Separating Temporal and Sacred Authority

Luther invoked a two-kingdoms theology, suggesting that Christians operate in two distinct, yet overlapping realms: one secular, the other sacred. In principle, the rulers of these two spheres (the princes and the Church) were not to interfere with each other. Luther had little confidence that earthly powers could or should be expected to provide moral guidance.[4] Furthermore, separate rules of conduct apply to each. In the sacred sphere, killing is banned; force would be unnecessary to govern true Christians. Realistically, few true Christians exist, so force is an unfortunate necessity in the secular sphere.[5] As a result, God ordains secular rulers – even non-Christian ones – to organize life on earth.[6] Christians owe obedience to their rulers, who in turn owe their subjects protection from harm. Thus, rulers have the right to use force to punish criminals, put down rebellions, and turn back invasions. Ultimately, "the coercive and violent functions of the state [are seen] as contingent upon the sinful nature of the world."[7]

This emphasis on the ruler's just authority legitimates defensive force used not only against invasion, but also against rebellion. Because earthly rulers are appointed by God, revolt is a sinful act of rebellion against God himself.[8] The conservatism of Luther's thought is evident in his condemnation of the 1525 peasant uprisings. Despite sympathizing with their cause, he believed that the peasants lacked just authority, and thus had no right to forcibly advance their claims.[9]

However, this condemnation of rebellion is not without nuance. The 1530 Diet of Augsburg declared that all Reformation heresy should be removed from the empire, by force if necessary. In response, Luther counseled that self-defense is distinct from rebellion, and urged Protestant soldiers not to obey imperial orders to forcibly suppress the movement.[10] So long as the Protestants did not use violence first, their physical self-defense against the temporal authorities' intervention should not be called rebellion.

Since the "two kingdoms" were separate, in this case the princes were guilty of overstepping their legitimate temporal authority by interfering in religion.

The limitation of princely authority to secular matters means that certain causes cannot be just. Possessing no authority over religion, secular leaders cannot use force to punish apostates or launch wars in the name of God. Thus, "military action [has] to be seen as a secular struggle, not as a religious crusade."[11] Luther therefore argued in 1526 that self-defense against the invading Turks was legitimate, yet condemned the crusading language that was in vogue. Not only did he doubt the "Christian" credentials of the European participants, but his vision of secular authority meant that the Turks had as much of a right to govern (and wage war) as anyone else.[12]

The limited authority of rulers reinforces a strong emphasis on individual conscience. Individuals are responsible for their own salvation, and thus must decide for themselves what is right or wrong in a given situation. When accounting for one's actions before God, responsibility cannot be denied simply because one was following orders. Conscientious objection is thus largely tolerated.[13]

In terms of *in bello* restrictions on conduct, Luther argued that if the cause is just, the necessary means are justifiable. In a just war of self-defense, "it is both Christian and an act of love to kill the enemy without hesitation, to plunder and burn and injure him by every method of warfare until he is conquered."[14] Nonetheless, Luther distinguishes between legitimate tactics of war and other violent acts (such as raping and pillaging) that often occur in wartime. While the enemy may be killed by nearly any means, the army should exercise self-control during and after the conflict.[15]

A limited concept of just war was accepted by most churches in this tradition. Early Lutheran confessions specifically referred to just war principles, upholding the right of the sovereign to wage war. Many daughter churches also accepted these principles. The Evangelical Lutheran Church in America, for example, argues that concern for one's neighbor makes it impossible to "rule out possible support for the use of military force."[16] Likewise, the Lutheran Church–Missouri Synod, asserts that "the maintenance of civic order at times requires the responsible application of force to the solution of social and political problems," tasking police and military forces with the responsibility.[17]

However, many denominations in this tradition are moving toward increasingly pacifistic positions. This shift began after World War I, when a "moral nausea" toward violence swept through Lutheran communities.[18] Dietrich Bonhoeffer and Reinhold Niebuhr, for example, were avowed pacifists through the 1920s, although both revised their views on the use of force in response to the threat posed by Hitler (Niebuhr even became a Christian realist). After World War II, the shift toward pacifism recommenced, as witnessed by the emergence of the Lutheran Peace Fellowship. This shift is inspired by the belief that the nuclear revolution has made limited war impossible, rendering it illegitimate to wage or threaten.

Integrating Temporal and Sacred Authority

Although John Calvin, like Luther, located the kingdom of God in the souls of believers (rather than any particular earthly kingdom), he entrusted earthly magistrates with providing both spiritual and civil care for their people, thus imagining a more theo-cratic system, with closely integrated sacred and secular authorities.[19] He believed God endowed rulers with the right to use force, which naturally included self-defense.[20] The government was also obligated to provide for the people's spiritual needs and to protect them from apostasy. Force could be used against individuals or groups whose religious beliefs and practices were dangerously deviant.[21] This led Reformed churches in "the direction of the crusade, partly because they became involved in the wars of religion and partly because of their theocratic concept of the Church."[22]

While Calvin himself did not advocate a doctrine of offensive war for the sake of reli-gion,[23] some of his philosophical descendants did. This idea is evident in the work of German theologians Johann Heinrich Alsted and Heinrich Bullinger,[24] as well as some seventeenth-century Puritans, such as William Gouge,[25] particularly during the English Civil War. These theologians justified force against outsiders who did not practice (the right kind of) Christianity. Two separate logics underpinned this belief.[26] First, Christians had a duty to spread their faith out of concern for nonbelievers' souls. If the disbelievers did not convert, they would be eternally damned, which arguably would be a fate worse than death. Second, the very existence of non-Christian peoples posed a risk to Christian travelers, who would be tempted to question their faith when faced with diverse beliefs. Lest they become lax, Christians should be constantly reminded of their duty to convert others.

The language of holy war has reemerged periodically. Some conservative Anglican priests argued during World War I that Germany should be showed little mercy, with the Bishop of London even calling for a "holy war."[27] More recently, it can be found in the rhetoric of some Evangelical churches in the United States, in support of the war on ter-ror and the war in Iraq.[28] This perspective defines the conflict as a fundamentally religious one, in the sense of both being driven by religious causes and being a direct judgment of God. Televangelist Pat Robertson, for example, declared the U.S. war on terror to be "a religious struggle … a clash of cultures … a clash of different ideologies."[29] Likewise, the National Association of Evangelicals proclaimed that September 11 "sharpened" the "spiritual and religious dimensions of global conflict," while cautioning that the use of "military force must be guided by the classical just-war principles."[30] Such claims are also often tied to an apocalyptic worldview, in which the Middle East – especially Israel and Iraq (Babylon) – play an important role in God's plan for the end of time.

The issue of rebellion was also significant for Calvin and other Reformed Protestants. Calvin suggested that Christians' duty was to obey and suffer in the face of tyranny.[31] Nonetheless, his condemnation of the abuse of power did make it possible for others inspired by him to conceive of rebellion under certain circumstances.[32] Although rulers derived their authority from God, they could forfeit their rights by turning away from God or becoming tyrants; in that case, rebellion would be legitimate as a last resort.

John Knox's theology, for example, encouraged Scottish rebellion against its Catholic queen. Although Knox spent time in Geneva, his revolutionary sentiments never received Calvin's official support. In the 1550s, he accepted a policy of nonresistance, which "although distasteful" was the "only option available."[33] Gradually, Knox came to accept the possibility of armed resistance against an "idolatrous ruler" for the ultimate "estab-lishment of a godly commonwealth ruled by a godly prince."[34]

Calvinist theology was also deployed in various other contexts, including Puritan rhetoric in both the English Civil War and the American Revolution. The seventeenth-century English Civil War was driven by an understanding of a "supposed divine mandate to reform the political order."[35] Although Queen Elizabeth I's reforms of the Church of England generated an "inclusive Calvinistic Protestantism," the Puritans – also Calvinist in outlook – united Presbyterians, Congregationalists, and Baptists in an effort to create a more radically Protestant church *and* state.[36] The American Revolution, while secular in its aims, also revealed the tension between the drive for political order and the right to rebellion against tyranny. Some Puritan preachers in the New World largely supported the Revolution, while in England many Anglican and Methodist religious leaders decried the rebellion.[37]

Conscientious objection is possible from the Calvinist perspective, but it is not purely a matter of individual conscience. If the prince is a true Christian, then he must be obeyed. Calvin asserts that "the Christian man, if according to the order of his country is called to serve his prince, not only does not offend God in taking up arms, but also fulfills a holy vocation, which cannot be reproved without blaspheming God."[38] One can refuse only if one knows with certainty that the prince has forfeited his God-given authority.[39]

Within the Reformed traditions, there has been a general acceptance of just war principles. For example, Article 23 of the 1648 Westminster Confession of the Presbyterian and Congregationalist traditions upholds the right of the rulers to use force, as does the 1677 London Baptist Confession of Faith.[40] Some churches in this tradition remain committed to a just war perspective, including the Christian Reformed Church (CRC). The CRC's 2006 synodical report on war and peace asserts that "members of the Christian Reformed Church who are pacifists or strong proponents for nonviolent action should respect the judgment of those who, out of obedience to God, serve as governing officials and participate in the conduct of war, even if their pacifist convictions lead them to plead with the soldier and the politician that 'there is a better way, a way of nonviolence and reconciliation.'"[41]

The Vietnam War sparked a period of deep introspection and debate about the ethics of conflict among all Protestant denominations in the United States. As a result of this soul-searching, some American reformed denominations began to shift from a theology of just war to "a positive theology of peace."[42] The establishment of the Presbyterian Peacemaking Program in 1980 is one result of this change. Although the position of the Presbyterian Church in Europe and North America cannot be described as pacifist, the emphasis has changed from an emphasis on just war to a focus on the demand for Christians to work for peace.[43] In 1993 the Japan Presbyterian Church went further, arguing in an official statement that since modern war "[leads] all of humanity to the brink of destruction," the denomination would renounce war, in keeping with the Japanese Constitution.[44] In 1985, the United Churches of Christ General Synod adopted a pronouncement as part of its basic teachings that "affirms the UCC to be a Just Peace church and defines Just Peace as the interrelation of friendship, justice, and common security from violence. It places the UCC General Synod in opposition to the [very] institution of war."[45] More modestly, the American Baptist Churches also established a peace-making program in 1980, calling for arms control and disarmament.[46]

Furthermore, Glen Harold Stassen, a Baptist theologian, has written several books on just peace.

The Anglican and Episcopal Communions, and their daughter churches, including the various Methodists, represent a melding of Lutheran and Calvinist theologies. Anglicans have historically afforded a "prominent place" to the concept of natural order in their political theories, reflecting a faith in natural law and the possibility of just government.[47] While these traditions still hold a just war perspective, many have edged closer to pacifism. The Anglican Lambeth Conference in 1930, for example, declared that "war as a method of settling international disputes is incompatible with the teaching and example of our Lord Jesus Christ," a position reaffirmed by the Conference in each subsequent decade.[48] Several others have begun to advocate just peace theory, including the Federal Council of Churches, the United Church of Christ, and the United Methodists.[49] This perspective begins with the assumption that war is always unjust, rather than asking how war could be justified or justly fought under certain circumstances. It also assumes that peace is possible; war is not the obvious result of a fallen human nature. This newly emerging tradition stresses cooperation, active peace making, and the efforts of the United Nations.

It should also be noted that there is a strong relationship between both the Lutheran and Calvinist families of Protestantism and the development of modern international law. Scholars trained in these traditions, including Grotius and Pufendorf, made major contributions to the formulation and codification of international law. Most of the mainstream denominations in these families have also issued statements in support of international law and the work of the United Nations.

Abdicating Secular Authority

The third broad grouping of Protestant denominations took a different approach to political authority, including the Anabaptists and Quakers.[50] Anabaptists include the Amish, Brethren, and Mennonites; the Quaker (Society of Friends) movement will also be considered here because of the similarity of its history and beliefs regarding government, although theologically, its roots are not Anabaptist.[51] Skeptical of the benefits of earthly powers, these denominations generally advocated withdrawing from the political realm.[52] Members were discouraged from participating in government work, and often from any interaction with the government at all (e.g., filing civil suits). The heavenly kingdom could be established on earth, but not via the earthly powers.

Many of these denominations took the stance that the use of force itself was outlawed by the New Testament. Christians were not allowed to kill under any circumstances. William Penn argued that the Christian use of force was "more condemnable" than that of non-Christians, since Christians had been ordered in the New Testament to love one another rather than to strike.[53] A combination of these first two justifications for pacifism can be found in the work of the modern Mennonite scholar John Howard Yoder.

Another reason for pacifism, reflecting discomfort with Christian involvement in earthly affairs, was that military service inherently put believers in the uncomfortable position of "serving two masters." Even in peacetime, the military could force believers to take oaths, salute flags, and work on the Sabbath.[54] Participation in government or military service could also encourage negative virtues, such as pride, a particular concern for the Quakers.[55] Another, more pragmatic reason for a pacifistic stance emerged at times when Anabaptist denominations faced government persecution. However, this pacifism actually often led to accusations of treason.

Conscientious objection for Anabaptists takes on a cast different from that of other Protestants. Rather than focusing on individual judgments of the justness of particular conflicts, Anabaptists adopted a blanket prohibition of the use of force. Under many governments, this eventually led to the creation of a special legal category of conscientious objection, available only to members of one of the "approved" peace churches.

Shifting Perspectives on Authority

There are two additional groupings that do not easily fit the schema developed thus far: the Restorationist (or Primitivist) movement and the Church of Latter-Day Saints. The Restorationist movement emerged in the nineteenth century and includes such diverse denominations as the Seventh-Day Adventists, the Churches of Christ, Pentecostals, and the Jehovah's Witnesses. These denominations interpret the Bible literally and weed out practices believed to have been invented by earlier formal churches.

In some ways, the Church of Latter-Day Saints (LDS) also conceives of itself as a Restorationist movement. However, because the LDS accepts the Book of Mormon as a revealed sacred text beyond the Bible, many Protestants do not recognize it as part of the same tradition, nor may many LDS members claim to be Protestants. Nevertheless, because the LDS emerged out of the Protestant theological milieu, with which it shares some core theological beliefs, it also bears consideration here.

Because Restorationist and LDS churches' beliefs about relationships with secular powers affect their judgments on the legitimacy of warfare, changes in such relationships have sometimes led to changes in their perspectives on the use of force.[56] The historical experience of the Seventh-Day Adventists is a case in point. The church's early pacifism was tied to the concern that military service would force participants not only to kill but to participate in many other sinful activities.[57] In the United States, as government and military policies became more flexible, Seventh-Day Adventists began to allow alternate service within the military itself, permitting service as medical personnel and chaplains.[58] Likewise, the Assemblies of God, the largest Pentecostal denomination, expressed views varying from a passively apocryphal interpretation of World War I to a general pacifism, before ultimately leaving the matter up to individual conscience.[59]

The experience of the Church of Latter-Day Saints similarly reveals that changes in the denomination's relationship with the United States government paralleled shifts in its attitude toward war. The LDS generally attempted to be conciliatory, "befriending that law which is the constitutional law of the land."[60] The Mormon Articles of Faith assert that members of the LDS "believe in being subject to kings, presidents, rulers, and magistrates, in obeying, honoring, and sustaining the law."[61]

Like the Bible, the Book of Mormon includes multiple perspectives on war, including pacifism and just war.[62] Alma 24 presents a community "embracing pacifism as a moral obligation realized in response to the gospel."[63] After their conversion, the Anti-Nephi-Lehis disavow violence, swearing that "they never would use weapons again for the shedding of man's blood; and this they did, vouching and covenanting with God, that rather than shed the blood of their brethren they would give up their own lives."[64] They then bury their weapons in the earth.[65] Their covenant is tested when the Lamanites attack. The Anti-Nephi-Lehis refused to resist and the Lamanites were so touched that they too threw down their swords and forswore violence.[66]

Yet as a whole, the Book of Mormon is not pacifist. Mormon's "attitude toward war, revealed in the structure of his account as much as in what it says, has remarkable parallels to classical just war theory."[67] Just cause consists of fighting "for their wives, and their children, and their houses, and their homes," and to prevent the enemy from taking "possession of any of our lands."[68] Revenge is not legitimate.[69] One Mormon author thus derives three just causes for participation in war: defense of liberty, defense of the state, and defense of another state that has been unjustly attacked.[70]

In practice, the LDS response to war has varied with the church's political relationship to the United States, ranging from the pacifism advocated by its founder, Joseph Smith, when the denomination was often persecuted as a sect,[71] to the adoption of a policy encouraging active citizenship. Thus, on the eve of the 1898 Spanish American War, LDS President George Cannon declared, "We should be equally willing, if it should be necessary, to lay down our lives for our country, for its institutions, for the preservation of this liberty that these blessings and privileges shall be preserved to all mankind."[72]

Since then, the LDS leadership has "condemned war and at the same time given instructions pertaining to the conduct of LDS involved in the conflict."[73] The church has not encouraged conscientious objection, even during the tumultuous Vietnam era: "The Church recognizes the right of anyone to conscientiously object.... [However] you can't use the Church as your justification for being a conscientious objector, because we do not recommend it."[74]

A Note on Evangelicalism and Fundamentalism

Evangelical denominations can be found within any of these three broad groupings, and evangelical believers can be found even within many mainline denominations. Furthermore, some evangelical churches are independent of any denominational affiliation.

Although the mainline/evangelical divide is commonly understood to be along the lines of "a Christianity interpreted either liberally or literally"[75] or along the distinction between American liberal and conservative politics, these correlations are imperfect and not evangelicalism's defining factors. Thus, for example, liberal evangelicals during the Cold War condemned nuclear deterrence strategy, while those on the right supported "peace through strength."[76]

Originating in Anglophone countries in the eighteenth century, evangelicalism is a movement that emphasizes that individuals' salvation – their access to heaven – depends on experiencing a personal, transformational relationship with Jesus (being "born again") as a result of recognizing the significance of his sacrifice on the cross, and that such born-again Christians have a duty to live lives that encourage others to accept Christianity.[77] The Bible is deemed inerrant, although not necessarily interpreted literally.

Evangelicalism does not speak with a single voice about the ethics of war. Evangelical denominations are not hierarchical, and therefore no single individual or group represents the whole. While evangelicals share many deeply held views about the importance of marriage and family, their views on the ethics of war diverge. This may partially explain why, despite evangelicals' prominent engagement with domestic social issues, they have remained relatively quiet about international politics.[78]

The diversity of evangelical approaches to war can be illustrated by Baptists' responses to the Iraq War. In 2003, the Ethics and Religious Liberties Commission of the Southern Baptist Convention, the largest Protestant denomination in the United States, argued that the Iraq War met just war criteria, with defense against weapons of mass destruction as a just cause, coupled with the right intent of liberating the Iraqi people.[79] Ultimately, the Southern Baptist Convention passed a resolution affirming that American leaders had acted justly, aiming to "restrain evil and punish evildoers through the power of the sword."[80]

Conversely, many of the predominately black Baptist denominations decried the Iraq War. The National Baptist Convention, USA, argued that "unnecessary and unjust war does not produce genuine peace, only death, suffering, more violence, and hate."[81] Likewise, delegates at the Progressive National Baptist Convention approved several resolutions calling for an end to the "unnecessary, unwise and destructive war in Iraq," which diverted resources away from programs for the poor and vulnerable.[82]

Evangelicalism, furthermore, needs to be distinguished from fundamentalism. While all fundamentalists are evangelicals, the reverse is not true.[83] In addition to a literal interpretation of the Bible, fundamentalists advocate cultural separation from the world.[84] While evangelicals generally believe all humans can potentially be saved, fundamentalists tend to believe in predestination. Perhaps as a corollary, fundamentalists are more pessimistic about the possibility of improving the human condition through politics.[85] Thus, while many other Protestants have championed the United Nations and international human rights law, fundamentalists are often vocal opponents of the creation of such a secular world order.[86]

Two common threads typify fundamentalist thinking about war. War is a divine punishment. And yet the millennialist view that wars are a symptom of the end times means that war itself is not shunned, since it might hasten the return of Christ.

For example, the Free Presbyterian Church (FPC) of Scotland deemed World War I an expression of divine wrath against the United Kingdom, yet encouraged its followers to join the war effort.[87] More recently, FPC ministers in the United States described September 11 as punishment for America's sins.[88] Thus, one prominent minister called on Americans not only to discontinue sinful behavior and policies at home, but also to remember that the "battle is not against some vague force called world terrorism … but … against the forces that set themselves up against God and His Christ," warning that some Islamic groups were "dedicated to the destruction of Christianity and therefore of America."[89] This perspective couples a focus on internal repentance and reform with an outward effort to defeat evil through both evangelism and military means.

As this short introduction illustrates, Protestant denominations differ as much among themselves in their beliefs about war as they do with other Christian traditions. These differences arise from differing theological perspectives and appear to be at least partially influenced by historical contingencies. The following sections present excerpts of some key source texts addressing the ethics of war in several Protestant denominations, arranged chronologically.

Sources

Protestant theologians draw from the same New Testament texts as Catholic and Orthodox thinkers, as well as the Old Testament texts referenced in Judaism. While the earliest Protestant reformers, especially Luther and Calvin, were trained in the Catholic tradition and were well aware of Ambrose, Augustine, and Aquinas, they rarely cite them specifically. Although such foundational theologians' works are highly respected by Protestants, their works do not carry doctrinal weight. Thus, the texts included here do not represent a "canon." Only biblical sources are seen as having such authority. This section is organized by century and, within that, by theological tradition, to reveal changes over time.

Europe was plagued with civil and interstate war during the early years of the Protestant Reformation. Amid such unrest and insecurity, it is not surprising that both Luther and Calvin expressed very conservative attitudes toward political power. As such, they focused on questions of legitimate authority, self-defense, and the soldier's duty to obey. Conversely, Menno Simons, their contemporary, upheld a radically pacifistic view, encouraging withdrawal from political life.

Martin Luther (1483–1546)

Martin Luther was a German monk who sparked the Protestant Reformation. He penned his foundational essay on the legitimacy of the soldier's profession in December 1526. That year, Emperor Charles V called on all Catholic rulers to forcefully suppress the Protestant heretics, who in turn organized an alliance of their own. Concurrently, the Ottoman Empire was threatening Europe following victories in Bohemia and Hungary. In this tense political atmosphere, Luther definitively urges his followers to actively engage in political life – including warfare. It should be recalled that Luther's attitude toward rebellion was ambivalent. Although he believed that the people had the right to use force in self-defense, he did not award them the right to use force first, or preemptively, to take the power of government into their own hands, believing that they lacked the legitimate authority to do so.

From: Martin Luther, "Whether Soldiers, Too, Can Be Saved" (1526)[90]

For the very fact that the sword has been instituted by God to punish the evil, protect the good, and preserve peace [Rom. 13:1–4, I Pet. 2:13–14] is powerful and sufficient proof that war and killing along with all the things that accompany wartime and martial law have been instituted by God. What else is war but the punishment of wrong and evil? Why does anyone go to war, except because he desires peace and obedience?

Now slaying and robbing do not seem to be works of love.... In truth, however, even this is a work of love.... [W]hen I think of how it protects the good and keeps and preserves wife and child, house and farm, property, and honor and peace, then I see how precious and godly this work is.... For if the sword were not on guard to preserve peace, everything in the world would be ruined because of lack of peace. Therefore, such a war is only a very brief lack of peace that prevents an everlasting and immeasurable lack of peace, a small misfortune that prevents a great misfortune.

What men write about war, saying that it is a great plague, is all true. But they should also consider how great the plague is that war prevents. If people were good and wanted to keep peace, war would be the greatest plague on earth. But what are you going to do about the fact that people will not keep the peace, but rob, steal, kill, outrage women and children, and take away property and honor? The small lack of peace called war or the sword must set a limit to this universal, worldwide lack of peace which would destroy everyone.

This is why God honors the sword so highly that he says that he himself has instituted it [Rom. 13:1].... For the hand that wields this sword and kills with it is not man's hand, but God's; and it is not man, but God, who hangs, tortures, beheads, kills, and fights. All these are God's works and judgments.

Luther then defines three types of conflicts: wars between equals, wars by a prince against his people, and wars by the people against the prince. He turns his attention particularly to the last category, relying on Romans 13:1–7 to condemn rebellion as typically against God's will.

From: Martin Luther, "Whether Soldiers, Too, Can Be Saved"[91]

Suppose that a people would rise up today or tomorrow and depose their lord or kill him. That certainly could happen if God decrees that it should, and the lords must expect it. But that does not mean that it is right and just for the people to do it. I have never known of a case in which this was a just action, and even now I cannot imagine any. The peasants who rebelled claimed that the lords would not allow the gospel to be preached and that they robbed the poor people and, therefore, the lords had to be overthrown. I answered this by saying that although the lords did wrong in this, it would not therefore be just or right to do wrong in return, that is, to be disobedient and destroy God's ordinance, which is not ours to do. On the contrary, we ought to suffer wrong, and if a prince or lord will not tolerate the gospel, then we ought to go into another realm where the gospel is preached, as Christ says in Matthew 10[:23], "When they persecute you in one town, flee to the next."

It is only right that if a prince, king, or lord becomes insane, he should be deposed . . . for he is not to be considered a man since his reason is gone. "That is true," you say, "and a raving tyrant is also insane; he is to be considered as even worse than an insane man, for he does much more harm.". . . A madman can neither do nor tolerate anything reasonable, and there is no hope for him because the light of reason has gone out. A tyrant, however, may do things that are far worse than the insane man does, but he still knows that he is doing wrong. He still has a conscience and his faculties. There is also hope that he may improve. . . .

If it is considered right to murder or depose tyrants, the practice spreads and it becomes a commonplace thing arbitrarily to call men tyrants who are not tyrants, and even to kill them if the mob takes a notion to do so. . . .

We dare not encourage the mob very much. It goes mad too quickly. . . . And it is better for the tyrants to wrong them a hundred times than for the mob to treat the tyrant unjustly but once. If injustice is to be suffered, then it is better for subjects to suffer it from their rulers than for the rulers to suffer it from their subjects. The mob neither has any moderation nor even knows what moderation is. . . .

From: Martin Luther, "Whether Soldiers, Too, Can Be Saved"[92]

Now perhaps you will say, "How can anyone possibly endure all the injustice that these tyrants inflict on us? You allow them too much opportunity to be unjust, and thus your teaching only makes them worse and worse. Are we supposed to permit everyone's wife and child, body and property to be so shamefully treated and always to be in danger? If we have to live under these conditions, how can we ever begin to live a decent life?". . .

In the first place, if you see that the rulers think so little of their soul's salvation that they rage and do wrong, what does it matter to you if they ruin your property, body, wife, and child? They cannot hurt your soul, and they do themselves more harm than they do you because they damn their own souls and that must result in the ruin of body and property. Do you think that you are not already sufficiently avenged?

In the second place, what would you do if your rulers were at war and not only your goods and wives and children, but you yourself were broken, imprisoned, burned, and killed for your lord's sake? Would you slay your lord for that reason? Think of all the good people that Emperor Maximilian lost in the wars that he waged in his lifetime. No one did anything to him because of it. And yet, if he had destroyed them by tyranny no more cruel deed would ever have been heard of. Nevertheless, he was the cause of their death, for they were killed for his sake. What is the difference, then, between such a raging tyrant and a dangerous war as far as the many good and innocent people who perish in it are concerned? Indeed, a wicked tyrant is more tolerable than a bad war. . . .

In the third place, if the rulers are wicked, what of it? God is still around, and he has . . . countless ways of killing. How quickly he can kill a tyrant! He would do it, too, but our sins do not permit it, for he says in Job [34:30], "He permits a knave to rule because of the people's sins." We have no trouble seeing that a scoundrel is ruling. However, no one wants to see that he is ruling not because he is a scoundrel, but because of the people's sin. The people do not look at their own sin; they think that the tyrant rules because he is such a scoundrel – that is how blind, perverse, and mad the world is! That is why things happened the way they did when the peasants revolted. They wanted to punish the sins of the rulers, as though they themselves were pure and guiltless. . . .

In the fourth place, the tyrants run the risk that, by God's decree, their subjects may rise up, as has been said, and kill them or expel them. For here we are giving instruction to those who want to do what is right, and they are very few. The great multitude remain heathen, godless, and un-Christian; and these, if God so decrees, wrongfully rise up against the rulers and create disaster. . . . The preservation of the rulers whom God has appointed is a matter that rests with God and in his hands alone. . . .

In the fifth place, God has still another way to punish rulers, so that there is no need for you to avenge yourselves. He can raise up foreign rulers, as he raised up the Goths against the Romans, the Assyrians against the Jews, etc. Thus there is vengeance, punishment, and danger enough hanging over tyrants and rulers, and God does not allow them to be wicked and have peace and joy. . . .

Now we will move on to the second point and discuss the question whether equals may wage war against equals. I would have this understood as follows: It is not right to start a war just because some silly lord has gotten the idea into his head. At the very outset I want to say that whoever starts a war is in the wrong. And it is only right and proper that he who first draws his sword is defeated, or even punished, in the end. . . . Worldly government has not been instituted by God to break the peace and start war, but to maintain peace and to avoid war. Paul says in Romans 13[:4] that it is the duty of the sword to protect and punish, to protect the good in peace and to punish the wicked with war. God tolerates no injustice and he has so ordered things that warmongers must be defeated in war.

From: Martin Luther, "Whether Soldiers, Too, Can Be Saved"[93]

Wait until the situation compels you to fight when you have no desire to do so. You will still have more than enough wars to fight and will be able to say with heartfelt sincerity, "How I would like to have peace. If only my neighbors wanted it too!" Then you can defend yourself with a good conscience. . . .

No war is just, even if it is a war between equals, unless one has such a good reason for fighting and such a good conscience that he can say, "My neighbor compels and forces me to fight, though I would rather avoid it." In that case, it can be called not only war, but lawful self-defense, for we must distinguish between wars that someone begins because that is what he wants to do and does before anyone else attacks him, and those wars that are provoked when an attack is made by someone else. The first kind can be called wars of desire; the second, wars of necessity. The first kind are of the devil; God does not give good fortune to the man who wages that kind of war. The second kind are human disasters; God help in them! . . .

Even though you are absolutely certain that you are not starting a war but are being forced into one, you should still fear God and remember him. . . . You ought not to think that that justifies anything you do and plunge headlong into battle. It is indeed true that you have a really good reason to go to war and to defend yourself, but that does not give you God's guarantee that you will win. Indeed, such confidence may result in your defeat – even though you have a just cause . . . for God cannot endure such pride and confidence except in a man who humbles himself before him and fears him. . . .

Our conclusion on this point, then, is that war against equals should be waged only when it is forced upon us and then it should be fought in the fear of God. Such a war is forced upon us when an enemy or neighbor attacks and starts the war, and refuses to cooperate in settling the matter according to law or through arbitration and common agreement, or when one overlooks and puts up with the enemy's evil words and tricks, but he still insists on having his own way. . . .

The third question is whether overlords have the right to go to war with their subjects. We have, indeed, heard above that subjects are to be obedient and are even to suffer wrong from their tyrants. Thus, if things go well, the rulers have nothing to do with their subjects except to cultivate fairness, righteousness, and judgment. However, if the subjects rise up and rebel, as the peasants did recently, then it is right and proper to fight against them. . . . Only it must be done in the fear of God, and too much reliance must not be placed on being in the right, lest God determine that the lords are to be punished by their subjects, even though the subjects are in the wrong. . . .

So much on these three points; now come the questions. Now since no king can go to war alone . . . the question arises whether a man ought to hire himself out for wages . . . and commit himself to serve the prince as the occasion may demand, as is customary. To answer this question we must distinguish various types of soldiers.

In the first place, there are some subjects who . . . are under obligation to aid their overlords with their body and property and to obey their lord's summons. This is especially true of the nobles and of those who hold property granted by charter from the authorities. . . . [T]hey have it, namely, as a loan from the emperor or the prince. Therefore they ought not use it to finance their own ostentatious display and riotous conduct, but be armed and prepared for war to defend the land and to maintain the peace. . . .

In Luke 2 [3:14] St. John the Baptist confirms the right of this first class to their pay . . . and says that they rightly do their duty when they help their lord make war. . . . When the soldiers asked him what they were to do, he answered, "Be content with your wages." Now if it were wrong for them to take wages, or if their occupation were against God, he could not have let it continue . . . but, as a godly,

Christian teacher, he would have had to condemn it and deter them from it. This is the answer to those who, because of tenderness of conscience ... profess that it is dangerous to take up this occupation for the sake of temporal goods, since it is nothing but bloodshed, murder, and the inflicting of all kinds of suffering upon one's neighbor.... These men should inform their consciences that they do not do this from choice, desire, or ill-will, but that this is God's work and that it is their duty to their prince and their God. Therefore, since it is a legitimate office, ordained by God, they should be paid and compensated for doing it, as Christ says in Matthew 10 [:10]....

Of course, it is true that if a man serves as a soldier with a heart that neither seeks nor thinks of anything but acquiring wealth, and if temporal wealth is his only reason for doing it, he is not happy when there is peace and not war. Such a man strays from the path and belongs to the devil, even though he fights out of obedience to his lord and at his call. He takes a work that is good in itself and makes it bad for himself....

A second question: "Suppose my lord were wrong in going to war." I reply: If you know for sure that he is wrong, then you should fear God rather than men, Acts 4 [5:29], and you should neither fight nor serve, for you cannot have a good conscience before God. "Oh, no," you say, "my lord would force me to do it; he would take away my fief and would not give me my money.... Besides, I would be despised and put to shame as a coward, even worse, as a man who did not keep his word and deserted his lord in need." I answer: You must take that risk and, with God's help, let whatever happens, happen. He can restore it to you a hundredfold, as he promises in the gospel, "Whoever leaves house, farm, wife, and property, will receive a hundredfold," etc. [Matt. 19:29].

In every other occupation we are also exposed to the danger that the rulers will compel us to act wrongly; but since God will have us leave even father and mother for his sake, we must certainly leave lords for his sake. But if you do not know, or cannot find out, whether your lord is wrong, you ought not to weaken certain obedience for the sake of an uncertain justice; rather you should think the best of your lord, as is the way of love, for "love believes all things" and "does not think evil," I Corinthians 13 [:4–7]. So, then, you are secure and walk well before God. If they put you to shame or call you disloyal, it is better for God to call you loyal and honorable than for the world to call you loyal and honorable....

The third question: "Can a soldier obligate himself to serve more than one lord and take wages or salary from each?" Answer: I said above that greed is wrong, whether in a good or an evil occupation.... Again, to take wages and serve for them is right in itself; it does not matter whether the wages come from one, or two, or three, or however many lords, so long as your hereditary lord or prince is not deprived of what is due him and your service to others is rendered with his will and consent....

The fourth question: "What is to be said about the man who goes to war not only for the sake of wealth, but also for the sake of temporal honor, to become a big man and be looked up to?" Answer: Greed for money and greed for honor are both greed; the one is as wrong as the other. Whoever goes to war because of this vice earns hell for himself. We should leave and give all honor to God alone and be satisfied with our wages and rations.

It is, therefore, a heathen and not a Christian custom to exhort soldiers before the battle with words like this, "Dear comrades ... be brave and confident; God willing, we shall this day win honor and become rich." On the contrary, they should be exhorted like this, "Dear comrades, we are gathered here to serve, obey, and do our duty ... for according to God's will and ordinance we are bound to support our prince ... even though in God's sight we are as poor sinners as our enemies are. Nevertheless, since we know that our prince is in the right in this case, or at least do not know otherwise, we are therefore sure and certain that in serving and obeying him we are serving God.... If God gives us victory, the honor and praise shall be his, not ours, for he wins it through us poor sinners. But we will take the booty and the wages as presents and gifts of God's goodness and grace to us, though we are unworthy, and sincerely thank him for them. Now God grant the victory! Forward with joy!"

John Calvin (1509–1564)

John Calvin was a French theologian who fled to Switzerland after the suppression of the Reformation in France. In 1536 he was invited to lead the Protestant movement in Geneva, participating in the city's governance. A decade before his arrival, Geneva had already established itself politically and religiously as an independent city, governed by a council anxious to hold its population to strict standards of public and private behavior. After two years, however, Calvin was exiled to Strasbourg due to conflicts with the ruling faction. In 1541, he rather reluctantly accepted an invitation to return to Geneva, believing it was God's will. Calvin lived out the rest of his life in Geneva, which gradually became theocratic, participating actively in its governance. Although Calvin had a great deal of respect for Luther, a dispute over the nature of the Eucharist ultimately split the Lutheran and Reformed branches of the Reformation. Calvin strongly influenced the theology of Heinrich Bullinger and John Knox, whose work will also be presented here. The *Institutes of the Christian Religion*, his most influential work, was first published in 1536, and Calvin continued to refine and expand it for the rest of his life.

From: John Calvin, *Institutes of the Christian Religion* (1536)[94]

IV.XX.II

Yet this distinction does not lead us to consider the whole system of civil government as a polluted thing, which has nothing to do with Christian men. Some fanatics ... do indeed boast and vociferate, that since we are dead with Christ to the elements of this world ... it is a degradation to us ... to be occupied with those secular and impure cares.... But as we have just suggested that this kind of government is distinct from that spiritual and internal reign of Christ, so it ought to be known that they are in no respect at variance with each other.... [T]his civil government is designed, as long as we live in this world, to cherish and support the external worship of God, to preserve the pure doctrine of religion, to defend the constitution of the Church, to regulate our lives in a manner requisite for the society of men, to form our manners to civil justice, to promote our concord with each other, and to establish general peace and tranquillity ... if such aids are necessary to our pilgrimage, they who take them from man deprive him of his human nature.

IV.XX.III

... At present we only wish it to be understood, that to entertain a thought of its extermination, is inhuman barbarism; it is equally as necessary to mankind as bread and water ... and far more excellent. For it not only tends to secure the accommodations arising from all these things, that men may breathe, eat, drink and be sustained in life ... its objects also are, that idolatry, sacrileges against the name of God, blasphemies against his truth, and other offences against religion, may not openly appear and be disseminated among the people ... in short, that there may be a public form of religion among Christians, and that humanity may be maintained among men....

IV.XX.IX

We see, therefore, that they are constituted the protectors and vindicators of the public innocence, modesty, probity, and tranquillity, whose sole object it ought to be to promote the common peace and security of all.... But as they cannot do this, unless they defend good men from the injuries of the wicked, and aid the oppressed by their relief and protection, they are likewise armed with power for the suppression of crimes, and the severe punishment of malefactors, whose wickedness disturbs the public peace....

X. But here, it seems, arises an important and difficult question. If by the law of God all Christians are forbidden to kill ... how can it be compatible with piety for magistrates to shed blood? But if we understand, that in the infliction of punishments, the magistrate does not act at all from himself, but merely executes the judgments of God, we shall not be embarrassed with this scruple. The law of the Lord commands, "Thou shalt not kill"; but that homicide may not go unpunished, the legislator himself puts the sword into the hands of his ministers, to be used against all homicides (Gen. ix. 6 Exod. Xxi. 12)....

Therefore, if princes and other governors know that nothing will be more acceptable to God than their obedience, and if they desire to approve their piety, justice and integrity before God, let them devote themselves to this duty. This motive influenced Moses, when, knowing himself to be destined to become the liberator of his people ... "he slew the Egyptian" (Exod. Ii. 12), and when he punished the idolatry of the people by the slaughter of three thousand men in one day (Exod xxxii. 26–28)....

Now, if it be true justice for them to pursue the wicked with a drawn sword, let them sheathe the sword, and keep their hands from shedding blood, while the swords of desperadoes are drenched in murders; and they will be so far from acquiring the praise of goodness and justice by this forbearance, that they will involve themselves in the deepest impiety. There ought not, however, to be any excessive or unreasonable severity, nor ought any cause to be given for considering the tribunal as a gibbet prepared for all who are accused. For I am not an advocate for unnecessary cruelty, nor can I conceive the possibility of an equitable sentence being pronounced without mercy....

XI. Now, as it is sometimes necessary for kings and nations to take up arms for the infliction of such public vengeance, the same reason will lead us to infer the lawfulness of wars which are undertaken for this end. For if they have been entrusted with power to preserve the tranquillity of their own territories, to suppress the seditious tumults of disturbers, to succor the victims of oppression, and to punish crimes, – can they exert this power for a better purpose, than to repel the violence of him who disturbs both the private repose of individuals and the general tranquillity of the nation; who excites insurrections, and perpetrates acts of oppression, cruelty and every species of crime? If they ought to be the guardians and defenders of the laws, it is incumbent upon them to defeat the efforts of all by whose injustice the discipline of the laws is corrupted.... For there is no difference, whether he, who in a hostile manner invades, disturbs, and plunders the territory of another to which he has no right, be a king, or one of the meanest of mankind: all persons of this description are equally to be considered as robbers, and ought to be punished as such. It is the dictate both of natural equity, and of the nature of the office, therefore, that princes are armed, not only to restrain the crimes of private individuals by judicial punishments, but also to defend the territories committed to their charge by going to war against any hostile aggression; and the Holy Spirit, in many passages of Scripture, declares such wars to be lawful.

XII. If it be objected that the New Testament contains no precept or example, which proves war to be lawful to Christians, I answer, first, that the reason for waging war which existed in ancient times, is equally valid in the present age; and that, on the contrary, there is no cause to prevent princes from defending their subjects. Secondly, that no express declaration on this subject is to be expected in the writings of the apostles, whose design was, not to organize civil governments, but to describe the spiritual kingdom of Christ. Lastly, that in those very writings it is implied ... that no change has been made in this respect by the coming of Christ. "For," to use the words of Augustine, "if Christian discipline condemned all wars, the soldiers who inquired respecting their salvation ought rather to have been directed to cast away their arms, and entirely to renounce the military profession; whereas the advice given them was, 'Do violence to no man, neither accuse any falsely; and be content with your wages' (Luke iii.14). An injunction to be content with their wages was certainly not a prohibition of the military life. But here all magistrates ought to be very cautious, that they follow not in any respect the impulse of their passions. On the contrary, if punishments are to be inflicted, they ought not to be precipitated with anger, exasperated with hatred, or inflamed with implacable severity: they ought, as Augustine says, 'to commiserate our common nature even in him whom they punish for his crime.' Or, if arms are to be resorted to against an enemy, that is, an armed robber, they ought not to seize a trivial occasion, nor even to take it when presented, unless they are driven to it by extreme necessity. For, if it be our duty to exceed what was required by that heathen writer who maintained that the evident object of war ought to be the restoration of peace, certainly we ought to make every other attempt before we have recourse to the decision of arms. In short, in both cases they must not suffer themselves to be carried away by any private motive, but be wholly guided by public spirit...."

XXIX. Finally, we owe these sentiments of affection and reverence to all our rulers, whatever their characters may be ... that we may learn not to scrutinize the persons themselves but may be satisfied with knowing that they are invested by the will of the Lord with that function, upon which he has impressed an inviolable majesty. But it will be said, that rulers owe mutual duties to their subjects.... [H]e who infers from this that obedience ought to be rendered to none but just rulers, is a very bad reasoner.... They are still subject, even to those who are wicked and unkind.... Wherefore, if we are inhumanly harassed by a cruel prince; if we are rapaciously plundered by an avaricious or luxurious one; if we are neglected by an indolent one; or if we are persecuted, on account of piety, by an impious and sacrilegious one, – let us first call to mind our transgressions against God, which he undoubtedly chastises by these scourges. Thus our impatience will be restrained by humility. Let us, in the next place, consider that it is not our province to remedy these evils, and that nothing remains for us, but to implore the aid of the Lord, in whose hand are the hearts of kings and the revolutions of kingdoms....

XXX. And here is displayed his wonderful goodness ... for sometimes he raises up some of his servants as public avengers, and arms them with his commission to punish unrighteous domination, and to deliver from their distressing calamities a people who have been unjustly oppressed: sometimes he accomplishes this end by the fury of men who meditate and attempt something altogether different. Thus he liberated the people of Israel from the tyranny of Pharaoh by Moses.... The ingratitude of the kings of Israel and Judah, and their impious rebellion, notwithstanding his numerous favors, he repressed and punished, sometimes by the Assyrians, sometimes by the Babylonians. These were all the executioners of his vengeance.... The former, when they were called forth to the performance of such acts by a legitimate commission from God, in taking arms against kings, were not chargeable with the least violation of that majesty with which kings are invested by the ordination of God; but being armed with authority from Heaven, they punished an inferior power by a superior one, as it is lawful for kings to punish their inferior officers. The latter, though they were guided by the hand of God in such directions as he pleased, and performed his work without being conscious of it, nevertheless contemplated in their hearts nothing but evil.

XXXI. But whatever opinion be formed of the acts of men yet, the Lord equally executed his work by them, when he broke the sanguinary scepters of insolent kings, and overturned tyrannical governments. Let princes hear and fear. But, in the meanwhile, it behooves us to use the greatest caution, that we do not despise

or violate that authority of magistrates, which is entitled to the greatest veneration, which God has established by the most solemn commands, even though it
reside in those who are most unworthy of it, and who, as far as in them lies, pollute it by their iniquity.

Heinrich Bullinger (1504–1575)

Heinrich Bullinger was a Swiss reformer influenced by Calvin. He had a great influence on both Puritan and Presbyterian thought regarding the role of the state, so it is
worthwhile to consider him here.[95] Unlike many of his contemporaries, Bullinger clearly
accepts religious causes as legitimate reasons for war.[96] In his view, the state had an obligation to provide for not only the physical needs of its subjects, but also their spiritual
ones. Thus, the magistrate could use violence to repress idolatry or apostasy.

From: Heinrich Bullinger, "A treatise or sermon of Henry Bullynger: much fruitfull and necessarye for this time, concernynge magistrates and obedience of subiectes: Also concernying the affayres of war and what scriptures make mention thereof" (1549)[97]

[T]his sword in the magistrates' hands hath two uses: either to punish trespassers
or else to repel and destroy our open enemies ... [such as] rebellious and seditious
citizens, and subjects. But here cometh about in many men's heads whether it be
lawful for magistrates to keep war. And I marvel that men can be so blind in a thing
so evident. For if it be lawful for magistrates by God's law to punish trespassers,
thieves and murders ... likewise is it lawful for them to invade and pursue with arms
rebels and seditious citizens, or any foreign enemy who so ever intend the same by
the color of war, that thieves and murderers do practice within the realm. ...

To put blame in this is not a sign of religious men but of timorous persons.
The pleasure in hurting, ... wild rebelling, greediness to get dominion ... be they
which be worthily repressed in war, and not only reproved, but also punished.
Against the violence of our adversaries, good men may rightfully war. ...

Thus ... it is lawful for magistrates to war. And by this we gather that subjects likewise may lawfully and without reprehension go and fight ... when they
be commanded by the magistrates so to do. But if it be so that the magistrate's
causes do set upon to slay the innocents ... in this case the magistrate's commandments are not to be obeyed.

Therefore let the magistrates take heed lest they abuse their authority. And
though it be lawful for the magistrates to keep war for just and necessary causes, yet
is war a most dangerous thing and bringeth with it heaps of infinite troubles. ...

How many times it happeneth that soldiers forget themselves, and break all
good order, provoking the mighty anger of God upon their heads ... ? ...

[I]t is requisite that princes first before all things do thoroughly consider the
causes of their wars. ... For either the magistrate is [forced to let] ... his realm

to be invaded with siege, then he must needs help and repulse his enemy. For it were too much unfaithfulness to forsake so disloyally his cities and fortresses in such extreme peril. Or else the magistrate by reason of his office be constrained to attempt war against incurable persons whom the sentence of the lord doth condemn and biddeth to bear down utterly without all peace. [Here Bullinger gives examples of Old Testament wars directly ordered by God.]

Hereto appertain also such wars achieved against Idolaters, and oppressors of the catholic faith, for true religion's sake. They be in a wrong dream which think no war ought to be attempted for religion.

The lord restrained Peter striking with the sword: ... he restrained him as an Apostle, he forbade not the magistrate the oversight of religion, but that he might defend the rite of our faith. If the magistrate may lawfully defend ... liberty, goods, bodily honesty and life ... how much more may he defend greater things, yea which be the greatest things of all? For what can be greater than true religion. Upon this we have an express commandment of the Lord in Deuteronomy, for the Lord commandeth any city under what magistrate so ever he be, which defileth from God and his worship, to be let upon with war and utterly to be subverted if it be stubborn....

Therefore the magistrates may lawfully defend their subjects and true religion against idolaters.

[There is] another cause which is alike. Some foreign and Barbarous adversary doth fly upon thy subjects, doth spoil them ... as the cruel wolves to the sheep, when not only thou hath not provoked them with any injuries, but moreover hast offered them right reasonable conditions of peace, than ought the magistrate to fight like a lion to preserve his people against the assaults of such malicious murderers....

Fourthly, it is lawful for the magistrate to fight in the defense of his confederate friends and aiders, for why may not a magistrate be at confederacy and [in] league with other nations so it be not in matters against the word of God in case they be ... oppressed [with] violence....

And the soldiers ... [who] herein obey their powers ... die gloriously and in a good state, in [so] dying for religion, for God's laws, for their country, their wives and children. Therefore all such as enter into war, and travail in the same, must not let their eye either upon filthy lust nor voluptuousness, as they lightly do when Jeopardy is past, but ... peace, public tranquillity, and the defense of truth and innocence must be all their mark which they shoot at: so that the wicked force being conquered, the victory got, and their enemies either repulsed or destroyed, true religion may flourish, judgment and equity, the church may flourish....

Therefore no war is lawful except it be against our adversaries and misordered rebels. Unjust wars be such as be made against our own fellows or men faultless, or in whom we see hope of amendment. Also unjust wars be they which be not inferred ... for any urgent cause.

All manner of ways ought to be assayed ... before we come to war. You must not seek to take in other men's bonds or limits [anything not] pertaining to your right. You must not oppress the liberties of other nations, neither yet of your own.... War is a remedy, but dangerous; a help, but pernicious, much like to the cutting of members. In case thy hand be on fire, and so thy arm be in danger to be burnt ... yet dost thee not cut away thy hand ... unless thou see ... no other help.... So neither is war to be set upon but where there is no other remedy, so yet that princes remember, they do nothing which after will be too late. For just wars be not repugnant to God's word in so much that it describeth to us the laws of warfare.... [Bullinger then sums up the rules presented in 20 Deuteronomy, arguing that the word of God serves as a field manual.]

Just laws no less ought to be kept in the midst of wars as in the midst of cities, the soldiers let them keep them in due order with all honesty, justice and holiness....

[L]et ever a Christian warrior be doing something, let him be courageous, faithful ... obedient to his captain ... not tender but hard, not cruel and fierce, but grave and gentle according as time doth serve. The thing that may be saved let him not destroy. But above all other especially let him not forget continually to pray unto God....

Let him seek for nothing more than for defense of his country, of laws, of religion, of justice, and of innocents.

Some here will marvel ... that I require these things of soldiers, which were wont in times past to be required of religious and professed men. As though soldiers were not also religious and professed to Christ, or as though only they may be profane and wicked, as in deed many of them be. [Bullinger here blames the poor morals of soldiers and statesmen for Europe's losses to the invading Ottoman Turks, the defeats representing divine punishment.]...

[N]ow we will discuss, whether it be lawful for Christians to bear office or not.... I bring here succinctly certain arguments, whereby a politick and Christian man against the furious dreams of the Anabaptists may understand, if he be called to office, that he may and ought to serve God well in keeping and well using his office....

For what things so ever be ordained of God to the health and safety of man, they be so seeming to a Christian man using them well and applying himself thereafter that if he refuse them, he is no Christian. For the greatest charge of a Christian is to set forward with all industry the safeguard and wealth of men, now the magistrate is ordained of no man, but of God himself, to the safeguard and protection of men.

John Knox (1510–1572)

John Knox was a Scottish clergyman, considered the founder of Presbyterianism. Originally a Catholic priest, he became involved in the movement to reform the Scottish Church and was exiled to England in 1549. There, he became a priest in the Church of England, and even chaplain to King Edward VI. After the Catholic Mary Tudor replaced Edward on the throne, however, Knox was forced to leave England. He then spent time in Geneva, where he met Calvin, whose theology markedly influenced him.

In 1559, Knox returned to Scotland, becoming embroiled in a rebellion against Mary of Guise, who served as regent for her daughter, Mary Stuart. Knox's theological influence on the rebels is clear, although his exact role in the movement is not.[98] After Mary of Guise's sudden death, the Scottish Parliament accepted a reformed confession of faith. In September 1561, Knox was summoned to an interview with the new queen, Mary Stuart. She accused him of fomenting rebellion against her because she was a woman and a Catholic. Knox retells this meeting in *The History of the Reformation of Religion*, boldly asserting subjects' right to rebel if their leaders overstep their authority.

From: John Knox, *The History of the Reformation of Religion within the Realm of Scotland* (1898)[99]

Queen Mary. "Ye think then that I have no just authority?"

John Knox. "Please Your Majesty learned men in all ages have ... most commonly disagreed from the common judgment of the world. Such also have they published, both with pen and tongue, and yet, notwithstanding, they themselves have lived in common society with others, and have borne patiently with the errors and imperfections which they could not amend.... Even so, Madam, am I content to do in uprightness of heart, and with testimony of a good conscience.... If the Realm finds no inconvenience from the government of a woman, that which they approve shall I not further disallow than within my own breast, but shall be as well content to live under Your Grace as Paul was to live under Nero. My hope is, that so long as ye defile not your hands with the blood of the Saints of God, neither I nor that book shall either hurt you or your authority." ...

Queen Mary. "But yet ye have taught the people to receive another religion than their princes can allow. How can that doctrine be of God, seeing that God commandeth subjects to obey their princes?"

John Knox. "Madam, as right religion took neither original strength nor authority from worldly princes, but from the Eternal God alone, so are not subjects bound to frame their religion according to the appetites of their princes. Princes are oft the most ignorant of all others in God's true religion.... If all the seed of Abraham should have been of the religion of Pharaoh, to whom they were long subjects, I pray you, Madam, what religion should there have been in the world? Or, if all men in the days of the Apostles should have been of the religion of the Roman Emperors, what religion should there have been upon the face of the earth? Daniel and his fellows were subjects to Nebuchadnezzar and unto Darius, and yet, Madam, they would not be of their religion.... Daniel did pray publicly unto his God against the expressed commandment of the King. And so, Madam, ye may perceive that subjects are not bound to the religion of their princes, although they are commanded to give them obedience."

Queen Mary. "Yea, but none of these men raised the sword against their princes."

John Knox. "Yet, Madam, ye cannot deny that they resisted, for those who obey not the commandments that are given, in some sort resist."

Queen Mary. "But yet, they resisted not by the sword?"

John Knox. "God, Madam, had not given them the power and the means."

Queen Mary. "Think ye that subjects, having the power, may resist their princes?"

John Knox. "If their princes exceed their bounds, Madam, no doubt they may be resisted, even by power. For there is neither greater honor, nor greater obedience, to be given to kings or princes, than God hath commanded to be given unto father and mother. But the father may be stricken with a frenzy, in which he would slay his children. If the children arise, join themselves together, apprehend the father, take the sword from him, bind his hands, and keep him in prison till his frenzy be overpast – think ye, Madam, that the children do any wrong? It is even so, Madam, with princes that would murder the children of God that are subjects unto them. Their blind zeal is nothing but a very mad frenzy, and therefore, to take the sword from them, to bind their hands, and to cast them into prison, till they be brought to a more sober mind, is no disobedience against princes, but just obedience, because it agreeth with the will of God."...

At length she said to John Knox: "Well then, I perceive that my subjects shall obey you, and not me. They shall do what they list, and not what I command...."

John Knox. "God forbid that ever I take upon me to command any to obey me, or yet to set subjects at liberty to do what pleaseth them! My travail is that both princes and subjects obey God. Think not, Madam, that wrong is done you, when ye are willed to be subject to God. It is He that subjects peoples under princes, and causes obedience to be given unto them. Yea, God craves of Kings that they be foster-fathers to His Church, and commands Queens to be nurses to His people. This subjection, Madam, unto God, and unto His troubled Church ... shall carry them to everlasting glory."

Menno Simons (1496–1561)

Menno Simons was born to a peasant family in the Netherlands. Trained as a priest, in the 1520s he began to question Catholic doctrine, and carefully studied the Bible, along with the works of Luther and Bullinger. Ultimately, he was swayed by the Anabaptist position and became one of the movement's most influential leaders and theologians. As a Radical Reformer, Simons based his theology strictly on the Bible, particularly the New Testament. He thus maintained that Christians are forbidden to kill under any circumstances – a decidedly pacifist position. In the "Testimony against John Van Leyden," Simons critiques the theology of a group of radical Anabaptists who had violently captured the city of Munster in an attempt to create a millennial kingdom.

From: Menno Simons, "Testimony against John Van Leyden" (1871)[100]

By the grace of God we will also write a little about warfare, that Christians are not allowed to fight with the sword, that we may unanimously leave the armor of David to the carnal Israelites....

Now we should not understand that the figure of the Old Testament is so applied to the truth of the New Testament, that flesh is understood as referring to flesh; but the figure must answer the truth; the image, the being, and the letter, the Spirit.

If we take this view of it we shall easily understand with what kind of arms Christians should fight, namely, with the word of God, which is a two edged sword....

If Christ fights his enemies with the sword of his mouth, if he smites the earth with the rod of his mouth, and slay the wicked with the breath of his lips; and if we are to be conformed unto his image, how can we, then, fight our enemies with any other sword?...

Here we are not taught to take up the carnal sword, or to repay evil with evil. But rather as Paul says at another place, "Recompense to no man evil for evil. ... If it be possible, as much as lieth in you, live peaceably with all men. Dearly beloved, avenge not yourselves; but rather give place unto wrath: For it is written, Vengeance is mine; I will repay, saith the Lord. Therefore if thine enemy hunger, feed him; if he thirst, give him drink; for in so doing thou shalt heap coals of fire on his head. Be not overcome of evil, but overcome evil with good," Rom. 12:17–21. And how can Christians fight with the implements of war?... Now, Christ Jesus was minded to suffer; thus, all Christians must be so minded.

Christ did not suffer Peter to defend him with the sword; how can a Christian, then, defend himself with the sword? Christ would drink the cup which the Father had given him; how then, can a Christian refuse to drink it? Matt. 26:51; Luke 22:50; Mark 14:47; John 18:11.

Or does any person expect to be saved by other means than those which Christ has taught us? Is not Christ the way, the truth, and the life?...

And if we are to take the prophets as an example to bear with persecution, then we must put on the apostolic armor, and the armor of David must be left behind. How would it comport with the word of God, that one who boasts of being a Christian, should lay aside the spiritual weapons and take up the carnal ones, for Paul says, "The servant of the Lord must not strive; but be gentle unto all men, apt to teach, patient; in meekness instructing those that oppose themselves ... ," 2 Tim. 24:26.

All of you who would fight with the sword of David, and be the servants of the Lord, consider these words, which show how a servant should be minded. If he is not to strive, how can he war? If he is to be gentle to all men, how can he then hate them and do evil unto them?... If he is to instruct in meekness those that oppose, how can he destroy them?

If he is to instruct in meekness those that oppose truth, how can he angrily punish those that do not yet acknowledge the truth?...

Christ has not taken his kingdom with the sword, but he entered it through much suffering. Yet they mean to take it by the sword! O, blindness of man! ... Therefore I admonish all beloved brethren, yea, I pray you by the mercy of God our Lord Jesus Christ, to give heed to the word of God, and do not forsake it....

Let every one of you guard against all strange doctrine, of the sword, of opposition and of other like things, which is nothing short of a fine cover, under which lies hidden an evil serpent which has blown its venom into many. Let everyone beware of it!

In contrast to the Lutheran and Reformed movements, the Anabaptists adopted strict pacifism. The Dordrecht Confession, adopted by Dutch Mennonite leaders in 1632, remains influential for many Mennonite and Amish believers today.

From: "Dordrecht Confession" (21 April 1632)[101]

Article XIII. Of the Office of Civil Government

We also believe and confess, that God has instituted civil government, for the punishment of the wicked and the protection of the pious; and also further, for the purpose of governing the world, countries and cities.... Wherefore we are not permitted to despise, revile or resist the same, but are to acknowledge it as a minister of God and be subject and obedient to it, in all things that do not militate against the law, will, and commandments of God.... That we are also to pray to the Lord earnestly for the government and its welfare, and in behalf of our country, so that we may live under its protection, maintain ourselves, and "lead a quiet and peaceable life in all godliness and honesty."...

Article XIV. Of Defense by Force

Regarding revenge, whereby we resist our enemies with the sword, we believe and confess that the Lord Jesus has forbidden His disciples and followers all revenge and resistance, and has thereby commanded them not to "return evil for evil" ... but to "put up the sword into the sheath," or, as the prophet foretold, "beat them into plowshares." Matt. 5:39, 44; Rom. 12:14; 1 Pet. 3:9; Isa. 2:4; Micah 4:3.

From this we see, that, according to the example, life, and doctrine of Christ, we are not to do wrong, or cause offense or vexation to anyone; but to seek the welfare and salvation of all men; also, if necessity should require it, to flee, for the Lord's sake, from one city or country to another, and suffer the "spoiling of our goods," rather than give occasion of offense to anyone; and if we are struck in our "right cheek, rather to turn the other also," than revenge ourselves, or return the blow. Matt. 5:39; 10:23; Rom. 12:19.

And that we are, besides this, also to pray for our enemies, comfort and feed them, when they are hungry or thirsty, and thus by well-doing convince them and overcome the evil with good. Rom. 12:20, 21.

As the Reformation swept across Europe in the sixteenth century, it met with particularly favorable political conditions in Great Britain, where eventually Protestantism, in the form of the Church of England, was enshrined as the state religion. The Thirty-Nine Articles, originally written in 1563, lay out Anglicanism's theological dimensions, which include Lutheran and Calvinist aspects. Ratified by Parliament in 1571, they have been consistently printed in the Book of Common Prayer of the Church of England. Revised versions are considered confessional documents in many churches of the Anglican communion, including the U.S. Episcopal Church. These articles also served as the basis for John Wesley's Articles of Religion, which remain official United Methodist Church doctrine. Article 37 deals with government and war.

From: Article 37, *The Book of Common Prayer* (1549)[102]

Where we attribute to the King's Majesty the chief government … we give not to our Princes the ministering either of God's Word, or of the Sacraments … ; but that only prerogative, which we see to have been given always to all godly Princes in Holy Scriptures by God himself; that is, that they should rule all estates and degrees committed to their charge by God, whether they be ecclesiastical or temporal, and restrain with the civil sword the stubborn and evil-doers. . . .

The Laws of the Realm may punish Christian men with death, for heinous and grievous offenses.

It is lawful for Christian men, at the commandment of the Magistrate, to wear weapons, and serve in the wars.

In the seventeenth and eighteenth centuries, several new Protestant denominations emerged. Although many of these denominations also established themselves on the European Continent, their roots were in the Anglican tradition. Two will be presented here. The Methodist movement, spearheaded by John Wesley, accepted the just war tradition. The Quakers, or Society of Friends, offered pacifism as an alternative.

John Wesley (1703–1791)

John Wesley was an Anglican clergyman who founded the Methodist movement. Rather than creating a new denomination, he imagined his project as a revivalist one, aimed at inspiring the public to a more passionate relationship with God. Indeed, he never broke with the established Anglican Church. The movement quickly spread through Great Britain and its American colonies. He did not support the colonists during the American Revolution, believing their cause was unjust, but after the revolution, he personally ordained ministers for the American Methodists, against the wishes of the Archbishop. In this moving sermon from 1757, Wesley decries war as the immoral product of humankind's fall.

From: John Wesley, "The Doctrine of Original Sin, According to Scripture, Reason and Experience" (1756–1757)[103]

10. But there is a still greater and more undeniable proof that the very foundations of all things, civil and religious, are utterly out of course in the Christian as well as the Heathen world. There is a still more horrid reproach to the Christian name, yea, to the name of man, to all reason and humanity. There is war in the world! War between men! War between Christians! I mean, between those that bear the name of Christ, and profess to "walk as he also walked." Now, who can reconcile war, I will not say to religion, but to any degree of reason or common sense?

But is there not a cause? O yes: "The causes of war," as the same writer observes, "are innumerable. Some of the chief are these: The ambition of princes; or the corruption of their ministers; difference of opinion; as, whether flesh be bread, or bread be flesh; whether the juice of the grape be blood or wine; what is the best color for a coat, whether black, white or gray.... Nor are there any wars so furious as those occasioned by such difference of opinions.

Sometimes two princes make war to decide which of them shall dispose a third of his dominions. Sometimes a war is commenced, because another prince is too strong; sometimes, because he is too weak. Sometimes our neighbors want the things which we have or have the things which we want: so both fight, until they take ours, or we take theirs. It is a reason for invading a country, if the people have been wasted by famine, destroyed by pestilence, or embroiled by faction; or to attack our nearest ally, if part of his land would make our dominions more round and compact.

Another cause of making war is this: A crew are driven by a storm they know not where; at length they make the land, and go ashore; they are entertained with kindness. They give the country a new name; set up a stone or rotten plank for a memorial; murder a dozen of the natives, and bring away a couple by force. Here commences a new right of dominion; ships are sent and the natives driven out or destroyed. And this is done to civilize and convert a barbarous and idolatrous people.

But, whatever be the cause, let us calmly and impartially consider the thing itself. Here are forty thousand men gathered together on this plain.... And these are going to shoot them through the head or body, to stab them, or split their skulls; and send most of their souls into everlasting fire, as fast as possibly they can. Why so? What harm have they done to them? O, none at all! They do not so much as know them. But a man who is king of France has a quarrel with another man, who is king of England. So these Frenchmen are to kill as many of these Englishmen as they can, to prove the king of France, is in the right.... What a method of proof! ... How shocking, how inconceivable a want must there have been of common understanding, as well as common humanity, before any two governors, or any two nations in the universe, could once think of such a method of decision! If, then, all nations, Pagan, Mohammedan, and Christian, do, in fact, make this their last resort, what farther proof do we need of the utter degeneracy of all nations from the plainest principles of reason and virtue?...

And meanwhile we gravely talk of the "dignity of our nature" in its present state.... And surely all our declamations on the strength of human reason, and the eminence of our virtues, are no more than the cant and jargon of pride and ignorance, so long as there is such a thing as war in the world.

Men in general can never be allowed to be reasonable creatures, till they know not war any more. So long as this monster stalks uncontrolled, where is reason, virtue, humanity? They are utterly excluded; they have no place; they are a name and nothing more. If even a Heathen were to give an account of an age wherein reason and virtue reigned, he would allow no war to have place therein. So Ovid of the golden age: "Steep ditches did not then the town surround, Nor glittering helm nor slaughtering sword was found; Nor arms had they to wield, nor wars to wage, But peace and safety crown'd the blissful age."

11. How far is the world at present from this state!

George Fox (1624–1691)

George Fox was one of the founders of the Religious Society of Friends, or Quakers. In this 1660 letter to King Charles II of England, he explains the Quaker commitment to nonviolence.[104] In so doing, he denies that they are guilty of any sedition or treason against the Crown, despite the Quakers' unwillingness to swear oaths and insistence on (illegal) unauthorized religious meetings. Seven hundred Quakers, including Fox himself, were released from prison after the King was convinced of their nonviolent intentions.

From: George Fox, *A journal or historical account of the life, travels, sufferings, Christian experiences and labour of love in the work of the ministry of that ancient, eminent and faithful servant of Jesus Christ, George Fox* (1694)[105]

Presented to the king the 21st day of the 11th Month, 1660.

Our principle is, and our practices have always been to seek peace, and ensue it, to follow after righteousness and the knowledge of God; seeking the good and welfare, and doing that which tends to the peace of all. We know that wars and fightings proceed from the lusts of men, as James iv. 1–3, out of which lusts the Lord hath redeemed us, and so out of the occasion of war. The occasion of war and the war itself (wherein envious men, who are lovers of themselves more than lovers of God, lust, kill, and desire to have men's lives or estates) ariseth from the lust. All bloody principles and practices we ... do utterly deny, with all outward wars, strife, and fighting with outward weapons for any end, or under any pretense whatsoever....

[W]e certainly know and testify to the world, That the Spirit of Christ, which leads us into all truth, will never move us to fight and war against any man with outward weapons, neither for the kingdom of Christ, nor for the kingdoms of this world.

First, Because the kingdom of Christ, God will exalt, according to his promise, and cause it to grow and flourish in righteousness, "Not by might, nor by power (of outward Sword) but by my Spirit, saith the Lord," Zech. iv. 6. So those that use any weapon to fight for Christ, or for the establishing of his kingdom or government, their spirit, principle, and practice we deny.

Secondly, We earnestly desire and wait, that (by the word of God's power, and its effectual operation in the hearts of men) the kingdoms of this world may become the kingdoms of the Lord, and of his Christ; and that he may rule and reign in men by his Spirit and truth; that thereby all people, out of all different judgments and professions, may be brought into love and unity with God, and one with another; and that all may come to witness the prophet's words fulfilled, who said, "Nation shall not lift up sword against nation, neither shall they learn war any more," Isa. ii. 4. Mich. iv. 3....

Since we, whom the Lord hath called into the obedience of his truth, have denied wars and fightings ... we can say to all the world, we have wronged no man, we have used no force nor violence against any man, we have been found in no plots, nor guilty of sedition. When we have been wronged we have not sought to revenge ourselves, we have not made resistance against authority; but wherein we could not obey for conscience sake, we have suffered the most of any people in the nation....

And whereas men come against us with clubs, staves, drawn swords, pistols cocked, and beat, cut and abuse us; yet we never resisted them, but to them our hair, backs, and cheeks have been ready. It is not an honor to manhood or nobility, to run upon harmless people, who lift not a hand against them, with arms and weapons.

Therefore consider these things, ye men of understanding; for plotters, raisers of insurrections, tumultuous ones, and fighters, running with swords ... one against another; we say, these are of the world, and have their foundation from this unrighteous world, from the foundation of which the Lamb hath been slain: which Lamb hath redeemed us from this unrighteous world; we are not of it, but are heirs of a world of which there is no end, a kingdom where no corruptible thing enters. Our weapons are spiritual, not carnal, yet mighty through God to the pulling down of the strong holds of sin and Satan, who is the author of wars, fighting, murder, and plots. Our swords are broken into plowshares, and spears into pruning-hooks.... Therefore we cannot learn war any more, neither rise up against nation or kingdom with outward weapons, though you have numbered us among the transgressors and plotters. The Lord knows our innocency herein....

Oh! friends! offend not the Lord and his little ones, neither afflict his people; but consider and be moderate.... Though we have suffered all along, because we would not take up carnal weapons to fight withal against any, and are thus made a prey upon because we are the innocent Lambs of Christ, and cannot avenge ourselves! These things are left upon your hearts to consider; for we are out of all those things, in the patience of the saints, and we know as Christ said, "He that takes the sword shall perish with the Sword," Matt., xxvi. 52. Rev. xiii. 10.

William Penn (1644–1718)

William Penn was the Quaker founder of the colony of Pennsylvania, established as a haven for English Quakers. He invited other persecuted sects from across Europe, vowed not to abuse the Native Americans, and established a democratic governing system. Deeply concerned with matters of peace and justice, in 1670 he wrote a treatise calling for European states to ally under a common government for the sake of peace.

From: William Penn, *An Essay Towards the Present and Future Peace of Europe* (1693–1694)[106]

What can we desire better than *Peace*, but the *Grace* to use it? *Peace* preserves our Possessions ... Our Trade is free and Safe, and we rise and lye down without

Anxiety.... But War ... seizes all these Comforts at once, and stops the civil Channel of Society. The Rich draw in their Stock, the Poor turn Soldiers, or Thieves, or starve: No Industry, no Building, no Manufactory, little Hospitality or Charity; but what the Peace gave, the War devours....

Section II: *Of the Means of Peace, which Is Justice, Rather Than War.*

As *Justice* is a Preserver, so it is a better Procurer of Peace than War. Tho' *Pax quaeritur bello* be an usual Saying, *Peace is the end of War*.... Yet the Use generally made of that expression shows us, that properly and truly speaking, Men seek their Wills by *War* rather than Peace, and that as they will violate it to obtain them, so they will hardly be brought to think of Peace, unless their Appetites be some Way gratified. If we look over the Stories of all Times, we shall find the Aggressors generally moved by Ambition ... more than Right....

[B]ut it is certain, that as War cannot in any Sense be justified, but upon Wrongs received, and Right, upon Complaint, refused; So the Generality of Wars have their Rise from some such Pretension. This is better seen and understood at Home; for that which prevents a Civil War in a Nation, is that which may prevent it Abroad, viz: *Justice*; and we see where that is notably obstructed, War is kindled between the *Magistrates* and *People* ... which, however it may be unlawful on the side of the *People*, we see never fails to follow, and ought to give the same Caution to Princes, as if it were the Right of the People to do it: Tho' I must needs say, *the Remedy is almost ever worse than the Disease*: The Aggressors seldom getting what they seek, or performing, if they prevail, what they promised: And the *Blood and Poverty* that usually attend the Enterprise, weigh more ... than what they lost or suffered.... Which *Disappointment* seems to be the Voice of Heaven, and Judgment of God against those violent Attempts. But to return, I say, *Justice is the Means of Peace*.... It prevents *Strife*, and at last ends it.... Thus *Peace* is maintained by *Justice*, which is a Fruit of *Government*, as *Government* is from *Society*, and *Society* from *Consent.*

Sect. III. *Government, Its Rise and End under all Models.*

... Government then is the *Prevention* or *Cure* of *Disorder* and the Means of *Justice*, as that is of *Peace*.... [Here Penn suggests that just as domestic laws permit the peaceful resolution of conflicts domestically, a pan-European system of laws could accomplish the same regionally.]

Sect. V. *Of the Causes of Difference, and Motives to Violate Peace.*

There appears to me but Three Things upon which Peace is broken, Viz: To *Keep*, to *Recover*, or to *Add. First*, to Keep what is Ones Right, from the Invasion of an Enemy; in which I am purely *Defensive. Secondly*, To Recover, when I think myself Strong enough, that which by Violence, I, or my Ancestors have lost by the Arms of a Stronger Power; in which I am Offensive; Or, *Lastly*, To increase my Dominion by the Acquisition of my Neighbor's Countries, as I find them Weak, and myself Strong. To gratify which Passion, there will never want some Accident or other for a Pretense: And Knowing my own Strength, I will be my own *Judge*.... [Here Penn lays out the details of his plan, addressing possible objections. Regarding the benefits, he begins as follows:]

Let it not, I pray, be the least, that it prevents the Spilling of so much *Humane and Christian Blood*: For a Thing so Offensive to God, and terrible and afflicting to Men ... must recommend our Expedient beyond all Objections.... And tho' the chiefest in Government are seldom personally exposed, yet it is a Duty incumbent upon them to be tender of the Lives of their People; since without all Doubt, they are accountable to God for the Blood that is spilt in their Service....

There is another *manifest Benefit* which redounds to *Christendom*, by this *Peaceable* Expedient, *The Reputation of Christianity will in some Degree be recovered in the Sight of Infidels*; which, by the many Bloody and unjust *Wars of Christians*, not only with them, but *one* with *another*, hath been greatly impaired. For, to the Scandal of that Holy Profession, *Christians*, that glory in their *Saviour's Name*, have long devoted the Credit and Dignity of it to their worldly Passions, as often as they have been excited by the Impulses of Ambition or Revenge. They have not always been in the Right: Nor has Right been the Reason of *War*: And not only *Christians* against *Christians*, but the same Sort of Christians have embrewed *their Hands in one another's Blood....* Yet their Savior has told them, *that he came to save, and not to destroy the Lives of Men*: To give and plant *Peace* among Men: And if in any Sense he may be said to send *War*, it is the *Holy War* indeed; for it is to send against the *Devil*, and not the *Persons of Men....*

[Penn's third, fourth, and fifth benefits are economic: peace is cheaper than war, allows money to be better invested for the common good, prevents the destruction of property, and makes travel and commerce easier.]

Another Advantage is, *The Great Security it will be to* Christians *against the Inroads of the* Turk, *in their most Prosperous Fortune....* [T]he *Grand Seignior* will find himself obliged to concur, for the Security of what he holds in *Europe*: Where, with all his Strength, he would feel it an Over-Match for him. *The Prayers, Tears, Treason, Blood and Devastation, that War has cost in* Christendom, *for these Two last Ages especially, must add to the Credit of our Proposal....*

The violence of the twentieth century – particularly the shock of the two world wars – inspired Protestant theologians to reevaluate their thinking about the ethics of war. While some continued to uphold a moderate just war position, others moved to the opposite extremes, expressing either increased tolerance for war, seen as a political necessity, or calling for increased international cooperation and peace.

Reinhold Neibuhr (1892–1971)

Reinhold Niebuhr was an American-born theologian who played an important role in shaping American public discourse. Following his graduation from Yale, he was ordained in 1915 by the Evangelical Synod of North America, which has a mixed Lutheran and Reformed heritage. Most famous for his Christian realism, here he argues against the pacifist stance taken by his brother, H. Richard Niebuhr (another prominent theologian), on the eve of World War II.

From: Reinhold Neibuhr, "Must We Do Nothing?" (30 March 1932)[107]

Dealing with a Sinful Nation

[My brother] could not have done better than to choose the Sino-Japanese conflict … in order to prove the difficulty, if not the futility, of dealing redemptively with a sinful nation or individual if we cannot exorcise the same sin from our own hearts. …

It is literally true that every recalcitrant nation, like every anti-social individual, is created by the society which condemns it, and that redemptive efforts which betray strong ulterior motives are always bound to be less than fully redemptive.

Inaction That Is Action

My brother draws the conclusion … that it is better not to act at all than to act from motives which are less than pure, and with the use of methods which are less than ethical (coercion). He believes in taking literally the words of Jesus. … He believes … that this kind of inaction would not really be inaction; it would be, rather, the action of repentance. …

This is an important emphasis particularly for modern Christianity with its lack of appreciation of the tragic character of life and with its easy assumption that the world will be saved by a little more adequate educational technique. … [I]t is the business of true religion to destroy man's moral conceit, a task which modern religion has not been performing. … A truly religious man ought to distinguish himself from the moral man by recognizing the fact that he is not moral, that he remains a sinner to the end. …

Shall We Never Act?

All this does not prove, however, that we ought to apply the words of Jesus, "Let him who is without sin cast the first stone," literally. If we do we will never be able to act. There will never be a wholly disinterested nation. Pure disinterestedness is an ideal which even individuals cannot fully achieve, and human groups are bound always to express themselves in lower ethical terms than individuals. … [N]o nation can ever be good enough to save another nation purely by the power of love. The relation of nations and of economic groups can never be brought into terms of pure love. Justice is probably the highest ideal toward which human groups can aspire. And justice … inevitably involves the assertion of right against right and interest against interest until some kind of harmony is achieved. If a measure of humility and of love does not enter this conflict of interest it will of course degenerate into violence. … But the ethical and spiritual note of love and repentance can do no more than qualify the social struggle in history. It will never abolish it.

An Illusory Hope

The hope of attaining an ethical goal for society by purely ethical means . . . without coercion . . . is an illusion. . . . My brother does not make the mistake of assuming that this is possible in social terms. . . . He understands the stubborn inertia which the ethical ideal meets in history. At this point his realistic interpretation of the facts of history comes in full conflict with his insistence . . . upon a religiously inspired moral perfectionism, and he resolves the conflict by . . . resorting to eschatology. The Christian will try to achieve humility and disinterestedness not because enough Christians will be able to do so to change the course of history, but because this kind of spiritual attitude is a prayer to God for the coming of his kingdom. . . .

What makes my brother's particular kind of eschatology impossible for me is that he identifies everything that is occurring in history (the drift toward disaster, another world war and possibly a world revolution) with the counsels of God, and then suddenly, by a leap of faith, comes to the conclusion that the same God, who uses brutalities and forces, . . . will finally establish an ideal society in which pure love will reign.

A Society of Pure Love Is Impossible

I have more than one difficulty with such a faith. I do not see how a revolution in which the disinherited express their anger and resentment, and assert their interests, can be an instrument of God and yet at the same time an instrument which religious scruples forbid a man to use. I should think it would be better to come to ethical terms with the forces of nature in history, and try to use ethically directed coercion in order that violence may be avoided. . . .

I find it impossible to envisage a society of pure love as long as long as man remains man. His natural limitations of reason and imagination will prevent him . . . from fully envisioning the needs of his fellowmen or from determining his actions upon the basis of their interests. . . . It is possible to envisage a more ethical society than we now have. It is possible to believe that such a society will be achieved partly by evolutionary process and partly by catastrophe in which an old order . . . is finally destroyed.

It is plausible also to interpret both the evolutionary and the catastrophic elements in history in religious terms and to see the counsels of God in them. But it is hardly plausible to expect divine intervention to introduce something into history which is irrelevant to anything we find in history now. We may envisage a society in which human cooperation is possible with a minimum amount of coercion, but we cannot imagine one in which there is no coercion at all – unless, of course, human beings become something quite different from what they now are. We may hope for a society in which self-interest is qualified by rigorous self-analysis and a stronger social impulse, but we cannot imagine a society totally without the assertion of self-interest and therefore without the conflict of opposing interests.

The Cost of Human Progress

I realize quite well that my brother's position both in its ethical perfectionism and in its apocalyptic note is closer to the gospel than mine. . . . I am unable to construct an adequate social ethic out of a pure love ethic. I cannot abandon the pure love ideal because anything which falls short of it is less than the ideal. But I cannot use it fully if I want to assume a responsible attitude toward the problems of society. . . . [A]s long as the world of man remains a place where nature and God, the real and the ideal, meet, human progress will depend upon the judicious use of the forces of nature in the service of the ideal. . . .

Life as Tragedy

To say all this is really to confess that the history of mankind is a perennial tragedy; for the highest ideals which the individual may project are ideals which he can never realize in social and collective terms. . . . The goal which a sensitive individual sets for society must therefore always be something which is a little outside and beyond history. Love may qualify the social struggle of history but it will never abolish it, and those who make the attempt to bring society under the dominion of perfect love will die on the cross. And those who behold the cross are quite right in seeing it as a revelation of the divine, of what man ought to be and cannot be, at least not so long as he is enmeshed in the processes of history.

Dietrich Bonhoeffer (1906–1945)

Dietrich Bonhoeffer, a doctor of theology, was ordained a Lutheran pastor, but Hitler's attempt to subvert the Lutheran church for nationalist purposes led him to participate in the emergence of the Confessing Church in 1933. Originally a pacifist, the growing horror of Hitler's Germany led him to tolerate violence under specific circumstances, and he sought himself to contribute to the fight against Hitler. In 1943, he became acquainted with plots to kill Hitler, and he was soon after, albeit on other grounds, arrested. Later charged with conspiracy for involvement with the planners of the 1944 assassination attempt against Hitler, he was ultimately executed in April 1945. In this selection from his *Ethics*, written before his arrest in 1943, he argues that an unconditional necessity – for example, to prevent other deaths – can make it not only legitimate, but also a duty, to kill another human being.

From: Dietrich Bonhoeffer, *Ethics* (1940–1943)[108]

Jesus Christ has made of the west a historical unit. . . . Even the wars of the west have the unity of the west as their purpose. They are not wars of extermination and destruction like the wars of pre-Christian times and those which are even today still possible in Asia. So long as they are to be western wars they cannot, therefore, ever be total wars. Total war makes use of all conceivable means which may possibly serve the purpose of national self-preservation. . . . Western wars have always distinguished between means of warfare which are permissible and rightful and those which are prohibited and criminal. It was belief in a just, divine government of the world which made it possible to dispense with the perhaps effective but certainly un-Christian practices of killing the innocent – torture, extortion, and the rest. War now always remained a kind of appeal to the arbitration of God, which both sides were willing to accept. It is only when Christian faith is lost that man must himself make use of all means, even criminal ones, in order to secure by force the victory of his cause. And thus, in the place of a chivalrous war between Christian peoples, directed toward the achievement of unity in accordance with God's judgment in history, there comes total war, war of destruction, in which everything, even crime, is justified if it serves to further our own cause, and in which the enemy, whether he be armed or defenseless, is treated as a criminal.... [Bonhoeffer then traces the political and social effects of the Protestant Reformation, arguing that the introduction of the idea of individual liberty laid the foundation for the French revolution, which further idealized and yet atomized the individual.]

The French Revolution created a new unity of mind in the west. This unity lies in the emancipation of man as reason, as the mass, as the nation. In the struggle for freedom these three are in agreement, but once their freedom is achieved they become deadly foes. Thus the new unity already bears within itself the seeds of decay. Furthermore, there becomes apparent in this an underlying law of history, namely that the demand for absolute liberty brings men to the depths of slavery....

By the loss of the unity which it possessed through the form of Jesus Christ, the western world is brought to the brink of the void.... Everything established is threatened with annihilation.... It is a decisive struggle of the last days.... It is, once again, a specifically western void, a rebellious and outrageous void, and one which is the enemy of both God and man....

In the political sphere the unscrupulous exploitation of the moment now goes by the false name of Machiavellism. The all-or-nothing gamble is called heroism.... Whatever is neither Machiavellian nor heroic can now be explained only as "hypocrisy," because there is no longer any understanding for the slow, laborious conflict between knowledge of the right and the necessities of the hour, the conflict which was the genuine political life of the west, with all its voluntary concessions and its authentically free responsibility.... Since there is no confidence in justice, whatever is useful is declared to be just.

In light of all the sins committed by the West, with the tacit permission of the churches, modern Christianity must confess its wrongdoing. From these confessions, we can derive an understanding of what obligations the Church has vis-à-vis the political world.

The Church confesses that she has taken in vain the name of Jesus Christ, for ... she has not striven forcefully enough against the misuse of this name for an evil purpose. She has stood by while violence and wrong were being committed under cover of this name....

The Church confesses that she has witnessed the lawless application of brutal force, the physical and spiritual suffering of countless innocent people, oppression, hatred and murder, and that she has not raised her voice on behalf of the victims and has not found ways to hasten to their aid. She is guilty of the deaths of the weakest and most defenseless brothers of Jesus Christ. . . .

The Church experiences in faith the forgiveness of all her sins and a new beginning through grace. For the nations there is only a healing of the wound, a cicatrization of guilt, in the return to order, to justice, to peace, and to the granting of free passage to the Church's proclamation of Jesus Christ. Thus the nations bear the inheritance of their guilt. Yet, through God's merciful governance in history, it may happen that what began as a curse may end as a blessing for them; out of power which has been wrongfully seized there may come justice and right; out of turmoil and insurrection there may come order; and out of bloodshed there may come peace. . . . This does not, of course, mean that the guilt is justified, or that it is removed or forgiven. The guilt continues, but the wound which it has inflicted is healed. . . . If he who wears the crown has gained it by wrongful means, but in the course of time has established justice, order, and peace, he cannot simply be compelled to renounce it. Nor can the conqueror who has led his subject lands into peace, prosperity and happiness simply be forced to give them up. For through the abdication of the crown or the abandonment of the conquered lands there might now arise still more disorder and still more guilt. In the life of the Church and of the faithful all continuity with past guilt is broken through atonement and forgiveness, but in the historical life of the nations it is maintained. The only question here is whether the wounds of this past guilt are in fact healed. . . . What happens here is the waiving of the demand that the guilty man shall fully expiate the wrong he has committed. It is recognized that what is past cannot be restored by any human might. . . . Not all the wounds inflicted can be healed, but what matters is that there shall be no further wounds. The law of retribution, "an eye for an eye and a tooth for a tooth" (Ex. 21.24), is the prerogative of God, the Judge of the nations. In the hands of men this law could only give rise to new disaster. This forgiveness within history can come only when the wound of guilt is healed, when violence has become justice, lawlessness has become order, and war has become peace. If this is not achieved, if wrong still rules unhindered and still inflicts new wounds, then, of course, there can be no question of this kind of forgiveness and man's first concern must be to resist injustice and to call the offenders to account for their guilt. . . .

The first right of natural life consists in the safeguarding of the life of the body against arbitrary killing. One must speak of arbitrary killing wherever innocent life is deliberately destroyed. But in this context any life is innocent which does not engage in a conscious attack upon the life of another and which cannot be convicted of any criminal deed that is worthy of death. This means that the killing of the enemy in war is not arbitrary killing. For even if he is not personally guilty, he is nevertheless consciously participating in the attack of his people against the life of my people and he must share in bearing the consequences of the collective guilt. And, of course, there is nothing arbitrary about the killing of a criminal who has done injury to the life of another; nor yet about the killing of civilians in war, so long as it is not directly intended but is only an unfortunate consequence of a measure which is necessary on military grounds. But it would be arbitrary to kill defenseless prisoners or wounded men who can no longer render themselves guilty of an attack on my life. It is arbitrary to kill an innocent man out of passion or for the sake of some advantage. All deliberate killing of innocent life is arbitrary. . . .

The destruction of the life of another may be undertaken only on the basis of an unconditional necessity; when this necessity is present, then the killing must be performed, no matter how numerous or how good the reasons which weigh against it. But the taking of the life of another must never be merely one possibility among other possibilities, even though it may be an extremely well-founded possibility. If there is even the slightest responsible possibility of allowing others to remain alive, then the destruction of their lives would be arbitrary killing, murder.

David O. MacKay (1873–1970)

David O. MacKay served as the ninth President of the Church of Latter-Day Saints. On the eve of Easter, celebrating Christ's triumph over death, McKay asks how Mormons can participate in the killing and violence associated with the "terrible conflict now raging."

From: David O. MacKay, "The Church and the Present War" (5 April 1942)[109]

War is basically selfish. Its roots feed in the soil of envy, hatred, desire for domination. . . . They who cultivate and propagate it spread death and destruction, and are enemies of the human race.

War originates in the hearts of men who seek to despoil, to conquer, or to destroy other individuals or groups of individuals. Self exaltation is a motivating factor; force, the means of attainment. War is rebellious action against moral order. . . .

War impels you to hate your enemies. The Prince of Peace says, Love your enemies. . . . War says, Injure and kill them that hate you. The Risen Lord says, Do good to them that hate you (Matt. 5:44). . . .

Thus we see that war is incompatible with Christ's teachings. The gospel of Jesus Christ is the gospel of peace. War is its antithesis, and produces hate. It is vain to attempt to reconcile war with true Christianity.

In the face of all this, I shall seem inconsistent when I declare that I uphold our country in the gigantic task it has assumed in the present world conflict, and sustain the Church in its loyal support of the government in its fight against dictatorship. . . .

Notwithstanding all this, I still say that there are conditions when entrance into war is justifiable, and when a Christian nation may, without violation of principles, take up arms against an opposing force.

Such a condition, however, is not a real or fancied insult given by one nation to another. . . .

Neither is there justifiable cause found in a desire or even a need for territorial expansion. . . .

Nor is war justified in an attempt to enforce a new order of government, or even to impel others to a particular form of worship, however better the government or eternally true the principles of the enforced religion may be.

There are, however, two conditions which may justify a truly Christian man to enter – mind you, I say *enter, not begin* – a war: (1) An attempt to dominate and to deprive another of his free agency, and, (2) Loyalty to his country. Possibly there is a third, viz., Defense of a weak nation that is being unjustly crushed by a strong, ruthless one. . . .

Paramount among these reasons . . . is the defense of man's freedom. An attempt to rob man of his free agency caused dissension even in heaven. . . . To deprive an intelligent human being of his free agency is to commit the crime of the ages. . . .

So fundamental in man's eternal progress is his inherent right to choose, that the Lord would defend it even at the price of war. Without freedom of thought, freedom of choice, freedom of action within lawful bounds, man cannot progress. The Lord recognized this, and also the fact that it would take man thousands of years to make the earth habitable for self-governing individuals. Throughout the ages advanced souls have yearned for a society in which liberty and justice prevail. Men have sought for it, fought for it, have died for it. . . .

A second obligation that impels us to become participants in this world war is loyalty to government.

We believe that governments were instituted of God for the benefit of man; and that He holds men accountable for their acts in relation to them, both in making laws and administering them, for the good and safety of society.

We believe that no government can exist in peace, except such laws are framed and held inviolate as will secure to each individual the free exercise of conscience, the right and control of property, and the protection of life.

The greatest responsibility of the state is to guard the lives, and to protect the property and rights of its citizens; and if the state is obligated to protect its citizens from lawlessness within its boundaries, it is equally obligated to protect them from lawless encroachments from without – whether the attacking criminals be individuals or nations. . . .

We believe that all men are justified in defending themselves, their friends, and property, and the government from the unlawful assaults and encroachments of all persons in times of exigency, where immediate appeal cannot be made to laws, and relief afforded.

Even though we sense the hellish origin of war, even though we feel confident that war will never end war, yet under existing conditions we find ourselves as a body committed to combat this evil thing. With other loyal citizens we serve our country as bearers of arms, rather than to stand aloof to enjoy a freedom for which others have fought and died. . . .

God bless them and others now registered awaiting the call to duty, and those serving in defense! . . . To all we say . . . [k]eep yourselves morally clean. Being soldiers or sailors is not justification for indulgence in vulgarity, intemperance, or immorality. Others may be impelled to do these things because of the beastliness of war, but you who hold the Priesthood cannot so indulge with impunity. For your own sweet lives, and for others who trust you, keep yourselves unpolluted. . . .

As seeds of future wars are often sown around the peace table, may the spirit of the gospel of Jesus Christ and not the spirit of retaliation and revenge actuate those who meet to determine peace terms. When that blessed occasion comes, may the representatives of the nations recognize the inalienable rights of peoples everywhere to govern themselves.

Paul Tillich (1886–1965)

Paul Tillich was a German Lutheran minister. After being dismissed from his university position in 1933 for his opposition to Hitler, Tillich was invited to Union Theological Seminary by Reinhold Niebuhr. In the following extract, Tillich argues against pacifism, asserting that force is necessary for the development of creative justice. Such justice is not based on a calculation of one's due (as in proportional justice), but rather arises out of love. It seeks to forgive and to reunite, to transform and to reconcile. Just wars are those fought to restore justice, to defend a political community, or even, in some cases, to create a new one. Yet just as the Church must avoid naïve pacifism, Tillich warns that it must also avoid support for militarism and empire, which are contrary to justice.

From: Paul Tillich, *Systematic Theology*, Vol. 3: "History and the Kingdom of God (1963)[110]

2. The Kingdom of God and the Ambiguities of Historical Self-Integration

. . . What is the relation of the Kingdom of God to the ambiguities of power? The answer to this question is also the answer to the question of the relation of the churches to power.

The basic theological answer must be that, since God as *the* power of being is the source of all particular powers of being, power is divine in its essential nature. The symbols of power for God or the Christ or the church in biblical literature are abundant. . . . The depreciation of power in most pacifist pronouncements is unbiblical as well as unrealistic. Power is the eternal possibility of resisting non-being. God and the Kingdom of God "exercise" this power eternally. But in the divine life – of which the divine kingdom is the creative self-manifestation – the ambiguities of power, empire, and control are conquered by unambiguous life.

Within historical existence this means that every victory of the Kingdom of God in history is a victory over the disintegrating consequences of the ambiguity of power.... In so far as democratization of political attitudes and institutions serves to resist the destructive implications of power, it is a manifestation of the Kingdom of God in history. But it would be completely wrong to identify democratic institutions with the Kingdom of God in history. This confusion, in the minds of many people, has elevated the idea of democracy to the place of a direct religious symbol and has simply substituted it for the symbol "Kingdom of God.".... [The churches'] judgment against power politics should not be a rejection of power but an affirmation of power and even of its compulsory element in cases where justice is violated ("justice" is used here in the sense of protection of the individual as a potential personality in a community). Therefore, although the fight against "objectivation" of the personal subject is a permanent task of the churches, to be carried out by prophetic witness and priestly initiation, it is not their function to control the political powers and force upon them particular solutions in the name of the Kingdom of God. The way in which the Kingdom of God works in history is not identical with the way the churches want to direct the course of history....

For the Christian churches this means that they must try to find a way between a pacifism which overlooks or denies the necessity of power (including compulsion) in the relation of history-bearing groups and a militarism which believes in the possibility of achieving the unity of mankind through the conquest of the world by a particular historical group. The ambiguity of empire building is fragmentarily conquered when higher political unities are created which, although they are not without the compulsory element of power, are nonetheless brought about in such a way that community between the united groups can develop and none of them is transformed into a mere object of centered control. This basic solution of the problem of power in expansion toward larger unities should determine the attitude of the churches to empire building and war. War is the name for the compulsory element in the creation of higher imperial unities. A "just" war is either a war in which arbitrary resistance against a higher unity has to be broken (for example, the American Civil War) or a war in which the attempt to create or maintain a higher unity by mere suppression is resisted (for example, the American Revolutionary War). There is no way of saying with more daring faith whether a war was or is a just war in this sense. This incertitude, however, does not justify the cynical type of realism which surrenders all criteria and judgments, nor does it justify utopian idealism which believes in the possibility of removing the compulsory element of power from history. But the churches as representatives of the Kingdom of God can and must condemn a war which has only the appearance of a war but is in reality universal suicide. One never can start an atomic war with the claim that it is a just war, because it cannot serve the unity which belongs to the Kingdom of God. But one must be ready to answer in kind, even with atomic weapons, if the other side uses them first. The threat itself could be a deterrent.

All this implies that the pacifist way is not the way of the Kingdom of God in history. But certainly it is the way of the churches as representatives of the

Spiritual Community. They would lose their representative character if they used military or economic weapons as tools for spreading the message of the Christ. The church's valuation of pacifist movements, groups, and individuals follows from this situation. The churches must reject political pacifism but support groups and individuals who try symbolically to represent the "Peace of the Kingdom of God" by refusing to participate in the compulsory element of power struggles and who are willing to bear the unavoidable reactions by the political powers to which they belong and by which they are protected. This refers to such groups as the Quakers and to such individuals as conscientious objectors. They represent within the political group the resignation of power which is essential for the churches but cannot be made by them into a law to be imposed on the body politic.

3. The Kingdom of God and the Ambiguities of Historical Self-Creativity

… A victory of the Kingdom of God creates a unity of tradition and revolution in which the unfairness of social growth and its destructive consequences, "lies and murder," are overcome.

They are not overcome by rejection of revolution or tradition in the name of the transcendent side of the Kingdom of God. The principal antirevolutionary attitude of many Christian groups is fundamentally wrong.… The chaos which follows any kind of revolution can be a creative chaos. If history-bearing groups are unwilling to take this risk and are successful in avoiding any revolution, even an unbloody one, the dynamics of history will leave them behind. And certainly they cannot claim that their historical obsolescence is a victory of the Kingdom of God. But neither can this be said of the attempt of revolutionary groups to destroy the given structures of the cultural and political life by revolutions which are intended to force the fulfillment of the Kingdom of God and its justice "on earth." It was against such ideas of a Christian revolution to end all revolutions that Paul wrote his words in Romans, chapter 13, about the duty of obedience to the authorities in power. One of the many politico-theological abuses of biblical statements is the understanding of Paul's words as justifying the anti-revolutionary bias of some churches, particularly the Lutheran. But neither these words nor any other New Testament statement deals with the methods of gaining political power. In Romans, Paul is addressing eschatological enthusiasts, not a revolutionary political movement.

The Kingdom of God is victorious over the ambiguities of historical growth only where it can be discerned that revolution is being built into tradition in such a way that, in spite of the tensions in every concrete situation and in relation to every particular problem, a creative solution in the direction of the ultimate aim of history is found.

In the United States, Tillich became a publicly influential theologian. While some theologians were pushed toward pacifism by their belief that nuclear weapons made limited war impossible, Tillich argued that the just war tradition can be upheld even within a nuclear world, while cautioning that most strategic uses of nuclear weapons are unconscionable and that first use of such weapons is always wrong.

From: Paul Tillich, "Seven Theses Concerning the Nuclear Dilemma," Chapter 18 (1961)[111]

1. Ethical problems underlie all political considerations. They become predominant when the political situation puts alternatives before the statesmen that cannot be escaped by compromise. They must anticipate them, even while negotiations aiming at compromises still are going on.

2. The ethical problem is not, as in discussions with older forms of pacifism, the rightness or wrongness of power-groups using force. The negation of this right, I am glad to say, did not come up in the present conversations.... It is, as I call it, creative justice – a justice whose final aim is the preservation or restitution of a community of social groups, subnational, or supranational.

3. The means for reaching this aim must be adequate to the aim: negotiation, diplomacy, war (if necessary), a peace that not only does not destroy but makes a new community possible. War occurs when a social group feels attacked and decides to defend its power to exist and the ultimate principles for which it stands (e.g., democratic freedom in this country).

4. The decision to enter a war is justified only if it is done in the service of creative justice. Each such decision, however, is not only political and military but also a moral risk.

5. In the light of the aim of intergroup justice, a war fought with atomic weapons cannot be justified ethically. For it produces destruction without the possibility of a creative new beginning. It annihilates what it is supposed to defend.

6. In the present situation this ethical principle leads to the following political-military preferences:

a. Defense – political and military – not only of its power to exist but also of its ultimate principles for itself and those who adhere to the same principles and who are likewise threatened, is a clear, ethical demand.

b. If such defense is in particular situations impossible with conventional weapons (as it would be in the case of Berlin and perhaps parts of Western Europe), even then this does not justify the use of atomic weapons; for they would not be the means of defense but of mere destruction of both sides.

c. Nevertheless, atomic armament is justified because it shows the potential enemy that radical destruction would take place on his side as much as on the other side if he attacks first with atomic weapons.

d. For the American strategy this means that no atomic weapon can be used before the enemy uses one, and even then not for "retaliation" but in order to induce him not to continue their use. (Practically, the very existence of atomic weapons on both sides is probably a sufficient deterrent.)

e. If this includes – as it very probably does – a temporary military retreat in Europe on our side (by no means a total surrender), this is a most ordinary phenomenon in most wars and can be redressed by the arrival of total Allied military power.

7. This suggestion makes, on the basis of ethical principles, a sharp distinction between the atomic weapons of total destruction (including the tactical atomic weapons) and

the so-called conventional weapons, that can be directed against the enemy army and its bases. Of course, the atomic weapons remain in the background, but our awareness of the social-ethical imperative must prevent us from ever using them first again.

David Jeremiah (b. 1941)

David Jeremiah is the independent evangelical pastor heading Shadow Mountain Community Church, one of the largest megachurches in California. He is also the host of several radio and television programs with a significant following among conservative evangelicals. At the time this article was written, his theology was more fundamentalist than it is now. The strategy of "defense through strength" advocated here was endorsed by many prominent evangelicals during the Cold War.

From: David Jeremiah, "Is War Ever in the Will of God?" (1982)[112]

[Jeremiah begins by describing the massive death toll that would follow a nuclear war.]

Can this be the will of God? How can a God who commands us to "love your enemies" and whose sixth command in the Decalogue is "thou shalt not kill" allow for war in His economy?...

The point is often made by the pacifists that, while the Old Testament is full of war, it is scarcely mentioned in the New Testament.... There is a reason for that, however. In the Old Testament, we have the development of a nation to produce a Savior, while in the New Testament, we have the development of an individual who has accepted that Savior. The one is national, the other is spiritual.... If God were writing a third Testament today, it would be full of wars and slaughters, because the world is now getting ready for the coming of a Judge and King....

Among the signs of the last days given by our Lord are "wars and rumors of wars" (Matthew 24:6; Mark 13:7; Luke 21:9, 21:24). Jesus accepts war as part of the world order and draws from it an impressive illustration of the exacting conditions of Christian discipleship.... He conceives of Himself as having come not to send peace on earth, but a sword (see Matthew 10:34)....

But why does God allow war?... God uses governments as vehicles to convey judgment.... Listen to the words of Paul in Romans 13:2–4:

Whosoever therefore resisteth the power, resisteth the ordinance of God; and they that resist shall receive to themselves judgment. For rulers are not a terror to good works but to the evil.... Do that which is good, and thou shalt have the praise of the same.... But if thou do that which is evil, be afraid, for he beareth not the sword in vain, *for he is a minister of God and avenger to execute wrath upon him that doeth evil.*[113]

... And God often uses wicked nations to judge nations that have known the advantage of His blessing. The Bible says of wicked Pharaoh, "Even for this same purpose have I raised thee up that I might show my power in thee, and that my name might be declared throughout all the earth" (Romans 9:17)....

It is this truth more than any other that ought to strike terror into the heart of every American. We of all nations have been blessed of God, but we have so violated that blessing that we are now ripe for the judgment of God upon us. And God will not hesitate to use the godless Russians as the rod of His anger against us.

What shall we do? Shall we begin to strengthen our defenses? Certainly ... America should have learned by now that baring our population to the Soviet sword has not caused them to do the same. While we cut back they built.... As much as we may be concerned about the buildup of nuclear arms, we must realize that the only hope we have of survival, humanly speaking, is to be as strong or stronger than our enemy....

War! Nobody likes to think about war, but the fact of the matter is that the way *not* to have war is to be so strong that nobody will dare take you on....

Shall we reinstitute the draft? Certainly. America should have learned by now that a volunteer army converts 60 percent of the defense dollar into recruitment costs, attracts less educated personnel, and turns our once disciplined armed forces into a band of mercenaries.

But our real defense as a nation rests in the spiritual convictions, character, and commitment of our citizenry. David discovered that fact and declared: "Some trust in chariots, and some in horses; but we will remember the name of the Lord our God" (Psalm 20:7).... We must return and repent and put our trust again in the God of our salvation. We must restore prayer to our lives, our homes, our churches, and our schools. We must remember from whence we are fallen and do again the first works: we must realize that while building a strong military, our trust must ultimately be in God. The danger of total faith in our military defense apart from God is as great as the danger of a second-rate military....

My position as a Christian American must be to work hard for a strong country capable of defending itself against any military aggression. At the same time I must pray for peace, peace that can be won without compromising the godly principles that made this land great. And all the while I am doing these things, I must keep an eye on the future, realizing that the only real and lasting peace will come when the Prince of Peace returns to set up His kingdom on earth.

Karl Barth (1886–1964)

Karl Barth, a Reformed theologian from Switzerland, reacted vehemently to the German government's effort to nationalize the Church in the 1930s. His protests cost him his position as a professor of theology in Bonn and he returned to Switzerland in 1935, where he volunteered for military service once war broke out. In *Church Dogmatics*, Barth tightly circumscribes the causes for which war may justly be fought but stops short of denying that war may ever be just. He also emphasizes the autonomy of the individual before God (and state), upholding the right to conscientious objection.

From: Karl Barth, *Church Dogmatics*, Vol. 3: *The Doctrine of Creation*, Part IV (1978)[114]

We conclude ... by turning to the problem of war. In older Christian ethics the question of the private duel was usually considered in this connexion.... After the shedding of so much blood, it has now come to be tacitly accepted as so much veritable nonsense, and ... is now obsolete. If only we had made the same progress in respect of war! ...

In this case, too, we shall begin by trying to stab our consciences awake in relation to certain illusions which may have been feasible once but cannot be entertained any longer.

1. There was a time when it was possible not only for monks and ecclesiastics but also for very wide circles of secular society to throw the problem of military action wholly on the so-called military classes. . . .

Those days have gone. To-day everyone is a military person, either directly or indirectly. . . . All nations as such, and all their members, have long since become responsible military subjects. . . . Each individual is himself the fatherland, the people, the state; each individual is himself a belligerent. Hence each individual must act when war is waged, and each has to ask whether the war is just or unjust. . . . It is an illusion to think that there can be an uncommitted spectator.

2. It has always been realized that war is concerned with the acquisition and protection of material interests. . . . In times past, however, it was easier to lose sight of the material aspect in all kinds of notions about the honor, justice, freedom and greatness of the nation as represented in its princely houses and rulers, or about the supreme human values at stake, so that something of the character of a crusade, of a religious or cultural war, could be conferred upon the conflict. . . . Political mysticism, of course, is still to be found; but it is now much more difficult to believe in it sincerely. . . .

3. It has always been realized that the main goal in war is to neutralize the forces of the enemy. But it has not always been seen so clearly ... that this goal demands ... quite nakedly and brutally the killing of as many as possible of the men who make up the opposing forces. In former days, this was concealed by the fact that the individual confronted an individual opponent and could thus think of himself as in an unavoidable position of self-defense in which it was his duty and right to kill. Today it is even better concealed by the fact that as a result of recent technical development the individual to a very large extent cannot even see his individual opponents as such. . . .

Today, however, the increasing scientific objectivity of military killing, the development, appalling effectiveness and dreadful nature of the methods, instruments and machines employed, and the extension of the conflict to the civilian population, have made it quite clear that war does in fact mean no more and no less than killing, with neither glory, dignity nor chivalry, with neither restraint nor consideration in any respect. . . . Much is already gained if only we do at last soberly admit that, whatever may be the purpose or possible justice of a war, it now means that, without disguise or shame, not only individuals or even armies, but whole nations as such, are out to destroy one another by every possible means. It only needed the atom and hydrogen bomb to complete the self-disclosure of war in this regard. . . .

[T]he soldier, i.e., the fighting civilian, stands in direct proximity to the executioner.... [I]t is only in this extreme zone, and in conjunction with other human acts which come dangerously near to murder, that military action can in certain instances be regarded as approved and commanded rather than prohibited....

It may be true that even in war many a man may save many things, and indeed that an inner strength may become for him ... more strong and genuine because a more tested possession. But it is certainly not true that people become better in war. The fact is that war is for most people a trial for which they are no match, and from the consequences of which they can never recover. Since all this is incontestable, can it and should it nevertheless be defended and ventured?

All affirmative answers to the question are wrong from the very outset ... if they do not start with the assumption that the inflexible negative of pacifism has almost infinite arguments in its favor and is almost overpoweringly strong....

There can be no objection to a general reckoning with war and Christian participation in it. Like the Christian recognition of the state, this is inevitable in any honest appraisal of what it means for the community to await its coming Lord amid the realities and laws of this passing eon. The objection is that these realities and laws have come to be rated more highly than ... the coming of the Lord.... The objection is that in a kind of panic at all costs to give the emperor or other ruler his due there has been a complete surrender of the wholesome detachment from this imperial or national undertaking which the early Church had been able [to find] in its own way and for good reasons to maintain. The objection is that there has been found for war a basic and general justification which through the centuries, and unfortunately with fresh vigor at the Reformation, Christianity has applied to the world, the state, the so-called powers that be, itself, and all its members.... The primary and supreme task of Christian ethics in this matter is surely to recover and manifest a distinctive horror of war and aloofness from it.

A first essential is that war should not on any account be recognized as a normal, fixed and in some sense necessary part of what on the Christian view constitutes the just state, or the political order demanded by God.... Especially the state must not be given *carte blanche* to ... [organize] mass slaughter in its dealings with other states.... The Church and theology have first and supremely to make this detached and delaying movement.... [I]f they do not say this first ... then at the striking of the last hour in the darkest of days they will be in no position ... authentically and authoritatively ... to issue a call to arms, to the political *opus alienum*. For they can do this only if they have previously held aloof, calling for peace right up to the very last moment....

What Christian ethics has to emphasize is that neither inwardly nor outwardly does the normal task of the state, which is at issue even in time of war, consist in a process of annihilating rather than maintaining and fostering life.... According to the Christian understanding, it is no part of the normal task of the state to wage war; its normal task is to fashion peace in such a way that life is served and war kept at bay. If there is a mistake in pacifism ... it consists in its abstract negation of war, as if war could be understood and negated in isolation and not in relation to the so-called peace which precedes it....

A peace which is no real peace can make war inevitable. Hence the first, basic and decisive point which Christian ethics must make ... is that the state, the totality of responsible citizens, and each individual in his own conduct should so fashion peace while there is still time that it will not lead to this explosion but make war superfluous and unnecessary ... it requires no great faith, insight nor courage to condemn war radically and absolutely, for no one apart from leaders of the armaments industry and a few high-ranking officers really believes that war is preferable to peace.... What does require Christian faith, insight and courage ... is to tell nations and governments that peace is the real emergency to which all our time, powers and ability must be devoted from the very outset in order that men may live and live properly, so that no refuge need be sought in war, nor need there be expected from it what peace has denied. Pacifists and militarists are usually agreed in the fact that for them the fashioning of peace as the fashioning of the state for democracy, and of democracy for social democracy, is a secondary concern as compared with rearmament or disarmament. It is for this reason that Christian ethics must be opposed to both. Neither rearmament nor disarmament can be a first concern, but the restoration of an order of life which is meaningful and just....

[In light of a pursuit of justice, the church should plead] for fidelity and faith in their mutual dealings as the reasonable presupposition of a true foreign policy, for solid agreements and alliances and their honest observance, for international courts and conventions, and above all, and in all nations, for openness, understanding and patience.... The Church can and should raise its voice against the institution of standing armies in which the officers constitute per se a permanent danger to peace.... [Yet] it exists in this eon. Hence it is not commissioned to proclaim that war is absolutely avoidable. But it is certainly commissioned to oppose the satanic doctrine that war is ... unavoidable and therefore right when it occurs, so that Christians have to participate in it....

Perhaps a state desires to expand politically, geographically, or economically.... Perhaps it thinks it necessary to rectify its internal conditions ... by external adventure.... Perhaps it feels that it is threatened by a shift in the balance of power among other states. Perhaps it thinks it sees in the internal conditions of another state, whether revolutionary or reactionary, a reason for displeasure or anxiety.... All this may well be so. Yet it certainly does not constitute a valid reason for setting one's own great or little war machine in motion, for sending out one's troops to the battlefield to kill and be killed. Such aims may be well worth striving for. But they are too paltry to be worth the terrible price involved in their realization by war. War for such reasons could always have been avoided. War for such reasons is an act of murder.... The Christian Church has to testify unambiguously that wars waged for such reasons are not just, and therefore ought not to be undertaken.

Even the existence or non-existence of a state does not always constitute a valid reason for war. It can sometimes happen that the time of a state in its present form of existence has expired, that its independent life has no more meaning nor basis, and that it is thus better advised to yield and surrender. . . .

Indeed, it is only in answer to this particular question that there is a legitimate reason for war, namely, when a people or state has serious grounds for not being able to assume responsibility for the surrender of its independence, or, to put it even more sharply, when it has to defend within its borders the independence which it has serious grounds for not surrendering. The sixth commandment is too urgent to permit of the justification of war by Christian ethics on any other grounds.

Why do we have to allow the possibility that in the light of the divine commandment this is a justifiable reason for war, so that a war waged for this reason must be described as a just war in spite of all the horrors which it will certainly entail? The obvious answer is that there may well be bound up with the independent life of a nation responsibility for the whole physical, intellectual and spiritual life of the people comprising it, and therefore their relationship to God. It may well be that in and with the independence of a nation there is entrusted to its people something which . . . they are commissioned to attest to others, and which they may not therefore surrender. It may well be that with the independence of the state, and perhaps in the form of the legally constituted society guaranteed by it, they would also have to yield something which must not be betrayed, which is necessarily more important to them than the preservation of life itself, and which is thus more important than the preservation of the lives of those who unfortunately are trying to take it from them. . . . Christian ethics cannot possibly deny that this case may sometimes occur. The divine command itself posits and presents it as a case of extreme urgency. . . .

A distinctively Christian note in the acceptance of this demand is that it is quite unconditional. That is to say, it is independent of the success or failure of the enterprise, and therefore of the strength of one's own forces in comparison with those of the enemy. . . .

We still have to consider . . . the same question with reference to the responsibility and decision of the individual. Thus far we have discussed it in relation to the state, war being an action undertaken by the state as a whole. On the Christian view, however, the state is not a strange, lofty and powerful hypostasis suspended over the individual, dominating him, and thinking, willing and deciding for him. To be sure, individuals are included in its jurisdiction and brought under its authority. Individuals are protected by it and owe allegiance to it. Yet in the very same process it is they who . . . bear responsibility for its condition, and for what is done or not done by it. . . . Hence the state cannot relieve the individual of any responsibility. . . . The state wages war in the person of the individual. In war it is he, the individual man or woman, who must prepare for, further, support and in the last analysis execute the work of killing. It is part of the responsibility that in so doing he must risk his own life. But the decisive point is that he must be active in the destruction of the lives of others. . . .

He personally is asked whether he hears the commandment and sees war in its terrible reality.... [H]e [is] finally asked whether, in the event of a true emergency arising in spite of everything for his nation or state, he is willing and ready ... to accept war and military training, to do so as a Christian ... in spite of all that it entails, shouldering personal responsibility not merely for being killed but for the much more horrible act of killing.... In all these aspects the question of war must be asked and answered as a personal question.... Killing is a very personal act, and being killed a very personal experience. It is thus commensurate with the thing itself that even in the political form which killing assumes in war it should be the theme of supremely personal interrogation....

The pacifist demand for the abolition of conscription ... is shortsighted. For conscription has the salutary effect of bringing home the question of war. War is an affair of the state and therefore of the totality of its subjects.... All citizens share responsibility for it both in peace and war.... To make military service once again something for mercenary or volunteer armies would be to absolve the individual from direct responsibility for war and to leave both war itself and the resultant "moral odium" ... to others.... The abolition of conscription would take the edge off this decision for those not personally affected. It would make it merely political rather than both political and personal. This could not possibly contribute to the serious discussion or solution of the problem of war. Pacifists, therefore, should be the very last to call for the abolition of conscription....

Although the state must claim it from the individual as a compulsory duty, and although its fulfillment is urgently prompted in the first instance by the relation of the individual to the state, it can finally be understood only as a question which is put to him and which no one can answer but himself. The state is not God, nor can it command as He does.... Hence it cannot be denied that in virtue of his relationship to God the individual may sometimes find himself compelled, even with a full sense of his loyalty as a citizen, to contradict and oppose what is thought right and resolved by the government or the majority....

Two formal presuppositions are essential if such refusal of military service by one or more individuals is to be accepted as imperative and therefore legitimate. The first is that the objector must accomplish his act of insubordination in the unity of his individual and personal existence with his existence as a citizen ... it cannot be merely a matter of ... keeping his own hands clean.... He must be convinced ... that by his opposition he stands and acts for the political community as willed and ordained by God, not denying the state but affirming it....

Second, the man who objects to military service must be prepared to accept without murmur or complaint the consequences of the insubordinate form of his national loyalty, the hostility of the government or majority ... and the penalty of his violation of the existing law and constitution.... He must act honestly and consistently as a revolutionary, prepared to pay the price of his action, content to know that he has on his side both God and the better informed state of the future, hoping to bear an effective witness to it today, but ready at least to suffer what ... his insubordination must now entail.

Stanley Hauerwas (b. 1940)

Stanley Hauerwas is an American theological ethicist. Most of his life, he has been affiliated with the United Methodist tradition; recently, he has identified himself as Anglican. He was greatly influenced by the Mennonite theologian John Yoder, and his work encourages Protestants to consider the implications of pacifism.

From: Stanley Hauerwas, "Peacemaking: The Virtue of the Church" (1985)[115]

If your brother sins against you, go and tell him his fault, between you and him alone. If he listens to you, you have gained a brother. But if he does not listen, take one or two others along with you, that every word may be confirmed by the evidence of two or three witnesses. If he refuses to listen to them, tell it to the church; and if he refuses to listen even to the church, let him be to you as a Gentile and a tax collector.... Then Peter came up and said to him, "Lord how often shall my brother sin against me, and I forgive him? As many as seven times?" Jesus said to him, "I do not say to you seven times, but seventy times seven" (Matthew 18:15–22).

This is surely a strange text to begin an article on peacemaking as a virtue. The text does not ... say if you have a grievance you might think about confronting the one you believe has wronged you. The text is much stronger.... It says if you have a grievance ... you are obligated to confront the one you believe has sinned against you. You cannot overlook a fault on the presumption that it is better not to disturb the peace. Rather, you must risk stirring the waters, causing disorder rather than overlook the sin.

But on what possible grounds could Christians, people supposedly of peace, be urged actively to confront one another? It seems out of character for Jesus to urge us to do so.... Yet I want to suggest that we will understand peacemaking as a virtue only when we see that such confrontation is at the heart of what it means to be a peacemaker....

It is interesting to note how seldom peacemaking is treated as a virtue. Courage, temperance, and even humility are usually acknowledged as virtues much more readily than is peacemaking. For many, peacemaking may sound like a "good thing," but they would be hesitant to call it a virtue. Peacemaking is usually seen more as a matter of political strategy than a disposition forming the self. Some people may even be peaceful, but that hardly seems a virtue....

Peacemaking is ... [a] virtue insofar as the church believes that peace (and a very particular kind of peace at that) is an essential characteristic of its nature.

As important as understanding why we rightly consider peacemaking a virtue is how we understand what kind of activity it is. It is in this context that the passage from Matthew is so important.... Normally we tend to think of peacemaking as the resolution of conflict rather than the encouragement of conflict. That such is the case, I suspect, is also one of the reasons that peacemaking, even if it is understood as a virtue, is not really all that appealing. Have you ever known anyone, yourself included, who would rush out to see a movie or play about peace?

We say we want peace, but in fact we know we love conflict and even war. Indeed, I suspect that one of the deepest challenges for those of us who call ourselves pacifists is that on the whole peace just does not seem very interesting to most people.... We want to work for peace, we like the struggle for peace, but the idea that peace might actually be achieved would actually scare us to death. For we associate peace with rest, but we fear that rest without conflict is but another name for death....

We simply have to admit that for most of us peace is boring.... Life needs movement, which most of us believe, rightly or wrongly, entails conflict....

But this text from Matthew puts the issue of peacemaking in quite a different light.... Jesus does not suggest that if you have a grievance against someone in the community it might be a good idea for you to "try to work it out." Rather ... you must go and speak to the one whom you believe has sinned against you. Such a speaking, of course, may well involve nothing less than confrontation.... [I]f reconciliation does not take place then you must "go public," taking witnesses with you. If that still is not sufficient, you must take the matter before the whole church.

Our first reaction to this text is to think that surely this procedure is far too extreme for most of our petty conflicts.... [W]ho wants to appear like someone who is too easily offended? No one likes people who tend to make mountains out of molehills, especially when they claim to be doing so only because of the "principle involved." Even more important, most of us learn that time heals all wounds, and thus we are better off waiting for some conflicts to die through the passage of time.

Yet Jesus seems to have been working with a completely different set of presuppositions about what is necessary to be a community of peace and peacemaking. It seems that peace is not the name of the absence of conflict, but rather, peacemaking is that quality of life and practices engendered by a community that knows it lives as a forgiven people. Such a community cannot afford to "overlook" one another's sins because they have learned that such sins are a threat to being a community of peace.

In response to renewed concerns about nuclear proliferation in the 1980s, several mainline denominations adopted just peace positions, including the United Methodist Church, the Presbyterian Church, and the United Church of Christ (UCC). The latter's General Synod labeled itself a "just peace church" in 1985. In addition to laying out the theological basis for a just peace, the UCC calls for nuclear disarmament and expresses support for international organizations and law. It further urges churches to support those who "out of individual conscience take the responsibility for such nonviolent extraordinary witnesses," such as becoming a conscientious objector, refusing employment in projects related to biochemical and nuclear weapons, and withholding taxes in protest of militaristic policies.

From: "Pronouncement on Affirming the United Church of Christ as a Just Peace Church" (1985)[116]

Since Just War criteria itself now rules out war under modern conditions, it is imperative to move beyond Just War thinking to the Theology of a Just Peace....

A Just Peace is grounded in God's activity in creation. Creation shows the desire of God to sustain the world and not destroy....

Just peace is grounded in covenant relationship. God creates and calls us into covenant, God's gift of friendship....

A Just Peace is grounded in the reconciling activity of Jesus Christ....

A Just Peace is grounded in the presence of the Holy Spirit. God sends the Holy Spirit to continue the struggle to overcome the powers ranged against human bonding. Thus, our hope for a Just Peace does not rest on human efforts alone.... A Just Peace is grounded in the community of reconciliation: the Just Peace Church....

Just Peace is grounded in hope. Shalom is the vision that pulls all creation toward a time when weapons are swept off the earth and all creatures lie down together without fear.... As Christians, we offer this conviction to the world: Peace is possible....

A just peace is a basic gift of God and is the force and vision moving human history.... God's activity in human history ... is understood through the Bible, church history, and the voices of the oppressed and those in the struggle for justice and peace. Nonviolent conflict is a normal and healthy reflection of diversity; working through conflict constructively should lead to growth of both individuals and nations.

Nonviolence is a Christian response to conflict shown to us by Jesus. We have barely begun to explore this little known process of reconciliation. Violence can and must be minimized, even eliminated in most situations.... War can and must be eliminated.

The State should be based upon participatory consent and should be primarily responsible for developing justice and well-being, enforcing law, and minimizing violence in the process.

International structures of friendship, justice, and common security from violence are necessary and possible at this point in history in order to eliminate the institution of war and move toward a Just Peace. Unexpected initiatives of friendship and reconciliation can transform interpersonal and international relationships and are essential to restoring community.

The Beachy Amish are an evangelical, fundamentalist group rooted in the Anabaptist tradition. Nonresistance – namely, not resisting a persecutor and instead responding with good – is one of their distinctive beliefs. They uphold the Dordrecht Confession of Faith and periodically publish statements outlining their positions on various issues. Although the Beachy Amish differ in practice quite markedly from many other conservative Anabaptist and even Amish orders, the following "Statement of Position" is included here as an example of a conservative Anabaptist theology of state and war.

From: Beachy Amish Mennonite Church, "Statement of Position on Peace, War, and Social Issues" (2004)[117]

I. Role of Government

We believe the government is duly ordained and instituted of God.... God has delegated to the government the authority "to execute wrath upon him that doeth evil."...

   We further believe the church and state are separate from each other. The church is responsible in the spiritual and moral realms ... the state ... for the civil and political realms. We view the state as having no Biblical authority to interfere with the church's spiritual responsibility.... The church on the other hand, must not resist, hinder, or obstruct the state's political function (Rom. 12:13).

II. Duty to the State

We believe in submission to every law of the land that does not violate the laws of God.... We invoke the blessings of God upon our national leaders and are thankful that under their administration laws have been made that allow the Christian to exercise a conscience void of offense....

   We believe taxes are a legitimate option of the state and are to be paid without resistance....

   We believe we cannot participate in any type of personal investments that directly support war efforts. We view these investments as being a violation of the Biblical principle of nonresistance.

III. Registration and Conscription

We look with disfavor upon military registration and conscription. Nevertheless, should these become mandatory, we can support alternative service under civilian or church administration.

   If any individual takes the position of non-cooperation to registration and the draft ... the constituency would consider this action valid only if the person manifests a deeply-held conviction based upon solid Biblical evidences.

   We believe conscription of women is a social and spiritual hazard. This would militate against women's Biblical role as "keepers at home" ... and against the God-ordained distinction between men and women....

IV. Military Service

We believe war and armed force are contrary to New Testament principles for Christians. Jesus has forbidden His disciples to engage in any form of revenge or resistance by such means. Christians are commanded to return good for evil....

   [I]t is inconsistent for Christians to participate in military service − whether combatant or non-combatant, whether in defense or offense.

In the event that our country becomes involved in war or violent conflict the Bible instructs us to maintain a spirit of Christian love and goodwill, avoid hatred and hysteria, and be obedient to all government laws and regulations that are not in conflict with Scriptural teachings. We are to turn the other cheek, rather than to retaliate.... If necessary, the Scriptures require us to flee or suffer the spoiling of our goods ... rather than to inflict injury on any person, even on an enemy....

[Sections V and VI explain that most civil defense activities and participation in the political system are inconsistent with service to God.]

VII. World Peace

We believe the Bible teaches that human efforts will never accomplish world peace.... Only the Prince of Peace can make wars to cease and strife to end....

VIII. Civil Rights

We believe that civil rights and equal treatment should be the right of all citizens. In our daily lives, we should continually demonstrate to all persons the untainted principles of peace and love taught and exemplified by Jesus....

We do not view organized marches, sit-ins, mass demonstrations and other coercive methods as Christian strategies for solving civil rights issues. We perceive nonviolent coercion as a form of external force, which frequently has the intent to harm through psychological undermining. Therefore, we disassociate ourselves from all protest demonstrations, peace marches, and other similar activities....

Among other Christian duties, we stress the following as ways for attaining civil rights and equal treatment of all persons:

(1) Love your neighbor – friend or foe – as yourself.

(2) Relieve physical needs with material aid.

(3) Avoid all bitterness and agitation.

(4) Present Christ in word and deed.

In the United States, the National Association of Evangelicals represents 40 denominations, millions of believers, and as much as 25 percent of the American electorate. While the state is still seen as having the right to use force for the sake of justice, the latest statement on civic responsibility focuses on a call for pro-active peace making.

From: National Association of Evangelicals, "For the Health of the Nation: An Evangelical Call to Civic Responsibility" (2004)[118]

We engage in public life because God created our first parents in his image and gave them dominion over the earth (Gen. 1:27–28).... Just governance is part of our calling in creation.

We also engage in public life because Jesus is Lord over every area of life. Through him all things were created (Col. 1:16–17).... To restrict our stewardship to the private sphere would be to deny an important part of his dominion and to functionally abandon it to the Evil One. To restrict our political concerns to matters that touch only on the private and the domestic spheres is to deny the all-encompassing Lordship of Jesus (Rev. 19:16)....

We know that we must wait for God to bring about the fullness of the kingdom at Christ's return. But in this interim, the Lord calls the church to speak prophetically to society and work for the renewal and reform of its structures.... This example will require us to demonstrate God's love for all, by crossing racial, ethnic, economic, and national boundaries. It will also often involve following Jesus' example by suffering and living sacrificially for others.

We Seek Peace and Work to Restrain Violence

Jesus and the prophets looked forward to the time when God's reign would bring about just and peaceful societies in which people would enjoy the fruits of their labor without interference from foreign oppressors or unjust rulers. But from the beginning, Christians have recognized that God did not call them to bring in God's kingdom by force. While all Christians have agreed that governments should protect and restore just and peaceful social orders, we have long differed on when governments may use force and whether we may participate in government-authorized force to defend our homelands, rescue others from attack, or liberate other people from oppression.

The peaceful settling of disputes is a gift of common grace. We urge governments to pursue thoroughly nonviolent paths to peace before resorting to military force. We believe that if governments are going to use military force, they must use it in the service of peace and not merely in their national interest. Military force must be guided by the classical just-war principles, which are designed to restrain violence by establishing the right conditions for and right conduct in fighting a war. In an age of nuclear and biological terrorism, such principles are more important than ever.

We urge followers of Jesus to engage in practical peacemaking locally, nationally, and internationally. As followers of Jesus, we should, in our civic capacity, work to reduce conflict by promoting international understanding and engaging in non-violent conflict resolution.

Richard Land (b. 1946)

Richard Land has served as president of the Southern Baptist Convention's Ethics and Religious Liberty Commission since 1988. He was appointed by President George W. Bush to the U.S. Commission on International Religious Freedom in 2001, and consistently reappointed to that position later by various senators. An ordained Southern Baptist minister, he is currently president of Southern Evangelical Seminary in North Carolina.

From: *The Divided States of America: What Liberals and Conservatives Are Missing in the God-and-Country Shouting Match!* (2007)[119]

Have we always been perfect? Of course not. But on the whole, we have a proven track record of extending to others the freedom and prosperity we have established and continue to enjoy. American influence has been a civilizing influence, a benign influence, a freedom-enhancing influence in the world.

This does not mean we have a license to act unilaterally at our whim. Most of the multilateral alliances defending freedom in the world today were built by the United States. It is no accident that the headquarters of the United Nations is in New York City. . . .

Sadly, sometimes these multilateral strategies don't work. The organizations become paralyzed by competing internal interests. . . . When these multilateral remedies are emasculated, the United States has an obligation to do what it can. That is not arrogant empire building. That is exceptionalism in the service of moral goals for global peace and security.

We are not omnipotent, and our resources are not limitless, but they are great. With those great resources and that great strength comes a particular responsibility to act multilaterally when we can, but unilaterally when we must, to fulfill what we believe is our destiny as a nation: to be the friend and defender of freedom at home and abroad. [Here, Land points to Bosnia and Rwanda as examples of the failure of multilateralism.] . . .

Without a sense of America's special role in the world, we are reduced to multilateral cooperation under global values created by multilateral committees. . . . Is American exceptionalism the "delusion" that we are different? Or is it the conviction that when we can do something to prevent horrible evils, and others won't act, we have an obligation to do so, based on the blessings God has poured out on us and the ability God has given us to do something about such evils?

I believe that if we do not act in such circumstances, we become morally culpable. Now, there are times when terrible things are happening, but the consequences of our intervention would be as horrible or even more horrible than what we're trying to stop: North Korea is a good example. Probably no country in the world is routinely committing more atrocities against its own people. . . . If we were to attempt to intervene militarily either unilaterally or multilaterally . . . [t]he disproportionate death toll among Koreans as well as Americans seeking to intervene would outweigh the intended good. . . .

The same thing would be true of any intervention in China. We know there is systematic abuse of human rights in China, but once again unilateral intervention by the United States must always be a last resort. Short of that, whenever people are having their rights or their lives trodden down, we have an obligation to express our concern, to do what we can to alleviate their suffering, and to help bring about their freedom. . . .

[W]hen we can act to fight great injustices, we have an obligation and a responsibility to do so. Genocide is taking place in Sudan. We could stop what's going
on in the Darfur region, and I believe we should – not necessarily with American
troops, but at minimum with American logistics and American leadership saying,
"We must do this...."

The Religious Left says that the Religious Right is pro-war. But sometimes war is
the least bad alternative – does that make you pro-war? Were those who wanted
to depose Hitler pro-war?

I believe that freedom is a universal longing of the human heart, and that as
a country we have to act on what we believe. Under certain conditions, war is
justified as a least-bad alternative. The first condition is that there is a just cause.
Our cause in Iraq is just; it may be one of the nobler things we have done in recent
history. We went to liberate a country that was in the grip of a terrible dictator
who had perpetrated horrible atrocities and crimes against humanity, against his
own people, and against his neighbors. We removed him, and we are giving the
Iraqis the ability to defend themselves and to build a stable democracy. We have a
responsibility and an obligation based on the blessings that have been showered
upon us to help others when we can.

NOTES

1 The Anglican arm of Protestantism combines aspects of Roman Catholic, Lutheran, and
   Calvinist thought, and theologically should be considered independent. Nonetheless,
   the Anglican and Lutheran approaches to governmental authority are similar, and hence
   they are grouped together here. Denominations derived from Anglicanism include the
   Church of Ireland, the Episcopal Church, the various Methodist denominations, and the
   Assemblies of God.
2 Calvinist denominations include Presbyterians, Congregationalists, and many Baptists.
3 Anabaptist denominations include Mennonites, Hutterites, Amish, and Brethren.
4 Lisa Sowle Cahill, *Love Your Enemies: Discipleship, Pacifism, and Just War Theory* (Minneapolis,
   Minn.: Augsburg Fortress, 1994), p. 104.
5 Martin Luther, "Temporal Authority: To What Extent It Should Be Obeyed," J. J. Schindel
   (trans.), in J. M. Porter (ed.), *Luther: Selected Political Writings* (Philadelphia: Fortress Press,
   1974), pp. 54, 56.
6 Luther, "Dr. Martin Luther's Warning to His Dear German People," Martin H. Bertram
   (trans.), in Porter (ed.), *Luther: Selected Political Writings*, p. 87.
7 Cahill, *Love Your Enemies*, p. 107.
8 Luther, "An Open Letter on the Harsh Book against the Peasants," Charles M. Jacob (trans.),
   in Porter (ed.), *Luther: Selected Political Writings*, p. 97.
9 Luther, "Admonition to Peace: A Reply to the Twelve Articles of the Peasants of Swabia," in
   Porter (ed.), *Luther: Selected Political Writings*, pp. 73, 78, 83.
10 Luther, "Dr. Martin Luther's Warning to His Dear German People," pp. 136, 139.
11 Martin E. Marty, "Can Soldiers Be Saved?," *Christian Century* 120 (2003), p. 47.
12 Luther, "On War against the Turk," Jacobs (trans.), in Porter (ed.), *Luther: Selected Political
    Writings*, pp. 123, 129.
13 Luther, "Whether Soldiers, Too, Can Be Saved," Jacob (trans.), in Porter (ed.), *Luther:
    Selected Political Writings*, p. 117.

14 Luther, "Temporal Authority: To What Extent It Should Be Obeyed," p. 66.

15 Martin Luther, "Lectures on Deuteronomy," in Jaroslav Pelikan (ed.), *Luther's Works*, volume 9 (St. Louis, Mo.: Concordia Publishing), 1960, p. 204. See also Luther, "Temporal Authority: To What Extent It Should Be Obeyed," p. 66.

16 Evangelical Lutheran Church in America, "For Peace in God's World," Social Statement Adopted 20 August 1995, p. 11, available at http://www.elca.org/What-We-Believe/Social-Issues/Social-Statements/Peace.aspx. To be clear, the ELCA is considered a mainline Protestant denomination; the LCMS is considered evangelical.

17 "Christian Citizenship: A Report of the Commission on Theology and Church Relations of the Lutheran Church – Missouri Synod," 26 May 1968, available at www.lcms.org/Document.fdoc?src=lcm&id=366.

18 Michael G. Thompson, "An Exception to Exceptionalism: A Reflection on Reinhold Niebuhr's Vision of 'Prophetic' Christianity and the Problem of Religion and U.S. Foreign Policy," *American Quarterly* 59:3 (2007), 835.

19 John Calvin, *Institutes of the Christian Religion*, vol. 2, Book 4, Chapter 20, Section 16 (4.20.16), John T. McNeill (ed.), vol. 21 (Philadelphia: Westminster Press, 1960), (4.20.4), p. 1496. See also Paul Mundey, "John Calvin and Anabaptists on War," *Brethren Life and Thought* 23 (1978), p. 244.

20 Calvin, *Institutes of the Christian Religion*, vol. 2 (4.20.11), p. 1499.

21 Ibid., vol. 2 (4.20.9), p. 1496.

22 Roland H. Bainton, *Christian Attitudes toward War and Peace: A Historical Survey and Critical Re-Evaluation* (New York: Abdingdon Press, 1960), p. 143.

23 In his commentaries on Joshua, Calvin argues that the Old Testament rules for Holy War are no longer applicable, since "no certain region marks out our precise boundaries; nor are we armed with the sword to slay all the ungodly...." See *Commentary on Joshua*, 23:13, available at www.ccel.org/ccel/calvin/calcom07.xxvi.ii.html. See also Mark J. Larson, "The Holy War Trajectory among the Reformed: From Zurich to England," *Reformation and Renaissance Review* 8 (2006), pp. 7–27.

24 Bullinger claimed that "they be in a wrong dream which think no war ought to be attempted for religion." See "A Treatise or Sermon of Henry Bullynger: Much Fruitfull and Necessarye for This Time Concernynge Magistrates and Obedience of Subjectes," in *Sermonum Decades Qinque*, Walter Lynne (trans.) (London: W. Powell, 1548), available at http://eebo.chadwyck.com. He also argued that the laws of war in 20 Deuteronomy "are still bidden to be kept." See "Sermon IX of the Second Decade," in *The Decades of Henry Bullinger* (Cambridge: Cambridge University Press, 1849), vol. 1, p. 380.

25 Gouge explicitly draws a parallel between Catholics and the ancient Amalakites, whom the Israelites were commanded to annihilate in Deuteronomy 25:17–19: "*Papists* to *Protestants* are as *Amalakites* to *Israelites*. We see therefore that no propinquity of country, kindred, neighborhood, or the like, can restraine their malice." Likewise, he argues that "some that outwardly professe the Christian Faith may be as great enemies to the true Faith, as plaine Infidels." He upholds offensive war as legitimate in the case of "maintenance of Truth and purity of Religion." William Gouge, *Gods Three Arrows* (London: George Miller, 1631), pp. 188, 213, 215.

26 See Joris van Eijnatten, "Religionis Causa: Moral Theology and the Concept of Holy War in the Dutch Republic," *Journal of Religious Ethics* 34:4 (2006), p. 616.

27 Charles E. Bailey, "The British Protestant Theologians in the First World War: Germanophobia Unleashed," *Harvard Theological Review* 77:2 (1984), pp. 211, 214.

28 Although there was broad support among evangelicals for the war, such a stance was far from universal. Some groups, such as the Sojourners or Evangelicals for Social Action, found U.S.

foreign policy immoral and imperialistic. Others rejected the war as part of an Illuminati conspiracy. See Martin Durham, "Evangelical Protestantism and Foreign Policy in the United States after September 11," *Patterns of Prejudice* 38 (2004), pp. 155–156.

29 Pat Robertson, "The Roots of Terrorism and a Strategy for Victory," Address to the Economic Club of Detroit, 25 March 2002.

30 National Association of Evangelicals, "For the Health of the Nation: An Evangelical Call to Civic Responsibility," 2004, available at http://www.nae.net/images/civic_responsibility2. pdf, pp. 1, 11.

31 Calvin, *Institutes of the Christian Religion*, vol. 2 (4.20.16), (4.20.29), pp. 1516, 1518.

32 Derek S. Jeffreys, "'It's a Miracle of God That There Is Any Common Weal among Us': Unfaithfulness and Disorder in John Calvin's Political Thought," *Review of Politics* 62 (2000), p. 114.

33 John Knox, *On Rebellion*, Roger A. Mason (ed.) (Cambridge: Cambridge University Press, 1994), p. xii.

34 Knox, *On Rebellion*, p. xiii.

35 Cahill, *Love Your Enemies*, p. 139.

36 Ibid., p. 140. Conversely, despite the bellicosity of a handful of Puritan preachers, Lowe draws on John Udall and others to argue that more frequently, "newly energized evangelicals found holy causes abhorrent and contrary to the gospel message." See Ben Lowe, "Religious Wars and the 'Common Peace': Anglican Anti-War Sentiment in Elizabethan England," *Albion: A Quarterly Journal Concerned with British Studies* 28 (1996), pp. 415–435.

37 While some ministers did use language reminiscent of holy war, many others relied on just war logics. See Melvin B. Endy, Jr., "Just War, Holy War, and Millenialism in Revolutionary America," *William and Mary Quarterly* 42:1 (January 1985), pp. 3–25.

38 John Calvin, *Brief Instruction for Arming All the Good Faithful against the Errors of the Common Sect of the Anabaptists*, 1544. Cited in Cahill, *Love Your Enemies*, p. 115.

39 Calvin, *Institutes of the Christian Religion* (4.20.32), p. 1520.

40 Article 23:2, "Of the Civil Magistrate," Westminster Confession, in *The Constitution of the Reformed Presbyterian Church of North America* (Pittsburgh, Pa.: Crown and Covenant, 2004), p. A-72. "London Baptist Confession of Faith," in William Joseph McGlothlin, *Baptist Confessions of Faith* (Philadelphia: American Baptist Publication Society, 1911), pp. 262–263.

41 Report of the Committee to Study War and Peace, Synod 2006, p. 26; available at www.crcna. org/site_uploads/uploads/resources/.../2006_warandpeace.pdf.

42 Donald K. McKim, *The Westminster Handbook to Reformed Theology* (Louisville, Ky.: Westminster John Knox Press, 2001), p. 167.

43 Ibid., p. 167.

44 Nelson Jennings, "Japan Presbyterian Church: Official Statement Concerning War," adopted at 1992 General Assembly. English translation authorized November 2002, available at http://church.ne.jp/yurinoki/choro/. See also J. Nelson Jennings, "A Call to Examine the 'Presbyterian Church in Japan's Statement Concerning War,'" *Presbyterion* 29 (2003), pp. 103–105. A similar position was advanced by the Nippon Sei Ko Kai (Japaneses Anglican Episcopal Church) in 2007. "An Open Letter from the Chubu Diocese of the Anglican/Episcopal Church in Japan," International Cooperation Committee, Chubu Diocese, Anglican Episcopal Church in Japan, 15 August 2007, available at http://www.anglicancommunion. org/acns/digest/index.cfm/2007/8/15/An-open-letter-from-the-Chubu-Diocese-of-the-AnglicanEpiscopal-Church-in-Japans.

45 Cited in Howard Schomer, "From 'Just War' to 'Just Peace': CPS and War Resistance among Congregationalists," *Mennonite Quarterly Review* 66 (1992), p. 612.

46 E. Glenn Hinson, "Baptist Attitudes toward War and Peace since 1914," *Baptist History and Heritage* (Winter 2004), p. 112. See also American Baptist Policy Statement on Military and Foreign Policy, 7022:3/89, available at http://www.abc-usa.org/Resources/resol/militpol. htm.

47 Dante L. Germino, "Two Types of Recent Christian Political Thought," *Journal of Politics* 21:3 (August 1959), p. 462.

48 Resolution 25, Lambeth Conference, 1930, available at http://www.lambethconference.org/resolutions/1930/1930–25.cfm. This resolution was also adopted by the Episcopal Church in 1931, and identical language found its way into section IV of the Amsterdam Statement of the World Council of Churches in 1948, as well as the *Book of Resolutions* of the United Methodist Church.

49 For example, the United Methodist Church's *Social Principles* recognize the legitimacy of the just war tradition while calling for increased attention to pacifism (Article 164 V, "The Political Community," available at http://www.umc-gbcs.org/site/c.frLJK2PKLqF/b.3713157/k. DE01/182164_The_Political_Community/apps/nl/newsletter.asp); the Church has also created a "Peace with Justice" program aimed at encouraging a just peace around the world. Stanley Hauerwas, a theologian long associated with the United Methodist Church, has also contributed significantly to the development of the just peace tradition.

50 Anabaptists emerged from the Radical Reform movement of the sixteenth century. Aiming to create Christian communities tied to a literal interpretation of the Sermon on the Mount, they rejected many customary practices that could not be specifically tied to scripture. The name derives from their practice of adult baptism: infants cannot be baptized, and adult converts from other denominations are rebaptized.

51 The Quakers are actually part of the Reformed movement, with roots in Calvinism.

52 J. Daryl Charles, "Between Pacifism and Crusade: Justice and Neighbor Love in the Just-War Tradition," *Logos* 8 (2005), p. 93.

53 Ibid., p. 101.

54 Ronald Lawson, "Onward Christian Soldiers? Seventh Day Adventists and the Issue of Military Service," *Review of Religious Research* 37 (1996).

55 William Penn, *No Cross, No Crown* (Philadelphia: Friends' Book Association, 1882), 1.7.1, pp. 100–101.

56 The Jehovah's Witnesses, however, have remained staunchly pacifistic, claiming that the New Testament explicitly forbids Christians from killing. Furthermore, their worldview emphasizes Christian participation in a heavenly, rather than earthly, kingdom. Witnesses thus refuse to participate in rituals (such as saluting national flags) that they feel unduly honor earthly governments. Consequently, Witnesses have faced persistent persecution in times of war. For example, in World War II, they faced intense discrimination in the United States, were outlawed in Canada, and were imprisoned or killed in Japan and Germany. See Chuck Smith, "War Fever and Religious Fervor: The Firing of Jehovah's Witnesses in West Virginia and Administrative Protection of Religious Liberty," *American Journal of Legal History* 43 (1999), pp. 133–151; Carolyn R. Wah, "Jehovah's Witnesses and the Empire of the Sun: A Clash of Faith and Religion during World War II," *Journal of Church and State* 44 (2002), pp. 45–72; M. James Penton, *Jehovah's Witnesses and the Third Reich: Sectarian Politics under Persecution* (London: University of Toronto Press, 2004). A similar theology motivates the pacifism of the Churches of Christ: Shelley L. Jacobs, "Pacifism in Churches of Christ in Western Canada during World War II and the Influence of Nashville Bible School," *Restoration Quarterly* 48 (2007), pp. 211–232.

57 Ronald Lawson, "Church and State at Home and Abroad: The Evolution of Seventh-Day Adventist Relations with Governments," *Journal of the American Academy of Religion* 64 (1996), pp. 279–311.

58 Lawson, "Church and State at Home and Abroad," p. 292.

59 Roger Robins, "A Chronology of Peace: Attitudes toward War and Peace in the Assemblies of God: 1914–1918," *Pneuma: The Journal of the Society for Pentecostal Studies* (1984), pp. 3–25.

60 Joseph Smith, *The Doctrine and Covenants of the Church of Jesus Christ of Latter-Day Saints* (Salt Lake City, Utah: Church of Jesus Christ of Latter-Day Saints, 1921), 98:6, p. 167.

61 Joseph Smith, *The Pearl of Great Price: Being a Choice Selection from the Revelations, Translations, and Narrations of Joseph Smith* (Salt Lake City, Utah: George Q. Cannon and Sons, 1891), p. 80.

62 Edwin Brown Firmage, "Violence and the Gospel: The Teachings of the Old Testament, the New Testament, and the Book of Mormon," *Brigham Young University Studies* 25:1 (1985), p. 11.

63 Firmage, "Violence and the Gospel," p. 15.

64 Alma 24:18; see also Alma 24:13. The Anti-Nephi-Lehis are a group of Lamanites converted by Aaron, one of the sons of Mosiah, according to the book of Alma. The term "Anti" in their name should not be understood to mean "in opposition to"; it is likely of Egyptian rather than Latin origin and may mean "belonging to." Thus, the name suggests the new converts' desire to join with Nephi and Lehi.

65 Alma 24:17.

66 Alma 24:24–25.

67 Firmage, "Violence and the Gospel," p. 17.

68 Mormon 2:23; Mormon 3:6.

69 Mormon 3:9, 14–16.

70 Daniel K. Judd, *Hard Questions, Prophetic Answers: Doctrinal Perspectives on Difficult Contemporary Issues* (Salt Lake City, Utah: Deseret Book, 2004).

71 Smith, *The Doctrine and Covenants of the Church of Jesus Christ of Latter-Day Saints*, 98:16, p. 167.

72 Quinn, "The Mormon Church," p. 359.

73 Mary Jane Woodger, "Commentary on the Leadership of the Church of Jesus Christ of Latter-Day Saints during the Vietnam War," *Journal of American and Comparative Cultures* 23:1 (2001), p. 54.

74 Hartman Rector, Jr., "Address at Brigham Young University," *The Daily Universe*, 16 November 1970, p. 1. Cited in Woodger, "Commentary on the Leadership," p. 58.

75 Martin Durham, "Evangelical Protestantism and Foreign Policy in the United States after September 11," *Patterns of Prejudice* 38:2 (2004), p. 146.

76 Martha Abele Mac Iver, "Mirror Images? Conceptions of God and Political Duty on the Left and Right of the Evangelical Spectrum," *Sociological Analysis* 51:3 (Autumn 1990), p. 289.

77 David W. Bebbington, *Evangelicalism in Modern Britain: A History from the 1730s to the 1980s* (New York: Routledge, 1989), p. 4.

78 "Profile: Silent Evangelical Support of Bush's Proposed War against Iraq," Morning Edition National Public Radio, 26 February 2003, available at http://www.npr.org/programs/morning/transcripts/2003/feb/030226.hagerty.html.

79 Richard Land, "The Time Has Arrived: Bush Policy on Iraq Meets Just War Criteria," Ethics and Religious Liberty Commission, Southern Baptist Convention, 6 February 2003, available at http://erlc.com/article/the-time-has-arrived/.

80 "On the Liberation of Iraq," Southern Baptist Convention, June 2003, available at http://www.sbc.net/resolutions/amResolution.asp?ID=1126.

81 "National Baptists Call for Withdrawal from Iraq, Intensification of Katrina Rebuilding," Baptist Peace Fellowship of North America, available at http://www.bpfna.org/home?archive_month=02&archive_year=2007&archives=Go&id=38139.

82 "Progressive Baptists Urge End to Iraq War," *Christian Century*, 5 September 2006, p. 14. A similar view was expressed by the Baptist Peace Fellowship of North America, a multiracial nondenominational organization. See "A Baptist Declaration in Opposition to Present U.S. Policies in Iraq," Baptist Peace Fellowship of North America, 2005, available at http://www.bpfna.org/home?search_string=Iraq&search=Go&id=25724.

83 George M. Marsden, *Understanding Fundamentalism and Evangelicalism* (Grand Rapids, Mich.: Wm. D. Eerdmans, 1991), p. 1.

84 Barry Hankins, *Evangelicalism and Fundamentalism: A Documentary Reader* (New York: New York University Press, 2008), p. 6.

85 Walter Russell Mead, "God's Country," *Foreign Affairs* 85:5 (September–October 2006), pp. 27, 29.

86 Ibid., 29. See also John Nurser, "The 'Ecumenical Movement' Churches, 'Global Order,' and Human Rights: 1938–1948," *Human Rights Quarterly* 25:4 (November 2003), pp. 841–881.

87 James Sinclair, "The War," *Free Presbyterian Magazine* 19:5 (September 1914), 167, cited in James Lachlan MacLeod, "'The Mighty Hand of God': The Free Presbyterian Church of Scotland and the Great War," *Bridges* 12:1 (Fall/Winter 2007), p. 22.

88 Neil Southern, "September 11: A Christian Fundamentalist Interpretation," *Political Theology* 9:2 (2008), p. 140.

89 Rev. Alan Cairns, "America's Day of Terror: What Is God Doing?," 16 September 2001, cited in Southern, "September 11," pp. 152, 150.

90 Luther, "Whether Soldiers, Too, Can Be Saved," in Porter (ed.), *Luther: Selected Political Writings*, pp. 102 and 103.

91 Luther, "Whether Soldiers, Too, Can Be Saved," in Theodore G. Tappert (ed.), *Selected Writings of Martin Luther, 1529–1546* (Philadelphia: Fortress Press, 1967), vol. 4, pp. 444, 445, 446.

92 Luther, "Whether Soldiers, Too, Can Be Saved," in Porter (ed.), *Luther: Selected Political Writings*, pp. 108–110, 113.

93 Luther, "Whether Soldiers, Too, Can Be Saved," in Tappert (ed.), *Selected Writings of Martin Luther, 1529–1546*, pp. 458–459, 461, 463, 465–466, 467–468, 469, 470–471, 472–473.

94 John Calvin, *Institutes of the Christian Religion*, John Allen (trans.) (Philadelphia Presbyterian Board of Publication and Sabbath School Work, 1902), vol. 2, pp. 634–635, 642–646, 660–661.

95 Andries Raath and Shaun de Freitas, "Theologico-Political Federalism: The Office of Magistracy and the Legacy of Heinrich Bullinger (1504–1575)," *Wesleyan Theological Journal* 63 (2001), p. 289. Indeed, Bullinger's *Decades*, popular with the Puritan faction, briefly was required reading for English clergy members in 1586. See James Turner Johnson, *The Holy War Idea in Western and Islamic Traditions* (University Park: Pennsylvania State University Press, 1997), p. 57. Johnson argues that the belief that war for religion was justified was commonplace in England during the period, influenced not only by Bullinger, but also by other Puritan and Presbyterian pastors.

96 See van Eijnatten, "Religionis Causa," pp. 609–635.

97 Heinrich Bullinger, "A treatise or sermon of Henry Bullynger: much fruitfull and necessarye for this time, concernynge magistrates and obedience of subiectes: Also concernying the affayres of war and what scriptures make mension thereof, whether christen powers may war against

their enemies. And whither it be laufull for a christyan to beare the office of a magistrate, and of the duety of souldiers with many other holsom instructions for captaynes [and] souldiers both," in *Sermonum decades qinque*, Walter Lynne (trans.) (London: W. Powell, 1549). Text modernized by V. O. Morkevicius.

98 Knox, *On Rebellion*, p. xxi.

99 John Knox, *The History of the Reformation of Religion within the Realm of Scotland*, Charles John Guthrie (ed.) (London: Adam and Charles Black, 1898), pp. 273, 277–279.

100 Menno Simons, "Testimony against John Van Leyden," in *The Complete Works of Menno Simmon*, Part I (Elkhart, Ind.: John F. Funk and Brother, 1871), pp. 434–437, 439–440.

101 From John H. Leith (ed.), *Creeds of the Churches: A Reader in Christian Doctrine, from the Bible to the Present*, 3rd ed. (Lexington, Ky.: Westminster John Knox Press, 1982), pp. 303–305.

102 United Church of England and Ireland, *The Book of Common Prayer* (Oxford: The University Press, 1865), pp. 534–535. Text modernized by V. O. Morkevicius.

103 John Wesley, "The Doctrine of Original Sin, According to Scripture, Reason and Experience: Part First, the Past and Present of Mankind," in *The Works of the Reverend John Wesley, A.M.*, 7 vols. (New York: Hunt & Eaton, 1839), vol. 5., pp. 511–513.

104 In May 1660, the English Civil War was brought to a close by the restoration of King Charles II to the throne.

105 George Fox, *A journal or historical account of the life, travels, sufferings, Christian experiences and labour of love in the work of the ministry of that ancient, eminent and faithful servant of Jesus Christ, George Fox* (Philadelphia: B. and T. Kite, 1808), vol. 1, pp. 523–527.

106 William Penn, *An Essay towards the Present and Future Peace of Europe* (Washington, D.C.: American Peace Society, 1912), pp. 2 – 7, 14, 17.

107 Reinhold Niebuhr, "Must We Do Nothing?," 30 March 1932, *Christian Century*, in Richard B. Miller (ed.), *War in the Twentieth Century: Sources in Theological Ethics* (Lexington, Ky.: Westminster John Knox Press, 1992), pp. 12 – 18.

108 Dietrich Bonhoeffer, *Ethics* (London: SCM Press, 1993), pp. 72–73, 81–82, 85, 87, 92–93, 96–97, 134–135.

109 President David O. McKay, during the Church of the Air Broadcast, 5 April 1942, Report of the 112th Annual Conference of the Church of Jesus Christ of Latter-Day Saints, available at http://scriptures.byu.edu/.

110 Paul Tillich, *Systematic Theology* (Chicago, Ill.: University of Chicago Press, 1963), vol. 3, pp. 385–389.

111 Paul Tillich, "Seven Theses Concerning the Nuclear Dilemma," in J. Mark Thomas (ed.), *The Spiritual Situation in Our Technical Society* (Atlanta, Ga.: Mercer University Press, 2002), pp. 197–198.

112 David Jeremiah, "Is War Ever the Will of God," *Fundamentalist Journal* 1:3 (November 1982), pp. 18–23, at 20–23.

113 Emphasis in original.

114 Karl Barth, *Church Dogmatics: The Doctrine of Creation*, Part IV, in G. W. Bromiley and T. F. Torrance (eds.) (Edinburgh: T & T Clark, 1961), vol. 3, pp. 450–468.

115 Stanley Hauerwas, "Peacemaking: The Virtue of the Church," in John Berkman and Michael Cartwright (eds.), *The Hauerwas Reader* (Durham, N.C.: Duke University Press, 2001), pp. 318–321.

116 United Church of Christ, Pronouncement on Affirming the United Church of Christ as a Just Peace Church, General Synod 15 Pronouncement, 85-GS-50, 1985, available at http://www.ucc.org/justice/peacemaking/pdfs/Just-Peace-Church-Pronouncement.pdf.

117 Beachy Amish Mennonite Church, "Statement of Position on Peace, War, and Social Issues," Peace and Service Committee, 2004, pp. 1–16, at pp. 9–10, 13–14, available at http://www.beachyam.org/Nonresistance.pdf. Emphasis in original.

118 National Association of Evangelicals, "For the Health of the Nation: An Evangelical Call to Civic Responsibility," 2004, pp. 2–3, 11–12, available at http://www.nae.net/images/content/For_The_Health_Of_The_Nation.pdf. Similar statements can be found from the World Evangelical Alliance's Peace and Reconciliation Initiative (WEAPRI), available at http://www.weapri.org/resource/.

119 Richard Land, *The Divided States of America: What Liberals and Conservatives Are Missing in the God-and-Country Shouting Match!* (Nashville, Tenn.: Thomas Nelson, 2007), pp. 201, 202–203, 204, 206.

SELECT BIBLIOGRAPHY

Bainton, Roland H., *Christian Attitudes toward War and Peace: A Historical Survey and Critical Re-Evaluation* (New York: Abingdon Press, 1960).

Barth, Karl, *Church Dogmatics: The Doctrine of Creation,* Part IV, G. W. Bromiley and T. F. Torrance (trans.) (Edinburgh: T & T Clark, 1961), vol. 3.

Berkman, John, and Michael Cartwright, *The Hauerwas Reader* (Durham, N.C.: Duke University Press, 2001).

Cahill, Lisa Sowle, *Love Your Enemies: Discipleship, Pacifism, and Just War Theory,* (Minneapolis, Minn.: Augsburg Fortress, 1994).

Calvin, John, *Institutes of the Christian Religion,* John T. McNeill (ed.) (Philadelphia: Westminster Press, 1960).

Judd, Daniel K., *Hard Questions, Prophetic Answers: Doctrinal Perspectives on Difficult Contemporary Issues* (Salt Lake City, Utah: Deseret Book, 2004).

McKim, Donald K., *The Westminster Handbook to Reformed Theology* (Louisville, Ky.: Westminster John Knox Press, 2001).

Miller, Richard B. (ed.), *War in the Twentieth Century: Sources in Theological Ethics* (Louisville, Ky.: Westminster John Knox Press, 1992).

National Association of Evangelicals, "For the Health of the Nation: An Evangelical Call to Civic Responsibility," 2004; available at http://www.nae.net/images/civic_responsibility2.pdf.

Porter, J. M. (ed.), *Luther: Selected Political Writings* (Philadelphia: Fortress Press, 1974).

Simons, Menno, *The Complete Works of Menno Simmon,* Part I (Elkhart, Ind.: John F. Funk and Brother, 1871).

Tillich, Paul, *Systemic Theology* (Chicago, Ill.: University of Chicago Press, 1963), vol. 3.

5

Sunni Islam

The readings that follow provide examples of Sunni Muslim discourse on matters of armed force. In this connection, a few introductory comments about the term "Sunni" are in order.

To begin: the qualifier "Sunni" distinguishes some Muslims from others, in this case the various Shi'i groups. The position of the latter is outlined elsewhere in this volume; with respect to armed force, the most important differences have to do with leadership, and thus with authority to order Muslim forces to fight. For Shi'i Muslims, such authority is often restricted to the designated Imam of the Age or, in his absence, his appointed representative. For Sunni Muslims, authority belongs to those who are selected though a process of consultation and to whom the Muslim community pledges loyalty. For many centuries, and thus for many of the scholars whose opinions are presented in the first part of this collection, this meant that authority for war rested with the Caliph (khalifa, one who "follows" in the way of the Prophet) or with his representative (usually the sultan, indicating possession of the requisite "power" to conduct war). In the modern period, when such historic political institutions no longer exist or are in question, authority for war constitutes a particularly contentious issue; the selections from contemporary Sunni discourse reflect this.

In addition to the question of authority, several other aspects of the qualifier "Sunni" are worth noting. The term is part of a longer phrase that may be translated as "the people who follow the example of the Prophet and who value the consensus of the Muslim community" (ahl al-sunna wa-l-jamā'a). "Sunni" is thus shorthand, pointing to the value placed on reports (a ḥadīth) of the words and deeds of the Prophet Muhammad, as well as to the ways the majority of Muslims think about the implications of his prophetic example for Muslim practice. The judgments presented in this volume point to this, with scholars and others presenting arguments about the justification and conduct of war that appeal to these sources (along with the Qur'ān).

The appeal to the consensus of the majority carries with it the further connotation that Sunni Muslim judgment represents a kind of establishment discourse. The best estimates regarding Muslim populations suggest that per-haps 80 to 85 percent of Muslims worldwide would describe themselves as Sunnis. As the modern selections indicate, however, the notion of consen-sus presents some difficulties at present. While disagreement among Sunni Muslims has always been possible, the social and political conditions of the twentieth and twenty-first centuries correlate with differences that are both wide and deep.

Part I: Classical Sources

Nesrine Badawi

Islamic Law in Sunni Islam

Understanding Islamic law as a codified system of law fails to take into account the dyna-mism and fluidity of the development of this legal system. Islamic law, as argued by many, developed as jurists' law. To help them develop a methodologically coherent approach to law, jurists gradually formulated a science called *uṣūl al-fiqh* (sources of jurisprudence). Although there are variations in the approaches to *uṣūl al-fiqh*, there are some sources that enjoy relative agreement over their authoritativeness, including:

Qur'ān: The primary source of Islamic law in general is the *Qur'ān*. It is regarded by Muslims as the infallible literal words of God transmitted to Prophet Muhammad (570–632 CE) to govern and regulate all aspects of Muslim life.

Sunna: The term *sunna* refers to any tradition. In Islamic law, the term eventually evolved to mean the traditions and practices of the Prophet, whether those traditions are reported as sayings, acts, or concurrence of other peoples' acts by the Prophet.

Ijmā' (consensus): Consensus of the *Umma* (Muslim community) is consid-ered an authoritative source of Islamic law. However, the group whose con-sensus is considered authoritative varied according to the various schools' interpretations.

Qiyās (analogical deduction): Since the textual sources mentioned above did not apply to each emerging situation, there was a sense of the need for a deductive tool that extrapolates rulings for newly emerging situations on the basis of simi-larity with situations addressed in textual sources.

Istiḥsān (juristic preference): Juristic preference has always been a subject of exten-sive debate in Islamic law, but jurists who uphold this form of reasoning argue that it is "nothing but a preferred form of legal argument based on *qiyās*, an argument in which a special piece of textual evidence gives rise to a conclusion different from what would have been reached by *qiyās*."[1]

Introduction

It is often emphasized that "Islamic law" refers to what the jurists have deemed to be law. The sources listed above were long considered to carry varying degrees of legal authority, even prior to detailed articulation of legal theory as developed by the jurists. In the absence of a system of legal authority by which the sovereign, who enjoyed central political authority, could enforce his will upon his subjects, Sunni Islamic jurisprudence was characterized by diversity and pluralism of legal thought. In practice, the different jurists offered competing interpretations of what might count as an expression of their interpretation of the divine will. Eventually, this diversity was formalized into distinctive schools of legal thought, or *madhāhib*. Modern scholars have disagreed on their accounts of the process that led to the emergence of multiple schools of jurisprudence. For example, Schacht emphasizes the regional factor as the primary reason for the divergences that arose between the schools of Ḥijāz[2] and Iraq, while others, Hallaq, for example, challenge this hypothesis and argue that schools originally developed around leading figures in Islamic jurisprudence who were accorded authoritative status by later generations.[3] Some of the early schools, for instance, the Ẓāhirī and the ʿAwzāʿī, are now widely considered to be extinct (i.e., to have no modern followers), while four schools are thought to comprise the dominant Sunni schools: the Mālikī, the Ḥanafī, the Shāfiʿī, and the Ḥanbalī.

Each school is typically described in terms of the sources that it is thought to prioritize: the *ḥadīth* and traditions of Medina in the case of the Mālikī school and prophetic *sunna* in the case of the Ḥanbalī school, while the Ḥanafī school is known for its employment of reasoning techniques. Mediating between the two approaches is the role usually accorded the Shāfiʿī school. The Ẓāhirī school is believed to have been the most adherent to literalist interpretations. It should be made clear, however, that such distinctions are extremely simplistic for a variety of reasons. First, the development of schools of jurisprudence was a gradual, long-term process that witnessed borrowing from other schools, which complicates the task of distinguishing the thought of any particular school. Additionally, schools disagree among themselves over the features of competing schools. For example, contrary to their opponents' criticisms of arbitrary reasoning reliant on personal views, the Ḥanafīs do not claim to resort to reasoning except in the absence of a text. Finally, there are wide disagreements within each school over a variety of issues, which further proves the limitation of such classifications.

Schools differ in their understanding of the sources of jurisprudence, or *uṣūl al-fiqh*. Whereas all give prime importance to the *Qurʾān* and the *sunna*, these schools disagree both over the authenticity of the different *ḥadīths* and over the relationship between those two sources in cases of conflict. Schools likewise diverge in the weight accorded to the deeds and words of the Prophet's companions, the definition of consensus, and the role of interpretive techniques such as *qiyās*. Even when scholars uphold the same theory of *uṣūl al-fiqh*, they sometimes reach alternative rulings with regard to a particular subject matter or branch of law (*furūʿ al-fiqh*).

Armed Conflict in Sunni Islam

Jihād is probably one of the most widely understood Arabic words around the world. The 9/11 attacks have brought the regulation of armed conflict in Islamic law to the forefront of public and academic life, with continuous attempts to expose the inherent "pacifist" or "violent" nature of Islam. But relatively few have truly attempted to understand the dynamics of the Sunni legal tradition that has produced this body of literature. It is too often that we witness selective reliance on a particular *Qur'ānic* text or a prophetic *ḥadīth* without attempting to address the complexity of those sources and understanding the long and diverse interpretive tradition dealing with them. Islamic jurisprudence has for centuries offered a sophisticated response to the textual sources and offered detailed normative discussions on armed conflict. This chapter provides an overview of the dominant Sunni school of jurisprudence and its approach to the regulation of armed conflict, on issues such as the legitimacy of *jihād*, the selection of targets and weapons, the treatment of captives, and limits on warfare within the Muslim community.

Sources of Islamic Jurisprudence and Armed Conflict

Conflict receives some level of prominent coverage in the *Qur'ān* with some verses arguably promoting fighting in the path of God and others instructing Muslims to uphold justice in their conflicts and to refrain from different forms of aggression. According to al-Zuḥaylī (b. 1932), a contemporary Muslim scholar, the *Qur'ān* contains more than a hundred verses denouncing aggression and forced conversion to Islam.[4] At the same time, there are other verses that were understood to promote a more offensive notion of warfare, calling on believers to fight nonbelievers wherever they may be and to strive for the advancement of Islam until it becomes the sole religion on Earth.

How those verses were coordinated varied from one jurist to the other. One approach has been to argue that the so-called sword verses, verses understood to promote offensive *jihād*, abrogated the other, "pacifist" verses. Proponents of this approach claim that most verses denouncing aggression were issued prior to the sword verses and that the *Qur'ānic* approach to conflict gradually moved from renunciation of violence and the exercise of self-restraint vis-à-vis oppressors to legitimating self-defense to finally demanding that Muslims fight to propagate their religion.[5] On the other side, a contrasting approach has maintained that the sword verses were excessively expanded by the early jurists to promote the notion of offensive warfare. For example, al-Qaraḍāwī (b. 1926) argues that the verse instructing Muslims "[to] slay the idolaters wherever you find them, and take them, and confine them, and lie in wait for them at every place of ambush"[6] was directed only against those infidels who had breached their agreements with the Prophet.[7] Shaltūt (1893–1963) similarly explains how the verse demanding that Muslims

> [f]ight those who believe not in God and the Last Day and do not forbid what God and his Messenger have forbidden such men as practice not the religion of truth,

being of those who have been given the Book – until they pay the tribute out of
hand and have been humbled.[8]

was uttered against enemies of the Prophet who had violated sworn agreements in an
attempt to abort his message.[9] To buttress this approach, these scholars quote numerous other verses that denounce aggression, such as, "If they withdraw from you, and
do not fight you, and offer you peace, then God assigns not any way to you against
them"[10] and "No compulsion is there in religion. Rectitude has become clear from
error."[11]

The passages cited above (and others like them) refer to rules governing the resort to
armed force. As to the regulation of actions within armed conflict,[12] the *Qur'ān* offered
little direct guidance apart from three specific areas: the treatment of persons captured
in war, deliberate destruction of property, and the rather detailed comments on dividing
up the spoils of war. Despite this relative silence, it is quite striking that the formative
medieval jurists nonetheless saw fit to discuss a broad range of issues relating to right and
wrong conduct in war. In doing so, they relied on general *Qur'ānic* directives, but also
(and especially) found guidance in the *sunna*.

The Prophet is reported to have participated in numerous battles while in Medina.
Those battles produced a rich body of relevant *sunna*. Beyond the directly relevant *sunna*
there is an even vaster pool of general prophetic *sunna* that provides ethical directives on
matters that may be interpreted as relating to warfare, such as the rejection of treachery.
But just as the *Qur'ān*, the *sunna* is complex and contain many seeming inconsistencies
from one passage to another. As a supplement, the jurists also appealed to the practice of
the Prophet's companions and the early Caliphs for further guidance.

In addition, the jurists made use of *istiḥsān* and *qiyās*. These sources provided deductive tools that allowed for a more sophisticated interpretation of the primary textual
sources (*Qur'ān*, *sunna*, and the practice of the companions). Nonetheless, some juristic schools advocated a stronger adherence to textual sources and shunned sources that
resorted to such interpretive techniques. Other schools, and some contemporary scholars, by contrast, have argued that the primary sources alone do not provide a sufficient
theoretical basis for navigating the complexity of situations experienced by Muslim communities. Since Islam is a universal religion, with its sources applying to all geographical
and temporal conditions, reliance on deductive techniques is necessary, they maintained,
to formulate an Islamic *ḥukm* (ruling) for widely different situations.

Regimes of Armed Conflict in Islamic Jurisprudence

Matters relating to armed conflict constitute one of the standard branches of Islamic
jurisprudence. This branch is typically divided into four main subcategories: fighting
non-Muslims, fighting apostates, fighting rebelling Muslims, and fighting bandits and
highway robbers. While some rules apply for all wars, the Islamic jurisprudential culture
distinguishes between these four groups and addresses each of them separately. The section below addresses these four regimes in a brief survey of the principles of Islamic laws
of armed conflict.

War against Non-Muslims

To designate the use of armed force against non-Muslims, *jihād* was the term most often employed in the writings of the classical jurists. While the term could have a purely spiritual meaning (struggling against inner, wayward desires – the so-called greater *jihād*), when it was applied specifically to war, *jihād* stood in contrast to other kinds of fighting, such as armed confrontations with fellow Muslims (often termed "*baghy*"). *Qitāl* (fighting) is the general term often used to refer to any conflict regardless of who the adversary is. There was considerable disagreement over the purpose of *jihād*, with most classical jurists maintaining that *jihād* should be conducted to ensure the propagation of religion,[13] and others stating that the purpose of *jihād* was essentially defensive.[14] Some of the jurists who believed the Muslim nation to be in a perpetual war with non-Muslim nations divided the world into two camps, *dār al-Islām* (Abode of Islam) and *dār al-ḥarb* (Abode of War). According to this view, it was always legitimate to launch war against the Abode of War, unless there was a truce with the Abode of War. Other jurists further added other categories of abodes, but the above-mentioned ones are the two primary categories, especially among those who adhere to offensive theories of *jihād*.

A detailed examination of the key texts used by proponents of offensive and defensive *jihād* is offered in Chapter 6, on Shi'ite Islam, whereas this chapter focuses primarily on juristic limitations on tactics employed in the conduct of armed conflict. Regardless of the purpose of *jihād*, scholars often devised specific rules to govern the conduct of warfare. These rules included stipulations on the treatment of persons living in enemy territory, restrictions on targeting and weaponry, and so on.

Jizya (*Poll Tax*)

Jizya is a very significant regime in Islamic law, a poll tax that entitles non-Muslim citizens to continue to inhabit their land and maintain their property. Expansion or limitation of the scope of *jizya* had direct implications, not only on the future of the person to whom the regime applied, but also on protection of that person's life, since many jurists believed that adult men who were not entitled to payment of *jizya* should be fought until they convert to Islam.

The primary *Qur'ānic* text addressing the *jizya* regime is verse 9:29:

> Fight those who believe not in God and the Last Day and do not forbid what God and His Messenger have forbidden – such men as practice not the religion of truth, being of those who have been given the Book – until they pay the tribute out of hand and have been humbled.[15]

Some jurists have argued that the verse clearly specifies the "People of the Book" as beneficiaries of the *jizya* regime and that all others should be fought until they convert. Those jurists claimed that the People of the Book included Jews, Christians, and Zoroastrians (also termed "Magi"), because the first two are explicitly referred to in Islamic sources as People of the Book and Zoroastrians are explicitly granted the right to pay the *jizya* in a prophetic tradition.[16] Other jurists, by contrast, relying on the same prophetic instruction to treat the Zoroastrians on par with the People of the Book, maintained that the instruction to fight non-Muslims until they convert was directed specifically at the idolaters of the Arabian Peninsula, with the implication that all other non-Muslims would be permitted to pay the poll tax by analogy with the Zoroastrians, thereby limiting forced conversion[17] to a smaller set of groups.

Targeting and Weapons

There was a consensus among formative and medieval jurists that women and children should not be deliberately targeted with harm in war. However, these jurists disagreed extensively over the other targetable categories. Many argued that all men of adult age (but not old) may be targeted in times of war because they have the ability to participate in fighting. As later detailed, others such as al-Shāfi'ī (766–820 CE) argued for an expansion of targetable categories beyond this limit, as they held that older men may also be killed. For support, al-Shāfi'ī cites a *ḥadīth* that relates how during the life of the Prophet an older man, who had provided military advice to the adversary, was justifiably killed.[18] Nonetheless, in another text the same author offers a more restricted view of targeting that states that Christian monks and priests should not be killed in wartime, although he states in yet another passage that these persons may be killed if they refuse to pay the *jizya*.[19] In a still more expansive view of targeting, Ibn Ḥazm (994–1064 CE) rejects any limitation on the legitimacy of killing all adult men regardless of their age or religious stature.[20] But on the other side of the spectrum, Ibn Qudāma (1146–1223 CE) and the Ḥanafīs, relying on other prophetic traditions, held that among men, the crippled, insane, and elderly should not be targeted with deliberate harm.[21]

War Captives

In line with premodern traditions of warfare in the Arabian Peninsula, captivation was not limited to those fighting on the enemy's side but extended to include other categories.[22] According to Ibn Rushd, there was a consensus among classical jurists that all infidels may be captured in wartime, including men, women, and children.[23] Only monks were considered to enjoy a special status, with some jurists arguing that these men of God should be left to practice their religion without any threat to their livelihood or freedom. The jurists also agreed that captured individuals could be enslaved and distributed as booty in the same manner as other spoils of war.[24] There was, however, extensive debate over the legitimacy of killing prisoners of war. Since women and children were not to be deliberately targeted, it was proscribed to kill them after captivation on the basis of prophetic traditions demanding that those two categories ought to be spared. With regard to men, views varied according to the different approaches. For example, as already noted, the Ḥanafīs held that insane, crippled, or old men who had been taken captive ought not to be killed. Al-Shāfi'ī offered a more expansive view (all adult male captives may be killed), as does Ibn Qudāma.[25] By contrast, other jurists were influenced by the following verse from the *Qur'ān*, which was taken to prohibit killing after captivation: "When you meet the unbelievers, smite their necks, then, when you have made wide slaughter among them, tie fast the bonds; then set them free, either by grace or ransom."[26]

Among the other jurists who discussed armed conflict, Mālik maintained that only dangerous war captives who continue to pose a threat to Muslims may permissibly be killed, whereas Ibn Ḥazm was entirely silent on this issue.[27]

Property

There was little doubt among the jurists that the acquisition of movable enemy property (spoils of war) should be deemed permissible under Islamic law; being a commonly held assumption, the legitimacy of this practice was rarely made the subject of explicit analysis. Most attention was directed instead to the rules that should be followed when warriors divided up spoils. One rule held that this division could take place only after one-fifth of the proceeds had been allocated to the *Imām* so as to cover administrative expenditures of the state.

Jurists, however, offered alternative approaches to the acquisition of immovable property because of the approach taken by 'Umar ibn al-Khaṭṭāb, the second Caliph and one of the most influential companions of the Prophet. After the conquest of southern Iraq, Ibn al-Khaṭṭāb decided that the inhabitants would be allowed to keep their land, with *kharāj* (a land tax) imposed on all owners.[28] The introduction of this practice led to an extensive debate among jurists regarding the most appropriate approach to lands that come under the domination of the Muslims. Whereas jurists such as al-Shāfiʿī continued to argue that the land ought to be treated as a spoil of war, much as other spoils of war,[29] Mālik held that immovable property was an endowment of the community, so that its revenues were to be dedicated to Muslim public services.[30] By contrast, the Ḥanafīs maintained continuity with the 'Umar tradition and argued that the original owners may keep the land and pay the *kharāj* tax.[31] As for Ibn Ḥazm, he took the more extreme position that the land was to be divided among the warriors unless they all agreed to give up their entitlements.[32]

Amān (Pledge of Safety)

Amān is a temporary pact of security whereby visitors from an enemy territory were conferred a certain level of protection from hostile acts (on life, liberty, and property) during their stay in the opposing community. Classical jurists agreed such a pact could be granted by Muslims to non-Muslims, and vice versa.[33] Concerning protection given to non-Muslims, the overwhelming majority of jurists agreed that an adult free man may grant *amān* to a non-Muslim and that such an *amān* was to be respected by the entire Muslim community. Once granted *amān*, these non-Muslims were guaranteed protection for the duration of their visit on Muslim territory, and if an *imām* wished to retract the *amān*, he was obliged to guarantee protection until the non-Muslim had been escorted away.

Jurists also examined the obligations of Muslims who had been granted *amān* in a non-Muslim territory. Most agreed that if a Muslim entered enemy territory on the basis of an *amān* contract granted by non-Muslims, guaranteeing his life and property, this agreement should be mutually respected, such that for the duration of his stay the Muslim would not be permitted to harm the non-Muslim enemies. For example, as later detailed, al-Shāfiʿī argued that Muslim men whose women and children had been taken captive were not allowed to free them by attacking their non-Muslim captors, if this would entail a violation of an *amān* agreement. It would be preferable, al-Shāfiʿī maintained, to ask for a retraction of the *amān* than to save the captives by its violation.

Baghy

The term *baghy* literally means transgression. However, as detailed below, it has been used in Islamic law in reference to rebellion by Muslims against a Muslim ruler. As the contemporary scholar Abou El Fadl has explained, classical Islamic sources of law did not articulate an explicit set of norms to regulate armed conflict within Muslim society.[34] In this area, jurists primarily relied on the practice of the fourth Caliph, ʿAlī ibn Abī Ṭālib. Appealing to the following *Qurʾanic* verse, he urged disputing Muslims to pursue the path of reconciliation. Muslims could take up arms against transgressors only when reconciliation had first been attempted and failed:

> If two parties among the believers fight each other, then make peace between them. But if one of them transgresses (*baghat*) against the other, then fight, all of you, against the one that transgresses until it complies with the command of God. But if it complies, then make peace between the two parties with justice and be fair, for God loves those who are fair and just. The believers are but a single brotherhood. So reconcile your two [contending] brothers, and fear God so that you will receive His mercy.[35]

Abou El Fadl further observes that the law of rebellion was first given detailed examination in the writings of al-Shāfiʿī, who nonetheless drew on the work of his predecessors.[36] Over time this theme became a necessary component of Islamic law treatises. Whereas many jurists thought that unjustified rebellion against a just *imām* is prohibited, they distinguish between the rightness or wrongness of rebellion and the protections rebels are entitled to. Most jurists argued that rebels enjoyed a special status under the law when their rebellion was based on a disagreement with the *Imām* over an interpretation (*taʾwīl*) of proper Islamic conduct. This status was to be upheld even if they were found to have erred in their reasoning, as long as their rebellion was not phrased as a mere pursuit of worldly objectives. The jurists generally agreed that the *Imām* should not fight dissenters unless they start to pose a threat to his rule and rebel. Once fighting has begun, rebels were to be fought under a legal regime that placed more restrictions on the conduct in battle than would be applicable in a war against non-Muslims. When the fighting has ceased and the rebels no longer pose a threat to the *Imām* (leader of a Muslim group; in the context of *baghy* jurisprudence, it refers to the political leader of the community, the Caliph), they should not be killed or taken as captives. Nor may their property be seized as booty. Furthermore, they were not to be held accountable for the damage they had inflicted in the course of battle. As later detailed here, jurists disagreed over the treatment of rebels who had fled in order to regroup and continue to fight. For example, the Ḥanafīs believed that such rebels could rightly be killed, and their weaponry used against them; al-Shāfiʿī, by contrast, was against such practices.

It should also be noted that most jurists said little or nothing about the norms that rebels should observe in their conflict with the just *Imām*. This created a lopsided system of law, whereby obligations were placed solely on the *Imām*. In so doing, the jurists may have worked under the assumption that a rebel was functioning outside the accepted legal framework of the Muslim polity; thus, in articulating norms, they directed their attention to the enforcer of the legal system, the Caliph or the *Imām*. However, it is also possible that the jurists, while addressing their discourse mainly to the legitimate authority, nonetheless assumed that all warring parties should be held to the same standard. After all, it seems highly unlikely that they would attempt to limit the powers of whomever they perceived as a just *imām*, while expanding the freedoms of those erroneously rebelling against him. The closest a jurist came to discussing this issue was Ibn Ḥazm, who maintained that rebels who resort to terrorizing tactics automatically become subject to the far more punitive regime of *ḥirāba*, detailed below.

Ḥirāba

Ḥirāba was the legal regime reserved for highway robbers and armed bandits who terrorized the Muslim public and disrupted their safety. Most jurists agreed that those who resorted to such tactics outside Muslim cities were to be called *muḥaribūn* (committers of *ḥirāba*). Some, like Mālik, argued that armed robbery inside cities also fell under this regime.[37] Jurists agreed that *muḥaribūn* must be fought and punished for their acts.[38] Punishment included execution, crucifixion, amputation of alternative arms and legs, and exile, as detailed in *Qur'ānic* verse 5:33. Despite its partial relevance, *ḥirāba* is not addressed in this chapter due to its classical limitation to criminal behavior.

Fighting Apostates

The jurists agreed on the legitimacy of fighting apostates; in this respect they appealed to the tradition of Abū Bakr (who succeeded the Prophet as the first Caliph). On the whole, the rules that governed war against non-Muslims were applicable also to the use of force against apostates, with the exception that no jurist allowed for the payment of *jizya* by apostates, since they were either to repent or to be killed. Apostate women were also to be killed, according to the majority of jurists, with the exception of the Ḥanafīs, who upheld the general prohibition of targeting women.

The Need for Alternative Interpretive Techniques: From Text to Context

Since textual sources are inherently indeterminate, juristic positions were often shaped by factors beyond the texts. As Islamic law developed into a sophisticated legal system, deductive techniques were devised in order to determine the most appropriate approach for treating the sources in a process often referred to as *uṣūl al-fiqh*. Each school (*madhhab*) maintained its own unique theory of *uṣūl al-fiqh*; however, as a result of individual jurists' perception of the socio-political reality, jurisprudence within each school often deviated from its declared jurisprudential techniques. A review of the prominent Sunni schools shows that those claiming strong adherence to the text did not show equal loyalty to their jurisprudential techniques. In fact, the more limited the jurisprudential theory of *uṣūl al-fiqh*, the more deviation can be witnessed in juridical reasoning. Ibn Ḥazm's theory of *uṣūl* claims the strictest faithfulness to the text and denies the role of many sources often relied on by other schools, thus preventing to some degree expansion of the jurist's freedom in utilizing the sources. But this theory did not prevent Ibn Ḥazm, the staunch critic of the ascent of non-Muslims to high-profile political positions, from manipulating the law of armed conflict to limit the inclusion of non-Muslims in Muslim communities. As is later detailed in this chapter, Ibn Ḥazm offered a creative but unconvincing analysis of the sources in order to limit the application of *dhimma* regime to non-Muslims. This he accomplished by introducing a novel condition for the application of this regime, recognition of Muhammad's prophethood by non-Muslims.

That is not to say that the so-called *ahl al-ra'y* (people of opinion, often referring to the Ḥanafis) were immune to the criticism of inconsistency. Contrary to detractors from the *ahl al-ḥadīth* camp, the Ḥanafi school never claimed to follow personal preference and disregard the text. As elaborated in their different *uṣūl* works, the Ḥanafis always claimed to uphold the *Qur'ān* and the prophetic *sunna*. Nevertheless, al-Shaybānī's denial of ransom as an alternative for captives disregards the *Qur'ānic* verse proposing ransom as an alternative. Such inconsistencies in the reasoning of the Ḥanafi school are further proof that the so-called distinction between *ahl al-ra'y* and *ahl al-ḥadīth* is often exaggerated, and on the whole the surviving *madhāhib* were more inclined to promote a restrictive textual interpretation of the law, even if such an inclination could be put into practice only with much difficulty.

Hegemony and the Islamic Empire

Many classical works were written at the height of Muslim hegemony, when the borders of the Muslim empire spanned Europe, Africa, and Asia. An examination of these works shows that they were written out of a concern to justify and indeed strengthen this hegemony by according liberty of action to Muslim armies. Despite the contention of Abou El Fadl, who argues that most jurists of the period had sought to achieve a balance between functionalism and morality in their approach to rules governing the conduct of the army,[39] a strong case can be made that functionalism was the more primary concern. Relaxing the regulations that would restrict the conduct of warfare seems to have been the primary intent of a majority of these jurists. That is not to say that there was no interest whatsoever in placing moral restrictions on warfare, even if such restrictions would negatively impact the Muslim military advantage. For example, as mentioned above, al-Shaybānī was keen to prohibit the killing of elderly men among the enemy, despite the existence of a prophetic *ḥadīth* that might be understood as promoting their killing. On his part such an interest cannot be attributed to anything but morality. Unlike women and children, who constituted a potential asset when taken into captivity, elderly men were probably of little or no benefit to the Muslim empire. Similarly, al-Shāfi'ī's and Ibn Ḥazm's prohibition of killing animals[40] is similarly triggered by a sense of obligation to preserve different forms of life. As noted by both jurists, there were certain regulations that ought to be respected even if these were likely to limit the damage inflicted by the army. When commenting on jurists who permitted animals to be killed in order to spite the enemy, he mockingly asked why those jurists did not also allow the killing of their women and children, since this would infuriate them even more.

But giving due consideration to morality did not prevent jurists from devising a system that could favorably support the Muslim empire in its dealings with non-Muslims. For example, as mentioned earlier, al-Shāfi'ī and Ibn Ḥazm were keen on limiting the application of the *jizya* regime. In the case of al-Shāfi'ī (a personal recipient of a share of the booty),[41] there is some evidence that he sought to expand the range of goods that could legitimately be confiscated as booty. By contrast, Ibn Ḥazm appears to have been more interested in ridding the Muslim empire of "fifth column" elements. This is evidenced by his sharp criticism of non-Muslims who had ascended to high positions in the Muslim territory of al-Andalus.[42] At any event, both jurists relied on *Qur'ānic* verses to prove that only People of the Book may "benefit" from the *jizya* regime. In so doing they were confronted with a rather problematic *ḥadīth* that permitted the Zoroastrians to pay the *jizya*. But unlike other jurists who took this *ḥadīth* to signify that all non-Arabs should be allowed to pay the *jizya*, they both went through a laborious and rather unconvincing analysis to prove that as the Zoroastrians were also (alongside Jews and Christians) People of the Book, other non-Muslim peoples could not partake of this "privilege."

For another example of the tendency to relax moral restrictions concerning war, one could again cite al-Shaybānī (749/50–805 CE), who makes little or no attempt to limit indiscriminate targeting of besieged cities. Nor does he take much care to ensure the protection of non-Muslim women and children from these indiscriminate tactics. By contrast, when the presence of Muslim children was explicitly envisioned, al-Shaybānī made clear that they should not be targeted with harm in the course of battle. While one would think, based on his method of reasoning, that both Muslims and non-Muslims should be sheltered from direct targeting, he seems more intent on expanding the powers of the army than on adherence to this principle if the damage was likely to be inflicted on non-Muslim protected categories. Indeed, al-Shaybānī's work contains one of the first formulations of *tatarrus* (shielding), which stipulates that if a non-Muslim enemy is shielded by untargetable categories (say, children), this should not stand in the way of military operations against such an enemy.[43] As Islamic law further developed, many jurists continued to uphold *tatarrus* when they argued that besieged cities could rightly be attacked regardless of the presence of such shields. However, later jurists failed to see the inconsistency of the early articulations of this legal tool and simply continued to reiterate it as an established principle, thereby lending it legitimacy. In failing to see this inconsistency in the early works, these later jurists lent legitimacy to a very questionable military tactic.

Decline of the Empire

For various reasons, the Islamic empire's power gradually started to wane, and many of its enemies started to pose a significant threat to its existence, at least in certain localities such as the Iberian Peninsula. The resulting sense of insecurity appears to have triggered a further loosening of restrictions on what could be done against non-Muslims, at least among some jurists. One of the clearest examples of this reaction was the work of Ibn Ḥazm. On witnessing the internal strife and pursuit of self-interest by rulers in the outlying Ṭā'ifa states (also referred to as petty states or party states), he argued strenuously against the appointment of *dhimmīs* (non-Muslims residing permanently in Muslim territory) to high-profile influential positions. Living through one of the most chaotic eras of Andalusī history, Ibn Ḥazm believed that this practice contributed to the degeneration of the Muslim empire, as on his view the *dhimmīs* were never keen on promoting Muslim interests. Thus, in light of the assumed potential contribution by *dhimmīs* to enemy war efforts, he proposed very strict limitations on their incorporation into the Muslim polity.

Another troubling issue facing Ibn Ḥazm was that Muslim rulers were fighting each other and calling on Christian neighbors as allies in their respective struggles.[44] His contempt for such a practice was reflected in his teaching on internal strife under Islamic law. He offers a very fluid system of *baghy* that allows the ruler to be considered a *baghī* (rebel) and a just rebel group considered the righteous group, *ahl al-ʿadl*.[45] In doing so, Ibn Ḥazm strips all warring parties of preassumed legitimacy. Only adherence to Islamic law could be the sole determinant of legitimacy. In this way he apparently hoped to delegitimize rulers who had associated themselves with Christians. By showing them to be rulers unworthy of trust, the pervasive internal strife among Muslim rulers, which depended on the military assistance of Christians, would be lessened.

Responsiveness to Accepted Social Structures

Scholarship was also, to a great extent, shaped by the social frameworks governing society at the time. In particular, juristic reasoning often reaffirmed the class and gender hierarchy accepted at the time. For instance, some scholars, including the Ḥanafī al-Shaybānī, maintained, on the basis of two prophetic traditions, that slaves should not receive a share of war spoils to which they would otherwise be entitled were it not for their special status. According to the first tradition, a slave who had asked the Prophet for a share of spoils received only something of meaningless value.[46] The second tradition is traced back to Ibn ʿAbbās, who said that the Prophet did not give slaves a share of spoils; instead they received only some compensation.[47] Scathingly criticizing this juristic position, Ibn Ḥazm argued that the Ḥanafīs often felt free to contradict Ibn ʿAbbās; moreover, the same author questioned the validity of the first tradition, on the ground that it was reported by an unknown transmitter.[48] Arguing against the view of al-Shaybānī and others like him, Ibn Ḥazm cites other prophetic traditions that prove the Prophet gave slaves a share of the booty.[49] It appears then that al-Shaybānī's neglect of these other traditions depends in large measure on his acceptance of the institution of slavery and perceptions of slave rights in Abbasid times.

Al-Shaybānī's works are also indicative of an engrained perception of gender roles. For example, he recognizes that a marriage conducted in the territory of war (i.e., outside the Islamic empire) should be regarded as valid once the couple had moved to the territory of Islam, "because such a marriage was lawful among them" (i.e., the infidels). On his account, this would obtain even if such marriages contravened Islamic laws, say, if the woman married without due observance of *ʿidda* (a stipulated waiting period) or if the man had already been divorced three times.[50] But, inversely, if a woman was remarried (while maintaining her first marriage) and then moved to the territory of Islam with her new husband, the marriage would not be recognized because "it is not lawful in any circumstance for a man to marry a woman who has another husband."[51] Whereas it is not clear what is meant by "any circumstance" here, obviously the idea of a woman being simultaneously married to two men was perceived as too repugnant to nature to the extent that it was unimaginable and unacceptable, leading to deviation from the rational attitude of inquiry into the initial legal status of the marriage.[52] Much like failure to observe *ʿidda* or to refrain from resumption of the marriage after three divorces, one would expect that the approach to polyandry under Islamic law and to its legitimacy should be analogous to the other forms of illegal marriage. But the pragmatic need to accept legitimacy of marriage contracts conducted in the territory of war could not, in this case, outweigh the perceived risk of accepting a marital relationship that offered women the privilege of multiple partnerships.

Relationship to Political Authority

Many jurists enjoyed a special relationship with the political authorities. For example, al-Shaybānī was twice appointed as a senior judge by the Abbasid Caliph Hārūn al-Rashīd (d. 809 CE), and Ibn Ḥazm was appointed as a minister by short-lived Umayyad rulers. Al-Shāfiʿī appears to have left a positive impression on al-Rashīd, who (as we earlier noted) ordered that al-Shāfiʿī, as a blood relative of the Prophet, should receive his share from the spoils of war. Finally, Ibn Qudāma is reported to have fought alongside Ṣalāḥ al-Dīn (1174–1193 CE, known in Western literature as Saladin) against the crusaders. But the juristic/political relationship was not one of linear alliance. For example, al-Shaybānī was dismissed by al-Rashīd for his determination to uphold an *amān* pact between al-Rashīd and a rebel group.[53] Al-Shāfiʿī got to meet al-Rashīd after his arrest for suspicion of *tashayyuʿ* (being a Shiʿite).[54] And Ibn Ḥazm was anything but an ally of the party kings, of whom he said:

> [B]y God, I swear that if the tyrants were to learn that they could attain their ends more easily by professing the religion of the cross, they would certainly hasten to profess it! Indeed, we see that they ask the Christians for help and allow them to take away Muslim men, women and children as captives in their land. Frequently, they protect [the Christians] in their attacks against the most inviolable lands and ally themselves with them in order to gain security.[55]

A close relationship with the political authorities appears to have left a strong imprint on the writings of at least some leading jurists. Al-Shaybānī, for instance, showed an interest in consolidating the power of the Caliph, not so much in an attempt to assert his reign, but rather to guarantee the power of the institution itself, both as a representative of the Muslim empire and as the leading domestic authority. In so doing, al-Shaybānī may have been motivated by a belief that centralized power was a necessary precondition to dominance in the "international" sphere. However, it is also possible that this was simply an outcome of exposure to a more authoritative political institution during Abbasid times. What is evident is that this objective seems to have dominated al-Shaybānī's work more than any other interest.

The emphasis on centralized authority is especially salient in al-Shaybānī's discussion of the division of spoils. He maintains, for example, that if a young slave (boy or girl) is captured and is likely to be given as spoil to one of the warriors, the one who has captured that slave is not permitted to free him or her, as it is not yet known with certainty that this particular slave will be apportioned to this particular warrior, even if the latter's share of booty exceeds the value of this slave.[56] This position is contrasted by al-Shaybānī to an analogically similar case in which a share of the booty is assigned collectively to a group of warriors by the *Imām* (the Caliph or whoever was assigned by the Caliph to head the raid). In this particular case, it is permitted for the warrior to offer manumission to the slave girl or boy before certainty of ownership. While acknowledging that the "the two situations are analogically the same," al-Shaybānī asserts that he would "prefer to abandon analogy and follow *istiḥsān* [juristic preference] and hold that the emancipation before the division of the spoil is not permissible."[57] The contrast between the two positions arises not from a difference with respect to the private property itself; it relates rather to the deference due to the authority of the *Imām*, whose judgment is needed to legitimize (or challenge) claims to property.

Al-Shaybānī's interest in the reinforcement and centralization of authority is also apparent in his approach to the regulation of conflict between public authority and Muslim rebels. Whereas the regime articulated by al-Shaybānī provided a degree of protection and legitimacy to rebels, he was also intent on maintaining the ruler's freedom of action. Thus, despite a heavy reliance on 'Alī's (the fourth rightly guided Caliph) conduct with rebels, including recognition of his unilateral promise to rebels ("Whoever flees [from us] shall not be chased, no [Muslim] prisoner of war shall be killed, and no wounded in the battle shall be despatched"[58]), al-Shaybānī nonetheless innovated by rather severely limiting which rebels could be entitled to protection and set as condition the nonexistence of another group of rebels "with whom refuge might be taken. But if a group of them has survived with whom refuge might be taken, then their prisoners could be killed, their fugitives pursued and their wounded despatched."[59] While little explanation is given for the introduction of this limiting condition, it seems intended to prevent such groups from reuniting with other rebels, thereby to continue the fight against the *Imām*. This same point is further reinforced when al-Shaybānī indicates how nondiscriminate weapons, such as catapults, inundation with water, and burning with fire, may permissibly be used against rebels while they would be prohibited in ordinary combat.[60]

The high respect accorded by al-Shaybānī to the Caliph's centralized authority can be highlighted by comparison with Ibn Ḥazm's position on rebellion. The latter deviates from the pragmatic approach that had then been adopted by most jurists in their treatment of *baghy*. Avoiding, like most of them, the question of the legitimacy of rebellion,[61] Ibn Ḥazm maintains that the juristic tradition's placing rebels under the category of *baghī* was ill founded, as the sources make no such assumption. Moreover, he maintains that the *Qurʾānic baghy* verse earlier cited does not distinguish, on the basis of political authority, between those who have transgressed and those who have been transgressed against. Political authorities could find themselves on either side of the equation, as could the rebels. In establishing this possible equivalence, Ibn Ḥazm seemed intent on subordinating both sides to a higher religious judgment. The *Imām* himself could be made subject to such judgment, thus resulting in his transfer from legitimacy to transgression if his acts were deemed to be inconsistent with God's laws and justice. Rebels, likewise, were subject to the same criteria. They were under obligation to conform to religious instruction and proper conduct, or otherwise they would lose the immunities that would otherwise be applicable to them.

Thus, in striking contrast to al-Shaybānī, Ibn Ḥazm showed little respect for men in power. He was particularly skeptical of their willingness to adopt tactics that would achieve their objectives, in utter disregard for the teachings of religion.

Classical Jurisprudence and the Regulation of Armed Conflict

This section details the views of five different jurists who discussed armed conflict under Islamic law. Four of the jurists represent the four Sunni schools of thought. The first, Mālik (d. 796 CE), is the founder of the Mālikī school. The work relied on below, *al-Mudawwana al-Kubra*, is a later compilation of his views. It contains "replies by Ibn [al-Q]āsim (d. 807 CE) according to the school of Mālik, or according to his own *ra'y*, to questions of Saḥnūn as well as traditions and opinions of Ibn Wahb (d. 813 CE)."[62] The second, al-Shaybānī,[63] is an immediate disciple of Abū Ḥanīfa. None of Abū Ḥanīfa's works survived, and representation of the Ḥanafī school at the time is best witnessed in the works of al-Shaybānī and Abū Yūsuf (another disciple of Abū Ḥanīfa). The third, al-Shāfiʿī, is the founder of the Shāfiʿī school. The fourth, Ibn Qudāma, is a renowned Ḥanbalī jurist who is often cited in militant manuscripts. The fifth, Ibn Ḥazm, is a representative of the extinct Ẓāhirī school, but his work is relied on because of the continued reference to his views in mainstream and militant works.

When Should Muslims Engage in War?

A Well-Articulated Theory of Jihād?
Most juristic works are surprisingly brief in their examination of the legitimacy of engagement in armed conflict. However, there is a general tendency to accept the legitimacy of offensive warfare for the promotion of religion. Al-Shāfiʿī probably offers the most sophisticated detailed legal opinion on the conditions for initiation of armed conflict with non-Muslims advocating conducting *jihād* to propagate the message of Islam.

From: al-Shāfiʿī, *al-Umm*, Vol. IV[64]

Exalted and Glorified God, rendered His religion, with which he sent His Apostle, God's blessings and peace be upon him, triumphant over all other religions, in that he made apparent to all who heard it that it is the Truth, and that all other religions are false.

And He made it triumphant in that the totality of disbelief is two religions; the religion of the People of the Book, and the religion of the unscriptured.* And God's Apostle, God's blessings and peace be upon him, vanquished the unscriptured until they adopted Islam, voluntarily and coerced, and he slew and enslaved the People of the Book until some of them adopted Islam, and some paid the *jizya*, humbled, and his command, God's blessings and peace be upon him, ruled them.

But the relative vagueness of other jurists in dealing with the issue of *jihād* does not necessarily indicate a stricter approach to the rules governing initiation of conflict. For example, Ibn Ḥazm touches briefly on the issue of initiation of *jihād* when addressing the matter of fulfillment of individual duty of *jihād*. But the list of *jihād*'s objectives is indicative of a view similar to that of al-Shāfiʿī.

From: Ibn Ḥazm, *al-Muḥalla*, Vol. VII[65]

And *jihād* is an obligation on all Muslims. If [a group of Muslims] fulfilled [its objectives] of defense against the enemy, invasion of the enemy territory's heart-

---

* Disbelievers with no recognized scriptural or religious tradition.

land, and protection of Muslim border cities, others would be relieved of the obligation.

Other Indications of Juristic Position on Jihād

Invitation to Convert to Islam

The brevity of the jurists on the objectives of *jihād* does not prevent the researcher from understanding the jurists' position on offensive *jihād*. For example, one way of understanding the juristic approach to the matter is to examine the jurists' positions on the need to invite people to join Islam before fighting. The fact that many jurists spent effort on detailing how and when infidels were to be invited to join Islam before fighting is, to some extent, an indication that they were willing to engage in an offensive war with the objective of propagation of the message of Islam. Whereas it can be, and has definitely been, argued that the objective of inviting non-Muslims to Islam was simply aimed at guaranteeing that the attacked party had been pacified, since conversion to Islam would be the primary indication the enemy is unlikely to show aggression against Muslims.[66] The fact still remains that jurists discussed and examined invitation to Islam as a condition for, rather than a general invitation to, peace or even a truce. The jurists whose work is examined in this chapter agree on a general need to familiarize the invaded enemy with the message of Islam before starting their mission, but they all agree that the need for invitation to join Islam is only commendable and can possibly be waived if the enemy army is already familiar with the message. If those invited to join the religion decide to accept the message of Islam, then they should not be fought in accordance with the Prophetic tradition cited below in al-Shāybanī's *Siyar*.

From: Mālik ibn Anas, *al-Mudawwana al-Kubra lī-al-Imām Mālik ibn Anas al-Aṣbaḥī*[67]

"He [Mālik] used to say I am of the opinion that the infidels should not to be fought until they are invited [to Islam]."

I said: "And they are not to be raided by night until they are invited [to Islam]?"
He said: "Yes."

I said: "And irrespective of whether we invaded them or whether they advanced upon us as invaders and entered our lands, we do not fight them, in Mālik's view, until we have invited them [to Islam]."

He said: "I have informed you of Mālik's opinion, and I did not ask him about that, and all these are alike to me."

I said: "And how is the invitation [to Islam] to be made, in the opinion of Mālik?"

He said: "I heard naught from Mālik in this regard, but we invite them to God and His Apostle, or to pay the *jizya* out of hand."

And Mālik said: "Additionally, with regard to those who are in the vicinity of [the entrances to the lands of the Byzantines], the invitation is discarded, due to their familiarity with what they are being invited to, their state of contempt and enmity to the religion and its adherents, and their long-standing opposition to and fighting against the armies [of Islam]. Then seek to take them unawares; the invitation [to Islam] would serve them only as a warning, to prepare themselves to fight the Muslims, and prevent the victory over them that the Muslims desire.

From: al-Shaybānī, *Siyar*[68]

And [the Apostle] said . . . [w]henever you meet your polytheist enemies, invite them [first] to adopt Islam. If they do so, accept it, and let them alone. You should then invite them to move from their territory to the territory of the émigrés [Madīna]. If they do so, accept it and let them alone. Otherwise, they should be informed that they would be [treated] like the Muslim nomads* [who take no part in the war] in that they are subject to God's orders as [other] Muslims, but they will receive no share in the *ghanīma* [spoils of the war, or in the *fay'*]. If they refuse [to accept Islam], then call upon them to pay the *jizya* (poll tax), if they do, accept it and leave them alone.

If the army [of Islam] attacks the territory of war and it is a territory that has received an invitation to accept Islam, it is commendable if the army renews the invitation, but if it fails to do so it is not wrong.

From: al-Shāfi'ī, *al-Umm*, Vol. IV[69]

It is obligatory to bid the infidels whom [we are obliged] to invite to Islam to [either] convert to Islam or to [pay] the *jizya*. As for he who has [already] received the invitation, Muslims have the right to slay him before he is invited [again] to Islam. And if they invite him to Islam, then that is their right, on the basis that if they have the right to leave off fighting him for an extended span of time, then postponing fighting him until he is invited is a [shorter span of time].

As for those who have not received the invitation of Muslims, it is not permissible to fight them until they are invited to [the] faith, if they are other than the People of the Book, or to [accepting] the faith or giving the *jizya* if they are of the People of the Book.

And I know of no one today whom the invitation to Islam has not reached, save that there be a nation of infidels behind our enemies who are fighting us. It is possible that there are people that we do not know of, for example behind the Byzantines, Turks, and Khazars that the invitation to Islam has not reached.

From: Ibn Qudāma, *al-Mughnī*, Vol. XIII[70]

He† said: "The People of the Book and the Magi are to be fought and are not to be invited to Islam, because the invitation has already reached them; and the idolaters are to be invited to Islam before they are warred against."

---

* Bedouins.
† The anonymous "he" in Ibn Qudāma's work refers to Aḥmad ibn Ḥanbal, the founder of the Ḥanbalī School.

As for his saying of the People of the Book and the Magi that they are not to be invited to Islam before the fighting, that is in general, because the invitation to Islam has propagated and spread, and there remain none among them who have not heard the invitation, save for the rare remote [individual].

As for his saying: "The idolaters are to be invited to Islam before they are warred against," that is not in general, because those whom the invitation to Islam has reached are not to be invited, [but] if any are found whom the invitation to Islam has not reached, they are to be invited to Islam before the fighting.

Similarly, if there is found among the People of the Book any whom the invitation to Islam has not reached, they are to be invited to Islam before the fighting.

Conducting a Truce with Non-Muslims

Moreover, the fact that some jurists such as al-Shāfiʿī and Ibn Qudāma were reluctant to acknowledge an open-ended truce with the enemy is indeed an assertion of an inclination toward perpetual war with this enemy until they have become Muslim, or have been subdued by payment of *jizya*.

From: al-Shāfiʿī, *al-Umm*, Vol. IV[71]

And if a group of infidels asks for a truce, the *Imām* may agree to a truce in the interest of the Muslims, in the hope that they [the group of infidels] become Muslims or pay the *jizya* without hardship [for the Muslims]. And he should not agree to a truce if there is no interest [to be attained]. And he should not conclude a truce with them [even if it is] in the interest of the Muslims, if it does not include payment of the *jizya*, for more than four months.

From: al-Shaybānī, *Siyar*[72]

I asked: If some of the inhabitants of the territory of war asked the Muslims to make peace with them for a specified number of years without paying tribute (*jizya*), do you think that the Muslims should grant the request?

He said: Yes, provided the Imām has considered the situation and has found that the inhabitants of the territory of war are too strong for the Muslims to prevail against them, and it would be better for the Muslims to make peace with them.

From: Ibn Qudāma, *al-Mughnī*, Vol. XIII[73]

It is not permissible to conclude a truce except for a reckoned and known span of time, based on what we have cited. Al-Qāḍī said: "What is apparent of Ahmed's words is that it is impermissible [to conclude a truce that extends] more than ten years," and that is the opinion chosen by Abu Bakr and al-Shāfiʿī's *madh-hab*,* because God's declaration to "slay the idolaters wherever you find them" is

---

* School of Jurisprudence

general, and the ten-year period was specified because the truce that the Prophet, God's blessings and peace be upon him, concluded with Quraysh on the day of al-Ḥudaybiya was of ten [years' duration].[74]

Classification of Enemies and the Jizya Regime

Who May Pay the Jizya

But Islamic jurisprudence was not interested in complete conversion of the other to Islam. Indeed, such a task would have been far from practically achievable. Jurists relied on the *Qur'ānic* text demanding that nonbelievers pay a poll tax or tribute to devise a sophisticated *jizya* regime allowing non-Muslims to continue to live in a territory that had come under the rule of Islam.

> Fight those who believe not in God and the Last Day and do not forbid what God and His Messenger have forbidden – such men as practice not the religion of truth, being of those who have been given the Book – until they pay the tribute out of hand and have been humbled.[75]

As is now clear from his position on waging *jihād*, al-Shāfiʿī was primarily interested in making Islam triumphant over other religions. He was keen to ensure hegemony of the Islamic regime, either by eliminating polytheism altogether or by subjugating the People of the Book through the *jizya* regime. To prove his argument that the *jizya* regime is reserved for People of the Book (Jews or Christians), he relies on the above-cited *Qur'ānic* verse and a prophetic *ḥadīth* instructing Muslims to fight infidels until they convert to Islam.

From: al-Shāfiʿī, *al-Umm*, Vol. IV[76]

And Exalted God revealed to His Apostle the command to fight the infidels from among the People of the Book, saying: "Fight those who believe not in God and the Last Day and do not forbid what God and His Messenger have forbidden. . . ."

And so Exalted and Glorified God distinguished, as he would, and none may dispute his command, between fighting idolaters, whom he commanded be fought until they convert to Islam, and fighting the People of the Book, whom he commanded be fought until they pay the *jizya* or convert to Islam.

God's Apostle, God's blessings and peace be upon him, said: "I was commanded to fight all people until they declare that there is no God but God." But these [people referred to in the *ḥadīth*] are the idolaters. And the people whom God has commanded to accept the *jizya* are the People of the Book. And the proof of this is what I have described concerning God's differentiation between these two kinds of fighting.

God's Glorified and Exalted command to fight the infidels until [prevailing] religion is God's [alone], and that they be slain wherever they are found until they repent, and perform the prayer, does not contravene Exalted and Glorified God's command that the People of the Book be fought until they pay the *jizya*. And neither verse abrogates the other, or one of the two *hadīths* the other, and all are to be found in what Glorified and Exalted God has revealed, and what was subsequently established by his Apostle in his *sunna*.

Al-Shāfiʿī said: "And if a man in ignorance says that God's command for [the payment of] the *jizya* abrogated his command to fight the infidels until they convert to Islam, it becomes possible for an ignorant one such as himself to say to him, 'Nay, the *jizya* was abrogated by [the command] to fight the infidels until they convert to Islam; but there is no abrogation of one by the other, and no contradiction [between them].'"

But jurists were confronted with a major challenge to any neat theory of distinction between different categories of nonbelievers on the basis of scripture. This arose because of a prophetic tradition that, as we have already mentioned, instructed Muslims to treat the Zoroastrians on a par with the People of the Book. Mālik and al-Shaybānī believed that the tradition indicated a distinction between nonbelievers on the basis of habitation/ethnicity; that is, Arabs were left with one of two alternatives, conversion or being killed, whereas non-Arabs had one of three alternatives: conversion, payment of the *jizya*, or being killed.

From: Mālik, *al-Mudawwana*, Vol. I[77]

I said: "Suppose that all nations accept to pay the *jizya* in exchange for being affirmed in their religion, should that be granted them or not, in Mālik's opinion?"

He said: "Mālik said that 'Uthmān Ibn 'Affān took the *jizya* from the Magi Berber.

"And Mālik said: 'Of the Magi, [you have] what you have heard of 'Abdul Raḥman Ibn 'Awf, that he said: "God's Apostle, God's blessings and peace be upon him, said: 'Follow the same *sunna* with them that you would follow with the People of the Book.'"'

"So all nations in this regard are as the Magi, in my opinion."

He said: "And Mālik was asked of the Fezzanese, who are a race from Abyssinia, and he said: 'I am of the opinion that they should not be fought until they are invited to Islam.'"

"Based on this statement made by Mālik, I am of the opinion that they should not be fought until they are invited [to Islam]; I am of the opinion that they are to be invited to Islam, and if they do not accept, they are to be invited to pay the *jizya* and be affirmed in their religion. If they agree, this is to be accepted from them."

This indicates Mālik's opinion on all nations; so if he said that the Fezzanese are to be invited [to Islam], then so too the [Slavs or Bulgars], the Avars, the Turks, and other non-Arabs who are not among the People of the Book.

From: al-Shaybānī, *Siyar*[78]

I asked: If the Arab polytheists refused to adopt Islam, do you think that they would be allowed to make peace with the Muslims and become Dhimmīs?

He replied: They should never be allowed to do so, but they would be invited to accept Islam. If they become Muslims, that would be acceptable on their part; otherwise, they should be forced to surrender because it has been related to us that such was the ruling and they should not [be treated] like other nonbelievers.

On the other hand, al-Shāfiʿī and Ibn Ḥazm argued that the sole reason for allowing the Zoroastrians to pay *jizya* was the scriptural foundation of their religion; consequently, all other non-Arabs were to be treated on par with the polytheist Arabs who had no scripture. Both jurists relied on a prophetic tradition instructing that the Magi receive the same treatment as the People of the Book to support their proposition.

From: al-Shāfiʿī, *al-Umm*, Vol. IV[79]

And the Magi followed a religion other than that of the idolaters, and were dissimilar from the Jewish and Christian People of the Book in some [aspects] of their religion, while the Jewish and Christian People of the Book disagreed on some [aspects] of their religion. And the Magi were on the periphery of the land, and the *salaf* (predecessors) of the Ḥijāz* knew not of their religion as they knew of the religion of the Christians and Jews until they came to know it, and they [the Magi] are – and Exalted God knows best – a People of the Book, joined in title, that they are "People of the Book" along with the Jews and Christians. . . .

And among this was reported of ʿAlī proof of what I have described, that the Magi are People of the Book, and proof that ʿAlī, may God ennoble his countenance, did not report that God's Apostle, God's blessings and peace be upon him, took the *jizya* from them [the Magi], save as People of the Book, nor did any [take the *jizya* from them save in recognition of their status as People of the Book] after him [the Apostle].

And if it were permissible to take the *jizya* from other than the People of the Book, ʿAlī would have said that the *jizya* is to be taken from them [the Magi] regardless of whether or not they are People of the Book. And I know of none among the Muslim *salaf* who declared it permissible to take the *jizya* from other than the People of the Book. . . .

God's Apostle, God's blessings and peace be upon him, declares, "Follow the same *sunna* with them that you would follow with the People of the Book."

Al-Shāfiʿī, may Exalted God have mercy upon him: "If it were a reliable [*ḥadīth*], then we would rule that the *jizya* should be taken from them because they are People of the Book, and not because it is said, if in fact he [the Apostle] said, 'Follow the same *sunna* with them that you would follow with the People of the Book,' – and Exalted God knows best – in the sense that their women are to be married and their slaughtered animals are to be eaten.

He said: "And if he meant all infidels other than the People of the Book, he would have said – and Exalted God knows best – 'Follow the same *sunna* with all infidels

---

* Arabian Peninsula.

that you would follow with the People of the Book,' but when he said 'Follow …
with them,' he specified them; and if he specified them, then others are in contradistinction [to this rule], and none are in contradistinction except for those who
are other than the People of the Book."

From: Ibn Ḥazm, *al-Muḥalla*, Vol. VII[80]

Naught is to be accepted from an infidel save Islam or the sword. Men and women
are, in this regard, alike, save for the People of the Book alone, and they are the
Jews, Christians, and the Magi only. For if they pay the *jizya*, they are affirmed on
that basis, and on being humbled.

And Abū Ḥanīfa and Mālik said: "As for those Arabs who are not among the People
of the Book specifically, it is either Islam or the sword. And as for the non-Arabs,
People of the Book or otherwise are alike, and all are affirmed on the basis of payment of *jizya*.

Abu Muḥammed [Ibn Ḥazm] said: "This is false, based on Exalted God's statement: 'Slay the idolaters wherever you find them, and take them, and confine
them, and lie in wait for them at every place of ambush. But if they repent, and
perform the prayer, and pay the alms, then let them go their way.' And Exalted
[God] said: 'Fight those who believe not in God and the Last Day and do not forbid what God and His Messenger have forbidden – such men as practice not the
religion of truth, being of those who have been given the Book – until they pay
the tribute out of hand and have been humbled.' So Exalted (God) did not distinguish Arab from non-Arab in both these rulings. And it has been verified that he
[the Apostle], peace be upon him, took the *jizya* from the Magi of Hajar, and thus
it was verified that they are among the People of the Book; had they not been so,
God's Apostle, God's blessings and peace be upon him, would not have contravened the scripture of his Exalted Lord."

But al-Shāfiʿī and Ibn Ḥazm were confronted with another obstacle to their claim of
inclusion of the Magi under the rubric of the People of the Book, which is effectively
a claim for exclusion of all other non-Arabs from the *jizya* regime, a regime definitely
perceived as a privilege in comparison with the other alternative. The challenge was the
general treatment of the Zoroastrians and whether or not they would be treated similar to the People of the Book in all other aspects of their life under the Muslim polity.
For example, the *Qurʾān* allowed Muslim men to marry women who belonged to the
People of the Book, but there was no existing tradition allowing Muslims to marry
Zoroastrian women. Ibn Ḥazm decided that his classification of the Zoroastrians as
a People of the Book should be upheld when addressing other areas of Islamic law,
thus allowing Muslim men to marry Magi women.[81] In contrast, al-Shāfiʿī appears
reluctant to allow his classification to influence other areas of the law. This led him
to create a subdivision within the category of People of the Book. On the one hand,
there were the Jews and Christians, whose women could be married. On the other
hand, there were the Zoroastrians, whose women should not be married. Al-Shāfiʿī
attempts to disguise the controversy of his claim by resorting to an assumed consensus

that Zoroastrian women are not to be married, but he fails to mention support for his claim of the existence of such consensus despite the fact that other jurists, such as Mālik and al-Shaybānī (who were both masters of al-Shāfiʿī), did not recognize them as a People of the Book.

From: al-Shāfiʿī, *al-Umm*, Vol. IV[82]

And I know of none who disagree that the womenfolk of the Magi are not to be wedded [by Muslims], nor are their slaughtered animals to be eaten, and so the consensus indicates that the rule concerning the People of the Book is twofold; that among them are those whose womenfolk can be wedded and whose slaughtered animals can be eaten, and those whose women are not to be wedded, and whose slaughtered animals are not to be eaten.

To avoid this controversy, Ibn Qudāma argued that the Zoroastrians had been treated as an exception due to the belief that they possibly had a scripture. This effectively created three legal categories of people: the clearly scriptured, the probably scriptured, and the unscriptured.

Ibn Qudāma, *al-Mughnī*, Vol. XIII[83]

The People of the Book and the Magi are to be fought until they convert to Islam or pay the *jizya* out of hand and are humbled; all others are to be fought until they convert to Islam.

In summation, the infidels are of three categories: The category of the People of the Book, and they are the Jews and Christians, and those who have taken the Torah and the Bible as scripture, such as the Samaritans, the Franks, and their like. The *jizya* is accepted from those, and they are affirmed in their religion if they pay it, due to Exalted God's saying: "Fight those who believe not in God and the Last Day and do not forbid what God and His Messenger have forbidden – such men as practice not the religion of truth, being of those who have been given the Book – until they pay the tribute out of hand and have been humbled."

[The second are] a category who have a semblance of scripture, and they are the Magi. The ruling pertaining to them is the same as that pertaining to the People of the Book in accepting the *jizya* from them, and affirming them [in their religion] by it, due to the declaration of the Prophet, God's blessings and peace be upon him: "Follow the *sunna* [with them] that you would follow with the People of the Book." And we know not of any disagreement between the learned pertaining to these two categories.

And a [third] category with no scripture, nor any semblance of scripture, and they are all save those [who fall in the aforementioned two categories], [i.e., they are the] idolaters, those who worship whatever they glorify, and all other infidels. The *jizya* is not accepted from them, and naught is accepted from them save conversion to Islam.

Obligations of Dhimmīs

Jurists also placed an obligation on the People of the Book or whoever was entitled to pay the *jizya*. Once the *jizya* was paid, these non-Muslims were believed to have signed a *dhimma* contract with the *Imām* that allowed them to live in Muslim lands, maintain their property, and enjoy protection as subjects of the *Imām*. But *jizya* payment signaled another important aspect of the contract, namely, *ṣighār* (humbling or subjugation). Whereas the *Qurʾān* is silent on what constituted *ṣighār*, jurists maintained that abiding by Muslim laws was a necessary constituent of the *dhimma* contract.

From: al-Shāfiʿī, *al-Umm*, Vol. IV[84]

And if the *Imām* surrounds a habitation before he takes its inhabitants captive, or if he manifestly vanquishes them and has not taken them captive, or if he is about to take them captive by encircling them in defeating them, and did not raid them due to their proximity, or their lack of numbers, or their great number, and his [forces'] strength, and they offer to pay the *jizya* if they are ruled by the laws of Islam, it becomes obligatory upon him to accept it from them.

And if they request that they pay [the *jizya*] without being ruled by the laws of Islam, he cannot do that, and he has to fight them until they convert to Islam or pay the *jizya* and are humbled by being ruled by the laws of Islam.

From: Ibn Ḥazm, *al-Muḥalla*, Vol. VII[85]

And "humbling" is that the law of Islam binds them, and that they make apparent naught of their disbelief, nor anything which is proscribed by the religion of Islam.

From: Ibn Qudāma, *al-Mughnī*, Vol. XIII[86]

It is not permissible to conclude a permanent *dhimma* contract, save with two conditions. The first: that they [the *dhimmīs*] commit to paying the *jizya* every year. The second: [that the *dhimmīs*] be bound by the laws of Islam, and that is to accept all that it enjoins upon them in terms of obligations or abandoning what is forbidden, due to Exalted God's declaration: "until they pay the tribute out of hand and have been humbled," and due to the Prophet's saying, God's blessings and peace be upon him, in the *hadīth* of Buraida: "Invite them to pay the *jizya*, and if they respond favorably, accept it from them and [keep] your hands from them."

Limitations on Dhimma Contracts

But jurists such as al-Shāfiʿī and Ibn Ḥazm were keen to limit the *jizya* regime for hegemonic interests (as discussed above). Accordingly, the two argued for more restrictive conditions that would have to be met in order for the People of the Book to be granted a *dhimma* contract. For example, al-Shāfiʿī held that only those (or their fathers) who had been People of the Book before the advent of Islam would be entitled to pay the *jizya*. Later converts to these monotheistic religions would be treated on par with the polytheistic infidels.

From: al-Shāfiʿī, *al-Umm*, Vol. IV[87]

The fundament upon which we base [our argument] is that the *jizya* is not to be accepted from any who take up the religion of the People of the Book, unless their parents or they themselves were of this religion before the revelation of the *Qurʾān*, and that it [the *jizya*] is to be accepted of all who remain as followers of their religion and the religion their fathers followed before the revelation of the *Qurʾān*, as long as they remain as followers of the religions from which the *jizya* is taken.

So if a Jew converts to Christianity, or Magianism, or if a Christian converts to Magianism, or a Zoroastrian converts to Christianity, or if any among them changes his religion to another religion from among [the religions of] the infidels which I have described, or to the denial of God's attributes, or otherwise, he is not to be slain, because the one to be slain is he who has left the true religion, which is Islam, for another.

And it is said [to the infidel who converts to another religion]: "If you return to your religion, we will take the *jizya* from you, and if you convert to Islam, we will absolve you from what you would have been expected to pay in [the] future, and we will take from you the portion of the *jizya*, which you were bound to pay until you became a Muslim or converted [to a different religion]. And if you convert to a religion besides Islam, we shall repudiate and expel you from the lands of Islam, because the territories of Islam are not a habitation for any save Muslims or those who have a covenant [with the Muslims], and it is not permissible for us to take the *jizya* from you while you follow a religion other than that which you followed when the *jizya* was first taken from you.

"And if we were to permit that, we would be permitting idolaters to become Christian today, or Jewish, or Magus, so that the *jizya* would be received from them, and the [obligation] to fight the infidels until they convert to Islam would be neglected."

Ibn Ḥazm offers even more restrictive conditions for *dhimma*. Most conditions advocated by Ibn Ḥazm have little or no textual basis despite his claim that he is a strong adherent of the Ẓāhirī literalist *madhhab*. First, he demands that the People of the Book acknowledge that Muḥammad is a prophet, which is arguably a requirement that fundamentally contradicts the belief system of many People of the Book. To prove his argument, he relies on an incident where a Jew acknowledged the prophethood of Muḥammad. Ibn Ḥazm argues that the incident supports his claim because the Prophet did not reprimand one of his companions for trusting the Jew when he called the Prophet by his name. But the same logic can be employed against Ibn Ḥazm's claim, since the Prophet did not reprimand the Jew for calling him by his name. In fact, the incident could arguably prove that the Prophet asserted the Jew's right to call him by his name as detailed below.

From: Ibn Ḥazm, *al-Muḥalla*, Vol. VII[88]

Thawbān, the freedman of the Apostle of God, God's blessings and peace be upon him, told him:* "I was with God's Apostle, God's blessings and peace be upon him, and a rabbi came and said: 'Peace be upon you, oh Muḥammed.' I pushed him so that he almost fell. He said: 'Why did you push me?' I said: 'Shouldn't you say "Oh Apostle of God"?' The Jew said, 'We call him by the name his family gave him.' So the Apostle of God, God's blessings and peace be upon him, said: 'My name is Muḥammed, which my family named me.'" And he recited the *ḥadīth*, adding at the end: "And the Jew said to him: 'Verily, you have spoken truth, and you are a prophet,' and he left."

And in this account, Thawbān, May God be pleased with him, struck the Jew for not saying "Apostle of God," and the Apostle of God, God's blessings and peace be upon him, did not denounce him for it. And therefore it is true that it is an obligatory right, as, if it had not been permissible he [the Apostle] would have denounced it, and the Jew said to him: "You are a prophet," and the Apostle of God, God's blessings and peace be upon him, did not oblige him to renounce his religion because of it.

And the *jizya* is not to be accepted from a Jew, a Christian, or a Magus, unless they acknowledge that Muḥammed is God's Apostle to us, and do not malign him, nor any part of the religion of Islam, based on the *ḥadīth* narrated by Thawbān, which we have previously cited, and based on exalted God's declaration: ". . . and thrust at your religion, then fight the leaders of unbelief; they have no sacred oaths," and that is the opinion of Mālik. He stated in the Mustakhraja:[89] "Whosoever from the *dhimmīs* states: 'Muḥammed was sent as an Apostle unto you, not unto us,' there is naught to be held against him." He said: "If he says: 'He was not a prophet,' he is to be slain."

Relief from the Jizya *Duty*

There is a general agreement by many jurists that women, children, and whoever was deemed by such jurists as belonging to a category of people who should not be killed willfully were relieved of the obligation to pay the *jizya*. This was because the *jizya* was levied primarily on persons whose lives could permissibly be taken. It was only by paying the *jizya* that their blood was inviolable.

From: Ibn Qudāma, *al-Mughnī*, Vol. XIII[90]

The *jizya* is not to be [imposed] upon a child, a madman, or a woman.

We know not of any disagreement among the learned about this, and it is also the opinion of Mālik, Abū Ḥanīfa and his companions, al-Shāfiʿī, Abu Thawr and Ibn al-Mundhir said: "I know not of any other who has disagreed with them."

---

* The transmitter of the *ḥadīth*.

> And the veracity of this [opinion] is attested to by the fact that 'Umar, may God be pleased with him, wrote to the leaders of the army to impose the *jizya*, but not to impose it on women and boys, and not to impose it on any save those who are old enough to shave.... [B]ecause blood money is taken to make their blood inviolable, and those [children, madmen, and women], their blood is inviolable without it [the paying of blood money].

But Ibn Ḥazm deviates from that agreement and argues that women ought to pay the *jizya* despite his claim that women may not be targeted intentionally. He also argues that humbling entails some level of constant inferiority within the Muslim state, such that People of the Book could not be allowed to employ Muslim servants, nor were they permitted to assume positions of power. No textual evidence was put forward by him to support this claim, however. This deviation seems to have resulted from his dislike of the practice whereby non-Muslims had ascended to positions of power in Muslim societies. In other words, Ibn Ḥazm's position on this matter is better interpreted as political rather than as based on an inference from the sources of the law.

From: Ibn Ḥazm, *al-Muḥalla*, Vol. VII[91]

And the *jizya* is equally compulsory, specifically upon those who have come of age, whether freemen among them or slaves, whether males or females, whether a destitute man or a wealthy monk, due to the statement of Exalted God: "until they pay the tribute out of hand and have been humbled." And there is no disagreement in that the religion obliges women as it obliges men, and there is no scriptural text indicating a difference between them in the payment of the *jizya*.

And "humbling" entails that they do no harm to a Muslim, nor take them as servants, and that none of them take a position of power in which their command would bind a Muslim.

Rules of Killing in War

Intentional Targeting

Most jurists agreed that there are restrictions on the intentional killing of particular categories of people in wartime. However, there was wide disagreement on who might count as an illegitimate target. Mālik, al-Shaybānī, and Ibn Qudāma prohibited killing people who were unable to fight, such as women, children, and the elderly, or even those who, by their role, were clearly uninterested in fighting, for instance, hired laborers and monks.

From: Mālik, *al-Mudawwana*, Vol. I[92]

I said: "Was Mālik of the opinion that slaying women, children, and old men in the Abode of War is reprehensible?"

He said: "Yes."

I said: "Was Mālik of the opinion that slaying monks is reprehensible?"

He said: "Yes, he was of the opinion that slaying monks secluded in cells and monasteries is reprehensible."

I said: "Do you suppose a monk should be slain?"

He said: "I heard Mālik say monks are not to be slain."

Mālik said: "And I am of the opinion that enough of their wealth is to be left to them to allow them to subsist. They should not take all their wealth and leave them with nothing to live off so that they would perish."

Ibn Wahb: "... When the Apostle of God, God's blessings and peace be upon him, dispatched a force, he would say: 'In the name of God, and in God's way: Do not transgress, do not commit treachery, do not mutilate, and do not slay children.'"

Mālik: "... God's Apostle, God's blessings and peace be upon him, forbade the band that slew Ibn Abū al-Ḥuqayq to slay women and children."

Mālik: "Additionally, of Nāfi', that the Apostle of God, God's blessings and peace be upon him, saw in some of his battles a slain woman, and he denounced that, and forbade that women and children be slain.". . .

[H]e* marched out with God's Apostle, God's blessings and peace be upon him, in a battle, in which Khālid Ibn al-Walīd was in the vanguard.

"Rabbāḥ and the companions of the Apostle, God's blessings and peace be upon him, passed by a slain woman, struck down by the vanguard. They stood around her, gazing upon her and wondering at her countenance, until God's Apostle, God's blessings and peace be upon him, caught up to them on his camel, so they parted around the woman.

"God's Apostle, God's blessings and peace be upon him, stood above her and said: 'Ah, this one should not have been fighting.'

"He said: Then he [the Apostle] looked into the faces of the crowd and said to one of them: 'Catch up to Khālid Ibn al-Walīd. He is not to slay a child or hired laborer.'"

From: al-Shaybānī, *Siyar* [93]

I heard the Apostle of God in the campaign against Banū Qurayẓa saying: "He [of the enemy] who has reached puberty should be killed, but he who has not should be spared."

He who related this tradition to Abū al-Zubayr, said that he had not reached puberty, so he was spared.

Whenever the Apostle of God sent forth a detachment he said to it: "Do not cheat or commit treachery, nor should you mutilate or kill children, women, or old men."

I asked: Do you think that the blind, the crippled, the helplessly insane, if taken as prisoners of war or captured by the warriors in a surprise attack should be killed?

He replied: [No], they should not be killed.

From: Ibn Qudāma, *al-Mughnī*, Vol. XIII[94]

If a fortress is conquered, males who have not reached puberty, grown facial hair, or reached the age of 15 are not [to] be slain.

---

* One of the Prophet's companions.

And the summation of this is that if the *Imām* is victorious over the infidels, it is not permissible for him to slay a prepubescent boy, and there is no disagreement on that.

And it was narrated by Ibn 'Umar, may God be pleased with him, "that God's prophet, God's blessings and peace be upon him, forbade the slaying of women and boys," unanimously agreed to be [an] authentic [*ḥadīth*], and because the boy becomes a slave in captivity, so slaying him would be destruction of property.

And if he is taken captive by himself, he becomes a Muslim, so to destroy him is to destroy one who can be made a Muslim.

The crippled, the blind, and monks are not to be slain. The disagreement in their regard is as the disagreement on the [slaying of] old men, and their evidence here is the same as there.

And our view of the crippled and the blind is that they are not combatants, and as such are similar to women. And in terms of monks, there is what was reported in the *ḥadīth* of Abū Bakr al-Ṣiddīq, may God be pleased with him, that he said: "And you will pass by a people in cells who have sealed themselves away within them. Leave them in their misguidedness until God takes them," and because they do not fight, in observance of their religion, and so are akin to those who cannot fight.... And slaves are not to be slain.

As for the sick man, he is to be slain if he is among those who, if they were [healthy], would have fought, because it is akin to slaying the wounded, unless his healing is despaired of, as then he is akin to the cripple and is not to be slain, because it is not feared that he may attain a condition in which he can fight....

As for the peasant who does not fight, he must not be slain, due to what was reported of 'Umar Ibn al-Khaṭṭāb, may God be pleased with him, that he said: "Be mindful of [the Will of] God in your treatment of peasants who do not make war on you."

By contrast, al-Shāfiʿī and Ibn Ḥazm proposed restrictions of a far more limited scope. Both jurists contended that the objective of *jihād* was not simply defensive – to fight those who fight Muslims – but also offensive, namely, the propagation of Islam. Accordingly, unless otherwise stipulated, as in the case of women and children, all other persons could be deemed legitimate targets in war. Accordingly, they dismissed the abovementioned viewpoint that prohibited the targeting of older men, hired laborers, monks, and peasants: all adult men could legitimately be targets of lethal attack.

From: al-Shāfiʿī, *al-Umm*, Vol. IV[95]

Those whom Glorified and Exalted Allah made it obligatory to fight until they pay the *jizya* are those who, when they came of age, [manifest] proof [of the veracity of Islam] was presented to them, but they left Glorified and Exalted Allah's religion and remained [followers of the religion] of their fathers from among the People of the Book.

And it is evident that those whom Allah commanded be fought over it [the *jizya*] are those who are fought; and they are adult males.

And it is not permissible for a Muslim to deliberately slay women and children, because God's Apostle, God's blessings and peace be upon him, forbade their slaying. It was reported to us ... that God's Apostle, God's blessings and peace be upon him, forbade those he dispatched to Ibn Abū al-Ḥuqayq from slaying women and children.

And the slaying of monks is to be eschewed, whether they are monks of the cells, or monks of the monasteries or deserts; all who seal themselves away for worship we eschew slaying them, in observance of the example of Abū Bakr, may God be pleased with him, and that is because, if it is within our rights to eschew slaying fighting men after overpowering them and [eschew] slaying men in some cases, then we are not held to be blameworthy by eschewing [slaying] the monks, God willing.

And indeed, we have stated this in [following an example], not through *qiyās*.* And if we claim that we eschew slaying monks because they are akin to noncombatants, then we would eschew slaying the sick when we raid them [the infidels], as well as monks, cowards, freemen, slaves and craftsmen who do not fight.

And if one were to ask: "What is the evidence that one who does not fight from among the infidels is to be slain?" it is to be said: "The companions of God's Apostle, God's blessings and peace be upon him, slew Darīd ibn al-Ṣama on the day of [the Battle of] Ḥunayn,[96] while he was prostrate in a litter and could not sit up, and was somewhere around 150 years old, and the Apostle of God, God's blessing and peace be upon him, did not denounce the slaying."

And I know of none among the Muslims who would denounce the slaying of infidel men other than monks. And if it were possible to denounce the slaying of those other than monks, on the basis that they are noncombatants, then captives would not be slain, nor would the immobile be [deliberately] wounded. And the wounded were dispatched in the presence of the Apostle of God, God's blessings and peace be upon him, including Abu Jahl ibn Hishām, who was dispatched by Ibn Masūd and others.

And if there was no evidence for eschewing the slaying of monks save what we have described, we would have despoiled them of all their property, in their cells and elsewhere, and left them nothing.

And peasants, hired laborers and old men are to be slain until they convert to Islam or pay the *jizya*.

In the above passages, al-Shāfi'ī is keen to advance his restrictive view of targeting, which led him to claim consensus on the permissibility of killing all adult men other than monks. As clarified from the above passages, al-Shaybānī and Mālik, both masters of al-Shāfi'ī, had prohibited the targeting of older men, and it is highly unlikely that al-Shāfi'ī was unfamiliar with their positions.

Moreover, monks appear to have been a problematic category for al-Shāfi'ī. While in the above passage he articulates a prohibition on killing them, later in the same

---

* Analogical deduction.

book he appears to reverse this position. This shift hinges on his interpretation of Abū Bakr's instructions, with the earlier passage maintaining that the jurist had placed them in the category of protected persons, a point that al-Shāfi'ī denied later. It is unclear which of the two positions was eventually held by al-Shāfi'ī, whose book, *al-Umm*, was revised and rewritten after he moved from Iraq to Egypt. Thus, both passages are cited below.

From: al-Shāfi'ī, *al-Umm*, Vol. IV[97]

For all those who are not Muslims and who inhabit the cells [monks], and others who follow the religion of the People of the Book, it must of necessity be either the sword, or the *jizya*.

On the day of [the Battle of] Ḥunayn, Durayd ibn al-Suna was slain at the age of 150 in a litter, and he was incapable of sitting up. This was mentioned to the Prophet, God's blessings and peace be upon him, and he did not denounce his slaying. And I know of no disagreement [on the subject of] monks, that they convert to Islam or pay the *jizya* or are slain. And the monks of the monasteries, cells, and homes are alike in this regard.

And I know of no [tradition] that establishes that Abū Bakr did otherwise. And if it was established, it would have been as though he had commanded them [the Muslim forces] to fight zealously [those] who fight them, and not to occupy themselves with remaining at their [the monk's] cells, as they are commanded not to remain at the [infidel's] fortresses, [but rather] to spread out, because they [the enemy's fortress] distract them [the Muslim forces], and to spread out because that is more injurious to the enemy, and not because fighting the inhabitants of the fortresses is forbidden to them, and because it is permitted to them [the Muslim forces] that they [inhabitants of the fortress] be left and not slain, then focusing on fighting those who fight them is more deserving of their attention.

From: Ibn Ḥazm, *al-Muḥalla*, Vol. VII[98]

And it is not permissible to slay their womenfolk, nor to slay those who have not reached puberty among them, unless one of the aforementioned fights so that a Muslim can find no salvation from him save by slaying him, in which case he is permitted to slay him. We have narrated ... that a slain woman was found in some of the Prophet's battles, God's blessings and peace be upon him, so God's Apostle, God's blessings and peace be upon him, denounced the slaying of women and boys. ...

And it is permissible to slay all – save the aforementioned – infidels, combatant or noncombatant, or merchant, or hired laborer (servant), or an old man, whether his advice [on military matters] is esteemed among them or not, or peasant, or bishop, or priest, or monk, or blind man, or cripple, with none spared. And it is also permissible to keep them alive; Exalted God said: "Slay the idolaters wherever you find them, and take them, and confine them, and lie in wait for them at every place of ambush."

Killing Untargetable Categories If They Fight

The restrictions imposed by jurists on targeting specific categories of people were far from static. On the mainstream view, individuals who were ordinarily counted among those protected would lose this immunity if they took part in armed hostilities. This participation was often expanded to include the provision of military advice and guidance, as well as other forms of support, psychological (morale boost to the fighting force or destruction of the morale of the adversary) or material, given to the enemy cause.

From: al-Shāfi'ī, *al-Umm*, Vol. IV[99]

And verily we eschew the slaying of their women and children based upon the report from God's Apostle, God's blessings and peace be upon him, that they are not among those to be fought. But if a woman or one who has not yet reached puberty fight, they [the Muslims] should not avoid smiting them with a weapon; this is because if one does not avoid [smiting] a Muslim who seeks to spill the blood of another Muslim, then the infidel woman or one who has not yet reached puberty among them [the infidels] [is] less deserving of being avoided [by Muslim warriors], as they would have abandoned the condition in which we were forbidden to slay them.

And if they are taken captive, or escape, or are wounded, and were among those who are not to be fought, then they are not to be slain, because they have departed from the condition in which the spilling of their blood was made permissible, and returned to the original ruling pertaining to them, that they are protected from being deliberately targeted for slaying.

From: Ibn Qudāma, *al-Mughnī*, Vol. XIII[100]

And whosoever among the aforementioned fights, it becomes permissible to slay them, because the Prophet, God's blessing and peace be upon him, on the Day of [the Battle of] Qurayẓa[101] slew a women who dropped a boulder on Maḥmūd Ibn Salma.

And whosoever among the aforementioned men is of [estimable] opinion [on military matters] and lends its aid in war, it becomes permissible to slay them, because Durayd ibn al-Suna was slain on the day of [the Battle of] Ḥunayn and he was an old man.

And if a woman stands among the ranks of the infidels or on their fortress and cursed the Muslims or exposed herself to them, it becomes permissible to fire upon her deliberately based on what Said reported: "... 'When God's Apostle, God's blessings and peace be upon him, laid siege to the people of al-Ṭā'if, a woman emerged and exposed her front, and she said: "Ah, this is beyond you; so shoot." So a man from among the Muslims shot her, and did not miss.'"

[I]t is likewise permissible to fire upon her if she collects arrows for them, waters them, or incites them to fight, because she would [come under the aegis] of the ruling on combatants, and such is also the rule for boys, old men, and all whom we are forbidden to slay among them [the infidels].

From: Ibn Ḥazm, *al-Muḥalla*, Vol. VII[102]

And it is not permissible to slay their womenfolk, nor to slay those who have not reached puberty among them, unless one of the aforementioned fights so that a Muslim can find no salvation from him save by slaying him, in which case he is permitted to slay him.

Killing Untargetable Categories during the Battle

Jurists also agreed that the accidental killing of women and children could be permitted, when this resulted as a side effect of using certain weapons on the battlefield. On this score there was a general consensus that even if fellow Muslims might thereby be harmed, such weapons could still be used. It should be noted, however, that jurists seemed keener on instructing the army to take precautions so as to protect fellow Muslims from harm, than on similarly protecting nontargetable infidels. This differentiation had little basis in the sources relied on, since killing within both categories was prohibited, apart from the accidental harm that was occasioned by measures needed to compel surrender. But the bias toward protection of Muslim life warranted more caution in jurisprudential litera-ture than the equally inviolable lives of women, children, and other categories perceived as untargetable. The situation most commonly envisioned by jurists was a besieged city that refused to surrender, and the subsequent use of mangonels and related weapons. As seen from passages below, the jurists were unequivocal in their support for the resort to indiscriminate weapons if children or any other inviolable persons were present, but they specifically instructed the army to attempt to avoid bringing harm on any Muslims who might be present in the besieged town.

Mālik, however, stands out as an exception to this position, as he is reported to have been reluctant to endorse indiscriminate targeting if Muslims or infidel children were present in a fortress. Nevertheless, Mālik's followers continued to assert that his tradition permitted the use of weapons that would harm indiscriminately.

From: Mālik, *al-Mudawwana*, Vol. I[103]

I said: "Suppose that men from among the infidels, in one of their fortresses, were besieged by the Muslims, and among them were Muslim captives they held. Should the fortress be burned down with those Muslim captives in it, or should the fortress be flooded?"

He said: "I heard Mālik when he was asked about a group of infidels at sea in their ships who took Muslim prisoners, and were then caught up by Muslims, and they wished to burn them and their ships with fire while the captives were in their ships.

He said: "Mālik said: 'I am not of the opinion that fire should be hurled at them,' and he forbade this.'

"Mālik said: 'God said to the people of Mecca: "Had they been separated clearly, then We would have chastised the unbelievers among them with a painful chastisement," meaning that the Prophet, peace be upon him, warded off [the painful chastisement] from the people of Mecca due to the presence of Muslims among them, and if the infidels had been separated clearly from the Muslims, he would have chastised them. That is the interpretation, and God knows best.'..."

I said: "Supposing that in this fortress besieged by us are the infidels' children and women, and it contains no Muslims. Should fire be set upon them so that the fortress is burned down, or should they be drowned?"

He said: "I know of nothing to recite in this regard, but I view that as reprehensible, and I do not like it."

I said: "Did you not tell me that Mālik said that there is nothing wrong with burning their fortresses and drowning them?"

He said: "That is when they are empty, and do not contain children. And that is permissible if it contains fighting men and they burn them. There is nothing wrong with that."

Ibn Wahb: "... Al-Ṣaʿb Ibn Jathāma said: 'Oh Apostle of God, our steeds in the chaos of the raid strike down the children of the infidels.' God's Apostle, God's blessings and peace be upon him, said: 'They are of them [the infidels],' or, 'They are with the fathers.'"

Ibn Wahb said: "And Hishām Ibn Saʿd told me similarly, of Ibn Shihāb."

Ibn Wahb: "Of Ismāʿīl ibn ʿAyāsh, who said: 'I heard our elders saying that the Apostle of God, peace be upon him, bombarded the people of al-Ṭāʾif with mangonels, and it was said to him: "Oh Apostle of God, there are women and children in it [the city]." So God's Apostle said: "They are of their fathers."'"

Unlike Mālik, al-Shaybānī argued that indiscriminate weapons could be utilized in a siege, regardless of the presence of slaves, women, old men, children, or Muslims. He justified such tactics on the basis that a total ban would halt most *jihād* operations, as protected persons were present in nearly all cities under attack. Al-Shaybānī did, however, express a need for greater caution when Muslim children were present; he accordingly instructed the army to avoid indiscriminate attacks if Muslim children were used as shields by the enemy.

From: al-Shaybānī, *Siyar* [104]

The army may launch the attack [on the enemy] by night or by day and it is permissible to burn [the enemy] fortifications with fire or to inundate them with water.

I asked: Would it be permissible to inundate a city in the territory of war with water[,] to burn it with fire or to attack [its people] with mangonels even though there may be slaves, women, old men, and children in it?

He [replied]: Yes, I would approve of doing all of that to them.

I asked: Would the same be true if those people have among them Muslim prisoners of war or Muslim merchants?

He replied: Yes, even if they had among them [Muslims], there would be no harm to do all of that to them.

I asked: Why?

He replied: If the Muslims stopped attacking the inhabitants of the territory of war for any of the reasons that you have stated, they would be unable to go to war at all, for there is no city in the territory of war in which there is no one at all of these you have mentioned.

I asked: If the Muslims besieged a city, and its people [in their defense] from behind the wall shielded themselves with Muslim children, would it be permissible for the Muslim [warriors] to attack them with arrows and mangonels?

He replied: Yes, but the warriors should aim at the inhabitants of the territory of war and not the Muslim children.

I asked: Would it be permissible for the Muslims to attack them with swords and lances if the children were not intentionally aimed at?

He replied: Yes.

I asked: If the Muslim [warriors] attack [a place] with mangonels and arrows, flood it with water, and burn it with fire, thereby killing or wounding Muslim children or men, or enemy women, old men, blind, crippled, or lunatic persons, would the [Muslim warriors] be liable for the *diyya** or the *kaffāra*?†

He replied: They would be liable neither for the *diyya* nor the *kaffāra*.

Al-Shāfiʿī's position on indiscriminate weaponry and tactics showed some ambivalence. On the one hand, he followed the same line of reasoning as al-Shaybānī, that is, in permitting indiscriminate measures when infidel women and children were present among the besieged enemy soldiers. But on the other hand, he showed himself more reserved than al-Shaybānī on the question of whether a town could be attacked when Muslims were present. However, he does indicate somewhat less reserve in another section of the same work, where he maintains that a Muslim army may be permitted to attack an enemy town despite the presence of infidel women, children, and captive Muslims, under the condition that every attempt is made to avoid bringing direct harm on these protected persons. It is noteworthy, however, that this qualification on the use of indiscriminate weapons in the presence of infidel women and children was brought up only when the situation also included the presence of captive Muslims.

From: al-Shāfiʿī, *al-Umm*, Vol. IV[105]

Al-Shāfiʿī said: "They are not to deliberately slay [the women and children], and it is permissible for Muslims to launch raids against them by night or day, and if they strike down any of the women or children, then neither blood money, nor retributive punishment, nor acts of expiation [are required].

---

* Blood money.
† Expiation or atonement.

"And if one were to ask: 'What is the evidence for this?' One would answer: 'It was reported to us ... that God's Apostle, God's blessings and peace be upon him, was asked of the infidel inhabitants of a habitation raided by night, and their women and children are struck down, and God's Apostle, God's blessings and peace be upon him, said: "They are of them."' And perhaps ... 'They are of their fathers.'"

Al-Shāfi'ī, may God have mercy upon him, said: "So if one were to say: 'God's Prophet, God's blessings and peace be upon him, said: "They are of their fathers,"' and it is said that no blood money, retributive punishment, or acts of expiation [are required]; if he says: 'Then why not deliberately slay them?' then it is to be said: 'Due to the Prophet's, God's blessings and peace be upon him, prohibition on deliberately [slaying them].' And if he were to say: 'Perhaps the two *hadīth*s are at odds?' then one would answer: 'Nay, their meaning is as I have described.' And if he were to say: 'What is the proof for what you have said?' one would say, God willing: 'If he has not forbidden night raids, it is understood that death might befall children and women.' And if he says: 'And did he [God's Apostle] raid by night or by day a people in their land, taking them at unawares?' one would say: 'Yes. It was reported to us ... that God's Apostle, God's blessings and peace be upon him, raided Banū al-Muṣṭaliq while they were at unawares and in comfort in al-Muraysi', and he slew the warriors and took the children captive.'"

And if the enemy entrench themselves on a mountain, in [a] fortress, trench or within palisades, or in anything else in which they can fortify themselves, there is nothing wrong with bombarding them with mangonels, catapults, fire, scorpions, and serpents, and all that they detest, and that they would breach the riverbanks to drown them or bury them [in a mudslide], irrespective of whether they have children, women, and monks with them, because the habitation is not inviolable, either by virtue of Islam [that the owners or inhabitants are Muslim] or by covenant.

And if one were to say: "What is the proof for what you say, when they have children and women among them, the slaying of whom is forbidden?" one would say: "The proof is that God's Apostle, God's blessings and peace be upon him, used mangonels or catapults against the people of al-Ṭā'if, and we know that among them were women and children, and that God's Apostle, God's blessings and peace be upon him, cut and burned down the property of the Banū al-Naḍīr."...

And if one were to say: "The prohibition [was revealed] after the burning of Banū al-Naḍīr's property," it is said to him, Exalted God willing: "It was prohibited because Exalted and Glorified God promised it [the property] to him [the Apostle], so burning it would be destroying his own property, and this is known, from a number of traditions, to the scholars of the prophet's battles."

And if one were to say: "Did he [God's Apostle] burn or cut down [property or orchards] after that?" it is said: "Yes, he cut down [date palms] in Khaybar, and that was after [the assault on] Banū al-Naḍīr, and in al-Ṭā'if, which was the last battle he led in which he was met with fighting."

And if one were to say: "How do you declare it permissible to fire mangonels and flame at a band of infidels among whom are children and women, whose slaying is prohibited?" it is said: "We declared it permissible based on what we have described, and because the Prophet, God's blessings and peace be upon him, launched a surprise attack on Banū al-Muṣṭaliq, and commanded that they be raided by night, [and their dwellings] burned, and it was known that there were children and women among them. This was because the habitation was an abode of idolatry, which is not inviolable. Indeed, what was prohibited was to deliberately target women and children for slaying, if their slayer can make them out individually, based on what was reported of the Prophet, God's blessings and peace be upon him.

If there were in the habitation Muslim captives or merchants granted *amān*, then I would be of the opinion that it is reprehensible [to use mangonels] against them, with what that entails of widespread burning and drowning, and similar [methods] that are not expressly prohibited. That is because it is not established that a habitation that is otherwise permissible to attack becomes forbidden due to the presence of a Muslim, whose blood is inviolable, within it, but I am of the opinion that it is reprehensible as a precaution, and because it is permitted to us to leave it be without attacking it, even if it had no Muslims in it.

And if we [choose] to attack it, we should attack it [with methods] other than those which [inflict] widespread damage from burning and drowning.

From: al-Shāfiʿī, *al-Umm*, Vol. IV[106]

If there are women, children and Muslim captives in the infidels' fortress there is nothing wrong with using catapults against the fortress, but not the homes inhabited by the inhabitants, unless the Muslims are in battle near the fortress, [in which case] there is nothing wrong with bombarding its houses and walls.

And if there are entrenched warriors within the fortress, the houses and fortifications are to be bombarded. And if they use Muslim or non-Muslim children as human shields while the Muslims are in battle, then there is nothing wrong with targeting the [infidel] warriors, but not the Muslims and children.

And if they [the Muslims] are not in battle, I favor that they [the infidels] be left alone until it is possible to fight them without their human shields.

Ibn Qudāma distinguishes between weapons that typically have indiscriminate effects, such as mangonels, and intentionally indiscriminate tactics such as burning a town or flooding a territory. He argues that mangonels are similar to arrows and lances; their use is permissible subject to military necessity. By contrast, burning and flooding are prohibited if alternative, discriminate tactics are available that would guarantee victory over the enemy. But Ibn Qudāma nonetheless adheres to the established tradition of double standard regarding the unintentional killing of protected persons. Whereas attacks may be carried out that result in side-effect harm to such persons on the enemy side, he emphasizes that Muslim fighters should refrain from shooting at the enemy when Muslim women and children are present, unless this is strictly necessary to assure the success of the operation.

From: Ibn Qudāma, *al-Mughnī*, Vol. XIII[107]

As for the enemy who is in one's power, it is impermissible to burn them with fire, and there is no disagreement on this of which we are aware.

And Abū Bakr used to command that the apostates be burned with fire, and Khālid Ibn al-Walīd did this by his command, but today, I know of no disagreement among people on this matter [being impermissible]. . . .

And alike is the ruling for breaching the river banks to drown them; if it is possible to defeat them otherwise, then it is impermissible [to drown them].

If this entails destroying women and children, whom it is forbidden to deliberately destroy, and if they cannot be defeated save by it [breaching the river banks], it becomes permissible, as do night raids, which entail the same [destruction of women and children], are permissible.

And it is permissible to use mangonels against them. And what is apparent of Ahmed's opinions is the permissibility [of their use], whether necessary or not, because the Prophet, God's blessings and peace be upon him, used mangonels against the people of al-Ṭā'if, and . . . because their [mangonels'] use in fighting is conventional, it is similar to the firing of arrows.

And if in war they use their women and boys as human shields, it becomes permissible to shoot at them, and to aim at combatants, because God's Prophet, God's blessings and peace be upon him, bombarded them with mangonels while women and boys were with them, and because if the Muslims had ceased [hostilities], it would have led to a stalling of the *jihād*, because once they [the infidels] had learned of this, they would have used them [women and boys] as human shields whenever they were in fear, so the *jihād* would end.

And it is [permissible] irrespective of whether the battle is joined or not, because the Prophet, God's blessing and peace be upon him, did not wait for the battle to be joined to fire [the mangonels].

And if they take a Muslim as a human shield, and there is no necessity to shoot at them because the war is not being waged, or because it is possible to defeat them without doing so, or to be secure from their menace, then it is impermissible to shoot at them. And if they [the Muslims] shoot at them, and a Muslim is struck, then he [the *Imām*] must undertake to pay his blood money.

And if necessity demands that they be shot at, out of fear for the Muslims, it becomes permissible to shoot at them because it is a state of necessity, and the intention should be [to strike down] the infidels.

And if there is no fear for the Muslims but they [the infidels] cannot be defeated without shooting at them, al-Awzā'ī and al-Layth said: "It is impermissible to fire upon them, due to God's declaration: 'If it had not been for certain men believers [and certain women believers whom you knew not, lest you should trample them, and there befall you guilt unwittingly on their account (that God may admit into His mercy whom he will), had they been separated clearly, then we would have chastised the unbelievers among them with a painful chastisement].'"[108]

Al-Layth said: "Forgoing the conquest of a fortress that it is possible to conquer is preferable to unjustly slaying a Muslim." And al-Awzāʿī said: "How can they [the Muslims] shoot at what they cannot see? Indeed, they are shooting at the children of the Muslims."

Ibn Ḥazm is relatively succinct on the issue of unintentional damage inflicted upon those who may not be intentionally targeted, women and children in his case, and simply argues that they may be killed during an indiscriminate night raid or during the battle itself, leaving open the question of resort to tactics that are by their nature indiscriminate.

From: Ibn Ḥazm, *al-Muḥalla*, Vol. VII[109]

So if they are unintentionally struck down during a night raid or in the tumult of battle, there is naught wrong in that. We have narrated … that God's Apostle, God's blessings and peace be upon him, was asked about the members of a household of the infidels raided by night, and their children and women are smitten, and he said: "They are of their fathers."

War Captives

Enslavement

It is commonly argued that Islam intended to abolish slavery gradually by prohibiting most justifications for enslavement other than those arising from armed conflict.[110] Moreover, the *Qurʾānic* text that reads: "When you meet the unbelievers, smite their necks, then, when you have made wide slaughter among them, tie fast the bonds; then set them free, either by grace or ransom, till the war lays down its loads"[111] makes no reference to enslavement, and there are numerous accounts that the prophet and the companions took slaves.[112] Jurists typically examined slavery in their discussion of the norms of war that were applicable to war captives. Slavery as an outcome of military conquest was a common practice in premodern times across the world. In this context, virtually all jurists permitted the enslavement of men, women, and children from among the defeated enemy. In fact, it is rather difficult to find any reference to a debate on the justifiability of this practice, since the issue appears to have been taken for granted. Debates focused rather on the proper treatment of enslaved captives, the permissibility of exercising grace vis-à-vis different categories of captives, as well as rules relating to the division of spoils.

From: al-Shaybānī, *Siyar*[113]

I asked: If the Dhimmīs violated their covenant and fought the Muslims, do you think that their status would be equivalent to that of the apostates who go over to the *dār al-ḥarb*?

He replied: Yes.

I asked: Would their women and children be taken as captives?

He replied: Yes.

From: al-Shaybānī, *Siyar*[114]

Do you think that the *Imām* should divide up the captives before the believers returned to the territory of Islam, if the believers need them?

He replied: No.

I asked: What should the *Imām* do with the captives if the believers do not need them? Should he sell them?

He replied: If I held that it would be permissible for the *Imām* to sell them [before the believers returned to the territory of Islam], I should hold that it would be permissible for him to divide them up [there].

From: al-Shāfiʿī, *al-Umm*, Vol. IV[115]

And if the idolaters or People of the Book are fought, they are to be slain, and their children and those who have not reached puberty among them, and their women, those who have reached puberty and those who have not, are taken captive, and they all became booty, with a fifth of them to be separated, and four-fifths divided upon those who rode against them on horseback or mounted.

And if they slaughtered and vanquished those whom they fought until they overwhelmed their lands, their homes and land are divided as one would divide dinars and dirhams; there is no difference.

From: al-Shāfiʿī, *al-Umm*, Vol. IV[116]

And if the *Imām* takes captive a group from the People of the Book and it includes their women and children, and they [the male infidels] ask him that they be released, along with their women and children, in return for paying the *jizya*, he cannot do so for their women and children, nor for their children and property under his control.

And if they ask him to pay the *jizya* at that time, it is not to be accepted from them because they have become spoils or booty.

From: al-Shāfiʿī, *al-Umm*, Vol. IV[117]

The children and women of monks are to be taken captive, if they are not themselves monks [or nuns]. And the basis for this is that Exalted and Glorified Allah declared the property of the infidels permissible [to take].

And if one were to say: "Then why do you not declare his [the monk's] property inviolable?" it is said, "As I do not declare the property of an infant or a woman inviolable, while I declare their blood inviolable."

And I favor that, if the women have become nuns, they are left [unmolested], as I would leave the men [unmolested].

From: Ibn Qudāma, *al-Mughnī*, Vol. XIII[118]

And if the *Imām* takes captives, he has the choice, if he is of the opinion [that it is fitting], to slay them, and if he is of the opinion [that it is fitting], to show grace to them and release them for nothing in exchange, and if he is of the opinion [that it is fitting], to release them in exchange for money to be taken from them, and if he is of the opinion [that it is fitting], to exchange them for [captured Muslims], and if he is of the opinion [that it is fitting], to enslave them. Whichever of these options he believes is most detrimental to the enemy and beneficial to the Muslims, he should do.

And the summation is that whosoever is taken captive from the people of the Abode of War is one of three things: one [category] is women and children, and it is impermissible to slay them, and they became slaves to the Muslims through captivity: "Because Allah's Prophet, Allah's blessings and peace be upon him, forbade the killing of women and children." [This *ḥadīth*] is agreed to be authentic. And he [the Apostle], peace be upon him, would enslave them if he took them captive.

The second: Men of the People of the Book and the Magi, who are affirmed [in their religion] by the *jizya*, and the *Imām* has one of four choices regarding them: Slaying them; showing them grace with nothing sought in exchange; exchanging them [for a ransom or Muslim captives]; and enslavement.

The third: Men of the Idolaters and others who receive no affirmation [in their religion] through payment of the *jizya*. The *Imām* has one of three choices regarding them: Slaying them, showing them grace, or [demanding a] ransom. It is not permissible to enslave them.

And it was reported that Aḥmad [was of the opinion that] it is permissible to enslave them, and that it is the opinion of [the] al-Shāfi'ī *madhhab*....

And as evidence for the permissibility of showing grace and demanding a ransom for their release, we have Exalted Allah's saying: "either by grace or ransom," and that "the Prophet, Allah's blessings and peace be upon him, showed grace ..., and said of the captives of [the Battle of] Badr: 'If Muṭ'im ibn 'Udaiy was alive and asked me for any of those stinkards, I would have freed them for him.'" And he took a ransom for the captives of [the Battle of] Badr, and they were seventy three men, 400 dirhams for every man of them. And on the day of [the Battle of] Badr, he exchanged one [infidel] man for two [Muslim men]....

And because each part of these parts may be more suitable in dealing with some captives – for among them may be a mighty one who would inflict great damage upon the Muslims, and his continued existence would be detrimental to them, and so slaying him would be more advantageous; and among them is the weak one who is wealthy, and so demanding a ransom for his release would be more advantageous; and among them is one who holds favorable opinions of the Muslims and it is hoped that showing him grace would lead to his conversion to Islam or to his helping the Muslims by freeing their captives or defending them, and so showing him grace is more advantageous; and among them is one who could be of benefit if kept to serve, as well as securing Muslims from his menace, so enslaving him is more advantageous, such as with women and children – and the *Imām* knows best where lies the greatest advantage, so this matter must be turned over to him.

And Exalted [Allah's] saying: "Slay the idolaters," is general, and does not abrogate specific verses, but is in fact applied to all save those excepted [i.e., those from whom the *jizya* is taken], and this is why they did not declare it prohibited to enslave them.

And as for the idolaters, there are two opinions regarding their enslavement: One is that it is impermissible, and this is the opinion of al-Shāfi'ī. And Abū Ḥanīfa said: "It is permissible [to do so to] non-Arabs, but not to the Arabs," based on his opinion regarding [whom] the *jizya* may be taken from.

And it is our opinion that he [the captive] is an infidel who cannot be affirmed through the [taking of the] *jizya* [from him], and so, like apostates, cannot be affirmed through enslavement, and we have cited evidence for this.

If this is established, then it is a matter of choosing the greatest advantage and exercising *ijtihād*,[119] and not a matter of choosing based on personal desires. Whenever he sees advantage in one of these parts, it is obligatory on him to select it, and it becomes impermissible to stray from it. And whenever he hesitates, then priority is given to slaying them.

And if the captives from the People of the Book ask to be released in exchange for paying the *jizya*, this is impermissible for their women and children, because they have become spoils of war through capture. As for the men, it is permissible, without removing the established options [for dealing with] them.

And as for those whom it is forbidden to slay, other than women and children, such as old men, the crippled, the blind and monks, it is impermissible to take them captive because slaying them is forbidden and there is no benefit in taking them.

From: Ibn Ḥazm, *al-Muḥalla*, Vol. VII[120]

And whosoever was enslaved from the people of war's young is a Muslim, regardless of whether he was enslaved with his parents, with one of them, or without them.

Killing Captives

Whether war captives could be killed was extensively discussed by jurists. Most prohibited the killing of women and children who had been taken captive. Mālik and al-Shāfi'ī did not allow for killing captives unless they were proven dangerous. On the other side of the spectrum, al-Shaybānī argued that captive men should not be ransomed or shown grace; they should rather be enslaved or killed. Ibn Qudāma claimed that all male captives could rightly be killed. Ibn Ḥazm was surprisingly silent on the matter despite his work being more recent than Mālik, al-Shaybānī, and al-Shāfi'ī, which means he must have been familiar with the debate on killing captives. It could be argued that this silence was triggered by Ibn Ḥazm's unwillingness to acknowledge the possibility of allowing men to live, unless they were People of the Book who had agreed to pay the *jizya*, but the above statement made by Ibn Ḥazm on a minor enslaved with both parents indicates acknowledgment of the possibility of enslaving adult men.

From: Mālik, *al-Mudawwana*, Vol. I[121]

I said: "Supposing the *Imām* took captives, did you hear Mālik say it was the Imām's prerogative, if he wishes, to smite their necks, and if he wishes, to let them live and take them as booty?"

He said: "I heard him say 'he who is to be feared is to be slain.'"

He said: "Did you see Mālik avoid addressing the slaying of those who are not to be feared among them, such as an old man or a child?

Saḥnūn said: "Did you not see what afflicted the Muslims from Abu Lu'lu'a? If he is one of those who despise the religion, who feel enmity toward its adherents and love its enemies, and it is feared that you will never feel secure from his menace, then that is the one to be slain. Other than that, they are the vitals, and for them the infidels fought; they are property, and are to be desired, and in them is the strength to fight idolatry.

From: al-Shaybānī, *Siyar*[122]

[A commander] wrote to [the Caliph] Abū Bakr inquiring whether a prisoner of war taken from the Rūm* might be ransomed. He replied that he should not be ransomed, even at the price of two mudds of gold, but that he should be either killed or become a Muslim. . . .

al-Ḥasan [b. al-Ḥasan al-Baṣrī] and 'Aṭā' b. Abī Rabāḥ, both of whom said: The prisoner of war should not be killed, but he may be ransomed or set free by grace.

However, Abū Yūsuf held that the opinions of al-Ḥasan and 'Aṭā' did not count for anything [on this matter].

He replied: If [the *Imām*] possesses surplus means of transport he should use it to carry [the captives]; if there is none he should see if there is any surplus means among the Muslims. If he finds such means he should get them to carry it with them of their own free will.

I asked: If neither the *Imām* nor the Muslims possess surplus means of transport but some [private] individuals among them [have their own means], should the *Imām* cause the spoil to be transported on the animals belonging to those particular persons?

He replied: Yes, provided those persons are willing to do so. Otherwise, the *Imām* should hire means of transport rather than force the owners of private means to carry the spoil. As to the captives, the *Imām* should oblige them to go on foot if they are able to do so.

I asked: And if they are unable to walk?

* The Byzantines.

He replied: He [the *Imām*] should kill the men and spare the women and children, for whom he should hire means for carrying them.

I asked: If male captives of war were taken from the territory of war, do you think that the *Imām* should kill all or divide them as slaves among the Muslims?

He replied: The *Imām* is entitled to a choice between taking them to the territory of Islam to be divided [among the warriors] and killing them [while in the territory of war].

I asked: Which is preferable?

He replied: [The *Imām*] should examine the situation and decide whatever he deems to be advantageous to the Muslims.

I asked: If killing them were advantageous to the Muslims, [do you think that the *Imām*] should order their killing?

He replied: Yes.

I asked: If all of them became Muslims, would he be entitled to kill them?

He replied: He should not kill them if they became Muslims, they should be regarded as booty to be divided among the Muslims.

From: al-Shāfiʿī, *al-Umm*, Vol. IV[123]

And if men who have reached puberty are taken captive, then the *Imām* decides whether to slay them, if the idolaters do not convert to Islam, or if the People of the Book do not pay the *jizya*, or to show them grace [release them for nothing in exchange], or to demand that they pay a ransom to go free, or exchange them for Muslim captives, or to enslave them. . . .

And if one were to say: "How is it that you applied one ruling to property, children, and women, and applied multiple rulings to the men?" It is to be said: "God's Apostle, God's blessings and peace be upon him, took captive the children of Banū al-Muṣṭaliq and Hawāzin and their women, and divided them as one would divide money. And God's Apostle, God's blessings and peace be upon him, took captive the men of [the Battle] of Badr, and there were among them those whom he showed grace with nothing in return, and there were those whom he took a ransom from, and those whom he slew.

From: al-Shāfiʿī, *al-Umm*, Vol. IV[124]

And he has the right, as he would, to slay, show grace, or demand a ransom for the release of their adult freemen specifically, because God's Apostle, God's blessing and peace be upon him, showed grace [to some captives], and demanded a ransom for the release [of other captives], and slew captives, and Exalted and Glorified God has made permissible the showing of grace and the demanding of a ransom for their release, saying: "smite their necks, then, when you have made wide slaughter among them, tie fast the bonds; then set them free, either by grace or ransom."

If infidels are taken captive, and they are in the power of the *Imām*, then there are two rulings [that can be] applied to them. As for the adult men, the *Imām* may slay them, or some of them, or may show them grace, or show some of them grace, and he is not obliged to compensate any for whichever alternative he selects, whether they [the captive infidels] were captured by the public or by an individual, or whether they surrendered conditionally, or whether [one of the Imām's] walis [lieutenants] captured them.

Al-Shāfi'ī said: "And he should not slay them unless by examining the circumstances of the Muslims [he determines] that [in so doing he] is strengthening Exalted and Glorified God's religion and weakening His foes, enraging and slaying them in every permissible fashion.

And he should not show them grace unless he sees reason to do so, [such as that] the conversion to Islam of one of those to whom he has shown grace is to be hoped for, or that he may turn the infidels away from the Muslims, or frustrate their plans against the Muslims, or terrify them in any way.

And if he does so [shows the captive infidels grace] for other reasons, I view it as reprehensible for him, and he is not obliged to compensate any.

And he also has the right to exchange them for Muslims; if he has the right to show them grace [by releasing them] with no benefit, then priority must be given to his gaining the benefit.

From: Ibn Qudāma, *al-Mughnī*, Vol. XIII[125]

And it was reported that al-Ḥasan, 'Aṭṭā' and Sa'īd Ibn Jubayr were of the opinion that slaying captives is reprehensible. They said: "If only he would show grace or demand a ransom for their release, as was done with the captives of [the Battle of] Badr, because Exalted God said: 'tie fast the bonds; then set them free, either by grace or ransom,' and [the Apostle] was given the choice between these two [options] after capturing [the infidels], none other."

And *ahl al-ra'y** said: "If he wishes, he can smite their necks, and if he wishes, he can enslave them; none other. And it is impermissible to show grace or demand a ransom for their release, for Exalted God said: 'slay the idolaters wherever you find them' after he said: 'then set them free, either by grace or ransom.'"

And 'Umar Ibn Abdul 'Azīz and 'Ayāḍ Ibn 'Uqba would slay captives....

As for slaying, it is because the Prophet, God's blessings and peace be upon him, slew the men of Banū Qurayẓa, and they were between 600 and 700, and on the day of [the Battle of] Badr, he executed al-Naḍir ibn al-Ḥārith and 'Uqba ibn Abū Mu'yaṭ, and he slew Abū 'Uza on the day of [the Battle of] Uḥud.

Property of the Enemy

Seizure of Property

Seizure of property belonging to the defeated enemy was approached in a manner very similar to enslavement. It was an accepted practice that required little or no justification. This

---

* People of opinion, referring to the Ḥanafīs.

was most often discussed when scholars considered the rules that should govern the division of war spoils among soldiers. Below is a representative sampling of passages on this topic.

From: Mālik, *al-Mudawwana*, Vol. I[126]

I said: "Supposing that the Muslims despoil [the enemy], does Mālik view it as reprehensible for them to apportion the spoils in the Abode of War?"

He said: "The matter for Mālik is that it should be apportioned in the Abode of War and sold."

He then said: "And Mālik argued in its favor and would say, 'They are more deserving of its licenses.'"

He said: "And Mālik said the spoils are to be apportioned and sold in the Abode of War."

From: al-Shaybānī, *Siyar*[127]

The one-fifth [share of the spoil] was divided in the time of the Apostle of God into five parts: one for God and the Apostle, one for the near of kin, one for the poor, one for the orphans, and one for the wayfarer.

The Apostle of God divided the spoil [of the campaign of Ḥunayn] at al-Ji'rāna after his return from al-Ṭā'if. As to Khaybar, the Prophet conquered it and his rule prevailed over it. So the Apostle of God divided up the spoils there before he left the town. He also divided the spoil of [the tribes of] Banū al-Muṣṭaliq in their land after he had conquered it.

I asked: If the *Imām* attacked an enemy territory and took possession of it, do you think that he should divide the land [among the warriors] as he divides the spoils of war?

He replied: The *Imām* is free either to divide the land into five shares. Distributing the four-fifths among the warriors who participated in conquering it, or not to divide it up [i.e., hold it as state-owned land] as [the Caliph] 'Umar did [in the case of] the land of al-Sawād of [southern Iraq].

From: al-Shāfiʿī, *al-Umm*, Vol. IV[128]

And as such, anything of the property of the infidels that is brought under control [of the Muslims], be it small or great, land, abode or otherwise, there is no difference, because it is booty, and Exalted and Glorified God's decree pertaining to booty is that it be divided into fifths.

And God's Apostle, God's blessings and peace be upon him, clarified that four-fifths are for those who rode against [the enemy] on horseback or mounted.

And if the Muslims take control of part of the infidels' territory so that it may be strengthened against the infidels, even if they do not meet the infidels in battle, then it is a conquered land that must be apportioned, with four-fifths apportioned to those who rode against [the enemy] on horseback or mounted, if there are dwellings upon it or if the land has value.

From: Ibn Qudāma, *al-Mughnī*, Vol. XIII[129]

It is permissible to apportion the spoils of war in the Abode of War ... because it is an issue for one to exercise *ijtihād* upon, so if the *Imām* rules regarding [the spoils] in a manner that concurs with the opinions of some of the scholars, his ruling is upheld.

And we have what was reported of Abu Ishāq al-Farāzī, who said: "I said to al-Awzā'ī, 'Did God's Apostle, God's blessings and peace be upon him, divide any of the spoils in Medina?' He said: 'I am not aware of that. People used to follow their spoils and divide them up in the land of their enemy, and God's Apostle would never return from a battle in which spoils were taken until he had divided them [the spoils] into fifths and apportioned them before returning; such was the case in the battles of Banū al-Mustaliq, Hawāzin and Khaybar.'"

And because the division is legitimate in each abode where it is permissible, as in the Abode of Islam, and because ownership was established there by vanquishment and capture, then its division is legitimate as though it were brought under control in the Abode of Islam.

From: Ibn Hazm, *al-Muhalla*, Vol. VII[130]

Whosoever slays one among the infidels has the right to despoil him of his property, small or great, whether the *Imām* has declared this or not, and irrespective of whether he killed him on the battlefield or caused his delayed death. If he [the person claiming to have killed the infidel] will not be believed except if he presents proof of his claim, and he has no proof, and fears that it shall be taken from him or that *khums*[131] will be levied on it, it is proper for him to conceal and hide it. And despoiled property is: the slain man's mount, his saddle, his bridle, all apparel, jewelry, and spurs upon him, any weapons with him, all the money in his belt or in his hand, or however else he has it.

Destruction of Property

At a time where military might was understood to emanate from the overall resources of the enemy community, many jurists were willing to acknowledge the legitimacy of destroying such property in wartime. In this connection, jurists were obliged to consider the prohibition that Abū Bakr had enjoined upon the Muslim army in the Levant, against cutting down or burning trees, or killing animals. This restrictive teaching was usually mitigated in a manner to avoid its general application to the regime of armed conflict. It was typically argued that these prohibitions applied specifically to warfare in the Levant, as this was a region that had been promised to the Muslims (to destroy property there would deprive Muslims of their rightful inheritance). The only exception in the jurisprudence reproduced below was from the pen of Ibn Qudāma, who argued that unless strictly necessary, or carried out as retaliation for enemy practice, trees and crops should not be destroyed.

Jurists gave special consideration to destruction wrought upon animals or anything that has a "soul." Al-Shāfi'ī and Ibn Hazm argued that it was prohibited to kill animals if they were not meant to be eaten, stating that whatever advantage might be gained from the killing was outweighed by the wrongness of the act. Ibn Qudāma's position oscillated between prohibition and recognition of the need to kill enemies' animals for military objectives, arguing that if there is no armed conflict, animals should not be killed even to spite an enemy, whereas during war it was permissible to kill animals, when necessary, in the heat of battle.

From: Mālik, *al-Mudawwana*, Vol. I[132]

"Was Mālik of the opinion that it is reprehensible to burn their villages and fortresses with fire or drown them with water?"

He said: "Mālik said there is nothing wrong with burning their villages and fortresses with fire and drowning them with water and ruining them."

Saḥnūn said: "And the basis of what was said of Abū Bakr, may God be pleased with him, of his prohibiting the chopping down of trees and ruining of buildings, is that this was not an act of consideration by Abū Bakr, may God have mercy upon him, toward idolatry and its adherents, nor protection of them, or warding [harm] from them, but rather he wished to show consideration of Islam and Muslims, and enfeeble idolatry. He hoped that it would become [property] of the Muslims; ruining it would weaken the Muslims, [by ruining] what he hoped would belong to the Muslims.

I said: "Cattle, sheep, beasts, food, weapons, and the property of the [Byzantines], their beasts, cattle, and food, and all that the Muslims cannot carry of their possessions, and their mounts that halt and refuse to go on.... What should they do with all these, in the opinion of Mālik?"

He said: "Mālik said: 'They should hamstring the mounts, or slaughter them, as well as the cows and sheep.'"

He said: "As for the possessions and weapons, Mālik said they are to be burned."

I said: "And the mounts, cattle, and sheep ... should they be burned after being hamstrung?"

He said: "I did not hear him say they should be burned."

He said: "And Mālik said of the man whose mount would not go on, that he should hamstring or kill it, and not leave it for the enemy to benefit from."

From: al-Shaybānī, *Siyar*[133]

I asked: If the believers in the territory of war capture spoil in which there are [animals such as] sheep, riding animals, and cows which resist them and they are unable to drive them to the territory of Islam, or weapons which they are unable to carry away, what should they do [with them]?

He replied: As to weapons and goods, they should be burned, but riding animals and sheep should be slaughtered and then burned.

I asked: Why should not [the animals] be hamstrung?

He replied: Because that is mutilation, which they should not do because it was prohibited by the Apostle of God. However, they should not leave anything that the inhabitants of the territory of war could make use of....

I asked: Do you think that it is objectionable for the believers to destroy whatever towns of the territory of war that they may encounter?

He replied: No. Rather do I hold that this would be commendable. For do you not think that it is in accordance with God's saying, in His Book: "Whatever palm trees you have cut down or left standing upon their roots, had been by God's permission, in order that the ungodly ones might be humiliated." So, I am in favor of whatever they did to deceive and anger the enemy.

From: al-Shāfiʿī, *al-Umm*, Vol. VII[134]

I asked Al-Shāfiʿī about a band who enter the Abode of War, should they tear down habitations, cut down fruit-bearing trees and burn them, and palm trees and [slay] cattle, or is all this reprehensible?

Al-Shāfiʿī, may God have mercy upon him said: "As for all that has no soul, such as fruit-bearing trees, habitations and otherwise, they may destroy it and tear or cut it down. And as for those which have a soul, none of them is to be slain, save what is permissible to slaughter, to eat.

So I said to him: "And what is the proof for this, when Abū Bakr found it reprehensible to tear down a habitation, cut down a fruit-bearing tree or burn date palms, or to slay a camel or a ewe, save for eating...."

Al-Shāfiʿī said: "That is from the *ḥadīth* of Mālik, [with a] broken [*isnād*],[135] and the people of the Levant may know it with a better chain of narration."

So I said to Al-Shāfiʿī: "And our companions have reported other than this of Abū Bakr, so with what would you counter it?"

So, he said: "With an authentic [*ḥadīth*] of God's Apostle, God's blessings and peace be upon him, that he burned the property of Banū al-Naḍīr, and cut and tore down [their property], and burned and cut down in Khaybar, and then cut down in al-Ṭāʾif, which was the last battle led by God's Apostle, God's blessings and peace be upon him, in which he fought."

So I said to Al-Shāfiʿī: "And how do you find it detestable to slay and burn that which has a soul, save for eating?"

He said: "By the *sunna*, that God's Apostle, God's blessings and peace be upon him, said: 'Whosoever slays a sparrow without just cause will be held to account for it.' It was said: 'And what is a just cause?' He said: 'To slaughter it and eat it, and not cut off its head and throw it away.' So I concluded that it is permissible to slay edible livestock save [those forbidden] in the Book [the *Qurʾān*] and the *sunna*; that is to hunt and eat it, or slaughter and eat it.

And it is forbidden to torture anything that has a soul.

From: Ibn Ḥazm, *al-Muḥalla*, Vol. VII[136]

And it is permissible to burn the trees of the infidels, their foodstuffs, their crops, and homes, and to tear them down. Exalted God said: "Whatever palm-trees you cut down, or left standing upon their roots, that was by God's leave, and that He might degrade the ungodly," and Exalted God said: "neither tread they any tread enraging the unbelievers, nor gain any gain from any enemy, but a righteous deed is thereby written to their account." And the Apostle of God, God's blessings and peace be upon him, burned the palm trees of the Banū al-Naḍīr which were on one side of the houses of Medina, and he knew that they would become the property of the Muslims someday. And we have narrated, of Abū Bakr al-Ṣiddīq, may God be pleased with him: "Do not cut down a fruit-bearing tree, do not destroy an inhabited building." And there is no admissible evidence from any alongside the Apostle of God, God's blessings and peace be upon him. Abū Bakr may have voluntarily chosen to make such a prohibition, because not doing so [destroying trees and homes] is also permissible, as indicated in the aforementioned verse.

It is not permissible to slay any of their animals whatsoever, not camels, nor cattle, nor sheep nor horses, nor chickens, nor pigeons, nor geese, nor camel herds, nor anything else, save for food alone, excepting pigs of all kinds, which are to be slain, and horses used in combat alone, and when, irrespective of whether the Muslims take them or not, the enemy would attain them, with the Muslims incapable of preventing it, or if they do not manage to attain it.

From: Ibn Qudāma, *al-Mughnī*, Vol. XIII[137]

And their trees are not to be cut down, nor their crops burned, unless they do so in our lands, and so this is done to them to force them to desist.

And the summation is that trees and crops are divided into three categories:

The first: What necessity dictates must be destroyed, such as those near their fortresses and which prevent them from being fought, or which they hide among from the Muslims, or if they [the Muslims] need to cut them down to widen the road or to allow them to fight, or to block up a watercourse, repair a road, or screen a mangonel or something else, or if they [the infidels] do so to us, so we do so to them to force them to desist; then [in those cases] it is permissible with no disagreement that we are aware of.

The second: That which the chopping down of would be harmful to the Muslims, because they would benefit from its remaining as animal fodder or for shade, or so that they eat from its fruit, or because it is not the established practice between us and our enemy to do so, and so if we were to do so to them, they would do so to us; this is forbidden due to what it entails of harm to the Muslims.

The third: Anything other than these two categories, which contains no harm to Muslims and no benefit save to enrage the infidels and harm them, there are two opinions:

The first: It is impermissible, based on the *ḥadīth* of Abū Bakr and his guidance, and a similar tradition reported and attributed to the Prophet, God's blessings and peace be upon him; and because it entails unmitigated destruction, then it is impermissible like slaying animals. This was the opinion of al-Awzāʿī, al-Layth, and Abū Thawr.

The second report is: It is permissible, and this was the opinion of Mālik, al-Shāfiʿī, Isḥāq and Ibn al-Mundhir. Isḥāq said: "Burning is a *sunna* if it is more damaging to the enemy, due to Exalted God's saying: 'Whatever palm-trees you cut down, or left standing upon their roots, that was by God's leave, and that He might degrade the ungodly.'"

And Ibn 'Umar reported that God's Apostle, God's blessings and peace be upon him, burned and cut down the palm trees of Banū al-Naḍīr, and this was at Būwayra, and Exalted God declared: "Whatever palm-trees you cut down...,"

And of al-Zuhrī, that he said: "Usāma told me that God's Apostle, God's blessings and peace be upon him, had given him guidance, saying: 'Raid Ubna by dawn and burn.'"

From: Ibn Qudāma, *al-Mughnī*, Vol. XIII[138]

And they are not to drown bees.

And the summation is that drowning or burning bees is impermissible in the opinion of most of the learned, including al-Awzā'ī, al-Layth, and al-Shāfi'ī. And Mālik was asked: "Should their beehives be burned?" He said: "As for bees, I know not [what the position should be regarding them]."

And the essence of the *madhhab* [school of jurisprudence] of Abū Ḥanīfa [on this matter] is its permissibility, because it enrages and weakens them [the infidels], and so is akin to slaying their beasts when fighting them.

And we have what was reported of Abū Bakr al-Ṣiddīq, may God be pleased with him, that he said to Yazīd ibn Abū Sufyān as he was giving him guidance when he dispatched him as a commander to fight in the Levant: "And do not burn bees or drown them."

And it was reported of Ibn Mas'ūd that he was met by his nephew returning from a raid, and he said: "Did you perhaps burn crops?" He said: "Yes." He said: "Did you perhaps drown bees?" He said: "Yes." He said: "Perhaps you killed a child?" He said: "Yes." He said: "Make your raids blameless [by refraining from such acts]." This was narrated by Sa'īd, and similarly from Thawbān.

And it is established of God's Apostle, God's blessings and peace be upon him, that he forbade the killing of a bee, and forbade that a beast be starved to death, and because it is a form of spreading corruption, it comes under the aegis of the Exalted's saying: "and when he turns his back, he hastens about the earth, to do corruption there and to destroy the tillage and the stock; and God loves not corruption"; and because it is an animal with a soul, it is impermissible to slay it to enrage the infidels, as with their women and children.

As for killing their beasts in other than a state of war to enrage them and bring ruin upon them, it is impermissible, irrespective of whether we fear they shall be taken or not, and this was the opinion of al-Awzā'ī, al-Layth, al-Shāfi'ī and Abū Thawr.

And Abū Ḥanīfa and Mālik said: "It is permissible because it entails enraging them and weakening their strength, and as such is similar to slaying them [the beasts] when we fight them."

And we have [as evidence] that Abū Bakr al-Ṣiddīq, may God be pleased with him, said in his guidance to Yazīd when he dispatched him as a commander: "Oh Yazīd, do not slay a child, nor a woman, nor an old man, and do not tear down habitations, do not chop down a fruit-bearing tree, nor [slay] a dumb beast, nor

a ewe, save for food, and do not burn bees nor drown them, do not commit perfidy, do not be cowardly." And because the Prophet, God's blessings and peace be
upon him, forbade that any beast be starved to death, because it is an inviolable
animal, and as such is similar to women and children.

As for the state of war, it is permissible to slay the infidels in any fashion possible,
as opposed to their condition when they are within the power [of the Muslims],
and this is why it is permissible to slay women and children in night raids and in
[fighting in] underground storehouses, if there was no intention to slay them individually, as opposed to their state if they are within [the Muslims'] power.

And slaying their beasts leads to slaying and defeating them.

Amān *(Pledge of Safety)*

Other than living in Muslim lands under the *dhimmī* regime, non-Muslims were allowed
temporarily to enter Muslim lands for trade or other purposes if they were granted a
pledge of safety (*amān*). Most jurists placed an obligation on Muslims not to infringe on
the life and property of a non-Muslim if before entering Muslim territory such a person
had been granted an *amān*. The legitimacy of the *amān* regime was treated as a given by
virtually all jurists; debate accordingly focused on problematic cases in which an *amān*
had not been clearly articulated or where other, competing interests came into play. To
deter occasions for treachery, most jurists adopted the position that error and ambiguity ought to be interpreted in favor of the non-Muslim. This regime was of particular
relevance in assessing the legality of military attacks against non-Muslims who were traveling on Muslim territory. Reference could also be made to *amān* in assessing military
action that was directed against Muslim civilians who were present in non-Muslim states.
For these reasons, discussion of *amān* has resurfaced in recent debates on Islamic militancy. In particular, there has been a debate on whether modern visas (granted either
by Muslim states to tourists and foreign workers or inversely by non-Muslim states to
Muslims) should be deemed a modern extension of *amān*.[139]

From: Mālik, *al-Mudawwana*, Vol. I[140]

"And Mālik was asked of [a] man from among the [Byzantines] whom the Muslims
meet, and he says: 'I have come to seek *amān*,' and they [the Muslims] say to him:
'You lie, you came up with that excuse when we captured you.'"

He said: "Mālik said: 'And how would they know? These are problematic matters.'

"Mālik said: 'And I am of the opinion that he is to be returned to his place of
security.'"

From: al-Shaybānī, *Siyar*[141]

I asked: If a Muslim army besieged a city whose inhabitants were well defended
and one of the Muslim [warriors] granted an *amān* to the inhabitants of that city,
do you think that his *amān* would be valid?

He replied: Yes.

I asked: What would be said to the inhabitants of the city?

He replied: Islam should [first] be offered to them; if they accept it they are entitled to the same rights and obligations as Muslims. If they refuse they should be asked to pay the *jizya*; if they agree it should be accepted and they should be left to themselves. If they refuse [to pay the *jizya*] they should be allowed to return to a place of security and fighting would be resumed.

I asked: If a *musta'min** from among the inhabitants of the territory of war enters the territory of Islam under an *amān* to trade and purchases a Muslim slave and thereafter returns with the slave to the territory of war, what would the status of the slave be?

He replied: He would be free from the moment [his master] entered with him into the territory of war.

I asked: Why?

He replied: Because [the slave] is a Muslim purchased in the territory of Islam. Do you not think that if the slave killed his master, took his property, and returned to the territory of Islam, everything that he had taken from his master, whether property or slaves, would be regarded as belonging to him and he would be a freedman and nothing would be held against him?[†]

I asked: Would it be lawful for that slave to kill his master?

He replied: Yes.

I asked: Would you not think that the sale contract [by virtue of which the unbeliever owned the Muslim slave] created a [state of security] (*amān*) between them?

He replied: No. That was the opinion of Abū Ḥanīfa. However, Abū Yūsuf and Muḥammad [b. al-Ḥasan] held that the slave would not become free [immediately after his entry into the territory of war] until the Muslims had taken him back by capture or he had returned to the territory of Islam against his master's will. Only in one of these two ways would the slave become free.

I asked: What would you think if a man from the inhabitants of the territory of war were apprehended in the *dār al-Islām* and claimed that he was an emissary and produced a letter from his ruler [to prove it]?

He replied: If it were established that the letter was from the ruler, the emissary would be entitled to an *amān* until he delivered his message and returned.

I asked: If a [Muslim] who entered the territory of war under an *amān* killed one of their men or seized some property or slaves and took it to the *dār al-Islām*, and thereafter the inhabitants of the territory of war became Muslims or *dhimmīs*,[‡] would you return to them any of the property which [the Muslim] had taken, or would he be liable for the property or the blood-money [of the unbelievers whom he killed]?

He replied: No.

---

[*] Person granted *amān*.

[†] The Ḥanafis believed in legal separation between the territory of Islam and the territory of war, with acts committed in the territory of war carrying no legal weight in the territory of Islam.

[‡] Thereby demanding protection of their life and property.

I asked: Why?

He replied: Because [the Muslims] did it in the *dār al-ḥarb*, where Muslim juris-diction is not operative.

I asked: Would you disapprove of [the Muslim's] committing such acts?

He replied: Yes, on the ground of his religion, I disapprove of his dealing treach-erously with them.

From: al-Shāfiʿī, *al-Umm*, Vol. IV[142]

And if minors or the insane grant *amān*, whether they fight or not, we do not acknowledge their *amān*. Also, if a *dhimmī* grants an *amān*, whether he fights or not, we do not acknowledge his *amān*. And if one of those grants an *amān*, and they [the infidels who have been granted the unrecognized *amān*] come out to us [in the belief that they have been granted] an *amān*, we should return them to their place of refuge and we do not infringe upon their property or lives, because they cannot distinguish between those in our army whose *amān* is acknowledged [and those whose *amān* is not].

From: al-Shāfiʿī, *al-Umm*, Vol. IV[143]

And if the enemy takes captive a Muslim man, and they release him, grant him an *amān*, and whether they entrust him with [part of] their land or not, then that *amān* granted him is to [provide the infidels] with security from him [the Muslim captive], and he should not slay them treacherously or betray them.

As for one who escapes by himself, he is entitled to escape, and if [they] catch up to him to take him, he has a right to defend himself, even if he slays the one who caught up to him, because what he [the Muslim] seeks is not *amān*, so he can slay him if he wishes and take his property if he [the pursuer] does not relinquish what he seeks [recapturing the Muslim].

And if the infidels take a Muslim captive and release him for a ransom to be paid at a subsequent time, and they obtain a pledge from him that if he does not pay the ransom he will return to captivity, he should not return to their captivity, and the *Imām* should not allow him to return if he so wishes.

And if they [the infidels] had refused to release him [until he pledged] to pay a ransom [after being released], he is not to pay them anything, because it is money that they had unjustly coerced him into paying.

If a body of Muslims enters the Abode of War with an *amān*, then the enemy is safe from them until they depart from them or the duration of their *amān* expires. They are not allowed to be unjust to them or to betray them. And if the enemy takes Muslim children and women captive, I do not favor that they [the Muslims with *amān*] should commit perfidy against the enemy, but I prefer that, if they are asked, they renounce the *amān*, and if they do, that they fight them [the infidels] for the Muslim children and women.

Ibn Ḥazm discussed *amān* only in the context of invalid *amān* agreements. On his under-standing, non-Muslims may never legitimately own Muslim property or Muslim slaves.

Thus, any *amān* agreement that allows for such ownership is a fortiori invalid. Despite the harsh tone adopted by Ibn Ḥazm apropos pledges involving the conferral of Muslim property to non-Muslims, his discourse nonetheless presupposes that *amān* is a valid legal regime that guarantees non-Muslims protection of their life and legitimate property.

From: Ibn Ḥazm, *al-Muḥalla*, Vol. VII[144]

If the people of war come to us as traders under *amān*, or messengers, or *musta'minūn*[145] seeking refuge, or to committing themselves to become *dhimmī*s, and we find in their possession Muslim or *dhimmī* captives, or female or male slaves belonging to Muslims, or Muslim or *dhimmī* property, all of that should be seized from them without compensation, with or without their consent.

And whosoever is a prisoner of the infidels, and agrees a covenant with them to pay a ransom [for his release], and is released, it is not permissible for him to return to them, nor to give them anything; and it is not permissible for the *Imām* to compel him to give them anything. And if he is unable to depart save by paying a ransom, it becomes obligatory upon the Muslims to ransom him, if he does not possess money sufficient to pay his ransom.

From: Ibn Qudāma, *al-Mughnī*[146]

And if a *ḥarbī*[*] enters the Abode of Islam with an *amān*, and deposits his property with a Muslim or a *dhimmī*, or lends it to them, and then returns to the Abode of War, we [should] examine [the situation]. If he entered [the Abode of War] as a merchant, a messenger, a tourist, or to fulfill a particular purpose and then returned to the Abode of Islam, then he is as the *dhimmī* who enters [the Abode of War] for those [reasons]. But if he enters [the Abode of War] to dwell therein, the *amān* is nullified [with respect to] his life, and upheld [with respect] to his property.

Whosoever enters enemy territory under *amān* should not betray them [by taking] their money.... As for betraying them, it is forbidden, because they have granted him an *amān* conditional on his not betraying them and securing them from himself, and even if this is not specified in the wording, it is understood from the meaning. And this is why he who comes to us from them with an *amān* and betrays us has violated his covenant. If this [*amān*] is proven, it is impermissible for him to betray them, because it is perfidy, and perfidy is not acceptable in our religion.

The Prophet, God's blessings and peace be upon him, said: "Muslims abide by their conditions." So if he betrays them, steals from them, or borrows something, it behooves him to return what he has taken to its owners.

And if its owners come to the Abode of Islam with an *amān* or in faith [as Muslims], he must restore it to them, or else send it to them, because he took it in a fashion which was forbidden to him, and it is compulsory for him to return what he took, as though he took a Muslim's property.

---

[*] Person from the Abode of War.

Baghy (*Rebellion*)

As noted earlier in this chapter, *baghy* was the legal regime that applied to Muslims who had formed a faction to rebel against a Muslim ruler. Rebellion, even if rejected in principle, was pragmatically regulated by jurists to accord rebels protection against the overly extreme tactics that might be employed against them by their ruler. Rebels were deemed to fall under the *baghy* regime if their disobedience had been permitted by a *ta'wīl* (religious interpretation). Jurists did not dwell very much on the conditions that might govern the validity of a *ta'wīl*; they seemed to assume that *baghy* would apply regardless of the ultimate validity of the underlying *ta'wīl*. In other words, even if the rebels erred in their interpretation, the fact that they believed they were acting in accordance with their religion constituted a legitimate *ta'wīl*. Rebels were sometimes designated *Khawārij*, a term that originally referred to the group of Muslims who had rebelled against 'Alī, the fourth Caliph, when he accepted arbitration between himself and Mu'āwīya, a rival who later assumed power as the fifth Caliph. In discussing *baghy*, most jurists held that only so much force could be used as was necessary to break the rebellion. Employing harsher tactics, so as to punish the rebels, was excluded. Mālik's account of rebellion was less developed than that of other jurists, since this area of law was arguably developed only later, by al-Shāfi'ī. Al-Shaybānī maintained that wounded rebels, or those in retreat, could be pursed and killed if they were found to be regrouping, as this would indicate their intent to resume hostilities. But al-Shāfi'ī and Ibn Ḥazm argued that retreating and wounded rebels should not be killed. With the exception of al-Shaybānī, jurists maintained that restrictions should be placed on the use of indiscriminate weapons against rebels. All jurists stated that once the rebellion ended, rebels under the *baghy* regime ought to be granted amnesty; their property should be returned to them; and they were not to be held liable for the damage they had caused to life and property.

General Directives on Fighting Rebels

From: Mālik, *al-Mudawwana*[147]

I said: "And of fighting the *Khawārij* ... what was Mālik's opinion of them?"

He said: "Mālik said of the Ibāḍiya, the Ḥarūriya [both factions of the *Khawārij*], and all those who would follow the vagaries of their desires: 'I am of the opinion that they are to be asked to repent, and if they repent [it is to be accepted], and if they do not, they are to be slain.'"

Ibn al-Qāsim said: "And Mālik said of the Ḥarūriya and their ilk that they are to be slain if they do not repent, if the *Imām* is righteous."

And this indicates that if they march out against a righteous *Imām* wanting to fight him, and advocating the beliefs that they hold, they are to be invited to [rejoin] the community and [uphold] the *sunna*, and if they refuse, they are to be fought.

He said: "And I asked Mālik of the tribal partisans who were in the Levant, [and] Mālik said: 'I am of the opinion that the *Imām* should invite them to cease their rebellion, and to a fair adjudication, and if they cease [that is to be accepted] and if not, they are to be fought.'"

From: al-Shāfi'ī, *al-Umm*, Vol. IV[148]

And Blessed and Exalted God said: "If two parties among the believers fight each other, then make peace between them. But if one of them transgresses against the other, then fight, all of you, against the one that transgresses until it complies with the command of God. But if it complies, then make peace between the two parties with justice and be fair; for God loves those who are fair and just. The believers are but a single brotherhood. So reconcile your two [contending] brothers, and fear God so that you will receive his mercy."

Al-Shāfi'ī, may God have mercy upon him, said: "Exalted and Glorified God mentioned the fighting of the two parties. Each of the rebelling parties rebels to a greater or lesser degree, if it has been described as rebelling, and Exalted God named them both as believers, and commanded that peace be made between them, and as such it is obligatory on all to call on the believers, if they are divided and wish to fight each other, not to fight, so that they may be invited to reconcile their differences . . . .

"And if it reverts, then none may fight it, because Exalted and Glorified God made it permissible to fight only while it rebels, until it reverts."

It was reported to us that 'Alī . . . [told the rebels], "Three rights you can claim from us: we do not forbid you to [pray] in the mosques of God, we do not deny you booty as long as you fight with us, and we will not fight you first. . . .

"'Umar ibn 'Abdūl 'Azīz* wrote [in reference to *Khawārij*] . . . 'If they curse me, curse them, or forgive them. And if they raise a weapon [against you], raise [a weapon] against them. And if they smite you, smite them.'"

Al-Shāfi'ī, may God have mercy upon him, said: "And all this we affirm. It is impermissible for Muslims to shed their blood due to their malignity, nor to deny [them] the spoils of war as long as they are subject to the laws of Islam and were their [the Muslims'] equals in waging *jihād* against the enemy, and they cannot be prevented from [entering] the mosques and markets."

From: Ibn Ḥazm, *al-Muḥalla*, Vol. XI[149]

Exalted God said: "If two parties among the believers fight each other, then make peace between them. But if one of them transgresses against the other, then fight, all of you, against the one that transgresses until it complies with the command of God. . . ." And thus fighting between Muslims is of two kinds: fighting rebels, and fighting those engaged in *ḥirāba*.

From: Ibn Qudāma, *al-Mughnī*, Vol. XII[150]

[The *Qur'ānic* verse starting with the phrase] "If two parties among the believers fight each other, then make peace between them. But if one of them transgresses against the other, then fight, all of you, against the one that transgresses until it complies

* An Umayyad Caliph whose piety and adherence to Islamic ethics are generally agreed on by most classical Muslim scholars.

with the command of Allah," [up] to His saying: "The believers are but a single brotherhood. So reconcile your two [contending] brothers," therein are five lessons. The first: that by rebelling they have not left [the fold of] belief, for He has named them believers. The second: that He has made fighting them obligatory. The third: that He has waived [the obligation to] fight them if they comply with the command of Allah. The fourth: that He has waived their liability for all that they destroyed in their fighting. The fifth: that the verse indicated the permissibility of fighting all who would withhold [by force or threat of force] any obligation [incumbent upon them].

Significance of Ta'wīl

From: Mālik, *al-Mudawwana*[151]

I said: "What distinguishes between blood spilled by those engaged in *ḥirāba* and *Khawārij*?"

He said: "Because the *Khawārij* rebelled based on an interpretation of religion, while those engaged in *ḥirāba* rebelled out of corruption and debauchery, with no interpretation."

From: al-Shaybānī, *Siyar*[152]

I asked: If a group of men were not *muta'awwils* [reliant on *ta'wīl*] but adventurers or the like who occupy a region and kill some of its [Muslim] inhabitants and capture their property and consume it, and thereafter [the forces of] the lawful authorities captured them, do you think that you would make a decision in favor of the owners of the property and those whose blood was shed against them?

He replied: Yes.

I asked: Why?

He replied: Because these are not regarded as *muta'awwils* but as marauding adventurers.

From: al-Shāfi'ī, *al-Umm*, Vol. IV[153]

And the verse indicates that fighting them [the rebels] is permitted in one situation [when they fight], and it does not permit [the taking] of their property, or any part thereof. As for bandits and those who slay without *ta'wīl* [a religious interpretation], irrespective of whether they are a group or individuals, they are to be slain in fulfilment of the [Qur'ānic] *ḥadd* punishment[154] and in retribution, in accordance with Exalted and Glorified God's ruling on murderers and *muḥāribūn*.*

From: Ibn Ḥazm, *al-Muḥalla*, Vol. XI[155]

And rebels are of two kinds, with no third: either a kind that has rebelled based on a religious interpretation, and in so doing have erred, such as the *Khawārij* and others

---

* Those who commit *ḥirāba*.

of like ilk who follow their whims in opposition to the truth; or a kind that desired the world for themselves and rebelled against the rightful *Imām*, or against one of a similar station. And if that faction transgresses to terrorizing the roads, or taking the property of those whom they encounter, or wantonly spilling blood, the ruling regarding them changes to the ruling regarding those engaged in *ḥirāba*.

So long as they do not do this, they remain under the ruling regarding rebels.

As for one who calls for enjoining good and forbidding evil, and that the *Qur'ān* and the *sunna* be paramount, and righteous rule: He is not a rebel; indeed, the *baghī* is he who opposes him – and through exalted God is success.

From: Ibn Qudāma, *al-Mughnī*, Vol. XII[156]

The fourth kind is a group from the Righteous who leave the *Imām*'s control, and who wish to depose him based upon a reasonable *ta'wīl*, and who are of such might that [the *Imām*] needs to muster the army to stop them. Those then, are rebels, the ruling concerning whom we relate in this chapter. And it is obligatory upon the people to aid their *Imām* in fighting the rebels, based upon what we cited at the beginning of the chapter, and because if they refrain from aiding him, the rebels would vanquish him and corruption [would] appear in the land.

Significance of the Number of Rebels

From: al-Shaybānī, *Siyar*[157]

I asked: If one or two men rebel against a city as *muta'awwils* [relying on *ta'wīl*] and fight and kill, but thereafter asked for an *amān*, do you think that they would be liable for anything they have done?

He replied: Yes.

I asked: Why?

He replied: Because they did not constitute a fighting force [as warriors] but would be regarded as highway robbers.

From: al-Shāfiʿī, *al-Umm*, Vol. IV[158]

And if a single man slays [another] based on a [religious] interpretation, or a band that does not rebel [slays a man], whether they subsequently become part of a rebelling band or not, it would be necessary to exact retribution from them for those they have slain, injured, or otherwise, as it would be [necessary to exact] from those who rebel with no basis in [religious] interpretation.

And if one were to say to me: "Why did you say of the rebelling faction that manifests enmity based on an interpretation, and that slays and ruins property, that it is absolved of retribution and compensation for ruined property, and yet if a man slays and destroys property based on an interpretation, you would exact retribution and compensation from him for the property?" I would say to him: "I found that Blessed and Exalted God said: 'Whosoever is slain unjustly, We have appointed to his next-of-kin authority; but let him not exceed in slaying,' and God's Apostle, God's blessings and peace be upon him, said [describing] what makes the blood of a Muslim permissible to shed: 'or to slay a soul [who did not slay] a soul.' And it was reported of God's Apostle, God's blessings and peace be upon him: 'whosoever slays a Muslim unjustly, he has led himself to retribution with his own hands.' And I found Exalted God had said: 'If two parties among the believers fight each other, then make peace between them. But if one of them transgresses against the other, then fight, all of you, against the one that transgresses until it complies with the command of God. But if it complies, then make peace between the two parties with justice and Be fair; for God loves those who are fair and just. The believers are but a single brotherhood. So reconcile your two [contending] brothers, and fear God so that you will receive His mercy.'" So Exalted and Glorified God mentioned fighting them, and did not mention that retribution should be exacted among [the both] of them.

So we have upheld retribution between Muslims based upon what Exalted and Glorified God has decreed in terms of retribution, and laid it aside [in the case of] those who rebel based on an interpretation, and we concluded that those Muslims from whom retribution is to be exacted are those who do not rebel based upon a religious interpretation, and so we extrapolated both rulings as we did.

Conduct during the Conflict

From: al-Shaybānī, *Siyar*[159]

It has also been related to us that [the Caliph] ʿAlī ibn Abū Ṭālib said in the Battle of the Camel:[160] "Whoever flees [from us] shall not be chased, no [Muslim] prisoner of war shall be killed, no wounded in battle shall be dispatched, no enslavement [of women and children] shall be allowed and no property [of a Muslim] shall be confiscated."

I asked: If there were two parties of believers, one of them is rebellious (party of *baghy*) and the other loyal (party of justice), and the former was defeated by the latter, would not the loyal party have the right to chase the fugitives [of the other party], kill their prisoners, and dispatch the wounded?

He replied: No, it should never be allowed to do so if none of the rebels has survived and no group remained with whom refuge might be taken; but if a group of them has survived with whom refuge might be taken, then their prisoners could be killed, their fugitives pursued, and the wounded dispatched.

I asked: Would it be objectionable to you if the loyalists shot [the rebels] with arrows, inundated [their positions] with water, attacked them with *manjanīqs** and burned them with fire?

He replied: No harm in doing anything of this sort.

I asked: Would a sudden attack at night be objectionable to you?

He replied: No harm in it.

---

* Mangonels.

From: al-Shāfi‘ī, *al-Umm*, Vol. IV[161]

"And that is why I said that the rebels are not to be raided by night before they are called upon [not to fight], because the *Imām* must call on them [not to fight], as Exalted and Glorified God commanded, before the fighting, and Exalted and Glorified [God] commanded that the transgressing party be fought, while naming it [its partisans] believers, until it complies with God's command....

Marwān ibn al-Ḥakam[162] ... said [to a descendant of ‘Alī]: "I have seen no one who was nobler in victory than your father. No sooner had we turned away [to flee] on the day of [the Battle of] the Camel than his herald called out: 'No retreater is to be slain, and none of the wounded is to be dispatched.'" ...

Al-Darawārdī said: "Ja‘far informed us, of his father, that ‘Alī, may God be pleased with him, would not take plunder, and that he would personally engage in battle, and that he would not slay the injured, nor slay those in retreat."

Al Shāfi‘ī, may Exalted God have mercy upon him, said: "And God made no exceptions in [demanding] compliance [with His command], so whether the one who complies is part of a faction or not, whenever he complies, and compliance is turning back from his rebellion, his blood becomes impermissible [to spill], and none of their retreaters [is] to be slain, ever, nor a captive, nor the wounded, under any circumstances, because they are now subject to a definition other than the one in which the [spilling] of their blood had become permissible, and as such."[*]

From: al-Shāfi‘ī, *al-Umm*, Vol. IV[163]

And if the war is ended, I am not of the opinion that their captives are to be imprisoned.

And I favor that [the Muslims] eschew doing that to them [using indiscriminate tactics], as long as the *Imām* sees no necessity to do so.

And the necessity to do so is when the *Imām* is confronting a band [of infidels] while he is in a fortified position, and they [the infidels] raid or burn his [fortress] or bombard it with mangonels or catapults or surround it, and he fears that those with him will be annihilated. If this, or any of this, is the case, I hope he would be able to bombard them with mangonels or fire, to defend himself or inflict retribution in kind.

From: Ibn Ḥazm, *al-Muḥalla*, Vol. XI[164]

And he who is taken prisoner from among the rebels, people's opinions on how to deal with him have differed: Should he be slain or not?

---

[*] Compliance refers to the term *fay’a*, which also means retreat. In this case, al-Shāfi‘ī is discussing permissibility of targeting a retreating rebel, arguing he may not be pursued regardless of whether he has a faction to retreat to and possibly resume fighting from or not.

Some of the companions of Abu Ḥanīfa said: "As long as the fighting continues, their prisoners are to be slain. But if the war ends, none of their prisoners [is] to be slain."

Abu Muhammad, God have mercy upon him, said: "And they cited as evidence that 'Alī, may God be pleased with him, slew Ibn Yathribī after capturing him."

And al-Shāfi'ī said: "It is not permissible in the first place to slay a prisoner from among them as long as the war continues, nor after the war is concluded" – and this opinion we affirm. The evidence for this: That it was verified that the Prophet, God's blessings and peace be upon him, said: "It is not permissible to spill the blood of a Muslim man, save for one of three reasons: disbelief after faith, adultery, or a life for a life."

And God made permissible the spilling of the blood of one who engages in *ḥirāba*, and the Apostle of God made permissible the spilling of the blood of one who [was punished by the *ḥadd* punishment for drinking alcohol] and then drank it a fourth time.

Thus, all those whom Scripture has declared that it is permissible to spill their blood, it is permissible to spill their blood. And all those whom Exalted God and his Apostle, God's blessings and peace be upon him, have not declared their blood permissible to spill, the spilling of their blood is forbidden.

From: Ibn Ḥazm, *al-Muḥalla*, Vol. XI[165]

If the rebels entrench themselves in a fortress which contains women and children, it is impermissible to cut off their food; quantities sufficient solely for the women and children and whomever is not among the rebels are to be allowed through; all else is to be denied them.

It is permissible to fight them with mangonels and by shooting. And it is impermissible to fight them with fire that would burn those inside who are not rebels, nor to flood them [in such a manner that nonrebels would] drown, due to Exalted God's saying: "Every soul earns only to its own account, no soul laden bears the load of another."

But if there are none inside save the rebels alone, then it is compulsory to deny them water and food until they submit; otherwise, they have slain themselves by their abstaining from righteousness.

And likewise it is permissible to kindle fires around them and leave them room to escape to the soldiers of righteousness, because that is a fire we have lit, but have not unleashed, and they are capable of escaping from it, if they so desire.

And it is impermissible to burn or drown them without leaving them room to escape, because Exalted God did not command this, nor did his Apostle, may God's blessing and peace be upon him, but rather commanded only that they be fought.

And it is not permissible that they be raided by night, unless it is to capture them. And as for those who do not fight, it is impermissible to slay them.

And through Exalted God is success.

From: Ibn Ḥazm, *al-Muḥalla*, Vol. XI[166]

They have differed also [on the permissibility or impermissibility] of executing their wounded. The ruling on their status is as the ruling on prisoners, because if a wounded man is in one's power, he is a prisoner, and if he is not in one's power and resists, then he is a rebel, as the rest of his companions.

From: Ibn Ḥazm, *al-Muḥalla*, Vol. XI[167]

Exalted God has obliged us to fight them until they revert to Exalted God's commandment. If they revert, it becomes impermissible for us to slay and fight them. If they turn and abandon their rebellion, returning to their homes, or dispersing from what they had been gathered for, then by abandoning their rebellion they have reverted to God's commandment. And if they revert to God's commandment, it is forbidden to slay them. And if it is forbidden to slay them, then there is no basis for holding them liable, and they owe us nothing then.

But if their turning is to evade being vanquished by the righteous – and they remain committed to their rebellion – then fighting them remains obligatory upon us, because they have not reverted to the commandment of Exalted God.

From: Ibn Qudāma, *al-Mughnī*, Vol. XII[168]

And the rebels are not to be fought with anything that causes widespread destruction, such as fire, mangonels, or flooding, if it is unnecessary [to do so], because it is impermissible to slay any who do not fight, and anything that causes widespread destruction afflicts those who fight and those who do not fight. But if necessity demands it, such as if the rebels surround them and they [the Muslims] cannot be saved except by bombarding them with something that causes widespread destruction, it becomes permissible [to do so]. And this is the opinion of al-Shafi'ī.

And Abū Ḥanīfa said: "If the *Khawārij* are entrenched, and the *Imām* needs to bombard them with mangonels, he can do so as long as they have an army, and as long as they are undefeated. And if the rebels bombard them [the Muslims] with mangonels and fire, it becomes permissible to bombard them with the like."

And the summation of the matter is that, if rebels desist from fighting, whether by reverting to obedience, or by casting down their weapons, or by being defeated as part of a faction or not, or by incapacitation through injury, sickness or capture, then it is impermissible to slay them, or to pursue [those among them who] retreat. And this was the opinion of al-Shafi'ī.

And Abu Ḥanīfa said that if they are defeated and they have no faction [that they are part of], then [they are to be treated] as we said. And if they have a faction they can seek refuge with, it is permissible to slay [those among them who] retreat and their captives, and to slay their wounded. And if they have no faction, they are not to be slain, but are to be beaten grievously and imprisoned until they abandon that which they were upon and resolve to repent. This was mentioned [pertaining to] the *Khawārij*, and a similar [report] was reported of Ibn 'Abbās.

And this [opinion] was chosen by some of the companions of al-Shāfi'ī, because if he [the *Imām*] did not slay them, they would assemble and then return to fight.

And we have [as evidence] what was reported of Ali, may Allah be pleased with him, that he said on the day of [the Battle of] the Camel: "None of the injured [is] to be slain, no veil to be torn aside, no door is to be opened; whosoever closes a door or his door, he is secure. None who retreat [is] to be pursued." A similar [report] was reported of 'Ammār.

And of Ali, may Allah be pleased with him, that he paid blood money from the Muslim's treasury [to the families of] a group that were slain while retreating. And of Abū Umāma, that he said: "I attended [the Battle of] Ṣiffīn, and they did not dispatch the injured, nor slay the retreater, nor despoil the slain."

And al-Qaḍī reported in his "*Sharḥ*," of Abdullah ibn Mas'ūd, that the Prophet, Allah's blessings and peace be upon him, said: "Oh Ibn Umm 'Abd, what is the ruling for those who rebel against my *umma* (nation)?" I said: "Allah and his Apostle know best." He said: "That their retreaters are not to be pursued, nor their injured dispatched, nor their captives slain, nor their booty apportioned."

And because the intention is to repel and stop them, and it has been achieved, it is not permissible to slay them.

Rebel Property

From: al-Shaybānī, *Siyar*[169]

I asked: If the loyal [army] acquired weapons, *kurā'*,* and other materials from the rebels, what would be done with them?

He replied: If any one of the rebels has survived, there would be no harm for the loyal army to use the weapons and *kurā'* against him; but when the war comes to an end, everything should be returned to its [original] owners. However, everything acquired, other than weapons and *kurā'*, should be returned to them [even] before the war comes to an end.

From: al-Shāfi'ī, *al-Umm*, Vol. IV[170]

Their property cannot be claimed [in the form of] a beast to be ridden, nor possession, nor a weapon to be fought with in their war, whether the [war] is ongoing or has concluded, nor anything else of their property, and whatever [ends up] with them [the Muslims fighting the rebels], of captured animals or weapons, they must return it to them [the rebels], and that is because it is permissible in fighting to [take] the property of the infidels who would concede it [the property]

---

* Ungulate animals.

if they come into [the Muslims'] power, but as for one who converts to Islam, he is to [suffer] the *ḥadd* punishment for banditry, adultery, or murder, but his property is not taken. So if he is fought in rebellion, his is a less serious condition, because if he ceases to fight, he is not to be slain.

From: Ibn Ḥazm, *al-Muḥalla*, Vol. XI[171]

When they disagreed, as we mentioned, it behooved us to examine the matter to learn the truth, that we may follow it, with Exalted God's aid. So we examined the proofs put forth by Abū Ḥanīfa, and his companions, that their weapons and mounts can be used as long as the war continues, and we found they had no evidence in the first place, not from the *Qur'ān*, nor from an authentic *sunna*, nor a weak one, nor from the saying of a companion, nor from consensus. And such is undoubtedly false.

God's Apostle, God's blessings and peace be upon him, said: "Your blood and your property is forbidden to you." And the weapons and mounts are property of theirs, and as such are forbidden to others. But the duty is to separate them from all that would aid them in their error, due to Exalted God's saying: "Help one another to piety and God fearing; do not help each other to sin and enmity."

And as such, it is manifestly true that leaving them to use their weapons to spill the blood of the righteous, and their mounts in fighting, is helping them to sin and enmity, and is forbidden by the text of the *Qur'ān*. And it is true that separating them from their weapons and mounts in the case of rebellion is helping to piety and God fearing.

As for using them [the rebel's weapons and mounts], it is impermissible based on what we have mentioned, unless necessity obliges it, in which case it becomes permissible.

From: Ibn Qudāma, *al-Mughnī*, Vol. XII[172]

As for spoils from their property and taking their offspring captive, we know of no disagreement among the Learned as to its impermissibility, and we mentioned the *ḥadīth* of Abū Umāma, and Ibn Mas'ūd, and because they [Muslim rebels] are inviolable, and what was declared permissible of the spilling of their blood and the taking of their property was done out of the necessity to repel and fight them, and all else remains under the original [ruling] of impermissibility.

Conducting a Truce with Rebels

From: al-Shaybānī, *Siyar*[173]

I asked: If the rebels want to enter into a peace agreement with the lawful authorities (the loyalists) for a specified number of days or for a month until they reconsider their position, would it be lawful to do so?

He replied: Yes, if this were advantageous to the loyalists.

From: al-Shāfiʿī, *al-Umm*, Vol. IV[174]

And if the rebels say, "Give us a reprieve, to reexamine our stance," I see nothing wrong with granting them a reprieve.

He said: "And if they say, 'Give us a reprieve for a while,' I am of the opinion that the *Imām* should exercise *ijtihād* on the matter, and if it is to be hoped that they will [comply with God's command], then I favor being patient with them."

From: Ibn Ḥazm, *al-Muḥalla*, Vol. XI[175]

And what if the rebels ask for a reprieve to reexamine their stance? If it is not a ruse, then he should grant them a reprieve for a period that would allow them to reexamine [their affairs] only. And that is the duration of time [necessary] only to invite them [to return to the fold] and present [the rebels] with undeniable proofs [that they are in error]; anything that exceeds that is impermissible.

From: Ibn Qudāma, *al-Mughnī*, Vol. XII[176]

And if they ask for a reprieve, he should consider their condition and inquire into their doings, and if it becomes apparent to him that their intention is to return to obedience and cognizance of the truth, he should grant them the respite.

Ibn al-Mundhir said: "This was the consensus of all of the Learned whose [opinions] I have memorized."

And if their intention [the rebels] is to gather to fight him [the *Imām*], and await reinforcement to strengthen them, or to deceive the *Imām* to take him unawares, and disperse his troops, he should not grant them the respite, [but rather] proceed to fight them because he cannot be assured that this will not become a means to vanquishing the Righteous. And that [granting the rebels a respite in the knowledge that it will be used to strengthen their position] is impermissible, even if they give him [the *Imām*] money to do so, because it is impermissible for him to take money to affirm them [the rebels] upon that which it is impermissible to affirm them upon.

And if they give him [the *Imām*] hostages to grant them a respite, it is impermissible to take them for that reason [that it would risk affirming the rebels on an illegitimate basis], and because it is impermissible to slay hostages for the perfidy of their people, and as such, there is no benefit to it [taking the hostages].

And if they [the rebels] have in their power captives from the Righteous, and gave [in exchange] hostages from among them [the rebels], the *Imām* should accept them, and triumph for the Muslims; and if they release the Muslim captives they hold, their hostages are to be released, and if they slay [the captives] they hold, it is impermissible to slay their hostages, because they are not to be slain for slaying [perpetrated] by others.

And if the war is concluded, the hostages are to be released, as the captives taken from among them are to be released.

And if the *Imām* fears the Righteous faction is too weak to confront them [the rebels], he should delay fighting them until he is able to overcome them, because he cannot be assured [that the Muslims] will not be annihilated and extirpated, and so he should hold off [fighting the rebels] until the Righteous are strengthened, and then fight them.

And if they [the rebels] ask him [the *Imām*] to grant them respite in perpetuity, and leave them be, and they would cease [to fight] the Muslims, it should be considered, and if he [the *Imām*] is not certain of his ability to overcome them, and fears that they will vanquish him if he fights them, he should leave them be.

And if he is strong enough to overcome them, it is impermissible to affirm them on that basis, because it is impermissible that some Muslims [be allowed] to abandon obedience to the *Imām*, and because their might cannot be secured, in such a manner that it [may] lead to the defeat of the Righteous *Imām* and those with him.

Liability for Damage to Life and Property

From: Mālik, *al-Mudawwana*[177]

I said: "What if the *Khawārij* rebel, and they shed blood and plunder, and then repent and cease their rebellion?"

He said: "It was reported to me that Mālik said that they are to be absolved from the shedding of blood, but as for plundered property, if they find something specific in their possession, they should take it, otherwise, they should not be held liable for any of this, even if they took money, because they have spent it, as per the interpretation, and that is what I heard."

From: al-Shaybānī, *Siyar*[178]

I asked: If the rebels repented and joined the loyalists, do you think that they should be held liable for whatever property or life they destroyed during the war?

He replied: No, unless something tangible remained which should be returned to its owners.

I asked: Would the same hold true for whatever property the loyalists had captured and consumed and would any blood they had shed be left unavenged – they would not be liable for that?

He replied: Yes [they would not].

I asked: If the rebels captured property or committed offenses before starting [a] rebellion or before they engaged in fighting, and the *Imām* thereafter made peace with them after they had rebelled on condition that he waive [all the said unlawful acts], do you think that this would be lawful?

He replied: No, it would not be lawful for the *Imām* to make peace with them on such [conditions]; on the contrary, they should be held liable for them.

From: al-Shāfiʿī, *al-Umm*, Vol. IV[179]

Al-Zuhrī said: "I lived through the first *fitna** with the companions of the Apostle of God, God's blessings and peace be upon him, and blood was shed and property pillaged, and there was no retribution [afterward] for [spilled] blood or [destroyed] property or for injuries inflicted on the basis of a [religious] interpretation, save [if] a man's specific property was found, it was returned to its owner."

Al Shāfiʿī said: "And this, as Al-Zuhrī has described it, is our opinion. In that *fitna*, blood was shed and in some cases the slayer and the slain were known, and property was destroyed, and people went on until the war was put to rest between them, and they were subject to [Ali's] rule, and I know not of any who exacted retribution from another, nor took compensation for property destroyed, and I know not of any disagreement among people on that any specific property taken during the rebellion and found [afterward], then its [original] owner is more deserving of it.". . .

And if . . . they [commit a crime] against Exalted and Glorified God's *ḥudūd*,[†] against people's blood, or otherwise, and then [adopt] a [religious interpretation], raise up an *Imām*, and rebel, and then ask that they commit to [ceasing violence] on condition that they be absolved of all or some of the [crimes] they committed before they [adopted] their [*taʾwīl*], it is not for the *Imām* to absolve them of any of it.

From: Ibn Ḥazm, *al-Muḥalla*, Vol. XI[180]

Abū Muhammad, may God have mercy on him, said: "And our position, as stated earlier, is that rebels are three types:[‡] A type [who rebelled] based on an interpretation that is unknown to many of the learned, like relying on a verse that was specified by another verse, or on a *hadīth* that was specified by another *hadīth*, or abrogated by another passage of scripture. And those, as we stated, are excused. Their legal position is similar to that of a ruler who exercises *ijtihād* and errs, slaying or destroying property or engaging in unlawful sexual relations based on his [erroneous] *ijtihād*, if the proof of his error is not presented to him. In this case, the blood money is to be paid by the state treasury, and not by the rebel or his paternal relatives, compensation for property is to be paid by whomever destroyed it, all their judgments are to be abrogated, and no *hadd* punishment is imposed on him for engaging in sexual relations that he did not know were unlawful, as long as he was unaware of the prohibition.

"The same applies to whomever, out of ignorance, relies on an interpretation that contravenes scholarly consensus, and proof of the error was not presented to him or did not reach him.

"As for one who relies on an inexcusable and vitiated interpretation that contravenes scholarly consensus and was not based on the *Qurʾān* and *sunna*, if

---

* Civil unrest.
† Specified punishments.
‡ Ibn Ḥazm earlier divides rebels into two types only.

evidence is brought forward to him and he understands it and he concocts an interpretation, and he is presented with evidence and shows stubbornness, then whoever slays in such a fashion should face retribution for the life [taken] or lesser injuries, and the *hadd* punishment is to [be] imposed on him for engaging in unlawful sexual relations, and he should pay compensation for destroyed property.

"The same applies to one who rises solely in pursuit of material gain, with no interpretation. In fact, such a one cannot be excused, because he willfully embarks on what he knows is prohibited.

"And in Exalted God is success."

From: Ibn Qudāma, *al-Mughnī*, Vol. XII[181]

Nor is it required of the rebels to pay compensation for what they have destroyed during the war, whether lives [taken] or property [destroyed]. And this was the opinion of Abu Ḥanīfa, and al-Shāfiʿī in one of his opinions. In the other [opinion of al-Shāfiʿī], they [are required] to pay compensation for those things....

As for what each has destroyed [of the lives or property] of the other, in other than a state of war, before or after it, then its destroyer is obliged to pay compensation for it. And this was the opinion of al-Shāfiʿī.

And that is why when the *Khawārij* slew Abdullah Ibn Khabbāb, Ali sent them a message: "Grant us the right of retaliation for Abdullah Ibn Khabbāb." And when Ibn Muljam slew ʿAlī outside of battle, retaliation was exacted upon him.

And is it imperative to slay the rebel if he slew one of the Righteous in other than battle? There are two perspectives. One: that it is imperative, because he slew with an unsheathed weapon and spread corruption in the land, and thus it is imperative to slay him, as with highwaymen. And the second: It is not imperative, which is the correct [opinion].

Conclusion

As seen in the selections reproduced above, classical Sunni jurisprudence on the regulation of armed conflict is a highly complex area of law that cannot be reduced to a single line of interpretation. There have been few systematic studies of this terrain, and even fewer that elaborate on the interplay of shifting historical context and the evolution of doctrinal diversity. Indeed, until we have a concrete understanding of this relationship, the classic juristic works will be subjected to arbitrary selection from mainstream and militant works alike, rendering both camps adversaries in an unwinnable debate over whose side is "truer" to the classical literature. Moreover, whereas contemporary authors usually present an overly restrictive conception of what is allowable in armed conflict under classical Islamic law, they are nonetheless commendable for their attempt at relating this law to the modern context. But unless authors consciously acknowledge the diversity (and thus the indeterminacy) of the underlying sources, their attempt at applying these sources to the present day will be vulnerable to the charge of selectivity. A reorientation of the field is sorely needed, one that recognizes the flexibility of the sources and their susceptibility to multiple, equally legitimate interpretations.

Part II: Contemporary Sources

John Kelsay

Classical Sunni judgments regarding the uses of armed force developed in the context of empire. While appeals to the notion of a unified territory of Islam always involved an act of imagination, the power of Muslim rulers and armies was undeniable.

By contrast, Sunni discussions about war in the modern age took shape in a situation characterized by loss of power. Beginning with the British domination of India in the eighteenth century, Muslim armies lost ground to a variety of European powers. The Allied defeat of the Axis powers in World War I proved decisive in this regard; the program of the elite group of officers led by Mustafa Kemal aimed decisively at modernization of the Turkish state, a part of that being the end of financial and other support for the Ottomans. With the demise of the sultanate, the last vestige of the old Sunni empire disappeared.

Loss of power engendered diverse forms of response, not least with respect to the historic law of war. Most Sunni authors in the modern era express a kind of reverence for the past. In that sense, the classical heritage outlined in Part I of this chapter retains a kind of validity, in the sense that the judgments associated with historic scholars such as al-Shafi'i stand as precedents, and any serious attempt to think about armed force in the modern era must refer to them. But what, exactly, is their import? In a new context, what do such precedents mean? Should Muslims adapt, working to develop new political and military institutions to replace those associated with the old imperial states? Or should Muslims resist, finding ways to engage in irregular or guerrilla fighting aimed at a restoration of Sunni power? Who decides?

In a way, the last of these questions looms over all others. Who speaks for Islam? As noted, almost all modern Sunni authors express a kind of reverence for the judgment of historic jurists (*ulama*). One of the most characteristic features of modern discourse, however, is the predominance of writers who are not members of the learned class. Certainly, there are exceptions. Scholars trained at al-Azhar and other historic institutions continue to issue *fatawa*, "opinions" in response to questions regarding Muslim practice, and believers listen to and respect these. But they do not constitute the last or even the most important word on matters of armed force or on many other subjects. From the late nineteenth century to the present, Sunni argument about war is characterized by the diversity of participants – and with that, by a diversity of viewpoints. Of these, the most striking and, in many cases, the most controversial contributions come from people best characterized as "activists." Beginning with Sayyid Ahmad Khan's reply to British presentations of the nefarious role played by Muslims in the Indian uprisings of 1857, intellectuals and community leaders motivated by concern for their people took it upon themselves to lead – usually with support from some portion of the *ulama*, but also in the face of opposition from that quarter.[182]

For many observers, this multivocal character of modern Sunni discourse about war suggests a crisis of authority, a judgment supported by the preponderance of writing about questions associated with the phrase "Islamic State." Are Muslims obligated to found such a political entity? If so, what should it look like? Would it have a constitution? Should its institutions be democratic? Or is the very idea of constitutional democracy antithetical to Islam, with its ideal of submission to the will of God? And in any case, should the struggle to establish a state involve armed force? One of the more important emphases of such writing has thus to do with questions about types of fighting associated with rebellion and resistance. Even, or perhaps one should say particularly, in the post-colonial order of states established following World War II, Sunni argument focused on these matters, as groups of Muslims struggled for liberation from Western influence, and then to establish new, Islamically legitimate patterns of order.

In this context, it hardly seems strange that many contemporary authors would reach back to recover one of the most difficult and controversial sets of precedents developed by classical *ulama*. This is the notion of fighting as an "individual duty," by which conditions of emergency lead to a suspension of ordinary measures of command and control. As several selections below suggest, appeals to this idea are particularly prominent in the work of more militant writers. Given the tendency of people arguing in this vein to support the use of tactics such as assassination and martyrdom operations (also known as "suicide bombings"), the arguments are serious, not least because they are consequential.

Our own proximity to such arguments ought not blind us to other parts of the story of modern Sunni judgments regarding war, however. The selections that follow display a variety of points of view. In one sense, these may be thought of as chapters, so that the arguments respond to very particular social and political contexts, and are thus aimed at equally specific audiences. Sayyid Ahmad Khan's comments in *The Loyal Mohammedans of India* (1860), for example, present classical Muslim judgments about armed force in response to British portrayals of Islam as uniquely prone to war. In doing so, he sought both to distinguish Islam from acts deemed rebellious and to suggest that overly harsh responses by imperial forces provided explanations for such acts. The intended audience is British, along with the class of Indian Muslims educated by or interested in British-Indian institutions. By contrast, the arguments advanced by Hasan al-Banna related to his leadership of the Muslim Brotherhood, a movement first organized as a popular response to the postwar opening in Egyptian politics created by British withdrawal in the 1920s. In that sense, al-Banna's activist understanding of *jihād* is an attempt to build pride and to foster a sense of unity in one of several parties attempting to define the new Egypt. In an analogous way, Mawdudi's treatise seems to be an assertion of the superiority of Muslim conceptions of warfare, responding first to claims that the faith no longer has anything useful to say about such matters, and second to a growing sense that Sunnis in the Indian subcontinent constitute a group for whom particularity is more important than considerations of the need to work with Hindus. In that connection, it is interesting that the essay, while well received by important leaders in Indian Islam in the 1930s, actually became more prominent when, following the establishment of Pakistan in 1948, Mawdudi became the ideologue for Jama'at-e Islami, one of the longest-standing Muslim parties in that country's political life.

As Mawdudi's role in the new state reminds us, World War II sparked important changes in the international system. As the era of European dominance waned, Muslims (along with others) became participants in the United Nations and other institutions in which international law provided norms related to the conduct of war. If Mawdudi's approach involved asserting the superiority of the Islamic way in politics and military matters, others thought it important to stress the agreement between historic tradition and contemporary international standards. In 1948, Mahmud Shaltut (1923–1963) published a treatise on the verses of the *Qur'ān* dealing with fighting. His argument that the sources of Islam indicate that the only just cause for war is defense, and thus that Muslim tradition as consonant with international law was controversial.[183] Shaltut did not stand alone, however. Here, a selection from Muhammad Hamidullah's (1908– 2002) oft-reprinted *Muslim Conduct of State* serves to illustrate a similar view, not only with respect to the verses of the *Qur'ān*, but by way of citing numerous precedents from the tradition of Sharia reasoning.

Muslim participation in the United Nations and other postwar institutions of international society has been steady and important. Nevertheless, developments in the Middle East and other historically Muslim areas, including conflicts between and within states, correlate with the rise of groups devoted to armed resistance. Soon after the June 1967 war during which Israeli troops took control of Jerusalem, the Palestine Liberation Organization would begin its long campaign aimed at securing Palestinian rights. While the official language of the PLO was secular, other groups would declare that their struggle for justice was inspired by Islamic norms. With respect to Sunni Islam, important examples include Islamic Jihad (Egypt), Hamas (which styles itself the Islamic movement for Palestinian liberation), and al-Qā'ida. The treatise known as *The Neglected Duty*, published in 1981, justified the participation of members of Islamic Jihad in the assassination of President Anwar Sadat. The Charter of Hamas tied Muslim precedents to armed struggle against Israel. And the leadership of al-Qā'ida, in particular Usama bin Laden (1957–2011), forged alliances with a variety of groups in claiming the mantle of Islamic tradition for an armed campaign aimed at changing the geopolitical order fostered by the United States and the international community. Our selections end with examples of arguments inspired by the claims and conduct of al-Qā'ida and other like-minded groups.[184]

The selections are thus ordered so as to tell a story, in which case the most striking fact seems to involve increasingly militant views. They may also be viewed as representations of continuing alternatives, however. In that sense, Muhammad Hamidullah's arguments for consonance between Muslim norms and international law builds on the view advanced by Sayyid Ahmad Khan. Themes from these writers are demonstrably present in the writing of Muslim advocates of democracy working today. Such people argue that the strategies and tactics advocated by those appealing to fighting as an individual duty (not least including the late Usama bin Laden) present a truncated version of Sunni Islam, based on a highly selective use of historic sources and displaying a remarkable ignorance about the facts of contemporary political life. As well, Muslim advocates of democracy represent at least an implicit criticism of al-Banna and Mawdudi – authors whose positions, while less militant than those of bin Laden and his contemporaries, nevertheless lend support to notions of Muslim particularity that make democratic practice difficult.

The variety represented in these selections, then, mirrors a Muslim conversation that takes place across space and time, and in which the positions advocated by an author writing in late nineteenth-century British India, whose interests are clearly apologetic, may be picked up by late twentieth- and early twenty-first-century authors working in Europe, North America, or the Middle East focused on the consonance of Islam with democratic ideals. Or again, arguments first developed in the initial steps of postcolonial nation building, and thus located in the formation of political parties, may be furthered in the texts of those who consider that such steps failed, because they were not radical enough. The story is one not only of development, but of continuing argument; and it is by no means clear where one may stand and say, "This is the modern Sunni position on war."

Islamic Norms in British India

Ahmad Khan (1817–1898) took part in a number of intellectual and political movements aimed at fostering Muslim (and more generally Indian) development in the context of British rule. Himself a recipient of a rather traditional Muslim education, he advocated a new type of Muslim institution, in which students would receive training in modern scientific and historical disciplines, as well as in classical Islamic scholarship. In writings such as *The Causes of the Indian Revolt*, Ahmad Khan sought to inform an English-speaking audience regarding the heritage and ideals of Islam. Along the way, he developed a unique position regarding armed struggle. As in this selection from "The Loyal Mohammedans of India" (1860), the point was to affirm historic judgments related to the conduct of fighting, as well as to suggest that British "protection" of Muslims provided a reason against rebellion. Among other features of the text, readers will note Ahmad Khan's adoption of standard (at the time) British terminology (e.g., "Mohammedans" instead of Muslims).

From: Ahmad Khan, "The Loyal Mohammedans of India"[185]

… I am no advocate of those Mohammedans who behaved undutifully, and joined in the Rebellion.…

[A]t the same time, I must deprecate that wholesale denunciation against the entire class of Mohammedans … which stains the pages of those who have written upon the events of 1857.…

Be it known that the object of a *jihād*[*] … is not to practice treachery and cruelty; and no sane man can, with the most distant approach to truth, apply that term to an insurrection characterized by violence, crime, and bloodshed, in defiance of, and utter disregard to, Divine commands. And further, a *jihād*, according to the principles of Mohammedan faith, really cannot take place under the present regime! The reason is, that the Mohammedans are living under the protection of their European rulers.…

---

[*] Altered from the original spelling "Juhad."

It is a strict and sacred command of our prophet to his followers, that when they wage war against their enemies, they are not to slay the women, nor children, nor the aged, nor the unresisting, nor those who demand quarter, even if they be *Kaffirs* [i.e., unbelievers].

Reclaiming *Jihād*

Ahmad Khan wrote in the context of British domination; as noted above, loss of power is one of the more persistent themes in Muslim writing from the middle of the eighteenth through the nineteenth and early twentieth centuries. Even as the demise of the Ottoman sultanate following World War I epitomized such loss, however, the first steps toward a lessening of British, and more generally European, power in the countries populated by Muslims created an opportunity for reassertions of Muslim political and military claims. Activists such as Hasan al-Banna (1906–1949) and Abu'l a'la Mawdudi (1903–1979) moved to fill this opening. Ahmad Kahn presented Islam as consonant with the norms of humanity in war. By contrast, al-Banna and Mawdudi claimed superiority for the Muslim way.

Hasan al-Banna, "On Jihad"

Probably written during the 1930s, "On Jihad" constitutes one of a number of "epistles" by which al-Banna offered instruction to members of the Muslim Brotherhood. Here, as throughout the text, al-Banna refers to historic precedents as a source of legitimacy. Significantly, he argues that given the contemporary circumstances of Muslim societies, such precedents indicate that *jihād* should be considered an individual duty. The goal is to enable the Muslim community to carry out its mission of calling human beings to Islam. When fighting becomes necessary in this regard, believers engaged in armed struggle observe the proprieties established by the Prophet and thus bear witness to the noble values of their faith.

From: Hasan al-Banna, "On Jihad" (ca. 1930s)[186]

Now you can see from all this how the men of learning, both those who employed independent judgment and those who strictly followed tradition, the earliest and the latest, agree unanimously that *jihād* is a communal obligation imposed upon the Islamic *umma* in order to broadcast the summons [to embrace Islam], and that it is an individual obligation to repulse the attack of unbelievers upon it. Today the Muslims, as you know, are compelled to humble themselves before non-Muslims, and are ruled by unbelievers. Their lands have been trampled over, and their honor besmirched. Their adversaries are in charge of their affairs, and the rites of their religion have fallen into abeyance within their own domains, to say nothing of their impotence to broadcast the summons [to embrace Islam]. Hence it has become an individual obligation, which there is no evading, on every

Muslim to prepare his equipment, to make up his mind to engage in *jihād*, and to get ready for it until the opportunity is ripe and God decrees a matter which is sure to be accomplished....

People have been for some time stigmatizing Islam because of the religious ordinance of *jihad* and the [divine] permission to wage war until the [message of] the precious *Qur'ānic* verse is fulfilled: "We shall show them Our signs in the farthest horizons and in themselves, until it is made clear to them that it is the Truth" (Q. 41:53). And now here they are acknowledging that it is the surest way to peace! God ordained *jihād* for the Muslims not as a tool of oppression or a means of satisfying personal ambitions, but rather as a defense for the mission [of spreading Islam], a guarantee of peace, and a means of implementing the Supreme Message, the burden of which the Muslims bear, the Message guiding mankind to truth and justice. For Islam, even as it ordains *jihād*, extols peace: the Blessed and Almighty said: "But if they incline toward peace, incline thou toward it, and put thy trust in God" [Q. 8:61]....

For when they fight, they do not instigate hostilities, nor do they behave licentiously, nor do they mutilate, nor do they steal or plunder property, nor do they commit rape, nor do they indulge in wanton destruction. In their warfare they are the best of fighters, just as in peace they are the most excellent of peacemakers ....

So also it is forbidden to slay women, children, and old men, and to dispatch the wounded, or to disturb monks and hermits, and the peaceful who offer no resistance.

Abu'l a'la Mawdudi, *Jihad in Islam*

First published in Urdu as a series of articles, *Al-Jihad fi'l Islam* came out in book form in 1930. At the time, Mawdudi was only beginning his long career. The selections that follow illustrate some of the most consistent themes in his writing, portraying *jihād* as struggle to establish, maintain, and defend a social-political order in which questions of policy are resolved with reference to divine guidance. As Mawdudi has it, this implies a comprehensive revolution in human affairs. If and when the struggle rises to the level of armed force, standard distinctions between offensive and defensive war do not apply. The most important requirement has to do with the intention to establish God's cause, which is by definition just.

From: Abu'l a'la Mawdudi, *Jihad in Islam* (1930)[187]

For the Cause of God": The Essential Condition

But the "Jihad" of Islam is not merely a "struggle"; it is a "struggle for the Cause of God.""For the Cause of God" is an essential condition for "*jihād*" in Islam....

The condition "in the cause of God" has been attached to "*jihād*" for the same reason. It strictly implies that when a person or a group arises to carry out a revolution in the system of life and to establish a new system in conformity with the ideology of Islam, he or they should keep no selfish motives in mind while offering sacrifices and executing acts of devotion for the Cause. The aim should not be to knock out an Emperor and occupy the vacant throne, i.e., to become a Caesar replacing another

Caesar. The objectives of the struggle should be completely free from the taint of selfish motives like gaining wealth or goods, fame and applause, personal glory or elevation. All sacrifices and exertions should be directed to achieve the one and only end, i.e., the establishment of a just and equitable social order among human beings; and the only reward in view should be to gain the favor of God. . . .

A World Revolution

It must be evident to you from this discussion that the objective of the Islamic "Jihad" is to eliminate the rule of an un-Islamic system and establish in its stead an Islamic system of state rule. Islam does not intend to confine this revolution to a single state or a few countries; the aim of Islam is to bring about a universal revolution. Although in the initial stages it is incumbent upon members of the party of Islam to carry out a revolution in the State system of the countries to which they belong, . . . their ultimate objective is no other than to effect a world revolution.

The Terms "Offensive" and "Defensive" Are Irrelevant

If you carefully consider the explanation given above you will readily understand that the two terms "offensive" and "defensive" by which the nature of warfare is differentiated are not at all applicable to Islamic "*jihād*." These terms are relevant only in the context of wars between nations and countries, for technically the terms "attack" and "defense" can only be used with reference to a country or a nation. But when an international party rises with a universal faith and ideology and invites all peoples as human beings to embrace this faith and ideology and admits into its fold as equal members men of all nationalities and strives only to dismantle the rule of an opposing ideology and set up in its place a system of government based on its own ideology, then in this case the use of the technical terms like "offense" and "defense" is not germane. Even if we stop thinking about these technical terms, the division of Islamic "Jihad" into offensive and defensive is not admissible. Islamic *jihād* is both offensive and defensive at one and the same time. It is offensive because the Muslim Party assaults the rule of an opposing ideology and it is defensive because the Muslim Party is constrained to capture state power in order to arrest the principles of Islam in space-time forces. As a party, it has no home to defend; it upholds certain principles which it must protect. Similarly, this party does not attack the home of the opposing party, but launches an assault on the principles of the opponent. The objective of this attack, moreover, is not to coerce the opponent to relinquish his principles but to abolish the government which sustains these principles.

Muslim Norms and International Law

Muhammad Hamidullah, Muslim Conduct of State

In his preface to the first (1941) edition of this work, the author writes of his experience as a young student of international law: "It struck me at once that what was taught us as international law was identical in many respects with the teachings of the books of *fiqh* and Muslim history." Hamidullah developed this idea and submitted the results for a doctorate at the University of Bonn in Germany. Subsequently reprinted in various editions (and translated into numerous languages), the work aimed primarily at Muslims involved with international institutions. The selection here, taken from the seventh edition (1977), deals with issues related to the conduct of war. The author quickly summarizes a number of standard precedents regarding targeting, weapons, and tactics. One notes that his comment about poison gases seems to contradict his assertions of the consonance between historic Muslim norms and international law. Where new forms of warfare suggest that historic rulings be updated, the author's argument involves an incorporation of the existing standards of the international community.

From: Muhammad Hamidullah, *Muslim Conduct of State* (1941)[188]

Acts Forbidden

In actual fight the following acts are forbidden to a Muslim army as regards enemy persons and property:

1. Unnecessarily cruel and tortuous ways of killing. The Prophet has said in this connection: "Fairness is prescribed by God in every matter; so if you kill, kill in a fair way."
2. Killing noncombatants: Combatants are only those who are physically capable of fighting. Women, minors, servants, and slaves who accompany their masters yet do not take part in actual fighting, the blind, monks, hermits, the very old, those physically incapable of fighting, the insane or delirious – these are authoritative examples thereof. . . .
3. Prisoners of war are not to be decapitated. . . .
4. Mutilation of men as well as beasts.
5. Treachery and perfidy.
6. Devastation, destruction of harvest, cutting trees unnecessarily.

Acts Permitted

. . . The enemy might be attacked with all kinds of weapons. In this matter ships and forts were regarded as the same. Of course unnecessary bloodshed is to be avoided. In the time of the Prophet, one comes across superior strategy and better tactics in the Muslim army, . . . [and] also new formations, new methods of defense. Ditch warfare was not known in Hijaz before the Prophet. The element of surprise was also included as much as possible, which diminished bloodshed and procured easy surrender. The Caliph Mu'awiya used incendiary materials in his marine expeditions. S.P. Scott records that the Muslims of Spain used in the seventh century of Hijrah what might be considered a crude form of cannon. During the Crusades the Muslims used a kind of marine mine. During the same time, Salahuddin managed to send his ships to ports besieged by Christians by placing pigs on the deck and clothing the sailors in Christian dress. An author of at least several hundred years ago mentions even poison gases. He says: . . . "As for acts of belligerency in war, like fires, smokes, prepared liquids and ill-smelling deadly odors (gases?), for causing damage to forts and castles and horrifying the enemy, they are permitted."

The name of the author is not known; the manuscript was copied in 123 A.H. Various formulae for the preparation of poisonous gases are given in another old MS. in Arabic. Attacks with smoke are mentioned and upheld by such an old author as Burhanuddin al-Margbinaniy (d. 616). Ash-Shaybani allows surprise attacks, burning forts and flooding them with water.

Instruments for producing terrifying and shrill sounds as a consternater were resorted to by Arabs and other Muslim peoples.... [Assassination] is allowed in Muslim law, and may perhaps be justified on the ground that often it diminishes greater bloodshed and discord, and it is resorted to as the lesser of two evils. In the life of the Prophet there are several clear instances of it. The expeditions dispatched by him against Abu'l Huqaiq, Ka'b ibn al-Ashraf, Abu Rafi and Sufyan ibn 'Anas were successful, and the one against Abu Sufyan failed to achieve the desired aim....

Air Warfare

... Naturally we have no classical literature to refer [to] on the laws of air warfare. The general principle enunciated elsewhere, however, holds good, that Muslims abide by the pacts and conventions they conclude. The international conventions on the laws of air are now parts of Muslim law, even if temporary, insofar as they have been adhered to by independent Muslim states. For these conventions, Oppenheimer's or any other modern Western book could be consulted, in order to ascertain the details of these modern laws.

Contemporary Armed Resistance

World Islamic Front, Declaration on Armed Resistance against Jews and Crusaders

This document first appeared on 23 February 1998, in *al-Quds al-Arabi*, an Arabic-language newspaper published in London. Sometimes described as Usama bin Laden's *fatwa*, the text was also signed by several other militant leaders and represented an alliance between bin Laden's al-Qā'ida and other groups. The Declaration begins with invocations of verses from the *Qur'ān* and selected *ḥadīth* reports, and then moves to a summary of the contemporary circumstance of Muslims, in which the United States and its allies are described as attacking Muslims "like people fighting over a plate of food." The judgment that follows is notable for its appeal to fighting as an individual duty, as well as its statement about targeting.

From: Usama bin Laden et al., *World Islamic Front Statement Urging Jihad against Jews and Crusaders* (1998)[189]

All these crimes and sins committed by the Americans are a clear declaration of war on Allah, his messenger, and Muslims. And *'ulama* have throughout Islamic history unanimously agreed that the *jihād* is an individual duty if the enemy destroys the Muslim countries. This was revealed by . . . the Shaykh of al-Islam in his books, where he said: "As for the fighting to repulse [an enemy], it is aimed at defending sanctity and religion, and it is a duty as agreed. . . . Nothing is more sacred than belief except repulsing an enemy who is attacking religion and life."

On that basis, and in compliance with Allah's order, we issue the following *fatwa* to all Muslims:

The ruling to kill the Americans and their allies – civilians and military – is an individual duty for every Muslim who can do it in any country in which it is possible to do it, in order to liberate the al-Aqsa Mosque and the holy mosque [Mecca] from their grip, and in order for their armies to move out of all the lands of Islam, defeated and unable to threaten any Muslim.

Yusuf al-Qaradawi

Al-Qaradawi (b. 1926) is one of the better-known contemporary interpreters of Islamic law. Educated at al-Azhar, his base of operations has for some years been in Qatar, where he makes use of television and other media to broadcast his opinions on a number of matters, including issues related to armed force. Associated with the Muslim Brotherhood, his opinions differ from those associated with al-Qāʿida. In particular, al-Qaradawi consistently speaks against attacks mounted in foreign countries (as in New York, London, and Madrid). With respect to Palestine, Iraq, and Afghanistan, however, he speaks in terms of fighting as an individual duty. The following selection exemplifies his reasoning.

From: Yusuf al-Qaradawi, "When Is Jihad an Individual Obligation?"[190]

First: If the enemy attacks a Muslim country, or if such an attack is reared and its signs are manifest (this situation is referred to as a "general call to arms"; that is when all Muslims are needed when the unbelievers enter and occupy Muslim land, or if they pose a threat to it and the danger thereto is expected), then it does not suffice for some Muslims of that land [to wage *jihād*] but not others, but rather, all must rise up to resist the invasion, each to the extent to which he is able. . . . This is in contrast to *jihād* in which it is Muslims who seek out and attack their foe. . . . And if the unbeliever's assault is greater than can be borne by the country under attack, then it becomes obligatory upon its nearest neighbors and the countries closest to them to join [the Muslims of the country under attack] with all they can muster, for *jihād* will have become an individual obligation upon them, and all other Muslim countries must supply them with all their needs of men, arms, and funds, until they vanquish their foe and drive out the invaders and exalt the word of Islam. . . . Similarly, if the people of a country are cowardly and abandon resisting the enemies of God and their own [enemies], it becomes obligatory upon those Muslims beyond them to rise up and repel the invasion and resist the enemy, because all Muslim land is the property of all Muslims, not the property of its residents alone, so if they are remiss in defending it, the obligation to defend Muslim land and the Abode of Islam is not lifted from those Muslims beyond them.

The second case in which *jihād* becomes an individual obligation: When the *Imām* calls an individual or specific group to arms, then *jihād* becomes an individual obligation upon them.... The third case: That a Muslim knows that the Muslim army needs him specifically, and that no one else can stand in his stead; for example if he has special experience not otherwise found within the fighting group, in training or tactics, weapons and ammunition.... The fourth case: When actually present in battle, it is impermissible to withdraw.... For his withdrawal at this point undermines the strength of the rest of the army....

Ayman al-Zawahiri

Al-Zawahiri (b. 1951) assumed the leadership of al-Qāʻida following the death of Usama bin Laden. Son and grandson of well-known scholars in Egypt, he became involved with those who claimed responsibility for the assassination of Anwar Sadat and served time in prison. Along with bin Laden, al-Zawahiri was one of the signatories of the World Islamic Front Declaration (see earlier). In the text below, he discusses the legitimacy of martyrdom operations ("suicide bombings"). The first question to be answered is whether an attack undertaken by such a person is legitimate – in particular, can a "suicidal" undertaking be distinguished from the sin of taking one's life? A second question flows from the fact that in many such operations, noncombatants are killed. Reasoning by way of analogy from various historic precedents, al-Zawahiri argues that both issues may be dealt with so that the tactic may be declared legitimate.

From: Al-Zawahiri, "Jihad, Martyrdom, and the Killing of Innocents"[191]

Permission for a Solitary Fighter to Attack a Great Number of Enemies in the Jihad

[Having cited a number of precedents, al-Zawahiri continues.] Based on the above, it becomes clear that there is no difference between the one who causes his own death through his own command ... or through his own actions ... or through the actions of another ... there is no difference whatsoever between the man who kills himself, or who plunges himself into the ranks of the enemy and they kill him, or who commands another to kill him – *provided that this is all done for the good and glory of Islam.*[192]...

[T]he deciding factor in all these situations is one and the same: the intention – is it to serve Islam [martyrdom], or is it out of depression and despair [suicide]?

Part Two: The Permissibility of Bombarding Infidels When Muslims and Others Who Are Not Permitted to Be Killed Are Dispersed amongst Them

[W]e conclude that the view of the *ulema* [is] condensed into three perspectives:

The first view: total prohibition, based on Malik and al-Awzaʻi.

The second view: total legitimacy with blood money and atonement [as the price], based on the words of the Hanafis, Ahmad, a number of Hanbalis, and the later Malikis.

The third view: based on the words of al-Shafi'i and the Hanbalis, permissibility to bombard the idolaters even if Muslims and those who are cautioned against killing are intermingled with them as long as there is a need or an obligation for Muslims to do so, or if not striking leads to a delay of the *jihād*. As for blood money and atonement, these are to be judged individually.

This [third] view is the one that we hold to, that is, permitting bombardments in order to expedite the *jihād* and never cause it delay.

'Abd al-Muni'm Mustafa Halimah (also known as Abu Basir al-Tartusi)

Al-Zawahiri's defense of martyrdom operations remains controversial. In this final selection, a Syrian-born scholar known for very conservative opinions voices criticisms of the tactic.

From: 'Abd al-Muni'm Mustafa Halimah, "Suspicions of Sin in Martyrdom or Suicide Attacks"[193]

More than five years ago, I spoke a few times about the law concerning martyrdom or suicide operations from a number of points of view, [but] to this day the brothers keep asking me the same questions, since they are not able to understand what I've said on this subject, as it is scattered among more than 1,000 responsa. Therefore, I have seen fit to repeat things I have said in those various and sundry responsa in one single article, in detail, in order to make it easier for those interested to read them and understand them.

I said, and I say: These actions are closer to suicide [*intiḥār*] than to martyrdom [*istishhād*] and they are forbidden because of sins they may potentially entail. . . .

The gravest [potential sin] is that . . . someone necessarily kills himself, which contradicts scores of unequivocal and conclusive Sharia texts. . . .

As for the arguments that have been used to prove that it is permitted for someone to kill himself in order to inflict heavy casualties on the enemy, like the proofs that it is permitted to be courageous and plunge into enemy lines . . . this [permission] does not allow one to kill one's self, but rather [permits one to enter into situations where] one is killed by the enemy or by someone else. . . .

One of the prohibitions the violation of which this action may entail is that it generally causes – as anyone can see – the killing of innocent civilians whose wrongful killing is prohibited by the Sharia, whether they be Muslims or non-Muslims. This is a danger that should not be taken lightly, but rather, one should take great pains to stay clear of it. . . .

[T]here is an authentic tradition that the Prophet said, "Beware not to commit the seven cardinal sins," one of which is "taking a life that Allah has made inviolable without justification." ...

NOTES

1 Wael B. Hallaq, *A History of Islamic Legal Theories: An Introduction to Sunni Uṣūl al-Fiqh* (Cambridge: Cambridge University Press, 1997), p. 108.

2 The Arabian Peninsula, or more accurately what is now Saudi Arabia.

3 See Wael Hallaq, "From Regional to Personal Schools of Law, a Re-evaluation," *Islamic Law and Society* 8:1 (2001), pp. 1–26.

4 Wahbaal-Zuhaylī, *Athār al-Ḥarb fī al-Fiqh al-Islāmī* (The Consequences of War in Islamic Jurisprudence), 3rd ed. (Beirut: Dār al-Fikr, 1981), p. 112.

5 Muḥammad ibn Idrīs al-Shāfiʿī, *al-Umm* (The Mother), Maḥmūd Mutrajī (ed.) (Beirut: Dar al-Kutub al-ʿIlmīya, 1993), vol. IV, pp. 219–221.

6 *Qurʾān* (9:5). Unless otherwise indicated, all translations of texts from the *Qurʾān* provided in this chapter are from *The Koran Interpreted*, Arthur J. Arberry (trans.) (New York: Macmillan, 1955).

7 Yūsufal-Qaraḍāwī, *Fiqh al-Jihād* (Jihād Jurisprudence) (Cairo: Maktabat Wahba, 2009), p. 288.

8 *Qurʾān* (9:29).

9 Maḥmūd Shaltuūt, *al-Qurʾān wa al-Qitāl* (*Qurʾān* and Fighting) (Cairo: Maṭbaʿat al-Naṣr, 1948), p. 31.

10 *Qurʾān* (4:90).

11 *Qurʾān* (2:256).

12 In international humanitarian law, justifications for the use of force are often referred to under the heading of *jus ad bellum*, whereas the rules governing the conduct of warfare are referred to as *jus in bello*, but in order to avoid exaggerating the similarity between international humanitarian law and Islamic laws of war, those terms are not here used to describe the rules for waging *jihād* and the rules of conduct in *jihād*.

13 Abū al-Walīd Muḥammad ibn Aḥmad ibn Muḥammad ibn Aḥmad Ibn Rushd (The Grandson), *Bidayāt al-Mujtahid wa Nihāyat al-Muqtaṣid* (The Distinguished Jurist's Primer), Farīd ʿAbdul ʿAzīzal-Jundī (ed.) (Cairo: Dār al-Ḥadīth, 2004), vol. I, p. 151.

14 For a survey of classical and modern literature rejecting offensive *jihād*, see Qarāḍāwī, *Fiqh al-Jihād*, pp. 373–339.

15 *Qurʾān* (9:29).

16 The Prophet is reported to have been asked about the treatment of the Zoroastrians and to have answered that they should be treated on par with People of the Book.

17 As later detailed in the chapter, the primary proponents of treating the Zoroastrians as People of the Book are al-Shāfiʿī and Ibn Ḥazm, while advocates of treating them as nonscripturaries are the Ḥanafīs and the Mālikīs. See Mālikibn Anas, *al-Mudawwana al-Kubra lī al-Imām Mālik ibn Anās al-Aṣbaḥī* (The Grand Document of the Imām Mālik ibn Anās al-Aṣbaḥī) (Beirut: Dār al-Kutub al-ʿIlmīya, 1994), p. 529; Al-Shāfiʿī, *al-Umm*, vol. IV, pp. 243–246; Muḥammadibn al-Ḥasan al-Shaybānī, *The Islamic Law of Nations: Shaybānī's Siyar*, Majid Khadduri (trans.) (Baltimore, Md.: John Hopkins University Press, 1966), p. 224; Ibn Ḥazm, *al-Muḥalla* (The Decorated), Aḥmad Muḥammad Shākir (ed.) (Beirut: al-Maktab al-Tijārī lī al-Ṭibāʿa wa al-Nashr, 1969), vol. VII, pp. 345–346.

18 Al-Shāfiʿī, *al-Umm*, vol. IV, pp. 340–341.

19 Ibid., pp. 340–341, 407. *Al-Umm* is known for providing contradictory views representing changes in his jurisprudential positions (or according to some providing evidence of later editing by his disciples).

20 Ibn Ḥazm, *al-Muḥalla*, vol. VII, p. 296.

21 Mūwaffaq al-Dīn Abī Muḥammad Abd Allāh ibn Aḥmad ibn Muḥammad Ibn Qudāma, *al-Mughnī* (The Sufficient) (Riyadh: Dār 'Ālam al-Kutub, 1999), vol. XIII, p. 180; al-Shaybānī, *Siyar*, pp. 91–92.

22 Reuven Firestone, *Jihad: The Origin of Holy War in Islam* (Oxford: Oxford University Press, 1999), p. 34.

23 Ibn Rushd, *Bidāyat*, p. 144.

24 Ibid.

25 Ibn Qudāma, *al-Mughnī*, vol. XIII, pp. 44–46.

26 *Qur'ān* (47:4).

27 Mālik, *al-Mudawwana*, vol. I, p. 501.

28 Al-Shaybānī, *The Islamic Law of Nations*, p. 101.

29 Al-Shāfi'ī, *al-Umm*, vol. IV, p. 257.

30 Ibn Rushd, *Bidāyat*, pp. 163–164.

31 Ibid.

32 Ibn Ḥazm, *al-Muḥalla*, vol. VII, p. 341.

33 Abū Ja'far Muḥammad Ibn Jarīr al-Ṭabarī, *Kitāb al-Jihād wa Kitāb al-Jizya wa Aḥkām Al-Muḥāribīn min Kitāb Ikhtilāf al-Fuqahā'* (The Book of *Jihād* and the Book of *Jizya* and the Rules on Committers of *Ḥirāba*), Joseph Schacht (ed.) (Leiden: Brill, 1933), p. 25.

34 Khaled Abou El Fadl, *Rebellion and Violence in Islamic Law* (Cambridge: Cambridge University Press, 2001), p. 61.

35 *Qur'ān* (49:9–10). Translated in Abou El Fadl, *Rebellion*, p. 37.

36 Abou El Fadl, *Rebellion*, p. 147.

37 Al-Ṭabarī, *Kitāb al-Jihād*, p. 244.

38 Ibid., p. 242.

39 Khaled Abou El Fadl, "Between Functionalism and Morality," in *Islamic Ethics of Life: Abortion, War and Euthanasia*, Jonathon Brockropp (ed.) (Columbia: University of South Carolina Press, 2003), p. 105.

40 Al-Shāfi'ī, *al-Umm*, vol. IV, pp. 245–246; Ibn Ḥazm, *al-Muḥalla*, vol. VII, pp. 345–346.

41 Aḥmad ibn al-Ḥasan al-Bayhaqī, *Manaqib al-Shafi'i*, Aḥmed Ṣaqr al-Sayid (ed.) (Cairo: Maktabat Dār al-Turāth, 1970), p. 152.

42 David Wasserstein, *The Rise and Fall of the Party-Kings: Politics and Society in Islamic Spain 1002–1086* (Princeton, N.J.: Princeton University Press, 1985), p. 231.

43 Al-Shaybānī, *Siyar*, pp. 101–102.

44 Wasserstein, *The Rise and Fall of the Party Kings*, p. 280.

45 Ibn Ḥazm, *al-Muḥalla*, vol. XI, p. 98.

46 Al-Shaybānī, *Siyar*, p. 81.

47 Ibid.

48 Ibn Hazm, *al-Muhalla*, vol. VII, p. 332.

49 Ibid.

50 Al-Shaybānī, *Siyar*, p. 183.

51 Ibid., p. 186.

52 Ibid., p. 187.

53 Ibid., p. 33.
54 Al-Bayhaqī, *Manāqib*, p. 107.
55 Ibn Ḥazm quoted and translated in Wasserstein, *The Rise and Fall of the Party Kings*, p. 280.
56 Al-Shaybānī, *Siyar*, p. 114.
57 Ibid., p. 116.
58 Ibid., p. 231. Clarifications in brackets added by translator.
59 Ibid., p. 232.
60 Ibid., p. 236.
61 Abou El Fadl, *Rebellion and Violence*, p. 215.
62 J. Schacht, "Mālik b. Anas," in *Encyclopaedia of Islam*, 2nd ed., P. Bearman, Th. Bianquis, C. E. Bosworth, E. van Donzel, and W. P. Heinrichs (eds.) (Brill Online, 2010), available at http://www.brillonline.nl/subscriber/entry?entry=islam_COM-0649.
63 Often referred to as Muḥammad.
64 Al-Shāfiʿī, *al-Umm*, vol. IV, p. 241. Al-Shāfiʿī's work cited in this chapter is translated by Aziz El-Kaissouni.
65 Ibn Ḥazm, *al-Muḥalla*, vol. VII, p. 291. Ibn Ḥazm's work cited in this chapter is translated by Aziz El-Kaissouni.
66 See, e.g., Yūsuf al-Qaraḍāwī, *Fiqh al-Jihād*, vol. I, p. 332.
67 Mālik, *al-Mudawwana*, p. 496. Mālik's work cited in this chapter is translated by Aziz El-Kaissouni.
68 Al-Shāybanī, *Siyar*, pp. 76, 95.
69 Al-Shāfiʿī, *al-Umm*, vol. IV, pp. 339–340.
70 Ibn Qudāma, *al-Mughnī*, vol. XIII, p. 29. Ibn Qudāma's work cited in this chapter is translated by Aziz El-Kaissouni.
71 Al-Shāfiʿī, *al-Umm*, vol. IV, p. 271.
72 Al-Shaybānī, *Siyar*, p.154.
73 Ibn Qudāma, *al-Mughnī*, vol. XIII, p. 155.
74 A truce agreement conducted between the Prophet and Quraysh in al-Ḥudaybiya near Mecca in 628 CE.
75 *Qurʾān* (9:29).
76 Al-Shāfiʿī, *al-Umm*, vol. IV, pp. 243–244.
77 Mālik, *al-Mudawwana*, vol. I, p. 529.
78 Al-Shaybānī, *Siyar*, p. 224.
79 Al-Shāfiʿī, *al-Umm*, vol. IV, pp. 245–246.
80 Ibn Ḥazm, *al-Muḥalla*, vol. VII, pp. 345–346.
81 Ibid., vol. IX, p. 445.
82 Al-Shāfiʿī, *al-Umm*, vol. IV, p. 260.
83 Ibn Qudāma, *al-Mughnī*, vol. XIII, p. 31.
84 Al-Shāfiʿī, *al-Umm*, vol. IV, p. 249.
85 Ibn Ḥazm, *al-Muḥalla*, vol. VII, p. 346.
86 Ibn Qudāma, *al-Mughnī*, vol. XIII, p. 207.
87 Al-Shāfiʿī, *al-Umm*, vol. IV, p. 260.
88 Ibn Ḥazm, *al-Muḥalla*, vol. VII, pp. 317–318.
89 A fundamental Mālikī text.
90 Ibn Qudāma, *al-Mughnī*, vol. XIII, p. 216.
91 Ibn Ḥazm, *al-Muḥalla*, vol. VII, p. 347.
92 Mālik, *al-Mudawwana*, vol. I, p. 499.
93 Al-Shaybānī, *Siyar*, pp. 87, 91–92, 101.

94 Ibn Qudāma, *al-Mughnī*, vol. XIII, pp. 175, 178, 180.

95 Al-Shāfi'ī, *al-Umm*, vol. IV, pp. 247–248, 337, 340–341, 406.

96 630 CE in Ḥunayn, close to Mecca.

97 Al-Shāfi'ī, *al-Umm*, vol. IV, pp. 407, 406.

98 Ibn Ḥazm, *al-Muḥalla*, vol. VII, p. 296.

99 Al-Shāfi'ī, *al-Umm*, vol. IV, p. 340.

100 Ibn Qudāma, *al-Mughnī*, vol. XIII, pp. 179, 141. Notice how the killing of Ibn al-Ṣama was interpreted differently by jurists. Whereas it is relied on by al-Shāfi'ī to prove that any old man may be killed, Ibn Qudāma relates to it as an exception to the general rule prohibiting targeting of older men, the exception being providing support to the enemy.

101 Battles with the Jewish clan of Banū Qurayẓa in Medina (627 CE).

102 Ibn Hazm, *al-Muḥalla*, vol. VII, p. 296.

103 Mālik, *al-Mudawwana*, vol. I, pp. 512–513.

104 Al-Shaybānī, *Siyar*, pp. 101–102.

105 Al-Shāfi'ī, *al-Umm*, vol. IV, pp. 337–338, 347.

106 Ibid., p. 409. It seems that al-Shāfi'ī, despite the enthusiasm for indiscriminate targeting in earlier passages, was aware of the contradiction of this position with a reluctance to allow casualties among Muslims. Hence, in the last passage, where there is a reference to the presence of non-Muslim women and children as well as Muslims, he adopts a more hesitant approach to the killing of these women and children.

107 Ibn Qudāma, *al-Mughnī*, vol. XIII, pp. 138–140, 141–142.

108 *Qur'ān* (48:25).

109 Ibn Ḥazm, *al-Muḥalla*, vol. VII, p. 296.

110 Abdullahi Ahmed An-Na'im, *Towards an Islamic Reformation: Civil Liberties, Human Rights and International Law* (Cairo: American University Press, 1992), p. 174. Al-Zuḥaylī, *Athār al-Ḥarb*, pp. 442–443.

111 *Qur'ān* (47:4–5).

112 An-Na'im, *Islamic Reformation*, p. 174.

113 Al-Shaybānī, *Siyar*, p. 219.

114 Ibid., pp. 97–98.

115 Al-Shāfi'ī, *al-Umm*, vol. IV, p. 335.

116 Ibid., p. 250.

117 Ibid., p. 341.

118 Ibn Qudāma, *al-Mughnī*, vol. XIII, pp. 44–47, 48, 49.

119 Juristic interpretation on the basis of knowledge of the sources and the school's methodology of interpretation.

120 Ibn Ḥazm, *al-Muḥalla*, vol. VII, p. 324.

121 Mālik, *al-Mudawwana*, vol. I, p. 501.

122 Al-Shaybānī, *Siyar*, pp. 91, 98, 100–101.

123 Al-Shāfi'ī, *al-Umm*, vol. IV, p. 335. It should be noted that al-Shāfi'ī's position on captives contradicts his position on targeting. Whereas he argues that adult male idolaters must be killed if they do not convert and adult scriptured men must be killed if they do not convert or agree to pay the *jizya*, he acknowledges ransom and grace as alternatives for captives. This contradiction portrays the arbitrariness of his claim that targeting rules ought to be independent from participation in combat.

124 Al-Shāfi'ī, *al-Umm*, vol. IV, pp. 250, 371.

125 Ibn Qudāma, *al-Mughnī*, vol. XIII, pp. 44–46.

126 Mālik, *al-Mudawwana*, vol. I, p. 503.

127 Al-Shaybānī, *Siyar*, pp. 77, 83, 99–100.

128 Al-Shāfiʿī, *al-Umm*, vol. IV, p. 257.

129 Ibn Qudāma, *al-Mughnī*, vol. XIII, p. 107.

130 Ibn Ḥazm, *al-Muḥalla*, vol. VII, p. 335.

131 The one-fifth share of the Umma.

132 Mālik, *al-Mudawwana*, vol. I, pp. 500, 524.

133 Al-Shaybānī, *Siyar*, pp. 98–99.

134 Al-Shāfiʿī, *al-Umm*, vol. VII, p. 390.

135 Chain of transmission.

136 Ibn Ḥazm, *al-Muḥalla*, vol. VII, p. 294.

137 Ibn Qudāma, *al-Mughnī*, vol. XIII, pp. 147–148.

138 Ibid., pp. 143–144.

139 See, e.g., Sayyid Imām ʿAbdul ʿAzīz, "Tarshīd Al-Jihād fī Misr wa Al-ʿĀlam, Al-Ḥalaqa al-Sābiʿa (A Minimalist Approach to Jihad in Egypt and the World-Episode Seven)," *al-Masrī al-Yawm*, 25 November 2007, p. 4; and Ayman al-Ẓawāhir, "al-Tabriʾa (Exoneration)," *As-Saḥab Media*, available at www.tawhed.ws/a?a=3i806qpo.

140 Mālik, *al-Mudawwana*, vol. I, p. 501.

141 Al-Shaybānī, *Siyar*, pp. 158–159, 160–161, 170, 191.

142 Al-Shāfiʿī, *al-Umm*, vol. IV, p. 405.

143 Ibid., pp. 353, 355.

144 Ibn Ḥazm, *al-Muḥalla*, vol. VII, pp. 306, 309.

145 People granted *amān*.

146 Ibn Qudāma, *al-Mughnī*, pp. 80, 152–153.

147 Mālik, *al-Mudawwana*, pp. 529–530.

148 Al-Shāfiʿī, *al-Umm*, vol. IV, pp. 303, 309.

149 Ibn Ḥazm, *al-Muḥalla*, vol. XI, p. 58.

150 Ibn Qudāma, *al-Mughnī*, vol. XII, p. 237.

151 Mālik, *al-Mudawwana*, p. 530.

152 Al-Shaybānī, *Siyar*, p. 250.

153 Al-Shāfiʿī, *al-Umm*, vol. IV, p. 308.

154 A *ḥadd* punishment is a punishment specifically stipulated in the textual sources.

155 Ibn Ḥazm, *al-Muḥalla*, vol. XI, p. 98.

156 Ibn Qudāma, *al-Mughnī*, vol. XII, p. 242.

157 Al-Shaybānī, *Siyār*, p. 247.

158 Al-Shāfiʿī, *al-Umm*, vol. IV, pp. 307–308.

159 Al-Shaybānī, *Siyar*, pp. 231–232, 236.

160 A battle between the fourth Caliph, Ali, and the Prophet's companion (including his wife Aisha), after the death of the third Caliph. The battle took place in 656 CE.

161 Al-Shāfiʿī, *al-Umm*, vol. IV, pp. 303, 308.

162 Umayyad fighting alongside Muʿāwiya.

163 Al-Shāfiʿī, *al-Umm*, vol. IV, pp. 311–312.

164 Ibn Ḥazm, *al-Muḥalla*, vol. XI, p. 100.

165 Ibid., pp. 116–117.

166 Ibid., vol. XI, p. 100.

167 Ibid., vol. XI, p. 101.

168 Ibn Qudāma, *al-Mughnī*, vol. XII, pp. 247, 252–253.

169 Al-Shaybānī, *Siyar*, p. 232.

170 Al-Shāfiʿī, *al-Umm*, vol. IV, p. 311.

171 Ibn Ḥazm, *al-Muḥalla*, vol. XI, p. 102.

172 Ibn Qudāma, *al-Mughnī*, vol. XII, p. 254.

173 Al-Shaybānī, *Siyar*, p. 234.

174 Al-Shāfiʿī, *al-Umm*, vol. IV, p. 311.

175 Ibn Ḥazm, *al-Muḥalla*, vol. XI, p. 116.

176 Ibn Qudāma, *al-Mughnī*, vol. XII, pp. 244–245.

177 Mālik, *al-Mudawwana*, p. 530.

178 Al-Shaybānī, *Siyar*, pp. 234–235, 240.

179 Al-Shāfiʿī, *al-Umm*, vol. IV, pp. 304, 309.

180 Ibn Ḥazm, *al-Muḥalla*, vol. XI, p. 107.

181 Ibn Qudāma, *al-Mughnī*, vol. XII, pp. 250, 251.

182 Sayyid Ahmad Khan, *The Causes of the Indian Revolt* (Lahore: Book House, 1970).

183 For reasons of space, Shaltut's essay is not included in this volume. It is available in Rudolph Peters, *Jihad in Classical and Modern Islam* (Princeton, N.J.: Markus Wiener, 1996), 59–102.

184 See *The Neglected Duty*, trans. Johannes J. G. Jansen (New York: Macmillan, 1986); the Hamas *Charter* is available in a translation by M. Maqdsi (Dallas, Tex.: Islamic Association for Palestine, 1990).

185 Ahmad Khan, "The Loyal Mohammedans of India," in *Writings and Speeches of Sir Syed Ahmad Khan*, Shan Mohammad (ed.) (Bombay: Nachiketa Publications, 1972), pp. 36, 43–44, 47.

186 Hasan al-Banna, *Five Tracts of Hasan al-Banna*, Charles Wendell (trans.) (Berkeley: University of California Press, 1975), vol. XX, pp. 150, 151, 154.

187 Abu'l aʿ laMawdudi, *Jihad in Islam* (Lahore: Islamic Publications, 1976), pp. 7, 8–9, 22, 25–26.

188 Muhammad Hamidullah, *Muslim Conduct of State*, 7th ed. (Lahore: SH Muhammad Ashraf, 1977), pp. 205, 225–227, 229.

189 Usama bin Laden et al., *World Islamic Front Statement Urging Jihad against Jews and Crusaders*, available at http://www.fas.org/irp/world/para/docs/980223-fatwa.html.

190 Yusuf al-Qaradawi, *Fiqh al-Jihad* (Cairo: Maktabat Wahbat, 2009), pp. 90–107. Translated by Aziz El-Kaissouni.

191 Raymond Ibrahim, *The al-Qaeda Reader* (New York: Broadway Books, 2007), pp. 156, 157, 168.

192 Emphasis in original.

193 ʿAbd al-Muniʾm Mustafa Halimah (Abu Baseer al-Tartousi), "Suspicions of Sin in Martyrdom or Suicide Attacks," posted 11 November 2005, accessed 20 December 2012, available at www.en.altartosi.com/suicide.htm.

SELECT BIBLIOGRAPHY

Abū Zahra, Muḥammad, *Al-ʿIlaqāt al-Dawliyya fī al-Islām* (International Relations in Islam) (Cairo: al-Dār al-Qawmīyya li al-Tibāʿa wal Nashr, 1964).

Ali, Shaheen Sardar, "Resurrecting Siyar through Fatwas? (Re)Constructing Islamic International Law in a Post-(Iraq) Invasion World," *Journal of Conflict and Security Law* 14:1 (2009), 115–144.

Al-Zuhaylī, Wahba, *Athār al-Harb fī al-fiqh al-Islāmī: Dirāsah Muqaranah* (The Effects of War in Islamic Jurisprudence: A Comparative Study), 2nd ed. (Damascus: Dār al-Fikr, 1981).

Bennoune, Karima, "As-Salāmu ʿAlaykum? Humanitarian Law in Islamic Jurisprudence," *Michigan Journal of International Law* 15 (1993–1994), 605–643.

Bonney, Richard, *Jihad: From Qur'an to Bin Laden* (New York: Palgrave Macmillan, 2004).

Brockopp, Jonathon (ed.), *Islamic Ethics of Life: Abortion, War and Euthanasia* (Columbia: University of South Carolina Press, 2003).

Cockayne, James, "Islam and International Humanitarian Law: From a Clash to a Conversation between Civilisations," *International Review of the Red Cross*, vol. 84, September 2002, accessed 20 March 2013, available at http://www.icrc.org/eng/resources/documents/misc/5fld2f.htm.

Cook, Michael, *Commanding Right and Forbidding Wrong in Islamic Thought* (Cambridge: Cambridge University Press, 2000).

El Fadl, Khaled Abou, *Rebellion and Violence in Islamic Law* (Cambridge: Cambridge University Press, 2001).

Evans, Carolyn, "The Double Edged Sword: Religious Influences on International Humanitarian Law," *Melbourne Journal of International Law* 6 (2005), 1–31.

Firestone, Reuven, *Jihad: The Origin of Holy War in Islam* (Oxford: Oxford University Press, 1999).

Freamon, Bernard K., "Martyrdom, Suicide, and the Islamic Law of War: A Short Legal History," *Fordham International Law Journal* 27 (2003), 299–369.

Hussain, Jamila, *Islam: Its Law and Society* (Sydney: Federation Press, 2003).

Johnson, James Turner, and John Kelsay (eds.), *Cross, Crescent and Sword: The Justification and Limitation of War in Western and Islamic Tradition* (New York: Greenwood Press, 1990).

Kelsay, John, *Arguing the Just War in Islam* (Cambridge, Mass.: Harvard University Press, 2007.

Kelsay, John, and James Turner Johnson (eds.), *Just War and Jihad: Historical and Theoretical Perspectives on War and Peace in Western and Islamic Traditions* (New York: Greenwood Press, 1991).

Kepel, Gilles, *Jihad: The Trail of Political Islam* (Cambridge, Mass.: Belknap Press of Harvard University Press, 2002).

Khadduri, Majid, *The Law of War and Peace in Islam: A Study in Muslim International Law* (London: Luzac, 1940).

Malekian, Farhad, *The Concept of Islamic International Criminal Law* (London: Graham & Trotman, 1994).

Malka, Haim, "Must Innocents Die? The Islamic Debate over Suicide Attacks," *Middle East Quarterly* 10:2 (2003), 19–28.

Peters, Rudolph, *Jihad in Classical and Modern Islam* (Princeton, N.J.: Markus Wiener, 2005).

Tibi, Bassam, *Islamism and Islam* (New Haven, Conn.: Yale University Press, 2012).

Van Engeland, Anisseh, "The Differences and Similarities between International Humanitarian Law and Islamic Humanitarian Law: Is There Ground for Reconciliation?," *Journal of Islamic Law and Culture* 10:1 (2008), 81–99.

6

Shi'ite Islam

Mohammad H. Faghfoory

The term "Shi'ite" existed during the time of the Prophet of Islam and denoted a number of pious Muslims who had an interest in intellectual, spiritual, and metaphysical issues and who had gathered around Ali ibn Abi Talib, the cousin and son-in-law of Prophet Muhammad.[1] When the Prophet passed away and the question of succession to him began to be discussed, Ali's supporters argued that he must succeed the Prophet not only as the political head of the Islamic state (i.e., Caliph) but also as religious and spiritual leader (Imām) of the community. They believed that before the Prophet passed away in 632 he had in fact appointed Ali as his successor. This claim was based on a number of Traditions of the Prophet accepted by all members of the Islamic community, Shi'ites and Sunnis alike, on the personal virtues and political qualities of Ali. The question, therefore, was not just who the legitimate successor of the Prophet was, but what role and function the successor to the Messenger was expected to perform. In other words, from the Shi'ite view dispute over succession to the Prophet was not a political one; rather, it was a disagreement over profound doctrinal and spiritual issues as well as over the nature of the Islamic state and society. However, while Ali and other family members of the Prophet were preparing for the burial of the Prophet's body, the senior members of the community in Medina gathered and elected Abu Bakr as the first successor to the Prophet. Thus the young Muslim community split and two branches of Islam, namely, Sunnism and Shi'ism, emerged.

Introduction

This chapter examines the Shi'i perspective on war and peace in a historical context. Its objective is to present a Shi'ite understanding of *jihad*[2] and to demonstrate how the Shi'ite clergy's views on war and peace can be translated into political action and impact the political behavior of Shi'i states and societies, and ultimately to show continuity and/or change in the Shi'ite jurists' understanding of war and peace. It is divided into seven parts. The first section is an introduction that examines the unique characteristics of the Shi'ite tradition and Shi'ite clergy – the *'ulama* – and the socio-economic and political foundations of their power. Sections two and three examine the sources of law in Islam and the *Qur'ānic* definition of the concept of *jihad*. The fourth section deals with the views of Shi'i jurists of the classical period on the types of war, followed by a discussion of jurists' opinions on war and peace and the role of the Twelfth *Imām* (the Mahdi) in the fifth section. The sixth section examines the rules of war, types of weapons, treatment of prisoners of war, and the rules concerning the ending of war. Finally, the seventh section provides a summary and conclusion and includes selections from primary sources to demonstrate how in the course of history Shi'i jurists and theologians interpreted the *Qur'ānic* injunctions, the *ḥadīth*, and the narrations of Shi'ite Imams, and the way that they articulated their own views on peace and war on the basis of guidelines presented in those sources.[3]

Before examining these issues, however, it is appropriate to present a few remarks about the Shi'ite tradition and explain the unique characteristics and the status of the *'ulama* within the Shi'i society. This will allow us to see how this status contributed to their understanding of the *Qur'ān* and *ḥadīth* and shaped their views on the legal and theological aspects of war and peace. It will also assist in the exploration of the role played by the *'ulama* in the course of history in preserving peace and/or promoting war.

Shi'ite Islam

Shi'ism, like Sunnism, is a part of Islamic orthodoxy. The term "Shi'ite" means "follower" or "partisan" and was used for the first time by the Prophet when he referred to a group of his companions who had gathered around his cousin and son-in-law Ali ibn Abi Talib. They included Salman, Miqdad, Abu Dhar, and 'Ammar, to whom the Prophet referred as Shi'ites of Ali.[4]

Ali was the cousin and son-in-law of the Prophet and the first male who accepted Islam when he was reportedly twelve or thirteen years old. For the next twenty-three years Ali served Mohammad sincerely and participated in major battles on the side of the Prophet. A man of special talent, Ali combined the rare qualities of a soldier and a metaphysician. He "personifies the combination of physical heroism on the field of battle with a sanctity wholly detached from the things of the world."[5] There are numerous traditions (*ḥadīth*) on the unique qualities and virtues of Ali narrated by Shi'i and Sunni scholars alike that explain the special status he enjoyed in the eye of the Prophet.[6] Of particular importance is a *ḥadīth* in which the Prophet called Ali as his brother (*akhi*), his legatee (*wasi*), and his successor (*khalifati*).[7]

In 632 the Prophet made his last pilgrimage to Mecca. On his way back to Medina on the 18th day of the month of Dhu'l Hajja (8 March), he stopped for noon prayer in Ghadir-i Khum, an oasis halfway between Mecca and Medina. After performing the prayer, he delivered a speech in which he outlined his will. This speech is commonly known as the *Ḥadīth Ghadiriyyah* whereby, according to Shi'ite belief, he appointed 'Ali as his successor:

> O people! This is the last stand I make in such a situation; so, listen and obey and submit to the command of God, your Lord, indeed God Majestic and Glorious is He, is your Master and Lord, then it is His Messenger and Prophet who is addressing you, then after me Ali is your Master and Imam by God's command, then the

Imamate will be from among my progeny, his offspring, till the Day they meet God and His Messenger.[8]

At another time on the same day and at the same location the Prophet delivered another speech, known as the *Ḥadīth al-Thaqlayn*, or the *Tradition Concerning Two Weighty Matters*. Both of these traditions are recorded as the parallel traditions (*aḥadīth-i mutawatir*) and acknowledged by both Shi'i and Sunni transmitters of *ḥadīth*. In this tradition, the Prophet said:

> O People! It seems the time that I shall be called is approaching and I shall answer that call. Behold, I am leaving you two weighty matters that if you cling upon both of them you shall not go astray after me. One is the Book of Allah, the other one my progeny (*'itrati*). These two shall not separate from each other till they join me by the pool of Paradise.[9]

The concept of Imamate that occupies such a central position in Shi'i Islam thus came into being. The Imamate embodies all temporal and religious-spiritual functions of the Prophet except the functions of prophethood and law making. It also includes the authority to interpret the *Shari'ah*, the *Qur'ān*, and the Tradition of the Prophet. The legitimacy of the Imamate is derived from the fact that such functions were given to Ali by the Prophet and by God's command. On the basis of this and similar traditions and the event in Ghadir-i Khum that took place three months before the death of the Prophet, the Shi'ites concluded that the Prophet had in fact appointed Ali as his successor and through him his eleven descendents from the line of Fatimah by virtue of their knowledge of the *Qur'ān* and authority to interpret the *Shari'ah*.

As the designated successor (*wali*) and spiritual heir (*wasi*) to the Prophet, according to Shi'ite belief 'Ali ibn Abi Talib is the pole of the Imamate and occupies a special place in Shi'i thought. He is also the founder of many fields of Islamic sciences, from theology to Arabic grammar, from political philosophy to Islamic art. He is in fact considered the first Muslim intellectual. Although the *Qur'ān* does not specifically address the question of the Imamate or Imam Ali's name, nonetheless, most commentators and scholars of the *Qur'ān* agree that seven verses were revealed concerning Imam Ali. These verses were reportedly revealed on specific occasions and in historical moments in the early days of Islam, or in relation to certain events or specific acts performed by Imam Ali.[10]

When Muhammad passed away in 10/632 some of his Companions and community leaders gathered together and elected Abu Bakr, a close companion of the Prophet, to act as the Prophet's successor and the head of the newly established Islamic state. According to the Shi'i view, Ali, his family, and followers were kept uninformed and while they were preparing for the burial of the Prophet's body, Abu Bakr accepted to become the first successor of the Prophet (*khalifah Rasul Allah*) despite the instruction the Prophet had given in Ghadir-i Khum.

The Function of the Imamate

It is beyond the scope of this study to examine the details of these developments that resulted in a split within the young Muslim community.[11] The majority who supported Abu Bakr's appointment called themselves Sunnis (i.e., those who follow the tradition [*sunna*] of the Prophet), while the minority group identified itself as the Shi'ites of Ali. In discussing the crisis that followed these developments and the differences between Shi'i and Sunni Muslims, historians often point to the question of succession to the Prophet as a purely political dispute. They argue that Ali and his party opposed the majority's decision for Abu Bakr's appointment because they failed to receive the support of the people. In the opinion of the majority, the consensus of the community and not kinship to the Prophet determined who must succeed the Prophet. In their view the office of Caliphate (i.e., the Prophet's political function) did not belong to the progeny of the Prophet. However from the Shi'i perspective, this crisis was not simply a struggle for power. The question was not who should succeed the Prophet but which kind of qualifications the successor to the Prophet should possess and which functions he should be expected to have. The Imamate embodies far more than just a political function. It includes the Prophet's religious-spiritual as well as his temporal functions. Reducing this dispute to merely a struggle for power between Ali and others disregards important theological, spiritual, and religious functions of the Imam.[12] Within the Shi'i universe, members of the household of the Prophet are believed to possess certain qualities that prepare them for the functions they perform. According to Shi'i beliefs, Ali was granted the knowledge of the *Qur'an* and its inward and outward meaning as well as the authority to interpret the law based on such knowledge. They believe that no other companion of the Prophet possessed these qualities. Ali is known to be the first Muslim intellectual, a legal scholar, calligrapher, theologian, and philosopher.[13] His wife, Fatimah, is considered the mother of all Imams. She has a status in Shi'ite Islam similar to that of Mary in Christianity and carried the honorific title of the virgin (*batul*) due to her extreme piety and virtuosity.

According to the Shi'ite historians, of the twelve Imams who guided the community after the death of the Prophet in 632, eleven were martyred in different ways. Some were assassinated (Ali), some were massacred along with their family members in the battlefield (Husayn), while others were either choked to death in prison or poisoned by the agents of the Caliphs (the Fourth through Eleventh Imams). The Twelfth Imam went into Occultation in 329/941.[14] These developments and especially the brutal massacre of Husayn, who was martyred along with all his family members in 61/680 at the hands of the Umayyad Caliph Yazid, place martyrdom in the center of Shi'i doctrine, second only to the concept of Imamate. It is in light of this event that most rituals, practices, and ceremonies in Shi'ite Islam have evolved during the last fourteen centuries. Husayn's martyrdom in particular provides a supreme example of his struggle to eradicate the moral and religious corruption of his time and reestablish Islamic orthodoxy and justice. It is a symbolic expression of atonement, the possibility of salvation, thus his function is similar to that of Christ and his martyrdom/crucifixion in Christianity. Shi'ites often call him by his honorific title of *Sayyid al-Shuhada*, the Master of all Martyrs.[15]

The tragic events of Karbala in 61/680 are always present in the collective memory of the Shi'ite community. This event has given martyrdom the highest honor one can achieve in the context of Shi'i doctrine. The martyr is portrayed as a person of strong faith and conviction, knowledge, legitimacy, and preparedness for self-sacrifice for the sake of God, religion, and the truth. The common theme in the lives of these Imams is that they rebelled against the decline of orthodoxy in their society and the growing corruption of the Caliphs who were willing to violate the *Shari'ah* and commit many forms of injustice to stay in power. A Shi'ite is regarded as a true follower of Husayn who emulates him in his fight against injustice and religious laxity and will continue the Imam's example until the end of time.

From the Shi'i perspective the Imams' claim to authority and legitimacy did not solely rest on kinship to the Prophet as some claimed. In addition to kinship and what the Prophet had said about his progeny,[16] the Imams' claim derived from their knowledge of the *Qur'ān* and Islamic revelation that the Messenger had taught Ali, and he in turn passed this knowledge on to his descendants.[17] In a sermon Ali alluded to the knowledge that the Prophet had taught him:

> Ask me about the Book of God. By God, there is no verse in the *Qur'ān* that I do not know [the time and place of its revelation] whether it was revealed at night or during the day, in the desert or in the mountains. There is no verse that I do not know where it was revealed and what subject it pertained to.

And:

> No verse was revealed to the Prophet (Peace be upon him) that he did not read to me, and did not have me write it with my own handwriting and taught me its meaning and interpretation.[18]

Ibn 'Abbas, who is one of the most reliable sources on the early years of Islamic history, tells us about Ali that:

> By God, there is nothing about the *Qur'ān* which he did not know. He was a scholar of exegesis and Hermeneutics of the *Qur'ān* (*Tafsir wa'l ta'wil*). I did not see anyone more skilled and better qualified to read [and understand] the *Qur'ān*.[19]

Closely associated with this knowledge and the essence of *Imamah* is the concept of *wilayah* in Shi'ism. According to Shi'ite belief, the Imam possesses not only temporal authority, but also spiritual authority and the power and function of *wilayah* delegated to him by the Prophet. From the spiritual point of view, the function of the Imam is identical to that of the Sufi master in Sunni Islam. A Shi'ite seeks to encounter his Imam, who is in fact none other than his inner spiritual guide (*Imam-i wujudik*). Indeed just as in Sufism[20] each master is in contact with the "Pole" of his age (*Qutb*); in Shi'ism all spiritual functions in every age are connected inwardly with the Imam.[21] It is important to note that the first eight Imams were all recognized as the Pole of their time by all Sufi orders – Shi'i and Sunni alike – and their names appeared in the chain of the masters (*silsilah*) of all orders.

According to a contemporary authority on Shi'ite tradition, during the first centuries of Islam, Shi'ite Imams taught and interpreted Islamic law and spirituality. They were the supreme scholars of exoteric and esoteric knowledge of Islam and masters of *Qur'ānic* sciences. One must remember that the founders of the four legal schools in Sunni Islam, namely, Abu Hanifah (d. 150/767) and Malik ibn Anas (d. 180/796), were both students of the Sixth Imam Ja'far al-Sadiq (d. 148/765), who trained Muhammad ibn Idris Shafi'i (d. 204/819) and Ahmad ibn Hanbal (d. 241/855). In the domain of the inner life, too, the Imams represented and defined Islamic spirituality and the inner meaning of revelation for the entire Muslim community. This is reflected in the respect for the *wilayah* of Imam 'Ali ibn Abi Talib and the recognition of his status as the Sufi *par excellence* by Shi'ites and Sunnis alike. The famous Prophetic *ḥadīth* "I am the city of knowledge and Ali is its gate" is a direct reference to the role of Imam Ali in Islamic spirituality. Some scholars assert that the two-pronged sword of Ali, the *Dhu'lfaqar*, alludes to his exoteric and esoteric functions that continued in the eleven descents of the Imam.[22] In fact, in the early centuries of Islamic history there was no distinction between Shi'ism and Sufism, and the line that separated the two was not defined clearly until after the death of the Eighth Imam 'Ali ibn Musa Rida in 203/817.

In the course of the history of Shi'ism the death of an Imam often created disputes about electing his successor. Consequently, splits occurred on a number of occasions and several branches emerged, the most populous branch being Twelve-Imam Shi'ism. Other branches include the Isma'ilis, which is the second largest branch, followed by Zaydis, Kaysaniyah, and several smaller branches. The Twelve-Imam Shi'ites represent over 85 percent of the world's Shi'ite population, who live in Iran, Iraq, Lebanon, India, and Pakistan, and smaller communities scattered throughout the world. It is Twelve-Imam Shi'ism that this chapter deals with in the coming pages.[23]

Foundations of the Shi'ite Clergy's Power

One of the most complex and perhaps least understood aspects of politics in the Shi'ite world is the interaction between the Shi'ite clergy, the state, and society at large. What factors have enabled the Shi'ite *'ulama* to play such a significant role in society and politics? To what extent did faith, socio-political factors, and group interest prompt them to play such roles? How did their views, interpretations, and relationship with the state and society resemble or differ from those of the Sunni *'ulama* and why? These questions are addressed in the first part of this chapter in order to create a historical context within which the juridical and theological views of the Shi'i clergy and their contributions to the literature on war and peace can be examined.[24]

The power of the Shi'ite *'ulama* is based on several factors. The first and foremost among these is the Shi'i doctrine itself, which legitimizes their position by recognizing them as representatives of the Twelfth Imam on earth.[25] A great deal of the Shi'i clergy's power and influence is derived from this representation and as a result of certain functions assigned to them in consequence. Those functions ranged from their full control over the judicial and educational systems, over pious foundations (*waqf*), properties, and collection and distribution of religious taxes and charities. These functions made them economically independent of the state and placed them in an intermediary position between the state and Shi'ite community. For example, unlike the Ottoman judicial system, which was also based on the *Shari'ah*[26] but included a large number of customary laws (*Qanun*), the judicial system of the Shi'ite territories remained predominantly religious until the third decade of the twentieth century. Every aspect of life, including politics, economic transactions, inheritance, marriage, and divorce, were regulated by the *Shariʿah* and controlled by the clergy. And since the *ʿulama* were the only authorized interpreters of the *Shariʿah*, their active participation in the implementation of the religious law was a given necessity.

The clergy performed some of these functions in the Sunni world as well, although Sunni *ʿulama* were dependent on the power of the state, especially during the Abbasid Caliphate (133–656/750–1258) and Ottoman rule (682–1342/1283–1922). After the consolidation of the Ottoman State and its expansion into the Arab world in the early years of the sixteenth century, gradually the Sunni *ʿulama* became fully integrated into the government administration and became subordinate to the state.[27] Indeed, the Chief Judge (*Qadi al-Qudat*) and the Shaykh al-Islam of Istanbul were directly appointed by the Sultan himself and were accountable to him alone. In contrast, during the same period under the Safavid state (907–1135/1501–1725), which controlled all of Mesopotamia and declared Shiʿism as the state religion, Shiʿi clergy became even more powerful. They grew more independent from the state by virtue of the increasing number of powerful positions they occupied, but more importantly by establishing economic independence from the government through their control over religious taxes, charities, and alms such as the "one fifth" (*Khoms*) and the Imam's share (*sahm-i Imam*).[28] Indeed, they became a state within the state.

Most of the clergy derived the greatest portion of their income from these sources and by administering pious foundations attached to the shrines and mosques, as well as through managing the wealth of orphans, minors, and widows. Any cleric who was a descendant of the Prophet Muhammad (*Sayyid*) was entitled to financial support by his community. Some members of the *ʿulama* were engaged in trade directly or through intermediaries, while others invested in urban property and land. Moreover, since commercial transactions were regulated by the *Shariʿah*, alliances were made frequently between the *ʿulama* and the bazaar merchants.[29] The *ʿulama* provided religious and spiritual guidance for the bazaar merchants and associated with guilds, often providing them with leadership in partnership with the leading merchants of a given business community. In return, merchants made generous contributions to the *ʿulama* in the form of alms, making them even more independent from the state.[30]

Sociologically speaking, the Shiʿite *ʿulama* made up a group that may be aptly called the intelligentsia and the educated elite, but unlike many modern intelligentsia they were not alienated from the masses of the people. As a social group they were characterized by a similarity of class background with which the rank and file members of the society could identify. They maintained contact with members of the community simply because this contact enhanced their power and prestige.

The *ʿulama*'s ties to the community made them credible in the eyes of the populace who entrusted them with deposits, guardianship of orphans and minors, the administration of private *waqf*, and supervision of the property of individuals. Indeed, in performing these functions the *ʿulama* claimed to fulfill the command of the Prophet, as he said, "The *ʿulama* are the guardians of those who are without protectors and in their hand is the enforcement of divine ordinance concerning what has been permitted or prohibited."[31] The significance of all these functions notwithstanding, the most important function of the Shi'i *'ulama* has been to teach people the principles of the faith, to protect Shi'ism, and to defend the Shi'i land.

With the claim of vice-regency of the Twelfth Imam, the place that the *'ulama* assigned to themselves was theoretically an intermediary position between the Imam and the community. This claim was based on their knowledge of and ability to practice *ijtihad*, whereas in the Sunni world the gate of *ijtihad* had been closed after the twelfth century.[32] The institutionalization of the concept of *taqlid* (emulation) under the leadership of Shaykh Muhammad Husayn Najafi Isfahani in 1262/1846 resulted in the creation of the office of the Supreme Source of Emulation (*marja'-i taqlid*), the highest position in Shi'i Islam. This position has played an important part in the political development of the Shi'ite world ever since its creation, acting sometimes in support of the state, sometimes against it. This development resulted in an even higher degree of political power for the *'ulama*.[33]

During the nineteenth century the Shi'i clerical establishment became like a state within a state in both Iran and Iraq. This was due to the weakness of the central government in Iran and the Ottoman control of the Shi'i shrine centers in Iraq, along with the increasing presence of European powers. One of the privileges the Shi'i clerical establishment acquired during this period was the right to remove a governor from his post if he did not comply with the demands of the chief clergy in the province. They also established control over any province or city whose governor they considered to be religiously or ethically unqualified. In addition, they were able to boycott company contracts with foreign governments and excommunincate (*takfir*) individuals and groups they identified as infidels or heterodox. Most important of all, they attained the right and authority to declare *jihad*.[34]

Implications of the Shi'i *'Ulama's* Status for Foreign Policy

The preceding discussion naturally leads us to reflect on the political behavior of the Shi'ite *'ulama* by taking into account their intermediary position in the social structure. Such a position has enabled them to act as an effective pressure group representing popular causes or expressing popular grievances and opposing the state with impunity. On some occasions they were appealed to by the people to voice their disapproval of certain policies or political leaders.[35] On other occasions they acted as an important channel of access by the government to the majority of the population. As such they could be used by the government as a propaganda mouthpiece for defending the government's interests and policies.[36]

The extent and scope of the involvement of the Shi'ite clergy in the domestic politics of Iran, Iraq, and Lebanon have been studied extensively.[37] Much less attention has been paid, however, to the manner in which the *'ulama* have used their power and prestige to influence the foreign policies of these countries, particularly in the developments that have led to wars in the past or the ways in which they may use their power to influence future foreign policy decisions and impose their views on issues of war and peace. Herein lies the main difference between the Shi'i and Sunni *'ulama* in terms of their ability to translate their views into action and to play an active part in the foreign policies of their respective lands.

One historical example of the *ulama*'s behavior in relation to our discussion is the position they took during the crisis between Iran and Russia that led to the first Russo-Persian war of 1218–1228/1804–1813. Mirza Bozorg Qa'im-Maqam, the minister and special adviser to Iran's Crown Prince 'Abbas Mirza Qajar, who lived in Azarbaijan and was the commander of Iran's armed forces, wrote letters to the leading Shi'i *ulama* in the shrine cities of Iraq asking them to issue a verdict (*fatwa*) and to declare *jihad*. Such powerful and prominent religious leaders as Shaykh Ja'far Najafi and Mulla Ahmad Naraqi wrote treatises on *jihad*. Mir Muhammad Husayn Khatoonabadi, the powerful Friday prayer leader (Imam Jum'ah) of Isfahan, wrote a treatise titled *Risalah ye-Jihadiyah Nasiriyah (Treatise on Jihad)*. Other *ulama* issued many such *fatwa*s for *jihad* and pressured the government to declare *jihad* against Russia. Qa'im Maqam collected those verdicts and compiled an anthology on *jihad* titled *Jihadiyah* and presented it to the Shah.[38] As a result, *jihad* was declared against Russia. Although the war ended in Iran's defeat and humiliation, the incident demonstrates the power of the *ulama* and the state's reliance on them in order to mobilize the population for war.

During the years that followed this defeat, the news of extensive abuse and ill treatment of Muslim populations in the newly conquered territories by the Russian armed forces reached the *ulama* in Najaf and Karbala. In response to public pressure the *ulama* began to discuss the possibility of issuing a verdict for *jihad* despite the reluctance of the ruling monarch, Fath 'Ali Shah Qajar. In the summer of 1826 when the Shah went for his summer retreat in Sultaniyah near the city of Zanjan, a number of important *ulama*, including Aqa Sayyid Muhammad Tabataba'i of Karbala, Mulla Ahmad Naraqi, and Mulla Muhammad Taqi Baraghani of Qazvin, held a meeting with him and demanded that he declare war on Russia. They threatened to take the initiative and declare *jihad* if the government did not do so. To show their seriousness they issued *fatwa*s and declared that *jihad* was obligatory and opposition to it was a sign of unbelief (*kufr*). The Shah complied and remained quiet. The outcome of the second war was even more disastrous than the first.[39]

On another occasion after the Persian conquest of Herat in 1856, the British, who were in control of Afghanistan, demanded payment of reparation to the people of Herat. This created a crisis during which the Persian *ulama* threatened the government to call for *jihad* if it complied with British demands. Their call provoked a public outcry, as demonstrated in the gathering at the Shah mosque in Tehran on 9 November. Public support for the *ulama* came from all parts of the country. Hajj Mirza 'Askari, the Imam Jum'ah of Mashhad, wrote a treatise titled *Risalah-ye Jihadiyah Nasiriyah (Treatise on Jihad)* in which he discussed the necessity of declaring *jihad* against the British if they invaded Persia. The British Foreign Office received news from Tabriz that *jihad* was proclaimed in January 1856.[40]

Similarly, the twentieth-century history of Iraq was marked by the anti-British activities of the Shi'i *ulama* when British authorities attempted to incorporate the holy cities of Najaf and Karbala into the administrative units introduced in August 1917. The *ulama*'s opposition to this measure and their activities to mobilize people against the British resulted in the formation of the Society of Islamic Movement (Jam'iyah al-nihdat al-islamiyah) and eventually led to the 1919 uprising in Kut al-Amarah. The *mujtahids* began to preach *jihad* in the mosques and sent agents among the tribes to mobilize the people into organized forces to fight the British. Then they issued *fatwa*s for *jihad* and a few of them, such as Ayatullah 'Abdullah Mazandarani, Shaykh al-Shari'ah Isfahani, Seyyed Mustafa Kashani and his son Seyyed Abu'lqasim, and the celebrated Ayatullah Muhammad Taqi Shirazi, issued *fatwa*s for *jihad* and personally participated in the war against the British.[41]

In the beginning of the twentieth century memories of the Tobacco uprising of 1891–1892 against the British were still rather fresh in the clerical circles.[42] This was followed by the Constitutional Revolution of Iran (1905–1906) in which the Shi'ite *'ulama* played an active part and threatened the Shah and his Russian supporters with *jihad*.[43] Then came a change of dynasty in 1921, which they supported, and this was followed by their participation in the crisis that resulted in the nationalization of the Iranian oil industry during the early 1950s. Finally, the Shi'ite *'ulama* played a leading role in the events that led to the 1978–1979 Iranian Revolution.[44] In all these events the *'ulama* threatened to declare *jihad*, and on each occasion their threats were taken seriously and were effective enough to force the government to retreat and comply with their demands.

Shi'i Clergy's Views on Peace and War

Shi'i jurists have defined *jihad* as a means to uphold "the strength of the foundations of Islam" and "one of the duties of Islam and one of its pillars."[45] There are of course many similarities between Shi'i and Sunni views on *jihad*. Similarities exist because of the common sources on which their views are based. Differences are the result of interpretations, perspectives, the environment, and even personal rivalries.

In Islamic perspective in general, there is a close connection between the concept of *jihad* and justice. There are several specific elements in the Shi'i conception of war/*jihad* that set it apart from the Sunni perspective. In Shi'ite Islam, extra emphasis is placed on justice in light of the events that have specifically shaped the Shi'i mindset, namely, the martyrdom of the grandson of the Prophet and the third Shi'ite Imam, Husayn ibn 'Ali in Karbala, in 81/680. This incident is seen as a cosmic event in Shi'ism and epitomizes the victimization of Imam Husayn in the hands of forces of evil and disbelief, hence his epithet *mazlum* (the victim of evil and injustice).

Another difference rests on the quality of the leadership of those who can invoke *jihad*. In Shi'ism the position of leadership belongs exclusively to the Imam or his representative. In the Sunni interpretation of *jihad* such function is the prerogative of the Caliph or sultan and the clergy provide justification and explanation for *jihad*.

The third difference is in identifying the enemy. While Sunni and Shi'i jurists agree that the infidels (*kuffar*[46]) are the most ardent enemies of Islam (i.e., external enemies), they differ on other categories of the enemies of Islam and Muslims. One such group is defined by the *Qur'ān* as *Ahl al-baghy*, that is, people who turn away from the truth and rebel against the legitimate ruler. Sunni jurists define *Ahl al-baghy* as those members of the Muslim community who revolt against the legitimate government. According to this view, it is the duty of Muslims to fight against all those enemies who threaten the existence of such a government, whether internal or external. At times this law was in fact used against Shi'ites. From the point of view of Shi'i jurists, however, *Ahl al-baghy* are those who rise against one of the twelve Imams. Other than these points of difference, in many respects a great deal of similarity exists between Shi'i and Sunni views on *jihad*.[47]

According to the injunctions of the *Qur'ān* and the Traditions of the Prophet, peace is a fundamental principle in Islamic political discourse. There are over one hundred verses in the *Qur'ān* that invite Muslims to peace, and recommend war only in self-defense.[48] The term *jihad* is used forty-four times in thirty verses in the *Qur'ān* and many times in the *ḥadīth* of the Prophet in a variety of meanings. One time *jihad* is specifically mentioned in chapter *al-Furqan* (25:52) as the *Greatest Jihad* (*jihad al kabir*) and denotes *intellectual jihad*. The other two kinds – that is, the *Greater jihad* (*jihad al-akbar*) and the *Lesser jihad* (*jihad al saghir*) are found only in the *ḥadīth* of the Prophet. The first denotes exerting oneself for spiritual *jihad* and self-purification, while the second connotes struggle to defend the *Dar al-Islam* by the use of force within the strict limits of the Islamic doctrine of just war, and respecting what we would today call the human rights of oneself and others.[49]

Out of thirty verses about *jihad* and its different meanings in the *Qur'ān*, only ten verses denote *war* and the necessity of fighting against infidels and heretics within a particular historical context when the Prophet fought against his opponents, especially those from the Quraysh Tribe of Mecca. That is the reason that none of these verses discusses the necessity of the presence of a government to declare *jihad*: the Prophet was present on all those occasions. One must differentiate between the injunctions of the *Qur'ān* about these particular wars and how Shi'i and Sunni jurists (*fuqaha*) apply these injunctions to all kinds of wars regardless of the historical context. While for the *Qur'ān*, *jihad* in its specific meaning of war is only defensive, some Shi'i *'ulama* and jurists speak also of an *offensive jihad* to fight against corruption on earth and with the purpose of commanding good and forbidding the reprehensible (*amr bi'l ma'ruf wa nahy 'an al-munkar*). In this sense they claim that *jihad* is not just a religious duty for every Muslim but also an ethical and moral obligation to defend and protect the orthodoxy of the Shi'ite faith and the honor of the community (the *ummah*). In so doing, therefore, they claim that they act in accordance with the injunctions of the *Qur'ān* regarding *jihad*. As deputies of the Twelfth Imam whose appointment is sanctioned by God alone, the Shi'ite clergy see it as their duty to carry on *jihad on his behalf*. We should bear in mind that not all Shi'i *'ulama* accept this interpretation, for there are at least four currents of thought among Shi'ite jurists and theologians regarding *jihad* as follows:

1. There are those jurists who believe that *offensive jihad* has always existed and will continue to exist in Islam and conclude that *war* for the purpose of spreading the faith is an indispensable principle of Shi'ite Islam.[50]

2. The second school advocates defensive war only when an Islamic state or land is attacked. Followers of this school argue that "There is no compulsion in religion" (2:256), that *offensive war* never existed in Islam with the intention to force people to enter Islam, and that *peace* is the central principle. In their view any kind of struggle to spread the faith or meet challenges and threats of unbelievers must be carried on through education and other peaceful means.

3. A third group consists of those jurists who believe that both *offensive* and *defensive* wars existed side by side in Islam and both kinds are as valid today as they were during the time of the Prophet.

4. Finally, the fourth school of jurists argue that *offensive* wars (i.e., *jihad*) were carried on during the time of the Prophet and the Infallible Imams (*ma'sumin*). However, in their absence only defensive *jihad* is permissible. Therefore, any discussion of *jihad* or offensive war in their opinion is irrelevant during the Period of Occultation. This view seems to be accepted by the majority of the Shi'ite *ulama* today. These positions are discussed in detail in the coming pages.

Another important issue examined in this study is the rules and laws regarding the conduct of war. Of special importance in this part are rules concerning respect for human dignity, resistance before foreign invasion, the timing of war, prohibition of inhumane acts and cruelty, types of weaponry, treatment of prisoners of war, protection of the environment and respect for nature, and cessation of hostilities and ending the war. The conclusion of this study is that the predominant view among the Shi'i *ulama*, especially in the contemporary period, is that Islam is a religion of peace, compassion, and submission to God. This conclusion profoundly impacts their position on the rules of engagement in and conduct of war and other issues related to *jihad*.

Recent Views on Peace and War in Shi'ite Circles

It is essential for contemporary Muslim jurists – Shi'ite and Sunni alike – to reexamine classical sources and the views of earlier jurists with a critical approach. They must reassess the conventional views that argued for the necessity of conducting annual *jihad* to spread Islam, treating the prisoners of war, attitude toward non-Muslims, the laws of war, and other related issues and present a contemporary reading of those sources to make them relevant to the political realities of the contemporary world. Important initial steps in this direction have already been taken by several contemporary Iranian religious scholars and jurists whose works are analyzed and presented in this study. In the following pages, some of those views will be discussed, and the conventional Shi'i jurists' views concerning the laws of war and peace are challenged. It is demonstrated that views held by many prominent jurists such as Shaykh Muhammd ibn Hasan ibn 'Ali Tusi, 'Allamah Abu Mansur Hasan ibn Mutahhar Hilli, and Shaykh Muhammad Hasan Najafi[51] did not really have any doctrinal justification or explanation, nor were they based on the narrations and writings of the Shi'ite Imams. Rather, as a contemporary Shi'i scholar demonstrates, their views were greatly influenced by the writings of Muhammad ibn Idris Shafi'i, the founder of the Shafi'i School of Law. To elaborate this argument, this study presents a new perspective on Shi'i perceptions of war and peace by examining the writings of three contemporary jurists and philosophers, namely, the late Ayatullahs Murtada Mutahhari and Ni'matullah Salihi Najafabadi, and Mostafa Mohaghegh Damad. These scholars base their writings on a critical analysis of Shi'i sources but also take into account the role of history, regional and international factors, and the necessity of safeguarding the security and territorial integrity of the Shi'ite lands.

The Islamic Revolution of 1978–1979 that resulted in the establishment of the Islamic government greatly increased the power of the Shi'ite *ulama*. The revolution transformed the power of the clergy from a position of observers and opinion leaders to that of political actors and decision makers. In addition to the immense power they had before, in the new environment the *'ulama* became ministers, military commanders, diplomats, legislators, and executives. The Islamic Revolution of Iran also inspired Shi'ites of Iraq and Lebanon and prompted them to organize. Developments in Iraq and Lebanon during the last two decades demonstrate the direct involvement of Shi'i clergy in the national politics of these states. Therefore, the writings and declarations of the Iranian *'ulama* are followed closely and emulated in Iraq and Lebanon as well. Since the revolution, the most important question has been the extent to which the clergy's religious and legal views must influence and determine their political actions and decisions. This question is posed also to present-day Iraq and, to a lesser extent, Lebanon, where Shi'ite power has increased to an unprecedented degree.

It is interesting to note that the behavior of the Iranian *'ulama* during the last three decades since the revolution demonstrates that they have been more concerned with concrete and practical interests of the state rather than with abstract laws or religious ideals. They have justified this new attitude on the basis of the *Qur'anic* injunctions that discuss the moral responsibility of the community to "command good and forbid the reprehensible" (3:104, 110, 9:71). These verses give the legitimate Islamic government the right to take measures against forces that threaten to break down the social order and security (106). The need for security of the Islamic state has therefore gained priority even over some prohibitions about times and places of fighting: "Fight not with them at the Inviolable Place of worship until they first attack you there, but if they attack you there then slay them" (2:291). This and other similar verses (2:194) are now exploited to show that the security needs of the Muslim community take priority over rules and regulations of a religious nature.[52]

Shortly after the establishment of the Islamic Republic the need for security and preservation of the state manifested itself in the establishment of the Council of Expediency (*showra-yi maslahat -i nizam*) headed by Ayatullah Hashemi Rafsanjani. Since then the question has no longer been who is the most learned and qualified *'alim* (religious scholar) to interpret the *Shari'ah*, but who can best identify, understand, and protect the Islamic state and its interests. Thus, since then the *'ulama* have been acting more like politicians than religious leaders. In fact, Ayatullah Khomeini, the leader of the revolution, was the first to introduce the concept of *expediency* into contemporary Shi'ite legal and political thought.[53] It was on the basis of this view that Khomeini refused to issue a *fatwa* for *jihad* during the revolution and also during the eight-year war with Iraq despite enormous pressure from lower ranking *mujtahids*. In addition, he proclaimed legal (*halal*) many practices that were religiously illegal (*haram*) or unpopular among the clergy prior to the revolution, including such controversial issues as women's participation in elections or the permissibility of consuming caviar-producing sturgeon fish because the export of caviar brought much needed foreign currency to the government treasury. Hence, the interests of the Islamic state gained priority over the abstract principles of Islamic law and Islamic ideals.[54] These and many other similar issues are discussed in the coming pages.

The final part of this chapter includes selections from important classical and modern legal and theological texts to show the richness and varieties of opinion among prominent Shi'i jurists of the classical period as well as contemporary scholars. It will demonstrate how the Shi'i *'ulama* interpreted the *Qur'anic* verses, the *hadith*, and the narrations of the Shi'i Imams and articulated their own views on the basis of their guide-lines to show continuity and/or change in their thoughts pertaining to peace and war in the Shi'ite tradition.

Sources of Law in Islam

The most important sources of law in Islam are the *Qur'ān*, the Traditions of the Prophet (*aḥadīth*), intellectual reasoning, and consensus attained by Islamic scholars of law. Obviously, not all of these sources stand on the same level of significance.

The first and most important source of law in Islam is the *Qur'ān*, the sacred book of Islam, which according to the Muslim view is the direct word of God revealed to the Prophet. It is "a world in which a Muslim lives. It is the central reality in the life of Islam."[55] All Muslims believe that the *Qur'ān* is mysteriously protected by God and is immune to change and distortion, for God says, "It is We who have sent down the Remembrance, and We watch over it" (15:9).

By virtue of being the word of God, the *Qur'ān* commands acts of worship in general terms. For example, it commands Muslims to perform daily prayer, fast, and pay alms, but it does not explain *how* to perform these duties. Therefore, to learn the details of these injunctions Muslims began to emulate the deeds of the Prophet and the conduct of the early Companions, as he said, "Perform daily prayer as you see I do."

From the Shi'ite perspective the household of the Prophet (the Imams) learned and followed his tradition in the most perfect manner and were the most trusted channel of transmission of the conduct of the Prophet. This quality enabled the Imams to inherit the knowledge of the manifest and nonmanifest meanings of the *Qur'ān* directly from the Prophet. Moreover, the belief in the infallibility of the Imams guaranteed that they did not commit error in understanding the injunctions and commands of the *Qur'ān*. The implications of this belief and its impact on the Shi'i understanding of the *Qur'ān* in the domains of law, religious practices, politics, and intellectual activities are obvious.

Originally, the science of *Qur'ānic* exegesis was founded by 'Ali ibn Abi Talib, the first Shi'ite Imam, and became the core discipline of Islamic learning. It was on the basis of guidelines established by Imam 'Ali that the science of commentary (*tafsir*) was born during the fourth/tenth century. It contributed immensely to the intellectual develop-ment of Muslim communities and gave birth to such disciplines as theology, jurispru-dence, Islamic art and calligraphy, politics, philosophy, and grammar.

The *Qur'ān* directs man toward intellectual understanding, reflection, meditation, and deliberation on the signs of God on earth.[56] In light of these injunctions and with the development of Shi'i jurisprudence (*fiqh*) during the fourth/tenth century under prominent jurists such as Muhammad ibn Ya'qub al-Kulayni (d. 328/939) and Abu Ja'far Muhammad ibn Hasan al-Tusi, known as *Shaykh al-Tai'fah* (d. 460/1068), the use of reason (*'aql*) became increasingly important in legal matters and the practice known as *ijtihad* came into being. *Ijtihad* is defined as "the process of arriving at judg-ments on points of religious law using reason and the principles of jurisprudence (*usul al-fiqh*)."[57] Its aim is to demonstrate as accurately as possible how the Imams would have decided in any particular legal case under similar circumstances.[58]

Based on the guidelines provided by Imam 'Ali, Shi'i commentators divide *Qur'ānic* verses into two categories. One category includes verses known as *Muhkam* (explicit and sound) and *Mutashabih* (implicit or similar), and the second category includes *nasikh* (abrogating) and *mansukh* (abrogated) verses. These classifications have had a profound impact on the Shi'i approach to jurisprudence and have given Shi'i law a great deal of flexibility, distinct from Sunni law. In the coming pages the ramifications of this approach and its impact on Shi'i understanding of the ethics of war and peace are discussed.[59]

It was mentioned that the *Qur'ān* speaks in general terms. Some of its verses pertain to Islamic law and jurisprudence and define how believers must act in accordance with the commands of the Sacred Book. These verses can be understood and interpreted in light of the tradition of the Prophet, that is, the Messenger's words and deeds (*hadīth* and *sunna*). These are in fact the first commentaries on the *Qur'ān*, followed by the writings and narrations of the Shi'ite Imams. Together they constitute the second source of Shi'i jurisprudence and explain and clarify the principles and injunctions of the *Qur'ān* for believers.[60] In our present study, in addition to major sources of Sunni *hadīth* a selected number of Shi'i collections of *ahadīth* have been chosen from among a number of sources to prevent confusion.[61] To put classical rulings in perspective, views expressed by some contemporary Sunni scholars such as Muhammad 'Abduh, Rashid Rida, and Shaykh Mahmud Shaltut are also examined. Among contemporary Shi'i scholars the works and ideas of such scholars as Murtada Mutahhari, Mostafa Mohaghegh Damad, and Ni'matullah Salihi Najafabadi are presented in order to demonstrate continuity and/ or change in the Shi'i views on the ethics of war and peace.

Intellectual reasoning (*'aql*) is a peculiarly important principle that constitutes the third source of Shi'i jurisprudence. It helps believers find solutions for problems they encounter in daily life in harmony with *Qur'ānic* injunctions and in accordance with reason and common sense. One is expected to comprehend and reach certainty in all matters of life – including legal matters – through demonstration (*burhan*) and dialectic (*jadal*).

Demonstration is "a proof whose premises are based on truth. Dialectic is a proof that all or some of its premises are based on observable and certain data." Both of these methods are employed in the *Qur'ān* (16:125). Through these processes, that is, deducing religious rulings according to conditions and rules described in jurisprudence, one practices *ijtihad*.[62] What makes this principle and the practice of *ijtihad* particularly important and relevant to our discussion is that "from 665/1226 the gate of *ijtihad* has been closed to scholars of the Sunni world,"[63] whereas in the Shi'ite world the gate of *ijtihad* remains open until the reappearance of the Twelfth Imam.

Finally, the fourth source of law is consensus (*ijma'*), that is, the consensus of scholars of law in legal matters. A legal decision reached through exchange of opinions and consultation among legal scholars must be in line with and include the opinion of the Twelfth Imam. From varying opinions the community finally arrives at a consensus (*ijma'*), which is considered to be the truth.[64]

Shi'i jurisprudents have based their legal decisions on the four sources described above, always practicing *ijtihad* in the process. As a result, they have been able to develop a large compendium of law that can be easily adapted to different circumstances and times, as well as respond to the changing environment and needs of the society without compromising principles of Islamic orthodoxy and orthoproxy. As we shall see in the coming pages, this peculiar aspect of Shi'i jurisprudence has had a profound impact – both positive and negative – on the Shi'i perception of the laws and ethics of war and peace.[65]

The Concept of *Jihad* in the *Qur'ān*

As we mentioned earlier, the *Qur'ān* is the first and most important source of Islamic beliefs and practices. There are about forty-four verses in the *Qur'ān* that deal with the concept of *jihad* and use the term to denote struggle, utmost effort, exerting oneself, and the like. In his authoritative work on the meaning of *Qur'ānic* terms, Raghib Isfahani uses the terms *jahd* and *juhd* to connote *extreme hardship* and *enduring hardship*.[66] In the famous Arabic dictionary *al-Munjid fi'l lughah*, the term *jihad* is defined as struggle and hardship beyond one's ordinary capacity.[67] A contemporary jurist states that the term *jhad* is used in the *Qur'ān* to denote a more general meaning than "fighting" or "war." In its most universal meaning it denotes striving on any undertaking, as is evident in the following verses of the *Qur'ān*: "But those who struggle in Our cause, surely We shall guide them in Our ways; and God is with the good-doers" (29:69). And: "And struggle for God as is His due" (22: 78).

Jihad is also used to denote war, but only as defensive war, preventive war, and war for the protection of the weak and the defenseless. As such it is defined as a measure to protect the Muslim community against injustice and violation.[68] Therefore, the context within which the term is used defines the nature and the cause of the struggle and determines if it is on the path of the good or evil.[69]

According to Murtada Mutahhari, "Any war aimed at self-defense, defense of the nation and humanity is always holy and good. Offensive war is not holy, but rather, is evil and illegitimate."[70] It is important to note that the translation of *jihad* as "holy war" by some Orientalist scholars of Islam has created a great deal of misunderstanding about its specific conditions and limitations and has caused much suspicion, negative perceptions, and antagonism about Islam and Muslims.

Some Western scholars have noticed this misinterpretation. Anne Mary Schimmel states:

> The widespread idea that Islam made its way through the world mainly through fire and sword cannot be maintained. To be sure, for a brief span of time it seemed as if *jihad* – the struggle for faith – might become the sixth "pillar of Islam." *Jihad* means "striving [in the path of God]"; the term "Holy War" goes back to the Crusaders who used it for their own undertaking; it is unknown in classical Islam.[71]

There are some other terms used in the *Qur'ān* that help us better understand the Islamic definition of the concept of war. Two such important terms are *qital* (fighting, war) and *fitnah* (revolt, uprising, plot, persecution, sedition, etc.). According to the celebrated commentator of the *Qur'ān* 'Allamah Seyyid Muhammad Husayn Tabataba'i, "*qital* means to kill someone who intends to kill you."[72] Some commentators have interpreted the term *fitnah* as it is used in Chapter 2:191 of the *Qur'ān* as infidelity and disbelief (*kufr*) against which one must fight. However, *fitnah* does not in fact mean infidelity. Rather, it denotes the persecution of Muslims, plotting against the Muslim community, imprisoning, torturing, or killing Muslims, and planning war against them:

> And fight in the way of God with those who fight you, but aggress not; God loves not the aggressors. And slay them wherever you come upon them, and expel them from where they expelled you; persecution is more grievous than slaying. (2:191)

Mutahhari argues that it is not wrong to translate or perceive *jihad* as war, for war is different from aggression. War is not always absolutely evil or condemnable in itself. To push an aggressor out of one's country is an honorable act and also one's duty. Defensive war particularly is a praiseworthy undertaking, in which members of the community are obligated to participate. In other words, he argues that defensive war is good and condoned and offensive war is evil and must be condemned. Therefore, if we choose to translate and use *jihad* as war, we must understand *jihad* as the *Qur'ān* defines it, that is, as defensive war. In other words, the *Qur'ān* does not prescribe *jihad* under all circumstances or without setting certain rules and conditions. Only if a war is defensive, *jihad* becomes an obligation to all able-bodied Muslims.[73]

After elaborating on the conditions of *jihad* Mutahhari describes the different kinds of *jihad* and circumstances in which *jihad* becomes permissible and legitimate.[74] They include fighting to defend one's life, family, property, country, and beliefs and values one considers sacred.[75]

In the coming pages, we return to the classification of war into defensive and offensive and examine the *Qur'ānic* verses relevant to each category. Here we must discuss another classification that a contemporary Shi'ite Iranian jurist, Mostafa Mohaghegh Damad, presents. Inspired by the classification work of the Egyptian scholar Shaykh Mahmud Shaltut, Mohaghegh Damad alludes to two kinds of *jihad* as follows:

1. Defensive *jihad* before foreign invasion, and,
2. Peaceful educational *jihad* for the propagation of the faith and the spread of Islam. This is often defined as "Call to Islam" and/or call toward God.[76]

This view is widely accepted by contemporary Muslim scholars and jurists. They argue that under no circumstances does the *Qur'ān* sanction war (*jihad*) to spread religion by force and impose Islamic faith on others. One can never impose religion on people, and that which is spread by force is not a genuine religion. Indeed, it leads to hypocrisy and ruins the faith.[77] In defense of this argument, it is maintained that there is not even a single verse in the *Qur'ān* that commands war and the use of force to convert non-Muslims to Islam.[78] Here the views of many contemporary Shi'i and Sunni jurists, especially Egyptian scholars at al-Azhar University, are identical.

In his refutation of offensive *jihad* to spread Islam, Mahmud Shaltut argues that Islam and its injunctions cannot be imposed on people by the use of force. He presents seven reasons to support his argument:

I. If the objective of *jihad* were to force all people to convert to Islam, why then would the *Qur'ān* prescribe *Jizya* on those who chose to remain in their ancestral faith in return for protection by the Islamic government?

II. There is no personal grace or social benefit in faith imposed by force.

III. There is not a single example in the tradition of the Prophet whereby a person entered Islam against his will, let alone was forced to enter Islam.

IV. The essence and the spirit of Divine revelation do not condone the use of force, as faith is based on love and compassion not force and compulsion. Rituals and outward aspects of religion can be imposed on a defeated nation by the use of force, but the seed of love and faith cannot be planted in hearts by force.

V. Imposing religion on a generation will affect future generations. How could religion be taught in an environment where faith is imposed on people forcefully? Spreading the teachings of religion is possible only if the present generation accepts religion willingly and trains future generations accordingly.

VI. Some Muslims may feel that God selected them to guide and purify non-Muslims of the world and keep them away from committing sins. To achieve this goal, they argue that all non-Muslims should convert to Islam even through the use of force, if necessary! This view asserts that it is the duty of all Muslims anywhere and at any time in history to carry on *jihad* against non-Muslims until they accept Islam. This view has found some adherents among followers of the Shafi'i School of Law, whereas [in the *Qur'ān*] Muslims are commanded to fight only in two circumstances, namely in defense of the community and removing corruption and *fitnah*.

VII. The behavior of governments in the Muslim world in certain episodes of Islamic history cannot necessarily be taken as Islamic, for they contradict the command of the *Qur'ān* and the Tradition of the Prophet.[79]

In short, the purpose of this brief discussion, Shaltut states, is to put forward the view that, arguably, the term *jihad* is not used in the *Qur'ān* and Islamic sources to denote exclusively fighting and war, let alone offensive war. Therefore, according to his view, *jihad* must not be translated or interpreted as "holy war" or offensive war against non-Muslims with the intention to convert them into believers of Islam. Rather, *jihad* must always be defensive in nature before foreign invasion. To spread Islam and its teachings among non-Muslims he advocates *religious-spiritual jihad* (*al-Da'wah ila'lLah*, Calling to God) or *al-Da'wah ila'lIslam* (calling to Islam). Therefore, one must not, he concludes, take seriously those who claim that a few verses in Chapter IX (Repentance) that were revealed in 9/631 – a year before the death of the Prophet – and that command Muslims to fight against non-Muslims and infidels condone offensive *jihad* and abrogate all previous verses regarding *jihad*.[80] If believing in God's unity is the right of every human being and must be defended like any other human right, a Muslim cannot fight with believing nations to impose Islam on them.[81] That is the reason, as one observer has stated, that all wars and battles conducted during the time of the Prophet and led by him were of a defensive nature.[82] Later 'Umar and many Caliphs after him argued that their military expeditions – including the conquest of Persia and India – were undertaken because of the provocative policies and threats of Persian kings and therefore were of the same nature as the wars conducted during the time of the Prophet.[83]

Islamic Perceptions of War and Peace

Before examining the circumstances in which an Islamic state can engage in a defensive or offensive war and analyzing the views of Shi'i jurists regarding this issue, a few introductory remarks must be made and some key concepts and terms clarified. These include the classification of the different types of war, the primacy of peace, freedom of religion, and, finally, the application of particular rules to universal situations and universal rules for particular situations.

In Islamic tradition in general and in Shi'ite Islam in particular *jihad* is comprised of four parts: *jihad* against the carnal soul, fighting against enemies of religion, struggle to revive a tradition of the Prophet, and struggle against invading enemies (i.e., defensive war). This classification is described in detail in all major Shi'i sources of law and politics. In all these situations the ultimate reward is martyrdom, for those who die in the path of God will go to heaven directly. Conversely, those who run away from the battlefield are guilty of a capital sin and will be punished severely on the Day of Judgment. The only virtue that is superior to martyrdom in a *jihad* is the struggle of scholars to discover and spread the truth, as the Prophet said, "on the Day of Judgment the ink of the scholars will outweigh the blood of the martyrs on the scales."[84]

Classification of the Types of War

It was pointed out earlier that Shi'i jurists have expressed a variety of opinions regarding war and *jihad* and have issued different verdicts on this subject. The most commonly accepted classification views *jihad* in terms of *offensive* and *defensive*. We shall discuss the meaning, conditions, and boundaries of each. Suffice it to mention here that there is no dispute regarding defensive *jihad* among jurists or theologians. They all unanimously consider it legitimate and participation in it a religious duty. Conversely, there are profound differences of opinion among them regarding offensive war. Three positions are particularly worth noting here that have been debated among jurists regarding the nature and timing, leadership and conditions for war, and the authority to declare war:

a. That offensive *jihad* never existed in Islam and the Tradition of the Prophet does not condone it. Therefore, offensive *jihad* is not permissible. Some say it is even *haram*, that is, forbidden according to Islamic law.
b. That offensive *jihad* is prescribed in Islamic law and the Tradition of the Prophet condones it. Therefore, it is permissible and as valid today as it was during the time of the Prophet.
c. That offensive war is prescribed in the *Shari'ah* and the Tradition of the Prophet and Shi'i Imams condone it. However, carrying on an offensive *jihad* is contingent on the physical presence of the Infallible Imam in the Islamic community.

There have always existed two basic and fundamentally different views regarding the nature of relationships between Islamic states and the non-Muslim world. One view considers war as *the central principle* that defines this relationship, while another view believes in the primacy of the principle of peace. There is a third current but less popular view that is attributed to Abu Hanifah and Zaydi Shi'ites that combines the two views above in consideration with factors such as geography, history, and the political situation. In other words, with regard to the neighboring countries of an Islamic state that may violate the state's territorial integrity or those who rebel against the Islamic state and cause anarchy and chaos, *war* is the central principle that defines the relationship; whereas with countries that have no common borders with an Islamic state and/or natural boundaries such as rivers and mountains that separate them, *peace* is the central principle in their relationship with the outside world. In the second case the propagation to spread Islam must be carried on through peaceful means such as education and guidance.[85]

Principality of Peace (Asalat-I Sulh)

We examine this principle later when we discuss defensive war and its details. However, due to its significance it is important to make a few remarks here. All jurists who reject offensive war and believe in defensive *jihad* insist that maintaining peace among nations is the norm and central rule in Islam. This state of being is interrupted only from time to time by wars. Ayatullah Salihi Najafabadi compares this to the human body:

> As the *Qur'ān* explains clearly,[86] the natural state of a human being is health and harmony. Illness is an accident that descends on the body and changes its equilibrium. Similarly, the natural state of human society is peace and harmony. War is an accident that falls on human society temporarily and destroys harmony and peace. Essentially, human conscience does not condone war and bloodshed and considers it cruel and unjustifiable.[87]

Other observers such as Mutahhari and Mohaghegh Damad have also emphasized the primacy of peace. Mutahhari cites verses of the *Qur'ān* and concludes that peace is in fact the true spirit of Islam.[88] Mohaghegh Damad mentions the names of a number of Shi'i and Sunni jurists and scholars who have expressed the same views regarding the centrality of peace in Islam.[89]

Freedom of Religion

There are numerous verses in the *Qur'ān* that deal with the issue of freedom of religion and opponents of offensive war often refer to them in their arguments and writings. It is appropriate to mention some of the most important and relevant *Qur'ānic* verses here:

> No compulsion is there in religion. Rectitude has become clear from error. (2:256)
>
> Call thou to the way of thy Lord with wisdom and good admonition, and dispute with them in the better way. Surely thy Lord knows very well those who have gone astray from His way, and He knows very well those who are guided. (16:125)

Surely We guided him upon the way whether he be thankful or unthankful. (76:3)

And if thy Lord willed, whoever is in the earth would have believed, all of them, all together. Wouldst thou then constrain the people, until they are believers? (10:99)

If We will, We shall send down on them out of heaven a sign, so their necks will stay humbled to it. (26:4)

To every one of you We have appointed a right way and an open road. If God had willed He would have made you one nation; but that He may try you in what has come to you. (5:48)

According to Mutahhari, all these verses, along with those that deal with peace and emphasize defensive war, bound and condition *jihad* and its definition.[90] Similarly, Ayatullah Najafabadi also condemns forcing non-Muslims to enter Islam. He states that

[I]nviting or guiding people to the straight path in its essence contains logic, advice, and good will and is never possible through the use of force and threat. That some jurists believe in the use of the sword to impose faith on people has no basis in the *Qur'ān* nor is it in harmony with reason and intellect. Such a view is irrational and must be rejected and universally condemned.[91]

In his monumental commentary on the *Qur'an*, 'Allamah Sayyid Muhammad Husayn Tabataba'i describes the meaning of the verse (2:256) where freedom of religion is addressed. According to him, compulsion (*ikrah*) means forcing one to do something one does not like or want to do. The verse clearly rejects imposing religion on people. Every religion consists of the knowledge of religion, its injunctions, commands, and rituals. Faith is a state of the heart in which force has no place. Force may be effective only in the realms of exoteric and outward aspects of religion, whereas heartfelt faith is based on perception and belief is based on the knowledge of religion. Ignorance is the absence of such knowledge. It is impossible to argue that ignorance could lead one to knowledge or that perception based on ignorance would result in judgment based on knowledge. Therefore, according to this argument, whether one interprets the verse as an engendering command (*amr-i takwini*) or prescriptive command (*amr-i taklifi*), it is not just a narration but an injunction on the basis of which a religious command can be constructed, a command that clearly rejects compulsion and the use of force to impose religion on people.[92]

Application of the Particular to the Universal

In relation to our discussion on war and peace, we must point out that two categories of verses exist in the *Qur'ān*. One group of verses deals with war in universal terms without mentioning any conditions and limitations for it. The second group includes verses that set certain conditions and limitations to war. Proponents of defensive war argue that the *particular* verses governing war place limitations on and create a context for those verses that deal with war in universal terms. This rule, which is called *application of the particular to the universal*, is observed in the domain of customary law and in the science of Principle (*usul*) as well. The following examples from the *Qur'ān*[93] may help us understand this rule better:

> And fight in the way of God with those who fight with you, but aggress not: God love[s] not the aggressors. (2:190)
>
> And slay them wherever you come upon them, and expel them from wherever they expelled you; for persecution is more grievous than slaying. (2:191)
>
> And fight them till there is no persecution and the religion is God's; then if they give over, there shall be no enmity save for evildoers. (2:193)
>
> Whoso commits aggression against you, do you commit aggression against him like as he committed against you; and fear you God, and know that God is with the godfearing. (2:194)

These verses in fact set conditions to the universal rules of war in Islam in the sense that they justify defensive war as a logical reaction and a just response to persecution, foreign invasion, and occupation of Muslim lands. Two contemporary Shi'i jurists, Ayatullah Mutahhari and Ayatullah Mohaghegh Damad, agree on this principle and set at least four conditions that define and limit *jihad*, as follows:

1. Fighting in the face of an enemy's attack.
2. Fighting to remove persecution and injustice.
3. Fighting to resist forceful imposition of a particular religion on people.
4. The primacy of peace, and condoning war only as a means of restoring peace.[94]

Both of these authorities agree that these verses that deal with *jihad* are not subject to abrogation by other verses, nor do they revoke other verses. Mohaghegh Damad adds that one cannot apply *particular* verses to all situations and argue in favor of war under all circumstances, for those verses limit war to a particular situation.[95]

Defensive War

There is a consensus among jurists and commentators of the *Qur'ān* that some of those verses of the *Qur'ān* that deal with war and *jihad* prescribe defensive war. Before examining those verses, however, it is appropriate to make some general remarks regarding war and discuss the intellectual and rational necessities of defensive war.

There is a strong argument for the position that warfare is not always unjust. Defense against aggression, the violation of a nation's territorial integrity, the plundering of its wealth, or the violation of its honor is a duty and an honorable act. When a nation or a community – religious or nonreligious, Muslim or non-Muslim – is attacked, it has the right to defend itself, its territory, honor, and freedom in any way or form it can. Those who reject *all* kinds of warfare indeed deny a natural right of every human being and nation to exercise such defense. In many traditions fighting on behalf of the weak and the defenseless and those who have been victims of injustice is viewed as a duty and a virtue. The following ten verses of the *Qur'ān* permit and in fact command Muslims to conduct defensive war when they are attacked by outside forces, although the number of verses dealing with this issue is indeed many more:

> And fight in the way of God with those who fight with you, but aggress not: God love[s] not the aggressors. (2:190)

While this verse condones war, arguably, it allows Muslims to fight only with those who attack them. It does not allow Muslims to initiate attack and start the war. It implicitly sets limits to the war efforts of Muslims and warns them to fight only the military forces of the aggressor and to respect and protect the civilians, women, elderly, and children, and also the environment and natural resources, in particular.

> The holy month for the holy month; holy things demand retaliation. Whoso commits aggression against you, do you commit aggression against him like as he committed against you; and fear you God, and know that God is with the godfearing. (2:194)

Most commentators agree that this particular verse was revealed specifically in reference to the Hudaybiyah[96] Peace Treaty that the Prophet Muhammad signed with the Quraysh tribe of Mecca. It allowed Muslims to defend themselves and fight back if the Quraysh attacked them during the months of Dhi'lqa'dah and Dhi'lhajjah, although the *Qur'ān* had declared these two as the forbidden months during which fighting was clearly prohibited. The verse also recognizes that, if attacked, Muslims have the right to defend themselves under all circumstances, but they are not allowed to start the war.

Evidence in support of defensive warfare is found in the verse that refers to the story of David and his defense before the attacking army of Goliath. God gave permission to his messenger to defend his kingdom, although his forces were weaker and far less in number:

> So they routed them, by the leave of God and David slew Goliath; and God gave him kingdom and wisdom, and He thought him such as He willed. Had God not driven back the people, some by the means of others, the earth had surely corrupted; but God is bounteous unto all things. (2:251)

And when people do not defend the poor, the weak, and themselves, God questions them, blames them, and commands them to fight in defense of women, children, and all those who cannot defend themselves:

> How is it with you, that you do not fight in the way of God, and for the men, women, and children who, being abased, say, "Our Lord, bring us forth from this city whose people are evildoers, and appoint to us a protector from Thee, and appoint to us from Thee a helper." (4:75)

In the following verse God commands Muslims to fight with those who persecute them or plot against them. The defensive nature of this command is clear, for it asks the Muslims to stop fighting as soon as their opponents stop persecuting them and/or fighting with them.

> And fight them till there is no persecution, and the religion is God's entirely; then if they give over, surely God sees the things they do; but if they turn away, know that God is your Protector – an excellent protector, an excellent Helper. (8:39)

In the following verses the *Qur'ān* commands Muslims to respect peace treaties with unbelievers but gives them permission to defend themselves when their opponents break the agreement and attack them:

> Will you not fight a people who broke their oaths and purposed to expel the Messenger, beginning the first time against you? Are you afraid of them? You would do better to be afraid of God, if you are believers. (9:13)

And:

> Leave is given to those who fight because they were wronged – surely God is able to help them – who were expelled from their habitations without right. (22:39)

Finally, the following verses discuss the necessity of military preparedness for war at all times as a means of frightening the enemy and deterring them from attacking Muslims.

> Make ready for them whatever strings of horses you can, to terrify thereby the enemy of God and your enemy, and others besides them that you know not; God knows them. And whatever you expend in the way of God shall be repaid to you in full; you will not be wronged. (8:60)

> And fight them till there is no persecution and the religion is God's; then if they give over, there shall be no enmity save for evildoers. (2:193)[97]

Offensive War

There are several opinions regarding the definition and nature of offensive war in Islam. According to some Shi'i and Sunni jurists, war is the most common type of contact and relationship that can ever exist between Muslims and infidels. They argue that it is obligatory for Muslims to fight against unbelievers when and where they find them. In their argument, this group of jurists recite certain verses and a few Traditions of the Prophet out of their proper contexts, and some even go a step further and claim that all Muslims except the Zaydi Shi'ites[98] are in consensus on this position.[99] From their point of view, *war* and not peace is a central principle in Islam.

A second opinion belongs to those jurists who argue that *peace*, and not war, is an essential principle in the *Qur'ān* and that peace defines the nature of the relationship between Muslims and their opponents. They often resort to the same group of verses and traditions as the first group but reject their interpretation on legal and theological grounds. They argue that there are other verses in the *Qur'ān* that limit and set conditions for war, or abrogate the verses the first group refers to in its argument. In the following pages we present the verses used by the first group in their writings, followed by a critique of their interpretation. We then proceed to present the second group's reasoning and the verses they use in their argumentation.

Verses referred to by the first group of jurists include the following:

> And slay them wherever you come upon them, and expel them from wherever they expelled you; for persecution is more grievous than slaying. (2:191)

Some jurists claim the above verse revokes all previous verses that were revealed regarding warfare. It commands Muslims to control themselves and avoid killing.[100] Others believe it commands Muslims only to expel the unbelievers from where they were expelled (i.e., Mecca).[101]

> And fight them till there is no persecution (*fitnah*) and the religion is God's; then if they give over, there shall be no enmity save for evildoers. (2:193)

A number of Shi'i jurists such as Muhsin Fayd Kashani and Muhaqqiq Ardabili define *fitnah* (persecution, sedition) as heresy and believe the main objective of war is to remove unbelief from the face of the earth.[102] Shaykh Tusi also accepts this interpretation on the authority of Imam Ja'far Sadiq narrated by Ibn Zayd, Mujahid, and Rabi.[103] A similar statement is also available in verse eight of chapter thirty-nine of the *Qur'ān*.

According to Tabataba'i, the following verses address *all* Muslims and declare it as their duty to participate in fighting (i.e., offensive war) against unbelievers.[104] The eminent nineteenth-century jurist Aqa Muhammad Hasan Najafi (1202–1266/1787–1850) also believed that these verses were revealed in relation to offensive war to spread the Islamic faith:[105]

> Prescribed for you is fighting, though it be hateful to you. Yet it may happen that you will hate a thing which is better for you; and it may happen that you will love a thing which is worse for you; God knows, and you know not. (2:216)

And:

> So let them fight in the way of God who sell[s] the present life for the world to come; and whosoever fights in the way of God and is slain, or conquers, We shall bring him a mighty wage. How is it with you, that you do not fight in the way of God, and for the men, women, and children who, being abased, say, "Our Lord, bring us forth from this city whose people are evildoers, and appoint to us from Thee a helper." The believers fight in the way of God, and the unbelievers fight in the idols' way. Fight you therefore against the friends of Satan; surely the guile of Satan is ever feeble. (4:74–76)

In the following verse God commands the Prophet to urge Muslims to fight against unbelievers. Some commentators believe that the verse is a clear command for offensive war and, therefore, an obligation for Muslims to fight unbelievers under all circumstances. However, they often ignore the particular condition and specific case the verse intended to address:[106]

> O Prophet, urge the believers to fight. If there be twenty of you, patient men, they will overcome two hundred; if there be a hundred of you, they will overcome a thousand unbelievers, for they are a people who understand not. (8:65)

Two well-known Shi'i jurists believe that the following verse abrogates all other earlier verses regarding peace with infidels.[107] Another observer considers it as a command to fight unbelievers:[108]

> Then, when the sacred months are drawn away, slay the idolaters wherever you find them, and take them, and confine them, and lie in wait for them at every place of ambush. But if they repent, and perform the prayer, and pay the alms, then let them go their way. (9:5)

The following verse was specifically utilized during the war with the Romans in the battle of Tabuk.[109] However, some jurists claim that it is a universal command and applies to all times and circumstances.[110] According to another source, the verse refers specifically to fighting those among the People of the Book (Christians, Jews, Zoroastrians, and Sabians), who under four conditions must be confronted and fought against.[111] Tusi claims that the verse commands Muslims to conduct war against those unbelievers and those who deny God's unity and the reality of the Day of Judgment:[112]

> Fight those who believe not in God and the Last Day and do not forbid what God and His Messenger have forbidden – such men as practice not the religion of truth, being of those who have been given the Book – until they pay the tribute out of hand and have been humbled. (9:29)

The next verse invites Muslims to unite in their fight against unbelievers and fight them as they are fought against. On the authority of Abu Bakr Asam,[113] Tabarsi claims that such a fight is eternal and continues generation after generation:[114]

> And fight the unbelievers totally even as they fight you totally; and know that God is with the godfearing. (9:36)

The following verses command Muslims to fight against unbelievers and condemn those who disobey. According to Tabarsi, these verses were revealed specifically in reference to the Battle of Tabuk, whereas Tabataba'i believes that it is a command for *jihad* in general and denotes utmost effort in the struggle against unbelievers under all circumstances:[115]

> O believers, what is amiss with you, then when it is said to you, "Go forth in the way of God; you sink down heavily to the grounds?" Are you so content with this present life, rather than the world to come? Yet the enjoyment of this present life, compared with the world to come, is a little thing. (9:38)

And:

> Go forth, light and heavy! Struggle in God's way with your possessions and your selves; that is better for you, did you know. (9:41)

The next four verses promise punishment for infidels and rewards in heaven for those who fight against unbelievers and who sacrifice their lives and wealth on the path of God. It calls Muslims to fight hard with them (struggle) and to rest assured that their efforts will not be in vain:

> O Prophet, struggle with the unbelievers and hypocrites, and be thou harsh with them, their struggle in hell – an evil homecoming! (9:73)

And:

> God has bought from the believers their selves and their possessions against the gift of Paradise; they fight in the way of God; till they are killed; that is a promise binding upon God in the Torah, and the Gospel, and the *Qur'ān*; and who fulfills his covenant truer than God? (9:111)

And:

> O believers, fight the unbelievers who are near to you, and let them find in you a harshness; and know that God is with the godfearing. (9:123)

However, once infidels are defeated and submitted, Muslims are commanded to stop fighting and/or killing them as well:

> When you meet the unbelievers, smite their necks, then, when you have made wide slaughter among them, tie fast the bonds. (47:4)

Jihad *and Offensive War in Traditions of the Prophet*

In addition to these verses of the *Qur'ān*, proponents of offensive war also resort to the Traditions of the Prophet to support their arguments. According to a *ḥadīth*, the Prophet is quoted as saying that "prayer, charity and *jihad* are the three works most beloved by God."[116] Two traditions are particularly cited more frequently than others. They are interpreted by some as acknowledging a constant state of war between Muslims and non-Muslims and allowing Muslims to conduct offensive wars against them. One is a tradition narrated on the authority of the Sixth Shi'ite Imam, Ja'far Sadiq. According to him, the Prophet said:

> All good lies in the sword and under its shadow. People will not be straightened except through [the] sword, and swords are the keys to Paradise.[117]

The second *ḥadīth* narrated in several variations and recorded in Bukhari reads as follows:

> I was commanded to fight people until they say *'La ilaha Ill'lLah* (There is no god but God). He who utters this formula indeed his life and possessions are protected, and their reckoning is with God.[118]

A different version of this *ḥadīth* is recorded on the authority of 'Abdullah ibn 'Umar[119] in two of the most authoritative sources of traditions, namely, in *Sahih al-Bukhari* and *Sahih al-Muslim*.[120] In both of these collections the formula "And Muhammad is His Messenger" and the command of obligatory performance of daily prayer and payment of alms are added. The original narrators of these two traditions were Malik ibn Anas and Abu Hurayrah, who are generally not considered by Shi'ite scholars of the *ḥadīth* to be the most trusted transmitters of the Prophetic traditions.[121] According to a contemporary observer, not only are the narrators of this *ḥadīth* rejected by Shi'i scholars, but also the meaning of this *ḥadīth* has been greatly distorted and misunderstood. Due to this one can argue that it is wrong to conclude from this *ḥadīth* that Islam and the Prophet condone the use of the sword to spread the message of Islam. Conversely, the Prophet says that he fights by the command of God. Once the enemies accept divine unity and utter the relevant formula, the war must stop for they are then considered Muslims, and their lives and properties must be respected and protected.[122]

To the *ḥadīth* of the Prophet we must add the narrations of the Shiʿite Imams in general and those dealing with *jihad* in particular. There is a wealth of information in this category of sources that gives any discussion of *jihad* a particularly Shiʿi character. One such narration attributed to the Fifth and Sixth Imams shows the supreme position *jihad* occupies in the Shiʿi tradition: "the root of Islam is prayer, its branch is almsgiving, and the top of its hump is *jihad* for the cause of God."[123] We refer to these sources several times in the following sections.

Concerning *Jihad* and War: Views of the Jurists

Opponents of Offensive War

In contrast to those jurists who justify and defend offensive war against unbelievers and those who persecute and subject Muslims to injustice, another group of jurists and theologians challenges the views of the advocates of offensive war and questions the validity of their arguments. In the past, the number of scholars in this group amounted to nearly as many as those in the first group, but in recent decades their views have found acceptance among an increasing number of scholars and jurists. As the most important representatives of this perspective we have selected three contemporary scholars – the late Ayatullahs Murtada Mutahhari and Salihi Najafabadi, and Mostafa Mohaghegh Damad – whose writings are easily accessible in several languages. Their arguments, language of discourse, and reasoning are more appealing and more easily understandable for contemporary readers. Not only are these individuals recognized authorities in jurisprudence, but they are also well-known scholars in fields such as philosophy and theology. They are also relatively well versed in contemporary history and international relations.

In his opposition to the arguments of the advocates of offensive war, Murtada Mutahhari states that if one takes the few verses in the *Qurʾān* that deal with war out of their proper historical context, one will be convinced that Islam seeks to be in a constant state of war with its opponents. In other words, on such a reading, one must admit that Islam commands Muslims to fight unbelievers under all circumstances, and therefore peace can never be established between an Islamic government and non-Muslims, let alone infidels. However, in reading and interpreting those verses we must bear in mind that the *particular* verses that deal with war in fact place limitations on and create a context for those verses that seem to deal with war in universal terms. Therefore, the rule that we discussed before, that is, the *application of the particular to the universal*, must be observed in the interpretation and application of such verses.[124]

As we have seen before, those verses mentioned in previous pages prescribe war against unbelievers without any conditions or limitations. There are many other verses, however, that discuss war and *jihad* with certain conditions and limitations, which can assist us in understanding when and under which conditions war is permissible (and even prescribed), and under which conditions it is not.[125] For example, the *Qur'ān* describes a number of these conditions under which Muslims have the right to resist and even fight with infidels:

a. When infidels attack Muslims and/or plot to fight against them;
b. When the enemy limits Muslims' religious activities including the right to introduce and spread Islam through education and other peaceful means; and
c. When the enemy systematically persecutes Muslims because of their religious beliefs and faith.[126]

In light of these conditions and taking into account the principle of freedom of religion so clearly emphasized in the *Qur'ān* as well as those verses that stress the necessity and significance of peace, we can arguably conclude that the *nature of war and* jihad *in Islam is essentially defensive*.[127]

In his introduction to *Jihad in Islam*, Ayatullah Salehi Najafabadi reiterates Mutahhari's position regarding the application of the above-mentioned rule to *Qur'ānic* verses in relation to war and peace. He makes an extremely courageous statement rarely seen in the writings of any jurist in Islamic history:

> During my career and after teaching advanced courses in jurisprudence I came to the conclusion that *jihad* as defined in the *Qur'ān* and elaborated in the Tradition of the Prophet is fundamentally very different from and often in contradiction with what jurisprudents have written in their books. For what the jurists say is that it is permissible to spread Islam through *jihad* and impose the religion by use of force, if necessary, even if there is no danger or threat against Muslims and the Islamic community from the unbelievers. They claim that this is a religious duty like daily prayer, fasting and other religious injunctions. This is despite the fact that the *Qur'ān* and the Tradition of the Prophet emphasize peace and friendly attitude and behavior toward unbelievers.[128] Therefore, we can clearly observe the difference between what they [the jurists] say and what we read in the *Qur'ān* and the Tradition.[129]

Najafabadi's conclusion is very important in itself. What is even more important is that he dismisses the views of proponents of offensive war as a Sunni, and not from a Shi'i perspective. He demonstrates that the views of both Sunni and Shi'i jurists regarding war and peace were deeply influenced by Imam Muhammad ibn Idri Shafi'i, the founder of the Shafi'i School of Law.[130] According to him, Imam Shafi'i once issued a verdict (*fatwa*) in which he claimed that verse 193 of chapter two[131] of the *Qur'ān* in fact abrogates all previous verses that set limitations and conditions to carry on a war against infidels and that it is permissible to fight against unbelievers even if they pose no threat to the Muslim community. This verdict greatly influenced Shi'i and Sunni jurists alike and was accepted by scholars in both communities.

Among the most important Shi'i scholars who accepted Imam Shafi'i's views were such luminaries as Shaykh Tusi, 'Allamah Hilli, and Muhammad ibn Makki 'Amili Jazini Shahid Thani. Among contemporaries, Ayatullah Kho'ie also accepted Shafi'i's verdict.[132]

According to Najafabadi, the view expressed in Imam Shafi'i's verdict was not an original one. It had been discussed and accepted by some earlier jurists such as 'Abd al-Rahman ibn Zayd ibn Aslam[133] and Rabi' ibn Anas.[134] Shafi'i simply repeated their views without mentioning their names or providing reference to their works. He asserts that Shafi'i, who was such a prominent jurist, must have known the weakness and limitations of his argument. The question is, why did he insist on an idea that arguably was not based on sound argument? What factors prompted a man such as Shafi'i to disregard the commonly accepted rules, not least the *application of the particular to the universal*, in commenting on the *Qur'ānic* verses? Why is it that this rule, which was applied to all other cases, was not applied to verses concerning *jihad*? Najafabadi states that the answer must be sought within the context of the political system, namely, the Abbasid Caliphate and their foreign policy. He concludes that verdicts like this were issued under political pressure by the Abbasid Caliphs. The need for new resources to meet the growing demands of an expanding empire prompted the Abbasid state to pressure jurists to provide religious justification for the state's expansionist policies. Shafi'i and other jurists simply had to yield to state pressure. Therefore, none of these verdicts and the expansionist policies resulting from them was in line with Islamic principles and the injunctions of the *Qur'ān*.[135] We do not know to what extent Shafi'i was subject to state pressure, but we know that during his time the idea of permissibility of war against unbelievers without any conditions prevailed, and he simply accepted and repeated that idea.[136] Najafabadi concludes that what the jurists compiled in the course of history as Islamic perceptions of war, and especially *jihad*, in fact contradicts the *Qur'ān* and Tradition of the Prophet. For God commands His Messenger to "Call people to the way of thy Lord with wisdom and good admonition, and dispute with them in the better way" (16:125).[137] The *Qur'ān* specifically states that "there is no compulsion in religion" (2:256) and that "Surely We guided him upon the way whether he be thankful or unthankful" (76:3).[138]

Najafabadi then proceeds to substantiate his claim by presenting a number of *aḥadīth* of the Prophet. According to him, whenever the Prophet appointed a military commander, he gave clear instructions to him regarding the treatment of infidels:

> When you encounter your enemies from among the infidels, offer them three choices and if they accept any one of the three refrain from attacking them and make peace with them. First, invite them to enter Islam. If they comply, accept it from them and avoid fighting them. If not, invite them to migrate. If they do so accept it from them and they shall have the status of the Immigrants. If they refuse to migrate, tell them that they will have the status of Bedouin Muslims and will be subjected to God's command like other Muslims. However, they will not get any share from the spoils of war except when they fight on the side of Muslims. If they refuse to accept Islam, demand from them to pay tax (*jizya*). If they agree to pay, accept it from them and hold off your hands. If they refuse to pay the tax, seek Allah's help and fight them.[139]

In another instruction addressed to 'Ali ibn Abi Talib when he was appointed to lead an expedition to Yemen, the Prophet outlined his views on the way Islam must deal with unbelievers:

> O 'Ali! Do not fight with anyone unless you call him to Islam first. By God if He guides even a single person with your hand, it is better for you than the entire world over which the sun rises and sets.[140]

It is obvious that *jihad* in this sense is not what the Shi'ite jurists have claimed. To the contrary, it is an invitation to Islam through peaceful means, education, and advice, and not through the power of the sword. The events that took place during the above expedition are recorded in history. According to Tabari:

> Prior to sending 'Ali, Khalid ibn Walid had been sent with a large army to invite [the] people of Yemen to enter Islam. For six months he accomplished nothing. The Messenger of God recalled Khalid and sent 'Ali to replace him and carry on the task. Khalid returned with all his forces except one person named Bara' ibn 'Azib. He says that "… when we arrived in Yemen and people were informed, they prepared an army to fight with 'Ali. We performed the morning prayer (*fajr*). 'Ali lined us up and facing the people of Yemen, he read the Prophet's letter to them. In a single day the entire members of the Hamdan tribe entered Islam."[141]

Let us now examine commentaries on the same verses we presented before and compare the conclusions drawn by both the opponents and proponents of offensive war.

I

> And fight in the way of God with those who fight you, but aggress not; God loves not the aggressors. And slay them wherever you come upon them, and expel them from where they expelled you; persecution is more grievous than slaying. (2:191)

Opponents of offensive war argue that this verse instructs Muslims on how to react in the face of persecution and enemy attack, but does not allow them to initiate war.[142] A prominent commentator emphasizes that the verse commands Muslims not to attack the enemy unless they are attacked first.[143] Najafabadi also warns Muslims not to initiate attack, for then they would be aggressors, and God does not like the aggressor.[144]

II

> And fight them till there is no persecution (*fitnah*) and the religion is God's; then if they give over, there shall be no enmity save for evildoers (*al-zalimin*). (2:193)

The key terms in this verse that pertain to war are *fitnah* and *al-zalimin*. *Fitnah* means not infidelity and/or heresy, but any kind of oppression, sedition, or plot such as taking over one's home or expelling one from his or her land.[145] Al-Suyuri considers Muslim expulsion from Mecca as an example of such *fitnah*.[146] Another important reminder to Muslims in this verse is that they should stop fighting as soon as the enemy stops being an aggressor.

III

> Prescribed for you is fighting, though it be hateful to you. Yet it may happen that you will hate a thing which is better for you; and it may happen that you will love a thing which is worse for you; God knows, and you know not. (2:216)

According to jurists who oppose offensive war, such as Najafabadi, this verse explains the collective obligation (*wajib kafa'i*) of all believers to defend the community when the enemy attacks.[147] Some even claim that this verse pertained only to the Companions of the Prophet.[148]

IV

So let them fight in the way of God who sell the life of this world for the world to come; and whosoever fights in the way of God and is slain, or conquers, We shall bring him a mighty wage. How is it with you, that you do not fight in the way of God, and for the men, women, and children who, being abased, say, "Our Lord, bring us forth from this city whose people are evildoers, and appoint to us from Thee a helper." The believers fight in the way of God, and the unbelievers fight in the idols' way. Fight you therefore against the friends of Satan; surely the guile of Satan is ever feeble. (4:74–76)

Opponents of offensive war maintain that verses 74 and 76 of this chapter denote a collective obligation of the community to defend itself, while verse 75 clearly alludes to defending the weak and the defenseless, including children and the elderly. This view is particularly emphasized by Mutahhari.

V

O Prophet, urge the believers to fight. If there be twenty of you, patient men, they will overcome two hundred; if there be a hundred of you, they will overcome a thousand unbelievers, for they are a people who understand not. (8:65)

Opponents of offensive war unanimously believe this verse makes fighting with the enemy contingent on being attacked. It commands Muslims to always be prepared to defend themselves.[149]

VI

Then, when the sacred months are drawn away, slay the idolaters wherever you find them, and take them, and confine them, and lie in wait for them at every place of ambush. But if they repent, and perform the prayer, and pay the alms, then let them go their way. (9:5)

This verse pertains specifically to those infidels who violated the peace treaty they had signed with the Prophet and who continued plotting against Muslims.[150] The verse before this clearly states that those who remained loyal to their promises and did not abate their rights or did not support anyone against Muslims must be respected and their rights must be acknowledged.[151]

VII

Fight those who believe not in God and the Last Day and do not forbid what God and His Messenger have forbidden – such men as practice not the religion of truth, being of those who have been given the Book – until they pay the tribute (*jizya*) out of hand and have been humbled. (9:29)

Among contemporary Shi'i jurists, Murtada Mutahhari has expressed the harshest criticism of the accepted view of earlier scholars and their interpretation of this verse. According to him, this verse commands Muslims to carry on war not with the People of the Book, but only against those among them who neither believed in God or His messengers, nor in any revealed religion altogether.[152] His argument is supported by Mohaghegh Damad, who states that this verse instructs Muslims to fight for the sake of the truth, justice, and God's religion rather than for worldly gains. Shaykh Mahmud Shaltut also defends this argument and adds that the injunction of this verse does not mean to impose Islam by force. If it were so, the People of the Book would not have been given a chance to choose between war and paying taxes.[153] We must also add that the tax (*jizya*) is not a poll tax, as it has been claimed, but is a tax in return for providing safety and security for the People of the Book and protecting their lives, honor, and wealth.[154]

VIII

And fight the unbelievers totally even as they fight you totally; and know that God is with the godfearing. (9:36)

The above verse makes war against infidels contingent upon being attacked by them, that is, if infidels are the initiators of aggression. Tabarsi argues that the verse in fact commands Muslims to fight against unbelievers *only* if they attack Muslims. In such a case it becomes a legitimate act of self-defense.[155] An important jurist of the Hanafi School of Law, Kamal ibn Humam, maintains that "[t]he war that we as Muslims have been commanded to fight in this verse is indeed a reaction to being attacked by unbelievers."[156]

IX

Some scholars believe that the verses below were revealed specifically in relation to the battle of Tabuk[157] when the Romans were contemplating war against Muslims. When their plan was discovered, Muslims initiated a preemptive attack on the Roman forces.[158]

Yet the enjoyment of this present life, compared with the world to come, is a little thing. (9:38)

Go forth, light and heavy! Struggle in God's way with your possessions and your selves; that is better for you, did you know. (9:41)

And:

> O Prophet, struggle with the unbelievers and hypocrites, and be thou harsh with
> them, their struggle in hell – an evil homecoming! (9:73)

X

Opponents of offensive war claim that the following two verses apply to all kinds of war,
offensive and defensive alike, and cannot be applied only to offensive *jihad*.[159]

> God has bought from the believers their selves and their possessions against the
> gift of Paradise; they fight in the way of God; till they are killed; that is a promise
> binding upon God in the Torah, and the Gospel, and the *Qur'ān*; and who fulfills
> his covenant truer than God? (9:111)

Both supporters of offensive war and those who oppose it agree that the following verse has a universal meaning and does not pertain to any specific kind of
war, defensive or offensive. It encourages believers to be prepared to sacrifice their
lives and possessions on the path of God, as the Torah and the Bible also promised
before.

> O believers, fight the unbelievers who are near to you, and let them find in you a
> harshness; and know that God is with the godfearing. (9:123)

XI

The following verse also makes war conditional in light of similar verses mentioned
before and commands Muslims to fight only those who fight with them. According to
Tabarsi, it also instructs Muslims to be prepared for defense under all circumstances
and emphasizes the necessity of military strength as a deterrent "to evoke awe and fear
in the heart of the enemy as a measure to prevent them from contemplating attacks on
them."[160]

> Now when you meet the unbelievers, smite their necks, then, when you have
> made wide slaughter among them, tie fast the bonds. Then set them free, either
> by grace or ransom, till the war lays down its loads. (47:4)

The verse above also concerns prisoners of war and rules and regulations regarding their
treatment, specifically in a war that unbelievers impose upon Muslims and that leaves
Muslims no other choice but to defend themselves.

Earlier in our discussion on war we narrated a few Traditions of the Prophet, to which
some jurists refer and with which they justify offensive war.[161] This practice was particularly accepted among Sunni jurists, and one such authority is Kamal ibn Humam,
who was a Hanafi jurisprudent. The two traditions he presents in his argument are the
following:

> Killing the infidels is obligatory even if they do not start the war.

And:

> I was commanded to fight people until they say 'La ilaha Ill'lLah (There is no god but God). He who utters this formula indeed his life and possessions are honored and protected, and his reckoning is with God.

In his interpretation, ibn Humam argues that according to these traditions, killing the infidels is not contingent on them starting the war; therefore, it is permissible to kill them whenever and wherever they are found.[162]

Since the transmitters of these traditions are not among the most reliable and authoritative scholars of *hadīth*, some Sunni and Shi'i jurists reject the conclusions and verdicts issued by them. Salihi Najafabadi argues that these traditions are also subject to the same rule as *Qur'ānic* verses, that is, the *application of the particular to the universal*. In other words, these traditions must be read and interpreted in light of other Traditions of the Prophet and in line with injunctions of the *Qur'ān*. Therefore, just as the conditional verses of the *Qur'ān* do, these traditions command Muslims to fight only if they are attacked by the enemy or the enemy starts the war first.[163]

Mohaghegh Damad believes that these traditions discuss the issue of war when it is necessary and unavoidable and not under all circumstances. They do not advocate forcing unbelievers to accept Islam.[164] According to him, whenever Imam 'Ali ibn Abi Talib faced his enemies, he commanded his army not to start the war until the enemy did so, telling them, "You have a proof for your claim to peace. You are on the side of the Truth. If you do not start the war, you will have another proof for your claim."[165]

Supporters of Offensive War

In the previous pages we examined briefly the opinions of Shi'i and Sunni jurists concerning different types of war and *jihad*. In the coming pages we discuss the historical processes of the formation of those views among traditional Shi'i jurists of earlier centuries. Moreover, we compare and contrast their views with the opinions of contemporary scholars of Islamic law to demonstrate continuity and/or change in Shi'i understandings of war and peace in light of the changing environment and within the context of contemporary political and social conditions.

As we observed in their interpretation of the *Qur'ān* and especially verses that addressed war and *jihad*, some jurists claim that *war* is a *central principle* of the Islamic doctrine and, therefore, that offensive war is as valid today as it was during the time of the Prophet. We identified this group of jurists as advocates of *offensive war*. In sharp contrast to them, some other jurists believe that *peace* and not war is central to the Islamic doctrine. Although the majority of jurists of the past centuries subscribed to one of these two currents, it is important to note that two other groups of jurists existed who disagreed with both of these views and held opinions of their own. Hence, the third group claimed that both offensive and defensive wars existed side by side during the time of the Prophet and are permissible until the end of time. Finally, followers of the fourth current, which is an exclusively Shi'i view, maintained that offensive war existed during the time of the Prophet; however, it is forbidden in the absence of the Prophet and during the period of Greater Occultation of the Infallible Imam (i.e., the Twelfth Imam).[166] As was mentioned before, all four groups base their arguments on their particular reading of the verses of the *Qur'ān*. In the following pages the views of each group are examined and its most important representatives are introduced. Following that, this chapter presents the views of contemporary Shi'i jurists and some conclusions are drawn.

As was discussed earlier, numerous verses in the *Qur'ān* and Traditions of the Prophet clearly demonstrate that offensive war with the objective of imposing Islamic faith is not permissible because the *Qur'ān* says, "There is no compulsion in religion."[167] Despite that, many early jurists claim that the most important form of *jihad* is one carried on for the spread of Islam among unbelievers and followers of other religions through the use of force. Such positions are in sharp contradiction with the statements of the *Qur'ān*, Traditions of the Prophet, and the narrations of the Shi'ite Imams. What follows are the opinions expressed by some of the leading jurists – both Shi'i and Sunni – articulated in their writings, which have formed the bulk of legal studies on the subject of war and peace.

The Views of Imam Muhammad ibn Idris Shafiʿi

In his monumental work entitled *Kitab al-Umm* (The Motherbook) Imam Shafi'i deals with legal issues that Islamic society faced at his time. Due to his eminence and scholarly standing he influenced his contemporary jurists, as well as future generations of legal scholars in the Sunni and Shi'i worlds alike, who accepted many of his verdicts.[168] One of the issues that profoundly impacted later jurists' views was his opinions on war and peace. According to Shafi'i, a short time after the migration of the Prophet (from Mecca to Medina in 622) by the grace of God many people joined him and formed a powerful community. As a result God made *jihad* an obligation for them, whereas before it was not. God said to them: "Prescribed for you is fighting, though it be hateful to you" (2:216), "And fight in the way of God with those who fight you" (2:190–193), "And struggle for God as is His due" (22:78), "and when you meet the unbelievers, smite their necks . . ." (47: 4), and "O believers, what is amiss with you, that when it is said to you, 'Go forth in the way of God. . .'" (9:38–39).

In other words, Shafi'i concluded that like obligatory daily prayer and fasting, fighting with unbelievers is also a command and an obligation, not realizing that the verses he cites to substantiate his conclusion set certain conditions for Muslims to fight with unbelievers. He claimed that all verses that set limitations for the above verses were abrogated by a single verse that commanded Muslims to "slay them wherever you come upon them, and expel them from where they expelled you; persecution is more grievous than slaying" (2:191).[169] This idea prevailed before Shafi'i; he simply narrated it without mentioning the sources of his narration.

The view expressed by Imam Shafi'i invites Muslims to fight all unbelievers even if they do not pose any threat to the Muslim community. It pays no attention to the first part of the verse that commands Muslims to "fight in the way of God *with those who fight you*, but aggress not; God loves not the aggressors."[170] Presumably, Shafi'i issued this verdict in light of certain political considerations of his time, namely, to justify the expansionist policies of the Abbasid Caliphate.[171] His view contradicts the statement of the *Qur'an* and Tradition of the Prophet. Later Sunni jurists and scholars, including the celebrated historian and commentator of the *Qur'an* Muhammad ibn Jarir al-Tabari, dismissed Shafi'i's argument and rejected his verdict.[172]

The Views of Kamal ibn Humam (790–861/1388–1457)[173]

In his authoritative text entitled *Fath al-Qadir lil 'ajiz al-faqir* (The al-Qadir Opening for Helpless Seeker), Humam states:

> War and fighting with unbelievers is obligatory for Muslims even if the infidels did not start the war. The *Qur'an* does not make war with infidels contingent upon starting war by them. Moreover, as recorded in Sahih al-Bukhari and Sahih al-Muslim,[174] the Prophet said that, "I was commanded to fight with people until they say 'There is no god but God' (*La ilaha Ill'ILah*)."[175]

As it is clear in this verdict, ibn Humam has followed Shafi'i by not taking into account the conditions and limitations that other verses place on verses he cites to support his conclusion. The reasons for rejecting his views are similar to the reasons that were presented in relation to Shafi'i's verdict. They both take *Qur'anic* verses out of their context and cite the portion of the verses that support their own argument.

The Views of Shaykh Tusi (385–460/995–1068)[176]

Known also by his honorific title of Shaykh al-Tai'fah ("Master of the Clan"), Tusi is one of the most outstanding Shi'i jurists and a leading spokesman of Shi'ism. He is widely acknowledged as a peerless authority on Islamic law by Shi'i and Sunni scholars alike. While in Najaf he associated frequently with Sunni jurists, who heavily influenced his legal writings. The impact of Tabari and 'Ali ibn 'Issa Rammani (d. 384/994) on his verdicts is particularly notable. In an environment dominated by the views of Sunni scholars it was only logical for him to follow their course, as his views on *jihad* are identical to those of the Sunni *'ulama*, especially Imam Shafi'i. In his monumental work, *al-Nihayah fi mujarrad al-fiqh wa'l fatwa* (The Ultimate Source on Principles of Jurisprudence and Legal Verdict), Tusi in fact repeats Shafi'i's verdict in *Kitab al-Umm* (The Motherbook) and states:

> *Jihad* against all infidels is obligatory for all Muslims. Unbelievers are divided into two categories. One group includes all unbelievers [in Islam]. Nothing short of accepting Islam is acceptable from them. If they refuse, they must be killed and

their offsprings captured and their properties confiscated. This rule does not apply to Jews, Zoroastrians, and Christians. If they pay obligatory tax (*jizya*) and decide to remain in their religion fighting with them is not permissible. Otherwise, the rule that applies to infidels applies to them as well and in such a case fighting with them is obligatory.[177]

It is strange enough that Shafi'i condones the capturing and killing of women and children. More shocking is the fact that Tusi follows him without criticism. Najafabadi strongly condemns Shi'i jurists after Tusi for repeating Tusi blindly and failing to see Tusi's argument in the context of the historical-political environment of his time, namely, the control of the (Sunni) Abbasid Caliphate. One can argue that had Tusi lived in a different time and environment, he would have expressed a different opinion. Therefore, Najafabadi does not accept the Tusi verdict and warns his fellow jurists not to emulate Tusi on this issue because his opinion (*ijtihad*) is not acceptable in our time and must be rejected.[178]

The Opinion of Muhammad ibn Ahmad ibn Idris Hilli (543–598/1149–1202)

Also known as Ibn Idris, Muhammad ibn Ahmad ibn Idris Hilli was the most prominent and most independent-minded Shi'i jurist whose critical approach to earlier scholars' views is well known. He commented on the writings of Shafi'i and Tusi, criticized them, and rejected many of their views.[179] However, with regard to the question of war and peace with unbelievers, Ibn Idris also took the same position as Shafi'i and Tusi. According to him, fighting with unbelievers is not permissible unless they refuse to enter Islam and accept its injunctions. Calling unbelievers to Islam must be carried out with the power of the sword. If they refuse, they must be fought with until they accept Islam or get killed.[180] This is in sharp contrast to the verse of the *Qur'ān* that clearly forbids war against peace-loving unbelievers:

If they withdraw from you, and do not fight you, and offer you peace, then God assigns not any way to you against them. (4:90)

The Views of Hasan ibn Mutahhar Hilli (648–726/1250–1308)

Considered one of the most remarkable Shi'i scholars of his time, Hilli wrote on a variety of subjects including theology and jurisprudence. Over 500 titles have been attributed to him. The best known among them are *Tadhkirah wa'l adhhan fi ahkam al-iman* (Treatise and Views on Laws of Religion), *Manahij al-yaqin* (The Paths of Certainty), *al-Bab Hadi 'ashar* (The Twelfth Gate: Principles of Shi'ite Theology), *Mukhtalaf al-fuqaha* (Diversity of Views among Jurists), and *al-Minhaj fi al-Ahkam* (The Path of the Laws of Transaction).[181]

In a section of his book *Tadhkirah wa'l adhhan fi ahkam al-iman* (Treatise and Views on Laws of Religion), Hilli deals with *jihad* and states:

It is the duty of Muslims to fight with those people against whom *jihad* is obligatory, and either to bring them to Islam or prevent their aggression. If they start the war, fighting with them is obligatory for Muslims. However, they must be called to accept Islam first and those among the enemy who enter Islam become free. Otherwise, Muslims must fight with them.[182]

Hilli is in fact following Ibn Idris and Sahykh Tusi without realizing that the *Qur'ān* sanctions such a *jihad* only if unbelievers threaten the security of the Islamic community. Hilli's verdict treats aggressors and peace-seeking unbelievers in the same manner.[183] A verdict similar to Hilli's was also issued by another prominent Shi'i jurist of the tenth/sixteenth century, namely, Muhammad ibn Makki 'Amili Jazini, also known as the Second Martyr.[184]

Mention must be made of three other important thirteenth/nineteenth- and fourteenth/twentieth-century Shi'i *'ulama*, namely, Muhammad Hasan Najafi,[185] Muhammad Husayn Tabataba'i (1321–1402/1903–1982),[186] and Ayatullah Sayyid Abulqasim Kho'ie.[187] Their views regarding the treatment of unbelievers and the permissibility of *jihad* with them must be examined.

Ayatullah Muhammad Hasan Najafi (1202–1266/1788–1850) was the author of the celebrated work on jurisprudence, *Jawahir al-kalam fi sharh-i sha'ayir al-islam fi Masa'il al-Halal wa'l-Haram* (Jewels of Words: Commentary on the Sharayi' al-Islam on the Lawful and Unlawful by Muhaqqiq Hilli).[188] In this book he makes two claims that must be addressed and criticized. First, he states that the notion of *jihad* denotes war against unbelievers and its objective is to force them to accept Islam. Second, he claims that the *Qur'ānic* verse 2:216 ("Prescribed for you is fighting, though it be hateful to you") was in fact revealed specifically about offensive war and commanded Muslims to fight against unbelievers without any conditions or limitations.[189] Regarding his first claim, as we explained earlier, *jihad* against unbelievers is permissible only if they violate the peace and start war against Muslims first. Concerning his second claim, we must take into account that verse 216 is followed by another verse that states:

> They will not cease to fight with you till they turn you from your religion if they are able, and whosoever from you turn from his religion and dies disbelieving, their works have failed in this world and the next, those are the inhabitants of Fire; therein they shall dwell forever. (2:217)

It is only in such a case that the command articulated in verse 216 applies; that is to say, fighting is prescribed only if unbelievers attack Muslims or attempt to turn them away from their religion. In such a case they should fight even if it be abhorrent to them.[190]

A more careful examination of the views expressed by these scholars indicates that they advocate offensive war in order to impose Islamic faith on unbelievers. In other words, they justify the use of the sword to spread religion. Their conclusions sharply contradict the injunctions of the *Qur'ān* that command the Prophet to "Call thou to the way of your Lord with wisdom and good admonition, and dispute with them in the better way" (16:125). In another verse, God says:

> "There is no compulsion in religion." (2:256)

And:

> "Surely We guided him upon the way whether he be thankful or unthankful." (76:3)

And:

> "Say: 'The truth is from your Lord; so let whosoever will believe and let whosoever will disbelieve.'" (18:29)

All these verses clearly mean that people cannot be forced to accept religion and that calling people to religion must be through reason, guidance, and education. Using force to impose religion on people and calling it "invitation" contradicts the words of God, as is demonstrated in the above verses.[191]

Like Najafi, Ayatullah Tabataba'i also condones offensive war as a means of spreading religion. According to him, Islam is a primordial religion and its mission is to guide man to the straight path.[192] As such it is the duty of Muslims to protect it before unbelievers. To fight for and defend Islam is a right and a duty that God assigned to man, as articulated in several verses of the *Qur'ān*:

> Had God not driven back the people, some by the means of others, there had been destroyed cloisters and churches, oratories and mosques, wherein God's Name is much mentioned. (22:40)

And:

> O believers, respond to God and the Messenger when He calls you unto that which will give you life. (8:24)

According to Tabataba'i, *jihad* is the right of a community to protect itself and its religion against unbelievers. It guarantees the protection of humanity from heresy. He goes one step further and argues that even the use of force to dominate over the enemies of Islam is permissible because war is the last resort to impose faith on those who refuse to believe in God by other means. This is a practice that even in civil societies governments undertake to force people to obey the laws of the state. Moreover, such a measure (imposing faith by force) takes place only in relation to the first generation in a society. Later generations just follow the way of their ancestors and become believers, forgetting that faith was initially imposed on their forefathers by force.[193]

In addition to the reasons we have already presented regarding the inadequacy of this argument and its incompatibility with the *Qur'ān*, as another scholar had argued, Tabataba'i does not give proper weight to the commands of the *Qur'ān* of "There is no compulsion in religion" (2:256) and "Say: 'The truth is from your Lord; so let whosoever will believe and let whosoever will disbelieve'" (18:29). These verses have never been abrogated and therefore are valid until the end of time. Moreover, his argument that *jihad* aims for the total destruction of heresy is not always valid because *jihad* is a natural reaction to the persecution of Muslims by infidels. As the *Qur'ān* has emphasized, "Leave is given to those who fight because they were wronged – surely God is able to help them" (22:39). One may ask why the Prophet signed a peace treaty in Hudaybiyah and did not fight to impose Islam on unbelievers while he could, or did not fight Meccans after he conquered the city, or signed a peace treaty with the Khoza'ah tribe that stipulated mutual defense before their common enemies.[194] Finally, Tabataba'i's argument that all governments punish their citizens if they disobey civil laws is irrelevant because such punishment occurs when citizens accept the authority and the laws of the state, and they would be punished only if they break the law, whereas unbelievers do not acknowledge the authority of Islam and the Islamic state, nor do they accept its law. If offensive war against such unbelievers were permissible, the Prophet would have fought against Meccan infidels when he conquered the city. Not only did he not fight them, but he declared that anyone who stays in his own house or takes refuge in a mosque would be immune from punishment.[195]

Another important contemporary Shi'i jurist, Ayatullah Sayyid Abulqasim Kho'ie, takes a similar position. In a chapter on *jihad* in his *Minhaj al-Salihin*, Kho'ie states that *jihad* is mandatory against three groups of non-Muslims. The first is unbelievers who are not among the People of the Book. It is obligatory to call them to Islam first. If they refuse, fighting with them is an obligation for Muslims. He presents certain verses of the *Qur'ān* that support his argument[196] and emphasizes that there is consensus among all jurists regarding this issue. The second group includes the People of the Book. It is an obligation for Muslims to fight with them until they enter Islam or accept to pay *jizya* as stipulated in the *Qur'ān* (9:29). The third group is the People of the Book who pay taxes without quarrel.[197] Thus, like other jurists whose views we examined before, Kho'ie also insists on the necessity of war to spread Islam.

The preceding discussion clearly demonstrates that during the classical period the majority of Sunni and Shi'i jurists supported offensive war against unbelievers. Some even went as far as insisting on the necessity of conducting *jihad* at least once a year. Thus, according to Tusi:

> The least that jurists expect from the Imam was to carry on war with unbelievers once a year so that the gate of *jihad* would not be closed. Since *jihad* is "sufficient necessity" (*wajib-i kafa'i*) the more frequent it is carried on, the more blessing and grace it will bring to the Islamic community.[198]

Shaykh Tusi, who was the first Shi'i jurist to express this opinion, must have realized that this view was indeed identical with the verdict of Shafi'i. The only difference was that in it the title of "Caliph" was replaced by "Imam." More astounding is the fact that later scholars, including such authoritative figures as Muhaqqiq Hilli, Muhammad Hasan Najafi, Muhammad ibn Makki al-'Amili al-Jazini, Zayn al-Din ibn Ali al-Juba'i, and 'Allamah Hilli, uncritically accepted this verdict and repeated it in their own writings. Despite all the changes that have taken place in the national and international political environment and the fact that many new laws have been introduced that prohibit aggression and offensive war, there are still some jurists in different Muslim countries who continue to repeat the idea of annual *jihad* and offensive war.[199] Some of these jurists even advocate *preemptive jihad* on the basis of a fabricated *ḥadīth* narrated by 'Abdullah ibn 'Umar, according to which the Prophet condoned preemptive attack on the Bani Mustalaq tribe. According to the well-known military historian Muhammad bin Umar al-Waqidi[200] and other scholars of *ḥadīth* such as Ibn Hisham, Shafi'i, and Tabari, this *ḥadīth* was fabricated and therefore preemptive *jihad* was never supported by the Prophet against the said tribe.[201] Unfortunately, some Sunni and Shi'i jurists have acknowledged the authenticity of this *ḥadīth* without verifying its chain of transmission and on the basis of that have issued verdicts supporting preemptive *jihad*.[202] They have been harshly criticized for this error by other scholars, as we discuss in the coming pages.

Supporters of Defensive War

Defensive war is defined by Muslims as a war that is imposed on a Muslim community or a Muslim nation. When a Muslim nation is persecuted or attacked by unbelievers, it is their God-given right to defend themselves, their land, and their honor. According to Mutahhari:

> It is in the nature of *jihad* to be defensive. *Jihad* is permitted only as a means of legitimate defense before aggression of the enemy and violation of a Muslim's integrity, honor, and territories. By the consensus of all Muslim jurists the first verse revealed to the Prophet in chapter 22 concerning *jihad* defines it as defensive war.[203]

Mutahhari argues that according to the *Qur'ān*, *jihad* can be undertaken by Muslims under only three circumstances: (1) to remove injustice and persecution of Muslims by infidels (22:39–40), (2) to resist expulsion from Muslim lands and annexation of Muslim lands by unbelievers (2:246), and (3) to defend Muslim lands and people when a war is imposed on them (2:190–191).[204] Mohaghegh Damad adds two other conditions that justify *jihad*. One is to defend and safeguard public order and security, the other to defend freedom of religion.[205] These two conditions are very original and we did not find them in any other source dealing with this issue.

Salihi Najafabadi, who is an ardent critic of offensive war, argues that *jihad* is a natural reaction of human beings to injustice and aggression, as the *Qur'ān* clearly maintains:

> Leave is given to those who fight because they were wronged – surely God is able to help them – who were expelled from their habitations without right. (22:39)

In his view under no circumstances in Islam is the use of force – much less carrying on *jihad* – permitted in order to impose religion on others, and the *Qur'ān* is quite clear on this point:

> No compulsion is there in religion. Rectitude has become clear from error. (2:256)

Another contemporary jurist has compiled a list of Shi'i and Sunni scholars who believe that *peace* with unbelievers must be a central principle in dealing with them. Among Sunni scholars of the classical period in this list are Malik ibn Anas, Tabari, Sufyan al-Thawri, Awza'i, Ibn Humam, Ibn Qayyim, and Ibn Taymiyah. Their view is supported by some prominent contemporary Sunni jurists as well, among them Rashid Rida, Muhammad 'Abduh, Ahmad Nar, 'Abd al-Rahman 'Azzam, Ibrahim Abd al-Hamid, and Abu'l 'Ala al-Mawdudi. Shi'i jurists who share this view include 'Allamah Hilli, Fadil Miqdad, and several others.[206] All these jurists, some of whom are among the most notable scholars in the Islamic intellectual tradition, reject offensive war. They do not even consider such war as *jihad* in the technical sense of the word. They argue that all verses of the *Qur'ān* that deal with war and *jihad* permit war only under certain conditions. They demonstrate that all wars in which the Prophet and Imam Ali personally participated were defensive in nature.[207] According to Mohaghegh Damad:

> For thirteen years while the Prophet lived in Mecca he adopted a peaceful policy toward his opponents and unbelievers. He never carried weapons with himself.

When he migrated to Medina and gave permission to his followers to carry arms, he did so only for self-defense. The wars he carried against such tribes as Huwazan and Thaqif were all defensive. "The wars he conducted against some Jewish tribes of Medina such as Binadir, Biqada'ah, and Biqinqa' were in response to their breach of peace agreement they had signed." The behavior of the Prophet in wars and peace all proves the primacy of peace over war in dealing with his adversaries.[208]

There is a minority group that takes a middle position between the supporters and opponents of offensive war. While this group acknowledges the defensive nature of war in Islam, it also claims that offensive war is as necessary today as it was earlier in Islamic history to keep the vitality of the Muslim community and help the spread of religion. This view is expressed as an ideal and therefore does not take the role of history and the political environment into consideration. These are the jurists who see the world divided into *Dar al-Islam* (the Abode of Peace) and *Dar al-Harb* (the Abode of War), and the two domains must be in a constant state of hostility and war. This position is in fact based on a lack of proper understanding of the terms used above. "This division itself is the result of offensive war mentality and not acceptable by reason and intellect. This is not legally acceptable because Islam has never commanded the massacre of unbelievers under any circumstances."[209]

The term *Dar al-Islam* is defined as the lands that are under Islamic rule, where Muslims are in the majority and where Islamic law is promulgated and practiced. Throughout Islamic history *Dar al-Islam* was juxtaposed with *Dar al-Harb*, defined as those territories that were inhabited by non-Muslims and administered by non-Muslim governments, where Muslims could not live and practice their religion freely, and where the law of Islam, the *Shari'ah*, was not the law of the land.[210] These definitions in fact describe the *legal* status of the territories under the rule of the Islamic government and the *Shari'ah* or territories outside the jurisdiction of the *Shari'ah* and of Islamic government. They make no reference to the nature of the relationship between the two abodes; therefore, they do not denote a state of constant hostility and war between them.

> According to the Islamic law of international relations, Muslims could make peace with countries outside of *Dar al-Islam* if they themselves were not threatened by them.[211]

There have been many occasions where Muslims have established peaceful relationships with friendly non-Muslim states on the basis of this principle. The best example is the relationship the Prophet established with the Christian Abyssinians at that time, who gave asylum to some Muslim refugees from Mecca in the early days of revelation. Other evidence of such relationships can be seen between Muslims and Christian Spain and the Hindus and Muslims in India. These examples clearly demonstrate that:

> In this domain the Islamic principles must not be confused with matters of political expediency and particular actions of this or that ruler over the age. What is important is to understand the Islamic principles involved.[212]

More confusion, misunderstanding, or misinterpretation exists regarding the *Dar al-Harb*. Islamic law requires Muslims to respect the laws of the land in which they live, but also insists that they be able to follow their own religious practices even under difficult circumstances. If that becomes impossible, they are advised to migrate to the "Abode of Islam."[213]

In addition to these two abodes, Muslim jurists divided the world into several subdomains such as *Dar al-Kufr* (Abode of Disbelief), which the Prophet had initially defined as the Quraysh-dominated society of Mecca, and *Dar al-Hudna* (Abode of Calm), the land of nonbelievers who live in a state of truce with Muslims. To these one might add *Dar al-'Ahd* or *Dar al-Sulh* (Abode of Treaty or Peace), which was invented by the Ottoman Empire to describe lands outside the Islamic world but ones in which Muslims could live and practice their religion freely. It refers to the Ottoman Empire's relationship with its Christian tributaries. Finally, mention must be made of two terms invented to describe the status of Muslims in the West, that is, *Dar al-Da'wah* (Abode of Invitation) and *Dar al-Amn* (Abode of Safety), which describe a region where the religion of Islam is spreading or is being introduced.[214] The existence of these legal terms and entities in fact demonstrates that Islamic understandings of relations with the non-Muslim world is not limited to war and peace alone, but that within the confines of the *Shari'ah*, a wide variety of possible relationships indeed exist.

Jihad and the Role of the Infallible Imam

Although our discussion has been carried out from a Shi'ite perspective, it has thus far examined the views of both Shi'i and Sunni jurists regarding *jihad*. We have demonstrated that for most of Islamic history, Shi'i and Sunni perceptions of war and peace were often identical or at least very similar to one another. If any differences existed between their understandings, they were minor and often a matter of interpretation. However, there is another opinion on *jihad* that is peculiarly Shi'ite and is absent in the Sunni legal discourse concerning war and peace. It originates from the Shi'ite belief in the concept of Imamate and pertains to the role and function of the Twelfth Imam. According to this view, declaration of *jihad* is contingent on the presence of the Infallible Imam in the Islamic community. In other words, *jihad* in the absence of the Imam is illegitimate. According to Ayatullah Muhammad Hasan Najafi (1202–1266/1788–1850), the author of the celebrated work on jurisprudence *Jawahir al-kalam fi Sharh-i Sharayi 'al-islam* (A Commentary on Sharayi), the legitimacy of *jihad* is contingent upon the command of the Infallible Imam who is practically in charge of the government and rules over the community of believers. This rule applies to offensive war alone in which the Imam directly or through his commanders issues an order for the war.[215] It is not applicable to defensive war, as defensive war is a natural reaction of the community in the face of aggression. Historically speaking, this situation never existed under any of the Imams except during the Caliphate of Imam Ali ibn Abi Talib, who ruled during 35–40/656–661.[216]

This rule is based on narrations recorded from Imam Ja'far al-Sadiq and several Shi'ite Imams[217] who lived in a hostile environment and under constant persecution during the Umayyad rule (41–133/661–750) and the first 190 years of the Abbasid Caliphate until 329/941 when the Twelfth Imam went into Occultation. During those centuries the state pursued an expansionist policy and conducted wars to find new resources to meet the needs of a growing population. Such wars were offensive in nature and were conducted for nonreligious purposes; nevertheless, in order to legitimize such wars and mobilize the masses Caliphs often gave them a religious coloring by declaring them as *jihad*. The Imams defied Caliphs and their policies and condemned their unorthodox behavior but also adopted a quietist attitude out of concern for their safety and the security of their followers. They devoted their lives to teaching and training students and other scholarly activities.[218]

During the Safavid period numerous treatises were written by jurists and theologians to demonstrate the legal or illegal nature of *jihad* in the absence of the Twelfth Imam. It was during this period that Shi'i jurists finally reached a compromise. They began to differentiate between two types of *jihad*, namely, offensive and defensive. They declared the defensive *jihad* obligatory for every able-bodied adult Muslim, while suspending offensive *jihad* during the period of Greater Occultation.[219]

Many among the most prominent Shi'i jurists and theologians indeed believe that the gate of *jihad* was closed with the Occultation of the Twelfth Imam in 329/941 and will remain so until his reappearance, and they have issued verdicts to that effect. Some have even eliminated discussion of *jihad* from their legal discourses and writing altogether. Mulla Muhsin Fayd Kashani,[220] for example, states, "Since during the period of Occultation [of the Twelfth Imam] *jihad* is not permissible and is dismissed, we do not see the need to discuss the rules of *jihad* in our discourse."[221] Among contemporary scholars, Ayatullah Ruhullah Khomeini, Mutahhari, and Salihhi Najafabadi have expressed similar opinions.[222]

The Laws of War

In the preceding pages we have demonstrated that selective interpretation of some verses of the *Qur'ān* and *ḥadīth* have led certain jurists to issue verdicts that are in contradiction with the commands of the *Qur'ān* and Traditions of the Prophet. This type of reading has portrayed the Islamic world as being in a perpetual state of war and conflict with unbelievers and even believing non-Muslims[223] and has impacted the Muslim jurists' definition of the rules of engagement during warfare.

Declaring War

The *Qur'ān* commands Muslims to fight in the path of God and for God's sake. It does not condone war for the sake of war, for revenge, or for military ambition and the expansion of the borders of the empire. As we mentioned before, unless Muslims are attacked by an enemy, under no circumstances does the *Qur'ān* allow them to start a war.[224] Declaration of war is the sole prerogative of the Caliph or Imam, who can delegate his authority, if he wishes, to his deputy or commander of the army. Going to war is allowed under the following conditions:

1. Defensive war in order to stop aggression of an enemy.
2. War in defense of an ally. If a Muslim state signs a treaty of friendship or a military pact with another nation that calls for joint defense in times of war, it can enter the war on the side of an ally even if it is a non-Muslim state.
3. Punitive war in order to end domestic revolts, though this is not considered *jihad*.
4. Preventive and/or preemptive war to repel aggression before it occurs.[225]

Except in the first and third cases, before a war is declared an ultimatum must be issued. In any case Muslims cannot start a war with infidels without proper warning and only after they reject the call to enter Islam or refuse to pay *jizya*.[226]

The Rules of Engagement

There are clear commands in Islamic law regarding the rules of engagement that explain in detail all permissible and forbidden acts that can be undertaken during warfare, and these are addressed below. As discussed previously, the *Qur'ān* allows Muslims to retaliate if attacked by enemy forces but does not permit excessive use of force and collective punishment. Killing noncombatants, especially women, children, the elderly, and the disabled, is strictly forbidden by the law.[227] In addition, destroying farms or orchards, polluting rivers, cutting trees, and all other kinds of violations of the sanctity of nature are banned.

Respect for the sanctity of time and space is also observed seriously in Islamic laws of war. The *Qur'ān* mentions (9:36) that during certain months of the year – that is, the first, the seventh, the eleventh, and the twelfth months (Muharram, Rajab, Dhi'l-qa'dah, and Dhi'lhajjah) – war is not allowed. Fighting is also prohibited in any sacred site, especially the *Ka'bah*,[228] mosques, churches, synagogues, temples, and all other religious sanctuaries. If the enemy takes refuge in a place of worship, it is the duty of a Muslim army to protect his life.

While the immunity of women, children, and other persons not participating in battle is a point clearly drawn within Shi'i jurisprudence, there was nonetheless some discussion of the possible exceptions. A particularly thorny problem arose apropos of the use of these innocents as human shields (*taturras*, taking shields). What should be done if the enemy interposes noncombatants between itself and the approaching line of battle? In fighting such an enemy should one surrender rather than do harm to persons who are presumed innocent under Islamic jurisprudence? Or inversely, would the enemy's unwarranted use of human shields permit action that results in the death of these innocents, however regrettably, under the principle of military necessity? Most jurisprudence leaned in favor of the second, more permissive option, as expressed for instance by Allamah Hilli (648–725/1250–1325):

> When women, children or some Muslim individuals are taken as a shield for protection by the enemy, in case the fire of war is aflame, one can make them a target.[229]

A somewhat more tempered statement may be found in the jurisprudence of Ibn Barraj (400–481/1009–1088):

> If in the state of *taturras*, the flame of war blazes up, making the enemy a target is permissible. Of course the children who are taken as a shield for protection are not made a target, but the enemy who lies behind the children is made into a target. If in such a state, children are slain, the slayer is not deemed culpable because this act has been performed out of necessity. It is evident that when the fire of combat is not kindled one can by no means shoot the children.[230]

Some jurists who discussed this issue found support in the practice of the Holy Prophet at the battle of Ta'if (*Qur'ān* 2:190), since on this occasion he used a catapult against the inhabitants of Ta'if while women and children were among them, thereby resulting in the death of these innocents.[231]

Another possible exception to the rule of noncombatant immunity concerned the case of "obscene exhibition" of women on battlefields.[232] Citing a *ḥadīth* that had been transmitted by Akramah, Allamah Hilli wrote:

> When the Prophet of Islam besieged the inhabitants of Ta'if, a woman appeared in the enemy's front and stripped off her garments and exhibited herself to the Muslim soldiers, whereupon the Prophet of Islam commanded that she should be shot by an arrow and then one of the Muslim soldiers cast an arrow toward her.[233]

A later jurist, Muhammad Najafi (1201–1277/1786–1860), has nonetheless argued that the chain of transmission of the above-mentioned *ḥadīth* is unreliable. Moreover, on substantive grounds he maintains that in such a situation the slaying of women is not permissible. Only should they wage war directly against Muslim troops can they be legitimately targeted.[234] Mohaghegh Damad comments that these two authors seem however to be talking at cross purposes, since Allamah Hilli speaks within the perspective of military necessity, while Najafi relies "mostly on the absolute and unrestricted nature of the preventive or prohibitive proofs (*al-addillah al-mani'ah*) and does not regard the problem as an instance of necessity."[235] Mohaghegh Damad concludes that even should women "revile Muslims or use opprobrious language" against their commander, this still "cannot be considered an instance of necessity and does not permit their slaughter."[236]

Restrictions on Weapons

Until the development of a technologically advanced and sophisticated war industry and the introduction of modern weaponry, Muslim jurists were not particularly concerned with the issue of weaponry. In fact, the degree of damage that old weaponry could inflict upon the body of combating forces, cities, and nature was very limited. Despite that, some Muslim jurists addressed these issues in their writings. For example, injury to the face and/or the use of weapons such as poisonous arrows that could inflict unnecessary pain or excessive injury were in fact declared forbidden.[237] Questions related to weapons have found more relevance in the contemporary world as the extent of destruction that modern military technology can inflict on man and nature has grown to an incredible extent. Of particular importance is the issue of thermonuclear, chemical, and other weapons of mass destruction that can be found in modern arsenals. Indeed, Islamic law unequivocally prohibits the use of weapons of mass destruction of any kind, including those that poison water sources and pollute the environment. To this end, Ayatullah Sayyid Ali Khamenei, currently the Supreme Leader of Iran, issued the statement below prohibiting the use of such weapons. Delivered to the First International Conference on Disarmament and Non-Proliferation (Tehran, 17–18 April 2010),[238] the last line is particularly significant as it expresses a religious condemnation of these weapons:

> The insistence of governments on keeping, aggrandizing, and enhancing the destructive power of these weapons whose only use is to frighten and terrorize the masses and to create a false kind of security based on averting an unavoidable mass destruction, has led to the continuation of the nuclear nightmare. Uncountable economic and human resources have been invested in an irrational rivalry so that each of the superpowers can reach an illusory capability of destroying their rivals and other inhabitants of the world, including their own ones.
>
> This deterrence policy, based on definite mutual destruction, has not without reason been called an idiocy....
>
> *In our view, besides nuclear weapons, all weapons of mass destruction, chemical or biological, are a serious threat to humanity. The Iranian people who have themselves been victim to chemical weapons feel more than any other nation the danger of producing and amassing this kind of weaponry and are ready to apply all of their capabilities to counter them.... We hold the use of these weapons to be* haram, *and consider it as the duty of all to strive for the protection of humanity from such a catastrophe* [emphasis added].[239]

Prisoners of War

One of the most controversial issues in the Islamic law of war and peace is the treatment of prisoners of war. The command of the *Qur'ān* is very clear on this issue:

> O Prophet, say to the prisoners in your hands: "If God knows of any good in your hearts He will give you better than what has been taken away from you, and He will forgive you; surely God is All-forgiving, All-compassionate." (8:70)

The tone of this verse reflects a kind and compassionate attitude toward prisoners of war. It is sympathetic to the condition of prisoners and implies that their captivity is temporary. Once a military operation is completed the *Qur'ān* commands Muslims to free prisoners out of generosity or, if they choose, in return for ransom:

> When you meet the unbelievers, smite their necks, then, when you have made wide slaughter among them, tie fast the bonds; then set them free, either by grace or ransom, till the war lays down its loads. So it shall be, and if God had willed, He would have avenged Himself upon them. (47:4)

In neither of the above verses nor in any other verse in the *Qur'ān* is there any command to kill prisoners of war or enslave them. In fact, kind treatment of prisoners was a way to capture their hearts and persuade them to enter Islam.[240] It is not understandable, therefore, why some jurists believed that prisoners of war must be killed or taken as slaves.[241] There is no verse in the *Qur'ān* or *ḥadīth* of the Prophet to condone such actions. In one case after the Battle of Badr where two prisoners, Nadr ibn Harith and 'Uqbah ibn Abi Mu'it, were killed by the order of the Prophet, it was because of the crimes they had committed in Mecca before the war and their captivity.[242] Despite all this evidence, many jurists have concluded that prisoners of war must all be killed and they have issued verdicts to that end. This conclusion is arguably based on their misinterpretation of verse five of chapter nine (Repentance) where God commanded the Prophet to smite the neck of unbelievers wherever he found them, not realizing that this particular verse was revealed exclusively in relation to those unbelievers *who broke their covenant with the Prophet and betrayed him* and does not apply to prisoners of war at all. Moreover, verse four of chapter 47 (Muhammad) soon abrogated the earlier command of verse five of chapter nine where God commanded the Prophet "then set them free, either by grace or ransom, till the war lays down its loads" (47:4). Salihi Najafabadi provides the names of those jurists who have issued verdicts on the basis of this misinterpretation of the *Qur'ānic* verses.[243] He also adds that Shaykh Tusi and many other Shi'i jurists who follow this conclusion were misled by several traditions narrated by unreliable transmitters such as Talhah ibn Zayd and several others who are not trusted by Sunni and Shi'i jurists and scholars of *ḥadīth*.[244]

As we mentioned before, Islamic law prohibits excessive use of force and any kind of physical and psychological torture and abuse of prisoners of war. As soon as the war ends, all prisoners are expected to be freed so that they can return home. The *Qur'ān* commands Muslims to free prisoners of war in exchange for Muslim prisoners, in return for ransom (*fidyah*), or out of generosity. On one occasion the Prophet freed those enemy forces taken prisoner in the Battle of Badr in return for ransom. The ransom he demanded was that each prisoner educate ten Muslim children and teach them how to read and write.[245]

Rules for Ending War

The concept of defensive war has gained increasing attention among many contemporary Sunni and Shi'i jurists and thinkers alike. A growing number of jurists have come to realize and agree that the natural state of human society is based on peace. War is the absence of peace caused by a transient struggle for power and wealth. Defense of the Islamic land before an aggressor is necessary, but once the aggressor is pushed back and defeated, fighting is no longer necessary and peace must be reestablished immediately. The *Qur'ān* clearly declares the end of war when the enemy lays down its arms, submits, or asks for peace: "And fight them till there is no persecution and the religion is God's; then if they give over, there shall be no enmity save for evildoers" (2:193).

While the *Qur'ān* emphasizes the necessity of Muslim military preparedness, this emphasis must be seen not as a desire for war but as a deterrent before any potential aggressor.[246] That is why as soon as the enemy shows willingness to end hostilities and asks for a cease-fire or peace, Muslim forces are obligated to stop the war and accept the enemy's request, granted that the enemy is sincere in its desire for peace and would not breach the cease-fire:[247] "And if they incline to peace, do thou incline to it; and put thy trust in God; He is the All-Hearing, the All-knowing" (8:61).

Summary and Conclusion

The notion of Islam prevalent in the West as the "religion of the sword" has helped to eclipse the inner and spiritual significance of the term *jihad*.[248] Its translation into European languages as "holy war" by virtue of its juridicial usage and the emergence of a number of extremist political groups in recent decades contending for power and using the term have also prevented an understanding of its traditional meaning.

Jihad in its most outward sense means the defense of the Islamic world from invasion and intrusion by non-Islamic forces. This call has been especially true when parts of the Islamic world began to be colonized. It must be remembered, however, that even in such situations *jihad* does not denote religious war but an attempt by a religion to protect itself from being conquered either by military and economic forces or by ideas of an alien nature. In the words of a prominent contemporary Shi'i scholar, "In all traditional religious and sapiential traditions justice is associated with truth, while truth itself is reality in the metaphysical sense. This fact is made clear in the double meaning of the Arabic term *al-haqq*, which means both truth and reality."[249]

Islam means submission to God's will. It also means peace. As a revealed religion it is a gift God gave man as a sign of His mercy.[250] Numerous verses of the *Qur'ān* call for fulfillment of God's will on earth, that is, to establish peace and understanding and to struggle for perfection and excellence on all levels.[251] To that end, Islam does not condone but limits war by including the question of war and peace in its sacred legislation:

> Islam bases itself upon the idea of establishing equilibrium in human soul and society, and such equilibrium is the basis upon which the soul takes its flight toward that peace which, to use Christian terms, "passeth understanding." If Christian morality sees the aim of the spiritual life and its own morality as based on the vertical flight toward that perfection and ideal which is embodied in Christ, Islam sees it in the establishment of an equilibrium, both outward and inward as the necessary basis for the vertical ascent.[252] That equilibrium is inseparable from the very name of Islam as being related to *salam* or peace and its preservation in this world requires continuous exertion. It means carrying out *jihad* at every stage of life.[253]

We mentioned that the *lesser jihad* is in fact the most outward meaning of the term and denotes the defense of the Islamic lands before foreign invasion. On a more limited level it also includes the socio-economic domain. The defense of one's rights, honor, and reputation is a *jihad*, as is the struggle for social justice. The struggle for improvement in one's living conditions, the development of projects for the improvement of the living conditions of the community, and the defense of the sanctity of nature are also a *jihad*.[254]

But more important than the *lesser jihad* is the reference to the *greater jihad* in the *ḥadīth* of the Prophet, that is, inward struggle against one's carnal soul and its desires and passions that destroy inner peace and equilibrium. Every Muslim is expected at every step of life to perform *jihad* to establish equilibrium first in his or her own soul, and only then in his or her immediate environment and the world:

> ... to wake up to that Divine Reality which is the very source of peace. The Prophet said, "Man is asleep and when he dies he awakens." Through inner *jihad* the spiritual man dies in this life in order to cease all dreaming, in order to awaken to that Reality which is the origin of all realities, in order to behold that Beauty of which all earthly beauty is but a pale reflection, in order to attain that Peace which all men seek but which can in fact be found only through the inner *jihad*.[255]

This study was undertaken to present a Shi'i perspective on peace and war and to demonstrate how Shi'i jurists understood and interpreted the concept of *jihad* as stipulated in the *Qur'ān* and *ḥadīth*. In the course of research and writing, it became clear to us that a unique and specifically Shi'i perspective does in fact exist, but in many ways it is very similar to the Sunni perspective. Indeed, on many issues related to war and peace Shi'i jurists accepted Sunni jurists' rulings and views. In particular, what was recognized as the Shi'i perspective after the last decades of the fifth/eleventh century was in fact a repetition of the views expressed by Imam Shafi'i, presented in Shi'i terminology, and accepted widely by later Shi'i scholars and jurists as "uniquely Shi'ite." Until very recently most Shi'i scholars in Iran and Iraq accepted those views without any attempt to reexamine or criticize them in light of new research or with consideration for the changes in the social, political, and intellectual environment of the Muslim world. In a sense, when it came to the question of war and peace, for many centuries Shi'i jurists in fact ceased to practice *ijtihad*. They did not reassess the views and writings of Sunni scholars nor of their own Shi'i predecessors independently of the authority and reputation of their authors, and in light of their *own* reading and understanding of the *Qur'ān* and *ḥadīth*. They even failed to investigate possible differences between Sunni and Shi'i views on *jihad* in light of Shi'i doctrine and principles such as the Imamate. Consequently, generation after generation repeated the same verdicts, changing only the language and the style of their presentation. It is for this reason that the efforts of a new generation of Shi'i scholars and jurists who try to critically examine classical texts and to challenge and reject the findings of scholars of past centuries must be acknowledged.

The Iran–Iraq War that started in 1980 brought this problem into the open. The war made the need for finding a specifically Shi'i formula to fight Saddam Hussein and/or negotiate for peace even more urgent and prompted these jurists to reassess many views and ideas of their predecessors. In fact, after several centuries of repeating earlier scholars' rulings in seminaries, a new generation of Shi'i jurists again began to practice *ijtihad* in relation to the question of war and peace. These scholars received the traditional education in seminaries in Qom and Najaf but were also exposed to modern education and research methodologies. Some of them knew at least one foreign language other than Arabic or had access to European sources in translation. In particular, the efforts of the three scholars whose views we referred to in the course of this study must be acknowledged for reviving *ijtihad* in the discussion of *jihad* in our time.

The most important and ground-breaking steps in this regard have been taken in Iran by three contemporary jurists and scholars, namely, Ayatullahs Murtada Mutahhari, Ni'matullah Salihi Najafabadi, and Mostafa Mohaghegh Damad. They had the courage to challenge and reject many ideas of earlier jurists on war and peace and especially *jihad* that for centuries had been accepted by the most authoritative jurists in the Shi'ite world as "uniquely Shi'ite." Rather than uncritically accepting the words of these jurists and eminent scholars, they argued that one must understand the commands of the *Qur'ān*, the *hadīth*, and narrations of the Imams in their proper context. One also must refer to one's intellect rather than repeat what scholars and jurists of earlier centuries have said. This is in fact what *ijtihad* is.[256] Throughout their writings these three scholars have demonstrated the flexibility of Shi'i jurisprudence by providing new interpretations of the *Qur'ānic* verses, Traditions of the Prophet, and the narrations of the Shi'ite Imams. They have shown that *peace* is the natural state of human existence and that within Islam, *peace* – and not war – is a central principle in dealing with the outside world. If war is important, it is because sometimes it is the only means to restore peace. This conclusion is in sharp contrast with the most widely accepted view among the earlier scholars who believed that *war* – and not peace – was the central Islamic principle in dealing with unbelievers or followers of other religions.

The result of this pioneering effort has indeed revealed that much of what was written by Shi'ite and Sunni jurists of past centuries indeed contradicts the guidelines of the *Qur'ān* and the Traditions of the Prophet. If a jurist such as Muhammad ibn Idris Shafi'i issued verdicts in support of offensive war, it was not because he failed to understand the injunctions of the *Qur'ān* and *hadīth* on *jihad*, but rather because he was blackmailed and pressured to provide religious justification for the policies of the Abbasid Caliphate. In other words, he interpreted the verses of the *Qur'ān* and the Traditions of the Prophet out of their specific historical context to serve the interests of the state. Because of his scholarly eminence and authority, later jurists did not dare to challenge or reject Shafi'i's views and simply repeated what he had stated. But the present generation does not have to follow their steps, for the implications of such juridical errors and short-sightedness for the image of Islam and Muslims have been far-reaching. One must admit that these jurists share a responsibility along with Orientalist scholars for portraying Islam as a religion of the sword; this is an image it has unfortunately come to have for many within the Islamic world and beyond its borders.

It is for these reasons that the efforts of the three scholars whose works we have introduced in this study, as well as those scholars of Islam who live and write outside the Islamic world, deserve special attention and recognition. Presumably, the views of these contemporary thinkers must have been accepted by many other Shi'i and Sunni jurists and scholars alike, for no one has come out to refute or even challenge them yet. Indeed, their initiatives might create a healthy environment for exchange of opinions between Shi'i and Sunni jurists and eventually lead to a consensus among them on the definitions of just war, peace, and *jihad*. These scholars all realize the destructive impact on Islam's image of such verdicts as the necessity of killing *all* infidels and carrying on offensive war at least once a year. They have started their own *jihad* to demonstrate that Islam is a religion of peace, acceptance, and tolerance, a religion in which force and compulsion have no place.

Remarks on the Selection of Primary Sources

The history of the development of Shi'i jurisprudence can be divided into at least nine periods. It is beyond the scope of this study to examine each period in detail. However, in order to place opinions expressed by different scholars at different times in a historical context, it is appropriate to present a brief sketch of each period as follows:

1. The formative period represented by the Shi'ite Imams from the time of Ali ibn Abi Talib to the time of Occultation of the Twelfth Imam (260–329/661–941). The Imams in fact laid the foundation of Islamic law by training a large number of students who afterward wrote on legal issues both in the Shi'i as well as Sunni circles. Of particular importance is the role of the Sixth Imam, Ja'far al-Sadiq, who trained Abu Hanifah (d. 767) and Malik (d. 796) directly, and through them Muhammad ibn Idris Shafi'i (d. 819) and Ahmad ibn Hanbal (d. 855). These jurists are considered the founders of the four Sunni Schools of Law after the death of Ja'far al-Sadiq in 765.
2. The age of the collectors and narrators of *hadīth* represented by Muhammad ibn Ya'qub Kulayni and Shaykh Muhammad ibn 'Ali ibn Babuyah, also known as Shaykh Saduq.
3. The period of the beginning of the practice of *ijtihad* by such jurists as Muhammad ibn Muhammad, also known as Shaykh Mufid.
4. This period marks the peak of the practice of *ijtihad* and its perfection represented by Shaykh Tusi.
5. The age of emulation (*taqlid*) and the decline of *ijtihad*.
6. The period of revival of *ijtihad* marked by the activities and writings of Muhammad ibn Idris Hilli, Shaykh Muhammad ibn Makki, and Shaykh 'Ali ibn Hasan, also known as Muhaqqiq Karaki, and Ja'far ibn Hasan ibn Muhaqqiq Hilli.
7. The Safavid period of the emergence of the Akhbari School of Shi'i Law. Muhammad ibn Murtada, also known as Fayd Kashani, was the most eminent jurist of this period who wrote about *jihad*.
8. The period of new interpretation represented by Muhammad Hasan ibn Baqir, also known as Sahib Jawahir and the author of *Jawahir al-kalam fi sharh-i sha'ayir al-islam (fi Masa'il al-Halal wa'l-Haram)* (Jewels of the Word: A Commentary on Sharayi', Legal Principles of Islam by Muhaqqiq Hilli).
9. The contemporary period that is marked by new approaches to jurisprudence and creative and new interpretations. The most important jurists of this period who wrote on the rules of *jihad* are Ayatullah Ruhullah Musavi Khomeini and Muhammad Taqi Bahjat.

The following statements have been selected from the most important Shi'i theological or legal sources on the ethics of war and peace written by jurists introduced above. To the best of my knowledge, this is the first time that any of these sources or selections

from them have been translated into English. The length of the materials dealing with
the issue of our interest varies from one source to another. In some cases, the author
mentions his views only in passing, in other cases they are discussed in great detail. With
the exception of the last source, the Treatise known as *jihadiyah* compiled by Mirza
Bozorg Qa'im Maqam, which is in Persian, all other sources have been translated from
Arabic.

There is a remarkable degree of continuity in the writings of Shi'i jurists and theologians of the classical period concerning *jihad*. Most of the views expressed are very
similar, and sometimes nearly identical. However, interpretations of each scholar and the
degree of emphasis on each aspect of *jihad* differ from one another, perhaps reflecting
the prevailing intellectual and religious environment.

Abu Jac'far Muhammad ibn Ya'qub al-Kulayni

Abu Jac'far Muhammad ibn Ya'qub al-Kulayni was born in the city of Rayy in Persia. He
traveled extensively and received his education in Rayy, Baghdad, and Qum. He died in
328/940. He is the most widely acknowledged Shi'i compiler of *hadīth*. His *Kitab al-
Kafi* is one of the four most important collections of Shi'i *hadīth*. The following excerpts
are selected from volume five of the *Book of Jihad*.

From: Abu Jac'far Muhammad ibn Ya'qub al-Kulayni, *Book of Jihad*, Vol. V (compiled between 309–329/921 and 940)[257]

So narrated Ali ibn Ibrahim from his father, and Ali ibn Muhammad al-Qasani
who both heard from Qasim ibn Muhammad who had heard from Sulayman ibn
Dawood al-Minqari who had heard from Fydayl ibn 'Ayyaz who said:

I asked Aba 'Abdullah (Husayn ibn 'Ali) to tell me about calling people to God
and *jihad* on His path, whether it is restricted to specific people and cannot be carried on except by them, is it impunible [if one chooses not to participate], or if it
cannot be carried except by those who believe in God and His Messenger (peace
be upon him).

I said, "Who are they?"

He said, "He who rises with God's condition, Majestic and Glorious is He, in
war and *jihad* he is one of the Mujahidun and he is allowed to call [people] to God.
However, he who does not rise [for *jihad*] in accordance with God's condition, he
is not allowed to participate in *jihad*, nor is he allowed to call people to God, until
he established in his soul that which was described about conditions of *jihad*."

I said, "May God have mercy upon you, can you explain that for me."

He said, "Indeed God, Praised and Most High, informed His Messenger in His
Book of the ways and rules of calling people to Him and described the [character-
istics of] callers. He ordained hierarchies and stations that describe one another
and reasons for one through others.

God, Most High and Praised, informed [His Messenger] that first one who in fact calls man to God and to obey His command is God Himself, [as He says] "... and God summons to the Abode of Peace, and He guides whomsoever He wills to a straight path" (The Noble *Qur'ān*, 10:25).

Then He praised His Messenger and said: "Call thou unto the way of your Lord with wisdom and good admonition, and dispute with them in the better way," that is to say with the *Qur'ān* (16:125). And do not call to God he who opposes God's command and calls [people] to other than what He commanded in His Book. God Said to His Messenger, "Indeed you are for guiding people to the straight path."

[True] believers are those who rise and observe conditions of faith as we described. That is why a person is not permitted to participate in war until he becomes oppressed. One will not become oppressed until one is a believer, he will not be a believer until he upholds the conditions of faith that God has placed on the shoulders of believers and those who fight on His path. When he meets all conditions God set, he will become a [true] believer, then he will become oppressed, and only then is he allowed to fight on God's path, as God says, "Sanction is given unto those who fight because they were wronged – surely God is able to help them" (22:39). And if one does not meet [the] conditions of faith perfectly, one is [the] oppressor and therefore not allowed to participate in *jihad* and call [people to God].

Shaykh Mufid (336–413/945–1025)

Muhammad ibn Nu 'man, also known as Shaykh Mufid, is among the first Shi'i jurists who combined intellectual life and the legal profession with practical experience. He often worked as an adviser to the kings of the Buyids, a Shi'ite dynasty that ruled over Persia between 322–446/934 and 1055. Mufid's views on *jihad* are available in Kitab al-Amali's work on jurisprudence that he dictated to his students. In this book he examines *jihad* mostly from an ethical dimension and as a pillar of Islamic faith. Unlike other jurists, he believes that offensive war *jihad* can be declared and carried out not only by the Infallible Imam but also by a qualified jurist, whose verdict he regards as valid as that of the Imam.

Shaykh al-Ta'ifah (Master of the Clan)

Muhammd ibn Hasan ibn 'Ali Tusi, also known as Shaykh al-Ta'ifah (Master of the Clan), was born in Khorasan in 385/995. He studied with Shaykh Mufid and Sayyid Murtada. After teaching in Baghdad for a while, he went to Najaf and established the most important Shi'i learning center of his time in that city. He was acknowledged as a peerless authority on Islamic law and jurisprudence by Shi'i and Sunni scholars and students. He died in Najaf in 460/1068. The following piece has been selected from *al-Nihayah fi mujarrad al-fiqh wa'l fatwa* (The Ultimate Book on the Pure Goal of Jurisprudence and Legal Verdict). This is one of the most important sources of Shi'i jurisprudence ever written. Tusi describes four conditions for *jihad*.

From: Shaykh al-Ta'ifah, *al-Nihayah fi mujarrad al-fiqh wa'l fatwa* (The Ultimate Book on the Pure Goal of Jurisprudence and Legal Verdict)[258]

1. *Jihad* is one of the pillars of Islam and an obligatory duty but it is also a sufficient necessity (*wajib-i kafa'i*) – that is, participation of some members of the society relieves others from taking part in it.
2. *Jihad* must be undertaken only under the leadership of the Infallible Imam. Therefore, in the time of Occultation, *jihad* is not permissible.
3. There are two categories of unbelievers [non-Muslim] against whom *jihad* may be carried out. One group accepts Islam, or does not accept Islam and chooses to fight. The other group includes Jews, Christians, and Zoroastrians [who are People of the Book who will remain in their religion but] accept to pay *jizya* (protection tax).
4. *Jihad* must be carried out as a last resort, and after inviting unbelievers to Islam. If they still refuse, then fighting is permitted against them.

In summary, *jihad* is not permitted unless by the command of a just Imam, that is, when a just Imam is present. *Jihad* is not permitted unless by his command, or by the command of whom he appoints, and he then calls them for *jihad*. In such a situation it becomes obligatory for the people to rise [for *jihad*]. If an Imam or the person he appoints is not present, fighting with the enemy is not permitted. *Jihad* under the command of unjust oppressive leaders or by the command of [a leader] other than the Imam is wrong and he who participates in it commits sin. If he participates in such a *jihad* he will not be rewarded.

Sharif Tahir ibn Zuhrah (d. 585/1189)

Sayyid 'Izz al-Din Hamzah, also known as Sharif Tahir ibn Zuhrah (d. 585/1189) was a descendent of the Sixth Shi'ite Imam, Ja'far al-Sadiq. His book, *Ghunyat al-nuzu'ila 'ilm a-lusul wa'-furu'* (A Compendium of Principles and Secondary Rules), is one of the oldest and most authoritative early Shi'i sources. The significance of this book is in the author's use of Sunni and Shi'i sources as well as the Traditions of the Prophet and narrations of the Imams. For information on the author and his book, see Sayyid Muhsin Amin 'Amili (d. 1282–1371/1865–1951), *A'yan al-Shi'ah* (The Notable Men of Shi'ites) (Beirut, 1403/1983), 2:249, 6:610–613, and Mohammad 'Ali Mudarris Khiyabani Tabrizi (d. 1371/1951), *Rayhanat al-adab* (Garden of Literature) (Tehran, 1369/1990), 7:551. The following passage describes individual qualifications for participation in *jihad*:

From: Sharif Tahir ibn Zuhrah, *Ghunyat al-nuzu' ila 'ilm a-lusul wa'-furu'*[259]

Qualifications to participate in *jihad*

As to the conditions under which *jihad* becomes an obligatory duty [for a believer] they include the following: He must be a free, [nonslave] male who has reached the age of adulthood, is in perfect mental and physical health, and has the power to fight and stand its consequences, can afford to fight and whom the just Imam or his designated appointee commands to fight when Islam, Muslims or their properties are threatened. Whenever one of these conditions [is] not met, *jihad* is no longer obligatory for him.

Muhaqqiq Hilli

Ja'far ibn Hasan, also known as Muhaqqiq Hilli, was born in 602/1205 in the city of Hillah in Iraq and received his education there and in Najaf. He gained prominence in scholarly circles and received the honorific title of Muhaqqiq, "Seeker of the Truth." He wrote extensively on legal and theological subjects. His most famous book, *Sharayi' al-Islam fi Masa'il al-Halal wa'l-Haram* (The Laws of Islam Regarding the Issues Related to Permissible and Forbidden Acts) received special attention, and many commentaries were written on it. He died in 676/1277. In this book he deals with *jihad* very briefly and classifies it with *ahkam*, that is, basic tenets of religion that define one's relationship with society. He makes declaration of and/or participation in *jihad* contingent upon the presence of the Twelfth Imam.

From: Muhaqqiq Hilli, *Sharayi' al-Islam fi Masa'il al-Halal wa'l-Haram* (The Laws of Islam Regarding the Issues Related to Permissible and Forbidden Acts)[260]

Jihad becomes obligatory only when the [Infallible] Imam is present, or a representative he may appoint on his behalf.

He would not decide for *jihad* or appoint anyone to lead it unless he sees that the interest of [Islam] necessitates *jihad*, or realizes that those who rise to defend are not able to do so except through the participation of all groups in the society.

Mulla Muhsin Fayd Kashani (d. 1091/1680)

Muhammad Muhsin ibn Murtada, also known as Mulla Muhsin Fayd Kashani, was a student of Sadr al-Din Shirazi (Mulla Sadra, d. 1050/1640) and became one of the most prominent eleventh-/seventeenth-century jurists, theologians, and philosophers of the Safavid period and the author of numerous works on jurisprudence, *hadith*, and

Qur'ānic commentaries and philosophy. He is particularly acknowledged and respected for his attempt to create harmony between philosophy, gnosis, and Islamic law. More than eighty of his works have been identified and published several times in Qom and Tehran.

From: Mulla Muhsin Fayd Kashani, *Kitab al-Wafi*, 15:84[261]

Defensive War

When a Muslim fears that harm may be inflicted upon him from the enemy it is an obligation for him to defend himself and remove that threat from his life. He has been commanded by God and His Messenger to fight in such a situation. Therefore, it is his duty to fight whenever there is a war against the just Imam for he acts upon God's command and the command of His Messenger in such a situation. Otherwise, it is not religiously permissible (*halal*) for him to initiate fighting.

Another verdict by Fayd Kashani found in his other work *Mafatih al-Sharayi'* clearly rejects the possibility of *jihad* in the absence of the Twelfth Imam, the Mahdi.

From: Mulla Muhsin Fayd Kashani, *Mafatih al-Sharayi'*, Vol. II (1042/1633)[262]

Jihad is necessary and obligatory for the protection of religion. It is essential for religion like commanding good and forbidding the reprehensible, collaborating in good deed and virtues, being chivalrous, judging among people in fairness and in accordance with the truth, upholding the laws of punishment and retribution, and other kinds of religious punishment.... This is the greatest pillar in religion and an important issue for which God appointed a messenger. If it is abandoned, messengership will be irrelevant, religiosity will decline, cracks will appear in religion, perversion will prevail, ignorance will spread, cities will be ruined, and people will be killed; We take refuge in God from all these.

Beware that *jihad* is to propagate and call [people] to Islam, and is specifically contingent upon the permission of the [Infallible] Imam. It will be dismissed during the time of [the Imam's] Occultation and that is the reason we do not bother to discuss it in this book.

Muhammad Hasan Najafi (1202–1266/1788–1850)

Muhammad Hasan Najafi was the author of the celebrated work on jurisprudence titled *Jawahir al-kalam fi sharh-i sha'ayir al-islam*. This is the most comprehensive collection of views and opinions of Shi'i scholars on jurisprudence. It has been recognized as a major reference for researchers and practitioners alike since its compilation was completed in 1231/1816.

From: Muhammad Hasan Najafi, *Jawahir al-kalam fi sharh-i sha'ayir al-islam* (Jewels of Words: Commentary on the Book of the Laws of Islam), Vol. XXI[263]

... There is no dispute among us [jurists] regarding *jihad*; rather, we are all in consensus about the kind of [*jihad*] that becomes obligatory in the said manner [offensive *jihad*] contingent upon the presence of the [Infallible] Imam and who is in charge of the government (*Imam mabsut al-yad*)[264] or whoever he appoints and extends his authority to him in order [to lead] *jihad*. The legitimacy of *jihad* is contingent upon this principle. It is reported on the authority of Bashir al-Duhhan [al-Kufi] who says, "I told Abi 'Abdullahh [Imam Husayn] (may God's greetings be upon him) I had a dream and in my dream I was telling you that war in the absence of an Imam – obedience to whom is an obligation – is forbidden (*haram*) like consuming the flesh of a dead animal, or blood, and you said to me "that is so." And Abi 'Abdullah said, "Yes indeed that is so, that is so."

... *Jihad* means one spending one's wealth and/or sacrificing one's life in fighting the infidels or rebellious people, or for spreading Islam, or observing the commands and injunctions of the faith. These explanations are for people to understand the universal meaning of the term. Any command that strengthens Islam and glorifies its majesty, therefore, is *jihad* and must be observed and is not limited to one specific meaning the term may denote.... However, there is no doubt that the main meaning of *jihad* is fighting with the infidels when they initiate attack against Islam, as God says in His Blessed Book, "Prescribed for you is fighting, though it be hateful to you" [2:216]. In such a case, this is itself a defensive war. However, driving away anyone who intends to kill a person, or take one's property, or violate one's privacy or honor is not typically called *jihad*.

As to the possibility of *jihad* in the absence of the Twelfth Imam, he says:

Fighting in defense of territories of Islam against an aggressor cannot be called *jihad*, but defense has its own rules regarding martyrdom, escaping from the front, and distributing bounties of war. I say that if all that was described takes place in the presence of an Imam or his appointee and even if it is defensive, it can then be considered *jihad* as it happened during the time of the Messenger of God when infidels attacked Medina.

There are several categories of *jihad*. One category is that which is initiated by Muslims to call [unbelievers] to Islam, and that is contingent upon this condition [i.e., the presence of the Imam]. This is a sufficient necessity (*wajib-i kafa'i*).

The second kind of *jihad* is the one Muslims undertake against unbelieving enemies who threaten Muslim territories, or those who intend to establish domination over Muslim lands (cities), enslave them, or take their properties. This kind of *jihad* is obligatory for every free Muslim or slave, every man and woman, healthy or unhealthy, blind or lame, and the like, if they are needed. This kind of *jihad* does not require the presence of an Imam or his permission. It is not limited only to those who decided to participate, but is obligatory upon any person who learns on the development of war and is not certain of the capabilities of those whom they intend to resist. It emphasizes the obligation of *jihad* upon those who are more qualified to fight.

The third kind of *jihad* is that when a Muslim [is settled] among infidels or captured by them, or given amnesty by them, he cannot trust his enemies and he fears his life. [In such a situation] it is permissible for him to defend himself in accordance with the possibilities of the situation. This kind of defense is unconditional and previously mentioned conditions do not apply to it.

Ayatullah Ruhullah Musavi Khomeini (1320h–1410h/1902–1989)

Ayatullah Ruhullah Musavi Khomeini was born in the village of Khomein near Tehran. He studied in Arak and Qum and at the age of twenty-two reached the rank of *ijtihad* and began to teach in Qum. In 1963 as a result of his antigovernment activities he was arrested and exiled to Iraq. For the next fifteen years he taught in Najaf while organizing opposition forces again the Pahlavi Regime. In 1978 he returned to Iran triumphantly as the undisputed leader of the Islamic Revolution that toppled the Shah's government and led to the establishment of the Islamic Republic. He wrote several works on different aspects of Islamic law and jurisprudence. His most important work is *Tahrir al-Wasilah* (A Clarification of Questions), which contains a detailed discussion of *jihad* entitled "Chapter on Defense." He goes far beyond any other jurist to this date and includes issues that are relevant to contemporary world politics.

From: Ayatullah Ruhullah Musavi Khomeini, *Tahrir al-Wasilah*, Vol. I, "Chapter on Defense" (1365/1986)[265]

This chapter is comprised of two parts. One part deals with the defense of Islamic territories and the second part examines the way it must be defended.

Part I

There are ten principles that must be taken into consideration in this regard.

1. If a Muslim country's territorial integrity or its borders are threatened by an enemy, it is obligatory to defend them with every possible means including the sacrifice of wealth and lives.
2. Such defense does not necessitate the permission of the [Twelfth] Imam or his presence (may God's greetings be upon him), nor the permission of his Special or General Deputies (*Na'ib al-khass* or *Na'ib al-'Amm*). In this case defense becomes an obligation for every adult in any way possible without restriction and condition.
3. If there is the possibility of humiliation and continued dominance of Muslim lands, annexation of Muslim lands or capturing Muslims as prisoners, defense will become an obligation by all means and in any way possible.

4. If Islamic lands are humiliated as a result of political domination of an enemy, or by economic factors that may lead to political and economic subjugation of Muslims and violation and weakening of Islam, in such situations, defense becomes obligatory in every possible way as well such as [through] negative resistance, boycotting consumption of [enemy] goods and/or stopping their use, and absolutely ending a relationship or transaction with them.

5. If any economic and commercial relations threaten Islam and Islamic lands of foreign political or spiritual dominance, or may result in colonization of Muslims or their lands, it is obligatory for all Muslims to avoid such relations and boycott them.

6. If a political relationship between Muslim governments and foreign ones results in their dominance over Muslim lands, their lives, or properties, or may result in Muslims' political subjugation, Muslim heads of states are forbidden from establishing such relationships. They should stop all such interactions and abolish such contracts. It will be obligatory for Muslims to guide such rulers and demand them to abandon such relations, even through negative resistance.

7. If one Muslim government is threatened by foreign invasion, it becomes obligatory for all Muslim governments to defend it by any means possible, as it becomes obligatory for all Muslims as well to defend that government.

8. If one Muslim government enters into a treaty that is against the interests of Islam and Muslims, it becomes obligatory for other Muslim governments to have that treaty abolished through political or economic means such as ending the diplomatic and commercial relationship with such a government. It will also become obligatory for other Muslims to resist such a government by any means possible such as negative resistance. From the point of view of Islam such treaties are considered null and void.

9. If one of the leaders of a Muslim government or a member of parliament becomes a channel or tool of foreign influence over a Muslim country politically or economically in such a way that territorial integrity of the Islamic world or a Muslim country's independence is threatened even in the future, such a leader is a traitor and must be removed from his position even if he assumed that position rightfully and through legal means. It is the duty of all Muslims to punish him even through negative resistance such [as] ending association and dealing with him and avoiding him in any possible way, striving to remove him from all political positions and depriving him from all social rights and privileges.

10. If in commercial relations with foreign governments or merchants there is a threat to the market of Muslims and their economic life, from the point of view of religious law (the *Shari'ah*) such relation is forbidden. It will become obligatory to end that relation. If such threat exists, it is the duty of religious leaders to boycott foreign products and trade with them in accordance with their capacity. It is also the duty of Muslims to follow religious leaders as it becomes obligatory for them all to end that relationship.

Part II

In the period of Occultation of the Twelfth Imam, the Possessor of Command and the King of the Age, may God expedite his return, his General Deputies (*Nuwwab-i*

'Amm) – that is, jurists who are qualified to judge and issue verdicts – will be in charge of implementing decisions and performing all other functions of the Imam, except his function of declaring *jihad*.

This position is identical with Shaykh Mufid's. Like Mufid, Khomeini also believed that *jihad* can be declared and carried out by the Infallible Imam but also by a qualified jurist, whose verdict he regards as valid as that of the Imam.

Ayatullah Muhammad Tqai Bahjat (1334–1388h/1916–2009)

Another contemporary 'alim who wrote on *jihad* is Ayatullah Muhammad Tqai Bahjat. His views regarding *jihad* are gathered in a book titled *Jami' al-Masa'il* (Qum, 1420/1999).

From: Ayatullah Muhammad Tqai Bahjat, *Jami' al-Masa'il* (Comprehensive Book of Fundamental Issues of Jurisprudence), Vol. II[266]

... *Jihad* is sufficient necessity (*wajib-i kafa'i*) – that is, participation of some members of the society relieves others from taking part in it. The number of people who must participate in such a *jihad* depends on the number and strength of the enemy (2:299).

Jihad becomes mandatory and legitimate only if the [Infallible] Imam is present or a deputy whom he assigns. His deputy is a just jurist (*faqih-i 'adil*) who can permit or forbid declaration of war of all kinds.

Offensive *jihad* is a war waged against unbelievers and is permitted under the above circumstances and only after infidels have been invited to enter Islam. Ordinarily, fighting is forbidden during the months of Rajab, Dhu'lqa'dah, Dhu'lhajjah, and Muharram except *jihad* against those who do not believe in this and violate the sanctity of these months. Defense against unbelievers is also exempt from this rule.

How the war must be fought against the enemy is for the deputy of the Imam who sets priority to decide. Of the two groups of infidels, the one which is closer in distance to Muslims must be fought against first unless a bigger danger threatens Muslims.

Also the strength and number of Muslim forces is decided in consideration with the number and strength of enemy forces.

It is necessary for Muslims to act with caution and construct shelters and means of protection, and grant the position of commanding of [Muslim] forces to a qualified leader who is gifted with intelligence, bravery and piety. He must be in close contact with Islamic centers and mosques within every community.

It is not permissible to initiate *jihad* against unbelievers before explaining to them the principles of Islam, their meaning and virtues. If they are among people who must pay protection tax (*jizya*) they must accept to pay taxes.

The objectives of Muslims to carry out war must be explained preferably to the chief commanders of unbelievers in a summarized fashion. If that is not possible, each [Muslim] fighter must do so to his opponent while he is engaged in fighting him.

The Russo-Persian War

During the first Russo-Persian War of 1218–1228/1804–1813, Mirza Bozorg Qa'im-Maqam, the minister and special adviser to the then Iran's Crown Prince 'Abbas Mirza Qajar wrote letters to the leading Shi'i *'ulama* in the shrine cities of Iraq asking them to issue a verdict (*fatwa*) and declare *jihad*. Such powerful and prominent religious leaders as Shaykh Ja'far Najafi, Mulla Ahmad Naraqi, and many others wrote treatises on *jihad*. Qa'im Maqam collected those verdicts and compiled an anthology on *jihad* titled *Jihadiyah* and presented it to the Shah.[267] As a result, *jihad* was declared against Russia. The collection properly reflects the *'ulama*'s mindset and their understanding of the domestic and foreign relations of Iran during the nineteenth century. The following selection is a summary of this treatise.

From: Qa'im Maqam, *Risalah-yi Jihadiyah Jihad* (The Lesser Treatise on *Jihad*)[268]

Know that there are two kinds of *jihad*. One is *jihad* for the purpose of calling unbelievers to Islam with the permission and approval of the Prophet, peace be upon him, or the [Infallible] Imam, or his Special Deputy (*na'yib-i Khass*).

The second kind of *jihad* is defensive, and that itself has several categories. One is *jihad* for protection of Islamic territories (*hifd-i baydah-yi islam*) at the time of invasion by unbelieving foreign forces who intend to annex Muslim lands [to their territories] and [exert] dominance over Muslims, to spread their beliefs and destroy Islam. The second kind in this category is *jihad* to stop and drive back unbelievers and prevent them from dominating over Muslims' lives and [ruin] their reputation. Another kind is *jihad* against a group of unbelievers who encounter Muslims and there is the possibility of their dominance over Muslims. Still another kind of *jihad* is to expel unbelievers from Muslim lands after they take it over. Protection of Islam means protecting Islamic land, regime, and sovereignty and independence. It can also mean protecting a Muslim ruler whose demise may lead to the weakening or destruction of Islam and dissension among Muslims. Some scholars have translated this term (*hifd-i baydah-yi islam*) as protecting the Muslim people. All of these kinds of *jihad* are in fact among the greatest pillars of Islam. *Jihad* is the most important duty after the basic duties of faith and religion, sometimes even more important than daily prayer. In fact preserving all injunctions and principles of Islam depends on this task.

A Tradition of the Prophet narrates that "Any one from among your people who goes out to fight on the path of God, every drop that falls from heaven will testify for him on the Day of Judgment." It is narrated that Imam Ali ibn Abi Talib said, "Indeed the best kind of death is dying with a thousand stroke[s] of the sword."

All Companions [of the Prophet] have emphasized defensive *jihad*. In such a situation it is obligatory for all Muslims to leave their families, children, and properties behind and struggle to protect Islamic land and remove the [threat] of God's enemies. Any person who may have a high position, wealth, or skill must sacrifice it for this purpose. The emphasis on this type of *jihad* [defensive] is stronger than other kinds. In this kind of *jihad* the presence of [the] Imam or his permission, or the presence of his special deputy is not necessary. Rather, *jihad* in such a situation is obligatory under the leadership of and obedience to whomever is qualified for leadership, regardless of the fact that he (the leader) is a just man or an oppressor, for the Imams have permitted, even declared it an obligation to obey any ruling king or sultan who can lead *jihad* in such a situation.

At this time his holiness Shaykh Muhammad Ja'far on behalf of the [Twelfth] Imam has given permission for *jihad* and has authorized His Majesty to prepare the population in Iraq, Fars, Azarbaijan, and Khorasan and fight for the protection of Islamic land and push the infidels out. By God Imam Husayn is present in this struggle and is calling you to help him. The Imam and Master of the Age [the Mahdi] is [in fact] the commander of this struggle. I [Shaykh Muhammad Ja'far] give permission for *jihad* and your obedience to Fath Ali Shah Qajar, may God protect him from what he fears, so that he would authorize his heir apparent who is the governor of Azarbaijan, namely Prince Abbas Mirza, to carry on *jihad*. Whoever does not help him will regret [it] later and will be deprived of the intercession of the Imam on the Day of Judgment.

Another *mujtahid* Aqa Sayyid Ali Mujtahid issued a *fatwa* (verdict) in Arabic which read, "It is obligatory for every adult to rise and fight against infidels and defend the Islamic land so that the infidels could not dominate over Muslims, their properties and lives." This great undertaking will not be possible except by the command of a wise leader who could mobilize the army. Since [at this time] the leadership of Muslims has been bestowed by the Almighty King of the universe to Fath Ali Shah Qajar, the honor of the kings of the Arab and non-Arab, it is incumbent upon him to take the responsibility for preparing the army and provid[ing] its logistics for *jihad*.

The same Aqa Sayyid Ali issued another verdict in Persian which read, "It is obvious to all Muslims of adult age that during the last several years Russian infidels have been invading Muslim lands from time to time and now are determined to take over Muslim territories. It is obvious that expansion of the faith and its glory is contingent upon the independence and sovereignty of the Islamic government [of Iran]. If any harm is inflicted upon this government by the [Russian] infidels obviously it will harm Islam. Therefore, I am addressing all adult Muslims, whether they live far from borders or in bordering provinces near the infidels, to use their utmost effort to push back the enemy. This is an obligation upon which all other religious duties depend. No one should be indifferent but must be determined to defend religion and the government in any way one can, whether by spending wealth or sacrificing life so that on the Day of Judgment one can respond to the Master of religion. Such an undertaking is impossible without a qualified leader. Therefore at this time while the government of Islam rests upon His Imperial Majesty Fath Ali Shah Qajar – may God make his kingdom eternal – he has authorized Prince Abbas Mirza to carry on *jihad*. Therefore, it is an obligation for all people of Iran to obey the command of the king and his Crown Prince. O Muslim people [of Iran] and Shi'ites of Ali! How can you allow Russian infidels to take over your land? How can you permit them to dominate over your properties, your honor, and your religion? How can you let them turn Muslim women into slaves of Russians? In accordance with the permission of these two deputies of the [Twelfth] Imam and verdicts of the *'ulama* of Islam it is obvious that *jihad* under the king to defend and protect Islamic land and Muslim life, property, and honor is a struggle and *jihad* on the path of God.

Participation in this *jihad* does not require [the] permission of parents. The only condition is one's physical ability. Therefore, it is obligatory to participate in this *jihad* as long as one is physically capable of fighting. No one is exempt from this duty. The parents of children and the insane are obligated to have them participate in this *jihad* as long as they are of adult age.

His Holiness, the Master of the Martyrs Imam Husayn never considered abandoning *jihad* out of fear of death or destruction of religion. Although he saw the huge number of enemy forces he did not fear to sacrifice his life to save religion. Now if Muslims fear losing their lives and flee before enemy forces hoping to reorganize for a new round of *jihad*, how would they be certain that they will win the next time? Therefore, Muslims must not be afraid to fight if the enemy forces are twice their number or even ten times more than their number. Under no circumstances however, it is permissible to kill children, the insane, women and the old members of the enemy forces, and their priests. If infidel forces surrender they must be protected and cannot be killed unless they betray the trust and plot or revolt against Muslim forces.

NOTES

1 Special thanks are due to Ayatullah Dr. Mostafa Mohaghegh Damad, who reviewed an earlier draft of this text; his perceptive and constructive comments on the selection of primary sources were most useful. This chapter also greatly benefited from verses of the *Qur'an* in an earlier article on *jihad* that was compiled in Persian by Dr. Abd al-Rahim Gavahi, based on a study by the late Ayatullah Salehi Najafabadi. I am indebted to both scholars for providing a context for the subject and for selecting relevant verses from the *Qur'an*. I am grateful to the support extended to me by the Noor Foundation in the process of writing this chapter and its preparation for publication. It goes without saying that the scholars and friends mentioned above are in no way responsible for any errors or shortcomings in the text and in my translation of the original sources. The responsibility of all such errors is solely my own. *Wa-min Allāh al-tawfīq wa-alayh -tuklan*.

2 Different meanings and interpretations of *jihad* will be explored later in the chapter.

3 Translation of *Qur'ānic* verses are taken from A. J. Arberry, *The Qur'an Interpreted* (New York: Touchstone, 1996). Occasionally I have consulted Marmaduke Pickthall, *The Meaning of*

the Glorious Qur'an, reprint (Tehran: Salehi Publishers, 1352/1973). Unless otherwise stated, all translations of Persian and Arabic texts are my own. In translating technical terms I have benefited greatly from works of other scholars and have mentioned the original Arabic in parentheses. Transliteration of terms and names has been done in accordance with the rules set by the Library of Congress.

4 Seyyed Muhammad Husayn Tabataba'i, *Shi'ite Islam*, Seyyed Hossein Nasr (trans., ed.), 2nd ed. (Albany: State University of New York Press, 1997), p. 39.

5 Frithjof Schuon, "Islam and the Perennial Philosophy," in Seyyed Hossein Nasr (ed.), *The Essential Writings of Frithjof Schuon* (Rockport, Mass.: Element Books, 1991), pp. 286–287.

6 For some of these *ahadīth*, see Tabataba'i, *Shi'ite Islam*, pp. 39 and 68.

7 Tabataba'i, *Shi'ite Islam*, p. 68.

8 For the text of this *hadīth* in Arabic and its English translation, see *Ghadir's Khutbah* (Rockville, Md.: Darul Salam Publications, 1999).

9 This *hadīth* has been recorded in numerous Shi'i and Sunni sources. For a reprint of the original Arabic text of this *hadīth*, see *Asrar al-hidayah fi anwar al-wilayah* (Secrets of Guidance in the Lights of Spiritual Authority), edited with an introduction by Nasir al-Din Kazemi Haqiqi (Tehran, 1384/2005), pp. 25–48.

10 For example, see the following unpublished manuscripts of commentaries on the *Qur'ān*: Ahmad ibn 'Abdullah Maybudi (d. 910/1504), *Tafsir-i Arba'in* (Commentary on Forty *Hadīth* in Persian); Isma'il ibn Ahmad Darir Nayshaburi (d. 430/1039), *Ma 'arij al-su'ul wa madarij al-ma'mul* (The Hierarchy of Principles); Qadi Muhammad ibn 'Abdullah Isfara'iyini, *al-Nasikh wa'l mansukh* (The Abrogating and the Abrogated [Verses of the *Qur'an*]); Qadi Sa'id Qumi (d.1130/1717), *Khazai'n al-anwar* (Treasures of Light). See also Muhammad Abdul-Rauf, *Imam Ali ibn Abi Talib: The First Intellectual Muslim Thinker* (Alexandria, Va.: Al Saadawi Publications, 1995), and Sulayman Kattani, *Imam Ali: Source of Wisdom and Might* (London: Muhammadi Trust, 1983). See also Ali ibn Abu Talib, *Nahj ul-Balagha* (Path of Eloquence), Askari Jafri (trans.), 12th ed. (New York: Islamic Seminary Publications, 1999).

11 Literature on the origins and development of Shi'ism has been growing rapidly in recent years. See, e.g., Henry Corbin, *Spiritual Body and Celestial Earth: From Mazdean Iran to Shi'ite Iran* (Princeton, N.J.: Princeton University Press, 1977); Etan Kohlberg (ed.), *Shi'ism* (Burlington, Vt.: Ashgate, 2003); Wilfred Madelung, *The Succession to Muhammad: A Study of the Early Caliphate* (Cambridge: Cambridge University Press, 1997); Moojan Momen, *An Introduction to Shi'i Islam: The History and Doctrines of Twelver Shi'ism* (New Haven, Conn.: Yale University Press, 1985); Maria Massi Dakake, *The Charismatic Community: Shi'ite Identity in Early Islam* (Albany: State University of New York Press, 2007); Arzina Lalani, *Early Shi'a Thought: The Teachings of Imam Muhammad al-Baqir* (London: I. B. Taurus in association with the Institute of Ismaili Studies, 2000). See also Yann Richard, *Le Shi'isme en Iran: Imam et revolution* (Paris: Librairie d'Amerique e d'Orient, 1980); Liyakat N. Takim, *The Heirs of the Prophet: Charisma and Religious Authority in Shi'ite Islam* (Albany: State University of New York Press, 2006). On Imam Ali's role in founding many fields of Islamic sciences and arts, see Jalaliyan, Habib'llah, *Tarikh-i tafsi-i Qur'an Karim* (A History of *Qur'ānic* Commentary Writing) (Tehran, 1378/1999); Martin Lings, *The Splendour of Islamic Art of Calligraphy and Illumination* (London: Thames and Hudson, 2005); Seyyed Hossein Nasr, *Islamic Art and Spirituality* (Albany: State University of New York Press, 1987), pp. 6–7, 17, 26; Reza Shah Kazemi, *Justice and Remembrance: Introducing the Spirituality of Imam Ali* (London: I. B. Taurus, 2006); Shaykh Abbas Qomi, *Muntahi al-Amal* (The Ultimate Goal) (Tehran, 1377/1998), esp. pp. 212–213; Sayyid Mohammad Baqir Hujjati, *Pazhuheshi dar Tarikh-i Qur'an-i Karim* (An Investigation into the History of the Noble *Qur'ān*) (Tehran, n.d.); Baha al-Din Khorramshahi, *Qur'an Shenakht* (Understanding

the *Qur'ān*) (Tehran, 1377/1998); Habibullah Jalaliyan, *Tarikh-i Tafsir-i Qur'an-i Karim* (A History of *Qur'ānic* Commentary Writing) (Tehran, 1378/1999); Ibn Abi'l-Hadid, *Sharh-i Nahj al-Balaghah* (Commentary on the Path of Eloquence Nahj al-Balaghah of Imam Ali ibn Abi Talib) (Beirut, 1965); Ibn Abi'l Hadid (d. 1258), who was the most prominent commentator on Ali's book *The Path of Elloquence*, describes it as "[b]elow the speech of the Creator but above the speech of the creatures."

12 On these debates, see Asma Asfaruddin, *Excellence and Precedence: Medieval Islamic Discourse on Legitimate Leadership* (Leiden: Brill Academic Publishers, 2002).

13 See Muhammad Abdul Rauf, *Imam Ali ibn Abi Talib: The First Intellectual Muslim Thinker* (Alexandria, Va.: Al Saadawi Publications, 1996), and Sulayman Kattani, *Imam Ali: Source of Wisdom and Might* (London: Muhammadi Trust, 1983). See also ' Ali ibn Abu Talib, *Nahj ul-Balagha* (Path of Eloquence).

14 On the Twelfth Imam and the Shi'i belief that his reappearance will coincide with the second coming of Christ, see Abdulaziz Sachedina, *Islamic Messianism: The Idea of the Mahdi in Twelver Shi'ism* (Albany: State University of New York Press, 1981), and Mostafa Vaziri, *The Emergence of Islam: Prophecy, Imamate and Messianism in Perspective* (New York: Paragon House, 1992).

15 Sayyid Jafar Shahidi, *Pazhuheshi Tazeh Piramoon Qiyam-I Husayni* (A New Investigation on the Uprising of Imam Husayn), 23rd ed. (Tehran: Daftar-i Nashr-i Farhang-i Eslami, 1378/1999); Mohammad Esfandiyari, *Ketabshenasi Tarikhi-ye Imam Husayn* (Tehran: Vezarat-I Farhang va Ershard-I Eslami, 1380/2001); Ni'matullah Salehi Najafabadi, *Shahid-i Javid Husayn ibn 'Ali*, 12th ed. (Tehran, 1380/2001); Abu Mikhnaf, Lut ibn Yahya, *Maqtal al-Husayn*, Husayn al-Ghaffari (ed.) (Qom, 1364/1985); Seyyed Jafar Shahidi, "The Significance of Ashura in Shi'i Islam," in Linda Clark (ed.), *Shi'ite Heritage: Essays on Classical and Modern Traditions* (New York: Global Scholarly Publications, 2001); Muhammad ibn Jarir Tabari, *The History of al-Tabari*, vol. xix, I. K. A. Howard (trans.) (Albany: State University of New York Press, 1990), pp. 125–126, 167–168; Momen, *An Introduction to Shi'i Islam*, p. 236. See also Mahmud Ayoub, *Redemptive Suffering in Islam* (The Hague: Mouton Publishers, 1978).

16 Some examples of these traditions are the following:

I am the city of knowledge and Ali is its gate.

Ali is of me and I am of Ali.

O' Ali! You are to me of the same rank and as [Prophet] Haroon was to Musa, but that there is no Prophet after me.

O' People, he who takes me as his master and leader (Mowla), so this Ali, is his master and leader.

Behold! The example of my household is like that of the Ark of Noah: He who embarks it, will be saved, and he who turns away from it, is doomed.

These traditions are taken from different volumes of the following source, ' Allamah Sayyid Muhammad Husayn Husayni Tehrani, *Imam Shinasi*, 15 vols. (Tehran: Hekmat Publishing, 1363/1984). Translations are my own. On examples of the Prophet's traditions regarding Ali and his progeny (the *Ahl al-Bayt*), see Tabataba'i, *Shi'ite Islam;* and Momen, *An Introduction to Shi'i Islam.* See also Wilferd Madelung *The Succession to Muhammad: A Study of the Early Caliphate* (New York: Cambridge University Press, 1997); Abu-Muhammad Ordoni and Muhammad Kazim Qazwini, *Fatimah, the Gracious* (Qum: Anssarian Publications, 1992).

17 See Sai'd A. Arjomand (ed.), *Authority and Political Culture in Shi'ism* (Albany: State University of New York Press, 1988).

18 Tabatabai, *Quran dar Islam*, 10th ed. (Qum, 1379/1999), pp. 27–32. See also Abu Jafar Muhammad Shaykh Saduq, known as ibn Babuyah, *Kitab al-Khisal*, p. 214, as quoted in Tehrani, *Nur-i Malakut-i Quran*, 4 vols. (Mashhad, 1368/1989). See Muhammad I. Ayati (ed.), *Tafsir-i Sharif-i Lahiji*, by Baha al-Din Muhammad Lahiji (Tehran, 1340/1961), introduction to vol. 4, p. 11.

19 'Ali ibn Abi Talib, *Nahj ul-Balaghah* (Path of Eloquence) (Qom: Kulalah Khavar, 1351/1972), discourse nos. 110, 125; Muhammad I. Ayati (ed.), *Tafsir-i Sharif-i Lahiji* (The Noble Commentary of Lahiji), Baha' al-Din Muhammad Lahiji (Tehran: Awqaf Foundation, 1340/1961), introduction to vol. IV, p. 11. See also 'Allamah Sayyid Muhammad Husayn Tabataba'i, *Qur'an dar Islam*, 10th ed. (Qum: Daftar-e Intesharat-e Islami, 1379/1999), pp. 27–32. Quotations translated by M. H. Faghfoory.

20 Sufism is the inner and mystical dimension of Islam. The origin of Sufism is the *Qur'ān* and the Tradition of the Prophet Muhammad. Like all other spiritual paths Sufism consists of doctrine, method, and practices. At the heart of the Sufi doctrine is knowledge of the oneness of God/ *Tawhid*. The goal of all Sufi practices is the realization of God in this world, here and now. See Seyyed Hossein Nasr, *Sufi Essays* (Albany: State University of New York Press, 1991); Seyyed Hossein Nasr, *The Garden of Truth: The Vision and Promise of Sufism, Islam's Mystical Tradition* (New York: HarpersOne, 2007); Shaykh Muhammad Ali Mu'adhdhin Khurasani, *Tuhfah-yi 'Abbasi, The Golden Chain of Sufism in Shi'ite Islam*, Mohammad H. Faghfoory (trans.) (Lanham, Md.: University Press of America, 2007); and Sayyid Muhammad Husayn Tabataba'i, *Kernel of the Kernel: Concerning the Wayfaring and Spiritual Journey of the People of Intellect* (*Lub-I Lubab*), Mohammad H. Faghfoory (trans.) (Albany: State University of New York Press, 2003).

21 Seyyed Hossein Nasr, *Sufi Essays*, chapter VIII.

22 For esoteric functions of Imams, see Mohammed Ali Amir-Moezzi, *The Divine Guide in Early Shi'ism: The Sources of Esotericism in Islam* (Albany: State University of New York Press, 1994). See also Sayyid Muhammad Baqir Sadr, *A Study on the Question of Al-Wilayah*, P. Haseltine (trans.). This treatise was first translated and published in India by P. Haseltine under the title *Shi'ism: the Natural Product of Islam* (n.d., n.p.). A new and revised edition was printed by Great Islamic Library, Tehran, 1982. See also Nasr, *Sufi Essays*.

23 On the Isma'ili branch of Shi'ism, see Farhad Daftary, *A Short History of the Isma'ilis: Traditions of a Muslim Community* (Princeton, N.J.: M. Wiener, 1998). See also Tabataba'i, *Shi'ite Islam*, pp. 75–84, and Momen, *An Introduction to Shi'i Islam*, pp. 45–60.

24 Most of the information in this section is taken from chapter 1 of Mohammad H. Faghfoory, "The Role of the *'Ulama* in Twentieth Century Iran with Particular Reference to Ayatullah Hajj Saiid Abu'l-Qasim Kashani," Ph.D. dissertation, University of Wisconsin-Madison, 1978. See also chapter 5 of Amin Banani, *The Modernization of Iran* (Stanford, Calif.: Stanford University Press, 1961); Hamid Algar, *Religion and State in Iran: The Role of the 'Ulama in Qajar Period: 1785–1906* (Berkeley: University of California Press, 1969), p. 14; Nikki Keddie, "The Roots of *'Ulama*'s Power in Modern Iran," *Studia Islamica* 29 (1969), 31–53.

25 The doctrine of occultation (*ghaybah*) is a cosmic event of eschatological significance in Shi'ism. According to Shi'ite belief the Twelfth Imam (the *Mahdi*) was the eleventh descendent of Imam 'Ali ibn Abi Talib. He went into occulation in 329/941 and his reappearance on earth will mark the beginning of the end of time. The timing of his reappearance will coincide with the second coming of Christ and is known by God alone. Sunni Islam also believes in the appearance of a savior at the end of time (the doctrine of Mahdism), but does not believe in the doctrine of occultation. It also differs with Shi'ism on the identity of the Mahdi and believes that he is not born yet. See Abdulaziz Sachedina, *Islamic Messianism: The Idea of the Mahdi in Twelver Shi'ism* (Albany: State University of New York Press, 1981).

26 Islamic law based on the *Qur'ān* and *ḥadīth*.

27 See Antony Black, *The History of Islamic Political Thought* (New York: Routledge, 2001), chapter 21. See also Huri Islamoglu-Inan (ed.), *Ottoman Empire and the World Economy* (Cambridge: Cambridge University Press, 2002); R. C. Repp, *The Müfti of Istanbul: A Study in the Development of the Ottoman Learned Hierarchy* (Oxford: Ithaca Press, 1986); Ahmed Uğur, *The Ottoman 'Ulema in the Mid-17th Century* (Berlin: K. Schwarz, 1986); and Madeline C. Zilfi, *The Politics of Piety: The Ottoman 'Ulema in the Postclassical Age 1600–1800* (Minneapolis, Minn.: Bibliotheca Islamica, 1988).

28 *Khoms* is a provision for an annual tax of one-fifth of one's net income and other assets. *Khoms* is expected to be paid to the descendants of the Prophet (the Sayyids), orphans, travelers, and the needy. See Momen, *An Introduction to Shi'i Islam*, pp. 179–180.

29 See Willem Floor, *Guilds, Merchants, and 'Ulama in Nineteenth Century Iran* (Washington, D.C.: Mage Publishers, 2009). See esp. chapters 5 and 6.

30 See Faghfoory, "The Role of the 'Ulama in Twentieth Century Iran," chapter 1; Banani, *The Modernization of Iran*, chapter 5; Algar, *Religion and State in Iran*, p. 14; and Keddie, "The Roots of 'Ulama's Power in Modern Iran," pp. 31–53.

31 As quoted in Ayatulah Muhammad Sangalaji, *Qadha dar Islam* (Judgment in Islam) (Tehran: Entesharat-e Danesh, 1960), p. 14.

32 In early centuries of Islam *ijtihad* was practiced extensively. Gradually, it fell out of favor especially after the Ash'arite school of theology gained dominance and Abu Hamid Ghazzali expressed doubts about its reliability, criticizing it for its potential to lead to errors in judgment. See Ignaz Goldziher, *Introduction to Islamic Theology and Law*, Andras Hamori and Ruth Hamori (trans.) (Princeton, N.J.: Princeton University Press, 1981), and Mohammad Hashim Kamaali, *Principles of Islamic Jurisprudence* (Cambridge: Islamic Texts Society, 1991). For a Shi'i perspective, see Momen, *An Introduction to Shi'i Islam*, p. 203. See also Ahmad Kazemi Moussavi, *Religious Authority in Shi'ite Islam* (Kuala Lampur: International Institute of Islamic Thought, 1996), p. 243.

33 Moussavi, *Religious Authority in Shi'ite Islam*, pp. 132–135. *Takfir*, or declaring one an infidel, was a practice that the 'ulama used against their opponents, particularly those who challenged the 'ulama's religious authority or power. See Faghfoory, "The Role of the 'Ulama in Twentieth Century Iran," pp. 24–25.

34 Kazemi, *'Ulama-yi Shi'ah va qudrat-i Siyasi* (Shi'ite Clergy and Political Power), pp. 140–147. For details of this event, see Abbas Amanat, *Pivot of the Universe: Nasir al-Din Shah Qajar and the Iranian Monarchy: 1831–1896* (Berkeley: University of California Press, 1997), pp. 277–303.

35 Nikki R. Keddie, "The Origins of the Religious-Radical Alliance in Iran," *Past and Present* 34 (July 1966), 72.

36 Algar, *Religion and State in Iran*, p. 24.

37 See, e.g., Mohammad H. Faghfoory, "The Role of the 'Ulama in Twentieth Century Iran," chapter 1. See also Banani, *The Modernization of Iran*, chapter 5; Algar, *Religion and State in Iran*, p. 14, and Keddie, "The Roots of 'Ulama's Power in Modern Iran," pp. 31–53.

38 Aqa Bozorg Tehrani, *al-Dhari'ah ila Tasanif al-Shari'ah* (A Descriptive Catalogue of Shia Books) (Beirut: Dar al-adwa, 1402/1983), vol. V, pp. 293–296. See also Rasool Ja'farian, *Mirza Bozorg Qa'im Maqam* (Tehran: Amir Kabir Publishers, 1380/2001), p. 82; and Momen, *An Introduction to Shi'i Islam*, p. 138.

39 For more information on this incident, see Momen, *An Introduction to Shi'i Islam*, p. 138.

40 For the text of this treatise, see H. Sa'idi (ed.), *Fasl Namah-ye Tarikh-e Mu'asir-e Iran* (Journal of Contemporary History of Iran) (Tehran: Institute for Studying the Contemporary History of Iran, Spring 1385/2006), pp. 235–243. FO 60/223, Sadr A'zam to Farrokh Khan (Diplomatic Report: From the Prime Minister to Iran's Ambassador in London, January 1865. See also FO,

Stevens to Clarendon (Baghdad, 2/28, 1857), London Public Records Office: "Reports from Iran." Special thanks to Dr. Willem Floor for putting this document at my disposal.

41 The details of these events and all *fatwa*s on *jihad* are available in a collection recently published in Tehran. See Mohammad Hasan Rajabi, *Rasa'il wa fatawa-ye Jehadi* (Treatises and Verdicts on Jihad) (Tehran: Political Studies and Research Institute, 1379/1999). For an exploration of the recent role of the Shi'i *'ulama* in Iraq, see Adeed Dawisha, *Iraq: A Political History from Independence to Occupation* (Princeton, N.J.: Princeton University Press, 2009).

42 Nikki R. Keddie, *Religion and Rebellion in Iran: The Tobacco Protest of 1891–92* (London: Cass, 1966); Firuz Kazemzadeh, *Russia and Britain in Iran: A Study in Imperialism* (New Haven, Conn.: Yale University Press, 1968). See also Ibrahim Taymuri, *'Asr-i Bikhabari ya Tarikhi-i Iimtiyazat dar Iran* (The Age of Ignorance or the History of Foreign Concessions in Iran) (Tehran: Iqbal Publishers, 1332/1953).

43 On the Constitutional Revolution of 1905–1906, see Janet Afary, *The Iranian Constitutional Revolution, 1906–1911* (New York: Columbia University Press, 1996).

44 On the Iranian Revolution of 1978–1979, see Janet Afary and Kevin Anderson, *Foucault and the Iranian Revolution: Gender and the Seductions of Islamism* (Chicago, Ill.: Chicago University Press, 2005); The Middle East Institute, *The Iranian Revolution at 30* (Washington, D.C., 2009); Mehdi Khalaji, *Apocalyptic Politics on the Rationality of Iranian Politics* (Washington, D.C.: Washington Institute for Near East Policy, 2008).

45 These are the views of Shaykh Mufid (d. 413/1022) and Abu Jafar al-Tusi (d. 460/1067), respectively. As quoted in E. Kohlberg, "The Development of the Imāmi Shi'i Doctrine of *Jihad*," *Zeitschrift der Deutschen Morgenlandischen Gesellschaft* 127 (1976), 64.

46 The word *Kufr* and its different forms (*kafir, kuffar, kafirun, kafara, kafaru*) is mentioned 470 times in the *Qur'ān* in several different meanings. In the context of the *Qur'ān* it means to cover the truth. A *kāfir* is a person who hides the truth of Islam and rejects Islamic faith. In other words, *kafir* is he who rejects belief in God and His unity, i.e., disbeliever or nonbeliever. On some occasions it is used to denote lack of gratitude toward God for His bounties. Followers of other traditions are not considered *kafir* as long as they believe in God and His unity as defined in each tradition. See, e.g., the following verses in the *Qur'ān*, 2:6, 2:89, 2:125, 2:152, 16:83, 26:18–19, 27:14, 47:7–8, 60:4, 57:20, 66:7.

47 Kohlberg, "The Development of the Imāmi Shi'i Doctrine of *Jihad*," p. 69.

48 See, e.g., 2:190, 2:192, 4:128, 22:39, and 60:8.

49 Robert D. Crane, "Maqasid al Shari'ah: A Strategy to Rehabilitate Religion in America," Roundtable, International Institute of Islamic Thought, Herndon, Virginia, 27 March 2009.

50 We define defensive war as one in defense of one's country, honor, and property. Mutahhari includes in his definition of defensive war the war intended to defend the victims of aggression by a powerful enemy. Such a war is also defined as preemptive war whose purpose is to push back the enemy before attack. Only in such cases is offensive war – that is, war without prior attack – permissible or even obligatory to all Muslims. Indeed, preemptive wars are defensive from one point of view but offensive from another. Military operations with the purpose of conquering land, imposing religion on nations, and plundering wealth are not justifiable and legitimate *jihad*, according to this view. Such wars are aggression and therefore not permissible. See Mutahhari, *Jihad*, pp. 24–25, 46–47. See also Salehi Najafabadi, *Shahid-i Javid Husayn ibn 'Ali*, pp. 82–85. For further discussion on this issue, see the section titled "Defensive War.".

51 Biographical information on these and other scholars is presented in the coming pages.

52 See Abdulaziz Sachedina, *The Just Ruler in Shi'ite Islam: The Comprehensive Authority of the Jurist in Imamite Jurisprudence* (New York: Oxford University Press, 1988), pp. 106–109.

53 For a discussion of the concept of *expediency* and its importance in Khomeini's political thought, see Sa'id Hajjarian, *Az Shahid-e Qudsi ta Shahid-i Bazari* (From a Divine Witness to a Bazari Witness) (Tehran: Kian Monthly Journal, 1380/2001), 69–122.

54 For an analysis regarding these developments, see Mehdi Khalaji, *Apocalyptic Politics: On the Rationality of Iranian Policy* (Washington, D.C.: Washington Institute for Near East Policy, Policy Focus 79, January 2008).

55 Seyyed Hossein Nasr, *Ideals and Realities of Islam*, revised ed. (Cambridge: Islamic Texts Society, 2001), pp. 29–56.

56 Tabataba'i, *Shi'ite Islam*, pp. 90–91.

57 Ayatullah Ja'far Subhani, *Doctrines of Shi'i Islam: A Compendium of Imami Beliefs and Practices*, Reza Shah-Kazemi (trans.) (London: I. B. Tauris, 2001), pp. 182–184. See also Momen, *An Introduction to Shi'i Islam*, pp. 183–187. See also Abulqasim Gorji, "Ijtihad," in *Islamic Encyclopedia* (Tehran: Islamic Encyclopedia Institute, 1373/1994), vol. VI, pp. 609; Hossein Modarresi, *An Introduction to Shi'i Law* (London: Ithaca Press, 1984); and "Rationalism and Traditionalism in Shi'i Jurisprudence: A Preliminary Survey," *Studia Islamica* 59 (1984), 141–158.

58 For the development of Shi'i commentaries, see Mohammad H. Faghfoory, "The Necessity of Studying Shi'i Commentaries on the *Qur'an*," *International Journal of Shi'i Studies* 1:3 (2003), 75–94.

59 'Allamah Seyyid Muhammad Husayn Tabataba'i, *Qur'an dar Islam*, revised ed. (Qom: Daftar-i Inteasharat-e Islami, 1386/2007). See also Ayatullah Ja 'far Subhani, *Introduction to the Science of the Qur'an*, Sleem Bhimji (trans.) (Stanmore: Islamic Education Board of the World Federation of KSMIC, 2006), esp. pp. 20–40.

60 For the most authoritative collection of Sunni ḥadīth, see Muhammad ibn Isma'il al-Bukhari, *Sahih al-Bukhari* (The Correct Book of *Ḥadīth*), Ludolf Krehl (ed.), 4 vols. (Leiden: E. J. Brill, 1862). Another edition was published in six volumes in Cairo in 1968. For Shi'i collection of ḥadīth, see Abu Ja'far Muhammad ibn Ya'qub al-Kulayni, *Usul al-Kafi* (Sufficient Principles [of Jurisprudence]), Ali Akbar Ghaffari (ed.), 8 vols. (Tehran: Dar al-Kutub al-Islamiyyah, 1983).

61 Among classical sources we have relied mostly on the writing of the following scholars: Kulayni, Shaykh Tusi, Ibn Idris, Hurr 'Amili, Abi Dawood, 'Allamah Hilli, Shahid Thani, Muhammad Hasan Najafi, Zumakhshari, Shaykh Saduq, Tabari, Waqidi, M.Baqir Majlisi. Among contemporary scholars we have use major writings of the following authors: Ayatullahs Tabataba'i, Nemooneh, Khomeini, Kho'ie. References are made to these sources throughout the text and a complete list of them is presented in the bibliography.

62 Tabataba'i, *Shi'ite Islam*, pp. 106–107. See also Subhani, *Doctrines of Shi'ite Islam*, pp. 182–183.

63 Ahmad ibn 'Ali al-Maqrizi, *al-Mawa'iz wa'l i'tibar bi dhikr al-khitat wa' athar* (Topographic and Historical Description of Egypt) (Cairo: Bulaq Publishers, 1270/1853), vol. II, p. 344; as quoted in Subhani, *Doctrines of Shi'ite Islam*, p. 183. See also Tabataba'i, *Shi'ite Islam*, p. 104.

64 Momen, *An Introduction to Shi'i Islam*, pp. 185–186.

65 For the consequences of the absence of *ijtihad* in Sunni jurisprudence, see Tabataba'i, *Shi'ite Islam*, p. 104; and Subhani, *Doctrines of Shi'ite Islam*, p. 185.

66 Abu al-Qasim Husayn ibn Muhammad al-Raghib al-Isfahani, *al-Mufradat fi Gharib al-Qur'an* (A Dictionary of Rare and Difficult Words of the *Qur'an*), S. M. Gilani (ed.) (Tehran, 1373/1954), *fitnah* entry, p. 290. See also pp. 58 and 174.

67 *Al-Munjid fi'l Lughah* (al-Munjid Dictionary of Arabic Language), 20th ed. (Beirut: Dar al-Mashriq, 1407/1986).

68 Mostafa Mohaghegh Damad, *Huquq-i bayn al-milal-i islami* (International Law in Islam) (Tehran: Markaz-e Nashr-e 'Ulum-e Islami, 1380/2001), pp. 92–93.

69 Salihi Najafabadi, *Jihad dar Islam*, 2nd ed. (Tehran: Nashr- e Ney, 1386/2007), p. 15.

70 Murtada Mutahhari, *Jihad*, 10th ed. (Tehran: Entesharat-e Sadr, 1377/1998), p. 43.

71 Anne Mary Schimmel, *Islam: An Introduction* (Albany: State University of New York Press, 1992), pp. 69–70.

72 Tabataba'i, *al-Mizan fi Tafsir al-Qur'an* (The Balance in Interpretation of the Qu'ran), (Qom: Entesharat-e Islami, 1350–1971), vol. II, p. 61.

73 Mutahhari, *Jihad*, p. 58.

74 Ibid., p. 38.

75 Ibid., pp. 40, 45, 63.

76 Mohaghegh Damad, *Huquq-i bayn al-milal-i islami* (International Law in Islam), p. 49.

77 Ibid., p. 49.

78 Tabataba'i, *al-Mizan fi Tafsir al-Qur'an* (The Balance in Interpretation of the *Qur'an*), p. 67.

79 Mahmud Shaltut, *al-Harb wa al-Salam fi al-Isalm* (War and Peace in Islam) (Cairo: n.p, n.d.), pp. 47–51. Shaykh Mahmud Shaltut (1893–1963) is a prominent Egyptian scholar of Islam and former rector of al-Azhar Islamic University (1958–1963). During his tenure he introduced Zaydi and Twelve-Imami Shi'i jurisprudence into the university curriculum and had all four Sunni Schools of Law recognize it as the fifth School of Law in Islam. For his biography and contributions, see Hunt Janin and Andre Kahlmeyer, *Islamic Law: The Sharia from Muhammad's Time to the Present* (Jefferson, N.C.: McFarland, 2007).

80 Mutahhari, *Jihad*, p. 58. See also Mohaghegh Damad, *Huquq-i bayn al-milal-i islami* (International Law in Islam), pp. 240–241.

81 Mutahhari, *Jihad*, pp. 73–75.

82 Ali Akbar Qurayshi, *Qamus-i Qur'an* (Dictionary of the *Qur'an*), 5:236.

83 ' Ali ibn Abi Talib, *Nahj ul-Balaghah* (Path of Eloquence), Fayd al-Islam (ed.) (Tehran: Kulalah Khavar, 1351/1972), pp. 442–446.

84 Ibn Bābawayhi as quoted in Kohlberg, "The Development of the Imami Shi'i Doctrine of *Jihad*," 66.

85 Mohaghegh Damad, *Huquq-i bayn al-milal-i islami* (International Law in Islam), pp. 92–93.

86 The *Qur'ān* commands the Prophet to initiate peace: "And if they incline to peace, do thou incline to it; and put thy trust in God" (8:61).

87 Najafabadi, *Jihad dar Islam*, p. 18.

88 There are over thirty verses regarding peace in the *Qur'ān*. See, e.g., verses 4:90, 4:128, 2:208, and 8:61.

89 The list of Sunni scholars includes such prominent scholars and jurists as Malik, Tabari, Sufyan al-Thawri, Ibn Taymiyah, Awza'i, Ibn Qayyim, and Kamal ibn Humam. Among Shi'i jurists he refers to Fadil Miqdad, 'Allamah Hilli, and a few others. See Mohaghegh Damad, *Huquq-i bayn al-milal-i islami* (International Law in Islam), p. 128.

90 Mutahhari, *Jihad*, p. 38.

91 Najafabadi, *Jihad dar Islam*, p. 52.

92 Tabataba'i, *al-Mizan fir Tafsir al-Qur'an* (The Balance in Interpretation of the Qu'ran), pp. 242–243.

93 See also verses 22:39, 2:194, 9:36, and many others.

94 Mutahhari, *Jihad*, p. 38. Mohaghegh Damad, *Huquq-i bayn al-milal-i islami* (International Law in Islam), pp. 110–111.

95 Mohaghegh Damad, *Huquq-i bayn al-milal-i islami* (International Law in Islam), pp. 110–111.

96 The Treaty of Hudaybiyya was signed between the Prophet as the head of the new Islamic state in Medina and the Quraysh tribe in the month of *Dhu'lqa'dah*, six years after *Hijrah/* March 628. On this treaty, see Martin Lings, *Muhammad: His Life Based on the Earliest Sources* (Rochester, N.Y.: Inner Traditions, 2006), pp. 257–262. See also Momen, *An Introduction to Shi'i Islam*, p. 7.

97 See the following verses in the *Qur'an*: "Had not God driven back the people, some by the means of others, there had been destroyed cloisters and churches, oratories and mosques, wherein God's Name is much mentioned. Assuredly, God will help him who help Him – surely God is All-strong, All-mighty," verse 22:40. See also verses 22:38 and 39. All commentators believe that these verses in fact define the meaning of defensive war and describe conditions under which it is permitted. See Mutahhari, *Jihad*, pp. 16 and 28.

98 On the Zaydi branch of Shi'ism, see Tabataba'i, *Shi'ite Islam*, pp. 76–79.

99 Ihsan al-Hindi, *Ahkam al-harb wa'l-Salam fi Dawlat al-Islam* (Laws of War and Peace in Islamic State) (Damascus: Maktabah al-Mustafa, 1414/1993), p. 124.

100 Jamal al-Din Miqdad ibn 'Abdullah al-Suyuri, *Kanz al-'Irfan* (Treasures of Gnosis), (Tehran: Dar al-nashid, 1343/1964), vol. I, p. 355.

101 Nasser Makarim Shirazi (ed.), *Tafsir-i Nemunah* (An Exemplary Commentary on the *Qur'an*), 21st ed. (Qom: Amir-Al-Momenin Seminary, 1386/2007), vol. II, pp. 13–14.

102 Muhaqqiq Ardabili, *Zubdat al-Bayan fi Ahkam al-Qur'an* (The Best Discourse on the Commands of the *Qur'an*), M. B. Behboodi (ed.) (Tehran: al-Maktabah al-Murtadawiyah, 1369/1980), p. 309.

103 Muhsin Fayd Kashani, *Tafsir-i Sadiq* (The Pure Commentary on the *Qur'an*), Shaykh Husayn A'lami (ed.) (Beirut, n.d.), vol. I, p. 229.

104 Tabataba'i, *al-Mizan fi Tafsir al-Qur'an* (The Balance in Interpretation of the *Qu'ran*), p. 164.

105 Aqa Muhammad Hasan Najafi, *Jawahir al-Kalam fi Sharh-i Kitab Sharayi' al-Islam* (Jewels of Words: Commentary on the Book of the Laws of Islam), new edition. (Beirut: Dar Ihya al-Turath al-Arabi, 1401/1981), vol. XXI, p. 4.

106 *The Glorious Qura'n*, Pickthal (trans.), notes on chapter 8, p. 163. This verse was revealed just before the Battle of Badr that broke out between Muslims and the Quraysh headed by Abu Sufyan. In this war the army of Quraysh outnumbered the Muslims and was better equipped. In the beginning of the war the Muslim army fought well, but the situation became very hard for them. The Prophet prayed, saying, "O God! If this little company is destroyed, there will be no one else in this land to worship you." Soon the above verse was revealed and the tide of the battle turned in favor of the Muslims. It was the bloodiest war the Muslims ever fought in which the Prophet also got injured and lost teeth. See Pickthal, pp. 163.

107 Abu Ali al-Fadl ibn Hasan al-Tabarsi, *Majma' al-Bayan* (Collection of Discourses), Husayn Nooru and Muhammad Mufattih (trans.) (Tehran: Intesharat-I Farahani, 1350/1972), vol. XI, p. 20.

108 Tabataba'i, *al-Mizan fi Tafsir al-Qur'an* (The Balance in Interpretation of the *Qu'ran*), vol. IX, p. 152.

109 The Battle of Tabuk took place in the month of October 630/Rajab 09. For the details of this battle, see Lings, *Muhammad: His Life Based on the Earliest Sources*, pp. 317–319.

110 Tabarsi, *Majma' al-Bayan* (Collection of Discourses), vol. XI, p. 66.

111 Al-Suyuri, *Kanz al-'Irfan* (Treasure of Gnosis), vol. I, p. 361.

112 Shaykh Tusi, *al-Tibyan fi Tafsir al-Qur'an* (*Qur'anic* Commentary Known as Tibyan), (Beirut: Dar Ihya al-Turath al-Arabi, nd.), vol. V, p. 203.

113 Abu Bakr 'Abd al-Rahman ibn Kaysan ibn Jarir al-Umawi (d. 201/817) was a well-known theologian of the Mu'tazilite school and a contemporary of the Abbasid Caliph al-Ma'mun (813–833).

114 Tabarsi, *Majma 'al-bayan* (Collection of Discourses), vol. XI, p. 85.

115 Ibid., p. 93. See also Tabataba'i, *al-Mizan*, vol. IX, p. 278.

116 This *ḥadīth* is narrated by Ibn Mas'ud and recorded in Bukhari in response to a man who asked the Prophet, "What deeds are the best?" See Sahih Bukhari, *Ḥadīth* #625, Book #93.

117 Muhammad ibn Hasan Hurr 'Amili (d. 1104/1693), *Wasa'il al-Shi'ah Ila Aḥadīth-ush-Shar'iah* (Shi'ite Guide to *Aḥadīth* Concerning Islamic Law) (Tehran: Dar al-Kutub al-Islamiyah, 1388/1968), vol. XI, p. 5.

118 Ibn Hajar al-'Asqalani, *Fath al-bari bi sharh-I Sahih al-Bukhari* (Revelations on Bukhari's [Collection of *Ḥadīth*]) (Cairo: Maktabah al-Bahiyyah, 1352/1933), vol. VI, p. 85.

119 The son of 'Umar ibn al-Khattab, the second Caliph after the death of the Prophet.

120 See 'Abd al-Majid Shartooti Azhari, *Sharh-i Arba'in ḥadīth* (Commentary on Forty *Ḥadīth*) (n.d., n.p.), p. 29.

121 'Abd al-Rahman ibn Sakhr Al-Azdi known as Abu Hurayrah (19–62/603–681) was a companion of the Prophet and transmitter of *ḥadīth*. He was particularly condemned due to his enigmatic personality. John Esposito (ed.), *The Oxford Dictionary of Islam* (Oxford: Oxford University Press, 2003), p. 5.

122 Mohaghegh Damad, *Huquq-i bayn al-milal-i islami* (International Law in Islam), p. 49.

123 Ahmad ibn Muhammad al-Barqi as quoted in Kohlberg, "The Development of the Imami Shi'i Doctrine of *Jihad*," 65.

124 Mutahhari, *Jihad*, pp. 26–27.

125 See, e.g., verses 2:190 and 9:36.

126 Mutahhari, *Jihad*, p. 8.

127 Ibid., p. 38. Emphasis added.

128 See, e.g, verse 60:8.

129 Najafabadi, *Jihad dar Islam*, pp. 10–12.

130 Muhammad ibn Idris Shafi'i was born in Gaza, Palestine, in 150/767 and was raised in Makkah. He founded the third School of Law in Sunni Islam known after his name. He died in 204/820 in Cairo where his tomb still stands. See Majid Khadduri, *Islamic Jurisprudence: Shafi'i's Risala* (Cambridge: Islamic Texts Society, 1987).

131 The verse reads as follows, "Fight them, till there is no persecution and the religion is God's, then if they give over, there shall be no enmity save for evildoers," 2:193.

132 Najafabadi, *Jihad dar Islam*, p. 12. Muhammad ibn Makki 'Amili Jazini, known as Shahid Thani (Second Martyr) was born in Jabal 'Amil in Lebanon in 911/1506 and was killed in 966/1559. He wrote on a variety of subjects dealing with theology, prayer, *ḥadīth*, and many works on jurisprudence. Over 79 books and treatises are attributed to him and are available in print. Among them are *Tamhid al-Qawa'id al-Usuliyah* (Preparation of the Rules and Principles) and a commentary on *Lam'ah al-Dimashqiyah* (Divine Flashes of Damascus), also known as *Sharh-i Lama'ah*, vol. I, p. 255, as quoted in Najafabadi, *Jihad dar Islam*, pp. 50–51.

133 An early transmitter of *ḥadīth* whose reliability in transmission has been questioned.

134 An early transmitter of *ḥadīth*. Anas ibn Malik quotes several traditions from him.

135 Najafabadi, *Jihad dar Islam*, pp. 39–42. He quotes Muhammad 'Abduh who had come to the same conclusion a century earlier in his commentary on the *Qur'ān*, known as *al-Minar*, 3rd ed. (Cairo: n.p., n.d.), vol. II, p. 216.

136 Najafabadi, *Jihad dar Islam*, p. 43; for examples of the influence of Shafi'i on Shi'i and Sunni jurists, see pp. 43–52.

137 Ibid., p. 52.

138 Ibid., pp. 52–53. See also verse 18:29.

139 Ibn Kathir, *Jami' al-Usul* (The Comprehensive Collection of Principles of Jurisprudence), vol. III, p. 201, as quoted in Najafabadi, *Jihad dar Islam*, p. 54.

140 Hurr 'Amili (d. 1104/1693), *Wasa'il al-Shi 'ah Ila Ahadith-ush-Shar'iah* (Shi'ite Guide to *Ahadith* Concerning Islamic Law), vol. XI, p. 30, as quoted in Najafabadi, *Jihad dar Islam*, p. 53.

141 Tabari, *Tarikh*, vol. II, p. 389, as quoted in Najafabadi, *Jihad dar Islam*, p. 55.

142 Muhsin Fayd Kashani, *Tafsi-i Safi* (The Pure Commentary on the *Qur'ān*), Shaykh Husayn A'lami (ed.), vol. I, p. 288.

143 Shaykh Tusi, *al-Tibyan fi Tafsir al-Qur'an* (*Qur'ānic* Commentary known as Tibyan), vol. II, p. 145.

144 Najafabadi, *Jihad dar Islam*, p. 21.

145 Muhaqqiq Ardabili, *Zubdat al-Bayanfi Ahkam al-Qur'an* (The Best Discourse on the Commands of the *Qur'ān*), M. B. Behboodi (ed.) (Tehran: al-Maktabah al-Murtadawiyah, 1369/1980), p. 308.

146 Al-Suyuri, *Kanz al-'Irfan* (Treasures of Gnosis), vol. I, p. 353.

147 Najafabadi, *Jihad dar Islam*, p. 51.

148 Fazl ibn Hasan Tabarsi, *Majma' al-Bayan* (Collection of Discourses), vol. II, p. 289.

149 Tabataba'i, *al-Mizan fi Tafsir al-Qur'an* (The Balance in Interpretation of the *Qu'ran*), vol. IX, p. 125.

150 Mohaghegh Damad, *Huquq-i bayn al-milal-i islami* (International Law in Islam), p. 107. See also Najafabadi, *Jihad dar Islam*, pp. 29–30

151 Nasir Makarim Shirazi, *Tafsir-i Nemoonah* (The Exemplary Commentary on the *Qur'an*), 44th ed. (Tehran, 1385/2006), vol. XXIV, p. 32.

152 Mutahhari, *Jihad*, pp. 5–10; see also p. 109.

153 Kate Zebiri, *Mahmud Shaltut and Islamic Modernism* (Oxford: Oxford University Press, 1993). See also Shaltut, *al-Harb wa al-Salam fi al-Isalm* (War and Peace in Islam), p. 47.

154 Mohaghegh Damad, *Huquq-i bayn al-milal-i islami* (International Law in Islam), p. 109.

155 Tabarsi, *Majma' al-Bayan* (Collection of Discourses), vol. XI, p. 85.

156 Ibid.

157 Mohaghegh Damad, *Huquq-I bayn al-milal-I islami* (International Law in Islam), p. 50, note 77.

158 Tabataba'i, *al-Mizan fi Tafsir al-Qur'an* (The Balance in Interpretation of the *Qu'ran*), vol. IX, p. 479.

159 Mohaghegh Damad, *Huquq-i bayn al-milal-i islami* (International Law in Islam), p. 108.

160 Tabarsi, *Majma' al-bayan* (Collection of Discourses), vol. I, pp. 242–243.

161 See the section in this chapter titled "Defensive War." See also Mohaghegh Damad, *Huquq-i bayn al-milal-I islami* (International Law in Islam), pp. 92–93.

162 Ibn Humam (258–336/872–948), *Fath al-Qadir* (al-Qadir Opening) (n.p., n.d.,), vol. V, p. 194. He was a well-known jurist of the Hanafi School of Law, Sufi master, and the chief judge in the city of Alexandria, Egypt.

163 Najafabadi, *Jihad dar Islam*, pp. 39–41.

164 Mohaghegh Damad, *Huquq-i Bayn al-milal-i eslami* (International Law in Islam), pp. 111–112.

165 Hurr 'Amili, (d. 1104/1693) *Wasa'il al-Shi 'ah Ila Ahadith al-Shar'iah* (Shi'itie Guide to *Ahadith* Concerning Islamic Law), vol. XI, p. 69 as quoted in Mohaghegh Damad, *Huquq-i bayn al-milal-i islami* (International Law in Islam), p. 112. See also Husayn Noori, *Mustadrik al-Wasa'il wa Mustanbit al-Masa'il al-Shari'ah* (Means of Documentation and Understanding Questions Related to Islamic Law) (Tehran: Dar al-Kutub al-Islamiyah), vol. XI, p. 86.

166 For the concept of Occulatation in Shi'ism, see Tabataba'i, *Shi'ite Islam*, pp. 210–214; Jassim M Hussain, *The Occulatation of the Twelfth Imam* (London: Muhammadi Trust, 1982), pp.

13–30; and Abdulaziz Sachedina, *Islamic Messianism, the Idea of Mahdi in Twelver Shi'ism* (Albany: State University of New York Press, 1981), pp. 152–166 and 172–79. See also Ali Amir-Moezzi, *The Divine Guide in Early Shi'ism* (Albany: State University of New York Press, 1994), pp. 133–139.

167   *Qur'ān* 2:256.

168   *Kitab al-Umm* (The Motherbook), his main surviving text that forms the foundation of the School of Law named after him, is a five-volume book published in Beirut (n.d.). A summarized version of it was compiled by Husain Abd al-Hamid in Cairo, titled *Mukhtasar Kitab al-Umm* (A Summary of the Motherbook). See Joseph Schacht, *The Origins of Muhammadan Jurisprudence* (Oxford: Clarendon Press, 1950); Majid Khadduri, *Islamic Jurisprudence: Shafi'i's Risala* (Cambridge: Islamic Texts Society, 1987). See also "The Book of the Amalgamation of Knowledge," in Aisha Y. Musa, *Ḥadīth as Scripture: Discussions on the Authority of Prophetic Traditions in Islam* (New York: Palgrave, 2008).

169   Shafi 'i, *Kitab al-Umm* (The Motherbook) (Beirut: Dar al-Ma'rifah, n.d.), vol. IV, p. 161.

170   Emphasis added.

171   Shafi 'i, *Kitab al-Umm* (The Motherbook), pp. 61–62. See also Najafabadi, *Jihad dar Islam*, pp. 39–41. The prominent Sunni jurist and once the rector of al-Azhar University in Cairo, Muhammad 'Abduh also believes that verdicts like this were issued under state pressure and out of the fear or persecution. See Najafabadi, *Jihad dar Islam*, pp. 41–42.

172   Muhammad ibn Jarir al-Tabari (223–311/838–923), *Jami' al-bayan fi ta'wil al-Qur'an* (Comprehensive Discourse on the Hermenutics of the *Qur'an*), commonly known as *Tafsir al-Tabari* (Tabar's Commentary) (Beirut: Matba 'ah Dar al-Fikr, 1416/1995), comments on chapter 2, verse 190. On his life and works, see *The History of al-Ṭabarī*, Yar-Shater (ed.), 40 vols. (Albany: State University of New York Press, 1986).

173   Kamal ibn Humam was born in Alexandria and received his early education in that city. He was a master of many sciences, including geometry, law, music, medicine, and law. He was also an eminent jurist of the Hanafi School of Law. He traveled extensively and finally settled in Cairo where he taught until his death. He has written extensively on legal issues and his most important books are *al-Tahrir fi usul* (Notes on the Principles of Jurisprudence) (Cairo, 1316/1899 and 1351/ 1933), *Zad al-faqir* (Provisions for the Poor Man) (Cairo, 1319/1899), and *Fath al-Qadir lil 'ajiz al-faqir* (The *al-Qadir* Opening for Helpless Seeker) (Lekhnow, 1292/1857). See M. H. Mu'adhdhin Jami, "Ibn Humam," in *Dai'rat al-Ma'arif-i Bozorg-i islami* (Great Encyclopedia of Islam) (Tehran, n.p.), vol. V, p. 74. See also *Lughatnamah yi- Dehkhoda* (The Dehkoda Dictionary) (Tehran: Dehkoda Foundation, 1378/1999).

174   Of all seven authoritative Sunni collections of the Tradition of the Prophet, these two are recognized as the most reliable and authentic.

175   Ibn Humam, *Fath al-Qadir lil 'ajiz al-faqir* (The *al-Qadir* Opening for Helpless Seeker), vol. V, p. 196, as quoted in Najafabadi, *Jihad dar Islam* p. 70.

176   Tusi studied and later taught in Baghdad. When the Mongols invaded Baghdad he fled to Najaf, and his presence there turned Najaf into a leading Shi'i learning center. He died in 460/1068. His most important work is *al- Tibyan fi tafsir al-Qur'an* (*Qur'anic* Commentary known as Tibyan) (Beirut: Dar Ihya al-Turath al-Arabi, n.d.); *al-Istibsar fi ma ikhtalafa min al-akhbar* (Insights into the Differences or Narrations), Sayyid Hasan Musawi (ed.), 3rd ed. (Tehran: Maktabat al-Islamiyah, 1390/1971). See also *al-Nihayah fi mujarrad al-fiqh wa'l fatwa* (The Ultimate Book on Principles of Jurisprudence and Legal Verdicts) (Qom: Entesharat-I Quds, n.d.), and *al-Mabsut fi'l fiqh* (A Comprehensive Book on Jurisprudence) (Tehran: al-Maktabah al-Mutadaviyah, 1387/1968). For his biography, see Aqa Bozorg

Tehrani, *al-Dhari'ah ila Tasanif al-Shari'ah* (A Descriptive Catalogue of Shia Books) (Beirut: Dar al-adwa, 1402/1983), vol. IV, p. 504.

177 Tusi, *al-Nihayah fi mujarrad al-fiqh wa'l fatwa* (The Ultimate Source on Principles of Jurisprudence and Legal Verdict), pp. 291ff.

178 Najafabadi, *Jihad dar Islam*, pp. 8 and 46–47: "Shafi'i's verdict is not based on any *Qur'ānic* verse, the practices of the Prophet or any historical precedent and must be seriously criticized and rejected"; see also p. 80.

179 Ibn Idris was born in the city of Hillah in Iraq. In his criticism of his fellow jurists he was relentless. He is credited for opening the way for critical thinking in legal matters. His most important books on jurisprudence include *al-Sara'ir al-hawi lit ahrir al-fatawi, Kitab al-Masa'il* (Secrets Surrounding the Writing of Legal Verdicts) and several other treatises. See Aqa Bozorg Tehrani, *al-Dhari'ah ila Tasanif al-Shi'ah* (A Descriptive Catalogue of Shi'a Books).

180 Ibn Idris, *al-Sara'ir al-hawi lit ahrir al-fatawi* (Secrets Surrounding the Writing of Legal Verdicts), lithograph edition (Tehran, n.p., n.d.), p. 156 as quoted in Najafabadi, *Jihad dar Islam*, p. 49.

181 Allamah Hilli was born and raised in Hillah, Iraq, and received his education in Najaf where he also taught. He spent some time in Persia, and as a result of his association with Uljaytu, the Mongol ruler of Persia at the time, the latter converted to Shi'ism.

182 See Hilli, *Tadhkirah, wa'l adhhan fi ahkam al-iman* (Treatise and Views on Laws of Religion), lithograph edition (Qum, n.d.), vol. I, p. 209, as quoted in Najafabadi, *Jihad dar Islam*, pp. 49–50.

183 Hilli, *Tadhkirah wa'l adhhan fi ahkam al-iman* (Treatise and Views on Laws of Religion), vol, I, p. 409.

184 See n. 98.

185 Known as Shaykh al-fuqaha (Master of Jurists), Najafi (d.1231/1816) was one of the most famous jurists of the nineteenth century and was highly acknowledged and respected for his mastery of Islamic sciences. Among his works are *Jawahir al-kalam fi sharh-i sharayi' al-islam (fi Masa'il al-Halal wa'l-Haram)* (Jewels of Words: Commentary on the Sharayi', the Book of the Legal Principles of Islam by Muhaqqiq Hilli), vol. XXI, pp. 11–19.

186 Sayyid Muhammad Husayn Tabataba'i was the most knowledgeable philosopher, jurist, and gnostic of twentieth-century Iran whose twenty-five-volume commentary on the *Qur'ān* is acknowledged widely as a standard commentary on the Sacred Book of Islam. For his biography, see Seyyed Hossein Nasr's translation and introduction to *Shi'ite Islam*. This is still the most authoritative book on Shi'ism in any European language.

187 Sayyid Abulqasim Kho'ie was born in the city of Khoy in Azarbaijan in 1899, and received his education in Najaf where he settled for the rest of his life until his death in 1992. After the death of Ayatullha Mohsin Hakim, Kho'ie was recognized as the Supreme Source of Emulation (*marja'-i taqlid*) by Shi'ites in Iran and Iraq with millions of followers. He established a charity foundation that carried on extensive religious, educational, and other projects throughout the Islamic world and Europe.

188 Reportedly, Najafi spent thirty years to complete this book. It is an indispensable source for any student of Shi'i jurisprudence and has been edited and published many times in Tehran, Beirut, and Najaf.

189 Najafi, *Jawahir al-kalam* (Jewels of Words), vol. XI, p. 4.

190 See Najafabadi, *Jihad dar Islam*, pp. 51–52.

191 Ibid., pp. 52–53.

192 See, e.g., verse 30:30.

193 Tabataba'i, *al-Mizan fi Tafsir al-Qur'an* (The Balance in Interpretation of the *Qu'ran*), vol. II, pp. 66–69.

194 Najafabadi, *Jihad dar Islam*, pp. 58–59.

195 Ibid., pp. 59–60.

196 E.g., verses 4:74, 8:39, 9:5, and 9:36.

197 Kho'ie, *Minhaj al-Salihin* (Path of the Righteous), 28th ed. (Qom: Entesharat-I Mehr, 1410/1990), vol. I, pp. 1–360.

198 This argument has been presented in one way or another in the writings and verdicts of jurists whose works we have discussed thus far. For a representative sample of this argument, see Tusi, *al-Mabsut fi'l fiqh* (A Comprehensive Book on Jurisprudence), vol. II, pp. 2 and 10.

199 This view is particularly present among the Sunni scholars. See, e.g., Sayyid Qutb, *Ma'alim fi al-tariq* (English as Milestones) (Chicago: Kazi Publishers, 1964), and Majid Khaddurie, *al-Harb wa'l-Slam fi Shar' al-Islam* (War and Peace in the Law of Islam) (New York, 1977).

200 Muhammad bin Umar al-Waqidi (130–210 H/747–825) was a transmitter of *hadith*, a jurist, and historian who functioned as the Chief Judge of Baghdad.

201 Najafabadi, *Jihad dar Islam*, pp. 86–92.

202 Among Sunni jurists who supported the idea of preemptive attack on the basis of this fabricated *hadith* are Ibn Homam, Shaykh Tusi, 'Allamah Hilli, and Najafi.

203 Mutahhari, *Jihad*, p. 39.

204 Ibid., pp. 8 and 18–19.

205 Mohaghegh Damad, *Huquq-i bayn al-milal-I islami* (International Law in Islam), p. 239.

206 For a complete list of these jurists, see ibid., pp. 127–129.

207 For a discussion of those wars, see Najafabadi, *Jihad dar Islam*, pp. 31, 34, 35–38, 55–56, and 72–82. See also Mohaghegh Damad, *Huquq-i bayn al-milal-I islami* (International Law in Islam), pp. 125–126, 135.

208 Ihsan al-Hindi, *Ahkam al-harb wa'l-salam fi dawlat al-islam* (The Rules of War and Peace in an Islamic State) (Damascus: Dar al-Munir lil-taba'ah wa'l-nashr wa'l-tawzi', 1993), p. 121.

209 The contemporary Sunni jurist Mahmud Shaltut and Shi'i scholar Mohaghegh Damad both reject this view and strongly condemn it as a sign of an unrealistic understanding of the capabilities of the Muslim world and its vital interests. See Shaltut, *al-Harb wa al-Salam fi al-Isalm* (War and Peace in Islam), p. 51, and Mohaghegh Damad, *Huquq-i bayn al-milal-i islami* (International Law in Islam), p. 115.

210 Seyyed Hossein Nasr, *The Heart of Islam: Enduring Values for Humanity* (San Francisco, Calif.: Harpers San Francisco, 2002), p. 163.

211 Nasr, *The Heart of Islam*, p. 164.

212 Ibid.

213 Ibid.

214 Sheikh Yusuf al-Qaradawi, "Interview with al-Sharq al-Awsat," 19 July 2003. See also Tariq Ramadan, *Western Muslims and the Future of Islam* (New York: Oxford University Press, 2005). On Ramadan's life and career, see Andrew F. March, "Reading Tariq Ramadan: Political Liberalism, Islam, and 'Overlapping Consensus,'" *Ethics and International Affairs* 21:4 (2007), 399–413, and Caroline Fourest, *Brother Tariq: The Doublespeak of Tariq Ramadan* (New York: Encounter Books, 2008).

215 Najafi, *Jawahir al-kalam fi Sharh-i Sharayi' al-islam (fi Masa'il al-Halal wa'l-Haram)* (Jewels of the Word: A Commentary on Sharayi', Legal Principles of Islam by Muhaqqiq Hilli), vol. XXI, pp. 13–14.

216 On the life and career of Imam 'Ali ibn Abi Talib, see Reza Shah Kazemi, *Justice and Remembrance: Introducing the Spirituality of Imam Ali* (London: I. B. Tauris Publishers, 2006); Ali Lakhani (ed.) *The Sacred Foundation of Justice in Islam* (Bloomington, Ind.: World Wisdom Publishing, 2006). See also Muhammad Abd al-Rauf, *Imam Ali ibn Abi Talib: The First Intellectual Muslim Thinker* (Alexandria, Va.: Al-Saadawi Publishers, 1995), and Sulayman Kattani, *Imam Ali: Source of Light, Wisdom, and Might* (London: Muhammadi Trust, 1983).

217 Muhammad b. Hasan al-Hurr 'Amili (d. 1104 /1693), *Wasa'il al-Shi'ah Ila Ahadith-ush-Shari'ah* (Shi'itie Guide to *Ahadith* Concerning Islamic Law), vol. XI, p. 35, as quoted in Najafabadi, *Jihad dar Islam*, p. 64.

218 In particular, the Fourth, Fifth, Sixth, Seventh, and Eighth Imams played a leading role in laying the foundations of the Islamic intellectual tradition. The Sixth Imam, Ja'far al-Sadiq, trained the founders of the first two Schools of Islamic Law, namely, Abu Hanifah and Malik, who in turn trained the founders of the Shafi'i and Hanbali Schools of Law. See Mohammad Ali Amir-Moezzi, *The Divine Guide in Early Shi'ism: The Sources of Esotericism in Islam*, David Streight (trans.) (Albany: State University of New York Press, 1994). See also Arzina R. Lalani, *Early Shi'i Thought: The Teachings of Imam Muhammad al-Baqir* (London: Institute for Ismaili Studies, 2004); Farhana Mayer (ed.), *Spiritual Gems: The Mystical Qur'an Commentary Ascribed by the Sufis to Imam Ja'far al-Sadiq* (Louisville, Ky.: Fons Vitae, 2009).

219 See Amir-Moezzi, *The Divine Guide in Early Shi'ism*, p. 135. For a bibliography of literature on these developments, see Tehrani, *al-Dhari'ah*, vol. V, pp. 296–298.

220 Muhammad ibn Murtada, known as Mulla Muhsin Fayd Kashani (1007–1090/1599–1680), was one of the most remarkable scholars of the Safavid era. A contemporary of Muhammad Taqi and Muhammad Baqir Majlisi, he was a student and son-in-law of Sadr al-Din Shirazi (Mulla Sadra). He wrote numerous works on jurisprudence, the science of principles, *hadith*, and *Qur'anic* commentary but is known for his writings on philosophy and metaphysics. He was also an eloquent poet, and his collection of poetry has been published several times in Tehran and Qom. See *Fayd Nameh: Essays in Memory of Mulla Muhsin Fayd Kashani* (Tehran: Entesharat-e Hekmat, 1385/2006).

221 Muhsin Fayd Kashani, *Kitab al-Shafi* (Book of Healing), vol. II, p. 73, as quoted in Najafabadi, *Jihad dar Islam*, pp. 66–67.

222 Ruhullah Khomeini, *Kita al-Bay'* (Book of Transaction) (Tehran-Qom: Mehr Publishers, 1385/2006), vol. II, p. 496.

223 See above for our discussion of the term *fitnah*. As we mentioned before, *fitnah* means not war, but trial, plot, sedition, persecution, revolt, and rebellion; not disbelief and heresy. 'Abdullah ibn 'Umar, one of the companions of the Prophet alludes to this term: "During the time of the Prophet we fought against the Quraysh because they persecuted, imprisoned and tortured Muslims. [By the command of the Prophet] we fought with them until they were defeated and their plots ended." On further elaboration of this term, see Abulqasim al-Husayn ibn Muhammad Raghib Isfahani, *Mufradat fi gharib al-Qur'an* (A Dictionary of Rare and Difficult Words of the *Qur'an*), S. M. Gilani (ed.) (Tehran, 1373/1954), *fitnah* entry. See section titled "The Laws of War".

224 *Qur'an* 2:19. See also Najafabadi, *Jihad dar Islam*, p. 20.

225 Mohaghegh Damad, *Huquq-i bayn al-milal-i islami* (International Law in Islam), pp. 261–262.

226 Najafi, *Jawahir al-kalam fi Sharh-i Sharayi' al-islam (fi Masa'il al-Halal wa'l-Haram)* (Jewels of the Word: A Commentary on Sharayi', Legal Principles of Islam by Muhaqqiq Hilli), vol. XXI, p. 51. See also *Ibn Mas'ud Kasani, Badayi' al-Sanayi'* (On Subtle Aspects

of [*Hanafi*] Jurisprudence) (Beirut: Dar al-Kutub 'Ilmiyah, 1406/1986), vol. VII, p. 100; Ali ibn Muhammad Mawardi, *al-Ahkam al-Sultaniyah* (Royal Commandments), p. 35; and Ibn Quddamah, *Mughni al-Muhtaj* (All One Needs to Know) (Beirut: Dar al-Kutub 'Ilmiyah, n.d.), vol. X, p. 385, as quoted in Mohaghegh Damad, *Huquq-i bayn al-milal-i islami* (International Law in Islam), p. 263.

227 *Qur'ān* 2:190 and 194.

228 Ka'bah is the most important pilgrimage site in Islam located in Mecca, Saudi Arabia. The original temple was built by Abraham, the patriarch of all Abrahamic religions. Making pilgrimage to Mecca at least once in a lifetime is an obligation for every Muslim who is physically capable of performing it and can financially afford it. See Seyyed Hossein Nasr, *Mecca, the Blessed, Medina, the Radiant: The Holiest Cities of Islam* (New York: Aperture, 1997). See also Omer Faruk Aksoy, *The Blessed Cities of Islam: Mecca-Medina* (Clifton, N.J.: Tughra Books, 2008).

229 *Yanabi' al-Fiqhiyah* (The Spring Sources of Jurisprudence); translated passage cited in Mostafa Mohaghegh Damad, *Protection of Individuals in Times of Armed Conflict under International and Islamic Laws* (New York: Global Scholarly Publications, 2005), p. 369.

230 *Yanabi' al-Fiqhiyah* (The Spring Sources of Jurisprudence); in Mohaghegh Damad, *Protection of Individuals in Times of Armed Conflict*, p. 369.

231 For a general discussion of this theme, as well as additional citations, see Mohaghegh Damad, *Protection of Individuals in Times of Armed Conflict*, pp. 368–373.

232 For discussion, see ibid., pp. 371–373.

233 *Tahrir al Ahkam* [*Al-Ahkam Al-Shariyah ala Madhhab Al-Imamiyah*] (Writing Legal Religious Injunctions in accordance with the Imami School of Law); translated passage in Mohaghegh Damad, *Protection of Individuals in Times of Armed Conflict*, pp. 371–372.

234 *Jawahir al-Kalem* (Jewels of Words), vol. 22, p. 76; paraphrased in Mohaghegh Damad, *Protection of Individuals in Times of Armed Conflict*, p. 372.

235 Mohaghegh Damad, *Protection of Individuals in Times of Armed Conflict*, p. 372.

236 Ibid.

237 Mohaghegh Damad quotes Muhammad Hamidullah, who cites a jurist named Khalil al-Maliki on this issue. See Muhammad Hamidullah as cited in ibid., pp. 399–400.

238 "Statement to the First International Conference on Disarmament and Non-Proliferation (Tehran, 17–18 April 2010)," Center for Preserving and Publishing the Works of Grand Ayatollah Sayyid Ali Khamenei, accessed 13 December 2012, available at http://farsi. khamenei.ir/message-content?id=9171. Passage translated by Dr. Sadrodin Mousavi Jashni. Emphasis added.

239 For more concerning restrictions on weaponry and other limitations on warfare, see Mohaghegh Damad, *Protection of Individuals in Times of Armed Conflict*, pp. 398–419.

240 Najafabadi, *Jihad dar Islam*, p. 152.

241 See, e.g., Ibn Quddamah, *Mughni al-Muhtaj* (All One Needs to Know), vol. X, p. 400.

242 It is reported that when Harith asked why they are going to kill him, he was told, "You persecuted and tortured the companions of the Prophet and violated the sacred precinct of the *Qur'ān*, that is the reason you are condemned to death." And when 'Uqbah asked the same question, the Prophet told him, "because of all your hostility against Islam and God's Messenger." See Waqidi as quoted in Najafabadi, *Jihad dar Islam*, pp. 151–152.

243 Najafabadi, *Jihad dar Islam*, pp. 152–155.

244 Ibid., pp. 158–158; see also pp. 199–213.

245 Waqidi, *Kitab al-Mughazi* (The Book of Prophet's Wars), as quoted in Najafabadi, *Jihad dar Islam*, p. 153.

246 "Make ready for them whatever force and string of horses you can, to terrify thereby the enemy of God and your enemy, and others besides them that you know not; God knows them" (*Qur'ān*, 8:60).

247 In fact verse 190 of chapter 2 of the *Qur'ān* clearly explains the rules and conditions under which war must begin, while verse 61 of chapter 8 discusses the conditions for cease-fire and peace. Interestingly, the rules and conditions of starting and ending wars in modern international law is profoundly impacted by and very similar to Islamic law of warfare. See Mohaghegh Damad, *Protection of Individuals in Times of Armed Conflict*, p. 274.

248 For an Orientalist understanding of this term, see Edward Said, *Orientalism* (New York: Vintage, 1978).

249 Nasr, "The Spiritual Significance of *Jihad*."

250 E.g., see the *Qur'ān*: "We have not sent thee, save as a mercy unto all beings" (21:107), and "O believers, enter the peace, all of you, and follow not the steps of Satan, he is a manifest foe to you" (2:208).

251 "Call thou to the way of thy Lord with wisdom and good admonition, and dispute with them in the better ways" (16:125).

252 Nasr, "The Spiritual Significance of *Jihad*."

253 Ibid.

254 One of the first projects started in Iran after the revolution of 1979 was the establishment of *jihad-i sazandigi*, that is, the "Reconstruction Crusade," a plan to introduce wide-ranging reforms into rural and poorer regions of the country.

255 Nasr, "The Spiritual Significance of *Jihad*."

256 See Mutahhari, *Jihad*, pp. 82–87; Najafabadi, *Jihad dar Islam*, pp. 12–14; and Mohaghegh Damad, *Huquq-i bayn al-milal-i islami* (International Law in Islam), pp. 114–126.

257 Abu Jac'far Muhammad ibn Ya'qub al-Kulayni, *Book of Jihad*, 6 vols. (Tehran, 1381/1961), vol. V, pp. 13–19. Translated by M. H. Faghfoory.

258 Shayk al-Ta'ifah, *al-Nihayah fi mujarrad al-fiqh wa'l fatwa* (The Ultimate Book on the Pure Goal of Jurisprudence and Legal Verdict), M. Faghfoory (trans.), 2nd ed. (Tehran, 1970), p. 289.

259 Sharif Tahir ibn Zuhrah, *Ghunyat al-nuzu' ila 'ilm a-lusul wa'-furu'* (A Compendium of Principles and Secondary Rules) (Qom: Imam Sadiq Publishing, 1997). Translated by M. H. Faghfoory.

260 Muhaqqiq Hilli, *Sharayi' al-Islam fi Masa'il al-Halal wa'l-Haram* (The Laws of Islam Regarding the Issues Related to Permissible and Forbidden Acts), vol. I, p. 278 (Najaf: Dar al-Adwa, 1389/1970, and Beirut: Dar al-Zahra, 1409/1989). Translated by M. H. Faghfoory.

261 Mulla Muhsin Fayd Kashani, *Kitab al-Wafi* (The Sufficient Book of Shi'ah *Ḥadīth*) (Qom: Ayatullah Najafi Publishing, 1362/1983), vol. XV, p. 84. Translated by M. H. Faghfoory.

262 Mulla Muhsin Fayd Kashani, "Mafatih al-Sharayi' " (Keys to Islamic Law), unpublished manuscript, 1042/1633 (Tehran University Central Library), vol. II, p. 50. A digital copy is available at the Ahl al-Bayt Digital Library in Qum. Translated by M. H. Faghfoory.

263 Muhammad Hasan Najafi, *Jawahir al-kalam fi sharh-i sha'ayir al-islam* (Jewels of Words: Commentary on the Book of the Laws of Islam) (1231/1816), vol. XXI, pp. 11–19. Translated by M. H. Faghoory.

264 This is a difficult term to translate into English. Literally, it means "he whose hands are extended," i.e., he who has full authority. In legal terms it refers to an Imam who is also in charge of the government, such as 'Ali ibn Abi Talib.

265 Ayatullah Ruhullah Musavi Khomeini, *Tahrir al-Wasilah* (A Clarification of Questions) (Tehran: Bi'that Foundation, 1365/1986), vol. I, pp. 483–487. Translated by M. H. Faghfoory..

266 Ayatullah Muhammad Tqai Bahjat, *Jami' al-Masa'il* (Comprehensive Book of Fundamental Issues of Jurisprudence) (Qum, 1420/1999), vol. II, pp. 299–310. Translated by M. H. Faghfoory.

267 See Aqa Bozorg Tehrani, *al-Dhari'ah ila Tasanif al-Shi'ah* (A Descriptive Catalogue of Shia Books) (Beirut: Dar al-adwa, 1402/1983), vol. V, pp. 293–296. See also Rasool Ja'farian, *Mirza Bozorg Qa'im Maqam* (Tehran, 1380/2001), p. 82.

268 *Risalah-yi Jahadiyah-yi Saghir* (The Lesser Treatise on Jihad) (Tehran, n.d.), pp. 9–11, 11–13, 15–17, 18–21, 22–25, 31–32, 64–70. This text was originally much longer and was written in a very formal and difficult language and style that prevailed in the literary and legal circles of Najaf and Qum. Qa'im Maqam prepared a summary of the longer version, simplified its style and language, and published it in a lithograph edition in 76 pages in Tehran in 1234/1819. In the mid-1960s the late Jahangir Qa'im Maqami, Iran's military historian wrote a long introduction to the text and reprinted that summary in Tehran.

SELECT BIBLIOGRAPHY

Cole, Juan, *Sacred Space and Holy War: The Politics, Culture and History of Shi'ite Islam* (London: I. B. Tauris, 2002).

Esposito, John L., *Unholy War: Terror in the Name of Islam* (New York and Oxford: Oxford University Press, 2002).

Fadlullah, Shakh Muhammad Husayn, *al-Islam wa Mantiq al-Quwwah* (Islam and the Logic of Power) (Beirut, 1402/1981).

Hindi, Ihsan, *Ahkam al-Harb wa'l-Salam fi Dawlat al-Islam* (The Rules of War and Peace in an Islamic State) (Damascus: Darr al-Munir Publisher, 1414/1993).

Ismail, A., "Gardens of the Righteous: Sacred Space in Judaism, Christianity and Islam," *Cross Currents* 52:3 (Fall 2002).

Khadduri, Majid, *War and Peace in the Law of Islam*, new ed. (Baltimore: Lawbook Exchange, 2006).

Mohaghegh Damad, Mostafa, *Protection of Individuals in the Time of Armed Conflict under International and Islamic Laws* (New York: Global Scholarly Publications, 2005).

Mutahhari, Murtada, *Jihad*, 10th ed. (Tehran, 1998/1377).

Nasr, Seyyed Hossein, "The Spiritual Significance of Jihad, in *al-Serat*," vol. IX, no. 1, January 26, 2006, available at http://www.al-islam.org/al-serat/default.asp?url=interior-nasr.htm.

Nasr, Seyyed Vali Reza, *The Shi'a Revival* (New York: W. W. Norton, 2005).

Shah-Kazemi, Reza, "Recollecting the Spirit of Jihad," Sacred Web Publishing, available at http://www.sacredweb.com/online_articles/sw8_shahkazemi.html.

Tabataba'i, Sayyid Muhammad Husayn, *Shi'ite Islam*, Seyyed Hossein Nasr (ed. and trans.) (Albany: State University of New York Press, 1975).

Takim, Liyakat N., *The Heirs of the Prophet: Charisma and Religiosity in Shi'ite Islam* (Albany: State Universiy of New York Press, 2006).

7

Hinduism

Kaushik Roy

An amalgam of philosophy and religious practice, from about 1500 BCE/BC, what is now known as Hinduism progressively became the dominant way of life (dharma) for the people living between the Indus river and the Arakan Yomas Mountains. Numerous gods and goddesses are recognized within this tradition. Thus it is by no means a monotheistic religion. Nor is Hinduism bound up with a single authoritative text, heroic figure, or hierarchical structure. Likewise, it is nearly impossible to identify a single coherent body of beliefs within Hinduism.[1] *Under this name there coexist a multitude of different orientations, such as Brahmanism, Vedantism, Vaishnavism, Shakti, and Tantra. More a way of life than a settled doctrine, scholars have long questioned whether the concept of "religion" has any meaningful application to Hinduism. For some, this names an artificial construct that emerged under the combined influence of British colonial Orientalism, Western education, and indigenous reform movements.*[2] *There is much truth in this assertion.*

However, it cannot be denied that Brahmanism as it emerged at the dawn of Aryan civilization in South Asia constitutes the core of Hinduism even today. Both George K. Tanham and Stephen Peter Rosen accept that Hinduism is closely linked with the caste system that still operates in the subcontinent even after two millennia.[3] *And throughout its different historical periods Hinduism has been identified with certain key texts: first the* Vedas *and the* Bhagavad Gita*, which are from the Vedic and epic periods, and then the dharmasastra literature (of which the* Manava-Dharmasastra *is the most significant text), which took root during the Common Era. After 900 CE, the growth of Hinduism was shaped by different commentaries on the above-mentioned sources. Finally, from the fifteenth century onward, two epics in particular, the* Ramayana *and the* Mahabharata*, came to acquire special significance.*

Unlike the Greco-Roman world and Chinese civilization one cannot find any treatises particularly devoted to warfare in the ancient Indian tradition. For that matter, historical texts by the ancient Indians are also more or less absent. Thus, ancient Indian Sanskrit literature has no equivalent of Herodotus' *Histories*, no military autobiographies like Julius Caesar's *Conquest of Gaul* and the *Civil War*, no biographies like that of Tacitus'

Agricola, and no campaign accounts like Arrian's *Campaigns of Alexander*. Although the kings of ancient India generated a number of royal eulogies (*prashastis*, which, according to Romila Thapar, functioned as royal biographies and provide some fragmentary historical evidence of the time),[4] most historical accounts of early India were written by foreigners and Buddhist travelers from China. The absence of proper historical literature can be attributed to the fact that the ancient Indians had little interest in history. Another argument could be that the brahmin intellectuals (*acharyas*) of ancient India were not interested in mundane, day-to-day activities. Rather, they focused on metaphysical concepts that constitute the core of Hinduism, such as *brahman* (the Hindu cosmic order, and the creator of the universe), *dharma* (righteous code of conduct), *karma* (activities in life that influence the cycle of rebirth), and *moksha* (the liberation of the soul).

Recent Interpretations of Classical Sanskrit Literature

Most interpretations of Vedic[5] literature focus on the ritual aspects of Hinduism and to some extent their metaphysical content. However, there are some exceptions. Wendy Doniger and Brian K. Smith write that the Vedic priestly rituals are governed by the values associated with the warrior class. In the *Vedas*,[6] they assert, self-aggrandizement and dominance were unabashedly embraced and unashamedly displayed in both ritual and secular domains. Violence and power are represented as part and parcel of the natural order. They accept that Vedic ideology is brutal and materialistic.[7] However, Doniger and Smith do not analyze the objectives and mechanisms regarding the use of force for political purposes.

The prevalent assumption of Western political scientists and historians is that ancient India lacked any concept of power politics and strategic theory due to the overwhelming influence of Hindu fatalism, which did not encourage long-term planning. Due to the influence of the caste system it is argued that a strong state failed to emerge, and in the absence of a state, one could not think of a standing army. Consequently, without a standing army, there could be no decisive battles. At best, the ancient Indian segmented polities engaged in ritualized battles known as "flower wars," which according to Western scholars were accompanied by intrigues and treacheries.[8]

Some Indian authors have attempted to turn the so-called Indian military weakness into moral supremacy over "brutal" Western civilization. Sarva Daman Singh and V. R. Ramachandra Dikshitar claim that a moral code for conducting warfare emerged during the Vedic and Epic[9] periods. The net result was humane warfare in ancient India.[10]

In recent times, some authors have tried to find elements of just war theory in classical Hinduism. The twin Hindu concepts of *dharmayuddha* (righteous war or just war) and *kutayuddha* (unjust war, involving trickery or deceit) are somewhat equivalent to the Christian concepts of just and unjust war.[11] Torkel Brekke asserts that unlike the Western theoreticians, the Hindu writers took very little interest in the moral conditions underlying the inception of war (what the Western literature terms *jus ad bellum*), particularly the issue of right authority. He continues that this was because the Hindu theoreticians made no distinction between private duels and public violence, nor between internal and external enemies.[12]

Francis X. Clooney asserts that Hindu religious philosophy somewhat addresses the issue of *jus ad bellum* through its underlying supposition that righteous activities are context-specific. Thus the king's duty was to rule the realm, and in pursuit of this task only the king had the legal authority of the scriptures to inflict pain by using force during situations of emergency. In so doing, the ruler must be conscious of using force proportionately and only as a last resort.[13] We will see that the materials selected from certain Hindu texts of ancient India discuss the issue of just use of force by the ruler in pursuit of *rajadharma* (duties of the righteous king).

Geopolitics and Classical Indian Strategic Thought

One component of the *rajadharma* is waging *yuddha*, that is, organized violence by the king directed against external and internal enemies. The division between external warfare (interstate war) and internal war (intrastate or civil war, now in many cases referred to as counterinsurgency warfare or low-intensity conflict) is a Clausewitzian one. Conceptualizing warfare into these two watertight compartments is also due to the peculiar Eurocentric development where small nation-states, each with a homogeneous ethnic populace, emerged after the Thirty Years' War. However, in Indian history large agrarian bureaucratic empires were the norm.[14] These huge Indian political entities were comprised of diverse religious and linguistic groups. Further, differing physical environments in various regions of the subcontinent accelerated the genesis of subnationalities. As a result, the central Indian governments had throughout history been engaged primarily in internal security campaigns.

India is bounded in the north by the Himalayas, in the east by the Arakan Yoma Mountains and forest, in the west by the Thar Desert, and in the northwest by the Hindu Kush and Pamir Mountains. Historically, military expeditions into these regions were physically impossible and economically ruinous. Hence, it made no sense for the central governments located in the fertile north Indian plains to push into the outlying regions. Rather, India offered a tempting target for the Central Asian steppe nomads across the northwest frontier. Vis-à-vis these external enemies, Indian rulers were concerned mainly with defensive rather than offensive warfare. Internally, however, and despite India's cultural unity, for most of the historical period, the subcontinent was divided politically into various warring states that fought incessantly against each other.

War and peace constituted an indivisible entity for the Brahmin intellectuals (*acharyas*).[15] From the perspective of the *acharyas*, routine administrative activities involved waging war and making peace; hence these two activities were inextricably yoked together. In this sense war and peace were not separable either conceptually or in practice. And the rulers of the subcontinent realized that if internal rebellion broke out during an external invasion, the regime would be doomed. In addition, foreign support for internal rebels could also subvert the indigenous regime. Thus, Indian political theorists such as Kautilya[16] and Kamandaka[17] emphasized the interconnections between interstate war and internal rebellions and the possibility that support for the internal rebels by an external enemy might result in escalation to war with the hostile foreign polity. It is to

be noted that only in the post–Cold War era have Western political and military theorists begun to realize the complex interconnections between conventional warfare and
counterinsurgency campaigns. After the events of 9/11, a number of Western military
theoreticians began advocating that armed stateless marginal groups constitute the principal threat to the state.[18] Proponents of what is often called Fourth Generation Warfare
not only speak of insurgents as the main threat to the existing societies, but also hint at
an evolving Fifth Generation Warfare. This warfare visualizes a small group of individuals or even a single individual conducting large-scale devastating terrorist-like strikes.[19]
Interestingly, Kautilya elaborates on how trained individual secret agents could raise a
commotion in the enemy kingdom. The linkages between internal warfare and external
war and the primacy of the former type of warfare are elucidated in the primary sources
of ancient India below.

The Textual Sources

Ancient India is typically defined as the period between the fall of the Indus Valley civilization (1500 BCE) partly due to the migration of the Aryans and the invasion of the Turks
during the ninth century CE. Some historians also categorize the period between sixth
and ninth centuries CE as the early medieval period. For our purposes, the literature of
ancient India can be categorized into three groups: Vedic literature, *dharmasastras*, and
works on *nitisastra*[20] or *arthasastra* traditions.[21] In the sections below, I have selected
passages from texts belonging to each genre. Since our concern here is the relationship
between warfare and religion, more importance is given to the *niti/arthasastra* literature
for the simple fact that it concentrates more on *yuddha/vigraha*[22] than the *dharmasastra*
literature. For the latter, warfare is of secondary importance.

While the *Bhagavad Gita* (henceforth *BG*) belongs to the genre of Vedic literature,[23]
Manu's *Manava-Dharmasastra* (henceforth *MD*) belongs to the *dharmasastra* literature.
And works by Kautilya and Kamandaka belong to the corpus of *niti/arthasastra* literature. The traditional Western division of secular and religious literature is not applicable
in the case of ancient Sanskrit literary works. While the Vedic literature emphasizes the
rituals, it also throws light on warfare between the Aryans and the non-Aryans and internal warfare between various Aryan tribes. The *dharmasastra* works provide insight not
only on the social, cultural, and religious customs but also on military laws. And the works
of *niti* literature, while paying lip service to *dharma*, concern themselves primarily with
statecraft, a context in which the army and warfare play a central role. Both Kautilya's
Arthaśāstra and Kamandaka's *Nitisara* are divided into several books and chapters. In
Kautilya and Kamandaka's case, several themes are mixed up in each of the books and in
some cases even within a chapter. In selections from these two texts that are presented
here, the original structure of the prose is maintained in order to preserve the originality
of these two authors. No separate work on military affairs exists because in the theoretical
paradigm of the *acharyas*, warfare is part and parcel of statecraft and statecraft is considered a component of *rajadharma*. However, there are some exceptions. The first military
technical treatise to emerge in ancient India was the *Dhanurveda* (science of archery), but
it has been lost. The first military technical treatise to survive is *Matanga-Lila* (Science of

War Elephants), which was composed in the beginning of the early Middle Ages (approximately 900 CE).

The primary source materials presented below are grouped into five sections arranged chronologically. The first contains selections from the *BG*. This section shows the duties of a warrior during *dharmayuddha*, in the context of an intra-Aryan struggle around 1200 BCE, and the issue of civil supremacy over the military. Excerpts from Kautilya's *Arthaśāstra* are presented in the second section, which displays *kutayuddha* in the context of an evolving large empire (ca. 300 BCE). Selections from the *MD* appear in the third section, which shows the swing of the pendulum back to *dharmayuddha* during the beginning of the Common Era. Manu's *MD* was on the one hand a Brahmanical reaction against the rise of new religions (Buddhism and Jainism) and on the other a critique of Kautilya's seemingly amoral approach to statecraft. This chapter's fourth section deals with Kamandaka's *Nitisara*. During the fifth or sixth century CE, Kamandaka realized that Manu's idealistic norms of warfare were inoperable, especially as nomadic tribes from the northwest frontier threatened the subcontinent. Thus, Kamandaka's *Nitisara* reverts back to Kautilya's *kutayuddha*, yet without totally neglecting the influence of the Brahmanical reaction. Hence, Kamandaka offers an attenuated version of Kautilya's *kutayuddha*. Finally, in a fifth section, the writings of Mohandas Gandhi are presented in their relation to the broader Hindu tradition on violence and warfare.

It is difficult if not impossible to date classical Hindu texts.[24] The identity of their authors is shrouded in mystery. While we know something about the background of Thucydides and Xenophon, we know almost nothing about the biographical details of Manu and Kamandaka. We do not even know the name of the author (or authors, if indeed there were several) of the *BG*. Concerning the *MD*, Doniger and Smith write that "Manu, like virtually all other religious texts, masks its true authorship and indeed must do so in order to posit effectively its own claims to transcendentally based and absolute truth. For religious discourse is always – and necessarily, if disingenuously – represented as anonymous (or as the direct and indirect 'word of God,' or the dictates of Manu, the 'first man,' either of which comes to the same thing."[25] This assertion could also be applied in the case of other ancient Indian texts. In fact, the *BG* is regarded as the dialogue between the great warrior Arjuna and the god Krishna. The fact that God himself gives advice to the warrior further raises the status of the text. More generally, in Hindu philosophy, the individual is subordinated to *brahman*, the collective will and ultimate reality. For this reason it is always the text and not the author that matters.

Regarding the nature of the texts, experts on Sanskrit literature are divided into two camps. Emphasizing textual criticism, one group argues that each text comprises several layers that were added by various nameless and faceless *rishis* (Hindu saints) over several centuries. The other camp argues, by contrast, that each text was authored by a genius or at best a gifted individual who was assisted by other writers. Then, during the process of oral transmission as well as the copying of the manuscripts, later authors and commentators contributed various interpolations. The contrast between these textual approaches is mentioned in the editor's comment, which usually appears as an introduction to the section preceding the text. By comparing and contrasting these texts within the evolving historical scenario, the core message of each can be clarified. Finally, it bears mention how in Sanskrit significant words such as *dharma*[26] and *raja* (Hindu king) have a range of meanings that are to be be understood in each particular case by placing the text in its historical context.

Key Themes in the Texts Selected

The *Rig Veda* provides us with fragmentary evidence about the progress of the Aryans in India from 1200 BCE onward, their internal divisions, and their wars with the Dravidians.[27] The wars between the Aryans and the Dravidians, two groups who had strong racial and cultural differences, were conducted with great brutality.

Warfare during the *Rig Vedic* period consisted mainly in cattle-lifting raids; during an enemy raid, the people and livestock took refuge in the *puras/durgas* (fortifications). However, in the later Vedic era, the nature of warfare was transformed. The armies of this period were comprised of foot soldiers equipped with spears, swords, and shields; warriors equipped with bows and arrows also fought from chariots. The *Mahabharata* portrays two armies (comprised of chariots and foot soldiers) fighting a decisive set piece for eighteen days until the army of the Kauravas was completely destroyed.[28] This challenges Victor Davis Hanson's assertion that the decisive battle was an invention of the Greek *polis* around 500 BCE, which with the passage of time became the "Western way" of warfare.[29]

The Mahabharata War occurred sometime between 1000 BCE and 850 BCE in the western Ganges Valley, in the land of the Kurus where the dominant form of political authority was Kshatriya[30] chiefship. Sorrow over the Battle of Kurukshetra as portrayed in the *Mahabharata* was due not merely to the death of kinsmen, but also to the death of the political order based on Kshatriya chiefships.[31] The war thus represented the end of an epoch and the beginning of the monarchical state in the middle Ganges Valley.

The *Mahabharata* epic probably came into existence between 500 and 300 BCE and is an example of hyperbole deliberately used by the poet to give the readers an idea of the immensity of the war. Mixing myth and history, the heroes of the epic are romanticized and mythicized by describing them as possessing superhuman/supernatural powers. The core of the *Mahabharata* is derived from Puru-Kuru war ballads, aboriginal myths, and Yadu sagas.[32]

Bhisma, one of the Kaurava warlords in the *Mahabharata*, explains that the earliest society was a utopian one. In the remote past there were neither laws nor kings nor social distinctions, and so people protected one another out of righteousness. However, with the slow decline of such virtues, laws were required and authority became vested in the *raja*. Hence emerged the concept of *rajadharma*, in which the notion of *danda* (coercive authority) became important.[33]

The word *dharma* is derived from *dhri*, which signifies how the cosmic order (including unchanging social relations) is upheld and sustained. During the Vedic period, the moral component of the term *rita* (representing order in both the cosmic world and natural world), writes D. Devahuti, was absorbed into the *dharma*. *Dharma* in Vedic literature is considered to be the moral law for inanimate objects and natural phenomena, an ethical and social standard of behavior for the people. Later, the term reflected the code of public duties for the king. The *Satapatha Brahmana* (composed around

900 BCE) equates *dharma* with truth. The *Upanishads* (ca. 700–600 BCE)[34] proclaim that with the help of *dharma*, even the weak can rule over the strong. The *Aitareya Brahmana* states that the king is the protector of *dharma*.[35] Bhisma, while explaining the emergence of kingship, says that in the absence of the king, the laws of the jungle prevail. Under the condition of *matsanyaya* (the chaos and political instability that result from the absence of a strong ruler), there is no protection of life, property, or maintenance of *dharma*.[36] Bhisma says that without a king, both public and private property will be threatened.[37] Kautilya, Manu, and Kamandaka utilize the concept of *matsanyaya* to justify the emergence of a strong ruler who, by wielding *danda*, will establish a rule of law in the land.

The *danda* represents not merely the apparatus for physical coercion but also the sanction of coercion and authority. *Danda* in ancient Indian literature is frequently referred to as the "rod of chastisement." Punishment is an important aspect of *danda* as the absence of *raja* raises the threat of anarchy. The killing of a king is not permissible as he is equated with the instrument of god on earth. It is further argued that in accordance with the *karma* doctrine, the king's fate after his death will take care of his unrighteousness and the subjects should therefore never take the law into their own hands. This notwithstanding, the banishment of a king was sometimes alluded to. Simultaneously, the *raja* is also warned that oppression of the *prajas* (subjects in the *rashtra* [polity]) might lead to rebellion.[38] However, the king, says Bhisma, is allowed to take one-sixth of the income of his subjects as a tribute for meeting the expenses of protecting them and could also appropriate the wealth of the rebellious subjects.[39]

V. M. Mohanraj argues that in the *BG* the king is equated with God to buttress the emerging monarchical states that slowly but steadily supplanted the tribal communes.[40] From an opposite point, Angelika Malinar asserts that in the *BG* Krishna is depicted as the highest god and the wielder of yogic power over nature. And this negates in Hinduism any concept of kingship that portrays the king as god. To my mind, Malinar's position is more acceptable. The king is made subordinate to the highest god as the god's earthly representative.[41] Torkel Brekke sums this up by arguing that the ancient Indian theory of kingship is somewhat ambivalent. There is an opposition between the view of kingship as divine, on one hand, and as a purely practical institution, on the other hand.[42] During the Later Vedic Age, the notions of divinity associated with the *raja* resulted in the transition to kingship. The amalgamation of divinity and the state structure in the monarchical form in the post-Vedic Age provided the *raja* with power qualitatively different from the *rajan* in the Rig Vedic Age. Then, a sizable chunk of the revenue went toward supporting the administrative infrastructure and the *bala* (army). Due to the emergence of the standing army, from 400 BCE, the sporadic cattle raids were replaced by systematic campaigns for conquest.[43] Overall, the message of *BG* is that the king should pursue his *dharma* by indulging in righteous warfare,[44] without considering the gains or losses to be accrued from such pursuits.

In general, the ancient Hindu theoreticians emphasize good governance. G. P. Singh claims that the word *raja* originated from *ranj* (one who pleases or satisfies the people). Surendra Nath Mittal says that the ancient Indian polity was based on the following trinity: sage, ruler, and the people.[45] The *Mahabharata* puts much stress on *rajadharma*, which means protection of the people of the *rashtra*.[46] Kautilya, Kamandaka, and Manu emphasize this point. For the ruthless Kautilya, the *dharma* of a king is to protect his kingship and kingdom by all possible means.[47] A useful explanatory parallel can be found in Aristotle's *Politics*, which differentiates between kingship and tyranny: while kings are motivated by the desire for the good of the subjects, tyrants are driven by lust for wealth and personal aggrandizement.[48] To an extent, Kautilya's *vijigīṣu* (ideal conqueror of the four corners of the earth) represents a kind of benevolent tyrant.

The first empire in India was established by the Nanda Dynasty (400–320 BCE). Its political economy was based on agriculture rather than pastoralism.[49] The Nandas were subsequently replaced by the Mauryas. At present, historians are divided into two camps regarding the nature of empires in ancient India. One side (especially Burton Stein, Aidan Southall, and Andre Wink[50]) holds that until the rise of the British Empire in the eighteenth century all of the polities in South Asia were segmented states. The other side (e.g., R. K. Mookerji and D. N. Jha[51]) claims that ancient India contained central-ized bureaucratic polities. Romila Thapar takes a middle position and asserts that the Maurya Empire was a quasi-centralized entity consisting of a metropolitan region/core, semi-periphery, and a periphery. While the control of the central government over the metropolitan/core region (Magadha) was intense and direct, over the semi-periphery central control was indirect. And over the periphery, which was most distant from the center, the emperor exercised a merely ritual *de jure* power. While Kautilya operated in the Maurya Age, Kamandaka belonged to the Gupta era. The post-Maurya states were weaker and the landowners emerged as powerful intermediaries between the distant and weakening central government and rural society.[52] A uniform administration was absent in these polities. The post-Maurya supraregional polities comprised several kingdoms held together under a loose hegemony.[53] Hence, Kamandaka gives more space to the necessity of handling the vassals by the *vijigīṣu* while waging both counterinsurgency campaigns and campaigns of external conquests.

Singh claims that the roots of the *maṇḍala* (circle of states) theory of statecraft could be traced back to the *Mahabharata*. The *maṇḍala* theory is primarily about the balance of power in the interstate system,[54] and it reached perfection under Kautilya, becoming his greatest legacy to Indian strategic theory. Although Manu disagrees with Kautilya regarding the role of *kutayuddha*, while writing about *rajadharma*, Manu borrows from Kautilya's *Arthaśāstra*.[55] The *Arthaśāstra* of Kautilya is referred to and quoted by numerous writers (such as Kamandaka, Bana, and Dandin) and in various works from the late third century CE until the eighth century CE, like the *Kamasutra* and *Panchatantra*. The *Panchatantra*, which was composed between the third and sixth century CE, pays homage to Kautilya as one of the greatest expounders of *rajadharma*. However, Bana, the author of *Harshacharita*, dislikes Kautilya's advocacy that the ends justify the means.[56] For both Kautilya and Kamandaka, the *maṇḍala* was comprised of twelve states. It is an arbitrary number to represent the various possible relationships in diplomatic affairs. The grand strategy propagated by Kautilya, Manu, and Kamandaka is that the objective of *vijigīṣu* is conquest in all directions (*digvijaya*), by either war or diplomatic coercion or both.[57]

A holy war for spreading the Hindu religion is an idea that is absent in classical Hindu literature. War in defense of religion was similarly absent for the most part, although a case can be made that some texts justify warfare to uphold *dharma* (which comprises both religion and the social structure based on *chaturvarna*[58]). Such wars are categorized as *dharmayuddha*. Broadly, the *acharyas* when writing on warfare focus on grand strategic aspects (or what in modern terminology is known as national security policy). Grand strategy could be defined as the amalgam of military, economic, diplomatic, and political assets mobilized for the security of a state. The *acharyas* highlight the relationship between the ruler and the army, the use of force and diplomacy, economic coercion, role of strategic intelligence, and so on.

Kautilya urges the importance of a well-paid standing army. The Mauryan standing army was larger than that of the Nandas. A large part of the state's revenue went toward supporting the Mauryan bureaucracy and the war machine.[59] Manu emphasizes the role of logistics in warfare. Kautilya, Manu, and Kamandaka note the importance of training and organizing the soldiers in *vyuhas*[60] while conducting battles. Hence, Stephen Peter Rosen's view that ancient Indian warfare was a disorganized melee[61] cannot be sustained.

It is true, however, that the ancient Indian *acharyas* did fail to give proper attention to the tactical-technical aspects of warfare. Over time this eroded the external security of the Indian states. In the Vedic era, the Hindu army consisted of foot soldiers and chariot warriors. During the Nanda Age, the *chaturanga bala*[62] emerged.[63] However, Kautilya overly emphasizes the role of elephants to the discredit of a mounted archery. One of the principal factors behind the success of the Sakas, Parthians, and the Kushanas was their better cavalry, their use of composite bows, and better bridles and saddles. Nevertheless, both Kautilya and Kamandaka continue to give importance to war chariots, which had already been proved obsolete during the Battle of Hydaspes in 326 BCE.[64]

Violence versus Nonviolence in Hindu Discourse

None of the Hindu theorists advocates nonviolence. Rather, they advocate various types of militarism: the *dharmayuddha* of Manu represents a moderate form of militarism, and the *kutayuddha* of Kautilya represents an aggressive militarism. After Kamandaka, ancient India did not generate any original literature on warfare and statecraft. This was probably because no pan-Indian Hindu empires emerged in India after 700 CE. The *Panchatantra* and the *Hitopadesa*, with the help of animal stories, and the *Kathasaritsagara*, through the aid of stories revolving around man-woman relationships, offer some ad hoc comments on statecraft but not much on warfare. From the tenth century onward, Islamic rule was established and Persian replaced Sanskrit as the court language. A few texts were written in Persian by Hindu chieftains who had entered the Mughal service. In the regional Hindu kingdoms, which were vassal states of the Mughal emperor, the *Ramayana* and the *Mahabharata* were translated into vernacular languages such as Bengali.

Popular vernacular literature is not included in this chapter as it was mostly concerned with social issues. The only exceptions to the genre of vernacular literature are *Sivabhrata*, an epic poem in Marathi that eulogizes the rise of Shivaji, the Maratha warlord in Maharashtra against the Mughals in late seventeenth century, and the *Maharashtra Purana*, a Bengali poem that depicts the chaos following the Maratha invasion of Bengal during the first half of the eighteenth century. The Mughal emperors (Akbar and Shah

Jahan, especially) had some of the Hindu classical texts translated, for instance, the *Mahabharata*, *Atharva Veda*, and *Upanishads*.[65] Since under Islamic and British rule, autonomous and expanding Hindu empires did not exist, Hindu texts on power-politics were also absent.

Hinduism witnessed a spurt of creative writings on warfare and peace at the beginning of the twentieth century. This was because at that time, the Hindus participated in the popular anticolonial movement directed against the British *Raj*. The last section has a selection of Mohandas Karamchand Gandhi's writings. It may seem odd to include Gandhi in an anthology dealing with the theorists of warfare. The logic behind the inclusion of the Mahatma's texts is to show the swing of the pendulum from *himsa* (jealousy and violence) to *ahimsa* (nonviolent response to injury). After 1947, political leaders of different parties reappropriated the traditional texts to justify their policies. Jawaharlal Nehru, the first Prime Minister of independent India, asserted that the core concept of his foreign policy, *Panchsheel*, the five holy principles, was derived from the pacific tendencies in Hinduism, particularly the principles of nonviolence that he attributed to Maurya Emperor Asoka (ruler from 268 to 233 BCE). Some outside observers have maintained in contradistinction to this view that the *realpolitik* of Nehru's diplomacy was in fact shaped by the concept of *kutayuddha*.[66]

Over the last decade a right-wing Hindu political organization known as the Bharatiya Janata Party (henceforth BJP) has demanded that India must increase its stockpile of nuclear weapons. The BJP justifies this policy by appealing to ancient texts, especially the *Mahabharata*, on grounds that such weapons are necessary to secure the safety of the Hindu realm. The BJP points out that Pakistan, besides possessing nuclear weapons, has also been conducting a *jihad*[67] in Kashmir. In response, the BJP leadership maintains that India needs "Hindu" bombs to safeguard the "Hindu *rashtra*" (state) from Pakistan. Moreover, in 2002, the BJP-led government initiated a secret project of using Kautilya's magnum opus *Arthaśāstra* as an ideological basis for conducting scientific research in the fields of chemical and biological warfare. However, for most of the time, the BJP and the *sadhu*s (Hindu holy men) associated with its sister organization, the Vishwa Hindu Parishad, have made selective use of Hindu texts to encourage communal riots against the Muslims of India. The BJP's objective is to use the insights from Classical Sanskrit texts in order to build Hindu world order (*Hindutva*). The hardliners within BJP concentrate their attention on harnessing Hinduism to the "nation"-building task through an emphasis on *shuddhi* (purification in the sense of conversion or reconversion to Hinduism). On the whole they show only marginal interest in conceptualizing warfare.[68] For this reason the incitement of communal riots against Muslims in India lies outside the scope of the present chapter.

Arjuna, the Reluctant Warrior: *Karma* Doctrine and the Beginnings of Military Professionalism

The *Bhagavad Gita* was first translated into English in 1795 and from this time until 2007, numerous versions have been published. In general, the interpreters of the *BG* are divided into two camps. Following the methods of textual criticism, one group argues that the text actually has several different layers: an epic layer, a theistic layer (Krishna's doctrine), and a nontheistic layer (Samkhya-Yoga, monism), and these layers emerged at different times. Another group of scholars, by contrast, hold that the text should be treated holistically. The reconstruction of textual history depends on internal criteria for detecting inconsistencies in the text such as changes in terminology, contradictory doctrines, and inconsistent use of personal pronouns. In reality, the methodology of the textual criticism depends mostly on the assumptions of the analysts. For instance, Malinar believes that the text-critical historical perspective should not be regarded as an alternative to the holistic view of the extant text; rather, it is best viewed as a helpful complement.[69] From our perspective, the core message in *BG* is the advice by charioteer-cum-God Krishna to the Pandava warlord Arjuna.

According to Mohanraj, the *BG* is an independent work that was probably composed around 400 BCE; later it was incorporated within the *Mahabharata*.[70] Taking the opposing viewpoint, Malinar asserts that the *BG* was composed not independently of this epic but in relation to it and even for it. She continues that the *BG* "became part of the epic in the course of its own textual history."[71] On her understanding, the *BG* emerged between the beginning of the Common Era and the second century CE.[72]

The *BG* represents a dialogue between Krishna and Arjuna, which is set against the background of the Mahabharata War. While Juan Mascaro provides a spiritual translation of the hymns of *BG*, Marxist scholars such as Mohanraj, Irfan Habib, V. Thakur, and Bandopadhyaya offer a materialistic interpretation of the same text. Mascaro asserts that Sanskrit literature is a sort of romantic literature interwoven with idealism and practical wisdom, and with a passionate longing for spiritual vision. The Mahabharata War represented, for Mascaro and Gandhi, the struggle between the forces of good and evil represented by the Pandavas[73] and the Kauravas.[74] Mascaro and Gandhi held that the *BG* represents the soul's great inner struggle against passions and desires. Victory is difficult, and sometimes, in the face of the body's demise, one hears of the soul's temptation to give up the struggle. It is made clear, however, that death is not the last word; it does not mean the end of everything.[75]

According to B. A. van Nooten, Hindu eschatology combines the doctrine of rebirth with the doctrine of *dharma*. *Karma* is the inexorable law that spans both life and death, operating from one lifetime to another, rewarding the just and making the evil suffer. On this account, a martial spirit pervades *Mahabharata*. It also illustrates how seemingly grand and magnificent human endeavors turn out to be astoundingly insignificant in the perspective of eternity.[76]

One scholar asserts that in the *Ramayana*, which is one of the epics, the afterlife is represented simply as the abode of death.[77] It is the case, however, that the *Upanishads* (composed roughly around 700–600 BCE) do discuss the transmigration of souls. In this connection we find Krishna in the *BG* (chapter 2, verses 11–38) commenting on the theory of *karma*. Later, in chapter 18, in hymns 41–44, Krishna elaborates the caste system of Vedic society. Basically, the theory is that after their bodily death all beings are born again in this world through their souls. This is possible because the soul is indestructible. The status of each person on rebirth is determined by the deeds performed in his or her previous life. Thus, an endless cycle of births and rebirths are established with souls taking one body after another.

Marxist scholars have often perceived a linkage between the exploitation of the Sudras (who were mostly agriculturists and comprise the lowest caste) by higher castes and the *karma* theory. Habib and Thakur assert that transmigration is a response to the immobility of the caste society where birth mattered most. One's position in the hereditary caste order could now be justified on the basis of one's own merit or fault in the previous life, that is, *karma*.[78] Bandopadhyaya asserts that unlike Greco-Roman society, the ruling class in ancient India did not use "raw" force to maintain internal order. Rather, the Brahmin–Kshatriya alliance used religion in a strategic manner to avoid peasant rebellions. And the principal component employed for establishing this hegemony of the ruling class was the *karma* theory. The origins of the *karma* doctrine in his view could be traced back to the *Purusha Sukta*[79] ideology of the *Rig Veda*. According to the *Purusha Sukta* ideology, the four hierarchical *varna*s in society were created by the original *Purusha*. The concept of the *brahman* of *Advaita Vedanta* as the creator and just governor of the universe, including the prevailing social order as developed in the *Upanishads*, is a modification of the *Purusha Sukta* ideology. The *Advaita Vedanta* thus takes Brahma,[80] the supreme creator, to be likewise the just distributor of wealth. The producing class of laborers is accordingly urged to remain steadfast in its occupational duties in a spirit of renunciation without any desire for improvement of their material conditions. Attachment to worldly affairs is considered to be false knowledge, and false knowledge leads to endless rebirths. The *BG* merely refined this ideology.[81]

In the *BG*, the blind Kaurava king Dhritarashtra asks his minister Sanjaya to tell him what is happening on the battlefield of Kurukshetra. Sanjaya repeats verbatim the dialogue between Krishna and Arjuna. The dialogue between Arjuna, the most famous warrior on the side of the Pandavas and Krishna, took place on the first day of the war before combat started. Just before the battle, Arjuna said to Krishna that he wanted to see all those who had come to participate in the battle. Krishna then drove forward and pulled up the chariot between the two armies. Arjuna then looked forward and saw his kith and kin armed to the teeth ready to kill and be killed. He was overcome with grief and despair. With tears in his eyes, Arjuna said that fratricide was repugnant to him and he did not want wealth and kingdom at the cost of killing his kinsmen. It seems that Arjuna was unnerved by the sight.[82]

Then, Krishna insists on Arjuna's duty as a Kshatriya. A Kshatriya who dies fighting attains *veeraswarga* (the right to go to heaven). Further, Krishna emphasizes the *karma* theory. According to this theory, the soul is immortal. Hence after the destruction of the body, the soul remains. Thus, in reality nobody dies. While the soul is immortal, the body is transient. Also one who is born is bound to die one day (i.e., destruction of the body and not the soul) and is bound to be reborn again. Krishna highlights to Arjuna *nishkamakarm* (doing one's duty selflessly). The right way of doing *karma* is to perform one's duty without thinking about the possible rewards in order to maintain the social structure. Krishna continues that if Arjuna fights with detachment, that is, he performs his *karma*, he would not commit any sin.[83] In contrast, the *Iliad* tells us that rage and revenge motivated Achilles to fight Hector.[84]

Narasingha P. Sil writes that Pythagoras and his followers believed in the immortality and transmigration of the human soul. They also accepted that the universe as a whole was a living organism. The cosmos was believed to be surrounded by a large quantity of air or breath permeating and providing life to the whole. Hence, according to Pythagoras, the breath or life of man and the breath and life of the infinite and divine universe were essentially the same. Before Pythagoras, the *Chandogya Upanishad* emphasized the identification of the microscopic *atman* (self, soul) with the macrocosmic *brahman* (supreme reality). The *Rig Veda* anticipated Pythagoras' assertion that the world is a divine and single whole. Thus, concludes Sil, both the early Greek and the Indian worldviews reflect an astonishing similarity in maintaining that a single substance – *arche* or *brahman* – forms the basis of all existence.[85] In the Platonic dialogue *Alcibiades I*, Socrates comments that a leader should follow the right course in spite of unwanted consequences. Applying the terminology of later moral philosophy, H. Syse identifies this perspective as a deontological approach to ethics.[86] Socrates makes clear that a war leader's actions have consequences for his soul and not merely for his body. A successful statesman or a king has a great soul that a decaying body can never conquer. Here, one finds parallels with the Hindu *atman* or *brahman* in Krishna's message.

Malinar writes that the *BG* is an attempt at balancing the contradictory claims of different levels of *dharma*. On this interpretation, Arjuna was torn between the kingship law (*kuladharma*), which demands that he should not kill his relatives, and the code of the Kshatriya Hindu warrior community, which demands that as a warrior he should never yield to the enemy on the battlefield. The *BG* also maintains a balance between the value of asceticism and social duties.[87] Applying categories from Western moral philosophy, J. N. Mohanty observes how something like the distinction between consequentialism (with its appeal to human psychology) and deontology (with its appeal to a metaphysics of the self in contradiction to nature) is reflected in Krishna's words and action within the *BG*.[88] Along these lines, N. Allen criticizes Krishna for ready acceptance of the warrior's duty to fight and not leaving any scope for conscientious objectors, and his failure to problematize the overall justice of the cause for which the warriors commit themselves to fight.[89]

Actually, this is arguably the strongpoint of the *BG*'s message. The *BG* does not allow any particular warrior (Arjuna) or even warrior community (Kshatriyas) the scope to challenge the ruler's decision to start a war. The right to decide whether a war is strategically and ethically correct falls exclusively within the purview of the *raja*. A Kshatriya has no say in this matter. However, once the decision to start *dharmayuddha* is taken, the issue of how to conduct the war depends on the Kshatriya. One of the chief components of modern military professionalism is subordination of the military to the political decision-making process. A professional military obeys the politician's right to start or stop a war, but once war is under way politicians do not engage in micro-management of the military operations.[90] On the other hand, a professional military is allowed autonomy in conducting warfare. This is the stuff of a modern professional civil-military relationship that has been developed in Western theory and practice over the last two centuries,[91] but which was already articulated in the *BG* over two thousand years ago.

In ancient India, military coups, unlike what was the case in the Roman Empire, were quite uncommon. While in the history of the Roman Empire, general after general became Caesar, in ancient Hindu India only one *senapati* (general/commander of the army), Pushyamitra Sunga, conducted a coup – which was against Brihadratha, the last Maurya Emperor in 187 BCE, thereby establishing the Sunga dynasty. Military coups were marginal in ancient Indian history because of the genesis of a professional civil-military relationship and a clear division of labor for the various *varnas* as propounded in the *BG*. Hence, Stephen P. Cohen's assertion that the British introduced civilian supremacy over the military in India after the eighteenth century needs to be challenged.[92]

From: *The Bhagavad Gita*, Chapter I[93]

Dhrita-rashtra

1. On the field of Truth, on the battle-field of life, what came to pass, Sanjaya, when my sons and their warriors faced those of my brother Pandu?

Sanjaya

2. When your son Duryodhana saw the armies of the sons of Pandu he went to his master*... and spoke to him these words:

3. See there, master, the vast army of the Pandavas well set in order of battle by the son of Drupada, your own wise pupil.

4. There can we see heroic warriors, powerful archers, as great as Bhima and Arjuna in battle....

6. ... See them all in their chariots of war....

12. To encourage Duryodhana, Bhisma, the glorious old warrior of the Kurus, sounded loud his war-cry like the roar of a lion, and then blew his far-sounding conch-shell.

13. Then the rumbling of war drums, the stirring sound of cymbals and trumpets, and the roaring of conch-shells and horns filled the sky with a fearful thunder....

19. At that fearful sound the earth and the heavens trembled, and also trembled the hearts of Duryodhana and his warriors.

20. The flight of arrows was now to begin....

Sanjaya

28. ... When Arjuna thus saw his kinsmen face to face in both lines of battle, he was overcome by grief and despair and thus he spoke with a sinking heart.

Arjuna

31. ... I cannot foresee any glory if I kill my own kinsmen in the sacrifice of battle....

34. Facing us in the field of battle are teachers, fathers and sons; grandsons [and] grandfathers....

35. These I do not wish to slay, even if I myself am slain....

From: *The Bhagavad Gita*, Chapter II[94]

Sanjaya

9. When Arjuna the great warrior had thus unburdened his heart, "I will not fight, Krishna," he said, and then fell silent....

---

* Instead of master, a better Indian term is *acharya*. This term refers to old scholar-warriors who trained and advised the princes in the theory and practice of warfare.

Krishna

11.... The wise grieve not for those who live; and they grieve not for those who die – for life and death shall pass away....

17. Interwoven in his creation, the Spirit is beyond destruction....

18. For beyond time he dwells in these bodies, though these bodies have an end in their time; but he remains immeasurable, immortal. Therefore, great warrior, carry on thy fight....

22. As a man leaves an old garment and puts on one that is new, the Spirit leaves his mortal body and then puts on one that is new....

31. Think thou also of thy duty and do not waver. There is no greater good for a warrior than to fight in a righteous war.

32. There is a war that opens the doors of heaven, Arjuna! Happy the warriors whose fate is to fight such war.

33. But to forgo this fight for righteousness is to forgo thy duty and honor: is to fall into transgression.

34. Men will tell of thy dishonor both now and in times to come. And to a man who is in honor, dishonor is more than death.

35. The great warriors will say that thou hast run from the battle through fear; and those who thought great things of thee will speak of thee in scorn....

37. In death thy glory in heaven, in victory thy glory on earth. Arise therefore, Arjuna, with thy soul ready to fight.

38. Prepare for war with peace in thy soul. Be in peace in pleasure and pain, in gain and in loss, in victory or in the loss of a battle. In this peace there is no sin....

47. Set thy heart upon thy work, but never on its reward. Work not for a reward; but never cease to do thy work.

From: *The Bhagavad Gita*, Chapter III[95]

Krishna

3. In this world there are two roads of perfection, as I told thee before, O prince without sin: Jñana Yoga,* the path of wisdom of the Sankhyas, and Karma Yoga, the path of action of the Yogis.

4. Not by refraining from action does man attain freedom from action. Not by mere renunciation does he attain supreme perfection....

6. He who withdraws himself from actions, but ponders on their pleasures in his heart, he is under a delusion and is a false follower of the Path.

7. But great is the man who, free from attachments, and with a mind ruling its powers in harmony, works on the path of Karma Yoga, the path of consecrated action.

---

* Performing certain *yogic* practice (involving austerity and rituals) by detaching oneself from mundane activities.

8. Action is greater than inaction: perform therefore thy task in life. Even the life of the body could not be if there were no action. . . .

19. In liberty from the bonds of attachment, do thou therefore the work to be done: for the man whose work is pure attains indeed the Supreme. . . .

24. If ever my work had an end, these worlds would end in destruction, confusion would reign within all: this would be the death of all beings. . . .

30. . . . Be free from vain hopes and selfish thoughts, and with inner peace fight thou thy fight. . . .

34. Hate and lust for things of nature have their roots in man's lower nature. Let him not fall under their power: they are the two enemies in his path.

From: *The Bhagavad Gita*, Chapter 5[96]

Krishna

2. Both renunciation and holy work are a path to the Supreme; but better than surrender of work is the Yoga of holy work.[*]

From: *The Bhagavad Gita*, Chapter 6[97]

Krishna

35. The mind is indeed restless, Arjuna: it is indeed hard to train. But by constant practice and by freedom from passions the mind in truth can be trained.

From: *The Bhagavad Gita*, Chapter 8[98]

Krishna

3. Brahman is the Supreme, the Eternal. Atman is his Spirit in man. Karma is the force of creation, wherefrom all things have their life.

From: *The Bhagavad Gita*, Chapter 10[99]

Krishna

34. I am death that carries off all things, and I am the source of things to come. . . .

From: *The Bhagavad Gita*, Chapter 11[100]

Krishna

33. Arise therefore! Win thy glory, conquer thine enemies, and enjoy thy kingdom. Through the fate of their Karma I have doomed them to die: be thou merely the means of my work.

---

[*] Performing righteous work is *karmayoga*. *Karmayoga* means performance of *karma*. It is superior to the renunciation of work.

From: *The Bhagavad Gita*, Chapter 18[101]

Krishna

8. And he who abandons his duty because he has fear of pain, his surrender is … impure, and in truth he has no reward.

9. But he who does holy work, Arjuna, because it ought to be done, and surrenders selfishness and thought of reward, his work is pure, and is peace.…

17. He who is free from the chains of selfishness, and whose mind is free from any ill-will, even if he kills all these warriors he kills them not and he is free.…

41. The works of Brahmins, Kshatriyas, Vaisyas and Sudras are different, in harmony with the three powers of their born nature.

42. The works of a Brahmin are peace; self-harmony, austerity and purity; loving-forgiveness and righteousness; vision and wisdom and faith.

43. These are the works of a Kshatriya: a heroic mind, inner fire, constancy, resourcefulness, courage in battle, generosity and noble leadership.

44. Trade, agriculture and the rearing of cattle is the work of a Vaisya. And the work of the Sudra is service.*…

59. If thou wilt not fight thy battle of life because in selfishness thou art afraid of the battle, thy resolution is in vain: nature will compel thee.

Kautilya's *Kutayuddha* and Empire Building

A debate regarding the authorship and dating of Kautilya's *Arthaśāstra* still rages among scholars. Ashok S. Chousalkar and Narasingha Sil assert that the *Arthaśāstra* was composed by Kautilya around the fourth century BCE.[102] Another school of thought asserts that the *Arthaśāstra* was composed around the third century CE[103] and was the creation of many individuals over several centuries.

The view that Kautilya the Maurya Minister did not compose the *Arthaśāstra* is based on the argument that *Arthaśāstra* refers to moderate-size states, while Chandragupta Maurya ruled over a large empire. The counterargument put forward by S. N. Mital and B. N. Mukherjee is that the concept of an empire in ancient India refers to a supraregional state that exercised suzerainty over other regional states. For maintaining suzerainty over the neighboring kingdoms, Kautilya brings in the concepts of *maṇḍala* theory and a *vijigīṣu* who is aspiring to be the ruler of the subcontinent (*sarvabhauma*). In such a scenario, one has to accept that the Maurya Empire was a weak state.[104] My understanding is that Kautilya speaks about the techniques that enable an ambitious ruler of a small kingdom (the future *vijigīṣu*) to become the ruler of the subcontinent and establish a large, centralized empire.

The expression *Kautilyarthasastra* at the end of each book, writes Mukherjee, ascribes the text to a person named Kautilya or to a school named after him. Mukherjee argues that the *Arthaśāstra* was composed during the Maurya age based on earlier and

---

* The Sudras tilled the land, but land ownership remained with the upper three *varnas*.

contemporary data. Mukherjee continues that a pre-Christian date for *Arthaśāstra* can be advocated on the basis of numismatic evidence. Kautilya refers to the minting of silver *pana* and copper *masaka* and *kakani*.[105] However, Kautilya never mentions the presence of silver *dramma* (*drachma*), which became popular in the northwest parts of the sub-continent during the second and first century BCE. Again, the *Arthaśāstra* never betrays knowledge regarding casting coins in mold, which became common during the second century BCE. The *Arthaśāstra* tells us about forging coins only by striking with the help of dies and hammer, a practice that was common before the second and first centuries BCE. In the first and second sections, the authorship of the *Arthaśāstra* is attributed to Kautilya. In the last section, the author is said to be Vishnugupta. Mukherjee suggests that Kautilya and Vishnugupta were the same person, with Vishnugupta as his personal name and Kautilya designating his subcaste (*gotra*).[106]

Kautilya's background is surrounded by mystery. The Buddhist *Mahavamsa* says that Brahmin Chanakya, after killing the ninth Nanda ruler Dhanananda, anointed Chandragupta Maurya as the ruler of *Jambudipa*.[107] The *Vishnu Purana* says that the Brahmin Kautilya exterminated the nine Nandas and then put Chandragupta Maurya on the throne. From the Buddhist and Jaina works and also the *purana*s it seems that Kautilya was insulted at the Nanda court. He then vowed to destroy the Nandas and took young Chandragupta as his protégé. Together they invaded the Nanda capital Pataliputra (Patna) but were defeated. Since the direct strategy of confrontation failed, they followed the indirect strategy. In accordance with this strategy, Kautilya and Chandragupta first decided to conquer the peripheral areas before moving against the core for the final overthrow of the Nanda ruler. This strategy constitutes one of the components of *kuta-yuddha*. *Mudraraksasa*, a political fiction by Vishakadatta composed between the fifth and ninth centuries CE, tells us that Chandragupta with Kautilya's help also requested the aid of Raksasa (a loyal minister of the Nandas) in overthrowing the Nanda Empire. Here is an example of winning over the high officials of the enemy, which Kautilya categorizes as *kutayuddha*. Kautilya is portrayed in the *Mudraraksasa* as *kutila*,[108] meaning a person of cunning genius (*kutilamati*).

Sil, like Mukherjee, concludes that Kautilya was the same person as Vishnugupta or Chanakya and that he lived around 350–275 BCE.[109] Just after the death of Alexander in 323 BCE, Chandragupta and Kautilya started fighting the Greeks. They assassinated two of Alexander's governors, named Nicanor and Philip.[110] It is probable that in 321 BCE, Chandragupta came to the Maurya throne and defeated Seleucus (Alexander's general who had succeeded in the eastern portion of the empire) in a battle near the Indus River around 305 BCE. In 303 BCE, Seleucus and Chandragupta signed a treaty. In accordance with this treaty, Seleucus was given 500 war elephants by Chandragupta and in return vacated Afghanistan to the Maurya Empire. There was a marriage alliance between these two royal families. Seleucus' daughter was married to Chandragupta.[111] The Maurya Empire established by Chandragupta continued to expand under his son Bindusara (293/7–272/68 BCE) and Chandragupta's grandson Asoka (268–232 BCE). After Asoka's death, the empire started to decline. The population of the Maurya Empire was 50 million and the capital Pataliputra was twice the size of Rome under Marcus Aurelius.[112] The Maurya Empire had several large populous cities, and for their defense the Maurya administration constructed several forts. Hence, Kautilya speaks much about *puras* and *durgas* in the *Arthaśāstra*.

Surya P. Subedi asserts that the concept of *dharma* is principally secular, as it deals with the maintenance of law and order rather than Hindu gods and goddesses. And Kautilya's *Arthaśāstra* is a prescriptive account for maintaining *dharma* in general and *rajadharma* in particular. Subedi writes that credit is due to Kautilya for coming up with a secular treatise on statecraft.[113] In Mukherjee's view, the *Arthaśāstra* of Kautilya is a practical handbook for governing a monarchical state. And in such a scenario, the management of finance plays a major role.[114]

The *Arthaśāstra* is divided into fifteen books. These books lay down general rules for the conduct of the king, give injunctions for the appointment of ministers and high priests, and enumerate other mechanisms for state security.[115] Kautilya recommends drastic measures against enemies, not because they are of a different religion, but in order to ensure the safety of the *rashtra*.[116]

Kautilya says that the state is made of seven constituent elements: king, ministers, forts, territory, treasury, army, and allies. This is also known as the *saptanga* (seven constituent elements) theory of *rashtra*. And of these seven elements, the king is considered to be the most important. In Chousalkar's view, Kautilya is not a supporter of the social contract theory regarding monarchy, which was expounded by the Buddhist thinkers. He continues that Kautilya sought to use the myth of social contract for the legitimization of royal authority.

Kautilya divides the *rashtra* into two divisions: the capital city and its environs, known as the *pura*, and the hinterland, known as the *janapada*.[117] *Pura* for him represented the interior regions, while *janapada* represented the outer regions of a kingdom. The outer regions also comprised rural regions, forests under the chieftains, and the realms ruled by the vassals.[118]

The *Aitareya Brahmana* emphasizes that a monarch should strive to establish a state with a unitary administration that should encompass all the land up to the sea. This is also the ideal of Kautilya's *vijigīṣu*.[119] The most important officials in the Kautilyan state were the *nayaka*,[120] director of factories, officer in charge of the frontier, *purohita* (Hindu priest), *senapati*, and the crown prince (*yuvaraj*). Overall, the *Arthaśāstra* speaks of a highly centralized administrative fabric.[121]

Kautilya's *vijigīṣu* is supported by three types of power: wise counsel (*mantrasakti*), valor, energy, and personal dynamism (*utsahasakti*). He likewise emphasized the combined might of financial and military resources (*prabhusakti*). Similar to sentiments expressed by his contemporaries Plato and Aristotle,[122] Kautilya would agree that the art of war must be pursued in order to secure peace.[123] However, for Kautilya, war is to be conducted for increasing the power of a state or at best to avert defeat in the hands of the enemy.

In Kautilya's paradigm, of all the possible disturbances, *kopa* (insurrection or revolt of the people) is the most serious. *Kopa* might occur in both the interior and the outer parts of the kingdom. *Kopa* in the core, asserts Kautilya, is always more dangerous than *kopa* in the periphery. *Kopa* represents the anger of the people against the ruling authority. It can arise from what are perceived to be the wrong policies of the ruler. Occasionally and more dangerously, ministers, the army, and foreign allies also get disgruntled. This, Kautilya cautions, can happen at the instigation of foreign powers as supported by treasonable elements. It is under such circumstances that discontent can escalate into internal warfare. This leads Kautilya to propose that the army and treasury be kept under the direct control of the monarch.[124] To prevent *kopa* in the cities and in the capital, Kautilya likewise proposes an internal surveillance mechanism. In his view, the tentacles of the state should go down deep in the society. He advocates that each big city or the capital should be divided into four wards, each under an administrative official known as a *sthanika*. Under each *sthanika*, there should be several junior administrative officials, known as *gopas*. Each *gopa* should look after ten to forty families and prepare lists of the persons under him with details regarding their gender, caste, occupation, levels of income, and so on.[125] In this spirit, Thapar recounts how the peasants in the Maurya Empire were disarmed in order to prevent them from undertaking armed rebellion.[126]

For the conduct of warfare, Kautilya emphasized the importance of soldiers' morale. To this end, tangible and intangible incentives should be provided. For example, pensions should be offered to the families of those who die on the battlefield. As part of *kutayuddha*, the *Arthaśāstra* speaks of manipulation of the soldiers by the *purohita* through acts of sorcery and black magic. Furthermore, special monetary rewards should be offered to personnel who would kill the enemy king or senior enemy commanders by especially risky missions. Kautilya even mentions biological warfare as part of *kutayuddha*. He displays a vast knowledge of herbs and drugs and speaks of the preparation and application of poisonous drinks containing liquid gold and mercury.[127]

From: *The Kauṭilīya Arthaśāstra*, Book I, "Concerning the Topic of Training," Chapter I, "Enumeration of Sections and Books"[128]

14. The mission of the Envoy, Fight with (the weapon of) Diplomacy, Assassination of (the enemy's) Army Chiefs, Stirring up the Circle of Kings, Secret Use of Weapons, Fire and Poison, Destruction of (the enemy's) Supplies, Reinforcements and Foraging Raids, Over-reaching (the enemy) by Trickery, Over-reaching (the enemy) by Force, Victory of the Single King, – these constitute the Twelfth Book "Concerning the Weaker King."

15. Instigation to Sedition, Drawing Out (the enemy) by means of Stratagems, Employment of Secret Agents, the Work of Laying Siege (to a Fort), Storming (a Fort), Pacification of the Conquered Territory, – these constitute the Thirteenth Book....

Kautilya's *Arthaśāstra* did not fall from heaven all of a sudden. The opening stanza of the *Arthaśāstra* says that this treatise on politics was composed by bringing together (consulting and synthesizing) the *arthasastras* written by former teachers such as Brhaspati and Usanas.[129] The science of *arthasastra* was thus developed from the fifth century BCE; its major concern was *artha* or material affairs of day-to-day governance.[130]

From: *The Kauṭilīya Arthaśāstra*, Part II, Chapter II[131]

4. "Economics and the science* of politics (are the only sciences)," say the followers of Brhaspati.

5. "For the Vedic lore is only a cloak for one conversant with the ways of the world."

---

* Instead of the term "science," I would use "knowledge system."

6. "The science of politics is the only science," say the followers of Usanas.

7. "For, with it are bound up undertakings connected with all the sciences."

8. "Four, indeed, is the number of the sciences," says Kautilya.

9. Since with their help one can learn (what is) spiritual good and material well-being, therefore the sciences (*vidyās*)* are so called....

11. Investigating, by means of reasoning, (what is) spiritual good and evil in the Vedic lore, material gain and loss in economics, good policy and bad policy in the science of politics, as well as the relative strength and weakness of these (three sciences), (philosophy) confers benefit on the people, keeps the mind steady in adversity and in prosperity and brings about proficiency in thought, speech and action.

12. Philosophy is ever thought of as the lamp of all sciences, as the means of all actions (and) as support of all laws (and duties).

From: *The Kauṭilīya Arthaśāstra*, Part II, Chapter III[132]

4. The law laid down in this Vedic lore is beneficial, as it prescribes the respective duties of the four *varṇas* and the four stages of life....

6. Those of the Kṣhatriya are: studying, performing sacrifices for self, making gifts, living by (the profession of) arms and protecting beings.

From: *The Kauṭilīya Arthaśāstra*, Part II, Chapter IV[133]

1. Agriculture, cattle-rearing and trade, – these constitute economics, (which are) beneficial, as they yield grains, cattle, money, forest produce and labor.

2. Through them, the (king) brings under his sway his own party as well as the party of the enemies, by the (use of the) treasury and the army....

5. "Therefore, the (king), seeking the orderly maintenance of worldly life, should ever hold the Rod lifted up (to strike).

6. "For, there is no such means for the subjugation of beings as the Rod," say the (ancient) teachers.

7. "No," says Kautilya.

8. For, the (king), severe with the Rod, becomes a source of terror to beings.

9. The (king), mild with the Rod, is despised.

10. The (king), just with the Rod, is honored.

11. For, the Rod, used after full consideration, endows the subjects with spiritual good, material well-being and pleasures of the senses.

12. Used unjustly, whether in passion or anger, or in contempt, it enrages even forest-anchorites† and wandering ascetics, how much more then the householders?

---

* Several branches of knowledge.
† "Anchorites" should be "authorities," i.e., forest chieftains.

13. If not used at all, it gives rise to the law of the fishes [big fish will eat smaller fish].

14. For, the stronger swallows the weak in the absence of the wielder of the Rod.

From: *The Kauṭilīya Arthaśāstra*, Part II, Chapter VIII, "Appointment of Ministers"[134]

25. "One, conversant with the science, (but) not experienced in practical affairs, would come to grief in (carrying out) undertakings."

For waging *kutayuddha* both against internal and external enemies, Kautilya emphasizes use of *chara* (spies). To preempt *kopa* (internal disturbances, armed uprisings, etc.), Kautilya recommends that the monarch should employ spies in large numbers. Besides the interception of messages and other such forms of intelligence, Kautilya focuses especially on human intelligence. Kautilya introduces the concept of *ubhayavetanas* (double agents) and emphasizes the use of female spies, all conversant in communicating through code language. The double agents are to operate independently in the enemy's territory, each being unaware of the other *ubhayavetanas* operating in the same enemy country, but all on the payroll of the *vijigīṣu*. Trained fortune-tellers and astrologers, these spies are to establish and maintain contact with the forest chieftains and other potential rebellious elements.[135] Kautilya supports the policy of employing *mlechchas*[136] as foreign spies for acquiring intelligence about the foreign enemies. The term *mlechchas* refers to the Greeks settled in northwest India and also the non-Hinduized forest tribes in peninsular India. Kautilya advises the spy establishment and the secret agents to operate on what we today call the "need to know" principle. He advocates the construction of small cells of secret agents (akin to present terrorist organizations such as Al-Qaeda). Even if one of the cells was infiltrated by the enemy counterintelligence department or if a cell was burst due to internal treachery, the other cells unknown to them could continue to operate. Kautilya encourages terrorist acts in enemy territory by the *vijigīṣu*'s secret agents. Kautilya says that by putting a house on fire or by poisoning somebody, a general commotion can be created and taken advantage of by the secret agents who could evacuate that place or vanish from that region. Kautilya advocates certain techniques that in modern military jargon are known as the Fourth and the evolving Fifth Generation Warfare.

From: *The Kauṭilīya Arthaśāstra*, Part II, Chapter XI, "Appointment of Persons in Secret Service"[137]

1. With the body of ministers proved upright by means of secret tests, the (king) should appoint persons in secret service … the apostate monk, the scheming householder, the seeming trader and the seeming ascetic, as well as the secret agent … the poison-giver and the begging nun.…

21. And he should pacify with money and honor those who are resentful for good reason, those resentful without reason, by silent punishment, also those who do what is inimical to the king.

22. And favored by the king with money and honor, they should ascertain the integrity of the king's servants.

From: *The Kauṭilīya Arthaśāstra*, Part II, Chapter XII, Section 8, "Rules for Secret Servants"[*][138]

2. Those in the land who are brave, have given up all (thought of) personal safety (and) would fight, for the sake of money, an elephant or a wild animal, are the bravoes.[†]

3. Those who are without affection for their kinsmen and are cruel and indolent are the poison-givers.

4. A wandering nun, seeking a (secure) livelihood, poor, widowed, bold, Brahmin (by caste) and treated with honor in the palace, should (frequently) go to the houses of high officers.

5. By her (office) are explained (similar offices for) the shaven nuns of heretical sects. These are the roving spies.

6. The king should employ these with a credible disguise as regards country, dress, profession, language and birth, to spy, in conformity with their loyalty and capability, on the councillor, the chaplain, the commander-in-chief, the crown prince … the chief of the palace guards … the director of stores, the magistrate, the commandant, the city-judge, the director of factories, the council of ministers, … the chief of the army staff, the commandant of the fort, the commandant of the frontier-fort and the forest chieftain, in his own territory.

7. Bravoes, (serving as) bearers of umbrella, water-vessel, fan, shoes, seat, carriage and riding animal, should (spy on and) ascertain the out-of-door activity of those (officers).

8. Secret agents should communicate that (information) to the (spy-) establishments.

9. Poison-givers, serving as cooks, waiters, bath attendants, … barbers, valets and water-servers, those appearing as hump-backs, dwarfs, … dumb, deaf, idiotic or blind persons, (and) actors, dancers, singers, musicians, professional story-tellers and minstrels as well as women should (spy on and) ascertain the indoor activity (of those officers)….

11. Assistants of the establishments should carry out the transmission of spied out news by means of sign-alphabets.[‡]

12. And neither the establishments nor these (assistants) should know one another.

13. In case of prohibition (of entry into the house) for nuns, (secret agents) appearing at the door one after another (or) appearing as the mother or father

---

[*] Instead of "secret servants," the proper translation should be "secret agents."

[†] By "bravoes," Kautilya means the desperadoes who functioned as shock troops, secret agents, and also volunteers in commando operations. "Braves" would be a better translation. Later, in Hindi, it became *bahadur* (heroes).

[‡] Code language.

(of servants in the house), or posing as female artists, singers or female slaves, should get the secret information that is spied out conveyed outside by means of songs, recitations, writings concealed in musical instruments or signs.

14. Or, a secret get-away (from the house should be made by the spies) by (taking advantage of a pretended) long illness or madness or by setting (something) on fire or [by] administering poison (to someone).

15. When there is agreement in the report of three (spies), credence (should be given).

16. In case of continuous mistakes on their part, "silent" punishment is (the means of) their removal.

17. And spies ... should live with enemies receiving wages from them, in order to find out secret information, without associating with one another.

18. They are "persons in the pay of both."

19. And he should appoint "persons in the pay of both," after taking charge of their sons and wives. And he should know such agents when they are employed by the enemies. And (he should ascertain) their loyalty through (spies of) their type.

20. Thus he should sow spies among the enemy, the ally, the middle king, the neutral king, as well as among the eighteen high officers of (each of) those (kings).

21. Humpbacks, dwarfs, eunuchs, women skilled in arts, dumb persons and different types of Mlechcha races (should be employed as spies)....

22. In fortified towns traders (should constitute) the spy establishments, on the outskirts of fortified towns ascetics, farmers and apostate monks in the countryside (and) herdsmen on the borders of the country.

23. In the forest should be placed forest-dwellers (such as) monks, foresters and others, – a series of spies, quick in their work, – in order to find out news of (the activity of) the enemy....

25. In order to discover espionage by enemies, he should station at frontiers principal officers, who are non-seducible, but are shown to be impelled by motives for action that are associated with seducible parties.

From: *The Kauṭilīya Arthaśāstra*, Part II, Chapter XIII[139]

1. When he has set spies on the high officials, he should set spies on the citizens and the country people....

14. And they should also find out rumors (spreading among the subjects).

15. And spies appearing as ascetics with shaven heads or with matted hair should ascertain the contentedness or discontentedness of those, who live on his grains, cattle or money, who help him with these in calamity or prosperity, who restrain a rebellious kinsman or region, (or) who repel an enemy or a forest chieftain.

16. He should favor those who are contented, with additional wealth and honor.

17. He should propitiate with gifts and conciliation those, who are discontented, in order to make them contented....

23. Spies appearing as fortune-tellers, soothsayers and astrologers should ascertain their mutual relations as well as their contacts with enemies or forest chieftains. . . .

26. In this way, the wise (king) should guard from the secret instigations of enemies those likely to be seduced and those not likely to be seduced in his own territory, whether prominent persons or common people.

From: *The Kauṭilīya Arthaśāstra*, Part II, Chapter 14[140]

3. One who has himself thwarted (someone), one who has committed a serious wrong, one who has become known for a sinful act, one frightened by punishment meted out to another with a like offense, one who has seized (someone's) land, one who is subdued by force, one in any (state) department who has suddenly amassed wealth, one hoping for a pretender from the (king's) family (coming to the throne), one disliked by the king, and one who entertains hostility toward the king, – this is the group of the frightened. . . .

6. Among them, he should cause instigation through spies appearing as holy men with shaven heads or matted hair, – of each person of the seducible party by that (spy) to whom he may be devoted. . . .

12. And he should win over the seducible in the enemy's territories by means of conciliation and gifts and those not seducible by means of dissension and force, pointing out (to them) the defects of the enemy.

From: *The Kauṭilīya Arthaśāstra*, Part II, Chapter 15[141]

6. One who divulges secret counsel should be extirpated.

Kautilya stresses the importance of fortifications. They are useful for conquering new territories, the pacification of occupied territory, and for coping with internal rebellions within the *vijigīṣu*'s *rashtra*. These forts can be built in the midst of natural lakes or on mountains. Depending on the local geography, Kautilya refers to the construction of moats, ramparts, and parapets. Generally, Kautilya refers to three wet moats. He refers to the drawbridge over the moat/ditch, which is to be drawn back when the fort is besieged. The widest moat is to be nearest the rampart and the narrowest one is to be farthest away from the rampart. Overall, the width at the bottom of a moat is one-third of the width at the surface. The surface of the moat is to be generally sloping in order to prevent enemy soldiers from climbing with ease. The wet ditch is filled with lotuses for aesthetic beauty and crocodiles to prevent the enemy soldiers from swimming across the obstruction. For protection of the fort, advises Kautilya, the garrison should be equipped with *sataghnis*, a machine that could kill 100 enemies at one single discharge.

From: *The Kauṭilīya Arthaśāstra*, Part II, Section 21, "Construction of Forts"[142]

1. In all four quarters, on the frontiers of the country, he should cause a nature-made fortress, equipped for fight, to be made: a water-fort (either) an island in

the midst of water . . . a mountain fort (either) consisting of rocks . . . (or) a desert fort (either) one without water and shrubs or a salty region, or a jungle fort (either) a marshy tract with water or a thicket of shrubs.

2. Among them a river fort and a mountain fort are places for the protectors of the country, a desert fort and a jungle fort are places for foresters or places of retreat in times of calamity.

3. In the center of the country, he should lay out . . . the headquarters for revenue, on a site recommended by experts in the science of building, at the confluence of rivers or on the bank of a lake that never dries up, either a (natural) lake or a (manmade) tank, round, rectangular or square or in accordance with the nature of the building site, with water flowing from left to right, a market town, served by a land-route and a water-route.

4. He should cause three moats to be dug round it, at a distance of one *danda*[*] from each other, fourteen, twelve and ten *dandas* broad, three-quarters or a half of the breadth deep, one-third (of the surface-breadth) at the bottom or square with the bottom, paved with stones or with the sides (only) built of stones or bricks, reaching down to (natural springs of) water or filled with water coming from elsewhere, with (arrangements for) draining excess water, and stocked with lotuses and crocodiles.

5. At a distance of four *dandas* from the moat, he should cause a rampart to be made out of the earth dug out, six *dandas* high, made compact, twice that in breadth, piled upward with a platform-like (flat) surface (at the top) or with a jug-like side, pounded by elephants and bullocks (and) having (on the sides) clusters of thorny bushes and poisonous creepers. . . .

7. On top of the rampart, he should cause a parapet to be built, double the breadth in height, built of bricks, from twelve *hastas*[†] upward up to twenty-four *hastas*, either odd or even in number (of *hastas* in height), with a passage for the movement of chariots, shaped like a palm-stem and with the top decked with "drums" and "monkey-heads."[‡]

8. Or, he should cause it to be made of stones, close knit with big slabs, but under no circumstances (should he have it) made of wood.

9. For, fire remains lurking in it.

10. He should cause turrets to be made, square with the breadth, provided with steps for going down, (of the) same (length) as the height, and at a distance of thirty *dandas* from each other.[§]

11. Midway between (every) two turrets, he should cause a tower to be built, with two stories inclusive of a hall, (and) one and a half times in length.

[*] Here *danda* means a unit of measurement, i.e., six feet.
[†] *Hasta* is a unit of measurement and equivalent to the length of a hand.
[‡] "Drums" and "monkey-heads" refer to stone covers for the fighters on the parapet.
[§] Kautilya is probably referring to the steps for going from the *attalaka* (turret) to the top of the parapet. The turret was comprised of planks attached to the outer edge of the parapet; through holes in the turret archers could shoot arrows at the enemy soldiers outside.

12. Between each turret and tower, in the center, he should cause to be erected a board, compact with planks having holes with coverings, as a place (from which to fight) for three archers.

13. In the intervening spaces, he should cause a "gods' way" to be made, two *hastas* in breadth and four times that in length, at the side.*...

30. The bridge should be equal (in width) to the opening and capable of being withdrawn. . . .

33. He should cause channels to be made for storing goods, one-third more in length (than the breadth).

34–35. In them should be stored stones, spades, axes, arrows and choppers, clubs and hammers, sticks, discuses, machines and "hundred killers," pikes prepared by smiths and bamboos with piercing points ... incendiary objects. . . .

The *vijigīṣu*'s state occupies the hub of the *maṇḍala*. Interstate relationships are based on the following policies: a treaty of friendship (*sandhi*), war (*vigraha*), inactive or passive policy (*asana*), surprise attack (*yana*), becoming a satellite state of a powerful state for survival (*samsraya*), and dual policy involving both peace and war (*dvaidhibhava*). The idea is that peace and war are the basic policies and the others are variations of these two.[143]

From: *The Kauṭilīya Arthaśāstra*, Part II, Book 6, "The Circle (of Kings) as the Basis," Chapter 1[144]

1. The king, the minister, the country, the fortified city, the treasury, the army and the ally are the constituent elements (of the state). . . .

11. Inherited from the father and the grandfather, constant, obedient, with the soldiers' sons and wives contented, not disappointed during marches, unhindered everywhere, able to put up with troubles, that has fought many battles, skilled in the science of all types of war and weapons, not having a separate interest because of prosperity and adversity shared (with the king), consisting mostly of Kshatriyas, – these are the excellences of an army.

From: *The Kauṭilīya Arthaśāstra*, Part II, Book 6, "The Circle (of Kings) as the Basis," Chapter 2[145]

1. Peace and activity constitute the source of acquisition and security. . . .

18. Beyond him, the ally, the enemy's ally, the ally's ally, and the enemy's ally's ally are situated in front in accordance with the proximity of the territories; behind, the enemy in the rear, the ally in the rear, the rear enemy's ally and the rear ally's ally (one behind the other).

---

* The *devapatha* (god's way/path) is for the protection of the parapet base on the outside and was made of wood fixed with copper strip.

19. One with immediately proximate territory is the natural enemy....

21. One with territory immediately proximate to those of the enemy and the conqueror, capable of helping them when they are united or disunited and of suppressing them when they are disunited, is the middle king.

22. One outside (the sphere of) the enemy, the conqueror and the middle king, stronger than (their) constituents, capable of helping the enemy, the conqueror and the middle king when they are united or disunited and of suppressing them when they are disunited, is the neutral king....

31. Power is (possession of) strength.

32. Success is (obtaining) happiness.

33. Power is threefold: the power of knowledge is the power of counsel, the power of the treasury and the army is the power of might, the power of valor is the power of energy.

34. In the same way, success is also three-fold: that attainable by the power of counsel is success by counsel, that attainable by the power of might is success by might, that attainable by the power of energy is success by energy.

From: *The Kauṭilīya Arthaśāstra*, Part II, Book 7, "The Six Measures of Foreign Policy," Chapter I[146]

2. "Peace, war, staying quiet, marching, seeking shelter and dual policy constitute the six measures," say the teachers.

3. "There are (only) two measures," says Vātavyādhi.

4. "For, out of peace and war the six measures come into being."

5. "These are really six measures, because of differences in the situations," says Kauṭilīya.

6. Among them, entering into a treaty is peace.

7. Doing injury is war.

8. Remaining indifferent is staying quiet.

9. Augmentation of (powers) is marching.

10. Submitting to another is seeking shelter.

11. Resorting to peace (with one) and war (with another) is dual policy.

12. These are the six measures of foreign policy.

13. When in decline as compared to the enemy, he should make peace.

14. When prospering, he should make war....

33. ... "My country, consisting mostly of martial people or fighting bands, or secure in the protection of a single entrance through a mountain-fort, a forest-fort or a river-fort, will be able to repulse the enemy's attack; or, taking shelter in an impregnable fort on the border of my territory, I shall be able to ruin the enemy's undertakings; or, the enemy, with his energy sapped by the troubles caused by a calamity, has reached a time when his undertakings face ruin; or, when he

is fighting elsewhere, I shall be able to carry off his country," he should secure an advancement by resorting to war. . . .

35. . . . "The ruin of the enemy's undertakings can be brought about by marching, and I have taken steps to secure the protection of my own undertakings," he should secure advancement by marching. . . .

37. Or, if he were to think, "I shall promote my own undertakings by peace on one side and ruin the enemy's undertakings by war on the other side," he should secure advancement through a dual policy.

38. Situated in the circle of constituent elements, he should, in this manner, with these six measures of policy, seek to progress from decline to stable condition and from stable condition to advancement in his own undertakings.

From: *The Kauṭilīya Arthaśāstra*, Part II, Book 7, "The Six Measures of Foreign Policy," Chapter 2[147]

5. For, he who resorts to the dual policy, giving prominence to his own undertakings, serves only his own interests, while he who takes shelter (with another) serves the interests of the other, not his own.

6. He should seek shelter with one whose strength is superior to the strength of the neighboring (enemy). . . .

8. For, union with one superior in strength is a great danger to kings, except when he is at war with an enemy. . . .

17. Or, taking shelter in a fort, he should resort to the dual policy. . . .

19. He should give support to the treasonable officers, the enemies and forest chiefs of both.

From: *The Kauṭilīya Arthaśāstra*, Part II, Book 7, "The Six Measures of Foreign Policy," Chapter 3[148]

1. The conqueror should employ the six measures of policy with due regard to his power.

2. He should make peace with the equal and the stronger; he should make war with the weaker. . . .

4. And (at war) with the equal, he brings about loss on both sides, like an unbaked jar struck by an unbaked jar.

5. (At war) with the weaker, he attains absolute success, like a stone with an earthen vessel.

6. If the stronger were not to desire peace, he should resort to the conduct of one submitting with troops or measures recommended for the weaker king. . . .

11. For, heroism born of grief and resentment makes one fight bravely like a forest fire. . . .

19. If he were to see success in his work by peace in one place and war in another, then even the stronger should resort to the dual policy.

From: *The Kauṭilīya Arthaśāstra*, Part II, Book 7, "The Six Measures of Foreign Policy," Chapter 4[149]

15. Or, when he were to see, "The enemy is in a calamity; or, a calamity of his constituent cannot be remedied by the remaining constituents; or, his subjects, harassed by his own army, or disaffected with him, are easy to entice, being weakened, without energy or divided among themselves; the enemy has his draught-animals, men, stores and fortifications reduced in consequence of fire, floods, disease, epidemic or famine," then he should make war and march....

17. Or, when he ... [is] to see that the fruit can be attained by a single person within a short time, then he should make war on the rear enemy and his ally and march.

18. In the reverse cases, he should make peace and march.

From: *The Kauṭilīya Arthaśāstra*, Part II, Book 7, "The Six Measures of Foreign Policy," Chapter 5[150]

1. In case the calamities of two neighboring princes are alike, (should one march) against the vulnerable king or the enemy? – in such a case, he should march against the enemy; after subduing him, against the vulnerable king....

3. (Should one march) against a vulnerable king in a serious calamity or the enemy in a light calamity? "He should march against the one in a serious calamity, because of ease (in subjugating)," say the teachers.

4. "No," says Kauṭilīya.

5. He should march against the enemy with a light calamity....

8. But the enemy with a light calamity, if not attacked, might easily overcome his calamity and go to the rescue of the vulnerable king, or might attack in the rear....

12. (When the choice is) between one with impoverished and greedy subjects and one with rebellious subjects, "He should march against the one with impoverished and greedy subjects; for, impoverished and greedy subjects easily yield themselves to instigations or harassment, not the rebellious who can be overcome by the suppression of their leaders," say the teachers.

13. "No," says Kauṭilīya.

14. For, impoverished and greedy subjects, when devoted to their master, remain steadfast in what is beneficial to the master or make the instigations futile, on the principle, "Where there is love, all qualities (are present)."

15. Hence he should march only against one with rebellious subjects.

16. (When the choice is) between a strong king unjustly behaved and a weak king justly behaved, he should march against the strong king unjustly behaved.

17. The subjects do not help the strong unjust king when he is attacked, they drive him out or resort to his enemy.

18. But the subjects support in every way the weak but just king when he is attacked or follow him if he has to flee. . . .

27. Subjects, when impoverished, become greedy; when greedy they become disaffected; when disaffected they either go over to the enemy or themselves kill the master.

28. Therefore, he should not allow these causes of decline, greed and disaffection among the subjects to arise, or, if arisen, should immediately counter-act them. . . .

31. The greedy, dissatisfied because of greed, willingly respond to the enemy's instigations.

32. The disaffected rise in revolt when there is an enemy attack.

Kautilya conceptualizes two types of warfare. Open war is *dharmayuddha*, whereas silent war and concealed war constitute *kutayuddha*. Silent war consists in sponsoring low-intensity operations (insurgencies) in the enemy kingdoms, and concealed war involves deceit, treachery, sudden attacks, night attacks, ambushes, and commando operations against the enemy's army as well as the forts.

From: *The Kauṭilīya Arthaśāstra*, Part II, Book 7, "The Six Measures of Foreign Policy," Chapter 6[151]

13. Wishing to over-reach an enemy, who is vicious, hasty, contemptuous, slothful or ignorant, he should create confidence with a treaty, saying "we are in alliance," without the fixing of place, time or object, and after finding the enemy's weak point, strike at him; this is (treaty) without stipulations. . . .

15. The wise (conqueror), making one neighboring king fight with another neighboring king, should seize the territory of another, cutting off his party on all sides. . . .

17. Of war, there is open war, concealed war and silent war. . . .

40–41. Open war is fighting at the place and time indicated; creating fright, sudden assault, striking when there is error or a calamity, giving way and striking in one place, are types of concealed warfare; that which concerns secret practices and instigations through secret agents is the mark of silent war.

Kautilya emphasizes the importance of time in conducting warfare. He equates the speed of mobilization with victory. While waging war, Kautilya prefers financial contributions from the allies as the best policy for the *vijigīṣu*, and incorporating the troops of the allies as the second best option. A small power whose policy could be shaped in accordance with the wishes of the *vijigīṣu* is preferable as an ally to a strong power who possesses the resources to follow an independent policy that might be contradictory to the expansionist policy of the *vijigīṣu*.

From: *The Kauṭilīya Arthaśāstra*, Part II, Book 7, "The Six Measures of Foreign Policy," Chapter 9[152]

12. As long as he helps, he becomes an ally; for, the characteristic of an ally is conferring benefit. . . .

18. As between a big ally mobilizing slowly and a small ally mobilizing quickly, "The big ally, mobilizing slowly, gives great prestige, and when he does mobilize, he secures the object," say the teachers.

19. "No," says Kautilya.

20. A small ally mobilizing quickly is preferable.

21. The small ally mobilizing quickly does not allow the time for action to pass, and because of his weakness becomes fit to be used at one's will, not so the other, with an extensive territory. . . .

28. The ally giving the help of money is preferable.

29. For, the use of money is made at all times, only sometimes that of troops.

30. And with money, troops and other objects of desire are obtained. . . .

50. As between a small but quick gain and a large gain after a long time, "The small but quick gain is preferable, if in consonance with the undertaking, the place and the time," say the teachers.

51. "No," says Kautilya.

52. A large gain after a long time is preferable, if not liable to disappear (and if) of the nature of a seed; in the reverse case, the former.

Kautilya prefers laying siege to an enemy fort to meeting the enemy army in a decisive battle. In Kautilya's paradigm, the acquisition of forts is more important from a strategic point of view than the destruction of enemy forces. Here, Kautilya differs from Carl von Clausewitz, who emphasizes decisive set-piece battles for destroying the enemy force.[153] Using Clausewitz's terminology, for Kautilya the enemy's center of gravity (*Schwerpunkt*) are his forts. Kautilya argues that conquest of the enemy's forts would enable the *vijigīṣu* to annex hostile territory.

From: *The Kauṭilīya Arthaśāstra*, Part II, Book 7, "The Six Measures of Foreign Policy," Chapter 10[154]

8. For, the acquisition of a fort brings about the protection of his own land and the repulsion of enemies and forest tribes. . . .

26. As between an enemy fit to be harassed and an enemy fit to be exterminated, acquisition of land from an enemy fit to be exterminated is preferable.

27. For, the king fit to be exterminated, being without support or with a weak support, is deserted by his subjects when, on being attacked, he wishes to flee taking with him the treasury and the army, not the one fit to be harassed, entrenched in a fort or supported by an ally.

28. Even of two kings entrenched in a fort, one in a land-fort and the other in a river-fort, the acquisition of land from one in a land-fort is preferable.

29. For, a land-fort is easy to besiege, to storm and to assault suddenly and does not allow the enemy to slip out.

30. A river-fort, however, causes double exertion. . . .

32. For, a river-fort can be conquered by means of elephants, bridges of wooden posts, embankments and boats....

33. A mountain-fort, however, is easy to protect, difficult to lay siege to, difficult to climb; and even if one (part) is breached, the destruction of all does not follow; and (there can be) throwing down of rocks and trees on those doing great damage.

From: *The Kauṭilīya Arthaśāstra*, Part II, Book 7, "The Six Measures of Foreign Policy," Chapter 11[155]

13. "As between the usefulness of a material forest and an elephant forest, the use of a material forest is the source of all undertakings and able to secure plenty of stores, the reverse is the use of an elephant forest," say the teachers.

14. "No," says Kautilya.

15. It is possible to plant many material forests in many tracts of land, not so an elephant forest.

16. For, the destruction of an enemy's forces is principally dependent on elephants....

18. As between land with people disunited and one with people in bands, that with people disunited is preferable.

19. One with people disunited becomes easy to enjoy, not susceptible to the instigations of others, is, however, unable to bear difficulties.

20. One with people in bands is the reverse of this, full of danger when there is a revolt.

From: *The Kauṭilīya Arthaśāstra*, Part II, Book 7, "The Six Measures of Foreign Policy," Chapter 13[156]

12. For, one attacking a righteous king is hated by his own people and by others, one attacking an unrighteous king is liked (by them)....

27. The enemy who helps is fit to be allied with, not the ally who has renounced his friendly feelings....

30. "For, in a fight with military operations, there is loss of prosperity for both sides because of losses and expenses.

31. For, even after winning, a king with his army and treasury depleted becomes a loser," say the teachers.

32. "No," says Kautilya.

33. Even with very great losses and expenses, the destruction of the enemy must be brought about....

41. When attacked, he should cause the rear of the attacker to be attacked by his ally and keep off the rear ally (of the attacker) from the attacker in the rear by the ally of his ally.

42. In this way, the conqueror should establish in the rear and in front, a circle (of kings) in his own interest, with the excellences of the constituent, called the ally.

43. And in the entire circle, he should ever station envoys and secret agents, becoming a friend of the rivals, maintaining secrecy when striking again and again.

44. The affairs of one, who cannot maintain secrecy, even if achieved with particular success, undoubtedly perish, like a broken boat in the ocean.

From: *The Kauṭilīya Arthaśāstra*, Part II, Book 7, "The Six Measures of Foreign Policy," Chapter 14[157]

1. When attacked by confederates in this manner, the conqueror should say to the one who is the principal among them, "With you, I would make peace; here is money and I shall be an ally, you will (thus) have a double advancement; it does not behoove you to let your enemies, masquerading as friends, [to] thrive at your cost; for, these, when grown powerful, will overthrow you yourself."...

11. Or, by whichever means any of them may be separated, by that he should secure him, or by means of conciliation, gifts, dissension and force....

14. If weak in a party, he should create a party of kinsmen and allies, or an unassailable fort.

15. For, one entrenched in a fort or supported by allies, becomes worthy of honor by his own (people) and by those of others....

23. A trade-route is the means of over-reaching the enemy.

24. For, along the trade route is made the carrying over of troops and secret agents (into enemy territory) and the purchase of weapons, armors, carriages, vehicles, as well as bringing in and taking out.

Like Sun Tzu, Kautilya emphasizes the importance of terrain in military operations.[158] Kautilya also warns that warfare should be conducted by taking the climate into account.

From: *The Kauṭilīya Arthaśāstra*, Part II, Book 7, "The Six Measures of Foreign Policy," Chapter 15[159]

6. Among those with an equal power of energy, superiority (comes) from the attainment of terrain suitable for one's own (mode of) fighting.

7. Among those with an equally suitable terrain, superiority (comes) from the attainment of a season suited to one's own (mode of) fighting.

8. Among those with equally suitable terrains and seasons, superiority (comes) from draught-animals, weapons and armors....

12. He should resort to that (fort) for these reasons: "I shall win over the enemy in the rear or his ally or the middle king or the neutral king; or, I shall cause his kingdom to be seized or destroyed by one of these, viz., his neighboring king, a forest chief, a pretender from his family and a prince in disfavor; or, by supporting the party of likely seceders, I shall raise a revolt in his fort, country or camp; or I shall kill him as I please, when he comes near, by the use of weapons, fire or poison ... I shall put him to losses and expenses on account of secret practices employed by myself; or, I shall succeed in gradually instigating (against him) the group of his allies or his army, when they are severely afflicted by losses, expenses and long marches...."

Kautilya speaks about the ethics of conquest. However, Kautilya's ethics is conditioned by his realist perspective. He warns the *vijigīṣu* that rapid conquest of too many kingdoms would threaten the other member states of the *maṇḍala* and might result in a coalition against the *vijigīṣu*. To prevent the emergence of such a coalition, after defeating the enemy king the *vijigīṣu* should designate one of the defeated king's relatives as a tributary ruler who would be dependent on the *vijigīṣu*'s favor for survival. And such a satellite kingdom should be gradually absorbed into the ever-expanding empire of the *vijigīṣu*.

From: *The Kauṭilīya Arthaśāstra*, Part II, Book 7, "The Six Measures of Foreign Policy," Chapter 16[160]

1. The strong king, desirous of conquering one causing harassment, though the terms of the treaty were accepted (by him), should march in that direction in which there is suitable terrain, suitable season and livelihood for his own troops, in which the enemy is without the refuge of a fort and without (protection in) the rear and the help of an ally. . . .

3. He should subjugate the weak by means of conciliation and gifts, the strong by means of dissension and force.

4. And he should secure the members (of the king's circle) who are immediately next to him and who are separated by one intervening state, by the exclusive use, the alternative use or the combined use of the (four) means. . . .

7. Making a demand for treasury, troops, land or inheritance by supporting one of these, viz., a neighboring prince, a forest chief, a pretender from the family and a prince in disfavour, – thus should he sow discord.

8. Subjugation of the enemy in open, concealed or silent war or through "means for taking a fort" – thus should he make use of force. . . .

24. And if any of them were to do him harm, he should proclaim his guilt and slay him openly.

25. Or, because of fright (likely) among others, he should act as in "infliction of secret punishment."

26. And he shall not covet the land, property, sons or wives of the slain one.

27. He should place in their appropriate positions even the members of his family.

28. He should place on the throne the son of one killed in action.

29. In this way, the princes surrendering to force remain loyal to his sons and grandsons.

30. But the circle (of kings), being frightened, rises to destroy one who were to kill or imprison those who have submitted and covet their land, property, sons or wives.

31. And those ministers,* who are under his control in their own lands, become frightened of him and resort to the circle.

32. Or, they themselves seek to take his kingdom or life.

---

* A proper translation of this term is "vassals."

33. And therefore, kings, protected in their own territories by means of conciliation, become favorably disposed toward the king, remaining obedient to his sons and grandsons.

From: *The Kauṭilīya Arthaśāstra*, Part II, Book 7, "The Six Measures of Foreign Policy," Chapter 17[161]

1. Peace, treaty, hostage, these are one and the same thing.

2. The creation of confidence among kings is (the purpose of) peace, treaty or hostage....

5. ... a surety or a hostage is of use only in this world, depending on strength....

24. Even in the matter of valor, the wise one overreaches the brave, as the hunter does the elephant....

32. When grown in strength, he should bring about the liberation of the hostage.

33. Secret agents disguised as artisans or artists, carrying out works in the proximity of the prince, should dig up a subterranean passage at night and carry away the prince....

43. Or, secret agents disguised as traders should administer poison to guards by selling cooked food and fruits....

46. Or, those disguised as traders should set fire to the market-place....

53. And agents appearing as foresters should direct (pursuers) to another direction when he is going in one.

From: *The Kauṭilīya Arthaśāstra*, Part II, Book 7, "The Six Measures of Foreign Policy," Chapter 18[162]

5. If the middle king were to desire to seize an ally of the conqueror* having the feelings of a friend, he should save the ally by rousing the allies of the ally and his own allies, and dividing his allies from the middle king.

6. Or, he should incite the circle:† "This middle king, grown very powerful, has risen for the destruction of all of us; let us join together and frustrate his expedition."

7. If the circle were to favor that, he should, by the suppression of the middle king, augment himself.

8. If it were not to favor, helping the ally with treasury and army, he should win over by conciliation and gifts one – the principal or the proximate – from among the kings inimical to the middle king, who, many in number, may be helping each other, or of whom, by winning over one, many would be won over, or who, being afraid of each other, would not rise....

10. Augmented in power in this way, he should suppress the middle king.

---

* By "conqueror" is meant *vijigīṣu*.
† While Kangle uses the term "circle," a better translation is circle of kings, i.e., *maṇḍala*.

11. Or, if place and time were to lapse, he should make peace with the middle king … or make a pact for an undertaking with the treasonable (officers of the middle king)….

23. If the middle king were to desire to seize his own enemy, he [the *vijigīṣu*] should help him with treasury and army, unseen….

25. Of the middle and the neutral kings, he should resort to the one who is liked by the circle of kings.*…

40. That ally who might do harm or who, though capable, would not help in times of trouble, he should certainly exterminate him, when trustingly, he comes within his reach.

From: *The Kauṭilīya Arthaśāstra*, Part II, Book 8, "Concerning the Topic of Calamities," Chapter 1[163]

2. A calamity of a constituent, of a divine or human origin, springs from ill luck or wrong policy….

38. Dependent on the fort are the treasury, the army, silent war … use of armed forces, receiving allied troops, and warding off enemy troops and forest tribes.

39. And in the absence of a fort, the treasury will fall into the hands of enemies.

40. For, it is seen that those with forts are not exterminated….

47. The army, indeed, is rooted in the treasury.

48. In the absence of a treasury, the army goes over to the enemy or kills the king….

56. When one has an army, one's ally remains friendly, or (even) the enemy becomes friendly.

From: *The Kauṭilīya Arthaśāstra*, Part II, Book 8, Chapter 2[164]

2. For the king, there is (danger of) revolt in the interior or in the outer regions….

4. Therefore, he should keep the power of the treasury and the army in his own hands.

Rather than launching a regular siege operation, which is bound to be costly and time-consuming, Kautilya urges the use of treachery and deception to eliminate the leaders of enemy forts. Without its leaders, the garrisons of such strongholds would surrender easily.

From: *The Kauṭilīya Arthaśāstra*, Part II, Book 13, "Means of Taking a Fort," Chapter 1[165]

17. Those who agree (to desert), he should endow with money and honor.

---

* The implication is that the *vijigīṣhu* should foment *bheda* between the *madhyama* and the *udasina*. *Madhyama* is the middle kingdom situated between the *vijigīṣu*'s realm and the hostile kingdoms. And *udasina* is a neutral king who might tip the military balance for and against the *vijigīṣu* by joining either the *vijigīṣu* or the latter's enemies.

From: *The Kauṭilīya Arthaśāstra*, Part II, Book 13, "Means of Taking a Fort," Chapter 2[166]

15. Or, an agent appearing as a holy man, finding shelter in (the temple of) an honored deity of the country, should, by frequent festivities, win over the chiefs among the constituents and gradually overreach the king....

20. Agents appearing as traders, coming with horses for sale, should invite the king to purchase or receive horses as a gift, and kill him while engrossed in inspecting the goods or when mingled with horses....

42. Or, secret agents should tempt the (enemy) greedy of money or ... rich widows (or) women possessed of great beauty and youth, taken to him....

43. When he agrees, they should, concealed in ambush, kill him with [a] weapon or poison at the time of the meeting.

44. Or, on the occasions of his frequent visits to holy men, mendicants, images of deities in sanctuaries and *stūpas*,* assassins, concealed in underground chambers or passages or inside hollow walls, should strike at the enemy.

Manu's Laws of *Dharmayuddha*

In 75 CE, a brahmin minister (*amatya*) of the last Sunga ruler deposed his master and established the Kanva dynasty, which lasted until 28 CE. The Bactrian Greeks established a short-lived Indo-Bactrian Empire in Punjab, which was destroyed by the Sakas in 130 BCE. By 80 CE, the Saka Empire in India spread across Punjab, Uttar Pradesh, and West India. The Sakas in turn were pushed into Saurashtra by the Parthians, who ruled parts of west and northwest India in the first century CE. Around 120 CE, the Parthians were eclipsed by the Kushanas.[167] In 226 CE, the Sassanians destroyed the Kushanas.[168] In central and west India, the Satavahanas were then the dominant power. However, none of these polities was a centralized pan-Indian entity on a par with the Maurya Empire.[169] Thapar claims that after the break up of the Maurya Empire, "[t]he monarchical system, which increasingly leaned on religious orthodoxy, tended to blur the concept of state, and instead loyalty was directed to the social order. The interdependence of caste and politics had gradually led to caste being accorded higher status than political institutions."[170] Social and ritual obligations in accordance with caste (*varna*) took precedence over the state. The Bactrian and Parthian rulers were considered as *mlechchas* by the Brahmin intellectuals because these foreigners patronized Buddhism rather than Hinduism.[171] Some Greeks who had settled in India accepted Vaishnavism and Saivasim.

The *sutra* literature emerged between 700 BCE and 300 CE. This literature deals mainly with religious matters. Also discussed are duties of the king and matters relating to criminal law.[172] In Manu's *Manava-Dharmasastra* (henceforth *MD*), military law

---

* Holy statues or places of worship.

figures as an additional topic of inquiry. The title *Manusmriti* was first used in 1503 CE. It emphasizes Manu's authorship. However, it is better to name this work the *Manava-Dharmasastra*, or "laws for human beings" especially prepared under Manu's guidance, a title that is attested before the sixteenth century.[173]

The ancient Sanskrit *acharya*s believed the Hindus of the subcontinent constituted the core of the world. They viewed the people outside Jambudvipa (ancient name of the subcontinent) as barbarians. P. V. Kane asserts that before the fourth century BCE, there was a work on *dharmasastra* composed by or attributed to Svayambhuva Manu. There was also a work on *rajadharma* by Pracetasa Manu. The *Mahabharata* and the *Arthasastra* refer to these works. The above-mentioned two works constitute the kernel of the *MD*, which was recast by Bhrgu between the second century BCE and the second century CE.[174] Patrick Olivelle asserts that the *MD* was composed by a single individual or probably by a committee of scholars under the chairmanship of a strong personality. Manu is not the real name of that gifted person. His original name is unknown. But we will follow tradition and call the author Manu. In all probability, he was a learned Brahmin from north India. Olivelle rejects the view that *MD* was the product of gradual accretions by countless people over several centuries because the work reflects a coherent structure and a style that could come only from the pen of a particular individual. Olivelle goes on to say that the code was initially written down.[175] While Tripathi, Doniger, and Smith accept that Manu's *MD* was composed around the beginning of the Christian era,[176] Olivelle asserts that the text was composed and written between the first century BCE and the second century CE.[177] Doniger and Smith claim that chapters 8 and 9 are later additions.[178] For our part, we are concerned mainly with chapter 7.

The brahmanical reaction constitutes the context in which Manu's *MD* was generated. One aspect of this reaction was that while both the Nanda and the Maurya dynasties were established by the Sudras, the Brahmins established the succeeding Sunga and Kanva dynasties. Compared with previous *dharmasastra* works, Manu accords much more importance and space to *rajadharma* in his compendium of laws.[179] Manu is trying to ward off the threat posed by the Sudras to the dominance of the Kshatriyas and the Brahmins. However, in order to maintain internal stability, Manu focuses on political legitimacy, as well as the use of force. Manu's policy is that the Brahmins should legitimize Kshatriya kingship and in return should receive the lion's share of material and nonmaterial rewards from the ruling regime. Manu uses *dharma* both in the general sense of righteousness and in the particular sense of social conduct and court laws. In Manu's universalistic text, political power is considered inferior to priestly ideals and rituals. Manu accepts the laws of *karma*. The ethical components of *dharma* for Manu are honesty (*asteya*), wisdom (*dhi*), steadfastness (*dhriti*), energy for a just purpose (*dama*), forgiveness (*kshama*), and purity, both mental and physical (*saucham*). Unlike Kautilya, Manu argues for the primacy of *dharma* in statecraft. Kautilya advocates that the king should pursue financial power (*artha*), sexual desire (*kama*), and *dharma* in a balanced manner, and these three are interdependent. Manu, by contrast, ordains that if *artha* and *kama* go against *dharma*, then the first two ought to be abandoned. In Manu's paradigm, the *dharma* of the Kshatriya is protection of the people, which in turn requires taxation of the *praja*s of the *rashtra*.[180] This sort of thinking evolved later into paternal despotism in Kamandaka's theory.

At the tactical level, Manu notes that in the absence of a strong cavalry, a ruler should not undertake aggressive campaigns but rather follow an appeasement policy toward the enemy. Manu's emphasis on the use of troops in battle formation for close quarter battle with the enemy challenges Western scholars such as Rosen, Wink, T. A. Heathcote, and George Tanham, who claim that ancient Indian warfare was merely a ritualized combat. Like Kautilya, instead of open attacks on the enemy's army, the *MD* prefers fortress warfare. Although Manu constructs a normative model for *dharmayuddha* during a battle, for siege warfare, Manu incorporates two elements of *kutayuddha*: pillaging the enemy's territory and surprise night attacks. At the strategic level, Manu notes the importance of coalition warfare with allies striving toward a common objective. Overall, Manu succeeded in coming out with a theory for maintaining internal order but failed to address the problem of external invasions by the *mlechchas*. Manu's normative model for conducting *dharmayuddha* reduced the combat-effectiveness of the Hindu armies. Archaeological references note the legacy of *MD*. An inscription of the Valabhi King Dharasena dated 571 CE reveals that the rules made by Manu were obeyed by this king.[181]

From: *Mānva-Dharmaśāstra* (Manu's Code of Law), Chapter 7, "The Law for the King"[182]

1. I will explain the Laws pertaining to kings – how a king should conduct himself, how he came into being, and how he can attain the highest success.

From: *Mānva-Dharmaśāstra*, Chapter 7, "The Law for the King": "Origin of the King"[183]

17. Punishment is the king; he is the male, he is the leader; he is the ruler; and, tradition tells us, he stands as the surety for the Law with respect to the four orders of life....

27. When a king administers Punishment properly, he flourishes ... but the king who is lustful, partial, and vile is slain by that very Punishment.

28. For Punishment is immense energy, and it cannot be wielded by those with uncultivated selves. It assuredly slays a king who deviates from the Law, along with his relatives....

31. Punishment can only be administered by someone who is honest and true to his word, who acts in conformity with the Treatises, who has good assistants, and who is wise.

Proper Behavior

32. Within his realm, he should act in accordance with the rules; upon his enemies, he should impose harsh punishments; toward his friends and loved ones, he should behave without guile; and to the Brahmins, he should show compassion....

35. The king was created as the protector of people belonging to all social classes and orders of life....

From: *Mānva-Dharmaśāstra*, Chapter 7, "The Law for the King": "Cultivating Virtue and Learning"[184]

43. From experts in the three Vedas, he should learn the triple Veda, the timeless science of government, logical reasoning, and the philosophy of self....

From: *Mānva-Dharmaśāstra*, Chapter 7, "The Law for the King": "Appointment of an Envoy"[185]

65. The army depends on the official; the enforcement of order, on the army; the treasury and the realm, on the king; and alliance and its reverse on the envoy.

66. For an envoy is the one who forges an alliance; and he is the one who splits allies apart.

From: *Mānva-Dharmaśāstra*, Chapter 7, "The Law for the King": "Constructing the Royal Fort"[186]

70. A fortress secured by a desert, a fortress with an earthen rampart, a fortress surrounded by water, a fortress protected by a forest, a fortress guarded by soldiers, and a fortress protected by a hill – finding safety in such a fortress, he should settle in a fort.

71. He should try his very best to find safety in a hill fortress; for the hill fortress, because of its numerous superior features, is the most excellent of them....

73. ... so his foes do not harm a king who has found safety in a fortress.

74. One archer positioned on a rampart can fight off a hundred, and one hundred can fight off ten thousand. On account of this, a fortress is most excellent.

75. It should be well supplied with weapons, money, grain, conveyances, Brahmins, artisans, machines, fodder, and water.

From: *Mānva-Dharmaśāstra*, Chapter 7, "The Law for the King": "Collectors and Supervisors"[187]

80. He should employ trusted officials to collect annual taxes from his realm, strictly follow tradition in his dealings with the population, and behave like a father toward his people.

From: *Mānva-Dharmaśāstra*, Chapter 7, "The Law for the King": "War and Warrior Ethic"[188]

87. When challenged by rivals – whether they are stronger, weaker, or of equal strength – as he protects his subjects, a king must never back away from battle, recalling the Law of Kshatriyas.

88. Refusal to turn back in battle, protecting the subjects, and obedient service to Brahmins – for kings, these are the best mean[s] of securing happiness.

89. When kings fight each other in battles with all their strength, seeking to kill each other and refusing to turn back, they go to heaven.

90. When he is engaged in battle, he must never slay his enemies with weapons that are treacherous, barbed, or laced with poison, or whose tips are ablaze with fire.

91. He must never slay a man standing on the ground, an effeminate man, a man with joined palms, a man with loose hair, a seated man, a man declaring "I am yours,"

92. a sleeping man, a man without his armor . . . a man without his weapons, a non-fighting spectator, a man engaging someone else,

93. a man with damaged weapons, a man in distress, a badly wounded man, a frightened man, or a man who has turned tail – recalling the Law followed by good people.

94. When a man is killed in battle by the enemy as he turns tail frightened, he takes upon himself all the evil deeds committed by his master. . . .

From: *Mānva-Dharmaśāstra*, Chapter 7, "The Law for the King": "War Booty"[189]

96. Whatever a man wins – chariot, horse, elephant, parasol, money, grain, livestock, women, all goods, and base metal – all that belongs to him.

97. A preemptive share, however, should be given to the king – so states the Vedic scripture; and the king should distribute among the soldiers anything that has not been won in single combat.

98. I have set forth above the eternal Law of warriors. . . . A Kshatriya must never deviate from this Law, as he kills his enemies in battle.

From: *Mānva-Dharmaśāstra*, Chapter 7, "The Law for the King": "Policies for Good Government"[190]

99. The king should seek to acquire what he has not acquired, preserve diligently what he has acquired, augment what he has preserved, and distribute what he has augmented on worthy recipients. . . .

101. What he has not acquired, he should seek to acquire with military force; what he has acquired, he should preserve with vigilance; what he has preserved, he should augment through profitable investments; and what he has augmented, he should distribute through gifts.

102. He should keep his military force in constant readiness, constantly display his might, constantly guard his secrets, and constantly probe his enemy's weaknesses.

103. The whole world stands in awe of the man who keeps his military force in constant readiness; it is with military force, therefore, that he should subdue all creatures.

104. He should always act without guile and never with guile; and, guarding himself well at all times, he should detect the guile employed by his enemies.

105. He must not let the enemy discover any weakness of his, but discover any weakness of the enemy; he should hide his limbs like a tortoise and conceal his own weak points. . . .

107. As he thus engages in conquest, he should bring under his control all the adversaries he encounters by the use of strategies beginning with conciliation.

108. If, after the employment of the first three strategies, they still do not submit, then he should undoubtedly subdue them by military force and in due course bring them under his control.

109. Among all four strategies beginning with conciliation, experts always recommend conciliation and military force for the enhancement of his realm. . . .

111. When a king in his folly oppresses his own realm indiscriminately, he is soon deprived of his kingdom and his life, along with his relatives.

112. As living beings destroy their lives by oppressing their bodies, so kings too destroy their lives by oppressing their realms.

113. He should observe this rule always in managing his realm, for when his realm is well managed, the king prospers with ease.

From: *Mānva-Dharmaśāstra*, Chapter 7, "The Law for the King": "Organization of the State"[191]

114. He should station well-supervised constabularies in the middle of two, three, and five villages, as also in the middle of one hundred villages for the protection of his realm.

115. He should appoint superintendents responsible for one village, for ten villages, for twenty villages, for one hundred villages, and for one thousand villages.

116. When troubles arise in a village, the superintendent of that village should, in due course, report them personally to the superintendent of ten villages, and he in turn, to the superintendent of twenty village[s].

117. The superintendent of twenty villages should report all that to the superintendent of a hundred villages, and he in turn should report them personally to the superintendent of a thousand villages.

118. The superintendent of a village shall avail himself of the food, drink, firewood, and the like that the villagers are required to supply daily to the king.

From: *Mānva-Dharmaśāstra*, Chapter 7, "The Law for the King": "Supervision of Officials"[192]

120. Their activities pertaining to the villages, as well as those undertaken by each individually, should be overseen vigilantly by another loyal officer of the king.

121. In each city he should appoint a general manager of all affairs. . . .

122. He should always make the circuit of all those officials personally and investigate their conduct within their jurisdictions thoroughly through resident spies;

123. for the king's officials, appointed to protect the people, often become swindlers seizing the property of others – he must protect his subjects from them.

124. When these evil-minded men extort money from people who have business with them, the king should confiscate all their property and send them into exile.

From: *Mānva-Dharmaśāstra*, Chapter 7, "The Law for the King": "Taxes and Duties"[193]

127. The king should levy taxes on traders after taking into consideration the price of purchase and sale, the distance of transport, maintenance and other expenses, and the cost of security.

128. The king should always assess taxes in his realm after careful consideration so that both he and those who do the work get their fair reward.

129. As leeches, calves, and bees eat their food a little at a time, so a king should gather annual taxes from his realm a little at a time.

130. Of livestock and gold, the king shall take a one-fiftieth share; and of grains, an eighth share, or a sixth or twelfth.

131. He shall also take a sixth share of trees, meat, honey, ghee,* perfumes, herbs, condiments, flowers, roots, fruits....

133. Even at the point of death, he shall never extract a tax from a Vedic scholar, nor shall a Vedic scholar living within his realm languish from hunger....

135. After ascertaining the man's learning and conduct, he should provide him with a means of subsistence consistent with the Law† and protect him in every way, as a father his own natural son.

136. When such a person practices the Law every day under the protection of the king, it augments the king's life span, wealth, and realm....

139. He must not cut off his own root and that of others through excessive greed; for by cutting off his own root, he does harm both to himself and to them.

From: *Mānva-Dharmaśāstra*, Chapter 7, "The Law for the King": "Protection of the Subjects"[194]

142. ... he should protect these subjects with care and vigilance.

143. When bandits abduct from his realm subjects screaming for help, while he and men in his service stand by – he is surely dead, he is not alive.

---

* Clarified butter.

† Rather than "law," I would translate this as "Vedic *dharma*." For the Sanskrit text, see *Manu's Code of Law, A Critical Edition and Translation of the Manava-Dharmasastra*, Patrick Olivelle and Suman Olivelle (ed. and trans.) (New Delhi: Oxford University Press, 2006), p. 636.

144. For a Kshatriya, the protection of his subjects is the highest Law; the enjoyment of the specified rewards binds the king to this Law.

From: *Mānva-Dharmaśāstra*, Chapter 7, "The Law for the King": "Meeting with Counselors"[195]

148. When common people, as they conspire, do not discover a king's plans, he will enjoy the entire earth, even though his treasury is empty. . . .

151. At midday or midnight, when he is not tired or worn out, he should reflect on these matters either in consultation with his counselors or alone – on Law, Wealth, and Pleasure,

152. and on how they may be acquired all together when they are in mutual opposition. . . .

155. on the activities of the buffer king*; on the conduct of the power hungry king; and on the activities of the neutral king and, with great diligence, of the enemy king.

From: *Mānva-Dharmaśāstra*, Chapter 7, "The Law for the King": "Constituents of the Circle"[196]

156. The above constituents, in brief, form the root of the circle of neighboring kings; eight others also have been enumerated, bringing the total, according to the tradition, to twelve. . . .

159. He should prevail over them by conciliation and the other strategies employed both separately and collectively, and by valor and policy. . . .

163. He should know that there are two kinds of alliance: the one is when both parties march together into battle with the same objective – it is of immediate significance; the other is its opposite – and it looks to the future.

164. Tradition records two types of war: the one is waged on one's own and for one's own ends, whether it is at a proper time or not; the other is occasioned when an ally has initiated the offensive.

165. Marching into battle is said to be of two types: the one is undertaken alone when an urgent situation has suddenly arisen; the other is undertaken in coalition with an ally.

166. Tradition records two types of remaining stationary: the one is undertaken when he is gradually weakened either by fate or due to his past deeds; and the other is undertaken as a favor to an ally. . . .

169. When he is convinced that his future dominance is certain and that any immediate disadvantage is slight, then he should resort to an alliance.

---

* Rather than "buffer king," I would translate this as "middle king," i.e., *madhyama*. See Sanskrit text in *MD*, Olivelle, p. 640.

170. When he believes that all his subjects are exceedingly content and that he himself is overwhelmingly powerful, then he should consider waging war.

171. When he believes in his heart that his own army is in high spirit and prosperous and that the opposite is true of his adversary, then he should march into battle against his enemy.

172. When he is weak in terms of mounted units and infantry, then he should diligently remain stationary, while gradually appeasing the enemy. . . .

174. When he has become extremely vulnerable to his enemy's forces, then he should quickly seek asylum with a strong and righteous king.

175. Should that king keep both his own subjects and the forces of his enemy in check, he should always serve him . . . with all his strength.

176. Even in that case, however, if he notices a liability resulting from his asylum, he should, even in that condition, resort to the good war* without hesitation.

From: *Mānva-Dharmaśāstra*, Chapter 7, "The Law for the King": "War"[197]

181. When the king launches a military expedition against the realm of an enemy, he should advance at a measured pace toward the enemy's fort. . . .

182. The king should start a military expedition during the auspicious month of Mārgaśirṣa (November–December), or toward the month of Phālguna (February-March) or Caitra (March–April), depending on the shape of his armed forces.

183. Even at other times when he foresees certain victory, he should undoubtedly declare war and launch the expedition, as also when a calamity has struck the enemy.

184. He should first make the necessary arrangements for his home territory, gather provisions for the expedition . . . secure a base for military operations, deploy spies suitably,

185. secure the three types of roads, and inspect the six divisions of his army – and only then march in battle formation. . . .

190. [He should] deploy on all sides platoons of reliable soldiers with whom signals have been arranged, who are adept both at holding their ground and at pressing an attack, and who are fearless and unwavering;

191. deploy a small group to fight in close quarters and freely spread out a large group; send them into battle arrayed in the needle and the thunderbolt formations;

192. fight with chariots and horses on level ground, with boats and elephants in marshy lands, with bows in areas covered with trees and shrubs, and with swords and shields on flat land. . . .

---

* Rather than "good war," "just war" is more appropriate.

194. After arraying the troops in battle formation, he should rouse them and inspect them closely; and he should monitor their behavior even when they are engaged in combat with enemy troops.

195. After laying siege to the enemy, he shall remain stationary – he should plunder his realm; constantly ruin his supplies of fodder, food, water, and fuel;

196. demolish reservoirs, ramparts, and moats; launch surprise assaults against him; frighten him at night;

197. foment sedition among the seditious; keep close watch over enemy activity … fearlessly launch the attack with the determination to win.

198. He should strive to triumph over his enemies through conciliation, gifts, and fomenting dissension, employed collectively or separately, but never through war.

199. Victory and defeat in battle are uncertain for the two combatants; he should, therefore, avoid war.

200. When the aforementioned three strategies fail, then let him, always on guard, pursue war in such a manner that he will triumph over his enemies.

From: *Mānva-Dharmaśāstra*, Chapter 7, "The Law for the King": "Conduct in Victory"[198]

201. After the victory, he should … grant exemptions; and issue proclamations of amnesty.

Kamandaka's Fusion: *Dharmayuddha* and a Watered-Down Version of *Kutayuddha*

The *Nitisara* of Kamandaka, also known as the *Kamandakiya-Nitisara*, is mostly based on Kautilya's *Arthaśāstra* and believed to be a revised and updated version of *Sukra-Nitisara*. Kamandaka's *Nitisara* was composed, in the view of G. P. Singh, around 400 CE during the reign of Gupta Emperor Chandragupta II (374–414 CE). It is thought that the *Sukra-Nitisara* was composed around the fourth century BCE.[199] Kamandaka himself states that he considers Vishnugupta as his *guru* (master). Kane writes that Kamandaka lived around the third century CE.[200] Devahuti claims that Kamandaka was a contemporary of Varahamihira, the astronomer and mathematician who lived around 550 CE, and that the *Kamandaka Nitisara* was composed between 450 and 550 CE.[201] However, P. C. Chakravarti assigns the eighth century CE as the date for Kamandaka's *Nitisara*.[202]

The *Brihaspati Sutra*, a work written just prior to Kamandaka's *Nitisara*, also falls within the genre of *arthasastra* literature. While the *Brihaspati Sutra* gives overt importance to the acquisition of financial assets by the king for maintaining strong rule,[203] Kamandaka, like Kautilya, includes politics and diplomacy along with wealth that enable the *vijigīṣu* to maintain strong rule. Both Kamandaka and Kautilya recommend

Lokayata (materialistic) philosophy and put less emphasis on ascetic principles and practices.[204]

Kamandaka, similar to Kautilya, accepts the *saptanga* theory of state.[205] Kamandaka frequently uses animal imagery in order to explain the various strategic scenarios and likewise emphasizes the daily training of the troops. Both Kautilya and Kamandaka refer to six types of troops: hereditary troops, mercenaries, guild levies, soldiers supplied by the feudatory chiefs and the allies, forest tribes, and troops captured and won over from the enemy. Both these authors refer to the existence of trading and craft guilds with their private soldiery, who were hired by the rulers during emergencies in order to meet both internal as well as external threats. Kautilya and Kamandaka also refer to the existence of predatory forest chieftains who might foment *kopa*.[206] For maintaining internal order, Kamandaka urges the king if necessary to act like *Yama*, the Hindu God of death. Kamandaka, like Kautilya, points out the linkages between internal disturbances and external dangers. Kamandaka elaborates the concept of paternal despotism. Kautilya also expounds the concept of paternal despotism when he says: "*sarvatra copahatan pitevanugrhniyat.*"[207] Kamandaka also criticized overtly militaristic rulers (in this case the *Ativigrahis*), just as Plato and Aristotle had criticized the Spartans.[208] In *sarga* (chapter) 9, verse 74, Kamandaka criticizes militarism. In *sarga* 12, verse 41, Kamandaka advises the *vijigīsu* that if possible he himself should never initiate an attritional campaign, as such an endeavor would dissipate his manpower and financial resources.

For Kamandaka, waging just war necessitates preventing any unnecessary harm to animals. Hence, Kamandaka criticizes a linkage between military training and hunting, by arguing that it is unethical to kill innocent animals for the purposes of enhancing military skill. However, at the same time, Kamandaka emphasizes the necessity of waging *kutayuddha* under certain circumstances, particularly as a means of limiting the impact of warfare. In his paradigm, the impact of regular warfare is much greater than the impact of *kutayuddha* on the fabric of society. Like Kautilya, Kamandaka argues that it is quite ethical for ambassadors (*dutas*) to function as spies in the foreign kingdoms. In *sarga* 12, verse 6, it seems as if Kamandaka is arguing against surprise attack; however, in *sarga* 19, verse 55, he advocates such actions. Akin to Manu, he even defends harming the civilian economy of the enemy kingdom as part of *kutayuddha*. And Kamandaka, like Kautilya, speaks of nocturnal raids. Kamandaka accepts the necessity of flank attacks as part of *kutayuddha* but like Manu notes that it is unethical to destroy the retreating enemy soldiers. Overall, while Kautilya wholly supports *kutayuddha*, Kamandaka is half-heartedly pushing the concept of *kutayuddha*.

At the tactical level, Kamandaka, like Kautilya, emphasizes the value of using elephants as battering rams in battle (his *prakasayuddha*,[209] which is a part of *dharmayuddha*). Despite the fact that the Central Asian nomadic tribes with their mounted archery ran roughshod over the armies of the Sungas and Kanvas, mounted archery was never a preferred method for either Kautilya or Kamandaka. The Guptas in order to check the Huns took to mounted archery. After the fall of the Guptas, India forgot all about horse archery and the Hindu *rajas* continued to wage internecine warfare with elephants as advocated by Kamandaka. One reason was that the ecology of India was not suitable for breeding good horses. Second, mounted archery could be performed creditably only by the steppe nomads. By the ninth century CE, the elephant-centric armies of the Hindus faced defeat against the mounted archery of the Islamic nomads.

From: *The Nītisāra by Kāmandaki, Sarga* 1[210]

9. . . . A king (by providing good government and ensuring all round prosperity) becomes the source of delight to his people. . . .

11. A king of righteous conduct, who governs the state justly and properly, and who (like a *vijigīṣu*, imbued with the policy of expansion), is capable of capturing enemy fortifications (*parapurañjayaṁ*), is acclaimed as the veritable *Prajāpati* (the Lord of all created beings) by his subjects.

12. An essential duty of the king is to protect the subjects of his dominion (*āyattam*), particularly their gainful occupations (*vārtā*, i.e., agriculture, cattle rearing and trade), which flourish only under royal protection. Disruption of economic vocations causes the most distressing condition of the people. . . .

14. A king should by all means protect his subjects, who in their turn contribute to his material prosperity (*pārthiva*, i.e., *kośa* or treasury, augmented by contribution from the subjects in cash and kind in the form of royal share or *bhāga*). . . .

15. A king, who governs justly conforming to the traditional laws (*nyāyapravṛttah*), acquires merits of *Trivarga* (three ends of life, viz., *Dharma, Artha* and *Kāma*) for himself as well as for his subjects, whereas his failure leads to total ruination. . . .

17. It is advisable therefore for a king to show due regard to righteousness . . . even in matters of acquisition of wealth. Because a kingdom flourishes only by means of righteousness. . . .

20. Acquisition of wealth by lawful means (by collection of revenue at standard rates etc.), its proper preservation and augmentation . . . and its judicious application in deserving cases (evidently for the welfare of the state), are the four-fold functions of a ruler.

21. Well versed in the laws of polity, possessing courage (valor) an ever-energetic king should exert for the attainment of prosperity. For, discipline (*vinaya*)* is the root of polity. . . .

40. A king (of unrestrained mind), given up to enjoyment of fleeting sensual pleasures, not only suffers from remorse when such enjoyment is over, but also runs the risk of subjugation (*grahaṁ*) by his enemies just as the elephant is entrapped (due to his own folly). . . .

65. A well disciplined (self-restrained) ruler following the prescriptions of the science of polity shines . . . by achieving . . . predominance in the . . . *maṇḍala*. . . .

71. A powerful ruler, apparently invincible, may be easily subjugated by his enemies for lack of self-restraint. But a weak ruler practicing self-restraint as prescribed in the *Śāstras*,† never suffers defeat.

---

* *Vinaya* means mental discipline and politeness.
† Ancient Sanskrit literature dealing with both religious and secular issues.

From: *The Nītisāra by Kāmandaki, Sarga 2*[211]

15. *Daṇḍa* stands for suppression (of anti-social elements by inflicting necessary punishments . . .). (As administration of justice is a function of the king), he is often identified with *Daṇḍa*. Hence the science dealing with *Daṇḍa* is called *Daṇḍanīti.* . . .

20. Use of arms and protection of all beings (in his dominion) are the occupations of the king (or the Kshatriyas), and cattle rearing, agriculture and trade are the means of subsistence of the Vaiśyas. . . .

32. *Ahiṁsā* (non-injury to beings), excellence of speech, truthfulness, purity (external and internal), mercy and forgiveness are the common duties of man of all castes. . . .

34. It is the king who (by the application of *daṇḍaśakti** . . .) leads the people to the practice of these rules in the proper manner; in the absence of . . . (the king) *Dharma* declines . . . ultimately causing destruction of the world or social order. . . .

36. Thus (ensuring the social order by supporting the *varṇas* and *āśramas*[†]) securing benefits for both the present existence and the next for himself and for his subjects, the self-possessed king holds the *daṇḍa* . . . impartially. . . .

37. Excessively rigorous punishments make the king repulsive to the people, whereas mild punishments make him contemptible. The best course is to award only just punishments (*yuktadaṇḍa*, proportionate to the gravity of [the] offense).[‡] . . .

39. Punishments should be just, in conformity with the *Śāstras* (legal texts) and conducive to the people (respecting their customs and traditions). When the mode of punishment does not infuriate the people, it brings about prosperity, otherwise due to excitement of the people the course of *dharma* is disrupted (*adharma* flourishes), ultimately causing ruin of the ruler.

40. In the world (society) people move about in different directions trying to push [their] own interests by devouring (usurping) others, as if out of greed for their flesh. . . . In the absence of *daṇḍa* (unless controlled and subdued by the king ...) *mātsyanyāya* (the law of fishes, the big fish swallows the smaller fry) prevails and the whole social order perishes.

From: *The Nītisāra by Kāmandaki, Sarga 4*[212]

1–2. The king . . . ministers, territory . . . *durga*, treasury . . . *caturaṅga*,[§] and allies . . . constitute the seven . . . limbs of the . . . *rājyam*. These elements are interrelated and interdependent, so much so that if any of them is out of order the whole system . . . breaks down. Hence careful attempts should be directed toward all round development of the elements collectively. . . .

---

* Coercive power.
† Educational institutions of the Brahmins.
‡ This is one of the indices of West European just war tradition.
§ This should be "*Chaturanga bala.*"

6–9. The qualities of a worthy ruler are the following – Nobility of his lineage, composure (in all circumstances, fair or foul), youthful vigor, good conduct, compassion, promptness (in executing royal business), consistency (in speech and action), truthfulness, rendering due service to the learned … gratefulness, faith in divine dispensations, intelligence, association with large hearted (liberal) men (and not with men of narrow outlook), possession of strong feudatories (*śakyasāmanta*, well able to assist the king in tackling the enemies), deep devotion (to spiritual and material affairs), farsightedness, energy, purity (internal and external), ambition (to effect expansion of territory and augmentation of wealth …), [the] power of self-restraint and piety….

15–19. Qualities enumerated below constitute … the personal possessions … of a king: – eloquence and frugality of speech (as necessary for refutation of others' arguments), memory … stately physical form (or domineering personality), strength (mental and physical), self-restraint … power of leadership, skill in the application of *daṇḍa* (coercive measures) … ability to win over the antisocial elements, steadiness during enemy action, knowledge of ultimate results or possible reactions … promptness in detecting the weak points of enemies, acquaintance with the laws of peace and war … observance of strict secrecy of decisions or counsels as well as actions … [the] ability to take advantages of place and time….

20. Adorned with these qualities (of head and heart) and well aware of the nature of men and matters … he who remedies all troubles of his subjects and governs them as a father unto them … is worthy of being a … ruler of [the] earth….

From: *The Nītisāra by Kāmandaki, Sarga* 5[213]

19. Deception, trickery, arrogance and cupidity should also be avoided by a dependent.* He should be respectful to the royal princes and king's favorites….

22. Whenever the king says "who is there," the dependent should promptly respond "I am here, kindly command me, my lord," and carry out the order properly and promptly (to the best of his abilities)….

80. A ruler, even if weak, should promote the interests of the trading class … (particularly of the importers of commodities), and not cause obstructions … to the free flow of it (by imposing embargo or tariff).

From: *The Nītisāra by Kāmandaki, Sarga* 6[214]

4. … Protection of the subjects is the greatest duty (*dharmaḥ*) of the king….

5. In performing his duties the king may have to adopt violent measures (i.e., inflict punishments, including capital punishment), to deal with dishonest … people dispassionately…. For that, no blame would lie with the king.

---

* Vassal ruler.

From: *The Nītisāra by Kāmandaki, Sarga* 8[215]

1. The king, securely settled in his fortified castle, possessing a flourishing treasury, a strong army and an efficient band of officers and counsellors, is regarded by the wise to be the master of the *maṇḍala*....

52. Friendship and enmity are born out of relevant causes.... Hence such causes as lead to the development of hostility should be ... (avoided).

53. The king (*vijigīṣu*) should take suitable measures to satisfy all his subjects throughout the dominion (including the newly acquired territories) and win their hearts over (by providing them with all possible amenities). Because when the king enjoys love and devotion of his subjects, no doubt he secures all round prosperity....

57. Destruction of enemy territory, forcing loss or waste of his powers, taking oppressive and harassing measures against him and his subjects, these are the four expedients to be adopted suitably by the *vijigīṣu* against his enemy, as recommended by experts in the science of polity....

58. Creation of disaffection and dissatisfaction in the enemy's dominion by covert use of *kośa* and *daṇḍa* ... and also by secret assassination of the *mahāmātras*, the *vijigīṣu* should oppress and harass his enemy kingdom.*

59. Action should be taken to exterminate the enemy (*ari*) ... if he is devoid of (adequately strong) fortifications, whose allies are weak themselves and enemies strong....

64. In the event of an invasion by a stronger foe, apprehending total annihilation, the *vijigīṣu* should provide resources (in the form of land or money or both) to the invader (in order to pacify him).

65. If on the liquidation of an enemy there is a chance of breaking out of hostility with another enemy (presumably a stronger one), the *vijigīṣu* should not ... liquidate his territory ..., but he should bring it under his control (by making it a dependency)....

68. Fish devours fish. So also unsuspected collaterals or relatives cut each other's throat....

71. The whole *Maṇḍala* (of twelve rulers) is composed of hostile and friendly powers and all of them are selfish (i.e., looking for their own interests). (As friendliness and hostility depend upon selfish motives, such feelings cannot be stable, that is, ever-shifting, according to circumstances). Hence perfect neutrality is hardly possible among them....

81. A *vijigīṣu* should not openly take the side of any one of his allies (lest others may be estranged from him out of envy). He himself should prevent them from being malicious against one another (or encourage a feeling or rivalry among them to gain his favors).

---

* I have modified the original translation. Here *kośa* means financial resources and *mahamatras* means important state officials.

From: *The Nītisāra by Kāmandaki, Sarga 9*[216]

50. Wealth or the resources of a state will not be unnecessarily exhausted if peace is concluded with a stronger adversary.... It may provide the weaker ruler to demonstrate his prowess in an opportune time....

53. [The] king (*vijigīṣu*) should not place too much reliance on his adversary even after concluding peace (i.e., he should not be complacent); rather he should mark time during the period of cessation of hostilities and strike him....

67. The assailed ruler should enter into secret alliances with the crown prince and principal officers (of the assailant king) in order to create dissension (in the ranks) of the assailant king of firm resolution (so that his resolution is slackened due to growing internal dissension ...).

68–69. He should also by offering money (bribes) and procuring forged documents (of sinister import) try to implicate the principal officers of the enemy state with false charges of corruption.

When an intelligent ruler is able to implicate the principal officers of the enemy with charges of corruption, the enemy, however formidable thinking faithlessness to be rampant in his own ranks, becomes inactive himself (i.e., does not care to risk a military expedition)....

72. (In order to prevent an imminent invasion by the enemy) the ruler should deploy spies in the guise of astrologers ... so that they would predict ... the dangerous results of the venture undertaken (which may dampen the spirit of the invader and his men for the time being at least).

73. In view of the fact that in a war loss of men and materials (*kṣaya*), heavy expenditure ... various difficulties ... and death of principal officers etc., are unavoidable, an intelligent ruler should carefully assess the probable losses and benefits and would not like to continue a war (i.e., call a truce) even by willing acceptance of some hardship, for, the consequences of war are always disastrous.

74. In [the] course of a war the ruler may in a moment have to suffer the loss of his wives, his own self, friends and allies and also his wealth. In consideration of constant anxiety and mental suffering resulting from wars an intelligent ruler should not indulge in frequent warfare (i.e., he should not be a warmonger (*ativigrahī*)....

76. A wise ruler when assailed should adopt the three well-known means of *sāma* (conciliation), *dāna* (offer of gifts) and *bheda* (sowing dissension in [the] enemy's ranks) and conclude peace with the assailant. If the assailant himself is desirous of peace, though of identical military strength, the ruler would do well to conclude peace with him from a distance (i.e., before he undertakes a march).

77. Armed with adequate defenses and a well-organized army, a wise ruler, if assailed, should deal furiously with the attacking enemy, so that the latter is made to suffer serious consequences. Only when the enemy is afflicted severely, will [he] ... sue for peace....

From: *The Nītisāra by Kāmandaki, Sarga* 10[217]

*Vigrahavikalpa**

1. Seized with revengefulness and agitated by feelings of resentment due to mutual harmful actions men take recourse to war (*vigraha*).

2. War is also resorted to by one aspiring after elevation of his status (aiming at overlordship) or one suffering from harassment at the hands of his enemies, provided his territorial and military resources and time are advantageous to him.

3–5. The sources (or causes) of war ... have been enumerated as follows: usurpation of the kingdom, abduction of women (of the royal family), occupation of forts and portions of territory, capture of ... (horses, chariots, etc.) as well as treasure ... or enticing away of the learned men and soldiers (by the enemy), (one's own) arrogance and false sense of pride, erosion of material resources (due to enemy action ...) infliction of damage to learning ... religion (or religious belief and institutions of the people) ... for the sake of friends (to render aid to them in their difficulties) ... interference or trespass into the dominion of one's dependents previously assured of protection, incitement or disaffection among the rulers of the ... [*maṇḍala*]....

6. To mitigate the evils of war breaking out on (any one or more of) the issues ... conciliatory measures of gifts (for appeasement) and restraint (on one's own self, *dama*) should be adopted. (The method of conciliation for an assailed ruler would be surrender or cession of a part of his territory in order to retain his hold on the rest; and for an assailant it would be restoration of status quo.)

7. ... But if the enemy indulges in destruction of material resources, counter-measures of inflicting similar damage to the resources of the enemy kingdom should have to be taken (so as to compel him to desist from hostilities)....

11. Hostility breaking out on the issue of assassination of an ally (by an assailant ruler) may be minimized (not by pursuing open war but) by the application of secret expedients ... or by employing spies and secret agents for ... [fomenting] panic and confusion in the enemy dominion....

14. A war with a strong power ... supported by other powers can be relieved by sowing dissension (*bheda*) among the parties through alluring offers, conciliatory gifts etc....

24–25. Hence a prudent king should embark upon such wars or expeditions as are prospective of immediate as well as future gains. He should carefully consider such undertakings only which may prove to be gainful in immediate and future times....

26. A ruler should avoid taking action under the influence of lust for wealth or for material pleasures in this world.... This being the view of the ... *Śāstras*....

---

* The decision to go or not to go for war. The term also means that once war is considered as an option, the decision to wage the type of war.

31. Territory, allies and wealth are the three likely gains in a war. So a ruler should embark upon a war when there is a clear prospect of these gains.

32. Gain of wealth is of course important, gain of an ally is more important than that, but the acquisition of territory is the most important of all gains. . . .

33. In a war with an adversary equal in all respects, the wise ruler should first apply the political expedients (*upāyān*), failing which, he may take up arms.

34. Even when a war is thrust upon him, the prudent king should try to pacify . . . [the enemy] by application of political expedients. As victory in war is always uncertain (*anitya*), it should not be launched upon without careful deliberation. . . .

38. A ruler has to bear the attack from a strong assailant by adopting the policy of the tortoise (that withdraws its limbs within its shell) (i.e., the ruler should withdraw from battle and take shelter within his own fortifications). It is only when time is found to be opportune that an intelligent king should strike at his enemy like a furious snake. . . .

39B. All men are selfish and they always strive for the success of their self-interests. . . .

40. (Having submitted to the strong adversary) a ruler should cultivate intimate relations with him to win his absolute confidence and earn his trust by superficially caring for his welfare, and thus know the enemy's plan and policies and get ready to fiercely attack him during the opportune moment. . . . *

44. Desirous of elevating the status of his already well-organized state and keeping himself well informed through the spies of the movements of his *maṇḍala* . . . a . . . *vijigīṣu* should wage war against his enemy with firm resolve and energy for achieving sure success.

From: *The Nītisāra by Kāmandaki, Sarga* 11[218]

13. When it is observed that the striking power . . . of both the *vijigīṣu* and his enemy is identical, the former undertaking a march should take recourse to *āsana* (encampment or laying a siege). . . .

35. For the purpose of union (i.e., in seeking shelter) a ruler should not trust even his own father (what to speak of others).

From: *The Nītisāra by Kāmandaki, Sarga* 12[219]

6. If a ruler acts in a way repugnant to the *Śāstras* and all of a sudden (. . . without due deliberation) falls upon an enemy, he can hardly get back without feeling the impact of the enemy's sword. . . .

7. Of the three *śaktis* (sources of power) *mantra-śakti* (the power of good counsel) is of greater significance than either *prabhāva* (. . . the power of the lord based on his treasury and army) or *utsāha śakti* (energy). . . .

---

* My translation of the passage is given above.

8. A lion, devoid of training in moral laws (*naya*, *nīti*), kills its prey by sheer brute force but a hundred of such lions are subjugated by a man of virtue of his intelligence and wisdom (i.e., *mantraśakti*)....

10. Desirous of acquisition (of territory or wealth), a ruler should undertake a march (against his adversary) finding the opportune time for it only after applying necessary political expedients.... Too much reliance on military power alone ... leads to repentance (*paścāttāpa*). (Because valor is successful if aided by reasonable judgment or *mantraśakti*.)...

15. One who proceeds with carefully calculated steps on the path of prudence after intelligent deliberations attains prosperity and position as high as the peak of a mountain....

41. Ministers out of their self interest desire a prolongation of wars, and a ruler who (acting on their counsel) adopts a prolongation of his actions, is played into their hands.

From: *The Nītisāra by Kāmandaki, Sarga* 13[220]

4. Under the commands of the ruler (*Vijigīṣu*) the ambassador would proceed to his destination (the enemy kingdom)....

5. He should cultivate friendship with [the] frontier guards (*antapālāh*)* and... (dwellers of forests) (of the enemy kingdom) and apprise himself of [the] river-routes and land-routes for the success of troop movements (of his lord)...

7. He (the ambassador) should collect information about the material resources of the enemy, forts, secret defence, their limitations ... and the strength of the treasury, military power and allies.†...

12. ... [T]he ambassador should keep [in] contact with the treacherous elements (... double agents, who accept remuneration from both sides), so that he may know (or identify) them whose allegiance (to their lord) is alienable, and incite them against their lord.

13. An ambassador should secretly communicate with the spies (of his own lord) stationed in places of pilgrimage, hermitages and temples in the guise of hermits pretending to study the *śāstras*....

22–23. The duties of an ambassador are said to be, – identification of enemies of the enemy, alienation of his friends and relatives, collection of information about the strength of his treasury and armed forces, winning over of his disaffected officers, frontier guards and foresters, and accurate knowledge of the topography of the enemy territory for the purpose of troop movements of his master....

26. Clever spies in the guise of mendicants, craftsmen and traders should move about (in the *maṇḍala*) collecting the views of all classes of men (within the state and without)....

---

* The officer in charge of the forest region or warden of the marches.
† My translation differs from that of the editor.

32. Spies are of two classes, viz., known (public or official agents) and secret (agents). Secret agents are referred to above and the official agents are the *dūtas* (or ambassadors)....

33. ... Even the ambassadors, who have the power of concluding peace (or otherwise) have to base their decisions on the information supplied by the spies.

From: *The Nītisāra by Kāmandaki, Sarga* 14[221]

29. It is from the secure shelter of the fort that intrigues and secret wars (*tuṣṇīyuddha*)* are conducted, necessary steps for amelioration of people's distress are taken, friends and foes are accommodated, and disturbances created by the (disaffected) feudatories and foresters are remedied.

From: *The Nītisāra by Kāmandaki, Sarga* 15[222]

2. A ruler, who is himself free from all *vyasanas*, is capable of remedying the *vyasanas* of (the component elements of) the state. But the *vyasanas* of the king cannot be remedied even by the thriving state....

12. ... When the ruler blends *daṇḍa* with *naya* (legal procedure) in dealing with the accused (*daṇḍya*) he is praised for being a *yuktadaṇḍa* or the right user of *daṇḍa*....

25. Physical exercise (in hunting expeditions) produces power of endurance (or strains) and immunity from indigestion, heaviness (due to growth of fat) ... hunting develops excellence in successfully hitting stationary or moving targets with darts.

26. These are said to be the benefits to be derived from hunting, which, of course are not acceptable to us.... For its inherent evil of killing (of animals) as such, it is a great *vyasana* (and should be shunned or forsaken).

From: *The Nītisāra by Kāmandaki, Sarga* 16[223]

4. The ruler should direct his march to conquer that part of the enemy territory which is rich in grains ... for loss of the grain stock will entail in loss of sustenance (by food supply for the enemy) and acquisition of (additional) resources for his own army....

19. About comparative seriousness of internal and external dangers (i.e., arising out of disaffection of internal elements and of external elements), the internal dangers are considered more potential of harm. Hence before marching out, the causes of internal disturbances should be properly remedied (by conciliation, rewards, etc.) and also of external factors by contributing to their welfare.

20. It is advised (by experts) that disaffection among the priests, ministers, princes, members of the royal family, commanders and chiefs of army contingents, stationed as they are within the capital, generate internal disturbances....

---

* Unjust war involving assassination, sudden attacks, etc.

21. Disaffection among provincial governors … (wardens of the marches) … (… chiefs of forest tribes) … leads to another kind of disturbances, viz., external disturbances….

22. By conciliation and other relevant means (reward or punishment) as well as by creating mutual disunion and dissension among them the disaffected parties, both internal and external, should be appeased (or subjugated)….

24. In spite of drainage of money (*vyaya*) an expedition likely to produce decisive gain and rich benefits within a (reasonably) short time … and likely to be conducive to the interests in future too, may be undertaken, but an expedition likely to involve in destruction (of men and animals) or *kṣaya* [financial ruin] must never be attempted.

From: *The Nītisāra by Kāmandaki, Sarga* 17[224]

11. A portion of the army ready with weapons led by the commander … should move round the camp area during the night (lest the enemy attempts a surprise attack).

From: *The Nītisāra by Kāmandaki, Sarga* 18[225]

2. Avoiding the use of the army in its full four complements (*caturaṅga balaṁ*), it is better to fight with the expedients of treasury and wise counsel … (… by *sāma* and *dāna*). Hence it would be wise to conquer (or win over) the enemy by duly deliberated expedients of *sāma* or conciliation and *dāna* (*kośa*) or gifts (or bribes).

3. Conciliation, gifts, (sowing) dissension, use of military power, display of deceitful tactics (*māyā*), neglect (*upekṣā*)… and conjuring tricks … are known to be the seven expedients….

8. *Bheda* (creation of dissension in the enemy camp), according to experts, is of three varieties, viz., generating loss of fellow feeling and affection (by sowing feelings of mutual distrust), fomenting mutual rivalries and clashes (*saṁgharṣa*), and causing worry and fear (… so that hesitation prevents taking any action)….

11. Against those persons who cause loss of lives and have become [a] source of anxiety to the common people, even if they are [the] king's favorites or relations, and such powerful men who cause obstruction to the growth of prosperity (of the state), secret methods of assassination (*upāṅgśudaṇḍa*) should be adopted.

From: *The Nītisāra by Kāmandaki, Sarga* 19[226]

54. When a *vijigīṣu* finds himself endowed with requisite powers and with [a] favorable situation as regards time and place, and the *prakṛti* or elements of the enemy disaffected and lacking in coordination … he may indulge in open war (*prakāśayuddha*), otherwise, i.e., the reverse being the condition, *kūṭayuddha* or deceitful war … should be adopted.

55. When the enemy forces are found to be unprepared (or resting in camps), and/or in unfavorable ground or situation … the *vijigīṣu* should take prompt steps for annihilating them (by surprise attack). Even if they are on their own ground

(favorable situation) steps should be taken for alienating them by harassment in their own land.

56. When the *vijigīṣu* is able to alienate the foresters and other border tribes (forces) of the enemy through bribes and harassments, the elements of state (*prakṛti*) of the enemy are also harassed, he should charge with his own heroic soldiers and annihilate the enemy.

57. With the demonstration of a frontal attack (as a ruse) and making the enemy firmly believe that (thus keeping the enemy forces engaged in that direction), the *vijigīṣu* should employ his heroic band of soldiers to charge swiftly (to surprise) the enemy forces from the rear.

58. In the same way making the enemy concerned about his rear (i.e., making the ruse of a rear attack and keeping the enemy engaged in that direction) the enemy may be assailed by frontal attack with the best of soldiers. Similar methods of *kūṭayuddha* may be adopted on either flank....

62. Enticing away the subjects of the enemy out of their fortifications and ... cities and markets, villages and pastures (through secret agents) the cool headed *vijigīṣu* should plunder and destroy the dominion of the enemy....

64. The enemy deeply addicted to hunting may be assailed upon within the forest by secret means (i.e., from a hidden place)....

65. When as a result of nocturnal encounters the enemy troops feel exhausted due to keeping awake at night and fall asleep or feel sleepy in daytime the *vijigīṣu* should suddenly fall upon them to annihilate them.

66. The enemy troops, wounded or exhausted (in serious combat) in the first half of the day, should be attacked for annihilation in the second half (i.e., before they could recuperate)....

69/1. The soldiers of the enemy who have turned their backs or have become hopeless of life or have lost their mobility (besieged from all sides) should not be struck down as they have (practically) surrendered....

70. The wise, cool-headed and energetic *vijigīṣu* should assail upon the enemy by the different methods (of *kūṭayuddha*) on the basis of reports and signals from similarly cool-headed secret agents about the movements of the enemy.

71. Thus the *vijigīṣu* should always adopt guileful tactics ... in annihilating his enemy, and by killing the enemy by deception, he will not be transgressing *dharma* ... (... for there is nothing unfair in war).

From: *The Nītisāra by Kāmandaki, Sarga* 20[227]

35. To meet the exigencies of war an expert warrior may be set up as a dummy (*muṇḍanikam*) of the king (so that his own forces may be inspired to feel the royal presence and the enemy's attention is diverted). War is the soul of the *nāyaka* (*vijigīṣu*), i.e., war depends upon the integrity of the *nāyaka* and without him (*a-nāyaka*) the army is annihilated....

41A. The intelligent ruler should plan his array of army considering the suitability of time and place.

42. ... *Maṇḍala vyūha* is almost a circular composition with attacking points on all sides (*sarvatomukha*). The composite array in which the different wings of the army charge simultaneously but separately is called *Asaṁhatavyūha*. ...

Prakāśayuddha (The Conduct of Open War)

55. Penetrating the enemy formation with either *pakṣa* (wing) of the army, and consolidating his central (*urasa*), the *vijigīṣu* should throw, i.e., employ the rest of the units to attack and besiege the enemy rank with his own *koṭi*[*] units.

56. Charging the outer flanks (*parakoṭi*) by both the *pakṣa* units, without disturbing his *pratigraha* (the reserve unit at the rear), or along with his reserve unit (*sapratigrahoḥ*), he should assail the rear flanks and bring pressure on the central part (of the enemy *vyūha*) in order to force them to surrender.

57. An energetic ruler should carefully array his forces in proper *vyūha* formation and with his own arrayed forces crush the forces of the enemy.

58. The ordinary, separated or detached, and corrupt soldiers of the enemy should be crushed by the ruler's own superior forces.

59. The superior forces of the enemy should be assailed by the doubly superior forces (of the *vijigīṣu*) and the ordinary soldiers by the superior. The consolidated units of the enemy should be liquidated by units of furious elephants.

60. The invincible elephants (of the enemy) should be charged by rutting elephants ... or captured by employing she-elephants ... mounted by expert riders.

61. The forces of the enemy should be crushed by tusker elephants ... covered by defensive iron network and attended by well-trained and energetic followers and expert warriors.

62. ... A ... (*vijigīṣu's*) victory depends on his elephant forces. Hence a ruler should always be endowed with a strong contingent of elephants.

Mohandas Karamchand Gandhi (1869–1948) on *Ahimsa*

Western theoreticians equate Mohandas Karamchand Gandhi's philosophy with nonviolent resistance. They argue that Gandhi showed the world a new way by discovering the quintessential principle inherent in Hinduism: nonviolence. Several Western commentators regard nonviolence as the salvation for the future.[228] And in their eyes, Gandhian philosophy as derived from Hinduism could provide a way out of the present violence-ridden world. In reality, Hinduism is anything but a nonviolent religion. The above four sections show how violence is often endorsed in classical Hindu texts. Viewed in light of this lineage, it must be acknowledged that Gandhian philosophy was the product of a particular historical context.

---

[*] Elite/special.

Gandhi was born on 2 October 1869, at Porbander (Gujarat state), into a family of Vaishya/Vaisya caste.[229] He was the youngest of three sons of Karamchand Gandhi, who was the Prime Minister of the princely states of Probander, Rajkot, and Vanakner. In 1882, Gandhi married, and six years later he sailed to England to study law, enrolling at Inner Temple, London. In 1893, Gandhi sailed to South Africa and dabbled in politics. The following year he established the Natal Indian Congress, an organization that aimed to end racial discrimination against the Indian community. In December 1899, he formed the Indian Ambulance Corps for service in the Boer War. At that time, Gandhi was a supporter of British imperialism. The British Empire, he believed, exercised a positive influence in the world; its defects could be amended by internal reforms.

Toward the end of the first decade of the twentieth century, Gandhi established a political technique that would transform the Indian National Congress (hereafter INC) into a mass movement that seriously threatened the British *Raj*. This political technique was *satyagraha*, a nonviolent movement based on the power of truth. In its engagement with the British, Gandhian *satyagraha* had two elements: negotiation and civil noncooperation.[230] On February 1918, three years after his arrival in India, Gandhi started *satyagraha* at Ahmedabad. However, by 18 April 1919, he suspended this practice due to an outbreak of violence. The following year at the Nagpur session, the INC adopted Gandhi's resolution to attain independence (*swaraj*) through nonviolence, and by December 1921, mass *satyagraha* was adopted. In response to the 12 February 1922 riots at Chauri Chaura, Gandhi yet again abandoned *satyagraha*. Gandhi relaunched the movement on 6 April 1930, and the British government responded by agreeing to negotiate for a partial devolution of power. These negotiations resulted in the 1935 Government of India Act. After the 1936–1937 elections, the INC formed governments in most of the provinces. However, when Governor-General Lord Linlithgow declared war against the Axis powers in 1939 without consulting the INC, on Gandhi's advice the Congress governments at the various provinces resigned from office. On 8 August 1942, Gandhi started the "Quit India" Movement, giving the call for *karenge ya marenge* (do or die) in order to achieve India's independence. When Gandhi and the top INC leadership were arrested, local members emerged and assumed leadership of the movement. Anticolonial action occurred most intensely in Bengal and Bihar, primarily because both areas were suffering from food shortages because of the war. Railroads were damaged and police stations were attacked. It was the biggest movement on the part of the INC, and the British *Raj* had to deploy fifty-seven infantry battalions to maintain order. It was clear to the *Raj* that they could hold India only by naked force. By late 1945, even that option was vanishing for the *Raj*, because the British military assets were highly depleted due to World War II and the beginning of the Cold War. The loyalty of the British-Indian Army was also becoming brittle. The Labour Government of Clement Attlee decided to divide and "quit" India. On 30 January 1948, a Hindu militarist named Nathuram Godse shot Gandhi. Gandhi died with his hands folded chanting "Hey Ram, Hey Ram" (Oh God, Oh God).[231]

Gandhi's use of Hindu religious terms and symbols to incite mass mobilization gradually alienated many Muslims. Most eventually deserted the INC in the late 1930s and joined the All India Muslim League. To a great extent this process was responsible for the partition of the subcontinent in 1947.[232]

In the section below, Gandhi's writings are arranged chronologically. Several themes emerge from them. Gandhi made no distinction between religion and politics. His approach is in tune with the line taken by the *acharyas* of ancient India that religion constitutes an inseparable component of *rajdharma*. The goal of politics (freedom/self-rule), as he understood it, was inseparable from religion. On 12 May 1920, Gandhi wrote that he was not trying to impose Hinduism on mass politics to achieve freedom from British rule. However, Gandhi himself admitted that his *ahimsa* was mainly derived from Hindu religious philosophy.

Gandhi's interpretation of the *BG* as an allegorical war between the forces of light and darkness is somewhat similar to the ancient *acharyas*' conception of the cosmos being maintained by a struggle between good and evil. Gandhi's essay dated 11 August 1920 considers the scope and power of *ahimsa*, a term that already figured in Kamandaka's *Nitisara*. In ancient Hindu literature, *ahimsa* had a meaning somewhat different from what is found in Gandhi's writings.[233] In the former, *ahimsa* designates killing under certain kinds of circumstances. It is thus related to the idea of self-sacrifice as well as the idea of sacrifice of animals in *Chandogya Upanishad*. It is true, however, that *ahimsa* was also associated with qualities such as austerity (*tapas*), benevolence (*dana*), integrity, and truthfulness, qualities later subsumed into Gandhian philosophy.

Gandhi's claim that India had in the past been a land of nonviolence is historically inaccurate. It was nonetheless an effective tool of persuasion. Although an idealist and moralist, Gandhi was also very much a realist. He employed *ahimsa* within a calculated political strategy to win freedom for India against Britain. He understood that *ahimsa* could be effective against the British only because they were commited to a "rule of law" that depended on cooperation with Indians.

One also finds the presence of military allegories in Gandhian *ahimsa*. Gandhi compared the leaders of the *ahimsa* struggle to the Duke of Wellington and other great generals of the British Empire. *Ahimsa* likewise demanded death from its followers if necessary, just as a military organization demands death from its personnel on the battlefield. Despite Gandhi's outward humility, he also had a large view of his place in history. He sometimes equated himself with the new India, just as Louis XIV had equated himself with France.

Challenging the Darwinian principle of the survival of the fittest Gandhi opposed Western materialism to Indian spiritualism. He advocated worldwide disarmament and vehemently opposed the possession of nuclear weapons. Even today, the antinuclear lobby in India derives moral support from Gandhi's views. Now, let us have a glance at Gandhi's writings in order to understand the philosophy behind his actions.

From: Mahatma Gandhi, *The Essential Writings of Mahatma Gandhi*, Vol. III: Non-Violent Resistance and Social Transformation, XIII Satyagraha – Non-Violent Resistance (2 September 1917)[234]

Satyagraha is not physical force. A *satyagrahi** does not inflict pain on the adversary; he does not seek his destruction. A *satyagrahi* never resorts to firearms. In the use of *satyagraha*, there is no ill-will whatever. *Satyagraha* is pure soul-force. Truth is the very

---

* One who follows *satyagraha*.

substance of the soul. That is why this force is called *satyagraha*. The soul is informed with knowledge.... "Non-violence is the supreme *dharma*" is the proof of this power of love.... In English there is a saying, "Might is Right." Then there is the doctrine of the survival of the fittest. Both these ideas are contradictory to the above principle....

We forget the principle of non-violence, which is the essence of all religions. The doctrine of arms stands for irreligion. It is due to the sway of that doctrine that a sanguinary war is raging in Europe.

From: Mahatma Gandhi, *The Essential Writings of Mahatma Gandhi*, Vol. I, "Saint or Politician?" (12 May 1920)[235]

... I have been experimenting with myself and my friends by introducing religion into politics. Let me explain what I mean by religion. It is not the Hindu religion, which I certainly prize above all other religions, but the religion which transcends Hinduism, which changes one's very nature, which binds one indissolubly to the truth within and which ever purifies....

It was in that religious spirit that I came upon *hartal*.* I wanted to show that it is not a knowledge of letters that would give India consciousness of herself, or that would bind the educated together. The *hartal* illuminated the whole of India as if by magic on the 6th of April, 1919.

From: Mahatma Gandhi, *The Essential Writings of Mahatma Gandhi*, Vol. II, "Non-Violence – The Law of Our Species" (11 August 1920)[236]

... I do believe that where there is only a choice between cowardice and violence I would advise violence.... I would rather have India resort to arms in order to defend her honor than that she should in a cowardly manner become or remain a helpless witness to her own dishonor. But I believe that non-violence is infinitely superior to violence, forgiveness is more manly than punishment. *Kshama virasya bhushanam*. "Forgiveness adorns a soldier." But abstinence is forgiveness only when there is the power to punish; it is meaningless when it pretends to proceed from a helpless creature.... But I do not believe India to be helpless. I do not believe myself to be a helpless creature. Only I want to use India's and my strength for a better purpose.

Let me not be misunderstood. Strength does not come from physical capacity. It comes from an indomitable will....

I am not a visionary. I claim to be a practical idealist. The religion of non-violence is not meant merely for the *rishis* and saints. It is meant for the common people as well. Non-violence is the law of our species as violence is the law of the brute. The spirit lies dormant in the brute and he knows no law but that of physical might....

I have therefore ventured to place before India the ancient law of self-sacrifice. For *satyagraha* and its off-shoots, non-cooperation and civil resistance, are nothing

---

* Strike.

but new names for the law of suffering. The *rishis*, who discovered the law of non-violence in the midst of violence, were greater geniuses than Newton. They were themselves greater warriors than Wellington. Having themselves known the use of arms, they realized their uselessness and taught a weary world that its salvation lay not through violence but through non-violence. . . .

However, being a practical man, I do not wait till India recognizes the practicability of the spiritual life in the political world. India considers herself to be powerless and paralyzed before the machine-guns, the tanks and the aeroplanes of the English. And she takes up non-co-operation out of her weakness. It must still serve the same purpose, namely, bring her delivery from the crushing weight of British injustice if a sufficient number of people practice it. . . . My life is dedicated to service of India through the religion of non-violence which I believe to be the root of Hinduism.

From: Mahatma Gandhi, *The Essential Writings of Mahatma Gandhi*, Vol. I, "Striving after *Moksha*" (1 November 1921)[237]

For me, even the effort for attaining *swaraj* [self-rule/independence] is a part of the effort for *moksha* [liberation/salvation].

From: Mahatma Gandhi, *The Essential Writings of Mahatma Gandhi*, Vol. I, "The Kingdom of Heaven" (3 April 1924)[238]

In the language of the *Gita* I want to live at peace with both friend and foe. . . . Thus it will be seen that for me there are no politics devoid of religion. They subserve religion. Politics bereft of religion are a death-trap because they kill the soul.

From: Mahatma Gandhi, *The Essential Writings of Mahatma Gandhi*, Vol. I, "One Step Enough for Me" (21 December 1925)[239]

When, thousands of years ago, the battle of Kurukshetra was fought, the doubts which occurred to Arjuna were answered by Shri Krishna in the *Gita*; but that battle of Kurukshetra is going on, will go on, forever within us, the Prince of Yogis, Lord Krishna, the universal *atman* [soul/brotherhood/humanity] dwelling in the hearts of us all, will always be there to guide Arjuna, the human soul, and our Godward impulses represented by the Pandavas will always triumph over the demoniac impulses represented by the Kauravas. Till, however, that victory is won, we should have faith and let the battle go on, and be patient meanwhile.

From: Mahatma Gandhi, *The Essential Writings of Mahatma Gandhi*, Vol. II, "Wars and Exploitation" (9 May 1929)[240]

This I know that if India comes to her own demonstrably through non-violent means, India will never want to carry a vast army, an equally grand navy and a grander air force. If her self-consciousness rises to the height necessary to give her a non-violent victory in her fight for freedom, the world values will have changed and most of the paraphernalia of war would be found to be useless.

From: Mahatma Gandhi, *The Essential Writings of Mahatma Gandhi,* Vol. II, "The Law of Love" (1 October 1931)[241]

For truth and non-violence are, to me, faces of the same coin.

From: Mahatma Gandhi, *The Essential Writings of Mahatma Gandhi,* Vol. II, "Axioms of Non-Violence" (12 October 1935)[242]

India had an unbroken tradition of non-violence from times immemorial. But at no time in her ancient history, as far as I know it, has it had complete non-violence in action pervading the whole land. Nevertheless, it is my unshakeable belief that her destiny is to deliver the message of non-violence to mankind. It may take ages to come to fruition. But so far as I can judge, no other country will precede her in the fulfilment of that mission.

From: Mahatma Gandhi, *The Essential Writings of Mahatma Gandhi,* Vol. II, "The Atom Bomb and Moral Strength" (25 April 1947)[243]

I hold that he who invented the atom bomb has committed the gravest sin in the world of science. The only weapon that can save the world is non-violence.

Conclusion

Despite Gandhi's abhorrence of nuclear weapons, India conducted a nuclear test at Pokhran in 1974. In 1998, the Bharatiya Janata Party (BJP) government conducted three nuclear tests under the ironic code name, "Buddha is smiling." Soon after, the BJP government declared that India should acquire a "triad" (nuclear weapons–equipped air force, ground force, and naval units). In the new millennium, the succeeding Congress government retained the policy of maintaining a nuclear triad despite the government's view of Gandhi as an ideological father figure. In spite of Gandhi's injunction that independent India should disband its armed forces and the military personnel should be used for cleaning the latrines of the *harijans,*[244] Nehru, Gandhi's closest disciple, maintained and expanded the armed forces after 1947. At present, the Indian Army in terms of manpower is the third largest in the world, and the armed forces consume about 3.5 percent of the gross national product.[245] Gandhian *ahimsa* may be expressed as ideological rhetoric, yet in the *realpolitik* worldview of India's strategic managers, it is believed to be practically inoperable. One could arguably conclude that *ahimsa* is a marginal trend in Hinduism and that the Hindu religion does permit engagement in organized violence, at least for purposes of self-defense.

42 Torkel Brekke, "Between Prudence and Heroism: Ethics of War in the Hindu Tradition," in Brekke (ed.), *The Ethics of War in Asian Civilizations: A Comparative Perspective* (London/ New York: Routledge, 2006), p. 116.

43 Thapar, *From Lineage to State*, pp. 63, 119, 126, 129.

44 Devahuti, *Harsha*, p. 116.

45 Singh, *Political Thought in Ancient India*, p. 35; Surendra Nath Mital, *Kautilya Arthaśāstra Revisited* (New Delhi: Centre for Studies in Indian Civilizations, 2004), p. vii.

46 Singh, *Political Thought in Ancient India*, p. 53.

47 Devahuti, *Harsha*, p. 116.

48 Neal Wood, "Xenophon's Theory of Leadership," in Everett L. Wheeler (ed.), *The Armies of Classical Greece* (Aldershot: Ashgate, 2007), p. 476.

49 Malinar, *Bhagavadgita*, p. 249.

50 Burton Stein, *A History of India* (New Delhi: Oxford University Press, 2004); Wink, "Sovereignty and Universal Dominion in South Asia," pp. 99–130; Aidan Southall, "The Segmentary State in Africa and Asia," *Comparative Studies in Society and History* 30:1 (1988), 52–82.

51 R. K. Mookerji, *Chandragupta Maurya and His Times* (Delhi: Motilal Banarasidas, 1960); Jha, *Early India*.

52 Thapar, *Penguin History of Early India*, pp. 174, 197, 208.

53 Devahuti, *Harsha*, p. 111.

54 Singh, *Political Thought in Ancient India*, pp. 120, 126.

55 *Manu's Code of Law, A Critical Edition and Translation of the Manava-Dharmasastra*, Patrick Olivelle (ed. and trans.) and Suman Olivelle (New Delhi: Oxford University Press, 2006), p. 24.

56 P. V. Kane, *History of Dharmasastra (Ancient and Medieval Religious and Civil Law in India)* (Poona: Bhandarkar Oriental Research Institute, 1968), vol. I, pp. 153, 177, 231.

57 Devahuti, *Harsha*, p. 135.

58 Organization of Hindu society on the basis of four castes: Brahmins, Kshatriyas, Vaishyas, and the Sudras.

59 Thapar, *Penguin History of Early India*, pp. 191, 195.

60 Deployment of the army in the battlefield.

61 Rosen, *India and Its Armies*, pp. 61–103.

62 Hindu army comprised four branches: infantry, cavalry, elephants, and chariots.

63 Kaushik Roy, *From Hydaspes to Kargil: A History of Warfare in India from 326 BC to AD 1999* (New Delhi: Manohar, 2004), pp. 35–58.

64 Kaushik Roy, *India's Historic Battles from Alexander the Great to Kargil* (New Delhi: Permanent Black, 2004), pp. 10–31.

65 M. Athar Ali, *Mughal India: Studies in Polity, Ideas, Society, and Culture* (New Delhi: Oxford University Press, 2006), pp. 173–182; Kaushik Roy, "Norms of War in Hinduism," in Popovski et al., *World Religions and Norms of War*, pp. 40–41.

66 Bharat Karnad, *Nuclear Weapons and Indian Security: The Realist Foundations of Strategy* (New Delhi: Macmillan, 2002), pp. xi–xxxvi, 1–65.

67 Holy war of Islam against the unbelievers.

68 Meera Nanda, *Breaking the Spell of Dharma and Other Essays* (Gurgaon: Three Essays Collective, 2007), pp. 1–3, 9–10; Jaswant Singh, *Defending India* (Basingstoke, Hampshire: Macmillan, 1999), pp. 290–291; Jaswant Singh, *A Call to Honour: In Service of Emergent India* (New Delhi: Rupa, 2006), pp. 111–150.

69 Malinar, *Bhagavadgita*, pp. 17, 30, 33–34.

70 Mohanraj, *Warrior and the Charioteer*, p. 30.

71 Malinar, *Bhagavadgita*, p. 33.

72 Ibid., p. 244.

73 The five Pancala/Panchala brothers: Yudhistira, Arjuna, Bhima, Nakula, and Sahadeva.

74 The one hundred sons of Dhritarashtra, the Kaurava King. The eldest son of Dhritarashtra was Duryodhana.

75 *The Bhagavad Gita*, Juan Mascaro (trans.) (London: Penguin, 1962), pp. x, xxv.

76 B. A. van Nooten, "Introduction," in William Buck, *Mahabharata* (Delhi: Motilal Banarasidas, 2006), pp. xvi–xvii, xxiii.

77 John Brockington, "Religious Attitudes in Valmiki's *Ramayana*," in Greg Bailey and Mary Brockington (eds.), *Epic Threads: John Brockington on the Sanskrit Epics* (New Delhi: Oxford University Press, 2002), p. 225.

78 Irfan Habib and Vijay Kumar Thakur, *The Vedic Age and the Coming of Iron c. 1500–700 BC* (New Delhi: Tulika, 2003), pp. 61, 65.

79 The original or first man from whose body the four castes emerged.

80 Hindu god of fire who created the cosmos.

81 Jayantanuja Bandopadhyaya, *Class and Religion in Ancient India* (New Delhi: Anthem, 2007), pp. 1–8, 51–100.

82 Mohanraj, *Warrior and the Charioteer*, pp. 39, 61–62.

83 Ibid., pp. 63–66, 71.

84 Lawrence A. Tritle, "Hector's Body: Mutilation of the Dead in Ancient Greece and Vietnam," in Wheeler (ed.), *The Armies of Classical Greece*, p. 342.

85 Narasingha P. Sil, *Kautilya's Arthaśāstra: A Comparative Study* (Kolkata/New Delhi: Academic Publishers, 1985), pp. 13–14.

86 Henrik Syse, "Plato, Thucydides, and the Education of Alcibiades," *Journal of Military Ethics* 5:4 (2006), 291, 295–296.

87 Malinar, *Bhagavadgita*, pp. 34, 227, 248.

88 Jitendra Nath Mohanty, *Theory and Practice in Indian Philosophy* (Calcutta: K. P. Bagchi, 1994), pp. 15–16.

89 Nick Allen, "Just War in the *Mahabharata*," in Richard Sorabji and David Rodin (eds.), *The Ethics of War: Shared Problems in Different Traditions* (Aldershot: Ashgate, 2006), p. 147.

90 Clausewitz famously spoke of the need "to subordinate the military point of view to the political" (quoted in Michael I. Handel, "Introduction," *Journal of Strategic Studies* 9:2–3 (1986), 24).

91 See Samuel P. Huntington, *The Soldier and the State: The Theory and Politics of Civil-Military Relations* (Cambridge: Harvard University Press, 1981).

92 Stephen P. Cohen, *The Indian Army: Its Contribution to the Development of a Nation* (1990; reprint, New Delhi: Oxford University Press, 1991).

93 English translation taken from *The Bhagavad Gita*, Juan Mascaró (trans.) (London: Penguin, 1962), pp. 3–6.

94 Ibid., pp. 10–13.

95 Ibid., pp. 17–20.

96 Ibid., p. 27.

97 Ibid., p. 34.

98 Ibid., p. 39.

99 Ibid., p. 50.

100 Ibid., pp. 55–56.

101 Ibid., pp. 80, 83–84.

102 Ashok S. Chousalkar, *A Comparative Study of Theory of Rebellion in Kautilya and Aristotle* (Delhi: Indological Book House, 1990), p. 8.

103 Mital, *Kautilya Arthaśāstra Revisited*, p. 15; Thapar, *Penguin History of Early India*, pp. 184–185.

104 Mital, *Kautilya Arthaśāstra Revisited*, pp. 24–25; B. N. Mukherjee, "Foreword: A Note on Arthasastra," in Sil, *Kautilya's Arthaśāstra*, p. viii.

further reflection he thought to himself: "It is not suitable that I, who have received the Precepts from the venerable Guru, should break them again." Three times he thought, "My life I will give up, but not the precepts!" and then he threw his knife away. Thereafter the huge viper let him go, and went somewhere else.

(III) The last kind of abstention is associated with the holy Path. It does not even occur to the Holy Persons to kill any living being.

The Renunciation of Temporal Power: The Case of Prince Siddhārtha

At the age of twenty-nine, the Buddha, then known by his lay name as Prince Siddhārtha, renounced temporal power in search of Buddhahood. Aware that temporal authority must impose physical punishment on wrongdoers, as well as use force to defend the nation from aggression, the Buddha thereby withdrew from any exercise of coercive legal measures, and abstained from all participation in violence and war.

Patience: The Foremost Practice of a Bodhisattva

The ideal of *bodhisattva*[6] functions as an important model for ethical actions in Buddhist societies. In the Mahāyāna (Great Vehicle) traditions, in particular, the ideal of *bodhisattva* plays a significant role even today. The *bodhisattvas* are beings who aspire toward enlightenment and work to reach for it by exercising virtues called "perfections." Theravāda traditions accept ten perfections: (1) generosity (*dāna*), (2) morality (*sīla*), (3) patience (*khanti*), (4) effort (*viriya*), (5) meditation (*dhyāna*), (6) wisdom (*prajñā*), (7) skillful means (*upāya*), (8) vow (*pranidhāna*), (9) strength (*bala*), and (10) knowledge (*jñāna*).

Among the 547 heuristic narratives in the collection of *Jātakas* in the Pāli canon, the *Khantivādi Jātaka* (no. 313 in the *Jātaka* and no. 28 in the *Jātakamālā*) highlights the unconditional practice of patience, even in the case of deliberate and provocative physical harm inflicted upon one's body.

From: *Jātaka or Stories of the Buddha's Former Births*, Book IV, No. 313, "Khantivādi-Jātaka"[7]

Once upon a time a king of Kāsi named Kalābu reigned at Benares. At that time the Bodhisatta came to life in a brahmin family endowed with eighty crores of treasure.... On the death of his parents, looking at his pile of treasure he thought: "My kinsmen who amassed this treasure are all gone without taking it with them: now it is for me to own it and in my turn to depart." Then he carefully selected persons, who by virtue of their almsgiving deserved it, and gave all his wealth to them, and entering the Himālaya country he adopted the ascetic life.... [H]e gradually made his way to Benares, where he took up his abode in the royal park.

Now one day King Kalābu being inflamed with strong drink came into the park in great pomp, surrounded by a company of dancers. Then he had a couch spread on the royal seat of stone, and lay with his head on the lap of a favourite of the harem, while the nautch girls* who were skillful in vocal and instrumental music and in dancing provided a musical entertainment.... And the king fell asleep. Then the women said, "He for whose sake we are providing music, is gone to sleep. What need is there for us to sing?" Then they cast aside their lutes and other musical instruments hither and thither, and set out for the garden....

At this moment the Bodhisatta was seated in this garden.... So these women in wandering about came upon him and said, "[L]et us sit down and hear somewhat from the priest who is resting at the foot of this tree, until the king awakes." Then they went and saluted him and sitting in a circle round about him, they said, "Tell us something worth hearing." So the Bodhisatta preached the doctrine to them.

Meanwhile the royal favourite with a movement of her body woke up the king. And the king on waking up, and not seeing the women asked, "Where are those wretches gone?" "Your Highness," she said, "they are gone away and are sitting in attendance on a certain ascetic." The king in a rage seized his sword and went off in haste, saying, "I will give this false ascetic a lesson." Then those of the women that were most in favour, when they saw the king coming in a rage, went and took the sword from the king's hand and pacified him. Then he came and stood by the Bodhisatta and asked, "What doctrine are you preaching, Monk?" "The doctrine of patience, Your Majesty," he replied. "What is this patience?" said the king. "The not being angry, when men abuse you and strike you and revile you." Said the king, "I will see now the reality of your patience," and he summoned his executioner. And he in the way of his office took an axe and a scourge of thorns, and clad in a yellow robe and wearing a red garland, came and saluted the king and said, "What is your pleasure, Sire?" "Take and drag off this vile rogue of an ascetic," said the king, "and throwing him on the ground, with your lash of thorns scourge him before and behind and on both sides, and give him two thousand stripes." This was done. And the Bodhisatta's outer and inner skins were cut through to the flesh, and the blood flowed. The king again asked, "What doctrine do you preach, Monk?" "The doctrine of patience, Your Highness," he replied. "You fancy that my patience is only skin deep. It is not skin deep, but is fixed deep within my heart, where it cannot be seen by you, Sire." Again the executioner asked, "What is your pleasure, Sire?" The king said, "Cut off both the hands of this false ascetic." So he took his axe, and placing the victim within the fatal circle, he cut off both his hands. Then the king said, "Off with his feet," and his feet were chopped off. And the blood flowed from the extremities of his hands and feet like lac juice from a leaking jar. Again the king asked what doctrine he preached. "The doctrine of

---

* The "nautch" (derived from Prakrit *nacca*, dancing) is an entertainment in India that primarily features professional dancing girls.

patience, Your Highness," he replied. "You imagine, Sire, that my patience dwells in the extremities of my hands and feet. It is not there, but it is deep seated somewhere else." The king said, "Cut off his nose and ears." The executioner did so. His whole body was now covered with blood. Again the king asked of his doctrine. And the ascetic said, "Think not that my patience is seated in the tips of my nose and ears: my patience is deep seated within my heart." The king said, "Lie down, false Monk, and thence exalt your patience." And so saying, he struck the Bodhisatta above the heart with his foot, and betook himself off.

When he was gone, the commander-in-chief wiped off the blood from the body of the Bodhisatta, putting bandages on the extremities of his hands, feet, ears and nose, and then having gently placed him on a seat, he saluted him and sitting on one side he said, "If, Reverend Sir, you would be angry with one who has sinned against you, be angry with the king, but no one else." And making this request, he repeated the first stanza:

Whoso cut off thy nose and ear, and lopped off foot and hand,
With him be wroth, heroic soul, but spare, we pray, this land.

The Bodhisatta on hearing this uttered the second stanza:

Long live the king, whose cruel hand my body thus has marred,
Pure souls like mine such deeds as these with anger ne'er regard.

And just as the king was leaving the garden and at the very moment when he passed out of the range of the Bodhisatta's vision, the mighty earth that is two hundred and forty thousand leagues in thickness split in two, like unto a strong stout cloth garment, and a flame issuing forth from Avīci* seized upon the king, wrapping him up as it were with a royal robe of scarlet wool. Thus did the king sink into the earth just by the garden gate and was firmly fixed in the great Hell of Avīci. And the Bodhisatta died on that same day. And the king's servants and the citizens came with perfumes and wreaths and incense in their hands and performed the Bodhisatta's obsequies.

The Origin of Kingship in the Aggañña Sutta

Buddhists do not have many stories that discuss the origin of the world and the birth of institutions such as kingship. Among the available works, the *Aggañña Sutta* stands out as one of the most important. It shows how kingship served as a crucial institutional framework for the protection of civil liberties and the establishment of law and order, while securing justice and producing a context for flourishing values, virtues, and ethics. The Buddhist explanation of the origin of kingship in the *Aggañña Sutta* has been quite influential in the development of Buddhist social philosophy. Its explanation gives a causal interpretation of the spread of crimes. It shows a close link between a lack of morals and the increase of criminality.

---

* Avīci is the lowest of the Buddhist hells and there is no intermission of suffering there.

From: *The Long Discourses of the Buddha: A Translation of the Dīgha-Nikāya*, Division Three: The *Patika* Division, "Aggañña Sutta: Sutta 27, On Knowledge of Beginnings"[8]

18. And then those beings came together lamenting: "Wicked ways have become rife among us: at first we were mind-made, feeding on delight ... and the rice grows in separate clusters. So now let us divide up the rice into fields with boundaries." So they did so.

19. Then, Vāseṭṭha, one greedy-natured being, while watching over his own plot, took another plot that was not given to him, and enjoyed the fruits of it. So they seized hold of him and said: "You've done a wicked thing, taking another's plot like that! Don't ever do such a thing again!" "I won't," he said, but he did the same thing a second and a third time. Again he was seized and rebuked, and some hit him with their fists, some with stones, and some with sticks. And in this way, Vāseṭṭha, taking what was not given, and censuring, and lying, and punishment, took their origin.

20. Then those beings came together and lamented the arising of these evil things among them: taking what was not given, censuring, lying and punishment. And they thought: "Suppose we were to appoint a certain being who would show anger where anger was due, censure those who deserved it, and banish those who deserved banishment! And in return, we would grant him a share of the rice." So they went to the one among them who was the handsomest, the best-looking, the most pleasant and capable, and asked him to do this for them in return for a share of the rice, and he agreed.

21. "The People's Choice" is the meaning of Mahā-Sammata, which is the first regular title to be introduced. "Lord of the Fields" is the meaning of Khattiya, the second such title. And "He Gladdens Others with Dhamma" is the meaning of Rājā, the third title to be introduced. This, then, Vāseṭṭha, is the origin of the class of Khattiyas, in accordance with the ancient titles that were introduced for them. They originated among these very same beings, like ourselves, no different, and in accordance with Dhamma, not otherwise.

> Dhamma's the best thing for people
> In this life and the next as well.

22. Then some of these beings thought: "Evil things have appeared among beings, such as taking what is not given, censuring, lying, punishment and banishment. We ought to put aside evil and unwholesome things." And they did so. "They Put Aside Evil and Unwholesome Things" is the meaning of Brahmin, which is the first regular title to be introduced for such people.

Yodhājīva: *One Who Earns Living by Warfare*

There are not many instances in the Pāli canon in which the Buddha discussed the lives of soldiers or matters related to warfare. Among the few found, the story of Yodhājīva found in the *Saṃyutta Nikāya* is an important one. The Pāli term *Yodhājīva* literally means "one who earns living by warfare."[9] It is the occupation of a mercenary or professional soldier.

From: *The Connected Discourses of the Buddha: A New Translation of the Saṃyutta Nikāya*, IV. The Book of the Six Sense Bases, "Yodhājīva"[10]

Then the headman Yodhājīva the Mercenary approached the Blessed One, paid homage to him, sat down to one side, and said to him: "Venerable sir, I have heard it said by mercenaries of old in the lineage of teachers: 'When a mercenary is one who strives and exerts himself in battle, if others slay him and finish him off while he is striving and exerting himself in battle, then with the breakup of the body, after death, he is reborn in the company of the battle-slain devas.' What does the Blessed One say about that?"

"Enough, headman, let it be! Don't ask me that!"

A second time and a third time Yodhājīva the headman said: "Venerable sir, I have heard it said by mercenaries of old in the lineage of teachers: . . . What does the Blessed One say about that?"

"Surely, headman, I am not getting through to you when I say, 'Enough, headman, let it be! Don't ask me that!' But still, I will answer you. When, headman, a mercenary is one who strives and exerts himself in battle, his mind is already low, depraved, misdirected by the thought: 'Let these beings be slain, slaughtered, annihilated, destroyed, or exterminated.' If others then slay him and finish him off while he is striving and exerting himself in battle, then with the breakup of the body, after death, he is reborn in the 'Battle-Slain Hell.' But should he hold such a view as this: 'When a mercenary strives and exerts himself in battle, if others slay him and finish him off while he is striving and exerting himself in battle, then with the breakup of the body, after death, he is reborn in the company of the battle-slain devas' – that is a wrong view on his part. For a person with [a] wrong view, I say, there is one of two destinations: either hell or the animal realm."

When this was said, Yodhājīva the headman cried out and burst into tears. [The Blessed One said:] "So I did not get through to you when I said, 'Enough, headman, let it be! Don't ask me that!'"

"I am not crying, venerable sir, because of what the Blessed One said to me, but because I have been tricked, cheated, and deceived for a long time by those mercenaries of old in the lineage of teachers who said: 'When a mercenary is one who strives and exerts himself in battle, if others slay him and finish him off while he is striving and exerting himself in battle, then with the breakup of the body, after death, he is reborn in the company of the battle-slain devas.'

"Magnificent, venerable sir! . . . From today let the Blessed One remember me as a lay follower who has gone for refuge for life."

From: *The Book of the Gradual Sayings* (*Aṅguttara-Nikāya*), The Book of the Fives: Chapter VIII, §V (75), "The Warrior (a)"[11]

Monks, these five kinds of warriors are found in the world. What five?

Monks, in one case there is the warrior who, just at the sight of the cloud of dust, loses heart and falters and stiffens not, nor is able to go down to battle. Monks, there is here this sort of warrior. This, monks, is the first kind of warrior found in the world.

Again, though another endure[s] (the sight of) the dust cloud, just on seeing a standard lifted up, he loses heart and falters and stiffens not, nor is [he] able to go down to battle. Monks, there is here this sort of warrior. This, monks, is the second kind....

Again, though another endure[s] the dust-cloud and the standard, at the sound of tumult he loses heart ... nor is [he] able to go down to battle. Monks, there is here this sort of warrior. This, monks, is the third kind....

Though another endure[s] the dust-cloud, the standard and the tumult, when struck in conflict he fails. Monks, there is here this sort of warrior. This, monks, is the fourth kind....

Then there is one who endures the dust-cloud, the standard, the tumult and the conflict; victorious in battle, winning the fight, he continues at the head of the battle. Monks, there is here this sort of warrior. This, monks, is the fifth kind of warrior found in the world.

Monks, these are the five kinds....

Even so, monks, these five kinds of persons, like warriors, are found among monks....

[T]here is the monk who endures the dust-cloud, the standard, the tumult and the conflict; victorious in battle, winning the fight, he continues at the head of the battle. And what to him is victory in battle?...

[H]is heart [being] ... free from the canker of lust, free from the canker of becomings, free from the canker of ignorance, and in the freedom comes the knowledge of that freedom, and he knows: Birth is destroyed; lived is the godly life; done is what had to be done; there is no more of this state. This to him is victory in battle.

Monks, just as the warrior endures the dust-cloud, the standard, the tumult and the conflict; and, victorious in battle, winning the fight, continues even at the head of the battle; like that, monks, I say, is this person. Monks, there is here this sort of person. This, monks, is the fifth kind of person, like a warrior, found among monks.

From: The Book of the Fives: Chapter VIII, The Warrior, §VI (76), "The Warrior (b)"[12]

Monks, these five kinds of warriors are found in the world. What five?

Monks, in one case a warrior, grasping his sword and shield, binding on his bow and quiver, goes down into the thick of the fight; and there he dares and strives; but others strike him as he dares and strives and overpower him. Monks, there is here this sort of warrior. This, monks, is the first kind of warrior found in the world.

Again, another, arming himself in like manner, goes down to the fight; and as he dares and strives the enemy wound him. And they bear him away to bring him to his relations; but while he is being carried by his kinsmen, ere he arrives, he dies on the way to his relations. Monks, there is here this sort of warrior. This, monks, is the second kind. . . .

Another . . . wounded by the enemy, is carried to his relations and they nurse him and care for him, but he dies of that hurt. Monks, there is here this sort of warrior. This, monks, is the third kind. . . .

Another . . . wounded by the enemy . . . nursed and cared for by his relations, is cured of that hurt. Monks, there is here this sort of warrior. This, monks, is the fourth kind. . . .

Then, monks, there is the soldier who, grasping sword and shield, binding on bow and quiver, goes down into the thick of the fight; victorious in battle, winning the fight, he continues at the head of the battle. Monks, there is here this sort of warrior. This, monks, is the fifth kind of warrior found in the world.

From: The Book of the Fives: Chapter XVIII, §VII (177), "Trades"[13]

Monks, these five trades ought not to be plied by a lay disciple. What five?

Trade in weapons, trade in human beings, trade in flesh,[14] trade in spirits and trade in poison.

Verily, monks, these five trades ought not to be plied by a lay-disciple.

From: *The Book of Kindred Sayings* (*Saṃyutta-Nikāya*), §§4, 5, "Two Sayings about War"[15]

Now the king of Magadha, Ajātasattu, son of the Accomplished Princess, mustering an army of cavalry and infrantry advanced into Kāsi against the king, the Kosalan Pasenadi. And the Pasenadi, hearing of the expedition, mustered a similar army and went to meet him. So they two fought one with another, and Ajātasattu defeated the Pasenadi, who retreated to his own capital, Sāvatthī.

And almsmen returning from their alms-round in Sāvatthī, came and told the Exalted One of the battle and the retreat.

Almsmen, the king of Magadha, Ajātasattu, son of the Accomplished Princess, is a friend to, an intimate of, mixed up with, whatever is evil.[16] The king, the Kosalan Pasenadi, is a friend to, an intimate of, mixed up with, whatever is good. But for the present the Pasenadi will pass this night in misery, a defeated man.

Conquest engenders hate; the conquered lives
In misery. But whoso is at peace
And passionless, happily doth he live;
Conquest hath he abandoned and defeat.

Now these two kings met again in battle, as is told in what is aforesaid.[17] But in that battle the Kosalan Pasenadi defeated Ajātasattu, son of the Accomplished Princess, and captured him alive. Then the Pasenadi thought: "Although this king injures me who was not injuring him, yet is he my nephew.[18] What if I were now to confiscate his entire army – elephants, horses, chariots and infantry – and leave him only his life?" And he did so.

And almsmen returning from their alms-tour in Sāvatthī, brought word of this to the Exalted One. Thereupon the Exalted One, understanding the matter in that hour, uttered these verses:

A man may spoil another, just so far
As it may serve his ends, but when he's spoiled
By others he, despoiled, spoils yet again.
So long as evil's fruit is not matured,
The fool doth fancy "now's the hour, the chance!"
But when the deed bears fruit, he fareth ill.
The slayer gets a slayer in his turn;
The conqueror gets one who conquers him;
Th' abuser wins abuse, th' annoyer, fret.
Thus by the evolution of the deed,
A man who spoils is spoiled in his turn.

From: *The Book of Kindred Sayings (Saṃyutta-Nikāya)*, §4, "Bowmanship"[19]

In an interview with the King Kosala, Pasenadi, at Sāvatthī the Buddha asked:

"What think you, sire? Suppose that you were at war, and that the contending armies were being mustered. And there were to arrive a noble youth, untrained, unskilled, unpracticed, undrilled, timid, trembling, affrighted, one who would run away – would you keep that man? Would such a man be any good to you?"

"No, lord, I should not keep that man, nor would such a man be any good to me."

"And would you say the same, sire, if such a man were a brahmin, or a merchant's son, or the son of a laborer?"

"Yes, lord."

"But what would be your opinion, sire, if the youth in question, to whichever social class he belonged, were trained, skilled, expert, practiced, drilled, bold, of steady nerve, undismayed incapable of running away? Would you keep that man? Would such a man be any good to you?"

"I should keep that man, lord, he would be useful to me."

"Even so, sire, is the case of a man, no matter what his social class, who has left the world and exchanged the domestic for the homeless life. He has abolished five qualities, and is possessed of five qualities. Given to him, a gift bears much fruit...."

Thus spake the Exalted One, and the Master added:

As [a] prince engaged in war would keep that youth
In whom he saw good bowmanship displayed
And mobile energy [*balaviriya*], and would not choose
Because of rank one craven and unfit,
So would the wise do reverence to him
Who, though of lowly birth, led [a] noble life
Of self-control and magnanimity.

From: *The Connected Discourses of the Buddha*, V, The Great Book, "Pointless Talk"[20]

Bhikkhus [monks], do not engage in the various kinds of pointless talk, that is, talk about kings, thieves, and ministers of state; talk about armies, dangers, and wars; talk about food, drink, garments, and beds; talk about garlands and scents; talk about relations, vehicles, villages, towns, cities, and countries; talk about women and talk about heroes; street talk and talk by the well; talk about those departed in days gone by; rambling chitchat; speculation about the world and about the sea; talk about becoming this or that. For what reason? Because, bhikkhus, this talk is unbeneficial, irrelevant to the fundamentals of the holy life, and does not lead to revulsion, to dispassion, to cessation, to peace, to direct knowledge, to enlightenment, to Nibbāna.[*]

From: *The Long Discourses of the Buddha*, *Brahmajāla Sutta*, Sutta 1, "What the Teaching Is Not"[21]

Short Section on Morality

1.8. "Abandoning the taking of life, the ascetic Gotama dwells refraining from taking life, without stick or sword, scrupulous, compassionate, trembling for the welfare of all living beings." Thus the worldling would praise the Tathāgata.[†]...

1.9. "Abandoning false speech, the ascetic Gotama dwells refraining from false speech, a truth-speaker, one to be relied on, trustworthy, dependable, not a deceiver of the world. Abandoning malicious speech, he does not repeat there what he has heard here to the detriment of these, or repeat here what he has heard there to the

---

[*] *Nibbāna* is the ultimate realization that appears as a result of complete cessation of all bondage, attachment, and craving.

[†] The *tathāgata* ("thus come" or "thus gone") is an epithet of the Buddha.

detriment of those. Thus he is a reconciler of those at variance and an encourager of those at one, rejoicing in peace, loving it, delighting in it, one who speaks up for peace. Abandoning harsh speech, he refrains from it. He speaks whatever is blameless, pleasing to the ear, agreeable, reaching the heart, urbane, pleasing and attractive to the multitude. Abandoning idle chatter, he speaks at the right time, what is correct and to the point, of Dhamma and discipline. He is a speaker whose words are to be treasured, seasonable, reasoned, well-defined and connected with the goal." Thus the worldling would praise the Tathāgata.

1.10. "The ascetic Gotama is a refrainer from damaging seeds and crops.... He avoids accepting gold and silver. He avoids accepting raw grain or raw flesh, he does not accept women and young girls, male or female slaves, sheep and goats, cocks and pigs, elephants, cattle, horses and mares, fields and plots; he refrains from running errands, from buying and selling, from cheating with false weights and measures, from bribery and corruption, deception and insincerity, from wounding, killing, imprisoning, highway robbery, and taking food by force." Thus the worldling would praise the Tathāgata.

Middle Section on Morality

1.13. "Whereas some ascetics and Brahmins ... remain addicted to attending such shows as dancing ... fairy-shows, acrobatic and conjuring tricks, combats of elephants, buffaloes, bulls, goats, rams, cocks and quail, fighting with staves, boxing, wrestling, sham-fights, parades, maneuvers and military reviews, the ascetic Gotama refrains from attending such displays."

1.14. "Whereas some ascetics and Brahmins remain addicted to such games and idle pursuits as ... dicing, hitting sticks, ... playing with ... bows... the ascetic Gotama refrains from such idle pursuits."...

1.17. "Whereas some ascetics and Brahmins remain addicted to such unedifying conversation as about kings, robbers, ministers, armies, dangers, wars, food, drink, clothes, beds, garlands, perfumes, relatives, carriages, villages, towns and cities, countries, women, heroes, street- and well-gossip, talk of the departed, desultory chat, speculations about land and sea, talk about being and non-being, the ascetic Gotama refrains from such conversation."...

1.19. "Whereas some ascetics and Brahmins remain addicted to such things as running errands and messages, such as for kings, ministers, nobles, Brahmins, householders and young men who say: 'Go here – go there! Take this there – bring that from there!' the ascetic Gotama refrains from such errand-running."...

Large Section on Morality

1.21. "Whereas some ascetics and Brahmins, feeding on the food of the faithful, make their living by such base arts, such wrong means of livelihood as palmistry, divining by signs, portents, dreams, body-marks, ... reading the finger-tips, ... skill in charms, ... foretelling a person's life-span, charms against arrows, knowledge of animals' cries, the ascetic Gotama refrains from such base arts and wrong means of livelihood."

1.22. "Whereas some ascetics and Brahmins make their living by such base arts as judging the marks of gems, sticks, clothes, swords, spears, arrows, weapons, women, men, boys, girls . . . , the ascetic Gotama refrains from such base arts."

1.23. "Whereas some ascetics and Brahmins make their living by such base arts as predicting: 'The chiefs will march out – the chiefs will march back,' 'Our chiefs will advance and the other chiefs will retreat,' 'Our chiefs will win and the other chiefs will lose,' 'The other chiefs will win and ours will lose,' 'Thus there will be victory for one side and defeat for the other,' the ascetic Gotama refrains from such base arts." . . .

1.25. "Whereas some ascetics and Brahmins make their living by such base arts as predicting good or bad rainfall; a good or bad harvest; security, danger; disease, health . . . the ascetic Gotama refrains from such base arts and wrong means of livelihood."

From: *The Anguttara Nikāya of the Sutta Piṭaka: Eka, Duka and Tika Nipāta*, III.ii.14, *"Rathakāra Vagga"*[22]

Even a pious and righteous universal monarch does not practice irresponsible sovereignty.

When this was said, a certain bhikkhu thus enquired from the Bhagavā: "Lord, who is this overlord of the monarch?"

"Law,"[23] replied the Bhagavā.

In this world a pious and righteous universal monarch, by supporting the law, honoring the law, reverencing the law, worshipping the law, as the banner of the law, the standard of the law, recognizing the supremacy of the law, provides due and lawful protection among his family members and personal attendants. . . .

This pious and righteous universal monarch having protected the family members and personal attendants, the attendant Kshatriyas, the army, the brahmans, householders, the residents of the districts, and provinces, the *samanas* [Pali for "recluses"] and brahmans and the animals and birds, rules in accordance with the laws. Such rules cannot be upset by any enemy whether human or animal.

Righteous and Unrighteous Wars: The **Sakka Suttas**

In relation to the battles between heavenly bodies, some of the early Buddhist discourses have focused on both righteous and unrighteous warfare. These canonical accounts indicate how individuals involved in fighting should adhere to accepted norms of war. Most important, no harm should be done to the innocent. While circumstances may compel groups to engage in war for self-defense, they should never engage in acts of cruelty. Those defeated or taken prisoner should be accorded protection. The following excerpts from the Pāli canon show the way that the issue of righteousness in battle is highlighted in the war between *suras* (gods) and *asuras* (fallen angels or Titans). In Buddhist mythology, *asuras* are a class of mythological beings who have fallen. They are classed as inferior deities. Their battle with the gods is a common topic in some Buddhist texts,[24] as is the case in the texts presented below. The chief of the gods was called Sakka and the chief of *asuras* was known as *asurinda*. Several *asuras* such as Vepacitti and Rāhu held the leadership of *asuras*.

From: *The Book of the Kindred Sayings*, Chapter XI, "The Sakka Suttas," §1, Suvīra[25]

... The Exalted One said: "In days gone by the Asuras [Titans] marched out against the gods. Then Sakka, ruler of the gods, called to Suvīra, son of the gods: 'These Asuras ... [have] come out against us. Go thou out to meet them.' 'So be it, lord,' responded Suvīra, son of the gods, but he played the slacker. Yea, twice and even thrice did Sakka summon him; and twice and even thrice with no better result."

From: *The Book of the Kindred Sayings*, Chapter XI, "The Sakka Suttas," §3, The Top of the Banner[26]

The Exalted One once, while at the Jeta Vana, addressed the brethren on this wise:

"Long ago, bhikkhus, a battle was raging between the gods and the Asuras. Then Sakka, ruler of the gods, addressed the Thirty-three Gods, saying: 'If in you, dear sirs, when ye are gone into the battle, fear and panic and creeping of the flesh should arise, look up at the crest of my banner. If ye do so, any fear and panic and creeping of the flesh that will have arisen will be overcome. If ye look not up to the crest of my banner, look up at that of Pajāpati, king of the gods, ... or at that of Varuṇa, king of the gods, ... or at that of Isāna, king of the gods, and any fear and panic and creeping of the flesh that will have arisen will be overcome.'

"Now, bhikkhus, in them that look up to the crest of one or other of these four banners, any fear and panic and creeping of the flesh that has arisen may be overcome, or again it may not. And why is this? Because Sakka, ruler of the gods, is not purged of passions, hate, or ignorance, is timid, given to panic, to fright, to running away."

From: *The Book of the Kindred Sayings*, Chapter XI, "The Sakka Suttas," §4, *Vepacitti*, or Forbearance[27]

Again, at the same place, the Exalted One addressed the brethren:

"Long time ago, bhikkhus, gods and Asuras were mingled in battle. And Vepacitti, ruler of the Asuras, addressed the Asuras, saying: 'If, dear sirs, in the battle now raging between gods and Asuras, the Asuras are victorious, the gods defeated, when ye have bound Sakka, ruler of the gods, hand and foot and neck, bring him before me into the City of the Asuras.'

"Sakka also, bhikkhus, ruler of the gods, addressed the Thirty-three Gods, saying: 'If, dear sirs, in the battle now raging between gods and Asuras, the gods are victorious, the Asuras defeated, when ye have bound Vepacitti, ruler of the Asuras, hand and foot and neck, bring him before me into the hall Sudhammā.'*

"Now in that battle, bhikkhus, the gods were victorious, the Asuras were defeated. And the Thirty-three Gods bound Vepacitti hand and foot and neck, and brought him before Sakka into the hall Sudhammā. And Vepacitti, thus bound, railed at and reviled Sakka as he entered and when he left the hall, with coarse and scurrilous words.

"Then, bhikkhus, Mātali, the charioteer, addressed Sakka, ruler of the gods, with the verse:

Now is it, Sakka, that thou art afraid,
Or because thou art weak that thou forbear'st,
When thou dost hear these speeches scurrilous
By Vepacitti cast into thy teeth?

Sakka:
Nay, not from fear nor weakness do I bear
With Vepacitti. How should any man
Who lacks not understanding, such as I,
Engage himself to bandy with a fool?

Mātali:
But fools may only wax ever more wroth
If there be none to put a stop to them.
Wherefore by heavy chastisement and sharp
Let the strong-minded man restrain the fool.

Sakka:
But in my judgment this alone avails
To stop [the railing of] a foolish man:
When he who has a mind alert, and sees
Another filled with rage, grows calm and still.

Mātali:
In this, that thou dost patiently forbear,
A grievous error, Vāsava, I see.

---

* Deities use the *Sudhammā-sabhā* (*Sudhammā*, hall) for their meetings.

For when the food doth fancy: "[I]t is from fear
He bears with me," the dolt will press you hard,
Like cow [that charges] more when you do flee.

Sakka:
O let him fancy as he will – or won't:
That I do bear with him because I fear.
'Mong highest matters of our spirit's growth
Nought ranks above forbearing patiently.
Yea, surely he that hath the upper hand
And beareth patiently with him that's down;
Ever to tolerate the weaker side:
This the supreme forbearance hath been called.
Whoso doth think the strength of fools is strength,
Will say of the strong man: A weakling he!
For the strong man whom righteousness doth guard,
To bandy words comes not into his thought.
Worse of the two is he who, when reviled,
Reviles again. Who doth not, when reviled,
Revile again, a twofold victory wins.

Both of the other and himself he seeks
The good; for he the other's angry mood
Doth understand and groweth calm and still.
He who of both is a physician, since
Himself he healeth and the other too,
Folk deem him fool, they knowing not the Norm.

"Verily this Sakka, bhikkhus, ruler of the gods, subsisting on the fruit of his own good works, and ruling over and governing the Thirty-three Gods, will be of those who commend forbearance and gentleness. Now in this Rule, bhikkhus, ye do enhance his virtue when ye who have gone forth under a Norm and Discipline so well proclaimed become forbearing and gentle."

From: *The Book of the Kindred Sayings*, Chapter XI, "The Sakka Suttas," §5, Victory by Speeches[28]

Another discourse at Sāvatthī:

"Long time ago, bhikkhus, a battle was raging between the gods and the Ausras. And Vepacitti, ruler of the Asuras, said to Sakka, ruler of the gods: 'Let the victory, ruler of the gods, be according to excellence in speech!'

"So be the victory, ruler of the Asuaras!

"Then bhikkhus, the gods and Asuras, arrayed their audiences, saying: 'These will judge what is well-spoken and what is ill-spoken.'

"Then Vepacitti said to Sakka: 'Recite thou a verse, ruler of the gods!' And Sakka replied: 'Thou, Vepacitti, art here the older god; speak thou a verse.'

"Then Vepacitti, bhikkhus, spoke this verse:

They that are foolish ever wax more wroth
If there be none to put a stop to them.
Wherefore by heavy chastisement and sharp
Let the strong-minded man restrain the fool.

"Now the Asuras, bhikkhus, applauded the verse spoken by Vepacitti; the gods remained silent.

"Thereupon Sakka spoke this verse:

But in my judgment this alone avails
To stop [the railing of] a foolish man:
When he who has a mind alert, and sees
Another filled with rage, grows calm and still.

"Now the gods, bhikkhus, applauded the verse spoken by Sakka; the Asuras remained silent.

"Then Sakka said to Vepacitti: 'Recite thou a verse, Vepacitti!'

Vepacitti:
In this that thou dost patiently forbear,
A grievous error, Vāsava, I see.
For when the fool doth fancy: "[I]t is from fear
He bears with me," the dolt will press you hard
Like [a] cow [that charges] more the more you flee.

"Now the Asuras applauded; the gods remained silent.

"Then Vepacitti said to Sakka: 'Recite a verse, ruler of the gods.' And Sakka spake these verses:

O let him fancy as he will – or won't:
That one doth bear with him because of fear. . . .

"Then the gods applauded the verses spoken by Sakka, the Asuras remained silent. Thereupon the audiences of gods and Asuras spoke thus:

"'The verses spoken by Vepacitti, ruler of Asuras, belong to the sphere of force and violence, of quarrelling, strife, and contention. The verses spoken by Sakka, ruler of the gods, belong to the sphere of persuasion and mildness, of concord, amity, and harmony. To Sakka, ruler of the gods, the victory by excellence of speech!'

"And thus, bhikkhus, did Sakka win the victory by excellence of speech."

From: *The Book of the Kindred Sayings*, Chapter XI, "The Sakka Suttas," §6, Nests[29]

Another discourse at Sāvatthī:

"Long time ago, bhikkhus, a battle was raging between the gods and the Asuras. And in that fight the Asuras conquered, the gods were defeated. And the defeated gods retreated toward the north, the Asuras pursuing them.

"Now Sakka, ruler of the gods, addressed Mātali, his charioteer, in the verse:

See that the chariot pole, O Mātali,
Keeps clear of nests 'mong the silk-cotton trees,
Let us choose rather to give up our lives
To Asuras than nestless make these birds.

"'So be it, lord!' said Mātali, and in obedience to Sakka he turned back the chariot with its team of a thousand thoroughly trained horses.

"Then, bhikkhus, the Asuras thought: 'The chariot of Sakka is now turned back, the devas will engage the Asuras in a second battle. And terrified, they retreated into the City of the Asuras.

"Thus, bhikkhus, was Sakka victor by righteousness."

From: *The Book of the Kindred Sayings*, Chapter XI, "The Sakka Suttas," §7, Not Treacherously[30]

Another discourse at Sāvatthī:

"Long time ago, bhikkhus, to Sakka, ruler of the gods, meditating in private, this idea arose in his mind: 'Whoever may be my enemy, even him I may not betray.'

"Then Vepacitti, ruler of the Asuras, discerning in [his] mind the mind of Sakka, came up to him. And Sakka saw him coming from afar, and seeing him, called out: 'Stop, Vepacitti, thou art my prisoner!'

"'That which was just now in thy mind, dear sir, renounce it not!'

"'Thou mayest swear, Vepacitti, that I will use no treachery.'"

Vepacitti:

The evil fruit that from false speaking comes,
The evil fruit from blasphemy of saints,
The evil fruit from perfidy to friends,
The evil fruit borne by ingratitude:
That evil fruit, O consort of Sujā,
He reaps who showeth treachery to thee.

From: *The Book of the Kindred Sayings*, Chapter XI, "The Sakka Suttas," §10, Seers of the Seaside, or *Sambara*[31]

Another discourse at Sāvatthī:

"Long time ago, bhikkhus, many seers, virtuous and lovely in character, were living together in leaf-huts on the seashore.

"Now at that time, bhikkhus, a battle was raging between the gods and the Asuras. And in those seers the thought arose: 'The gods are righteous, the Asuras are unrighteous. There may be danger even for us from the Asura. What if we were now to go to Sambara, lord of Asuras, and ask for a pledge of safety?' Then those Rishis [seers], as quickly as a strong man might stretch out his bent arm, or bend his arm stretched out, vanished from their leaf-huts on the seashore and appeared before Sambara. Then, bhikkhus, those Rishis, virtuous and lovely of character, addressed Sambara, lord of Asuras, in a verse:

We Rishis, come to Sambara,
Entreat of him a safety-pledge.
Do as thou listest. Give that we
In peril or in safety dwell.

Sambara:
Safety is not for such as ye!
Who Sakka serve choose ill their time.
To you entreating safety-pledge,
Terror is all that I do give.

The Rishis:
And dost thou only peril give
To us who ask for safety-pledge?
Lo! then accepting this from thee,
May never-dying fear be thine!
According to the seed that's sown
So is the fruit ye reap therefrom.
Doer of good [will gather] good,
Doer of evil evil [reaps].
Sown is the seed and planted well.
Thou shalt enjoy the fruit thereof.

"Then, bhikkhus, those Rishis, virtuous and lovely of character, having laid a curse on Sambara, ruler of the Asuras, as a strong man might stretch out his bent arm . . . , vanished from the presence of Sambara and reappeared in their leaf-huts on the seashore. But Sambara, on whom those Rishis had laid a curse, that very night woke up thrice seized with terror."

The Buddha and War

The earliest systematic literary corpus of Buddhism, the Pāli canon, is relatively free of texts that may be effectively used as a basis for developing a "just war" theory. In this sense the canon offers no parallel to what may be found, for instance, in the Christian tradition, with influential texts supporting the idea of just war, such as Gratian's *Decretum* or Thomas Aquinas' *Summa Theologiae*.[32] Nevertheless, war was a fact of life even in the Buddha's lifetime, and there are plenty of references to warfare in Buddhist literature that narrate instances in which various kings waged war against one another.

The Historical Buddha's Interventions in War

The historical Buddha did not just preach the importance of peace; on two occasions, he personally intervened to prevent war. The first occasion was when King Ajātasattu wished to invade the Vajjian Kingdom. The second was when his relatives were about to wage war against each other over the distribution of water from the Rohinī River.

Prior to invading the Vajjians, King Ajātasattu sent his Prime Minister Vassakāra ("rain maker") to receive the Buddha's advice so that he could secure success in his military ambitions. The king asked Vassakāra to remember everything the Buddha said. In conversation with Vassakāra, the Buddha discouraged the king from waging war by saying that the Vajjians cannot be defeated as long as they abide by the seven welfare conditions that the Buddha had taught them. After hearing this advice the king abandoned his invasion of the Vajjian Kingdom for the time being.

From: *Dialogues of the Buddha, "Mahā Parinibbāna Suttanta"*: The Book of the Great Decease, Chapter 1[33]

1. ... The Exalted One was once dwelling in Rājagaha, on the hill called the Vulture's Peak. Now at that time Ajātasattu, the son of the queen-consort of the Videha clan, the king of Magadha, had made up his mind to attack the Vajjians; and he said to himself, "I will strike at these Vajjians, mighty and powerful though they be, I will root out these Vajjians, I will destroy these Vajjians, I will bring these Vajjians to utter ruin!"

2. So he spake to the Brahmin Vassakāra (the Rain-maker), prime-minister of Magadha, and said:

"Come now, Brahmin, do you go to the Exalted One, and bow down in adoration at his feet on my behalf, and inquire in my name whether he is free from illness and suffering, and in the enjoyment of ease and comfort and vigorous health. Then tell him that Ajātasattu, son of the Vedehī, the king of Magadha, in his eagerness to attack the Vajjians, has resolved, 'I will strike at these Vajjians, mighty and powerful though they be, I will root out these Vajjians, I will destroy these Vajjians, I will bring these Vajjians to utter ruin!' And bear carefully in mind whatever the Exalted One may predict, and repeat it to me. For the Buddhas speak nothing untrue!"

3. Then the Brahmin Vassakāra, the Rain-maker, hearkened to the words of the king, saying, "Be it as you say." And ordering a number of state carriages to be made ready, he mounted one of them . . . and went to the Vulture's Peak . . . and then alighting and proceeding on foot to the place where the Exalted One was. On arriving there he exchanged with the Exalted One the greetings and compliments of politeness and courtesy, sat down respectfully by his side (and then delivered to him the message even as the king had commanded).

4. Now at that time the venerable Ānanda was standing behind the Exalted One, and fanning him. And the Blessed One said to him: "Have you heard, Ānanda, that the Vajjians foregather often and frequent the public meetings of their clan?"

"Lord, so I have heard," replied he.

"So long, Ānanda," rejoined the Blessed One, "as the Vajjians foregather thus often, and frequent the public meetings of their clan; so long may they be expected not to decline, but to prosper."

(And in like manner questioning Ānanda, and receiving a similar reply, the Exalted One declared as follows the other conditions which would ensure the welfare of the Vajjian confederacy.)

"So long, Ānanda, as the Vajjians meet together in concord, and rise in concord, and carry out their undertakings in concord – so long as they enact nothing not already established, abrogate nothing that has been already enacted, and act in accordance with the ancient institutions of the Vajjians, as established in former days – so long as they honor and esteem and revere and support the Vajjian elders, and hold it a point of duty to hearken to their words – so long as no women or girls belonging to their clans are detained among them by force or abduction – so long as they honor and esteem and revere and support the Vajjian shrines in town or country, and allow not the proper offerings and rites, as formerly given and performed, to fall into desuetude – so long as the rightful protection, defense, and support shall be fully provided for the Arahants among them, so that Arahants from a distance may enter the realm, and the Arahants therein may live at ease – so long may the Vajjians be expected not to decline, but to prosper."

5. Then the Exalted One addressed Vassakāra the Brahmin and said:

"When I was once staying, O Brahmin, at Vesālī at the Sārandada Shrine, I taught the Vajjians these conditions of welfare; and so long as these conditions shall continue to exist among the Vajjians, so long as the Vajjians shall be well instructed in those conditions, so long may we expect them not to decline, but to prosper."

"We may expect then," answered the Brahmin, "the welfare and not the decline of the Vajjians when they are possessed of any one of these conditions of welfare, how much more so when they are possessed of all the seven. So, Gotama, the Vajjians cannot be overcome by the king of Magadha; that is not in battle, without diplomacy or breaking up their alliance. And now, Gotama, we must go; we are busy and have much to do.". . .

26. At that time Sunīdha and Vassakāra, the chief ministers of Magadha, were building a fortress at Pātaligāma to repel the Vajjians, and there were a number of fairies who haunted in thousands the plots of ground there. Now, wherever

ground is so occupied by powerful fairies, they bend the hearts of the most powerful kings and ministers to build dwelling-places there, [and fairies of middling and inferior power bend in a similar way the hearts of middling or inferior kings and ministers].

27. And the Blessed One, with great and clear vision, surpassing that of ordinary men, saw thousand of those fairies haunting Pātaligāma. And he rose up very early in the morning, and said to Ānanda: "Who is it then, Ānanda, who is building a fortress at Pātaligāma?"

"Sunīdha and Vassakāra, lord, the chief ministers of the Magadha, are building a fortress there to keep back the Vajjians."

War for Water: The Buddha's Mediation

On another occasion the Buddha intervened to prevent war when he mediated a dispute between his relatives. As narrated in the *Kuṇāla-Jātaka*, a conflict arose between the Śākyas (on his paternal side) and the Koliyas (on his maternal side). The dispute concerned the distribution of water of the Rohiṇī River. This river divided their territories and its water was crucial for agriculture. After their respective claims proved irreconcilable, the armed forces of the two sides gathered along the river to wage war. When the Buddha learned of this, he intervened. His words were effective in demonstrating the futility of warfare. He thereby prevented unnecessary bloodshed.

From: *Kuṇāla-Jātaka*[34]

This was a story told by the Master, while dwelling beside lake Kuṇāla, concerning five hundred Brethren who were overwhelmed with discontent.... The Sākiya and Koliya tribes had the river Rohiṇī which flows between the cities of Kapilavatthu and Koliya confined by a single dam and by means of it cultivated their crops. In the month Jeṭṭhamūla[35] when the crops began to flag and droop, the laborers from among the dwellers of both cities assembled together. Then the people of Koliya said, "Should this water be drawn off on both sides, it will not prove sufficient for both us and you. But our crops will thrive with a single watering; give us then the water." The people of Kapilavatthu said, "When you have filled your garners with corn, we shall hardly have the courage to come with ruddy gold, emeralds and copper coins, and with baskets and sacks in our hands, to hang about your doors. Our crops too will thrive with a single watering; give us the water." "We will not give it," they said. "Neither will we," said the others. As words thus ran high, one of them rose up and struck another a blow, and he in turn struck a third and thus it was that what with interchanging blows and spitefully touching on the origin of their princely families they increased the tumult. The Koliya laborers said, "Be off with your people of Kapitavatthu, men who like dogs, jackals, and such like beasts, cohabited with their own sisters. What will their elephants and horses, their shields and spears avail against us?" The Sākiya laborers replied, "Nay, do you, wretched lepers, be off with your children, destitute and ill-conditioned fellows, who like brute beasts had their dwelling in a hollow jujube tree (*koli*). What shall their elephants and horses, their spears and shields avail against us?" So they went and told the counselors appointed to such services and they reported it to the princes of their tribes. Then the Sākiyas said, "We will show them how strong and mighty are the men who cohabited with their sisters," and they sallied forth, ready for the fray. And the Koliyas said, "We will show them how strong and mighty are they who dwelt in the hollow of a jujube tree," and they too sallied forth ready for the fight. But other teachers tell the story thus, "When the female slaves of the Sākiyas and Koliyas came to the river to fetch water, and throwing the coils of cloth that they carried on their heads upon the ground were seated and pleasantly conversing, a certain woman took another's cloth, thinking it was her own; and when owing to this a quarrel arose, each claiming the coil of cloth as hers, gradually the people of the two cities, the serfs and the laborers, the attendants, headmen, counselors and viceroys, all of them sallied forth ready for battle." But the former version being found in many commentaries and being plausible is to be accepted rather than the other. Now it was at eventide that they would be sallying forth, ready for the fray. At that time the Blessed One was dwelling at Sāvatthi, and at dawn of day while contemplating the world he beheld them setting out to the fight, and on seeing them he wondered whether if he were to go there the quarrel would cease, and he made up his mind and thought, "I will go there and, to quell this feud, I will relate three Birth Stories, and after that the quarrelling will cease. Then after telling two Birth Stories, to illustrate the blessings of union, I will teach them the Attadaṇḍa Sutta and after hearing my sermon the people of the two cities will each of them bring into my presence two hundred and fifty youths, and I shall admit them to holy orders and there will be a huge gathering.". . .

[The Buddha] went by himself and sat cross-legged in the air between the two hosts. And seeing it was an occasion to startle them, to create darkness he sat there emitting (dark-blue) rays from his hair. Then when their hearts were troubled he revealed himself and emitted the six-colored rays. The people of Kapilavatthu on seeing the Blessed One thought, "The Master, our noble kinsman, is come. Can he have seen the obligation laid upon us to fight? Now that the Master has come, it is impossible for us to discharge a weapon against the person of an enemy," and they threw down their arms, saying, "Let the Koliyas slay us or roast us alive." The Koliyas acted in exactly the same way. Then the Blessed One alighted and seated himself on a magnificent Buddha throne, set in a charming spot on a bed of sand, and he shone with the incomparable glory of a Buddha. The kings too saluting the Blessed One took their seats. Then the Master, though he knew it right well, asked, "Why are ye come here, mighty kings?" "Holy Sir," they answered, "we are come, neither to see this river, nor to disport ourselves, but to get up a fight." What is the quarrel about, sires?" "About the water." "What is the water worth?" "Very little, Holy Sir." "What is the earth worth?" "It is of priceless value." "What are warrior chiefs worth?" "They too are of priceless value." "Why on account of some worthless water are you for destroying chiefs of high worth? "Verily, there is no satisfaction in this quarrel, but owing to a feud, sire, between a certain tree-sprite and a black lion a grudge was set up, which has reached down to this present aeon," and with these words he told them the Phandana Birth.

The Origin of Social Problems, the Decline of Morals, and the Wheel Turner King

The discourse on *The Lion's Roar on the Turning of the Wheel*, known as the *Cakkavatti-Sīhanāda Sutta*, belongs to the collection of *The Long Discourses of the Buddha* (The *Dīgha-Nikāya*). It is a quite popular Pāli canonical text among Theravāda Buddhist societies in South and Southeast Asia because of its analysis of social problems. Its doctrinal content (i.e., explanation of poverty and its relationship to the origin of conflict, violence, and war) has contemporary relevance for understanding issues in modern society. The text's causal analysis of social problems (poverty and the like) has attracted a wide readership today among practicing Buddhists (laymen and scholars). The *Cakkavatti-Sīhanāda Sutta* is focused on the ideal of a wheel-turning monarch,[36] namely, one who observes the Buddha's teaching (*dhamma*) and who provides care for those in poverty. The way the wheel-turning monarch secures power and imposes his authority in a nonviolent manner by using some military metaphors and parading with a fourfold army has led some to argue that the very notion of the wheel-turning monarch itself potentially contributes to a development of just war theories in Buddhism.

From: *The Long Discourses of the Buddha: A Translation of the Dīgha-Nikāya*, Sutta 26, "*Cakkavatti-Sīhanāda Sutta*: The Lion's Roar on the Turning of the Wheel"[37]

2. "Once, monks, there was a wheel-turning monarch named Dalhanemi, a righteous monarch of the law, conqueror of the four quarters, who had established the security of his realm and was possessed of the seven treasures. . . .

"He has more than a thousand sons who are heroes, of heroic stature, conquerors of the hostile army. He dwells having conquered this sea-girt land without stick or sword, [but rather] by the law. . . ."

3. . . . "[A]fter many hundreds and thousands of years, King Dalhanemi said to a certain man: '. . . whenever you see that the sacred Wheel-Treasure has slipped from its position, report it to me.' . . . And after many hundreds and thousands of years the man saw that the sacred Wheel-Treasure had slipped from its position. Seeing this, he reported the fact to the King. The King Dalhanemi sent for his eldest son, the crown prince, and said: '. . . I have heard [one] say that when this happens to a wheel-turning monarch, he has not much longer to live. . . . You, my son, take over control of this ocean-bounded land.'. . . [S]even days after the royal sage had gone forth, the sacred Wheel-Treasure vanished."

4. "Then a certain man came to the anointed Khattiya King and said, 'Sire, you should know that the sacred Wheel-Treasure has disappeared.' At this the King was grieved. . . . He went to the royal sage and told him the news. And the royal

sage said to him: 'My son, you should not grieve or feel sad at the disappearance of the Wheel-Treasure . . . now, my son, you must turn yourself into an Ariyan wheel-turner. And then it may come about that, if you perform the duties of an Ariyan wheel-turning monarch . . . the sacred Wheel-Treasure will appear to you. . . .'"

5. "'But what, sire, is the duty of an Ariyan wheel-turning monarch?' 'It is this, my son: Yourself depending on the Dhamma, honoring it, revering it, cherishing it, doing homage to it and venerating it, having the Dhamma as your badge and banner, acknowledging the Dhamma as your master, you should establish guard, ward and protection according to Dhamma for your own household, your troops, your nobles and vassals, for Brahmins and householders, town and country folk, ascetics and Brahmins, for beasts and birds. Let no crime prevail in your kingdom, and to those who are in need, give property. And whatever ascetics and Brahmins in your kingdom have renounced the life of sensual infatuation and are devoted to forbearance and gentleness . . . , if from time to time they should come to you and consult you as to what is wholesome and what is unwholesome . . . , you should listen, and tell them to avoid evil and do what is good. That, my son, is the duty of an Ariyan wheel-turning monarch.'"

"'Yes, sire,' said the King, and he performed the duties of an Ariyan wheel-turning monarch. And as he did so, on the fast-day of the fifteenth, when he had washed his head and gone up to the veranda on top of his palace for the fast-day, the sacred Wheel-Treasure appeared to him, thousand-spoked, complete with felloe, hub and all appurtenances. Then the King thought: 'I have heard that when a duly anointed Khattiya king sees such a wheel on the fast-day of the fifteenth, he will become a wheel-turning monarch. May I become such a monarch!'"

One modern commentator has stated that the *Cakkavatti-Sīhanāda Sutta* can function as a potential just war text.[38] The way the monarch follows the wheel with his fourfold army is seen as a demonstration of his military might.

6. "Then, rising from his seat, covering one shoulder with his robe, the King took a gold vessel in his left hand, sprinkled the Wheel with his right hand, and said: 'May the noble Wheel-Treasure turn, may the noble Wheel-Treasure conquer!' The Wheel turned to the east, and the King followed it with his fourfold army. And in whatever country the Wheel stopped, the King took up residence with his fourfold army. And those who opposed him in the eastern region came and said: 'Come, Your Majesty, welcome! We are yours, Your Majesty. Rule us, Your Majesty.' And the King said: 'Do not take life. Do not take what is not given. Do not commit sexual misconduct. Do not tell lies. Do not drink strong drink. Be moderate in eating.' And those who had opposed him in the eastern region became his subjects.

7. "Then the Wheel turned south, west, and north. . . . Then the Wheel-Treasure, having conquered the lands from sea to sea, returned to the royal capital and stopped before the King's palace as he was trying a case, as if to adorn the royal palace."

The *Cakkavatti-Sīhanāda Sutta* also explains how the neglect of *dhamma* can affect the welfare of the state.

8. "And a second wheel-turning monarch did likewise ... and a seventh king also...."

9. "Then a man came to the King and said: 'Sire, you should know that the sacred Wheel-Treasure has disappeared.' At this the King was grieved and felt sad. But he did not go to the royal sage and ask him about the duties of a wheel-turning monarch. Instead, he ruled the people according to his own ideas, and, being so ruled, the people did not prosper so well as they had done under the previous kings who had performed the duties of a wheel-turning monarch. Then the ministers, counsellors, treasury officials, guards and doorkeepers, and the chanters of mantras came to the King and said: 'Sire, as long as you rule the people according to your own ideas, and differently from the way they were ruled before under previous wheel-turning monarchs, the people do not prosper so well. Sire, there are ministers ... in your realm including ourselves, who have preserved the knowledge of how a wheel-turning monarch should rule. Ask us, Your Majesty, and we will tell you!'"

10. "Then the King ordered all the ministers and others to come together, and he consulted them. And they explained to him the duties of a wheel-turning monarch. And, having listened to them, the King established guard and protection, but he did not give property to the needy, and as a result poverty became rife."

The *Cakkavatti-Sīhanāda Sutta* points out the importance of caring for the needy. It thus highlights the alleviation of poverty as a moral task of good governance. The text vividly explains how violence readily arises when social issues such as poverty are not addressed in a forward-looking manner.

"With the spread of poverty, a man took what was not given, thus committing what was called theft. They arrested him, and brought him before the King, saying: 'Your Majesty, this man took what was not given, which we call theft.' The King said to him: 'Is it true that you took what was not given – which is called theft?' 'It is, Your Majesty.' 'Why?' 'Your Majesty, I have nothing to live on.' Then the King gave the man some property, saying: 'With this, my good man, you can keep yourself, support your mother and father, keep a wife and children, carry on a business and make gifts to ascetics and Brahmins, which will promote your spiritual welfare and lead to a happy rebirth with pleasant result in the heavenly sphere.' 'Very good, Your Majesty,' replied the man...."

12. "Then people heard that the King was giving away property to those who took what was not given, and they thought: 'Suppose we were to do likewise!' And then another man took what was not given, and they brought him before the King. The King asked him why he had done this, and he replied: 'Your Majesty, I have nothing to live on.' Then the King thought: 'If I give property to everybody who takes what is not given, this theft will increase more and more. I had better make an end of him, finish him off once for all, and cut his head off.' So he commanded his men: 'Bind this man's arms tightly behind him with a strong rope, shave his head closely, and lead him to the rough sound of a drum through the streets and squares and out through the southern gate, and

there finish by inflicting the capital penalty and cutting off his head!' And they did so."

13. "Hearing about this, people thought: 'Now let us get sharp swords made for us, and then we can take from anybody what is not given [which is called theft], we will make an end of them, finish them off once for all and cut off their heads.' So, having procured some sharp swords, they launched murderous assaults on villages, towns and cities, and went in for highway-robbery, killing their victims by cutting off their heads."

14. "Thus, from the not giving of property to the needy, poverty became rife, from the growth of poverty, the taking of what was not given increased, from the increase of theft, the use of weapons increased, from the increased use of weapons, the taking of life increased – and from the increase in the taking of life, people's life-span [and] ... beauty decreased...."

With the escalation of immoral behavior, including excessive greed, violence, and lack of respect for ascetics, Brahmins, and parental figures, the average life span is said to be reduced to a mere ten years.

19. ... "And with them, the ten courses of moral conduct will completely disappear, and the ten courses of evil will prevail exceedingly: for those of a ten-year life-span there will be no word for 'moral,' so how can there be anyone who acts in a moral way? Those people who have no respect for mother or father, for ascetics and Brahmins, for the head of the clan, will be the ones who enjoy honor and prestige. Just as it is now the people who show respect for mother and father, for ascetics and Brahmins, for the head of the clan, who are praised and honored, so it will be with those who do the opposite."

20. ... "Among them, fierce enmity will prevail one for another, fierce hatred, fierce anger and thoughts of killing, mother against child and child against mother, father against child and child against father, brother against brother, brother against sister, just as the hunter feels hatred for the beast he stalks...."

21. "And for those of a ten-year life-span, there will come to be a 'sword-interval' of seven days, during which they will mistake one another for wild beasts. Sharp swords will appear in their hands and, thinking: 'There is a wild beast!' they will take each other's lives with those swords. But there will be some beings who will think: 'Let us not kill or be killed by anyone! Let us make for some grassy thickets or jungle-recesses or clumps of trees, for rivers hard to ford or inaccessible mountains, and live on roots and fruits of the forest.' And this they will do for seven days. Then, at the end of the seven days, they will emerge from their hiding-places and rejoice together of one accord, saying: 'Good beings, I see that you are alive!' And then the thought will occur to those beings: 'It is only because we became addicted to evil ways that we suffered this loss of our kindred, so let us now do good! What good things can we do? Let us abstain from the taking of life – that will be a good practice.' And so they will abstain from the taking of life, and, having undertaken this good thing, will practice it. And through having undertaken such wholesome things, they will increase in life-span and beauty. And the children of those whose life-span was ten years will live for twenty years."

22. "Then it will occur to those beings: 'It is through having taken to wholesome practices that we have increased in life-span and beauty, so let us perform still more wholesome practices. Let us refrain from taking what is not given, from sexual misconduct, from lying speech, from slander, from harsh speech, from idle chatter, from covetousness, from ill-will, from wrong views; let us abstain from three things: incest, excessive greed, and deviant practices; let us respect our mothers and fathers, ascetics and Brahmins, and the head of the clan, and let us persevere in these wholesome actions.'"

"And so they will do these things, and on account of this they will increase in life-span and in beauty."

Poems from the Dhammapada: *The Historical Buddha's Teachings on Hatred, Revenge, Conquest, and Punishment*

The *Dhammapada* is an early Buddhist text of 423 poems with brief summaries of the Buddha's teachings organized into twenty-six chapters according to popular themes such as mind, self, punishment, anger, righteousness, and happiness. It is a Pāli canonical text belonging to the *Khuddakanikāya* and also available in other ancient languages such as Gāndhārī. It has been translated into many Asian and Western languages. The first complete translation of the *Dhammapada* in a European language was the Latin version (1855) of Michael Viggo Fausbøll (1821–1908), the pioneering Danish Pāli scholar. This translation became the basis for the first complete English translation, by Max Müller (1823–1900), which was published in 1881 as volume 10 of the series *Sacred Books of the East*. Today, however, in the English language alone, there are many popular and scholarly translations, which have attempted to capture with doctrinal accuracy the content and poetical aesthetics of the Buddha's poetry.[39]

Pāli poems quoted from the *Dhammapada* constitute the most popular Buddhist literature today in circulation in Theravāda Buddhist societies of South and Southeast Asia. Theravāda monastic preachers recite them as poems in sermons to capture the attention of worshippers and to focus their minds on a particular religious theme or instruction. Popular speakers such as politicians and statesmen often cite verses from the *Dhammapada* to promote the practice of nonviolence. For example, the Minister of Finance in the Government of Ceylon (1948–1953), Junius Richard Jayawardene (1906–1996), who later became the first Executive President of Sri Lanka (1978–1989), delivered a powerful speech at the conference for a Peace Treaty with Japan (San Francisco, 6 September 1951). Jayawardene, urging that Japan be pardoned for its wartime aggression,[40] cited one of the most famous verses of the *Dhammapada* (verse 5):

Not by enmity are enmities quelled,
Whatever the occasion here.
By the absence of enmity are they quelled.
This is an ancient truth.

Today in Sri Lanka young Buddhist novices memorize verses of the *Dhammapada* as a compulsory part of monastic training. In fostering the virtues associated closely with

Buddhism, the *Dhammapada* has played a significant role in perpetuating the cultural and religious canons in Buddhist societies. The verses cited below demonstrate a few of its many sayings on violence, punishment, and war. At the same time, it highlights core Buddhist values such as self-control and generosity.

From: The *Dhammapada*, I[41]

3. "He reviled me! He struck me!
He defeated me! He robbed me!"
They who gird themselves up with this,
For them enmity is not quelled.

4. "He reviled me! He struck me!
He defeated me! He robbed me!"
They who do not gird themselves up with this,
For them is enmity quelled....

6. Others do not realize
"We here are struggling."
Those who realize this – for them
Are quarrels therefore quelled.

From: The *Dhammapada*, Chapter VIII, The Thousands (*Sahassa-vaggo*)[42]

103. He, truly, is supreme in battle,
Who would conquer himself alone,
Rather than he who would conquer in battle
A thousand, thousand men.

104. Better, indeed, oneself conquered
[Rather than] these other folk.
Of a person who has won himself,
Who is constantly living in self-control,

105. Neither a god nor a *gandhabba*,[*]
Nor Māra[†] together with Brahmā[‡]
Could turn the victory into defeat
Of a living being like that.

---

[*] The term *gandhabba* refers to a celestial musician of the orchestra at the banquets of the deities.
[†] Māra refers to the god of death.
[‡] Brahmā refers to the chief of deities.

From: The *Dhammapada*, Chapter XVII, Wrath (*Kodha-vaggo*)[43]

221. Wrath one would leave behind,
Measurement one would abandon, every fetter transcend.
Who clings not to name and form, and possesses no thing,
Upon that one miseries do not fall.

222. Who can hold back arisen wrath,
Like a swerving chariot,
That one I call "a charioteer,"
Any other one is merely a reins-holder.

223. With absence of wrath one would conquer the wrathful one;
With good, one would conquer the bad one;
With giving, one would conquer the stingy one;
With truth, the one speaking falsehood.

224. Let one tell the truth, let one not be angry.
Asked, let one give even when one has but little.
By these three factors,
One would go into the presence of the gods.

An Early Buddhist Conception of Dharmayuddha *(Righteous War)*

In the Indian religious traditions, the Sanskrit term *dharmayuddha* is often used to designate a "holy" or "righteous" war. In classical Hindu literature including that of the *Bhagavadgītā*, the concept of *dharmayuddha* became quite a prominent and influential theological justification for waging war.[44] By contrast, in the early Buddhist literature of the Pāli canon, the term *dharmayuddha* was hardly ever used. It does nonetheless appear in a work called the *Ummagga Jātaka*, although in this case the meaning and usage of *dharmayuddha* is somewhat different from what may be found in the *Bhagavadgītā*. Given the importance of the *Ummagga Jātaka* in defining a Buddhist ethics of warfare, a brief account of the work's literary context is in order.

The *Ummagga Jātaka* appears as section 546 of *The Jātaka*. The major spokesperson in this *Jātaka* narrative was a wise man named Mahausada ("Great Remedy"). It is understood that he was none other than the Buddha himself, born as a prince in a previous life. With its focus on the wisdom (Skt. *prajñā*) of the *bodhisattva*, the *Ummagga Jātaka* is one of the longest and most popular *Jātakas* in the Theravāda Buddhist world.

For an exploration of Buddhist attitudes to war and in particular to better understand the very restricted conception of warfare in early Buddhism, this is a valuable text. The term *dharmayuddha* arises in a discussion of tactics that may be used to prevail in battle. To illustrate the *bodhisattva*'s perfection of skill-in-means (Skt. *upāyakauśalya*), the text explains how a war may be waged in both a pragmatic and righteous manner. A battle between King Brahmadatta and King Vedeha provides the concrete setting for the text's treatment of *dharmayuddha*. The point is to explain how the *bodhisattva* was exceptionally skilled in countering the cunning strategy of his adversary. So effective is the *bodhisattva*'s skill that he is able to win the battle without needing to have his army fight.

The *Ummagga Jātaka* speaks of *dharmayuddha* in order to explain how the employment of skillful strategies will achieve victory while at the same time rendering resort to large-scale violence unnecessary. As an instance of such a strategy, a story is told about the traditional custom of greeting elders, and how this custom was artfully employed to defeat an enemy prior to any engagement in battle. In the following excerpts, the Pāli term *dhammayuddha* is rendered as "The Battle of Justice."

From: *Ummagga Jātaka*, "The Battle of Justice"[45]

And again the foolish old Brahmin said, "My lord! it will be a great disgrace to us all if they say that the great king Brahmadatta, with his hundred kings and the armies, unable to capture kind Vedeha, fled away defeated. Now, think not my lord, that Mahausadha Pandit is the only wise man. I too possess great wisdom, and I shall defeat him in one way."

"If there is a way, tell me what it is."

"I shall fight the Battle of Justice," replied Kevatta.

"What is this Battle of Justice?"

"O great king! Listen to me!" said Kevatta, "the two armies shall not fight, but when the two Pandits of the two kings appear in one place, if one of them bows before the other, the defeat shall be assigned to the king whose Pandit has saluted, and victory to the one whose Pandit has received the salutation. Mahausadha Pandit does not know of this plan of mine. I have grown old with years, whereas Mahausadha is but a youth. Being a good mannered man who knows to respect his elders, he will, when he sees me, naturally salute me! Then King Vedeha will certainly be defeated. Having thus defeated King Vedeha, we shall return, for there will be no disgrace in doing so. This is what is called the "Battle of Justice."

The Bosat, hearing of this device too as before, thought, "If by this plan I yield to Kevatta, I am much to blame."

In the meantime King Brahmadatta saying: "O Professor! That is a very good plan!" sent a messenger to King Vedeha, by the postern gate, announcing that there would take place on the morrow a Battle of Justice, and the failure to comply would be regarded as a defeat.

Hearing this King Vedeha called the Bosat and acquainted him of it. And the Bosat – the pleasure of the inhabitants of the whole universe – saying, "Very well, my lord," caused an arena for the Battle of Justice to be formed outside the western gate.

Nevertheless, the hundred warriors who were with the various kings not knowing what the consequences might be, took their stand round Kevatta in order to protect the Bosat. King Brahmadatta and the hundred kings reaching the arena of the Battle of Justice, were looking toward the east, expecting the Bosat, like men who on an auspicious day unanimously look toward only one direction, eagerly expecting to see the New Moon. The foolish Kevatta too, stood looking toward the East muttering:

"He is getting late! Time is passing by!"

That morning the Bosat – the Teacher of the three worlds, who has brought the earth under his lotus-like feet – having bathed himself with sixteen pots of sweet-scented water, attired in a silken cloth worth a *lakh*[*] of gold coins and decked with all ornaments; and then, after partaking of the delicious and dainty dishes prepared by Amara Devi, went to the gate of the Palace in a great procession, and announced his arrival to the king, who said:

"Let my son come in immediately!"

Thereupon he entered the Palace, saluted the king, and stood on one side; and when the king inquired, "Well, son Mahausadha," he replied:

"I am going for the Battle of Justice!"

The king then continued, "Son what can I do for you?"

"My lord! I wish to deceive Kevatta by means of a gem; may it therefore please Your Majesty to let me have the eight-sided gem?"

"Son! Do you need my permission to get it? Take it!" said the king.

Then the Pandit took in his hand the gem that had been given to him in his former birth by Sakra, the King of Gods, and saluting the king, went down from the Palace. Attended by the thousand warriors born on the same day as himself, and followed by a whole army, seated in a magnificently decorated chariot drawn by two white steeds worth ninety thousand pieces of gold, he reached the gate, at the time of the midday meal.

Now, Kevatta eagerly waited, expecting the Pandit's arrival every moment, and gaping with his neck craned in the direction from which the Pandit should come, with the result of his neck looked like that of a crane. His body was bathed in sweat caused by the rays of the sun, which was like the glory and majesty of the Bosat. And the Bosat, attended by his retinue of elephants and horses, that surged on the streets like the angry sea inundating the earth, caused the gate to be opened, and driving out from the city, alighted from the chariot and stepped toward the arena of the Battle of Justice, in majesty, like unto a roused lion with mane erect. The hundred kings, beholding the beautiful personality of the Bosat applauded a hundred times with joy, saying, "O! Is this the son of the millionaire Siriwaddhana, Pandit of the 'Great Remedy' who is second to none in wisdom in all Jambudipa?"

The Pandit, like Sakra, who started off to the battle with Titans attended by the gods of the Two Heavens, advanced up to Kevatta, taking with him the eight-sided

[*] A *lakh* is an amount of 100,000.

gem. The Brahmin Kevatta, seeing the Bosat, was fascinated, and, unable to stand where he was, advanced to meet him, and said:

"O Mahausadha Pandit! We are both Pandits. I am surprised why you have not sent me a present, after I have come and waited here so long for you. Please tell me, why have you failed in this mark of respect for me?"

"Excuse me Pandit, all the time I was searching for a present that should be worthy of you, and I have today found this gem. Accept it; it is a peerless gem!"

And Kevatta seeing the gem that was shining in the hands of the Pandit, thought in happy emotion:

"This Pandit has brought a gem for me," and saying "If so, please give it," he stretched out his hands.

And the Bosat, too, saying, "Then take it," stretched out his hand and let the gem fall on the tips of the Brahmin's fingers. Now the Brahmin could not support the heavy gem with his finger-tips, and it fell on the ground and rolled on to the feet of the Bosat. Then the Brahmin, anxious to possess the gem, bent down toward the feet of the Bosat to pick it up. Seeing this, the Bosat held the Brahmin's neck firmly with one hand, and the loins with the other, so that he could not raise his bowed head, and saying:

"Get up, professor! Get up! I am younger enough to be your grandson; do not bow down before me! Do not worship me!" and rubbed the Brahmin's face against the rough ground, and made his face as red as a shoe flower; then seizing him by the throat, cast him off, exclaiming, "You fool! did you think you could get a bow from me?"

Kevatta fell to the ground six fathoms off, and rising up, ran away wiping the sand. The gem was picked [up] by the Bosat's men; and the voice of the Bosat, crying, "Get up professor! Do not worship me," was heard above the din of the great armies.

All the people applauded and waved cloths above their heads, clapping their hands and shouting aloud:

"Shame! Shame! Kevatta Brahmin has worshipped the feet of Mahausadha Pandit!"

Now all the people, including King Brahmadatta and the hundred kings saw Kevatta bending down at the feet of Mahausadha Pandit, and overcome with mortal fear at the sight of their wise champion worshipping at the feet of the foe, which signified their utter defeat and put their lives at stake, mounted their chargers which galloped as fast as their feet could carry them to Uttara Pancala. Seeing their flight, all the retinue of the Bosat cried:

"Look! King Brahmadatta and the hundred kings are flying for life with their routed army!"

At this noise the panic of the kings increased by leaps and bounds. They fled, fled for life. The great army was scattered, and each man looked only for his personal safety in flight. As they ran, the Bosat's men shouted all the more. Our lord, Our Savior, the Mine of Mercy, without ordering a pursuit of the defeated foes, returned to the city attended by his men.

King Brahmadatta flew a distance of twelve *gawwas*[46] with the army, which had been scattered into individuals in spite of its great numbers. The shameless Kevatta mounted his horse and followed the army spitting blood from his mouth and wiping the gore from his forehead. And when he came up with the army he cried from his seat on horse-back, "Friends! Stop! Stop! I did not worship the son of the cultivator. Halt! Halt!"

But in spite of his cry the army fled away without halting, saying:

"You wicked, mean, dirty, despicable, ugly and silly fool of a Brahmin! After boasting that you would go to fight a Battle of Justice, you bowed down before a person young enough to be your grandson. Have you not committed the lowest act that would bring shame even to the meanest of men? You fool! Don't speak nonsense. You villain!"

In such abusive terms the army reviled Kevatta, and turning a deaf ear to [his] words, refused to stop their flight.

Buddhist Warfare in India and Sri Lanka in the Post-canonical Era

The long history of Buddhism in Asia shows that quite a few Buddhist rulers have been involved in national as well as international wars. Some have secured their political power through fierce military conquest. It is not uncommon to find such rulers forswearing resort to force, once their power has been consolidated. This section provides inscriptional evidence showing how some kings eventually renounced violence. In this connection, Emperor Aśoka (ca. r. 268–232 BCE) provides an exemplary illustration of a king who first engaged in military conquest but then subsequently espoused nonviolence.

Emperor Aśoka's Renunciation of Violence and War

In Indian history, Emperor Aśoka (also known as King Priyadarśī) stands out as a paradigmatic Buddhist king who has been emulated by later royals across Asia, as well as by some modern politicians. In the Buddhist traditions of South and Southeast Asia, Emperor Aśoka is often held up as the exemplar of a righteous king. As the historical record testifies, to become king, Aśoka had first to wage war against his own siblings. Moreover, he likewise waged war against his neighbors and successfully conquered the competing states. In doing so, he was able to create a vast empire, the first one in ancient India. After his exposure to Buddhism, however, he changed his way of life and the way he ruled his empire. Committing himself to nonviolence, he created a kingdom in which righteousness was advanced as a key feature of statecraft. Most attribute the transformation from violence to nonviolence in Emperor Aśoka's life to the influence of Buddhist teachings. In the course of his reign, he left many inscriptions throughout the land that communicated to the public his vision of the state, its policies, and the principles of righteous government. These inscriptions show how he professed the importance of peace and religious tolerance. They testify that beyond human affairs nonviolence was extended even toward animals. Buddhists throughout Asia still celebrate Aśoka's legacy and take him as the model of a righteous ruler.

From: Aśoka, "Against Aggression and Tension between States: Kalinga Edict II"[47]

Whenever something right comes to my attention, I want it put into practice and I want effective means devised to achieve it. My principal means to do this is to transmit my instructions to you.

All men are my children. Just as I seek the welfare and happiness of my own children in this world and the next, I seek the same things for all men.

Unconquered peoples along the borders of my dominions may wonder what my disposition is toward them. My only wish with respect to them is that they should not fear me, but trust me; that they should expect only happiness from me, not misery; that they should understand further that I will forgive them for offenses which can be forgiven; that they should be induced by my example to practice Dharma; and that they should attain happiness in this world and the next.

I transmit these instructions to you in order to discharge my debt [to them] by instructing you and making known to you my will and my unshakable resolution and commitment. You must perform your duties in this way and establish their confidence in the King, assuring them that he is like a father to them, that he loves them as he loves himself, and that they are like his own children.

Having instructed you and informed you of my will and my unshakable resolution and commitment, I will appoint officials to carry out this program in all the provinces. You are able to inspire the border peoples with confidence in me and to advance their welfare and happiness in this world and the next. By doing so, you will also attain heaven and help me discharge my debts to the people.

This edict has been inscribed here so that my officials will work at all times to inspire the peoples of neighboring countries with confidence in me and to induce them to practice Dharma.

From: Aśoka, "The Objectives of Inculcation of Dharma"[48]

For many hundreds of years in the past, slaughter of animals, cruelty to living creatures, discourtesy to relatives, and disrespect for priests and ascetics have been increasing.

But now, because of King Priyadarśī's practice of Dharma, the sound of war drums has become the call to Dharma [rather than to war], summoning the people to exhibitions of the chariots of the gods, elephants, fireworks, and other divine displays.

King Priyadarśī's inculcation of Dharma has increased, beyond anything observed in many hundreds of years, abstention from killing animals and from cruelty to living beings, kindliness in human and family relations, respect for priests and ascetics, and obedience to mother and father and elders.

The practice of Dharma has been promoted in this and other ways. King Priyadarśī will continue to promote the practice of Dharma. His sons, grandsons, and great-grandsons to the end of time will ever promote the practice of Dharma; standing firm themselves in Dharma, they will instruct the people in Dharma and moral conduct.

For instruction in Dharma is the best of actions.

The practice of Dharma is impossible for the immoral man. To increase this practice, even to forestall its diminution, is laudable.

The Righteous King Who Gave Away His Head: The Challenges for a Righteous King in Statecraft

The story of King Sirisaṅgabō (r. ca. 247–249 CE) presents vividly the Buddhist notion of a righteous king. Legends, a variety of narratives, and temple paintings illustrate the challenges that such a ruler will potentially face in the actual conduct of statecraft. In the history of Buddhist kingship in Sri Lanka, the life of King Sirisaṅgabō epitomizes how *ahimsā* (nonviolence) functions in the real political world. In ancient Ceylon, *ahimsā* was valued, and some ethically inspired rulers such as King Sirisaṅgabō went out of their way to practice Buddhist precepts on nonviolence to the letter. The existing narratives, in both Sinhala and Pāli, show that King Sirisaṅgabō sacrificed his life for the good cause that he believed in. This commitment to the ideal of a *bodhisattva*, who is driven by virtues such as compassion, later came to occupy a central place in the Mahāyāna Buddhist narrative of the *mahāsattva* (great being) who gave away his life to feed the hungry cubs.[49] The narrative of King Sirisaṅgabō portrays him unwilling to employ any violence whatsoever. The "royal innocence" visible in this narrative stands in sharp contrast to Machiavellian theories of statecraft and most contemporary understandings of good governance. Although the political efficacy of his righteous actions and state policies is open to doubt, as a religiously inspired narrative his example still exercises a significant influence on the devotional public. The post-canonical Pāli chronicle *The Mahāvaṃsa* described him as an individual "rich in compassion" (36:94) who, rather than bringing "harm to others" (36:92), willingly exiled himself into the forest. The Pāli chronicles of Sri Lanka recorded that he was willing to give his head to the aggressive brother, Goṭhakābhaya, who dethroned him earlier.[50] The life and reign of King Sirisaṅgabō illustrates his adoption of Buddhist principles such as nonviolence to statecraft, but also his failure when he was met with an exceptionally ruthless aggressor. Rather than championing self-defense, the story of King Sirisaṅgabō illustrates how the ideal of a righteous and truthful life was understood by Buddhists in ancient Sri Lanka.

From: Mahānāma Thera, *The Mahāvaṃsa, or The Great Chronicle of Ceylon*, Chapter XXXVI, The Thirteen Kings: 73–97[51]

The king, who was known by the name Sirisaṃghabodhi, reigned two years in Anurādhapura, keeping the five precepts.

In the Mahāvihāra he set up a beautiful *salākā*-house.[*] When the king heard that the people of the island were come to want by reason of a drought, he himself, his heart shaken with pity, lay down on the ground in the courtyard of the Great Thūpa, forming the resolve: "Unless I be raised up by the water that the god shall rain down I will nevermore rise up from hence, even though I die here." As the ruler of the earth lay there thus the god poured down rain forthwith on the whole island of Laṅkā, reviving the wide earth. And even then he did not yet rise up because he was not swimming in the water. Then his counsellors closed up the pipes by which the water flowed away. And as he now swam in the water the pious king rose up. By his compassion did he in this way avert the fear of a famine in the island.

At the news: "Rebels are risen here and there," the king had the rebels brought before him, but he released them again secretly; then did he send secretly for bodies of dead men, and causing terror to the people by the burning of these he did away with the fear from rebels.

A yakkha[†] known as Ratakkhi, who had come hither, made red the eyes of the people here and there. If the people did but see one another and did but speak of the redness of the eyes they died forthwith, and the yakkha devoured them without fear.

When the king heard of their distress he lay down with sorrowful heart alone in the chamber of fasting, keeping the eight uposatha vows,[‡] (and said): "Till I have seen the yakkha I will not rise up." By the (magic) power of his piety the yakkha came to him. To the king's (question): "Who art thou?" he answered: "It is I, (the yakkha)." "Why dost thou devour my subjects? Swallow them not!" "Give up to me then only the people of one region," said the other. And being answered: "That is impossible," he came gradually (demanding ever less and less) to one (man) only. The (king) spoke: "No other can I give up to thee; take thou me and devour me." With the words: "That is impossible," the other prayed him (at last) to give him an offering in every village. "It is well," said the king, and over the whole island he decreed that offerings be brought to the entrance of the villages, and these he gave up to him. Thus by the great man, compassionate to all beings, by the torch of the island was the fear [of] pestilence brought to an end.

The king's treasurer, the minister Goṭhakābhaya, who had become a rebel, marched from the north against the capital. Taking his water-strainer with him the king fled alone by the south gate, since he would not bring harm to others.

A man who came, bearing his food in a basket, along that road entreated the king again and again to eat of his food. When he, rich in compassion, had strained the water and had eaten he spoke these words, to show kindness to the other: "I am the King Samghabodhi; take thou my head and show it to Goṭhābhaya, he will

---

[*] The *salākā*-house (P. *salākagga*) is the place in which food received by a monastery is distributed to monks using the *salākā* (ticket) system.

[†] *Yakkha* (P.) is a demon.

[‡] The *uposatha* (P.) vows are the eight precepts observed by the laity on the day of the quarter moon.

give thee much gold." This he would not do, and the king to render him service gave up the ghost even as he sat. And the other took the head and showed it to Goṭhābhaya and he, in amazement of spirit, gave him gold and carried out the funeral rites of the king with due care.

The Post-canonical Justifications of War and Military Conquest

In the section above on "Warfare in the Early Buddhist Traditions," it was shown, from an examination of early Pāli canonical texts, that the teachings of the Buddha afford little if any justification for engagement in war. The picture that emerges from the post-canonical chronicle literature is, however, quite different. One of the most important texts in this connection is the *Mahāvaṃsa* (*The Great Chronicle*). Written in Pāli, it is among the most popular and influential post-canonical chronicle texts. It is a literary source of historical value for understanding affairs of Buddhism in Sri Lanka and India. Composed by Mahānāma Thera, a Buddhist monk who lived in the unstable, political context of sixth century (CE) Sri Lanka, the *Mahāvaṃsa* alludes to some possible justifications for war. The work contains thirty-seven chapters that outline the history of Buddhism from the Buddha's three visits to Sri Lanka several centuries before the common era to the reign of King Mahāsena (ca. 274–301 CE).[52]

In light of its national significance, the *Mahāvaṃsa* continues to be updated regularly, even today, often with the support of the Sri Lankan government. Attention is often directed to the *Mahāvaṃsa*'s account of a battle that was fought between the Sinhala Prince Duṭṭhagāmaṇi (Gāmaṇī, the Ferocious, ca. 161–137 BCE) and the Tamil ruler Elāra. However, before we discuss this battle, it is important to contextualize the story in order to highlight its meaning and draw out its importance for our engagement with the ethics of war in the Buddhist tradition.

The *Mahāvaṃsa* illustrates how as a young man, Prince Gāmaṇī ridiculed his father, Kāvantissa, King of Ruhuna (also referred to as Tissa), for refusing to wage war against Elāra, the Dravida King of Anurādhapura, who had seized the throne. In Chapter XXIV, "The War of the Two Brothers," Gāmaṇī says to his father,

> "I will make war upon the Damiḷas."[53] The king, to protect him, forbade him, saying: "The region on this side of the river is enough." Even to three times he sent to announce the same (reply). "If my father were a man he would not speak thus: therefore shall he put this on." And therewith Gāmaṇī sent him a woman's ornament. And enraged at him the king said: "Make a golden chain! with that will I bind him, for else he cannot be protected."
>
> Then the other fled and went, angered at his father, to Malaya, and because he was wroth with his father they named him Duṭṭhagāmaṇī [the angry Gāmaṇī].

Upon the death of the king, Duṭṭhagāmaṇī returned to Mahagama,

> ... and caused himself to be consecrated king. He sent a letter to his brother (asking) for his mother and the elephant [Kaṇḍula]. But when after the third time he did not receive them he set forth to make war upon him. And between those two

there came to pass a great battle in Cūḷaṅgaṇīya-piṭṭhi:[54] and there fell many thousands of the king's men.

Although the two brothers are later reconciled, Duṭṭhagāmaṇī continues on his quest to slay King Elāra:

When the King Duṭṭhagāmaṇī had provided for his people and had had a relic put into his spear[55] he marched, with chariots, troops and beasts for riders, to Tissamahārāma, and when he had shown favor to the brotherhood he said: "I will go on to the land on the further side of the river to bring glory to the doctrine [of the Buddha]. Give us, that we may treat them with honor, bhikkhus [monks] who shall go on with us, since the sight of the bhikkhus is blessing and protection for us." As a penance the brotherhood allowed him five hundred ascetics; taking this company of bhikkhus with him the king marched forth, and when he had caused the road in Malaya leading hither to be made ready he mounted the elephant Kaṇḍula and, surrounded by his warriors, he took the field with a mighty host. With the one end yet in Mahāgāma the train of the army reached to Guttāhalaka.

Arrived at Mahiyaṅgaṇa he overpowered the Damiḷa Chatta. When he had slain the Damiḷas in that very place he came then to Ambatitthaka, which had a trench leading from the river, and (conquered) the Damiḷa Titthamba; fighting the crafty and powerful foe for four months he (finally) overcame him by cunning, since he placed his mother in his view.

When the mighty man marching thence down (the river) had conquered seven mighty Damiḷa princes in one day and had established peace, he gave over the booty to his troops....

When the monarch heard (that it was said:) "Not knowing their own army they slay their own people," he made this solemn declaration: "Not for the joy of sovereignty is this toil of mine, my striving (has been) ever to establish the doctrine of the Saṃbuddha.[56] And even as this is truth may the armour of the body of my soldiers take the color of fire." And now it came to pass even thus.

Making his way closer to Anuradhapura, Duṭṭhagāmaṇī marches through to Vijitanagara, letting loose his elephant Kaṇḍula upon King Elāra's general, Nandhimitta, along the way:

When the elephant came to overpower him, Nandhimitta seized with his hands his two tusks and forced him on his haunches.... When the king had (thus) put them both to the test he marched to Vijitanagara. Near the south gate befell a fearful battle between the warriors....

The Damiḷas shut the gate and the King [Elāra] sent thither his men.... The city had three trenches, was guarded by a high wall, furnished with gates of wrought iron, difficult for enemies to destroy. Placing himself upon his knees and battering stones, mortar and bricks with his tusks did the elephant attack the gate of iron. But the Damiḷas who stood upon the gate-tower hurled down weapons of every kind, balls of red-hot iron and molten pitch. When the smoking pitch poured on his back Kaṇḍula tormented with pains, betook him to a pool of water and dived there....

When the King Elāra heard that King Duṭṭhagāmaṇī was come to do battle he called together his ministers and said: "This king is himself a warrior and in truth many warriors (follow him). What think the ministers, what should we do?" King Elāra's warriors, led by Dīghajantu, resolved: "Tomorrow will we give battle." The King Duṭṭhagāmaṇī also took counsel with his mother and by her counsel formed thirty-two bodies of troops. In these the king placed parasol-bearers and figures of a king; the monarch himself took his place in the innermost body of troops.

When Elāra in full armor had mounted his elephant Mahāpabbata he came thither with chariots, soldiers and beasts for riders. . . .

King Duṭṭhagāmaṇī proclaimed with beat of drum: "None but myself shall slay Elāra." When he himself, armed, had mounted the armed elephant Kaṇḍula he pursued Elāra and came to the south gate (of Anurādhapura).

Near the south gate of the city the two kings fought; Elāra hurled his dart, Gāmaṇī evaded it; he made his own elephant pierce (Elāra's) elephant with his tusks and he hurled his dart at Elāra; and this (latter) fell there, with his elephant.

When he had thus been victorious in battle and had united Laṅkā under one rule he marched, with chariots, troops and beasts for riders, into the capital. In the city he caused the drum to be beaten, and when he had summoned the people from a *yojana*[57] around he celebrated the funeral rites for King Elāra. On the spot where his body had fallen he burned it with the catafalque,* and there did he build a monument and ordain worship. And even to this day the princes of Lanka, when they draw near to this place, are wont to silence their music because of this worship.

When he had thus overpowered thirty-two Damiḷa kings Duṭṭhagāmaṇī ruled over Laṅkā in single sovereignty.

Contesting Widespread Misinterpretations of Duṭṭhagāmaṇī's Weapon

Recently, there has been considerable academic debate about King Duṭṭhagāmaṇī's battle with Elāra. As one scholar has pointed out, "Duṭṭhagāmaṇī is yet a most complex character whose actions, especially in war, would seem an outright affront to the Buddhist sensibility . . . the contradiction inherent in a Buddhist king who would go so far as to place a relic of the Buddha in his battle lance and call for a company of 500 monks to escort his troops to war."[58] Duṭṭhagāmaṇī's alleged use of a relic in his spear is recorded in the *Mahāvaṃsa* 25.1: "When the King Duṭṭhagāmaṇī had provided for his people and had had *a relic put into his spear*[59] he marched, with chariots, troops and beasts of riders, to Tissamaharama." The translators of the text [Geiger and others] maintain that the "spear" functions as "a royal standard" that was always "carried before the prince."[60] However, this translation (the idea of placing a relic of the Buddha in the spear) has caused some significant controversy. For instance, Dhammavihari Thera has argued[61] that Geiger's translation of the above sentence is quite misleading. In the early years of Sri Lanka, as Buddhism was the main religion of the Sihalas, "Whoever ruled the

---

* A catafalque is a decorated wooden frame that supports a coffin.

land had to be a defender of the faith of the people." As Duṭṭhagāmaṇī goes out to war with the invader, he has to take with him what was symbolic of the cause for which he was fighting. So in his own symbol of royalty, *namely the royal scepter which was carried ahead of him wherever he went*, he had the relics of the Buddha deposited [*kunte dhātum nidhāpetvā, Mahāvaṃsa* 25.1]. Dhammavihari Thera further explains that the sentence "*kunte dhātuṃ nidhāpetvā*" was mistranslated "by an early Buddhist scholar monk of Sri Lanka [Hikkhaduwe Sri Sumangala Nayaka Thera, 1912], and followed without question by equally eminent lay professors has led to calamitous results." "[I]n translating the Pāli noun *kunta*, he first used the identical term *kuntaya* in Sinhala [Ch. 25.1] and at its second occurrence at Ch. 26.9, he translates it as *kuntāyudhaya*, i.e. the weapon *kunta*. This, we are compelled to call *a grave error* [113] *of very serious consequences.*[62] This has enabled later writers on Sri Lankan history to give the national and religious consciousness of the day an unfortunately malicious slant." This error has, in the eyes of Dhammavihari Thera, led to a masking of the true reasons that Duṭṭhagāmaṇī had gone into battle, namely, that he was battling "against the foreign invader who was wrecking Buddhism and its cultural heritage in the island. It was necessarily a war of defense and liberation. He was going to fight it out like a gentleman. Even his treatment of dead Elāra who fell in battle establishes this beyond doubt. We are quite certain that he would not descend so low as to carry relics of the Buddha in a spear-like killer weapon or *āyudhaya.*"[63]

A Southeast Asian Narrative of Buddhist Warfare and Justice

The Thai Victory over Burmese Invasions

In the sixteenth century, Thailand witnessed many wars. King Naresuan (also known as Naresvara), who reigned from 1590 to 1605, was a heroic figure in Thai history. He was at the center stage of war campaigns beginning in 1585. At that time, he was barely thirty years old. Thais were besieged continuously from all sides: by combined forces of the Burmese and their allies in the north, by the Khmer in the east, and by pirates from the sea.

Throughout their history, Thais witnessed continual Burmese invasions. Prince Naresuan managed the successive Burmese invasions from 1585 to 1593 that took place during the reign of his father, King Maha Thamam Racha. Naresuan ascended to the throne in 1590. The final Burmese assault took place only three years later, in early 1593.

Successful wars fought by King Naresuan reaffirmed the survival of the Thai nation. He re-established the Thai kingdom in Ayutthaya in the seventeenth century, having first defeated the Burmese, who possessed significant military power. However, the next century saw the renewal of their attack and the destruction of the city of Ayutthaya in 1767.

During a dangerous battle with the Burmese, it is said that the generals of the Siamese troops could not catch up with King Naresuan, whose elephant and a handful of foot-soldiers were caught among larger troops of the Burmese prince. Against all odds, with wit, courage, and fighting skills, King Naresuan won the decisive battle over the Burmese and declared independence for Ayutthaya.

After returning from the battle, King Naresuan consulted the chief monk on how to punish the generals who had abandoned him. The chief monk's reply is relevant. His response changed the course of action of the king. The monk explained that the failure of the generals was an occasion for the greater glory of the king. Without support from his generals, the king was nonetheless able to win the battle, having used his superior skill to achieve victory. His victory under such precarious conditions testified to the greatness of the king. Hearing the chief monk's response, the king pardoned his generals, who thereby escaped capital punishment.

From: H.R.H. Prince Damrong Rajanubhab, *A Biography of King Naresuan the Great* [64]

Naresuan returned to the capital, still feeling cheated of the chance to attack and utterly rout the Burmese invaders, which he had succeeded in doing the previous time they invaded. He attributed this outcome to his commanders, who failed to obey his orders to keep pace with him so that they could all engage in the offensive simultaneously. He therefore had the royal judges consider these cases and deliver judgments according to the military code. The judges deliberated and handed down their verdicts. Si Sai Narong was found guilty of disobeying a royal command, losing his advantage and falling back while leading his men on the battlefield. Chakkri, Phra Khlang, Thep Arachun, Phichai Songkhram and Ram Khamhaeng were found guilty of negligence in failing to obey the order to keep pace with the king. The judges declared that the punishment for all six should be execution....

On 30 January, which was the day prior to the holy day, Patriarch Wannarat of Pa Kaeo Monastery and twenty-five monks of the Royal Ecclesiastical Council had an audience with the king. According to custom, they inquired about the battle fought by the king. The counselors listened as the king recounted everything – from the beginning up through his victory over the Heir Apparent in elephant-back combat. The following passages are quoted from the Thai annals.

The patriarch asked:

As My Lord of Accumulated Merit [the king] has gained a victory over his enemies, whatever could be the reason that penalties have been imposed on all these officers?

Naresuan replied:

These commanders feared the invaders more than they feared me. They left us two brothers to brave it alone, to go into the midst of the enemy forces and ultimately to engage in elephant-back combat with the Heir Apparent. Only after my victory did matters come aright. Only then did I see their faces. I was not yet fated to die. But what if that had not been the case? Our country would now be in the hands of the Peguans! These are the reasons why I meted out punishments according to the military code.

The patriarch then said:

Upon reflection, I do not think that these officers lacked any fear of My Lord. I think these events occurred merely to make manifest the miraculous nature of My Lord's honor – like that of the Lord Buddha on the day of his Enlightenment, when he sat at dusk, undefeated, beneath the sacred Bodhi tree....

Suppose the Lord Buddha had a retinue of deities, and suppose he used this retinue to gain his victory. In such a case, there would have been nothing miraculous about the event. It so happened, however, that he sent all the immortals scurrying away, leaving only himself alone....

Suppose that you two brothers had gone out together with an enormous armed legion and defeated the Burmese Heir Apparent. That would not have looked like a miracle, and it could not have brought you honor in the eyes of all the greater and lesser kingdoms of the world. My Lord of Accumulated Merit, do not feel alarmed or hurt. All this has come to pass, truly just as I have stated, so that all the deities, who are your guardians, could demonstrate your honor.

Upon hearing the broad response delivered by the patriarch and his allusions to the sacred name of the Lord Buddha, and reflecting upon the grace of this name, the king felt his heart uplifted in a sublime way, and he rejoiced. Raising his hands and bringing them together in a prayerful manner above his head, he said:

Amen! Amen! Your Holiness's observations are profoundly appropriate.

Observing that the king's anger had abated, the patriarch continued:

We Royal Ecclesiastical Counselors feel that these condemned officials have committed profound wrongs. But they have been in the royal service ever since the reigns of your father and your grandfather, and they have subsequently served you, in exactly the same way that pious Buddhists have been followers of our great Teacher. Given these considerations, we ecclesiastics request royal pardon for these men, this time, so that they may continue to serve and honor you.

In reply, Naresuan said:

I shall grant Your Holiness's request. But first, I shall send them to attack and capture Tenasserim and Tavoy, as a means of redeeming themselves.

Patriarch Wannarat replied:

Such use of them in going out to attack another land is entirely at My Lord's pleasure. For all of us, who are monks, it is not our concern.

Modern Articulations of Buddhist Warfare

The twentieth and twenty-first centuries mark an important phase with regard to Buddhist involvement in warfare. Several countries having a Buddhist majority population, such as Japan, Korea, Sri Lanka, and Vietnam, faced civil, national, or international wars. Cambodia was completely devastated by the genocidal atrocities of the Khmer Rouge, who were followers of the Communist Party of Kampuchea, a totalitarian regime led by Pol Pot (1928–1998) that ruled Cambodia from 1975 to 1979. Sri Lanka, likewise, was engaged in a civil war that involved fierce fighting between the Sri Lankan government forces and the Liberation Tigers of Tamil Eelam (LTTE) guerrilla army. Having started in 1983, the war came to an end when the LTTE was defeated in May 2009. Also significant is the Muslim insurgency in southern Thailand, which has made Buddhists acutely aware of the threat arising from terrorism. Since 1959, with the Chinese occupation of Tibet and the Dalai Lama's exile to India, Tibetans have similarly been faced with increasing violence.

Vietnamese Buddhist monks, in particular, have played an important role in the development of an ethical response to war in the modern period, through their use of nonviolent means and self-sacrifice. To draw the world's attention to the Vietnam War and the sufferings of the Vietnamese people under Ngo Dinh Diem's oppressive regime, Thich Quang-Duc committed an act of self-immolation in Saigon on 11 June 1963.[65] Several other monks subsequently followed his example. Self-immolation arose as the dramatic extension of the more common monastic practice by which Mahāyāna Buddhist monastics burn a small spot on their body as testimony to their religious devotion. While it is often taken to be a manifestation of defeat or loss of hope, self-immolation is increasingly coming to be viewed as the expression of great compassion, on a par with what one would expect of a *bodhisattva*.

Thich Nhat Hanh (b. 1926) is a very influential Buddhist thinker of the late twentieth and twenty-first century. He is a Vietnamese scholar monk and a poet who has shaped a generation of engaged Buddhists around the world. His early contribution lies in the efforts of peace making in Vietnam when the country was caught in a long-lasting war with the United States. Thich Nhat Hanh reflects on the repercussions of this act in his book *Vietnam: Lotus in a Sea of Fire* (1967). Thich Nhat Hanh spoke for the numerous Vietnamese who had little or no voice in the public arena but who were eager to preserve Vietnam's traditional identity as an Asian and Buddhist culture. His proposal provides an early articulation of an "engaged" Buddhism.

From: Thich Nhat Hanh, *Vietnam: Lotus in a Sea of Fire* (1967)[66]

After twenty years of war, Vietnamese society now approaches the ultimate in disintegration. The needless killing and dying that occur every day, the destruction of property, and the venal use of money to erode human values have resulted in widespread doubt and frustration among the Vietnamese. . . . In such a situation the peasants, who constitute up to 90 percent of the country's population, turn for help to their religious leaders. They, then, in turn, are all but forced to act: the Buddhist population may often be found complaining about their spiritual leaders' silence in the face of the nation's suffering.

In a river current, it is not the water in front that pulls the river along, but the water in the rear that acts as the driving force, pushing the water in front forward. The image may serve to explain the engagement of the Unified Buddhist Church in worldly affairs, and help to reveal the nature of reality in present-day Vietnam. Objective conditions in Vietnamese society have compelled the Buddhist religion to engage itself in the life of the nation. To explain that engagement otherwise, as

by the militancy and ambition for power of a few monks, leads to tragic oversim-
plication of the whole matter. . . .

During the Buddhist crisis in 1963, the Overseas Vietnamese Buddhist
Association received from Saigon an important and voluminous document on
these cases of persecution. . . .

According to this document, there were in the province of Quang Ngai alone
seven cases in which the local administration forced Buddhists to receive instruction in the personalist doctrine and to convert to Roman Catholicism, eight cases
of the misuse of public power to force the Buddhist population to convert, and one
case of falsely accusing a Buddhist monk of Communist affiliation and of arresting and imprisoning him. . . . In the province of Phu Yen, there were fifteen cases
of forced conversions, three cases of calumny and threatened liquidation directed
against the Buddhist population, three cases of arrest, torture, and liquidation,
one case of the live burial of two Buddhists in the same tomb. . . .

[T]he people of Vietnam generally are fed up with the whole absurd war, and
if there are those who still fight valiantly in the National Liberation Front, it is
because they are convinced it is the only way to secure their independence, and
not because of any ideological alignment. Anyone standing for a further extension of the war would not be considered by the people themselves as a part of the
Vietnam community or as one who understood or shared its sufferings.

From: Thich Nhat Hanh, *Vietnam: Lotus in a Sea of Fire* (1967), A Letter Addressed to the Rev. Dr. Martin Luther King, Jr., June 1, 1965[67]

The self-burning of Vietnamese Buddhist monks in 1963 is somehow difficult for
the Western Christian conscience to understand. The press spoke then of suicide,
but in the essence, it is not. It is not even a protest. What the monks said in the
letters they left before burning themselves aimed only at alarming, at moving the
hearts of the oppressors, and at calling the attention of the world to the suffering
endured then by the Vietnamese. To burn oneself by fire is to prove that what one
is saying is of the utmost importance. There is nothing more painful than burning oneself. To say something while experiencing this kind of pain is to say it with
utmost courage, frankness, determination, and sincerity. During the ceremony
of ordination, as practiced in the Mahāyāna tradition, the monk-candidate is
required to burn one or more small spots on his body in taking the vow to observe
the 250 rules of a *bhikshu*, to live the life of a monk, to attain enlightenment, and
to devote his life to the salvation of all beings. One can, of course, say these things
while sitting in a comfortable armchair; but when the words are uttered while
kneeling before the community of *saṅgha* and experiencing this kind of pain, they
will express all the seriousness of one's heart and mind, and carry much greater
weight.

The Vietnamese monk, by burning himself, says with all his strength and determination that he can endure the greatest sufferings to protect his people. But why

does he have to burn himself to death? The difference between burning oneself and burning oneself to death is only a difference in degree, not in nature. A man who burns himself too much must die. The importance is not to take one's life, but to burn. What he really aims at is the expression of his will and determination, not death. In the Buddhist belief, life is not confined to a period of 60 or 80 or 100 years: life is eternal. Life is not confined to this body: life is universal. To express will by burning oneself, therefore, is not to commit an act of destruction but to perform an act of construction, that is, to suffer and to die for the sake of one's people. This is not suicide. Suicide is an act of self-destruction, having as causes the following: (1) lack of courage to live and to cope with difficulties; (2) defeat by life and loss of all hope; (3) desire for non-existence (*abhaya*).

This self-destruction is considered by Buddhism as one of the most serious crimes. The monk who burns himself has lost neither courage nor hope; nor does he desire non-existence. On the contrary, he is very courageous and hopeful and aspires for something good in the future.

Controversial Representations of Buddhist Thought

In closing this chapter, it is important briefly to identify two figures in the Buddhist tradition who have expressed sentiments in relation to Buddhism and the use of armed force that can arguably be seen as contradictory to the traditional tenets of the religion. Bhikkhu Kittivuddho, a widely respected Buddhist monk from a prominent Buddhist establishment in Bangkok, is known, for example, for his publicly articulated rhetorical war against the communists in the late 1970s.[68] Kittivuddho was a master rhetorician and his controversial statements have a specific historical and political context. They can be seen to reflect an unstable period in Thai history when a "militant" form of Buddhism began to rise. Two statements of Bhikkhu Kittivuddho have drawn the attention of scholars. The first, most widely known "militant" statement is: Killing communists is not really killing. The second statement is: The Buddha allowed killing. This second statement is more injurious, from a traditional Theravada Buddhist point of view, since it seems to misrepresent the original content of the Pāli text and, therefore, the Buddha's words.[69]

A similarly controversial figure is the Ven. Elle Gunavaṃsa. He is a radical Buddhist monk whose creative, poetic compositions have been identified as militant and warlike. His poems and songs were intimately connected with the civil war between the government of Sri Lanka and the Tamil Tigers (LTTE). Ven. Gunavaṃsa was influenced by his teacher, the late Ven. Baddegama Vimalavamsa (1913–1993), whose teaching is associated with post-independent Sri Lankan patriotism and nationalism. One of Elle Gunavaṃsa's collections of songs – *War Songs for Armed Forces* (*Bala Senagaṭa Samara Gī*)[70] – was allegedly used to "boost soldier morale in battle"[71] in the early 1990s. Prominent Sri Lankan vocalists sang the songs that he composed, and the Sri Lankan Broadcasting Cooperation published as *Bala Senagaṭa Samara Gī*. Highlighting the odd combination of "militancy and music"[72] in the creative work of this Sri Lankan Buddhist monk, Gananath Obeyesekere wrote: "[T]he ones who have been influenced by Muslim ideas of jihad are very few in number, the exception being Elle Gunavaṃsa, a monk, who believes that those soldiers who die for the motherland will achieve nirvana."[73] Richard Gombrich, a prominent scholar of Theravāda Buddhism, highlighting Ven. Gunavaṃsa's "militancy of personality,"[74] commented as follows: "Elle Gunavamsa seems to defy all traditional monastic norms by composing songs for soldiers to sing in battle.... The idea that defending the motherland (not, note, defending Buddhism) may lead one to *nirvana* – albeit only in a future life – is certainly alien and repulsive to the mainstream of Buddhist tradition."[75] Since the late 1970s, Ven. Gunavaṃsa has influenced soldiers and politicians with his songs for soldiers in the battlefield. In *The Work of Kings: The New Buddhism in Sri Lanka*, H. L. Seneviratne has translated some of his songs that deal with the theme of war. A few of them highlight a variety of concerns of Buddhist society in the context of war.[76] Commenting on the issues that Ven. Gunavaṃsa's songs raise, Seneviratne says:

> Even in translation, which waters down the effect of these songs, the sentiments expressed are strongly exclusivist and xenophobic. The militancy Elle Gunavamsa exudes in conversation is powerfully condensed in them. The landscape is familiar: religion, country, and race; the sword that should not be sheathed unless it is smeared with blood; the recurring evocation of Dutugamunu, his brave mother, and his superhuman ten soldiers ... the songs are set to stirring martial music, with a predominance of wind instruments and percussion which recalls the traditional war drums (*gaman hevisi*). The statements that connect the dominant theme of violence with images of religion and worship – that fighting accrues enough merit to reach Nirvana, that the country, religion and race are the speaker's Triple Gems – are startling.[77]

The intense debate surrounding Ven. Gunavaṃsa highlights the tensions within Sri Lankan society (and Buddhism) about war. On the one hand we find those who favor a strong militancy associated with Sri Lankan nationalism, and on the other those critics who charge that such expressions of a militant ethos are very much in conflict with the tenets of Buddhism.

Conclusion

This chapter on warfare in the Buddhist traditions of South and Southeast Asia has reproduced and commented on a variety of primary sources in Pāli and Sinhala. It has sought to open a window on Theravāda Buddhist approaches to the ethics of war. Similarly, but more briefly, it has explored some material in Thai and Vietnamese. The range of ideas on war and the related ethical concerns have proven to be considerably varied, a reflection of the diverse historical, religious, national, social, and cultural contexts of the different Theravāda Buddhist communities. Cutting through all of these accounts is a serious concern with the dignity of human life. Some of these texts strongly suggest that measures must be taken to protect innocent lives and property in circumstances of war and that proper means of warfare should be encouraged, giving priority to justice and righteousness.

NOTES

1 These organizations include the Jātika Hela Urumaya (National Sinhala Heritage) Party, National Movement against Terrorism, Janatā Vimukti Peramuṇa (People's Liberation Front), and Dēsahitaiśī Jātika Vyāpāraya (Patriotic National Movement).

2 Pāli is one of the two ancient Prakrit languages of India, which was used in the writings of early Buddhist tradition found in the Pāli canon of Theravāda Buddhists.

3 The term *arahant*, often translated as the "worthy one," refers to the Buddhist saint in Theravāda Buddhism who has achieved the ultimate goal of religious aspiration, *nibbāna*.

4 Jainaism was contemporary to Buddhism and maintained an absolute nonviolent position.

5 The exact origin of the Five Precepts is not known. They embrace some pre-Buddhist ideas and form the basis of Buddhist way of life. Their formulation as disciplinary rules is found throughout Buddhist scriptures. *Buddhist Scriptures*, Edward Conze (trans.) (Middlesex: Penguin, 1986), pp. 70–73.

6 The Sanskrit term *bodhisattva* (P. *bodhisatta*; Sin. *bōsat*) means a "being who aspires Buddhahood."

7 The *Jātaka* is considered relatively late in origin as a collection of Buddhist scriptures. From E. B. Cowell (ed.), *The Jātaka or Stories of the Buddha's Former Births*, H. T. Francis and R. A. Neil (trans.) (Oxford: Pali Text Society, 1995), vol. III, pp. 26–28.

8 This text belongs to an early part of the Buddhist canon. *The Long Discourses of the Buddha: A Translation of the Dīgha-Nikāya*, Maurice Walshe (trans.) (Boston: Wisdom Publications, 1995), pp. 412–413.

9 This is the translation of *"yuddhena jīvikaṃ kappanako."* *The Connected Discourses of the Buddha: A New Translation of the Saṃyutta Nikāya*, vol. II, Bhikkhu Bodhi (trans.) (Oxford and Somerville: Pali Text Society and Wisdom Publications, 2000), p. 1449, note 339.

10 Ibid., pp. 1334–1335.

11 *The Book of the Gradual Sayings* (*Aṅguttara-Nikāya*), E. M. Hare (trans.) (London: Pali Text Society, 1934), vol. III, pp. 72–77.

12 Ibid., p. 77.

13 Ibid., p. 153.

14 According to the commentary to the *Aṅguttara-Nikāya*, "trade in flesh" includes activities such as breeding and selling pigs or deer.

15 *The Book of the Kindred Sayings* (*Saṃyutta-Nikāya*), Part I, Caroline A. F. Rhys Davids and Suriyagoda Sumangala Thera (trans.) (London: Pali Text Society, 1917), pp. 109–110.

16 Ajātasattu, the king of Magadha, is known to have committed one of the five gravest crimes (*ānantarikakamma*), whose karmic fruits immediately follow – parricide of his father King Bimbisara – under the influence and encouragement of his supporter, Devadatta, the Buddha's cousin and enemy.

17 It seems they have gone to battle four times.

18 Ajātasattu's mother was a sister of Pasenadi, the King of Kosala.

19 *The Book of the Kindred Sayings* (*Saṃyutta-Nikāya*), Part I, pp. 123–124.

20 *The Connected Discourses of the Buddha*, p. 1843.

21 *The Long Discourses of the Buddha: A Translation of the Dīgha-Nikāya*, Maurice Walshe (trans.) (Boston: Wisdom Publications, 1995), pp. 68–72.

22 *The Aṅguttara Nikāya of the Sutta Piṭaka: Eka, Duka and Tika Nipāta*, Edmund Rowland Jayetilleke Gooneratne (trans.) (reprint, Galle: Lankaloka Press, 1913), pp. 132–133.

23 As written in the original commentary, "Law – which comprises the ten meritorious qualities that appertain to a king."

24 The fight between *suras* and *asuras* called *devā-sura-sangāma* (battle between gods and Titans) occurs in identical terms in several Pāli canonical texts such as *Dīgha-Nikāya* II.285, *Samyutta-Nikāya* I.222, *Samyutta-Nikāya* IV.201, *Samyutta-Nikāya* V.447, *Majjhima-Nikāya* I.253, and *Anguttara-Nikāya* IV.432. The rebirth as an *asura* was considered as one of the four unhappy rebirths.

25 *The Book of the Kindred Sayings* (*Samyutta-Nikāya*), Part I, pp. 279–280.

26 Ibid., pp. 281–282.

27 Ibid., pp. 283–286.

28 Ibid., pp. 286–287.

29 Ibid., p. 288.

30 Ibid., pp. 288–289.

31 Ibid., pp. 292–293.

32 See Chapter 2 of this book for the relevant texts from Gratian and Thomas Aquinas.

33 *Dialogues of the Buddha*, T. W. Rhys Davids and C.A.F. Rhys Davids (trans.) (London: Pali Text Society, 1977), pp. 78–81, 92.

34 *The Jātaka or Stories of the Buddha's Former Births*, E. B. Cowell and H. T. Francis (trans.) (Oxford: Pali Text Society, 1995), vol. V, pp. 219–220.

35 May and June.

36 The Pāli term *cakka* refers to the wheel. The monarch who rules with righteousness is known as a wheel-turning monarch (*cakkavatti-rājā*). The expression of the turning the wheel of *dhamma* (*dhammacakka*) is used to explain the first sermon of the historical Buddha. Turning the wheel is a symbolic gesture of acting fairly and naturally by taking into consideration the circumstances and opportunities of the time.

37 *The Long Discourses of the Buddha: A Translation of the Dīgha-Nikāya*, Maurice Walshe (trans.) (Boston: Wisdom Publications, 1995), pp. 395–403.

38 Tessa J. Bartholomeusz, *In Defense of Dharma: Just-War Ideology in Buddhist Sri Lanka* (London: Routledge Curzon, 2002).

39 The most recent English translation that emphasizes the poetical aspects of the *Dhammapada* is Valerie J. Roebuck (ed.), *Dhammapada* (London: Penguin, 2010).

40 V. L. B. Mendis, *Foreign Relations of Sri Lanka: From Earliest Times to 1965* (Dehiwela: Tisara Prakasakayo, 1983), pp. 385–387.

41 *The Dhammapada*, John Ross Carter and Mahinda Palihawadana (trans.) (New York: Oxford University Press, 1987), pp. 94–96.

42 Ibid., pp. 183–185.

43 Ibid., pp. 270–272.

44 See Chapter 7 of this book for more on the concept of *dharmayuddha* in Hindu thought and practice.

45 *Ummagga Jātaka*, David Karunaratne (trans.) (Colombo: M. D. Gunasena, 1962), pp. 120–124. The original text can be found in Munidasa Kumaratunga, *Ummagga Jātakaya* (Colombo: M. D. Gunasena, 1979), pp. 100–104 (no. 26 episode).

46 *Gawwa* (*gavva*) is an Indian measure of distance, approximately four miles (a league).

47 From *The Edicts of Aśoka*, N. A. Nikam and Richard McKeon (ed. and trans.) (Chicago, Ill.: University of Chicago Press, 1959; reprint, 1978), pp. 53–54.

48 Ibid., pp. 31–32.

49 *Buddhist Scriptures*, Edward Conze (trans.) (Middlesex: Penguin Books, 1986), pp. 24–26.

50 Mahānāma Thera, *The Mahāvamsa, or The Great Chronicle of Ceylon*, Wilhelm Geiger and Mabel Haynes Bode (trans.) (Colombo: Ceylon Government Information Department, 1950), ch. 26: 9–97, pp. 260–261.

51 Ibid., pp. 261–263.

52 In later periods, the writing of the *Mahāvaṃsa* continued and came to be known as the *Cūlavaṃsa*, a name coined by a prominent German Indologist Wilhelm Ludwig Geiger (1856–1943).

53 Tamils; that is, Gamāṇi wishes to wage war against the representatives of Elāra.

54 There are references to this war at Cūlaṅgaṇī in later sections of this chapter.

55 There are recent debates on the exact meaning of this usage of "spear." See the interpretation of Ven. Dhammavihāri as elaborated upon later in this section.

56 "Perfectly Awakened One."

57 *Yojana* is an ancient measurement of distance equal to four *gavvas*, or fifteen miles. Some computations make a *yojana* thirteen or nine miles, others make it about five miles (B. Clough, *Sinhala English Dictionary* (Colombo: Wesleyan Mission Press, 1892), p. 516).

58 Alice Greenwald, "The Relic on the Spear: Historiography and the Saga of Duṭṭhagāmaṇī," *Religion and the Legitimation of Power in Sri Lanka*, Bardwell L. Smith (ed.) (Chambersburg, Pa.: Anima Books, 1978), p. 13.

59 Emphasis added to highlight the controversial sentence that is discussed below.

60 Mahānāma Thera, *The Mahāvaṃsa, or The Great Chronicle of Ceylon*, p. 170, note 1.

61 See Dhammavihari Thera, *Critical Studies on the Early History of Buddhism in Sri Lanka* (Dehiwela: Buddhist Cultural Centre, 2003).

62 Emphasis in original.

63 For further elaboration of this controversy, see Thera, *Critical Studies on the Early History of Buddhism in Sri Lanka*, pp. 113–124.

64 H.R.H. Prince Damrong Rajanubhab, *A Biography of King Naresuan the Great*, Kennon Breazeale (trans. and ed.) (Samutprakan and Bangkok: Toyota Thailand Foundation and the Foundation for the Promotion of Social Science and Humanities Textbooks Project, 2008), pp. 73–76.

65 Thich Nhat Hanh, *Vietnam: Lotus in a Sea of Fire* (New York: Hill and Wang, 1967), p. 1.

66 Ibid., pp. 2–3, 28, 31.

67 Ibid., pp. 106–107.

68 Charles F. Keyes, "Political Crisis and Militant Buddhism in Contemporary Thailand," in *Religion and Legitimation of Power in Thailand, Laos, and Burma*, p. 148.

69 See, e.g., ibid., pp. 153–161.

70 In translating the Sinhala title of this collection of songs, differing from H. L. Seneviratne, who translates it as "Memory Songs for the Soldiers" (H. L. Seneviratne, *The Work of Kings: The New Buddhism in Sri Lanka* (Chicago, Ill.: University of Chicago Press, 1999), p. 244), I emphasize the meaning of the Sinhala term *samara*, which means "war" and "battle," according to Clough's *Sinhala English Dictionary*, p. 664.

71 Seneviratne, *The Work of Kings*, p. 244.

72 Ibid., p. 242.

73 Gananath Obeyesekere, "Buddhism, Ethnicity and Identity: A Problem of Buddhist History," *Journal of Buddhist Ethics* 10 (2003), available at http://www.buddhistethics.org/10/obeyesekere-sri-lanka-conf.html#n1.

74 Seneviratne, *The Work of Kings*, p. 242.

75 Richard Gombrich, "Is the Sri Lankan War a Buddhist Fundamentalism?," in *Buddhism, Conflict and Violence in Modern Sri Lanka*, Mahinda Deegalle (ed.) (London: Routledge, 2006), p. 37.

76 See, e.g., Seneviratne, *The Work of Kings*, pp. 272–276.

77 Ibid., pp. 244–245.

SELECT BIBLIOGRAPHY

Deegalle, Mahinda, "Is Violence Justified in Theravāda Buddhism?," *Ecumenical Review* 55:2 (2003), 122–131.

Deegalle, Mahinda (ed.), *Buddhism, Conflict and Violence in Modern Sri Lanka* (New York: Routledge, 2006).

Deegalle, Mahinda, "JHU Politics for Peace and a Righteous State," in Mahinda Deegalle (ed.), *Buddhism, Conflict and Violence in Modern Sri Lanka* (London: Routledge, 2006), pp. 239–243.

Deegalle, Mahinda, "Buddhist Monks and Political Activism in Sri Lanka," in P. Broadhead and D. Keown (eds.), *Can Faiths Make Peace? Holy Wars and the Resolution of Religious Conflicts* (London: I. B. Tauris, 2007), pp. 134–148.

Deegalle, Mahinda, "Creating Space for the Non-Buddhists in Sri Lanka: A Buddhist Perspective on the Other," in A. Rambachan, A. R. Omar, and M. T. Thangaraj (eds.), *Hermeneutical Exploration in Dialogue: Essays in Honour of Hans Ucko's 60th Birthday* (Delhi: ISPCK, 2007), pp. 114–127.

Deegalle, Mahinda, "Norms of War in Theravada Buddhism," in V. Popovski, Gregory M. Reichberg, and N. Turner (eds.), *World Religions and Norms of War* (Tokyo: United Nations University Press, 2009), pp. 60–86.

Gombrich, Richard, "Is the Sri Lankan War a Buddhist Fundamentalism?," in Mahinda Deegalle (ed.), *Buddhism, Conflict and Violence in Modern Sri Lanka* (London and New York: Routledge, 2006), pp. 22–37.

Greenwald, Alice, "The Relic on the Spear: Historiography and the Saga of Duṭṭhagāmaṇī," in Bardwell L. Smith (ed.), *Religion and the Legitimation of Power in Sri Lanka* (Chambersburg, Pa.: Anima Books, 1978), pp. 13–35.

Johnston, Douglas, and Cynthia Sampson (ed.), *Religion: The Missing Dimension of Statecraft* (Oxford: Oxford University Press, 1994).

Mendis, V. L. B. *Foreign Relations of Sri Lanka: From Earliest Times to 1965* (Dehiwela: Tisara Prakasakayo, 1983), pp. 385–387.

Obeyesekere, Gananath, "Buddhism, Ethnicity and Identity: A Problem of Buddhist History," *Journal of Buddhist Ethics* 10 (2003), available at http://www.buddhistethics.org/10/obeyes-ekere-sri-lanka-conf.html#n1.

Tikhonov, Vladimir, and Torkel Brekke (eds.), *Buddhism and Violence: Militarism and Buddhism in Modern Asia* (New York: Routledge, 2013).

9

Chinese and Korean Religious Traditions

Vladimir Tikhonov

During a large part of the first millennium BCE, before the second century BCE, a variety of philosophical and political traditions rivaled each other in China, but the dominant religious and political tradition after the second century BCE and until the beginning of the twentieth century in both China and Korea was heavily based on Confucian teachings. Confucianism envisions society as a vertically structured organic entity – and extension of a large patriarchal family – in which the rulers are entitled to "civilize" the ruled through imposition of ethical norms, ritual, and music. Confucianism prioritizes socio-political stability and thus favors "soft" governance, allowing the ruled to preserve their traditional clan structures or local autonomy and strongly disapproving of excessive military expenses.

Introduction

For East Asian political thought, especially after the maturing of the Confucian and Taoist traditions (fifth to third centuries BCE), warfare was an inherently contradictory subject. On the one hand, it was commonly agreed that, in practical terms, the welfare and the very existence of the state depended on its military capabilities. On the other hand, the agrarian polities of the region tended to focus on the inescapable negative consequences of any, even successfully prosecuted, war – that is, disturbances in the agricultural cycle due to war-related mobilizations and decrease in the numbers of taxpayers and corvée[1] laborers due to the inevitable losses of human resources. In ideological terms, the darker side of war was often described as a breakdown of the "harmonious" societal order based on highest Confucian values such as "humaneness" (Ch. *ren*, Kor. *in*).[2] War was thus seen as a catastrophic event – even if unavoidable and in certain situations desirable.[3] To mitigate this contradiction, East Asian thinkers often conceptualized war as an extension of criminal justice. "Righteous war" was seen as a just punishment reserved for "evil rulers" who misgoverned their states, rebels, "outer" barbarians, and other real or potential disturbers of the "normal" societal order. In this way, a "just" war was redefined as a way toward a restoration of cosmic and societal harmony rather than a cause of its breakdown.[4] In this connection, the moral qualities of both war-making politicians (kings and their ministers) and soldiers (especially high-ranking officers) were crucial. "Just" war was expected to be prosecuted by "just" people.

In the period when the classical East Asian traditions were formed – the Spring and Autumn (770–476 BCE) and Warring States (475–221 BCE) epochs of Chinese history – endemic interstate warfare was one of the major features of socio-political life. Ancient Sinitic states commanded huge conscript armies (up to 500,000 strong) – conscription being understood as part of the corvée obligations – who were armed by the fourth to the third centuries BCE with iron weapons. In some battles, the losses were momentous even by modern standards – the battle of Fei (233 BCE, in present-day Jinzhou, Hebei Province, China), in which the troops of the state of Zhao routed the invading army of Qin, cost the latter more than 100,000 men. For later historians, while brutality is inherent to any war, some episodes of interstate warfare during the Warring States epoch characterized the most brutal behavior possible. An earlier battle between Qin and Zhao troops, the battle of Changping (260 BCE, in the vicinity of present-day Gaoping, Shanxi Province, China), ended in Qin victory and the triumphal slaughter of ca. 450,000 surrendered Zhao troops, who were presumably buried alive. This is quite possibly one of the largest known massacres of prisoners of war in the whole premodern history of the world.[5] As warfare came to be a defining trait of the socio-political order by the beginning of the Warring States epoch, different schools of philosophical and political thought used it as a benchmark while positioning themselves against one another.

The school of Mohists, for example, distinguished itself by advocating defensive warfare only as a matter of principle, while tolerating offensive warfare in some cases for the "pacification of unruly barbarians."[6] The Confucian school, which came to dominate the statecraft of China – and, largely, the whole region – during and after the time of the Han Empire (206 BCE–220 CE), was generally moderate in its approach to warfare, defining it as a last resort in the cause of restoring an unjustly disturbed cosmic and social order, while emphasizing the role of "humane governance" in both preventing warfare from occurring and in order for a war to be prosecuted both "justly" and successfully.[7] While differing from Confucians in their principal "noninterference" approach to the business of statecraft, Taoists used to show quite similar attitudes toward warfare, routinely described as a sometimes inescapable calamity. Similar to Confucians, they also saw fighting as a field for the demonstration of one's degree of spiritual maturity – the ability to win by "becoming one with Tao" and following the inherent logic of things, in their case.[8] Much more pro-war and activist was the attitude of the Legalists, whose teachings formed the basis for the official governing ideology of the first unified empire in China's history, the Qin Empire (221–206 BCE). They viewed war as the main business of the state and one of the chief social mobility channels – the soldiers were to be promoted, all the way to the highest ranks, in accordance with the number of enemy heads they acquired in battle. While Confucians wished wars to be won by "virtue," Legalists saw battlefield bravery rather as an extension of the desire for reward and fear of punishment. One thing they had in common with their Confucian opponents, however, was the belief that the results of the war directly reflected the general quality of the domestic administration in a given state. War, in this scheme, was a vital part of statecraft in general.[9]

The importance of warfare led to the emergence of a special genre of literature devoted exclusively to the matters of war. Some of best-known classics of this genre – including Sun Zi's world-famous treatise, *Art of War* (*Sun Zi Bing Fa*), as well as *Wei Liaozi* or *Six Secret Teachings of Tai Gong* (*Tai Gong Liu Tao*) – seem to have originated in the Warring States epoch, while some others are more likely to date from later periods. Seven books of this genre, known as "military classics," were canonized in the eleventh century CE and were later included in most encyclopedias of military matters. Most of those books, undoubtedly influenced by Confucian moralism, tended to set strict criteria for a "legitimate" war – it was supposed to lead to peace and a "triumph of humaneness," and it was to be prosecuted in a way that would be least harmful to noncombatants, also on the enemy's territory. Such reasoning led to the idea that the best way of solving a situation of interstate hostility was to avoid fighting and either overwhelm the adversary by the sight of good government, wealth, and power of one's state or – in less Confucian spirit – prevail through intrigues and political machinations (e.g., encouraging discord at the court of the inimical kingdom). Another non-Confucian feature of the "military classics" was the commonly advocated strict separation between the king and military authority; in wartime, the general should be obeyed as if he were a person with absolute power. Generals were even encouraged to ignore the monarchical orders once they were deemed unhelpful or directly harmful for battlefield successes. Given the all-encompassing nature of kingly authority in the classical political thought of China, this attempt to distinguish military affairs as a separate societal field is highly remarkable. It is important to remember, however, that the authority of the general had to be buttressed by a uniform bureaucratic system of disciplinarian authority inside the military. Absolute obedience was valued much more than personal bravery, and a victory gained at the cost of disobeying a general's orders could well lead to punishment rather than promotion.[10]

While victory gained in violation of a general's orders was strictly disapproved of, warfare by deception was actively promoted. The encouragement of a wide use of intrigues and spies was, paradoxically enough, related to the idea that a "legitimate" war should not overburden the populations of either participant country. It was understood that "winning without a fight" (by fanning the discord and disruption at the court of the enemy monarch and inducing the downfall of his regime) or by a blitzkrieg was impossible without activating a vast spying network and practicing deception – hence the emphasis on intelligence operations and cunning.[11] The principle of the protection of noncombatant populations did not translate, however, into lenience toward soldiers and officers. The punishments were harsh, especially for the deserters; in cases where deserters returned to their families, it was recommended to have the whole families punished collectively to prevent any further occurrences of desertion. In a similar fashion, the whole unit could expect execution in the case of failing to report on desertion or any other delinquency by one of its members. The harshness stemmed, in part, from the common recognition that war making is abnormal and basically foreign to human nature. "People tend to love life and hate death" was a popular saying, while on the battlefield they were to willingly choose death if necessary. To force them into making such an unnatural choice, an elaborate system of rewards and punishments was needed, and most "military classics" go into subtle details in their descriptions of the optimal stimuli system for the military men. In most cases, these stimuli systems tended to synthesize the Confucian belief in the efficiency of "humane government" with the Legalist penchant for using fear of chastisement and desire for reward as the main incentives. The generals were expected to showcase their morality by sharing the hardships of war on an equal footing with their underlings – but also to establish their "dignity" by mercilessly punishing the wrongdoers.[12]

In the history of Imperial China, during the Han Empire period and after, discussions on the ethical issues of warfare as such were generally a rarity. It was universally accepted that, following the guidance of the "military classics," the noncombatants and surrendered enemy troops were to be allowed protection; it was also widely accepted that, as a matter of fact, such "niceties" were largely impractical while dealing with "barbarians" (in particular, nomadic peoples on the Chinese northern frontier) or rebels. Excessive or unnecessary warfare was deplored, often in poetical form, as the Confucian literati considered it their duty to express their anguish about the unnecessary sufferings of the conscript soldiers. The sufferings of the "Others" – especially if they were "frontier barbarians" – typically attracted much less attention. Minimalist approaches (focusing on defensive warfare) and maximalist approaches (promoting Chinese expansion, especially into the steppe regions) to the perennial fight against nomadic "barbarians" were hotly debated, but in most cases from fiscal rather than humanitarian perspectives. Massacres committed by the imperial troops in the wars against nomads – for example, the notorious slaughter of up to one million Dzungar tribal people during the conquest of what is known as Xinjiang Province today (1755–1759)[13] – were often mentioned by historians, but rarely in a critical context, although the wisdom of the overspending on the conquest of a largely barren area with almost indefensible borders was often questioned. All in all, a certain consensus on war seems to have been reached by the time of the Han Empire. It was understood to be an unpleasant, but inevitable part of Confucian statecraft, to be prosecuted in harmony with the general moralist principles of Confucian political theory, but simultaneously allowing ample room for a variety of exceptions, which, in the end, could make a mockery out of all the Confucian declarations of "humaneness."

Chinese military classics were on the obligatory reading list for the traditional Korean elite as well. Warfare in traditional Korea included the wars between (proto-)Korean states, the wars against the states and tribes deemed "barbaric" (nomadic dynasties of China and Japan were supposed to belong to this category), suppression of rebels, and armed conflicts with "proper" Chinese dynasties, the last of which was a war between the (proto-)Korean kingdom of the Silla and Tang Empire that ended in 676 with Silla's victory and successful consolidation of his control over the territory of the Korean Peninsula to the south of the river Taedong. "Legitimacy" was an important requirement for "proper" warfare: in the wars between the (proto-)Korean peninsular states, it was essential for all the combatants to persuade their own people, as well as Chinese dynasties to which these states used to pay formal "tribute," that they waged "just wars" in order to "liberate" the peoples of the neighboring states from the "misrule" of their dynastic rulers. It was also ideologically important to emphasize that the wars were being waged for the sake of eventual peace: "the war to end all wars" was a central, recurrent ideological theme. Of course, the (proto-)Korean states involved in conflicts with peninsular rivals also tended to stress that they, unlike their rivals, protected noncombatants, treated prisoners humanely, and welcomed defectors, providing them with jobs matching their abilities. The wars against "barbarians" were thought to be "legitimate" by default as long as the "barbarians" refused to submit to the "civilizing influence" of the Korean rulers. The punitive expeditions against "barbarians" were often accompanied by damage to noncombatants, but that was rarely considered a worthy subject for criticism. The crushing of rebels was supposed to be followed by rather ruthless reprisals against the (suspected) leaders and activists, while the rank-and-file participants in a rebellion could hope for mercy, as long as they were content to "full-heartedly submit" themselves to the "civilizing influence" of their monarchs. In the times of Korea's longest living traditional dynastic state, the Chosŏn monarchy (1392–1910), military affairs were seen as an important part of the administration: many long-sighted literati were anxious about possible future attacks, especially by the Japanese (particularly after the Japanese invasion of 1592–1598, which dealt enormous damage to the country's economy and society), and vigorously debated the possible countermeasures, which often involved the provision of military training for common-ers. "Unity of agriculture and military affairs" was, in fact, one of the ideals of Korea's traditional Confucian statecraft.[14]

Warfare in the Canonical Philosophic Literature of Ancient China

An examination of the corpus of China's pre-Qin classics (i.e., the canonical texts with their fundamentals dating back earlier than the mid-third century BCE) suggests that warfare constituted an important part of the general administration of state affairs. The interstate wars were habitually classified into legitimate "punitive expeditions" (*taofa*), and the "clashes" (*zhengdou*) between the rulers, of doubtful legitimacy but endemic in the times when central authority was weakened. The legitimacy of "punitive expedi-tions" was guaranteed by the fact that they were to be initiated by the right author-ity – by either the "Son of Heaven" (*tianzi*), the legitimate dynastic ruler over "all under the Heaven" (all the substates constituting what is known as China now) or one of his vassals operating on his behalf. "Clashes" between the unruly vassals of the "Son of Heaven," which lacked proper authorization and arose presumably out of the greed and vanity of the petty local rulers, were, on the contrary, seen as an important sign of the general socio-cosmic disharmony. A legitimate "punitive expedition" was admin-istrative as well as a ritual act – it would often be launched in a solemn atmosphere, preceded by sacrifices and royal edicts elaborating the "crimes" of the potential objects of "punishment" and presumably altruistic aims of the reprisals the authorities were to undertake.

As philosophical thinking was gradually developing after the sixth to fifth centuries BCE from the erstwhile, more practical or ritualistic approaches to statecraft, warfare – its visible cruelty standing in open contradiction to all these eloquent declarations about "humaneness" and "ritual propriety" that were so important for the ancient political thought of China – became an essential object for critical reflection. Confucians, whose conservative utopia envisioned the clan-based local communities being left by a patriar-chal, "humane" state to govern themselves following the supposedly "benevolent" and "ethical" standards of antiquity, were also remarkably conservative in their approach to warfare, especially in view of the hardships the conscription of men and the mobilization of goods for the war effort could impose on the population. However, the "legitimate" wars against rebels, usurpers, "inhumane" (and thus "illegitimate") rulers, and "barbarians" were all actively supported. Confucian thinkers such as Xunzi (ca. 312–230 BCE) who deeply interested themselves in military affairs tended to extrapolate general Confucian moral norms into the army's specific sphere of activity, emphasizing the "humaneness" of the general and his officers as the key to battlefield success. Legalists, on the other hand, tended to extrapolate specific military norms to social and political affairs in general, envisioning an ideal society as a military-like top-down structure ruled by the desire for award and fear of punishment. A Legalist classic, *Book of Lord Shang* (*Shangjunshu*), ascribed to Shang Yang (fourth century BCE), a political adviser known for his attempts to put into practice some of the crucial themes of Legalist theory, privileges war, together with agriculture, as the "main foundation of the state." Mohists, with their famous ideas of "universal love" – that is, disregarding the degree of familial or personal affinity and caring about "everybody under Heaven" to a similar extent – and with their well-known aversion for offensive warfare, seem on the surface to be the exact opposite of the Legalist bellicosity and barrack-state ideals. However, the Mohist vision of the peaceful "unified world" was predicated on the "Son of Heaven" achieving not only political but also mental unification of the universe – that is, inducing *all* people of the world to use the same "correct" standards of value judgment. The universal peace, thus, was seen as achievable only on making everybody more or less like one another – the utopia inherently much more totalitarian than what was implied by the Legalists' rather practical, down-to-earth advice on privileging the best soldiers. Mohist peacefulness, in addition, did not imply total pacifism; both defensive warfare and "legitimate pacification of barbarians" were approved of as long as the world was still failing to reach the ultimate stage of full unification of thought and behavior.

Successful Completion of Zhou's "Punitive Expedition" against the Shang Dynasty

One of the landmark events of China's early history was the downfall of the Shang dynasty, overthrown by the Zhou lineage and the tribal confederation it mustered, at some point around 1045–1040 BCE. This act by Zhou king Wu (personal name Fa) remained as an archetypical "just war" in Chinese – and broader East Asian – tradition. The war against Shang's supposedly "immoral and cruel" last king Zhou (a homonym with no connection to the Zhou lineage) was understood to be legitimate since the Zhou lineage was seen as endowed with the Mandate of Heaven (*tianming*) – the rightful authority sacredly bestowed on every new dynasty by the supreme sacerdotal entity, Heaven. Shang's mandate was understood by later historians and philosophers – who mostly tended to endorse Zhou's claim to legitimacy – to be withdrawn by Heaven as a consequence of the violent misrule by Shang's last ruler, tyrant Zhou. Thus, a "legitimate war" was, in the last instance, seen as a continuation of Heaven's providential ordering of human affairs – a sacred act.

From: "The Book of History (*Shujing*)," Chapter 23, "The Successful Completion of War" (ca. fourth century CE)[15]

1. In the first month, the day *ren-chen*[16] immediately followed the end of the moon's waning. The next day was *gui-shi*, when the king in the morning marched from Zhou to attack and punish Shang.

2. In the fourth month, at the first appearance of the moon, the king came from Shang to Feng, when he hushed all the movements of war, and attended to the cultivations of peace. He sent back his horses to the south of mount Hua,[17] and let loose his oxen in the open country of Tao Lin,[18] showing the empire that he would not use them again.

3. On the day *ding-wei*[19] he sacrificed in the ancestral temple of Zhou, when the chiefs of the imperial domain, and of the Dian, Hou and Wei domains[20] all hurried about, carrying the dishes. Three days after, he presented a burnt-offering to Heaven, and worshipped toward the mountains and rivers, solemnly announcing the successful completion of the war.

4. After the moon began to wane, the hereditary princes of the various States, and all the officers, received their appointments from Zhou.

5. The king spoke to the following effect: "Oh! ye host of princes, the first of our kings founded the State and commenced our territory. The duke Liu[21] was able to consolidate the merits of his predecessor. But it was the King Tai[22] who laid the foundations of the imperial inheritance. Then King Qi[23] was diligent for the royal House; and my deceased father, King Wen, completed his merit, and received the great decree of Heaven to soothe the regions of the great bright land. The great States feared his strength; the small States cherished his virtue. In nine years, however, the whole empire was not collected under his rule, and it fell to me, who am but a little child, to carry out his will.

6. Detesting the crimes of Shang, I announced to great Heaven and the sovereign Earth, to the famous hill and the great river, by which I passed, saying, "I, Fǎ, the principled, king of Zhou, by a long descent, am about to have a great righting with Shang. Zhou, the king of Shang, is without principle, cruel and destructive to the creatures of Heaven, injurious and tyrannical to the multitudes of the people, chief of the vagabonds of the empire, who collect about him as fish in the deep, and beasts in the prairie. I, who am but a little child, having obtained the help of virtuous men, presume reverently to comply with the will of God, to make an end of his disorderly ways. The great and flowery region, and the wild tribes of the south and north, equally follow and consent with me.

7. Reverently obeying the determinate counsel of Heaven, I pursue my punitive work to the east, to give tranquillity to its men and women. Its men and women bring their baskets full of azure and yellow silks to show forth the virtue of us the kings of Zhou. Heaven's favors stir them up, so that they come with

8. their allegiance to our great State of Zhou. And now, ye spirits, grant me your aid, that I may relieve the millions of the people, and nothing turn out to your shame!"

9. On the day *wu-wu*[24] the army crossed the ford of Meng; on the day *gui-hai*[25] it was drawn up in array in the borders of Shang, waiting for the gracious decision of Heaven. On the day *jia-zi*,[26] at early dawn, Zhou led forward his hosts like a forest, and assembled them in the wilderness of Mu. But they would offer no opposition to our army. Those in the front inverted their spears, and attacked those behind them, till they fled, and the blood flowed till it floated the pestles about. Thus did King Wu once don his arms, and the empire was greatly settled. He overthrew the existing government of Shang, and made it resume its old course. He delivered the count of Qi[27] from prison, and raised a tumulus over the grave of Bi Gan.[28] He bowed in his carriage at the gate of Shang Rong's[29] village. He dispersed the treasures of the Lu Dai,[30] and distributed the grain of Zhu Jiao,[31] thus conferring great gifts throughout the empire, and all the people joyfully submitted.

10. He arranged the orders of nobility into five, assigning the territories to them on a threefold scale. He gave offices only to the worthy, and employments only to the able. He attached great importance to the people's being taught the duties of the five relations of society, and to take care for food, for funeral ceremonies, and for sacrifices. He showed the reality of his truthfulness, and proved clearly his righteousness. He honored virtue, and rewarded merit. Then he had only to let his robes fall down, and fold his hands, and the empire was orderly ruled.

Legalist Apology of the War

A Legalist classic, *The Book of Lord Shang*, made the case for maximizing the effectiveness of state rule by forcing the people to concentrate their energies on agriculture and military service and violently suppressing anybody with the potential to rival the state authority – be it local notables or Confucian philosophers, with their preaching of "humane," less assertive, and more permissive statehood. From being just a part of state administration, warfare was elevated by the Legalists into the basic model for all the spheres of statecraft.

From: Shang Yang, *The Book of Lord Shang* (ca. late fourth century BCE)[32]

The means, whereby a ruler of men encourages the people, are office and rank; the means, whereby a country is made prosperous, are agriculture and war. Now those, who seek office and rank, never do so by means of agriculture and war, but by artful words and empty doctrines. That is called "wearying the people." The country of those, who weary their people, will certainly have no strength, and the country of those, who have no strength, will certainly be dismembered.

Those, who are capable in organizing a country, teach the people that office and rank can only be acquired through one opening, and thus, there being no rank without office, the state will do away with fine speaking, with the result that the people will be simple; being simple, they will not be licentious. The people, seeing that the highest benefit comes only through one opening, will strive for concentration, and having concentration, will not be negligent in their occupations. When the people are not negligent in their occupations, they will have much strength, and when they have much strength the state will be powerful. But now the people within the territory all say that by avoiding agriculture and war, office and rank may be acquired, with the result that eminent men all change their occupations, to apply themselves to the study of the *Odes* and *History* and to follow improper standards; on the one hand, they obtain prominence, and on the other, they acquire office and rank. Insignificant individuals will occupy themselves with trade and will practice arts and crafts, all in order to avoid agriculture and war, thus preparing a dangerous condition for the state. Where the people are given to such teachings, it is certain that such a country will be dismembered. . . .

But now, those who run a state, for the most part, overlook what is essential, and the discussions at court, on government, are confused and efforts are made to displace each other in them; thus the prince is dazed by talk, officials confused by words, and the people become lazy and will not farm. The result is that all the people within the territory change and become fond of sophistry, take pleasure in study, pursue trade, practice arts and crafts, and shun agriculture and war and so in this manner the ruin of the country will not be far off. When the country has trouble, then, because studious people hate law, merchants are clever in bartering and artisans are useless, the state will be easily destroyed.

Indeed, if farmers are few, and those who live idly on others are many, then the state will be poor and in a dangerous condition. Now, for example, if various kinds of caterpillars, which are born in spring and die in autumn, appear only once, the result is that the people have no food for many years. Now, if one man tills and a hundred live on him, it means that they are like a great visitation of caterpillars. Though there may a bundle of the *Odes* and *History* in every hamlet and a copy in every family, yet it is useless for good government, and it is not a method whereby this condition of things may be reversed. Therefore the ancient kings made people turn back to agriculture and war. For this reason it is said: "Where a hundred men farm, and one is idle, the state will attain supremacy; where ten men farm and one is idle, the state will be strong; where half farms and half is idle, the state will be in peril." That is why those, who govern the country well, wish the people to take to agriculture. If the country does not take to agriculture, then, in its quarrels over authority with the various feudal lords, it will not be able to maintain itself, because the strength of the multitude will not be sufficient. Therefore the feudal lords vex its weakness and make use of its state of decadence; and if the territory is invaded and dismembered, without the country being stirred to action, it will be past saving. A sage knows what is essential in administrating a country, and so he induces the people to devote their attention to agriculture. If their attention is devoted to agriculture, then they will be simple, and being simple, they may be made correct. Being perplexed it will be easy to direct them, being trustworthy, they may be used for defense and warfare. Being single-minded, opportunities of deceit will be few and they will attach importance to their homes. Being single-minded, their careers may be made dependant on rewards and penalties; being single-minded, they may be used abroad.

Mohist Condemnation of Offensive Warfare

The book of Mo Zi (Tsu), which contains the discourses traditionally ascribed to the founder of the Mohist School, Mo Zi (ca. 471–391 BCE), is known as one of the first explicit statements against offensive warfare in human history. Mo Zi was thought to be a skilled carpenter himself, and a large number of his followers, whose efforts were instrumental in posthumously compiling the book of Mo Zi, were also drawn from the ranks of the artisans and other petty townsfolk. Largely echoing the commonsensical worldview of people from this social stratum – those who tended to suffer from conscription, excessive taxation, and the general destructiveness of warfare and who had very little to gain from battlefield victories – the book of Mo Zi declares offensive warfare both a criminal enterprise (since it involved large-scale manslaughter) and an unnecessary burden on the commoners. Together with war, Mo Zi also opposed all other kinds of unnecessary and burdensome state expenses, including elaborate funerals and ritual music. It did not mean, however, that he and his followers were not spirit believers themselves. Indeed, one of the reasons they opposed wartime manslaughter was that killing humans, who were to take care of the spirits and sacrifice to them, was also contemptuous of the spirits. However, the book of Mo Zi simultaneously praises the semi-legendary "punitive expeditions against barbarians" by the model "sage emperors" of China's canonized antiquity. The descriptions of these expeditions – for example, "sage emperor" Yu's grand battle against the "unruly" Miao tribes – are peppered with mythological details that were to assure the public that the "just war" was actively assisted by Heaven and the spirits. While some offensive wars were seen as "crimes against Heaven," some were regarded as Heavenly sanctioned – and even Heavenly assisted. Defensive warfare – in which both Mo Zi himself and many of his followers were considered experts – was also seen as virtuous.

From: Mo Tsu, "Against Offensive Warfare" (ca. mid-fourth century BCE)[33]

If a man enters an orchard and steals the peaches and plums, everyone who hears about it will condemn him, and if those above who administer the government catch him they will punish him. Why? Because he injures others to benefit himself. When it comes to carrying off dogs, swine, chickens, and piglets, the deed is even more unrighteous than entering an orchard to steal peaches and plums. Why? Because the loss to others is greater. It shows a greater lack of benevolence and is a more serious crime. When it comes to breaking into another man's stable and seizing his horses and cows, the deed is even more unrighteous than carrying off dogs, swine, chicken, and piglets. Why? Because the loss to others is greater, and if the loss is greater, it shows a greater lack of benevolence and is a more serious crime. And when it comes to murdering an innocent man, stripping him of his clothing, and appropriating his spear and sword, the deed is even more unrighteous than breaking into a stable and seizing someone's horses and cows. Why? Because the injury to others is even greater, and if the injury is greater, it shows a greater lack of benevolence and is a more serious crime. Now all the gentlemen in the world know enough to condemn such acts and brand them as unrighteous. And yet when it comes to the even greater unrighteousness of offensive warfare against other states, they do not know enough to condemn it. On the contrary, they praise it and call it righteous. Is this what it means to know the difference between righteousness and unrighteousness?

If someone kills one man, he is condemned as unrighteous and must pay for his crime with his own life. According to this reasoning, if someone kills ten men, then he is ten times as unrighteous and should pay for his crime with ten lives, or if he kills a hundred men he is a hundred times as unrighteous and should pay for his crime with a hundred lives. Now all the gentlemen of the world know enough to condemn such crimes and brand them as unrighteous. And yet when it comes to the even greater unrighteousness of offensive warfare against other states, they do not know enough to condemn it. On the contrary, they praise it and call it righteous. Truly they do not know what unrighteousness is. So they make a record of their wars to be handed down to posterity. If they knew that such wars were unrighteous, then what reason would they have for making a record of their unrighteous deeds to be handed down to posterity? . . .

Everyone agrees that the ways of the sage kings constitute a standard of righteousness. Yet many of the feudal lords of today continue to attack and annex their neighboring states. They claim they are honoring righteousness, but they fail to examine the truth of the matter. . . .

[W]hen the benevolent men of ancient times ruled the world, they strove for amicable relations among the large states, united the world in harmony, brought together all within the four seas, and led the people to serve and honor the Lord on High, the sacred mountains and rivers, and the spirits. Many were the benefits they brought to mankind, and great was their success. Therefore Heaven rewarded them, the spirits enriched them, and men praised them. . . .

But the rulers and feudal lords of today are not like this. . . .

[C]lad in strong armor and bearing sharp weapons, they set off to attack some innocent state. As soon as they enter the borders of the state, they begin cutting down the grain crops, felling trees, razing walls and fortifications, filling up moats and ponds, slaughtering the sacrificial animals, firing the ancestral temples of the state, massacring its subjects, trampling down its aged and weak, and carrying off its vessels and treasures. . . .

[T]hey are massacring the subjects of Heaven, driving out the spirits of their ancestors, overthrowing their altars of the soil and grain, and slaughtering their sacrificial animals. This brings no benefit to Heaven on high. Is it intended then to benefit the spirits? But to murder men is to wipe out the caretakers of the spirits, to cause the spirits of the former kings to suffer neglect, to oppress the subjects of the state and scatter its people. This brings no benefit to the spirits in the middle realm. . . .

In ancient times the three Miao tribes were in great disorder and Heaven decreed their destruction. The sun came out at night and for three days it rained blood. A dragon appeared in the ancestral temple and dogs howled in the marketplace. Ice formed in summertime, the earth split open until springs gushed forth, the five grains grew all deformed, and the people were filled with a great terror. Kao Yang gave the command in the Dark Palace, and Yü in person grasped the jade staff of authority and set out to subdue the ruler of the Miao. Amidst the din of thunder and lightning, a spirit with the face of a man and the body of a bird came bearing a jade baton to wait upon Yü. The general of the Miao was felled by an arrow, and the Miao army thrown into great confusion. After this their power waned. When Yu had conquered the three Miao, he marked off the mountains and rivers, separated those things which pertained to above and below, and clearly regulated the four extremities of the world, so that neither spirits nor people committed any offense, and all the world was at peace. This was how Yü launched an expedition against the ruler of the Miao.

Mencius and the Conditional Acceptance of Warfare

Mencius (Meng Zi, ca. 372–289 BCE), a known opponent of Mo Zi, was one of the most influential interpreters of Confucian teachings in the period of antiquity. While his renowned belief in the natural human propensity to do good was not necessarily completely irreconcilable with the Mohist ideal of "universal" (i.e., undiscriminating) love, his vision of the ideal, affection-based community was more traditionalist – for him, the moral commitments toward one's parents, one's clan, and one's state were certainly more important than the abstract love toward the rest of humanity. In relation to war, his attitudes were not fully dissimilar to those of the Mohists, but they were certainly much less radical. "Excessive," "unnecessary," or "unjust" wars were firmly rejected as both inhumane and burdensome for the general populace, whose well-being Mencius considered the foremost criterion of good governance. "Just wars" – sanctioned by the authority of the "Son of Heaven" or necessitated because of the misrule of the monarchs on the receiving edge of "punitive expeditions," which Mencius habitually called "royal corrections" – were, however, regarded as completely legitimate. While Mohists tended to see only defensive warfare or the expeditions against "barbarians" as largely "just," Mencius defined a "just war" in a broader way, legitimizing many of the military conflicts waged by what he considered the proper authority – either the "Son of Heaven" or those acting on his behalf.

From: *The Works of Mencius*, Book 7, Part 2
(ca. late fourth century BCE)[34]

1-1. Mencius said, "The opposite indeed of benevolent was the king Hûi of Liang! The benevolent, beginning with what they care for, proceed to what they do not care for. Those who are the opposite of benevolent, beginning with what they do not care for, proceed to what they care for."

1-2. Kung-sun Ch'âu said, "What do you mean?" Mencius answered, "The king Hûi of Liang, for the matter of territory, tore and destroyed his people, leading them to battle. Sustaining a great defeat, he would engage again, and afraid lest they should not be able to secure the victory, urged his son whom he loved till he sacrificed him with them. This is what I call – 'beginning with what they do not care for, and proceeding to what they care for.'"

2-1. Mencius said, "In the 'Spring and Autumn' [Annals] there are no righteous wars. Instances indeed there are of one war better than another.

2-2. "'Correction' is when the supreme authority punishes its subjects by force of arms. Hostile States do not correct one another."

3-1. Mencius said, "It would be better to be without the *Book of History* than to give entire credit to it.

3-2. "In the 'Completion of the War,'* I select two or three passages only, which I believe.

3-3. "'The benevolent man has no enemy under heaven. When the prince the most benevolent was engaged against him who was the most the opposite, how could the blood of the people have flowed till it floated the pestles of the mortars?'"

4-1. Mencius said, "There are men who say – 'I am skilful at marshalling troops, I am skilful at conducting a battle!' – They are great criminals.

4-2. "If the ruler of a State love[s] benevolence, he will have no enemy in the kingdom.

4-3. "When Tang was executing his work of correction in the south, the rude tribes on the north murmured. When he was executing it in the east, the rude tribes on the west murmured. Their cry was – 'Why does he make us last?'

4-4. "When king Wû punished Yin, he had only three hundred chariots of war, and three thousand life-guards.

4-5. "The king said, 'Do not fear. Let me give you repose. I am no enemy to the people!' On this, they bowed their heads to the earth, like the horns of animals falling off.'

4-6. "'Royal correction' is but another word for rectifying. Each State wishing itself to be corrected, what need is there for fighting?"

Xun Zi and the Confucian Vision of "Humane Warfare"

Xun Zi (Hsün Tsu) (ca. 312–230 BCE) was a junior contemporary of Mencius and one of his main opponents inside the Confucian school. While Mencius made a point out of his optimistic vision of human nature as inherently inclined toward goodness, Xun Zi, in a much soberer and more pessimistic tone, held that humans are full of egoistic desires and normally tend to commit evil acts if they need to do so to satisfy their desires. That was exactly why they were to be corrected by the elites – beginning from the "sage emperors" of antiquity down to the rulers and learned gentlemen of Xun Zi's own days. To correct human nature, lavish rituals might be necessary – and at this point Xun Zi was an ardent opponent of the Mohists, who primarily thought of such rituals in terms of the burden

---

* By this is meant "The Successful Completion of War," the chapter from *The Book of History* cited above.

they imposed through excessive taxation. Aside from rituals, Xun Zi emphasized education and "just wars" as important methods of correcting the human world's inherently evil tendencies. "Just war" was regarded by his school as vital enough to have an entire chapter (No. 15, according to the traditional sequence), entitled "Debating Military Affairs" ("Yi Bing"), devoted to the ways of "Confucian warfare": how to practice the Confucian virtues (benevolence, etc.) in a way that uplifts the spirit of the troops and guarantees victory, and how to conduct a "just war" in a "virtuous" way. Protection of noncombatants and surrendered enemy troops was duly emphasized, also as an important difference between a "just war" (which Xun Zi, not too dissimilar to either Mo Zi or Mencius, saw as a "correction" or "punitive expedition") and chaotic and illegitimate warfare between the profit-obsessed state rulers.

From: Hsün Tsu, "Debating Military Affairs" (ca. late third century BCE)[35]

... From what I have heard of the way of the ancients, the basis of all aggressive warfare and military undertaking lies in the unification of the people.... If the officers and people are not devoted to their leaders, even the sages Tang or Wu could not win victory. The one who is good at winning the support of his people is the one who will be good at using arms. Therefore what is really essential in military undertakings is to be good at winning the support of the people....

As for the relations between superior and inferior under the rule of a benevolent man, the various generals will be of one mind, and the three armies of the state will work together. Subjects will serve their lord and inferiors will serve their superiors like sons serving a father or younger brothers serving an elder brother. They will be like hands held up to guard the face and eyes, arms clasped to protect the breast and belly....

He who treats his officers well will be strong; he who does not will be weak. He who loves his people will be strong; he who does not will be weak. He whose government decrees are trusted will be strong; he whose government decrees are not trusted will be weak. He whose people are unified will be strong; he whose people are not unified will be weak.... He who uses his soldiers with caution will be strong; he who uses them rashly will be weak. He whose strategies proceed from a single source will be strong; he whose strategies proceed from several sources will be weak. This is the abiding rule of strength and weakness....

Obedience to orders is counted first; achievements are counted second. To advance when there has been no order to advance is no different from retreating when there has been no order to retreat; the penalty is the same. The king's army does not kill the enemy's old men and boys; it does not destroy crops. It does not seize those who retire without a fight, but it does not forgive those who resist. It does not make prisoners of those who surrender and seek asylum. In carrying out punitive expeditions, it does not punish the common people; it punishes those who lead the common people astray. But if any of the common people fight with the enemy, they become enemies as well. Thus those who flee from the enemy forces and come in surrender shall be left to go free....

The righteous man acts in accordance with what is right, and for that reason he hates to see men do wrong. He takes up arms in order to put an end to violence and to do away with harm, not in order to contend with others for spoil. Therefore, where the soldiers of the benevolent man encamp they command a godlike respect; and where they pass, they transform the people. They are like the seasonable rain in whose falling all men rejoice.

Warfare in the Historical Records and Literature in China and Korea

Confucian exhortations about the avoidance of unnecessary warfare notwithstanding, warfare was endemic in Chinese history, both before the short-lived Qin Empire (221–206 BCE) unified diverse Chinese kingdoms and after that period. The huge empire with its diverse population, surrounded by a variety of heterogeneous tribes and states on all its land borders, was constantly busy suppressing uprisings, expanding, or defending itself from ambitious challengers from the outside. It is perhaps no accident that China boasts some of the most important inventions in the worldwide history of military technology, including the crossbow (*nu*, developed by the mid-fifth century BCE), gunpowder (*huoyao*, invented by the mid-ninth century at the latest), guns (the earliest proto-guns, "fire lances," *huoqiang*, were in use in China by the mid-tenth century), and even prototypes of modern flamethrowers and rockets. In Korean history after 676, when the territory of the Korean Peninsula to the south of the river Taedong was successfully unified by a (proto-)Korean state, Silla, warfare was much more sporadic but doubtless played an important historical role – the damage done by the Japanese invasion of 1592–1598, for example, was so huge that it took approximately a century to restore Korea's predominantly agrarian economy to prewar levels.

The importance of war meant that it was often represented in both fictional and nonfictional accounts. In fiction as well as in history, representations of warfare tended to serve, first and foremost, as lessons. The nature of the lessons could be moral: Confucian generals were to show their ethical qualities, or lack thereof, on the battlefield, the task of the historian being to immortalize the lesson for the sake of posterity. Literary descriptions of war frequently tended to be rather didactic as well; the extreme situation of fighting and dying forming a useful backdrop emphasizing the depths of loyalty and wisdom – or disloyalty and stupidity – in human hearts and minds. One consequence of such a didactic tendency was that many portrayals of battlefield scenes often lost their vividness and detail. It was not violence per se but the ethical qualities of those thrown into the violent circumstances that were romanticized. Perhaps one exception was the accounts dealing with the world of outlaws and bandits. Lively descriptions of blows, blood gushing from wounds, agony, and painful death were seemingly seen as sufficient entertainment for the undemanding lower-class public. It is not, however, that the gore was seen as simply entertaining stuff. In high-level Confucian poetry, for example, the unreasonably frequent conscriptions, excessive "punitive expeditions," and painful death waiting for so many peasant recruits was seen as an important part of "people's suffering" in general – such suffering being what the "humane" Confucian administrators were in principle to alleviate. It is not easy, however, to find a single literary text explicitly pitying the "barbarians" to be targeted by the imperial "corrections." "Barbarians" were certainly not fully dehumanized in classical Chinese literary discourse but were still seen as an inferior – and external – category of "people"; their suffering counted incomparably less than the suffering of one's own people.

General Li Guang, a Confucian Warrior

Li Guang (d. 119 BCE) was a general of the Han Empire (206 BCE–220 CE) whose primary claim to fame was his personality rather than battlefield achievements. It is not that the latter were completely lacking – General Li scored a number of serious successes in the battles against Xiongnu nomads (who inhabited the territory of present-day Mongolia), then the main enemy of the Han Empire in the north. However, General Li's neglect of the necessary precautions and formal procedures of expedition preparation and accounting significantly worsened his official record – he was often outnumbered by his nomadic enemies, and even if his troops managed to kill enough adversaries to earn some distinction, his disregard for the routine reporting of his successes to his higher-ups was to destroy his chances for promotion. Despite his failure to fit the standards of the imperial military routine, General Li acquired considerable popularity for his unmatched bravery, magnanimousness, calm in the face of death, and keen sense of honor. His life ended, in fact, with him choosing to commit suicide rather than to suffer the disgrace of a formal court-martial. It is not that the great warrior never himself experienced the pangs of conscience, however. As his biography by the Han Empire's great historian, Sima Qian (ca. 145 or 135 BCE–86 BCE), did not fail to notice, his own conscience was tormented by his memories of breaking an important precept of a Confucian warrior: slaughtering some of the surrendered "barbarian" enemies.

From: Sima Qian, "General Li Guang" (91 BCE)[36]

In the fourteenth year of Emperor Wen's reign (166 BCE) the Xiongnu entered the Xiao Pass in great numbers. Li Guang, as the son of a distinguished family, was allowed to join the army in the attack on the barbarians. He proved himself a skillful horseman and archer, killing and capturing a number of the enemy, and was rewarded with the position of palace attendant at the Han court. . . .

When Emperor Jing came to the throne, Li Guang was made chief commandant of Longxi; later he was transferred to the post of general of palace horsemen. At the time of the revolt of Wu and Chu, he served as a cavalry commander under the grand commandant Zhou Yafu, joining in the attack on the armies of Wu and Chu, capturing the enemy pennants, and distinguishing himself at the battle of Changyi. But because he had accepted the seals of a general from the king of Liang without authorization from the Han government, he was not rewarded for his achievements when he returned to the capital.

Following this he was transferred to the post of governor of Shanggu Province, where he engaged in almost daily skirmishes with the Xiongnu. The director of dependent states Gongsun Kunye went to the emperor and, with tears in his eyes, said, "There is no one in the empire to match Li Guang for skill and spirit and yet, trusting to his own ability, he repeatedly engages the enemy in battle. I am afraid one day we will lose him!" The emperor therefore transferred him to the post of governor of Shang Province....

When Li Guang went out on expeditions to attack the Xiongnu, he never bothered to form his men into battalions and companies. He would make camp wherever he found water and grass, leaving his men to set up their quarters in any way they thought convenient. He never had sentries circling the camp at night and beating on cooking pots, as was the custom, and in his headquarters he kept records and other clerical work down to a minimum. He always sent out scouts some distance around the camp, however, and he had never met with any particular mishap....

Li Guang was completely free of avarice. Whenever he received a reward of some kind, he at once divided it among those in his command, and he was content to eat and drink the same things as his men. For over forty years he received a salary of 2,000 piculs,* but when he died he left no fortune behind. He never discussed matters of family wealth. He was a tall man with long, ape-like arms. His skill at archery seems to have been an inborn talent, for none of his descendants or others who studied under him were ever able to equal his prowess. He was a very clumsy speaker and never had much to say. When he was with others he would draw diagrams on the ground to explain his military tactics or set up targets of various widths and shoot at them with his friends, the loser being forced to drink. In fact, archery remained to the end of his life his chief source of amusement.

When he was leading his troops through a barren region and they came upon some water, he would not get near it until all his men had finished drinking. Similarly he would not eat until every one of his men had been fed. He was very lenient with his men and did nothing to vex them, so that they all loved him and were happy to serve under him....

Li Guang was once chatting with Wang Shuo, a diviner who told men's fortunes by the configurations of the sky, and remarked on this fact. "Ever since the Han started attacking the Xiongnu, I have never failed to be in the fight. I have had men in my command who were company commanders or even lower and who did not even have the ability of average men, and yet twenty or thirty of them have won marquisates† on the strength of their achievements in attacking the barbarian armies. I have never been behind anyone else in doing my duty. Why is it I have never won an ounce of distinction so that I could be enfeoffed‡ like the others? Is

---

* In the original, the traditional Chinese measure of weight, *dan* (lit. "stone"), is used. One *dan* in Han dynasty time approximately equaled 31 kg. An annual salary of two thousand *dan* was the highest possible one, paid only to the top civil and military officials.

† The nobility title *hou*, often translated as "marquis" in the European languages, was the second highest, after that of *gong* ("duke"). Under the Han dynasty, it was bestowed both on the relatives of the imperial house and on the selected meritorious officials, civil and military.

‡ That is, given one of the five nobility ranks.

it that I just don't have the kind of face to become a marquis? Or is it all a matter of fate?"

"Think carefully, general," replied Wang Shuo. "Isn't there something in the past that you regret having done?"

"Once, when I was governor of Longxi, the Qiang tribes in the west started a revolt. I tried to talk them into surrendering, and in fact persuaded over 800 of them to give themselves up. But then I went back on my word and killed them all the very same day. I have never ceased to regret what I did. But that is the only thing I can think of."

"Nothing brings greater misfortune than killing those who have already surrendered to you," said Wang Shuo. "This is the reason, general, that you have never become a marquis!"...

The Grand Historian remarks: One of the old books says, "If he himself is upright, those under him will act without being ordered to; if he himself is not upright, they will not obey even when ordered."[37] It refers, no doubt, to men like General Li.

I myself have seen General Li – a man so plain and unassuming that you would take him for a peasant, and almost incapable of speaking a word. And yet the day he died all the people of the empire, whether they had known him or not, were moved to the profoundest grief, so deeply did men trust his sincerity of purpose. There is a proverb which says, "Though the peach tree does not speak, the world wears a path beneath it." It is a small saying, but one which is capable of conveying a great meaning.

Cai Xi and the War by Deception

While killing helpless captives (the exception being "barbarians"), in violation of previously given guarantees, was regarded as unworthy for a Confucian warrior, the use of deception, especially in the wars against "barbarians," was taken more or less for granted. The logic here was that they were perceived as "criminals" of sorts, and the use of deception in a punitive manner against "foreign criminals" was nothing to be ashamed of. On the contrary, a successful "punitive expedition," which owed its success to artful deception used against the barbarian enemy, was seen as a merit to be officially rewarded. The account below is a memorial written in 853 by a junior scholar, Li Qi. He sought to establish that the honor of having successfully conducted one such deception operation – against rather defenseless Uighur refugees who were camping in close proximity to Tang Empire (618–907 CE) borders – was to be given to a low-ranked soldier, Cai Xi, rather than his commander, General Liu Mian, who had seemingly rather unceremoniously "appropriated" the merits of his underling. While the Uighur Empire was an ally of Tang before its collapse in 840, which was caused by a Kirghiz invasion and internal conflicts, the Uighur refugees who approached the Tang borders after the collapse were seen as a "barbarian horde" to be controlled and, if possible, eliminated. Of special attention to the soldiers of Tang was a Tang princess, Taihe, who married an Uighur ruler before the collapse of his state, in 821. As is shown in the account below, she was to be rescued, while the Uighur "savages" were to be lured within striking distance and then attacked, defeated, and slaughtered.

From: Li Qi, "The Account of Cai Xi" (853)[38]

Cai Xi is, in his own words, an assistant general. The origin of his family is unknown; from their [known] beginnings their descendants ["posterity" in the original], down to Xi, have lived in the Zhenwu Army [administrative unit] in the north.[39] [Xi] was a student of fencing; he was calm and brave, and achieved distinction through his fondness for unusual strategies. At first, before anyone knew of him, he behaved recklessly. He got into a fight with someone and [apparently] killed him. At that time, since the [later] Minister of Works Liu Mian had been made Military Governor of Zhenwu while serving as Right Vice-Director of the Department of State Affairs, he heard of [the matter] and had Xi imprisoned. [Cai Xi] was about to be executed by whipping, but in the night the "dead" man revived. Thus Xi escaped death; [instead] he was banished to do garrison duty at the frontier for several years. Mian [later] was transferred to guard Hedong.[40]

At the beginning of [the reign of Emperor] Wuzong (r. 840–846), the Xiongnu[41] violated the border. [The emperor] ordered that troops be sent out from Mian's [circuit of] Hedong and from other circuits to attack them. When Xi heard that there was an incident at the border, he wished to avail himself of [the situation] to establish merit, so he escaped from the place where he was working and came to beseech Mian....

... Mian considered him resolute and upright, and ordered that he be placed among the soldiers of the government army. When they reached Daning, they heard that the Xiongnu already had entered the border at Zhenwu. At this time the Taihe Princess had been abroad [among the northern nomads] for many years; [the government troops] also heard that [the military officials of] Zhenwu wanted to rescue the princess. Mian was afraid that the princess would be taken by [the military officials of] Zhenwu, and for this they would obtain great merit. He schemed and planned, but did not know what to do, nor could his generals and officers come up with a plan. Xi then requested permission to pretend to be pursuing ... escaped criminal(s) and so reach the Xiongnu camp to sow doubt among them, causing them to enter the border at Hedong. Mian strongly approved of this plan, and so sent Xi on his way.

When Xi arrived at the place where the Xiongnu [were camped], he spread the word: "Those who guard Zhenwu wish to kill you all. In Hedong, Vice-Director of the Department of State Affairs Liu is Pacification Commissioner. If you do not shift [your camp] you surely will be destroyed by the forces of Zhenwu." There were those among the Xiongnu who, having heard these words, hurried to Ningwu [to submit]. [The remainder] subsequently shifted as divisions and regiments, and arrived at [the area] west of Quyue City. They were already at the border of Hedong, [but] still were more than two hundred tricents (*li*)* from the government army.

---

* Tricent (*li*) is a traditional measure of length equivalent to 300 paces, ca. 500 meters.

When Xi returned and reported to Mian, [the latter] wanted to memorialize to the throne [concerning the matter], but feared an imperial edict [requiring] prisoners as evidence. Xi again [acted on Liu Mian's behalf and] captured twelve prisoners and fifteen horses. The commander (i.e., Liu Mian) then wrote [a memorial] concerning the matter. After the emperor had learned of it, there were repeated imperial edicts ordering [Mian] to obtain the princess. Mian was distressed that the camp of the Xiongnu was [still so] far away; he wanted them to come closer, but again could not [think of a way to bring this about]. Xi then requested permission to enter their territory with goods and provisions to entice them [to approach nearer]. Mian agreed with him. . . .

Xi . . . met with their minister. . . . The minister . . . said, "We would go to the Tang now, but fear that your superiors will deceive us. If you truly welcome us and encourage us to come, then swear a weighty oath with us." Xi said, "Generally those who take an oath are anxious and so there are myriad complications. Xi's oath-taking is different from this." He then stretched out his hands in front of the minister and asked him to cut off his left hand at the wrist in order to take the oath. His complexion was unchanged and his speech was quite resolute. The minister did not agree [to cut off Xi's left hand] and said, "Now, if you will cut open [the flesh above] your heart for me so that blood comes forth, and then drink it yourself, this will suffice to earn my trust." Xi then let blood flow from [the flesh] above his heart into a vessel and swore an oath, saying, "If I duplicitously mislead you into entering the Tang border, then may Heaven strike me dead – boil me alive and mince me for pickling." After he had finished speaking, he drank all the blood that was in the vessel. The Xiongnu then trusted him, and so shifted their camp to the valleys and mountains of the frontier north of Yunzhou. . . . Xi . . . lied to the *chanyu*,[42] saying to him that at Yunzhou and Shuozhou he would obtain more goods and provisions for the foreigners. Therefore he was then able to return home. He told Mian everything. . . . [He added that] if Mian would obtain the princess, he certainly should take advantage of the moment and go quickly. Mian agreed and ordered his high-ranking military officers . . . all to go with Xi to the *chanyu*'s camp. They surrounded it and soundly defeated [the Xiongnu]. Xi rushed into the camp and helped the princess onto a horse. . . . The princess was sent to Hedong, and the whole of the affair was ascribed to Liu Mian. . . . [Xi's] achievements and strategies subsequently were obscured and were not made known. And yet the destruction of Xiongnu by [the forces of] Hedong and the settling and clearing of the border dust up to now had their origins in the strength of Xi's strategies.

Zhuge Liang and the Confucian Ideal of the "Pacification of the Barbarians"

While the Confucian *realpolitik* included the practical use of deception, especially against the supposedly unworthy non-Chinese counterparts ("barbarians"), a much nobler ideal of a Confucian warrior was upheld not only in elite scholarship but in popular culture as well. This ideal made warfare part and parcel of a larger paradigm of Confucian moral politics – the "ethical warriors" were supposed to "civilize" their opponents, first emotionally moving them by a display of "humaneness" and "propriety" and eventually persuading them to accept the political and ethical superiority of the central "civilizing subject" of the Universe – the Chinese Confucian state. The ideal may be compared, in a general typological way, to the various "hearts and minds" counterinsurgency strategies of the post-1945 Western powers. One of the best-known literary descriptions of a "charm offensive" is found in China's famous classical novel, *The Romance of the Three Kingdoms* (*Sanguo Yanyi*, compiled around the fourteenth century), chapters 87–90. The protagonist there is an idealized Confucian warrior: renowned minister and strategist Zhuge Liang (181–234), from the kingdom of Shu (today's Sichuan Province in China). These chapters deal with Zhuge Liang's 225 campaign, against both rebellious local officials in the southern borderlands of the Shu kingdom and their tribal ally, the "barbarian" *man* tribes. A famous story incorporated into these chapters tells us that Zhuge Liang captured and subsequently released a *man* tribal leader, Meng Huo, seven times, in full knowledge that the "barbarian" was bent on continuous resistance, just in order to demonstrate the "moral superiority" of the Chinese "pacificators." In the end, this psychological war ("fight with sentiments") strategy was said to pay off – Meng Huo ended up swearing allegiance to the Shu kingdom. After "pacifying" the region, Zhuge Liang left and entrusted the administration to the local tribal leaders who were supposedly overwhelmed enough by Zhuge's show of leniency. While the novel should not be treated as a historical source, and some of its descriptions of the "kindness" of the Shu army appear heavily exaggerated, it is also undeniable that in many cases "hegemony," in Gramscian terms – that is, willing submission to authority seen as legitimate and well intended, rather than simple domination – was the aim of the Chinese "pacification" campaigns.

From: Lo Kuan-chung, *Romance of the Three Kingdoms*, Chapter 87 (ca. fourteenth century)[43]

[I]n the third year [of Beginning Prosperity (225 CE)], the news came [from Yizhou] to the capital that a host of *Mans* [tribesmen] had invaded the south and were laying waste [to] the country, and that the Prefect of Chienning, a man of an honorable and even noble family, had joined them. Already two districts had yielded to the invaders, but a third was staunchly holding out. The three rebels, [Yong Kai, Gao Ding, and Zhu Bao] who had joined the invaders, were now acting as guides and assisting in the attack on Jungch'ang, which had remained faithful. Wang K'ang, the Prefect of Jungch'ang, ably seconded by Lu K'ai, one of his subordinates, was making a desperate effort to defend the city with only its ordinary inhabitants as fighting men. The position was very desperate.

When this news came, K'ung-ming [Zhuge Liang's courtesy name] went into the palace and thus memorialized to his lord, "The contumacy of the *Mans* is a real danger to our state. I feel it incumbent upon me to lead an expedition to reduce the barbarians to obedience. . . .

"This country of the *Mans* is distant and mostly uncivilized. To reduce them to reasonableness will be difficult, and I feel I ought to go. When to be harsh and when to show leniency are matters to be decided on at the moment, and instructions cannot be easily given to another."...

Chiang Yuan was Councillor of the expedition. Fei Wei was Recorder; Tung Chueh and Fan Chien were Historians; Chao Yun and Wei Yen were Generals; Wang P'ing and Chang I were Deputy Generals and leaders of the fighting men. Beside these were officers originally belonging to Shu, and the whole force was fifty legions....

The Prefect of Jungch'ang then came out of the city and welcomed K'ung-ming, and, when he had made his entry into that city, he called Wang K'ang and asked who had aided him in the defense. The Prefect said, "The safety of this city is due entirely to Lu K'ai." So Lu was called. He came and bowed. K'ung-ming said, "Long since I heard of you as a remarkable man of this district. We are greatly indebted to you for its safety. Now we wish to conquer the *Mans*, have you any advice to offer?" Lu K'ai then produced a map of the country and presented it, saying, "From the time of my appointment, I have felt certain that the southern men [tribal people] would rise against you, and so I sent secret agents to map out the country and find the strategic points. From that information I prepared this map, which I call 'An Easy Scheme to Conquer the *Mans*.' I beg you, Sir, to accept it, as it may be of use." Then K'ung-ming took Lu K'ai into his service as adviser and guide. With his help he advanced and penetrated deeply into the country.

While the army was advancing, there came a messenger from the Court. When he appeared, K'ung-ming saw it was Ma Su, and he was clothed in white. He was in mourning for his brother, Ma Liang, who had just died. He had come by special command of the Emperor with gifts of wine and silk.

When the ceremonies proper on receipt of a mandate from the Emperor had been performed, and the gifts distributed as instructed, Ma Su was asked to remain to talk over matters.

K'ung-ming said, "I have His Majesty's command to conquer these *Mans*. I hear you have some advice to offer, and I should be pleased if you would instruct me."

"Yes; I have one thing to say that may be worth thinking over. These people refuse to recognize our supremacy because they think their country is distant and difficult. If you should overcome them today, tomorrow they would revolt. Wherever your army marches they are overcome and submit, but the day you withdraw the army and attack Ts'ao P'ei they will renew their attack. In arms even it is best to attack hearts rather than cities; to fight with sentiment is better than to fight with weapons. It will be well if you can win them over." "You read inmost thoughts," said K'ung-ming. Then Ma Su was retained with the army as adviser, and the army marched on....

The King of the *Mans* was sitting in his tent when the scouts told him that his three chiefs had been captured and their armies scattered. It made him very angry, and he quickly got his army ready to march. Soon he met Wang P'ing, and, when the armies were arrayed, Wang P'ing rode out to the front. The flaunting banners of his foes then opened out, and he saw their ranks. Many captains were on horseback. In the middle was the king, who advanced to the front. He wore a golden, inlaid headdress; his belt bore a lion's face as clasp; his boots had pointed toes and were green; he rode a frizzy-haired horse the color of a hare; he carried at his waist a pair of swords chased with the pine-tree device.

He looked haughtily at his foes, and then, turning to his captains, said, "It has always been said that Chuko Liang is a wonderful soldier, but I see that is false. Look at this array with its banners all in confusion and the ranks in disorder. There is not a weapon among all the swords and spears better than ours. If I had only realized this before I would have fought them long ago. Who dares go out and capture a Shu captain to show them what sort of warriors we are?"

At once a captain rode toward the leader, Wang P'ing. His name was Huanmangyachang; his weapon was a huge headsman's sword, and he rode a dun pony. Riding up to Wang P'ing, the two engaged.

Wang P'ing only fought a short time, and then fled. The king at once ordered his men in quick pursuit, and the men of Shu retreated a score or so of *li* before the *Mans* were near enough to fight. Just as the *Mans* thought their enemies were in their power, a great shouting arose and two cohorts appeared, one on either flank, and attacked. The *Mans* could not retreat, and as another force under Kuan So also turned upon them, the *Mans* were surrounded and lost the day. Menghuo and some of his captains fought their way out and made for the Chintai Mountains. The men of Shu followed and forced them forward, and presently there appeared, in front, Chao Yun. . . .

The king and his followers were taken to the main camp, where K'ung-ming was waiting with wine and meat ready for the captives. But his tent was now guarded by a seven-deep force of men all well armed with glittering weapons, beside the lictors bearing the golden axes, a present from the Emperor, and other insignia of rank. The feather-hatted drummers and clarion players were in front and behind, and the Imperial Guards were extended on both sides. The whole was very imposing and awe-inspiring.

K'ung-ming was seated at the top of it all and watched the captives as they came forward in crowds. When they were all assembled, he ordered their bonds to be loosed, and then he addressed them.

"You are all simple and well-disposed people who have been led into trouble by Menghuo. I know your fathers and mothers, your brothers and wives, and your children are anxiously watching from the doorways for your return, and they are cut to the quick now that the news of defeat and capture has reached their ears. They are weeping bitter tears for you. And so I will set you all free to go home and comfort them."

After they had been given food and wine and a present of grain, he sent them all away. They went off grateful for the kindness shown them, and they wept as they thanked K'ung-ming.

Then the guards were told to bring the King before the tent. He came, bound, being hustled forward. He knelt in front of the great leader, who said, "Why did you rebel after the generous treatment you have received from our Emperor?"

"The two Ch'uan [River Lands] belonged to others, and your lord took it from them by force, and gave himself the title of 'Emperor.' My people have lived here for ages, and you and your . . . [cohorts] invaded my country without the least excuse. How can you talk of rebellion to me?"

"You are my prisoner; will you submit or are you still contumacious?"

"Why should I submit? You happened to find me in a narrow place; that is all."

"If I release you, what then?"

"If you release me I shall return, and when I have set my army in order, I shall come to fight you again. However, if you catch me once more, I will submit."

The King's bonds were loosed; he was clothed and refreshed, given a horse and caparisons, and sent with a guide to his own camp.

After having scored several decisive victories over the *man* forces that involved the use of the mine-like explosive devices that burned alive a large army of the "barbarians," and having captured and released Meng Huo seven times, Zhuge Liang was in the end able to persuade the "*man* King" to submit himself voluntarily and full-heartedly to Shu:

"Seven times a captive and seven times released!" said the King. "Surely there was never anything like it in the whole world. I know I am a barbarian and beyond the pale, but I am not entirely devoid of a sense of propriety and rectitude. Does he think that I feel no shame?"

Thereupon he and all his [followers] fell upon their knees and crawled to the tent of the Commander-in-Chief and begged pardon, saying, "O Minister, you are the majesty of Heaven. We men of the south will offer no more opposition."

"Then you yield?" said K'ung-ming.

"I and my sons and grandsons are deeply affected by your all-pervading and life-giving mercy. Now how can we not yield?"

K'ung-ming asked Menghuo to come up into the tent and be seated, and he prepared a banquet of felicitation. Also he confirmed him [Menghuo] in his [kingship] ... and restored all the places that had been captured. Everyone was over-whelmed with K'ung-ming's generosity, and they all went away rejoicing.

Du Fu and the Confucian Abhorrence of the Horrors of War

War, especially against the borderland "barbarians," was acknowledged as a necessity in Confucian statecraft discourse; but, as is made clear by all the major Confucian thinkers beginning with Confucius and Mencius, excessive and unnecessary wars were to be avoided. The main reason for this was the burden that war-related conscriptions and requisitions imposed on the commoners, the paternalist "care" for whom was supposed to be the cornerstone of Confucian statecraft. The losses that were caused by these unneeded and excessive wars were believed to potentially harm the state as well – the peasant families in which breadwinners were consumed by the borderland wars were no longer in a position to pay the taxes that the government continuously demanded. A major task of a conscientious, Confucian intellectual was either to prevent such misuses of the military or at least to express protest once the misuse took place. One of the strongest possible ways of protesting was through literary means. It was believed that a literary text, especially poetry, possessed the needed persuasive strength to prevent similar, unwholesome developments in the future. One of the best known literary works expressing grief over the burdens of warfare is the *Ballad of the War Chariots* (*Bing Che Xing*, composed around 750) by Du Fu (712–770), a Tang Dynasty official and arguably one of the greatest poets China ever produced. Generally, Du Fu's works are known for their compassion toward the victims of socio-political injustice and misrule and for their penetrating sorrowfulness. The *Ballad of the War Chariots* may be read as "protest literature" of sorts, but the protest here is solidly grounded in foundational Confucian values.

From: Du Fu, *Ballad of the War Chariots* (ca. 750)[44]

The jingle of war chariots,
Horses neighing, men marching,
Bows and arrows slung over hips;
Beside them stumbling, running
The mass of parents, wives and children
Clogging up the road, their rising dust
Obscuring the great bridge at Hsienyang;
Stamping their feet, weeping
In utter desperation with cries
That seem to reach the clouds;

Ask a soldier: Why do you go?
Would simply bring the answer:
Today men are conscripted often;
Fifteen-year-olds sent up the Yellow River
To fight; men of forty marched away
To colonize the western frontier;
Village elders take young boys,
Do up their hair like adults
To get them off; if they return
It will be white with age, but even then
They may be sent off to the frontier again;

Frontiers on which enough blood has flowed
To make a sea, yet our Emperor still would
Expand his authority! Have you not heard
How east of Huashan many counties
Are desolate with weeds and thorns?
The strongest women till the fields,
Yet crops come not as well as before;

Lads from around here are well known
For their bravery, but hate to be driven
Like dogs or chickens; only because
You kindly ask me do I dare give vent
To grievances; now for instance
With the men from the western frontier
Still not returned, the government
Demands immediate payment of taxes,

But how can we pay when so little
Has been produced?

Now, we peasants have learned one thing:
To have a son is not so good as having
A daughter who can marry a neighbor
And still be near us, while a son
Will be taken away to die in some
Wild place, his bones joining those
That lie bleached white on the shores
Of Lake Kokonor, where voices of new spirits
Join with the old, heard sadly through
The murmur of falling rain.

General Yun Kwan and the "Pacification" of the Jurchen

The ideal of a "just war" in ancient or medieval Korea largely followed general Confucian guidelines. "Pacifications" of rebels or "barbarians" were usually thought to be "just" by default, but to cement the argument on the justice of a given campaign, a more detailed and nuanced argument might also be required. In the case of "anti-barbarian" expeditions, for example, it might be important to make clear that the territory currently held by the "barbarians" either formerly belonged to one of the (proto-)Korean states or found itself in a vassal or tributary relation with them. Then, it was essential to emphasize that the Korean Confucian state acted as an aggrieved party – that a "punitive expedition" was just a response to the "barbarian" incursions against Koreans. In this way, it might be thought as a continuation of domestic criminal justice by military means. It was also vital to assure that the victory was swift, that is, that the war in question was not disproportionally burdensome for the Korean population. All these elements were seen as present in the successful 1107 expedition against the Jurchen tribes (ancestors of the Manchus) that populated much of the borderland zone between what is now North Korea and China. The expedition, led by a noted aristocratic official Yun Kwan (d. 1111) took several months to accomplish and ended in a decisive victory for the presumably 300,000-strong army (the figure seems to be exaggerated) of the Korean Koryŏ Dynasty (918–1392). Around 6,000 "barbarians" were reported to have been killed and 50,000 were captured alive. Historically, the net result of the expedition was almost insignificant, since in a couple of years almost all the territory conquered by Yun Kwan had to be returned to the "barbarians" in return for a peace agreement; it was too burdensome to defend it. The account of the expedition below, written immediately after its completion by one of its participants, an aristocratic official named Im Ŏn, suggests, however, a triumph. The "barbarians," subjugation of whom was one of the important foreign political aims of Koryŏ, were at last shown their proper place in the universe dominated by the Confucian monarchies. An important point also made by Im Ŏn in the context of the Confucian logic of "just war" was that the 1107 expedition was an expression of the king's filial piety – King Yejong (r. 1105–1122) having continued the unfinished undertaking of his father, King Sukchong (r. 1095–1105), in the matter of "meting out the punishment to barbarians."

From: Im Ŏn, "Memorial on Victory at Yŏngju"
(From *Koryŏ sa* 96:19b–22a) (1107)[45]

The Jürchens are inferior to our country in strength and size, but in reconnoitring our frontier in King Sukchong's tenth year [1105] they took advantage of our unguarded moment and attacked us, killing people and enslaving many others. King Sukchong, in indignation, marshalled troops to punish them in the name of justice, but regrettably, the king died before he could launch the attack.

The present king, Yejong, mourned for three years, but on completing his funeral obligations he said to his officials, "The Jürchens, who were once under Koguryŏ[46] rule, lived in a community to the east of a spring on Mount Kaema. For many years, they brought tribute, and in return benefitted profoundly from our ancestors' blessings. Then suddenly and unjustifiably they betrayed us, causing the deep indignation of my deceased father. I have heard the ancient saying that one who is filial will continue his father's goals to their satisfactory completion. Fortunately I have now completed three years of mourning. If I am to conduct state affairs properly, how can I not raise the banner of righteousness, vanquish the immoral, and erase the shame of my father?"

Thereupon he appointed Custodial Grand Instructor and Executive of the Royal Secretariat Yun Kwan to be grand marshal of the expeditionary force and appointed Administrator of the Security Council, Hallim Academician, and Royal Transmitter O Yŏnch'ong to be deputy marshal. They led three hundred thousand elite troops, taking complete responsibility for the pacification.

Lord Yun was heroic in waging the campaign....

Lord O, a man greatly respected by his contemporaries, was naturally cautious. In handling affairs, he always considered each matter three times. Thus in carrying out his well-planned strategy, he never failed....

On entering enemy territory, the three [Koryŏ] armies became so greatly incited that one person became the equal of one hundred. They overcame their foes as easily as breaking down a rotten stump or wedging down bamboo. They beheaded more than six thousand. Laying down their bows and arrows, more than fifty thousand of the Jürchens surrendered at the front. One cannot estimate the number of the enemy who fled north in desperation, having lost their hope and fighting spirit. Alas, because of their stubbornness and foolishness, the Jürchens disregarded their strength and size and thus destroyed themselves in this manner.

Their territory covers three hundred *ri* square, reaching in the east to the Eastern Sea, in the northwest to Mount Kaema, and south to Changju and Chŏngju. But its mountains and rivers are beautiful and its land is fertile, so much so that our people could settle there. Since it was originally occupied by Koguryŏ, monuments and sites from that kingdom still remain. The territory that Koguryŏ had once lost is now recovered by the present king. How can this not be Heaven's will?

Confucian Officials in War Trouble: Yu Sŏngnyong's Memoirs on Japanese Invasion

Warfare in traditional Korea was not, however, restricted to the triumphal campaigns against "barbarians" of the kind described above. "Barbarians" – Mongols, Manchus, Japanese, and others – invaded Korea, too, and among all these invasions the Japanese incursion in 1592–1598 was especially painful. This invasion – known in Korea as the Imjin War (*imjin* is the cyclical name of the year 1592) – was led by Toyotomi Hideyoshi (1536–1598), the unifier of Japan, who wished to invade Korea and, subsequently, Ming Dynasty–ruled China in order to cement domestic political unity, give a meaningful job to the multitudes of samurais left redundant by the completion of the internecine warfare in Japan, and potentially extend the influence of unified Japan over the neighboring parts of the Asian continent. The approximately 200,000-strong Japanese army, equipped with Portuguese muskets, was eventually repelled by the combined Korean-Chinese forces, but the economic damage done to Korea was enormous. Full recovery arguably took a century. Ming China was also crucially weakened by the war-related overspending, and soon succumbed under the rebel assaults, eventually giving way to the reunification of China by the Manchu Qing Dynasty (1644–1911).

Enormous war-related damage was one topic, but perhaps even not the most important topic dealt with in the voluminous Korean literature on the Imjin War. Barbarity was, after all, more or less expected from "Japanese barbarians" who were traditionally seen in Confucian Korea as being significantly lower on the "civilization ladder" than the Chinese or Koreans themselves. What interested the Confucian literati who experienced the war – such as Yu Sŏngnyong (1542–1607), the Supreme Commander and Chief State Counselor during the war – was the behavior of officials and soldiers on their own side. Both the instances of praiseworthy behavior – magnanimity and inner calm in the face of danger, willingness to sacrifice one's personal interests and, ultimately, one's life, care about one's underlings, and so on – and the cases when the "virtue" of the Confucian officials did not measure up to the demands of a national emergency were to be recorded for posterity, as a lesson in both morality and statecraft. It is not accidental that Yu entitled his memoirs *The Book of Corrections* (*Chingbirok*), as the main task in his writing was to draw both ethical and institutional lessons from the war. The fragment below is a narrative on the calm, composed, and responsible behavior shown by one of Yu's close friends, the noted official and scholar Kim Sŏng'il (1538–1593), who was appointed in 1592 as a recruiting officer in the Kyŏngsang Province in the southeastern part of Korea. That region initially took the brunt of the Japanese offensive.

From: Yu Sŏngnyong, *The Book of Corrections: Reflections on the National Crisis during the Japanese Invasion of Korea, 1592–1598* (1604)[47]

The king ordered Kim Sŏng'il, provincial army commander of the right for Kyŏngsang province, to be arrested, but acquitted him before he was brought to Seoul for trial. Subsequently, he appointed Kim as recruiting officer, and appointed Yu Sung'in, district magistrate of Haman, as provincial army commander of

Kyŏngsang province. Prior to this event, when he arrived in Sangju, Kim Sŏng'il heard the news that the enemy had already crossed our border. He ran his horse day and night trying to get to the military headquarters; and on his way, he ran into Cho Taegon and exchanged official seals and warrants.

In the meantime, the enemy had already captured Kimhae and, dividing their army, had started plundering the villages in Right Kyŏngsang province. Kim launched out against the Japanese, but as his troops approached their enemy, his officers and soldiers became scared and tried to run away. Kim dismounted his horse and sat down on a chair, showing no signs of fear. He sent for Yi Chong'in and said to him, "Since you are a brave warrior, you should not run away from the enemy." At that moment, one of the enemy soldiers with an iron mask dashed forward to attack, wielding his sword. Yi Chong'in ran his horse to meet his opponent and killed him by shooting an arrow. Watching this man killed, the enemy did not dare advance further and ran away.

As Kim Sŏng'il was about to reassemble the scattered troops and devise strategies to stop the advancing enemy, sending out notices to all districts, the king remembered that Kim had made a false report on the possibility of the Japanese invasion after he had been to Japan as his ambassador.[48] The king believed that Kim should be held responsible for misleading the court and bringing about the current crisis. Therefore, he ordered the lieutenant (*tosa*) of the State Tribunal (Ŭigŭmbu) to arrest Kim and bring him to Seoul. It seemed that the situation was so serious for Kim that no one could tell what would happen to him.

Governor Kim Su of Kyŏngsang province went to see him off on the road when he heard of Kim's arrest. However, Kim Sŏng'il neither changed his expression nor said a word in relation to his personal affairs. Urging the governor to repulse the enemy, he seemed to be concerned only about the national crisis. Ha Chayong, and old *yamen*[49] attendant who happened to be standing by Kim, was deeply moved by Kim's attitude and remarked, "The man is truly a loyal subject. Showing no sign of sorrow over his impending death, he is only worried about his country."

When Kim Sŏng'il arrived in Chiksan, the wrath of the king relented. He came to know that Kim had won the hearts of the people in his region and sent down orders to pardon him. Furthermore, he appointed Kim recruiting officer (*ch'oyusa*) of Right Kyŏngsang province with the purpose of raising a civilian army to repulse the enemy. The king also appointed Yu Sung'in to provincial army commander, jumping over the regular order of promotion, as a reward to the outstanding contributions he had made during the battles.

Conclusion

Confucianism is no longer explicitly used as official ideology in East Asia, but the justifications used for the sake of legitimizing warfare in the region today are implicitly based on Confucian assumptions. Reference to *realpolitik* only is not enough to make a war licit; instead, the war has to be placed within the context of the world system interpreted in terms of "moral politics." For example, South Korea's participation in the U.S. invasion of Vietnam (in 1965–1973, more than 300,000 South Korean soldiers served in Vietnam) was justified in terms of "anti-communist solidarity" with and "gratitude" toward the United States for having "saved" South Korea from the North Korean assault during the Korean War (1950–1953). In reality, however, this participation resulted from the zeal of South Korean authorities to earn hard currency, modernize the military, and obtain some leverage over U.S. policies in the region; U.S. authorities, in turn, were motivated by a desire to reduce American casualties in a unpopular foreign war.[50] Communist leaders of modern East Asia such as Mao Zedong (1893–1976) operated on the surface with the Marxist-Leninist concepts of "unjust" (imperialist, colonialist) and "just" (liberational, people's) wars, but were also continuing the Confucian tradition of the moralization of politics defining the makers of "unjust" wars as first and foremost "immoral" (rather than historically "reactionary"). At the same time, in the spirit of the Confucian tradition, the populations ("peoples' masses") governed by the "immoral" rulers were given a choice of joining the camp of the "liberational" war – by solidarizing with the international Communist movement.[51] A moralistic approach to the soldierly virtues remained in force – it is perhaps telling that the most famous soldier in the history of the People's Republic of China is Lei Feng (1940–1962), who never fought on the battlefield but posthumously became a propaganda icon due to the alleged altruism shown in his daily life as well as his absolute devotion to the Communist Party and to Mao's personality as expressed in his diary.[52] Emphasis on "loyalty" and high ethics as the main qualities of a good soldier (or officer) seems to be especially strong in North Korea (Democratic People's Republic of Korea), where the Confucian background of the official ideology is perhaps more evident than in China or South Korea.[53] However, the implicit Confucian assumptions for the discourse on war and war-related behavior are common for China and South Korea as well.

NOTES

1 Corvée is unpaid labor usually imposed by the state on the nonprivileged members of the society. It was known in many ancient and medieval societies (Egypt, Roman Empire, France before the Revolution, etc.) and was practiced by the Chinese states from the mid-second millennium BCE and until the end of the traditional dynastic statehood (Xinhai Revolution of 1911–1912). Typically, during the Tang Dynasty (618–907), peasants were conscripted for obligatory labor for twenty days annually. Conscription for military service was understood as a part of commoners' corvée obligations in the broad meaning of the term.

2 Hereafter, *pinyin* is used as the standard Romanization system for Chinese terms, and the McCune-Reischauer system is used for Korean. However, some of the works used or cited in this chapter use either the Wade-Giles system (which was in wide use before the International Organization for Standardization adapted *pinyin* as the international standard in 1982) or other systems for Chinese Romanization. For example, translations by James Legge (whose translation of *The Book of History* is cited below) use an original system that is basically similar to Wade-Giles but exhibits some minor differences.

3 See, e.g., the emphasis on the tragic, catastrophic nature of war in ancient Chinese military classics: Ralph Sawyer and Mei-Chūn Sawyer, *The Seven Military Classics of Ancient China* (Boulder, Colo.: Westview Press, 1993), pp. 55–56, 256–259.

4 Mark Lewis, "The Just War in Early China," in Torkel Brekke (ed.), *The Ethics of War in Asian Civilizations: A Comparative Perspective* (New York: Routledge, 2006), pp. 185–201.

5 Ssuma Chien, William Nienhauser (trans. and ed.), *The Grand Scribe's Records* (Bloomington: Indiana University Press, 1994), vol. 5, pp. 119–121; Ralph Sawyer, "Chinese Strategic Power: Myths, Intent and Projections," *Journal of Military and Strategic Studies* 8:4 (2006), 1–64; Marvin Whiting, *Imperial Chinese Military History: 8000 BC–1912 AD* (San Jose, Calif.: Writers' Club Press, 2002), pp. 85–86.

6 Chris Fraser, "The Mohist School," in Bo Mou (ed.), *Routledge History of World Philosophies: History of Chinese Philosophy* (New York: Routledge, 2009), pp. 137–164.

7 Robert Ginsberg, "Confucius on Ritual, Moral Power, and War," *Peace and Change* 3:1 (1975), 17–21.

8 Bai Tongdong, "How to Rule without Taking Unnatural Actions: A Comparative Study of the Political Philosophy of Lao Zi," *Philosophy East and West* 59:4 (2009), 481–502

9 Don Handelman, "Cultural Taxonomy and Bureaucracy in Ancient China: the Book of Lord Shang," *International Journal of Politics, Culture and Society* 9:2 (1995), 263–293.

10 Krysztof Gawlikowsky, "The School of Strategy (Bing jia) in the Context of Chinese Civilization," *East and West* 35:1–3 (1985), 167–210.

11 Sawyer and Sawyer, *The Seven Military Classics of Ancient China*, p. 87.

12 Mark Lewis, *Sanctioned Violence in Early China* (Albany: State University of New York Press, 1990), pp. 107–108.

13 Frederick Starr, *Xinjiang, China's Muslim Borderland* (New York: M. E. Sharpe, 2004), pp. 61–62.

14 On the institutional history of the military in Chosŏn Korea, see James Palais, *Confucian Statecraft and Korean Institutions: Yu Hyŏngwŏn and Late Chosŏn Dynasty* (Seattle: University of Washington Press, 1996), pp. 92–115, 391–579.

15 *The Chinese Classics*, J. Legge (trans.) (Hong Kong: University of Hong Kong Press, 1960 [1893–1895]), vol. 3, pp. 306–316. Definitions added by the author of the chapter. The original source is *The Book of History* (*Shujing*), China's most ancient collection of historical documents. It is widely assumed that the original, basic text of this collection was already known in the fourth to third centuries BCE. The text most widely used now – and translated by James Legge – is, however, thought to be compiled, very possibly on the basis of older originals and prototypes, in the early fourth century CE, when it was presented by a certain scholar, called Mei Ze, to the Jin Dynasty (265–420) court, as purportedly the "most authentic" text of *The Book of History*.

16 The twenty-ninth year in the Chinese lunar sexagenary cycle. The same cycle was used for the calculation of days as well.

17 A mountain located in what is Shaanxi Province in modern China, traditionally considered sacred.

18 "Peach Forest," presumably in the northwest of modern Hunan Province, China.

19 The forty-fourth year (or day) in the sexegenary cycle.

20 The space "under the heaven" was, in theory, divided into five domains in ancient China. The central, imperial, domain, was to be directly ruled by the "son of Heaven." Such peripheral domains as that of Hou ("marquis" is often used to translate this feudal rank in ancient China) or Wei were to be ruled by the feudal lords.

21 One of the semi-legendary ancestors of the Zhou royal house.

22 Another royal ancestor, King Wu's putative grand-grandfather.

23 King Wu's assumed grandfather.

24 The fifty-fifth year (or day) in the sexagenary cycle.

25 The sixtieth (last) year (or day) in the sexagenary cycle.

26 The first year (or day) in the sexagenary cycle.

27 A Shang noble supposedly imprisoned for his principled opposition to King Zhou's misrule.

28 An uncle of tyrant Zhou, who was remembered as a loyal and wise minister, undeservedly put to death by his tyrannical lord.

29 Another loyal retainer of Shang's downfall period, who was known to have committed suicide since the tyrant Zhou did not listen to his advice.

30 A gallery supposedly built by tyrant Zhou for his mistress, with ample use of precious stones.

31 "Giant Bridge," the grain storage of tyrant Zhou.

32 *The Book of Lord Shang*, J. J. L. Duyvendak (trans.) (London: Arthur Probsthain, 1963), pp. 185–187.

33 "Mo Tsu: Against Offensive Warfare," in *Basic Writings of Mo Tzu, Hsün Tzu, and Han Fei Tzu*, B. Watson (trans.) (New York: Columbia University Press, 1967), pp. 50–61.

34 "Book 7, Part 2," in *The Works of Mencius*, J. Legge (trans.) (Oxford: Clarendon Press, 1895), pp. 477–478.

35 Hsün Tsu, "Debating Military Affairs," in *Basic Writings of Mo Tzu, Hsün Tzu, and Han Fei Tzu*, pp. 56–69.

36 Sima Qian, *Records of the Grand Historian: Han Dynasty II*, B. Watson (trans.) (New York: Renditions – Columbia University Press, 1993), pp. 117–129.

37 The citation is from *Analects* (*Lunyu*), ascribed to Confucius and his disciples, and known as the key text of the Confucian canon (Xiii, 6).

38 Li Qi, "The Account of Cai Xi," in *Hawaii Reader in Traditional Chinese Culture*, Michael Drompp (trans.), V. H. Mair et al. (eds.) (Honolulu: University of Hawaii Press, 2005), pp. 370–373.

39 The vicinities of Hohhot in today's Chinese province of Inner Mongolia.

40 Present-day Yuncheng in Shanxi Province, China.

41 Xiongnu, the old "barbarian" enemies of the Han Empire, are used here as a literary metaphor for the Uighurs.

42 The title of the Xiongnu supreme ruler (which was never used by Uighurs but is used here as a metaphoric name for a "barbarian" ruler).

43 Lo Kuan-chung, *Romance of the Three Kingdoms*, C. H. Brewitt-Taylor (trans.) (Boston: Tuttle, 2002), vol. 2, pp. 299–309, 346.

44 "Ballad of the War Chariots," in Du Fu, *Selected Poems*, R. Alley (trans.) (Hong Kong: Commercial Press, 1977), pp. 12–13.

45 Im Ŏn, "Memorial on Victory at Yŏngju" (From *Koryŏ sa* 96:19b–22a), H. H. W. Kang and E. J. Shultz (trans.), in *Sourcebook of Korean Civilization*, P. H. Lee (ed.), vol. 1 (New York: Columbia University Press, 2003), pp. 301–302.

46 A (proto-)Korean state that existed from ca. first century until 668, occupying the northern part of the Korean peninsula and a part of the Jilin, Liaoning, and Heilongjiang Provinces in today's Northeast China. It was destroyed by a coordinated attack of the Chinese Tang forces and another (proto-)Korean state, Silla (based on the southern part of the Korean peninsula).

47 Yu Sŏngnyong, *The Book of Corrections: Reflections on the National Crisis during the Japanese Invasion of Korea, 1592–1598*, Choi Byonghyon (trans.) (Berkeley: University of California Press, 2002), pp. 55–56.

48 It happened in 1590, and Kim Sŏng'il's position on the low likelihood of a Japanese invasion was undoubtedly influenced by the general line of the court fraction he belonged to – the Easterners – who opposed what they perceived as overspending on defense. The episode is also

narrated in Yu's memoirs: *The Book of Corrections: Reflections on the National Crisis during the Japanese Invasion of Korea, 1592–1598*, pp. 28–30.

49 Kor. *amun*, local government's office.

50 Frank Baldwin, "America's Rented Troops: South Koreans in Vietnam," *Bulletin of the Concerned Asian Scholars* 7:2 (1975), 33–40.

51 See, e.g., Mao's pronouncement (14 September 1939) on the "character" of the Second World War: "The Second Imperialist War"; available at http://www.marxists.org/reference/archive/mao/selected-works/volume-6/mswv6_33.htm.

52 See his famed diary: Lei Feng, *Lei Feng riji* (Diary of Lei Feng) (Hong Kong: Zhaoyang Press, 1969). See excerpts from a Chinese hagiographical account of Lei's life in Patricia Ebrey (ed.), *Chinese Civilization: A Sourcebook* (New York: Free Press, 1993), pp. 442–446.

53 On the importance of "loyalty" in the North Korean hagiography of war heroes, see O Sŏngho and Sin Hyŏnggi, *Pukhan Munhaksa* (History of North Korean Literature) (Seoul: P'yŏngminsa, 2000), pp. 149–153.

SELECT BIBLIOGRAPHY

Bai, Tongdong, "How to Rule without Taking Unnatural Actions: A Comparative Study of the Political Philosophy of Lao Zi," *Philosophy East and West* 59:4 (2009), 481–502.

Baldwin, Frank "America's Rented Troops: South Koreans in Vietnam," *Bulletin of the Concerned Asian Scholars* 7:2 (1975), 33–40.

Ebrey, Patricia (ed.), *Chinese Civilization: A Sourcebook* (New York: Free Press, 1993).

Feng, Lei, *Lei Feng riji* (Diary of Lei Feng) (Hong Kong: Zhaoyang Press, 1969).

Fraser, Chris, "The Mohist School," in Bo Mou (ed.), *Routledge History of World Philosophies. History of Chinese Philosophy* (New York: Routledge, 2009), pp. 137–164.

Gawlikowsky, Krysztof, "The School of Strategy (Bing jia) in the Context of Chinese Civilization," *East and West* 35:1–3 (1985), 167–210.

Ginsberg, Robert, "Confucius on Ritual, Moral Power, and War," *Peace and Change* 3:1 (1975), 17–21.

Handelman, Don, "Cultural Taxonomy and Bureaucracy in Ancient China: the Book of Lord Shang," *International Journal of Politics, Culture and Society* 9:2 (1995), 263–293.

Lewis, Mark, *Sanctioned Violence in Early China* (Albany: State University of New York Press, 1990).

Lewis, Mark, "The Just War in Early China," in Torkel Brekke (ed.), *The Ethics of War in Asian Civilizations: A Comparative Perspective* (New York: Routledge, 2006), pp. 185–201.

Lo, Ping-cheung, "Warfare Ethics in Sunzi's *Art of War*? Historical Controversies and Contemporary Perspectives," *Journal of Military Ethics* 11:2 (2012), 114–135.

Palais, James, *Confucian Statecraft and Korean Institutions: Yu Hyŏngwŏn and Late Chosŏn Dynasty* (Seattle: University of Washington Press, 1996).

Sawyer, Ralph, "Chinese Strategic Power: Myths, Intent and Projections," *Journal of Military and Strategic Studies* 8:4 (2006), 1–64.

Sawyer, Ralph, and Sawyer, Mei-Chün, *The Seven Military Classics of Ancient China* (Boulder, Colo.: Westview Press, 1993).

Sin Hyŏnggi, O Sŏngho, *Pukhan Munhaksa* (History of North Korean Literature) (Seoul: P'yŏngminsa, 2000).

Ssuma Chien, and William Nienhauser (trans. and ed.), *The Grand Scribe's Records* (Bloomington: Indiana University Press, 1994), vols. 1–9.

Starr, Frederick, *Xinjiang, China's Muslim Borderland* (New York: M. E. Sharpe, 2004).

Tikhonov, Vladimir, and Torkel Brekke (eds.), *Buddhism and Violence: Militarism and Buddhism in Modern Asia* (New York: Routledge, 2013).

Whiting, Marvin, *Imperial Chinese Military History: 8000 BC–1912 AD* (San Jose, Calif.: Writers' Club Press, 2002).

Zedong, Mao, "The Second Imperialist War" (14 September 1939); available at http://www.marxists.org/reference/archive/mao/selected-works/volume-6/mswv6_33.htm.

10

The Religious Traditions of Japan

Soho Machida

Religion in Japan has arisen from an amalgamation of different traditions, the most important of which are arguably Shinto, Buddhism, and various forms of folk belief. Even though the majority of contemporary Japanese do not necessarily show a keen interest in religion, it remains true that these religious traditions have formed the core of Japanese culture over the centuries. Today, religion still substantially affects daily life through rituals and festivals and by informing the thought and fundamental values of the Japanese people.

Introduction: Peaceful versus Militant Buddhism

Within Buddhism many forms and traditions of subtle variations all coexist simultaneously, and Buddhism in Japan is no exception. Buddhism was formally introduced into Japan in the sixth century. Its endorsement by the aristocracy contributed to its eventual acceptance throughout Japan. The reception of Buddhism among the Japanese people is partially due to the ease of integrating Buddhism with the preexisting culture shaped by the indigenous religion of Shinto.[1]

Rather than strictly observing a single belief, the Japanese reconciled the differences between the two, forming an amalgamation of beliefs and traditions. The two never perfectly coalesced and thus produced an unsystematized and complicated relationship. The phenomenon of reconciliation between the two religions and their inextricable relationship provides perspective into the manner in which Buddhism would interact throughout several aspects of Japanese society and culture historically, not just with respect to Shinto. The beliefs and practices of Buddhism would evolve within Japan to become permanently linked to several unique facets of Japanese culture but without ever having permeated deeply enough to penetrate beyond the established culture.

Buddhism is, at its root, a religion of peace. War lies so far from the fundamentals of Japanese Buddhism that there is an implicit understanding that there are no moral justifications for armed conflict or for any violence at all. Basic Buddhist understanding is that suffering, often in the forms of jealousy, greed, and hatred, is caused by the egoistic desire for power and pleasure. Thus, Buddhists put special emphasis on the minimization of suffering by advocating benevolence, philanthropy, and the cessation of hatred. What results is a fundamentally pacifistic religion. How Japanese Buddhism could nonetheless at some critical junctures in the nation's history give support to the invasion of neighboring countries and the commission of wartime atrocities is explored below.

From: *The Dhammapada*, Chapter 8, "Better Than a Thousand"[2]

Better than a thousand useless words is one single word that gives peace.

Better than a thousand useless verses is one single verse that gives peace.

Better than a hundred useless poems is one single poem that gives peace.

The *Dhammapada* is an anthology of aphorisms traditionally credited to the Buddha.[3] One of the most popular scriptures of Buddhism, many of its teachings revolve around the development of self-control and a peaceful frame of mind. Agitation, resentment, jealousy, and distrust are obstructions in the path to enlightenment, and Buddhism teaches that situations in which these sentiments arise are best avoided through verbal control.

From: *The Dhammapada*, Chapter 17, "Forsake Anger"[4]

Forsake anger, give up pride. Sorrow cannot touch the man who is not in the bondage of anything, who owns nothing.

He who can control his rising anger as a coachman controls his carriage at full speed, this man I call a good driver: others merely hold the reins.

Overcome anger by peacefulness; overcome evil by good. Overcome the mean by generosity; and the man who lies by truth.

Speak the truth, yield not to anger, give what you can to him who asks: these three steps lead you to the gods.

The wise who hurt no living being, and who keep their body under self-control, they go to the immortal *nirvana*, where once gone they sorrow no more.

As a way of achieving this level of control, a strong emphasis is placed on developing the ability of objective self-reflection. While monotheistic religions often implement their doctrines through religious leaders who act as agents of the word of God, Buddhism, in principle, encourages the practice of its doctrines through self-discipline. Buddhist philosophy begins with the individual.

From: *The Dhammapada*, Chapter 8, "Better Than a Thousand"[5]

If a man should conquer in battle a thousand and a thousand more, and another man should conquer himself, his would be the greater victory, because the greatest of victories is the victory over oneself; and neither the gods in heaven above nor the demons down below can turn into defeat the victory of such a man.

If month after month with a thousand offerings for a hundred years one should sacrifice; and another only for a moment paid reverence to a self-conquering man, this moment would have greater value than a hundred years of offerings.

If a man for a hundred years should worship the sacred fire in the forest; and if another only for a moment paid reverence to a self-conquering man, this reverence alone would be greater than a hundred years of worship.

Whatever a man for a year may offer in worship or in gifts to earn merit is not worth a fraction of the merit earned by one's reverence to a righteous man.

To conquer oneself is to attain full comprehension of one's own tendencies and to enrich those who bring peace and quell those who do not. Cessation of hatred and the consequent spirit of forgiveness lie at the root of this objective.

From: *The Dhammapada*, Chapter 1, "Contrary Ways"[6]

1. What we are today comes from our thoughts of yesterday, and our present thoughts build our life of tomorrow: our life is the creation of our mind.

If a man speaks or acts with an impure mind, suffering follows him as the wheel of the cart follows the beast that draws the cart. . . .

3. "He insulted me, he hurt me, he defeated me, he robbed me." Those who think such thoughts will not be free from hate. . . .

5. For hate is not conquered by hate: hate is conquered by love. This is a law eternal.

6. Many do not know that we are here in this world to live in harmony. Those who know this do not fight against each other.

A harmonious communal relationship is the ideal result of Buddhist practice, and this is understood to be achieved through the reciprocation of individual inner peace. Thus, each individual is encouraged to discover that peace on his or her own, without letting him- or herself be compelled or influenced by the forces of society.

From: *Mahāparinibbāna Sutta* (ca. fourth century AD)[7]

So, Ānanda, you must be your own lamps, be your own refuges. Take refuge in nothing outside yourselves. Hold firm to the truth as a lamp and a refuge, and do not look for refuge to anything besides yourselves. A monk becomes his own lamp and refuge by continually looking on his body, feelings, perceptions, moods, and ideas in such a manner that he conquers the cravings and depressions of ordinary men and is always strenuous, self-possessed, and collected in mind. Whoever among my monks does this, either now or when I am dead, if he is anxious to learn, will reach the summit.

The upholding of collective harmony and attainment of inner peace through self-reliance: these are the characteristic practices of Buddhism. Apart from their denunciation, destructive forces such as violence and war are given no mention in the pacifistic teachings of Buddhism.

Indeed, its emergence in Japan did instill a deep appreciation for benevolence and tolerance among the Japanese. This was attributable in part to the legendary prince regent Shōtoku Taishi (572–622 CE), considered one of the greatest patrons of Buddhism in Japanese history.

From: Shōtoku Taishi, *The Seventeen-Article Constitution* (ca. 604)[8]

Forget resentment, forsake anger, do not become angry just because someone opposes you. Everyone has a mind, every mind comes to a decision, and decisions will not always be alike. If he is right, you are wrong; if you are not quite a saint, he is not quite an idiot. Both disputants are men of ordinary mind; who is decisively capable of judging an argument between them? If both are wise men or both foolish men their argument is probably a vicious circle. For this reason, if your opponent grows angry, you had better be all the more cautious lest you too should be in error. Although you might think you are quite right, it is wiser to comply with the other man.

Yet history paints an unfortunate truth that contradicts the Buddhist influence on the Japanese people. Not only did wars become frequent, but also they became increasingly violent over the course of history, reaching a gruesome apex in World War II.

Beginning in China in the Second Sino-Japanese War and then throughout Southeast Asia and the islands of the Pacific, the Japanese military killed hundreds of thousands of people as a way of displaying its military dominance. A particularly notorious example of their brutality was the Nanking Massacre of 1937. In *The Rape of Nanking* (1997), Iris Chang provides a disturbingly pictorial description of the atrocities that were claimed to have occurred in the massacre. Sadly, this sort of brutality was not unique to Nanking, as similar war crimes are believed to have occurred throughout the greater Pacific War, as explained by Edwin P. Hoyt in *Japan's War: The Great Pacific Conflict 1853–1952* (1987). Intolerance of foreigners in Japan, which had been brewing since the 1860s when the country emerged from isolation, grew during the early 1900s more rapidly than ever before, sparked by its conflicts with China (the First Sino-Japanese War) and Russia (the Russo-Japanese War), as well as World War I.

At some point over the course of four major wars and millions of casualties, one would expect there to be strong outcries from the Buddhist communities of Japan and that at some level the sheer prevalence and popularity of Buddhism as a peaceful religion would inhibit public inclination toward war and intolerance. However, as a religion originally foreign to Japan, the nonviolent tenets in Buddhism never overcame the nationalistic pride nurtured by the indigenous religion of Shinto but only helped to pacify the Buddhist communities of Japan into supporting the war. Standing alongside the state as fervent advocates of war, Buddhism was wholly transformed from a pacific into a militant religion. Defenseless against government repression, Buddhist leaders agreed to support the war so as not to incur a reaction that would threaten their way of life. Thus, under the Meiji regime, certain Buddhist sects chose to position themselves closer to the government in the case that the government might once again decide to uproot Buddhism in Japan. Particularly in the years leading up to and during World War II, leaders from various Buddhist sects not only approved but also outwardly came forward to encourage Japanese support for military expansion, while being well aware of the casualties that would result.

An example is seen in the following excerpt from *Bukkyō no Sensō Kan* (The Buddhist View of War, 1937), a book written by Zen[9] scholars Hayashiya Tomojiro (1886–1953

CE) and Shimakage Chikai (1902–1983 CE). The work attempts to tie together Buddhist doctrines and the militaristic interests of the state by masking and reinterpreting the fundamental contradiction between the two, thereby maintaining the validity of a war for the greater good. Such works also exemplify the intent of Buddhist scholars who sought to gain prestige and recognition for supporting war and its cause in order to avoid being targeted by the government.

From: Shimakage Chikai and Hayashiya Tomojiro, *The Buddhist View of War*[10]

In order to establish eternal peace in East Asia, arousing the great benevolence and compassion of Buddhism, we are sometimes accepting and sometimes forceful. We now have no choice but to exercise the benevolent forcefulness of "killing one in order that many may live" (*issatsu tashō*). This is something which Mahayana Buddhism approves of only with the greatest of seriousness....

The reason that Buddhism hasn't determined war to be either good or bad is that it doesn't look at the question of war itself but rather to the question of the war's purpose. Thus, if the war has a good purpose it is good, while if it has a bad purpose it is bad. Buddhism doesn't merely approve of wars that are in accord with its values; it vigorously supports such wars to the point of being a war enthusiast.

The Buddhist understanding of war as advocated by its leaders in the 1930s held that in conquering foreign soil Japan would ultimately bring about peace and stability for those countries. In this way, military expansion was deemed an act of benevolent patronage as opposed to self-interested invasion. The decision to support war, however, was never approved by Buddhist communities in order to promote religious conversion. Buddhism had already obtained a ubiquitous presence throughout Asia and furthermore no such interest existed in Buddhist ideology.

Examining the historical role of Buddhism in Japan, however, shows several dynamic factors that contributed to the relative ease with which the religion was used to convince – and arguably was manipulated into convincing – the nation to support militaristic doctrines that were entirely opposed to that of the original teachings of Buddhism.

The Doctrine of Nonduality

Historically, Buddhist teachings never appear to have been fully understood or, perhaps more accurately, never pensively considered by the Japanese public because of the ambiguous nature of the Buddhist religion itself. This apathy alone is a partial explanation as to why a peaceful, Buddhist sensibility never seemed to have prevailed among the Japanese during their militant era.

Like many of its Eastern counterparts, Buddhism differs greatly from the religions of the West in its absence of a single God of judgment and the lack of strict moral codes by which one is told to live. Instead, the focus lies in the attainment of a self-awakening that allows one's escape from the continuous cycle of suffering of which all living beings are believed to be a part. This cycle is known in Buddhism as *samsara*. The cessation from *samsara*, however, is an experience that transcends everyday consciousness and cannot find in language a sufficient means of expression.

The self-awakening that leads to this linguistically intangible state is commonly referred to as *nirvana*. In *nirvana* one is freed from desire and aversion, and thereby from suffering altogether. While most must endure countless cycles of death and rebirth in *samsara*, one who has achieved *nirvana* is liberated from that cycle and is never reborn again. On death, such a person leaves the *samsaric* experience, not to a place such as heaven, but to a state of being that transcends all worldly concepts, including that of existence and nonexistence. This state is fully grasped only by those who have experienced *nirvana*. An example of such a person is Takuan Sōhō (1573–1646), a highly revered monk of the Rinzai Zen sect who describes this state in his widely popular treatise, *The Unfettered Mind*.

From: Takuan Sōhō, *The Unfettered Mind* (1632)[11]

Long ago, the World Honored One went into the Snowy Mountains, and after passing six years in suffering, became enlightened. This was the enlightenment of the True Self. The ordinary man has no strength of faith, and does not know the persistence of even three or five years. But those who study the Way are absolutely diligent for ten to twenty years, twenty-four hours a day. They muster up great strength of faith, speak with those who have wisdom, and disregard adversity and suffering. Like a parent who has lost a child, they do not retreat a scintilla from their established resolution. They think deeply, adding inquiry to inquiry. In the end, they arrive at the place where even Buddhist doctrine and the Buddhist Law melt away, and are naturally able to see "This."

Penetrating to a place where heaven and earth have not yet divided, where Ying and Yang have not yet arrived, I quickly and necessarily gain effect means to set one's eye on the place that existed before heaven became heaven and earth became earth, before Ying and Yang came into being. It is to use neither thought nor reasoning and to look straight ahead. In this way, the time of gaining great effect will surely arrive.

The "This" of which Takuan speaks is also referred to in Buddhism as "oneness." It in fact has many labels because of the inadequacy of language in giving it an appropriate name. A parallel can be drawn with the concept of the "way," "one," or "*Tao*," the central teaching of Taoism. Though Taoism was never formally introduced as an independent religion in Japan, for centuries it was in very close connection with Buddhism in China. Originally imported from China, Japanese Buddhism has retained the concept of *Tao* and related notions. Much like oneness, the *Tao* can be given no true name.

From: Lao Tzu, *Tao Te Ching* (ca. eighth century BC)[12]

The way that can be spoken of
Is not the constant way;

The name that can be named
Is not the constant name.
The nameless was the beginning of heaven and earth;
The named was the mother of the myriad creatures.
Hence always rid yourself of desires in order to observe its secrets;
But always allow yourself to have desires in order to observe its manifestations.
These two are the same
But diverge in name as they issue forth.
Being the same they are called mysteries,
Mystery upon mystery –
The gateway of the manifold secrets.

The influence of Taoism on Buddhism cannot be overstated. Just as in Buddhist *oneness* and *samsaric* escape, the essence of *Tao* transcends worldly concepts: it is of something before heaven and earth, life and death, existence and nonexistence.

From: Lao Tzu, *Tao Te Ching*[13]

There is a thing confusedly formed,
Born before heaven and earth.
Silent and void
It stands alone and does not change,
Goes round and does not weary.
It is capable of being the mother of the world.
I know not its name
So I style it "the way."
I give it the makeshift name of "the great."
Being great, it is further described as receding,
Receding, it is described as far away,
Being far away, it is described as turning back.
Hence the way is great; heaven is great; earth is great; and the king is also great.
Within the realm there are four things that are great, and the king counts as one.
Man models himself on earth,
Earth on heaven,
Heaven on the way,
And the way on that which is naturally so.

As exemplified by both the Buddhist and Taoist explanations of their respective teachings on oneness and *Tao*, the essence of Buddhism is extraordinarily difficult to envision from an intellectual standpoint. For this reason the common people of Japan have not achieved a holistic understanding of the most vital teachings of Buddhism. Only its tangible aspects – festivals, funerals, and related rituals – are practices that people have "religiously" followed. In response to this inexplicability, Japanese Buddhism in each of its sects has had to provide signs and signals to direct its followers down a path, while leaving its destination undefined and shrouded in an appealing mysticism.

A particular concept on which Japanese Buddhists focused in presenting the religion was that of nonduality. A fundamental Buddhist understanding is that the apparent predisposition of human nature to compare and to define things as opposites is only a perception, and by ceasing this dualistic way of thinking, one becomes closer to achieving *samsaric* escape. Indeed, the causes of suffering – desire and aversion – are simply another form of dualism that one must eradicate in order to attain enlightenment.

The dualities of human perception are well described in the historically popular *Holy Teaching of Vimalakīrti* (ca. second century AD), a Mahayana[14] scripture that outlines how the understanding of nondualism enables the entrance into enlightenment. The text has been widely translated, studied, and taught by Japanese Buddhists through the ages. "Vimalakīrti" of the title refers to a man (and *bodhisattva*[15]) who is believed to have lived around the time of the Buddha (Siddharta Gautama, sixth to fifth century BCE). The "Dharma-Door of Nonduality" chapter lists dualistic ways of thought that Vimalakīrti himself had to overcome in order to enter into nonduality.

From: *The Holy Teaching of Vimalakīrti*, Chapter 9, "The Dharma-Door of Nonduality"[16]

Then, the Licchavi Vimalakīrti asked those bodhisattvas, "Good sirs, please explain how the bodhisattvas enter the Dharma-door of nonduality!"

The bodhisattva Dharmavikurvaṇa declared, "Noble sir, production and destruction are two, but what is not produced and does not occur cannot be destroyed. Thus the attainment of the tolerance of the birthlessness of things is the entrance into nonduality."

The bodhisattva Śrīgandha declared, "'I' and 'mine' are two. If there is no presumption of a self, there will be no possessiveness. Thus, the absence of presumption is the entrance into nonduality."

The bodhisattva Śrīkūṭa declared, "'Defilement' and 'purification' are two. When there is thorough knowledge of defilement, there will be no conceit about purification. The path leading to the complete conquest of all conceit is the entrance into nonduality."

The bodhisattva Bhadrajyotis declared, "'Distraction' and 'attention' are two. When there is no distraction, there will be no attention, no mentation, and no mental intensity. Thus, the absence of mental intensity is the entrance into nonduality."

The bodhisattva Subāhu declared, "'Bodhisattva-spirit' and 'disciple-spirit' are two. When both are seen to resemble an illusory spirit, there is no bodhisattva-spirit, nor any disciple-spirit. Thus, the sameness of natures of spirits is the entrance into nonduality."

The bodhisattva Animiṣa declared, "'Grasping' and 'nongrasping' are two. What is not grasped is not perceived, and what is not perceived is neither presumed nor repudiated. Thus, the inaction and noninvolvement of all things is the entrance into nonduality."

The bodhisattva Sunetra declared, "'Uniqueness' and 'characterlessness'" are two. Not to presume or construct something is neither to establish its uniqueness nor to establish its characterlessness. To penetrate the equality of these two is to enter nonduality.

The bodhisattva Tiṣya declared, "'Good' and 'evil' are two. Seeking neither good nor evil, the understanding of the nonduality of the significant and the meaningless is the entrance into nonduality."

The bodhisattva Siṃha declared, "'Sinfulness' and 'sinlessness' are two. By means of the diamond-like wisdom that pierces to the quick, not to be bound or liberated is the entrance into nonduality.". . .

The bodhisattva Dāntamati declared, "'Life' and 'liberation' are dualistic. Having seen the nature of life, one neither belongs to it nor is one utterly liberated from it. Such understanding is the entrance into nonduality.". . .

The bodhisattva Parigūḍha declared, "'Self' and 'selflessness' are dualistic. Since the existence of self cannot be perceived, what is there to be made 'selfless'? Thus, the nondualism of the vision of their nature is the entrance into nonduality.". . .

The bodhisattva Puṇyakṣetra declared, "It is dualistic to consider actions meritorious, sinful, or neutral. The non-undertaking of meritorious, sinful, and neutral actions is not dualistic. The intrinsic nature of all such actions is voidness, wherein ultimately there is neither merit, nor sin, nor neutrality, nor action itself. The non-accomplishment of such actions is the entrance into nonduality.". . .

The bodhisattva Maṇikūṭarāja declared, "It is dualistic to speak of good paths and bad paths. One who is on the path is not concerned with good or bad paths. Living in such unconcern, he entertains no concepts of 'path' or 'nonpath.' Understanding the nature of concepts, his mind does not engage in duality. Such is the entrance into nonduality."

These examples of nonduality are constituents of the broader, intangible concept of oneness, but as individual ideas that use familiar terms they are more easily grasped than if we take them together as a whole. Of those, "self" and "nonself" and "life" and "death" are especially scrutinized in Japanese Buddhism. This is apparent in all the popular Buddhist sects of Japan, including the Tendai, Shingon, and Nichiren sects. It was, however, the introduction of two new sects, Pure Land and Zen, that had a particularly significant influence on Japanese social philosophy by presenting the doctrine of nonduality in a way that could more easily be accepted and applied by ordinary people in Japan.

Pure Land Buddhism was fundamentally different from other Buddhist teachings during the time of its rise in the tenth and eleventh centuries. Pure Land, or *Jodo*, teachings insist on absolute devotional worship of the Amida, a Buddha of a bygone era who had promised that all who call on his name shall be granted admission to a place of rebirth known as the "Pure Land." Thus, *Jodo* followers practice *nembutsu*, the repetitive incantation of Amida's name, *Namu Amida Butsu*. The spread of this practice is largely attributed to the pioneering efforts of Hōnen (1132–1212 CE), a monk originally of the Tendai sect who believed that the attainment of enlightenment was too challenging for most people and that they were better off devoting themselves to the grace of the Amida. Hōnen summarized his teachings in *The One Page Testament*. The "Original Prayer" refers to Amida's vow that all shall be accepted to the Pure Land granted they call on his name.

From: Hōnen, *The One Page Testament*[17]

By Nembutsu* I do not mean such practice of meditation on the Buddha as is referred to by the wise men of China and Japan, nor is it the recitation of the Buddha's Name which is practiced as the result of study and understanding as to the meaning of Nembutsu. It is just to recite the Name of Amida, without doubting that this will issue in the rebirth of the believer in the Pure Land. Just this, no other considerations, are needed. Mention is often made of the threefold heart and the four modes of practice, but these are all included in the belief that rebirth in the Pure Land is most conclusively assured by "Namu-Amida-Butsu." If one imagines something more than this, he will be excluded from the blessings of the two holy ones, Amida and Shakyamuni, and left out of the Original Prayer. He who believes in the Nembutsu, however learned he may be in all the teachings of Shakyamuni, should behave like an ignoramus who knows nothing, or like a simple-hearted woman devotee; avoid pedantry, and recite the Buddha's Name with singleness of heart.

Unsurprisingly, other sects did not welcome his simplified methods because they contradicted some of the basic Buddhist teachings of the time. One of these Pure Land teachings is the absolute reliance on an otherworldly power, which defies the self-discipline and self-development emphasized by the other sects. The second is the fervent promotion of a rebirth in the Pure Land, which is conceptually very different from self-attained enlightenment. Its simplicity, however, though a cause for disquietude among non-*Jodo* monks, was the reason for its popular reception among laypersons. In addition, the belief in a higher power was readily accepted, as the worship of superiors and emperors was a traditional aspect of Japanese culture. D. T. Suzuki (1870–1966), a renowned modern philosopher of Buddhism, provides further insight on the appeal of the Pure Land sect.

From: D. T. Suzuki, *Japanese Spirituality*[18]

For most of us spirituality cannot send forth its essential light because the intellect stands in the way. That is why Pure Land Nembutsu is the practice of those who "know nothing." In one sense, since spirituality has an immediacy that is emotional or sensory, when we speak of "simple-hearted women" and so on, we are liable to imagine spirituality as something instinctive, completely shorn of intellectuality. But as has been repeated over and over, spiritual insight holds its significance within itself. For those "ignorant and unlettered" this has an all the more incomprehensible charm. That is why the Nembutsu was so readily accepted among the common people.

Despite the simplicity of the *nembutsu* practice, its foundation still remains the doctrine of nonduality. As is alluded to in Hōnen's *One Page Testament*, the correct practice of *nembutsu* is achieved through the complete emptiness of mind, and emptiness is achieved

---

* *Nembutsu* is a Japanese term that derives from the Sanskrit term *buddhānusmṛti*, or "mindfulness of the Buddha," which refers to the practice of reciting Amida Buddha's name ("*Namu Amida Butsu*") within the context of Pure Land Buddhism.

only through the cessation of dualistic thinking. The lack of intellectual reasoning placed behind Pure Land *nembutsu* gives it its allure to laypersons, but at the most basic level the product of its practice is attainment of Buddhist oneness, the same as that of all other Buddhist methods. D. T. Suzuki once again elaborates this point.

From: D. T. Suzuki, *Japanese Spirituality*[19]

When, after cutting off all ideas of good and evil, yes and no, all actions at all times become one with the calling of the Name, that is the practice of single-minded Nembutsu. It then becomes a Nembutsu of all acts. Though people of the orthodox groups may explain *senju* (exclusive) Nembutsu in many ways, it is all dogmatic finery. *Senju* Nembutsu is not one act chosen from among others; to say that it signifies absolute Nembutsu would be in more accord with the true intent of both Hōnen and Shinran. It is Nembutsu seen from spiritual insight itself, and it is Japanese. When instead of conceptually following the historical Nembutsu, one sees the Nembutsu of Amida's Original Prayer directly with the awakening of his own individual spirituality, it is felt clearly and intimately. This is Hōnen's "Nembutsu of plain wood." Intellectually-minded priests have an unfortunate habit of discussion and argument for their own sake. Even this would not be bad in some instances, but for one who would confront life's truth the Nembutsu must be spoken with spiritual insight, in "plain wood."

Note that this "spiritual awakening" does not refer to one's entrance into the Pure Land. It signifies rather the state of ultimate clarity, of oneness and nonduality. Hōnen and his disciples simply provided a more convenient vehicle for the Japanese people to understand this Buddhist philosophy. Pure Land reinforced the preexisting Japanese emphasis on faith in a higher ideal, and in addition, by simplifying Buddhist doctrines it became an essential means to spread the teachings of Buddhism to the common people.

The counterpart to Pure Land *nembutsu* is *zazen*, a primary practice of Zen, the other Buddhist sect that significantly augmented the collective Japanese faith in Buddhism. *Zazen* signifies the act of meditative sitting, the position by which the Buddha Shakyamuni himself had achieved enlightenment. While performing *zazen*, just as when reciting *nembutsu*, the aim is the cessation of dualistic thinking. Again, the fundamental principle of nondualism remains the same. The following excerpt describing the nondualistic nature of *zazen* is from the *Fukanzazengi* (Universal Recommendation of Zazen), written by the Zen master Dōgen (1200–1253 CE), who was responsible for pioneering the Sōtō Zen school in Japan.

From: Dōgen, *Fukanzazengi*[20]

Cast aside all involvements and cease all affairs. Do not think of good or bad. Do not administer pros and cons. Cease all movements of the conscious mind, the gauging of all thoughts and views....

Think of not-thinking. How do you think of not-thinking? Without thinking. This in itself is the essential art of zazen.

More so than any other sect, Zen promotes self-discipline and independence in achieving enlightenment. Thus, much of its teachings focus on the idea of understanding oneself, and in doing so learning how to sever the consciousness of self. This is taught throughout the *Shōbōgenzō* (Treasury of the True Dharma Eye), another work by Dōgen that is considered to be a primary scripture for Sōtō Zen.

From: Dōgen, *Shōbōgenzō* (1235)[21]

To practice and confirm all things by conveying one's self to them, is illusion; for all things [dharmas] to advance forward and practice and confirm the self, is enlightenment....

To learn the Buddha Way is to learn one's self. To learn one's self is to forget one's self. To forget one's self is to be confirmed by all things [dharmas]. To be confirmed by all dharmas is to effect the dropping off of one's own body-and-mind and the mind-and-body of others as well.

When the consciousness of self and others is erased, the duality of life and death, and even good and evil, also disappears. However, directly or indirectly, this sort of thinking prepared the philosophical basis of the neglect of moral codes when fighters engaged in acts of killing. "To forget one's self" or "the dropping off of one's own body-and-mind" in Zen meditation is a beautiful way to reach enlightenment through the negation of egoism. By the same token, however, it can unwittingly foster blind devotion to authority and a willingness to sacrifice oneself for a cause without critical thought to the underlying political context.

From: Dōgen, *Shōbōgenzō*[22]

When you simply release and forget both your body and your mind and throw yourself into the house of the Buddha, and when functioning comes from the direction of the Buddha and you go in accord with it, then with no strength needed and no thought expended, freed from birth and death, you become Buddha. Then there can be no obstacle in any man's mind.

The nonduality of life and death and the "forgetting" of the "self" work hand-in-hand with another vital practice of Buddhism: that of self-sacrificing benevolence. For one who is on the path of Buddhahood, the triviality of "self" and "death" translates into an unbound philanthropy. The value of philanthropy in Buddhism is made apparent in the following account of Dōgen's mentor, Myōan Eisai (1141–1215), the priest responsible for introducing Rinzai Zen to Japan. The story emphasizes the virtue of self-sacrifice for the betterment of others, a virtue considered of such value that one is taught not to have qualms in the act of giving even at the risk of condemnation or death.

From: Dōgen, *Shōbōgenzō*[23]

When the late Abbot [Eisai] was still at Kenninji monastery, a poor man once came and said, "My family is so destitute that they have had nothing to cook for several days. Myself, my wife, and our three children are on the verge of starvation. For pity's sake, please help us!" At the time there was in the Abbot's quarters nothing whatever – no food, no clothing, no money – for him to give away, and he was almost at the end of his wits. There was, however, some beaten copper which was to be used in making a halo for the statue of the Lord of Healing. He took it and broke it up in his hands. Then, tying it in a little package, he gave the copper to the poor man. "Exchange this for food and save your family from starvation." The man went away overjoyed.

But some of the Abbot's disciples criticized his action, saying, "This was no less than the halo of the Buddha statue. Giving it to a layman constitutes the crime of using what belongs to the Buddha for one's own private purposes. Isn't that wrong?"

"You are right," the Abbot replied, "but just consider the will of the Buddha. He sacrificed his very flesh and limbs for the sake of all mankind. If some men are about to die of starvation, would he not want us to give the whole Buddha figure to save them? Even if I should go to Hell for this crime, I would want to save people from starvation." Such loftiness of purpose is well worth reflecting upon. You students should keep this in mind.

There was another time when his disciples observed to the Abbot that the site of the Kenninji monastery buildings was too close to the river, so close, in fact, that in years to come the monastery would be likely to suffer flood damage. The Abbot told them, "Do not worry about the damage our monastery may suffer in years to come. The first temple of the Buddha, in the Jetavana Park of India, has now disappeared and only stone ruins remain. Nevertheless the merit of building a temple or monastery should not be lost sight of. To practice the way of the Buddha in such a place, if only for six months or a year, is a work of enormous merit."

Thinking back on this, the building of a temple or monastery seems indeed to be the greatest undertaking of a man's life. It is only natural that one should want it to endure for all time. And yet this did not keep him from realizing in the depths of his soul a very profound truth, which is well worth remembering.

In congruence with self-sacrifice, the way of Buddhahood is true and absolute dedication beyond rational thinking. Religious experience based on nondualistic, nonanalytical perception can open the door to blind devotion for dubious causes. Especially when "loftiness of purpose" as shown in this text is overlapped with nonconditional fidelity to higher authority such as the emperor or the lord, it can mobilize the public to wrong directions. People could be persuaded that their self-sacrificial acts may guide them to eternal glory after life, as some suicidal terrorists today reportedly believe.

From: Dōgen, *Shōbōgenzō*[24]

The concerns of the disciple of Buddhism are different from those of the ordinary man. During the lifetime of the Abbot of Kenninji, it once happened that there was no food for those in the monastery. At that time, however, a patron of the monastery invited the Abbot to visit him, and then presented him with a roll of silk as an offering. Overjoyed, the Abbot took it with him back to the monastery and turned it over to the steward, saying, "Use it to buy food for the morrow."

Just at that time, however, there was a layman who, seeing this, went up to the Abbot and begged, "I have a desperate need for two or three rolls of silk. If you have anything at all, I would deeply appreciate it." The Abbot thereupon took back from the steward what he had just turned over to him, and gave the silk to the layman while the steward and all the other monks watched in amazement. Later the Abbot said to them, "You all probably think it was a rash thing for me to do. But it occurred to me that the inmates of this monastery have all dedicated themselves to the way of the Buddha, and even if they should have to go without food for a day, or perhaps even starve to death, they would still have no cause for complaint. So if by this means the distress of some layman should be relieved in a time of dire need, each of you should regard it as a work of personal gratification and merit." Truly this is the sort of thing that reflects an enlightened mind.

It should be noted that the dedication described above closely parallels what may be found in Confucian teachings. In fact, the philosophies of Zen, Pure Land, and Japanese Buddhism as a whole were greatly influenced by schools of thought outside Buddhism, specifically Confucianism and Taoism. Confucianism in particular had been incorporated in Japanese social and political philosophy from before the introduction of Buddhism in the sixth century, and even the Buddhist teachings that were brought to Japan inherently contained Confucian philosophy because of the syncretism of the two in China.

An important influence of traditional Confucianism on Buddhism was the emphasis on sacrifice and duty. This is taught in Confucius' descriptions of how an ideal gentleman ought to act in front of his superiors. Consequently, religious devotion is sometimes replaced by fanatic obedience even to cult leaders, as we have seen in the extreme case of the Aum Shinrikyo sect, led by Asahara Shoko. In 1995 he and his devoted followers used sarin gas to attack passengers in the Tokyo subway.

From: *The Analects of Confucius*, Book I (ca. 550 BCE)[25]

The Master said, If a gentleman is frivolous, he will lose the respect of his inferiors and lack firm ground upon which to build up his education. First and foremost he must learn to be faithful to his superiors, to keep promises, to refuse the friendship of all who are not like him. And if he finds he has made a mistake, then he must not be afraid of admitting the fact and amending his ways.

From: *The Analects of Confucius*, Book X[26]

When his prince sends him a present of food, he must straighten his mat and be the first to taste what has been sent. When what his prince sends is a present of uncooked meat, he must cook it and make a sacrificial offering. When his prince sends a live animal, he must rear it. When he is waiting upon his prince at mealtimes, while his prince is making the sacrificial offering, he (the gentleman) tastes the dishes. If he is ill and his prince comes to see him, he has himself laid with his head to the East with his Court robes thrown over him and his sash drawn across the bed. When the prince commands his presence he goes straight to the palace without waiting for his carriage to be yoked.

In obediently and earnestly serving superiors, one is able to attain inner peace. This parallels the attitude that many Buddhist monks display with regard to their religious superiors.

From: *The Analects of Confucius*, Book IX[27]

The Master said, I can claim that at Court I have duly served the Duke and his officers; at home, my father and elder brother. As regards matters of mourning, I am conscious of no neglect, nor have I ever been overcome with wine. Concerning these things at any rate my mind is quite at rest.

As with the attainment of Buddhist enlightenment, diligence in work is a necessary step in grasping the Confucian Way. The high standards of the Japanese work ethic are partially due to this Buddhist-Confucian appreciation of professional diligence in secular life. One is encouraged to seek spirituality within mundane life in the Japanese tradition.

From: *The Analects of Confucius*, Book IX[28]

The Master said, The case is like that of someone raising a mound. If he stops working, the fact that it perhaps needed only one more basketful makes no difference; I stay where I am. Whereas even if he has not got beyond leveling the ground, but is still at work, the fact that he has only tilted one basketful of earth makes no difference. I go to help him.

Through this dedication and diligent work, one attains a true understanding of self. The emphasis on self-reflection, as well as on self-control, is of as much importance in the Confucian ideal as it is in Buddhism.

From: *The Analects of Confucius*, Book XII[29]

Once when Fan Ch'ih was taking a walk with the Master under the trees at the Rain Dance altars, he said, May I venture to ask about "piling up moral force," "repairing shortcomings" and "deciding when in two minds"? The Master said, An excellent question. "The work first; the reward afterwards"; is not that piling up moral force? "Attack the evil that is within yourself; do not attack the evil that is in others." Is not this "repairing shortcomings"?

"Because of a morning's blind rage
To forget one's own safety
And even endanger one's kith and kin"
is that not a case of "divided mind"?

The mark of a person who truly lives with the dedication and self-insight advocated in these teachings is a willingness to sacrifice oneself in the name of duty, in much the same way as an ideal Confucian "gentleman" would. Though a Buddhist sacrifice is usually discussed in relation to philanthropy, the absence of the fear of death is the same in a Confucian sacrifice of righteousness and duty.

From: *The Analects of Confucius*, Book XIV[30]

... One who, when he sees a chance of gain, stops to think whether to pursue it would be right; when he sees that (his prince) is in danger, is ready to lay down his life; when the fulfillment of an old promise is exacted, stands by what he said long ago – him indeed I think we might call "a perfect man."

Fulfillment of duty is given the utmost value in the Confucian tradition. That is why this tradition was a significant factor in the establishment of feudalism in China, Korea, and Japan during premodern times.

From: *The Analects of Confucius*, Book VIII[31]

The Master said, Be of unwavering good faith, love learning, if attacked be ready to die for the good Way.

Death for the protection of the superiors' honor was always taken to be a heroic act. And if their own honor was defamed, Japanese warriors practiced *hara-kiri* (stomach-cutting, ritual suicide by disembowelment) to prove their innocence. Death for the sake of honor was greatly admired within ancient Confucian-based societies. This mentality eventually developed into the suicidal attacks that were carried out by the Kamikaze pilots in World War II.

From: *The Analects of Confucius*, Book XIX[32]

Tzu-chang said, A knight who confronted with danger is ready to lay down his life, who confronted with the chance of gain thinks first of right, who judges sacrifice by the degree of reverence shown and mourning by the degree of grief – such a one is all that can be desired.

The impartiality with which Confucian and Buddhist teachings view death is common among many Eastern religions. This is the same for Taoism, which views life and death together as a constituent of the greater *Tao*.

From: *Tao Te Ching*[33]

When going one way means life and going the other means death, three in ten will be comrades of life, three in ten will be comrades of death, and there are those who value life and as a result move into the realm of death, and these also number three in ten. Why is this so? Because they set too much store by life. I have heard it said that one who excels in safe-guarding his own life does not meet with rhinoceros or tiger when traveling on land nor is he touched by weapons when charging into an army. There is nowhere for the rhinoceros to pitch its horn; there is nowhere for the tiger to place its claws; there is nowhere for the weapon to lodge its blade. Why is this so? Because for him, there is no realm of death.

Under the influence of Confucian and Taoist thought, much of Zen doctrine focuses on self-discipline, diligence, and sacrifice, facets that later become apparent in the militaristic mentality of Meiji Japan (1868–1912 CE). In congruence with self-sacrifice, the way of Buddhahood is that of true and absolute dedication beyond rational thinking. Religious experience based on nondualistic, nonanalytical perception intrinsically bears the danger of blind devotion for wrong causes. During the time of its introduction and development, however, Zen was most noted for its enormous influence in the cultivation of the arts. It was able to do this because unlike the other popular Buddhist teachings, it did not focus on the momentary experience of enlightenment and instead encouraged the practice of understanding the "self" in everyday activities. As Dōgen taught, learning how to "forget one's self" and ceasing deliberate consciousness is the way to be "confirmed by all things." It was understood that this practice did not have to be limited to *zazen* but was indeed applicable in all activities.

The freely applicable nature of this philosophy, however, was manipulated in a manner that is undoubtedly far from what the original teachings had intended. This all began with the philosophical union between Buddhism and a particularly common art in feudalistic Japan: *Bushido*, or the "way of the warrior."

The Spirit of Warriors

The *samurai* warriors, who were the military nobility of preindustrial Japan and effectively a militant wing of the state, were strongly influenced by Buddhism in their practice of obedience, self-discipline, and sacrifice, the defining concepts of the *samurai* spirit. Few writings describe the *samurai* way as well as the *Hagakure*, a collection of commentaries compiled by Tsuramoto Tashiro based on conversations he had with his *samurai* master, Yamamoto Tsunetomo (1659–1719), a Buddhist monk who had formerly been a retainer of the Nabeshima Domain of Kyushu. The *Hagakure* was compiled in the early 1700s, during the peaceful Tokugawa Era (1615–1867 CE) when the role of the *samurai* shifted from fighting to administrative tasks. Dismayed over the diminishing warrior role, Tsunetomo articulated the ideals of a true *samurai* through an appeal to the strict military code of his lord and his predecessors. This short excerpt from the *Hagakure* summarizes the defining characteristics of the *samurai* spirit.

From: Yamamoto Tsunetomo, *Hagakure*[34]

When Nakano Takumi was dying, his whole house gathered and he said, "You should understand that there are three conditions to the resolution of a retainer.

They are the condition of the master's will, the condition of vitality, and the condition of one's death."

The *Hagakure* provides an enduring reflection of these ideologies. It is particularly famous for its emphasis on the glorification of death in the *samurai* culture. As is seen from the following passage, the cult of death was deeply entrenched in *samurai* mentality.

From: Yamamoto Tsunetomo, *Hagakure*[35]

Although it stands to reason that a samurai should be mindful of the Way of the Samurai, it would seem that we are all negligent. Consequently, if someone were to ask, "What is the true meaning of the Way of the Samurai?" the person who would be able to answer promptly is rare. This is because it has not been established in one's mind beforehand. From this, one's unmindfulness of the Way can be known.

Negligence is an extreme thing.

The Way of the Samurai is found in death. When it comes to either/or, there is only the quick choice of death. It is not particularly difficult. Be determined and advance. To say that dying without reaching one's aim is to die a dog's death is the frivolous way of sophisticates. When pressed with the choice of life or death, it is not necessary to gain one's aim.

We all want to live. And in large part we make our logic according to what we like. But not having attained our aim and continuing to live is cowardice. This is a thin dangerous line. To die without gaining one's aim *is* a dog's death and fanaticism. But there is no shame in this. This is the substance of the Way of the Samurai. If by setting one's heart right every morning and evening, one is able to live as though his body were already dead, he gains freedom in the Way. His whole life will be without blame, and he will succeed in his calling.

However, simple indifference toward death reflects only incomplete adherence to strict *samurai* discipline. Alluding to his lord's grandfather (one Nabeshima Naoshige), Tsunetomo expresses his belief that the true power of the *samurai* is maximized by having a complete disregard for death, which is best achieved by suppressing rational thought during battle.

From: Yamamoto Tsunetomo, *Hagakure*[36]

Lord Naoshige said, "The Way of the Samurai is in desperateness. Ten men or more cannot kill such a man. Common sense will not accomplish such great things. Simply become insane and desperate.

"In the Way of the Samurai, if one uses discrimination, he will fall behind. One needs neither loyalty nor devotion, but simply to become desperate in the Way. Loyalty and devotion are of themselves within desperation....

"When on the battlefield, if you try not to let others take the lead and have the sole intention of breaking into the enemy lines, then you will not fall behind others, your mind will become fierce, and you will manifest martial valor. This fact has been passed down by the elders. Furthermore, if you are slain in battle, you should be resolved to have your corpse facing the enemy."

The glorification of death was applied to the counterpart to dying, the act of killing. Tsunetomo does not fail to emphasize the deftness, as well as the inclination, that a *samurai* should have when it comes to the taking of another's life.

From: Yamamoto Tsunetomo, *Hagakure*[37]

Yamamoto Kichizaemon was ordered by his father Jin'emon to cut down a dog at the age of five, and at the age of fifteen he was made to execute a criminal. Everyone, by the time they were fourteen or fifteen, was ordered to do a beheading without fail. When Lord Katsushige was young, he was ordered by Lord Naoshige to practice killing with a sword. It is said that at that time he was made to cut down more than ten men successively.

A long time ago this practice was followed, especially in the upper classes, but today even the children of the lower classes perform no executions, and this is extreme negligence. To say that one can do without this sort of thing, or that there is no merit in killing a condemned man, or that it is a crime, or that it is defiling, is to make excuses. In short, can it not be thought that because a person's martial valor is weak, his attitude is only that of trimming his nails and being attractive?

If one investigates into the spirit of a man who finds these things disagreeable, one sees that this person gives himself over to cleverness and excuse making not to kill because he feels unnerved. But Naoshige made it his orders exactly because this is something that must be done.

Last year I went to the Kase Execution Grounds to try my hand at beheading, and I found it to be an extremely good feeling. To think that it is unnerving is a symptom of cowardice.

It was unsurprising that this exaltation of both dying and killing was utilized by the modern Japanese military to encourage young Kamikaze pilots for their suicidal attacks. It is also well known that Mishima Yukio (1925–1970), a renowned novelist who committed *hara-kiri* after a failed coup d'état to restore the traditional powers of the emperor, was one of the most enthusiastic readers of the *Hagakure*.

From: Yamamoto Tsunetomo, *Hagakure*[38]

It is said that every time Ōki Hyōbu's group gathered and after all their affairs were finished he would say, "Young men should discipline themselves rigorously in intention and courage. This will be accomplished only if courage is fixed in one's heart. If one's sword is broken, he will strike with his hands. If his hands are cut off, he will press the enemy down with his shoulders. If his shoulders are cut away, he will bite through ten or fifteen enemy necks with his teeth. Courage is such a thing."

Vitality, both mental and physical, was an important facet in the actualization of this *samurai* ideology of death. Meditation was common practice among the *samurai* in achieving this, much in the same way that *nembutsu* and *zazen* were the meditative practices of Pure Land and Zen in the pursuit of nonduality in life and death.

From: Yamamoto Tsunetomo, *Hagakure*[39]

Meditation on inevitable death should be performed daily. Every day when one's body and mind are at peace, one should meditate upon being ripped apart by arrows, rifles, spears and swords, being carried away by surging waves, being thrown into the midst of a great fire, being struck by lightning, being shaken to death by a great earthquake, falling from thousand-foot cliffs, dying of disease or committing *seppuku*[40] at the death of one's master. And every day without fail one should consider himself as dead.

There is a saying of the elders that goes, "Step from under the eaves and you're a dead man. Leave the gate and the enemy is waiting." This is not a matter of being careful. It is to consider oneself as dead beforehand.

People will become your enemies if you become eminent too quickly in life, and you will be ineffectual. Rising slowly in the world, people will be your allies and your happiness will be assured.

In the long run, whether you are fast or slow, as long as you have people's understanding there will be no danger. It is said that fortune that is urged upon you from others is the most effective.

Miyamoto Musashi (1584–1645), the legendary swordsman of the seventeenth century, further elaborates the codes by which a *samurai* ought to live in *The Book of Five Rings*, his treatise on *samurai* philosophy and the art of swordsmanship. His teachings strongly emphasize the paramount importance of mind over technique. His focus on eliminating desire and dependency on others, and on curtailing intimate association with them, illustrates the strong discipline and mental vitality that one must practice in order to fulfill the principles of the *samurai*. Though it is important to note that Miyamoto Musashi avoided the direct incorporation of Buddhism in *The Book of Five Rings* and in fact in the following excerpt encourages one not to depend on gods and Buddhas, there is a very apparent philosophical parallel between Zen Buddhism and his teaching on self-reliance, discipline, and the acceptance of death.

From: Miyamoto Musashi, *The Book of Five Rings*, "The Way of Walking Alone"[41]

Do not turn your back on the various Ways of this world.
Do not scheme for physical pleasure.
Do not intend to rely on anything.
Consider yourself lightly; consider the world deeply.
Do not ever think in acquisitive terms.
Do not regret things about your own personal life.
Do not envy another's good or evil.
Do not lament parting on any road whatsoever.

Do not complain or feel bitterly about yourself or others.
Have no heart for approaching the path of love.
Do not have preferences.
Do not harbor hopes for your own personal home.
Do not have a liking for delicious food for yourself.
Do not carry antiques handed down from generation to generation.
Do not fast so that it affects you physically.
While it's different with military equipment, do not be fond of material things.
While on the Way, do not begrudge death.
Do not be intent on possessing valuables or a fief in old age.
Respect the gods and Buddhas, but do not depend on them.
Though you give up your life, do not give up your honor.
Never depart from the Way of the martial arts.

The philosophical similarities with *Bushido* made Zen a natural fit for the *samurai*. This reality was well understood by the aforementioned Rinzai Zen monk, Takuan Sōhō. His most famous treatise, *The Unfettered Mind* (1632), is a collection of writings specifically on the application of Zen Buddhism to the martial arts. Here he affirms the value of the enlightened mind, or "right-mindedness," by comparing it to life and wealth.

From: Takuan Sōhō, *The Unfettered Mind*[42]

There is nothing dearer to us than life. Whether a man be rich or poor, if he does not live out a long life, he will not accomplish his true purpose. Even if one had to throw away thousands in wealth and valuables to do so, life is something he should buy.

It is said that life is of small account compared with right-mindedness. In truth, it is right-mindedness that is most esteemed.

Nothing is more precious than life. Yet, at the moment when we must throw away this valued life and stand on right-mindedness, there is nothing more highly esteemed than right-mindedness.

Looking carefully at the world, we can see that there are many people who throw away their lives lightly. But do you suppose one person in a thousand would die for right-mindedness? It would seem that among the humble servant class, contrary to what you might expect, there are many who would. Yet it would be difficult for people who think themselves wise to do the same.

As I was saying such things half to myself while passing a long spring day, a certain man came up and said something like this:

"While wealth truly pleases our hearts, having life is the greatest wealth of all. So when it comes to the moment of reckoning, a man will throw away his wealth to keep his life intact. But when you think that a man will not hesitate to throw away the life he so values for the sake of right-mindedness, the value of right-mindedness is greater than life itself. Desire, life and right-mindedness – among these three, isn't the latter what man values most?"

However, simply dying a courageous death does not in itself imply a death of right-mindedness. Takuan Sōhō acknowledges that countless *samurai* died in the name of duty and honor, but that many of them did so with the agenda of personal gain. By reinforcing the value of right-mindedness and connecting it to the *samurai* spirit, Takuan Sōhō created an even higher ideal for which warriors can live and die, bolstering their devotion to *Bushido* and the martial arts.

From: Takuan Sōhō, *The Unfettered Mind*[43]

Is there one person in a thousand who would die like this? If there were one person in a thousand, then there would be a hundred in a hundred thousand, and for any eventuality there would be a hundred thousand men available.

In truth, one hundred right-minded men would be hard to find.

Regardless of the epoch, whenever the country was in disorder, there might be five to seven thousand corpses after a battle. Among them were men who met the enemy and made names for themselves. Others were struck down by the enemy without anyone's noticing. All of these men would seem to have died for right-mindedness, but many of them did not. Many died for name and for profit.

The first thought is of doing something for fame; the second is to think of establishing a name, and later of receiving land and coming up in the world.

There are people who accomplish notable feats, attract fame and come up in the world. There are those who die in battle. There are among the older samurai those who would make a name for themselves in the next battle so as to leave it to their descendants in their old age; or if they did not die in battle, they would try to leave both name and estate. All these take their lives lightly, but all are concerned with name and profit. Theirs is a hot-blooded death born of desire. It is not right-mindedness.

Those who receive a kind word from their lord and devote their lives to him also die a death of right-mindedness. But there are none who would value right-mindedness even though it is what should be valued most. So those who throw away their lives for desire, and those who hold their lives dear and expose themselves to shame belong with those who take right-mindedness lightly, whether they live or die.

Equally emphasized by Takuan Sōhō was the nonduality of "self" and "no-self." The *samurai* culture of obedience required that duty should be placed before self-interest, and this coincides with the "forgetfulness of 'self'" in Zen. Likewise, the *samurai* practice of discipline is analogous to the self-discipline that is sought in Zen for the understanding of the "non-duality of 'self' and 'no-self.'" Takuan Sōhō provides insight on the meaning of "no-self," which he refers to here as "True Self," and its association with martial arts.

From: Takuan Sōhō, *The Unfettered Mind*[44]

The *me* of "the enemy does not see me" refers to my True Self. It does not mean my perceived self.

People can easily see the perceived self; it is rare for them to discern the True Self. Thus I say, "The enemy does not see me."

I do not see the enemy. Because I do not take the personal view of the perceived self, I do not see the martial art of the enemy's perceived self. Although I say, "I do not see the enemy," this does not mean I do not see the enemy right before my very eyes. To be able to see the one without seeing the other is a singular thing.

Well then, the True Self is the self that existed before the division of heaven and earth and before one's father and mother were born. This self is the self within me, the birds and the beasts, the grasses and the trees and all phenomena. It is exactly what is called the Buddha-nature.

This self has no shape or form, has no birth, and has no death. It is not a self that can be seen with the aid of your present physical eye. Only the man who has received enlightenment is able to see this. The man who does see this is said to have seen into his own nature and become a Buddha.

For those who have achieved right-mindedness and gained understanding of these non-dualities, effective performance in battle comes naturally. In understanding nonduality, a *samurai* is able to perceive his surroundings objectively. Thus he finds perfection in the way of the warrior.

From: Takuan Sōhō, *The Unfettered Mind*[45]

Well then, the accomplished man uses the sword but does not kill others. He uses the sword and gives others life. When it is necessary to kill, he kills. When it is necessary to give life, he gives life. When killing, he kills in complete concentration; when giving life, he gives life in complete concentration. Without looking at right and wrong, he is able to see right and wrong; without attempting to discriminate, he is able to discriminate well. Treading on water is just like treading on land, and treading on land is just like treading on water. If he is able to gain this freedom, he will not be perplexed by anyone on earth. In all things, he will be beyond companions.

The accomplished man means the man accomplished in the martial arts.

He uses the sword, but not to kill others means that even though he does not use the sword to cut others down, when others are confronted by this principle, they cower and become as dead men of their own accord. There is no need to kill them.

He uses the sword and gives others life means that while he deals with his opponent with a sword, he leaves everything to the movements of the other man, and is able to observe him just as he pleases.

When it is necessary to kill, he kills; when it is necessary to give life, he gives life. When killing, he kills with complete concentration; when giving life, he gives life with complete concentration means that in either giving life or taking life, he does so with freedom in a meditative state that is total absorption, and the meditator becomes one with the object of meditation.

Without looking at right and wrong, he is able to see right and wrong; without attempting to discriminate, he is able to discriminate well. This means that, concerning his martial art, he does not look at it to say "correct" or "incorrect," but he is able to see which it is. He does not attempt to judge matters, but he is able to do so well.

If one sets up a mirror, the form of whatever happens to be in front of it will be reflected and will be seen. As the mirror does this mindlessly, the various forms are reflected clearly, without any intent to discriminate this from that. Setting up his whole mind like a mirror, the man who employs the martial arts will have no intention of discriminating right from wrong, but according to the brightness of the mirror in his mind, the judgment of right and wrong will be perceived without his giving it any thought.

Treading on water is just like treading on land, and treading on land is just like treading on water. The meaning of this will not be known by anyone unenlightened about the very source of mankind.

If the fool steps on land like he steps on water, when he walks on land, he is going to fall on his face. If he steps on water like he steps on land, when he does step onto water, he may think he can actually walk around. Concerning this matter, the man who forgets about both land and water should arrive at this principle for the first time.

If he is able to gain this freedom, he will not be perplexed by anyone on earth. According to this, the martial artist who is able to gain freedom will not be in a quandary about what to do, regardless of who on earth he comes up against.

In all things, he will be beyond companions means that as he will be without peer in all the world, he will be just like Shakyamuni, who said, "In Heaven above and Earth below, I alone am the Honored One."

True Self and the nonduality of life and death are advocated in a similar manner in Pure Land Buddhism. Though Zen was of greater popularity due to its emphasis on self-discipline and simple practicality, the *nembutsu* of Pure Land Buddhism was still a well-utilized practice among the *samurai*. This can be seen in the following text from the medieval monk Honen (whose thought we have already discussed above):

From: *Hōnen Shōnin Gyōjo Ezu* (**The Biographical Paintings of Saint Hōnen**)[46]

The original vow of [the] Amitābha is not concerned whether one's predisposition is good or evil, or whether the religious practice is more or less. Since it does not depend upon the purity or impurity of the body, or time, place or opportunities, the occasion of death is of no consequence. Even sinners, as sinners, are eligible for rebirth in the Pure Land, if they should invoke the name of Amitābha. This is the miracle of the original vow. As for those born into the families of warriors, who fight in war and lose their lives therein, if they only should invoke the name of Amitābha, they would be assisted by the original vow and would be welcomed by Amitābha into the Pure Land. This you should never doubt.

Hōnen's advocacy of Amida's unconditional power of salvation was easily manipulated for the justification of nonmoral conduct in later Pure Land Buddhists. In fact, the moral dilemma between devotional faith and self-conscious behavior (that many Buddhists faced) became one of the most serious theological issues to arise in Japanese religious history. Suzuki Shōsan (1579–1655), a *samurai*-turned-monk of the seventeenth century, was just as much an advocate of *nembutsu*.

From: Suzuki Shōsan, *Roankyō*[47]

There are two ways of saying Nembutsu: To think to become Buddha by saying the Nembutsu is an act of karmic transmigration. In reality, the correct way is to recite away all passions by means of Nembutsu. Therefore, one does not generally become Buddha through Nembutsu; if one recites away these passions one knows that one's fundamental self is Buddha. Nevertheless, thoughts that you will become Buddha after death and the like are all post-mortem thirsts.... The only way for you is to cast aside all things "Namu-Amida-Butsu" "Namu-Amida-Butsu," regulate your respiration, continually study death, say the Nembutsu for all your worth, and die a peaceful death. You must simply do single-minded Nembutsu.

You must simply employ the Nembutsu with singleness of purpose, without distractions, until you are detached from self. To be detached from self means to learn death while repeating "Namu-Amida-Butsu" "Namu-Amida-Butsu," and to be enlightened as to the matter of death. I know that you too must cherish your individual self greatly, but it is not a difficult or lengthy matter, just use up the self with Nembutsu.

The "single-mindedness" to which Shōsan refers is a principle readily applicable to the *samurai* when in battle. Pure Land Buddhism taught that if a man is to be freed of the distractions of "self," life, and death, he must single-mindedly practice *nembutsu*. This single-minded focus directly parallels the "rushing-in" mentality of a warrior going into battle. As Miyamoto Musashi teaches, a warrior should free his mind of technical detail and attack with clarity and directness.

From: Miyamoto Musashi, *The Book of Five Rings*[48]

All things being the same, mine is a Way in which it is important that you attack vigorously and directly, chasing your opponents around, making them jump back and confusing them, and gaining the victory with certainty.

This principle applies as well in martial arts situations involving large numbers. All things being the same, it is an essential point of the martial arts that you are intent on rushing into your opponents quickly with a large number of men, and crushing those opponents immediately.

When people in this world study these things, they ordinarily learn parrying, dodging, withdrawing and evading. But these draw their minds from the Way, and allow them to be pushed around by others. Because the Way of the martial arts is direct and true, it is essential that you be intent on pursuing others, and subjugating them with true principles. You should investigate this thoroughly.

As is apparent in the words of the *samurai* and monks discussed, there was a strong influence of Buddhism in the *Bushido* culture. That this influence had occurred so pervasively seems in obvious contradiction to the pacifistic nature of the religion. However, the implication in the teachings of influential Zen practitioners such as Takuan Sōhō and Suzuki Shōsan is that the fundamentals of the religion were of less concern than its successful propagation. This pattern was apparent from the time of the very introduction of the religion to Japan. This is made abundantly clear in Myōan Eisai's endorsement of Zen, which is directed not necessarily to the people of the country, but rather to the leaders of the state.

From: Myōan Eisai, *The Propagation of Zen for the Protection of the Country* (1198)[49]

Great is Mind. Heaven's height is immeasurable, but Mind goes beyond heaven; the earth's depth is also unfathomable, but Mind reaches below the earth. The light of the sun and moon cannot be outdistanced, yet Mind passes beyond the light of sun and moon. The macrocosm is limitless, yet Mind travels outside the macrocosm. How great is Space! How great the Primal Energy! Still Mind encompasses Space and generates the Primal Energy. Because of it heaven covers and earth upbears. Because of it the sun and moon move on, the four seasons pass in succession, and all things are generated. Great indeed is Mind! Of necessity we give such a name to it, yet there are many others: the Highest Vehicle ... the Peerless Bodhi, the Way to Enlightenment as taught in the *Laṅkāvatāra Sūtra*, the Treasury of the Vision of Truth, and Insight of Nirvana. All texts in the Three Vehicles of Buddhism and in the eight treasuries of Scripture, as well as all the doctrines of the four schools and five denominations of Zen are contained in it. Shākya, the greatest of all teachers, transmitted this truth of the Mind to the golden-haired monk [Kāshyapa], calling it a special transmission not contained in the scriptures. From the Vulture Peak it moved to Cockleg Cave, where it was greeted with a smile. Thus with the mere twist of a flower a thousand trees were made to bloom; from one fountainhead sprang ten thousand streams of Truth.

As in India, so in China this teaching has attracted followers and disciples in great numbers. It propagates the Truth as the ancient Buddha did, with the robe of authentic transmission passing from one man to the next. In the matter of religious discipline, it practices the genuine method of the sages of old. Thus the Truth it teaches, both in substance and appearance, perfects the relationship of master and disciple. In its rules of action and discipline, there is no confusion of right and wrong.

After the Great Master [Bodhidharma] sailed by way of the South Seas and planted his staff of Truth on the banks of [the] East River in China, the vision of the Law soon made its appearance in Korea and the Oxhead School of Zen from North China made its way to Japan. Studying it, one discovers the key to all forms of Buddhism; practicing it, one's life is brought to fulfillment in the attainment of enlightenment. Outwardly it favors discipline over doctrine, inwardly it brings the Highest Inner Wisdom. This is what the Zen sect stands for.

In our country the Divine Sovereign shines in splendor and the influence of his virtuous wisdom spreads far and wide. Emissaries from the distant lands of South and Central Asia pay their respects to his court. Lay ministers conduct the affairs of government; priests and monks spread abroad religious truth. Even the truths of the Four Hindu Vedas are not neglected. Why then reject the five schools of Zen Buddhism?

There are, however, some persons who malign this teaching, calling it "the Zen of dark enlightenment." There are also those who question it on the ground that it is "utter Nihilism." Still others consider it ill-suited to these degenerate times, or say that it is not what our country needs. Or else they may express contempt for our mendicant ways and our alleged lack of documentary support for our views. Finally there are some who have such a low opinion of their own capabilities that they look upon Zen as far beyond their power to promote. Out of their zeal for upholding the Law, these people are actually suppressing the treasures of the Law. They denounce us without knowing what we have in mind. Not only are they thus blocking the way to the gate of Zen, but they are also ruining the work of our great forebear at Mt. Hiei [Saichō]. Alas, alas, how sad, how distressing!

It is for this reason that I venture to make a general survey of the Three Vehicles for consideration of philosophers today, and to record the essential teachings of our sect for the benefit of posterity.

Eisai understood that if his school of thought was to be successful in Japan, it had to be endorsed in consideration of the political interests of the sovereign.[50] In Eisai's time, state interests were focused on national security, thus he provided a justification for the application of Zen among the *samurai*, the military class of feudal Japan.

What Eisai may not have realized, however, was that these applications would be exploited some 700 years later by the leaders of the "imperial forces."

From: Ministry of Education, *Fundamentals of Our National Polity* (1937)[51]

Bushidō: *Bushidō* may be cited as showing an outstanding characteristic of our national morality. In the world of warriors one sees inherited the totalitarian structure and spirit of the ancient clans peculiar to our nation. Hence, though the teachings of Confucianism and Buddhism have been followed, these have been transcended. That is to say, though a sense of obligation binds master and servant, this has developed into a spirit of self-effacement and of meeting death with a perfect calmness. In this, it was not that death was made light of so much as that man tempered himself to death and in a true sense regarded it with esteem. In effect, man tried to fulfill true life by way of death. . . .

The warrior's aim should be, in ordinary times, to foster a spirit of reverence for the deities and his own ancestors in keeping with his family tradition; to train himself to be ready to cope with emergencies at all times; to clothe himself with wisdom, benevolence, and valor; to understand the meaning of mercy; and to strive to be sensitive to the frailty of Nature. Yamaga Sokō [1622–1685], Matsumiya

Kanzan [1686–1780], and Yoshida Shōin [1830–1859] were all men of the devoutest character, who exercised much influence in bringing *bushidō* to perfection. It is this same *bushidō* that shed itself of an outdated feudalism at the time of the Meiji Restoration, increased in splendor, became the Way of loyalty and patriotism, and has evolved before us as the spirit of the imperial forces.

The Modernization of Japan and the Emergence of Nationalism

The Meiji Restoration in 1868 saw the opening of the country, long in isolation, to foreign trade. This paved the way for the modernization of Japan. When the demand for natural resources was conjoined with the nationalism that was then developing in the country, there resulted a strong impetus for militarist territorial expansion. This led first to the Sino-Japanese War of 1894–1895, in which the Meiji government fought China for control over Korea. Lasting nine months, the war revealed to the whole world how Japan's industrial progress had supported a dramatic increase in its military strength. The victory further inflated Japanese self-confidence and nationalistic pride. When tensions grew between Japan and Russia over control of Manchuria in the short years after the Sino-Japanese War, Japan was less than hesitant in initiating a war against Russia (the Russo-Japanese War of 1904–1905).

Japanese victory came yet again with relative ease, despite the conflict being of far greater scale than the war against China. The effect of this war on global public opinion was immense, as this marked the first time since the Mongol invasions of the thirteenth century that an Asiatic country had defeated a Western nation. Increasing its military spending after the war, and with its participation in World War I just nine years later, Japan became a serious presence as a militant nation from the international standpoint. Moreover, because of its limited participation in World War I, Japan suffered minimal casualties and capital losses, allowing it significant economic and political gains.[52]

With the end of World War I, the preoccupation of leading Western nations with their own affairs allowed Japan an unhindered focus on further expansion into China.[53] A major stepping-stone for Japan was the successful invasion of Manchuria in 1932, which gave it a puppet state in continental Asia that provided much-needed raw materials as well as a strategic position against Russia. The initial invasion eventually snowballed into the Second Sino-Japanese War, which included the aforementioned Nanking Massacre and other atrocities committed by Japan in the greater Pacific War.

Imperial Japan's violent conquests were fueled politically by the country's entrance as a militant power in the international arms race, and economically by the desperate need for financial security in the face of the Great Depression and Japan's own growing industries. The second factor became of even greater significance in the late 1930s when Western nations began limiting their trade with Asian nations. This pressure was further augmented in 1940 and 1941 when the United States initiated sanctions against Japan, including a strict embargo on oil and raw materials related to the manufacture of weaponry.[54] Insulted by these restrictions and pressured to take action, Japan began actualizing its plans to stand up against the Western powers. Pearl Harbor and other Western territories in the Pacific came under attack beginning in December 1941.

That Japan's political and economic needs took the form of military aggression can be attributed to the social mentality of the Japanese during that time. A strong sense of nationalism had been developing in Japan since the end of the Tokugawa Era, and was inflated with each new military victory. The nationalistic attitude of the public was an enormous benefit for the military interests of the state and garnered support from the Buddhist communities as well. Buddhist schools were able to convincingly endorse war to the public by appealing to the philosophical union of Buddhism and the samurai spirit.

From: Ministry of Education, *Fundamentals of Our National Polity*[55]

The Martial Spirit: And then, this harmony is clearly seen also in our nation's martial spirit. Our nation is one that holds *bushidō* in high regard, and there are shrines deifying warlike spirits.... But this martial spirit is not [a thing that exists] for the sake of itself but for the sake of peace, and is what may be called a sacred martial spirit. Our martial spirit does not have for its objective the killing of men, but the giving of life to men. This martial spirit is that which tries to give life to all things, and is not that which destroys. That is to say, it is a strife which has peace at its basis with a promise to raise and to develop; and it gives life to things through its strife. Here lies the martial spirit of our nation. War, in this sense, is not by any means intended for the destruction, overpowering, or subjugation of others; and it should be a thing for the bringing about of great harmony, that is, peace, during the work of creation by following the Way.

Another key factor conducive to the religious endorsement of war was the unbounded respect and sense of duty that the Japanese expressed toward their emperor. This reverence for the imperial family is something that had existed since the beginnings of written Japanese history and was a direct result of mythologies of the second major indigenous religion of Japan, Shinto. A distinctive characteristic of the religion is its belief in a multitude of gods (*kami*). The exact number remained unspecified, but was nonetheless traditionally said to be eight million. "God," however, is an inadequate translation of the word *kami*, whose true meaning is as vague as the vastness of the number of things to which it refers. The term is often applied for things in nature but is used liberally for all things that are considered beautiful and inspirational, be it animals, objects, ancestors, or even living individuals. The emperor received particular recognition in this connection, as he was considered to be the direct descendant of the *kami* who created Japan.

The Shinto myths that gave rise to this belief are recorded in the *Kojiki* and *Nihongi*, two of the oldest written works in Japanese history. Their content revolves around Shinto mythology and includes descriptions of the nation's birth and its roots in the imperial family. Although both texts were written by the rulers of the time to secure their own political interests, they have nevertheless helped to define Japanese perceptions of the country's origins since their inscription in the eighth century.

The *Kojiki*, completed in 712 CE, is considered one of the oldest and most monumental literary works of Japan. The *Kojiki* is highly valued for its descriptions of ancient

Japan and its Shinto traditions, which are otherwise very difficult to find, as Shinto was largely based on oral tradition. The *Nihongi*, an equally important book written eight years after the *Kojiki*, is the more extensive and detailed of the two. While containing fewer references to the mythological deities, it provides much historical detail about the eighth century and its emperors.

The following excerpts, from Aston's translation of the *Nihongi*, illustrate the beginnings of the imperial line. The first story describes the descent of the August Grandchild from heaven, whom the Heaven-Shining-Deity sends down to rule Japan. The Heaven-Shining-Deity, or Amaterasu, is one of the most recognized *kami* in Shinto belief and is the daughter of Izanagi and Izanami, the deities who created the islands of Japan. The August Grandchild is the direct grandson of Amaterasu.

From: *Nihongi*[56]

"All the Central Land of Reed-Plains is now completely tranquilized." Now the Heaven-Shining-Deity gave command, saying: "If that be so, I will send down my child." She was about to do so, when in the meantime, an August Grandchild was born, whose name was called Ama-tsu-hiko-hiko-ho-no-ninigi no Mikoto. Her son represented to her that he wished the August Grandchild to be sent down in his stead. Therefore the Heaven-Shining-Deity gave to Ama-tsu-hiko-hiko-ho-no-ninigi no Mikoto the Three Treasures, viz. the curved jewel of Yasaka gem, the eight-hand mirror, and the sword Kusanagi, and joined to him as his attendants Ame no Koyane no Mikoto, the first ancestor of the Naka-tomi; Futo-dama no Mikoto, the first ancestor of the Imbe; Ame no Uzume no Mikoto, the first ancestor of the Sarume; Ishi-kori-dome no Mikoto, the first ancestor of the mirror-makers; and Tamaya no Mikoto, the first ancestor of the jewel-makers; in all Gods of five *be*. Then she commanded her August Grandchild saying: "This Reed-plain-1500-autumns-fair-rice-ear Land is the region which my descendants shall be lords of. Do thou, my August Grandchild, proceed thither and govern it. Go! and may prosperity attend thy dynasty, and may it, like Heaven and Earth, endure forever.

Four generations down the line of the August Grandchild, His Augustness Kami Yamoto Ihare-biko, also known as Jimmu, is born, who becomes the first emperor of Japan. In the following, Jimmu, along with his elder brother, His Augustness Itsu-se, venture into the country in the hopes of finding a suitable dwelling from which to rule the nation. Though His Augustness Itsu-se dies in battle, the younger Jimmu eventually succeeds in the pacification of the empire. The Prince of Tomi mentioned below is one of the primary villains in the brothers' adventures. Nigi-hayabi is a god of unknown origins.

From: *Kojiki*[57]

So then His Augustness Nigi-hayabi waited on and said to the august child of the Heavenly Deity: "As I heard that [thou], the august child of the Heavenly Deity, hast descended from Heaven, I have followed down to wait on thee."

Forthwith presenting to him the heavenly symbols, he respectfully served him. So His Augustness Nigi-hayabi wedded the Princess of Tomi, sister of the Prince of Tomi, and begot a child, His Augustness Umashi-ma-ji.... So having thus subdued and pacified the savage Deities, and extirpated the unsubmissive people, [His Augustness Kamu-yamato-ihare-biko] dwelt at the palace of Kashibara near Unebi and ruled the Empire.

The following passage from the *Nihongi* is a more elaborate description of Jimmu's conquest of Eastern Japan and his rise to the throne. It is important to note how the emperor is described as a direct descendant of the *kami*, and he is praised for establishing order within the nation.

From: *Nihongi*[58]

The Emperor Kami Yamato Ihare-biko's personal name was Hiko-hoho-demi. He was the fourth child of Hiko-nagisa-take-u-gaya-fuki-aezu no Mikoto. His mother's name was Tama-yori-hime, daughter of the Sea God. From his birth, this Emperor was of clear intelligence and resolute will. At the age of fifteen he was heir to the throne. When he grew up, he married Ahira-tsu-hime, of the district of Ata in the province of Hyūga, and made her his consort. By her he had Tagishi-mimi no Mikoto and Kisu-mimi no Mikoto.

When he reached the age of forty-five, he addressed his elder brothers and his children, saying: "Of old, Our Heavenly Deities Taka-mi-musubi no Mikoto, and Ō-hiru-me no Mikoto, pointing to this land of fair rice-ears of the fertile reed-plain, gave it to Our Heavenly ancestor, Hiko-ho-no ninigi no Mikoto. Thereupon Hiko-ho no ninigi no Mikoto, throwing open the barrier of Heaven and clearing a cloud-path, urged on his superhuman course until he came to rest. At this time the world was given over to widespread desolation. It was an age of darkness and disorder. In this gloom, therefore, he fostered justice, and so governed this western border. Our imperial ancestors and imperial parent, like gods, like sages, accumulated happiness and amassed glory. Many years elapsed. From the date when Our Heavenly ancestor descended until now is over 1,792,470 years. But the remote regions do not yet enjoy the blessings of imperial rule. Every town has always been allowed to have its lord, and every village its chief, who, each one for himself, makes division of territory and practices of mutual aggression and conflict.

"Now I have heard from the Ancient of the Sea that in the East there is a fair land encircled on all sides by blue mountains. Moreover, there is there one who flew down riding in a Heavenly Rock-boat. I think that this land will undoubtedly be suitable for the extension of the Heavenly task, so that its glory should fill the universe. It is, doubtless, the center of the world. The person who flew down, was, I believe, Nigi-haya-hi. Why should we not proceed thither, and make it the capital.

"All the Imperial Princes answered, and said: "The truth of this is manifest. This thought is constantly present to our minds also. Let us go thither quickly." This was the year Kinoe Tora of the Great Year.

The year Tsuchinoto Hitsuji, Spring, 3rd month, 7th day. The Emperor made an order saying: "During the six years that Our expedition against the East has lasted, owing to My reliance on the Majesty of Imperial Heaven, the wicked bands have met death. It is true that the frontier lands are still unpurified, and that a remnant of evil is still refractory. But in the region of the Central Land there is no more wind and dust. Truly we should make a vast and spacious capital, and plan it great and strong.

"At present things are in a crude and obscure condition, and the people's minds are unsophisticated. They roost in nests or dwell in caves. Their manners are simply what is customary. Now if a great man were to establish laws, justice could not fail to flourish. And even if some gain should accrue to the people, in what way would this interfere with the Sage's action? Moreover, it will be well to open up and clear the mountains and forests, and to construct a palace. Then I may reverently assume the Precious Dignity, and so give peace to My good subjects. Above, I should then respond to the kindness of the Heavenly Powers in granting Me the Kingdom, and below, I should extend the line of the imperial descendants and foster right-mindedness. Thereafter the capital may be extended so as to embrace all the six cardinal points, and the eight cords may be covered so as to form a roof. Will this not be well?"

Thus begins the reign of the imperial family, and both the *Kojiki* and the *Nihongi* provide a chronological genealogy of the emperors that follow in the form of myths and stories. These stories are often used to glorify the emperor's role in maintaining a successful empire. Known also for its strong infusion of Confucian political theory, the *Nihongi* portrays the role of the emperor as a provider whose primary responsibility is to foster the welfare and prosperity of the people. This idea is exhibited no more clearly than in the benevolent characterization of the sixteenth emperor, Nintoku (313–399).

From: *Nihongi*[59]

4th year, Spring, 2nd month, 6th day. The Emperor addressed his ministers, saying: "We ascended a lofty tower and looked far and wide, but no smoke arose in the land. From this We gather that the people are poor, and that in the houses there are none cooking their rice. We have heard that in the reigns of the wise sovereigns of antiquity, from everyone was heard the sound of songs hymning their virtue, in every house there was the ditty, 'How happy are we.' But now when We observe the people, for three years past, no voice of eulogy is heard; the smoke of cooking has become rarer and rarer. By this We know that the five grains do not come up, and that the people are in extreme want. Even in the Home provinces there are some who are not supplied; what must it be in the provinces outside of Our domain?"

3rd month, 21st day. The following decree was issued: "From this time forward, for the space of three years, let forced labor be entirely abolished, and let the people have rest from toil." From this day forth his robes of state and shoes did not wear out, and none were made. The warm food and hot broths did not become sour or putrid, and were not renewed. He disciplined his heart and restrained his impulses so that he discharged his functions without effort.

Therefore the Palace enclosure fell to ruin and was not rebuilt; the thatch decayed, and was not repaired; the wind and rain entered by the chinks and soaked the coverlets; the starlight filtered through the decayed places and exposed the bed-mats. After this the wind and rain came in due season, the five grains produced in abundance. For the space of three autumns the people had plenty, the praises of his virtue filled the land, and the smoke of cooking was also thick.

7th year, Summer, 4th month, 1st day. The Emperor was on his tower, and looking far and wide, saw smoke arising plentifully. On this day he addressed the Empress, saying: "We are now prosperous. What can there be to grieve for?" The Empress answered and said: "What dost thou mean by prosperity?" The Emperor said: "It is doubtless when the smoke fills the lands, and the people freely attain to wealth." The Empress went on to say: "The Palace enclosure is crumbling down, and there are no means of repairing it; the buildings are dilapidated so that the coverlets are exposed. Can this be called prosperity?" The Emperor said: "When Heaven establishes a Prince, it is for the sake of the people. The Prince must therefore make the people the foundation. For this reason the wise sovereigns of antiquity, if a single one of their subjects was cold and starving, cast the responsibility on themselves. Now the people's poverty is no other than Our poverty; the people's prosperity is none other than Our prosperity. There is no such thing as the people's being prosperous and yet the Prince in poverty."

Imperial deification and other Japanese customs rooted in Shinto beliefs persisted throughout history despite the dominance of foreign philosophies, specifically Buddhism and Confucianism. This is largely because Shinto was never displaced by the continental religions, but rather incorporated within them. This was necessary for the success of Buddhism and Confucianism, because the Japanese place particular weight on tradition and would not have welcomed ideas that significantly differed from their own. Fortunately for these two foreign religions, their adaptable nature and a sufficient similarity of their philosophies with Japanese tradition allowed for the relative ease of their assimilation. Buddhism and Shinto over the course of history were combined into one, which further secured Shinto customs as a relevant part of Japanese life. The continued, underlying reverence of the Japanese people for their emperor is largely owed to this amalgamation.

Though at times latent in the shadow of Buddhism, the undying relevance of Shinto permitted its resurrection into the mainstream whenever it was convenient for ruling authorities. Two prominent examples of this occurred each in the thirteenth and eighteenth centuries. The first was spurred by the successful defense against the Mongol invaders. Twice, the more experienced and better equipped Mongols tried to invade Japan, but in both of these attempts, occurring in 1274 and 1281 CE, tropical storms ravaged Mongol warships and led to Japanese victory. It is of little surprise that the timeliness of these storms generated much inspiration for the Japanese. These storms were interpreted as divine interventions and came to be known as *kamikaze*, or "wind of the gods." Kitabatake Chikafusa (1293–1354 CE), a prominent supporter of Shinto beliefs, was conveniently able to utilize this inspiration to rekindle the idea of Japan as a unique nation whose emperor is of divine descent.

From: Kitabatake Chikafusa, *The Records of the Legitimate Succession of the Divine Sovereigns*[60]

Japan is the divine country. The heavenly ancestor it was who first laid its foundations, and the Sun Goddess left her descendants to reign over it forever and ever. This is true only of our country, and nothing similar may be found in foreign lands. That is why it is called the divine country.

Kitabatake Chikafusa's notion of "the divine country" became an invincible driving force for Japanese troops who were committed to defending the divine lineage of the Imperial family. They believed that something miraculous would happen in the last moment whatever desperate situations they were put in. When Japanese soldiers were discovered about thirty years after World War II in the jungles of Guam and The Philippines, it took some time for them to accept the fact that Japan had lost the war.

The beginnings of Japan in some ways resemble the Indian descriptions, telling as it does of the world's creation from the seed of the heavenly gods. However, whereas in our country the succession to the throne has followed a single undeviating line since the first divine ancestor, nothing of the kind has existed in India. After their first ruler, King People's Lord, had been chosen and raised to power by the populace, his dynasty succeeded, but in later times most of his descendants perished, and men of inferior genealogy who had powerful forces became the rulers, some of them even controlling the whole of India. China is also a country of notorious disorders. Even in ancient times, when life was simple and conduct was proper, the throne was offered to wise men, and no single lineage was established. Later, in times of disorder, men fought for control of the country. Thus some of the rulers rose from the ranks of the plebeians, and there were even some of barbarian origin who usurped power. Or, some families after generations of service as ministers surpassed their princes and eventually supplanted them. There have already been thirty-six changes of dynasty since Fu-hsi, and unspeakable disorders have occurred.

Only in our country has the succession remained inviolate, from the beginning of heaven and earth to the present. It has been maintained within a single lineage, and even when, as inevitably has happened, the succession has been transmitted collaterally, it has returned to the true line. This is due to the ever-renewed Divine Oath, and makes Japan unlike all other countries.

It is true that the Way of the Gods should not be revealed without circumspection, but it may happen that ignorance of the origins of things may result in disorder. In order to prevent that disaster, I have recorded something of the facts, confining myself to a description of how the succession has legitimately been transmitted from the Age of the Gods.

The second outstanding revival of Shinto customs occurred in the eighteenth century through the National Learning movement, a nationwide study of ancient Japanese literature. Though initially inspired by academic interest, the movement later became a means to inflate the sense of national pride and to strengthen the domestic religion against the growing popularity of foreign philosophies.

One of the most recognized scholars who participated in the growth of the National Learning movement was Motoori Norinaga (1730–1801). He is best known for his work in annotating the *Kojiki*, which until then had been widely disregarded because of the difficulty of its language. As it was written in a time when Japanese existed as a largely oral tradition, the *Kojiki* used Chinese characters to phonetically articulate the Japanese language, which resulted in a very difficult read. By essentially translating the *Kojiki* so that it could be better understood in the more modern era, Norinaga was able to create a primary scripture for the Shinto religion. Norinaga's extensive research on the *Kojiki* helped to revitalize the perception of Japanese superiority during the Tokugawa Period (1603–1867 CE). Shinto's role in advocating the national identity served as an immensely powerful tool for secular authorities to ignite the martial spirit of militant Japan.

Secular versus Religious Authority

From ancient times, Shinto theocracy had been particularly easy to exploit. An oral tradition of anecdotal myths with no true religious scriptures or recognized origins, Shinto was open to reinterpretation and arguably manipulation by the very recipients of Shinto worship themselves, the emperor and his court. Their assumed superiority allowed the sovereign significant political leverage over religious authorities. Hence, from the beginnings of Japanese history, authorities from religious communities, however influential they might be, could not amass the power of those who governed the nation.

Buddhism was very much under the influence of political authorities. The initial promulgation of the religion was made possible because of its popularity among the aristocracy and not because there was a religious need among the people.[61] As a result of this position of dependency, Buddhist communities have repeatedly conceded much control to secular authorities over the course of Japanese history. An example of this was the system of *danka seido*, which enabled the government to maintain its grip over religious activity. Originally an arrangement whereby individual households were affiliated with local Buddhist temples, this system underwent drastic changes during the Tokugawa Era when it was used as a means to register and effectively monitor all citizens. For the temples and their monks, government support of the system provided financial security, but their dependence on the state reduced the role of Buddhism as a spiritual guide for the people.[62]

Secular authority was further reinforced by the group-oriented mentality of Japanese culture. This mentality pre-dates written history and the influence of foreign religions. Its origins can be traced back to the farm-based communities of prehistoric Japan. In these close-knit societies, members depended greatly on one another for the success of their own rice fields, necessitating their cooperation and mutual caretaking. Furthermore, the limitations of cultivable land and the year-long maintenance required by rice-based agriculture entailed that families should reside in fixed locations. This strengthened the bond within these communities over a number of generations. In these family-like societies, the under-standing of an individual was that any harm done to the greater group would be reflected back to him or her.[63] This reduced the idea of the individual and prioritized the importance of the group. This, in turn, gave rise to the "nation-first" mentality of the Japanese.

The apex of religious suppression and nationalism was seen at the start of the Meiji Era (1868–1912 CE) in the form of the *haibutsu kishaku* movement[64] and the establishment of State Shinto. The former is literally translated as the abolishment and destruction of the Indian-originated Buddha and his teachings. In a violent move to abolish all foreign religions, the state used sheer force to destroy thousands of temples and coerce monks into giving up their faith. This was all done to pave the way for the formation of a new, government-directed religion called State Shinto. Though "Shinto" is part of its name, State Shinto had little connection with traditional Shinto other than the practice of imperial deification. State Shinto was effectively a political vehicle put together and uti-lized by the government to consolidate the nation and create a society of obedient mili-tary supporters. Though the public was eventually given back their right to the freedom of religion, by then the forceful show of intimidation by the state prevented Buddhist authorities from standing up against State Shinto.

From: Ministry of Education, *Fundamentals of Our National Polity* (1937)[65]

Loyalty and Patriotism: Our country is established with the emperor, who is a descendant of Amaterasu Ōmikami, as her center, and our ancestors as well as we ourselves constantly have beheld in the emperor the fountainhead of her life and activities. For this reason, to serve the emperor and to receive the emperor's great august Will as one's own is the rationale of making our historical "life" live in the present; and on this is based the morality of the people.

Loyalty means to reverence the emperor as [our] pivot and to follow him implic-itly. By implicit obedience is meant casting ourselves aside and serving the emperor intently. To walk this Way of loyalty is the sole Way in which we subjects may "live" and the fountainhead of all energy. Hence, offering our lives for the sake of the emperor does not mean so-called self-sacrifice, but the casting aside of our little selves to live under his august grace and the enhancing of the genuine life of the people of a State. The relationship between the emperor and the subjects is not an artificial relationship [which means] bowing down to authority, nor a relationship such as [exists] between master and servant as is seen in feudal morals.... The ideology which interprets the relationship between the emperor and his subjects as being a reciprocal relationship such as merely obedience to authority or rights and duties, rests on individualistic ideologies, and is a rationalistic way of thinking that looks on everything as being in equal personal relationships. An individual is an existence belonging to a State and her history which forms the basis of his ori-gin, and is fundamentally one body with it....

From the point of individualistic personal relationships, the relationship between sovereign and subject in our country may [perhaps] be looked upon as that between non-personalities. However, this is nothing but an error arising from treating the individual as supreme, from the notion that has individual thoughts for its nucleus, and from personal abstract consciousness. Our relationship between sovereign and subject is by no means a shallow, horizontal relationship such as implies a correlation between ruler and citizen, but is a relationship springing from a basis transcending this correlation, and is that of "dying to self and returning to [the] One," in which this basis is not lost. This is a thing that can never be understood from an individualistic way of thinking. In our country, this great Way has seen a natural development since the founding of the nation, and the most basic thing that has manifested itself as regards the subjects is in short this Way of loyalty....

Harmony: When we trace the marks of the facts of the founding of our country and the progress of our history, what we always find there is the spirit of harmony. Harmony is a product of the great achievements of the founding of the nation, and is the power behind our historical growth; it is also a humanitarian Way inseparable from our daily lives. The spirit of harmony is built on the concord of all things. When people determinedly count themselves as masters and assert their egos, there is nothing but contradictions and the setting of one against the other; and harmony is not begotten. In individualism it is possible to have cooperation, compromise, sacrifice, etc., so as to regulate and mitigate this contradiction and the setting of one against the other; but after all there exists no true harmony. That is, a society of individualism is one of clashes between [masses of] people ... and all history may be looked upon as one of class wars. Social structure and political systems in such a society, and the theories of sociology, political science, statecraft, etc., which are their logical manifestations, are essentially different from those of our country which makes harmony its fundamental Way....

Harmony as in our nation is a great harmony of individuals who, by giving play to their individual differences, and through difficulties, toil and labor, converge as one. Because of individual differences and difficulties, this harmony becomes all the greater and its substance rich. Again, in this way individualities are developed, special traits become beautiful, and at the same time they even enhance the development and well-being of the whole.

There were, however, movements by Buddhists against the state's aggressive campaign for war and its distortion of religious belief. One such organization was the Shinkō Bukkyō Seinen Dōmei (Association for Newly Emerging Buddhist Youths) a group of inspired young Buddhists who saw the moral danger in the incorporation of Buddhism with the increasingly militaristic government of the 1930s.

From: *Butsuda o Seoite Gaitō e* (Spreading of Buddhist Teaching on the Streets)[66]

This is an age of suffering. Our compatriots are seeking affection, yet have had no choice but to struggle. The masses of people seek bread, but are fed repression. To escape or to fight, today the entire world is moving about in confusion and financial difficulty.

In such an age, what should Buddhists be aware of, what contribution should they be making to society? The majority of Buddhists, intoxicated with an easy peace of mind, don't even think about these questions. Through Buddhism these Buddhists possess the highest principles available for the guidance of human beings, yet what contact do they have with the lives of the masses? Furthermore, these Buddhists claim that "religion transcends class differences and values harmony." However, in reality their role is that of an opiate, and they are therefore cursed by the masses and incite the moral indignation of young Buddhists.

This present situation is something that genuine believers cannot bear. However, when we look to already existing sectarian organizations for reform, we are forced to recognize just how serious their corrupt traditions and degeneration are. Faced with this situation, we have no choice but to resolutely propose a movement to revitalize Buddhism. A revitalized Buddhism must be based on self-reflection. It must deny currently existing Buddhism which has already lost its capacity for confrontation while, at the same time, calling on all Buddhists to return to the Buddha. A revitalized Buddhism must recognize that the suffering in present-day society comes chiefly from the capitalist economic system and must be willing to cooperate in a fundamental reform of this system, working to preserve the well-being of the masses. We must revolutionize bourgeois Buddhism and change it to a Buddhism for the masses. A revitalized Buddhism must intensify its speculation and research in an attempt to clarify Buddhist culture for the new age and bring about world peace.

Sadly, the organization's anti-war outcries were smothered by the state before it could take any real effect with the public. The organization's chairman, Senō Girō (1889–1961), was arrested just five years after the formation of the group for his "unpatriotic" stance against the government, and during his imprisonment was eventually forced to confess to charges of treason.[67] Though others in the Buddhist community also voiced their opposition to the war during these years, they too were eventually quelled by the police, often getting prosecuted or in some cases mysteriously disappearing.

It was under this totalitarianism that Buddhism was morally expected to oppose militarism. Already having experienced the violence of the *haibutsu kishaku* in 1868, Buddhist schools needed little persuasion in taking sides with the state, if just for their own protection. Zen, Pure Land, and indeed all schools came forward to endorse the national polity and its militarism, each using the concepts of Buddhist discipline, obedience, and sacrifice as their ethical basis.

In sum, the forgoing has sought to show how Buddhism, despite its strong orientation toward peace, tolerance, and preservation of life, never penetrated Japanese culture to the point that peace was effectively prioritized over compliance with the sovereign. A secular mindset, superficially colored with Buddhist motifs, prevailed most often in practice. Under the influence of preexisting Japanese social tendencies, the moral foundations of Buddhism were accordingly subordinated to the expediency of the state. There resulted a set of outwardly Buddhist teachings that, in contradiction with the inner ethos of the religion, condoned and sometimes even encouraged the most extreme forms of violence.

NOTES

1 It is understood that Shinto was adopted in Japan during the establishment of the Yamato dynasty around the fourth century AD. A further elaboration of Shinto can be found in the section on "The Modernization of Japan and the Emergence of Nationalism" in this chapter.

2 *The Dhammapada: The Path to Perfection*, Juan Mascaró (trans.) (Harmondsworth: Penguin Books, 1973), p. 50.

3 The Buddha's proper name being Siddhartha Gautama (463–383 BCE). He is also referred to as the Buddha Shakyamuni, which means "Sage of Shakyas," the name of his original tribe.

4 *The Dhammapada*, Mascaró (trans.), p. 68.

5 Ibid., p. 50.

6 Ibid., p. 35.

7 *Mahāparinibbāna Sutta* translation taken from *The Buddhist Tradition in India, China and Japan*, William Theodore de Bary (trans.) (New York: Vintage Books, 1972), p. 29.

8 Translation of *The Seventeen-Article Constitution* attributed to Prince Shōtoku taken from Hajime Nakamura, *Ways of Thinking of Eastern Peoples: India-China-Tibet-Japan* (Honolulu: University of Hawaii Press, 1985), p. 383.

9 The term *zen* originates from the Sanskrit word *dhyāna*, which means "meditate" or "meditative state." Zen is a school of Mahayana Buddhism that emphasizes experiential enlightenment through meditation.

10 Tomojirō Hayashiya and Chikai Shimakage, *Bukkyō no Sensō Kan*, translation taken from Brian Daizen Victoria, *Zen at War*, 2nd ed. (Lanham, Md.: Rowman & Littlefield Publishers, 2006), pp. 87 and 88.

11 Takuan Sōhō, *Fudōchishinmyōroku* (The Unfettered Mind), William Scott Wilson (trans.) (Tokyo: Kodansha International, 2002), pp. 114–115.

12 Lao Tzu, *Tao Te Ching*, D. C. Lau (trans.) (Harmondsworth: Penguin Books, 1963), p. 57.

13 Ibid., p. 82.

14 Mahayana (literally, "great vehicle") is one of two major branches of Buddhism in existence today, the other being Theravada. The form of Buddhism found in Japan is Mahayana Buddhism.

15 In general a bodhisattva refers to an enlightened (*bodhi*) essence or being (*sattva*). In Mahayana Buddhism a bodhisattva refers to an individual who is able to reach nirvana but delays doing so in order to save suffering beings.

16 *The Holy Teaching of Vimalakīrti: A Mahāyāna Scripture*, Robert A. F. Thurman (trans.) (University Park: Pennsylvania State University Press, 1976), pp. 73–76.

17 Translation of *Ichimaikishōmon* (One Page Testament) taken from D. T. Suzuki, *Japanese Spirituality* (*Nihon-teki reisei*), Norman Waddell (trans.) (New York: Greenwood Press, 1972), p. 138.

18 Suzuki, *Japanese Spirituality*, pp. 137–138.

19 Ibid., p. 137.

20 Translation of Dōgen Zenji, *Fukanzazengi* taken from David Edward Shanner, *The Bodymind Experience in Japanese Buddhism: A Phenomenological Study of Kūkai and Dōgen* (Albany: State University of New York Press, 1985), p. 163.

21 Translation of Dōgen, *Shōbōgenzō* taken from Keiji Nishitani, *Religion and Nothingness*, Jan Van Bragt (trans.) (Berkeley and Los Angeles: University of California Press, 1982), pp. 107–108.

22 Translation of Dōgen Zenji, *Shōbōgenzō* taken from Shanner, *The Bodymind Experience in Japanese Buddhism*, p. 172.

23 Translation of Dōgen Zenji, *Shōbōgenzō* taken from *Sources of Japanese Tradition*, Ryusaku Tsunoda, William Theodore de Bary, and Donald Keene (comp.), 2 vols. (New York: Columbia University Press, 1958), vol. 1, pp. 248–249.

24 Ibid., p. 249.

25 *Analects of Confucius*, Arthur Waley (trans.) (New York: Vintage Books, 1938), p. 85.

26 Ibid., p. 150.

27 Ibid., p. 142.

28 Ibid.

29 Ibid., pp. 168–169.

30 Ibid., p. 183.

31 Ibid., p. 135.

32 Ibid., p. 224.

33 *Tao Te Ching*, Lau (trans.), p. 111.

34 Yamamoto Tsunetomo, *Hagakure: The Book of the Samurai*, Williams Scott Wilson (trans.) (Tokyo: Kodansha International, 2002), p. 124.

35 Ibid., pp. 17–18.

36 Ibid., p. 45.

37 Ibid., pp. 102–103.

38 Ibid., p. 107.

39 Ibid., pp. 164–165.

40 Another name for *hara-kiri*.

41 Miyamoto Musashi, *Gorinsho* (The Book of Five Rings), William Scott Wilson (trans.) (Tokyo: Kodansha International, 2001), pp. 35–37.

42 Takuan Sōhō, *The Unfettered Mind*, pp. 68–69.

43 Ibid., pp. 73–74.

44 Ibid., pp. 113–114.

45 Ibid., pp. 115–118.

46 Translation of Hōnen, *Hōnen Shōnin Gyōjo Ezu* taken from Nakamura, *Ways of Thinking of Eastern Peoples*, p. 365.

47 Translation of Suzuki Shōsan, *Roankyō* taken from Suzuki, *Japanese Spirituality*, pp. 142–143.

48 Musashi, *The Book of Five Rings*, p. 161.

49 Myōan Eisai, *Kinzen Gokokuron* in *Taishō daizōkyō*, vol. 80 in *Sources of Japanese Tradition*, Tsunoda et al. (comp.), vol. 1, pp. 236–237.

50 *Sources of Japanese Tradition*, Tsunoda et al. (comp.), vol. 1, p. 235.

51 Ministry of Education, *Kokutai no hongi* (Fundamentals of Our National Polity), in *Sources of Japanese Tradition*, Tsunoda et al. (comp.), vol. 2, pp. 284–285.

52 W. Scott Morton, *Japan: Its History and Culture*, 3rd ed. (New York: McGraw-Hill, 1994), p. 183.

53 Daniel Marston (ed.), *The Pacific War Companion: From Pearl Harbor to Hiroshima* (Oxford: Osprey Publishing, 2005), p. 20.

54 Ibid., p. 26.

55 *Fundamentals of Our National Policy* translation taken from *Sources of Japanese Tradition*, Tsunoda et al. (comp.), vol. 2, p. 283.

56 *Nihongi* translation taken from *Sources of Japanese Tradition*, Tsunoda et al. (comp.), vol. 1, pp. 17–18.

57 *Kojiki: Records of Ancient Matters*, Basil Hall Chamberlain (trans.) (Tokyo: Charles E. Tuttle, 1981), pp. 177–178.

58 *Nihongi* in *Sources of Japanese Tradition*, Tsunoda et al. (comp.), vol. 1, pp. 64–66.

59 Ibid., pp. 66–67.

60 *Jinnō Shōtō-ki* translation taken from *Sources of Japanese Tradition*, Tsunoda et al. (comp.), vol. 1, pp. 273–274.

61 Nakamura, *Ways of Thinking of Eastern Peoples*, p. 525.

62 Joseph M. Kitagawa, *On Understanding Japanese Religion* (Princeton, N.J.: Princeton University Press, 1987), p. 211.

63 Nakamura, *Ways of Thinking of Eastern Peoples*, p. 413.

64 *Haibutsu kishaku* means the expulsion of Buddhism from Japan. The most well-known historic event took place in 1868 when the Meiji government sought, through official policy, to create an ideological separation between Shinto and Buddhism, with the aim of promoting Shinto as the only national religion. During this period many temples, images, and texts were destroyed. Likewise, many monks were forced to return to secular life.

65 *Kokutai no hongi* translation taken from *Sources of Japanese Tradition*, Tsunoda et al. (comp.), vol. 2, pp. 280–283.

66 Inagaki Masami, *Butsuda o Seoite Gaitō e* translation taken from Victoria, *Zen at War*, p. 67.

67 Victoria, *Zen at War*, p. 73

SELECT BIBLIOGRAPHY

De Bary, William Theodore, *The Buddhist Tradition in India, China and Japan* (New York: Vintage Books, 1972).

Kitagawa, Joseph M., *On Understanding Japanese Religion* (Princeton, N.J.: Princeton University Press, 1987).

Machida, Soho, *Renegade Monk: Hōnen and Japanese Pure Land Buddhism*, Ioanis Mentzas (trans.) (Berkeley: University of California Press, 1999).

Marston, Daniel (ed.), *The Pacific War Companion: From Pearl Harbor to Hiroshima* (Oxford: Osprey Publishing, 2005).

Morton, W. Scott, *Japan: Its History and Culture*, 3rd ed. (New York: McGraw-Hill, 1994).

Nakamura, Hajime, *Ways of Thinking of Eastern Peoples: India-China-Tibet-Japan* (Honolulu: University of Hawaii Press, 1985).

Nishitani, Keiji, *Religion and Nothingness*, Jan Van Bragt (trans.) (Berkeley: University of California Press, 1982).

Shanner, David Edward, *The Bodymind Experience in Japanese Buddhism: A Phenomenological Study of Kūkai and Dōgen* (Albany: State University of New York Press, 1985).

Tikhonov, Vladimir, and Torkel Brekke (eds.), *Buddhism and Violence: Militarism and Buddhism in Modern Asia* (New York: Routledge, 2013).

Victoria, Brian Daizen, *Zen at War*, 2nd ed. (Lanham, Md.: Rowman & Littlefield, 2006).

11

Sikh Tradition

Torkel Brekke

Sikhism originated with the religious sage Guru Nanak, who was born in Punjab in 1469 and died in 1539. Guru Nanak founded what is often known in India as a panth, *that is, a path to religious realization, a new religious movement. Nanak was followed by nine Sikh gurus, the last of whom was Guru Gobind Singh, the founder of the Khalsa, or the community of the pure (baptized Sikhs). The communal religious life of the Sikhs takes place in houses of worship called* gurdwaras *(literally, "the Guru's door"), and it centers on the sacred book called the* Guru Granth Sahib, *which was compiled in the late 1600s. In modern times, Sikhism has spread to many parts of the globe through migration, and Sikhs have made visible cultural contributions to societies on most continents.*

Introduction

The focus of Sikhism is a belief in God, called The Timeless One (*Akal Purakh*). Sikhs believe that God is the creator and sustainer of the universe and that God is immanent in all of creation. As an Indian religion, Sikhism affirms *transmigration*, the continued rebirth after death of some essential part of living beings. The goal of Sikhism is to achieve union with God through meditation on the divine name (*nam*), which is the eternal presence of God in creation. If human beings devote themselves to remembrance of the divine name (*nam simaran*), they will achieve complete peace in their union with God and thereby stop the painful cycle of rebirth. Guru Nanak was followed by nine other gurus. The tenth, Guru Gobind Singh, died in 1708 during a period marked by clashes with the armies of the Mughal Empire. Two of the texts included in this chapter are authored by him, according to the Sikh tradition.

Thus, Sikhism is a fairly young religion with a well-defined beginning. It has a collection of scriptures and a rather limited number of followers compared with world religions such as Christianity or Islam. The number of Sikhs is comparable to the number of followers of the Jewish tradition, but with just five centuries of history. This makes it both easier and more difficult to give a good picture of Sikh ethics in general and Sikh ethics of war in particular. It is easier in the sense that the number of relevant texts and authors are fewer than in the Christian or Islamic traditions. Moreover, although there are several important lines of division within Sikhism, the diversity represents nothing like the proliferation of sects and denominations within Christianity. On the other hand, the task is more difficult because little research has been done on Sikhism compared with the world religions. Several British scholars of the nineteenth century translated the Sikh scriptures and wrote monographs on the Sikhs. Among the most famous was Joseph D. Cunningham's *A History of the Sikhs: From the Origin of the Nation to the Battles of the Sutlej* (1849) and the English translation of the *Adi Granth* produced by the German missionary Ernest Trumpp in 1877. Still, the academic study of the history of Sikhism as a religious and literary tradition, and the ethnographic study of contemporary Sikhism, was established quite recently. The modern academic study of Sikhism is closely associated with a limited number of scholars such as W. H. McLeod, Pashaura Singh, J. S. Grewal, and Gurinder Singh Mann. It is impossible to read the learned works of these scholars without being struck by the number of questions still to be answered concerning the history and development of the Sikh community and its teachings.

The Gurus and Their Teachings

Although both Islam and Hinduism were dominant religions in India in Guru Nanak's days, his thought was mainly influenced by the worldview and the theological ideas found in the traditions we can include under the heading of "Hinduism." More specifically, Guru Nanak belonged to a milieu of religious seekers called *Sants*. The Sant tradition of North India was a mix of religious movements that opposed the ritualism and conventional patterns of orthodox Hinduism. Important elements in Sant religiosity were the devotional religion focused on the greatest of the Hindu gods, Vishnu, and the practice of yoga. In addition, the mystical theology of the Muslim Sufi saints had a certain influence on this milieu.[1] The core message of Sant religiosity was love. The devotees must love God with intensity and they must seek God not through conventional rituals, offerings, pilgrimages, or following traditional authority, but rather through inward meditation and unselfish devotion. God was sovereign, formless, eternal, and ineffable, and he was also immanent in His creation and could be found inside one's own heart through the right techniques and state of mind. This was the teaching that Guru Nanak promoted to his group of followers, and this interior, devotional religion continues to be the core of Sikhism.

The gurus that followed Nanak contributed in different ways to developing Sikhism as a religious community. The self-consciousness of Sikhism as a *political* community developed from the fifth guru, Arjun (b. 1563, guru 1581–1606). This development is closely connected to the political history of South Asia. Emperor Akbar died in 1606 and left the Mughal throne to his son Jahangir, who was less tolerant of non-Muslim communities. Guru Arjun was martyred in 1606 and his son Hargobind started building a Sikh army to resist Mughal oppression. According to Sikh tradition, he also extended the authority of the gurus to include political matters. This is expressed in the donning of two swords: one represented spiritual authority (*piri*) and the other represented temporal authority (*miri*). With the accession of Mughal Aurangzeb to the throne in 1658, relations with the authorities in Delhi became increasingly complicated and Aurangzeb would prove to be an enemy of the Sikhs.

The conflict with the Mughals reached a peak under the tenth guru, Gobind Singh (1666–1708). He was the son of the ninth guru, the martyr Tegh Bahadur, who was executed by Aurangzeb in Delhi in 1675. Guru Gobind Singh was born in 1666 in Patna. In the "Bachitar Natak" Gobind states, "When the Lord commanded I took birth in this dark-age (*kaliyuga*)."[2] In other words, he considered himself to have been born to carry out God's plan on earth, that is, to spread the true religion (*dharma*), thereby resisting tyranny and false religion. As a boy he was taken to Punjab for his education and he later assumed guruship at his capital in Anandpur. From the point of view of the great Mughal Aurangzeb in Delhi, the Sikh leader was one among a number of rebellious chieftains at the fringes of the vast Islamic empire. In 1699, on Baisakhi Day (i.e., the first day of the month of Baisakh), Gobind invited every Sikh to join him, and he founded the *Khalsa* (a religious order) by baptizing five loyal followers and giving them the name Singh. As an expression of this rebirth and initation into the order, its members are required to wear five symbols: uncut hair and beard (*kes*), carrying a comb (*kangha*), wearing knee-length breeches (*kachh*), wearing a steel bracelet (*kara*), and carrying a saber (*kirpan*).

The founding of the *Khalsa* meant the creation of a new relationship between the guru and his followers. It also meant the introduction of a code of conduct, the *rahit*. This is regarded as one of the most crucial events in Sikh history. At the same time, the Mughals decided that Guru Gobind Singh was a threat to the empire. This resulted in the siege of Anandpur in 1701 and the Battle at Chamkaur in 1704. The battle at Chamkaur is a key historical focus for modern Sikh discussions of the *dharma yudh*, the just war, as we will see.

Sacred Scripture and History

To understand the essence of Sikh theology and religiosity we need to look at the holy book of the Sikhs, as this is the center of their religious activity. Much of the historical research on Sikhism has focused on the sacred text *Adi Granth*, also known as the *Guru Granth Sahib* (literally, "the respected guru-book"). Compiled in 1604 and canonized a century later, this scripture contains about 3,000 compositions of the six Sikh gurus and like-minded poets and bards in the Sikh courts, spread over more than 1,400 pages in modern printed versions of the text.

The preservation of historical manuscripts from the sixteenth century has made it possible for scholars to reconstruct a compilation history of the *Guru Granth Sahib* that is quite unique in comparison to many other religions.[3] Sikh historiography recounts how the first Sikh guru, Guru Nanak, had a religious experience in his late twenties and set out on extensive travels to refine and spread his message before he settled in Kartarpur (Punjab) and established a community of Sikhs. It is commonly held that Guru Nanak ensured the preservation of his teaching by committing his compositions to writing in the Gurmukhi script (literally, "the mouth of the guru") and establishing a succession line of human gurus, who operated as spiritual leaders of the Sikh community during an era of two hundred years. Guru Nanak's poetry seems to have been collected in a manuscript (the *Harshahai pothi*) that was created in the 1530s. A major step in the evolution of the Sikh scripture was taken in 1604 when the fifth guru, Guru Arjun (1563–1606), compiled the compositions of the first five Sikh gurus as well as religious hymns by like-minded Hindu and Muslim poet-saints (*bhagats*) of different sectarian traditions in a new manuscript (the *Kartarpur Pothi*). A century later, the canon was sealed after the hymns of the ninth guru, Guru Tegh Bahadur (1621–1675), had been added to the Sikh scripture, which was now entitled *Adi Granth* (literally, "the original book"). In 1708, the tenth guru, Gobind Singh, declared the scripture to be the eternal Guru of the Sikhs. This decision signaled the end of a succession line of human gurus, since the scripture, hereafter called the *Guru Granth* with an added suffix of reverence (*Sahib*), succeeded to the office of guru and was endowed with the spiritual authority to guide the Sikhs.

Given these events in the Sikh tradition, the majority of Sikhs take the *Guru Granth Sahib* to be a collection of their historical Sikh gurus' divinely inspired utterances and teachings, simultaneously as they understand it to be their living guru. Wherever the Sikhs have settled in the world, scripture occupies the center of their devotional assemblies. In the Sikh place of worship (the *gurdwara*, or the "Guru's door") the scripture is placed daily on an elevated throne before worshippers. Hymns from the text are recited with devotional singing, accompanied by oral expositions. When religious Sikhs embark on new enterprises in life or have queries regarding ethical standpoints and acts, they turn to the scripture and search for moral guidance and support.

The early Sikh teaching presented in the gurus' poetic language presumes the existence of a divine will and order (*hukam*) that is embedded in the creation of all living things and keeps the cosmos going. Human beings are bound to the cycle of births and rebirths. However, they are also given a unique opportunity to break from this transmigration and attain liberation (*mukti*). According to a central theme in the *Guru Granth Sahib*, the self-centeredness of humans keeps them alienated from God and entangled with the material world. Lust, anger, greed, worldly attachment, and egoism are considered to be five vices that confuse us and create self-centeredness. For the Sikh gurus the internal struggle of humans is primarily a combat against vice. This is acccomplished by submitting to the divine will and engaging in devotion to God. The term *gurmukh* (literally, a "guru-oriented person") is used to designate the liberated state of an individual who has come to possess the godly virtues of truth, compassion, contentment, humility, and love. Such a person, moreover, fears only God and is thus fearless in the world. By contrast, the *manmukh* is the self-oriented and self-willed person who remains deluded by the world. It is precisely within this spiritual framework that the theme of war arises in the Sikh scripture.

The Sikh gurus, however, did not limit their writing to spirituality but also expressed ideas about the ideal society and expected norms for rulers. The vision presented in *Guru Granth Sahib* is a society based on divine justice without oppression of any kind. Like the characteristics of a redeemed *gurmukh*, a worthy ruler is one who is obedient to God's will, has conquered the five vices, and humbly serves the people with truth, justice, compassion, and forgiveness. For example, in one hymn Guru Nanak writes: "He alone, who is worthy of the throne, sits on the throne. He is such a page of the Lord; who by Guru's instructions has silenced the five demons."[4]

The Sikhs are well aware of the sometimes violent nature of their relations with the Indian state, whether under the rule of the great Mughal Aurangzeb in the early 1700s or under Prime Minister Indira Gandhi, who was assassinated by her Sikh bodyguards after she had ordered an armed assault on the Golden Temple in 1984. The Sikh tradition presents the comparative ethics of war with a very topical example, for it is a tradition of ethical reasoning that is still alive and relevant to politics. The Sikh tradition of just war (*dharam yudh*) has been kept alive by the Sikhs' keen sense of being a special people with a distinct identity and by their recurrent conflicts with the state authorities in Delhi. The violent conflicts between the Khalistan movement[5] and the Indian state in the early 1980s made questions of legitimate rule and violence an urgent question for many Sikhs, insofar as the conflict affected them so directly.

The *Guru Granth Sahib* (First Compiled in the 1680s)

As the primary source to early Sikh beliefs and ethics, the *Guru Granth Sahib* provides a tapestry with images of war, battles, and warriors both in a mythical past and in the time of the Gurus. However, this text is not a manual with explicit prescriptions for a Sikh code of conduct in warfare. Rather, images of war and warriors are used in this religious poetry primarily as linguistic metaphors to articulate the spiritual teaching of the early gurus about the internal struggles in human life. Political concepts seem to be employed first and foremost in a metaphorical sense, with the aim of praising the divine, providing vivid images of guru-oriented people, and teaching how humans face inner struggles in life. In this context, the ideal warrior is a spiritually advanced person who is liberated from selfish attachments and fears only God. In modern times, many Sikh exponents of the *Guru Granth Sahib* would, however, maintain that an early conception of war was developed by the gurus and that some of the scriptural references to war were meant to signify actual combat in the physical world.

The language of the *Guru Granth Sahib* does in fact contain a rich vocabulary relating to war, weapons, and brave heroes. The terms "warrior" and "hero" (*sūr/sūrā*) recur frequently as epithets for God, as seen below in hymns by Guru Arjun. In other hymns the same word operates as a metaphor for guru-oriented persons, that is, the spiritual and heroic "warriors" who have control of their own minds, fear only God, and have subjugated the vices by following the guru's teaching. Guru Arjun fully exploits the image of warfare when describing the strength of a congregation of saintly people who are immersed in devotion to the divine. But in a sense "warrior" is also employed to designate the attraction of vice. Guru Arjun thus speaks of the human emotional attachment to the world as a destructive warrior on the battlefield who even entices the gods and crushes other powerful beings.[6] Similarly, Guru Arjun presents the five vices as powerful "fighters" (*sūrbīr*) to be seized and controlled by humans.[7]

Starting with the first, positive sense, the following passages illustrate how the early Sikh gurus used the word "hero" or "warrior" (*sūra*) for saintly people in their compositions.

From: *One Hymn by Guru Nanak* (1469–1539)[8]

O my infinite and Unequalled Lord, Thou art from the very beginning and the beginning of ages.

O primordial and immaculate Lord, Thou art my Beloved Spouse. I reflect on the way to unite with the True One, and fix I my attention in the True One.

For many ages there was inky darkness and the Creator-Lord sat in trance. Then there were only Thy True Name, Thy True glory and the greatness of Thy True throne. In the True age, truth and contentment permeated the human bodies. In truth and Thee, O Deep and Unfathomable True Lord, the mortals then remained absorbed. The True Lord assays the mortals on the touchstone of truth and issues True commands. True and content is my Perfect True Guru. He alone is a hero,* who believes in the Guru's word.

He, who submits to the command of the commandant obtains true seat in the True Court.

From: *Four Hymns by the Fifth Guru*, Guru Arjun (1563–1606)[9]

He alone, who is imbued with God's love in this age, is said to be a warrior.† Everything is under his control, who, by the Perfect True Guru's grace, conquers his self.

Sing thou the Lord's praise with deepest love.

They, who seek Lord's refuge and meditate on His Name, are blended with the Lord. Pause.

The feet of God's slave abide within my mind, and in their association, my body is rendered pure. O Treasure of mercy, bless Nanak with the dust of Thine serf's feet. This alone is the source of peace for him. . . .

The saints are the succourers of the soul and are the ferry-men to cross the terrible world-ocean. O Nanak, know them to be the highest of all, as they cherish love for the Lord's Name.

They, who know the Lord, swim across. They are the heroes and they alone, the warriors.‡ Nanak is a sacrifice unto those who by uttering God's Name land on the shore.[10] . . .

Within the world, the mortal is engrossed in doubt and realizes not the Incomprehensible Lord, Ineffable is whose discourse.

He, whom the Lord instructs, understands Him. Him the Lord cherishes like His child. If man abandons *mammon*,§ then he can abandon it not. If he amasses it, then the fear of losing it haunts his mind. He, whose honor the Lord protects in the midst of this *mammon*, is a saint and over the head of such a saint, I wave the fly-brush.**

---

* *Sūra.*

† *Sūra.*

‡ *Sūre se bīr.*

§ Money, worldly goods.

** The fly-brush (*chauri*) is a whisk waved over the holy book as a symbol of royalty.

He alone is a warrior who remains dead in life.[11]. . .

All the saints are an unconquerable army of the heroes, who have doused their body with the coat of arms of humility.

The recitation of the Lord's praises are their weapons and shelter and the Guru's word is the shield in their hands.

To realize the Lord's path, is their riding the horses, chariots and elephants.

They walk fearlessly amidst the army of their enemies and charge them with the Lord's praises.

They conquer the whole world and overwhelm the five thieves as well, O Nanak.[12]

From: *Three Hymns by the Third Guru*, Guru Amardas (1479–1574)

The Perfect one, Himself unites one with the True Guru and through his instruction he makes him a very powerful warrior.

The Guru fixes man's mind with the True Lord, who blessing him with glory, unites Him with Himself. Within our very home is He, the True Lord.

Rare is the one, who realizes this by the Guru's grace.[13]. . .

Valiant and the most distinguished are the persons, who grapple with their mind.

They who recognize their own self ever remain united with their God.

This is the glory of the theologians, that they remain absorbed in their own mind.

They embrace the True Lord's meditation and mount to the Reverend Master's mansion. They, who conquer their mind by the Guru's grace; they conquer the whole world.[14]. . .

Creating both the sides, He, the One Lord, is pervading both. Spreading the gospel of the Vedas* He has brought about strife between the two.

Attachment and [detachment] are the two sides and it is the faith that discriminates between the two.

False and worthless are the egocentrics. Verily lose they in the Lord's court. They, who practice the Guru's instruction, are the Lord's warriors, who have stilled their lust and wrath.

They, who are, embellished with the Name, enter into the True Lord's mansion. The saints, who love the True Name, are pleasing to Thee, O Lord.

They, who serve their True Guru unto them I am a sacrifice.[15]

The following two texts are examples of compositions in which the fifth guru, Guru Arjun, gives God the epithet of a great warrior (*sūra*):

I beg of all the saints to give me a commodity. I make a supplication and abandon my ego. *Lakhs*† of times I am [a] sacrifice unto them and pray for the grant of the

---

* The Vedas are the holy scriptures of the Hindus.
† In the Indian numeral system *lakh* means 100,000.

dust of saint's feet. Thou, O' Lord! art the donor and Thou the mighty destiny scribe. Thou art Omnipotent and ever the peace-giver. All are blessed by Thee. Do Thou make my lifetime, fruitful.

They whose home body is rendered pure by Thine sight, conquer the arduous soul fort. Thou art the giver and Thou the powerful designer of chances. None is as great a warrior as Thou.[16]. . .

There is but One God. By True Guru's grace is He obtained. O God, the Lord of the world and the Destroyer of pain, I seek the refuge of Thine feet. Bless Thou me, Thy serf, with Thine Name. O Lord, show mercy unto me; save me by Thine grace and taking me by the arm, pull me out of the well. Pause.

The man is blinded by lust and wrath, he is fettered by worldly attachments and his body and its clothes are full of many sins. Without the Lord, no one else is the man's protector. O, accomplished protecting Warrior; make me utter Thine Name.

O, Lord the Purifier of sinners and the Savior of big and small creatures, even the expounders of Vedas have not found Thy limit. My Lord is an ocean of virtues and peace and the mine of jewels. Nanak sings the praise of the Lover of His devoted servants.[17]

Fearing no one in the world but only God is another central theme in the gurus' religious poetry and a quality of the ideal guru-oriented person and the warrior. In one hymn Guru Nanak describes how all of creation, including the warriors and heroes, exists in fear of God:

In Lord's fear wind and breeze ever blow. In Lord's fear flow *lakhs* of rivers. In Lord's fear fire is forced to perform labor. In Lord's fear the earth is trampled under burden. In Lord's fear the cloud moves head-long. In Lord's fear Dharamraj (Righteous Judge) stands at His door. In Lord's fear is restrained the sun and in Lord's fear the moon. They travel myriads of miles without an end. In Lord's fear are the men of miracles, Buddhas, the demigods and the Yogis. In Lord's fear is stretched the sky. In Lord's fear are the warriors and the very powerful heroes. In Lord's fear multitudes come and go. The Lord has written the writ of His fear on the heads of all. Nanak, the True Formless Lord alone is fearless.[18]

In a more negative sense, Guru Nanak mentions how fighting battles is akin to other human activities that do not please God. He emphasizes how uttering the divine name is alone truly pleasing to God:

The Lord is pleased not by making music, tuning musical instrument[s] and reading the Vedas. Through wisdom, knowledge and Yoga, he is pleased not. The Lord is pleased not by ever feeling sorrow. He is pleased not with beauty, wealth and revelments. He is pleased not by wandering naked at the places of pilgrimage. By giving gifts and alms, the Lord is softened not. Sitting outside alone in wilderness, He is softened not. Fighting to death as a warrior in a battle, the Lord is melted not. Becoming the dust of the feet of many, He is melted not. The account of hearty love alone is writ there. O Nanak, if one utters the True Name, the Lord is supremely pleased.[19]

The following is an example of a hymn in which Guru Nanak seems to emphasize that the duty of all, including the warriors, is to be immersed in meditation of the divine name regardless of their social duties in the world:

> The way of union with the Lord is the way of Divine knowledge. With the Brahmans*
> the way is through the Vedas.
> Khatri's way is the way of bravery and of the Sudras, the way is the service of
> others.
> The duty of all is the duty of the One Lord's meditation, provided one cares to
> know this secret.
> Of him Nanak is a slave. He Himself is the Immaculate Lord.
> The One Lord is the God of all gods. He is the soul of their godliness.
> If any one knows the mystery of the soul and the Omnipresent Lord; of him, Nanak
> is the slave. He Himself is the Immaculate Lord.[20]

In the *Guru Granth Sahib* the real fight and struggle is within humans. In one composition Guru Arjun exemplifies this killing (*mare*) of the duality and ego in humans:

> He, who kills this, is a hero.
> He, who kills it, is perfect.
> He, who kills it, obtains glory.
> He, who kills it, is freed from suffering.
> Rare is such a person, who kills and casts off his duality.
> Killing it, he enjoys the union of the King. Pause.
> He, who kills it, has no fear.
> He, who kills it, is absorbed in the Name.
> He, who kills it, has his desire quenched.
> He, who kills it, is approved in [the] Lord's Court.
> He, who kills it, becomes wealthy.
> He, who kills it, becomes worthy of honor.
> He, who kills it, is rendered a celibate.
> He, who kills it, attains to salvation.
> The advent of him, who kills it, is of account.
> He, who kills it, is stable and opulent.
> He, who kills it, is indeed very fortunate.
> He, who kills it, is wakeful, night and day.
> He, who kills it, is emancipated in life.
> He, who kills it, has pure way of life.
> He, who kills it, is a good divine.

---

* Brahmans are the people who belong to the high, priestly castes. They have certain religious roles and privileges in Hindu society.

He, who kills it, is the visualizer of the Lord.
Without killing this love of another, man becomes not acceptable, even though he may perform millions of rituals; worship and austerities.
Without killing it, one's being born ceases not.
Without killing it, man escapes not from death.
Without killing it, one obtains not Divine comprehension.
Without killing it, impurity is not washed off.
Without killing it, everything remains defiled.
Without killing it, everything is an entanglement.
Unto whom, the treasure of kindness becomes merciful, he secures release and attains all perfection. He, whose duality has been destroyed by the Guru, says Nanak, is the Lord's contemplator.[21]

Two popular and oft-cited hymns, which many Sikhs believe legitimize the use of violence for a righteous cause and are interpreted as referring to real physical fights, are written by the saint-poet Kabir. According to professional exegetes in Punjab, these hymns were used to justify political action during the 1980s:

The battle-drum beats in the mind's sky, aim is taken and the wound is inflicted. They, who are the warriors, enter the battle-field. Now is the time of combat. He alone is known to be a warrior, who fights for the sake of his religion. He dies cut piece by piece, but deserts not the battle-field, ever.[22]

Kabir has structured this composition after different consonants and vowels in the alphabet and therefore the verse is rather short and starts with "Y."

Y – If Thou know anything, then, destroy thy evil-intellect and subdue thy body hamlet. Being engaged in battle, if thou fleest not away, thou shalt go by the Name of a hero.[23]

A professional exegete connected to a Sikh Missionary College in Roopar (Punjab) explained in an interview in January 2010 that the following hymns by Guru Nanak can legitimize a resort to violence by someone who has been unjustly insulted and thereby dishonored:

He alone lives within whose mind that Master abides. O' Nanak! none else is really alive. If someone lives, he shall depart dishonored. All, that he eats, is forbidden. Imbued with the pleasure of the intoxication of authority and revelments of riches, the mortal dances shamelessly. Nanak, he is beguiled and defrauded. Without the Lord's Name, he loses his honor and departs.[24]

In one composition Guru Nanak explains how gods and kings in a legendary past lost their power because they were arrogant, full of pride, and had often forgotten about God:

Brahma indulged in ego, and he understood not the Lord.
Faced with the calamity of the loss of Vedas, he did repent.
Whoever remembers the Lord, his soul is propitiated.
So heinous is the pride in this world.
The Guru effaces the ego of him whom He meets. Pause.

Bal the King, in the pride of wealth and inflated with excessive load of pride performed gratuitous feasts.

Bereft of Guru's counsel, he had to go to the underworld.

Hari Chand gave alms and earned renown.

Without the Guru, he found not the limit of the Inscrutable Lord.

The Lord Himself misleads and Himself imparts understanding.

Evil intellected Harnaksh* committed wicked deeds.

The Pervading Lord Master is the destroyer of pride.

The Lord showered His benediction and saved Prahlad.† Foolish and unwise Ravana‡ forgot the Lord.

Ceylon together with his head was plundered.

He indulged in ego, and was without Guru's love.

The Lord killed thousand-armed Arjan, the demons Madh Kaitab, and buffalo like Mahkhaswa.

Seizing him, God tore up Harnaksh with nails.

The demons were slain without the practice of Lord's meditation.

The demons Jara Sandh and Kaliaman were destroyed.

Rakatbej and Kal Nem, demons were annihilated.

Slaying the demons, the Lord saved the Saints.

Himself, the Lord, as the True Guru meditates on His Name.

Because of duality God slew the devils.

For their true devotion the Lord saved the Guru-wards.

Sunk in ego, Daryodhna§ lost his honor.

He did not realize the Pervading Lord Creator.

He, who teases God's slave himself putrefies in pain.

Janmeja did not realize the Guru's Word.

Lured by doubt, how could he find peace?

By forgetting the Lord, even for an instant man has to repent afterward.

Kans, Kes, and Chandur had no equal.

Without knowing the Omnipresent Lord, they lost their honor, Sans the Lord of the Universe, none can save the mortal.

Without the Guru, self-conceit cannot be effaced.

---

* Harnakash or Harnaksh is a variant of the name "Hiranyakashipu." The latter is the father of Prahlada (see next footnote) in Hindu mythology.
† Prahlad or Prahlada is a well-known mythological figure in both Hinduism and Sikhism. He is the perfect devotee of God.
‡ Ravana is a well-known demon in Indian mythology.
§ This is a variant of the name "Duryodhana." Duryodhana is a great warrior and villain of the Hindu *Mahabharata* epic.

By Guru's instruction, faith, composure, and God's Name are procured.

Nanak, by singing the praises of the Lord, the Name is obtained.[25]

The following text illustrates how the first guru, Guru Nanak, commented on the first Mughal invasion in 1526, and the atrocities that ensued. The hymn has sometimes been interpreted as if Guru Nanak were a political writer of his time, with the implication that the Mughals won the battle because of their superior weaponry (they worked no miracles but still the religious leaders failed to halt them). Still, the main point of this composition seems to be to praise God, who is all-powerful.

Where are those sports, stables and horses?

Where are the drums and bugles? Where are those sword-belts and chariots? Where are those scarlet uniforms?

Where are those mirrored finger-rings and beautiful faces, which are no longer seen here.

This world is Thine and Thou art the Lord of Universe.

In a moment Thou establishest and disestablishest. Thou distributest wealth as Thou pleasest. Pause.

Where are those houses, gates, seraglios* and mansions and where are those beautiful caravanaries?

Where is that comfortable couch enjoying damsel, by seeing whom one would get no sleep?

Where are those betel-leaves,† betel-sellers and charming fairies? They have vanished like the shadow.

For this wealth many are ruined and it has disgraced many.

Without misdeeds it is not amassed, and it departs not with the dead.

He, whom the Creator Himself destroys, him, He first deprives of virtue.

When they heard of invasion of Emperor Babar, then, millions of religious leaders failed to halt him.

He burned houses, resting places and strong palaces and the princes, cut into pieces, he caused to roll in dust.

No Mughal became blind and no one wrought any miracle.

There raged a battle between the Mughals and Pathans and the sword was wielded in the battle-field. They, the Mughals, aimed and fired their guns and they, the Pathans attacked with their elephants.

They, whose letter has been torn in God's court, must die, O my brethren. There were the women of Hindus, Muslims, Bhattis and Rajputs.

The robes of some were torn from head to foot, and some had their dwellings in the cremation ground.

* The living quarters of wives and concubines.
† The betel-leaf has been used as a stimulant in South Asia for a long time. Today it is normally chewed with arecan nuts, and sometimes tobacco, as *paan*.

How did they, whose majestic husbands came not home, pass their night?

The Creator, of Himself, acts and causes others to act. To whom should we complain?

Weal and woe, O God, are according to Thy will. To whom should man go to wail?

The Commander issues His command and is pleased. Nanak, the mortal obtains, what is destined for him.[26]

Next are introduced two popular *gurbani* hymns by Guru Nanak, which have often been advanced as justification for the claim that a conception of militant martyrdom was developed early in the Sikh tradition and by the first guru.

If thou yearnest to play the game of love, step on to my path, with thy head placed on the palm of thy hand.

And, once thou settest thy feet on this Path, then lay down thou thy head and mind not public opinion.[27] . . .

Come mates, let us meet and contemplate over the True Name. Let us bewail over our body's (soul's) separation from the Lord and remember Him.

Let us cherish the Lord and keep an eye on the Path. We, too have to go there.

He, who creates, also destroys. All that takes place is in His will.

Whatever He has done, that has happened. How can we give the command? Come and meet me, O maids; let us take the True Name.

O people, let us not call death bad. There is hardly any such person, who knows how to die.

Serve, thou, thy Omnipotent Lord.

Thus, thy path in the Yond shall be easy to tread.

If thou go by the easy route, then shalt thou gather fruit and receive honor in the world beyond.

If thou go with the offering of meditation, then shalt thou merge in the True Lord and thy honor will be approved.

Thou shalt obtain place in the Master's mansion, be pleasing to Him and enjoy revelments with love.

If one knows how to die, O people then, death would not be called bad.

Fruitful is the dying of the brave persons,[*] whose death is approved by the Lord (die for a good cause).

Hereafter, they alone are acclaimed as warriors,[†] who receive true honor in the Lord's court.

They depart with honor, obtain glory in the Lord's court and suffer not pain in the next world. Deeming the Lord but One, they dwell upon Him and then gather reward. The Lord is such, by serving whom, the fear is dispelled. Indulge thou not in ego and abide within thyself. The Knower Himself knows everything.

---

[*] *Munasām sūriām.*
[†] *Sūre.*

Profitable is the dying of the brave persons, whose death is approved by the Lord.

Says Nanak, who should we wail for, O Sire, when this world is but a play?

The Lord watches His craftsmanship and gives thought to His creation.

He, who has created the universe, gives thought to His creation.

He, who has created, alone knows.

The Lord Himself sees, Himself understands and Himself realizes He His will.

He who has made all this deal alone knows it. Infinite is His beauty.

Says Nanak, whom should we weep for, O father. This world is but a play.[28]

The *Dasam Granth* (Mid-Eighteenth Century)

The *Dasam Granth* is an important text for an understanding of Sikh ideas in the eighteenth century. It is a collection of diverse literary materials heavily influenced by Hinduism. For instance, texts about the goddess Chandi in the *Dasam Granth* (such as the Chandi Charitra Ukti Bilas, the Chandi Charitra, and the Var Sri Bhagauti Ji Ki) are poems about the struggle between gods and demons taken from the Hindu mythic repertoire.

In the *Dasam Granth*, special significance must be given to the text called "Bachitar Natak," traditionally regarded as the guru's autobiography. The battles described in the "Bachitar Natak" follow the model of the heroic battles found in epic Hinduism. The "Bachitar Natak" does not really touch on moral questions except when the author explains the terrible consequences of abandoning the guru as the strong Mughal Army is closing in. Those who turn away from the feet of the guru will be ridiculed in this world and end up in hell, as the text explains over a number of verses.[29] Another important section of the *Dasam Granth* is the "Zafarnama." This is supposedly a letter written by Guru Gobind Singh to the Emperor Aurangzeb shortly after the Battle at Chamkaur. A translation of this text is herein included in its entirety

Much work remains to be done on the sources for the life of Guru Gobind Singh, as Gurinder Singh Mann has pointed out, and we may expect a more complete picture of the life and times of the tenth guru to appear in the future.[30] In fact, Mann has suggested that the attribution of compositions in the *Dasam Granth* to the guru is based on a twentieth-century misinterpretation of the title *Sri Mukhvak Patishai* found in the compositions.[31]

From: "Bachitar Natak"[32]

We enter the "Bachitar Natak" in Section V, where we hear how Guru Nanak, the first guru, entered the world to spread the Dharma.

Guru Nanak spread Dharma in the Iron age and put the seekers on the path.
Those who followed the path propagated by him, were never harmed by the vices.[33]

In the following verses we are told about Guru Tegh Bahadur, who was the ninth guru and the father of Guru Gobind Singh. Tegh Bahadur is central to Sikh ideals of martyrdom. According to tradition he was beheaded by Aurangzeb in Delhi because he refused to convert to Islam. By this act of defiance he supported a group of Hindus who had sought his assistance against aggressive attempts at conversion by the Mughal emperor.

> He protected the forehead mark and sacred thread (of the Hindus) which marked a great event in the Iron age.
>
> For the sake of saints, he laid down his head without even a sigh.
>
> For the sake of Dharma, he sacrificed himself. He laid down his head but not his creed.
>
> The saints of the Lord abhor the performance of miracles and malpractices....
>
> Breaking the potsherd of his body on the head of the king of Delhi (Aurangzeb), He left for the abode of the Lord.
>
> None could peform such a feat as that of Tegh Bahadur.[34]

After describing the line of gurus preceding him, Guru Gobind Singh arrives at his own birth. This extract is from Section VI of the text.

> When the Lord ordered me, I was born in this Iron age.[35]

Then Guru Gobind Singh explains how all other prophets, such as Muhammad and several Hindu saints, have failed. In the following verse, the poet asserts that both Muslims and Hindus are mistaken in their beliefs:

> Someone studies the Quran and someone studies the Puranas.
>
> Mere reading cannot save one from death. Therefore such works are vain and do not help at the time of death.[36]...
>
> When the Lord Willed, I was born on this earth.
>
> Now I shall narrate briefly my own story.[37]

Section VII relates briefly Guru Gobind Singh's own story, his birth and early life. Then, in Section VIII, we are told about how the guru was forced to employ violence to defend himself against attackers. In the following two verses there is explicit reference to the hero Drona, one of the key persons in the great Hindu war-epic the *Mahabharata*. This shows how Sikh warrior poetry was influenced by the wider traditions of Hindu literature.

> Maharu got enraged and with frightening expression killed brave Khans in the battlefield.
>
> The godly Daya Ram, filled with great ire, fought very heroically in the field like Dronacharya.[38]

In the next verses, we hear of a battle between Guru Gobind Singh and his enemies. There is a reference to Lord Krishna, which is another sign of the porous boundaries between Hinduism and Sikhism before modern times. Toward the end of this section the Guru mentions that he moves to Anandpur. This would be his capital until he was forced to flee when the great army of the Mughal emperor Aurangzeb besieged the town.

Kirpal in rage, rushed with his mace and struck it on the head of the tenacious Hayaat Khan.

With all his might, he caused the marrow [to] flow out of his head, which splashed like the butter spattering out of the pitcher of butter broken by Lord Krishna.

Then Nand Chand, in fierce rage, wielding his sword struck it with force.

But it broke. Then he drew his dagger and the tenacious warrior saved the honor of the Sodhi clan.

Then the maternal uncle Kirpal, in great ire, manifested the war-feats like a true Kshatriya.

The great hero was struck by an arrow, but he caused the brave Khan to fall from the saddle.

Sahib Chand, the valiant Kshatriya, killed a bloody Khan of Khorasan.

He slew several graceful warriors, with full force; the soldiers who survived, fled away in order to save their lives. . . .

There in great fury, a warrior Hari Chand, very skillfully took position in the battlefield.

He discharged sharp arrows in great range and whosoever was struck, left for the other world.[39] . . .

The warriors struck with arrows became red with blood.

Their horses fell and they left for heavens. . . .

In the hands of blood-thirsty Khans, there were the Khorasan swords, whose sharp edges flashed like fire.

The bows shooting out volleys of arrows twanged, the splendid horses fell because of the heavy blows.

The trumpets sounded and the musical pipes were played, the brave warriors thundered from both sides.

And with their strong arms struck (the enemy), the witches drank blood to their fill and produced dreadful sounds. . . .

How far should I describe the great battle?

Those who fought attained martyrdom, thousands fled away.[40] . . .

The hill-chief spurred his horse and fled, the warriors went away without discharging their arrows.

The chiefs of Jaswal and Dadhwal, who were fighting (in the field), left with all their soldiers.

The Raja of Chandel was perplexed, when the tenacious Hari Chand caught hold of the spear in his hand.

He was filled with great fury, fulfilling his duty as a general; those who came in front of him, were cut into pieces and fell (in the field).

Then Najabat Khan came forward and struck Sango Shah with his weapons.

Several skillful Khans fell on him with their ams and sent Shah Sangram to heaven. . . .

The brave warrior Sango Shah fell down after killing Najabat Khan.

There were lamentations in this world and rejoicing in heaven.[41] . . .

After regaining consciousness from the swoon, Hari Chand shot his arrows with unerring aim.

Whosoever was struck, fell down unconscious, and leaving his body, went to the heavenly abode.

He aimed and shot two arrows at the same time and did not care for the selection of his target.

Whosoever was struck and pierced by his arrow, went straight to the other world. . . .

Hari Chand, filled with rage, drew out his bow, he aimed and shot his arrow, which struck my horse.

He aimed and shot the second arrow towards me, the Lord protected me, his arrow only grazed my ear.

His third arrow penetrated deep into the buckle of my waist-belt.

Its edge touched the body, but did not cause a wound, the Lord saved his servant.[42] . . .

When the edge of the arrow touched my body, it kindled my resentment.

I took the bow in my hand and aimed and shot the arrow.

All the warriors fled, when a volley of arrows was showered.

Then I aimed the arrow on a warrior and killed him.

Hari Chand was killed and his brave soldiers were trampled.

The chief of Kot Lehar was seized by death.

The hill-men fled from the battlefield, all were filled with fear.

I gained victory through the favor of the Eternal Lord (KAL).

We returned after victory and sang songs of triumph.

I showered wealth on the warriors, who were full of rejoicings. . . .

When I returned after victory, I did not remain at Paonta.

I came to Kahlur and established the village Anandpur.

Those, who did not join the forces, were turned out from the town.

And those who fought bravely were patronised by me.[43]

The "Zafarnama"

We now move to a different section of the *Dasam Granth*, the "Zafarnama." The tradition attributes this to a letter written by Guru Gobind Singh to the Mughal emperor.

Keeping in mind the important reservations about the literary history of Sikh scriptures from the time of Guru Gobind Singh, this sheds light on the tenth guru and his followers in the period around the creation of the *Khalsa*. One of the main contentions of the guru against the Mughal emperor in his letter is that the emperor is a breaker of promises and therefore not a truly religious man. Aurangzeb's generals had promised the guru and his followers safe passage if they left their stronghold of Anandpur, but the Mughal forces attacked the Sikhs once they were outside the walls of the town. In the "Zafarnama," Guru Gobind Singh famously asks the emperor how he could possibly resist when his forty Sikh warriors were engaged by a Mughal army of 100,000 men.

The immediate intention of the letter from the guru to Aurangzeb is to make the emperor realize that his generals have fought an unjust battle against the Sikhs and to convince the emperor to enter into talks with the Sikhs on an equal footing. These were high ambitions for a leader in Guru Gobind Singh's position after the battle, to say the least. As evidence for the "unjust" conduct of the Mughal generals, Guru Gobind Singh made reference to the letters in which the emperor's generals had granted him safe passage from Anandpur Sahib. The guru insists that according to the religious ideals of Islam, the Mughal ruler must now himself travel to Guru Gobind Singh's place of refuge in order to have talks. The guru writes that he is in a position to guarantee the safety of the emperor, if he should come to the village, as the people of the area, the Brars, are his subjects and accept his word. Although Guru Gobind Singh is first and foremost a great and righteous warrior, in Sikh tradition his life is also tied to the theme of martyrdom. All his four sons were killed at Chamkaur or in the aftermath of the battle.

From: Guru Gobind Singh, "Zafarnama"[44]

[Opening Invocation of God]

Eternal, gracious, wonderful,
Kind Comforter, Deliverer,
Protector, Giver who supports,
Sustainer who fulfills desires,
Giver of goodness, King and Guide,
Unequalled and unparalleled,
Who needs no royal pomp and show,
The Lord whose grace grants heaven's bliss,
Transcendent, mighty, manifest,
Generous in His immanence,
Most pure and gracious Cherisher,
Whose kindness nurtures every land,
Lord of all lands, greater than great,
Supremely fair, kind Nourisher,
All-knowing Guardian of the weak,
Foe-smiter who protects the poor,
Law-keeper, Prophet of the Book,
Truth-knower, Seat of excellence,
Great Wisdom-seeker who knows all,

Truth-Knower who is manifest,
Omniscient Ruler of the world,
God solves all problems, knowing all,
And in His total knowledge makes
All actions in the world occur.

[The Loss of Anandpur]

Let God the One be witness that
I place no trust upon this oath.
No trust at all have I in him
Whose Bakhshis and Divans speak false,
For those who trust Koran-sworn oaths
Will finally be put to shame.
One whom the royal phoenix shades
Escapes the crow's designing grasp.
The lion's cover keeps him safe,
Goats, sheep and deer are kept at bay.
Had I sworn even secretly,
I never should have moved one step.

[The Battle of Chamkaur]

But how could forty starving men
Resist the onslaught of that horde?
They broke their oath and suddenly
Attacked with arrows, swords and guns.
Surrounded, with no choice, in turn
I too attacked with bow and gun.
When matters pass all other means,
It is allowed to take up arms.
Why should I trust Koran-sworn oaths?
What need had I to take that route?
Had I seen through his foxiness,
They'd not have made me go that way.
To kill or capture ill beseems
A man who swears on the Koran.
In sudden fierce attack they rushed,
Like swarming insects, clad in black.
One arrow drowned in blood all those
Who dared to leave their wall's defense,
For only those who stayed behind
Stayed safe from arrows and from shame.
When I saw Náhar come to fight
He tasted my swift arrow's point.
He fled, and so did many Khans

Who'd boasted loud before the fight.
Another Afghan joined the fray,
Swift as a flood, a shaft, a shot.
He launched repeated brave attacks,
Some planned with care, some wildly rushed.
His onslaughts brought him many wounds,
He killed two men, then lost his life.
That cursed Khwaja dared not fight,
But cowered back behind the wall.
Ah, had I seen his face, how quick
I should have shot his sins away!
On both sides, struck by shaft and shot,
Many fell prey to sudden death.
The arrows and the bullets rained,
The earth was stained bright poppy-red.
The heads and limbs piled everywhere
Seemed polo balls upon a pitch.
The world was filled with mighty noise
From twanging bows and crackling shots.
The whistling of those vengeful shafts
Made even heroes lose their wits.
But what could bravery achieve
When forty faced that countless host?
The veiling of the world's bright lamp
Brought forth the shining lord of night.
True keepers of Koran-sworn oaths
Are safely guided by the Lord,
So did the Foe-Destroyer bring
Me forth unharmed, with hair untouched.

[Address to Aurangzeb]

That promise-breaker – I knew not –
Was fond of lucre, false in faith,
Unrighteous and unpracticing,
For God or Prophet without care.
All those who to their faith are true
Will keep the promises they make.
There is no trusting him, though he
Calls on Koran and God the One.
For all his strong Koran-sworn oaths,
I will not trust him in the least.
For had I trusted him at all
I should have made my way to you.
It is your duty to observe

That promise sworn by God to me.
If you were before me, Sire,
Then all would be at once revealed.
It is your duty now to act
In keeping with the words you wrote.
Your letter and your message gave
Assurances which should be kept.
For promises are made to keep,
Nor should the tongue belie the heart.
Your Kazi* said you'd keep your word,
If you were true, you should have come.
Do you still need that first Koran-sworn oath?
I'll send it, and you'll see it says:
"*In Kangar first you may remain,*
But then the two of us should meet.
There is no risk for you this way,
All the Bairars are ruled by me.
Come and let us converse direct
And let me show you favor too.
Come, take a horse to suit high rank
And rich estates besides as gifts."
I am, my lord, your humble slave
Ready to serve at your command.
Once I receive your orders, I
Shall readily present myself.
As you adore the One True God
Be prompt in this affair of mine.
Adore Him, and do not oppress
Any man at another's word.
Though from your throne you rule the world
Your justice strangely suits a king.
Strange is your justice, strange – alas –
Your faith-observance too, I fear!
How strange, how strange are your decrees!
False promises cause only harm.
Do not have others cruelly killed –
The sword of fate may slay you next.
Pay heed now, as you fear the Lord,
Who feels no need or gratitude.
He is the fearless King of kings,
Heaven and earth's true Sovereign,
The Lord of earth and heaven, God

---

* Islamic expert in law; judge. Often written as *qadi*.

Who makes the world and all it holds.
Protecting ants and elephants,
He smites the heedless, guards the weak.
Immune to flattery and need,
His name is Guardian of the poor.
Unbending and unparalleled,
He is the Guide who shows the way.
Be true to your Koran-sworn oath,
Perform the promise which you made.
Let love of wisdom be your guide,
And boldly see this matter through.
Then what if my four sons are slain?
This coiled serpent still remains.
To put out sparks is no great deed
Should this stir up a circling fire.
How well sweet-tongued Firdausi* said:
"Hastiness is the devil's work."
Be present with your witness, Sire,
Upon that day I come to you.
Do not forget, for else God will
Most certainly forget you too,
But if you gird your loins for this,
The Lord will grant to you His grace.
The best of acts is righteousness,
The best of lives is knowing God.
These many grievous acts of yours
Show me you do not know the Lord.
Nor does the Lord of grace know you –
No care has He for all your wealth.
Hundreds of your Koran-sworn oaths
Cannot inspire my slightest trust.
I'd not have come to you this way –
The Prince's call alone draws me.

[Conclusion]

Hail Aurangzeb, great king of kings,
Fine horseman, masterly in craft,
Of fair appearance and bright mind,
Great lord and master of the realm,
Skilled both in policy and war,
Lord of the cauldron and the sword,
Brilliant in mind and fair in form,

* Persian poet.

Divider of the empire's wealth,
Mighty in giving, firm in fight,
Angelic, star-like majesty,
Great Aurangzeb, world-emperor
But like Darius[*] far from faith!
I was the idol breaker when
I slew those hill-idolators.
See how fate's faithless cycles turn
Behind the backs of those they harm.
See too the holy power of God
Which lets one man defeat whole hosts.
The Friend's support unarms all foes,
For giving is the Giver's task.
He guides and grants deliverance,
Instructing tongues in how to praise.
He blinds the foe before he acts
And brings the helpless forth unhurt.
All who stay true to Him enjoy
The mercy of the Merciful.
Those hearts which strive to serve Him best
Obtain the shelter of the Lord.
How can his enemy deceive
A man with whom the Guide is pleased?
Attacked by many thousands, he
Rests safe in the Creator's care.
You look to armies and to gold –
We look to thanking God who knows
Your pride in rule and wealth is matched
By our trust in the Deathless Lord.
Since all in turn must leave, be not
Misled in this short stay serai.[†]
See how fate's faithless cycles turn
Over this world and all it holds.
Use not your strength to harm the weak
Nor chisel at your promises.
However many troops they lead,
No foe harms him whom God befriends.
Nor will a thousand arts allow
A foe to harm one hair of his.

[*] Achaemenid emperor, sixth and fifth century BC.
[†] Station where travelers can rest.

The *Rahit-namas*

As we have observed, there is not much in the way of moral advice or precepts in the *Guru Granth Sahib*. If we are looking for rules of behavior for Sikhs of the *Khalsa* on the field of battle we might instead turn to the code of conduct (the *rahit*), laid out in the class of texts known as the *rahit-nama*. The most valuable source for this tradition is W. H. McLeod's work on the six *rahit-namas* of the eighteenth century. These are the *Tanakhah-nama*, the *Prahilad Rai Rahit-nama*, the *Sakhi Rahit ki*, the *Chaupa Singh Rahit-nama*, the *Desa Singh Rahit-nama*, and the *Daya Singh Rahit-nama*. Of these the *Tanakhah-nama* is the oldest and simplest in form; it may have been composed in the second decade of the eighteenth century. The eighteenth century was a time of conflict with the Mughals. Thus, the *rahit-namas* of this period contain negative views of Mughal rule and, by implication, of Muslims in general, who are referred to as *malecchans* (Sanskrit, *mleccha*, meaning barbarian) or *turak* (Turk).

From: The *Tanakhah-nama* (attributed to Nand Lal, a leading author attached to Guru Gobind Singh's court, early eighteenth century)[45]

44. He is a Khalsa who in fighting never turns his back....

44a. He is a Khalsa who slays Muslims....

48. He is a Khalsa who fights face to face....

50. He is a Khalsa who destroys the oppressor....

51. He is a Khalsa who fights his enemy....

53. He is a Khalsa who is always fighting battles.

He is a Khalsa who carries weapons....

From: The *Rahit-nama* of Bhai Desa Singh (late eighteenth century)[46]

45. ..."Intoxicating liquor may be taken before battle, but there should be no mention of it at other times. In battle the Singh should roar [like a lion]. Fighting them face to face he defeats the Muslims (*malechhan*).

46. In battle let [the Khalsa] never be defeated. He should forget sleep, [remaining ever alert] to fight the Muslim (*turak*). Let him with determination do the deeds of a Kshatriya, crying "Kill! Kill!" [as he fights] in the battle.

47. Fear not, for many are fearlessly fighting. Sustain the spirit [which declares]: "I shall kill the enemy!" Those [Khalsa] who die in the course of a battle shall certainly go to paradise.

48. He who defeats the enemy in battle will find his glory resounding the whole world over. Stand firm, therefore, in the fiercest of conflicts. Never turn and flee from the field of battle.

49. If anyone fears fighting in battles let him earn his sustenance by such activities as agriculture.

Sant Jarnail Singh Khalsa Bhindranwale

In the early 1980s, Punjab was ravaged by conflict between groups of armed insurgents and the Indian authorities. The conflict culminated with an attack on the Golden Temple in Amritsar on 3–6 June 1984. Prime Minister Indira Gandhi, who had ordered the attack, was later assassinated by her Sikh bodyguards as revenge. This in turn led to pogroms against civilian Sikhs in Delhi and other parts of India. In this section we include extracts from the speeches of the most famous leader of the insurgency, Sant Jarnail Bhindranwale (1947–1984). Most Sikhs today would agree that Bhindranwale was not in any way representative of Sikh political ideals. However, considering the national and international repercussions of the Punjab insurgency, his ideas deserve a place in this book. In a speech of 13 April 1983, he warned Sikhs to prepare for an attack by government forces.

From: *Struggle for Justice*, "Speech #7: Government Is Planning to Attack Harmandar Sahib" (1983)[47]

In that eventuality, at various places, in the villages as in the cities, wherever there is a critic of Satguru Guru Granth Sahib, or one who dishonored sisters and daughters, or one who rejoices in this dishonor, or one who creates rifts among us, kill them wherever they are, punish them. This is my firm request of you. You must not hesitate at that time. . . . So long as they hold back from such action, we shall hold back too. Beyond Mecca, everything is wilderness to a Muslim, after Harmandar Sahib, for the Sikh all is wilderness.

Bhindranwale seems to have believed that the Sikhs were engaged in a just war, a *dharam yudh* against their enemies. In a speech of 27 March 1983 he appealed to his followers to stay peaceful until the Golden Temple itself was invaded by the Government.

From: *Struggle for Justice*, "Speech #6: Stay Peaceful but Be Prepared: Act Only If Harmandar Sahib Is Attacked" (1983)[48]

. . . We have to maintain peace, we have to obey orders. So long as the Government confines its activities to outside [of Harmandar Sahib], definitely stay cool because we are engaged in the *Dharam Yudh Morcha*.[49] . . .

However, when at any time, on any day, the Government enters the boundary of this complex to destroy its sanctity, let me appeal most strongly to the entire Sikh congregation – to all of you who live in villages, towns and in the entire country – that when you learn that they have entered the boundary of the complex and attacked then it will be your responsibility everywhere to kill every critic of the Guru and every enemy of the Sikh Nation. At that time there should be no hesitation on your part.

Sikh Shadat

Here we include two extracts from a modern magazine, *Sikh Shadat* (Sikh Martyrdom), published in Punjab. The aim of the magazine is to make Sikhs more conscious of their religious and ethnic identity. Many of the contributors to the magazine write about the conflicts between Sikhs and the Indian state. Several important issues are touched on in the two extracts here. In the first, the writer asks whether the battle at Chamkaur was a just war.

From: *Sikh Shadat* (Sikh Martyrdom) (2005)[50]

Was the war of Chamkaur *dharm yudh*? Yes, it was *dharm yudh*. If *dharm yudh* is when politics is removed and the principles of the Guru are present then it is *dharm yudh*. But what is the meaning of war? What is the real definition? *Britannica Encyclopaedia* says that war is a fight between political groups. If politics is removed it will be a small fight between thieves and smaller groups. The only aim of that war is to rob. But here Guru Gobind Singh is fighting that kind of *dharm yudh* which is totally different from the world wars. At the same time he created Khalsa in order to reach the aim of *dharm yudh*.

In the second extract, the author uses the story about the wars of the tenth guru to discuss the nature of the warfare of Guru Gobind Singh.

... There was only love and love in the *dharm yudh* of Guru Gobind Singh. There was no sign of revenge and hatred in his wars. That is why the Guru Sahib never gave the name violence to his wars. Violence is related to hatred and anger and is for revenge. Those Mogul emperors who martyred Guru Arjan Sahib, cut the head of Guru Tegh Bahadur, martyred many Sikhs, the four *sahibzadian*, the five beloved,[*] the forty mukhtian[†] and Beant Singh, their hands were full of blood. Even if this happened Guru Gobind Singh agreed to have a conversation with the emperor king Aurangzeb and that proves clearly that the Guru ji had no hatred, anger or desire to take revenge in his heart. In the war of Bhangani he fought against the mountain kings and then in the war of Nadaun he helped them. That proves that Guru ji never fought with anger and hatred but with good behavior. Whoever suffered cruelty, he fought for them. When someone complained about Bhai Khania for giving water to the enemy and the wounded then Guru ji called him in to ask for a reason. He answered "Maharaj I did not see any enemy. According to your teaching I see God's soul in all." The true Guru praised him and embraced him. He gave medicine and told him to not only give water but also give aid.

---

[*] The first five Sikhs to be initiated as members of the *Khalsa*.
[†] Forty martyred soldiers fighting with Guru Gobind Singh called the "liberated ones" (Sanskrit, *mukti*, liberated)

Conclusion

This chapter has reproduced and discussed extracts from traditional and modern sources relevant to Sikh ideas and norms concerning war, beginning with the *Guru Granth Sahib*, the most holy book of the Sikhs. In this and subsequent texts it became clear that the language of war, killing, and fighting was used in several different ways, and given several different meanings, by the Sikh gurus. Often these terms referred to spiritual processes of overcoming delusions and vice rather than actual violence. From the *Dasam Granth* we included extracts from the "Bachitar Natak" and the entire "Zafarnama." In the "Bachitar Natak," one could easily detect the influence of Hindu literature and religion on the heroic battle scenes describing Guru Gobind Singh's encounters with his enemies. The "Zafarnama" was a letter referring to the dramatic events of the clash between the tenth guru and the Mughal army. The process of codifying rules of conduct (*rahit*) began under the tenth guru, and we have accordingly included short extracts about conduct in battle taken from some of the texts called *rahit-namas*. Also included were extracts from two modern sources: speeches of the militant leader Bhindranwale and material from the magazine *Sikh Shahadat*. Obviously, these sources cannot be compared to the sacred scriptures in significance or authority. Still, the modern sources are important because they show how some Sikhs have drawn on traditional notions of martyrdom and just resistance against tyranny in order to legitimize struggle against the Indian state.

In conclusion, we may say that Sikhism never developed a systematic theory of just or legitimate war, as was the case in Christianity and Islam. Viewing themselves as a persecuted minority through history, Sikhs have generally approved of war as a defensive measure. Thus its legitmation was never a great problem. The statement from the "Zafarnama" sums up the matter succinctly: "When matters pass all other means, it is allowed to take up arms."

NOTES

1 H. W. McLeod, *Guru Nanak and the Sikh Religion* (Delhi: Oxford University Press, 1978), p. 151f.
2 *Sri Dasam Granth Sahib*, Surindar Singh Kohli (trans.) (Birmigham: Sikh National Heritage Trust, 2003), vol. 1, p. 153.
3 See Pashaura Singh, *The Guru Granth Sahib: Canon, Meaning and Authority* (New Delhi: Oxford University Press, 2000), and Gurinder Singh Mann, *The Making of the Sikh Scripture* (New York: Oxford University Press, 2001).
4 Manmohan Singh (trans.), *Guru Granth Sahib*, 8 vols. (Amritsar: Golden Offset Press, 1996), vol. 6, p. 1039.
5 The Khalistan movement was an insurgency movement of the 1970s and 1980s consisting of several militant groups working for Sikh homeland called Khalistan.
6 Singh, *Guru Granth Sahib*, vol. 8, p. 1358.
7 Ibid., vol. 2, p. 404.
8 Ibid., vol. 6, p. 1023.
9 Ibid., vol. 4, p. 680.
10 Ibid., vol. 6, p. 929.
11 Ibid., vol. 6, p. 1019.

12 Ibid., vol. 8, p. 1356.

13 Ibid., vol. 6, p. 1060.

14 Ibid., vol. 6, p. 1089.

15 Ibid., vol. 7, p. 1280.

16 Ibid., vol. 1, p. 99.

17 Ibid., vol. 4, p. 683.

18 Ibid., vol. 3, p. 464.

19 Ibid., vol. 7, p. 1237.

20 Ibid., vol. 8, p. 1353.

21 Ibid., vol. 2, pp. 237–238.

22 Ibid., vol. 6, p. 1105.

23 Ibid., vol. 2, p. 342.

24 Ibid., vol. 1, p. 142.

25 Ibid., vol. 2, pp. 224–225.

26 Ibid., vol. 3, pp. 417–418.

27 Ibid., vol. 8, p. 1412.

28 Ibid., vol. 4, pp. 579–580.

29 *Sri Dasam Granth Sahib*, Jodh Singh and Dharam Singh (trans.), 2 vols. (Patiala: Heritage Publications, 1999), vol. 1, pp. 198–202.

30 See in particular his "Sources for the Study of Guru Gobind Singh's Life and Times" and "Facsimiles of Core Compositions in the Earliest Manuscripts of the *Dasam Granth,*" *Journal of Punjab Studies* 15:1, 2 (2008) (Special Issue on Guru Gobind Singh), 227–285.

31 Mann, "Sources for the Study of Guru Gobind Singh's Life and Times," p. 258 and note 141.

32 "Bachitar Natak,"in *Sri Dasam Granth Sahib*, Kohli (trans.), pp. 53–62.

33 Ibid., pp. 53–54.

34 Ibid., p. 54.

35 Ibid., pp. 54–55.

36 Ibid., p. 58.

37 Ibid., p. 59.

38 Ibid., p. 60.

39 Ibid.

40 Ibid., pp. 60–61.

41 Ibid., p. 61.

42 Ibid., pp. 61–62.

43 Ibid., p. 62.

44 "Zafarnama," in *Teachings of the Sikh Gurus*, Christopher Shackle and Arvind-pal Singh Mandair (ed. and trans.) (New York: Routledge, 2005), pp. 139–144.

45 W. H. McLeod, *Sikhs of the Khalsa: A History of the Khalsa Rahit* (Delhi: Oxford University Press, 2005), p. 284.

46 Ibid., p. 300.

47 *Struggle for Justice: Speeches and Conversations of Sant Jarnail Singh Khalsa Bhindranwale* (Ohio: Sikh Educational and Religious Foundation, 1999), p. 87.

48 Ibid., p. 72.

49 Literally, a campaign that is a just war.

50 Anonymous, *Sikh Shahadat*, vol. 11, January 2005, pp. 13 and 45. The extracts from the *Sikh Shadat* have been translated by Dr. Kristina Myrvold and a translator who wishes to remain anonymous.

SELECT BIBLIOGRAPHY

Brekke, Torkel, "Between Prudence and Heroism: Ethics of War in the Hindu Tradition," in Torkel Brekke (ed.), *The Ethics of War in Asian Civilizations* (London: Routledge, 2005), pp. 113–144.

Fenech, Louis, *Martyrdom in the Sikh Tradition: Playing the "Game of Love"* (Delhi: Oxford University Press, 2005).

Mann, Gurinder Singh, *The Making of Sikh Scripture* (New York: Oxford University Press, 2001).

Mann, Gurinder Singh, "Sources for the Study of Guru Gobind Singh's Life and Times," *Journal of Punjab Studies* 15:1, 2 (2008) (Special Issue on Guru Gobind Singh), 227–285.

McLeod, W. H., *Guru Nanak and the Sikh Religion* (Delhi: Oxford University Press, 1978).

McLeod, W. H., *The Chaupa Singh Rahit-Nama* (Dunedin: University of Otago Press, 1987).

McLeod, W. H., *Who Is a Sikh? The Problem of Sikh Identity* (Delhi: Oxford University Press, 2002).

McLeod, W. H., *Sikhs of the Khalsa: A History of the Khalsa Rahit* (Delhi: Oxford University Press, 2005).

Singh, Fauja (ed.), *The City of Amritsar: An Introduction* (Patiala: Publication Bureau Punjabi University, 1990).

Singh, Jasmer, *Sri Guru Granth Sahib: A Descriptive Bibliography of Punjabi Manuscript* (Patiala: Publication Bureau Punjabi University, 2005).

Singh, Pashaura, *The Guru Granth Sahib: Canon, Meaning and Authority* (New Delhi: Oxford University Press, 2000).

Singh, Pashaura, *The Bhagats of the Guru Granth Sahib: Sikh Self-Definition and the Bhagat Bani* (New Delhi: Oxford University Press, 2003).

Index